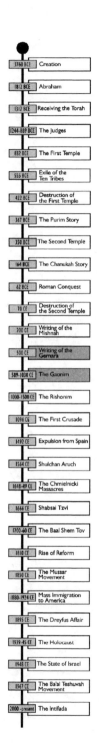

3760 BCE	Creation
1812 BCE	Abraham
1312 BCE	Receiving the Torah
1244-889 BCE	The Judges
832 BCE	The First Temple
555 BCE	Exile of the Ten Tribes
422 BCE	Destruction of the First Temple
367 BCE	The Purim Story
350 BCE	The Second Temple
164 BCE	The Chanukah Story
62 BCE	Roman Conquest
70 CE	Destruction of the Second Temple
200 CE	Writing of the Mishnah
500 CE	Writing of the Gemara
589-1030 CE	The Gaonim
1000-1500 CE	The Rishonim
1096 CE	The First Crusade
1492 CE	Expulsion from Spain
1564 CE	Shulchan Aruch
1648-49 CE	The Chmielnicki Massacres
1666 CE	Shabsai Tzvi
1700-60 CE	The Baal Shem Tov
1810 CE	Rise of Reform
1850 CE	The Mussar Movement
1880-1924 CE	Mass Immigration to America
1895 CE	The Dreyfus Affair
1939-45 CE	The Holocaust
1948 CE	The State of Israel
1967 CE	The Ba'al Teshuvah Movement
2000-present	The Intifada

Miraculous Journey

Miraculous Journey

*A complete history
of the Jewish people from
Creation to the present*

RABBI YOSEF EISEN

The Zolty Edition
TARGUM/FELDHEIM

Published by
TARGUM PRESS, INC.
22700 W. Eleven Mile Rd.
Southfield, MI 48034
E-mail targum@netvision.net.il
Fax 888-298-9992
www.targum.com

Distributed by
FELDHEIM PUBLISHERS
208 Airport Executive Park
Nanuet, NY 10954

Printing plates, "Frank," Jerusalem

Printed in Israel

The Zolty edition
of *Miraculous Journey*
has been made possible by the generosity
of

Dr. Paul and Wendy Zolty

of Atlanta, Georgia.

And to Zebulun he said, "Rejoice O Zebulun in
your excursions and Issachar in your tents."
(Deuteronomy 33:18)

May God bless them in all their endeavors.

לזכר נשמת

אבי מורי ר׳ דוד בן ר׳ אפרים יהושע
י״ט אייר תשל״ח
Rabbi David Eisen

אמי מורתי פיגל בת ר׳ שלמה
שמיני עצרת תשנ״ט
Mrs. Faigel Eisen

אחי ר׳ אפרים יהושע בן ר׳ דוד
כ״ז שבט תשל״ו
Shia Eisen

חמותי
רחמה עלקא וויטיל בת ר׳ משה חיים
ה׳ טבת תשל״ג
Mrs. Eleanor Rosenbloom

ר׳ מרדכי דוד בן ר׳ שמואל

מרת רחל בת ר׳ שלמה דוד

מאיר בן אלפרעד

חוה בת יעקב

שמואל קמנצקי
Rabbi S. Kamenetsky

2018 Upland Way
Philadelphia, Pa 19131

Home: 215-473-2798
Study: 215-473-1212

בעז"ה יום ג' ויגש תשפ"ה לפ"ק

לכבוד הרב הגאון ר' ... שליט"א

אתי בזה אשר שמעתי הטיב עליו

גם ה' נתן לו מדות טובות מנה מדה שינף הוא

יהיו לכבוד לכם וגם לתועלת רבים מחה שינף הוא

ונתן לו חין לאחרין למיטרח ... מן הבריות

מראש וכן מראה לבבו ... את הבחינן

אם יזכה ליתן ... פעם ...

ונכונו ...

וזכה לחיים טובים ...

ומברך ...

דורה ...

Rabbi Reuven Feinstein
131 Bloomingdale Rd.
Staten Island, New York 10309

ראובן פיינשטיין
ראש הישיבה
מתיבתא תפארת ירושלים ד'סטעטן אײלענד

Rabbi Yosef Eisen, one of the outstanding talmidim of the Yeshiva of Staten Island, has written a history text book based on the perspective of Chazal.

While still in Yeshiva, Rabbi Eisen demonstrated his scholarship and knowledge in Torah and history. He is a talented and gifted educator, a veteran of many successful years in the day school movement, inspiring his students to greater heights in Torah and Avodas HaShem. Through Rabbi Eisen, they are able to experience history from a Torah prospective.

Rabbi Eisen has incorporated his vast knowledge of historical facts and his ability to convey them without compromising the eternal truth of Torah teachings and values. He has masterfully compiled them into a history text book filling a void that was not addressed until now. I am sure that this text book will be an invaluable tool to teachers and students alike.

May HaShem give him the strength to author additional books for various class levels.

B'Birchas HaToarh

Rabbi Reuven Feinstein
Rosh HaYeshiva
Yeshivas Staten Island

RABBI MOSHE FEINSTEIN זצ"ל
Founder

RABBI REUVEN FEINSTEIN
Rosh Hayeshiva

RABBI GERSHON WEISS
Menahel-Ruchni

RABBI YISRAEL H. EIDELMAN
Executive Vice-President

20 Av, 5761

Dear Rav Yosef, Shlita:

I have read with great interest, enjoyment, and satisfaction, a chapter of your proposed history textbook for the classroom based on your experience in teaching this subject to high school students and adults. I always knew that you are blessed with an encyclopedic mind and a profound, deep understanding of Torah. However, reading this sample of yours in Jewish history, I discovered that you are also blessed with a wonderful pen in the English language and with a knack for presenting historical facts in a very interesting, enjoyable way. There is no doubt that since HaShem blessed you with these capabilities you should endeavor to produce a concise book of Jewish history, as this is of utmost importance for students in our generation. A clear picture of *Klal Yisrael,* beginning with the Exodus from Egypt and Revelation at Sinai until our day, and seeing the uninterrupted chain of a vibrant, intelligent, and yes, a stubborn people journey through 3000 years of world history clinging to their Torah even at the point of sacrificing their lives for the truth, will strengthen a student's *Emunah* in *Torah min HaShomayim* and *Hashgocha Pratis*. At the same time, students will learn the story of the miraculous survival of an unarmed nation despite the efforts of mighty empires to annihilate it, a phenomenon that has baffled many non-Jewish historians.

Therefore, I say אזל וחזק . Use your G-d-given talents to bring light and understanding to our people, and HaShem should be with you that only the absolute truth should emanate from your pen.

ג'רשון וויס
Your Rebbi,

Gershon Weiss

RESIDENT DIVISION OF

EXECUTIVE OFFICES: 141-7 EAST BROADWAY   NYC 10002 / (212) 964-2830

Congregation Poale Zedeck

אך יי ארביצו גא רעל

November 16, 2000

**Rabbi
Yisroel
Miller**

Spiritual Leader

Rabbi Joseph Eisen is well known as a talmid chochom and master mechanech, and his shiurim in Jewish history appeal to all ages in our community. Rabbi Eisen's history textbook will be an important sefer for our children's mosdos, and it will also provide adults with a deeper understanding of the life and the Mesorah of the Am HaTorah.

Rabbi Yisroel Miller

6318 Phillips Ave.
Pittsburgh, PA
15217-1808
tel. (412) 421-9786
fax (412) 421-3383

Contents

Acknowledgments xxv

Introduction: Why Study Jewish History? 1

1: Creation to Egyptian Slavery 5

Creation 5 • Adam and His Mission 5 • From Adam to Noah 5 • The Flood 6 • After the Flood 6 • Creation and the Jewish Calendar 7 • The Age of the Earth 8 • Is the Torah Racist? 10 • Idolatry 11 • Abraham and the Rise of Judaism 11 • Isaac 12 • Jacob 14 • Joseph 17

2: From Slavery to Monarchy 18

Slavery in Egypt 18 • The Exodus 19 • Purpose of Slavery in Egypt 20 • Miracles of the Exodus 20 • Archaeology and the Torah 21 • Receiving the Torah 22 • The Forty Years in the Desert 24 • Conquest of the Land of Israel 25 • The Seven Nations of the Land of Israel 25 • The *Mishkan* and the Permissibility of *Bamos* 26 • The Period of the Judges 27 • The Era of the Monarchy 29 • King Saul 29 • Saul's Pursuit of David 30 • Saul's Suicide 30

3: The Kingdoms of Israel and Judah 32

King David 32 • King Solomon 33 • Rehoboam and the Division of the Kingdom 33 • Jeroboam 33 • The Kingdom of the Ten Tribes 34 • Exile of the Ten Tribes 34 • The Ten Tribes Today 35 • The Kingdom of Judah 35 • Idolatry 37 • *Bamos* 38 • Prophecy 38 • Manasseh 39 • Josiah 39 • Jehoiakim 40 • Jehoiachin 40 • Zedekiah 41 • The Destruction of the First Temple 41 • Gedaliah 42

4: Babylonian Exile to the End of the Biblical Era 44

Benefits of Babylonian Exile 44 • The Jews in Babylon 44 • The Fiery Furnace 45 • Evil Merodach 45 • Jeremiah's Seventy-Year Prophecy 46 • The Handwriting on the Wall 46 • Darius I 47 • Cyrus 47 • King Ahasuerus 48 • Lessons of the Purim Story 48 • Building the Second Temple 50 • Ezra 51 • Nehemiah 52 • Problems Faced by Ezra and Nehemiah 52 • *Anshei Knesses HaGedolah* 52 • The End of Prophecy 55 • Review of the Major Events after the Destruction of the Temple 55 • The Discrepancy Between the Rabbinic and Secular Dates 56 • The Samaritans 57

5: The End of Prophecy to the Chanukah Miracles 58

After Malachi 58 • Shimon HaTzadik 59 • Alexander the Great 59 • Antigonos Ish Socho 60 • Division of Jewish Powers 60 • The Septuagint 61 • The First Unresolved Halachic Dispute 61 • The Spread of Greek Culture 62 • Seleucid Rule 63 • Antiochus IV 63 • Chonyo, Jason, and Menelaus 63 • Events that Sparked the Hasmonean Revolt 64 • Antiochus' Evil Decrees 64 • Matisyahu 65 • The Revolt 66 • The Miracle of Chanukah 67 • The Holiday of Chanukah 68 • The Wars Following the Chanukah Miracle 69

6: The Hasmonean Dynasty 71

The Hasmoneans 71 • Jochanan Hyrcanus 71 • Jannai 72 • Queen Shlomis 72 • Jewish Society During this Period 73 • Roman Conquest 75 • Herod 75 • Hillel 77 • Beis Shammai and Beis Hillel and the Proliferation of Disputes 78 • Yeshu 79

7: The Destruction of the Second Temple 81

The Procurators 81 • The Spiritual Cause of the Destruction 82 • King Agrippas 82 • The Procurators Return 83 • Jewish Disunity 84 • Kamtza and Bar Kamtza 85 • Vespasian's Campaign of Conquest 86 • Life in Jerusalem 86 • The Mission of Rabbi Jochanan Ben Zakkai 87 • Titus Destroys the Beis HaMikdash 89 • Titus' Victory March 90 • Masada 91 • The Year of the *Churban* 92 • Josephus 92 • Suicide in Jewish Law 93

8: From Yavneh to the Writing of the Mishnah 95

Comparing the Two Destructions 95 • Yavneh 95 • Rabbi Jochanan ben Zakkai 97 • Roman Emperors after Vespasian 98 • Disputes

Between the Sages 99 • *Bo Bayom* 101 • Trajan 101 • Hadrian 102 • Bar Kochba 104 • The Downfall of Betar 104 • *Shaas Hashmad* 105 • *Asarah Harugei Malchus* 106 • Acher 108 • Breakaway of the Christians 108 • Matters Improve 109 • Rabbi Shimon bar Yochai 110 • Rabbi Judah HaNasi 111 • Writing the Oral Law 111 • Writing the Mishnah 112 • The Mishnah 112 • Other Writings of the Tannaim 113 • The Generations of the Tannaim • 113

9: The Amoraim 115

The Passing of an Era 115 • Trends in Jewish Life 115 • Torah Life in Babylon 116 • The Third Century 117 • Relations with the Gentiles in Babylonia 118 • Amoraim of Eretz Yisrael 119 • Christianity Begins to Dominate 119 • The Jerusalem Talmud 120 • Fixing the Jewish Calendar 120 • Abaye and Rava 121 • The Arrangement of the Babylonian Talmud 122 • Sealing the Babylonian Talmud 122 • The Rabanan Savoroi 123 • The Babylonian Talmud 124 • Generations of Amoraim 125

10: The Gaonic Era 126

The Gaonim and Their Times 126 • Accomplishments of the Gaonim 127 • The Rise of Islam 128 • Arab-Jewish Relations 129 • Bustenai 131 • The Karaite Sect 132 • Enactments of the Gaonim 133 • The Siddur Expanded 133 • Biblical Scholarship 134 • Eldad HaDani 135 • The Khazars 135 • The Great Calendar Dispute 136 • The First Pure Halachic Works 137 • Rabbi Achai Gaon 137 • Rabbi Amram Gaon 138 • Rabbi Saadiah Gaon 138 • Rabbi Sherira Gaon 139 • Rabbi Hai Gaon 139 • Changes in Jewish Life 140 • The Four Captives 140

11: The Rishonim 142

The Rishonim 142 • Accomplishments of the Rishonim 142 • Rishonim vis-à-vis the Gaonim 143 • Growth of Jewish Communities in France and Germany 143 • Italy 144 • The Jews Come to Spain 144 • The Golden Age of Spanish Jewry 145 • Sephardim and Ashkenazim 146 • Spanish Jews in Secular Pursuits 147 • Shlomo Ibn Gabirol 149 • *Dikduk* 149 • Ashkenazic Poetry 150 • Ashkenazim and Kabbalah 151 • Jewish Community Life in Germany 152 • Customs of Worms, Germany 152 • Jewish Community Life in Spain 155

12: Twenty-Five Great Rishonim 157

Rabbi Chananel 158 • Rabbi Gershom Meor Hagolah 159 • Rabbi Yitzchak Alfasi 160 • Rabbi Nassan of Rome 161 • Rabbi Bachya ibn Pakudah 161 • Rabbi Shlomo ben Yitzchak — Rashi 162 • Rabbi Abraham ibn Ezra 165 • Rabbi Judah HaLevi 166 • Rabbi Shmuel ben Meir — Rashbam 167 • Rabbi Jacob ben Meir — Rabbeinu Tam 167 • Rabbi Moshe ben Maimon — Rambam 168 • Rabbi Abraham ibn David — Raavad III 172 • Rabbi Zerachiah HaLevi 173 • Rabbi David Kimchi 173 • Baalei Tosafos 173 • Rabbi Moshe Ben Nachman — Ramban 174 • Rabbi Jonah 176 • Rabbi Meir of Rothenberg 176 • Rabbi Asher ben Yechiel — Rosh 177 • Rabbi Menachem Meiri 178 • Rabbi Shlomo ben Aderes — Rashba 178 • Rabbi Yom Tov ibn Ashvili — Ritva 178 • Rabbi Nissim — Ran 179 • Rabbi Jacob ben Asher 179 • Rabbi Israel Isserlein 180

13: Persecutions 181

Early Christian Anti-Semitism 181 • The Crusades 182 • Anti-Jewish Discrimination 187 • Jewish Money Lending 188 • Popular Anti-Jewish Beliefs 189 • The Blood Libel and Ritual Murder 189 • Desecration of the Host 192 • Jews as Devils 192 • The Jewish Smell 193 • The Wandering Jew 193 • Polluted Jewish Blood 193 • Well Poisoning 193 • Jewish World Conspiracy 194 • Jewish Stubbornness 194 • Jewish Laziness 194 • Expulsions 195 • Burning the Talmud 195 • The Disputation of Ramban 196

14: The End of Spanish Jewry 198

Christian Spain 198 • The Pogroms of 1391 198 • Mass Conversion 199 • Prominent Jewish Apostates 199 • The Disputation at Tortosa 200 • The Converts' Dilemma 201 • The *Conversos* Gain Power 202 • Resentment Toward the *Conversos* 202 • Ferdinand and Isabella 203 • The Inquisition Comes to Spain 203 • Procedure of the Inquisition 204 • Tortures 204 • Punishments 205 • Torquemada 206 • The Holy Child of La Guardia 207 • The Myth Today 207 • The Decree of Expulsion 208 • The Expulsion • 208 • The Trip 209 • Where Jews Went 210 • Reasons for the Tragedy 210 • 500 Years Later 210

15: The Early Acharonim (the 1500s) 212

New Torah Centers 212 • Tzefas 212 • The Arizal 212 • Rabbi Joseph

Karo and *Beis Yosef* 214 • *Shulchan Aruch* 214 • The Attempt to Revive *Semichah* 215 • Rabbinic Opposition 215 • David HaReuveni 216 • Shlomo Molcho 216 • Donna Gracia Mendes and Don Joseph Nasi 217 • The Printing Press 218 • Censorship 218 • The *Shtadlan* 219 • The Protestant Reformation 219 • The First Ghettoes 220 • Poland 221 • Torah Life 222 • Rabbi Moshe Isserles (Rema) 222 • Maharsha 222 • Rabbi Shlomo Luria (Maharshal) 223 • Rabbi Joel Sirkes and Rabbi Meir of Lublin 223 • *Vaad Arba Aratzos* 224 • Jewish Economic Activity 225 • The Shtetl 225 • Maharal of Prague 225 • Prague 226 • Other Torah Centers 226

16: The 1600s 227

Great Turmoil 227 • Amsterdam 227 • Jewish Heretics 228 • Baruch Spinoza 228 • The Jews Return to England 229 • The New World 229 • The Jews Come to New York 230 • Great Sages of the 1600s 230 • The Taz and the Shach 231 • Rabbi Yom Tov Lipman Heller 231 • The Chmielnicki Massacres 231 • Jewish Reaction 232 • Shabsai Tzvi 233 • The Aftereffects 235 • Yiddish 235 • Jewish Last Names 237

17: The 1700s 238

Great Changes 238 • The *Aliyah* of Rabbi Yehuda HaChasid 238 • Rabbinic Controversies 239 • Rabbi Yaakov Emden versus Rabbi Yonoson Eybeschutz 239 • Rabbi Yaakov Emden versus Rabbi Moshe Chaim Luzzatto (Ramchal) 240 • The *Get* of Cleves 241 • Great Scholars of the 1700s 241 • Rabbi Eliyahu Kramer (Gra) 243 • The Rise of the Chassidic Movement 245 • Rabbi Israel Baal Shem Tov 245 • The Maggid of Mezeritch 246 • Rabbi Schneur Zalman of Liadi 248 • The Conflict Between Chassidus and Its Opponents (Misnagdim) 249 • Bans and Counterbans 251 • The Split Widens 252 • The Russians Intervene 252 • The Pale of Settlement 253 • Jews in America 253 • Chassidic *Aliyah* to Eretz Yisrael 254

18: The Darkness of Enlightenment 255

Europe Enters the Modern Age 255 • The French Revolution 255 • Napoleon 256 • Napoleon's Great Sanhedrin 256 • Assimilation in Germany — Moses Mendelssohn 257 • Emancipation 259 • The Backlash 259 • Karl Marx 259 • The Beginning of Reform Judaism 260 • The Maskilim 261 • The Salons 261 • Fighters against Reform — Rabbi Samson Raphael Hirsch 262 • Rabbi Yaakov Ettlinger 264 • Chasam Sofer 264 • Rabbi Akiva Eiger 265 • Rabbi Meir Leib ben Yechiel Michael (Malbim) 266 • Reform in America 267 • The Conservative Movement 268 • Fighters against Reform in America 269 • Jews in Secular Pursuits 270 • In America 270 • The Rothschilds 270 • Sir Moses Montefiore 272

19: Life under the Czars in the 1800s 275

Russian Society 275 • Russia Acquires Many Jews 275 • Czar Nicholas I and the Cantonist Decree 279 • Other Decrees of Czar Nicholas I 282 • Alexander III 283 • The Pogroms 283 • Other Discrimination 286 • *The Protocols of the Elders of Zion* 286 • The *Haskalah* 287 • Hebrew *Haskalah* 288 • Yiddish *Haskalah* 289 • Reasons for *Haskalah*'s Success 289 • The Vilna versus Slavita *Shas* Controversy 290

20: Religious Jewry's Response 292

The 1800s — a Difficult Divine Test for the Jewish People 292 • The Yeshivah Movement 292 • Volozhin 292 • Other Lithuanian Yeshivos 293 • Non-Lithuanian Yeshivos 294 • Chassidic Yeshivos 294 • Rabbi Chaim Soloveitchik 295 • The Mussar Movement — Problems in Lithuanian Society 296 • Rabbi Israel Salanter 297 • The Principles of Mussar 298 • Rabbi Israel's Saintliness 299• Rabbi Israel's *Talmidim* 300 • The Kelm School of Mussar 301 • The Slabodka School of Mussar 302 • The Novarodok School of Mussar 302 • Opposition to Mussar 304 • In the Yeshivah World 305 • The Chassidic World — Chassidus Expands 305 • Polish Chassidus 305 • The Kotzker Rebbe 307 • Kotzker Disciples 307 • Kotzker Sayings 308 • Other Chassidic Centers 308 • The Rebbes of Lubavitch in the 1800s 310 • The Chafetz Chaim 311 • Chacham Yosef Chaim 312

21: Places Old and New 313

Eretz Yisrael 313 • *Hovovei Zion* and *Bilu* 314 • The Roots of Zionism 315 • Theodore Herzl 317 • The First Zionist Congress 318 • Uganda 319 • The Second Aliyah 319 • Religious Opposition to Zionism 320 • Mizrachi 322 • Arab Opposition to Zionism 323 • Socialism 324 • The Bund 324 • Immigration to America 325 • The Trip on Land 326 • The Sea Voyage 327 • Arrival in America 328 •

Life in America 328 • Jobs 329 • Spiritual Life 329 • Rabbis 332 • New York Chooses a Chief Rabbi 332 • Rabbi Bernard Drachman 334 • Rabbi Herbert S. Goldstein 335

22: The Beginning of the Twentieth Century through World War I 337

Unrest in Russia 337 • The Kishinev Pogrom 337 • The Jerusalem Talmud Forgery 338 • The Dreyfus Affair 339 • Anti-Semitism in France 339 • Alfred Dreyfus 340 • The Affair Begins 340 • The Degradation of Dreyfus 341 • The Aftermath 341 • The Beilis Blood Libel Trial 342 • Labor Unions 343 • Agudath Israel 344 • Anti-Semitism in England and America 345 • World War I 346 • The Jews of Palestine During World War I 347 • The Balfour Declaration 348

23: The Aftermath of World War I 350

Great Change 350 • The Treaty of Versailles 350 • Russia Becomes Communist 351 • Supports of Torah in Russia 354 • Birobidzhan 355 • England Creates the Map of the Modern Middle East 355 • The British Change Their Policy 356 • The Arabs Riot 357 • A Bitter Enemy Arises 357 • The Riots Continue 358 • Jewish Political Activity in Palestine 359 • The Labor Party 361 • The Revisionist Zionists 361 • Religious Zionism 362 • Non-Zionist Jews 362 • Political Assassinations 363 • Torah Grows in Eretz Yisrael 364 • Jewish Life in Poland 1918–1939 364 • Jewish Population Distribution in Poland 366 • Political and Cultural Activity 367 • Religious Life in Poland 368 • Chassidic Life 369 • Beth Jacob 369 • *Daf Yomi* 370 • The Lithuanian Yeshivos 370 • Non-Lithuanian Yeshivos 372 • Jewish Life in Hungary 372 • The Community 375 • American Jewish Economic Life Between the Wars 375 • The Immigrants' Children 377 • Secular Culture 378 • American Philanthropy 379 • Community Relations Organizations 380 • Politics 381 • Demographics 381 • Religious Life 382 • Young Israel 382 • Kashrus 383 • Anti-Semitism in the United States 383 • Henry Ford 384 • Father Charles Coughlin 384 • The Sephardic World 385 • Political Activity 387 • Anti-Semitism 388 • Jewish Populations on the Brink of World War II 388

24: Introduction to the Holocaust 389

Zachor! 389 • Why Did the Germans Kill Jews? 390 • The Burning Question: Why Did It Happen? 392 • The Torah's Paradigm of Jewish History 395 • The 2,000-Year Pattern of Jewish Exile 396 • Four Approaches to Understanding Why the Holocaust Happened 397 • Why Did 1.5 Million Innocent Children Die in the Holocaust? 399 • The Enormity of the Holocaust 399 • The Spiritual Loss 401 • G-d's Consolation — the Rebuilding 401 • Hitler's Hatred of Jews 402

25: Prelude to the Holocaust 404

European Anti-Semitism 404 • In Germany 404 • Why Germany Produced the Holocaust 405 • Modern Backdrop to the Holocaust 406 • Germany Becomes One 406 • World War I 407 • The Aftermath of Defeat 407 • Anarchy 407 • Adolph Hitler 408 • Nazi Gains 409 • Hitler Seizes Power 410 • Early Anti-Jewish Measures 410 • The Nuremberg Decrees 411 • Why Jews Did Not Leave 412 • Nazi Leaders 412 • Nazi Propaganda 413 • The Nazi Olympics 415 • German Expansion 416 • Czechoslovakia 417 • The Events Leading up to *Krystallnacht* 417 • Jewish Refugees 420 • The Ill-Fated Voyage of the *St. Louis* 421 • Attitudes Toward Refugees 422 • Could an Independent State of Israel in the 1930s Have Helped? 425 • Germany's Euthanasia Program 426 • Hitler's Demands on Poland 427 • The Hitler-Stalin Pact 427 • Jewish Reaction 427 • Secret Provisions of the Treaty 428 • Divine Providence 428

26: The Horrors Begin in Poland 429

Hitler Attacks Poland 429 • The Establishment of Ghettoes 431 • Life in the Warsaw Ghetto 432 • Religious Life in the Ghetto 435 • The *Judenrat* 437 • The Ghetto Police 439 • German Victories 440

27: The Large-Scale Massacres 442

The German Invasion of the Soviet Union 442 • Planning the Final Solution 442 • The *Einsatzgruppen* 444 • The Wannsee Conference 450 • The Trains of Death 451 • The Death Camps 453 • Arrival at the Camps 454 • The Gassing 455 • The *Sonderkommandos* 458 • Hiding the Crimes 460 • A Day in the Life of a Camp Worker 462 • Auschwitz 464 • The Selection 466 • Life in Auschwitz 466 • Medical Experiments 467 • 1942 467

28: Spiritual and Physical Resistance 469

A Canard Used Against the Victims 469 • Overwhelming German Power 469 • Fear of Reprisals 470 • German Deceptions 470 • Futility of Resistance 471 • An Unprecedented Foe 472 • Physical Resistance 472 • The Warsaw Ghetto Uprising 473 • Spiritual Resistance 474 • Commemorating Resistance 478 • Righteous Gentiles 479 • Diplomats 480 • Raoul Wallenberg 481 • Chiune Sugihara 481 • Carl Lutz 482 • Feng Shan Ho 482 • Righteous Individuals 483 • *Zegota* 485

29: The Fate of Jews in Various Countries 487

Poland 487 • The Soviet Union and the Baltic Nations 489 • Romania 489 • Germany 490 • Austria 491 • France 492 • The Netherlands 493 • Czechoslovakia 493 • Greece 494 • Hungary 494 • Denmark 499 • Bulgaria 501 • Italy 502 • Albania 502 • The Channel Islands 503 • Japan 504

30: Rescue Efforts During the Holocaust 506

A Sorry Record 506 • Public Opposition 506 • Governmental Opposition 509 • American Jewish Response to the Holocaust 510 • Attempts at Rescue 514 • Peter Bergson 515 • Orthodox Rescue Efforts 516 • Zeirei Agudath Israel 517 • Va'ad Hatzalah 518 • Escape from Auschwitz 519 • The Kasztner Train 520 • The Sternbuch-Musy-Himmler Negotiations 521 • Bombing Auschwitz 521 • The Dispute 521 • The Pope and the Holocaust 523

31: The Final Days of the Holocaust 525

The Death Marches 525 • The Liberation 526 • The Survivors 527 • Punishment of the Perpetrators 529 • The Nuremberg Trials 529 • The Eichmann Trial 530 • Other Trials 530 • Economic Exploitation 531 • Post-Holocaust Germany 531 • The Swiss and the Holocaust 532 • Holocaust Denial 533 • The Effects of the Holocaust on the Jewish People 535

32: The Establishment of the State of Israel 536

Palestine During World War II 536 • The Germans Approach Palestine 536 • British-Jewish Cooperation Ends 537 • The Three Jewish Resistance Groups 538 • Jewish Refugees 540 • The *Exodus* 540 • Britain Consults the United Nations 541 • The Fighting

Begins 543 • Jerusalem 543 • Deir Yassin 544 • The Proclamation of the State of Israel 545 • The Early Stages of the Battle 545 • The First Cease-Fire 547 • The *Altalena* Incident — Jew vs. Jew 548 • The Second Round of Fighting 548 • The Bernadotte Mission 548 • The Last Fighting 549 • Israel after the War 549 • The Palestinian Refugees 550 • Religious Reaction to the State of Israel 551 • Agudah Participates in the State of Israel 552 • Israel's First National Elections 553 • The Law of Return 553 • Divine Providence in the Establishment of Israel 554

33: The 1950s 555

The Great Immigration to Israel 555 • The Treatment of the Sephardim 556 • The Yemenite Jews 557 • German Reparations 558 • The Kasztner Trial 559 • The Sinai War of 1956 560 • Israel's Economic Position Improves 561 • Soviet Jewry 562 • Torah Life in America 563 • Torah Umesorah 564 • Beth Jacob 564 • Chinuch Atzmai 565 • Chassidic Communities 565 • Jewish Demographic Trends in the 1950s 567 • Yeshiva University 568 • Intermarriage 568

34: The 1960s 569

Cataclysmic Upheaval 569 • The Silent Holocaust 569 • The Civil Religion of American Jews 570 • Black Anti-Semitism 571 • The Orthodox World 571 • The *Ba'al Teshuvah* Movement 572 • The Palestine Liberation Organization (PLO) 573 • The National Water Carrier 574 • Eli Cohen 574 • The Six-Day War 575 • Prelude to the War 575 • The *Hamtanah* Period 576 • Day One — Monday, June 5 577 • Day Two — Tuesday, June 6 577 • Day Three — Wednesday, June 7 578 • Day Four — Thursday, June 8 578 • The *Liberty* Incident 579 • Day Five — Friday, June 9 579 • Day Six — Saturday, June 10 579 • Results of the War 580 • UN Resolution 242 581 • The War of Attrition (1967–70) 581 • The Soviet Union 582 • Vatican II 582

35: The 1970s 583

Far-Reaching Change 583 • Soviet Jewish Emigration 583 • The *Ba'al Teshuvah* Movement Expands 585 • The Feminist Movement 587 • American Orthodox Jewish Life and Culture 588 • Agudath Israel 589 • American Torah Life 592 • Torah Life in Israel 593 • Torah Leaders in Israel 594 • The Conservative and Reform

Movements 595 • Jewish Settlement in the Conquered Territories 596 • The 1973 Yom Kippur War 597 • The War Begins 597 • The Turning Point 599 • Results of the War 601 • The Palestinians and Terrorism 601 • United Nations Anti-Semitism 603 • Zionism Is Racism 603 • The Entebbe Rescue 604 • The Likud Election Victory 605 • Sadat Visits Israel 606 • Peace with Egypt 606

36: The 1980s 608

Setting the Tone 608 • A New Era 608 • Affluence 609 • Religious-Secular Tension 610 • In America 611 • Radicalization of the Islamic World 612 • Soviet Jewry 613 • Bombing Iraq's Nuclear Reactor 614 • The Lebanon War (1982) 614 • New Religious Parties 617 • The Rescue of Ethiopia's Jews 618 • Arab Terror 619 • The *Intifada* 619

37: Recent Times 621

Great Turmoil 621 • Changing of the Guard 621 • American Jewish Demographics 621 • The Fall of the Soviet Union 623 • Non-Jewish Immigration to Israel 623 • Ethiopian Immigration 624 • The First Gulf War 624 • The Oslo Accords 625 • Peace with Jordan 628 • Negotiations with Syria 628 • The Goldstein Shooting 629 • Homicide Bombings 629 • Oslo B 630 • The Rabin Assassination 631 • The Hasmonean Tunnel Riots 631 • The Wye Accords 632 • More Secular-Religious Tension 632 • Israeli Withdrawal from Lebanon 633 • The Failed Camp David Talks 634 • Media Distortions 635 • Anti-Semitism Increases 636 • The Pope Visits Israel 636 • American Orthodoxy 637 • 9/11 638 • The Israeli Economy 639 • Gulf War II 640 • The Road Map 640

Notes 641

Hebrew Bibliography 677

Bibliography 679

Index 689

Acknowledgments

Publishing *Miraculous Journey* would be impossible without the efforts of many people. A special appreciation to Rabbi Isser Pliner, former principal of Hillel Academy in Pittsburgh, Dr. Carey Balaban, and Mr. Sandy Riemer, for their moral support while this project was in its infancy.

Numerous people and organizations generously supported this book's publication, and I would like to thank them: Mr. and Mrs. Parke Americus, Mr. and Mrs. Jay Angel, Mr. and Mrs. Chaim Balsam, Mr. and Mrs. Joseph Berger/Congregation Torath Chaim of Pittsburgh, B'nai Emunah Congregation of Pittsburgh, Mrs. Evelyn Bloom, Dr. and Dr. David Brent, Dr. and Mrs. Yaakov Guterson, Mr. and Mrs. Leroy Harris, Dr. and Mrs. Alan Itskowitz, Dr. and Mrs. Emanuel Kanal, Dr. and Mrs. Michael Kentor, Kollel Bais Yitzchak of Pittsburgh, Dr. and Dr. Barry Levine, Dr. and Dr. Frank Lieberman, Miss Tova Mendelson, Mr. and Mrs. David Nadoff, Mrs. Shoshana Nudel, Mr. and Mrs. Brad Perelman, Mr. and Mrs. Joel Pfeffer/Congregation Poale Zedeck of Pittsburgh, Mr. and Mrs. Murray Pfeffer, Dr. and Mrs. Dean Pollack, Mr. and Dr. Joel Posin, Rabbi and Mrs. Avraham Rodkin, Rabbi and Mrs. Mordechai Rosenberg, Rabbi and Dr. Amiel Rosenbloom, Mr. Joshua Rosenbloom, Rabbi and Mrs. Yaakov Rosenstein, Mr. and Mrs. Larry Rubin, Mr. and Mrs. Alex Sassoon, Mr. and Mrs. Mark Seigle, Mr. and Mrs. Norman Sindler, Mr. and Mrs. Mitchell Small, Mr. and Mrs. Alan Tombosky, Dr. and Mrs. Hirsh Wachs, Dr. and Mrs. Dennis

Wayne, Dr. and Mrs. Ben Zimmer, and Dr. and Mrs. Yitzchok Zlochower.

I realize that there are individuals who helped sponsor this book after it went to the printer and as a result could not be mentioned here. Your contributions are not forgotten!

I would like to express special gratitude to Dr. and Mrs. Paul Zolty, whose very significant assistance played the major role in making this project a reality. *Yasher koach!*

Rabbi Joseph Elias, dean of Rika Breuer's Seminary and head of Torah Umesorah's Zechor Yemos Olam Program, generously shared his sagacious advice in reviewing the chapter on understanding the Holocaust. The expression goes, "Time is worth more than money," especially the priceless time of a *gadol*.

Dr. Abby Mendelson is a master of the writer's craft, and his skillful editing is apparent on every page. It has been a pleasure to work with him. His son Elie artfully designed the graphic layout of this book, making it a pleasure to read.

My *rabbeim* at the Yeshiva of Staten Island, Rabbi Reuven Feinstein, *rosh yeshivah*, Rabbi Gershon Weiss, and Rabbi Chaim Mintz, have inspired me with their Torah wisdom and *middos tovos*, and I am eternally indebted to them.

Kollel Bais Yitzchak of Pittsburgh, its *rosh kollel* Rabbi Aharon Kagan, and the *chavrei hakollel*, have been a constant source of *chizuk* in many ways.

Thank you to Rabbi Moshe Dombey and the staff of Targum Press for their great expertise in producing this book and for their business integrity.

My family deserves much appreciation for putting up with the long hours of researching and writing. May we see much *nachas* from each other.

"To man belongs the arrangements [of thoughts] in his heart, but from Hashem comes the tongue's reply" (Proverbs 16:1). *Hakaras hatov* to Hashem for giving me the ability to take the raw thoughts of my mind and put them in writing. May He inspire me for many years to continue the greatest calling of a Jew as expressed in *Ahavah Rabbah*: *"Lilmod ul'lameid lishmor v'laasos es kol divrei salmud Torasecha b'ahavah* — To learn and to teach, to guard and to perform, all the words of Your Torah's teaching with love."

"For I am G-d, I do not change; you are the children of Jacob, you will not cease to be."

(Malachi 3:6)

"In every generation they rise up to finish us, and the Holy One, Blessed be He, saves us from their hand."

(Passover Haggadah)

"All things are mortal but the Jew; all other forces pass but he remains. What is the secret of his immortality?"

(*The Complete Essays of Mark Twain*, Doubleday, 1963, p. 249)

"Finally, the book gave me the chance to reconsider objectively, in the light of a study covering nearly 4,000 years, the most intractable of all human questions: what are we on earth for? Is history merely a series of events whose sum is meaningless? Is there no fundamental difference between the history of the human race and the history, say, of ants? Or is there a providential plan of which we are, however humbly, the agents? No people have ever insisted more firmly than the Jews that history has a purpose and humanity a destiny."

(Paul Johnson, *A History of the Jews*, p. 2)

"History records no other people like the Jews...by every sociological law they should have disappeared from the stage of history a long time ago, as did all ethnic groups before them who were uprooted from their native land or, alternately, were conquered and assimilated by stronger groups."

(Klaus P. Fischer, *The History of an Obsession*, p. 21)

Introduction

WHY STUDY JEWISH HISTORY?

The Torah states: "Remember the days of the world, understand the years of generations gone by. Ask your father, and he will tell you; your elders, and they will relate it to you" (Deuteronomy 32:7). *Miraculous Journey* attempts to fill a glaring need: a comprehensive treatment of the entire sweep of Jewish history, from Creation to the present, written from a Torah point of view. As such, *Miraculous Journey* focuses on Jewish history from a traditional perspective while at the same time not neglecting pertinent secular and contemporary sources. We are given the mission of understanding our past, not out of a sense of nostalgia or curiosity, but rather to apply yesterday's lessons to today's times.[1] As such, the lesson is clear: our history must be viewed through the lens of Jewish tradition as taught by our sages and elders. That lens is polished and clear. We can trace an unbroken chain back to Sinai and beyond. Although spiritual achievement and Torah greatness have declined precipitously since those days,[2] we are still inextricably linked to the giants of the past. Their story is our story, and their heritage is our heritage to pass on to future generations.

Our tradition is unequivocal: the Scriptures are Divinely written with complete objectivity. The sins and failings of the Jewish people as a whole, as well as of individuals including the very greatest leaders, are placed under a glaring spotlight and harshly exposed.[3] No other historical or religious document is written in such a manner. Ancient records portray rulers as infallible, omitting or distorting their foibles and defeats. Even modern historians are not immune to subjectivity — World War II is taught very differently in Japanese schools than in American ones.

At this point, we can appreciate the greatest of all miracles — the inexplicable survival of the Jewish people through exiles, persecutions, holocausts, and assimilation.[4] Historians throughout the generations have been baffled and amazed by this incredible

THE SIX MAJOR PERIODS OF JEWISH HISTORY

Name of Period	Time of Period	Prominent Personalities
1. Biblical	1–3448 (3760-312 BCE)	Adam, Noah, Abraham, Moses, David, Mordecai
2. Tannaim	3448–3960 (312 BCE–200 CE)	Hillel, Shammai, Rabbi Akiva
3. Amoraim*	3960–4360 (200–600 CE)	Rav, Shmuel, Abaye, Rava
4. Gaonim	4349–4790 (589–1030 CE)	Rabbi Saadiah Gaon, Rabbi Hai Gaon
5. Rishonim	4760–5260 (1000–1500 CE)	Rashi, Rambam, Ramban
6. Acharonim	5260–present (1500 CE–present)	Rabbi Joseph Karo, Baal Shem Tov, Vilna Gaon, Chafetz Chaim, Rabbi Moshe Feinstein

* Includes Rabanan Savoroi

phenomenon.[5] To Jews, however, there is no mystery at all — G-d has promised that the Jewish nation is eternal.

Because *Miraculous Journey* exclusively employs a traditional Torah framework, subjects such as the age of the Earth, dates of historical events, even the dating system itself, are in accordance with accepted Rabbinic and Midrashic authorities. These differ significantly in many cases from generally accepted secular dates.

Chapter 1

CREATION TO EGYPTIAN SLAVERY

C REATION: "In the beginning, G-d created the heavens and the earth" (Genesis 1:1). With these words, the history of the Jewish people and the world begins. Unlike the belief of many ancient and modern philosophers, who say that the earth always existed, the Torah declares two things: that the world was created from nothing and had a sudden beginning. Furthermore, Creation was not, as is erroneously claimed, "a cosmic accident," but rather the world was created with a plan and a purpose.[6]

ADAM AND HIS MISSION: Adam was created not as a wild, illiterate savage, but as a sophisticated, intellectually mature adult.[7] Had he passed the difficult test of not eating of the Tree of Knowledge, the ultimate purpose of Creation would have been achieved — the triumph of Good over Evil — and the splendor of the Messianic age would have been ushered in. The world would have achieved spiritual perfection and would experience eternal, unlimited Divine reward. After Adam's sin, however, the struggle for perfection would become long and protracted, fraught with many seemingly insurmountable obstacles and hardships.[8] This episode taught mankind that G-d takes a continued, active interest in the affairs of the world, and that human beings are responsible for their actions.

FROM ADAM TO NOAH: The ten generations from Adam to

Noah continued mankind's downward spiral, with events hurtling inexorably toward the total spiritual degradation of the Flood. Adam's son Cain committed history's first murder, Adam's grandson Enoch introduced the evil of idolatry, and Lamech began men's exploitation of women and created the climate for immorality.[9] Thus these three most severe sins became implanted into human nature at a very early stage. Instead of channeling his awesome intellect and creativity toward beneficial purposes, man misused and corrupted his G-d-given talents. Jabal discovered the science of animal husbandry, and his brother Jubal was the father of music. Yet both of these discoveries were intended to further the cause of idol worship.[10] Tubal Cain developed iron tools — and became the world's first arms dealer.[11] Clearly, from the outset science and technology were harnessed toward the pursuit of evil.

THE FLOOD: By the year 1656, mankind had so corrupted the world that it had to be destroyed and rebuilt anew. Only eight righteous people remained — Noah; his wife; their three sons, Shem, Ham, and Japheth; and their wives. They were chosen to be the survivors of the Flood and to reconstitute the world, thus illustrating the importance of the righteous individual. Stories of a worldwide flood abound among many far-flung cultures: the Chinese, Mayans, Greeks, Babylonians, and many others all relate the story of the destruction of humans and animals, save for a selected few survivors on board a ship. Physical evidence of a giant deluge exists all over the world. For example, whale and walrus bones are found in Michigan and Georgia, thus indicating the presence of the ocean over the North American continent.[12] Likewise, fossils of fish and sea creatures are found on high elevations, including Mount Everest. The Flood itself lasted a complete solar year.[13]

AFTER THE FLOOD: Noah and his three sons became the forerunners of the seventy primary nations. In fact, the Talmudic term for human beings is *B'nei Noach*, Sons of Noah.[14] (It is commonly held that Shem was the ancestor of the Semitic peoples,

Ham the Negroid race, and Japheth the Caucasians. However, the noted historian Rabbi Berel Wein is of the opinion that Shem, Ham, and Japheth each gave birth to all the different races and ethnic groups.)[15] This period saw the rise of the *Dor HaHaflagah*, the Generation of the Tower. King Nimrod, the world's first dictator (whom some identify with Hammurabi),[16] organized the people in the construction of a tower that would supposedly reach the heavens. Its purpose was to demonstrate man's self-aggrandizement and independence from G-d.[17] For the first time, the rights of the individual were subjugated to the needs of the state or project. The Midrash relates that if a brick fell and broke during construction there was a great hue and cry, whereas if a human fell to his death no concern was shown.[18] (Some ideas never die: one of the Russian Czars was quoted as saying that soldiers can always be replaced, but lost land can never be regained.) Since society was pooling its talents and resources in the pursuit of evil, G-d intervened, interrupting the project by splitting mankind into different linguistic groups. However, a terrible precedent was set, one that would realize its most horrific fruition in Nazi and Communist societies.

SOME IMPORTANT DATES:
    930 — Death of Adam
    1656 — The Flood
    1948 — Birth of Abraham
    1996 — *Dor HaHaflagah*

CREATION AND THE JEWISH CALENDAR: Rabbinic tradition states that Creation began on the 25th day of Elul, culminating in the creation of Adam on the first day of Tishrei (Rosh HaShanah).[19] There is a difference of opinion as to whether the first five days of Creation count as Year One, and the creation of Adam begins Year Two; or whether Year One dates from the first Rosh HaShanah of history, the creation of Adam. This is not a purely theoretical issue, but rather has great halachic significance. In the land of Israel, farmers observe the mitzvah of *shmittah*, which means that every seventh year no agricultural work may be done. Our present dating system bases its calculations on Adam beginning Year Two. Therefore, *shmittah* was observed in 5761 and will be observed every seven years after that. However, if Adam begins Year One, then 5760 was the proper *shmittah* year. (See *The Jewish Observer*, "Mystery of the Missing Years," January, 1994, for an explanation of the calculation of *shmittah*.)

Another area of halachah in which this issue impacts is the dating of documents. A *get* (bill of divorce) is invalid if an improper date is used. The standard form of a *get* states: "In the year X, according to the count that we calculate." The actual year entered in the *get* is based on Adam's creation being Year Two, and the phrase "according to the count that we calculate" is inserted in case our dating system is incorrect and Adam begins Year One. The document will be valid whichever year is actually correct, because the date as described is unquestionably accurate. Although our current calendar is based on Adam beginning Year Two, Biblical events are dated in the Talmud on the basis of Adam beginning Year One. (See Talmud *Avodah Zarah* 9b, Schottenstein Mesorah edition, note 9.)

THE AGE OF THE EARTH: In 1859, Charles Darwin published *The Origin of Species by Means of Natural Selection*. This book introduced the theory of evolution, which proposed that all plant and animal life arose from lower forms by a process of natural selection acting on random genetic variations. While the Greek philosopher Aristotle had earlier arranged animals on a Great Ladder of Nature from simple to complex, until the time of Darwin many Christian scientists still maintained that some sort of natural ladder or progression was an indication of a plan by a conscious Creator. Darwin's idea that life arose from random processes and natural selection provided a way for scientists, and others, to dispense with the idea of a conscious Creator.

While the Darwinian theory of evolution is widely taught today as standard scientific dogma, many prominent scientists have recognized that evolutionary theory is both unproven and unprovable, and have expressed their misgivings that belief in evolution has become a secular religion rather than a scientific principle. Said Harold C. Uray, a Nobel Prize winner in chemistry: "All of us who study the origin of life find that the more we look into it, the more we feel that it's too complex to have evolved anywhere. *We all believe as an article of faith that life evolved here from dead matter on this planet* [italics in original]. It is just that its complexity is so great that it is hard for us to imagine that it did."[20]

Similarly, G. Marsden wrote in *Nature*, 1983: "Evolution is sometimes the key mythological element in a philosophy that functions as a virtual religion."[21] Richard Dawkins, a prominent British zoologist wrote: "Darwin makes it possible to be an intellectually fulfilled atheist."[22] In a lecture given at the American Museum of Natural History, Colin Patterson, a senior British paleontologist, asked his audience, "Can you tell me anything you know about evolution, any one thing, that is true? I asked this question of the evolutionary morphology seminar in the University of Chicago, a very prestigious body of evolutionists, and all I got was silence for a long time and eventually one person said, 'I do know one thing — it ought not to be taught in high school.' "[23]

In the popular mind, evolutionary theory has been associated with the idea that the earth is billions of years old. However, ideas about the age of the earth (geochronology) and the universe are based on methods from the physical sciences. For example, scientific methods for determining the age of rocks and fossils are based upon the rates of decay of radioactive isotopes. These methods assume that the current rate of decay occurred at all times, so that ages can be estimated directly (*Encyclopaedia Britannica*, 1991, vol. 19, pp. 748–773). However, the Talmud tells us that this assumption is incorrect: the universe was created with the appearance that it was already aged and possessing resources that would normally take millions of years to develop.[24] There is no argument between Torah and fact: the issue is so-called scientific interpretation.

Due to the popularity of evolutionary theory, many people

feel that there is an irreconcilable difference between traditional Jewish belief and science. However, we must distinguish between theory and actual science. Scientific truth does not contradict the Torah. The ancient sages were well versed in such diverse fields as embryology,[25] medicine,[26] and astronomy. For example, rabbinic tradition gives the time between one new moon and the next as 29.53059 days. Thousands of years later, scientists at NASA, using sophisticated satellites and computers, determined the interval to be 29.530588 days, an insignificant difference of .000002![27] (The rabbis themselves wrote that their calculation is not exact.) The hostility between science and religion stems from the Middle Ages, when the Catholic Church felt threatened by scientific knowledge and sought to suppress it. Judaism believes that the universe was created in one instant, thousands, not billions, of years ago. Scientific evidence points to the Big Bang, a moment in which the universe exploded from a small drop. Furthermore, both fossil and geological evidence do not contradict the Torah's dating system. Rabbinic tradition teaches us that this world is built on layers of earlier worlds.[28] One difficulty is that the cataclysmic events of the Flood wreaked havoc with the interior of the Earth.[29]

Following traditional Jewish thought, the Jewish calendar is based on the six days of creation being normal 24-hour periods. The calculation of Rosh Chodesh and Rosh HaShanah is based on the recurring *molad*, the monthly rebirth of the moon. This calculation begins from Creation and assumes a normal time span of six days.[30]

IS THE TORAH RACIST?: Racists who believe that the Torah relegates blacks to a position of inferiority have misinterpreted the well-known story of Noah cursing his son Ham with servitude. In fact, until recently the Mormon Church based its exclusion of black people on this Biblical episode. In reality, no such conclusion can be drawn. The Torah specifically states that G-d *blessed* Ham, thus rendering any curse ineffective.[31] It was Ham's son Canaan, who may have been either white or black, who was cursed.

(Ham's son Kush, who is assumed to be black, was specifically *not* cursed.) Jews accept converts without regard to skin color or race. The Torah's view of racism may be summed up in the succinct saying of the Mishnah: "Adam was created single so that no human should be able to claim, 'My ancestor is greater than yours.' "[32]

IDOLATRY: Scripture is replete with descriptions of bizarre idolatrous rituals as well as admonitions against idol worship. Maimonides traced the historical development of this aberration from the times of Adam's grandson Enoch. Maimonides writes that the origin of idolatry stems from a noble, but erroneous, misconception: we honor G-d by honoring His servants, such as the heavenly bodies, similar to the way that an earthly ruler is honored when respect is shown to his appointed officials. Eventually, this practice of honoring G-d's servants evolved into full-scale worship of the forces of nature on their own merit, and the existence of the true G-d became virtually forgotten.[33] Elaborate rituals sprang up around the idols. Orgies, fertility rites, and human sacrifice were common, at times widespread. Great temples were constructed, and idolatrous icons and statuettes abounded in every home. Further, unlike the true G-d, the pagan gods were seen as capricious beings who had to be propitiated with sacrifices, possessed every human vice, and were totally unconcerned with man's moral and ethical development. Because of idol worship, a spiritual torpor reigned over the world until the advent of Abraham.

ABRAHAM AND THE RISE OF JUDAISM: Abraham faced struggles that no other person experienced before or since. As a result of successfully overcoming these challenges, he became the father of the Jewish people. When yet a child, without the positive role models of parents, teachers, and society, he discovered the existence of G-d entirely on his own.[34] At great personal risk, he introduced the major principles of monotheism to a world in which the concept did not exist. Ordered by the wicked King Nimrod to recant his beliefs, Abraham refused, even when threatened with death. His staunch refusal was all the more remarkable, considering that Abraham had never received communication from G-d and thus had no idea of being saved or of earning eternal reward in the next world. Miraculously, Abraham emerged from Nimrod's fiery furnace unscathed.[35]

Later, Abraham left his hometown, Ur, in southern Iraq, and settled in the land of Israel, where he taught multitudes the Jewish concept of G-d. He is One, Abraham said, timeless, incorporeal, benevolent, and demands moral and ethical behavior from mankind. At the age of seventy,[36] Abraham received a prophetic vision in which G-d promised that Abraham would become the forerunner of a nation totally devoted to G-d's service, and that this nation would inherit the land of Israel. The promise was realized when at age ninety Abraham's wife Sarah gave birth to his son Isaac.

G-d tested Abraham's faith ten times. The greatest of these challenges was the *Akeidah*, the command to offer Isaac as a sacrifice. Aside from the personal tragedy of losing his son, Abraham faced the total destruction of his life's work. First, Abraham's greatest desire was to establish a nation that would continue his G-dly mission, a dream that would not be realized if Isaac perished. Second, Abraham would be revealed as a charlatan and a fraud. Indeed, for many years Abraham preached that G-d abhors human sacrifice, and suddenly he would stand accused of that very same crime! Nevertheless, Abraham responded to G-d's command with alacrity. At the last moment, as Abraham held the knife above the neck of his bound son, G-d told Abraham to desist and gave him the promise of eternal survival, which has sustained the Jewish people to this day. Countless Jews throughout the generations have emulated Abraham and Isaac, and have given up their lives, when necessary, *al kiddush HaShem*, to sanctify G-d's name. Abraham died in 2023 at the age of 175.

ISAAC: Isaac's history was very different than that of his father. Unlike Abraham, Isaac was born in the land of Israel, and lived and died there. Unlike his father, a master teacher, Isaac saw as his life's mission the solidifying of the spiritual foundation of the Jewish people through internal self-perfection. Therefore, he did not reach out to the masses in the manner of Abraham, although Issac did not entirely neglect outreach activities.[37] When there was a famine, Isaac settled in the Philistine area of southwestern Israel. A remarkable episode took place there, one that is a portent for the Jewish experience throughout the exile: the story of Isaac and the wells. The following chart displays the striking similarities between Isaac's life and future events and also illustrates the concept of *maaseh avos siman l'banim*: the events of our forefathers' lives are a paradigm for those of their descendants.

Isaac died in 2228 at the age of 180.

Verse in Genesis (Chapter 26)	Parallel in Jewish History
v. 1 — "And there was a famine in the land...and Isaac went to Abimelech the king of the Philistines, to Gerar."	Jews migrate to a new land seeking economic opportunity
v. 12–13 — "And Isaac planted in that year, and he found in that year a hundredfold, and G-d blessed him. And the man became greater and greater, until he was exceedingly great."	Jews prosper beyond the level of the native inhabitants
v. 14 — "And he had much sheep and cattle and many workers, and the Philistines were jealous of him."	Newfound Jewish wealth provokes animosity of host nation

v. 15 — "And all the wells that his father's servants dug...the Philistines stopped up and filled them with earth."	Anti-Jewish discrimination
v. 16 — "And Abimelech said to Isaac, 'Go from us for you are too powerful for us.' "	Expulsion
v. 19–21 — "And Isaac's servants dug a well... And the shepherds of Gerar fought over it, saying 'the water is ours...' "	Persecution
v. 22 — "And he moved from there and dug another well and they did not fight over it..."	Jews find peace in another place
v. 26–28 — "And Abimelech came to him... And Isaac asked them, 'Why do you come to me after you hated and expelled me?' And they replied, 'We have seen how G-d is with you...and we wish to make a treaty with you.' "	Jews are invited back not because they are liked but because they are economically advantageous
v. 29 — "Lest you do evil with us, just as we have not touched you and have only done good to you."	Anti-Semites deny ever mistreating Jews

JACOB: Of all the Patriarchs, the Torah devotes the most space relating the events of Jacob's life. More than any individual in Scripture, Jacob typifies the Jewish people in exile. He is the greatest personification of *maaseh avos siman l'banim*, a most important concept that teaches us the vicissitudes of this long exile are not haphazard coincidences, but rather are carefully orchestrated Divine events that first appeared in the dawn of our history.[38] Just as Jacob only understood the meaning of his suffering at the end of his life, so too will the Jewish people finally realize the significance of their trials and tribulations at the time of the Messianic Era.

Jacob was born in 2108, when Isaac was sixty years old. At the age of fifteen, he purchased the birthright from his twin brother Esau. This meant that Jacob's branch of the family would be the nucleus of a nation that would devote itself to the service of G-d. When Jacob was sixty-three, an event took place that would have major ramifications in Jewish history. At his mother Rebecca's command, Jacob impersonated his brother and received from Isaac the blessings meant for Esau. Bestowal of these blessings meant that Isaac validated Jacob's birthright and that he was designated as the builder of the eternal Chosen People. Esau realized what he had forfeited and developed a virulent hatred toward Jacob.

This implacable enmity has been passed down throughout the generations and is the source of anti-Semitism.[39] The Roman Church, descended from Esau, saw itself as the New Israel, replacing the Jewish people whom G-d had supposedly rejected, Heaven forbid. The Nazis, too, viewed themselves as the Master Race whose mission it was to eradicate the memory of the Jewish people.

Not all attacks on the Jewish people's special status are so brazen. In today's egalitarian society, the concept of the Chosen People has been greatly misunderstood. First, the meaning of "chosen" is that Jews have a covenantal relationship with G-d to bring the world to spiritual perfection by keeping the Torah's commandments and serving as spiritual role models, the proverbial light among the nations. Second, the covenantal relationship carries no notion of racial superiority, for any person may join the Jewish religion and become a member of the Chosen People regardless of race, color, or national origin.[40]

After receiving Isaac's blessings, Jacob fled his brother's anger and settled in his uncle Laban's house, where he worked for twenty years. Here he married his four wives, who gave birth to eleven sons, who in turn became the ancestors of the Tribes of Israel. (The twelfth son, Benjamin, was born after Jacob left Laban.) An episode took place here that bears an uncanny resemblance to the Jewish experience throughout the ages:

After leaving Laban's house, Jacob wrestled with Esau's guardian angel and defeated him, Jacob sustaining an injury to

Verse in Genesis (Chapters 30–31)	Parallel in Jewish History
v. 30:30 — "You [Laban] had very little before I came, but since then it has increased and become very substantial."	Jews build up country
v. 30:43 — "The man [Jacob] became tremendously wealthy."	Jews prosper in exile
v. 31:1 — "And he heard that Laban's sons were saying, 'Jacob has taken *everything* belonging to our father and has become rich by taking our father's property.'"	Jews accused of exploiting country despite earning their wealth honestly
v. 31:7 — "'Your father swindled me and changed his mind about my pay at least ten times, but G-d would not let him harm me.'"	Jews prosper despite all restrictions and discriminatory laws
v. 31:36–42 — "Jacob argued with Laban, 'What is my crime?...What did you find from your house?...Never once did I take a ram from your flocks as food.'"	Jews try to prove their innocence to their anti-Semitic accusers
v. 31:43 — "Laban replied, 'The daughters are my daughters, the flocks are my flocks. All that you see is mine!'"	Jewish entreaties fall on deaf ears

his thigh in the process. This event foreshadowed what would transpire to the Jews in exile. The Jewish people survive, but suffer both physical and spiritual injuries.[41] Tragically, countless numbers of Jews have perished throughout the ages, and countless others have been lost through assimilation, but the Jewish people have survived. When Jacob encountered Esau, who had come to kill our Patriarch, Jacob, through a combination of humility and diplomacy, emerged unscathed. Jacob's behavior toward Esau is described at great length in the Torah and has served as the example par excellence of how Jews are supposed to deal with an enemy that has physical superiority.[42] Jacob died in 2255 at the age of 147. With the birth of his twelve sons, the foundation of the Jewish people was finally set.

JOSEPH: "All that happened to Jacob happened to Joseph" (*Rashi*, Genesis 37:2). The events of Joseph's life likewise reverberate throughout Jewish history. Rabbinic tradition teaches that as a punishment for the ten brothers' sale of Joseph, ten great sages, including Rabbi Akiva, were brutally executed by the Romans.[43] The wife of Potiphar falsely imprisoned Joseph in Egypt on trumped-up charges of immorality; likewise, Christians in the Middle Ages killed their own children and accused innocent Jews of ritual murder, and in the United Nations, Israel stands accused of the most heinous crimes by nations such as Syria and Iraq, who have massacred countless numbers of their own citizens. In addition, Joseph's rise to power in Egypt is the first of many cases of Jews succeeding in a foreign country. Joseph died in Egypt in 2309 at the age of 110, having served as the Divine conduit for bringing Jacob's family to Egypt to escape hunger in the land of Israel.

Chapter 2

FROM SLAVERY TO MONARCHY

SLAVERY IN EGYPT: At first, the family of Jacob entered Egypt as honored, invited guests. With the passage of time, however, things turned drastically worse. Not long before Jacob's family arrived, the Egyptians threw off the yoke of a foreign occupier, the Asiatic Hyksos people.[1] As a result, Egypt became a xenophobic society. When the Jews began multiplying rapidly and penetrating all areas of Egyptian society,[2] a great backlash ensued.

The following chart notes the similarities between Egyptian slavery and the Nazi Holocaust:

Verse in Exodus	Event in the Holocaust
1:7 — "The Israelites were fertile and prolific and their population increased."	Jews prosper in Germany
1:8 — "A new king, who did not know of Joseph, came into power over Egypt."	Hitler assumes power in Germany
1:9–10 — "He announced to his people, 'Behold the Israelites are becoming too numerous and strong for us. We must deal wisely with them. Otherwise, they will join our enemies and drive us from the land.' "	Hitler claims the Jews are a threat to Germany and strong measures must be taken against them

1:11–12 — "They appointed officers to crush their spirits with hard labor. They [Israelites] built cities... And they [Egyptians] became disgusted because of the children of Israel."	Discrimination: the Nuremberg Laws distinguished between duties of citizens (Aryans) and state subjects (Jews)
1:13–14 — "And the Egyptians forced the Israelites to do back-breaking work. They embittered their lives with difficult labor."	Slave labor, ghettoes, dehumanization
1:16, 22 — "And the king of Egypt said... 'If a son is born you shall kill him.'"	Extermination
2:23 — "And the king of Egypt died, and the Israelites groaned and cried out." (Rashi comments that Pharaoh became ill and used blood of Jewish children as a cure.)	Nazi medical experiments on Jews

THE EXODUS: There are several figures given for the length of the Egyptian exile. Genesis 15:13 mentions 400 years, while Exodus 12:40 puts its duration at 430 years. The Midrash arrives at another three numbers: 210, 116, and 86. The following list places each number in proper perspective: [3]

Year 2018 — At the *Bris Bein Habesarim* (Covenant between the Parts), G-d tells Abraham that his descendants will be exiles in Egypt for 400 years. This is 430 years before the Exodus.

Year 2048 — Isaac is born. The 400 years of exile date from his birth.

Year 2238 — Jacob's family comes to Egypt. This is 210 years before the Exodus.

Year 2332 — Egyptian slavery begins after the death of Levi, the last of Jacob's sons. This is 116 years before the Exodus.

Year 2362 — The most intense persecution, which lasts eighty-six years, begins when Miriam, the sister of Moses, is born. Her name means "bitter" in Hebrew.

Year 2448 — The Exodus.

PURPOSE OF SLAVERY IN EGYPT: The long servitude had a positive effect on the character of the nation in several ways. First, the Jewish people developed a sense of gratitude toward G-d and therefore readily accepted the Torah. In the absence of such a national mood, Moses would have had to debate the pros and cons of adopting the Torah's lifestyle with each individual Jew.[4] Second, a Jew is constantly duty-bound to keep the mitzvos; Egyptian slavery provided the requisite sense of subservience to a master.[5] Third, Jews learned to sympathize with disadvantaged people. Numerous commandments require the Jew to part with his hard-won earnings and share them with others. The Torah often mentions in connection with such precepts, "And you shall remember that you were slaves in Egypt; therefore, I command you to do this thing."[6] Even Jews who strayed from Jewish observance have still exhibited this basic Jewish characteristic and have been active in founding the labor-union, socialist, and civil rights movements, and in establishing hospitals and charitable foundations.

MIRACLES OF THE EXODUS: The period of the Exodus was a time of spectacular, open miracles witnessed by millions of Jews and Egyptians and unprecedented in history before or since. Ramban[7] explains that at the formation of the Jewish religion, miracles of such magnitude were necessary to prove the existence of G-d beyond a shadow of a doubt. If the Jews who received the Torah did not experience G-d personally, they would not have transmitted the Torah to future generations and Judaism would have died out, G-d forbid. Therefore, once the veracity of the Torah rested on solid foundations, there was no need for G-d to perform further miracles to satisfy every skeptic. In the words of the historian, Paul Johnson:

"The stories of the plagues of Egypt, and the other wonders and miracles which preceded the Israelite break-out, have so dominated our reading of Exodus that we sometimes lose sight of the sheer physical fact of the successful revolt and escape of a slave-people, the only one recorded in antiquity. It became an overwhelming memory for the Israelites who participated in it. For those who heard, and later read, about it, the Exodus gradually replaced the Creation itself as the central, determining event in Jewish history. Something happened at the frontiers of Egypt that persuaded the eyewitnesses that G-d had intervened directly and decisively in their fate. The way it was related and set down convinced subsequent generations that this unique demonstration of G-d's mightiness on their behalf was the most remarkable event in the whole history of nations" (*A History of the Jews*, p. 26).

ARCHAEOLOGY AND THE TORAH: In the nineteenth century, German Bible scholars led by Julius Wellhausen developed the spurious study known as Biblical Criticism. Influenced by anti-Semitism,[8] they said that the stories of Genesis and Exodus were myths, written many years after the traditional date of the giving of the Torah. However, "truth sprouts from the ground" (Psalms 85:12), and modern scientific archaeology has completely refuted this theory. Recent discoveries include:

1) Excavations made at Ur, Abraham's birthplace, show a city with a sophisticated level of culture, contradicting the theory that the ancestors of the Jews were desert savages.[9]

2) Tablets at Nuzi contain patriarchal-type names, such as Abram, Jacob, Leah, Laban, and Ishmael. Issues such as childlessness, divorce, inheritance, and birthrights are dealt with in a similar fashion as in Genesis. In the words of Paul Johnson: "All this Genesis material dealing with the problems of immigration, of water wells and contracts and birthrights, is fascinating because it places the patriarchs so firmly in their historical setting, and testifies to the Bible's great antiquity and authenticity."[10]

3) Egyptian hieroglyphics and pictorial representations in tombs show one of the pharaohs investing his vizier with linen garments, a royal signet ring, and a special gold neck chain. This is exactly the way Joseph was honored by Pharaoh (Genesis 41:42). Egyptian records also speak of a man of Semitic origin rising to power at the royal court.[11]

4) A papyrus from Rameses II's reign, Leiden 348, states: "Distribute grain rations to the soldiers and to the Habiru who transport stones to the great pylon of Rameses,"[12] corresponding to the facts presented in the biblical narrative.

5) The Ipuwer Papyrus, Leiden 344, is an Egyptian account of plagues striking the country. It mentions the plagues of blood, hail, death of cattle, and vast numbers of people dying. Mention is also made of a population fleeing.[13] Of course, Jews throughout the ages have always relied upon the Tanach, the Scriptures, as interpreted by the rabbinic sages, as the true and complete account of historical events. In this age of skepticism, however, it is important for those who respect non-Jewish sources to make use of secular testimony.[14]

RECEIVING THE TORAH: Seven weeks after the Exodus, the defining moment in Jewish and world history arrived. In total unity,[15] unequaled before or since, the Jewish people lovingly agreed to accept the Torah, and the purpose of creation thus was realized.[16] Their decision was not based on impulse or mass hysteria. Instead, it was a conscious, rational choice made with a full understanding of the great ramifications that would come about as a result of this undertaking. The three million Jews who received the Torah were intelligent, highly critical human beings who could not have been forced or bamboozled by Moses into accepting the Torah. At Sinai, the entire Jewish people attained the prophetic level of Moses when G-d directly transmitted the first two commandments to them face-to-face.[17] (Moses transmitted the other eight of the Ten Commandments.) The magnitude of the moment, when the Jews became G-d's people, was indelibly sealed into the Jewish soul for all time.

Matan Torah is the basis of Jewish belief. The claim of a public, national revelation distinguishes Judaism from all other religions. The Torah repeatedly exhorts the Jewish people not to forget what each had *personally* seen and to transmit it to his and her children. If the parents had not individually witnessed such a cataclysmic event, they would not have believed it, and would never have taught their children something they thought to be false.[18] While it is certainly possible for parents to teach lies to their children if they are *legends* the parents believe that happen to be false, or if the lies are fallacious *ideals* the parents believe, such as Communism, nevertheless parents will never wittingly teach their children something they know to be patently untrue. Furthermore, such a transmittal of fallacious information simply could not occur over scores of generations literally all across the globe. The famous author James Michener, in *The Bridge at Andau*,[19] writes that students began the Hungarian Revolution of 1956 because in school they learned the falsified Communist history of their country, while their parents taught them the truth at home. The contradiction between truth and falsehood inspired them to revolt.

It is obvious from the Torah itself that it is a Divine and not man-made document. The Torah commands that Jewish farmers in the land of Israel refrain from planting every seventh year, *shmittah*. After every seven *shmittah* cycles, *yovel*, the fiftieth Jubilee year, follows, thus making two consecutive years in which agricultural activity is proscribed. The Torah then *guarantees* that there will be sufficient crops in the sixth year to last the following three years.[20] No human, no matter how powerful, would be so foolish to make such a promise. In another example, all Jewish men are required to visit the Holy Temple in Jerusalem on the holidays of Pesach, Shavuos, and Sukkos, thereby leaving the borders undefended. The Torah then assures the Jewish people that no enemy will dare to attack.[21] Once again, no human would — or could — make such a promise. When discussing the formation of a Jewish army on the battlefield, the Torah commands that all soldiers who are afraid should return home.[22] Historically, nations have always tried to recruit as many soldiers as possible and have unremittingly punished draft-dodgers. Once again, no human has ever said such a thing — especially in time of war.

Concurrent with the Written Law (the five books of the Torah), G-d transmitted the oral explanations (*Torah sheba'al peh*) to Moses.[23] It is evident from many mitzvos that such oral explanations are necessary. For example, the Torah prescribes the death penalty for working on the Sabbath, but does not define exactly what work is. In regard to Yom Kippur, the Torah says, "Any soul who does not afflict itself will be cut off (*kares,* spiritual extinction) from its people" (Leviticus 23:29). As with work, the Torah does not define affliction. On Succos, Jews are commanded to take the "fruit of a beautiful tree" (ibid. 40). While there are certainly many beautiful fruit-bearing trees, the oral tradition specifies which one is proper for the mitzvah. It is only the oral tradition as transmitted by G-d to Moses that defines thirty-nine major categories of labor prohibited on the Sabbath, affliction on Yom Kippur as fasting, and the fruit of the beautiful tree as the *esrog* (citron). Perhaps the most famous example of the oral tradition elucidating the written Torah is the verse "An eye for an eye" (Exodus 21:24), which does not call for maiming an injurer but instead for assessing monetary payment for injuries accrued.

Clearly, Western civilization bases its morals and ethics on the Torah. In the ancient world, however, the Torah's ideals were revolutionary. Concepts such as respect for human life, monotheism, social welfare, and the rights of such disadvantaged people as widows and slaves simply did not exist. Even worse, human sacrifice was prevalent, and in many societies, such as the Greek, Chinese, and Eskimo, female or deformed infants were killed or left to die. In some American Indian tribes, widows were robbed of all their possessions and left to freeze outdoors.[24] With time, the Torah's ideals have spread throughout the world. Indeed, the Torah is the perennial global best-seller, having been translated into every language on Earth.

THE FORTY YEARS IN THE DESERT: The generation that lived in the desert was the greatest in Jewish history, experiencing constant miracles including the manna, clouds of glory, and the constant manifestation of G-d's Divine Presence, the *Shechinah*, in the Tabernacle, the *mishkan*. All the Jews' physical needs were miraculously fulfilled, enabling them to use their utmost ability to learn the entire Torah from Moses, the greatest teacher in Jewish history. Over a forty-year period they only committed ten sins, but G-d judged the Jewish people harshly, commensurate with their greatness, and they were not permitted to enter the land of Israel. They did not have a slave mentality, as many erroneously claim, but instead were intelligent, thinking people who constantly criticized Moses and argued with him over anything not meeting their approval. To this day, the Jewish people constantly yearn to recapture the splendor of those times, as King Solomon so eloquently expresses in the Song of Songs (1:2): "Communicate Your innermost wisdom to me again in loving closeness."

CONQUEST OF THE LAND OF ISRAEL: After the death of Moses in 2488, his disciple Joshua led the Jewish people into the land of Israel. The campaign of conquest took seven years, and the division of the land among the tribes took another seven years.[25] Great miracles, such as the walls of Jericho collapsing, accompanied the fighting, but the most spectacular of all was Joshua's stopping the sun at Gibeon. This event is so famous that it is recorded in the lore of peoples around the world, including the American Indians, Chinese, and Greeks.[26] In all, thirty-one kings were subdued, although the Jews did not conquer the entire Promised Land. Joshua also set up the Tabernacle at Shiloh in 2502, which lasted 369 years. Joshua died in 2516.

THE SEVEN NATIONS OF THE LAND OF ISRAEL: The Torah exhorts the Jewish people to annihilate the Seven Nations: men, women, and children, everyone down to the very last infant. To the Western mind, this seeming ethnic cleansing seems barbaric, reminiscent of the Nazi extermination of the Jews. However, there are several very important distinctions that must be made. What if a parent or a physician knew the future of a newborn infant — and that that future was Joseph Mengele, standing at the train ramp in Auschwitz, selecting Jews for the gas chambers. Killing such an infant would be doing a great service for mankind. Of course, under normal circumstances, since no one knows the future, no one has the right to take someone's life.

In the case of the Seven Nations, however, G-d Himself tells the Jewish people to execute these nations based on His knowledge of what will transpire. G-d knew that these nations were the most depraved on earth, killing and torturing children in the most savage idolatrous rituals.[27] Since immorality and corruption completely permeated their society,[28] any contact would be most detrimental to the Jewish people — as was sadly borne out by history.[29] Joshua first presented the Seven Nations with three choices.[30] If they accepted the Seven Noachide Laws, the basis of a civilized society, they would be permitted to remain in the Land. Of the seven, only the Gibeonites availed themselves of this option. Those who did not accept the Noachide Laws were given the opportunity to leave, and the Girgashites did so, fleeing to Africa. (This historical fact was memorialized in a tablet called the Girgashite Stone, unearthed in North Africa. Inscribed on it are the words "We fled from Joshua the robber.") Finally, Joshua presented the remaining nations the choice to fight — and to face the consequences if defeated. They chose to fight — and were conquered. Nevertheless, even when killing out the nations, the Jewish people did not torture or degrade them, as the Nazis later did to the Jews.

THE *MISHKAN* AND THE PERMISSIBILITY OF *BAMOS*: The Torah prohibits offering sacrifices outside the Holy Temple (*mishkan*) on a private altar, or *bamah* (pl. *bamos*).[31] This was not a constant prohibition, and according to rabbinic tradition did not apply at certain times in Jewish history.[32] An understanding of this issue is essential when studying the books of Samuel and Kings. The following chart outlines the permitted and forbidden times for *bamos*:

Place of Central Tabernacle	Duration	Status of *Bamos*
The Desert	39 years (2449–2488)	Forbidden
Gilgal	14 years (2488–2502)	Permitted
Shiloh	369 years (2502–2871)	Forbidden
Nob	13 years (2871–2884)	Permitted
Gibeon	44 years (2884–2928)	Permitted
Jerusalem	410 years (2928–3338)	Forbidden

Bamos became permanently forbidden with the erection of the Holy Temple at Jerusalem. Therefore, sacrifices may not be offered today even though there is no Beis HaMikdash.

THE PERIOD OF THE JUDGES (*SHOFTIM*): The era of the Judges, which lasted 355 years (2516–2871),[33] was a most unique period in Jewish history. The Jews functioned without a central government for this entire era, with but two breakdowns in society: Micha's graven image and Gibeah's concubine. (By contrast, in 1977, in New York City, the lights went out for several days, and police were unable to patrol effectively. Countless numbers of business establishments were ransacked in a wild orgy of looting.)

Perhaps the period was so tranquil because of the great stature of the Judges — Chief Rabbis who held no political or governmental power and whose positions were not transferred to their sons. In 355 years there was only one grab for power: Abimelech ben Gideon ruled three years. Indeed, so exemplary was the Judges' rule that a king was unnecessary to enforce the Torah's laws. In addition, the collective conscience of the Jewish people united them in combating such deviancies as Micha's graven image and Gibeah's concubine.

However, since the Jewish people did not completely follow the Torah's admonition to expel the Seven Nations from the Land, some Jews became influenced by their neighbors' idol worship. As a result, from time to time the Jews were subjugated by neighboring countries. When they repented, G-d defeated their enemies. This cycle of spiritual backsliding and hostile oppression, followed by repentance and long periods of peace, occurred repeatedly during this era. Even during times of foreign invasion, however, the Jews continued to be protected by Divine Providence. In addition, a different nation conquered the Land each time, for a country that invades and occupies another and is forced to withdraw will be utterly ruthless if it succeeds in reconquering the land it lost.[34] The only exception was the Philistines, who, despite controlling the Jews numerous times, treated them relatively well. The easy treatment was due to the pact that Abraham and the Philistine king Abimelech concluded, forbidding each nation to mistreat the other.

There were many famous Judges, including:

Ehud: Left-handed warrior (a rarity). Judged eighty years. Defeated Moab.

Deborah: A female judge and one of the seven female prophets. She defeated the mighty Sisera.

Gideon: Defeated Midian. Refused to become king when offered.

Jephthah: Defeated Ammon. Upon returning victorious from the battlefield, he vowed to offer to G-d the first thing that left his home. Alas, his daughter came out first.

Ivtzan: Identical to Boaz. He married Ruth and is the ancestor of King David.

Samson: A Nazirite who performed supernatural feats with his Divine strength. He defeated the Philistines.

Eli: Judge and High Priest. He died when the Philistines destroyed the Tabernacle at Shiloh and captured the Holy Ark.

Samuel: Judged eleven years (2871–2882), ten years on his own and one year in conjunction with King Saul. Considered the last (and greatest) of the Judges, and the first of the Prophets.

THE ERA OF THE MONARCHY: Toward the end of Samuel's life, the Jewish people asked him to appoint a king, a request seemingly prompted by noble considerations. To enforce the laws of the Torah, keep the tribes united, prevent the kind of religious backsliding that had occurred during the time of the Judges, and organize an army, the Jewish people felt they needed a king. However, while the Torah indeed commands the Jewish people to appoint a king, asking for a monarch at that point in time was wrong.[35] In truth, the Jewish people should have waited until that current system of self-government had completely stopped working. In addition, having a temporal monarch would subject the Jewish people to natural forces and diminish the obvious manifestation of Divine Providence. Worst of all, the Jews did not want a king in order to fulfill the Torah's command; instead, they demanded a king so that they could be like the surrounding nations. As such, the early and presumptive institution of royalty was a disaster for the Jewish people. Corrupt monarchs split the nation, introduced idolatry on a large scale, and caused both the destruction of the First Temple and the Babylonian Exile.

KING SAUL: Saul is one of the most tragic figures in Scripture, a man who had a very difficult role to play. Sadly, due to several errors — which, although relatively minor, were judged very harshly by G-d — Saul's vast potential went unrealized. In fact, because he did not heed Samuel's instructions to obliterate totally the nation of Amalek, Saul lost his throne. As a result, he fell into a deep melancholy, relentlessly pursuing David, his designated successor. When faced with imminent capture by the

Philistines, Saul committed suicide on the battlefield. His rule lasted three years (2881–2884).[36] In summing up his career, the sages wrote: "Had David been Saul, and had Saul been David, G-d would have destroyed many Davids for his sake."[37]

SAUL'S PURSUIT OF DAVID: The sages listed five transgressions committed by Saul.[38] Interestingly enough, pursuing David is not one of them. This fact can be understood through a story related in the Talmud: Shimon HaTzadik, a High Priest in the days of the Second Temple, designated his younger son Chonyo as his successor. Chonyo voluntarily declined in favor of his older brother Shimi. However, although Chonyo had relinquished the position willingly, he was still jealous of the honor Shimi enjoyed and so devised a plan to remove his older brother from office. Chonyo told Shimi, who was ignorant of Temple procedure, that in honor of his inauguration he should wear women's garments. Shimi did so, and when the enraged onlookers saw such a sacrilege committed in proximity to the Altar, they wanted to execute Shimi. However, upon finding out that Chonyo had duped Shimi, they pursued Chonyo, who fled to Egypt.

Discussing this story, the sages remarked: "If even someone who voluntarily refuses a high position is so jealous, then surely one who loses an office he previously had would find it intolerable." Rabbi Yehoshua ben Perachiah commented: "Before I assumed high office, if anyone would have suggested that I take a prestigious position, I would have tied him in front of a lion. Now that I have the office, if someone would tell me to relinquish it, I would pour a pot of boiling water on his head. For Saul did not desire monarchy, but once he had it, he wanted to kill David." Removing a person from a position he held is tantamount to killing him, and it is human nature to try to prevent it from happening. Therefore, Saul is held relatively blameless for his pursuit of David.[39]

SAUL'S SUICIDE: Ordinarily, suicide is a grave sin, the equivalent of murder. A suicide forfeits his share in the World to Come and is buried at the edge of the cemetery. Saul's suicide, however, was permissible for several reasons.[40] Normally, even if a person is in a bleak situation, he should not lose hope of Divine rescue — G-d's salvation can come in the blink of an eye. Saul's situation was different, for Samuel had informed him prophetically that the king would die in the war with the Philistines. Furthermore, it would be a great *chilul HaShem* (desecration of G-d's Name) if the Jewish king were captured and tortured. Saul also feared that when his subjects realized he was captured, they would try to free him — despite overwhelming odds — thereby resulting in many deaths. Therefore, given the extraordinary circumstances, Saul properly took his own life. (Nevertheless, some rabbinic opinions hold that suicide is forbidden under all circumstances, and that Saul therefore acted improperly.)

Chapter 3

THE KINGDOMS OF ISRAEL AND JUDAH

KING DAVID: David was the greatest of the kings and the quintessential example of what a Jewish monarch should be.[1] He ruled for forty years (2884–2924), seven years in Hebron and thirty-three years in Jerusalem. David conquered Jerusalem in 2891 and made it the capital of the Jewish state, a status it has enjoyed since. Previously, Jerusalem was a non-Jewish Jebusite city.

No one in Scripture suffered as much as David. From the day he was anointed king by Samuel, he knew only tribulation, persecution, and humiliation, yet he could still say, "The Lord is my shepherd; I shall not want."[2] His psalms have captivated the hearts of the Jewish people for all time, enjoying the greatest familiarity next to the *Chumash*. Every noble emotion utilized in the service of G-d is encapsulated in the book of Psalms.

As king, David received a promise from G-d unique in the annals of mankind: the monarchy is his forever. No matter how corrupt his descendants become, they cannot lose it.[3] In the future, the Messianic redeemer will be from David's lineage. Although he is mentioned more than 1,000 times in Scripture — more than any other individual[4] — Bible critics doubted his existence until recent excavations revealed pottery inscribed with his name. David died at the age of seventy.

KING SOLOMON: Solomon ruled from 2924–2964, his reign constituting the Golden Age of the Jewish people. Wealthy, powerful, numerous, and united, under Solomon the Jewish people controlled all of Eretz Yisrael and dominated many lands beyond. Nevertheless, the seeds of destruction were planted during Solomon's reign. As the wisest of all men, he wrongly felt that the Torah's laws regarding monarchy did not apply to him.[5] Consequently, he amassed great wealth, acquired many horses, and married many women, all actions expressly prohibited by the Torah. Although his non-Jewish wives converted,[6] they also introduced idolatrous practices that became entrenched in Jewish society. Despite the troubling aspects of his monarchy, Solomon has vast achievements to his credit. He built the First Temple in 2928;[7] composed the Scriptural books of Proverbs, Ecclesiastes, and Song of Songs;[8] and instituted the rabbinic injunctions of *netilas yadayim*, the ritual washing of hands before a meal, and the Sabbath *eruv*.[9] Solomon died at the age of fifty-two.[10]

REHOBOAM AND THE DIVISION OF THE KINGDOM: Unfortunately, Rehoboam, Solomon's son and successor, did not possess even a fraction of his father's wisdom. When the people asked that he lighten their tax burden, he rejected the advice of his sages to acquiesce in their request, instead adopting the counsel of his youthful advisors to impose even harsher strictures. In response, the people revolted against Rehoboam's rule and appointed Jeroboam, of the tribe of Ephraim, as their ruler. Thus the Jewish people split into two monarchies: the Northern Kingdom, known as the Kingdom of Israel, or the Ten Tribes; and the Southern Kingdom, encompassing the tribes of Judah, Benjamin, and Levi. The Ten Tribes controlled the more fertile areas of the north and most of Eretz Yisrael, while the Kingdom of Judah included the spiritual centers of Jerusalem and the Beis HaMikdash.

JEROBOAM: A brilliant scholar and eminent personality, Jeroboam's character flaws caused him to create an irreversible rift among the Jewish people. Jeroboam realized that a threat to his legitimacy would arise when his people traveled to the Beis

HaMikdash on holidays. According to Jewish law, only the Davidic king may be seated in the Temple Courtyard, thus demonstrating Jeroboam an impostor.[11] He therefore posted guards at the borders to prevent access to the Temple. To compound his break with Jerusalem, Jeroboam set up shrines at Dan and Bethel, placed golden images of calves in them, and proclaimed new holidays. Although his motives for instituting these changes were political and not religious, these shrines spearheaded a new idolatrous cult among the Ten Tribes, which eventually destroyed them spiritually. Even when G-d offered him reward in Heaven second only to David's, Jeroboam refused to repent, as he could not bear not being the best.[12] His great potential squandered, he is held up as the prime example of "One who sins and leads many people astray."[13]

THE KINGDOM OF THE TEN TRIBES: Led by their rulers, who were universally wicked, the people of the Ten Tribes sank into a morass of idolatry and materialism. King Ahab's Phoenician wife Jezebel introduced the Baal cult, which ate at the very fabric of society. Despite the fact that the vast majority of the Ten Tribes kept the Torah, and the presence of such great prophets as Elijah, Elisha, Hosea, Amos, and Jonah, the people were virtually beyond salvation. Nevertheless, G-d continued to provide them with opportunities for repentance. Not even material or territorial blessings — as when Jeroboam II (3113–3153) enlarged the territory of the Ten Tribes to the greatest extent in Jewish history, even beyond the conquests of David and Solomon[14] — could sway the Ten Tribes from their disastrous course. Alas, the people did not repent, and the final decline began. In one final move, Hosea ben Elah, the last king of the Ten Tribes, removed the guards preventing the people from going to the Beis HaMikdash. However, they did not seize even this opportunity, and their lack of desire deprived them of all previous excuses for not worshipping at the Temple. Sadly, their fate was sealed.[15] The Kingdom of the Ten Tribes lasted 241 years, from 2964–3205.

EXILE OF THE TEN TRIBES: This traumatic event, which ripped away more than 80 percent of the Jewish people, the largest proportional loss in Jewish history, occurred in three stages over an eighteen-year period. First, in the year 3187, the tribes of Reuben, Gad, and half of Manasseh were taken into Assyrian captivity. Thus the tribes that had chosen in the time of Moses to live farthest from the spiritual center of the Jewish people were the first to be taken away. At this point, observance of *yovel* became impossible because it is contingent on the twelve tribes all residing in their ancestral lands.[16] As such, *yovel* became the first of many commandments that could not be fulfilled due to external circumstances. Shalmanessar, king of Assyria, completed the expulsion of the Jewish people in 3205.

THE TEN TRIBES TODAY: Few historical mysteries have fired the imaginations of people as much as the fate of the Ten Tribes. While countless legends have sprung up about them over the centuries, even today many groups claim descent from the Ten Tribes. Indeed, Jewish tradition teaches us that no tribe is extinct, and that these tribes will all be reconstituted in the days of the Messiah.[17] At the time of the expulsion, some were settled in Judah and had been even before the split, while others, in order to be able to worship at the Beis HaMikdash, came after Jeroboam broke away.[18] Some time later, the prophet Jeremiah journeyed to the lands east of Eretz Yisrael and brought back some of the Ten Tribes.[19] Even in Talmudic times, nearly 1,000 years after the exile, individuals were still able to trace their ancestry back to the Ten Tribes.[20] Regardless of where the Ten Tribes might be today, and despite this and other expulsions, the prophet Isaiah assures the Jewish people of a bright future: "And it will be on that day a great shofar will be blown, and those that are lost in Assyria and cast away in the land of Egypt will come and bow to G-d at the Holy Mount in Jerusalem" (Isaiah 27:13).

THE KINGDOM OF JUDAH: Unlike the kings of the Ten Tribes, who were all wicked, the twenty Davidic monarchs who ruled after Solomon ranged from extremely righteous individuals, such as Hezekiah and Jotham, to such grossly wicked personalities as

Manasseh and Jehoiakim. Although spiritual standards were higher in Judah than in the Ten Tribes, due to the presence of the Beis HaMikdash, idolatry eroded society and was a major factor in the destruction of the Temple. The Kingdom of Judah lasted 454 years (2884–3338), 133 years longer than the Kingdom of the Ten Tribes. Prominent Judean kings and queens include:

Rehoboam: His misguided policies caused the split of the kingdom.

Asa: Ruled forty-one righteous years, destroyed idols, brought prosperity.

Jehoshaphat: A very righteous king who committed a fatal error when he took Ahab's daughter, Athaliah, for his son Jehoram.

Athaliah: She exterminated the entire royal family except for the infant Joash, who was hidden in the Temple. Ruled as queen for six years and was fanatically idolatrous. She was slain in a coup engineered by the *kohen gadol*, the high priest, who anointed Joash and placed him on the throne.

Joash: A tragic figure, he started off as a righteous king and oversaw the repair of the Temple; later, however, he imagined himself to be divine and died a wicked man. When the prophet Zechariah rebuked him in the Beis HaMikdash, Joash ordered his men to kill the prophet. The murder was an enormous national crime and had terrible ramifications later in Jewish history.[21]

Uzziah: A righteous king, he made a tragic mistake in thinking that the king could officiate in the Beis HaMikdash. As Uzziah approached the altar to burn incense, he was stricken with *tzara'as*, a skin condition that renders one ritually impure. In accordance with Torah law, Uzziah was banished outside Jerusalem and abdicated the throne in favor of his son Jotham.

Jotham: Considered by the Talmud to be one of the greatest people of all time,[22] he is the exemplar of the son who honors his father. Upon assuming the throne during Uzziah's lifetime, Jotham demonstrated respect for his father by issuing all royal proclamations in Uzziah's name as long as the man lived.

Hezekiah: The greatest of the Judean kings since David, he did what no other king was able to do: eliminate the individual *bamos*. Spreading Torah knowledge throughout the land, until even young children knew the complicated laws of ritual purity,[23] Hezekiah's engineers bored the Siloam Tunnel through solid rock to assure Jerusalem a water supply. During his reign the Ten Tribes were exiled, and a few years later the Assyrian king Sennacherib captured much of Judah and surrounded Jerusalem. Upon the advice of the prophet Isaiah, Hezekiah refused to surrender — and in a single night the entire Assyrian army of nearly 200,000 men was struck dead by G-d. Sennacherib, virtually the sole survivor, returned home and was assassinated by his sons. (While Bible critics have ridiculed this story, excavations of Assyrian ruins have confirmed it.) Later Judean kings appear in chapter 4.

IDOLATRY: Throughout Tanach, the Jewish people are taken to task for the sin of idolatry. Despite the stern admonitions, the overwhelming majority of the Ten Tribes — and certainly Judah — did not worship idols. Even those who did were also Torah-observant Jews in all other respects. Ahab, for example, the idolatrous king of the Ten Tribes, kept a kosher kitchen.[24] Currently, by contrast, it is almost impossible to find an average religious Jew walking into a church to celebrate Mass. However, in the times of the First Temple, even great scholars were subject to the extraordinary temptation of idolatry. At that time, too, people felt no contradiction in their behavior: they could pray the afternoon Minchah service to G-d, take out a statuette during the customary short break between Minchah and the evening Maariv service, bow to it, and then return to synagogue for Maariv! How could they do so? So that people could be tested in their faith, G-d permitted idols seeming powers. Therefore, as the spiritual level of the Jewish people declined after the destruction of the first Beis HaMikdash, and idolatry would be too great a temptation for the average person to resist, G-d removed the inclination toward it.[25] Nevertheless, idolatry was only removed from Jews who have some connection with Judaism; those who grow up with no Jewish background can fall prey to it.[26] Sadly, today there are many Jews who are caught up in Christian, Hindu, or other pagan cults.

BAMOS: A constant criticism in Tanach, even of the righteous kings of Judah, was that they did not uproot the practice of offering sacrifices to G-d on private altars outside the Temple. While still forbidden, this sin stands as a testament to the great spirituality of those generations. Today, of all the sins a person has a desire to commit, offering sacrifices on *bamos* must rank near the bottom. In those days, however, people felt a palpable closeness and awareness of G-d's presence and wanted to have a strong, personal connection with the Divine. These spiritual giants felt that they were capable of achieving this at any time and in any place, and so did not feel that the Beis HaMikdash, with its hierarchy of priests, was necessary to commune with G-d. Here, the people made the tragic mistake of letting their emotions, no matter how noble, rule them; they did not realize that closeness to G-d must be achieved on His terms and with His rules, and not any other way.[27]

PROPHECY: For 1,000 years, from 2448–3448, prophecy was highly prevalent among the Jewish people. During this time, there were more than one million prophets, both men and women; nevertheless, only prophecies necessary for all time were recorded: forty-eight men and seven women.[28] A person could only become a prophet if he or she was of great intellectual stature and was recognized by his or her generation as being extremely righteous. To this end, the Great Sanhedrin, the Supreme Court comprised of the seventy-one greatest Torah scholars of the Jewish people, subjected persons who claimed to have had prophetic revelations to a rigorous examination process. In accordance with Torah law, charlatans were executed, thus preventing many impostors from arising.[29]

Once a prophet was certified as true, all his words had to be heeded. If it was necessary, the prophet was even permitted to suspend a Torah law temporarily, with the exception of idolatry. In a contest with the Baal priests to prove them wrong, Elijah, for example, offered a sacrifice outside the Temple.[30]

All told, a prophet's main function was to make the people aware of their faults and the future consequences of their actions. He also anointed kings and prophetically advised monarchs on such matters as going to war and forging alliances. In addition, the prophets played a major role in transmitting Torah from generation to generation.[31] This aspect, however, was due to their being the leading Torah scholars of the Sanhedrin and not specifically because they were prophets, for a prophet was not permitted to decide Torah law through prophecy.[32] In chapter 4 the termination of prophecy is discussed.

MANASSEH: Although King Hezekiah raised the spiritual level of the Jewish people to its highest degree since the days of David, his wicked son Manasseh undid all his work. His disastrous reign of fifty-five years introduced paganism on a national level and created a mass movement to imitate the surrounding nations' idolatrous ways. (Previously, idol worship was only on an individual basis.) Manasseh also ruthlessly suppressed any dissent, and even executed the great prophet Isaiah, perhaps his harshest critic.[33] Although Manasseh repented later in life, the damage he caused was irreversible. His son Amon followed him, and during his short, two-year rule actually outdid his father in wickedness. To demonstrate his contempt for G-d, Amon burned Torah scrolls and placed an idol in the *Kodesh HaKodashim*, the holiest part of the Beis HaMikdash.[34]

JOSIAH: This highly righteous monarch represented the last hope to save both the kingdom and the Temple from Divine wrath. During his thirty-one-year reign, Josiah almost single-handedly forestalled the destruction. Initiating a national *teshuvah* (repentance) movement, and nearly eradicating idol worship in his kingdom, Josiah also made badly needed repairs in the Beis HaMikdash and purified it from all vestiges of idolatry. At the end, realizing that destruction was imminent, Josiah also hid the Holy Ark and several other sacred objects to prevent them from falling into enemy hands.[35] Along with the prophet Jeremiah, Josiah brought back remnants of the Ten Tribes from their exile in the East.[36]

Finally, Josiah's tragic death was a calamity of such major proportions that it is commemorated for all time in the special Tishah B'Av service, the *Kinnos*. In order to attack Assyria, Pharaoh Necho, the king of Egypt, requested Josiah's permission to allow Egyptian troops safe passage across the land of Israel. Because G-d had promised the Jewish people that when they do His will, "A sword will not pass through your land" (Leviticus 26:6), implying that even a force not intent upon invasion would not enter Eretz Yisrael, Josiah refused. Josiah was convinced that the people were righteous, and had even sent detectives all over the land to eradicate idols. Nevertheless, some people employed ingenious methods to conceal them — a fact which Josiah did not know. The Prophet Jeremiah did, understanding also that the Jewish people were not on the lofty spiritual level Josiah imagined them to be. As such, Jeremiah advised Josiah to allow the Egyptians to pass through. Unfortunately, Josiah did not heed Jeremiah's advice and forcibly attempted to prevent the Egyptians from crossing Israel. The king was killed in battle, and with his death the last opportunity to stop the destruction evaporated.[37] Josiah died in 3316, twenty-two years before the Temple's destruction.

JEHOIAKIM: He was the worst of all the kings of Judah. During his reign, Babylon (Iraq), after overthrowing Assyria, became the dominant power in the Middle East. In 3319, Babylon's King Nebuchadnezzar conquered Eretz Yisrael, allowing Jehoiakim nominal independence while in reality making him a vassal. When Jehoiakim chafed under Babylonian rule and rebelled, Nebuchadnezzar executed him in 3327 and installed Jehoiakim's son Jehoiachin on the throne.

JEHOIACHIN: While he ruled only three months, nevertheless Jehoiachin presided over a major event in Jewish history. Eleven years before Nebuchadnezzar destroyed the Temple, he took Jehoiachin into Babylonian exile, along with 1,000 of the era's greatest Torah scholars. This momentous event, known as *galus hacheresh vehamasger*, the exile of the "artisans and gatekeepers" (II Kings 24:14) and explained in the Talmud as a reference to outstanding Torah scholars, was a Divine blessing in disguise.[38] Because these scholars were well treated in Babylon, they were able to set up a thriving Jewish community, with the infrastructure necessary to lessen the traumatic adjustment of the later exiles. Indeed, Babylon became a major Torah center for the next 1,500 years. This first wave of exiles took along earth from Eretz Yisrael and used it to build a special holy synagogue — *Bei Kenishta D'Shaf Veyasiv* — to recapture some of the Holy Land's sanctity.[39]

ZEDEKIAH: This tragic figure was the last king of Judah. Although he was personally righteous, he did not try to challenge the powerful, wicked noblemen, and as a result the first Beis HaMikdash was destroyed during his reign.[40] On the tenth of Teves 3336, two and a half years before the destruction, the Babylonians surrounded Jerusalem and besieged it. This tragic event is marked today by the fast of the tenth of Teves. In Jewish law, this fast day alone shares a special status with Yom Kippur in that it is never postponed. (Fasting is generally forbidden on the Sabbath.) According to the calendar, the tenth of Teves cannot fall on the Sabbath; however, if it could, the Jewish people would still fast.[41] However, the tenth of Teves is the only fast that can occur on Friday, and unlike other fast days, the fast is observed. Why of all fasts does this have such special significance? In general, the beginning of a tragedy is considered particularly severe.

THE DESTRUCTION OF THE FIRST TEMPLE: On the ninth of Tammuz, 3338 (the seventeenth of Tammuz, according to another opinion),[42] Nebuchadnezzar's legions breached the wall of Jerusalem. One month later, on the ninth of Av, Tishah B'Av, the Babylonian army burned the Beis HaMikdash. Zedekiah's sons were killed in front of him, and he was blinded and taken in chains to Babylon. Nebuzaradan, the chief executioner of Babylon, slaughtered myriads of Jews in the Beis HaMikdash as revenge for the murder of the Prophet Zechariah many years before.[43] Although the Jews were treated well once they arrived in Babylon, they suffered terribly until they arrived. While traveling the dismal road of exile, the Jews were cruelly tormented by the Arabs, who fed them salty fish and then gave the thirst-crazed Jews empty, air-filled canteens, causing many of them to die.[44] Many of the horrific events of this period are recorded in the Midrash and the *Kinnos*.

Scripture is replete with references to the *churban*, the destruction. The book of Lamentations, *Eichah*, composed by the prophet Jeremiah and read on the night of Tishah B'Av, graphically describes the travails of the Jewish people. Psalm 137 expresses the anguish of the Levites when ordered to play the Temple's sacred music for King Nebuchadnezzar: "How can we sing the songs of G-d on foreign soil? If I forget thee, O Jerusalem, let my right hand forget [its strength]." In great sorrow, they cut off their thumbs so as to be unable to entertain the heathen king with Divine sacrificial tunes.[45] The Haftarah of the second day of Rosh HaShanah contains the famous verse, "Rachel weeps for her children, for they are no more," along with the Divine promise that "the children will return to their borders." At traditional Jewish weddings, the groom puts ashes on his forehead, and a glass is broken under the *chupah*, the wedding canopy, to fulfill the verse, "If I do not lift Jerusalem above all my joy."[46]

GEDALIAH: After destroying the Beis HaMikdash and exiling many Jews, Nebuchadnezzar allowed a small farming element to remain in Eretz Yisrael. Gedaliah, a righteous man, was appointed governor over them, and a Babylonian garrison maintained order. When informed of a plot to unseat him, Gedaliah ignored it, not taking steps to protect himself. This inaction, criticized by the sages, resulted in tragedy.[47] On the second day of Tishrei, Jews assassinated Gedaliah. In retaliation, Nebuchadnezzar drove the rest of the Jews to Babylon and Eretz Yisrael was desolate for fifty-two years.[48] The Fast of Gedaliah commemorates this tragic event. (Although Gedaliah was killed on the second of Tishrei, that day is Rosh HaShanah, so the fast is pushed to the third day of Tishrei.)

Chapter 4

BABYLONIAN EXILE TO THE END OF THE BIBLICAL ERA

BENEFITS OF BABYLONIAN EXILE: This exile, although very traumatic, nevertheless was of great benefit to the Jewish people. There were no more corrupt kings or nobility — in Babylon the Torah scholars had complete power. Moreover, the Babylonians were not anti-Semites per se; while they only wanted to destroy Judah as an independent political power, they harbored no ill feelings toward the Jewish religion. Consequently, Jews were given their own cities, where earlier exiled Jews welcomed them warmly. The Talmud tells us that G-d chose Babylon as the place of exile for several reasons: Aramaic, the language of Babylon, was very similar to Hebrew. Abraham was born in Babylon, so the Jews were not regarded as foreigners. And it was easy to make a living from the abundant date trees. All told, then, life was pleasant for the Jews once they reached Babylon.[1]

THE JEWS IN BABYLON: Despite the relative ease of their exile, the Jews reacted in vastly different ways. Some of them, traumatized by the shock of heathens conquering Jerusalem, an occurrence they had previously deemed impossible, despaired of a future redemption, saying that G-d had severed His relationship with the Jewish people.[2] Others settled down comfortably and planned to assimilate. Accordingly, the prophet Ezekiel addressed both of these concerns. To the first group, he shared his prophetic visions of the Heavenly chariot and the Third Eternal Temple, telling them that G-d did not forsake them.[3] He also revived the dry bones in the Valley of Dura, symbolizing the rejuvenation of the Jewish people. To the second group, he burst out with fiery denunciations, saying that G-d will never allow the Jewish people to assimilate.[4] Nevertheless, many Jews did assimilate, and some even rose to prominence at Nebuchadnezzar's court. Daniel was appointed governor over the realm, while Hananiah, Mishael, and Azariah also attained high positions in the government.

THE FIERY FURNACE: King Nebuchadnezzar set up a giant statue and ordered each captive nation to send representatives. When his band struck up a tune, everyone was supposed to bow to the statue; those that refused would be tossed into a fiery furnace. Hananiah, Mishael, and Azariah, the Jewish delegates, consulted the prophet Ezekiel as to the proper course of action. Since the statue was not erected for idolatrous purposes, but only to honor the king, it would seem that Jewish law permitted bowing to it.[5] However, the three Jews decided that they would demonstrate that only G-d possesses unlimited power. Their plan was to refuse to prostrate before the statue, thereby defying Nebuchadnezzar publicly. Ezekiel, however, knowing that the punishment for such actions was death, instructed the three not to be present at the ceremony; if they went, he said, they should not expect G-d to save them miraculously.[6] Nevertheless, the three appeared, and when they proudly stood tall as everyone else bowed down, they were cast into the furnace. A spectacular miracle occurred, witnessed by the vast multitudes: the three walked out of the furnace without even being singed! After witnessing this great *kiddush HaShem*, the nations of the world gained a new respect for G-d and the Jewish people.

EVIL MERODACH: After a reign of forty-five years, Nebuchadnezzar died and was succeeded by his son Evil Merodach. This king treated the Jews favorably and released the former Judaic king Jehoiachin from prison. Subsequently, Jeconiah bore children in Babylon, thereby preserving the Davidic line and uplifting the spirits of the exiled Jewish people, who realized that this venerable house had not been destroyed by the exile. Hundreds of years later, there were still individuals who could trace their ancestry to this royal family.

JEREMIAH'S SEVENTY-YEAR PROPHECY: Jeremiah foretold that the Jewish people would be redeemed from their Babylonian exile after seventy years. "For thus said G-d: 'When seventy years are completed for Babylon, I shall remember you...to return you to this place' " (Jeremiah 29:10). However, Jeremiah did not clarify how those seventy years were to be calculated. The gentile kings who dominated the Jews awaited the fulfillment of this prophecy with great trepidation. Although these kings were all idolaters, they realized that Jeremiah was a prophet of the supreme G-d and that his words would indubitably come true. At the time, there were three possibilities as to when the seventy years began, but only one interpretation was correct. Two monarchs calculated the starting point erroneously and brought disaster upon themselves.

THE HANDWRITING ON THE WALL: Evil Merodach ruled twenty-three years, then his son Belshazzar assumed the throne in the year 3386. In 3389, the third year of his reign, he realized that seventy years had elapsed since Nebuchadnezzar's domination of the Jewish people in 3319. Assuming that the seventy-year period was up, and that the Jewish people would never leave exile, Belshazzar decided to celebrate. At his lavish feast, he demonstrated his contempt for G-d by drinking from the holy vessels that his grandfather Nebuchadnezzar had plundered from the Beis HaMikdash.[7] Suddenly, a hand appeared and wrote a mysterious inscription on the wall: *Mene, Mene, Tekel, Upharsin.* These words were written in a strange script and in an acrostic form;[8] thus they were seemingly indecipherable. Nevertheless, Daniel interpreted the words as follows: *Mene, Mene*: G-d has counted the days of Belshazzar's kingdom, and they are numbered. *Tekel*: G-d has weighed Belshazzar on the scales of justice and has found him guilty. *Upharsin*: His kingdom will be broken up and given to Persia and Media. On that very night, Belshazzar was killed, and the Babylonian Empire came to an end.

DARIUS I: In 3389, Darius the Mede became monarch of the Persian-Median Empire, the new world power. He was very favorably inclined toward the Jewish people and appointed Daniel chief minister of the realm. Jealous of Daniel's high position, Darius' other officials plotted to rid themselves of the king's favorite minister. As such, they convinced Darius to enact a law saying that any person who prays to anyone other than the king will be thrown into a den of lions. As a committed Jew, Daniel openly prayed three times a day facing Jerusalem. Reluctantly, the king threw Daniel into the lions' den. G-d performed a miracle, and although the lions had been especially starved beforehand, they did not touch Daniel. Since it was the first night of Pesach, G-d transported the Prophet Habbakuk to the lions' den, and he and Daniel conducted the Seder in full view of the lions.[9] When Daniel emerged unscathed from the den, a greatly relieved Darius threw the plotting ministers and their families into the den instead, such being the system of justice in those times. Even before the ministers and their families hit the ground, the lions tore them to pieces. After ruling but one year, Darius died in 3390.

CYRUS: Darius' successor is known in world history as Cyrus the Great, and Jewish history likewise considers him to be an extraordinary person, albeit for different reasons. Cyrus permitted the Jews to go to Jerusalem and rebuild the Beis HaMikdash; indeed, his famous proclamation to that effect is the very last verse of the Bible: "Thus said Cyrus, king of Persia: 'Hashem, G-d of Heaven, has given to me all the kingdoms of the earth, and He has commanded me to build Him a Temple in Jerusalem, which is in Judah. Whoever there is among you of His entire people — may G-d be with him, and let him go up' " (II Chronicles 36:23).

This remarkable personality missed an opportunity to play a unique role in Jewish and world history. Had Cyrus personally involved himself in bringing the Jews back to Eretz Yisrael and building the Beis HaMikdash, he would have ushered in the Messianic Era.[10] Two hundred years before Cyrus was born, Isaiah predicted the king's reign, mentioning him by name.[11] Bible critics, uncomfortable with such an accurate prophecy, try to say that there were three prophets named Isaiah, and that the third one lived during the time of Cyrus. However, the language and style of the book of Isaiah strongly indicate that there was only one author. Cyrus ruled for three years, 3390–3393.

KING AHASUERUS: The king of the Purim story was a rabid anti-Semite.[12] Upon the instigation of the Samaritans, bitter enemies of the Jews residing in the land of Israel, he halted the construction of the Temple. Ahasuerus, too, miscalculated the end of the seventy years, figuring them from 3327, the date that Nebuchadnezzar exiled the 1,000 Jewish sages. In the year 3395, the third year of his reign, believing that the seventy years had passed without Jewish redemption, Ahasuerus made his famous feast. (Although only sixty-eight years elapsed from 3327, Ahasuerus reckoned partial years of previous kings as full years. That was not an error, as the Talmud reckons the reign of monarchs in a similar way. His mistake was the starting point for the seventy years.) Disaster then struck when, drinking from the holy vessels of the Beis HaMikdash, he ordered the execution of his queen Vashti.[13] The ensuing story of Purim is well known, and the following chart gives the dates for the major events of the book of Esther. Note that the Purim story unfolds over a fourteen-year span, from 3393–3406.

LESSONS OF THE PURIM STORY: The entire story was a hidden miracle — no seas split, no fire rained from heaven. Such an event becomes the prototype for Jewish survival in the present exile. Indeed, in this form Purim presents Jewish history as a jigsaw puzzle — no one sees how each piece fits in until the end. In the present exile, then, people only see the surface of things, not the deeper un-

Year of Ahasuerus	Major Events of Megillas Esther	Day of Month (if applicable)
1	The Megillah begins	—
3	Ahasuerus makes his parties	—
7	Esther becomes queen	—
12	Haman makes decree to kill the Jews	13 Nisan
12	Jews fast for three days	13, 14, 15 Nisan (another opinion: 14, 15, 16 Nisan)
12	Esther goes to Ahasuerus and invites him to her first party	15 Nisan
12	Ahasuerus cannot sleep, Haman builds gallows	Night of 16 Nisan
12	Mordecai rides on horse Esther's second party Haman is hanged	Day of 16 Nisan
13	Jews all over the realm, including the capital Shushan, kill their enemies	13 Adar
13	Jews in Shushan kill their enemies	14 Adar
13	Jews outside Shushan rest and celebrate	14 Adar

13	Jews in Shushan rest and celebrate	15 Adar
14	Mordecai and Esther establish Purim as an official holiday	—

derlying significance, just as in the Megillah. (In the late 1800s, the French archeologist Marcel Dieulefoy unearthed the ruins of the Persian palace at Susa after it had been buried for more than 2,000 years. He declared that only someone who was familiar with its layout must have written the descriptions of the palace in the book of Esther. Dieulefoy's statement gave the lie to the Bible critics who claimed that the Purim story was fabricated.)[14]

BUILDING THE SECOND TEMPLE: When Cyrus granted permission to build the Beis HaMikdash, 42,360 Jews, led by Zerubabel, a grandson of Jehoiachin, and the prophets Haggai, Zachariah, and Malachi, came to Jerusalem and began the work. At first they rebuilt the Altar, for Jewish law permits offering sacrifices on the Temple Mount even if the Temple building is not in existence.[15] Construction was stopped by Ahasuerus and did not continue during his lifetime. Shortly after the end of the Purim story, in 3406, Ahasuerus died and was succeeded by Darius II, his Jewish son through Esther. Two years later, in 3408, the Jews were given permission to resume work on the Beis HaMikdash. This was exactly seventy years after the destruction of the first Beis HaMikdash in 3338 and is the true interpretation of Jeremiah's seventy-year prophecy.[16]

After four years, in the year 3412, the second Beis HaMikdash was completed. Although its sanctity was not equal to the first Beis HaMikdash — the Holy Ark was missing, along with several other sacred objects[17] — it became the spiritual center of the Jewish people. Despite their reverence for the new Holy Temple, numerous physical attributes reminded the Jewish people of its lower status. Spikes were attached to the roof to prevent birds from alighting — something unnecessary in the first Beis HaMikdash, for birds sensed its great holiness and did not rest there.[18] In addition, a representation of the Shushan skyline was placed over the entrance to the second Beis HaMikdash, reminding the Jewish people of their status as subjects of the Persian Empire.[19]

EZRA: "If Moses had not preceded him, G-d would have given the Torah to the Jewish people through Ezra" (Talmud, *Sanhedrin* 21b). Although he was a strong and charismatic leader, only 1,500 Jews answered Ezra's call to join him on the trip to Eretz Yisrael. No *leviim* came along, and Ezra penalized their tribe for the lack of interest shown by depriving them of the right to receive *maaser rishon*, the 10 percent tithe that farmers in the land of Israel must give the *leviim*. There are two opinions in the Talmud as to the exact nature of this penalty. One opinion holds that before they were punished, the *leviim* had the exclusive right to receive the *maaser rishon*, but that after the penalty the *kohanim* (priests) also became eligible to get it. The other opinion maintains that even before the penalty a farmer had the option to give the tithe to either *kohanim* or *leviim*, whereas after Ezra's penalty he could only give it to *kohanim*.[20]

When this great teacher journeyed to the land of Israel, he found widespread ignorance and weak observance of Torah. Consequently, he forced the small percentage of intermarried Jews to divorce their non-Jewish spouses and began a successful campaign of mass Torah education. In addition, Ezra decreed ten enactments aimed at improving the quality of Jewish life both materially and spiritually. Among these decrees was the requirement to read the Torah in the synagogue on Mondays, Thursdays, and Sabbath afternoon. He also ensured that peddlers selling cosmetics and other women's items make the rounds of outlying settlements, thereby making such things available to women living in these isolated areas.[21]

Rabbinic tradition states that once again the Jewish people

squandered a golden opportunity — if they would have made *aliyah* to Eretz Yisrael en masse, G-d would have ushered in the Messianic Era.[22]

NEHEMIAH: In the year 3426, Nehemiah received authority from the Persian king to become governor over the Jews in Jerusalem. Upon arrival, he found the community in miserable condition and that the wall of the city has been burned down. Undaunted, Nehemiah rebuilt the wall in several weeks. (This is not the present wall around the Old City of Jerusalem, which was built by the Turks in the 1500s.) Appalled by commercial activity on the Sabbath (which, although not forbidden by the Torah if no writing is done, nevertheless is not within the spirit of Sabbath), Nehemiah stopped it and instituted rules of *muktzah*, items whose handling on the Sabbath is forbidden.[23]

PROBLEMS FACED BY EZRA AND NEHEMIAH: The issues that Ezra and Nehemiah encountered in Eretz Yisrael bear a striking resemblance to the problems faced there in modern times. For example, Eretz Yisrael was a poor, barren land, and the vast majority of Jews preferred to live in the relative comfort of foreign countries. Torah observance was weak, particularly in keeping the Sabbath, and many Jews were ignorant of Torah laws. Terrorism was rampant: the book of Nehemiah describes the struggles combating Arabs and other nations who tried to sabotage rebuilding Jerusalem's wall.

ANSHEI KNESSES HAGEDOLAH: Approximately fifty years before prophecy terminated in 3448, a body of 120 of the greatest Torah scholars assumed the spiritual leadership of the Jewish people. This august assembly, led by Ezra, functioned as the Sanhedrin of the nation. Although scholars disagree as to whether all 120 sages served on the Court simultaneously, or the Sanhedrin was composed of its normal quorum of seventy-one members while the others were alternates,[24] nevertheless all agree that the *Anshei Knesses HaGedolah*, the Men of the Great Assembly, was the greatest scholarly assembly in the history of the Jewish people. Membership was composed of prophets and non-prophets: among its more prominent members were Mordecai, Daniel, Ezra, Nehemiah, Haggai, Zachariah, Malachi, and Shimon HaTzadik. These eminent rabbis realized that Jewish society was changing irrevocably. The era of prophecy, in which the Jewish people received direct Divine communication, was about to come to a close. In addition, the majority of Jews would live in a state of exile outside the land of Israel. The awesome responsibility of leading the Jewish people during this difficult transitional period and facing the challenges of an uncertain future weighed heavily on their shoulders. Therefore, the Great Assembly effected far-reaching enactments that guide the Jewish people to this day, enabling the nation to survive spiritually during the long, dark exile. The major accomplishments of the Men of the Great Assembly include:

Formalizing the text of the prayers and blessings. *Tefillah,* or prayer, is one of the Torah's 613 commandments. However, the Torah does not specify specific texts. Originally, people composed their own informal supplications and praises to G-d, with synagogues serving as the place for public Torah readings, which require a quorum of ten male adults. Unfortunately, due to the vicissitudes of exile, the spiritual level of the Jewish people declined to the point where they could not compose proper prayers. Understanding this situation, the *Anshei Knesses HaGedolah* enacted a formal prayer service containing all the spiritual states that a Jew is supposed to attain during prayer. By reciting the prescribed text, any Jew could ideally access the mystical, Kabbalistic levels that prayer accomplishes. A common prayer book also united the Jewish people — to this day, the order of prayers for Jews from Poland to Yemen is basically identical.[25]

Abolishing the desire for idolatry. Idol worship was a major scourge during the First Temple era. The sages, realizing that the Jewish people were not on a sufficiently high spiritual level to cope with the desire to worship idols, fervently prayed to G-d to remove this urge from the Jewish people. Miraculously, He assented to their request.[26] In later times, under Greek and Christian rule, Jews generally worshiped idols to gain acceptance by the ruling power and not out of any inner conviction. However, since the world was created in balances, G-d replaced the desire to worship idols with atheism, which was not prevalent in biblical times.

Arranging the Oral Law. From the time of Moses, the Oral Law was meticulously preserved and accurately transmitted throughout the generations. However, this great body of information was not taught with any formal text. The 120 scholars used precise wording and systematized the Oral Law into tractates and subjects. Scholars memorized this material, which later became the basis of the written Mishnah.[27]

Creating rabbinic customs and decrees. It is important to understand that the rabbis did not create a new Rabbinic Judaism to replace the old observances. The laws of the Torah remained unchanged; however, since spiritual levels were weakening, the sages adopted preventive measures to forestall greater religious backsliding. Authority to do so was based on a verse in the Torah (Leviticus 18:30) that enjoins Torah leaders to enact safeguards to preserve mitzvah observance.[28] Clearly, rabbinic decrees were not imposed in an autocratic, tyrannical manner, but rather with the full agreement of the Jewish people.[29] Decrees that did not have the assent of the majority of Jews, or that were deemed too difficult to follow, were revoked.[30]

Sealing the Scriptures. To ensure that no charlatans could claim Divine revelation and lead the Jewish people astray, the *Anshei Knesses HaGedolah* sealed the Bible (Tanach).[31] Henceforth, no material could be added or subtracted. Although all this material was accurately passed down throughout the generations, there was a danger that it would eventually be forgotten. First, the sages decided which writings to include in the Scriptural canon and which to leave out. The precise order of the Biblical books was also determined at this time.[32]

Tanach was split into three categories: *Torah, Neviim,* and *Kesuvim.* The Torah, the Five Books of Moses, possesses the greatest sanctity of the Scriptures. Every word of these books was directly dictated to Moses by G-d.[33] (The Talmud discusses the authorship of the last eight verses of the Torah, those dealing with the death of Moses.)[34] The sages of the Great Assembly also clarified the proper spelling, pronunciation, and musical cantillation (*trop*) of the Torah's words.[35]

The *Neviim* are Divine messages received by a prophet and recorded in the prophet's own words.[36] Some prophets recorded their prophecies, while others only transmitted them orally. The *Kesuvim* are not formal prophecies, but were written by their respective authors with Divine inspiration (*ruach hakodesh*). After the 120 sages collected the mass of written and oral material, they finished some incomplete books and wrote others in their entirety.

As a result of their great endeavor, the Jewish Bible is accurate down to the last detail, with virtually no conflicting versions. (There is a question regarding the spelling of the word "*dakah*" in Deuteronomy 23:2; its meaning is the same with either variant.)

THE END OF PROPHECY: With the passing of the last prophet, Malachi, in 3448, the 1,000-year era of prophecy came to a close.[37] Two factors caused this cessation: first, the Jewish people were not on the exalted spiritual level required for prophets to exist.[38] Second, prophecy functions in Eretz Yisrael (and in exceptional circumstances, elsewhere) and most Jews lived outside the Land.[39] From that point, no person would be able to proclaim, "So speaks G-d"; those who claimed prophetic revelation were immediately recognized as frauds. However, the Jewish people were not bereft of spiritual leadership: G-d would continue to guide Torah leaders, albeit in a more indirect manner.[40]

REVIEW OF THE MAJOR EVENTS AFTER THE DESTRUCTION OF THE TEMPLE:

1) *Churban Bayis Rishon*, Destruction of the First Temple

2) Assassination of Gedaliah

3) Hananiah, Mishael, and Azariah in the fiery furnace

4) Handwriting on the wall

5) Daniel in the lions' den

6) Cyrus

7) The Purim story

8) Building of the Second Temple

9) Ezra and the *Anshei Knesses HaGedolah*

10) Nehemiah

11) End of prophecy

SOME IMPORTANT DATES:

3327 — *Galus Hacheresh Vehamasger*

3338 — *Churban Bayis Rishon*

3393–3406 — The story of Purim

3408–3412 — Construction of the Second Temple

3413 — Ezra comes to Jerusalem

3448 — End of prophecy

THE DISCREPANCY BETWEEN THE RABBINIC AND SECULAR DATES: A major difference exists between the traditional rabbinic date for the destruction of the First Temple and the date given by secular historians. Traditional sources, based on the second-century rabbinic work *Seder Olam*, place the destruction in the year 3338, or 422 BCE. Secular historians date this event as occurring in 587 BCE, or 165 years earlier than the rabbinic date. This gap between the two chronologies narrows between twenty and twenty-five years at the time of Alexander's conquests, with secular sources dating it 334 BCE and traditional ones 312 BCE, and virtually disappears at the destruction of the Second Temple, with just a one- or two-year difference.

The source for this discrepancy is the time frame assigned to the Persian-Median period. Talmudic sages state that there were four Persian-Median kings, Darius I, Cyrus, Ahasuerus, and Darius II, spanning fifty-two years (3390–3442 or 370–318 BCE). Conventional, or secular, chronology, based on the works of Herodotus, a Greek historian, and cuneiform inscriptions found at excavations of ancient Persian palaces, indicates that there were more than ten Persian kings over a 207-year period. Volumes have been written trying to solve this historical conundrum, but the rabbinic tradition is regarded as authentic.[41] Nevertheless, secular dating unfortunately creeps into Jewish life. In 1996, the State of Israel celebrated Jerusalem 3000, based on the secular date of 1004 BCE for King David's conquest of Jerusalem. For Torah-observant Jews, however, it was only Jerusalem 2865.

THE SAMARITANS: When the Assyrians exiled the Ten Tribes, the conquerors brought in a foreign people called Cutheans to populate the vacated territory. These people were idol-worshipers, and G-d sent lions to decimate them. Out of fear of the lions, the Cutheans converted to Judaism, but the rabbis of the Talmud debated whether their conversion was valid or not.[42] The Cutheans' Torah observance was spotty — extremely strong in some areas, but very weak or nonexistent in others.[43]

Settling in the Samaria region of Eretz Yisrael, over time the Cutheans became known as Samaritans. Fearing that the Jews returning from Babylonian exile would reclaim their ancestral lands, the Cutheans became bitter enemies of the Jewish people, even going so far as to attempting to sabotage the construction of the Second Temple. Disguising their evil intentions, the Cutheans offered to help build the Temple. Realizing the Cutheans' real goal, the Jews rebuffed their proposed aid. Stung by this rejection, the Cutheans convinced Ahasuerus that the Jews wished to foment rebellion against Persian rule, so he suspended construction.

On a number of occasions during the Second Temple Era, the Cutheans were anathema to the Jewish people. Finally, when the rabbis of the Talmud discovered that the Cutheans were worshiping idols and not keeping the commandments, the sages expelled the Cutheans from the Jewish fold and declared them to be gentiles.[44] Although most of the Cutheans eventually died out, a small group exists today, living around Mount Gerizim in Israel. While they have ancient scrolls that bear some resemblance to the Five Books of Moses, these descendants of the ancient Cutheans have no connection to the Jewish people.

Chapter 5

THE END OF PROPHECY TO THE CHANUKAH MIRACLES

AFTER MALACHI: With the passing of the last prophets, a glorious era came to an end for the Jewish people. No longer would a human be able to proclaim, "So says G-d." The great spiritual inspiration gained through contact with a prophet,[1] and the absolute knowledge of one's Divinely ordained mission in life — on both personal and national levels — as communicated directly by G-d's chosen messenger, was no more. However, there was no break in the flow of Torah transmission, for the era of prophecy blended smoothly into the era of the Tannaim, the sages of the Mishnah.[2] Shimon HaTzadik, the first Tanna and the last member of the *Anshei Knesses HaGedolah*,[3] received the Torah tradition from his teachers, the last prophets, and faithfully continued the holy task of guiding the Jewish people. Although prophecy no longer existed, G-d compensated the Jewish people by granting the Tannaim extraordinary insight and depth of understanding in all areas of Torah, and by inspiring the Tannaim to crystallize and systematize the corpus of Torah law into the written Mishnah.[4] Yet the Tannaim only built on the knowledge of their predecessors. This fact may be compared to Einstein's discovery of the Theory of Relativity. Although many books have been written on the subject, and new implications of the theory are still being discovered, they are all based on Einstein's original work. The same is true of the Mishnah.

SHIMON HATZADIK: In 3448, the Jewish people entered a time of great turbulence, both in the spiritual and material realms. Prophecy had come to a close, and Alexander the Great was conquering the known world. Fortunately, a great leader, Shimon HaTzadik, deftly steered the people through uncharted waters. As *kohen gadol* and head of the Sanhedrin, he embodied both religious and political power. (In the absence of the monarchy, the *kohen gadol* represented the nation to the outside world. Previously, it was a purely religious office.) Indeed, he was so fair, just, and beloved that Shimon was one of very few people to receive the appellation "*HaTzadik*" — the Righteous — after his name.

The Talmud relates that five miracles occurred in the Beis HaMikdash during his tenure.[5] First, the red string that was hung in the Beis HaMikdash during the Yom Kippur services turned white, symbolizing Israel's purity. Second, on Yom Kippur two sacrificial goats were designated — one to be offered in the *Kodesh HaKodashim*, one to be cast off a cliff. The *kohen gadol* drew lots in each hand to determine which goat should be used for which purpose. During Shimon HaTzadik's forty-year tenure, the lot indicating the goat to be offered in the *Kodesh HaKodashim* always turned up in his right hand, a sign of Divine favor. Third, every evening a full night's supply of oil was put into each lamp of the Menorah. Miraculously, the oil put into the western lamp burned for twenty-four hours, demonstrating the constant presence of G-d in the Beis HaMikdash. Fourth, although each *kohen* received only a small portion of the *lechem hapanim* (the showbread), he felt satiated as if he had eaten a full meal. Fifth, the fire on the altar burned steadily without constant addition of wood. Sadly, after Shimon HaTzadik's death, miracles of such magnitude were no longer manifest in the Beis HaMikdash.

ALEXANDER THE GREAT: In 3448,[6] Alexander marched through the land of Israel, bringing Persian rule to an end. Filled with trepidation, the Jews sent a delegation of *kohanim* led by Shimon HaTzadik, all dressed in their priestly raiments. Upon approaching Alexander, they were astounded when the great conqueror prostrated himself before Shimon! When asked the reason for such inexplicable behavior, Alexander replied that before his battles a vision of Shimon appeared to him promising victory.[7] After arising, Alexander promised to treat the Jews benignly. In appreciation, the Jewish people honored Alexander in two very special ways. First, all male *kohanim*[8] (according to some opinions, all male Jews)[9] born that year would be named Alexander. Second, a new dating system for documents would be instituted, one based on Alexander's rule. This system was known as *minyan shtaros* and lasted more than 1,000 years.[10]

ANTIGONOS ISH SOCHO: The leading disciple of Shimon HaTzadik, and the Jewish people's new Torah leader, Antigonos, taught the famous credo: "Do not serve G-d on condition of reward."[11] While this simply means that one's Divine service should be free of ulterior motives, two of his students, Tzadok and Beothus, misconstrued these words to mean that there is no eternal reward. They therefore denied the validity of the Oral Law and the authority of the sages to interpret the Torah, and founded the breakaway sects, the *Tzadokim* and *Baithusim*, the Sadducees.[12] This highly contentious group constantly disparaged the Oral Torah and Torah-observant Jews, and was the source of much tragedy and strife.

DIVISION OF JEWISH POWERS: Shimon HaTzadik held absolute power over the Jewish people. Unfortunately, his descendants were not of sufficient stature to be similarly entrusted with the reins of government. In addition, after the death of Alexander, his surviving generals jockeyed for power, and conditions became unstable in Eretz Yisrael. For a vast payment, Joseph ben Tuvia, a highly corrupt man, obtained the taxation franchise from the ruler. Predictably, his exorbitant taxes bled the people dry. Eventually, even the exalted position of *kohen gadol* was turned into a purely political office, one entirely devoid of spirituality, and was sold to the highest bidder. In response to these deteriorating conditions,[13] the Sanhedrin established two leadership positions: the *nasi*, or president of the Sanhedrin, who represented the Sanhedrin in political affairs; and the *av beis din*, or dean of the Sanhedrin, who was its leading halachic spokesman. The holders of these two offices were known as *zugos*, pairs.[14] The Mishnah in *Avos* lists five generations of *zugos*, beginning with Yose ben Yoezer and Yose ben Yochanan, and continuing through Shammai and Hillel, representing a span of some 200 years.

THE SEPTUAGINT: In 3515,[15] Eretz Yisrael was under the sway of the Egyptian Ptolemaic kings. Ptolemy II Philadelphus, a great lover of books and wisdom, painstakingly acquired a vast library. Knowing of the great fame of the Torah, he ordered seventy-two sages to come to Alexandria. When they arrived, he isolated each one to prevent collaboration, and demanded that they translate the Torah into Greek. Divinely inspired, they all provided identical translations,[16] especially for verses that if understood literally could easily be misconstrued. For example, the verse which literally reads "And they saw the G-d of Israel" (Exodus 24:10) was translated "And they saw the glory of the G-d of Israel," which is indeed figuratively accurate, for no human can see G-d directly.[17]

While the assimilated Jews of Alexandria rejoiced at the opportunity to display Jewish wisdom to the Greeks, the rabbis viewed this event as an unmitigated disaster for the Jewish people[18] — for putting holy words in the hands of non-Jews who did not understand the Torah's inner meanings turned the Jewish Bible into ordinary literature. Sadly, history has borne out the sages' fears. Christians have distorted and falsified Scripture to comply with their own theology and justify their persecution of the Jewish people. Even now, missionaries entrap countless Jews with spurious interpretations of the Bible.

THE FIRST UNRESOLVED HALACHIC DISPUTE (*MACHLOKES*): For more than 1,000 years, since the giving of Torah at Sinai, scholarship was on such a high level that no halachic question was left undecided. After an issue was debated, analyzed, and voted on, there was complete unanimity and clarity in the decision. However, in the days of Yose ben Yoezer and Yose ben Yochanan, the initial *zugos*, the first unresolved dispute arose. The case involved the permissibility of leaning one's hands (*semichah*) on a sacrificial animal on *yom tov*, a holiday.[19] The question was whether the mitzvah of *semichah* should be performed despite the prohibition of exerting pressure on an animal on *yom tov*. Despite the fact that only one dispute arose among the countless facets of Jewish law, and even that one was a relatively minor rabbinic issue, the Talmud viewed this event as a disastrous drop in Torah scholarship.[20]

THE SPREAD OF GREEK CULTURE: The ancient Greeks were a brilliant people whose advances in mathematics, science, literature, philosophy, architecture, and government form the basis of much of Western civilization and thought today. The Olympic Games, for example, feature many of the sporting events of ancient Greece, while the Olympic Flame is lit at Mount Olympus, in Greece, signaling the beginning of competition. Alexander, a great proponent of Greek culture, spread it throughout his vast conquests, building Greek cities containing vast libraries, beautiful temples, and impressive gymnasiums.

By and large, the conquered nations welcomed the Greeks' superior and very attractive culture, and had no problem incorporating the Greek gods into their pantheons of idols. The Jews, however, viewed Greek influence as a major threat. Jewish youth flocked to the entertainments, at which athletes competed naked. Some Jews even attempted to undo their circumcisions surgically, which the Greeks encouraged because they considered circumcision a blemish on the supposedly perfect human body. Even worse, after sporting events, participants offered sacrifices to the Greek gods. Following such practices, a number of Jews adopted Greek names and mores, studied Greek literature and philosophy, and cast off Torah observance. These Jews became known as *Misyavnim*, or Hellenists, and looked with disdain at their religious, less modern brethren. Jews also moved to Greek centers, such as Alexandria, a major Hellenist city where Jews attained great affluence and rapidly assimilated. Alexandria was also the location of Chonyo's temple, where Jews offered sacrifices to G-d, violating the law of sacrificing outside the Beis HaMikdash. This temple lasted several hundred years.[21]

SELEUCID RULE: In 3562, after 114 years,[22] Eretz Yisrael passed from Ptolemaic rule to the control of the Seleucid (Syrian-Greek) kings. During this time, the Hellenists gained more power and influence. While relations between the Jews and the early Seleucid kings were generally amicable, there was one notable exception: Seleucus IV. Upon being told by Hellenists that the treasury of the Beis HaMikdash contained vast sums of money, he attempted to plunder the Holy Temple. One of his trusted officers, Heliodorus, entered the Beis HaMikdash, and despite the desperate entreaties of the *kohen gadol*, approached the treasury. Miraculously, a heavenly apparition of a rider appeared, striking Heliodorus to the ground. When Heliodorus recovered, he offered a sacrifice in reverence to G-d, and upon returning to Seleucus convinced him to leave the Beis HaMikdash alone.

ANTIOCHUS IV — THE ANTIOCHUS OF CHANUKAH: In 3586, Antiochus assumed the Seleucid throne. This monarch saw as his life's mission spreading Greek culture and religion throughout his empire. While his visions of grandeur caused him to take the title "Epiphanes" (the Great), behind his back his subjects called him "Epimanes" (the Mad) for his undignified behavior at court. Regardless of his behavior, the Hellenist Jews were delighted with Antiochus, seeing a great opportunity to usurp the office of *kohen gadol*, which they previously had not controlled.

CHONYO, JASON, AND MENELAUS: At this time the *kohen gadol* was a righteous man named Chonyo, a nickname for Yochanan. His Hellenized brother Jason, the Greek version of Joshua, bribed Antiochus with vast sums of money to be appointed in Chonyo's place. Once installed as *kohen gadol*, Jason built a gymnasium close to the Temple Mount. Sadly, many of the *kohanim* and Jewish youth flocked to the hedonistic entertainments provided by Jason, complete with offering sacrifices to the

Greek gods. However, these activities were not enough for the more extreme Hellenists, who wanted to uproot Judaism entirely. Jason's associate Menelaus, who may not even have been a *kohen*,[23] bribed Antiochus with even greater amounts of money to depose Jason and appoint Menelaus himself as *kohen gadol*. Once in power, Menelaus stole the holy vessels of the Beis HaMikdash to raise the vast sums he needed to pay his bribe. When Chonyo protested this brazen behavior, Menelaus had him murdered. The Sanhedrin then sent a delegation to Antiochus accusing Menelaus of great excesses, but Menelaus bribed the king's advisors and had the sages executed.

EVENTS THAT SPARKED THE HASMONEAN REVOLT: While Antiochus was abroad fighting the Egyptians, a rumor spread among the Jews that he had died in battle. Jason, taking advantage of this report, attacked Jerusalem, massacred many Jews, and drove Menelaus from power. However, Antiochus returned to Jerusalem, incensed at Jason's affront to his authority. The king massacred some 40,000 Jews, restored Menelaus to power, and despoiled the Beis HaMikdash of all remaining holy vessels, including the Golden Table and Menorah. Encouraged by the Hellenists, Antiochus also instituted harsh decrees aimed at destroying the Jewish religion, effectively plunging the Jewish people into a terrible spiritual exile in their own country. Indeed, the three years (3594–3597) of Antiochus' evil decrees are among the blackest in Jewish history, despite the fact that the Jews dwelled in their land and the Beis HaMikdash was still standing.[24]

ANTIOCHUS' EVIL DECREES: After plundering the Beis HaMikdash, Antiochus turned it into a pagan temple. The Divine service was abolished, and statues of Greek idols were set up. On 25 Kislev 3594, hogs were offered on the altar to Greek gods. Possession of the Scriptures was forbidden, and any Jew found studying them was cruelly executed. Observance of the Sabbath, Rosh Chodesh, and circumcision was punishable by torture and death.[25] Why did the Greeks object so greatly to these three mitzvos? Clearly, Sabbath, new moons, and circumcision represented the ultimate challenge to the Greek worldview that man is the center of the universe and solely determines right and wrong. Cessation of work on Sabbath is a reminder that G-d is in control of nature. Proclaiming Rosh Chodesh, upon which the festivals, times of Divine closeness, are based, shows that time is not merely a mundane procession of moments, but is instead infused with holiness through the authority granted by the Torah to the Sanhedrin. And circumcision teaches that the purpose of the human body is to serve G-d, and not to be indulged and glorified for its own sake — ideas in direct contrast to Greek philosophy. As a final insult, in order to attack the sanctity of the Jewish family, the Greeks decreed that prior to her wedding a bride must be violated by the local Greek official — in some ways the single most abhorrent edict of all.[26]

Many Jews died resisting these terrible decrees. Women caught circumcising their children were executed in gruesome fashion, along with their innocent infants and entire families. An elderly rabbi, Elazar, was killed for refusing to eat pork — indeed, for refusing to eat kosher meat and pretend it was pig's flesh. A woman, Chanah, allowed her seven sons to die horribly in her presence rather than submit to idol worship.[27] The distraught mother then hurled herself off a roof. Stories such as these fired the Jewish people, giving them the fortitude to withstand the terrible persecutions and to revolt.

MATISYAHU: The leader of a prominent priestly family known as the Hasmoneans, Matisyahu may have been a *kohen gadol* or a descendant of one.[28] In addition to that aspect of his lineage, there are several possibilities for the origin of the name Hasmonean. It might come from the town Hashmon, where this family originated. It is similar to the Hebrew word *hashmanim* (Psalms 68:32), meaning nobles. It was merely a family surname.[29] As is well known, Matisyahu's family also became known as Maccabees, which has several meanings. It is an acronym for the verse (Exodus 15:11), "*Mi Chamochah ba'eilim Hashem?*" meaning, "Who is like You among the heavenly powers, O G-d?"

It represents the initial letters of the words **M**atisyahu **K**ohen **b**en **Y**ochanan. It is the Hebrew word for hammer: *makav*.[30] Regardless of the origin of the family's given and acquired names, Matisyahu had five sons: Judah, Shimon, Jochanan, Jonathan, and Elazar. Hoping to escape Greek scrutiny in the large city of Jerusalem, they fled to the small hamlet of Modiin.

THE REVOLT: Clearly, the revolt against the Greeks was not for national independence. Babylonians, Persians, and Egyptian Ptolemies all controlled Eretz Yisrael, yet the Jews never attempted to overthrow their rule. Only when the Greeks made Torah observance virtually impossible did the Jews fight.

The revolt began when a Greek garrison arrived in Modiin. Gathering all the Jews to the town square, the Greeks ordered Matisyahu to offer a hog to the Greek deities. He refused, exhorting the townspeople to be steadfast against the forces antithetical to Torah. When a renegade Jew approached the pagan altar in order to offer the sacrifice himself, Matisyahu killed him and the surrounding Greek soldiers. Proclaiming *"Mi Lashem eilai"* (Exodus 32:26) — "Whoever is for G-d join me!" — with other loyal Jews Matisyahu ran to the hills and began a guerrilla campaign against the Greek oppressors. Shortly afterward, Matisyahu, who was aged, died, leaving the leadership of the small but determined Jewish forces to his son Judah. Eventually, the Jews gathered 6,000 ill-equipped troops and began attacking the Greeks and their Hellenist Jewish supporters.

Soon, the Greeks realized the threat to their rule and sent armies to crush the incipient uprising. Despite having inferior forces, at Shechem Judah defeated a Greek army under Appolonius. Another army led by Seron met the same fate at Beis Horon.

At this point, the enraged Antiochus sent an army of 40,000 infantry and 7,000 cavalry, led by his best general, Lysias, against Judah. Camped at Emmaus, the vast force faced the 3,000 Jewish soldiers Judah mustered together. Facing suicidal odds of 1:16, where 3:1 odds are usually needed to avoid defeat, before going into battle at Mitzpah, Judah and his men fasted and prayed to G-d. That night the Greeks split their forces, one arm attempting a surprise raid on the Jewish camp. However, Judah anticipated such an attack and himself organized a surprise attack on the sleeping troops left in the Greek camp, killing them, and capturing their stores. Realizing that their supply base was destroyed, the remaining Greek soldiers fled the battlefield.

Lysias made one more attempt to destroy the Jewish army. A year later, he assembled a force of 60,000 infantry and 5,000 cavalry, and marched on Beis Tzur. There, Judah met him with a force of 10,000 men. With faith in G-d, the Jews attacked first and killed 5,000 enemy soldiers. Seeing the grim determination of the Jews, who would never surrender, Lysias returned home to his capital, Antioch. Meanwhile, King Antiochus died in Persia of a horrible disease, regretting to the end that he had begun fighting the Jews.

THE MIRACLE OF CHANUKAH: A triumphant Judah entered Jerusalem and the Beis HaMikdash. He and his forces spent several weeks in the Holy Temple, removing the idols, making necessary repairs, and reconstructing the defiled altar. Finally, on 25 Kislev 3597 (164 BCE), three years to the day after hogs had been offered on the altar, the *kohanim* were ready to resume the sacrificial service. As the new golden Menorah was not yet ready, a Menorah of iron spikes was set up.[31] However, they found but one jar of oil, sealed with the *kohen gadol*'s stamp attesting to its purity, an amount sufficient for only one day's lighting. Nevertheless, the *kohanim* lit the oil, and it miraculously burned for a full eight days until new oil could be processed. Overjoyed at this sign of Divine favor, the Jews celebrated spontaneously for eight days. A year later, the Sanhedrin ordained the eight-day festival of Chanukah to commemorate the great miracle of the oil for all time.[32]

Despite the fact that all authorities agree to the fact of the Chanukah miracles, there are two opinions for the date and nature of the Chanukah victory. The first opinion holds that the

Chanukah miracle occurred in 3597, while it took another twenty-five years of warfare until the Jews enjoyed total independence.[33] The second opinion states that the miracle happened in 3622, at the end of all the battles, when the Jewish people became free of Syrian-Greek domination.[34]

THE HOLIDAY OF CHANUKAH: Incredibly, most of the Chanukah events are reported by secular sources. Midrashim mention the wars only in a very general way, focusing instead on the anti-Torah decrees and the heroism of the Jews who gave their lives to avoid transgression. The only Talmudic reference to the Chanukah story is a brief passage in the Talmud (*Shabbos* 21b), which asks, "What is the reason for Chanukah?" Rashi explains that the Talmud is trying to identify the miracle on which the holiday is based. The Talmud continues: "When the Syrian-Greeks entered the Sanctuary, they contaminated all the oil in the Temple. When the Hasmoneans defeated them, the Jews searched and found only one flask of oil with the *kohen gadol*'s seal still intact. It contained only enough oil to light the Menorah for one day. However, a miracle occurred and the oil burned for eight days. The following year, these eight days were established as holidays with respect to reciting Hallel and thanksgiving" (*Al HaNissim*). In the Talmud, therefore, no mention is made of the cataclysmic battles and political upheavals.

However, Josephus, *Sefer HaMakkabim*, and *Megillas Antiochus*, the three secular sources upon which much of our knowledge of Chanukah is based, focus on the battles and not on the miracle of the oil. Why is there such a major disagreement regarding the events' historicity and importance? Perhaps the sages did not consider the details of the victory sufficiently important to record. To their way of thinking, while military prowess and independence are fine, Chanukah celebrates a spiritual victory, one exemplified by the miracle of the oil. Nevertheless, the miracles of "delivering the strong in the hands of the weak" are alluded to in a general sense when Jews offer thanks to G-d in the *Al HaNissim* prayer.

THE WARS FOLLOWING THE CHANUKAH MIRACLE: Although the Hasmoneans succeeded in reconstituting the Temple service and having the anti-Torah decrees rescinded, the Syrian-Greeks and their Hellenist allies remained very powerful. Another twenty-five years of fierce battles ensued until the land was totally free. During these wars, all of Matisyahu's sons, except for Shimon, lost their lives. First, Judah subdued the small, hostile border nations. However, apprehensive of the Jews' growing strength, Antiochus V Eupator, son of Antiochus Epiphanes, invaded Eretz Yisrael with a force of 100,000 infantry, 20,000 cavalry, and 32 battle-trained elephants, the tanks of those days, all commanded by his chief of staff Lysias. Elazar, seeing a decorated elephant, mistakenly thought it was bearing the king. He attacked it, but was killed when the elephant's mortally wounded body fell on top of him. At that point, with Jerusalem about to fall to the enemy, Divine providence intervened. Lysias, hearing of an insurrection against Antiochus back home in Antioch, urged Eupator to conclude a peace treaty with the Jews and return to his capital to quell the coup attempt.

Antiochus, however, did not rule long afterward. His uncle Demetrius seized power and executed both Antiochus and Lysias. Renegade Jewish Hellenists, seeing an opportunity to crush Judah Maccabee, encouraged the new king to invade Eretz Yisrael. These Hellenists also murdered Yose ben Yoezer, who along with Yose ben Yochanan were the Torah leaders of the Jewish people during the years of Greek oppression. A new Syrian-Greek general, Nicanor, invaded with 35,000 soldiers, and was opposed by only 3,000 Jewish defenders. Enraged by the resistance, Nicanor vowed to raze the Beis HaMikdash, but the Jews wiped out his army and killed him. Then, to demonstrate what happens to blasphemers against the House of G-d, the Jews hung Nicanor's head, fingers, and toes on the gates of Jerusalem.[35] Ensuing battles were fought, but G-d helped Judah hold off the vastly superior foreign and Hellenist forces.

Finally, political infighting within the Seleucid Empire caused the Syrian-Greeks to abandon their hope of subduing the

Jewish people. Shimon, the last Maccabee survivor, eliminated the last Hellenist strongholds, bringing total independence to Eretz Yisrael in 3622.

Chapter 6

THE HASMONEAN DYNASTY

THE **HASMONEANS:** Shimon, the last surviving son of Matisyahu, became the leader of the Jewish people in 3622. He was the forerunner of the Hasmonean royal dynasty, which lasted 103 years until Herod wiped it out.[1] The early Hasmonean rulers were righteous people who were careful not to assume the title of monarch. However, it is an old adage that power corrupts, and eventually the Hasmoneans usurped the throne, disregarding the tradition that only a descendant of King David may be called king. (Indeed, Ramban writes that G-d destroyed the family in retribution for that act.)[2] In addition, the enormous power and wealth generated by their position caused the Hasmoneans to identify increasingly with the Sadducees, many of whom were also rich and powerful. As a result, the Hasmoneans began persecuting and even murdering Torah-observant Jews, thereby earning the Jewish people's enmity. Finally, and worst of all, the Hasmoneans fought wars for self-aggrandizement, ruthlessly crushing anyone even suspected of not supporting their rule.

JOCHANAN HYRCANUS: Jochanan Hyrcanus ruled for thirty-one years (3625–3656)[3] after the death of his father Shimon. Generally righteous, Jochanan enacted several decrees to improve the spiritual level of the people, the most famous of which was the requirement of tithing any produce about which there was a doubt as to whether the necessary tithes had already been removed (*demai*).[4] However, Jochanan committed a severe error that had drastic implications for the Jewish people. Upon conquering the neighboring people of Edom, he compelled them to convert to Judaism, contradictory to the Jewish law expressly forbidding forced conversions.[5] Later, Herod, himself a converted Edomite, caused terrible suffering for the Jewish people. According to some historical opinions, Jochanan even became a Sadducee at the end of his life, and is the person referred to in the Talmudic statement: "Do not believe in yourself until the day you die, for Jochanan served as *kohen gadol* for eighty years and in the end became a Sadducee."[6] His son Aristobulus ruled for a year and was the first Hasmonean to proclaim himself king.[7]

JANNAI: Jannai ruled twenty-seven years (3657–3684)[8] and completely identified with the Sadducees, even going so far as to persecute Torah sages. The Talmud relates that Jannai made a thanksgiving feast after a successful war and invited Torah sages.[9] At that point, the Sadducees saw an opportunity to eliminate the sages, and told Jannai to don the priestly garments of the *kohen gadol* before all those at the party. Aghast, one of the rabbis told the king to remove the garments, as there was a question whether Jannai was a legitimate *kohen*. Upon investigation, the rumor was found to be false, but the Sadducees used the occasion to convince Jannai that the sages opposed his rule. Thereafter, Jannai killed many Torah sages, and the rest went into hiding. Sadducees then dominated the Sanhedrin, while true Torah scholars lost all positions of influence. In another sacrilege, when Jannai was officiating as *kohen gadol* in the Beis HaMikdash on the holiday of Sukkos, he poured the sacrificial water on his feet instead of the altar. The enraged onlookers pelted him with their holiday *esrogim* (citrons), whereupon Jannai's soldiers massacred 6,000 Jews in the Temple courtyard.[10] He also murdered more than 50,000 Jews on other occasions.[11]

QUEEN SHLOMIS: Also known as Salome and Shlomtzion, Shlomis was Jannai's wife and ruled for nine years (3686–3695). A thoroughly righteous woman, her rule was marked by great peace and prosperity. As the best period of the Second Temple era, Divine favor was manifest in Eretz Yisrael. For example, it rained only on Friday nights, when people stayed home, and wheat kernels grew as large as ox kidneys.[12] Together with her brother Shimon ben Shatach, Shlomis removed the Sadducees from both the Sanhedrin and all positions of power, replacing them with Torah sages. At this time, Yehudah ben Tabbai and Shimon ben Shatach became *av beis din* and *nasi* of the Sanhedrin, respectively. (One opinion in the Talmud, however, maintains that their offices were reversed.)

In order to restore order, people who had committed crimes, particularly murder, were put to death.[13] In addition, the sages enacted decrees to improve the spiritual life of the Jewish people. When the traditional method of education — fathers teaching Torah to their children at home — became weakened, for example, Joshua ben Gamla instituted a system of public education, setting up schools for children at six.[14] Shimon ben Shatach was active as well, making it easier for a woman to collect her *kesubah* (marriage settlement) upon divorce or her husband's death.[15] In addition, as witchcraft, a sin that the Torah punishes by death, was very prevalent at that time, Shimon ben Shatach also executed many witches.[16]

JEWISH SOCIETY DURING THIS PERIOD: There were four groups of Jews during much of the Second Temple era: Pharisees, Sadducees, *Amei Haaretz*, and Essenes. The Pharisees, known as *Perushim*, or *Chaverim*, consisted of the sages and the vast majority of the Jewish people who were loyal to the Torah and followed the sages.[17] This group was called *Perushim*, which means separate, because they were careful not to come in contact with people who may not have been ritually pure.

The Sadducees, or *Tzadokim* (for followers of the apostate Tzadok), were a wealthy and very powerful minority who wielded great political influence out of proportion to their numbers. Clearly and overtly demonstrating their disbelief in the rabbinic interpretations of the Oral Law, they deliberately perverted Torah practice. For example, Sadducee *kohanim gedolim* offered the incense of Yom Kippur by first placing it on the coals of a pan outside the *Kodesh HaKodashim* and then bringing it inside, thereby flouting Torah law that specifies the reverse.[18] By so doing, the *kohen gadol* would invariably die. Nevertheless, the Sadducees were so set on proving Torah wrong that they persisted in their incorrect practices. In fact, the Talmud states that more than 300 *kohanim gedolim* served during the Second Temple, in contrast to only eighteen for the First Temple, although each sanctuary lasted for approximately the same amount of time.[19]

On Sukkos, Sadducee *kohanim* would refuse to pour sacrificial water on the altar, because this particular service was part of the oral tradition not explicitly mentioned in the written Torah.[20] In addition, Sadducee-controlled courts interpreted the verse (Exodus 21:24) "An eye for an eye" literally, instead of its traditional meaning that damages require monetary payment.[21]

On Pesach, specifically on the second day of the holiday, the Torah requires a grain sacrifice, called the *omer*, to be offered. The Torah uses the term "The day following the Sabbath" (Leviticus 23:15) in referring to the *omer*, which the Oral Law interprets as the day following the first day of Pesach, regardless of what day of the week that is. However, the Sadducees followed the literal meaning of the verse and brought the *omer* on a Sunday.[22]

In addition, and clearly most heinous, the Sadducees were not merely a heretical group. Instead, they seized every opportunity to persecute the sages.

Amei Haaretz (singular, *Am Haaretz*), literally people of the earth, were observant Jews[23] who were not educated in the intricate laws of ritual purity and separating tithes (*maaser*). As a result, Jews who scrupulously kept these laws could not come into physical contact with the *Amei Haaretz* or eat their food. This social ostracism, necessary as it was, caused great resentment between the Pharisees and *Amei Haaretz*.[24] Despite such ill feelings, however, the *Amei Haaretz* generally followed the sages.

By contrast, the Essenes were a small splinter group that lived in isolated desert caves and practiced extreme asceticism in ways that had no basis in Jewish law. Some historians speculate that Yeshu (Jesus) may have been a member of this group. In 1947, scrolls were found in caves at Qumran containing apocalyptic visions that may have had Essene origins.

ROMAN CONQUEST: Sadly, upon her death, the golden years of Shlomis came to an end. Almost immediately, civil war broke out for the right of succession between her two sons Hyrcanus and Aristobulus. As the bitter conflict dragged on with no end in sight, the brothers committed an unimaginable blunder that led to the end of Jewish independence — ultimately to the destruction of the Beis HaMikdash. In 3698, the brothers asked Pompey of Rome to mediate their dispute. Pompey, until that time uninterested in the land of Israel, sensing Jewish weakness and political instability, promptly marched into Jerusalem and conquered it.[25] (Although the Romans had exerted influence over the Jews even during the period of Jewish independence,[26] they did not specifically meddle into Jewish affairs.)

As conqueror, Pompey put the weaker brother Hyrcanus on the throne as a figurehead while imprisoning the more dangerous Aristobulus. Real power, however, was in the hands of the Roman lackey, the Edomite Antipater. Thus, Jochanan Hyrcanus' misguided policy of forcibly converting the Edomites bore bitter fruit. The Romans abolished the Sanhedrin[27] and destroyed some cities. Although Julius Caesar (later assassinated in 3717, or 44 BCE) restored the Sanhedrin and some territory, his successors Cassius and Marc Anthony further oppressed the Jews. As such, the Torah leaders of the time, Shemaya and Avtalyon, encouraged the sages to leave politics and not be involved in governmental affairs.[28]

HEROD: In 3725,[29] the Romans installed Antipater's son Herod as king of the Jews, and his wicked rule was a blow from which the Jewish people would not recover. As a descendant of Edomite slaves who had Hasmonean masters, Herod realized that the majority of the Jewish people would never accept him as a legitimate king. Therefore, in order to give the appearance of legitimately occupying the Hasmonean throne, he exterminated the entire Hasmonean family, leaving but one young girl whom he intended to marry. However, the maiden committed suicide,[30] bringing the Hasmonean line to an end after 103 years.[31]

Aside from being cruel, Herod was also extremely paranoid, imagining plots against him although none existed. He murdered thousands of Jews, especially sages, and did not spare even his closest family members. As an avid admirer of Roman culture, Herod entered into a frenzy of grandiose construction projects, building palaces, amphitheaters, and other structures at Jerusalem, Masada, Herodion, and other locations; some of his creations still exist today. In addition, Herod built the great seaport of Caesarea, along with smaller cities, populating them with Greeks and Romans. The great prominence of foreigners in the Herodian demographic had the effect of making the Jewish people feel like strangers in their own land.

Nevertheless, Herod had one positive achievement to his credit. Following the advice of the sage Bava ben Buta, Herod refurbished the Beis HaMikdash, making it into a magnificent edifice.[32] Currently, for example, the massive stones of the Western Wall are still known as Herodian stones, dating back to this period. (It is important to note that while the Beis HaMikdash was being reconstructed, the sacrificial service continued uninterrupted because the altar was left in place.) Herod's motives were not altogether altruistic, however, for when the Beis HaMikdash was completed he ordered the Roman eagle placed on the front gate. When some outraged sages removed it, Herod had them burned alive.[33]

At the end of his life, as he lay dying with a fatal illness, Herod commanded that on the day of his death many Jews be executed, so that the Jews should mourn and not rejoice. Fortunately, this order was not carried out. Herod died in 3757 and was succeeded by his son Archelaus, who ruled for nine years and continued his father's wicked legacy. Eventually, the Romans deposed Archelaus and took direct control of the Jewish people. Eretz Yisrael was then ruled by local Roman governors, called procurators, who were in turn overseen by the regional Roman official in Syria, the proconsul.

HILLEL: Although the sages had removed themselves from overt participation in the government, they realized that due to Roman meddling in the Sanhedrin the spiritual life of the nation was being compromised. In consequence, the sages decided that they, rather than the Sanhedrin, should appoint the *nasi*. Hillel, born in Babylon and a maternal scion of the House of David,[34] was proclaimed *nasi* in 3728,[35] a position that included the right to pass on the title to his descendants. Indeed, the House of Hillel produced fourteen generations of great leaders,[36] spanning nearly 400 years, and guiding the Jewish people through some of their most difficult times.

Hillel and his Torah colleague Shammai were both disciples of Shemaya and Avtalyon as well as the last of the *zugos*. (The five generations of *zugos* were Yose ben Yoezer and Yose ben Yochanan, Yehoshua ben Perachiah and Nitai HaArbeli, Yehudah ben Tabbai and Shimon ben Shatach, Shemaya and Avtalyon, and Hillel and Shammai.)[37] Hillel and Shammai were revered by the Jewish people, so much so that even the evil Herod feared to harm them. In addition, Hillel's devotion to Torah study was legendary. Once, unable to afford a yeshivah entrance fee, he crawled up to the skylight in order to hear the lecture and was nearly frozen to death by accumulating snow.[38] He was also possessed of great character traits. His reputation as being impossible to anger, for example, was such that someone bet 400 dinars — a very large sum — that he could cause Hillel to lose his temper. Try as he might, the man could not anger Hillel — and so lost the bet![39] Hillel is also the author of the famous saying: "What is hateful to you do not do unto others."[40]

In terms of Jewish law, Hillel's best-known enactment is the *prozbul*, a document that a creditor writes before the end of *shmittah* assigning collection of his loans to a court. (In *shmittah*, the Torah cancels all private debts. Because of the chilling effect such cancellation has on commerce, and because debts to a court are never cancelled, Hillel created a mechanism to keep the Jewish economy alive.)[41] Hillel's partner Shammai, also a paragon of virtue, taught, "Greet every person with a cheerful face."[42] He was also a fearless upholder of the Torah's honor, standing up to Herod[43] and brooking no mockery of Judaism. (The Talmud, in a famous story, contrasts the strict approach of Shammai and the gentle approach of Hillel regarding potential converts who appeared before them displaying mocking attitudes toward Judaism.)[44]

BEIS SHAMMAI AND BEIS HILLEL AND THE PROLIFERATION OF DISPUTES: Shammai and Hillel themselves only disagreed in three cases.[45] However, due to increased Roman persecution, their disciples were unable to analyze new situations as deeply as Jewish scholars once could. As a result, the emerging scholars broke off into two schools of thought, known as Beis Shammai and Beis Hillel, and wound up disputing more than 300 cases. This beginning of large-scale argumentation (*machlokes*) is viewed by the Talmud as a sad diminution in Torah scholarship, which, due to the lack of clarity, had drastic results for the Jewish people.[46] Although these two schools disagreed about many issues, the scholars personally treated each other with great love and respect.[47] Because of such fine behavior, and because the scholars' sole motivation was to understand G-d's will as reflected in the Torah, and not to engage in personal self-aggrandizement, the Mishnah describes the disputes of Beis Shammai and Beis Hillel as being "for the sake of Heaven."[48]

In most cases, Beis Shammai is stricter while Beis Hillel takes a more lenient approach.[49] In addition, the Talmud rules in favor of Beis Hillel in virtually all situations.[50] One of the more famous disputes involves the number of lights kindled on each night of Chanukah: Beis Shammai holds that eight lights are lit on the first night and one less each night afterward, while Beis Hillel is of the opinion that one light is lit the first night and one more each succeeding night.[51]

It is fitting that Beis Shammai and Beis Hillel are called the first Tannaim, or scholars of the Mishnah. And their longevity is unmatched, for these two schools of sages spanned five generations over a period of approximately 200 years.[52] (Although all the sages from Shimon HaTzadik on are technically considered Tannaim, due to Beis Hillel's and Beis Shammai's frequent appearance in the Mishnah, the term is commonly used to describe the rabbis following Shammai and Hillel themselves.)

YESHU: When viewed in Jewish terms, Yeshu, or Jesus, the central personality in the Christian religion, is a figure shrouded in much doubt and uncertainty. His story comes mainly from Christian writings, which themselves were not based on eyewitness accounts but instead were legends recorded by people who lived generations after the events supposedly took place.[53] Indeed, all references to Yeshu in Josephus, a contemporary historian, are viewed by many scholars as Christian interpolations.[54]

According to the Christians, Yeshu was born in 4 BCE and died in 29 CE after the Jews delivered him to the Romans for execution. Talmudic sources[55] also refer to a person called Yeshu; however, there are many differences between Yeshu in the Talmud and Yeshu in Christianity. First, the Talmud says that the Sanhedrin killed him, whereas Christians say the Jews delivered him to the Romans, who then put him to death. Second, according to Christian sources Yeshu was crucified, which is not — and never has been — one of the modes of execution mandated by Jewish law. Third, the Talmud states that Yeshu was close to the political regime, while Christians believe that the government despised him, considering him an outsider. Fourth, Christians say Yeshu was tried on the eve of Pesach and executed on Pesach, with the so-called Last Supper being a Pesach Seder. However, the Talmud writes that because trials may not be held on the eve of a festival,[56] and executions may not be carried out on a festival itself,[57] Yeshu was actually executed before Pesach. Fifth, Talmudic sources place Yeshu at the time of Yehoshua ben Perachiah, who lived at least 130 years before the time of the

Christian Yeshu's supposed birth. Based on the evidence, then, it appears that there is no record of the Christian Yeshu in either Jewish or secular contemporary sources.

Further, the Christian belief that the Jews are eternally cursed for their complicity in Yeshu's death is recorded in their Bible and is the basis of Christian anti-Semitism. Countless numbers of innocent Jews have been massacred for this supposed crime in the last 2,000 years — most recently during the Holocaust — which could not have been possible without centuries of built-up Christian hatred of Jews. Although the Pope recently absolved the Jews for the death of the Christian god, the myth of Jewish complicity is still widely believed among Christians. Indeed, every ten years the Oberammergau passion play, a major tourist attraction, is performed in Germany. The story of Yeshu's trial and execution is reenacted with spectacular acting and pageantry, including the statement from the book of Matthew attributed to the Jews, that "His blood be on us and on our children." All told, no single person has ever caused as much suffering to the Jewish nation as the man upon whom the Christian religion is based.

Chapter 7

THE DESTRUCTION OF THE SECOND TEMPLE

THE **PROCURATORS**: After deposing Herod's son Archelaus in 6 CE (3765), the Romans imposed direct rule on Eretz Yisrael through procurators. These officials were rapacious and corrupt, and as their behavior increasingly worsened they drove the Jews into revolt against Rome. Indeed, complete Roman callousness toward Jewish religious sensitivities over the years had exacerbated tensions between Romans and Jews to the breaking point. As but one example, Roman procurators confiscated the priestly garments of the *kohen gadol*, releasing them for Jewish use only on Yom Kippur. Pontius Pilate, one of the worst procurators, brought statues of the Roman emperor into Jerusalem, only removing them when thousands of protesting Jews prostrated themselves in front of Pilate's residence, ready to be trampled by his soldiers if Pilate did not comply.

On festivals, when great masses of Jews came to sacrifice at the Beis HaMikdash, they were met by jeering Roman soldiers, who had been stationed in the Temple courtyard in defiance of Jewish law excluding gentiles from such holy areas. At one time, the insane Roman emperor Caligula decreed that a statue of himself be placed in the Beis HaMikdash — then strictly ordered his proconsul Petronius to enforce the ruling. As Petronius approached, tens of thousands of Jews beseeched him to reconsider. Touched by the sight of so many people willing to die for their beliefs, Petronius recanted. The furious emperor instructed him to commit suicide; however, providentially Caligula died, and the noble Petronius was saved.

The procurators also provoked the people into open resistance, then using the rebellion as an excuse to further oppress so-called Jewish criminals. Jewish murder and robbery became commonplace as society began to crumble. To make matters even worse, a revived Sadducee movement bribed the avaricious procurators and gained control of both the Beis HaMikdash and the Sanhedrin.

THE SPIRITUAL CAUSE OF THE DESTRUCTION: The Talmud states that needless hatred among Jews led to the *churban Bayis Sheini*, the destruction of the Second Temple.[1] Civil war between the brothers Hyrcanus and Aristobulus also divided Jews into different factions and led to Roman rule. Eventually, Jewish society was splintered by groups that hated each other — and even fought among themselves. Such strife tore apart Jewish cohesiveness, which, if it had existed, would have successfully resisted Roman infiltration into all areas of life.

At that time, extremist groups of Jews, known as Zealots, arose. Not only were they violently opposed to Roman rule, they also murdered Jews who disagreed with the Zealots' views. In addition, Jewish criminals, known as *sicarii*, prowled the roads and extorted wealth from whomever they could. By 30 CE, forty years before the *churban*, matters spiraled so out of control that the Sanhedrin stopped judging capital cases.[2] Similarly, the Talmud relates that the signs of Divine favor so prevalent in the Beis HaMikdash during the time of Shimon HaTzadik were completely reversed.[3] As but one example, the doors of the Sanctuary opened of their own accord, ominously symbolizing the future Roman entry to destroy the inner sanctum.

KING AGRIPPAS: Despite all the turmoil, a ray of hope still shone for the Jewish people. Herod's grandson Agrippas grew up in Rome and was a childhood friend of the future Emperor Claudius. Upon assuming the throne, Claudius appointed Agrippas King of the Jews.

Despite his Roman upbringing, Agrippas, who ruled 41–44 CE, identified with the Jewish people and their sages. In addition, several of his actions showed his humility and earned him the love of the nation. On Shavuos, Agrippas brought his *bikkurim* (first fruits) to the Beis HaMikdash, humbly carrying them on his shoulder like an ordinary pilgrim.[4] Once, when traveling, his retinue encountered a bridal procession at a crossroads, and Agrippas permitted it to precede him.[5]

In the Beis HaMikdash once again on Sukkos, Agrippas read the Torah scroll, in fulfillment of the mitzvah that the Torah must be read by the king every seven years (*hakhel*). When he came to the verse that states a king must be appointed "from among your brothers" (Deuteronomy 17:15), which requires the monarch to be of Jewish descent, Agrippas broke out in tears, for he was of Edomite ancestry. The people mollified Agrippas by shouting, "You are our brother!" However, the Talmud severely criticizes the Jewish people for such flattery, for Torah law may not be distorted or falsified for any reason. Rather, the Jews present should have remained silent.[6]

Tragically, Agrippas' benevolent reign lasted but a short time. Because the Greek residents of Caesarea were alarmed at his favorable treatment of their bitter enemies, the Jews, when Agrippas visited Caesarea he was poisoned. With his death passed the last chance to save the country and the Beis HaMikdash.

THE PROCURATORS RETURN: After Agrippas' death, the country returned to rule by the procurators. These officials were far worse than their predecessors, and the worst procurator of all was Florus, who came to power in 64 CE. His brutal policies were the direct cause of the Jewish revolt against Roman rule, which began in 66 CE.

Florus' attempts to goad the Jews into violent acts, which in turn would both invite severe Roman reprisals and cover up

Florus' own many indiscretions, succeeded. In Caesarea, riots broke out when Greeks attempted to prevent Jews from attending synagogue on the Sabbath. Florus refused to intervene, and when offered a sizable bribe by the Jews, took the money but did not come to their aid. On another occasion, when Jews responded to Greek mocking of their religion, he threw a number of Jews into prison. In Jerusalem, Florus attempted to rob the Temple treasury. Some youths walked about the city with charity boxes, calling out, "Charity for poor Florus!" An enraged Florus demanded that the leaders of the city hand over those who had insulted him. When the hapless Jews told him that they could not identify the perpetrators, Florus sent his soldiers on a rampage throughout Jerusalem, killing and crucifying 3,600 men, women, and children.

Attempting peace, the Jewish people marched respectfully toward Florus' troops. However, the soldiers refused to acknowledge the Jews' motives, instead attacking them and attempting to seize the Beis HaMikdash. The Jews then besieged the Roman soldiers, who left the city. This skirmish in Jerusalem, in the year 66 CE, marked the beginning of the war against Rome. Afterward, uprisings against Roman rule, encouraged by the Zealots, broke out throughout the land.

The Romans, shocked by Jewish intensity and the initial success of the revolt, saw it as a threat to their rule — not only in Eretz Yisrael, but also throughout the empire where news of the struggle was rapidly spreading. The Romans therefore felt that the incipient uprising must be crushed at all costs. As such, Jewish success in battle also proved fatal for many Jews living throughout the Roman Empire. Riots broke out in Alexandria, Damascus, and elsewhere, resulting in the butchery of countless thousands of Jews. For example, all the Jews of Caesarea were either massacred, expelled from the city, or sold into slavery.

JEWISH DISUNITY: Sadly, instead of uniting to meet the common danger, the Jews splintered into factions that continually fought each other. There were three major groups:

The Friends of Rome were led by wealthy, assimilated Sadducees who desired Roman rule, both to preserve their wealth and power and to weaken the Jewish religion and the sages who maintained it.

The Moderates comprised the majority of the people and the Torah sages. While not favorably inclined to Roman rule, they correctly realized that resisting what was then the world's sole superpower would lead to unmitigated disaster. As such, the Moderates repeatedly tried to communicate to the Romans that their quarrel was not with Roman rule but rather with the wicked procurators. However, the Moderates' efforts were thwarted at every step by other Jewish factions.

The Zealots were made up largely of young toughs who desired an independent Jewish state at all costs, and who operated under the illusion that they could victoriously fight the mighty Roman Empire.

As the struggles continued, the Friends of Rome and the Zealots fought for control of Jerusalem. To further their cause, the Zealots took the astounding step of inviting Edomite mercenaries into Jerusalem, who then perpetrated frightful massacres upon the defenseless populace. Even after taking control of the city, the Zealots fought among themselves for sole rule of Jerusalem. Extremist Zealots, called *biryonim*, burned the stores of food and fuel, which had been sufficient to last twenty-one years of siege,[7] meaning that the then-starving populace would have no choice other than to fight. Following such horrific events and extreme Jewish folly, leading to Jewish self-destruction in Jerusalem, the Roman general Vespasian told his troops that G-d was a better general than he, conferring victory on the Romans without risk.[8]

KAMTZA AND BAR KAMTZA: The Talmud relates that this famous, tragic episode led to the destruction of Jerusalem.[9] A wealthy Jerusalemite made a lavish feast and commanded his servant to invite his friend Kamtza. However, the servant confused Kamtza with Bar Kamtza, who was the host's bitter enemy. Upon noticing Bar Kamtza at the party, the enraged host publicly ordered him to leave. Mortified, Bar Kamtza offered to defray the cost of the entire banquet, but the host refused and personally ejected Bar Kamtza.

Furious that the rabbis attending the meal did not protest his treatment, Bar Kamtza told the Romans that the Jews were rebelling against their rule. In addition, he told the Romans to send a sacrifice to the Beis HaMikdash, in keeping with the Roman tradition of offering such sacrifices, and to entrust the safekeeping of the animal to him.

While on the road, Bar Kamtza inflicted a tiny blemish upon the sacrifice, not noticeable to Roman eyes. Although the *kohanim* wanted to offer the animal anyway, due to the danger involved in insulting the Romans, a distinguished sage prevailed upon them not to do so. Since sacrifices offered on behalf of the emperor and Rome were thereby suspended, Josephus writes that this incident was the basis of war with Rome.[10]

VESPASIAN'S CAMPAIGN OF CONQUEST: In 67 CE, the veteran Roman general Vespasian invaded Eretz Yisrael with four outstanding legions, including the X Legion, the most distinguished of all Roman legions. In addition, Vespasian brought the latest weapons of war, including catapults, siege towers, and battering rams. His strategy was to conquer the land, moving down from the Galilee in the north, thereby isolating Jerusalem. Wisely, he left the heavily defended capital for last.

The city of Sepphoris, with its strategic fortifications, surrendered to the Romans without lifting a hand in self-defense. Vespasian then marched through the Galilee, easily capturing such important towns as Tiberias, Gamla (in the nearby Golan Heights), and Gush Chalav. After forty-seven days of fierce battle, the Romans scaled the walls of the presumably impregnable fortress at Jotapata, massacring 40,000 Jewish defenders.

After completing the conquest of the north, Vespasian turned south and west, conquering the Mediterranean seacoast, and all inland areas, finally besieging Jerusalem in 68 CE.

LIFE IN JERUSALEM: Rival Zealot factions, ruthlessly executing anyone suspected of wishing to negotiate with Rome, held the be-sieged city. Starvation was rampant, even among the very wealthy. The Talmud tells the story of Martha bas Beothus, an upper-class woman who never walked in the street but always rode in a carriage, and who was accustomed to eating only the fin-est foods. After sending her servant on a fruitless search for an ever-dwindling supply of inferior food, Martha decided to walk out and see what she could find. After accidentally stepping on some refuse, she was so nauseated that she became fatally ill. As Martha was dying, she threw all her gold and silver into the street, proclaiming its worthlessness, but no one bothered to col-lect the treasure.[11]

Meanwhile, there was turmoil in Rome, as several emperors were proclaimed and deposed in 69 CE. As the Roman Senate searched for a successor who could bring stability to the empire, Vespasian, one of the contestants, maintained the siege of Jeru-salem, biding his time and awaiting developments in Rome.

THE MISSION OF RABBI JOCHANAN BEN ZAKKAI: As Jerusa-lem hurtled toward its inevitable destruction, the sages made a last effort to negotiate with the Romans to save something of the Jewish people and the Jewish religion. Rabbi Jochanan ben Zakkai, the leading Torah scholar in Jerusalem, secretly ap-proached his nephew, Zealot head Abba Sikra, requesting safe conduct out of the city.[12]

When public exit became impossible, because the Zealot forces executed anyone attempting to leave, Abba Sikra proposed that Rabbi Jochanan feign sickness, then have his students spread a rumor that the great sage had passed away. Because Jewish law forbids keeping a dead person overnight in Jerusa-lem, Rabbi Jochanan was placed in a coffin, along with some de-caying meat, and carried by trusted disciples. (An outsider would quickly realize that a coffin carrying a live person is lighter than if it contained a corpse — hence the term dead weight.) Rabbi Jochanan's followers all prayed that the ruse would succeed. Ev-erything worked according to plan until the coffin approached the city gates. There, the Zealot guards demanded to stab the body to insure that it was actually dead. At that point, Abba Sikra intervened, telling the guards that it was disrespectful to stab the dead rabbi, and Rabbi Jochanan's students were permitted to take the coffin out of the city.

Out of sight of the guards, Rabbi Jochanan left his coffin and approached the Roman camp. Upon meeting with Vespasian, Rabbi Jochanan greeted the general with the salutation due an emperor, predicting that Vespasian would be so crowned. As they were conversing, a messenger arrived from Rome with the news that the Senate had indeed proclaimed Vespasian emperor.

Impressed by Rabbi Jochanan's prescience, Vespasian, in a spirit of magnanimity, granted him three wishes. Realizing that Vespasian would refuse to spare the Beis HaMikdash, Rabbi Jochanan requested something that seemed insignificant to the Romans, but was crucial to Jewish survival. (There is an alternative opinion in the Talmud that criticizes Rabbi Jochanan for not asking Vespasian to spare the Beis HaMikdash.)[13]

Indeed, Rabbi Jochanan knew that the Jewish people could outlast the loss of their land, and even the loss of their Beis HaMikdash, but that without Torah sages the nation would die. As such, Rabbi Jochanan uttered four of the most famous words in Jewish history: *"Ten li Yavneh vechachameha"* — Give me Yavneh and its scholars. Vespasian, having no opposition to a group of rabbis studying Torah in an obscure hamlet, readily acquiesced to the request, allowing the sages to assemble at Yavneh even prior to the destruction of Jerusalem. (Fifty years later, the Romans regretted their colossal mistake, realizing that Torah is indeed the key to Jewish survival.)

Rabbi Jochanan also asked that the Romans spare the family of the *nasi*, and that physicians heal the sage Rabbi Tzadok, who fasted forty years hoping to invoke Divine mercy and forestall the impending destruction. Both these requests were answered as well. In all, the farsightedness of Rabbi Jochanan has preserved the Jewish people to this day: Rome is long gone, but the Jewish people are still studying the teachings of the Yavneh sages.

TITUS DESTROYS THE BEIS HAMIKDASH: Leaving for Rome to assume power, Vespasian transferred control of the army to his son Titus. After Pesach 70 CE, the final battles for Jerusalem began.[14] The emaciated Jews fought bravely and tenaciously, but Roman assault teams eventually overwhelmed them.

On the seventeenth of Tammuz, the Romans broke through the walls of Jerusalem. The fast day of 17 Tammuz marks this and other tragedies that occurred on that day throughout history.[15]

On the ninth of Av, Tishah B'Av, the Romans entered the Beis HaMikdash late in the afternoon, setting it on fire. Josephus graphically describes the carnage:

> As the flames caught, a fearful cry welled up from the Jews, who rushed to the rescue, caring nothing for their lives... Around the altar were heaps of corpses, while streams of blood flowed down the steps of the sanctuary... While the Temple was in flames, the victors stole everything they could lay their hands on, and slaughtered all who were caught. No pity was shown to age or rank, old men or children, the laity or priests — all were massacred. As the flames roared up, and since the Temple stood on a hill, it seemed as if the whole city were ablaze. The noise was deafening, with war cries of the legions, howls of the rebels surrounded by fire and sword, and the shrieks of the people. The ground was hidden by corpses, and the soldiers had to climb over heaps of bodies in pursuit of the fugitives.[16]

The Beis HaMikdash started burning late on Tishah B'Av, and burned throughout the entire day afterward. For this reason, Rabbi Jochanan was of the opinion that the tenth of Av be designated as a fast day. However, because the Beis HaMikdash began to burn on the ninth of Av, other rabbinic authorities fix the fast then. Current practice accepts the latter view.[17] Nevertheless, Rabbi Jochanan's view is also taken into account, as the mourning practices of the Nine Days commence at the beginning of the month of Av and end midday on the tenth.[18]

After the destruction, the Romans emptied the Temple treasuries, with gold becoming so commonplace that its price dropped by 50 percent. Drunk with victory, the soldiers entered the Temple courtyard, offered sacrifices to their gods, and praised Titus. Titus himself entered the *Kodesh HaKodashim*, committed a lewd and despicable act, and disdainfully slashed the holy curtain, the *paroches*, with his sword. Miraculously, blood spurted from the curtain, causing Titus to believe that he had killed the Almighty, G-d forbid.[19]

The destruction was so complete that only the Western Wall, the *Kosel HaMa'aravi*, was left standing, for G-d had promised that the Holy Temple would never be entirely destroyed. After the fall of the Temple, the Romans spent the next four weeks crushing the remaining resistance; by the seventh of Elul they had complete control of Jerusalem. Thousands of captured Jews were executed, while those that remained alive envied the dead, for the survivors were sent to the mines of Egypt or became gladiators, fighting each other or wild beasts for the amusement of the Romans. Finally, so many Jews were available as slaves that there was no need for slave markets. Overall, Jewish casualties were enormous — more than one million killed in Jerusalem alone, with nearly 100,000 taken captive.[20]

TITUS' VICTORY MARCH: Having completed his sack of Jerusalem, Titus departed for Rome, taking hundreds of Jewish captives carefully chosen for their height and appearance. To the roar of cheering crowds, the Jewish prisoners marched through the imperial city, bearing holy Temple vessels, including the Menorah. Arriving at the temple of Jupiter, one of the rebel leaders was publicly beheaded, and another thrown into prison.

To commemorate the victory, a monument was constructed, which still stands today. The Arch of Titus, depicting the scene of Jewish captives carrying the holy objects of the Beis HaMikdash, was complemented by coins minted to commemorate the great Roman victory over the Jews. With Emperor Vespasian on the front, the coin's reverse depicts a weeping woman with bound hands, symbolizing the Jewish people, with a Roman legionnaire standing haughtily nearby. The caption reads JUDEA CAPTA — Judah is captured.

MASADA: After the Jewish nation was conquered, one stronghold still held out — the seemingly impregnable fortress of Masada, standing on a high hilltop in the Judean desert. Built as a palace by King Herod, Masada had its own water supply, food stores, and even a *mikvah*, a ritual bath, constructed according to all rigorous legal standards.

Approximately 1,000 Zealots — men, women, and children — occupied the mountaintop fort, hoping to outlast the might of Rome. As the Jews held out atop Masada, Roman Legion X methodically constructed adjacent earthworks, and on top of these a high tower, from which they operated their battering rams and hurled missiles into the fortress. Although the Jewish defenders courageously repulsed the Romans, eventually the attackers were ready to storm the outpost. On the first day of Pesach, 73 CE, Elazar ben Yair, the Zealot leader, delivered an impassioned speech imploring the Jews to take their lives rather than submit to Roman slavery. A suicide pact was drawn up, and men slew their wives and children before killing themselves. When the Romans entered Masada, they were greeted by an eerie silence. Two women and five children, who had hidden to avoid the mass suicide, told them what had happened. Filled with respect for the Jews' dogged determination, the Romans did not celebrate their hard-won victory.

With the fall of Masada, all Jewish resistance in Eretz Yisrael came to an end.

As important as the Masada events are in Jewish history, it is interesting to note that the entire episode is not recorded in Talmudic or Midrashic sources; instead, events are reported only in Josephus' narrative. Why did the sages not record it? Although no one is certain, perhaps the sages did not consider suicide for the sake of independence, or to avoid slavery, a worthy ideal.

Despite the lack of authentic Jewish sources about Masada, there is no doubt that momentous events occurred there. Even today, more than 1,900 years later, the outlines of both the besieging Roman camp and the siege wall surrounding Masada remain clearly visible.

THE YEAR OF THE *CHURBAN*: There are several opinions as to which year the destruction of the Beis HaMikdash occurred. Rashi gives the date as 3828, or 68 CE,[21] while Tosafos hold that it took place in 3829 or 69 CE.[22] Josephus, on whom secular histories of this era are based, says it happened in 70 CE.

Part of the differences in opinion stem from alternate readings of the Talmud. Rashi and Tosafos dispute the meaning of the statement[23] that the Second Temple lasted 420 years. Rashi holds that the *churban* took place in the 420th year after the Temple was built: adding 420 to 3408 (the date of construction) yields 3828, or 68 CE. However, Tosafos understand that the 420-year duration of the Second Beis HaMikdash means 420 complete years; therefore, one year must be added to the calculation, which comes out to 3829, or 69 CE. Finally, Josephus' opinion does not contradict Tosafos, as there are two methods for dating Jewish years. First, the five days before the creation of Adam are Year Zero, and Adam's creation marks Year One. Second, those initial five days are Year One, and Adam's creation begins Year Two. Tosafos use the former opinion, while Josephus follows the latter.

Current dating of the Jewish calendar assigns a year to the five creation days, hence the date of 3830 or 70 CE. However, Rashi's date of 3828 is difficult to understand. Rabbinic tradition states that the Beis HaMikdash was destroyed in the year after *shmittah*, the sabbatical year.[24] Jewish law states that *shmittah* occurs in any year divisible by seven. Accordingly, 3829 (Tosafos) or 3830 (Josephus) was a year after *shmittah*. However, the year 3828, the year according to Rashi's view, is not a year after *shmittah* in either calendar calculation. (For a fuller treatment of this subject, see *History of the Jewish People: The Second Temple Era*, Mesorah Publications, pp. 213–214.)

JOSEPHUS: Josephus Flavius, the Jewish secular historian of the Second Temple era, is a figure of great controversy. Some traditional Jewish historians defend him passionately, saying that his actions and writings were motivated by what Josephus himself considered best for the survival of the Jewish people.[25] Others are equally adamant in proclaiming him to be an opportunistic traitor who fawned on the Romans for self-preservation, and whose history is full of distortions.[26]

Born in 37 CE, Josephus was a *kohen* who, as a young man, traveled to Rome and became enamored of Roman culture. During the war against Rome, he commanded the fortified city of Jotapata. Realizing that defeat was imminent, Josephus hid in a cave with other fighters. When the Jews in the cave decided on a suicide pact, Josephus arranged matters to remain alive. Surrendering to the Romans, he convinced Vespasian that he would be valuable as a Roman spokesman to the Jews. Traveling with the Roman army on their road of conquest, Josephus constantly harangued the Jewish defenders, telling them of the futility of resistance.

After the war, as a friend of Vespasian and Titus, Josephus settled in Rome, where he wrote historical works with a pro-Roman slant. However, his Jewish sentiments do sometimes appear in his work, which includes *The Jewish War*, describing Jewish history from the Maccabees to the downfall of Masada; *The Jewish Antiquities*, a history from Creation to the outbreak of war with Rome; and *Contra Apion*, a spirited defense of Judaism in response to the anti-Semitic Greek writer Apion.

On many occasions, the writings of Josephus contradict Talmudic and Midrashic tradition. For example, he writes that he, and not Rabbi Jochanan ben Zakkai, negotiated with Vespasian, and that Titus did not want to destroy the Beis HaMikdash; instead, his soldiers simply got out of control. Josephus also slanders the Pharisees, the sages and their followers. Mainstream opinion is that if Josephus records events, such as Masada, that do not appear in traditional sources, he can be believed. Nevertheless, Josephus' ideas must be discounted if he contradicts accepted Talmudic or Midrashic sources.

SUICIDE IN JEWISH LAW: A very severe transgression, suicide is considered tantamount to murder. A suicide forfeits his share in the World to Come (*Olam Haba*)[27] and is buried in a separate area of the cemetery. Unless it can be assumed that the suicide was deranged at the time of his death, no mourning rites are held for him.[28] However, some rabbinic opinions hold that suicide to avoid being tortured into sinning is greatly meritorious.[29] As such, the Talmud relates the story of 400 boys and girls who, while being taken to Rome for immoral purposes, jumped into the sea and drowned themselves.[30] In the times of the Crusades, parents killed their young children and themselves to prevent them from being forcibly baptized. The stories of some of these martyrs are immortalized in the *Kinnos* and other prayers. According to those opinions, suicide to avoid transgression is highly proper. (The permissibility of killing one's children to prevent their conversion is an issue that is hotly debated by the great Rishonim. See *Daas Zekeinim MiBaalei HaTosafos* on Genesis 9:5 for a discussion of this most difficult issue.) However, suicide for national pride, such as at Masada, is not part of this category.

Chapter 8

FROM YAVNEH TO THE WRITING OF THE MISHNAH

C OMPARING THE TWO DESTRUCTIONS: *Churban Bayis Sheini* was far more disastrous for the Jewish people than the destruction of the First Temple.[1] The Babylonians who destroyed the first Beis HaMikdash did so for purely political motives; they harbored no feelings of hate toward Jews per se. The Romans, however, who were fueled by anti-Semitic writings and actions of Syrians and Greeks, and the long-running Jewish revolt, despised the Jews for many years before the *churban*. After the first destruction, the Babylonian exile was a relatively benign experience, for the conquerors deported the Jews en masse to Babylon. As a result, the Jews were all concentrated in one general area, making it much easier for them to regroup and rebuild their communities. The Romans, however, scattered the Jews throughout their vast empire, beginning the great Jewish Diaspora. After the first destruction, the prophet Jeremiah had proclaimed that the Beis HaMikdash would be rebuilt after seventy years. However, Roman exile brought with it no such harbinger of hope. Quickly, it became apparent to the Jewish people that a dark, seemingly endless exile lay ahead.

YAVNEH: Providentially, G-d had prepared the cure before the blow. Before the Roman destruction, Rabbi Jochanan ben Zakkai, a great and indefatigable leader, laid the foundation of

Jewish survival. With Roman assent, he brought the nation's greatest Torah sages to Yavneh, established a great yeshivah, and reconstituted the Sanhedrin. Free of Sadducees, Herodians, Hellenists, corrupt kings, *kohanim gedolim*, and nobility, all of whom had abandoned the Jewish people in the time of their distress, the sages had the people's sole allegiance. As such, the Sanhedrin at Yavneh had several vital tasks to accomplish:

Many halachic issues had not been decided in the tumultuous years before the *churban*, notably the disputes between Beis Shammai and Beis Hillel. At Yavneh, the Academy ruled in favor of Beis Hillel in virtually all cases.[2]

As the last eyewitnesses told of the terrible events, and over time as they passed away, the Yavneh sages were concerned that Temple matters were in danger of being forgotten. As such, they recorded the laws of the Temple service, as well as the Beis HaMikdash's layout.[3]

The sages also created a uniform prayer service for the Jewish people. Although prayers such as the *Amidah* already existed during Temple times,[4] these prayers were not written down, and different versions began to be part of general use. In addition, the sages of Yavneh added *Velamalshinim* to the weekday *Shemoneh Esrei*, making a total of nineteen benedictions.[5] This addition was created to counteract growing Christian influence, for the early Christians were Jews who were indistinguishable from their Torah-observant brethren and were having a pernicious influence on the Jewish people. Here, the Christians' refusal to recite this blessing helped identify them. Finally, the scholars of Yavneh also revised the *Amidah* to reflect the loss of the Temple, changing the text from praying for the survival of the Beis HaMikdash and Jerusalem to supplications for their restoration.

Since political action on behalf of the Jews was necessary, the sages of Yavneh, whom the Romans believed represented the Jewish people, sent delegations to Rome to advocate for Jewish needs. In addition, since thousands of Jews were held captive in Rome, the rabbis redeemed them wherever possible, sometimes expending vast sums for this purpose.[6]

Rabbi Jochanan ben Zakkai: A distinguished disciple of Beis Hillel,[7] the elder statesman of the sages was universally acclaimed. Although not of the dynastic family of Hillel, Rabbi Jochanan ben Zakkai acted as *nasi* in Yavneh until Rabban Gamliel, the son of the previous *nasi*, came of age. Contrary to the charge made by secular historians, during Rabbi Jochanan's tenure a new Rabbinic Judaism did not appear and Torah did not change. Instead, Jewish observance continued as before, without the sacrificial services then impossible to carry out. However, so that the Jewish people would not forget the Beis HaMikdash over time, Rabbi Jochanan made several enactments:

In the time of the Beis HaMikdash, the *esrog, lulav, hadasim,* and *aravos* were used as ritual objects in the Beis HaMikdash all seven days of Sukkos, as mandated by the Torah (Leviticus 23:40), but only on the first day everywhere else. Rabbi Jochanan decreed that the four species be used all seven days worldwide, thereby perpetuating the memory of the Beis HaMikdash.[8]

In Temple times, on the second day of Pesach, the *omer* sacrifice was offered, thereby permitting consumption of new grain. In the absence of this sacrifice, the Torah nevertheless permits eating that year's crop immediately on the morning of the second day. However, to remember the Temple, Rabbi Jochanan forbade eating the grain the entire second day. Rabbi Jochanan's reasoning was as follows: following the advent of Messiah, the possibility exists that the Third Temple could be rebuilt at any time; unwittingly, people would not realize that when the Beis HaMikdash is rebuilt they must wait for the *omer* to be offered to eat, and would instead erroneously begin eating the new grain on the morning of the second day of Pesach.[9] Not only did this enactment preserve an important law, it also elevated hope for the imminent return of the future Beis HaMikdash.

In addition, Rabbi Jochanan stipulated that the shofar be sounded in Yavneh when Rosh HaShanah occurs on the Sabbath. Normally, due to a concern that one might inadvertently carry the shofar into the street, thus violating the Sabbath, rabbinic law forbids sounding the shofar on the Sabbath. In Temple times, Sabbath shofar sounding was permitted at the site of the Great Sanhedrin, which met adjacent to the Beis HaMikdash. In order to invest the Great Sanhedrin of Yavneh with the necessary prestige needed for its decisions to be honored by the Jewish people, Rabbi Jochanan gave the court equal status to its earlier counterpart.[10]

Having trained Rabban Gamliel to assume his rightful inheritance as *nasi*, Rabbi Jochanan then moved to the distant town of Beror Chayil, so that Rabban Gamliel could make decisions without being perceived in Rabbi Jochanan's shadow.[11]

ROMAN EMPERORS AFTER VESPASIAN: Vespasian died several years after the *churban*, and was succeeded by his son Titus, whose rule was marked by great benevolence. When the famous eruption of Mt. Vesuvius and other disasters occurred during his reign, Titus emptied the imperial coffers to aid the populace. How did his unspeakable cruelty give way to such kindness? Although scholars differ on the subject, Titus' change in personality was likely due to a degenerative condition caused by a gnat eating away at his brain. According to the Talmud,[12] Titus was punished in such an unnatural manner because he blasphemed the Almighty when he destroyed the Beis HaMikdash.

In 81 CE, after a two-year reign, Titus died and was succeeded by his brother Domitian, a vicious anti-Semite. Troubled by the Jewish success at Yavneh, the new emperor's constant harassment forced the assembly to disband.[13] Also plotting to exterminate the Jews throughout the empire, Domitian's decree was forestalled due to the intervention of a sympathetic Roman senator, who gave his life to annul the edict.[14] In 96 CE, after Domitian's assassination, Nerva, an emperor more favorable to the Jews, ascended to the throne. Relaxing many of the discriminatory decrees against the Jews, Nerva also repealed the annual tax that Jews had to pay to the temple of Jupiter.

DISPUTES BETWEEN THE SAGES: The instability caused by the temporary breakup of the Yavneh assembly resulted in a number of disputes that created dissension among the Torah scholars. While such disharmony was both real and strong, the sages disagreed with one another only because each felt that his course of action was best for the nation as a whole. Personal animosity, or desire for honor, played no role in the opposing viewpoints, as the various episodes clearly indicate. Among these disputes are three famous incidents, two between Rabban Gamliel and Rabbi Joshua, and one involving Rabban Gamliel and Rabbi Eliezer.

As *nasi*, Rabban Gamliel felt that even the greatest scholars must scrupulously adhere to decisions reached at Yavneh; otherwise, a disastrous fragmentation of the Jewish people would take place.[15] Further, he felt that at such a traumatic time the Jewish people needed especially strong leadership. Despite Rabban Gamliel's thoughts, the other sages felt that laws promulgated during the dispersion of the Yavneh academy were not binding.[16] In addition, they thought that the Jewish people would be better served by rulings achieved through a consensus of opinions, rather than imposed from above.[17] Finally, these sages felt that it was forbidden for any rabbinic authority to follow what he knew to be incorrect if the matter had not been voted on by a full Sanhedrin.

The first episode concerned Rabban Gamliel and other sages who disagreed with Rabbi Eliezer regarding the ritual purity of a certain type of oven. In fact, Rabbi Eliezer was so convinced that he was correct that he invoked supernatural phenomena to prove his point. A stream outside the yeshivah began flowing backward, and the walls of the study hall began to move inward. Unimpressed, the other sages told him that miracles do not decide halachic issues. Not giving up, Rabbi Eliezer asked G-d Himself to concur with his view, and a voice came from heaven stating that Rabbi Eliezer's opinion should be followed, as he was the greatest of the rabbis. Despite this impressive evidence for Rabbi Eliezer, the sages refused to relent, taking the entire incident as a Divine test to see whether they would back down from a decision reached by majority vote.[18] Sadly, the sages also excommunicated Rabbi Eliezer. Despite feeling he was correct, Rabbi Eliezer observed the ban, demonstrating his great humility.[19]

One year, Rabban Gamliel, the *nasi*, and Rabbi Joshua, the *av beis din*, disputed the proper day for Rosh HaShanah. Accordingly, Yom Kippur came out on a different day in each sage's calculation. While not openly rejecting Rabban Gamliel's Yom Kippur, Rabbi Joshua planned to observe his own date quietly.[20] However, Rabban Gamliel commanded Rabbi Joshua to appear in court on Rabbi Joshua's supposed Yom Kippur, carrying his wallet and walking stick in violation of Rabbi Joshua's own calculations. Upon being told by his colleagues that Rabban Gamliel has jurisdiction over the calendar, Rabbi Joshua complied with the order. In a great display of respect for Rabbi Joshua, Rabban Gamliel rose to greet him, embraced him, and called him "my teacher, who is greater than I in Torah wisdom."[21]

There was a disagreement between Rabban Gamliel and Rabbi Joshua as to whether or not reciting the evening prayer (Maariv) is obligatory. Rabban Gamliel held that Maariv is obligatory, while Rabbi Joshua was of the opinion that it is optional. (Currently, Jewish practice mandates Maariv as an obligation.)[22] When a student asked Rabbi Joshua for a private ruling on the matter, Rabbi Joshua told him Maariv was optional. Upon hearing that Rabbi Joshua told others to follow his opinion, Rabban Gamliel confronted Rabbi Joshua, who, in order to preserve the peace, denied his involvement in the matter.

Sensing that Rabbi Joshua was trying to evade the issue, Rabban Gamliel forced him to stand during the *nasi*'s lecture at the yeshivah. Stung by Rabban Gamliel's continuing humiliation of Rabbi Joshua, the people — not the sages — decided to depose Rabban Gamliel as *nasi*. However, a suitable candidate was needed to replace him, and this was not a simple matter. Obviously, Rabbi Joshua could not assume Rabban Gamliel's position, as such a move would indicate the greatest disrespect to

Rabban Gamliel. Others were unacceptable for other reasons. Due to his undistinguished lineage, for example, and the fact that the people would not sufficiently respect him, Rabbi Akiva could not fill the spot.

Eventually, Rabbi Elazar ben Azariah, but eighteen years old, was tapped for the job. Would the Jewish people follow such a young man? As an answer, G-d made a miracle and turned Rabbi Elazar's hair white like someone aged seventy. Eventually, Rabban Gamliel asked forgiveness of Rabbi Joshua, and was reinstated as *nasi*, sharing the position with Rabbi Elazar ben Azariah. Here, the Talmud notes Rabban Gamliel's great integrity, for during the entire time he was deposed, Rabban Gamliel took part in all the halachic discussions at the yeshivah, sitting among the disciples and accepting Rabbi Elazar ben Azariah's authority.[23]

BO BAYOM: On the day that Rabbi Elazar ben Azariah was appointed *nasi*, many students were admitted to the yeshivah. As a result of the ensuing discussions, all undecided halachic issues were resolved. Laws clarified on that day are prefaced in the Mishnah with the phrase *Bo Bayom*. The *Mishnayos* of tractate *Eduyos* were also taught that day.[24] Among the subjects discussed in *Eduyos* are six disputes of Beis Shammai and Beis Hillel that had not been incorporated into the body of the oral Mishnah; cases in which, contrary to usual practice, Beis Shammai takes the lenient approach while Beis Hillel is strict; and instances in which Beis Hillel retracted their opinion in favor of that of Beis Shammai.

TRAJAN: The emperor Trajan, who succeeded Nerva from 98–117 CE, was a vicious anti-Semite, and the Jews suffered terribly through his long reign. Dreaming of extending the Roman Empire beyond the countries Alexander the Great had conquered, even to fabled India, Trajan knew that Babylon, heavily populated by Jews, lay in his path. The Babylonian Jews found themselves in a terrible dilemma: Should they resist the Romans, thereby endangering all the Jews in the Roman Empire, or should they not fight alongside their Babylonian country-men to repulse Trajan, and thereby be accused of treason? Alarmed at the prospect of all the world's Jews falling under Roman domination, the Jews of Babylon chose to fight. Consequently, although the Romans conquered Babylon, they held it only a short time.

Infuriated by the Jewish role in Trajan's defeat, the anti-Semitic Greeks of Alexandria, Egypt, assisted by Roman troops, instigated pogroms against the Alexandrian Jews, the largest Jewish population of any city in the Roman Empire. Many Jews had assembled for prayer at the Great Synagogue, which was so vast that sextons standing with flags indicated the time to respond Amen to the blessings. At prayer, the Jews were massacred to the last person.[25]

When the Jews of Cyprus and Libya discovered what had happened to the empire's largest and wealthiest Jewish community, they readied themselves to resist the inevitable attacks. Taking their preparations as a sign of incipient revolt, Trajan sent Roman legions to assist the Greeks in wiping out the Jews. To this day, church historians, full of malice toward Jews, have distorted these events, stating that the Jews both attempted a general uprising against Rome and engaged in wholesale massacres of Greeks and Romans. However, papyrus writings of that period indicate that the Greeks were the instigators.[26]

During Trajan's rule, the sages had to leave Yavneh and met secretly. Convening surreptitiously in the town of Lod, in the attic of the Nitzah family, their meetings are recorded in the Talmud as *B'Aliyas Beis Nitzah B'Lud.*[27] At this time, Trajan appointed a special governor for Eretz Yisrael, Quietus, who caused so much anguish that to commemorate the intense suffering the sages forbade brides to wear crowns.[28] He was so hated that the date of Quietus' removal from office was celebrated annually.

HADRIAN: If Trajan was horrible, he was benign compared to his successor Hadrian, who of all the Roman emperors was the single worst ruler of the Jewish people. Remarkably, though, Hadrian began his reign favorably inclined to the Jews. Roman oppression of Jews throughout the empire ceased, and the Sanhedrin was permitted to reconvene openly, this time in the town of Usha in the Galilee. Hadrian even gave permission to rebuild the Beis HaMikdash.

Understandably, excitement in the Jewish world reached a fever pitch. Vast sums of money were gathered, and multitudes of Jews streamed toward Eretz Yisrael. However, the Samaritan inhabitants of the land, long-time foes of the Jews, were terrified by the possibility of a Jewish rejuvenation. Convincing Hadrian that a Jewish rejuvenation would spark a revolt, the Samaritans advised Hadrian to retract his magnanimous gesture. Not willing to change his mind openly, Hadrian allowed the Jews to rebuild the Beis HaMikdash, but stipulated that it could not be in its original place. Since Jewish law precisely fixes the site of the Temple,[29] this decree was tantamount to a revocation of the promise.

Greatly dismayed at having their hopes so cruelly dashed, many Jews began talking openly of revolt, and it took the valiant efforts of the great sage Rabbi Joshua to ameliorate the people's anger. The turning point was his parable of a bird that removes a bone stuck in a lion's throat, then demands a reward. The lion replies that the ability to boast of sticking one's neck into a lion's mouth and escaping unscathed is itself the greatest reward. Likewise, Rabbi Joshua continued, Jews should be grateful that they are not being persecuted, and therefore not demand too much from the Romans. Mollified, the people accepted Rabbi Joshua's logic, and calm was temporarily restored.[30]

Over time, however, Hadrian realized that the mitzvos of the Torah, rather than national independence, were the backbone of the Jewish people — and he set out to break it. Indeed, Hadrian took several steps that convinced the Jewish people that there was no alternative to rising up against an oppressor bent on destroying them spiritually. First, Hadrian built a temple to Jupiter on the site of the Beis HaMikdash, and then began constructing a new Roman city, naming it Aelia Capitolina, on the ruins of

Jerusalem. To accomplish his aims, Hadrian completely ploughed over the remnants of Jerusalem, thereby removing all traces of the former Jewish presence. Like the destruction of the Holy Temple itself, this tragedy also occurred on Tishah B'Av,[31] and is one of the reasons for the fast. In a departure from previous Roman policy, Hadrian also decreed against the observance of key mitzvos: *bris milah*, the Sabbath, and *taharas mishpachah*, family purity.[32] As in the times of Antiochus, this blow against the Torah sparked the second great Jewish revolt against Rome.

BAR KOCHBA: This revolt began as small, spontaneous clashes between Jews and Roman forces. Jews were hiding in caves in order to be able to perform the mitzvos.[33] When discovered by Roman soldiers, they resisted, in some cases successfully. Eventually, a great warrior, Shimon ben Kozba, united the disparate armed Jewish groups into a cohesive fighting force, which then captured Jerusalem from the Romans. Ben Kozba further proclaimed himself as the Messiah,[34] and had the backing of the greatest sage of his time, Rabbi Akiva, along with many other sages. Shortly, Ben Kozba became known as Bar Kochba, which means son of a star, based on a verse in the Torah (Numbers 24:17) that likens the Messiah to a star.

However, other sages felt strongly that Bar Kochba was not the Messiah, and two incidents vindicated them. First, before one of his battles, Bar Kochba blasphemously proclaimed: "G-d, if you choose not to help us, at least do not come to the aid of our enemies," thereby implying that the Jews could be victorious without Divine assistance. On another occasion, Bar Kochba suspected that his saintly uncle, Rabbi Elazar HaModai, knew military secrets. Enraged, Bar Kochba confronted the elderly Rabbi Elazar, kicking him and causing his death.[35] Their hopes dashed, the Jews then called Bar Kochba "Bar Koziba," meaning son of a lie. All told, Bar Kochba ruled in Jerusalem for two and a half years,[36] with minted coins commemorating his rule.[37]

THE DOWNFALL OF BETAR: Aghast at the success of the Jewish uprising, Hadrian committed all his forces to crush the revolt. Julius Severus, a top general, was recalled from far-off Britain to head the Roman army.[38] Slowly, despite meeting fierce resistance from Bar Kochba's troops, the Romans reconquered Jerusalem and much of the country. Finally, Bar Kochba fled to the fortified city of Betar. On Tishah B'Av,[39] 133 CE,[40] after nine years of war, the Romans conquered Betar, effectively ending all Jewish resistance. Hundreds of thousands of Jews were slaughtered by the vengeful Romans in Betar alone. With virtually no survivors,[41] rivers of Jewish blood flowed for miles to the sea, and the Romans were able to fertilize their fields for seven years using their victims' blood.[42] Jewish bodies were not buried, but were used as fences for fields, in a chilling premonition of Nazi practice. Bar Kochba also died, either executed by the sages for making false Messianic claims,[43] or during the final battle for Betar.[44]

SHAAS HASHMAD: As would occur 1,800 years later, the Romans embarked on implementing the Final Solution to the Jewish problem in Eretz Yisrael, and the destruction became worse than at the time of the *churban*. A Roman official, Tinneas Rufus, ransacked Eretz Yisrael, killing countless numbers of Jews and selling others as slaves throughout the Roman Empire. All anti-Torah edicts were reinforced, and performance of any mitzvah was punished by torture and death.[45] Indeed, this period of time, among the worst in Jewish history, is described in the Talmud as *Shaas Hashmad* — a time of full-fledged warfare against the Jewish religion. Events became so dire that, although Jewish law normally mandates that one may violate any transgression — other than idolatry, adultery, and murder — to save one's life,[46] at such a time it is prescribed that one must give his life rather than transgress even the smallest Jewish custom, including those not established halachically. To make matters worse, the Romans, realizing that the Torah sages are the moral center of the Jewish people, hunted them down ruthlessly. (Centuries later, the Nazis would follow the same tactics.)[47] Many scholars were executed, and others fled to safety in Babylon.

In order to eradicate any vestige of Jewish connection to Eretz Yisrael, the Romans renamed it Palestina, after the previous Philistine inhabitants. Currently, this name survives as Palestine, and is likewise used instead of Eretz Yisrael to deny any Jewish connection to the land.

ASARAH HARUGEI MALCHUS: Ten great sages were brutally tortured and executed by the Romans. Although two of them were killed at the time of the *churban*, and the others during *Shaas Hashmad*, all ten are grouped together in the liturgy of Tishah B'Av[48] and Yom Kippur[49] (The Midrash states that all ten were killed as a Divine, national punishment for the sale of Joseph by his ten brothers.)[50] Several Midrashic versions exist as to the identity of the ten sages, including:

Rabbi Akiva: The greatest of the Tannaim, Rabbi Akiva approached the level of Moses.[51] Of humble origins, and a descendant of converts,[52] Rabbi Akiva was an ignorant shepherd up until the age of forty. However, his wealthy employer's daughter, Rachel, saw his refinement of character[53] and potential for greatness,[54] and proposed to marry him if he would study Torah. Her father, not in favor of the marriage, forbade the couple the use of his property, and as a result they lived in abject poverty. So that he could study properly, Rachel sent Rabbi Akiva away and did not see him for twenty-four years, until he returned as a great sage accompanied by 24,000 disciples.

As a true sage, Rabbi Akiva indefatigably served the Jewish people, traveling all over the Jewish world to aid outlying communities in spiritual need, and to raise funds for the poor and for Torah institutions.[55] At that time, he suffered a tragedy that would have broken a lesser man — the eradication of his life's work. All 24,000 students died in a Divine plague for not showing each other proper respect.[56] (Since this misfortune occurred during the seven-week period between Pesach and Shavuos, it is customary for Jews to observe some mourning practices during that time.)[57] Undaunted, Rabbi Akiva taught five new students, who became the nucleus of the Torah leadership for the next generation.

In a famous story related in the Talmud,[58] Rabbi Akiva publicly flouted the Roman decree against Torah study. The Romans arrested him, then flayed his flesh with iron combs. Impervious to the pain, Rabbi Akiva recited the *Shema*, joyously anticipating the opportunity to sanctify G-d's Name with his life. As he was pronouncing the word *Echad*, which signifies the unity of G-d, Rabbi Akiva's soul departed. Although his murder was a tragedy, Rabbi Akiva's sacrifice has served as an inspiration for countless Jewish martyrs throughout the centuries.

Rabbi Hananiah ben Tradyon: When Rabbi Hananiah ben Tradyon was caught teaching Torah in public, the Romans decided to make an example of him. Accordingly, Rabbi Hananiah was wrapped in a Torah scroll, which was then set afire. As if this torture were not sufficient, strips of water-soaked wool were placed on his body to prolong his agony. While his distraught students looked on helplessly, Rabbi Hananiah inspired them with his famous utterance, "The parchment is burning but the letters are flying off," meaning that enemies can crush the Jewish body but not the spirit. Although Rabbi Hananiah refused to shorten his life by breathing in the fumes, he did consent when asked by the executioner if he should remove the wool. Deeply moved by the spiritual greatness he was witnessing, the Roman official took off the wool and then jumped into the fire himself. Through his courageous act, the executioner also attained eternity in Heaven.[59]

Rabbi Judah ben Bava: To prevent the emergence of a new generation of Torah scholars, the Romans outlawed *semichah*, rabbinic ordination. This draconian law called for a severe punishment — the execution of all parties involved in any *semichah*, and leveling the towns in the area. Nevertheless, in order to keep *semichah* alive, Rabbi Judah took five disciples to a mountainous, uninhabited area and ordained them. Constantly on the alert for such transgressions, the Roman forces rapidly approached them. Heroically, Rabbi Judah sent his students away but refused to flee — as his body was riddled by 300 spears.[60]

Rabbi Shimon ben Gamliel HaNasi and Rabbi Yishmael

Kohen Gadol: These two martyrs were slain during the time of the *churban*, sixty-five years before the others. When each sage begged to be killed first, so as not to witness the execution of his distinguished colleague, the Romans sadistically cast lots, and Rabbi Shimon was murdered first. As Rabbi Yishmael was bemoaning the loss of his close friend, the executioner's daughter, attracted by the rabbi's physical beauty, implored her father to keep him alive. When the Roman refused, his daughter asked instead that Rabbi Yishmael's facial skin be removed so that she could always gaze at its beauty. This unspeakably barbaric request was fulfilled, and Rabbi Yishmael's face was skinned while he was still alive.[61] As a further insult, the skin was kept in Roman storage, to be worn by legions for good luck during battle.[62] Rabbi Yishmael's face was also displayed in a ceremony performed once every seventy years in the streets of Rome to celebrate the ascendancy of Esau over his brother Jacob.[63]

According to the Yom Kippur liturgy, the other five martyrs are Rabbi Elazar ben Shamua, Rabbi Haninah ben Hachinai, Rabbi Jeshevav the Scribe, Rabbi Judah ben Damah, and Rabbi Hutzpith HaMeturgeman. The Midrash describes the gruesome manner in which the Romans killed each one.

ACHER: Originally known as Elisha ben Abuyah, the mentor of the famed Rabbi Meir was profoundly troubled by the horrific events of his time, much as people today are troubled by the Holocaust. Rejecting the concept of reward in the next world,[64] Elisha abandoned Jewish observance, openly committing many transgressions to demonstrate his disbelief.[65] As such, he became known as Acher, the Other One, due to his radical change of heart. Although Rabbi Meir kept a connection to his erstwhile mentor, other sages ostracized him, and Acher became the prime example of a great Torah scholar gone astray.

BREAKAWAY OF THE CHRISTIANS: The original Christians were Jews who acted Jewishly in all respects except for their belief in Yeshu. Eventually, the Christians realized that the Jewish people would not accept their idolatrous beliefs, and decided to introduce their religion to the Gentile world. Instrumental in this endeavor was a Jew named Paul, with whom the major tenets of Christianity originate. In order to make Christianity palatable to non-Jews, Paul taught that the Torah's commandments do not have to be kept; instead, faith in Yeshu was all that mattered.

Paul traveled all over the Roman Empire, attracting many converts to Christianity, a new religion which borrowed ideas from the Torah, some of its morals and ethics, and some rituals, which Paul combined with pagan rites. Not content with rewriting basic Judaism, Paul also claimed that the gentile Christians supplanted the Jews as G-d's chosen people, and that the Christian New Testament had replaced the Torah. He also taught that the Jews killed Yeshu and could be saved only if they turn to his worship. Such teachings, although not the sole basis for Christian anti-Semitism, played a significant role in the way post-Pauline Christians viewed the Jewish people. As two scholars put it:

> Those who believe Paul taught such ideas are able to cite many passages from his own writings in support of their interpretation. If they are right, he must be held responsible for the theological anti-Judaism that soon grew up in the Church and proved to be the ancestor of later anti-Semitism. In any case, since his writings so eloquently set forth the Christian myth, inherently anti-Jewish as it turned out to be, he can hardly escape all responsibility for the implications that later generations found in it.[66]

> So when it comes to the question of the origin of Christian hatred for Jews, Paul is at the story's center. His letters, as the oldest extant Christian writings, show him at his most flawed. His rage, prejudice, and self-obsession are as evident as his courage, gentleness, and faith.[67]

By 100 CE, Christianity was an exclusively non-Jewish religion.

MATTERS IMPROVE: After Hadrian's death in 138 CE, the Romans gradually relaxed the heavy yoke of oppression. As a gesture, they permitted interment of the vast number of corpses at

Betar; the day this took place, the fifteenth of Av, was subsequently observed as a joyous occasion.[68] Miraculously, the bodies had not decayed, and in commemoration the sages added the benediction *HaTov VeHaMeitiv* in *Birkas HaMazon*, Grace after Meals, thanking G-d for His great kindness.[69]

Although the Romans also stopped enforcing the anti-Torah decrees, they were not officially rescinded. Realizing that the possibility existed of the Romans suddenly reimposing the hated edicts, the sages worked assiduously to have them overturned, and eventually succeeded.[70] In addition, the Romans began a rebuilding program for Eretz Yisrael, and the Jewish community was strengthened by the arrival of Babylonian Jews. Despite the better conditions, it still was too dangerous for the hereditary *nasi*, Rabbi Shimon ben Gamliel, to adopt a leadership position. As a result, the Sanhedrin remained leaderless. Providentially, though, help came from a most unexpected source — the Romans themselves.

RABBI SHIMON BAR YOCHAI: This renowned Tanna, an outstanding disciple of Rabbi Akiva, was a staunch critic of the Romans. In a famous episode recorded in the Talmud,[71] several sages were discussing Roman rule. Rabbi Judah Berabbi Ilai praised it, while Rabbi Shimon bar Yochai scathingly criticized it. Upon hearing of the conversation, the Romans sentenced Rabbi Shimon to death, whereupon he fled and hid in a cave for thirteen years. Grateful to Rabbi Judah Berabbi Ilai for his support, the Romans commanded that the Jews promote him. Seizing the opportunity, the sages appointed Rabbi Judah as leader of the Sanhedrin. Clearly, they could not call Rabbi Judah *nasi*, as this title would arouse Roman ire. Nevertheless, the Jewish people had a recognized leader at a most critical time.

For his part, Rabbi Shimon bar Yochai was known as a great Kabbalist and the authorship of the mystical work, the *Zohar*, is attributed to him. His tomb at Meron in the Galilee attracts thousands of pilgrims, especially on Lag B'Omer, the anniversary of his death.

RABBI JUDAH HANASI: A descendant of Hillel, Rabbi Judah HaNasi was the compiler of the Mishnah and the last of the Tannaim. Due to his great stature, he was known simply as Rabbi, or Rabbeinu HaKadosh.[72] Developing a personal closeness with the emperor, Marcus Aurelius Antoninus, Rabbi recognized the emperor as an upstanding individual who loved learning, even studying Torah.[73] Because of his friendship with Antoninus, Rabbi was able to assume the role of *nasi* openly. In fact, the Talmud states that from the time of Moses until Rabbi, no other individual embodied in himself supreme greatness in Torah scholarship, wealth, and political power as did Rabbi.[74] Further, G-d imbued Rabbi with all these qualities to enable him to write the Mishnah and have it accepted by all Jews. Finally, Rabbi recapitulates a recurring theme in Jewish history: during times of oppression, when something of supreme importance needs to be accomplished, G-d grants short periods of respite. Such was the case with Rabbi.

WRITING THE ORAL LAW: Before the times of Rabbi, it was forbidden to write a public record of the Oral Law,[75] although notes for private use were permitted.[76] This prohibition existed for several reasons.[77] First, because new situations always arise, writing down the Oral Law would limit its scope. Second, just as any complex body of knowledge, such as surgery, cannot be learned from textbooks alone but also requires interaction with a master teacher, so, too, the Oral Law cannot be optimally understood without a live rebbe to give it meaning. Third, Gentiles could claim it as their own, saying they are the chosen Jewish people, much as they have attempted to do based on their translation of the Bible. Without the oral interpretation of the Written Torah, it remains a sealed book, thus forestalling such claims. All those important ideas to the contrary, Rabbi realized that benign Roman rule was only temporary. Eventually, times would become unstable again, and Jews would scatter throughout the world. It was thus necessary for every Jew to have a guidebook spelling out the major points of all the mitzvos. Based on a Scriptural verse that permits the leading sages to suspend a Torah prohibition in cases of national emergency,[78] Rabbi recorded the Oral Law for posterity.

WRITING THE MISHNAH: Taking advantage of the favorable political climate, Rabbi convened all the Torah scholars in Eretz Yisrael. Over a period of many years, each subject was painstakingly analyzed, with legislation left undecided from previous generations written into law and incorporated into the Mishnah.[79] There are two major opinions as to Rabbi's role in the authorship of the Mishnah. One view is that the bulk of the material in the Mishnah — basic wording and arrangement of tractates — already existed long before Rabbi's time.[80] This view holds that Rabbi's role was to take this oral material, write a standard, universal text, add some explanatory comments, and resolve matters disputed by the sages of his times and those immediately preceding him. Another opinion is that Rabbi both composed the actual wording of the Mishnah, and divided it into orders, tractates, and chapters.[81] According to both opinions, Rabbi based his work on the teachings of Rabbi Meir and Rabbi Akiva, the most succinct and easiest scholarship to understand.[82] In most cases, Rabbi recorded their opinions anonymously, indicating that they are normative rulings (*stam mishnah*).[83]

THE MISHNAH: Although Rabbi wrote and disseminated the Mishnah, it is a guidebook, albeit one written in cryptic form whose explication requires a rebbe, a mentor. Further, because a particular *mishnah* may apply only in special circumstances, one may not decide halachah (Jewish law) based on a *mishnah*.[84] As Rabbi devised it, the Mishnah is broken into six orders, 63 tractates, 525 chapters, and 4,224 *mishnayos*. The six orders are *Zeraim*, which discusses prayer and agricultural laws; *Moed*, about the Sabbath and holiday laws, fast days, and mourning regulations; *Nashim*, pertaining to women, including marriage and divorce; *Nezikin*, on money matters and court procedure; *Kodashim*, centering on sacrificial law and kashrus; *Taharos*, ritual purity, including *mikvah* and family purity (*Hilchos Niddah*). Rabbi concluded the Mishnah in 190 CE.

OTHER WRITINGS OF THE TANNAIM: Since the Mishnah was written very concisely, a vast body of knowledge remained that was left out. This material was also assembled by Rabbi and his disciples and recorded separately in volumes known as *Mechilta* (Midrash on the Book of Exodus), *Safra* (also known as *Toras Kohanim*, Midrash on Leviticus), and Sifri (Midrash on Numbers and Deuteronomy), *Beraisos*, and *Tosefta*. These Midrashic works are halachic in nature, giving the Scriptural sources for many of the laws found in the Mishnah. Midrashim also exist that are homiletical, such as *Midrash Rabbah* on Genesis. *Beraisos* are lengthier commentaries on the Mishnah, while *Tosefta* is an appendix to the Mishnah.[85]

THE GENERATIONS OF THE TANNAIM: There were five generations of Tannaim, 30 BCE–200 CE. Some major Tannaim in each generation include:

Generation One: (Before the *churban*) Beis Shammai, Beis Hillel, Rabbi Shimon ben Gamliel the *nasi*, Rabbi Yishmael the *kohen gadol*.

Generation Two: (Yavneh) Rabbi Jochanan ben Zakkai, Rabban Gamliel the *nasi*, Rabbi Joshua, Rabbi Eliezer ben Hyrcanus, Onkelos.[86]

Generation Three: (Betar) Rabbi Akiva, the other seven martyrs.

Generation Four: (After Betar) Rabbi Meir, Rabbi Shimon bar Yochai, Rabbi Judah Berabbi Ilai, Rabbi Shimon ben Gamliel the father of Rabbi.

Generation Five: Rabbi Judah HaNasi — seventh in line from Hillel.

The generations of the House of Hillel from father to son, each of whom acted as *nasi*:[87]

Hillel
Rabbi Shimon I
Rabban Gamliel I (*HaZaken*)

Rabbi Shimon II (one of the ten martyrs)

Rabban Gamliel II of Yavneh

Rabbi Shimon (III) ben Gamliel (the Rabbi Shimon ben Gamliel often mentioned in the Mishnah)

Rabbi Judah HaNasi

His sons: Rabban Gamliel (III) and Rabbi Shimon (IV), the last Tannaim.[88]

Chapter 9

THE AMORAIM

THE PASSING OF AN ERA: Rabbi died about 200 CE, and the Talmud[1] describes his final moments, death, and massive funeral in great detail, something it does not do for any other sage. The outpouring of grief at Rabbi's passing indicated that the Jewish people realized the spiritual grandeur of the Tannaim was coming to a close. Afterward, the leading Torah scholars were known as Amoraim, or interpreters, in contrast to Tannaim, the teachers of the Oral Law. For their part, the Amoraim explained the rulings of the Tannaim, applying them to new situations, but never disagreeing with their teachers. It is axiomatic to students of the Talmud that if an Amora contradicts a Tanna, the Amora's opinion is refuted — unless the Amora can back up his statement with another Tanna's opinion. Although such a methodology was never adopted as a formal edict, Torah scholars of that time presumed it to be obvious. Following them, throughout history the Jewish people have instinctively realized who its paramount sages are and when an era has ended. As in the times of Rabbi, Torah leaders do not campaign for their position; public acclaim accords it to them.

TRENDS IN JEWISH LIFE: Shortly after the Mishnah was completed, significant changes began to take place in Jewish life. As a result of rising instability in the Roman Empire, life in Eretz Yisrael became increasingly precarious for Jews. As local Roman commanders ruled without the moderating influence of the central government, an increasing number of sages moved to Babylonia, which became the central focus of Jewish life. During the period of the Tannaim, when the incessant persecutions caused the Jews of Eretz Yisrael to forget some laws, Babylonia hosted great Torah scholars who constantly infused the sages of Eretz Yisrael with true Torah leadership.[2] Nevertheless, the *chachamim* (scholars) of Eretz Yisrael were still the main deciders of Jewish law, utilizing the authority invested by the Sanhedrin in Israel. In rabbinic accounts from the Tannaic period, there is virtually no mention of Torah life in Babylonia.

With the advent of the Amoraim, however, the Sanhedrin and *nasi* began to play increasingly diminished roles in Torah life, eventually passing out of existence. Rabbi's grandson, Rabbi Judah Nesiah, the ninth *nasi* of the House of Hillel, was the last person to be accepted by all Jews as *nasi*.[3] Afterward, the *kehillah*, or local Jewish community, assumed greater institutional importance, with each *kehillah*'s leaders deciding halachah for their own community at times when no national consensus was reached.[4] In addition, people had complete allegiance to the *chachamim*; there were no deviant groups.

TORAH LIFE IN BABYLON: As the community grew, Babylonian Jewry developed unique Torah and political institutions. Twice yearly, during the months of Adar and Elul, many Jews took advantage of a break in the agricultural cycle to attend great Torah convocations led by leading scholars, known as *Yarchei Kallah*. A specific topic was chosen in advance, giving everyone the opportunity to prepare questions and pose new cases. Due to the vastness of the crowd, it was impossible to hear the speakers, so scholars were strategically positioned throughout the area, offering a simultaneous translation of what was being taught.[5] In describing the splendor of the gathering, the Talmud relates that when the assembled people stood up, the dust that was shaken off their garments blocked out the sun.[6] Similarly, the gentiles of the city in which the *Yarchei Kallah* was held were criticized for not being sufficiently inspired to convert.[7]

Unlike Roman rule in Eretz Yisrael, the Babylonian government allowed the Jews total autonomy over internal affairs. The political leader of the Jews in Babylon, known as the *resh galusa*, or head of the exile, was invariably a direct descendant of King David (paternally, at least, in contrast to the *nasi* of Eretz Yisrael, who descended from King David maternally).[8] The *resh galusa* possessed both judicial and police power;[9] in addition, some *rashei galusa* were great scholars and righteous individuals. Mar Ukba, for example, performed great acts of charity,[10] and Rav Huna, his father and a contemporary of Rabbi, was one of more than sixty important sages carrying the name Huna.[11] The best-known *resh galusa* was the famous Bustenai, who lived in the seventh century. Other *rashei galusa,* however, were evil, terrorizing the people. In one case, the *resh galusa*'s people poisoned a scholar whose halachic opinion they disliked, even though it concerned only a minor matter.[12] All told, the position of *resh galusa* lasted hundreds of years, until the tenth century, finally falling out of practice when Babylon lost its status as the center of world Jewry.[13]

THE THIRD CENTURY: The generation of sages following the death of Rabbi was a bridge between the Tannaim and Amoraim.[14] Several of Rabbi's prominent disciples, most notably Rav, were considered as both Tannaim and Amoraim. Although he himself was not mentioned in any *mishnah*, Rav had the right — which he rarely exercised — to dispute a *mishnah* as a Tanna.[15] Two other students of Rabbi, Rabbi Chiyya and Rabbi Oshiya, compiled an authoritative compendium of all *beraisos.* Indeed, the Talmud states that any *beraisa* not taught by these two sages is not reliable.[16]

Rav, originally known as Abba Aricha, was Rabbi's outstanding disciple. Given the name Rav, similar to that of his teacher Rabbi, it illustrated that his greatness was unembellished by titles. Rav also had a reputation for not having spoken an unnecessary word during his entire life, and not walking even a short distance without wearing tefillin.[17] When he traveled to Babylon,

Rav did not settle in the main Jewish city of Nahardea, but moved instead to the town of Sura, then a spiritual wasteland. With tireless effort, Rav revived Jewish life in Sura, and it became the seat of a great yeshivah, one of two major Torah centers in Babylonia, rivaling only Nahardea.

Rav also composed several well-known prayers, such as *Vatodienu* in *Shemoneh Esrei* when a holiday occurs on Saturday night; major portions of the Rosh HaShanah Mussaf *Amidah*; and *Yehi Ratzon*, the introductory prayer recited when the upcoming month is announced on the Sabbath before Rosh Chodesh.

Shmuel, a famous contemporary of Rav, was the head of the Nahardea yeshivah. An accomplished astronomer, he is quoted as saying, "The pathways of the sky are as familiar to me as the streets of Nahardea."[18] As such, Shmuel's astronomical calculations continue to play a significant role in the Jewish calendar.[19] Distinguished study partners, Rav and Shmuel dispute hundreds of cases in the Talmud, with halachah decided according to each one's area of expertise. The Talmud rules according to Rav in ritual prohibitions and such practices as kashrus, the Sabbath, and prayers, while Shmuel's opinion is followed in matters of monetary law.[20]

RELATIONS WITH THE GENTILES IN BABYLONIA: Generally, life for the Jews in Babylonia was peaceful, as Roman or Christian anti-Semitism was not a factor there. When there were troubles, they were usually short-lived and local. In the middle of the third century, fire-worshipers known as Zoroastrians gained power in Babylonia, and outlawed lighting fires at certain times.[21] The Talmud rules that in such a situation one may light Chanukah candles on his table rather than exposing them to public view.[22] It also permitted moving a candle out of sight on the Sabbath, an act normally prohibited by *muktzah* regulations.[23] One major event did not have Jewish origins: when the city of Nahardea was destroyed in a war, its famous yeshivah relocated in Pumbeditha.

AMORAIM OF ERETZ YISRAEL: Although most sages lived in Babylonia, there still was a sizable Torah community in Eretz Yisrael. The leading sage during the third century was Rabbi Jochanan, who died in 259 CE.[24] His yeshivah, in Tiberias, was the last of the Great Sanhedrin's ten locations before it ended.[25] The Talmud describes Rabbi Jochanan as having exceptional beauty, with only the lack of a beard keeping him from being counted among the most beautiful men who ever lived.[26] Sadly, his personal life was very tragic — his ten sons died in his lifetime — but rather than wallowing in self-pity, Rabbi Jochanan used his situation to comfort other bereaved parents.[27] Rabbi Jochanan also laid the framework for the Jerusalem Talmud, *Talmud Yerushalmi*,[28] but was unable to finish the work. It was continued by his disciples.

A contemporary of Rabbi Jochanan, Rabbi Shimon ben Lakish was better known as Resh Lakish. This remarkable personality began as a robber who was persuaded by Rabbi Jochanan to channel his energies into studying Torah. Eventually becoming Rabbi Jochanan's brother-in-law, Resh Lakish and Rabbi Jochanan disputed many points of law, and the halachah follows Rabbi Jochanan in all but three cases.[29] Another prominent scholar in Eretz Yisrael was Rabbi Abahu, who resided in the Roman city of Caesarea. The Talmud relates that Rabbi Abahu's beauty was a reflection of the Patriarch Jacob.[30] Greatly respected by the Roman authorities,[31] Rabbi Abahu used his influence to help his people.[32]

CHRISTIANITY BEGINS TO DOMINATE: In 323 CE, the Roman Emperor Constantine declared Christianity to be the official religion of the Roman Empire. As a result, Christianity, which had grown from humble beginnings, became the dominant religion of the world. Persecution of the Jews rapidly followed, as the new creed left no room for other belief systems, a contrast to the relatively benign tolerance of the formerly pagan empire. In particular, the Christians were incensed at the success of Judaism in attracting numerous converts from throughout the Roman Empire, continuing a trend that had begun in the times of the Tannaim.[33] In 325 CE, at the Council of Nicea, the Christians laid down the basic tenets of their faith. Severing all connections with Judaism (such as fixing the date of Easter to coincide with Pesach), the Christians also incorporated many anti-Semitic doctrines into official Church dogma. Later, when the Roman Empire split into East and West, Eretz Yisrael fell under control of the Eastern Byzantine Empire. At that time, the Christians built churches in Eretz Yisrael in Jerusalem, Bethlehem, and Nazareth, all sites associated with the founding of their religion. They also constructed a church on the Temple Mount.

THE JERUSALEM TALMUD: Due to severe Christian persecution, much of Jewish life in Eretz Yisrael came to a halt, and as a result the *Talmud Yerushalmi* was not completed. Dating from the middle of the fourth century, it is on just four sections of the Mishnah: *Zeraim* (which has no Babylonian Talmud except for tractate *Berachos*), *Moed, Nashim,* and *Nezikin.* Small excerpts also exist on part of tractate *Niddah,* in *Taharos.* Some opinions maintain that the *Talmud Yerushalmi* also once existed on the order of *Kodashim*[34] but was lost. In any event, the *Talmud Yerushalmi* is considerably shorter than its Babylonian counterpart, and employs a terse, difficult Aramaic. As such, its study has never been as prized as that of the Babylonian Talmud, remaining the province of specialized scholars. (For example, the *Yerushalmi* was never on the curriculum of the great yeshivos throughout history.) In cases of disputes between the two Talmuds, the Babylonian Talmud is followed.[35]

FIXING THE JEWISH CALENDAR: Traditionally, there was no set Jewish calendar as currently exists. Rather, as empowered by the Torah, the Great Sanhedrin calculated Rosh Chodesh and the holidays on a monthly basis.[36] In that system, a combination of eyewitness sightings of the new moon and mathematical calculations were taken into account. Leap years were added as necessary to ensure that Pesach always occurred in the spring.[37] At that time, incredibly precise calendar computations were only disclosed to selected scholars to ensure that the Sanhedrin retained control of the calendar.[38] This act was deemed necessary to prevent fragmentation of the Jewish people, which would surely result if there were competing calendars. Due to Roman persecution, it became progressively difficult to maintain the old system.

However, Divine providence intervened, and as on numerous other occasions the Jewish people were given a brief respite when an important matter needed to be accomplished. A new Roman emperor arose, Julian the Apostate, who was both anti-Christian and favorably inclined toward the Jews in Eretz Yisrael. Realizing that this peaceful time would not last, Hillel II, the last *nasi* of the House of Hillel, convened the Great Sanhedrin in the year 359 CE (4119).[39] These sages, the last to have *semichah*, created the fixed calendar in use today. They also publicized the previously secret method of calculation, so that everyone could realize the calendar's veracity. According to the calendar, all holidays, days of Rosh Chodesh, and leap years were set until the Jewish year 6000, which Jewish tradition accepts as being the last date for the arrival of the Messiah and the concurrent reinstitution of the ancient calendar system.[40] (It was not necessary to fix the day of the Sabbath, because that is Divinely set, unlike the festivals that were fixed by the Sanhedrin.)[41] Shortly afterward, Julian died, the persecutions resumed, and the Sanhedrin and *semichah* went out of existence.

ABAYE AND RAVA: The best known of all Amoraim lived in the middle of the fourth century.[42] Because Abaye's father died before he was born, and his mother died giving birth to him, Abaye was raised by Rabbah, the leading Torah sage of the time.[43] Interestingly, the Talmud considers Abaye fortunate for not having parents, because the mitzvah of honoring parents is extremely difficult to fulfill properly.[44] As for Rava, his power of concentration was legendary: the Talmud relates that while studying he sat on his fingers, causing them to bleed profusely, but he did not realize it.[45] Their disputes are found throughout the entire Talmud, to such an extent that the Talmud is often called "the discussions of Abaye and Rava."[46] Halachah follows Rava in all but six cases,[47] one of which is a fairly common occurrence: the case when one finds an object without identifying marks, which the owner has not yet realized is missing but who will surely despair of recovering it when he does notice that it is missing. Abaye, whose opinion is followed, says that the finder may not keep it, while Rava allows him to.[48] One of their disciples was Rav Papa, who had ten sons who became Torah scholars. It is customary when completing the study of a Talmudic tractate to mention all ten of Rav Papa's sons to invoke their memory.[49]

THE ARRANGEMENT OF THE BABYLONIAN TALMUD: By the middle of the fourth century, Christian persecution in Eretz Yisrael caused the remainder of the sages to immigrate to Babylonia.[50] For the first time since the Babylonian Exile nearly 800 years previously, all Torah scholarship was concentrated in one area. Led by Abaye and Rava, this august assembly debated new cases, analyzing decisions and explanations of earlier Amoraim, checking them for inconsistencies, and provided explanatory comments on the Mishnah. These discussions were fixed in a formalized lexicon, and form the bulk of the Babylonian Talmud.[51] At first, however, this material was not written down, and each topic was not assigned its place in a text.[52] This task was left for the codifiers of the Talmud, Rav Ashi and Ravina II.

SEALING THE BABYLONIAN TALMUD: Once again, G-d granted the Jewish people a period of tranquility before times became bad, in order to facilitate a monumental task — in this case, sealing the Babylonian Talmud. As in the days of Rabbi Judah HaNasi, Rav Ashi, the leader of the Jewish people, had the three qualities necessary for this endeavor: supreme political power granted him by the Babylonian authorities, universal recognition as the greatest Torah scholar of the era, and unsurpassed wealth.[53] As such, he spent close to sixty years in conjunction with other sages editing the voluminous material known as the Gemara, making a first draft and then a final copy.[54] At that time, not only were the halachic conclusions written down, but also the argumentation of previous generations of Amoraim up to his own time.[55] Unlike the Mishnah, the Gemara was written in great detail, to facilitate understanding from the text itself.[56]

In many ways, the Gemara clarifies the Mishnah, establishing which halachic opinions are binding, providing derivations for the laws, and teaching moral lessons in the form of homilies and stories.[57] After Rav Ashi passed away in 426 CE, Ravina II, who died in 500 CE, continued the final editing and halachic writing.[58] At that point, the Jewish people accepted that the Babylonian Talmud, composed of the Mishnah and the Gemara, was the final halachic authority. No one could decide any matter contradictory to the Talmud, and all future decisions had to be based on it.[59] To this day, the sine qua non of an observant Jew is his adherence to the Talmud, and one who denies any teaching of the Talmud is considered a heretic.[60]

THE RABANAN SAVOROI: In the middle of the fifth century widespread religious persecution broke out in Babylonia, instigated by Persian fanatics. Fortunately, the major work of redacting the Babylonian Talmud had been finished. At that time there remained some relatively minor editing — resolving issues that Rav Ashi and Ravina II had left open, and adding such explanatory notes as the first page of tractate *Kiddushin*[61] and the two-dot quotes preceding portions of the *mishnah* under discussion.[62] The sages responsible for this work, coming after the Amoraim, were known as Rabanan Savoroi (the explainers), and the Talmud assumed its final form during their time.[63] Simultaneously, 500–589 CE, the Jewish people underwent severe tribulations in Babylonia — and it was only due to the efforts of the Rabanan Savoroi that Torah was successfully transmitted during such turbulent times.[64] Some of the Rabanan Savoroi include Rabbi Sama, Rabbi Rechumi, Rabbi Aina, and Rabbi Simona. During their time, the so-called minor tractates of the Talmud were completed, including *Maseches Soferim* and *Maseches Semachos*.[65] In all, the Rabanan Savoroi's total additions to the Babylonian Talmud comprise less than 2 percent of the text.[66]

It had been a long journey, from oral arrangement by Abaye and Rava, to major writing by Rav Ashi, final halachos by Ravina II, resolution of unresolved issues by the early Rabanan Savoroi, and finally clarifications and introductory remarks by the later Rabanan Savoroi. The Babylonian Talmud was complete.

THE BABYLONIAN TALMUD: Known simply as the Talmud, the Babylonian Talmud covers almost all of the orders of *Moed, Nashim, Nezikin,* and *Kodashim. Zeraim* and *Taharos* are represented by only one tractate each, *Berachos* and *Niddah* respectively. A monumental work of scholarship, the Babylonian Talmud has become the heart and soul of the Jewish people. Even the word scholarship is defined as one's knowledge of the Talmud. Its study has given Jews many things, not the least of which is succor and strength to withstand all vicissitudes of life.

An all-encompassing work, the Talmud discusses not only law and ethics but also such practical matters such as investment strategy[67] and unhealthful practices.[68] Its eclectic topics range from the equitable distribution of profits in a partnership[69] to the state of the world in the Messianic Era.[70] Humorous anecdotes are related, such as the story of the man who boxed his friend's ear and was fined half a *zuz* (a type of coin). However, since the boxer had only a one-*zuz* coin, and his friend had no change, he boxed his friend's ear again and told him to keep the change.[71] Heartbreaking stories are also told, such as the terrible suffering of the Jewish people at the time of the destruction of the Second Temple.[72] Perhaps because of its greatness, throughout the generations the Talmud has been the target of anti-Semites, who knew that to destroy the Talmud is to destroy the Jewish people. It was publicly burned in the Middle Ages and again by the Nazis. For example, in 1940, the Reich Security Main Office sent the following directive to German authorities in Poland:

The continued emigration of Jews from Eastern Europe to the West spells a continued spiritual regeneration of world Jewry, as it is mainly the Eastern Jews who supply a large proportion of the rabbis, Talmud teachers, etc., owing to their orthodox-religious beliefs, and they are urgently needed by Jewish organizations active in the United States."[73]

Transmitted with remarkable accuracy over the generations, the Talmud has survived the inevitable mistakes that creep in due to hand copying such vast material. To this day, Jews spend countless hours engrossed in its study, with many scholars devoting their lives to immersion in the sea of Talmud. A popular system of study, known as *daf yomi*, was instituted in 1923. Participants study one page each day, completing the Talmud's 2,711 pages in seven and a half years. A massive worldwide celebration is held at the end of the cycle, when many thousands of Jews gather in such immense arenas as New York's Madison Square Garden and Nassau Coliseum, with others following on satellite hookups or staging their own celebrations.

GENERATIONS OF AMORAIM: There were seven generations of Amoraim in Babylonia and four in Eretz Yisrael. The Babylonian Amoraim ranged from 200–500 CE, including:[74]

In Babylon:

Generation 1: Rav, Shmuel, Rabbi Chiyya, Rabbi Oshiya
Generation 2: Rav Huna, Rabbi Judah, Rabbah bar bar Hana
Generation 3: Rav Chisda, Rav Sheshes, Rav Zera
Generation 4: Rabbah, Rav Joseph
Generation 5: Abaye, Rava
Generation 6: Rav Papa, Rav Nachman bar Yitzchak
Generation 7: Ravina I, Rav Ashi, Ravina II

In Eretz Yisrael (c. 200–350 CE):

Generation 1: Rabbi Jochanan, Resh Lakish.
Generation 2: Ulla, Rabbi Abahu
Generation 3: Rabbi Ami, Rabbi Asi
Generation 4: Rav Zevid

Chapter 10

THE GAONIC ERA

THE **G**AONIM AND **T**HEIR **T**IMES: The leaders of the two major Babylonian yeshivos at Sura and Pumbeditha were known as Gaonim, Hebrew for "magnificent." The Gaonic period spanned nearly 450 years, from Rabbi Chanan of Ashkaya, the first Gaon, in 589, to Rabbi Hai Gaon, the last Gaon, in 1038.[1] Throughout the Jewish world, these two Gaonim were universally regarded as the final halachic authorities. All told, there were more than eighty Gaonim during this period, about most of whom there is little or no information, other than their names.[2]

Also, not much is known about Jewish life in general during these several hundred years, as no historical records were kept and no archaeological evidence has been unearthed in Babylonia (Iraq). Similarly, secular history is scanty, this being the so-called Dark Ages. While most of the world's Jews still lived in Babylonia, there began a gradual but very significant emigration to Europe, North Africa, and other parts of Asia. Such a migration is unique in Jewish history, for it marks the only time that large numbers of Jews left a country without a sudden reason to emigrate, such as from Egypt at the Exodus, Eretz Yisrael at *churban Bayis Rishon*, Spain at the Expulsion, Russia during the pogroms of 1880–1920, and Europe after the Holocaust.

In Babylonia, rabbinic power was concentrated in the hands of the Gaonim, while political power was under the domain of the government-approved *resh galusa*. This arrangement led to frequent conflict, as the *rashei galusa* would often attempt to encroach upon the prerogatives of the Gaonim, and the Gaonim would try to curb the harmful influences of the *rashei galusa*. On rare occasions, there also was disagreement between Sura and Pumbeditha regarding who should have the preeminent role in halachic matters. However, the vast majority of the time cordial relations existed between the two academies.

ACCOMPLISHMENTS OF THE GAONIM: Even after the Talmud was completed, its understanding still remained largely inaccessible to all but accomplished scholars. Often, the Talmud debates an issue at length without reaching a definite conclusion. The Gaonim filled a vital need by developing new forms of Torah scholarship, including anthologies of laws grouped by subject matter culled from all over the Talmud, with all debates and reasoning removed, thus making it easy to locate a halachah. In addition, the Gaonim published responses to halachic questions posed from all over the Jewish world, thereby demonstrating the application of Talmudic law to new situations. These Gaonic correspondences became known as *Shaalos Uteshuvos*, questions and answers, and greatly popularized this new genre of Torah study. Many thousands of compilations of *Shaalos Uteshuvos* have been published since Gaonic times. A direct descendant of these Gaonic masterpieces is the famous eight volumes of *Shaalos Uteshuvos Igros Moshe* by the world-renowned halachic authority Rabbi Moshe Feinstein, of blessed memory. Such contemporary issues as the halachic permissibility of heart transplants [3] and the use on the Sabbath of lenses that darken in sunlight [4] are discussed in detail, all based on principles enunciated in the Talmud.

The Gaonim also wrote the first authorized siddur, prayer book, replacing what had been an oral transmission of the service. They also authored works explaining basic Jewish philosophy and belief, making this important area of learning accessible to all. Previously, these concepts were scattered throughout the Scriptures and Talmud, and were very difficult to approach in a systematic manner. So great was their scholarship, in fact, that there is a discussion among later rabbinic authorities as to whether the rulings of the Gaonim are considered unimpeachable such as those of the Talmud.[5]

THE RISE OF ISLAM: During the Gaonic Era, an event of monumental effect on world history occurred, which at the time was very beneficial to the Jewish people. By the early 600s the outlook for the physical survival of the Jews was bleak. Christianity held sway over both the Eastern and Western Roman Empires, with Jews under its rule constantly persecuted. In 613, the Roman Catholic Visigoth rulers of Spain expelled all Jews who did not convert. In Babylonia, fanatical anti-Jewish Persian rulers closed many yeshivos and instituted decrees outlawing Jewish practices.

However, G-d directs the affairs of empires for the benefit of the Jewish people.[6] In Arabia, the same as the current Saudi Arabia, an illiterate merchant named Mohammed claimed prophetic revelations. He preached that the pagan Arabs should believe in one G-d, and accept Mohammed as His prophet. Hoping to attract Jews to his new belief, he incorporated some Jewish practices into his new religion, such as a fast day similar to Yom Kippur and prayer toward Jerusalem. The Jews of Mecca, Mohammed's hometown, rejected Mohammed's overtures, feeling that Islam had nothing to offer them, and the Arabs there, too, did not heed his call. After being forced to flee Mecca, Mohammed gathered a following in Medina, and then conquered Arabia. Angry at the Jews for not adopting his faith, he severed his connection to Jewish belief. Yom Kippur was replaced by the fast of Ramadan, and prayer was directed toward Mecca. Mohammed also vituperatively attacked the Jews in his holy book, the Koran. By the mid 600s, Muslim Arab soldiers swept through much of the Middle East, North Africa, and Europe, spreading Islam over vast territories. The Caliph Omar conquered Eretz Yisrael and built the present-day Mosque of Omar (Dome of the Rock) on the Temple Mount in 638.

ARAB-JEWISH RELATIONS: The Jews and the Christians under the rule of Islam were subject to varying conditions, dependent on the place and the period. Both religions were present in Arabia before the advent of Mohammed, although Islam demanded the acceptance of the new religion only by the pagans and not by the Jews and Christians. In certain places, the Islamic rulers habitually employed Jews and Christians in higher government positions. Over time, special restrictions were applied to the Jews and Christians, including the Covenant of Omar, which laid down laws under which a *dhimmi*, or non-believer, was allowed to live under the rule of Islam. Some of these measures also meant imposing special taxes, wearing distinctive yellow cloth badges, and prohibiting religious practices in public. (This latter restriction is still enforced in Saudi Arabia, where non-Islamic U.S. soldiers must conduct their religious ceremonies privately.)

Actual persecution of non-Muslim religions took place during the Middle Ages and under the rule of the Berber dynasty of the Almohads, but these practices did not spread to all areas under Muslim rule. Indeed, the level of persecution of Jews often depended on the caprices of a particular ruler. Overall, however, the single worst place in the Islamic world for Jews was Yemen. There, persecution occurred constantly for hundreds of years, with periodic pogroms killing thousands of Jews. At times, Jewish life little but was abject slavery. For example, Jews had to clean the city latrines and clear the streets of animal carcasses, even on the Sabbath. Fatherless Jewish children under the age of thirteen were often taken from their homes and given to Muslims to be raised in their faith. Sadly, much of this persecution lasted into modern times.

The high point of Jewish-Arab relations occurred from 900 to 1200 CE, and it is hardly coincidence that Jewish culture flowered in the Arab world at the time that Islamic civilization was at its apogee. For a few centuries, Greek humanism and Islamic universalism combined with a dynamic mercantile economy to produce a relatively open society. At such times, Muslims and non-Muslims could participate, if not on an entirely equal footing, at least with near equality in those spheres of activity that were not specifically religious — in the marketplace, scientific and intellectual circles, and civil service. Such activities were most prevalent in Spain, and to a lesser degree in Babylonia.

There, the Muslim majority felt sufficiently secure, and was suitably prosperous, not to be overly concerned with enforcing the humility of the non-Muslim minority. Indeed, Muslims and non-Muslims lived in close proximity, with no ghettoes. While most Jews lived in their own quarters near their synagogues, their neighborhoods were rarely exclusively Jewish. While day-to-day contacts between Muslims and non-Muslims were generally quite amicable, intimate social relationships were rare. Indeed, one's religious community was the principal arena for social life and activity; furthermore, the cordiality of interfaith relationships was tenuous. In fact, Muslims could be deeply offended when Jews rose too high or became too conspicuous in government service; at such times, there were almost always disastrous results for the Jews.

Generally, however, the Jews got along better with the Muslim Arabs than with the Christians. References in the Koran to Jews being the People of the Book, along with Jewish and Islamic belief in a common G-d, caused Muslims to look upon Jews with less hostility than did Christians. In addition, Arabs shared a love of learning with the Jews, and needed the Jews to administer the Arabs' vast conquests. For the Muslims, as long as the Jews realized that Islam ruled supreme, and that they were *dhimmi*, second-class citizens, relations were frequently cordial.

In modern times, though, Judaism and Islam have been at loggerheads. The rise of political Zionism, and the existence of the State of Israel, is regarded by many Muslims as an affront to their religion, which once again assigns Jews *dhimmi* status. Saudi Arabian maps of the Middle East demarcate the borders of Israel, but describe the country as Palestine. For many Muslims, it is simply inconceivable to accept Jewish rule in Eretz Yisrael, which they regard as holy Arab land. In addition, the Shiite branch of Islam, which stresses martyrdom and the Muslim obligation of *jihad* (holy war) to rid the land of infidels, has imbued the Arabs with a fierce sense of fanaticism, embodied in such tactics as homicide bombing. To this way of thinking, no sacrifice is too great, and no struggle too long, to end Jewish sovereignty in so-called Zionist-Occupied Palestine.

BUSTENAI: The most famous of all *rashei galusa*, Bustenai's birth and life is the stuff of many legends, some of which may be true.[7] In the late 500s, a fanatical Persian ruler of Babylonia embarked on a campaign to exterminate the House of David. Eventually, the entire family was wiped out, leaving only one pregnant woman in hiding whose dead husband was of the Davidic dynasty. One night, the tyrant dreamed that he was chopping down trees in an orchard, when an elderly man grabbed his axe and threatened to kill him for destroying the garden. The tyrant pleaded for his life, promising to stop the destruction. Upon awakening, he was greatly troubled by his dream, and sought out a Jewish scholar to interpret it. The king was told that the man in his dream was King David, threatening to punish him for wiping out his descendants. Hearing this, the king promised to treat well any survivors of King David. As such, the pregnant woman came out of hiding and was given quarters in the palace. When her child was born, he was named Bustenai, which is Persian for "orchard."

Once, as a youth, Bustenai was standing before the king when a fly alighted on Bustenai's forehead and stung him, causing him to bleed. Yet Bustenai did not attempt to chase away the insect. Amazed at such self-control, the king asked him the reason for such behavior. Bustenai replied that it is the tradition of members of the House of David that, when standing in front of a ruler, they did not make a move without being granted permission. In commemoration of this episode, the seal of King David's descendants subsequently bore the image of a fly.

Bustenai was thereafter appointed *resh galusa*, and he used his influence to strengthen Jewish life throughout Babylonia. When the Arab Caliph Ali conquered Babylonia, he reconfirmed Bustenai as *resh galusa*, giving him one of the daughters of the captured Persian king as a wife. This woman converted sincerely, married Bustenai, and bore him several children. In addition, Bustenai raised a family from a native Jewish woman. On numerous occasions, there were attempts by the native Jewish wife's descendants to impugn the Jewish lineage of Bustenai's children from his Persian wife, but the rabbinic authorities always ruled that her conversion was valid.[8] A number of the Persian wife's descendants went on to become *rashei galusa*.

THE KARAITE SECT: In the mid-700s, the *resh galusa*, Shlomo, died childless. Logically, the elder of his two nephews, Anan, should have inherited the position. However, the Gaonim of the time had reason to doubt Anan's character and beliefs, and despite being intellectually superior to his younger brother, Anan was passed over. Anan then declared himself *resh galusa*, and the Muslim authorities, which had confirmed the Gaonim's choice for *resh galusa*, imprisoned Anan for rebellion. Awaiting execution, Anan, by claiming to be a member of a breakaway Jewish sect, was able to convince the Caliph to release him. Upon release, Anan founded the Karaite movement, which basically was a resurrection of the Sadducean heresy.

The Karaites, like the Sadducees before them, only accepted the Written Torah, rejecting the Oral Torah and all rabbinic interpretation. To reinforce their position, they even took the name *Karaim*, Hebrew for written verses (*mikrah*). Due to their literal reading of Exodus 35:3, which forbids lighting fires on the Sabbath, the Karaites spent the Sabbath in the dark, not eating hot food. In response, Jews loyal to the Torah adopted the custom of eating hot *cholent* on Sabbath afternoon, demonstrating that they adhered to rabbinic tradition, which taught that one may keep food warm on Sabbath if cooked beforehand.[9] At first, Anan's movement gained a sizable following, but eventually lost much of its popularity. Nevertheless, the movement has had remarkable longevity. Small pockets of Karaites existed in Lithuania even into the early 1900s, and Israel today maintains a tiny Karaite community.[10]

ENACTMENTS OF THE GAONIM: Throughout their time, the Gaonim made a number of decrees to enhance Jewish life. For example, under Talmudic law a widow or divorcee may only collect her *kesubah* (marriage settlement) from landed property belonging to her former husband. This decree was based on the fact that in that time virtually all Jews owned real estate, which was the best collateral for a debt. However, in Gaonic times Jews became involved less in agriculture and more in commerce. In response to the changing conditions, then, the Gaonim enacted that movable property could also be mortgaged for the *kesubah*. (The Gaonim's decision was based on a Talmudic statement that allows such action in exceptional localities where movables were the major source of commerce.)

When this lack of real estate became the rule rather than the exception, the Gaonim extended the Talmud's ruling to all places,[11] a prophetic move which has served the Jewish people well through its many exiles. Another decree instituted by the Gaonim, commemorating the tragic passing of Rabbi Akiva's 24,000 students, is the custom of observing a level of national mourning by not allowing weddings during the *Omer* period, between Pesach and Shavuos.[12] In later times, such mourning practices were expanded to restrict shaving and haircuts as well.[13]

THE SIDDUR EXPANDED: The prayer service as enacted by the *Anshei Knesses HaGedolah*, and as recorded in the Talmud, is relatively short. Not being satisfied with what was essentially the bare minimum, many Jews felt that the rite should be enlarged, an act permitted by the Talmud in certain areas of the service.[14] In addition, as the long exile dragged on, with no end in sight, people desired a lengthier prayer service with which to beseech G-d for personal and national salvation.[15] At that time, individual *chazzanim* (prayer leaders), as well as great scholars, composed original prayers, some of which became accepted by the nation and assumed the status of *minhag* (custom), later becoming codified into law.

The most famous of these composers was Rabbi Elazar

HaKalir, the son of the Tanna Rabbi Shimon bar Yochai, according to tradition.[16] Writing extremely intricate compositions, Rabbi Elazar had a total command of Hebrew and Torah — and both are required to understand the prayers. Many of his pieces still exist, especially in the Rosh HaShanah, Yom Kippur, and special Sabbath and festival *machzorim* (seasonal prayer books). In addition, much of the *Selichos, Kinnos,* and *Hoshanos* services are also based on Rabbi Elazar HaKalir's work. Indeed, during Gaonic times this genre of synagogue liturgy became extremely popular and the great burst of creativity in poetic prayer lasted hundreds of years. These prayers, known as *piyutim*, or liturgical poems, rhymed and were arranged according to the *alef-beis*, the Hebrew alphabet. Authors also encoded their names into the text of their compositions.

However, there was criticism about adding these prayers for three reasons. First, many *piyutim* were written to be said at points in the service where interruptions are normally forbidden, such as during the benedictions of *Yotzer Or*, and during the *chazzan*'s repetition of the *Amidah*. Second, some scholars felt that a number of words in the *piyutim*, particularly those of Rabbi Elazar HaKalir, were linguistic flights of fancy which did not exist in Hebrew.[17] Third, *piyutim* addressed to angels could mislead people into believing that these angels should be worshipped in their own right, which is idolatry. Regardless of the concerns and criticisms, however, *piyutim* became accepted by general consensus, and now form a major portion of the siddur, enriching Jewish prayer services immeasurably.

BIBLICAL SCHOLARSHIP: While most of world Jewry resided in Babylonia during the Gaonic era, a small but significant community still existed in Eretz Yisrael. Indeed, the town of Tiberias became renowned for its biblical scholars, known as Masoretes. These sages worked tirelessly to record the proper punctuation and musical cantillation of all the verses in Scripture. To that point, this body of knowledge had existed as oral tradition, but due to the dispersal of Jews to far-flung areas, it was in danger of being forgotten. Indeed, because the Torah and prophetic scrolls read publicly during synagogue services have no vocalization marks, the real danger existed that conflicts in pronunciation could lead to distorted translations. Therefore, the system of vowels in use today was developed, along with the musical signs indicating the proper tune for each word. The most famous of the Masoretes was Aharon ben Asher, who lived in the tenth century. After much research, he painstakingly compiled a codex of the Bible, considered authoritative by Maimonides, who based many of his laws regarding Torah scrolls on it.[18]

A contemporary of Ben Asher was Ben Naftali, who disagreed with Ben Asher in several hundred instances, almost all involving pronunciation or placement of musical signs. For example, the pronunciation of the word Issachar, one of Jacob's sons, is *Yisaschar* according to Ben Asher, but *Yisachar* according to Ben Naftali.[19] While current practice regards Ben Asher as authoritative in virtually every instance,[20] Ben Naftali's pronunciation of *Yisachar* is customarily followed. A copy of Ben Asher's work was in Aleppo, Syria, for many hundreds of years. Although 25 percent of the manuscript was destroyed, the rest was brought to Israel, where it exists today.[21]

ELDAD HADANI: In the 800s, a traveling merchant, claiming descent from the tribe of Dan, made his rounds in many Jewish communities. Calling himself Eldad HaDani, he told of an independent Jewish kingdom in Africa consisting of four of the lost ten tribes. He also taught previously unheard-of halachos, particularly regarding kosher slaughter of animals. Among the new laws he stated are if one slaughters without reciting a blessing beforehand, or without a head covering, or if the slaughterer is under the age of eighteen or over the age of eighty, the animal is not kosher.[22] (Current practice does not follow this stringent view.) While some scholars regarded Eldad as authentic, others viewed him as totally unreliable.[23]

THE KHAZARS: It is commonly believed that the State of Israel is the first independent Jewish country in nearly 2,000 years. However, incredibly enough, a powerful Jewish kingdom known as Khazaria flourished during the Gaonic era and lasted several hundred years. In the eighth century, a people known as Khazars converted to Judaism and created a nation in a large area of the Caucasus, what is today southern Russia. According to the twelfth-century Spanish scholar Rabbi Judah HaLevi in his book the *Kuzari*, Khazar King Bulan invited representatives of the Jewish, Christian, and Islamic faiths to debate the merits of their respective beliefs, planning to adopt the religion of the winner. Details of the debate are recorded in the *Kuzari*, along with Bulan's decision to convert his kingdom to Judaism.

Although differing opinions exist among historians as to whether this disputation actually took place, based on archaeological evidence all agree that a Jewish Khazar kingdom existed. The Khazars followed traditional Judaism and had contact with other Jews. The Khazar king, known as the *kagan*, by law had to be a Jew. The Khazars waged war with surrounding nations, frequently emerging victorious. However, by the tenth century, constant battles with Russian tribes greatly weakened Khazaria, and the kingdom collapsed. Many Khazar Jews were killed, while others converted to their conquerors' beliefs. Nevertheless, most Khazars retained their Jewish faith and joined other Jewish communities, particularly in Poland and Ukraine. Today, the Khazars are integrated into Jewish life and are unrecognizable.[24]

THE GREAT CALENDAR DISPUTE: In 920 CE, a controversy erupted that threatened to tear Jewish society apart. Aharon ben Meir, the head of the Jewish community of Eretz Yisrael, used a technical rarity to dispute the generally accepted calendar for the year 4681 (920–921).[25] According to his calculation, Pesach 4681 fell on a Sunday, while the prevalent opinion in Babylonia was that it fell on Tuesday. Basing his ideas on a Talmudic passage that delegates authority in calendar matters to the sages of Eretz Yisrael, Ben Meir instructed the Jews of Eretz Yisrael to celebrate Pesach on Sunday. Meanwhile, the Jews of Babylonia began the holiday on Tuesday. This sorry state of affairs lasted for two years, until, realizing that the cohesiveness of the Jewish people was in danger if people would continue observing different dates for festivals, Rabbi Saadiah Gaon, the leader of Babylonian Jewry, decisively proved that Rabbi Aharon ben Meir was incorrect. The matter died, and never again was there a calendar controversy in the Jewish world.

THE FIRST PURE HALACHIC WORKS: Two Gaonim wrote the first volumes dedicated solely to halachic decisions. Rabbi Yehudai Gaon authored *Halachos Pesukos*, which groups laws by topic. Blind and unable to write, the book was actually written by his disciples. Rabbi Shimon Kayara composed *Halachos Gedolos*, commonly known as the *Behag*, which arranges laws according to the order in the Talmud. Both works are considered the foundation of all subsequent halachic codifications.

MAJOR GAONIM

RABBI ACHAI GAON: Rabbi Achai Gaon lived in the 700s and wrote *Sheiltos DeRabbi Achai*. The book, arranged according to the weekly Torah portion, has each week's section divided into four parts. First, there is a general overview of laws based on that week's parashah. Second, there is a question posed on halachic practice, the *sheilta* related to the subject of the week. Third, there are moral lessons for the week. Fourth, there is a response to the *sheilta*. For example, in the beginning of the volume, on *Parashas Bereishis* in connection to the Torah's mention of the Sabbath, Rabbi Achai discusses laws of honoring the Sabbath, quoting inspirational selections from the Talmud regarding the greatness of the day. The *sheilta* ponders the question of whether someone fasting on Friday may continue his fast up to nightfall, even though he is entering the Sabbath in an unpleasant state. Rabbi Achai's response is that the fast is indeed completed until nightfall. According to tradition, Rabbi Achai wrote in such an easy, non-scholarly style because he had a son who was not interested in exerting himself in his studies, and the Rabbi believed that this book would help the son gain basic Torah knowledge.[26]

RABBI AMRAM GAON: Living in the 800s, Rabbi Amram Gaon compiled the first official siddur, on which all subsequent prayer books are based. Responding to a request from a distant community, Rabbi Amram wrote a detailed siddur for the weekdays and all holidays, including the laws of prayer. Although various versions evolved, such as *Nusach Sefard, Nusach Ashkenaz,* and *Nusach Ari,* all follow the basic format laid down by Rabbi Amram.

RABBI SAADIAH GAON: Born and raised in Egypt, and living in the 800–900s, Rabbi Saadiah Gaon was the only non-Babylonian to hold the post of Gaon throughout the hundreds of years of the Gaonim. While in his twenties, he became famous throughout the Jewish world when he wrote a book decisively refuting the Karaite movement. Utilizing a complete command of Hebrew and Scriptures to defeat the Karaites, Rabbi Saadiah directly caused the Karaites to lose much of their great appeal. Several years later, he settled the dispute over the calendar by conclusively proving that Rabbi Aharon ben Meir was incorrect. Realizing his unparalleled greatness, the *resh galusa* appointed the thirty-six year old Saadiah as Gaon of the yeshivah of Sura.

However, this idyllic state of affairs did not last long. Rabbi Saadiah opposed the *resh galusa*'s ruling on a complicated case, and when the two could not reach an agreement a great conflict erupted. Rabbi Saadiah excommunicated the *resh galusa*, and the *resh galusa* imposed a ban on Rabbi Saadiah. Eventually, Rabbi Saadiah had to flee from the *resh galusa*, going into hiding for seven years.

During that time, Rabbi Saadiah wrote many books, the most famous of which was *Emunos VeDeos*, the first work ever to organize the basic beliefs of Judaism in one place. Approaching Jewish belief from a rational viewpoint, Rabbi Saadiah wrote that because three million people witnessed G-d's giving the Torah at Mount Sinai, and then transmitted it to succeeding generations, it is a certainty that G-d did indeed give the Jews the Torah at Mount Sinai. Eventually, Rabbi Saadiah and the *resh galusa* reconciled their differences, and Rabbi Saadiah was reinstated as Gaon. Nevertheless, the entire episode took a great toll on him. After five years, at the age of fifty, Rabbi Saadiah passed away, and was greatly mourned by Jews everywhere. His epitaph could be one of his most famous sayings: "Our nation is a nation only because of the Torah." [27]

RABBI SHERIRA GAON: In the 900s, together with his son Rabbi Hai Gaon, Rabbi Sherira Gaon wrote great numbers of responsa, many of which have survived.[28] His magnum opus, however, is the *Iggeres DeRabbi Sherira Gaon*, a detailed analysis of the transmission of the Oral Law and rabbinic authorities, traced for some 1,000 years, from the Tannaim to his own time. Virtually all extant knowledge of this time, particularly that of the Amoraim, Rabbanan Savoroi, and Gaonim, is based on this book. Rabbi Sherira lived to be 100, and died under mysterious circumstances. Differing opinions exist as to whether he was executed by the Babylonian king, died in prison, or passed away naturally.[29]

Upon Rabbi Sherira's death in 1006, his son Rabbi Hai was installed as Gaon. The following Sabbath, several changes were made in the Torah and Haftarah readings. For example, the verse "Let G-d...appoint a man over the congregation" (Numbers 27:16), referring to Joshua's succession of Moses, was added to the weekly Torah reading. The regular Haftarah was replaced by a passage dealing with the death of King David and his son Solomon's accession to the throne. The last verse was changed from "And Solomon sat upon the throne of his father David, and his kingdom was firmly established" (I Kings 2:12) to "And Hai sat upon the throne of his father Sherira, and his kingdom was firmly established." [30]

RABBI HAI GAON: Rabbi Hai Gaon, who died in 1038, was the last and greatest of all Gaonim.[31] During his lifetime, Rabbi Hai attracted thousands of students from all over the Jewish world, from as far away as Europe. Unlike the earlier Gaonim, Rabbi Hai traveled to faraway Jewish communities, including Rome, spreading Torah learning on an unprecedented scale. So great was his teaching that many of Rabbi Hai's disciples became the leaders of the succeeding generation.[32] In terms of his scholarship, many of Rabbi Hai's responsa and writings are extant, dealing to a great extent with rules of commerce, such as oaths, deposits, and terms of sale. In explaining numerous remarkable stories found throughout the Talmud, Rabbi Hai took a rational approach, writing that many of the tales are parables and allusions to various concepts, and are not to be taken literally.[33] With Rabbi Hai Gaon's passing, the Gaonic Era came to a close, and Babylonia concomitantly lost its status as the Jewish people's supreme Torah center.

CHANGES IN JEWISH LIFE: After 1038, no one in Babylonia was of the stature of Rabbi Hai Gaon and able to take his place. As a result, Jews in faraway communities turned to their local rabbis for halachic guidance. In addition, as people began supporting their own community institutions, financial contributions from Jews worldwide to the Babylonian yeshivos slowed to a trickle. Sura and Pumbeditha became shadows of their original greatness, gradually going out of existence. In their stead, many new Torah centers sprung up, and for the first time in Jewish history no one place was considered the national halachic center. As each Jewish settlement developed independently, diverse customs evolved, leading to the proliferation of *minhagim* (local practices) in areas not legislated by normative halachah.

THE FOUR CAPTIVES: In the mid-900s, an incident took place that caused Torah scholarship to spread in many different areas. Four distinguished scholars traveled together on a fundraising mission for their institutions. According to some historians, they departed from Babylonia, while according to others they traveled from Italy.[34] Regardless, on the way pirates captured their ship. Realizing the value of their captives, the pirates did not harm the rabbis, but brought them to different Jewish communities to be redeemed. One of the captives, Rabbi Chushiel, was sold in Kairouan, in Tunisia, and helped develop it into a major Torah center. Rabbi Shemariah was redeemed in Egypt and settled there. Rabbi Moshe, along with his wife and young son Chanoch, wound up in Cordova, Spain. The fourth scholar, whom some say was Rabbi Nassan HaBavli,[35] was taken to France. Although at that time it must have appeared as a tragedy to the scholars involved, in actuality it was a Divine method of spreading Torah throughout the Jewish world.

Chapter 11

THE RISHONIM

THE RISHONIM: The successors to the Torah tradition of the Gaonim were known as the Rishonim, or early scholars, to distinguish them from the later Torah authorities called Acharonim. Spanning ten generations over approximately a 500-year period, the Rishonim led the Torah world from 1000 to 1500 CE, during which time Jewish life underwent enormous changes. Babylonia ceased being the major Torah center, and no other place would ever hold that distinction. Instead, many centers of learning sprung up, with none being the ultimate voice for world Jewry. In addition, the period of the Rishonim saw the rise of Roman Catholic domination of Western Europe, which included the great persecutions of the Jews, culminating in the Spanish Expulsion of 1492.

ACCOMPLISHMENTS OF THE RISHONIM: The scholarly and literary output of the Rishonim is staggering, with virtually all current Biblical and Talmudic scholarship based on their work. Hundreds of brilliant scholars wrote vast commentaries on the Bible, Talmud, halachah, and Jewish philosophy. In addition, much of the current liturgy draws from *piyutim* composed by rabbinic poets clearly imbued with a spirit of holiness. Amazingly, much of this work was accomplished during times of extreme persecution and tragedy, thereby fulfilling G-d's promise to the Jewish people (Deuteronomy 31:21) that despite all the horrors they will endure, the Torah will never be forgotten. Today, the Rishonim are held in such great esteem that it is unthinkable for any later scholar to dispute their decisions or interpretations. In fact, since their times, 500 years of study and many thousands of books and commentaries have been devoted to analyzing and interpreting every nuance of a Rishon's words. Indeed, such reverence is accorded to the Rishonim that any serious student knows that one does not say, "Rashi was wrong," or "Rambam made a mistake," but rather, "We must attempt to figure out what they are trying to teach us."

RISHONIM VIS-À-VIS THE GAONIM: Compared to the writings of the Rishonim, the output of the Gaonim is quite scanty — despite their greater Torah scholarship. The relatively few Gaonic publications may be due in part to the loss of much Gaonic material over the centuries. However, a famous Rishon, the Meiri,[1] explains that "They [the Gaonim] were well-versed in the entire Torah and Talmud as one is fluent in reading the *Shema*; therefore, they saw no need to write lengthy commentaries, for in their few words lay all the intermediate steps." In modern terms, the Gaonim are like a faster computer. Interestingly, a similar phenomenon manifests itself with the *Shaalos Uteshuvos* of Rishonim and Acharonim. Questions posed to a Rishon such as the Rashba are usually answered in a paragraph or two, while those found in the *Igros Moshe* of Rabbi Moshe Feinstein often take many pages to answer. A great deal of the latter's length is devoted to explaining how the decision was reached, which the Rashba simply assumes as a matter of course.

GROWTH OF JEWISH COMMUNITIES IN FRANCE AND GERMANY: Even during the Gaonic era, new Jewish communities were arising and achieving prominence. In the eighth century, Emperor Charlemagne asked the Caliph of Babylonia to send him a Torah scholar to strengthen European Jewish spiritual life. Acquiescing to this request, the Caliph sent Rabbi Machir to Narbonne, France. Rabbi Machir and his descendants then proceeded to build Narbonne into a major Torah center that lasted hundreds of years.[2] (According to some historians, one of the Four Captives also strengthened the French Jewish community.) In the tenth century, Charlemagne's grandson Charles imported from Italy to Germany Rabbi Moshe of the famous Kalonymous family. Aside from Cyrus the Great, these are the only two instances of non-Jewish rulers inviting Jews to their countries in order to improve Jewish spiritual life. Usually, Jews were welcomed to a new land only for the economic boon that they could bring.

ITALY: Jews came to Italy during the time of Roman rule of Eretz Yisrael. After *churban Bayis Sheini*, Titus also brought successive waves of Jews as prisoners and slaves. A considerable number of these Jews subsequently gained their freedom and became the nucleus of many Jewish communities throughout Italy. Strangely enough, despite dwelling in the center of Roman and later Catholic rule, it appears that the Jews of Italy fared better than those of outlying areas. A famous Italian Jewish family, for example, the Kalonymous clan, spanned several hundred years. Members of this family wrote numerous *piyutim*, which figure prominently in the Ashkenazic Yom Kippur rite. Most famous of these is the lengthy description of the *kohen gadol*'s Temple service (the *Avodah*), which is recited during Mussaf.

THE JEWS COME TO SPAIN: Although Jewish legend has Jews arriving in Spain at *churban Bayis Rishon*, or even during the reign of King Solomon, historians feel that they arrived at the time of *churban Bayis Sheini*.[3] Indeed, a third-century gravestone has been found in Spain bearing the unmistakably Jewish name Salomonula. Until the fifth century, Spain was under Roman rule, and conditions for Jews were benign. However, the situation changed drastically with the Visigoth conquest, which brought strict Christian rule to Spain. In the seventh century, the Visigoths decreed that all Jewish children must be raised as Catholics, and in an ominous portent of events 900 years in the future, declared that only Catholics might reside in Spain. Plans were made to confiscate the Jews' property and sell them into slavery.

However, a providential event took place that dramatically

changed the course of Jewish history. The Moorish Arabs conquered Spain in 711, bringing a welcome respite for the Jews. While the Muslims swept through Spain with ease, driving the Christians in a headlong retreat into the northern mountains, the Moors committed a fatal mistake when they did not completely expel the Christians from Spain. Brooding in their mountain redoubts, the Christians planned the Holy *Reconquista*, or reconquest, of Spain for Christianity. For hundreds of years, this vision was tenaciously transmitted to successive generations. Over an 800-year period, the Christians slowly drove the Muslims from the land, culminating with the conquest in 1492 of Granada, the last Arab stronghold.

THE GOLDEN AGE OF SPANISH JEWRY: From 950 to 1150 CE, under tolerant Arab rule, the Jews of Spain entered into an era of splendor, both spiritually and materially. As the Muslim conquerors needed help in administering their new land, they eagerly sought Jewish expertise in both commerce and governance. In addition, the Arabs shared a love of learning with the Jews, which manifested itself in the fields of philosophy, medicine, mathematics, astronomy, and poetry. While Christian Europe sank into the Dark Ages, Muslim Spain developed into a modern, pluralistic society, where all beliefs were tolerated. Sophisticated cities were built featuring paved streets, piped water, and exquisite gardens and palaces. Cordova, Toledo, and Granada became major centers of learning, where mathematicians, scientists, and poets perused scholarly volumes in world-class libraries.

Given both freedom and riches, Spain rapidly became the largest Jewish community in the world. Spanish Jewry produced dazzling Torah scholars, poets who wrote some of the most inspiring sacred pieces of the liturgy, philosophers whose writings remain as classic as when they were written, and grammarians who laid down the basic rules of Hebrew. In the secular realm, Jews became diplomats, generals, prime ministers, scientists, and secular poets. Sadly, the Golden Age came to a halt in 1147, when fanatic Almohad Muslims invaded Spain from North Africa. To avoid being offered a choice between conversion to Islam or death, many Jews fled to the Christian north of Spain. So great was Jewish life in Spain that such a favorable climate for Jews would not exist again until the twentieth-century United States.

SEPHARDIM AND ASHKENAZIM: Although Jewish legend traces the origin of the Ashkenazim to the tribe of Benjamin,[4] and the Sephardim to the tribe of Judah, it appears that the division took place gradually over several hundred years, culminating during the eighth to tenth centuries. At that time, world Jewry lived under two great empires — the Muslim Arab-ruled areas of the Middle East, North Africa, and Spain; and the Christian-ruled Roman Empire in Europe and Asia Minor, itself divided into the Holy Roman Empire in the west and Byzantium in the east.

Over hundreds of years Jews traveled to all areas of the Roman Empire, both as slaves after *churban Bayis Sheini* and the fall of Betar, and as free men seeking economic opportunity. Likewise, Jews under Arab rule were encouraged by the new rulers and traveled throughout the lands conquered by the Arabs, who needed the Jews to help administer the newly occupied lands. By the ninth century, the Islamic world had undergone a great transformation, from a concatenation of wild desert tribes to peoples living in sophisticated urban centers of commerce and learning, such as Baghdad and Cordova. Indeed, the growth of a mercantile economy weakened traditional agrarian societies. Many Jews abandoned the fields and farms of Babylonia, which they had tilled for centuries, and went forth to take advantage of many new and exciting opportunities. Thus, the Jews of both the Roman Empire and the Islamic Empire developed into unique Ashkenazic and Sephardic cultures, reflecting the influences of their respective rulers.

Spain became the center of the Sephardic world, influencing communities in North Africa, Eretz Yisrael, Babylonia, and the Middle East, while Germany, Northern France, and Italy were the bastions of the Ashkenazim. Due to its location, Southern

France, or Provence, was the crossroads of the two schools of thought, although Provence tended to follow Sephardic practice. While both groups were loyal to the same Torah, important differences arose between them in three major areas:

Different customs arose between the two groups. Divergent *minhagim* arose, particularly in the prayer service. Indeed, the origins of today's *Nusach Sefard* and *Nusach Ashkenaz* come from this time period.

Methods of learning diverged as well. Ashkenazim employed a unique analytical approach to the Talmud, as embodied in the commentary of the great Tosafists, while the Sephardim usually focused on halachic works, as evinced in the great halachah compendiums of the Rif and Rambam. (Of course, there were Sephardic Talmudic commentators, such as Rashba and Ritva, and Ashkenazic halachists, such as Maharam MiRothenberg.)

The Jewish attitude toward secular studies varied as well. Sephardic scholars studied science, literature, and philosophy, and wrote non-sacred poetry, while such practices were completely absent among the Ashkenazim. This difference was due largely to the cultural milieu in which each group lived. In Spain, such studies were in vogue, while in France and Germany these studies did not exist. For their part, Sephardic scholars felt that secular studies were important both to enhance one's understanding of Torah and to gain the respect of the non-Jewish world. Some Sephardic scholars also had creative drives that naturally channeled themselves into secular pursuits. To the contrary, Ashkenazic scholars lived in a world of brute ignorance, where they had very little interaction with gentile society. As such, all of these scholars' talents were devoted exclusively to Torah. To this day, the issue of what role, if any, secular disciplines should play in understanding Torah, and to what extent Jews should involve themselves with the outside world, has been fiercely debated among Jews.[5]

SPANISH JEWS IN SECULAR PURSUITS: During the Golden Age Spanish Torah scholars rose to prominence in many different fields, becoming ministers, generals, poets, and grammarians. In the tenth century, Chisdai ibn Shaprut became the personal physician and prime minister to the Arab caliph of Spain. Ibn Shaprut's responsibilities included overseeing the collection of custom duties on merchandise entering Spain, and negotiating treaties with foreign countries. Utilizing his international connections, Ibn Shaprut was able to secure more favorable treatment for Jews throughout the civilized world. Utilizing his vast wealth to support Babylonian yeshivos and many other Jewish communities, Ibn Shaprut even redeemed Rabbi Moshe ben Chanoch when that renowned scholar was brought to Spain on a pirate ship. Later Ibn Shaprut encouraged Rabbi Moshe to set up his own yeshivah, thus building up the quality of Torah study in Spain. Finally, on hearing of the powerful Jewish Khazar kingdom, Ibn Shaprut proposed an alliance and received a positive reply. Unfortunately, the plan never reached fruition.

In the eleventh century, Shmuel ibn Joseph, a disciple of Rabbi Moshe ben Chanoch, caught the attention of the vizier (prime minister) of the caliph. Shmuel was a master calligrapher and linguist of the Arabic language, and when the vizier saw Shmuel's masterful work, the vizier appointed Shmuel his personal secretary. On his deathbed, the vizier told the caliph that Shmuel was responsible for all the advice the vizier had given the caliph. Seeing that Shmuel was a suitable replacement, the caliph appointed him vizier, and Shmuel became known to the Jews as Shmuel HaNagid, the prince. Shmuel then became the general of the Arab armies, fighting many successful battles. At home, Shmuel continued in the tradition of Ibn Shaprut, showing concern for Jews everywhere and supporting Torah scholars with his vast wealth. Himself a Torah scholar of note, Shmuel wrote the Talmudic commentary *Mavo HaTalmud*. He also was a prolific poet, both in religious and secular realms. In one of his poems, Shmuel takes issue with the practice of loud Talmudic argumentation in the synagogue, comparing it to the braying of animals.[6] (Current practice does not follow this view.)

A brilliant man, Shmuel's adroitness in dealing with his detractors was legendary. Once, for example, while walking with the caliph, an Arab insulted Shmuel HaNagid. While the caliph ordered Shmuel to cut out the offender's tongue, instead Shmuel befriended the Arab and showered him with gifts. On another occasion, Shmuel and the caliph were taking a stroll, and the same Arab heaped praise on Shmuel. In anger, the caliph asked Shmuel why his order was not carried out. Shmuel's wise reply was that he did indeed cut out the Arab's bad tongue and replaced it with a good one. When Shmuel died, his son Joseph became the new *nagid*. Unfortunately, Joseph did not possess his father's wisdom. Joseph's lavish lifestyle and condescending attitude toward Arabs brought him many enemies. A pogrom broke out in his hometown of Granada, and Joseph and many other Jews were killed.

SHLOMO IBN GABIROL: One of the most famous poets of the Golden Age, Shlomo ibn Gabirol composed the immortal *Adon Olam*, which compares G-d's omniscient glory with His benevolent, personal concern for all people. Ibn Gabirol's *Keser Malchus*, a classic of Hebrew language and belief, is recited in some congregations on Yom Kippur. In fact, Ibn Gabirol was universally recognized as great — so much so that the great commentator Ibn Ezra called Ibn Gabirol "the master of verse."[7] In addition, Ibn Gabirol wrote a book discussing such elemental issues as G-d and the human condition, employing a strictly philosophical viewpoint and not resorting to Scripture or other traditional sources.[8] The book, written in Arabic under a pen name, was translated into Latin. The Catholic Church, unaware of the book's Jewish origins, adopted it as a religious primer — while at the same time some Jewish sages attacked the book. Sadly, Ibn Gabirol had many enemies, and had to wander from place to place. According to legend, an Arab poet killed him out of jealousy for Ibn Gabirol's great poetic acumen.

DIKDUK: The study of Hebrew grammar (*dikduk*) became very popular during the Golden Age. Among the most famous grammarians are Menachem ibn Saruk, his student Yehuda ibn Chiyug, and Donash ibn Labrat. A protege of Ibn Shaprut, Menachem wrote the *Machberes*, the first book exclusively devoted to rules of *dikduk*. This landmark work posited that Hebrew words can have roots (*shorashim*) of one to five letters, an idea to which Ibn Chiyug strenuously objected, claiming that all words possess a three-letter root. (Popular Hebrew grammar adheres to this position, although some scholars prefer a one- to four-root idea.)

Despite disagreeing with Menachem, Ibn Chiyug defended his teacher against the attacks of Donash ibn Labrat, who wrote a competing Hebrew grammar text. Indeed, the conflict became so acrimonious that at one point supporters of Donash accused Menachem of harboring Karaite beliefs because he explained words in the Torah according to their simple meaning and not following rabbinic tradition. (For example, they took issue with Menachem's translation of *melikah*, the nipping of the head of a bird sacrifice, as a form of ritual slaughter.)[9] Ibn Shaprut cut off Menachem's financial support, and Menachem was even physically attacked. Despite all the acrimony, Jewish tradition regards both disputants as legitimate, and Rashi quotes both Menachem and Donash in his commentary on the Torah.[10] Donash is the author of the Sabbath song *"Dror Yikra"* and the introduction to *Birkas HaMazon* recited during the wedding week (*sheva berachos*), *"Devai Hosair."*

ASHKENAZIC POETRY: Although not nearly as prolific as their Sephardic counterparts, Ashkenazim nonetheless made very important contributions to *piyutim*. One of the highlights of the Rosh HaShanah and Yom Kippur services is the recital of *Unesaneh Tokef*, which describes the process of Heavenly judgment in stark, chilling terms. The prayer was composed by the tenth-century sage, Rabbi Amnon, and has a remarkable story behind it, one which offers a picture of the power of Christianity at that time.

Rabbi Amnon, who lived in Mainz, Germany, was a close confidante of the ruler. After repeated entreaties to adopt the

Christian religion, Rabbi Amnon, in order to distance himself from the duke, told him that he would give the duke a reply in three days. Upon leaving the duke, Rabbi Amnon felt extremely distraught that he gave even an impression of renouncing Judaism. Instead of returning to the court, Rabbi Amnon spent three days in fasting and prayer, not appearing at the appointed time. Enraged, the duke ordered that if Rabbi Amnon refused to convert his arms and legs be cut off one by one. Rosh HaShanah was approaching, and the crippled and dying Rabbi Amnon asked to be taken to the synagogue. During the Mussaf service, he asked the *chazzan* to wait while he composed the *Unesaneh Tokef*. Upon concluding, he returned his pure soul to his Creator. Shortly afterward, Rabbi Amnon appeared in a dream to one of his disciples, and requested that the prayer be disseminated throughout the Jewish world. Since that time, *Unesaneh Tokef* has become universally accepted.

Another Ashkenazic poet, Rabbi Shimon HaGadol, also lived in tenth-century Mainz. One of his compositions for the second day of Rosh HaShanah contains the words *"Kel chanan nachaloso."* Legend ascribes a fascinating story to these words. Rabbi Shimon's young child Elchanan was kidnapped by the Church, and brought up as a Christian. Rising higher and higher in the Church hierarchy, he reached the level of pope. The new pope then enacted a decree of expulsion against the Jews, which Rabbi Shimon, as the leading Jewish spokesman, attempted to forestall. While meeting the pope, the two became involved in a game of chess. When the pope made a move in a certain position, Rabbi Shimon exclaimed that he once taught that move to his long-lost son. As the conversation continued, Rabbi Shimon realized that the pope was his son Elchanan. Father and son were tearfully reunited, and the pope disappeared and rejoined the Jewish people.

ASHKENAZIM AND KABBALAH: The study of Kabbalah became popular among Ashkenazic scholars of the Middle Ages, particularly in Germany. A well-known Kabbalistic personality was the twelfth-century Rabbi Judah HaChasid, whose best-known work, *Sefer Chassidim*, approaches halachah both from Kabbalastic and non-Kabbalistic sources. The book won popular acclaim, and is revered to this day. Among Rabbi Judah's most famous enactments are that enemies should not be buried in the same row in the cemetery, and that a man should not marry a woman who has the same name as his mother.[11] (Currently, a bride with the same name simply adds a name.)

JEWISH COMMUNITY LIFE IN GERMANY: During the times of the Rishonim, Jews did not live in officially sanctioned ghettoes, but lived instead primarily in their own quarter of major towns. In Frankfurt, Germany, for example, the Jewish section was known as the Judengasse, while in England there was a Little Jewry Lane in Oxford and a Jewbury district in York. At that time, Jews were in constant, daily contact with their gentile neighbors , interacting with the nobility, burghers, merchants, and peasants. The Jews hired gentiles for all sorts of labor, both skilled and unskilled, and also purchased goods from gentiles that the Jews themselves did not produce, such as wood, bricks, paints, and flour.[12] When fire threatened a town, a frequent occurrence in those days, Jews and non-Jews banded together to extinguish it, even on the Sabbath if necessary. In all, despite the lack of relationships between German Jews and non-Jews on the social and intellectual levels, there was considerable interaction between them economically.

A specially appointed government judge, known as the Judge of the Jews, handled legal disputes between Jews and non-Jews. At times, there was even a mixed court, consisting of two Jews appointed by the community and two non-Jews appointed by the town council. Toward the end of the fifteenth century, regular municipal courts assumed this function, as non-Jewish merchants falsely accused the Jews' judge of taking bribes.[13]

CUSTOMS OF WORMS, GERMANY: Worms was one of the oldest Jewish communities in Europe, and is best known for being the town where Rashi spent a good part of his life. In the 1600s, a learned individual by the name of Juspa Shammas recorded the ancient customs of Worms. These *minhagim* provide a fascinating window on life in an ancient Ashkenazic community.

The *shammas* (synagogue sexton) was responsible for the arrangement and performance of the davening (prayers). He woke men for services — at 4:30 a.m. in the summer, and daybreak in the winter (7:00–8:00 a.m.). Using a special gavel, the *shammas* knocked on those selected windows and doors in the center of the street so that the sound carried to all the houses. As he knocked, he called out "*Schulen, Schulen*" (come to the synagogue). This duty was carried out faithfully in all seasons, regardless of weather.

As it was described in contemporary documents, "First, he knocks upon his own house, the house of the *shammas*. He then approaches the outer building, next to the women's section of the synagogue, and knocks a second time. Next, he enters the synagogue and recites [the introductory prayer] *Mah Tovu*. He remains in his place while reciting *Ashrei*. Subsequently, he proceeds to the house of the head of the rabbinical court and knocks. He then walks to the lower gate, on the east side of the street, and opens the large gate and the small doorway within it. He continues until he reaches the upper gate, on the west side of the street, visiting the designated houses and knocking on doors as he walks... He also opens the upper gate."[14] The meticulous attention paid to seemingly minor details of procedure bespeak an ancient ritual that was reverently kept unchanged for centuries.

Another duty of the *shammas* was to maintain a communal oven in his house where the townspeople stored their Sabbath *cholent* pots. On Sabbath morning, the *shammas* left services shortly before they concluded in order to assist people in removing their pots from the oven. (Carrying them home was permissible, for medieval communities all constructed an *eruv* for this purpose.)

Among the rabbi's duties was to punish or fine recalcitrant members of the community. On occasion, proclamations of bans against individuals were issued in the synagogue. (Most medieval communities had but one synagogue.) As is customary today, the rabbi delivered special sermons on the Sabbaths before Pesach and Yom Kippur. The rabbi was provided with a home, and was exempt from all community and property taxes. He was also given a special seat in the synagogue, facing east on the northern side toward the *bimah*, the platform on which the Torah is read. The rabbi's jurisdiction extended to the towns surrounding Worms, and he was expected to visit them periodically.

Community members were selected to become *parnassim* and *gabbaim*. *Parnassim* were responsible for the administrative affairs of the community, such as overseeing the assessment of families' income for tax purposes and enforcing community decisions, while *gabbaim* collected each family's charity obligation.

A boy who turned thirteen on Sabbath was not permitted to read the Torah in the synagogue but was required to wait to the next Sabbath, for the community did not consider him to be bar mitzvah until one day had passed following his thirteenth birthday.

On Purim, before the night and day Megillah readings, young boys paraded around both the men's and women's sections, wearing masks and holding torches at night. Young girls donned their holiday attire, dressing up as Queen Esther. They also paraded around the synagogue in a manner similar to the boys.

Juspa's recording of engagement, marriage, and circumcision ceremonies indicates that despite the everyday struggle for survival, and occasional persecutions, the Jews of Worms had an ample livelihood. A bridegroom sent lavish gifts to his bride, banquets and feasts were abundant, and marriage ceremonies were held in the communal wedding hall. Circumcisions were attended by many of the congregation's members with great rejoicing.

Juspa also records the rare occasions when individuals transgressed the law. For example, a *kohen* who was a Sabbath desecrator was ordered to descend from the platform on which the *kohanim* bless the congregation on holidays. Juspa also mentions the extraordinary rabbinic ban placed throughout the year on playing cards, dice, or any other type of game, except for chess, and except for Chanukah.

Shedding light on an important issue of his day (and for all time), Juspa exhorted the leaders of the community to ensure that Jewish businessmen be scrupulously honest with gentiles. Jews who peddled their wares in the city were not to act in a way to cause the non-Jews to complain about unfair competition. Men and women were not to dress boastfully or immodestly, so as not to attract the attention of gentiles.[15]

From Juspa's descriptions, it is clear that Worms was a close-knit, peaceful community, maintaining its customs for many hundreds of years. In general, life in Ashkenazic communities was peaceful up until the times of the Crusades, thereby enabling the Jews to develop both in Torah and material well-being.

JEWISH COMMUNITY LIFE IN SPAIN: During the Golden Age of Spain, and the earlier part of subsequent Christian rule, Spanish Jews enjoyed greater freedoms than did Jews anywhere else in the world. Indeed, along with Christians and Muslims, the Spanish Jews were recognized as belonging to a separate and distinct religious and national group whom it suited the monarchs to treat favorably. On the whole, Jews were free to trade or engage in such crafts or professions as they chose, while money lending was never regarded as a typically Jewish occupation. In Spain, then, the Jews were weavers, tailors, furriers, blacksmiths, saddlers, potters, boilermakers, merchants, and shopkeepers. As there were no restrictions on Jews owning land, they cultivated fields and vineyards. Jewish artisans produced elegant filigree silver, with their best customer the Catholic Church. On El Medio Street in Saragossa, where Jewish shops lined both sides of the narrow passage, the Jews crafted leather shoes that were renowned throughout Spain. (This is still a street of shoemakers and repairers, albeit non-Jewish, who work out of tiny shops.)[16] Jews were also famed artists who produced stunning illuminated manuscripts, such as Passover Haggadahs, which possess great value today.

On Thursdays, market days, Jews exhibited their wares in open-air markets. One market sold grain; another silk, famed for its high quality; and a third market sold general wares, including kosher meat, which, as today, was prized by non-Jews.

Jews lived in their own quarters, known as *juderias*, a number of which have been preserved in Spain and can be seen today. The streets were a maze of narrow alleyways, with hygiene primitive by today's standards. Stinking garbage was piled high at every turn of the road. Latrines were nonexistent, except among the rich, whose palaces sometimes bordered rivers, where elementary piping systems dumped waste directly into the water. Rats were at home everywhere.

The *aljamas*, Jewish communities, possessed extensive powers of self-government. In some communities, there were officers whose job it was to watch for and apprehend individuals found violating halachah. The Jewish courts were empowered to impose bans of excommunication, corporal punishment, and in some cases the death penalty, which was usually carried out by the king. Disputes between Jews and non-Jews were handled fairly by courts composed of representatives of both faiths. In all, although there was discrimination from time to time, Jewish life in Spain during this period was generally peaceful and prosperous.

Chapter 12

TWENTY-FIVE GREAT RISHONIM

Name/ Acronym	Genera- tion*	Origin	Country
R. Chananel	1	Sephardic	Tunisia
R. Gershom	1	Ashkenazic	Germany
R. Yitzchak Alfasi	2	Sephardic	Morocco, Spain
R. Nassan (Aruch)	2	Ashkenazic	Italy
Ibn Pakudah	2	Sephardic	Spain
Rashi	3	Ashkenazic	France, Germany
Ibn Ezra	3	Sephardic	Spain
R. Judah HaLevi	3	Sephardic	Spain
Rashbam	4	Ashkenazic	France
Rabbeinu Tam	4	Ashkenazic	France
Rambam	5	Sephardic	Spain, Egypt
Raavad III	5	Provence	France

R. Zerachiah HaLevi	5	Provence	France
R. David Kimchi	6	Provence	France
Baalei Tosafos#	6	Ashkenazic	France, Germany
Ramban	7	Sephardic	Spain, Eretz Yisrael
R. Jonah	7	Sephardic	Spain
R. Meir of Rothenberg	7	Ashkenazic	Germany
R. Asher (Rosh)	8	Ashkenazic	Germany, Spain
Meiri	8	Provence	France
Rashba	8	Sephardic	Spain
Ritva	9	Sephardic	Spain
R. Nissim (Ran)	9	Sephardic	Spain
Baal HaTurim#	9	Ashkenazic	Germany, Spain
R. Y. Isserlein	10	Ashkenazic	Germany, Austria

Name of commentary. *Based on R. M. Bergman, Mavo Shearim, p. 68

R ABBI CHANANEL (tenth–eleventh centuries, Sephardic): The son of Rabbi Chushiel, one of the Four Captives, and a disciple of Rabbi Hai Gaon,[1] Rabbi Chananel is considered the bridge between the Gaonim and the Rishonim. Under his aegis, Kairouan in Tunisia developed into a major Torah center. In recognition of his great stature, his commentary (where extant) is printed on every Talmud page alongside those of Rashi and Tosafos, an honor accorded to very few scholars. In addition, Rabbi Chananel revived the regular study of the Jerusalem Talmud, which had suffered neglect, and frequently referred to it in his commentary. As a scholar, he influenced disciples both in the Sephardic and Ashkenazic worlds, including Rabbi Yitzchak Alfasi of North Africa and Rabbi Nassan of Rome. Exceedingly wealthy, Rabbi Chananel supported Torah scholars both at home and abroad. After his death, nine daughters and no sons survived him, and Kairouan declined as a Torah center, disappearing in the twelfth century during the Arab persecutions.

RABBI GERSHOM MEOR HAGOLAH (tenth–eleventh centuries, Ashkenazic): Another disciple of Rabbi Hai Gaon,[2] Rabbi Gershom's famous enactments, known as *Cherem DeRabbeinu Gershom*, continue to have a great impact on Jewish life. The best known of these is the dictum that a man may not be married to two women simultaneously, an act permissible according to biblical law. The reason for his enactment was to prevent strife between the two wives, which seemed to be a problem in Rabbi Gershom's time.[3] Although this decree was originally set to expire in the year 5000 (1240 CE), Ashkenazic Jews extended the restriction, thus giving it the force of eternal Jewish law.[4]

Another decree, related to the first, is the limitation of the husband's power to divorce his wife. Under biblical law, a divorce may be effected against her will. However, at that time, due to the increasing abuse of this rule by men who arbitrarily divorced their wives,[5] Rabbi Gershom took this step to protect women. An exception is the much-misunderstood *heter meah rabbanim*, a dispensation given by 100 rabbis in three countries for a man to marry a second wife while still technically married to the first one. Such an exception is only performed in extremely limited circumstances, such as when the wife committed adultery, in which case the Torah prohibits the marriage to continue. If, at that point, the wife refuses to receive a *get*, a divorce document, one may be written for her and deposited with a Jewish court. She is then notified that any time she wishes, she may receive the *get* and be free of the marriage. Then, and only then, may the husband initiate the *heter meah rabbanim* process, which allows him to remarry.[6] Clearly, this process is not a method for a husband to escape marriage while leaving his lawful wife in limbo.

A third of Rabbi Gershom's decrees is that one may not read sealed letters sent to another person. Although such reading is also forbidden under the biblical injunction against gossip ("*Lo selech rachil b'amecha*" — Leviticus 19:16),[7] to emphasize its severity Rabbi Gershom imposed a *cherem*, a ban, on such behavior. It then became customary to write on the outside of letters the Hebrew acronym *Upagin Deragmah*, based on a verse in Ecclesiastes 10:8, which stands for "One who breaks a fence [a ban] of Rabbi Gershom should be bitten by a snake."[8] Rabbi Gershom also enacted the decree that if a Jew converted to Christianity and subsequently repented, he should be welcomed back to the community and not encounter any discrimination. Rabbi Gershom's disciples were the teachers of Rashi.

RABBI YITZCHAK ALFASI (eleventh century, Sephardic): A disciple of Rabbi Chananel, Rabbi Yitzchak Alfasi is popularly known by the acronym of his name, the Rif, and Alfasi is after the Moroccan city of Fez where he headed a large yeshivah. In contrast to other Sephardic scholars who often devoted attention to secular studies, Rif exclusively focused on Torah study. As a result, he became the greatest sage of his time.

One of the three halachic authorities on whom contemporary Jewish law is based, along with Rambam and Rosh, Rif, with his monumental work *Alfasi*, made a unique contribution to the study of halachah. Based on the language and style of the Talmud, the *Alfasi* is an abridgement of all laws currently applicable. While the work retains the frame of a topic as it appears in the Talmud, *Alfasi* deletes the Talmud's discussions and digressions. For example, in the *Alfasi* the 156 pages of tractate *Shabbos* are reduced to sixty-seven pages. When a matter is left undecided in the Talmud, as is often the case, the *Alfasi* decides the halachah, giving the reasoning behind every verdict. Accordingly, the Rif's magnum opus won the acclaim of all Jewry. (In recent times, the Chafetz Chaim published an *Alfasi*-style commentary, known as *Likutei Halachos*, on the Talmudic tractates dealing with laws that do not currently apply, such as sacrifices and ritual purity.) Printed in standard editions of the Talmud after the conclusion of each tractate, the *Alfasi* is surrounded on the page by a number of commentaries, which vary according to the tractate being discussed. At an old age, Rif moved to Spain, where he died. His main disciple was Rabbi Yosef ibn MiGash, the teacher of Rambam's father.

RABBI NASSAN OF ROME (eleventh century, Ashkenazic): Rabbi Nassan wrote the *Aruch*, the first dictionary of obscure words in the Talmud, grouped in alphabetical order. The work was accepted by all scholars, both Sephardic and Ashkenazic, and is quoted by Rashi and Tosafos.[9] In the course of defining words, the *Aruch* gives new insights into Talmudic topics, some of which are accepted as definitive halachah. For example, in discussing the word *heses*, an oath imposed by the rabbis of the Talmud in specific instances, the *Aruch* describes the elaborate procedure taken by the court in administering a biblical oath. When a litigant swears a biblical oath, a coffin is brought into the room, sackcloth and dirt are spread around, balloons are popped, and candles are lit and then extinguished. The one swearing holds a Torah scroll, and a shofar is blown as the oath is taken. (Currently, due to the severity of possibly swearing falsely, there is great reluctance to impose such oaths in court, and only rabbinic oaths, which are less severe, are administered.)[10] The *Aruch* remains immensely popular to this very day.

RABBI BACHYA IBN PAKUDAH (eleventh century, Sephardic): Author of *Chovos HaLevavos*, or Duties of the Heart, a work dealing with commandments based on the mind and emotions, such as love of G-d and trust in G-d, Rabbi Bachya has had a lasting effect on the Jewish people. Although the first portion of the book, *Shaar HaYichud*, is not commonly studied today, due to its reliance on unfamiliar forms of philosophy, the rest of the work remains as fresh and relevant as when it was first written. Originally composed in Arabic, and translated into Hebrew in the twelfth century by the famous Ibn Tibbon family of translators, in recent times it has been adapted into an easier Hebrew known as *Lev Tov*. Regarded as a basic primer of Jewish thought, *Chovos HaLevavos' Shaar HaBitachon* is the definitive text on the delicate balance between the belief that one's income is predetermined by G-d and the obligation to work for a living.

RABBI SHLOMO BEN YITZCHAK — RASHI (1040–1105, Ashkenazic): The famous name Rashi stands for **R**abbi **Sh**lomo **Y**itzchaki, or *Rabban Shel Yisrael*, the teacher of the Jewish people. The appellation Teacher of the Nation has been given to a select few leaders throughout Jewish history, among them Moshe Rabbeinu (Moses) and Rabbeinu HaKadosh (Rabbi Judah HaNasi). Rashi stands in such august company because no other individual in the last 1,800 years has played such a major role in making the Torah's wisdom accessible to as many Jews.

A number of well-known legends surround Rashi's birth and life. Rashi's father, Rabbi Yitzchak, was a diamond merchant. Once, he came into possession of a spectacular gemstone that the Church wanted as a centerpiece for a statue. Despite much pressure, and promises of incredible sums of money, Rabbi Yitzchak refused to sell the diamond. When Church officials lured him onto a boat and threatened him with death if he refused to sell, only then did Rabbi Yitzchak agree to part with the precious stone. While standing on deck, he took it out as if to give it to them, then craftily he faked tripping. When the stone slipped out of his hand and into the water, a Heavenly voice proclaimed, "You gave up a material diamond for My honor, and you will receive a spiritual diamond in its place!"

While Rashi's mother was pregnant with him, she was walking in the narrow street of the Jewish quarter when a nobleman's carriage came hurtling toward her at high speed. In desperation, she pressed against the wall, which miraculously contracted, making an indentation for her to back into.

Toward the end of Rashi's life, Crusaders embarked on their conquest of the Holy Land. Godfrey of Bouillon, one of the Crusader leaders, had heard of Rashi's greatness, and asked him whether his crusade would be successful. Reluctantly, Rashi told Godfrey that he would indeed conquer Jerusalem but rule over it a very short time, and eventually return to Troyes with only three horsemen. Incensed, Godfrey told Rashi that if he returned with four riders, he would kill all the Jews of France.

Events transpired exactly as Rashi had foretold. Godfrey captured Jerusalem, but ruled it very briefly, and was driven from Eretz Yisrael. Arriving at the gate of Troyes, he realized that he had four horsemen. Gleefully anticipating his revenge upon Rashi, Godfrey entered the city. As the fourth rider came under the gate, a massive stone fell from the archway, killing him and his horse. Filled with awe, Godfrey arrived at the Jewish quarter, only to be told that Rashi had passed away.

Separating fact from legend, Rashi was born in 1040 in Troyes, France, and studied under the great scholars of both his hometown and Worms, Germany. His major teacher was Rabbi Jacob bar Yakar, whom Rashi quotes on numerous occasions in his commentary on the Talmud.[11] Rashi's father, also a scholar of note, is also quoted by his illustrious son.[12] Upon returning to his hometown at age twenty-five, Rashi was already recognized as a major scholar. Refusing to support himself through the rabbinate, Rashi went into the wine business, while simultaneously opening a yeshivah that attracted the best minds of the Ashkenazic world. His three daughters, Miriam, Rachel, and Yocheved, married great Torah scholars, and their sons were among the great Ashkenazic Torah sages known as the *Baalei Tosafos*. Rashi died in 1105, at the age of 65. In Worms, Germany, the small synagogue in which Rashi studied and taught was carefully preserved for hundreds of years, until the Nazis destroyed it.

Rashi's commentary on *Chumash*, the Five Books of Moses, was immediately accepted as authoritative by all Jews, both Sephardic and Ashkenazic, during the author's lifetime, usually not the case for Torah works. It remains the premier commentary on the *Chumash* — so much so that it is simply unthinkable to study *Chumash* without Rashi. Indeed, from a young age every Jew is introduced to Rashi's unique blend of interpretations, midrashim, laws, insights, and grammatical rules. As such, both the Torah's personalities and commandments are viewed through Rashi's lens. At the same time that the schoolchild studies Rashi on his level, the greatest scholars grapple with the profundity of his commentary. Indeed, hundreds of books have been written delving into the meaning of Rashi's explanations. In fact, the first Hebrew book ever printed, in 1474 CE, was a *Chumash-Rashi*. In addition, Rashi also wrote a commentary on *Neviim* and *Kesuvim*, which, although not as extensive as his work on *Chumash*, is also regarded as vital.

Along the same lines, Rashi's commentary on the Talmud is indispensable: simply, without Rashi, the Talmud would remain a closed book to all but the most accomplished scholars. Even more so, by ensuring that every Jew would be exposed to this major repository of Torah learning, it is safe to assume that Rashi assured the spiritual survival of the Jewish people. Going line by line, Rashi's explanation of the Talmud guides the student deftly through the often-tortuous text. With uncanny ability, Rashi anticipates how the lack of seeming clarity concerns a student each step of the way; often, with a single word or phrase, he sheds much valuable light on an entire topic. Simultaneously, the most accomplished scholars laboriously pore over the same words, unearthing previously unseen, intricate Talmudic analyses. In the words of the Meiri: "One word of Rashi provides the answers to bundles of questions."[13] As such, none of the thousands of commentaries written throughout Jewish history has remotely approached his skill in using the same language to reach all levels of understanding.

Appearing throughout most of the Talmud, Rashi's commentary elucidates all the tractates except for *Nedarim*, *Nazir*, and parts of *Pesachim*, *Bava Basra*, and *Makkos*, which were either lost or interrupted by his death. As a Frenchman, Rashi frequently used Old French words to illustrate technical words or concepts. Other languages, such as German[14] and Arabic,[15] also appear in his commentary. Finally, Rashi's humility also shines forth in his writings; he is never ashamed to say that he doesn't understand the meaning or source of something. (Rabbi Akiva Eiger, for example, points out more than forty places in the Talmud where Rashi states that he does not know something.)[16]

Aside from his commentaries, Rashi also wrote responsa and composed *piyutim*. He also created the introductory piece to the *selichos* of *Erev Rosh HaShanah* (*selichah* 23). Near the end of his life, the ravages of the Crusades struck the Jews, and some of Rashi's writings reflect the travails of those times. Interestingly, many Ashkenazic Jews trace their lineage to Rashi, and through him to the Tanna Rabbi Jochanan HaSandlar and even King David.

RABBI ABRAHAM IBN EZRA (twelfth century, Sephardic): One of the great biblical commentators, Ibn Ezra's life was filled with tragedy, including the fact that most of his sons died, and one converted to Islam but later repented. All his business ventures having ended in abject failure, he once remarked, "If I sold candles, the sun would stop setting, and if I sold burial shrouds, people would stop dying." Ibn Ezra traveled the length and breadth of the Jewish world, from England in the west to Persia in the east, coming in contact with myriad Sephardic and Ashkenazic scholars.

In his commentary, Ibn Ezra tried to adhere to the simple meaning of the text without resorting to complex Midrashic explanation. In particular, he focused on the grammatical structure of the words and verses. He was also very caustic, especially regarding those who distort the meaning of the text, such as the Karaites, sparing no humor in refuting their viewpoint. For example, in Genesis 29:17, the verse states that Leah's eyes were tender or tearful (*rakos*). Ibn Ezra quotes a Karaite named Ben Ephraim, who explains the word as a contraction of *arukos*, meaning long-eyed. On this, Ibn Ezra comments, "Ben Ephraim explains the word *rakos* as missing the letter *alef*, but his name is missing an *alef*." Instead of Ben Ephraim, Ibn Ezra renders it Ben Parim, which in Hebrew means son of cows. Ibn Ezra also wrote *piyutim*, and works on philosophy, grammar, and astronomy.

RABBI JUDAH HALEVI (eleventh–twelfth centuries, Sephardic): One of the greatest Hebrew poets and philosophers of all time, Rabbi Judah was a disciple of the Rif and excelled in Torah and secular pursuits, specializing in medicine (in accordance with the times). His religious poetry was so renowned that the great Spanish scholar Rabbi Judah al-Charizi wrote: "Rabbi Judah HaLevi is the right hand of poetic song. He entered the gates of poetry, cleaned out its treasures, and locked the door when he left. All subsequent poets did not reach the dust of his feet."[17] Rabbi Judah composed the Sabbath song *Yom Shabason* and the well known *kinnah* for Tishah B'Av, "*Tzion Halo Tishali*" (*kinnah* 36). In this eloquently moving prayer, the author pours out his love and passion for the Holy Land, writing, "How can food and drink be pleasant for me, when I see that enemies have ravaged you... How can the sun's light be enjoyable in my eyes, while I see ravens consume your flesh."

In addition, Rabbi Judah authored the *Kuzari*, a classic work on Jewish philosophy. Based on the tale of a Khazar king who has representatives of the Christian, Muslim, and Jewish faiths debate their respective beliefs, the *Kuzari* demonstrates how, when the Jewish scholar presents his case rationally, the king adopts the Jewish faith. For example, when G-d teaches the Ten Commandments, He writes (Exodus 20:2): "I am the Lord your G-d who took you out of the land of Egypt." Upon being questioned by the king as to why G-d didn't describe Himself as the Creator of the Universe, the Jewish scholar replied that G-d referred to an event that the Jewish people personally experienced — therefore making G-d and His Torah more credible. Also a primary source for an issue of great halachic relevance, the *Kuzari* discusses the Torah's date line, which affects Sabbath observance. (According to Rabbi Judah, it is 90 degrees east of Jerusalem, or the eastern coast of China.)[18]

Throughout his life, Rabbi Judah dreamed of settling in the Land of Israel. He coined the famous phrase, "My heart is in the East, but I am in the farthest West." At an advanced age, he set out for Eretz Yisrael. Legend has it that upon reaching Jerusalem and beholding the Temple Mount, he rolled on the ground in ecstasy and composed *"Tzion Halo Tishali."* At that moment, an Arab horseman saw him and trampled him to death.

RABBI SHMUEL BEN MEIR — RASHBAM (eleventh–twelfth centuries, Ashkenazic): A grandson of Rashi and one of his premier disciples, Rashbam completed Rashi's commentary on two Talmudic tractates — the tenth chapter of *Pesachim* and the final 148 pages of *Bava Basra*. This commentary, which appears on the Talmudic page in place of Rashi, is considerably longer than that of Rashi. For example, on *Bava Basra* 29a, Rashi uses two words to comment on a phrase of Gemara, while Rashbam takes up four lines. Rashbam also wrote a commentary on *Chumash* which adheres closely to the literal text. There, he writes that although the sages of the Mishnah and Talmud derived many teachings embedded in the verses of the *Chumash*, all based on various rules of interpretation, nevertheless each passage must also be understood according to its plain meaning.[19]

Known for his great piety, as Rashbam walked the streets he focused his eyes downward so as not to see anything improper. Once, he was about to enter a wagon, not noticing that it was being pulled by a mule and a horse, an act forbidden by the Torah. Fortunately, his brother walked by and notified him just in time.[20] As a scholar, the Rashbam appears several times in the *Tosafos* commentary on the Talmud,[21] although not as frequently as the better-known Tosafists.

RABBI JACOB BEN MEIR — RABBEINU TAM (twelfth century, Ashkenazic): A younger brother of Rashbam, he became known as Rabbeinu Tam based on a verse (Genesis 25:27) that describes Jacob as *tam*, perfect. The main founder of the Tosafist school, whose method of study became the basis of all advanced Talmudic learning for the past 900 years, Rabbeinu Tam specialized in comparing and contrasting seemingly contradictory Talmudic texts and resolving them by painstakingly unearthing the halachic principles underpinning each. Frequently, Rabbeinu Tam disagrees with Rashi's interpretation of a Talmudic discussion, with the best known of these disputes regarding the placement of the *parshiyos* (Scriptural verses written on small parchment rolls) in the tefillin pair.[22] Current practice is to wear Rashi's tefillin, although many people don Rabbeinu Tam's tefillin as well.[23] Considered the greatest Talmudist of his generation, Rabbeinu Tam was judged even greater than Rambam in scholarship.[24]

As a leader, Rabbeinu Tam also enacted decrees affecting Jewish life. In response to the horrific blood libel in the city of Blois on 20 Sivan 1171, he decreed that day to be a public fast. Currently, although fasting is not required on 20 Sivan, pious individuals do fast and recite a special prayer service.[25] Rabbeinu Tam also ordained that once a *get* has been given to a woman, under penalty of *cherem* no one may question its validity.[26] Perhaps the most well-known of Rabbeinu Tam's halachic opinions is that nightfall does not commence until seventy-two minutes after sunset.[27]

He, too, experienced the horrific fury of the Crusades. In 1146, a mob entered Rabbeinu Tam's home, robbing his possessions and wounding him grievously. In mortal danger, Rabbeinu Tam's life was spared due to the entreaties of a nobleman, who promised the attackers that he would convert Rabbeinu Tam to Christianity. (The nobleman did not fulfill his promise.) When Rabbeinu Tam died, the sense of communal loss was so great that one of his students, a *kohen*, stated that had he been present at the funeral, he would have allowed himself to become *tamei* (ritually impure) through contact with the coffin, an act normally forbidden to a *kohen*.[28] (There are instances where such an action is permitted, however.)

RABBI MOSHE BEN MAIMON — RAMBAM (1135–1204, Sephardic): Of all the Rishonim, none are as famous in both the Jewish and general worlds as the Rambam. In contrast to other

Rishonim, the events of his life are very well known. Born in Cordova, Spain, while yet a youth, the Rambam's family, along with thousands of other Jews, fled Almohad-controlled Muslim Spain for the relative safety of the Christian part of the country. A few years later, the Maimon family moved again, to Morocco. Fleeing further persecution, they wound up in Eretz Yisrael and then moved to Egypt, where Rambam finally settled. Thereafter, much misfortune struck the Rambam's family. After his father's death, his younger brother David supported the Rambam's Torah study by dealing in precious stones. However, David died at sea, taking with him his entire fortune, leaving the Rambam with the burden of supporting both his own and his brother's family. Specializing in medicine, the Rambam became the ruler's personal physician. Although his medical duties took up his time from early morning until past midnight, the Rambam still managed to produce works of unsurpassed brilliance. Among his incredible output, his best-known writings are as follows:

Mishnah Torah. The Rambam's magnum opus, this monumental halachic compendium is unique among all writings of the Rishonim. Generally, halachic works were written regarding laws applicable after the destruction of the Beis HaMikdash. *Mishnah Torah*, however, covers the entire gamut of Torah law, including sacrifices, ritual purity, monarchy, and *yovel*, even though these precepts had not been performed for more than a thousand years. All this material is covered in a clear, flowing Hebrew, making the book a pleasure to study — even, or especially, for people of limited background.

Unlike other authors of compilations of Jewish law, Rambam gives no sources for his decisions. As such, his intention was for *Mishnah Torah*, unburdened as it is by lengthy explanations, to become the handbook of every Jew. Ironically, instead of becoming every Jew's handbook, *Mishnah Torah* has become the sine qua non of Talmudic scholarship. Hundreds of volumes have been written on it, a process that continues today. Based on a seeming omission or addition of a single word in *Mishnah Torah*'s explanation of a topic, advanced scholars expend great effort in extrapolating myriads of novel insights. In the yeshivah world, the mark of a distinguished scholar is his ability to clarify *ah shvere Rambam* (a difficult passage in *Mishnah Torah*.)

Peirush HaMishnayos. This commentary on the Mishnah, a massive work written while the Rambam was fleeing from place to place, was composed in Arabic and subsequently translated into Hebrew by the famous Ibn Tibbon family. An explanation of each *mishnah* in the six orders of *mishnayos*, the Rambam touches on many indirectly related topics, such as the reason for the sequence of each tractate in its respective order, a record of the transmission of the Oral Law to the leaders of each generation from Moses to Rav Ashi, and the thirteen basic beliefs of Judaism, the *Ani Maamin.*

Sefer HaMitzvos. Also written in Arabic, this work is an enumeration of the 613 mitzvos of the Torah. In the introduction, Rambam enumerates fourteen rules for determining what Divine commands are to be listed. For example, a precept that only applied for a limited time, such as the prohibition of approaching Mount Sinai at the Giving of the Torah (Exodus 19:12), is not counted. Particular laws of a mitzvah are not counted separately, such as fashioning the Holy Ark, the Table, and the Menorah, which are included in the commandment to build the Beis HaMikdash. In several instances, other Rishonim disagree with Rambam's list of mitzvos. For example, based on the first of the Ten Commandments, "I am the Lord thy G-d" (Exodus 20:2), Rambam states that belief in the existence of G-d is a positive commandment. Ramban, however, holds that belief in G-d precedes all mitzvos and is not to be counted as a mitzvah per se, for belief is the basis of all observance.[29]

Moreh Nevuchim. A treatise on Jewish philosophy written in Arabic, *Moreh Nevuchim* deals with philosophical concepts that are foreign to the Western mind, although sections do discuss such important topics as the nature of prophecy, clarification of verses that ascribe physical characteristics to G-d (such as "the hands of G-d" and "G-d was angry"), and the significance of the different Divine names found in the Bible. Along with Rambam's other Arabic writings, and a number of books written in that language by other scholars, *Moreh Nevuchim* was translated into Hebrew by the famous Ibn Tibbon family of translators over several generations in the twelfth and thirteenth centuries.

Iggeres Teiman. "A Letter to the Jews of Yemen" was written at a time when the Yemenite Jews were under the sway of fanatical Arabs who offered them the choice between conversion to Islam or death. Told by a local rabbi that they must submit to death, many Jews fell into a state of abject despair. In *Iggeres Teiman*, Rambam emphatically ruled that the Torah did not require martyrdom, because Islam, unlike Christianity, believes in one G-d. As such, the Jews of Yemen were instructed to adopt Islam outwardly, while remaining loyal Jews in the privacy of their homes. When the pressure abated, Rambam wrote, they should return to open Jewish observance. The Jews followed this ruling and remained faithful. (In the 1800s, the Jews of Mashad, Iran, were faced with the same situation and responded in a similar manner.) Thereby, the Rambam became regarded as the savior of Yemenite Jewry.

A number of the Rambam's writings became very controversial. Unhappy with the Rambam's practice of not adducing sources for his rulings in *Mishnah Torah*, many scholars felt that no one possessed the authority to issue such decisions. *Moreh Nevuchim* also came under intense fire, as many great rabbis felt that the Aristotelian philosophy contained within was contrary to Jewish belief. (Indeed, some 600 years later the great Vilna Gaon stated that the study of philosophy caused Rambam to err.)[30] A storm also broke out over Rambam's view that *techiyas hameisim*, the resurrection of the dead, will be an entirely spiritual existence,[31] an idea which many distinguished scholars felt was in flagrant contradiction of the accepted principle that resurrection involves a physical state. Although Rambam subsequently wrote a treatise demonstrating that he believed in a physical resurrection as well, the controversy did not abate. Nevertheless, later generations completely vindicated all of the Rambam's writings.

Aside from his major works, as a highly prolific author many of the Rambam's other, less-familiar writings exist, although regrettably much has also been lost. Aside from his greatness in Torah scholarship, Rambam was also known as a brilliant physician. As such, perhaps the best known of his medical writings is the diet and lifestyle prescribed in chapter four of *Hilchos Deos* in *Mishnah Torah*. For example, the Rambam writes, a person should avoid certain foods, not overeat, and get eight hours of sleep at night. Rambam then guarantees that if a person follows his instructions, then he "will not be sick his entire life and will die at a ripe old age, unless he was born with a weak constitution or dies suddenly of an external factor."[32]

Rambam himself died in 1204, greatly mourned by Jews and non-Jews alike. In 1985, in honor of the 850th anniversary of his birth, the United Nations Educational, Cultural, and Scientific Organization (UNESCO) held a giant Rambam conference attended by scholars and dignitaries worldwide, including Jews and Arabs. Inscribed on the Rambam's tombstone in Tiberias, Israel, is the fitting statement, "From Moshe to Moshe none has arisen like Moshe."

RABBI ABRAHAM IBN DAVID — RAAVAD III (twelfth century, Provence): One of three sages called Raavad, he was known as "the critic" for his sharp disagreements with the Rif and especially the Rambam. Clearly, the Raavad did not engage in personal attacks; rather, his sole motivation was to fight for the truth of Torah as he understood it. Therefore, on many occasions he praised the Rambam, agreeing with his decisions. In one instance, Raavad notes that Rambam achieved a great accomplishment in compiling such a masterful work.[33] However, when Raavad disagreed with Rambam, he spoke strongly. In one place, Raavad stated that the words of the Rambam are "*lo nahir velo tzahir velo bahir*" (don't make sense), while elsewhere he states that Rambam is simply incorrect.[34] Raavad composed numerous scholarly works, many of which were lost. His treatise on the halachos of family purity and *mikvah* form the basis of many of these laws today. At the time, Raavad was held in such great esteem that *kohanim* were permitted to attend his funeral.

RABBI ZERACHIAH HALEVI (twelfth century, Provence): Rabbi Zerachiah wrote critical glosses on the Rif, which are included in the Rif's standard editions. These glosses, called either *HaMaor HaGadol* or *HaMaor HaKatan*, depending on the tractate under discussion, are combined as the *Baal HaMaor*. In response, Raavad and Ramban defended the Rif, the Ramban titling his rebuttal *Milchamos HaShem*, the Wars of G-d. Interestingly, both these commentaries are also found on the printed Rif page. (Parenthetically, the *Baal HaMaor* and *Milchamos HaShem* are written in extremely difficult and terse language, challenging even the most accomplished Torah scholars.) Although Rabbi Zerachiah often disagreed with the Rif, he regarded him with the greatest respect, in one instance stating, "We may rely on the Rif and Rashi, who are two great pillars [of wisdom]."[35]

RABBI DAVID KIMCHI (twelfth–thirteenth centuries, Provence): Popularly known as the Radak, he is the author of a basic commentary on *Neviim* and some *Kesuvim*, printed in the standard *Mikraos Gedolos* text. A famous statement of Radak is his observation in Jeremiah 1:5 that a prophet is born with an innate inclination toward prophecy. Likewise, he says, if a person excels in a given area, it is due to a combination of inborn traits and subsequent training.

BAALEI TOSAFOS (twelfth–thirteenth centuries, Ashkenazic): *Tosafos* (additions) is the name given to notes of scholarly analysis on the logic of the Talmud and Rashi's explanation of it; the scholars involved in this form of learning are known as the Baalei Tosafos. These sages, largely centered in the Ashkenazic strongholds of Northern France and Germany, were also found in England, Austria, and Central Europe (corresponding to the present-day Czech Republic). A *Tosafos* is usually written in question and answer form, much in the manner of the Talmud itself, attempting to resolve contradictions between Talmudic tractates, problems in Talmudic logic, and difficulties with Rashi's understanding of a topic. On some occasions, *Tosafos* will clarify an unfamiliar subject, or if two Talmudic sages possess the same name will identify the particular scholar. Occasionally, *Tosafos* will rule on halachic issues.

Many collections of *Tosafos* exist, and it is unclear why the *Tosafos* found in current editions of the Talmud were printed while others were not, especially since not all tractates possess *Tosafos* from the same author. Major Tosafists included Rabbeinu Tam, Rabbi Yitzchak HaZaken (known as the Ri), Rabbi Yitzchak ben Asher (the Riva), Rabbi Judah ben Nassan (Rivan), Rabbi Yitzchak ben Meir (Rivam), and Rabbi Eliezer of Touques. A number of Tosafists were sons-in-law and grandsons of Rashi. For Talmudic analysis, studying *Tosafos* is essential; otherwise, one's understanding of the Talmudic topic is superficial — and suspect. Not uniform, *Tosafos'* comments on a subject can run from one word to two sides of a page. On one occasion, at the end of a discussion taking up a full side, *Tosafos* remarks, "Let's not dwell too long on this topic."[36]

RABBI MOSHE BEN NACHMAN — RAMBAN (1194–1270, Sephardic): Also known as Nachmanides, Ramban was one of the most prolific Rishonim. A few of his better-known writings include:

Commentary on the Torah. This lengthy, classic work plumbs the depths of the *Chumash*, focusing both on its open, philosophical, and hidden, Kabbalistic lessons. While Ramban's Commentary is a major source for subsequent works of Kabbalah, two of its most famous non-Kabbalistic statements are that the purpose of all existence is for mankind to recognize G-d as its creator, and that G-d does not perform miracles in all generations to satisfy every nonbeliever.[37] After Rashi's commentary on *Chumash*, Ramban's is most indispensable.

Additions to the Rif. Although Rabbi Alfasi wrote a halachic code for virtually all laws that apply today, he left out several topics. By compiling the laws of vows, firstborn humans and animals, and the separation of *challah*, and by copying the format of the Rif, Ramban completed the Rif's work. As noted, Ramban also wrote *Milchamos HaShem*, defending the Rif against the attacks of Rabbi Zerachiah HaLevi.

A critique of Rambam's listing of the mitzvos. In a number of instances, Ramban takes issue with Rambam's list of the 613 mitzvos and substitutes other commandments. For example, Ramban holds that it is a mitzvah for every Jew to live in Eretz Yisrael, something that Rambam omits in his mitzvah tabulation.[38]

Novellae on Talmudic tractates. Ramban's commentary exists on a number of Talmudic tractates, his work reflecting the analytical approach of the Ashkenazic Tosafists, whose method of study became popular in Spain. Previously, Sephardic scholars focused on producing purely halachic commentaries. In contrast to other, similar explanations of the Talmud, such as Rashba and Ritva, Ramban's language is terse and requires much effort to understand.

Shaar HaGemul (The Gate of Reward). Shaar HaGemul is a lengthy, brilliant exposition of such difficult topics as good and evil, suffering, the nature of Heavenly reward and punishment both in this world and in the afterlife, and the principles of G-d's judgment of the world. Study of this trailblazing work is absolutely essential for a Jew to strengthen his faith in G-d; fortunately, the well-known scholar Rabbi Charles Chavel translated this and many other writings of Ramban into English.

Iggeres HaRamban. An ethical letter Ramban sent to his son, *Iggeres HaRamban* opens with the sound advice that whatever the situation one should speak calmly to all people at all times. A popular classic, many people have the custom of reciting the *Iggeres* monthly, weekly (according to Ramban's own instruction to his son), even daily. Ramban told his son that every day he read the letter, his prayer requests would be answered by G-d.

In 1263, Ramban was forced to debate Christian priests publicly, whom he soundly defeated. Afraid of the inevitable retaliation of the Church, Ramban fled to Jerusalem. In a letter to his family in Spain, he wrote that the holy places are in a state of destruction, with Jerusalem in the worst condition of all. Seeing that the Jewish community there consisted of only two people, Ramban built a synagogue, the famous Ramban Synagogue in the Old City, and convinced a group of Jews to move to Jerusalem.[39] Since then, Jerusalem has had a constant Jewish presence. Ramban died in Eretz Yisrael in 1270, his burial place unknown.

RABBI JONAH (twelfth–thirteenth centuries, Sephardic): The author of *Shaarei Teshuvah*, one of the most important Mussar (ethics) texts of all time, Rabbi Jonah wrote his magnum opus as penance for attacking some works of Rambam. Divided into four sections, *Shaarei Teshuvah* discusses the twenty steps required for total repentance, the motivation necessary to repent, a detailed list of the positive and negative commandments in ascending order of severity, and the different levels of Heavenly atonement. A famous ruling in *Shaarei Teshuvah* is that one must forfeit his life rather than embarrass another person publicly, as shaming someone in public is akin to murder.[40] However, other halachic authorities do not hold this opinion.[41]

RABBI MEIR OF ROTHENBERG (thirteenth century, Ashkenazic): Regarded as the leading Ashkenazic halachic authority of his generation, when Rabbi Meir attempted to flee oppression in Germany, he was caught by the emperor's agents and imprisoned. When the emperor demanded a huge ransom from the Jewish community for his release, they were willing to pay, but Rabbi Meir refused to consider the proposal. Despite the loss to the community of his leadership and the weakening of his Torah study, Rabbi Meir feared that such ransoms would set a bad precedent: any time an unjust ruler needed money he could kidnap a leading Torah authority.[42] Although his students were permitted to visit him and study, heroically Rabbi Meir remained in prison for the last seven years of his life. Afterward, the vengeful emperor kept Rabbi Meir's remains in prison another fourteen years, perhaps the only instance in history of someone remaining incarcerated after his death. Finally, a wealthy Jew named Alexander Vimpen redeemed the body for a great sum, asking only that he be eventually buried near the great rav, a request that was honored. As a result of Rabbi Meir's self-sacrifice, the government no longer captured great sages for ransom. In addition, Rabbi Meir played a major role in the development of current halachah. His major disciple, the Rosh, is one of the three authorities on which the *Shulchan Aruch* is based. Rabbi Meir's numerous *Shaalos Uteshuvos* are also considered authoritative.

RABBI ASHER BEN YECHIEL — ROSH (thirteenth–fourteenth centuries, Ashkenazic): Along with the Rif and Rambam, Rabbi Asher, known as the Rosh, is one of the three pillars of halachah. Born in Germany, he assumed leadership of Ashkenazic Jewry at a time of terrible persecution. Fearing a fate similar to Rabbi Meir of Rothenberg, Rosh fled to Spain, settling in Toledo and becoming the leader of Spanish Jewry. Of all the Rishonim, Rosh stands unique in becoming the recognized leader of both strains of the Jewish people. While in Toledo, Rosh established a yeshivah that introduced the Ashkenazic method of the Tosafists to the Sephardim.

Rabbi Asher's most famous work, the halachic digest compiled on many Talmudic tractates, is printed at the end of each tractate. A masterful analysis of both Sephardic and Ashkenazic authorities on each topic, Rosh appended the conclusion he felt was correct. Due to its impartial recording of all opinions, the commentary won wide acceptance, and is regarded as indispensable to the understanding of how halachah evolves from the Talmud.

Another of Rosh's masterpieces, *Orchos Chaim L'Rosh*, is a guidebook to ethical living. Containing both practical and moral advice — such as don't act in a rush,[43] ask forgiveness for reciting the benediction of *Selach Lanu* (a prayer requesting forgiveness) without concentration,[44] and don't attempt to reason with a crazy person, because your words will be ridiculed[45] — in many yeshivos a set portion of *Orchos Chaim L'Rosh* is recited daily during the month of Elul as preparation for Rosh HaShanah and Yom Kippur.

RABBI MENACHEM MEIRI (thirteenth–fourteenth centuries, Provence) The author of the monumental *Beis HaBechirah* on many Talmudic tractates, the Meiri composed a commentary so unique in that it systematically explains each topic in a logical progression, from simpler concepts to more difficult ones. One of the more easily understood commentaries of the Rishonim, *Beis HaBechirah* was not discovered until relatively recent times. As a result, its halachic conclusions do not carry the weight of other Rishonim who have undergone an acceptance process over time.[46] (Many other manuscripts of Rishonim are being found, particularly in the archives of the Vatican, and the same rule applies to them.)

RABBI SHLOMO BEN ADERES — RASHBA (thirteenth–fourteenth centuries, Sephardic): A disciple of Rabbi Jonah and Ramban, Rashba became the rabbi of Barcelona. Regarded as the greatest halachic authority in Spain, and one of the greatest of his generation, Rashba received countless questions from all over the Jewish world — and many of his responses have been preserved. All Jews accepted Rashba's decisions, and they play a prominent role in the development of contemporary halachah. In order to counteract the rampant secularism then present in Spain, one of his most famous rulings is a ban on the study of philosophy and science until the age of twenty-five. Only Rambam's writings, and the study of medicine for professional purposes, were exempted from the ban. Rashba also wrote a commentary on many Talmudic tractates that is regarded as essential to serious study.

RABBI YOM TOV IBN ASHVILI — RITVA (fourteenth century, Sephardic): A disciple of Rashba, Ritva wrote a Talmudic commentary that is required for any aspiring scholar. In his commentary on the Haggadah, he described the question of the wicked son — "What is the purpose of this work for you?" — as meaning, "Why must we recite this lengthy Haggadah service? Let's get to the meal already!" There is doubt regarding some of his writings — certain commentaries attributed to Ritva are certainly those of other scholars, while some novellae of other scholars were actually written by Ritva.[47]

RABBI NISSIM — RAN (thirteenth–fourteenth centuries, Sephardic): The author of a commentary on the Rif that is printed alongside the Rif in many tractates, the Ran's explanation of tractate *Nedarim* is printed on the Talmudic page in place of *Tosafos*. The primary source for understanding *Nedarim*, which lacks the standard commentaries of Rashi and Tosafos, one of Ran's famous statements is that in the First Temple era, the Jewish people studied the Torah solely for intellectual pleasure and did not treat it with the respect due the word of G-d.[48] Rabbi Nissim also wrote *Derashos HaRan*, a key work on the fundamentals of Jewish belief.

RABBI JACOB BEN ASHER (thirteenth–fourteenth centuries, Ashkenazic): A son of Rosh, he is known as Baal HaTurim after the name of his most famous commentary. Rabbi Jacob collected the great mass of halachic opinions, both Sephardic and Ashkenazic, and rearranged it according to topic. Titling the massive work *Arbaah Turim*, or Four Rows, after the four rows of precious jewels that adorned one of the *kohen gadol*'s priestly garments (Exodus 28:17), it was popularly known as the *Tur*. Divided into four sections, *Orach Chaim* is on the laws of prayer, the Sabbath, and the holidays; *Yoreh Deah* contains the laws of kashrus, family purity, mourning, and miscellaneous halachos; *Even HaEzer* discusses marriage, divorce, and other related issues; and *Choshen Mishpat* deals with monetary laws and judicial procedure. Containing more than 1,600 chapters, along with commentaries, the *Tur* runs to ten folio-sized volumes. Discussing all opinions on a topic in a systematic progression, culminating with Rabbi Jacob's own opinion, due to its diversity and layout the *Tur* won quick acceptance and became the basis for the later *Shulchan Aruch*, closely patterned on the *Tur*. Rabbi Jacob also wrote a commentary on *Chumash* that has remained very popular as well.

Rabbi Israel Isserlein (fourteenth–fifteenth centuries, Ashkenazic): Living in the tenth and last generation of the Rishonim, Rabbi Israel Isserlein's treatise, *Terumas HaDeshen*, is considered a vital halachic work.

Overall, it is remarkable, when studying the origins of contemporary halachah, to note how many great Rishonim made vital contributions to its development. By the year 1500, Jews instinctively realized that an era had passed, and that all subsequent scholars would be vastly inferior to the great Rishonim.

Chapter 13

PERSECUTIONS

Although hatred of the Jewish people had been a part of Christianity from its inception, the full virulence was not felt until the end of the eleventh century. During the high Middle Ages, Christian anti-Jewish passion reached its zenith. So strong was the anti-Semitism that many of the attitudes Christians developed regarding Jews clearly led hundreds of years later to the Holocaust — and are still widely felt today.

EARLY CHRISTIAN ANTI-SEMITISM: With the triumph of the Church during the reign of Constantine, for the first time Jews found themselves in a wholly Christian world. The Church, believing that Judaism was a rival to Christianity, saw many enlightened pagans and Christians attracted to the Jewish faith. Indeed, from the early contact between Jews and Romans hundreds of years before, there had been a stream of converts to Judaism throughout the empire, at times reaching considerable proportions. Unlike the pagan Roman empire, which was generally tolerant in matters of religion, the new Christian Roman Empire claimed to represent the only true faith — meaning that Judaism, and Jews, were an anathema.

In the fourth century, Constantine decreed that Jews could not prevent their coreligionists from converting to Christianity, and could not accept converts. Another law affected Jewish slave owners, stipulating that if a Jew circumcised his slave in accordance with Torah law, the slave gained his freedom. Later, the death penalty was prescribed for circumcision. In later centuries, Christian Roman law forbade Jews from holding public office or officers' rank in the military.

Theologically, the early Church Fathers laid the groundwork for much of subsequent Christian anti-Semitism. St. John of Chrysostom, known as "The Golden Mouth" for his eloquence as a preacher, called the Jews "godless, idolaters, child-murderers, [guilty of] stoning the prophets, and committing ten thousand crimes." Gregory of Nyssa added that Jews are "Murderers of the lord, assassins of the prophets, rebels and detesters of G-d, companions of the devil, [a] race of vipers, darkeners of the mind, Sanhedrin of demons, accursed, detested, enemies of all that is beautiful."

THE CRUSADES: In general, the Church found Muslim control of Christian holy places in Eretz Yisrael intolerable, especially when reports came from Jerusalem of harassment of Christians visiting the holy sites. As such, in 1095 Pope Urban II called for an army of Christians to conquer Eretz Yisrael from its Muslim rulers. Indeed, that Christians viewed Islam as a threat was hardly new. In the eighth century, for example, Muslims captured Spain and made inroads into France, before being defeated by Charles Martel's Frankish army. Slowly, the Christians fought back, beginning the reconquest of Spain. When the legendary Spaniard El Cid retook the important Spanish city of Valencia from the Muslims, the Christian world was greatly encouraged, feeling that the time was ripe to strike at the Muslim world. In addition, the Church saw as its mission spreading Christian rule, which they termed the "Kingdom of G-d," over the heathen infidels.

On a more secular level, the possibility of attaining great wealth through conquest was a strong attraction. Northwestern Europe had been devastated by bad harvests in the autumn of 1095, and the crusading impulse rescued many serfs and landowners from desperate economic straits. The population had markedly increased in the previous century, and a spirit of restlessness took hold among the masses. Many people were tantalized by the prospect of adventure, riches, and being part of something great and noble.

Political considerations also played a major role in the Pope calling for a Crusade. There were disputes between the Pope and secular rulers regarding the limits of the Church's authority. Princes and tribes also often fought among themselves. Therefore, a campaign — a crusade — against a common enemy would unite the warring peoples of Europe under the Pope's rule, thereby unifying the Eastern and Western Churches.

Although the Pope viewed the Crusades as a campaign led by a professional, well-trained army, the excursion rapidly evolved into a mass movement, with an estimated 100,000 people dropping everything to join. As a proportion of the European population, a comparable response today would be well over a million people "taking the cross," as it was known. In addition, the Church provided a further incentive by promising that whoever took part in the endeavor would earn a special place in heaven. From that moment, participants were known as Crusaders, after the French word for the crosses affixed to their garments.

The First Crusade started out from France in 1095. In order to remain in the good graces of the Crusaders, French Jews supplied funds and food for the journey. However, when some of the Crusaders reached Germany, their mood changed drastically. Among many Crusaders the feeling grew rapidly that before they attacked the heathens in far-off Palestine, there were infidels much closer to home with whom they should contend.

In May, 1096, in a period of four weeks frenzied bands of Crusaders struck the Jewish communities of Speyer, Worms, Mainz, and Cologne. The Jews were offered the option of conversion to Christianity or death; the vast majority chose the path of *kiddush HaShem*, sanctification of G-d's name. Rather than submit to forced conversion, in many cases Jews killed their wives and children, and then themselves. In the words of one of the *Kinnos* recited on Tishah B'Av: "Who can see it and not cry/As the child is slaughtered, the father recites the *Shema*/ Has such been seen or heard before?"[1] Estimates of the toll taken on the Jewish communities range from 3,000 to 10,000 deaths.

These heroic martyrs have been immortalized in Jewish history as saintly people who reached the highest spiritual levels. In the *Selichos* service for the eve of Rosh HaShanah, Jews implore G-d to remember those who sacrificed their lives: "The bloods of fathers and sons touched, the bloods of merciful women and their children touched, the bloods of brothers and sisters mixed, the bloods of grooms and brides, wise men and wise women, pious men and pious women, elderly men and women, young men and women, all mingled. O land, do not conceal their blood!"[2]

Undaunted, unstoppable, the Crusaders conquered Eretz Yisrael, reaching Jerusalem in 1099. Once there, they gathered all the Jews of Jerusalem into the central synagogue and set it afire. Other Jews, who had climbed to the roof of Al-Aksa mosque on the Temple Mount, were caught and beheaded. The Crusader leader, Godfrey of Bouillon, wrote to the Pope, "If you want to know what has been done with the enemy found in Jerusalem...our people had their vile blood up to the knees of their horses." After this victory, the Crusaders retained control of Jerusalem for close to 100 years.

Although compared to later tragedies the loss of Jewish life was relatively small, with the main devastation occurring in but four Rhineland towns, the First Crusade has generally been regarded by Jews as a disaster of epic proportions. The period of counting the *omer*, between Pesach and Shavuos, when the massacres occurred, became fixed in Jewish law as a time for mourning. A prayer commemorating the martyrs, *Av HaRachamim*, was added to the Sabbath morning services and is recited weekly, except on joyous occasions. Several *Kinnos* were composed remembering these events and became part of the Tishah B'Av service. There are several reasons why the First Crusade has been given such prominence, while other, seemingly far greater tragedies have not:

The four towns destroyed were major Torah centers of Ashkenazic Jewry. Although Jews resettled and rebuilt these communities, and Ashkenazic Torah centers flourished, the greatness of these cities' martyred scholars was lost forever — a theme that appears prominently in the *Kinnos*.

The Crusades set a dangerous precedent — the rise of organized, popular, anti-Jewish uprisings.[3] Although both the Pope and the local authorities were generally opposed to the Crusaders' excesses in Germany, these leaders' hostility to Jews caused them to remain apathetic to Jewish suffering, thus they generally did not intervene.[4] After the First Crusade, instances of mob persecution occurred regularly. Therefore, the Crusades can be seen as the source for much of subsequent Christian persecution. In keeping with the traditional Jewish viewpoint, that the beginning of a tragedy is noted,[5] the events of the Crusades are commemorated.

As the events of the Crusades and the victory in Jerusalem renewed religious fervor everywhere, among the masses, Christian consciousness became greatly heightened. In this new religious climate, traditional anti-Jewish teachings became magnified — and were augmented by new beliefs regarding Jews.

In contrast to previous anti-Jewish outbreaks, in which the primary aim was plunder, the Crusades introduced a new element to Christian anti-Jewish assaults: the ideology of total annihilation.[6]

In the words of the historian Salo Baron:

The trail of blood and smoldering ruins left behind in the Jewish communities from France to Palestine...for the first time brought home to the Jewish people, its foes and friends, the utter instability of the Jewish position in the western world...from the First Crusade on, anti-Jewish persecutions exercised a dangerously contagious appeal, which in periods of great emotional stress degenerated into mass psychosis transcending national boundaries.[7]

The Second Crusade began in 1146, and struck Jews in France and Germany, including some of the towns destroyed in the First Crusade. A monk named Rudolph told the Crusaders that it was their duty first to kill the Jews at home before proceeding to Palestine. St. Bernard, the Crusade's official preacher (assigned that role by the Pope) tried to stop the killings by citing the Church's traditional view that the Jews must be preserved until the return of Yeshu, when they will supposedly serve as witnesses to their own crimes. Although many Jews were killed, compared to the First Crusade, the loss of life in the Second Crusade was far less extensive.

The Third Crusade, launched in 1189–90, greatly affected the Jews of England. Jews had first arrived in England in 1066 with William the Conqueror from northern France. The new community thus had had a comparatively artificial origin, and possessed a remarkable homogeneity, being composed almost entirely of financiers and their dependents. A type of late medieval Jewry in composition and occupation, the English community was also typical because of its close subjection to royal control.

While the community originated in the main in northern France, of which it was a cultural, linguistic, and economic offshoot, a minority came from Germany, Italy, and Spain — with one or two individuals coming from Russia and the Muslim countries. By the middle of the twelfth century, Jewish communities were found in most of the greater English cities, Lincoln, Winchester, York, Oxford, Norwich, and Bristol. Nevertheless, the London community was always the most important.

In the course of the twelfth century, however, anti-Jewish feeling began to infect the country. In 1130, London's Jews were fined the then-enormous sum of 22,000 pounds because one of them had supposedly killed a sick man. The world's first recorded blood libel took place at Norwich in 1144, and was imitated at Gloucester in 1168. (The horrendous anti-Jewish tactic was then exported outside England.) In 1188, a tax of one-fourth the value of its movable property was levied upon all London Jewry. According to the rough contemporary estimate, the amount raised was 60,000 pounds, compared to 70,000 pounds raised from the general population.

While the English Jewish community was not large, numbering perhaps several thousand at most, its financial importance was out of proportion to its numbers. As they did elsewhere, British Jews specialized in money lending, dispensing vast sums to ordinary people, noblemen, even the Crown. Aaron of Lincoln (c. 1125–1186) was the greatest English capitalist of his day, whose financial aid made possible the completion of several English monasteries, abbeys, and secular buildings. On Aaron's death, the Exchequer set up a special department to deal with his property and credits.[8]

In 1189, a crowd attacked a delegation of Jews attending the coronation of Richard the Lionheart at Westminster Abbey in London. From there, pogroms broke out in London and spread through many towns. In the city of York, for example, 150 Jews barricaded themselves in a castle known as Clifford's Tower and valiantly resisted the mob. On the Sabbath before Pesach, the Jews, realizing their situation was hopeless, heeded the advice of their spiritual leader, the Tosafist Rabbi Yom Tov of Joigny, and committed mass suicide. When the frenzied crowd scaled the fortress later that day, they discovered seven Jews who had hid — and massacred them. (In 1981, during excavations for a parking lot, an ancient Jewish cemetery was discovered in York, and the bodies were reburied elsewhere.) The jubilant crowd then burned the records of the considerable debts owned to the Jews. Although there is no reliable source for the custom, Jews traditionally have not lived in York, or even spent a night there, since the massacre. Clifford's Tower still stands, and a plaque commemorates the horrific event that took place there.[9]

ANTI-JEWISH DISCRIMINATION: Church and governmental authorities imposed many restrictions on the Jews. Princes declared the Jews to be slaves of the crown, a punishment that carried a blessing, as the Jews then received royal protection. However, while the Jews' own personal liberty was preserved, they faced exorbitant taxation. Further, when a Jew died, his estate was seized by the king. In 1215, at the Fourth Lateran Council, Pope Innocent III enacted a number of anti-Jewish decrees, the most famous of which was that Jews must wear distinctive clothing. The purpose of this decree was to prevent friendships, and possibly intermarriage, from occurring between Christians and Jews. The ruling, borrowed from a seventh-century Islamic decree, did not specify what form the distinctive Jewish dress should take. Local authorities required them to wear a so-called badge of shame, a yellow circle symbolizing the Jews' alleged love of gold. The Nazis later changed this yellow circle to a yellow star. In England, Jews were required to wear the insignia of the Two *Luchos*, or Tablets of the Law. The Vatican Council also decreed that Jews could not hold any public office that would place them in a position of superiority over Christians, an edict also copied by the Nazis.[10]

JEWISH MONEY LENDING: Numerous factors caused the association of Jews with this highly unpopular occupation. The consolidation of a continent-wide European identity, a mark of Charlemagne's reign in the ninth century, brought the close of what remained of Jewish citizenship rights dating to Roman antiquity. Immediately, Jewish communities became dependent on the benevolence of princes, bishops, and popes, who all thought of themselves as owning Jews. The rights of the evolving feudal system, as limited as they were for peasants, were not extended to Jews.

Over time, with the coming of money-based economies, Jewish communities became necessary as financial centers. As much precious metal had been withdrawn from circulation and converted into ecclesiastical and state regalia, European money sources were drying up. After the First Crusade, the Italian city-states had developed a flourishing international trade with the Muslim countries, further depleting the money supply. The Jews, however, retained supplies of capital from previous successes in international trade. However, there was not much business they could do with it other than lend it to those who needed it. In addition, since Jews were more mobile than Christians, they were a ready source of currency exchange.

As Christian commercial activity expanded in the Middle Ages, Jews were forced out of many occupations they previously engaged in, including crafts, trade, and international commerce.

The rise of Christian-only crafts guilds both created a Christian monopoly and eliminated Jewish competition. Further, as Jews could not own or farm land, they were increasingly forced into the one occupation that the Church forbade its adherents — lending money at interest rates high enough both to pay the exorbitant taxes imposed on them[11] and to cover their losses when a debtor defaulted. As such, the Jews obtained a reputation as bloodsuckers, an image that survives to this day. Such circumstances are responsible for the unfortunate and undeserved reputation for exceptional financial expertise and greed that has clung to Jews into modern times.[12]

POPULAR ANTI-JEWISH BELIEFS: In the Middle Ages, many delusional beliefs about Jews gripped the European masses, some of which were later modernized by the Nazis. There were at least ten such superstitions,[13] traces of which can still be found today.

1) THE BLOOD LIBEL AND RITUAL MURDER: In 1144, in Norwich, England, a twelve-year-old child named William disappeared in Thorpe's Wood, a forest near the town, and was found dead. A Jewish convert to Christianity, a monk named Theobald, testified that the Jews tortured the child, stabbed him, and nailed him to a cross, reenacting Yeshu's death. Since this event took place around Pesach, and the Christian days of Good Friday and Easter, rumors spread that the Jews needed to sacrifice a Christian child on Pesach. William quickly became St. William, the first of many Christian child martyrs, and his tomb became a popular site for religious pilgrimages. As Christianity became more fixated on the power of Yeshu's blood, considering it even as the *korban Pesach*, Jews were accused of slaughtering Christian children in order to obtain their blood for matzo and red wine of the seder. Pesach then became a dread time for Jews in Europe, for fanatic priests would whip up the masses into frenzied mobs.

Unlike the accusation of usury, which had a semblance of truth, the blood libel was completely false. Jewish law, as is well known, prohibits the consumption of even the smallest amount of blood, and not even one blood libel was proven to be true. Frequently, Christians killed one of their own children and tried to plant the body in a Jewish house. Although the popes repeatedly stated that this accusation was false, it remained entrenched in the mind of the general Christian public for centuries.

The ritual murder charge even appears in classic English literature. The great medieval English writer, Geoffrey Chaucer, relates such a story in his Canterbury Tales. The Prioress' Tale tells of a little Christian child who happily sang Christian hymns as he walked. Chaucer describes what happened when the child walked through the Jewish quarter of town:

> The serpent, our first foe, who has his nest
> Of hornets in Jews' hearts, puffed up and said,
> "O Hebrew people, is it for the best
> That a mere boy, just as he likes, should tread
> Your street, and bring contempt upon your head,
> And sing to such a purpose, for a cause
> That is against the reverence of your laws?"

> From this time on the cursed Jews conspired
> This innocent boy out of the world to chase.
> A murderer for their purposes they hired
> Who in an alley had a secret place,
> And as he went by at his childish pace,
> This Jew seized on him, and held him fast, and slit
> His neck, and threw his body in a pit.

> Into a privy they threw the boy, I say,
> A place in which these Jews purged their entrails.
> O cursed people, unchanged since Herod's day,
> What think you that your foul design avails?
> Murder will out, for certain; it never fails,
> The more so when the honor of G-d's name
> May spread! The blood cries on your deed of shame!

The distraught mother, after much searching, found the

child in the pit. Miraculously, the child, even with his throat slit, began to sing hymns. The amazed Christians called for the magistrate:

> The magistrate at once put every Jew
> To death with torment and with shamefulness.
> He spared not one that of this murder knew.

> He would not palter with such wickedness.
> "He that deserves ill, he shall have no less,"
> And so he ordered that wild horses draw
> Their flesh, and then he hanged them by the law.

The child instructed the monks how to cause him to stop singing. After the child died again, he was buried as a holy martyr in a special tomb. Referring to another such child, Chaucer concluded:

> Young Hugh of Lincoln, you who were also
> Slain by accursed Jews, notoriously,
> For it was a little while ago
> Pray for us; in our fitful errancy...

From Norwich, the blood libel rapidly spread all over Europe. In 1171, after the Jews of Blois, France, were executed on account of such an accusation, Rabbeinu Tam declared the twentieth of Sivan as a fast day. In all, more than 150 accusations of ritual murder are recorded, many leading either to massacre or expulsion of the Jews. From the 1200s to the 1400s, most of these cases occurred in Germany. Later, the blood libel moved to Poland and Russia. In 1840, a famous blood libel took place in Damascus, Syria, and in 1913, the notorious Beilis blood libel trial was conducted in Russia. The Nazis made it a cornerstone of their anti-Jewish propaganda. In 1946, the Kielce blood libel broke out in Poland, killing numerous Jews, including Chaim Hirschman, one of two survivors of the Belzec death camp, which itself took 600,000 victims. Sadly, the blood libel is still believed in many parts of the world, even in the United States.[14]

Tourists still visit the Child-Devouring Fountain in Berne, Switzerland (Kinderfresserbrunnen), dedicated to a young boy who vanished from the city in 1294, prompting a pogrom that killed all Berne's Jews.[15] In the words of the Catholic historian Edward Flannery, "The ritual murder calumny stands in the judgment of history as the most monstrous instrument of anti-Jewish persecution in the Middle Ages."[16]

2) DESECRATION OF THE HOST: In 1215, the Church announced the dogma of transubstantiation, meaning that the consecrated wafers (host) and sacramental wine consumed by Christians represented the body and blood of Yeshu. Soon Jews were accused of stealing wafers from churches and torturing them by sticking pins in them, thus crucifying Yeshu again. According to some reports, blood gushed from such wafers as they moaned in agony. Other accounts had the hosts flutter in the air, producing butterflies, angels, and doves.[17] The entire matter would be laughable, except that more than 100 such accusations were made, resulting in the massacre of countless Jews. In 1298, a notorious Jew-hater named Rindfleisch spread the calumny throughout Germany and Austria. Within a short period of time, 150 Jewish communities were destroyed, causing the deaths of more than 100,000 Jews.

3) JEWS AS DEVILS: The association of the Jews with the devil can be detected in the Christian Bible, which describes the devil as the father of the Jews. In the Middle Ages, when superstition was rampant, the devil was a terrifying reality to the masses of Christians. Jews were portrayed in woodcuts as pigs (*Judensau*), depicted as swarthy and hook-nosed, and presumed to have a tail and horns. Jews were seen as sorcerers and magicians, expert in the black arts of the occult. The Nazi newspaper *Der Sturmer* reproduced a number of such woodcuts, reinforcing this belief in modern times. Many eyewitnesses report that Germans regularly asked: "Are you Jews? You are human beings who work! Where are your horns?"

4) THE JEWISH SMELL: Since the Jews were associated so closely with the devil, they were believed to share his characteristics, notably his smell of sulfur. If Jews did not smell of it, Christians claimed they used Christians' blood to rid themselves of it. Indeed, the belief about a unique Jewish odor was so powerful that it not only persisted throughout the ages, but also became the object of study by Nazi scientists.[18]

5) THE WANDERING JEW: The Christian Bible relates that Yeshu cursed a Jew, who had mocked him, to endless wandering. The mythical Wandering Jew became known by the name of Ahasverus (sic), and reports of his sighting spread throughout Europe for hundreds of years. In 1602 a German Lutheran minister published *Brief Description and Tale of a Jew Named Ahasverus*, and the book became so popular that it went through fifty editions in just a few years.[19] This myth, too, has persisted throughout the ages. The Wandering Jew was reported in Upper New York State in 1898. In 1940, a man believing himself to be the Wandering Jew visited the New York Public Library and had his borrower's card printed as T. W. Jew.[20]

6) POLLUTED JEWISH BLOOD: Christians in the Middle Ages believed that the Jews were sickly and weak people, possessing blood diseases that could only be cured by an infusion of Christian blood. Thus, the Jews were always looking for opportunities to intermarry with pure Christians and pollute their lineage. This canard became the most powerful of all Nazi beliefs about the Jews, and it was employed as a justification for annihilating the entire Jewish people.

7) WELL POISONING: In the mid-1300s, the Black Death swept throughout Europe, decimating perhaps 50 percent of the population. Jews, too, were greatly affected, although not to the same degree as the Christians, due to traditional Jewish emphasis on personal cleanliness and burial of their dead. Soon a rumor spread that Jews brought about the plague by poisoning wells. Although Pope Clement issued a papal bull contradicting the allegation, and numerous rulers stated likewise, the superstitious Christian masses believed that the plague was the work of the devil through his children, the Jews.

The populace also believed that the Black Death was Divine punishment for their sins. Christian penitents, known as flagellants, went from town to town, whipping themselves with iron rods until the flagellants bled, all to expiate their sins and those of the people. After performing in city squares to the awed attention of the populace, they then led the people against the real villains, the Jewish well poisoners. In countless communities, especially in Germany, nearly all the Jews lost their lives.

8) JEWISH WORLD CONSPIRACY: This belief, which is still quite prevalent today, originated in the Middle Ages. It was claimed that a council of rabbis from Spain met secretly every year to cast lots regarding which city should supply the Christian victim for the annual sacrifice required by the Jewish religion. Later, this myth changed the Jewish goal from human sacrifice to world financial domination, as found in the nineteenth-century publication of the notorious *Protocols of the Elders of Zion*. Currently, this lie is being spread by Arab regimes into countries that have had little or no previous encounters with Jews.

9) JEWISH STUBBORNNESS: Naturally, the Jews were seen as a stubborn people for absolutely refusing to convert and accept Yeshu as the Messiah. Such a refusal was particularly infuriating to the Christians, who believed that the Second Coming of Yeshu was contingent upon the Jews accepting Christianity. Thus, as the Jews were seen as blocking the Final Redemption, special effort has been expended through the ages to enable them to see the so-called light of Christianity, either by the Jews' own volition or by force.

10) JEWISH LAZINESS: This accusation charged that Jews did not engage in productive occupations, preferring instead to live off honest Christian labor by engaging in money lending and shady transactions. (For their part, Christians were invariably seen as productive farmers and craftsmen.) What was conveniently forgotten was that Jews were not permitted any form of manual labor. Of course, the myth that Jews become rich at the expense of hard-working, poor Christians has persisted to today, and is strongly held by many people.

EXPULSIONS: During the Middle Ages, the Jews were expelled at one time or another from virtually every country in Europe. Many times, they were driven out of a city and had to seek sanctuary in another town. Usually, these expulsions, even from entire countries, were not permanent, and the Jews were able to return after several years — sometimes even sooner than that. However, when the Jews were expelled from England in 1290, they were not permitted to return until the late 1600s. (It is interesting to note that William Shakespeare, who caricatured Jews as rapacious in *The Merchant of Venice*, may have never seen a Jew.) Of course, the most famous of all expulsions is known as The Expulsion — the forced departure of the Spanish Jews in 1492.

BURNING THE TALMUD: Christians had long believed that the Talmud was the main obstacle to Jews believing in Christianity. A Jewish apostate, Nicholas Donin, told the Pope that the Talmud contained insults to the Christian religion. In France, on the order of the Pope, many volumes of the Talmud were seized. In 1240, King Louis IX (later St. Louis) ordered the Talmud put on trial. Jewish representatives were permitted only to defend themselves, not to advance positive proofs for their position. Not surprisingly, the Talmud was declared guilty, and in 1242 twenty-four wagonloads of Talmudic volumes were publicly burned in Paris. As each book was painstakingly handwritten and could not be easily replaced, it was a disaster of massive proportions for French Jewry. Indeed, Torah scholarship rapidly declined, and France never again regained its prominent position as a Torah center.

In line with the Jewish principle that spiritual destruction is the greatest tragedy, Rabbi Meir of Rothenberg composed an elegy for the burned Talmud that became part of the Tishah B'Av *Kinnos*. Sadly, Jewish infighting regarding Rambam's works also played a major role in this tragic event. Some overzealous Jews denounced the Rambam's writings to the Church, and once the Church determined that his books should be burned, it was only a small step until all Jewish books were consigned to the flames. Pious individuals observe the day on which the Talmud was burned, Friday of *Parashas Chukas*, as a fast day. [21]

THE DISPUTATION OF RAMBAN: Religious disputations between Jews and followers of other religions first appear in biblical times. Abraham debated belief in one G-d with King Nimrod and his followers. Elijah's confrontation with the prophets of Baal had elements of a religious debate. Numerous sages of the Mishnah and Talmud were forced to participate in religious discussions with pagans or Jewish Christians.[22] Josephus recorded a debate with the anti-Jewish Greek Apion, calling it *Contra Apion*. With the rise of Christianity, such debates became more frequent, especially from the twelfth century. Rishonim such as Radak, Meiri, Rabbeinu Tam, and Rashba were compelled to take part in such discussions. The most famous such debate was the Ramban's disputation. It is unique in that it was the fairest and best recorded of all such incidents.

In 1263, in the Spanish city of Barcelona, Ramban was ordered by King James I of Spain to debate publicly the Jewish religion with Church officials. The king agreed to Ramban's request that he be allowed to speak his mind freely, as long as he did not denigrate Christianity. There were four sessions held over a week, and they were well attended by both Jews and Christians, including the king. Ramban kept a record of the debate, which has survived.[23] There were four main issues:

First, the Christians tried to prove from Tanach that Yeshu is the Messiah, and that he had already come, and then asked why the Jews did not believe so. Ramban refuted their seeming proofs from the Scriptures and argued cogently that if the Jews of Yeshu's time, who heard and saw him personally, did not believe in Yeshu and had remained faithful Jews, how could any different course of action be expected from Jews 1,200 years later?

Second, in response to Christian belief that Yeshu is the Messiah, Ramban referred to numerous biblical passages that state that the Messiah will bring peace to the world and unite humanity to follow the true faith. However, Ramban argued, since the time of Yeshu Christianity had not ruled the world, for the Muslims were more powerful than the Christians. In addition, rather than there being peace, much blood had been spilled in warfare, especially in the Christian nations.

Third, Ramban demonstrated how the Christian belief in the Trinity and Yeshu's birth could not be believed by any thinking Jew. The Trinity is outright idol worship, for it is belief in three gods, while the Virgin Birth is wholly foreign to Jewish tradition and logic. Interestingly, Christian missionaries still attempt to convince Jews of the truth of their religion, and the refutation of their so-called proofs is exactly the same as the Ramban used more than 700 years ago.

Fourth, the Christians argued that mankind is condemned to hell because of the sin of Adam and Eve, and that only belief in Yeshu can save it from that fate. Ramban argued that such an assertion could not be proven, for anyone can say what he likes regarding the next world. Belief in Yeshu does not change suffering and the death decreed on humanity in this world, which indeed would have been a powerful proof for Christianity's veracity. Ramban further argued logically that G-d would not cause one person's soul to suffer because of another's sins.

At the conclusion of the debate, the king presented Ramban with 300 gold coins and stated that he had never heard anyone so wrong defend his case so well. However, that is hardly the end of the story. A week after the debate, the king came to the Barcelona synagogue to lecture on Christianity — a lecture at which Jewish attendance was mandatory. Having more or less defeated the Church, Ramban, to escape Catholic wrath, had to flee Spain. He immigrated to Eretz Yisrael, where he died in 1270.

Chapter 14

THE END OF SPANISH JEWRY

C**HRISTIAN SPAIN**: In the middle of the twelfth century, fanatical Almohad Muslims overran Southern Spain, causing a massive Jewish exodus to the Christian North. At first, the Christians proved to be as tolerant to Jews as were the Muslim rulers of the Golden Age. However, in the thirteenth century matters began to deteriorate. By the mid-1200s, the Christians had nearly completed the *reconquista*, with only Granada and its environs in Southern Spain remaining in Muslim hands. As a result, the Christians felt that the Jews were not as important to their cause as previously. In the 1300s, the situation worsened drastically. The Black Death struck Spain, and rumors of Jewish responsibility spread through the country. In response to the disaster, both Christian religious consciousness and open anti-Semitism increased. Spaniards also increasingly resented Jewish financial success. In addition, there was a power struggle between two contestants for the Spanish throne, and the Jews backed the losing side. By 1391, the atmosphere was so tense that even a tiny spark could have set off a major conflagration. Tragically, that is what happened.

THE POGROMS OF 1391: Ferrand Martinez, a vicious, Jew-hating priest, traveled throughout the country, calling on Christians to attack the Jews. Although the Pope and the king tried to restrain him, Martinez's popularity only increased. In June 1391, riots broke out in Seville, rapidly spreading through the country. In

Valencia, a pogrom began when Christian youths entered the Jewish quarter to taunt Jews. During the ensuing scuffle, a Christian child was accidentally killed, bringing the entire Christian population in a frenzied rage into the Jewish streets. By the time the riots died down — a full two months later — 50,000 Jews were dead, and numerous, ancient communities were completely destroyed. It was a blow from which Spanish Jewry would never recover.

MASS CONVERSION: During the riots, Jews were offered the option of conversion to Christianity or death. Sadly, for the first time in Jewish history, large numbers of Jews converted, both under immediate coercion and in fear of future pressure. In 1411, a priest, Vincente Ferrer, later to become St. Vincent, embarked on a major mission to secure even more Jewish converts. He traversed all of Spain, preaching in synagogues, holding a Torah scroll in one hand and a cross in the other, while a howling mob stood outside. His glib style and facile theological arguments attracted thousands of converts in each place. Estimates put the number of Jews who converted during these two great waves, 1391 and 1412, as high as 400,000.[1]

There are several reasons why Spanish Jews became Christians in such large numbers. First, many Jews did not want to give up their comfortable lifestyles and prestigious positions in Spanish society. Second, the Jews felt that because Spain, the last bastion of the Jewish world, had turned so inhospitable, there was no hope for the future of the Jewish people. Shattering the illusion "it can't happen here" simply crushed the Spanish Jews. Third, there was the widespread feeling that insincere conversion to Christianity was not such a bad thing, and that the Jews would revert to Jewish practice as soon as the pressure was off. Alas, the Jews did not realize that after conversion there would be no turning back.[2]

PROMINENT JEWISH APOSTATES: A shocking phenomenon occurred in Spain — the conversion to Christianity of prominent

Torah scholars. The most infamous of these was the rabbi of Burgos, Solomon HaLevi, who became Pablo de Santa Maria. Rising to the position of bishop in the Catholic Church, he persecuted Jews with fiery zeal. Playing a major role in enacting decrees that degraded unconverted Jews, such as forcing them to wear coarse sackcloth upon which was sewn a red badge of shame, Santa Maria also forbade Jewish men to trim their beards. Another scholarly convert was Joshua HaLorki, who became Maestre Geronimo de Santa Fe. Faithful Jews disparagingly called him the *Megadef*, the blasphemer, an acronym of his Christian name. He forced Jews to debate Christians under circumstances extremely disadvantageous to the Jews.

THE DISPUTATION AT TORTOSA: In 1413, the Pope ordered the Jews of Spain to send representatives to the Spanish city of Tortosa for a religious disputation.[3] The Pope personally attended, along with cardinals and bishops and the Jewish apostate Joshua HaLorki. Thirteen rabbis represented the Jews, most notably Rabbi Joseph Albo, who wrote the important book on Jewish belief called *Sefer HaIkkarim*. HaLorki, who personally knew all the rabbis, informed them that the debate would center on one point only: whether Yeshu fulfilled the prophecies ascribed by the Tanach regarding the Messiah. To bolster his false arguments, HaLorki falsified Talmudic texts, and tried to apply literal logic to Aggadic statements of the Talmud that Jewish tradition states can only be understood on a deeper level. Since the Jewish delegates were not permitted to offer any replies that the Christians could find offensive, which included virtually everything, the Jews rapidly lost heart. After close to two years, the Christians closed the debate, claiming victory.

Meanwhile, while the rabbis were at Tortosa, Vincente Ferrer moved through their leaderless communities, gaining many converts. Angry at the rabbis who refused to concede his so-called victory, the Pope enacted severe restrictions against the Jews. Among these were prohibitions to study the Talmud, the exclusion of Jews from almost all professions, and a requirement that Jews attend sermons given by Christian priests. Despite being ostracized from society and reduced to utter poverty, many Jews courageously held steadfast in their beliefs. Yeshivos and Torah scholars existed in Spain up to the time of the Expulsion of 1492.

THE CONVERTS' DILEMMA: After the fury of the pogroms and anti-Jewish decrees abated, many converts desired to return to Judaism. Alas, this was not possible according to Christian law. The Pope ruled that only those Jews who were dragged to the baptismal font vehemently protesting their opposition were permitted to rejoin the Jewish faith. Anyone who converted under threat of harm, and surely those who accepted baptism in anticipation of threats, were considered by the Church to be full-fledged Christians. Reversion to Jewish practice was considered heresy, which was punishable by death. These *conversos* lived in limbo, despised by both Jews and Christians. Jews looked down on them for forsaking Judaism, and Christians saw them as insincere, which many were.

Even while outwardly professing Christian belief, many *conversos* retained Jewish laws, privately mocking the Christian religion. However, Jewish religious observance gradually faded. For example, it was impossible for *conversos* to circumcise their sons; if the heretical act were discovered, it would lead to death. Similarly, since these Jews were unable to provide their children with a Torah education, their children grew up with just a smattering of Jewish knowledge. By 1492, the third generation *conversos* were overwhelmingly Christian, with lingering traces of Judaism. Faithful Jews attempted to bring the *conversos* back to Torah observance, but the Jews' efforts were stymied by the Church's ruling that anyone causing a Christian to leave the fold would incur the death penalty. Nevertheless, many *conversos* did not sever all links to Judaism, and observed some mitzvos, despite the dangers involved. Often, the Inquisition caught them, and they died *al kiddush HaShem* saying *Shema Yisrael*.

Many halachic responsa were written regarding the Jewish

status of the *conversos*, an issue that became pertinent when a number of them managed to leave Spain and join Jewish communities elsewhere. Eventually, those who remained behind assimilated into the Spanish people and became full-fledged gentiles. However, even today there are people in both Spain and South America who light candles in a hidden room on Friday night, ascribing it to an ancient family custom.

Among the Jews, these converts and their descendants were known by the name of *Anusim*, the forced ones, for many of them had adopted Christianity under duress. The general Spanish population was less charitable, using the pejorative term Marranos to describe them. In the words of a prominent historian: "The word Marrano is an old Spanish term dating back to the early Middle Ages and meaning swine. The word expresses succinctly and unmistakably all the depth of hatred and contempt which the ordinary Spaniard felt for the insincere neophytes by whom he was now surrounded."[4] As on so many occasions throughout Jewish history, assimilation proved not to be the answer to the Jews' problems.

THE *CONVERSOS* GAIN POWER: Under Spanish law, the *conversos*, as full-fledged Christians, were subject to none of the discrimination professing Jews faced. The *conversos* intermarried with the noblest Christian families, including the royal house. Eventually, it became difficult to find a Spanish family without *converso* blood, a situation that still exists today. The *conversos* rapidly occupied the top jobs in the country. *Conversos* and their children became integral to the government, judiciary, army, universities, even the Church itself. They held all the financial levers of power, from administering the treasury to tax collection, and greatly dominated Spanish life.

RESENTMENT TOWARD THE *CONVERSOS*: In 1449, in Toledo, riots broke out against *converso* tax collectors, which soon spread to other cities. Laws were promulgated barring *conversos* from all prominent positions, despite the fact that such a ban was contrary to Christian teachings prohibiting discrimination against any adherent of the faith. At that point, Spaniards were divided into two groups: Old Christians, who were untainted with Jewish blood, and New Christians, which included *conversos* and anyone with *converso* lineage. Spaniards began priding themselves on their *limpiezza de sangre*, or pure gentile blood, as opposed to the *mala sangre*, the bad blood of the *conversos*. Proof of pure ancestry was required of one aspiring to any prestigious post. Anti-Semitism then took a new historical twist — changing from a religious hatred to a racial one. Thus, this new hatred prepared the ground for the secular racism of modern anti-Semitism.[5]

FERDINAND AND ISABELLA: Spain's various provinces were riven by lawlessness and ethnic tensions that threatened to tear the country apart. In 1469, Ferdinand of Aragon (who had *converso* ancestry[6]) married Isabella of Castille, uniting the two most powerful Spanish regions under one royal family. The couple became known as *los reyos catholicos*, the Catholic Sovereigns. While Ferdinand was driven by love of money, Isabella was motivated by religious fanaticism, having been raised in a convent as a pious Catholic. The royal couple restored law and order, uniting Spain, making it a powerful country. Two major problems remained — the *converso* issue and the completion of the *reconquista*. Despite Ferdinand's power and lineage, anti-*converso* feelings remained at a fever pitch, with the people demanding a resolution of the issue.

THE INQUISITION COMES TO SPAIN: The Inquisition did not originate in Spain and did not originally target Jews. In the 1200s, the Pope established the Holy Inquisition against Depraved Heresy to deal with breakaway Christian sects. It remained relatively powerless, as secular rulers, suspicious of papal meddling in their own internal affairs, did not allow it access to their countries. In a period of more than 200 years, very few heretics were burned at the stake. In 1481, however, after extracting a promise from the Pope that the Inquisition would remain under the Crown's control, thus ensuring that confiscated assets of heretics would revert to the throne, Ferdinand and Isabella established the Inquisition in Seville. While it is commonly assumed that the Inquisition was brought to Spain out of a concern that Jews were trying to influence *conversos* to leave the Christian fold, one prominent historian is of the opinion that by 1481 Jewish consciousness was virtually nonexistent among the *conversos*, and that Jews did not attempt any such outreach.[7] Rather, he believes, the Inquisition was an outgrowth of the attitudes of Spain's Old Christian population. In the words of one Spanish historian, "The Inquisition was a genuine expression of the soul of the Spanish people."

PROCEDURE OF THE INQUISITION: Once the court was set up, a thirty-day grace period was granted in which voluntary confessions of wrongdoing received light sentences, such as small fines. However, a confessor had to agree to spy on his friends and relatives, and if he did not produce evidence, he would be under suspicion as a heretic and could receive the death penalty. Naturally, this system encouraged great corruption, for people fabricated false evidence against others either out of fear, jealousy, and hatred, or to receive a reward. To make matters worse, any accused person was not permitted to know the identity of his accusers, or even the evidence, and thus had no way to refute the charges, which were always believed by the court. Defense counsel was allowed, but was virtually impossible to obtain, because defending heresy was also considered heretical and punishable by death, thus discouraging any potential advocates.

The Inquisition publicized signs of heretical behavior for faithful Christians to watch for and report, including changing linens on Friday, buying vegetables before Pesach, blessing children without making the sign of the cross, fasting on Yom Kippur, and refraining from work on the Sabbath. Interestingly enough, Jews who never converted to Christianity were not under the jurisdiction of the Inquisition, and could practice their religion freely and openly. It was only *conversos* who were considered heretics for forsaking the Christian creed and practicing Judaism.

TORTURES: If the Inquisitors could not obtain a confession from a suspected heretic, they employed torture to extract one. Interestingly, as gruesome as these tortures were, they were designed not to spill blood, a practice forbidden under Christian law. In the rope torture, for example, the victim's hands were tied behind him, and the rope was connected to a pulley. Weights were attached to the victim's legs, and he was raised to the ceiling. When he was suddenly lowered, his arms and legs were painfully dislocated. The water torture consisted of laying a wet cloth over the prisoner's mouth and nostrils and running a small stream down his throat. As the victim gagged and pulled the cloth into his throat, it was yanked away, causing excruciating pain. Torture by fire was also employed, in which the victim's feet were smeared with a flammable material and held near a fire, causing a slow, painful burning.[8] If the accused fainted during interrogation, a physician standing nearby revived him; if the official administering the torture caused the victim to die, he was not held responsible. Overall, no person was safe from the clutches of the Inquisition — even children and pregnant women underwent these horrific tortures.

PUNISHMENTS: The penalties imposed by the Inquisition included monetary fines, confiscation of all property, public humiliation, and flogging. Most severe of all punishments were the death sentences. Since the Church did not spill blood, but only saved souls, the victims were handed over to the secular authorities for execution. Bloodless deaths were preferred, such as strangling and burning alive. Periodically, an *auto-de-fé* (act of faith) was held, in which all the victims of an area were punished together. These became great public spectacles, taking on a holiday atmosphere, as people brought their families to watch the proceedings and jeer the victims. Condemned people wore yellow *sanbenitos*, cloaks with red crosses and the letter X painted on them. Those given the death penalty wore tunics with paintings of flames and devils. The procession marched through the town to the burning area where the judges sat. The cases involving lesser penalties were judged first, then those receiving strangulation before burning, and finally those condemned to be burned alive.

The first *auto-de-fé* was held in 1481, and the last in 1731 when an old woman was accused of "being influenced by the Devil, after which she laid eggs with prophecies written on them."[9] In 1680, the most spectacular of all *autos-de-fé* was held to celebrate the wedding of King Carlos and his bride. At that time, the Inquisition spread to Spanish and Portuguese colonies in the New and Old Worlds, with victims burned in Havana, Cuba; Mexico City, Mexico; Buenos Aires, Argentina; and Goa, India. After 350 years, the Inquisition was finally abolished in 1834. In all, more than 400,000 people were accused of heresy, with 30,000 of those put to death.[10]

TORQUEMADA: In 1483, Queen Isabella's personal confessor, the Dominican priest Tomas de Torquemada, was appointed head of the Inquisition. Of *converso* origin,[11] Torquemada was a fanatic Jew-hater who was wholly incorruptible. Unlike other monks, he kept his vows of poverty, never eating meat, not wearing linen near his body, or sleeping on anything softer than a board. It was precisely his complete zeal to the cause of Christianity that made Torquemada such an implacable foe. He personally turned the Inquisition into the terrifying institution it would become. Under his administration, the Inquisition amassed enormous assets confiscated from its victims, much of it used to finance the war to conquer the last Muslim stronghold of Granada.

Quickly, Torquemada began taking steps to weaken the unconverted Jewish community and eventually expel it from Spain. In 1485, he forced all rabbis, under pain of death, to report *conversos* who were practicing Judaism, and to pronounce a rabbinic curse on any Jew who failed to notify the Inquisition of such behavior. This cruel edict badly split the Jews of Spain. Alarmed by the greatly increasing power of the Inquisition, that year a group of *conversos* plotted to kill the inquisitor of Saragossa, Pedro de Arbues, hoping to begin a popular uprising against the Inquisition. However, the assassination had the opposite effect.

The townspeople were enraged, rampaging through the streets, killing many *conversos*. All the conspirators were caught and executed, and the Inquisition grew even stronger.

THE HOLY CHILD OF LA GUARDIA: In 1486, Torquemada petitioned Ferdinand and Isabella to expel the Jews from Spain, but they refused. Therefore, Torquemada needed to create a sensation in order to poison the atmosphere, stir public wrath against the Jews, and force their expulsion. In 1490, the Inquisition fabricated the tale of the Holy Child of La Guardia. Several Jews and *conversos* were accused of kidnapping a seven-year-old boy in the town of La Guardia and taking him to a cave, cutting out the child's heart, and using it in magical rites designed to overthrow Christian Spain and turn it into a Jewish country. Although no body was ever found, under torture all the defendants admitted to the charges. In late 1491, for the first time unconverted Jews were burned at the stake in a spectacular *auto-de-fé*, which people traveled many days to witness. (Before being killed, the Jews were punished spiritually by being excommunicated from the Catholic Church, to which they had never belonged.) Torquemada wasted no time in sending reports of the episode all over Spain, whipping the populace into an even greater anti-Jewish frenzy.

THE MYTH TODAY: The myth of the Holy Child of La Guardia entered the history of Spain, where it helped keep anti-Semitism alive for centuries. Missing details of the "Holy Child's" name, age, birthplace, and place of murder were obligingly provided by willing contributors. (The embarrassing lack of a corpse was attributed to the child's body ascending to heaven, along with his soul.) In 1989, a book on the history of Spain quoted the story as justification for the expulsion of the Jews. In 1993, the author Erna Paris visited La Guardia and described what she saw:

> The church stands in glorious tribute to the Holy Child, patron saint of La Guardia, whose feast day has just passed. A statue of the child graces an alcove, and votive candles burn brightly at his feet. A priest approaches, eager to talk about his church's

claim to fame. The child, I learn, was five years old and his name was Juan. He was kidnapped by the Jews and crucified. This act, says the priest, was the ultimate reason for the expulsion of the Jews from Spain. The cave where he was martyred is not far from here. I may see it if I wish, he says, smiling.

"Is the story true?" I ask the priest.

"Well," he replies slowly, "the Jews did admit to taking the child into the cave. I suppose that is all we can know," he concludes, turning his head away.[12]

THE DECREE OF EXPULSION: In January 1492, after a campaign of nearly 800 years, the Christians conquered Granada, the last Muslim outpost in Spain, bringing the *reconquista* to an end. Ironically, Rabbi Isaac Abarbanel, the famous Jewish scholar and Spanish finance minister, directed the war. Spain was finally united under one sovereign and one religion, and the Jews were no longer needed to help fight. On March 31, 1492, Ferdinand and Isabella signed the Edict of Expulsion in the Alhambra Palace in Granada, giving Jews until the end of July to leave the country. Justification for the decree was that the "Jews are instructing them [*conversos*] in the ceremonies and observances of their religion, seeking to circumcise them and their children, giving them prayer books, supplying them with matzo on Passover, and kosher meat throughout the year." Legend has it that Don Isaac Abarbanel offered his entire enormous fortune to the Catholic kings if they would rescind the decree. Ferdinand, who loved money above all else, was about to accept the proposal. Suddenly, Tomas de Torquemada burst into the room, waving a golden crucifix. He angrily threw it on the ground, screaming, "The Jews sold Yeshu for money, and you want to sell him again!" The pious Catholic Isabella told the Jews that the deal was off.

THE EXPULSION: A Catholic priest, Andres Bernaldez, vividly describes the Jews' departure: "Within the terms fixed by the edict of expulsion, the Jews sold and disposed of their property for a mere nothing. They went about asking Christians to buy and found no buyers. Fine houses and estates were sold for trifles; a house was exchanged for a mule, and a vineyard given for a little cloth or linen. The rich Jews paid the expenses of the departure of the poor, practicing toward each other the greatest charity, so that they would not become converts. In the first week of July they took the route for quitting their native land, great and small, old and young, on horses and in carts. They experienced great trouble; some falling, others rising; some dying and others being born; some being stricken with illness. Christians along the way persuaded them to be baptized, but those who converted were very few. The rabbis encouraged them and made the people sing and play instruments to enliven them and keep up their spirits."[13]

Historians estimate that anywhere from 100,000 to 300,000 Jews departed. The last Jews left Spain on Thursday, August 2, 1492, Tishah B'Av. Christopher Columbus (who may have been a descendant of *conversos*) was supposed to leave for America that day, but could not because the harbor was full of fleeing Jews. Undaunted, he departed the next day, eventually discovering a continent that would prove hospitable for Jews in the future. Clearly, even when striking the Jewish people, G-d lays the foundation for future salvation.

According to Rabbi Joseph Yaavetz, one of the exiles, many of the Jews leaving Spain were the humble folk who had a simple faith untainted by philosophical musings. A large number were women, who, as in the forty years of wandering in the desert, professed unquestioning loyalty to the Torah.[14] Among the great rabbis who left was Don Isaac Abarbanel, who departed despite assurances from the monarchy that he had permission to stay without converting to Christianity. He left behind nearly his entire fortune and settled in Italy, where he died in 1508.

THE TRIP: Finding a new home was not easy, and many Jews died from the rigors of the journey. Some ships were overloaded and sank; others caught fire on the high seas. Unscrupulous captains threw Jews overboard or robbed them of all their possessions. Jews were sold to pirates as slaves or dropped on uninhabited islands off the coast of Africa to attempt to survive.[15] A number of Jews returned to Spain, where they were baptized immediately upon landing, and then closely watched by the Inquisition. Travelers on land were killed by robbers, attacked by wild animals, or wandered about until they died of hunger, disease, or exposure.

WHERE JEWS WENT: Many Jews went to Portugal, adjacent to Spain with a similar climate and culture. However, this was only a temporary haven, for in 1497 Portugal embarked on a program of forced conversion. Later, the Inquisition came to Portugal as well, and the Jews either left the country or converted. Others left for North Africa, Italy, and Western Europe. Some even wound up in such Ashkenazic countries as Germany and Poland, becoming culturally Ashkenazic. A large number settled in Turkey, whose ruler extended a welcome to the Jews. The Turkish sultan was quoted as saying, "Can such a king be called wise and intelligent — one who impoverishes his country and enriches my kingdom?"[16]

REASONS FOR THE TRAGEDY: As the single greatest tragedy to strike the Jewish people since the Roman era, the Spanish Expulsion sent shock waves throughout the Jewish world. People searched for ways to understand such a harsh Divine decree. Rabbis who themselves had been expelled from Spain attempted to provide answers. Among the reasons given were lack of observance of some mitzvos, particularly in the area of *tznius*, modesty between men and women;[17] excessive study of non-Jewish philosophy, which weakened Jewish faith in times of crisis; mass conversions, beginning in 1391, which had previously never happened on such a large scale; flaunting of wealth and power by upper-class Jews, arousing much jealousy among non-Jews and leading to widespread anti-Semitism; and unfathomable Divine decree.[18]

500 YEARS LATER: On March 31, 1992, 500 years to the day after the Edict of Expulsion was signed, King Juan Carlos of Spain stood in the main synagogue of Madrid, wearing a skullcap, flanked by his wife, Queen Sofia, and the president of Israel, Chaim Herzog. What he said is very revealing: "May hate and intolerance never again cause desolation and exile. Let us be capable of building a prosperous and peaceful Spain based on concord and mutual respect. What is important *is not an accounting of our errors* [emphasis added] or successes, but the willingness to think about and analyze the past in terms of our future, and the willingness to work together to pursue a noble goal."[19] In other words, the king did not apologize for the Expulsion, for to do so would be unfaithful to Spanish history, which views uniting the country under Christian rule a most noble endeavor. However, the Expulsion decree was legally rescinded, and Jews may now live freely in Spain.

Chapter 15

THE EARLY ACHARONIM
(the 1500s)

NEW **TORAH CENTERS**: The Talmud states that G-d does not smite the Jewish people unless He has previously prepared a remedy.[1] Great Torah centers, most notably in Eretz Yisrael, Turkey, and Poland, arose to replace the destruction of the Spanish communities. Indeed, the Spanish Expulsion marks the approximate beginning of the age of the Acharonim, or later Torah scholars. Jews universally recognized that the era of Torah scholarship of the caliber of the Rishonim had irrevocably passed. Consequently, virtually no Acharon of the last 500 years has disputed the words of a Rishon.

TZEFAS: In the 1500s, the town of Tzefas in Eretz Yisrael hosted a great concentration of leading Torah luminaries. Scholars such as Rabbi Joseph Karo, Rabbi Yitzchak Luria (Arizal), Rabbi Chaim Vital, Rabbi Moshe Cordovero, Rabbi Jacob Berav, Rabbi Moshe Alshich, and Rabbi Shlomo Alkabetz (composer of the famous Sabbath song *Lecha Dodi*) made their home in this tiny hamlet in the north of Israel. Some of these scholars were among those expelled from Spain. As many of these sages were giants of Kabbalah, Tzefas became the major center of this kind of Torah study.

THE ARIZAL: Rabbi Isaac Luria (1533–1572) has a unique distinction — he is the only person in Jewish history to have the appellation *zal* (*zichrono livrachah*, of blessed memory) appended to his name. A glimpse of his greatness may be found in the words of Rabbi Chaim of Volozhin, quoting his teacher, the illustrious Gaon of Vilna: "What can we possibly say about G-d's holy one, a man of G-d, so holy and so fearsome, to whom mysteries of wisdom were revealed, and whose understanding wondrously grew ever greater from the time he merited the revelation of Elijah the Prophet?"[2] Acknowledged as the greatest sage of his time, Arizal is considered the father of contemporary Kabbalah.

Kabbalah, which literally means "receiving," is the mystical understanding of the Torah that G-d taught Moses at Sinai. Due to the possibility of spiritual harm coming to those who study it without the proper level of understanding, this discipline was carefully transmitted over the generations only to disciples deemed worthy of its revelation.[3]

The primary Kabbalistic work is the *Zohar*, written by the Tanna Rabbi Shimon bar Yochai. This book lay hidden for more than 1,000 years, until it was discovered by a thirteenth-century Spanish Kabbalist.[4] However, by deeply expounding on its hidden secrets it was Arizal who brought the *Zohar* to the forefront of Jewish consciousness, and his thoughts became the basis of all subsequent study of Kabbalah. Although Arizal did not write down any of his teachings, his disciples, led by Rabbi Chaim Vital, recorded them for posterity. Arizal's own prayer service, known as *Nusach Ari*, is based on Kabbalistic secrets and is followed today by Chabad Chassidim. Arizal passed away at thirty-eight, having accomplished an incredible amount in such a short lifetime.

Beginning in the Middle Ages, and especially after the times of Arizal, Kabbalah penetrated all areas of Jewish life, and in numerous cases even influenced halachic practice. As a measure of its influence, an entire avenue of Jewish thought opened up for masses of Jews, who although unable to plumb the depths of Kabbalah, nonetheless had their spiritual horizons broadened immeasurably. Through some of the darkest eras of the Jewish people, even up to current times, Kabbalah has fortified Jews with the realization that their sufferings had meaning and were part of a Divine plan for the rectification of the world. Today, many areas of Jewish observance are greatly influenced by Kabbalah, especially the laws and customs of Rosh HaShanah and Yom Kippur, the elaborate ritual of preparing a body for burial (*taharah*, or purification), and many funeral and bereavement practices.

RABBI JOSEPH KARO AND *BEIS YOSEF*: At age four, Rabbi Joseph Karo (1488–1575) left Spain with his family, settling in Turkey and growing up there. Reaching great spiritual heights, he was Divinely inspired to write a halachic work that would serve the needs of the Jewish people. Based on the *Arbaah Turim* written by Rabbi Jacob ben Asher, Rabbi Karo's massive *Beis Yosef* took twenty years to complete. Filling a crucial need, the multi-volume work systematically detailed all Jewish law, quoting all relevant opinions on a topic and rendering a final ruling based on consensus. During the creation of *Beis Yosef*, Rabbi Karo moved to Tzefas, where he finished the work.

SHULCHAN ARUCH: Rabbi Karo also wrote the monumental *Shulchan Aruch*, patterned on the *Beis Yosef* and the *Arbaah Turim*. A compilation of all Torah laws applicable today, *Shulchan Aruch* is written in a much-shortened format, leaving out the debates and differing opinions. While both books spread quickly throughout the Jewish world, there were three criticisms of *Beis Yosef* and *Shulchan Aruch*. First, it was said that since Rabbi Karo was Sephardic, the books overly reflected that practice. Second, people could commit errors in Jewish practice by looking in the books and deciding law rather than consulting a rabbi. Third, Torah scholarship would become too easy if all the sources were laid out so plainly. The great Polish scholar Rabbi Moshe Isserles (Rema) addressed the first concern by adding notes to *Shulchan Aruch* where Ashkenazic practice differed. As far as the other concerns, with the passage of time people realized that rather than these books lessening Torah scholarship, they increased it, and that rabbis still had to be consulted for direction of proper practice. Indeed, so greatly accepted have Rabbi Karo's works been that for centuries an observant Jew has been defined by strict adherence to the laws of *Shulchan Aruch*. Rabbi Karo also wrote *Kesef Mishnah*, a basic text for understanding Rambam's *Mishnah Torah*.

THE ATTEMPT TO REVIVE *SEMICHAH*: *Semichah*, rabbinic ordination, was instituted by Moses and transferred in an unbroken chain from teacher to student until the fourth century, when Roman persecution forced its cessation. More than a mere formality, this form of ordination is biblically required for the Sanhedrin to convene and judge many types of cases, especially involving capital punishment and *malkos*, lashes.[5] In 1538, based on a statement of Rambam that if a majority of sages of Eretz Yisrael wish to confer *semichah* on one of their colleagues they may do so (and that sage may grant *semichah* to those who bestowed it upon him),[6] an attempt was made to revive *semichah*. In this manner, it was believed, the Sanhedrin could be reconstituted. Rabbi Jacob Berav, one of the great scholars of Tzefas, felt that the restoration of the Sanhedrin was necessary to deal with complicated halachic problems caused by the Spanish Expulsion, and to enhance the prestige of Torah scholars at such a traumatic time for the Jewish people. As such, Rabbi Jacob Berav received *semichah* from the rabbis of Tzefas, and then gave it to several scholars, including Rabbi Joseph Karo.

RABBINIC OPPOSITION: Rabbi Jacob Berav's plan met with vehement opposition from many scholars, most notably Rabbi Levi ben Chaviv (Ralbach), who although granted *semichah* by Rabbi Jacob Berav, refused to accept it. Ralbach opposed *semichah* for numerous reasons, including the fact that not all the rabbis in Eretz Yisrael had been consulted, especially those in Jerusalem and of Ashkenazic background. In addition, Ralbach said that Rambam's statement was his own personal opinion, as he himself stated, and might not be halachically reliable. Most important, reviving *semichah* was an innovation, and if the great scholars of the previous 1,000 years did not see fit to take such action, it should not be done at this time. This last argument continues to be a very powerful one, and is the major reason why new ideas and so-called improvements in Jewish practice, no matter how attractive they might appear, are not easily implemented. Shortly thereafter, *semichah* died out. (The *semichah* granted to rabbis today is only an acknowledgement that one has studied certain areas of Jewish law and is qualified to render halachic decisions.) By the end of the 1500s, Tzefas ceased being a Torah center, and many of its great scholars are buried in the famous cemetery nearby.

DAVID HAREUVENI: Since many Jews felt that the Spanish Expulsion was a harbinger of the Messianic Era, the time was ripe for dubious characters to make such claims. One such person was David HaReuveni, who in 1524 arrived in Rome on a white horse with two attendants and was granted a meeting with the Pope. Claiming to be an ambassador of the Tribe of Reuben, one of the lost Ten Tribes of Israel, HaReuveni proposed an alliance between the Ten Tribes and the Christians to conquer Eretz Yisrael from the Muslims. Intrigued by the idea, the Pope sent David HaReuveni to Portugal to gain the assent of the Portuguese king. In Portugal, the king cordially received HaReuveni, and the spirits of the oppressed *conversos* soared. However, fearing the consequences of a Jewish revival, the Portuguese king ordered HaReuveni to leave the country. Eventually, he wound up in Germany, where the emperor imprisoned him. Although it is not definite, in all probability HaReuveni died in jail.

SHLOMO MOLCHO: While David HaReuveni was in Portugal, he attracted the attention of a brilliant *converso* named Diego Perez, who by age twenty-one had risen to great power at the king's court. Upon meeting HaReuveni, Diego decided to circumcise himself and adopt Judaism openly. Although HaReuveni tried to dissuade Diego, he went ahead, nearly killing himself in the process. Taking the name of Shlomo Molcho, Diego left Portugal and studied Torah, especially Kabbalah, under many great scholars, mainly in Tzefas. Feeling that his life's mission was to usher in the

Messianic Era, Diego traveled throughout Jewish communities exhorting the populace to repent. At times, he claimed to be Elijah the Prophet, who will herald the arrival of the Messiah. When Diego came to Germany, the emperor arrested him, offering him a choice between conversion to Christianity or martyrdom. Diego chose the latter and was burned at the stake, professing his desire to give his life *al kiddush HaShem*. To this day, Diego — Shlomo Molcho — remains a very enigmatic figure. On the one hand, he performed the greatest act a person can do: offering his life for G-d's sake. On the other hand, he made false Messainic claims, either intentionally or delusionally, that demoralized many Jews when the claims were not fulfilled.

DONNA GRACIA MENDES AND DON JOSEPH NASI: These two *conversos* utilized their great power and wealth to help Jews in many places. Donna Gracia escaped from Portugal to Belgium, along with her nephew Don Joseph Nasi, taking much of their wealth with them. In the city of Antwerp, Donna Gracia managed the family's international banking house, thus making important connections in many countries. Don Joseph married his cousin, Donna Gracia's daughter, and entered the banking business. Unable to practice Judaism openly in Belgium, in 1553 they fled to Turkey, where Don Joseph became the sultan's closest advisor. In 1561, the Turkish government gave Don Joseph permission to start a Jewish settlement in the city of Tiberias in Eretz Yisrael. A wall was constructed around the city, silkworm trees were planted, and plans were made for industries that would support many Jews. However, for unknown reasons, the project failed.

Don Joseph also used his influence at the sultan's court to help Jews in danger. When the Church arrested *conversos* in the Italian city of Ancona, Don Joseph convinced the sultan to write a letter to the Pope threatening harm to Christians in Turkey if the Jews were not released. Undaunted by the threat, the Pope freed only Jews who were Turkish citizens, and burned twenty-five other Jews at the stake. In response, Don Joseph organized an economic boycott of Ancona, which was backed by the leading halachic authority of the time, Rabbi Joseph Karo. Upon Don Joseph's death, thousands of Jews attended his funeral and mourned for their great benefactor.

THE PRINTING PRESS: The advent of printing with movable type created a revolution in the Torah world. *Sefarim* became widely available, and many scholars were encouraged to publish their works, thus greatly disseminating Torah knowledge. Due to easily reprintable books, disasters such as the burning of the Talmud in France in 1242 would have a diminished effect on the Jewish people. Not surprisingly, the first Hebrew book printed was a 1474 *Chumash* with Rashi's commentary. In 1484, the first volume of the Talmud, tractate *Berachos*, was printed in Soncino, Italy. Nevertheless, despite the greater availability of *sefarim*, they were quite expensive, and often a city had but one complete set of the Talmud. One great Talmudic scholar of the 1700s, the Pnei Yehoshua, lamented the fact that he could not write novellae on tractate *Kerisos* because the volume was not in his town. Still, over a 400-year period, the Talmud was printed fifty-six times. The last printing, the Vilna edition, was completed in 1886, and remains the most accurate, authoritative edition, and is the one in current use.

CENSORSHIP: Sadly, throughout Jewish history, Jews themselves have been responsible for perpetrating some of the greatest harm upon the Jewish people. In the Middle Ages and onward, Jews who converted to Christianity told the Christians the falsehood that the Talmud contains statements offensive to Christianity. As a result, through numerous printings of the Talmud, censors, both Christians and apostate Jews, were appointed to expunge any statements they felt were blasphemous. The deleted material ranged from single words to entire paragraphs. In particular, three pieces in tractate *Sanhedrin* discussing Yeshu, on pages 43a, 67a, and 107b, were stricken. Jews did manage to record the missing material in a slim volume called *Chesronos HaShas*, thus saving it for posterity. Further, in numerous editions of the Talmud tractate *Avodah Zarah*, which deals with laws of idolatry, was printed without a title page so to escape the censor's attention. Throughout the Talmud and other Jewish works, the word *min*, meaning heretic, was changed to *tzadoki*, Sadducee, so that no one might think Christians were implied. Frequently, the censors were wholly ignorant of Hebrew, and changed words even where no offense to Christians could be imagined. For example, the phrase *min kitniyos*, which means types of beans, was changed to *akum kitniyos*, meaning idolatrous beans, because the censors thought *min* meant a Christian heretic.[7]

THE *SHTADLAN*: The Hebrew word *l'hishtadel* means to make an effort, and its derivative, *shtadlan*, was commonly used to describe Jews in the Middle Ages and onward who used their influence at a ruler's court to ameliorate anti-Semitic decrees. One of the most famous *shtadlanim* was the legendary Rabbi Joselman of Rosheim, who lived in Germany in the 1500s. On countless occasions, he risked his life to save his fellow Jews. Once, an apostate Jew named Pfefferkorn informed the German emperor that the Talmud was insulting to Christians and must be burned. The emperor ordered that the Jews surrender their Gemaras to Pfefferkorn, who would review and burn them if he found incriminating material. Joselman enlisted the aid of many non-Jews, including the great philosopher Johann von Reuchlin, convincing them that the Talmud meant no harm to Christians. Joselman then made a personal appearance before the emperor, causing him to rescind the decree.[8] Another time, Dominican priests attempted to convince Emperor Charles V, ruler of both Spain and Germany, to extend the jurisdiction of the Inquisition to German Jews. Risking being burned at the stake, Joselman traveled to Spain and succeeded in getting the emperor to disregard the priests.[9]

THE PROTESTANT REFORMATION: Martin Luther, who lived in the 1500s and sparked the movement against the Catholic Church that resulted in the Protestant Reformation, started out friendly to the Jewish people. Hoping to attract Jews to his new brand of Christianity, Luther stated that the Catholics' mistreatment of the

Jews was a crime against G-d's Chosen People. However, when Luther realized that the Jews would not become Lutherans, he reversed himself and spewed forth foul anti-Semitic venom. Luther's statement "the Jews are our pest and misfortune" was copied almost verbatim by the Nazis. He recommended:

First, to set fire to their synagogues or schools.

Second, I advise that their houses also be razed and destroyed.

Third, all their prayer books and Talmudic writings, in which such lies, cursing, and blasphemy are taught, be taken from them.

Fourth, I advise that their rabbis be forbidden to teach.

Fifth, I advise that safe conduct on the highways be abolished completely for the Jews.

Sixth, I advise that all cash and treasure of silver be taken from them.

Seventh, let whoever can, throw brimstone and pitch upon them. Let them be driven like mad dogs out of the land.[10]

Some historians are convinced that Martin Luther, considered the first great national prophet of Germany, not only outdid all previous Christian anti-Semites, but also, in his outbursts of hatred, was the first major step to the Holocaust.[11] At the Nuremberg trials in 1946, for example, Julius Streicher, the editor of the vicious anti-Semitic Nazi newspaper *Der Sturmer*, stated that if he is on trial, then Martin Luther should also be in the dock with him.[12] Indeed, reading Luther's diatribes against the Jews, it is difficult not to agree with Streicher. To its credit, in 1994 the Lutheran Church repudiated Luther's anti-Semitic words, calling them false.

THE FIRST GHETTOES: Although no official edict required it, in the Middle Ages the Jews lived in separate quarters. Finally, in 1516 in Venice, Italy, the Jews were ordered to relocate to the site of an ironworks factory, thus creating the first ghetto. (Ghetto is the Italian word for iron foundry.) Rapidly, ghettoes sprung up all over Europe. Generally, the ghettoes were located in the most run-down part of town. For example, in Rome, the ghetto was on the banks of the Tiber River, which flooded frequently. Walls were constructed around the ghetto, Jews were locked in at night, and Christians were paid to watch the walls.

Physical life in the ghetto was very difficult. As the Jewish population grew, overcrowding became severe. Houses were built tall and thin, as there was no room for expansion. Fires spread quickly, and on numerous occasions entire ghettoes were destroyed. However, spiritual and communal life was greatly enhanced in the ghetto. Jews moved closer together, and could share their joys, tragedies, and goals with each other. Rabbis and synagogues were within close proximity and easily accessible. A spirit of sharing, lending, and *chessed* (lovingkindness) pervaded the atmosphere. The Sabbath and holidays were intensely spiritual and uplifting. In addition, the ghetto walls shut out alien influences, and afforded the Jews a sense of security and protection.

POLAND: In the 1500s, the territory known as Poland encompassed areas of the present nations of Poland, Lithuania, Belarus, Ukraine, and Russia. According to legend, Jews traveling eastward from Germany in the 900s received a Heavenly message *po-lin*, which is not only the Hebrew name for Poland, but also means "settle here." Settle they did, minting coins with Hebrew inscriptions in Poland as early as the 1100s. At first, Jews traveled to Poland to escape persecution and the ravages of the Black Death. Later, Jews came from the south and east, possibly remnants of Khazar Jews. Polish kings, needing people to inhabit their vast territories, and realizing the economic boon that Jews bring to a country, welcomed them. Indeed, despite occasional outbreaks of anti-Semitism, life in Poland was far more pleasant for Jews than anywhere else. The Polish cities of Cracow, Warsaw, Poznan, Kalisz, Brisk, and Grodno became major Jewish centers. By 1500, between 20,000 and 30,000 Jews lived in Poland. At the end of the 1500s, Great Poland contained fifty-two Jewish communities, Little Poland had forty-one, and the eastern regions eighty.[13] During the 1600s, it is estimated that four-fifths of the world's Jews resided there.[14]

TORAH LIFE: By the 1500s, Ashkenazic Poland became the Torah center of world Jewry, a position it held until the Holocaust. Producing the greatest scholars, yeshivos, and *sefarim,* Poland played a dominant role in Torah scholarship up to the contemporary era. Great movements within traditional Judaism, such as Chassidus and Mussar, originated in Poland. Due to the relative absence of oppression, and the complete lack of assimilation with the unattractive, backward Polish culture and society, Jewish spiritual life flourished in Poland. Even ordinary people spent many hours studying Torah, creating a society where Torah was paramount. Some great Polish scholars of the 1500s include:

RABBI MOSHE ISSERLES (REMA): Born in Cracow, Rema was regarded as the leader of Ashkenazic Jewry. His greatest accomplishment was his critical notes on the *Shulchan Aruch* of Rabbi Joseph Karo. The *Shulchan Aruch* reflected Sephardic practice, and in numerous instances Ashkenazic custom differed. Rema humbly called his notes *Mapah,* a tablecloth for the *Shulchan Aruch,* the set table. He pointed out where Ashkenazim diverged, thus enabling them to be loyal to their traditions but also benefit from Rabbi Joseph Karo's masterpiece. Incredibly, Rema wove his notes into the text of the *Shulchan Aruch,* thus preserving the integrity of the original work. Sephardim read the *Shulchan Aruch* without Rema's notes, while Ashkenazim read the same text with those notes, and both readings make perfect sense. No other author in history can boast of such a literary accomplishment. Rema died in Cracow, and his grave and synagogue still exist today, miraculously surviving the Holocaust unscathed.

MAHARSHA (Moreinu Harav Rav Shmuel Aidels): This scholar, financially supported by his wealthy mother-in-law Aidel, took her name as an honorific. Maharsha's commentary on the Talmud is the sine qua non of absolute logic, and its study is required for clear understanding of Gemara, and particularly of *Tosafos.* The Chazon Ish, the leading Lithuanian scholar in Eretz Yisrael of the twentieth century and who passed away in 1953, wrote that if one does not study Maharsha's work, he has but a superficial knowledge of the topic at hand.[15] Maharsha also wrote a commentary on the non-legal passages (Aggadah) of the Talmud, which, although written in a very different style, is indispensable for understanding those sections. A glimpse of some of the social and religious problems of Polish Jewry in the 1500s can be seen in a famous statement of Maharsha, yet the issues he raises bear an uncanny resemblance to current times:

> Many people are unaware of the intricate laws of the Sabbath, and constantly violate it. On Saturday nights, many Jews see it as a religious obligation to waste time in frivolous pursuits, and awaken on Sunday too late to recite the *Shema*. During school vacations, youths spend vast amounts of time in the street in purposeless pursuits. Everyone wants to flaunt their wealth by building palatial mansions, wearing expensive clothing, and [engaging] in all manners of conspicuous consumption. People are dishonest in monetary affairs, and rabbis who speak out regarding the excesses of society are scorned.[16]

RABBI SHLOMO LURIA (MAHARSHAL): This eminent scholar, a contemporary of Rema and Maharsha, also wrote a commentary on Talmud in which he frequently disagrees with Maharsha. One of Maharshal's well-known works, *Yam Shel Shlomo*, is a halachic compendium on many Talmudic tractates. A very famous ruling contained therein is the requirement that a Jew must sacrifice his or her life rather than falsify even one word of the Torah.[17]

RABBI JOEL SIRKES AND RABBI MEIR OF LUBLIN: Rabbi Joel, popularly known as the Bach after his analysis of the *Tur* called *Bayis Chadash*, is one of many Acharonim called by the title of his most important scholarly work rather than by his name. For example, Rabbi Israel Meir Kagan is known as the Chafetz Chaim, the title of his masterpiece on the laws of *lashon hara* — evil gossip. Rabbi Meir, called Maharam, is best known for his commentary on the Talmud. Maharam's commentary is similar to that of Maharsha, but is written is a much simpler style. Maharam, too, plays an important role in understanding the topic at hand.

VAAD ARBA ARATZOS: With the permission of the authorities, about 1520 the Jews of Poland organized an umbrella organization known as *Vaad Arba Aratzos*, the Council of the Four Lands. Rabbis were chosen from the four major Polish provinces — Great Poland, Little Poland, Volhynia, and Podolia. For a time, rabbis from Lithuania also participated, and the council was known as *Vaad Chamesh* (five) *Aratzos*. The *Vaad* met twice a year, in Lublin after Purim, and in Yaroslav before Rosh HaShanah. As these two cities were major market centers, they attracted many merchants and scholars. Major litigation was decided then, such as disputes between merchants or towns, along with the determination of which areas would pay what proportion of the king's taxes on the greater Jewish community. By consent of each area's representatives, decrees applicable to all Polish Jewry were also enacted. As such, the *Vaad* had enormous prestige, and was considered not only the de facto Jewish parliament, but also a replica of the Great Sanhedrin.[18] As an example of the far-reaching powers of the *Vaad*, one pronouncement states:

> It is forbidden for any Jew to rent the collection rights for taxes on whiskey or any other taxes from the king. One who violates this shall be excommunicated from this world and the next, and has no connection to the Jewish people. His bread and wine should be considered as that of non-Jews, his slaughter is invalid, no Jew should marry his children and no rabbi should officiate at such a ceremony, and he should not be afforded a Jewish burial. All the curses written in the Scriptures should take effect on him until he repents of his evil ways.[19]

Another ordinance of the *Vaad* prohibited rabbis from offering payment to obtain a rabbinical position. The Polish government abolished the *Vaad* in 1764.

JEWISH ECONOMIC ACTIVITY: In the 1300s, King Casimir the Great invited Jews to Poland, giving them special economic privileges reconfirmed by subsequent Polish kings. Not restricted by any discriminatory laws, Jews became the middle class of Poland, filling a gap in a Polish society that was composed of wealthy landowners and landless serfs. Jews became horse and cattle traders, cloth dyers, metal workers, artisans, tailors, and jewelers. They owned taverns, lent money, managed the vast estates of the noblemen (the infamous *poritzim* of many Jewish tales), and collected taxes. Such a complete Jewish dominance of Polish economic life aroused great resentment among the gentile population, an antipathy augmented by the people's fervent Christianity. These attitudes would later have disastrous ramifications for the Jews of Poland.

THE SHTETL: The word "shtetl" is from the Yiddish for "small town," and in Poland many Jews wound up settling in tiny hamlets, both to escape the overcrowding of the large cities and to band together in the vast stretches of the wild eastern provinces. Due to the tranquil surroundings and isolation from alien influences, shtetl life was conducive to intense Torah study and spiritual achievement; indeed, many of the greatest scholars were products of the shtetl. Over time, the greatness of the Eastern European Jews was realized in the shtetl, and the beauty of its lifestyle, and spiritual grandeur, were a source of strength until the shtetls were irrevocably destroyed in the Holocaust.

MAHARAL OF PRAGUE: One of the most famous Jewish thinkers of all time, Rabbi Judah Loew, more commonly known as Maharal, held several prestigious rabbinical posts, most notably in sixteenth-century Prague. Best known for the Kabbalistic creation of a golem, a clay being with human characteristics who aided Rabbi Loew in combating blood libels and other plots against the Jews, the Maharal's prolific literary output combined aspects of both philosophy and Kabbalah, and influenced both the Mussar and Chassidic movements. Maharal's writings are still popular today, having lost none of their profound intellectualism or timeless appeal. A statue of Maharal was erected in Prague in 1917 and still stands today.

PRAGUE: Known as a mother city of the Jewish people, over hundreds of years Prague boasted one of the greatest Jewish communities in Europe. From the time of the Rishonim, many great scholars lived in Prague. The city's most famous site is the Altneushul, built in 1265 and stands as the oldest synagogue in Europe. The name Altneu may come from the Hebrew *al tnai*, meaning "on condition," signifying that the synagogue was built with the understanding that it would only be used until the Messianic era, when Jews would return to Eretz Yisrael. Maharal was rabbi in this synagogue, and the golem is supposedly buried under a pile of discarded sacred objects (*sheimos*) in the attic, which for hundreds of years Jews have not entered. Other famous shuls are the Pinkas and Klaus synagogues, both hundreds of years old. The ancient Jewish cemetery has rows of bodies sixteen deep due to the limited burial space, and contains some of the gravesites of Prague's most famous rabbis. The city escaped destruction during World War II, and the Nazis, who planned to establish the Museum of the Extinct Jewish Race in Prague after they destroyed the Jewish people, left the Jewish quarter intact.

OTHER TORAH CENTERS: In the 1500s, Frankfurt, Germany; Salonika, Greece; and Constantinople and Smyrna, Turkey, were all major Torah centers. These cities were heavily populated by Jews and attracted great scholars, who welcomed the challenges of prestigious rabbinical posts. These cities also contained printing presses for the dissemination of Torah works. Other areas of significant Jewish population at the time included Italy, Germany, Holland, and North Africa.

Overall, the 1500s were a time of great change and enormous accomplishment in the Jewish world. It was a century in which the foundation of Jewish life for the next several hundred years was set.

Chapter 16

THE 1600s

GREAT TURMOIL: The 1600s saw great changes in the Jewish world. New Jewish centers sprang up, and Jews spread far and wide. Ashkenazic Jews began to play a dominant role in Torah scholarship, producing great rabbis and educated laymen, while the Sephardic world fell far behind. Jewish demographics also began to shift dramatically in favor of the Ashkenazim. In the twelfth century, it is estimated that Sephardim outnumbered Ashkenazim 15:1 (1.5 million Sephardim to 100,000 Ashkenazim). By 1500, the ratio had dropped to 2:1 (one million Sephardim to 500,000 Ashkenazim), and at the end of the 1600s, Sephardim and Ashkenazim stood even at one million apiece. Afterward, Ashkenazim increased at a spectacular rate, while the Sephardic population remained static.[1] By century's end, too, Jews were rocked by the terror of the Chmielnicki massacres and the trauma of the Shabsai Tzvi messianic movement. In addition, new heresies arose that would have a major damaging effect upon the Jewish people.

AMSTERDAM: After 1581, when Holland declared independence from Spain, many *conversos* left Spain and Portugal, settling in Amsterdam. Enjoying religious tolerance, along with protection of life and property, the Sephardim prospered greatly, engaging in numerous industries, especially diamonds, which Jews virtually dominated. In addition, Jews controlled 25 percent of the famous Dutch East India Company.[2] Sephardic merchants built up a trading empire on a scale previously unimaginable, making important contributions to the development of Holland as a major mercantile center. Jewish traders spread throughout North and South America, Africa, India, and Southeast Asia.[3] However, this great economic success came at the cost of spiritual development. Due to their constant involvement in business, the Sephardim of Amsterdam had no time for Torah study. Merchants who traveled to remote outposts rapidly shed their religious observance, for there was no Jewish community or infrastructure in those places.

JEWISH HERETICS: In Amsterdam, a *converso* named Uriel da Costa publicly preached against basic Jewish beliefs, such as the validity of the Oral Law and immortality of the soul. When he published heretical books, the rabbis of Amsterdam excommunicated him. In 1640, he recanted his views, and, after receiving thirty-nine lashes, was permitted to rejoin the community. Da Costa also had to lie on the threshold of the synagogue, where the congregation stepped over him and spat on his face. Unable to bear the experience, he committed suicide shortly afterward.

BARUCH SPINOZA: This notorious heretic caused untold harm to the Jewish people by teaching a philosophical system that ran completely counter to all that Judaism stands for. Efforts were made to convince Spinoza to stop espousing his poisonous views, but these failed. Consequently, when Spinoza was put on trial by the Jewish council, witnesses testified in his presence that he had no intention of recanting. When in 1655 he published a book denying the Divine origin of the Torah, the rabbis of Amsterdam placed a public *cherem* on him. Such drastic measures are taken only in extreme cases and only with great reluctance, and Spinoza has the dubious distinction of being the last person in Jewish history to be excommunicated in such a spectacular way.

The rabbinic pronouncement reads in part: "Spinoza should be excommunicated and cut off from the nation of Israel. Let him be accursed by day and by night, in his lying down and his rising up, in going out and coming in. May G-d never pardon him, and raze out his name from under the sky. All are admonished that none should converse with him in any manner, do him any service, abide under the same roof with him, or approach within four cubits [6–8 feet] of him."[4]

Today, visitors to the Spanish-Portuguese Synagogue in Amsterdam see Spinoza's name crossed out from a list of the congregation's membership.[5] Sadly, the rabbis realized all too well the terrible spiritual destruction wreaked by Spinoza. As the father of the secular discipline of Biblical Criticism, and his own philosophical system, which are both still studied today, Spinoza led countless Jews away from their heritage.

THE JEWS RETURN TO ENGLAND: Jews were expelled from England in 1290. A small *converso* community settled there in the 1500s, but they could not practice Judaism openly. With the rise of Puritan rule in England in the mid 1600s, an opportunity presented itself for Jews to return. Among other things, Puritans advocated a return to the Tanach, and the Lord Protector of England, Oliver Cromwell, was favorably inclined to the Jewish people as the nation of the Bible. On a more practical level, Cromwell realized that Jewish businessmen in England would help England compete with rival Holland for commercial ascendancy. In light of these issues, a great rabbi in Amsterdam, Rabbi Manasseh ben Israel, petitioned Cromwell to allow Jews back into England. The rabbi told the Bible-loving Puritans that according to Daniel (12:7), the Messianic age would only begin when the Jews are scattered all over the world. As the French name for England is Angleterre, which means the end of the earth, Daniel's prophecy would be fulfilled only when Jews returned to England. Convinced by this argument, Cromwell presented it to Parliament, which initially resisted the measure. However, as the *conversos* already in England were allowed to practice Judaism on an unofficial basis, small numbers of Jews were admitted into England informally. In the 1660 Restoration, when Charles II became King of England, he repaid Jews who had supported him in exile by officially allowing Jews into England. Thereafter, the community expanded rapidly.

THE NEW WORLD: Jews fleeing Spain and Portugal to those countries' colonies in the New World were hunted down by the Inquisition. *Autos-de-fé* took place in Havana, Cuba; Lima, Peru; and Mexico City, Mexico; among other places.[6] However, Jewish communities also sprang up in the area of Brazil that was under benign Dutch rule. In 1654, Portuguese forces defeated the Dutch in Brazil, and the Jews had to scatter. Most of them settled in Caribbean and West Indies islands not under Spanish or Portuguese rule, such as Jamaica, Barbados, and Curacao.

THE JEWS COME TO NEW YORK: In 1654, a shipload of twenty-three Jewish refugees from Brazil arrived in New York, what was then New Amsterdam. The anti-Semitic governor, Peter Stuyvesant, ordered them to leave, saying that he did not wish to admit members of a "deceitful race whose abominable religion worshiped at the feet of Mammon." When letters arrived from the Dutch West India Company authorizing the Jews to stay, Stuyvesant imposed harsh restrictions on them. The Jews were not permitted to build a synagogue, own land, or engage in certain occupations. A special tax was imposed on them for not serving in the militia, to which they were forbidden. Understandably, the Jews appealed to the courts and the government in Holland, and the restrictions were withdrawn. Asher Levy, a prominent merchant, won the right for Jews to serve in the militia like other citizens and had all discriminatory taxes removed. With the British conquest in 1664, the city was renamed New York, and Jews received full and equal rights. A smaller Jewish community opened in 1677 in Newport, Rhode Island. It, like New York, was composed almost entirely of assimilated, Sephardic Jews.

GREAT SAGES OF THE 1600s: In 1622, Rabbi Isaiah Horowitz, having served in numerous prestigious communities in Poland, Germany, and Prague, made *aliyah* to Eretz Yisrael, where he became rabbi of Jerusalem and composed his major work, *Shnei Luchos HaBris*. This treatise is a compendium of the 613 mitzvos, approaching them from both Kabbalistic and ethical angles. It became an immediate favorite, is studied to this day, and has been reprinted many times. Known as the *Shelah HaKadosh*, it is one of only four books given such an accolade of *kadosh* — holiness. (The other three are the *Zohar HaKadosh, Or HaChaim HaKadosh*, and *Alshich HaKadosh*.)[7]

THE TAZ AND THE SHACH: Rabbi David HaLevi, a great Polish scholar, is known as the Taz after his great commentary on *Shulchan Aruch*, called *Turei Zahav*. Rabbi Shabsai HaKohen of Lithuania also wrote a commentary on *Shulchan Aruch*, called *Sifsei Kohen*, and like the Taz he became known as the Shach after the initials of his commentary. Both commentaries are staples in the study of *Yoreh Deah*, the section of *Shulchan Aruch* dealing with laws of kashrus, and an understanding of *Shach* and *Taz* is required in order to receive rabbinic ordination. Taz also wrote a commentary on *Orach Chaim*, and Shach wrote a major one on *Choshen Mishpat*, renowned for its profound scholarship and length.

RABBI YOM TOV LIPMAN HELLER: This distinguished scholar served as rabbi of Prague and other communities. With a life full of suffering and hardship, including numerous occasions when enemies spread slanderous reports about his supposed disloyalty to the government, Rabbi Heller was condemned to death by the king, and only escaped by paying a large ransom and leaving Prague. He is best known for his analytical commentary on the Mishnah, *Tosafos Yom Tov*, printed as a basic commentary in standard editions of the Mishnah. Some editions of the Mishnah have an abridgement of *Tosafos Yom Tov*, known as *Ikkar Tosafos Yom Tov*. Rabbi Heller died in 1654.

THE CHMIELNICKI MASSACRES (1648–49): Chafing under the rule of the Polish nobility, the Ukrainian people's resentment was twofold: they were lowly serfs tied to the land, and their Orthodox Christianity was at variance with the Poles' Roman Catholicism. However, the Ukrainians' anger flared most against the Jews. Jews ran the estates of the nobility, and were charged with collecting taxes from the serfs. These highly unpopular duties aroused enormous hatred of the Jews, the people whom the Ukrainians dealt with directly. Bogdan Chmielnicki, one of the most murderous oppressors of the Jews of all time, led a Cossack and peasant revolt against Polish rule. In one year, 1648–49, hundreds of Jewish communities throughout Eastern Poland and Ukraine were destroyed and their inhabitants massacred. Of those Jews not butchered, many were sold by the Cossacks' Tatar allies into slavery in Mediterranean countries. Those Jews were actually fortunate, for local Jewish communities often redeemed them. After attaining their freedom, some of the Polish Jews settled in nearby countries and became culturally Sephardic.

The unspeakably savage Cossacks subjected the Jews to horrible deaths, their cruelty surpassing anything in Jewish history up to that point. Jews were skinned alive and thrown to the dogs. Pregnant women had their fetuses cut out, and live cats were sown inside their bellies. Children were roasted in front of their parents, who were then forced to eat them.[8] On 20 Sivan, 1648, the 6,000 Jews of Nemirov were slaughtered and drowned. Cossacks desecrated the Torah scrolls by trampling them, then making shoes of them. (Later, the Nazis acted in the same way.) It is estimated that more than 300 communities were destroyed and 100,000 Jews killed.[9] Due to constant battles between the Swedes, Russians, and Poles, further massacres of Jews occurred during the next ten years, with matters not subsiding until 1660. These terrible events became known as *Gezeros Tach Vetat*, the Decrees of 5408 and 5409. (*Tach Vetat* stand for those Jewish years, corresponding to the secular years 1648–49.)

JEWISH REACTION: Whenever possible, Jews resisted physically and were able to save lives. Most of the time, however, there was no effective defense against overwhelmingly superior armed forces, and Jews met their deaths heroically *al kiddush HaShem*. In 1650, the *Vaad Arba Aratzos* enacted several decrees to commemorate the tragedy. The twentieth of Sivan was adopted as a public fast day.[10] Music was forbidden at weddings for a year, wearing fancy clothing for three years, and strict limits were put on the number of guests one was permitted to invite for festive occasions. Ashkenazic Jews tried to understand the Divine reason for the horrors inflicted upon them, the ferocity of which surpassed even the Expulsion from Spain. The renowned sage Rabbi Yom Tov Lipman Heller, author of the Tosafos Yom Tov, felt that the tragedy was Heavenly retribution for the sin of talking in synagogue during prayer services.[11] Regardless of the reason, surviving Jewish communities banded together to cope with the masses of destitute, homeless refugees, while rabbinic authorities dealt with the great number of halachic questions regarding *agunos*, women who were not certain of the whereabouts of their husbands. Many precedents were set in these difficult laws.

SHABSAI TZVI: Not surprisingly, the terrible suffering of the Jewish people heightened messianic aspirations, with the Jews grasping at any idea that might bring an end to their travails. Consequently, the time was ripe for impostors to make messianic claims. As such, the messianic fervor started by Shabsai Tzvi and his followers became the greatest and most pernicious false messianic movement in Jewish history since the time of Bar Kochba.

Born in Turkey in 1626, Shabsai Tzvi claimed to be born on Tishah B'Av, the date of the destruction of both Temples and traditionally believed to be the birthday of the Messiah. At a young age, he displayed great brilliance, and became an accomplished Talmudic and Kabbalistic scholar. Between 1642 and 1648 he lived in semi-seclusion and began to display character traits that psychologists describe as manic-depressive. As Shabsai also exhibited periods of normal behavior, his followers explained his irrational moments as Divine inspiration.

At this time, Shabsai began violating Jewish law, explaining his actions by saying that according to Kabbalah his sins were actually righteous deeds. When reciting blessings, for example, he often pronounced the name of G-d literally, which is forbidden. According to halachah, the Divine Name *yud-kay-vav-kay* must be read *alef-daled-nun-yud*,[12] and one who reads it as written forfeits his portion in the World to Come.[13] Shabsai also ate forbidden fats, *chelev*, claiming that they elevated the Divine sparks embedded in the animal. Because of these actions, the rabbis of Smyrna, his hometown, expelled him in 1654.

After his expulsion, Shabsai visited a number of Jewish communities in the Mediterranean area, his great charisma causing him to attract numerous followers. There, Shabsai further transgressed halachah by celebrating the holidays of Pesach, Shavuos, and Sukkos all in one week, and by coining a new blessing *Mattir Asurim*, praising G-d for permitting what is forbidden. Shabsai also married a Torah scroll under a wedding canopy, with a full nuptial celebration. Expelled once again, he visited Jerusalem, where he attracted further adherents by exhibiting normal behavior and displaying his great scholarship. In 1664, he married Sarah, a woman of ill repute, justifying his behavior by comparing himself to the prophet Hosea, who was commanded by G-d to do something similar.

The Sabbatean messianic movement began in earnest in 1665, when Shabsai Tzvi met Nathan of Gaza, a young scholar and Kabbalist who suffered from delusions. Nathan convinced Shabsai to make Messianic claims, with Nathan adopting the role of Elijah the Prophet, whom Jewish tradition believes to proclaim the arrival of Messiah. This heretical movement unfortunately spread quickly, causing countless Jews in Eretz Yisrael and the Sephardic Mediterranean lands to sell their possessions in anticipation of the triumphant journey to the Holy Land. From the Mediterranean basin, the hysteria spread to Holland and Germany, where assimilated Jews repented, and descendants of *conversos* returned to their Jewish roots. Benedictions for the Messianic King were even recited in many synagogues. In 1666, excitement heightened when Shabsai Tzvi abolished the fast days of 17 Tammuz and Tishah B'Av, declaring them instead to be days of joy. In Turkey, Shabsai also captivated people when he slaughtered the *korban Pesach*, roasted it in its fat, and ate it. These sins, punishable by *kares* (spiritual extinction), were explained as capturing the inner essence of the Torah. Strong, reasonable rabbinic opposition was swept aside in the frenzy, with those showing disbelief in the so-called Messiah hounded and reviled.

One courageous rabbi, the great Rabbi Jacob Sasportas of Amsterdam, fearlessly spoke out against the messianic craze, stating that the true Messiah would not deviate one iota from the Torah and halachah. As such, he published a book, *Tzitzas Novel Tzvi*, refuting all the arguments of the Sabbateans. Although Rabbi Sasportas was largely ignored, and was even forced into exile by the followers of Shabsai Tzvi, Rabbi Sasportas was nevertheless influential in combating the spread of the movement.

From Western Europe the movement swept into the Ashkenazic heartland of Poland and the Ukraine, where the bloodied and battered Jews eagerly embraced the heresy. Even great rabbis were caught up in the atmosphere of anticipation — so much so that by 1666 nearly all of the world's Jews were followers of Shabsai Tzvi.

Concerned by a possible threat to his rule, the Turkish sultan arrested Shabsai in February 1666. However, Shabsai was placed in comfortable surroundings and permitted to receive visitors. In September, having heard that Shabsai wanted to depose him, the sultan offered him the choice between conversion to Islam or death. Renouncing Judaism, Shabsai took the name Aziz Mehmed Effendi. The sultan gave him a pension and eventually sent him to Albania, where Shabsai died in 1676.

THE AFTEREFFECTS: Their deepest hopes cruelly dashed, Jews everywhere reacted to the news of Shabsai's apostasy with shock and disbelief. Nathan tried to explain that Shabsai's seeming conversion was all part of the messianic plan, but this outright lie was not believed. Many Jews retreated within themselves, finding solace in the eternal truths of the Torah. Others turned away from Judaism, discarding their Torah observance. Fearing a backlash from the government, rabbis, especially in Turkey, forswore any previous support of the campaign. In religious life, a movement against the study of Kabbalah began to take hold. Nevertheless, spinoff Sabbatean messianic movements appeared from time to time, although none had the effect of the original craze.

YIDDISH: Although the origins of the Yiddish language are unclear, it may have originated about 1,000 years ago.[14] The first Jews to speak Yiddish were the Ashkenazim of France and Germany. As such, Ashkenazic Jews adapted words from French and German into a new usage, Yiddish, which became sanctified through being used exclusively by Jews.[15] (Sephardim developed their own special language, Ladino, based on Spanish, which also possesses sanctity.) By the 1600s, use of Yiddish had expanded greatly, being the language of Eastern European Jews, who generally did not speak Polish, Lithuanian, Russian, or Ukrainian. At the time, Torah study, sermons, and everyday conversations took place in Yiddish, while *Lashon HaKodesh*, the holy language of biblical Hebrew, was reserved for prayer and writing scholarly works. Yiddish was especially employed in popular books for people not familiar with Hebrew. The most famous of these was the *Tzena Urena*, written for women, discussing the weekly Torah portion and related laws. A number of popular prayers for women, known as *techinos*, also were written in Yiddish. Yiddish names for children became widespread, especially for girls.

As Western European Jews assimilated, they stopped speaking Yiddish, and the language became the exclusive province of Eastern European Jews, who developed their own Yiddish dialects. In all, roughly 85 percent of Yiddish words are of German extraction, 10 percent originate from Hebrew, and 5 percent come from such Slavic languages as Polish.[16] Two major dialects of Yiddish developed, which still exist today — the northeastern European Jews of Lithuania, northern Poland, and Belarus spoke one version, while the southeastern Jews of southern Poland, the Ukraine, Romania,

Word	Northern	Southern
Reuvain (a name)	ROO-VAIN	REE-VIN
Sefer (book)	SAY-FER	SI (long I) -FER
Numen (name)	NU (as in up)-MEN	NOO-MEN
Mehl (flour)	MEHL	MAIL
Broit (bread)	BRAIT (as in braid)	BROIT (as in broil)

and Hungary, who comprised the majority of Yiddish speakers, utilized another dialect. See the chart for some examples of differences in pronunciation between southerners and northerners (these differences also affect spoken Hebrew).

JEWISH LAST NAMES: During biblical and Talmudic times, Jews did not have last names. In the 1200s and 1300s, names began to make a frequent appearance among Sephardic Jews, and by the late 1400s Jews in Italy began adopting last names to facilitate commerce. By the 1600s, German surnames were widespread in the Ashkenazic world. At that time, Jews were permitted to choose their last names, and their origins are quite fascinating. Sources for last names include acronyms. The name Sachs, for example, comes from *Zera Kedoshim Shmo* — child of holy martyrs.[17] There are descriptive names, too: Gelbard, for example, means yellow beard. Place names, too, were used — Epstein, Bachrach, Leipzig, Berliner, Breslau, and so on. House signs became names as well. In the Frankfurt Ghetto, for example, the name Rothschild came from the red shield displayed on the family's house.[18] Occupations were names, as well. Becker, for example, means a baker; Farber a dyer. Names honored a woman, too, such as Pearlman and Estrin, or remembered a father, like Jacobson, Davidowitz. A *kohen* took the name Cohen or Katz, while a Levite would adopt Segal or Levin. Later, in Germany, authorities gave surnames to Jews, and bribes were offered to the naming officials so as not to impose bad names upon them. Capricious bureaucrats sometimes saddled Jews with derogatory last names, such as Eselkopf, a donkey's head, Taschengrieger, a pickpocket, and Galgenstrick, a gallows rope. In many towns in Hungary, Jews were assembled in the town square, divided into four groups, and given the names Weiss, Schwartz, Gross, and Klein, white, black, big, and little, respectively.[19]

Chapter 17

THE 1700s

GREAT **CHANGES**: The 1700s, particularly the second half of the century, saw far-reaching changes in Jewish life. Most important, there was a veritable explosion in both the number of Torah scholars and the quality of their scholarship, previously so grievously affected by the Chmielnicki ravages. New movements and ideas, both adhering to Jewish tradition and deviating from it, arose and developed. For the first time in hundreds of years, a large number of Jews began to fulfill the ancient yearning to live in the Land of Israel. Great controversies erupted, some involving the greatest rabbis of the times. In the world at large, this, too, was a time of great upheaval. The American and French Revolutions, and the Age of Enlightenment, forever changed the face of European society — and also had an enormous influence on the Jewish world as well. The famous Yiddish saying, "As the Gentile world goes, so, too, does the Jewish one," was fully realized.

THE *ALIYAH* OF RABBI YEHUDA HACHASID: In 1700, the great scholar and tzadik Rabbi Yehuda HaChasid set out from Poland with thirty families to settle in Eretz Yisrael. Along the way, many people were inspired to join, swelling the number of hopeful *olim* to 1,500. However, in accordance with the Talmudic statement that Eretz Yisrael can only be acquired with suffering, they encountered many problems.[1] First, 500 of the travelers died from the hardships of the journey, never reaching the shores of the Holy Land. Within a week of arriving in Eretz Yisrael, the seemingly indefatigable Rabbi Yehuda HaChasid suddenly passed away, leaving the Ashkenazic community leaderless. Rampant poverty and the difficulty of earning a living then caused a number of people to return to Europe. In addition, Polish Jews were unfamiliar with the Sephardic and Arab culture of the region, making it difficult to do business and form relationships. The climate of Eretz Yisrael, too, in which rain does not fall for six months, plus frequent droughts and epidemics, were conditions to which the European Jews had extreme difficulty adapting.

Eventually, the Ashkenazic community of Jerusalem fell deeper and deeper into debt to rapacious Arab landowners. When, in 1720, the Ashkenazim were unable to repay the astronomical sums owed, the Arabs destroyed the Old City synagogue of Rabbi Yehuda HaChasid. At that time, Ashkenazic Jews were either imprisoned or fled the city, and the Arabs forbade Ashkenazic Jews from living in Jerusalem, a ban that was in effect for 100 years. The destroyed synagogue is a famous landmark in the Jewish Quarter today. An arch was built over the site, and it is known as the Churvah Shul.

RABBINIC CONTROVERSIES: Aside from the great dispute between the Chassidim and the Misnagdim to follow, there were three major rabbinic controversies. First, Rabbi Yaakov Emden versus Rabbi Yonoson Eybeschutz. Second, Rabbi Yaakov Emden versus Rabbi Moshe Chaim Luzzatto (Ramchal). Third, the *get* of Cleves. Scholars on each side of these controversies acted out of pure motives, feeling that what they did was for the sake of the Jewish people. However, as happens so often in these kinds of matters, lesser people became involved, some wanting personal gain and others seeking a fight, and things ballooned out of control.

RABBI YAAKOV EMDEN VERSUS RABBI YONOSON EYBESCHUTZ: It is important to realize the atmosphere of the time in which this dispute took place. After the debacle of Shabsai Tzvi, the study of Kabbalah was deeply frowned upon, for it was Shabsai Tzvi's expertise in this area that led people astray. As a result, anyone engaging in this discipline faced much suspicion and hostility. Rabbi Yaakov Emden, a great scholar, was especially vigilant in combating any perceived Sabbatean influences.

In 1750, a prodigious, world-recognized scholar, Rabbi

Yonoson Eybeschutz, accepted the rabbinate of the major German cities of Altona, Hamburg, and Wandsbeck. While there, he wrote amulets for sick people containing Kabbalistic formulae that were supposed to advance a patient's health. Rabbi Yaakov Emden obtained one of these amulets and claimed that if certain letters were transposed, it would read "In the name of G-d and His Messiah Shabsai Tzvi." A great controversy ensued, with many prominent rabbis taking sides. Eventually, unscrupulous people entered the fray, even involving the ruler of the area in the dispute. Rabbi Yonoson was forced to vacate his rabbinical post and suffered much persecution. The matter finally ended when Rabbi Yonoson died in 1764, and Rabbi Yaakov passed away in 1776. Since then, Jews have viewed both of the disputants as being motivated solely for the honor of G-d, with no right or wrong in this issue.

RABBI YAAKOV EMDEN VERSUS RABBI MOSHE CHAIM LUZZATTO (RAMCHAL): Rabbi Luzzatto was born in Italy, and at a young age became a great Torah scholar. A great Kabbalist, his profound insights attracted selected disciples. Due to the great fear of a recurrence of Sabbateanism, Rabbi Luzzatto fell under suspicion. Forced to stop teaching Kabbalah and leave his native Italy, Rabbi Luzzatto moved to Amsterdam, where he continued studying Kabbalah. Rabbi Yaakov Emden vehemently attacked him for this study, and Ramchal immigrated to Eretz Yisrael, where he died in 1747 at age forty.

In his brief lifetime, Ramchal published many great works, including the Mussar classic *Mesillas Yesharim*, a step-by-step guide to reach the highest levels of saintliness. The primary book for the study of Mussar, time has not dulled its message. After its publication, the Vilna Gaon stated that if the author were alive, the Gaon would have traveled on foot to meet him. The Gaon himself paid a hefty sum for a copy of the *sefer*, and reviewed it many times.[2] Among Ramchal's other philosophical and Kabbalistic works are *Derech HaShem, Daas Tevunos,* and *Kalach Pischei Chochmah*, all of which are highly popular today. A famous theme of Ramchal, which runs throughout his *sefarim*, is that the purpose of creation is for G-d to do the greatest good to the beings He made.[3]

THE *GET* OF CLEVES: In 1766, a great controversy regarding a *get* took place, involving some of the greatest rabbis of the time. (Interestingly, the Vilna Gaon did not voice his opinion.) Fortunately, others did not intervene in the quarrel, so it was conducted in a civil manner.

A young couple married on a Thursday, and on the Sabbath the husband fled, taking his entire dowry. He was found the next day and rationalized his strange behavior by saying that he was seized by an inexplicable fear. Several days later, he demanded to divorce his wife, saying he had to flee the country because his life was in danger. The rabbinical court of Cleves, Germany granted the divorce, whereupon the man sailed to England. When the strange story spread, numerous rabbis considered the *get* invalid, because the husband's bizarre behavior qualified him as a *shoteh*, a mentally incompetent individual who may not divorce his wife. Other rabbis disagreed, saying that the husband's actions did not categorize him as a *shoteh*.[4] Ultimately, the validity of the *get* was upheld, but as a result of the extensive scholarly discussion regarding the case, there was much clarification regarding what behaviors cause a person to be considered a *shoteh*, a matter of great relevance today.

GREAT SCHOLARS OF THE 1700S: Rabbi Chaim ben Attar, known as the Ohr HaChaim HaKadosh, was born in Morocco. As indicated by his title, he was a great scholar and tzadik, and many miracles were attributed to him. Immigrating to Eretz Yisrael, he eventually settled in Jerusalem. Although he was Sephardic, he inspired Ashkenazic settlement in Jerusalem. Rabbi Chaim's most famous *sefer, Ohr HaChaim* on *Chumash*, has achieved universal popularity. He is buried in Jerusalem, and his tomb is known as a site where prayers are answered.

Rabbi Tzvi ben Yaakov Ashkenazi was born in the Czech Republic. Moving to Salonika, he became known by the Sephardic title Chacham Tzvi. However, he kept the name Ashkenazi to reflect his Ashkenazic origins. Rabbi Tzvi is the author of *Shaalos Uteshuvos Chacham Tzvi*, one of the basic works of responsa. His son was the famous Rabbi Yaakov Emden.

Rabbi Yaakov Yehoshua Falk wrote the commentary *Pnei Yehoshua* on many Talmudic tractates. When he was young, a tragic explosion killed his wife and daughter, and buried him under the rubble of a collapsed house. Rabbi Yaakov vowed that if he escaped, he would devote his life to writing an in-depth commentary on the Talmud. Miraculously, he found an opening through the debris and survived. The *Pnei Yehoshua*, according to its author's testimony, was a product of great exertion in Torah study in fulfillment of the promise. It is regarded as a basic Talmudic commentary, and is studied in yeshivos worldwide.

Rabbi Aryeh Leib Ginzburg is the author of *Shaagas Aryeh* on part of the first section of *Orach Chaim*. This work is immensely popular, and its section on the laws of tefillin is the basis for many a bar mitzvah boy's *pshetel*, a customary Torah discourse delivered on the occasion.

Rabbi Aryeh Leib HaKohen Heller wrote the monumental *Ketzos HaChoshen* on *Choshen Mishpat*, the section of *Shulchan Aruch* dealing with monetary laws. In contrast to the *pilpul* style of learning that was popular then in Poland, which emphasized sharp, often fanciful comparisons between Talmudic texts, the *Ketzos HaChoshen* is a paradigm of straightforward logic.[5] It clearly delineates the essential principles of Talmudic topics, shedding light on many seemingly contradictory laws and disparate passages. Although its author was not from Lithuania, *Ketzos HaChoshen* became the quintessential *sefer* of the *Litvishe derech*, Talmudic study employed in the great Lithuanian yeshivos. The *sefer* retains its premier status today.

Other works by the same author include *Avnei Miluim* on *Even HaEzer*, the section of *Shulchan Aruch* that discusses marriage and divorce, and *Shev Shmaatsa*, a rigorous, all-encompassing analysis of seven major Talmudic topics. Both these *sefarim* are also basic staples of the yeshivah curriculum. All of this material was produced under the most extreme conditions. Rabbi Aryeh Leib was so poor that the table in his house consisted of a wide board supported by barrels, and during the cold winter months he had to write under a pillow to prevent the ink from freezing.[6]

Rabbi Yecheskel Landau was a rabbi in a number of cities, notably Prague. His encyclopedic *Shaalos Uteshuvos Noda B'Yehudah* is a masterpiece of this genre, and his decisions set precedents in many halachic areas, particularly complicated laws of *agunos*, women whose husbands have disappeared.

In addition, Rabbi Yecheskel made numerous decrees to curb conspicuous consumption and displays of wealth, both prevalent at the time. As chief rabbi, Rabbi Yecheskel had the power to enact such decrees and enforce them, a situation which clearly does not exist today. At bar mitzvahs, he said, only ten men could be invited, besides the family and out-of-town guests. Beef, duck, or chicken could be served, but not two such dishes together. No fancy desserts were allowed, either. For weddings, no more than four musicians might play, and but fifteen men and six women, besides close relatives, could attend the banquet. If one paid a large sum for communal taxes, he might serve whatever food he desired, but he had to use simple dishes. Women could not leave the ghetto wearing ostentatious clothing.[7]

RABBI ELIYAHU KRAMER — THE GAON OF VILNA (GRA) (1720–1797):

A faint glimpse of the Gaon's unparalleled greatness may be seen in some of the statements of both his contemporaries and succeeding generations of scholars: "Great among giants." "Since the times of the Rabanan Savoroi and the Gaonim [1,000 years earlier], no man of such all-encompassing greatness has arisen." "There are unique individuals in every era, but not in every field of wisdom. However, to be so elevated that one is unique in every field, unique in knowledge of the revealed Torah, the hidden Torah, in piety, holiness, and purity, in the attainment of the very highest levels, in every area of intellect and wisdom, in mathematics, grammar, algebra, etc., such wondrous excellence was impossible even for the greatest men of earlier generations. Only our great teacher merited such a level!"[8]

The great *rosh yeshivah*, Rabbi Aharon Kotler, founder of the Lakewood Yeshiva, said that it is beyond human ability to fathom the Gaon's greatness.[9] The Chazon Ish wrote: "We regard the Gaon as being in the line of Torah transmission of Moshe, Ezra, Rabbi Judah HaNasi, Rav Ashi, Rambam, and the Gaon, through whom Torah was revealed. He shed light on matters that had never been illuminated before, and is considered as one of the Rishonim."[10] Of all scholars, Gra alone is given the title "the Gaon."

The events of the Gra's life are well known. At the age of three, he already knew the entire *Chumash* by heart. At seven, he gave an original, complex Talmudic lesson in the main synagogue of Vilna. He began studying Kabbalah when he was eight, and mastered Tanach and Talmud with their most difficult commentaries. At eleven he undertook to finish the entire Talmud by the morning of Simchas Torah. By nightfall of the holiday, he still had two of the hardest tractates left — *Zevachim* and *Menachos*, a total of 230 pages. Eliyahu studied them that night, and to the disbelief of a great scholar who was watching, was able to take a rigorous oral examination on the material, answering all questions perfectly.

The Gaon's piety matched his incomparable intellectual abilities. Sleeping four half-hour periods daily, his lips murmured words of Torah even then. His diet consisted of two olive-sized pieces of dry bread soaked in water, in the morning and at night. (The Gaon discouraged his disciples from following such a regimen, saying that he was able to do it only because he had a strong constitution.) Every Yom Kippur, he repented for the amount of time that — in his estimation — he wasted not studying Torah. The total came to three hours annually, or 30 seconds per day.

The Gaon also emphasized straightforward logic in his learning. Devoting great effort to establishing correct versions of many *sefarim* of previous generations, he corrected copying errors that had crept in over the years. As the leading Kabbalist of his generation, he also authored many works of Kabbalah, and revealed many matters previously unknown. In all, such acts would have been questioned were they performed by any other person, but the Gaon's lifestyle and studying preferences were not disputed, for everyone knew that he was in a category of his own, personifying the greatness of Torah.

At roughly forty, the Gaon stopped writing his Torah thoughts and began cultivating select disciples, including students of Kabbalah. At the Gaon's request, Rabbi Chaim of Volozhin, the greatest of the Gaon's students, established the first modern yeshivah. As such, the Gaon is seen as the father of the Yeshivah Movement, and the tradition of Lithuanian Torah scholarship traces to him. In 1797, at the age of seventy-seven, the Gaon passed away. In his final moments, he clutched his tzitzis and tearfully remarked that he was saddened to leave a world where a mitzvah such as tzitzis could be performed so easily. He also regretted not being able to impart much of his wisdom to his students.

THE RISE OF THE CHASSIDIC MOVEMENT: After the debacle of Shabsai Tzvi, the Jewish people were at a low ebb. Scholars were able to find comfort in Torah, but the masses of unlettered Jews felt spiritually adrift. G-d, in His great kindness, provided the Jewish people with the means to revitalize their lives. Chassidus, a new movement, took age-old Jewish traditions and presented them in a novel way. Although greatly opposed in its formative years, Chassidus proved to be a force that rejuvenated the Jewish people and ultimately preserved the majority of Eastern European Jews from the ravages of assimilation. Chassidus fortified the Jewish people both on external and internal levels. Externally, chassidic emphasis on beards, *peyos* (ear locks), and distinctive Jewish dress helped reduce the attractiveness of the outside world. Internally, the profound teachings of Chassidus inspired individual Jews, making them realize that they were important and part of something noble, and their joyous performance of mitzvos infused daily life with great meaning.

RABBI ISRAEL BAAL SHEM TOV: The founder of Chassidus, known as the Besht, is shrouded in legend and mystery. Born either in 1698 or 1700 in Okup, Ukraine, he was orphaned at a very young age. As a youth, he went alone on excursions into the fields, woods, and mountains, communing with G-d. Soon, the Besht became proficient in Kabbalah, but concealed his scholarship for many years. At the age of thirty-six, the Besht revealed himself as a spiritual leader, quickly becoming famous as a great tzadik and performer of miracles. Although the Besht did not write his teachings, his disciples published them after his death.

His major principles of Chassidus are that a Jew should attempt to feel close to G-d (*deveykus*) in all his actions, even the most mundane. Prayer and mitzvos should be done with fiery enthusiasm and joy, which is superior to fasting and self-affliction. G-d is good; therefore, even things that may appear to be evil contain a spark of holiness. Even the simplest Jew's deeds, if performed with sincerity, equal those of the greatest scholars. The importance of a tzadik, or rebbe, is central — one who serves as the conduit to bring G-d's closeness to those unable to achieve it on their own. A person should view himself as having no importance, only existing to serve the Creator and fulfill His mission on earth. These profound ideas, so basic to Judaism today, spread rapidly through the Jewish people, attracting not only the masses but also even some of the greatest scholars of the time. However, some scholars became bitterly opposed to the new movement, fearing a resumption of Sabbateanism. The Besht passed away in 1760.

THE MAGGID OF MEZERITCH: Rabbi Dov Ber of Mezeritch, the Besht's chief disciple and successor, was the man most responsible for the development of Chassidus into a major force. Before he was involved in Chassidus, Rabbi Dov Ber was one of the major scholars of his times, both a great tzadik and Kabbalist. Although virtually any rabbinical post could have been his, he chose to be a *maggid*, a traveling preacher, going from town to town inspiring Jews to better their ways. Eventually, he became lame and was unable to walk. Although Rabbi Dov Ber was reluctant at first, he was convinced to go to the Baal Shem Tov for a cure. Upon meeting the Besht, Rabbi Dov Ber was inspired by his greatness to stay in Mezhibuzh, the Besht's town, and became his leading disciple.

Realizing that Chassidus could be spread most effectively if he could attract great scholars, the Maggid worked for a twelve-year period — from 1760, when he succeeded the Besht, until 1772, when he passed away — training some of the generation's leading sages in the ways of Chassidus. In turn, each individual spread Chassidus to many, each becoming the forerunner of a chassidic court. Some of the Maggid's more famous disciples were Rabbi Yaakov Yosef, Rabbi Aaron of Karlin (Stolin), Rabbi Elimelech of Lizhensk, the Chozeh of Lublin, the Kozhnitzer Maggid, the Maggid of Chernobyl, Rabbi Levi Yitzchak of Berdichev, Rabbi Shmelke of Nikolsburg, the Apter rebbe, and Rabbi Schneur Zalman of Liadi, the first rebbe of Chabad-Lubavitch. Within a short time, much of Eastern Europe came under the influence of the Maggid of Mezeritch.

Rabbi Yaakov Yosef was the senior disciple of the Besht, although he did not inherit the mantle of leadership. In 1780, he published *Toldos Yaakov Yosef*, which was the first written record of the Besht's teachings. The book was largely responsible for spreading the message of Chassidus.

Rabbi Elimelech of Lizhensk, the famed Rebbe Reb Meilach, was the catalyst for the spread of Chassidus throughout Poland and Hungary, and his disciples were the forerunners of the great chassidic dynasties of those lands. Together with his famous brother Rabbi Zushe, they became students of the Maggid of Mezeritch, spending three years in self-imposed exile to purify themselves. (This was once a common practice of greatly righteous men. The incognito, rootless wandering from place to place removed all possible self-conceit and refined their characters.) Traveling from village to village, they spread the ideals of Chassidus. Rabbi Elimelech is buried in Lizhensk, Poland; his tomb is a center for pilgrimages.

Rabbi Levi Yitzchak, the Berdichever, is known as the de facto defense attorney of the Jewish people for his impassioned entreaties to G-d to overlook the Jews' sins and see only their good. A famous story typifies this attitude: Once, a wagon driver was greasing his wagon while saying his morning prayers and wearing his tefillin. When the shocked people criticized this outlandish behavior, Rabbi Levi Yitzchak remarked, "G-d! Look at your great people! Even when engaged in such mundane activities, a Jew still prays to You!"[11]

The Chozeh of Lublin, Rabbi Yaakov Yitzchak Horowitz, was a disciple of both the Maggid and Rabbi Elimelech. Called the Chozeh, or Seer, because he was able to gaze into the depths of a person's soul, during his lifetime almost all of Poland was brought under the umbrella of Chassidus, becoming the world's largest chassidic center until the Nazis destroyed its Jews.[12]

Rabbi Nachman of Breslov had a unique distinction among chassidic leaders — he was a direct descendant, a great-grandson, of the Besht. He and his Chassidim became very controversial within the Chassidic movement itself, having both bitter detractors and ardent supporters. When Rabbi Nachman died in 1810, his followers did not appoint a successor, thereby becoming known as the so-called dead Chassidim. However, Breslover Chassidus is alive and vibrant today, particularly in Israel, and Rabbi Nachman's major work *Likutei Moharan* remains very popular. His gravesite in Uman, Ukraine, attracts thousands of Jews, particularly on Rosh HaShanah.

Rabbi Avraham Yehoshua Heschel, the Apter rebbe, was one of the most important figures of the Chassidic movement. His greatness was so recognized that he was able to establish his court in Mezhibuzh, the town where the Besht galvanized people to Chassidus. The Apter rebbe, known for his complete love and devotion to the Jewish people, tirelessly sought to combat both anti-Semitic decrees and assimilation. Before his death, he instructed his children to write on his gravestone only "He loved Jews." The Apter rebbe is buried next to the Besht.

RABBI SCHNEUR ZALMAN OF LIADI (1745–1812): Known as *der alter Rebbe*, Rabbi Schneur Zalman was the founder of Chabad Chassidus. (Chabad is an acronym for **Chochmah, Binah, Daas,** which means Wisdom, Understanding, and Knowledge.) Rabbi Schneur attempted to establish a systematic, intellectual base for Chassidus, interweaving the teachings of the Besht and the Maggid with those of the earlier scholars and Kabbalists such as Arizal. He eventually became the leading chassidic figure in Russia.

A scholar of enormous proportions, at thirty Rabbi Schneur had already studied the entire Talmud in depth, with all the commentaries of the Rishonim and Acharonim, a full sixteen times. Constantly studying Torah day and night, he stood in order to keep awake.[13] As a young man, Rabbi Schneur became attracted to the chassidic path of the Maggid of Mezeritch, and eventually became a major disciple.

In 1770, the Maggid gave Rabbi Schneur the task of re-editing the *Shulchan Aruch*, as many new decisions had been rendered since Rabbi Joseph Karo's original 200 years before. In addition, the original version of *Shulchan Aruch* had become too difficult for the average person to consult. Rabbi Schneur's new edition, known as the *Rav Shulchan Aruch*, addressed both these problems, became recognized as a major contribution to halachah by all Jews, and is still considered the final halachic authority among Chassidim.

Despite these great contributions, Rabbi Schneur's magnum opus is the *Tanya*, in which he laid down the principles of Chabad Chassidus. After twenty years, the work was published in 1796, and immediately made a profound impression in the chassidic world. Reaction among Lithuanian Chassidim was especially favorable, due to the fact that its author was a great Lithuanian scholar, and that the *Tanya* appealed to the intellect of the Lithuanians, generally higher than that of other Eastern European Jews.[14] However, other Chassidim felt that the Kabbalistic concepts revealed in the *Tanya* would be harmful to simple, unscholarly Jews.[15] The controversy threatened to split the chassidic world in two, with permanent damage only averted due to Rabbi Levi of Berdichev and Rabbi Nachman of Breslov mediating the dispute. Since then, through the efforts of Chabad Chassidim, the *Tanya* has been printed countless times in many languages.

Rabbi Schneur also published a new prayer book based on the traditions of Arizal. Combining elements of both *Nusach Sefard* and *Nusach Ashkenaz*, the siddur uses *Nusach Ari* and has become standard in Chabad Chassidus. Accompanying the siddur is a commentary based on the teachings of Kabbalah and Chassidus. Rabbi Schneur also left a number of other important works.

THE CONFLICT BETWEEN CHASSIDUS AND ITS OPPONENTS (MISNAGDIM): In order to understand the intensity of this conflict, it is important to remember that the specter of Shabsai Tzvi still cast a long shadow over the Jewish people. In the mid 1700s, when Jacob Frank claimed to be a reincarnation of Shabsai Tzvi and founded the Frankist movement, there was a recurrence of Sabbateanism in Eastern Europe. Although its membership was limited to several hundred, the Frankists still caused great harm to the Jewish people. In the city of Kamenitz, for example, they told church leaders that the Talmud contained blasphemies. The result was that the Talmud was publicly burned, a chilling reenactment of the Middle Ages. Eventually, Jacob Frank and his followers converted to Christianity, parallel to Shabsai Tzvi's conversion to Islam.[16] As a result, the study of Kabbalah became even more suspect, and great hostility was shown to those who did not follow accepted thinking. In addition, rabble-rousers became involved in this dispute, leading to a far more tragic spread of the conflict than the disputants had envisioned.

By 1771, Chassidus had developed into a dynamic force. During that winter, there was a severe epidemic in Vilna that took the lives of several hundred young children. The ensuing soul-searching for a Divine reason for the tragedy focused on the Chassidim, whose different practices, it was felt by some, were the cause of the fearsome Heavenly retribution.[17] Led by the Vilna Gaon, the chief opponent of the Chassidic movement, chassidic works were publicly burned, and some of its members were forced to renounce their beliefs. Shortly after, a ban was placed on all Chassidim. The Misnagdim based their actions on five claims:

First, the Chassidim were seen as separating from the community. The Chassidim established separate houses of worship, known as *shtieblach*, rather than praying at community synagogues. In an age when small, independent houses of worship were not the norm, such behavior was seen as creating a schism among Jews, possibly leading to a recurrence of Shabsai Tzvi.

Second, the Chassidim were accused of improper behavior at prayer. Misnagdim scorned and ridiculed chassidic prayer. Chassidim were taken to task for frivolous actions during prayer, such as jumping, fervent dancing, and even somersaulting! In actuality, only a small minority of Chassidim were involved in such excessive displays.[18] In addition, the Chassidim were also accused of interrupting the prayer service with chants at points where halachah forbade such actions. Also cited by the Misnagdim was the chassidic disregard for the established times of prayer, and the change from the traditional *Nusach Ashkenaz* to *Nusach Ari*.

Third, the Chassidim were accused of having Sabbatean tendencies. To the Misnagdim, the chassidic view of the tzadik or rebbe smacked of Shabsai Tzvi. In Chassidus, the tzadik presumed to have extraordinary powers, including being the link between the ordinary Jew and G-d, and being able to perform supernatural feats. Misnagdim saw this not only as detracting from the primacy of Torah scholarship and halachah, but also leading to charismatic hero worship. In actuality, virtually all the chassidic leaders of the time were tzaddikim as well as Torah scholars of the highest magnitude.

Fourth, the Chassidim were accused of having misplaced priorities. Chassidim were faulted for stressing prayer and joyous ritual at the expense of Torah study, which is the greatest of all mitzvos. Consequently, simple devotion of unlearned people was placed on a par with the learning of the greatest scholars. Misnagdim also felt that Chassidim put too much emphasis on the study of Kabbalistic texts, such as the *Zohar*, and neglected more traditional Talmudic learning.

Fifth, the Chassidim were accused of general improprieties. Chassidim were said to act strangely in public, partaking of excessive liquor and tobacco during their frequent parties. It was also claimed that numerous violations of Torah law occurred at chassidic get-togethers. Unfortunately, the dread of Shabsai Tzvi was so powerful that rumors and allegations of anything considered out of the norm were magnified out of all proportion. In such an atmosphere, dialogue became impossible.

BANS AND COUNTERBANS: In 1772, the Misnagdim of Vilna and other communities placed a ban — signed by the Vilna Gaon — on the Chassidim. All the above accusations were brought up, and Misnagdim were told to excommunicate them. A further ban that year rendered meat slaughtered by Chassidim not kosher. Against the wishes of the Maggid of Mezeritch, the Chassidim responded with a ban of their own against the Misnagdim. In 1775, Rabbi Schneur Zalman and Rabbi Menachem Mendel of Vitebsk, the two foremost chassidic scholars of that time, traveled to Vilna in an attempt to meet with the Gaon and explain to him that Chassidus was a legitimate expression of Judaism. However, for reasons never made public, the Gaon refused to meet with them. Over the next several years, things quieted down, and gradually the Chassidic movement gained many new adherents.

THE SPLIT WIDENS: In 1780, the chassidic treatise *Toldos Yaakov Yosef* was published. Feeling greatly threatened, Misnagdim reacted swiftly and furiously. The book was publicly burned, and all the previous bans were reiterated. As the Chassidic movement grew, its opposition intensified. New bans prohibiting anyone from sheltering Chassidim, and other restrictions, were promulgated in 1786 and repeated over the next ten years. In 1797, when the Vilna Gaon passed away during Sukkos, some Chassidim in Vilna gathered privately for the traditional *simchas beis hashoeva* celebration. Misnagdim believed that the festivities were greater than usual in order to mark the Gaon's death,[19] while the Chassidim claimed that they were unaware of the Gaon's passing.[20] In the superheated climate, violence broke out. After the burial of the Gaon, some of his followers undertook to avenge the master's honor. Edicts were read in Vilna's synagogues proclaiming that Chassidim were not part of the Jewish people, and that the Gaon had lamented before his death that the battle had not yet been won.

THE RUSSIANS INTERVENE: Up to that point, the conflict was confined to the Jewish community. However, a new and dangerous element became involved: the czarist government. (Considerable controversy exists as to who caused the government to meddle into the affair; there continues to be much disagreement on this issue.) Reports submitted to the Russian government accused Rabbi Schneur Zalman of illegally sending funds to Eretz Yisrael, then controlled by Russia's archenemy Turkey, and of being the leader of the Chassidic movement, seen as a threat to the czarist regime. The czar's officers arrested Rabbi Schneur Zalman, holding him in prison for fifty-three days. On the nineteenth of Kislev of 1798, Rabbi Schneur Zalman was found innocent of both charges and released. Chabad Chassidim continue to celebrate this day with much festivity. Rabbi Schneur Zalman was arrested once more, in 1800, but was quickly freed. Gradually, matters settled down, as both sides realized that they had a common interest in ameliorating the anti-Semitic decrees of the czar, which badly threatened the Jewish people.

THE PALE OF SETTLEMENT: In 1772, Poland was partitioned between Russia, Austria, and Prussia, eventually disappearing as an independent nation. Russia, which had a longstanding policy of prohibiting Jewish settlement, suddenly acquired vast numbers of Jews. Anxious to prevent Jewish expansion into Russia, the czar restricted Jews to the areas between the Baltic and the Black Seas, essentially the western part of the empire. Certain classes of Jews deemed useful to the regime, such as medical professionals, were exempted from the decree, and in many instances Jews were able to bribe capricious government officials for residency permits. However, the vast majority of Jews in the Russian Empire were crammed into the Pale of Settlement, which held a majority of the Jewish people into the twentieth century.

JEWS IN AMERICA: By 1700, there were roughly 300 Jews in America; this number grew to 2,500 by the American Revolution of 1776. Up to 1720, the Jews were exclusively of Spanish and Portuguese descent; afterward, Ashkenazim from Central and Eastern Europe arrived. The Jews settled in New York City, Philadelphia, Charleston, Savannah, and Newport.[21] The first synagogue, New York's Shearith Israel, was built in 1728.[22] Philadelphia's Mikveh Israel, the oldest continuous Jewish service in America, was established in 1740.[23] Touro Synagogue, in Newport, was built in 1764, and is the oldest synagogue in the United States. It has been designated a National Historic Landmark by the United States government and is still currently in use.

The new American Jews had no Torah learning and eventually assimilated. A few learned individuals did exist, most notably Rabbi

Raphael Karigal. Born in Eretz Yisrael, his travels brought him to Newport, Philadelphia, and New York, and he acted as an unofficial rabbi in all three places. Gershom Mendes Seixes, born in New York in 1745, also served a number of communities, including performing many ritual circumcisions. He was one of the invited clergy at the inauguration of President George Washington in 1789.[24]

During the Revolution, Jews served on both the American and British sides, although the majority of Jews favored independence. Haim Solomon of Philadelphia, deputy treasurer of the United States, bankrupted himself paying the republic's bills and died a pauper. (Recently, his descendants sued the United States for principal and interest over a 200-year period, claiming that the money was a loan. However, the United States court ruled that since Haim Solomon gave a gift, no payment was due.)

CHASSIDIC *ALIYAH* TO ERETZ YISRAEL: In 1757, the Besht's brother-in-law, Rabbi Avraham Gershon Kitover, emigrated from Poland to Eretz Yisrael, settling in the city of Hebron. (At that time, Ashkenazic Jews were not able to dwell in Jerusalem.) The only Ashkenazic Jew in Hebron, upon visiting Jerusalem he wept when he saw the churches and the mosques. While reciting *Kinnos* on Tishah B'Av, he fainted several times. In the 1770s, the small trickle of Chassidim moving to Eretz Yisrael turned into a large tide. (Rabbi Schneur Zalman was the first major figure to set out for Eretz Yisrael. However, when the Lithuanian Chassidim needed his leadership, he returned home.) The Chassidim in Israel faced all the problems of the settlers during the times of Rabbi Yehuda HaChasid. However, their love for Eretz Yisrael was so great that they stayed — while discouraging others from settling there. Later, some disciples of the Vilna Gaon also made *aliyah*. Both groups settled in the four holy cities of Eretz Yisrael — Jerusalem, Tzefas, Tiberias, and Hebron. There, they became the nucleus of the Ashkenazic settlement of Israel.

In addition, the latter half of the 1700s saw the rise of secularism in the Jewish world, which led to the defection of great numbers of Jews from Torah observance, as will be presently discussed.

Chapter 18

THE DARKNESS OF ENLIGHTENMENT

E UROPE ENTERS THE MODERN AGE: The *Zohar* (*Parashas Vayeira* 117), based on a verse in Genesis 7:11, states that during the sixth century of the sixth millennium (5500–5600, or 1740–1840), there will be a Divine outpouring of wisdom on humanity. Indeed, this was a time of incredible achievement in Torah wisdom. Similarly, in the secular world great changes began to take place in the social, political, and technological spheres. Change occurred, and is occurring, at a dizzying pace, altering both Jewish and gentile societies forever.

THE FRENCH REVOLUTION: As one historian succinctly phrased it, "When France sneezed, Europe caught a cold." Inspired by the American Revolution, in 1789 the French people overthrew the monarchy and established a secular republic. The supremacy of the Catholic Church was nullified, and all people were regarded as equal. In 1791, after a heated debate, the French National Assembly granted citizenship to Jews. However, equality came at a bitter price: Jews were expected to abandon their traditional, religious way of life and become full-fledged Frenchmen. In the words of one of the deputies: "There cannot be a nation within a nation. Everything for the Jews as individuals; nothing for them as a people."[1] A mass defection from Torah life began, and virtually all French Jews abandoned observance.

NAPOLEON: The great French emperor sought to solve the so-called Jewish Problem by granting the Jews rights in order to assimilate them. As such, throughout Europe Napoleon's conquering soldiers broke down the walls of the ghettoes. In 1798, in Bonn, Germany, a remarkable scene took place: Christians and Jews marched together to the ghetto walls, carpenters used their tools to break down the gates, and in a dramatic act proclaiming brotherhood and equality for all, the ghetto walls were shattered. In Italy, French troops, young Jews, and Italians all threw down the ghetto gates with their bare hands. Jews in France were expected to become what was known as Frenchmen of the Mosaic persuasion. Jews were no longer to be governed by the Torah and their rabbis; religion would only apply to private relationships and personal morality, not to maintain a unique Jewish society. Jews were also supposed to abandon hope for a Messianic redemption in the Land of Israel, and to regard France as their permanent fatherland. From France, these ideas spread throughout Western Europe.

When Napoleon invaded Russia in 1812, a number of chassidic leaders welcomed the prospective easing of czarist oppression. However, Rabbi Schneur Zalman of Liadi, the first Lubavitcher rebbe, took a much different view, which was ultimately upheld by history: "If Napoleon wins, the Jews will prosper both materially and socially, but they will deteriorate spiritually. If the czar is victorious, the ancient discrimination will continue, but Jews will draw closer to their Father in Heaven."[2] As such, the rebbe instructed his Chassidim to do all they could to help the Russian army, and a number of them rendered invaluable service to the czarist cause by spying on the French invasion forces.

NAPOLEON'S GREAT SANHEDRIN: In 1807, Napoleon assembled what he called a Sanhedrin to legislate officially the status of Jews in the new French state, and to have its decisions accepted by Jews everywhere. Rabbi David Sinzheim, a distinguished Torah scholar and the rabbi of Strasbourg, France, led the seventy-one delegates. They were presented with twelve provocative questions, among them the validity of mixed marriages, the Jewish position on usury (which troubled Napoleon greatly), and whether Jews both considered France their country and would fight to defend it. To the last question, they enthusiastically answered, "Unto death!" The other questions, however, they answered in a diplomatic manner, being careful not to offend the mighty French emperor. Regarding intermarriage, they replied that such unions are not recognized by religious law, but are binding according to the civil laws of France. The Sanhedrin also tactfully reminded the emperor that this was also the position of the Catholic Church.[3] With the decisions of the Sanhedrin, the Jews of France renounced rabbinical jurisdiction, unique nationhood, and the hope of a return to Eretz Yisrael. From that point on they were Frenchmen in France.

However, Torah-observant Jews regarded the Sanhedrin's deliberations as a farce. For their part, gentiles saw the Sanhedrin as an open gathering of a secret cabal of international Jews who meet in order to destroy Christian society. As such, this negative view stirred memories of the supposed Jewish conclaves that were rumored to meet each year to choose the city from which a Christian child would be ritually murdered. Thus, the image of a worldwide Jewish conspiracy was given great credence.[4]

As happens on so many occasions throughout Jewish history, Jews operated under the illusion that assimilation was the solution to their problems. However, the Sanhedrin's renunciations of Jewish tradition did not win for the Jews of France the promised full acceptance as Frenchmen. On the contrary, during the course of the nineteenth century, anti-Semitism grew dramatically in France, taking on the secular, racist view that no amount of assimilation or conversion could change the inherent evil of the Jew. In the view of a prominent historian, "When the ghetto walls fell, and the Jews walked out into freedom, they found they were entering a new, less tangible, but equally hostile ghetto of suspicion. They had changed ancient disabilities for modern anti-Semitism."[5] Of course, this is the Divine plan to ensure that the Jewish people would never totally assimilate.

ASSIMILATION IN GERMANY — MOSES MENDELSSOHN (1729–1786): While personally a religious Jew, Mendelssohn introduced ideas that led to the mass defection of German Jews from Torah observance. Although he did not intend so, Mendelssohn ultimately was responsible for the twin influences of Reform and baptism of German Jews, and the spiritual destruction of a major portion of the Jewish people to this very day. In the words of the historian, Paul Johnson:

> The truth is, there was much of it [Judaism] in which he simply did not believe: the idea of the Chosen People, the mission to humanity, the Promised Land. The idea that the whole of a culture could be contained in the Torah was to him absurd. The Jew should worship at home, and then, when he went out into the world, participate in the general European culture.[6]

Clearly, Mendelssohn felt that the Torah was only a book of rituals and observances, but moral and ethical behavior should be determined by human reason according to the ideals of the Enlightenment. He believed that secular culture in many ways was superior to the Torah, and that Jews should cease being a unique people and instead incorporate secular values into their lives. With these ideas, he spurned many basic Jewish beliefs. For example, the first *mishnah* in *Avos* introduces the ethical imperatives of the tractate by stating "Moses received the Torah at Sinai" to teach us that even laws which seem to be universal human values find their sources only in the Torah.[7] The Torah writes (Leviticus 20:26): "And I have separated you from the nations to be Mine." Jews derive their culture only from the Torah, as it states: "Delve into [the Torah] and continue to delve into it, for everything is in it." [8]

Mendelssohn's close friend, the gentile German dramatist Gotthold Lessing, produced a play called *Nathan the Wise* that introduced Mendelssohn's idealized Enlightenment Jew to great numbers of Jews and Germans. For his part, Mendelssohn wrote a commentary on the *Chumash* in classical German, but using Hebrew letters, in order to introduce Jews to the beauties of the German language and accelerate their integration into German society.[9] At the heart of Mendelssohn's philosophy was the idea, which would so tragically be disproved, that the more Jews would be like the Germans, the more they would be liked by the Germans.

EMANCIPATION: During the 1800s, laws were passed throughout the various German states granting equal rights to the Jews. They entered universities, the military, and all professions, achieving great success. Between 1800 and 1810, one-tenth of German Jews purchased what Heinrich Heine, a non-observant Jew who became Europe's most widely acclaimed poet, called "the ticket of admission to European culture" in the form of baptism.[10] Throughout the 1800s this number became a flood, reaching 250,000.[11] Clearly, German culture exerted a very powerful pull on the Jews, as both groups shared a number of similar values: a strong sense of family, hard work, commitment to religion, and great respect for education.

THE BACKLASH: The Jews, however, never achieved full acceptance. In 1819, the *Hep! Hep!* anti-Jewish riots broke out in a number of German cities. (*Hep!*, the battle cry of the rioters, is an acronym for the Latin words "*Hierosolyma Est Perdita*," Jerusalem is destroyed.)[12] A growing number of German intellectuals began preaching the idea of the German *Volk*, a mystical people based on an ancestral fatherland and common blood ties, which of course excluded the Jews. Richard Wagner, the famous German classical composer, wrote operatic music, the *Ring* cycle, which harked back to a pagan, Teutonic Germany untouched by Jewish culture. A century later, his music captivated the Nazis, as Adolph Hitler wrote, "Whoever wants to understand Nazi Germany must know Wagner."[13] At the same time, the English-German writer Houston Stewart Chamberlain wrote that Jews are a dangerous race, and his books found a wide audience in Germany. In 1879, a German journalist, Wilhelm Marr, founded the League of Anti-Semites to combat Jewish influence in Germany, thus coining the familiar phrase "anti-Semitism."

KARL MARX (1818–1883): Descended from rabbis on both sides of his family, the young Karl was baptized into the Lutheran Church at five and raised as a Christian. Eventually, he grew to despise all religion, but hated Judaism most of all. (Indeed, his anti-Jewish writings became the basis of Communist persecution of the Jews in the former Soviet Union.) Marx wrote:

"What is the profane basis of Judaism? Practical need, self-interest. What is the worldly cult of the Jew? Haggling. What is his worldly god? Money. Very well: then in emancipating itself from huckstering and money, and thus from real and practical Judaism, our age would emancipate itself."[14] Marx, unfortunately, took his place in a long line of former Jews who slandered their own people in the gentile world, as the Prophet Isaiah states (49:17): "Those that break and destroy you come from your midst."

THE BEGINNING OF REFORM JUDAISM: Understandably, many Jews found conversion to Christianity unacceptable, but still wished to be a part of gentile culture. As such, they felt that by discarding much of the Torah they deemed to be irrelevant, and resembling Christians as much as possible, their process of assimilation would be quickened. Accordingly, in 1810 Israel Jacobson opened a Reform temple and celebrated the Festival of the Jewish Reformation. A choir of Jewish and Christian boys and girls sang prayers and hymns in German, accompanied by an organ, while the children's parents and friends, Jewish and gentile, were in attendance. Church bells pealed, and Jacobson announced that, from then on, Judaism would follow the spirit of the times.[15] Followers of Reform called their houses of worship temples to emphasize their connection to the Judaism of the Bible rather than that of the rabbis and the Talmud.[16] As with all deviant anti-Torah movements — beginning with Korach, and later the Sadducees and Karaites — Reform Judaism denied the G-d-given authority of the sages to interpret the Torah. However, unlike other movements that often offered a stricter, more literal interpretation of the Torah than did the sages, the Reform movement only sought to cast away as much of Torah observance as possible.

As such, the Reform movement first focused on changing the traditional prayer service that had been followed for hundreds of years, whose customs have the force and sanctity of *minhag Yisrael din hu*, accepted Jewish law. To begin with, the Reformers removed as irrelevant one of the *Yekum Purkan* prayers, recited in the synagogue on Sabbath, which invokes Divine mercy for the Torah scholars of Eretz Yisrael and Babylon.[17] Once the wall had been breached, a flood of Reform innovations in the siddur and in synagogue practice took place, and Reform temples began to resemble Protestant churches. In the 1840s, several Reform rabbinical assemblies rejected the authority of the Talmud. Some leaders even claimed that the *Chumash* itself is subject to human criticism, and that observance of its ritual commandments, such as kashrus, circumcision, and holidays, is optional.

THE MASKILIM: Maskilim, or secularly enlightened Jews, were a group with similar goals to Reform Jews, but employing different methods to achieve them. Whereas the Reform movement wanted to blur the distinction between Jew and gentile in matters of observance, the Maskilim wanted to show the outside world that Judaism is a universal faith and not a collection of alien beliefs. To this end, in 1819 they set up an organization called The Society for Jewish Culture and Science. Its founder, Leopold Zunz, investigated Jewish history and practices utilizing a modern, scientific, critical approach, completely denying the Divine uniqueness of the Jewish people. In the words of the German philosopher Nietzsche, once it became possible to study scientifically the history of a religion, it was already dead.[18] Heinrich Graetz, one of the Society's members, wrote a multivolume Jewish history in which he claimed that the sages invented much of the Oral Law to further their own ends. The implication of all this pseudo-scholarship was that if the Oral Law was largely man-made and subject to change, it could also be amended in modern times. The Society disbanded after five years, and several of its prominent members converted to Christianity.

THE SALONS: As Jews became more secularly educated and wealthy, they opened up salons throughout Germany and France where they freely mingled with upper-class gentiles. Attractive Jewish women, who used their beauty, intelligence, and wealth to break down traditional barriers to socialization and intermarriage, typically ran these salons. In the words of a prominent historian: "The Jews used education as a lever to success, and because they became rich, because they were talented, brilliant, witty, interested in the theater, music, literature, the Christian intelligentsia found itself drawn to the Jewish salons. After an inspiring Mass on Sunday morning, it was wonderful to relax in the elegant, sophisticated atmosphere of a Jewish drawing room where one could meet royalty, aristocracy, and the latest celebrities of stage, arts, and letters."[19]

FIGHTERS AGAINST REFORM — RABBI SAMSON RAPHAEL HIRSCH (1808–1888): Widely regarded as the savior of religious German and Western European Jewry, Rabbi Hirsch realized that he had to use the tools of the Enlightenment to fight Reform and inspire the younger generation to uphold the Torah staunchly despite being exposed to Western culture. He envisioned the philosophy of *Torah im derech eretz*, Torah with the way of the world. This concept stated that for the Jew, the Torah and its commandments are the source of all wisdom, culture, and values, and that no compromise with Torah values could be brooked. Secular knowledge, Rabbi Hirsch said, only has meaning when it is utilized in the service of the Torah. In the words of a prominent scholar:

> *Torah im derech eretz* was not meant by Rabbi S. R. Hirsch to sanction our thorough involvement — immersion — in the larger society, even if accompanied by religious zeal and strict observance of halachah. Such a course ignores the laws of sociology that govern cultural assimilation. What he had in mind was the 'Toraization' of the prevailing cultural and educational material *within* our Torah society.[20]

Rabbi Hirsch wrote numerous works in beautiful, literary German explaining timeless Torah truths in modern, Western terminology. His revolutionary approach electrified the German Jewish world, and inspired many to be proud of their Jewish heritage while living in a world without ghetto walls. *The Nineteen Letters* conveyed in a highly intellectual manner the Orthodox rebuttal to Reform, and the relevance of the Torah to modern times. Rabbi Hirsch's copious commentaries on *Chumash* and *Nach* helped the enlightened Jew relate to the eternal words of our holiest books. *Horeb*, an explanation of the mitzvos of the Torah, showed the modern Jew how the Divine precepts are the framework of a structure of unsurpassed beauty and grandeur. These and other works have been translated into English, and they remain every bit as relevant today as in the mid-1800s. Rabbi Hirsch also set up an educational system in which students were given intensive Torah studies and a thorough secular education, preparing them for the challenges of German society. This system of education has been followed in American day schools, which function in a similar environment.

In 1851, Rabbi Hirsch was Chief Rabbi of Moravia, a major Austro-Hungarian province containing 50,000 Jews. Meanwhile, the city of Frankfurt, Germany, a famed center of Torah scholarship for hundreds of years, had fallen under Reform dominance. Under German law, all Jews had to belong to one community. The handful of observant Jews remaining in Frankfurt formed a religious society, which was permitted by law. However, they did not have their own synagogue building. Needing help, this group of 100 Jews invited the German-born Rabbi Hirsch to be their spiritual leader. To the amazement of all, Rabbi Hirsch accepted this position to go to what was then a spiritual backwater. Then, painstakingly, he rebuilt Frankfurt as a prominent Torah center.

In 1876, the German government passed a new law allowing any Jew to secede from his community and form a new one. The official Frankfurt Jewish community, although dominated by Reform, did not control Orthodox institutions. However, many religious Jews felt it would be harmful to secede; one reason given was fear of not having use of the communal cemetery, which, although used by all Jews, was under Reform auspices. Secession would deprive Orthodox Jews of the right to be buried near their ancestors. Although not all rabbinic opinions agreed, Rabbi Hirsch encouraged a small number of his congregants to break off all institutional contact with Reform, so as not to give any appearance of credence to its heresy.[21] His courageous decision was known as *Austritts Gemeinde*. Rabbi Hirsch's proud, break-off community existed until the 1930s, when Nazi persecution forced it to relocate to the United States. Today, it is located in New York City and known as the Breuer's Kehillah, for Rabbi Breuer, Rabbi Hirsch's son-in-law, who carried on its traditions. Breuer's continues to play a leading role in American Jewish life.

RABBI YAAKOV ETTLINGER: Known as the Aruch LaNer, after his classic commentary on the Talmud, the German-born Rabbi Ettlinger played a leading role in combating the spread of Reform. A tireless fighter, he attended university, as did many German rabbis who felt that they must gain secular knowledge in order to influence their fellow Jews more strongly. However, before any lecture, Rabbi Ettlinger prayed to G-d that he not be negatively influenced by any heretical ideas that he might hear.[22] Rabbi Ettlinger became the leading halachic authority in Germany. When the Reform movement convened in 1844 and made their heresy official, Rabbi Ettlinger wrote a lengthy letter of protest, which ultimately was signed by hundreds of Western European rabbis and widely disseminated. Rabbi Ettlinger passed away in 1872.

CHASAM SOFER: Rabbi Moshe Sofer, known as the Chasam Sofer, after the title of his Torah writings, was born in Frankfurt in 1762. Serving as rabbi in several communities, including the prestigious posts of Mattersdorf and Pressburg (today Bratislava), Chasam Sofer fought Reform in Austria-Hungary and was directly responsible for the salvation of Orthodox life. By establishing a school in Pressburg that taught hundreds of students, Rabbi Sofer created the largest yeshivah in hundreds of years. Aside from size, the Pressburg yeshivah was unique in a number of ways. Rigorous examinations were given periodically, courses in public speaking were offered, and students were required to spend time studying with laymen. Subjects such as Tanach and grammar, traditionally neglected in yeshivah curriculums, were stressed. As a result of this well-rounded approach, Pressburg graduates were able to fill numerous rabbinical posts throughout Hungary, thereby denying those pulpits to the Reform movement. Although Reform eventually made great strides in Hungary, it was not able to wreak the same havoc that it did in Western Europe.

In addition, Chasam Sofer fought tenaciously against even the smallest change in Jewish customs. He coined the famous phrase "*Chadash asur min HaTorah*" taken from the Mishnah[23] and meaning that the new crop of grain (*chadash*) is biblically forbidden for consumption before the time of the *omer* offering (the sixteenth of Nisan). Chasam Sofer's play on these words was that Torah law forbids *Chodosh*, any new innovation. In addition, regarding association with followers of Reform, he wrote: "If we had the power, in my opinion, we should thoroughly expel such people from our community. We should forbid anyone to marry into their families so that they do not draw anyone after them. We would be by ourselves and they would be by themselves."[24] Basing himself on Talmudic precedent, Chasam Sofer decided that even if a significant portion of the people would abandon the faith, not even the smallest part of Judaism can be compromised.[25] Chasam Sofer died in 1839.

RABBI AKIVA EIGER (1761–1837): This contemporary of Chasam Sofer also battled Reform in his home country of Austria. However, Rabbi Akiva Eiger is better known for being the leading Torah personality of his generation. A prolific writer, he is famed for the supreme logic and profound depth of his writings. One of his well-known works is *Gilyon HaShas*, a collection of brief notes that appear on the standard Talmudic page, indicating their importance. Frequently these comments end with "This matter needs thought" (*Tzarich iyun*), "This matter needs much thought" (*Tzarich iyun gadol*), or "May G-d enlighten my eyes" (*V'HaShem yair einai*). Scholars expend much effort in determining the relative severity of a problem based on the nuances of Rabbi Akiva Eiger's words.

In addition, Rabbi Akiva Eiger's kindness, humility, and devotion to Torah and mitzvos were legendary. Once, when he was riding in a wagon in a snowstorm, the driver had to fix an axle and his feet became wet. When he re-entered the coach, Rabbi Akiva Eiger handed him a dry pair of socks, saying they were extra. Later, the driver saw that the rabbi was wearing shoes without socks. Rabbi Akiva Eiger told him, "If your feet are wet, they're extra for me." Once, at Seder, one of his guests spilled wine on the clean tablecloth. Immediately, Rabbi Akiva Eiger surreptitiously tipped his own cup, remarking that the table must be unsteady — and saving his guest any possible embarrassment.

Rabbi Akiva Eiger served as the rabbi in the town of Markish Friedland and then in Posen. His salary in Markish Friedland sheds light on typical financial arrangements for rabbis in those times. Aside from a monthly stipend, and money for special rabbinic functions, he received a free dwelling, flour, and wine for Pesach according to his family's needs, a *lulav* and *esrog* for Sukkos, the right to teach four students at community expense, and an annual supply of candle-tallow. Rabbi Akiva Eiger left behind a large family, and has many descendants today.

RABBI MEIR LEIB BEN YECHIEL MICHAEL (MALBIM) (1809–1879): This unique scholar fought Reform in Romania, where he was chief rabbi. Angered by his resolute stand against their heresy, adherents of Reform falsely denounced him to the authorities. Malbim escaped death only by outside intervention and by promising to leave Romania. Persecuted by assimilationists, who saw him as a threat to their ideology, he moved from rabbinical post to rabbinical post. At one point, he was even considered for Chief Rabbi of New York, but refused the position.

Malbim especially fought Reform in the one area they felt superior to Orthodox Jews: the study of Tanach, which traditionally was not studied as intensely as Talmud. He wrote a monumental commentary on *Chumash* and *Navi*, which stand out among all other commentaries. Malbim's major principle is that there are no repetitious phrases in the Bible, and those words or expressions that sound alike are really adding profound new concepts to the verse. Countless times throughout Tanach, Malbim demonstrates this idea in a beautiful, intellectually satisfying manner. He also highlights the inextricable relationship of the Written and Oral Laws, and proves how the interpretations of biblical verses in the Talmud and Midrash are indicated in the text itself. With his material, observant Jews were able to show how Tanach is a source of great intellectual depth and grandeur of expression. Malbim's commentary remains a timeless classic, opening up the inner essence of Tanach.

REFORM IN AMERICA: Although the Reform movement wreaked great havoc in Western Europe, its greatest success in destroying traditional Judaism came in the United States. Unlike Europe, America had no established Jewish communities or institutions, and so Reform was able to create a stranglehold on Jewish life, which would prove disastrous for the great waves of future immigration. In 1840, there were 15,000 Jews in America, a number that swelled to 150,000 by the eve of the Civil War,[26] with virtually all the immigrants assimilated German Jews. Their de facto leader, and the most important nineteenth-century Reformer, was Isaac Mayer Wise. In every possible way, he struck at the Divine origin of the Torah, especially ridiculing the mitzvah of *chalitzah*, a ceremony in which a childless widow removes a ritual shoe off the foot of her brother-in-law and spits before him on the ground. Wise dropped observance of the second day of festivals, customarily observed outside Eretz Yisrael, using the spurious argument that America is the new Promised Land and is not considered exile. (Needless to say, merchants were very pleased with this innovation.) Wise then introduced all the German reforms in the synagogue, only differing in the use of English for prayers, and creating a revised siddur, *Minhag America*.[27]

In 1873, Wise organized the scattered Reform temples around the country into an umbrella organization known as the Union of American Hebrew Congregations (UAHC). Two years later, he founded Hebrew Union College, in Cincinnati, to train Reform clergy. UAHC soon gained great power and the loyalty of vast numbers of American Jews. In 1885, at the Pittsburgh Platform, American Reform formally rejected all Torah laws "such as are not adapted to the views and habits of modern civilization," including rules on diet, ritual and family purity, and dress. The Pittsburgh

Platform further proclaimed that Jews were no longer a nation but a religious community, denied life after death, and presented the concept of the Messianic Age not as a return to Eretz Yisrael, but rather as the search for social justice, in which all religions shared equally.[28] By 1880, there were about 300,000 Jews in the United States, largely Americanized, affluent, and Reform.

THE CONSERVATIVE MOVEMENT: In 1887, a group of Jews, angered by the deviations of the Reform movement (for example, at the first graduation of Hebrew Union College in 1883, in what became known as the Treifah Banquet, shrimp, frog legs, clams, and milk and meat were served),[29] wanted change, yet did not want to be completely Torah observant. They opted for a compromised, watered-down version of Torah Judaism, which became known as Conservative Judaism. This purely American spinoff from traditional Judaism experienced enormous growth, and eventually overtook Reform in numbers of temples and adherents. Their rabbinical school became known as the Jewish Theological Seminary (JTS), and the famous professor Solomon Schechter became its head in 1902. Conservative temples were joined in an organization called United Synagogues of Conservative Judaism (USCJ).

While retaining more observances than Reform Jews, the Conservative movement also denies the Divine origin of the Torah, thus adopting a heretical philosophy. A sad result of this deviation is that halachah is viewed as arbitrarily man-made; therefore, it is presumed that Torah law can be universally changed to fit the times. The most egregious example of this attitude is the Conservative movement's official dispensation to drive to synagogue on the Sabbath, predicated on the erroneous belief that in the modern era synagogue attendance overrides Sabbath observance. Currently, much tension exists between the Reform and Conservative movements on one side, and Orthodox Judaism on the other. The non-observant groups want recognition as legitimate expressions of Judaism, something that Orthodox Jews, in the spirit of the great nineteenth-century German rabbis, cannot afford them.

FIGHTERS AGAINST REFORM IN AMERICA: Due to the very small number of learned Jews in the United States, and the lack of a community structure, the struggle against Reform in America in the 1800s was much more difficult than in Europe. Nevertheless, some courageous individuals fought for upholding the Torah. Isaac Leeser of Philadelphia, a man of prodigious energy, produced the first Jewish translation of the Tanach in English, completed English translations of the Ashkenazic and Sephardic siddurim, founded a Jewish newspaper, and wrote textbooks for Jewish schools, all in the spirit of Torah-true Judaism.

German-born Rabbi Abraham Joseph Rice arrived in the United States in 1840, the first distinguished Torah scholar to settle in the country. Accepting a rabbinical post in Baltimore, he immediately joined Isaac Leeser in the struggle against wholesale abandonment of the Torah's commands. Rabbi Rice's scholarship was unmatched by any person in the Reform camp, and his writing inspired his and succeeding generations to remain loyal to their tradition and faith. However, the trend toward permissiveness was overwhelming, even in Rabbi Rice's own synagogue, and he resigned in 1849. His farewell speech is an indication of his greatness, and is the supreme fulfillment of the Torah's exhortation to a rabbinic judge: "You shall fear no man."[30]

> I am aware that my sermons have caused me much trouble and grief. My outspokenness has oftentimes disturbed my peace and serenity. Yet, an inner voice, which you may call conscience, speaks to me and says: Be yourself! Act according to the obligations of your calling! My conscience further says to me: It is your rabbinic responsibility, your professional obligation, to teach the right path of our religion, regardless of the consequences to yourself. One must be prepared to sacrifice comfort and tranquility and even abandon one's occupation if need be, in the interest of truth. One should not be afraid to speak openly against the wealthy and influential, the powerful, regardless of the consequences.[31]

After his resignation, Rabbi Rice opened a dry goods store.

Throughout his American rabbinical career, Rabbi Rice bemoaned the fact that he had no scholarly companionship, and that he was virtually a lone voice in a spiritual wasteland. Only his sense of mission kept him from leaving America for more hospitable Torah climes. Rabbi Rice died in 1862. Although not well known today, his pioneering work paved the way for the eventual flourishing of Orthodox life in the United States.

JEWS IN SECULAR PURSUITS: As the outside world beckoned, Jews excelled in many secular fields, almost invariably at the cost of their Torah observance and Jewish faith. Sigmund Freud developed the principles on which modern psychology is based. During the reign of Queen Victoria, Benjamin Disraeli, who was baptized into the Church of England at age twelve, became Prime Minister of England and helped England become a great colonial power. Gustav Mahler, after converting to Roman Catholicism, became music director of the prestigious Vienna Opera House, the most important post in German music. Albert Einstein was the father of modern physics. Many other Jews excelled in politics, art, literature, theater, music, science, and especially medicine. Eventually, these achievements caused great resentment in the non-Jewish world, which felt itself overrun by Jews.

IN AMERICA: In the mid-1800s, German Jews became a powerful force in American business. Lazarus Strauss began his career as a wandering peddler in Georgia. He then opened a small store that eventually became two great department stores — Macy's and Abraham & Strauss. The founder of Gimbel's department store began as a dry goods salesman in Indiana. In California Gold Rush towns, Levi Strauss peddled pants, which became known as Levi's, the first designer jeans in history. Julius Rosenwald developed a very successful mail-order firm, Sears Roebuck and Company. During the Civil War, Jews prospered by being bankers, contractors, and clothing suppliers.

THE ROTHSCHILDS: For more than a century, the name of this world-famous international banking family served both as a positive symbol of Jewish wealth, influence, and philanthropy among the Jewish people, and as a negative, sinister symbol to anti-Semites who used it as tangible proof of an international Jewish banking conspiracy. The origin of this surname comes from the 1500s in the Frankfurt ghetto, where a red shield (*Rothschild* in German) adorned the family's house. A famous legend explains the Rothschild family's wealth. Mayer Amshel Rothschild was a small-time dealer in old coins. In 1806, while fleeing Napoleon's army, a prominent German ruler entrusted his fortune to Rothschild's care. When the French troops entered Rothschild's house, he gave them his entire wealth, also giving them the impression that it was the ruler's. Meanwhile, he had safely hidden the ruler's money. When matters settled down, the ruler returned, thinking that his fortune had been lost. However, Mayer Amshel returned it to him with interest. Greatly impressed by Mayer Amshel's self-sacrifice, the ruler recommended Rothschild's firm to all his fellow noblemen.[32]

Regardless of origin, the Rothschilds made a colossal fortune by investing in such highly risky ventures as bullion transfer (subject to theft), government bonds (regimes could collapse), and investment management for exiled rulers. They also profited immensely by investing in the British textile industry. During the American Civil War, the Rothschilds invested in American government bonds,[33] albeit a relatively small investment. The bulk of the family's holdings were in Europe: Mayer Amshel's five sons established bank branches in London, Paris, Naples, Vienna, and Frankfurt. Between 1815 and 1914, the Rothschilds owned what was easily the largest bank in the world. Indeed, no individual today owns as large a share of the world's wealth as the Rothschilds did in the mid 1800s.[34]

As such, the Rothschilds' immense wealth enabled them to obtain titles of European aristocracy. They added the noble prefixes of "von" in Germany, "de" in France, and, the greatest prize of all, "sir" when they secured an English peerage. The family married almost exclusively among itself, with only female Rothschilds permitted to marry outsiders — but on express condition that the husbands would not inherit the family fortune.[35] Although no Rothschilds converted, most of them assimilated. A notable exception was Wolf Rothschild of Frankfurt, who strongly supported Rabbi Samson Raphael Hirsch. Baron Edmund de Rothschild of Paris played a major role in establishing and sustaining some of the early Jewish settlements in Eretz Yisrael.

In the 1900s, due to changing global economic realities, the influence of the Rothschilds diminished. During World War II, although the Nazis did not capture any family members, the Germans were able to expropriate what remained of the Rothschild wealth in Nazi-ruled countries. However, most of the Rothschild holdings were beyond the Nazis' grasp. At the present, the family is completely nonreligious, and a number have intermarried with non-Jews. The family's wealth is concentrated mainly in the London-based bank, N. M. Rothschild & Sons.

SIR MOSES MONTEFIORE (1784–1885): Unlike many other Jews who achieved distinction in the non-Jewish world, this great British Jew remained proudly Torah-observant. After amassing a personal fortune at a young age (he was Nathan M. Rothschild's brother-in-law), Montefiore devoted the rest of his long life to helping his fellow Jews. Montefiore's upstanding religious observance, devotion to concerns of his people, and personal integrity won him the admiration of all Jews and the respect of the gentile world. Appointed sheriff of London, he was later knighted by Queen Victoria, great honors normally not bestowed upon Jews.

In 1840, the infamous Damascus blood libel, the first such incident in the Muslim world, broke out in Syria. A Catholic monk and his Muslim servant disappeared, and some Christians spread the rumor that the Jews had killed them to use their blood on Pesach. Several Jews were arrested, and after undergoing excruciating torture, they confessed to the crime. Syrian authorities also seized sixty-three Jewish children, in order to extort the location of the hiding place of the victims' blood from the children's mothers.[36] The French government stated its belief in the ritual murder charges. Anti-Jewish riots erupted, prompting protest from numerous nations, including the United States. To ameliorate conditions, Montefiore himself led a delegation of distinguished Jews and non-Jews to the sultan, convincing him to issue an official denunciation of the charges. All the surviving accused Jews were released, and Montefiore returned home to a hero's welcome.

A case where Montefiore's efforts resulted in failure was the Mortara Affair. In 1858, the Catholic Church abducted a six-year-old Italian Jewish boy, Edgardo Mortara, on the grounds that his family's Christian domestic servant had baptized him. The child was taken to a convent where he was given a Catholic upbringing. The unfortunate parents vehemently protested, and the incident provoked an international outcry, but the Pope remained adamant. Montefiore traveled to Rome in an unsuccessful attempt to gain the child's release. When Edgardo became an adult, he was offered the freedom to return to his family and religion, but decided instead to become a Catholic priest. Montefiore also traveled to Morocco, Romania, and Russia, where he interceded with high government officials, including the czar himself, to lessen anti-Semitic decrees. A legend is told that in Poland a ruffian chased after his carriage, shouting the pejorative Polish epithet for a Jew, "*Zhid.*" Montefiore stopped the carriage and handed the Polish youth a gold coin, saying: "Around the world, people call me 'Sir,' 'Baron,' and 'Knight.' However, you have addressed me by my most honorable title — 'Jew!' "

Montefiore made seven arduous trips to Eretz Yisrael, the last one at the age of ninety. He gave vast sums of money to impoverished Jews there, and in order to provide a source of income for the Jewish inhabitants, attempted to develop agricultural colonies and industry. Montefiore founded the first Jewish settlement in Jerusalem outside the walls of the Old City, and the neighborhood was named Yemin Moshe for him. As a source of employment, he also built the famous windmill that dominates the skyline. Montefiore also cleaned the area around *Kever Rachel*, which had accumulated debris over the years, and built the famous dome over the tomb. One time, he entered Temple Mount, assuming that Jewish law permitted it. When afterward he was informed that he had committed a great transgression, he allowed himself to be publicly humiliated, letting rabbis drag him across a room while sitting in a chair. His 100th birthday was celebrated as a public holiday by Jewish communities the world over, and noted by Queen Victoria. Montefiore died in 1885, age 101.

Chapter 19

LIFE UNDER THE CZARS
IN THE 1800s

RUSSIAN SOCIETY: Life in Russia was very different from that in Western Europe. The Enlightenment passed Russia by, leaving Russia with a medieval feudal system unchanged over hundreds of years. More than 90 percent of the people were illiterate peasants, bound as serfs to the nobility's vast estates. The Russian Orthodox Church held complete religious sway over the land, regarding Muslims, pagans, and especially Jews as alien outsiders. At the head of government the czar ruled by divine appointment, wielding absolute power with no parliament — or press, or populace — to answer to. Politically, too, Russia's defeat of Napoleon ensured that progressive ideals would not take root in the country.

RUSSIA ACQUIRES MANY JEWS: Until the later 1700s, Russia had a relatively small Jewish population. With the successive partitions of Poland from 1772–1795, Russia acquired more than one million Jews. By the end of the nineteenth century, this number had swelled to more than five million Jews, comprising by far the largest Jewish population in the world. Alarmed at the prospect of Jewish competition to Russian merchants, Czar Alexander I restricted the Jews to twenty-five western provinces, including Lithuania, Poland, White Russia, and Ukraine. Known as the Pale of Settlement, the area comprised 1,000 miles by 300 miles, taking final form in

1812. Much of the land was uninhabitable, causing severe over-crowding. Successive czars contracted the Pale even further, making a difficult situation impossible. The Jews of the Pale lived largely in small towns called shtetlach, and their life was one of grinding, unalleviated poverty. In the words of someone who grew up in a shtetl during the 1880s:

> Anyone accustomed to the American standard of living who might have come to Neshwies in those days and walked through its unpaved and unlighted streets, looked into its small, unventilated, and often overcrowded wooden houses, devoid of all plumbing or the simplest precautions against contagious diseases of an epidemic character, would have pronounced the town unbelievably poor, dirty, criminally ignorant as to hygiene, and altogether lifeless. Indeed, he would have wondered how its six to eight thousand inhabitants managed to live at all.[1]

Another shtetl resident recalls the old days:

> When I say "poverty" I mean a situation such as is hardly thinkable in [America] our land of plenty. It was nothing unusual to have been occasionally without bread in the house. To obtain it, we either had to borrow a slice from a neighbor or buy a loaf on credit. It often happened that there was not a match in the house to kindle a stove or light the petroleum lamp, if there was wood in the stove or kerosene in the lamp... Most of the time our home consisted of one or one and a half rooms and kitchen. The latter was shared most of the time with another tenant. If you asked how we managed — well, we just managed; even if I told you, you would not understand. Our food was sparse and simple. We often did not have enough wooden spoons with which to consume it when we were all together. Our bread was made of coarse corn meal, not the fancy corn bread we know here as a delicacy, but a huge coarse loaf. A piece of white bread was a rare treat. Potatoes, beans, and other vegetables furnished the diet. Milk was a rarity, as were eggs. Meat was only for Shabbos.[2]

Despite the unceasing poverty (or perhaps because of it), spiritual life was rich indeed. Religious education was universal for shtetl Jews, irrespective of social or economic position. A description of the primary role of Torah study in the shtetl:

What other nation has a lullaby to the effect that "study is the best of wares"? At the birth of a child, the school children come and chant the *Shema* in unison around the cradle. The child is taken to school for the first time wrapped in a tallis (prayer shawl). School children are referred to as "sacred sheep," and a mother's pet name for her little boy is *mayn tsadikl* (my little saint). Hence, one is ready to sell all household belongings to pay tuition. Women work all their lives to enable their husbands to devote themselves to study. One shares his last morsel of food with a *yeshivah bachur* (young student). And when the melancholy sweet tone of Talmudic study penetrates the poor alleys, exhausted Jews on their pallets are delighted, for they feel they have a share in that study. Study was a song of longing, a pouring out of the heart before the Merciful Father, a sort of prayer, a communion and an ardent desire for a purified world.[3]

The Sabbath was an oasis of joy in a harsh world. Families scraped together their meager earnings during the week in order to afford better food for the holy day. The house was cleaned, and everyone washed and wore fresh clothing for the Sabbath. Just how the Sabbath was prepared for and enjoyed by a struggling shtetl family is depicted in moving detail:

For this holy day Molke would buy...flour to bake challah. She would have dough to take off to make noodles for soup and a kugel, to make pancakes for the children, and enough twisted challahs to last through the Sabbath. Then she would get some fish and horseradish, for without fish the Sabbath would lose one custom. Then of course there was meat, or if there was enough money, chicken. She would also have a tzimmes of carrots, and when Simcha came home, usually Friday about noon, if he had a good week and could afford it, he would go out and buy a bottle of wine.

Molke before sunset would light four candles stuck in a candelabrum, put on a clean, ironed dress and a silk kerchief on her head, turned in back of her ears. With satisfaction, a sense of accomplishment and devotion, she would put her hands over the lighted candles, close her eyes, and *bensh licht* (recite her opening Sabbath prayers). The children would stay near her, and it seemed as if a Divine spirit filled the room. When she ended she said "Good Shabbos" and the children answered "Amen."

When Simcha returned from the synagogue he would repeat "Good Shabbos" and everybody would say "Amen." The table was set; the candles threw a dim light over the room. The white tablecloth glimmered and the lights showed two challahs covered with a hand-embroidered cloth, the bottle of wine and glasses around it — knives, forks, and spoons, all were on the table. Simcha washed his hands, opened the bottle, filled the bigger glass, put it in the palm of his hand, and said Kiddush, the blessing of G-d for the Sabbath. He then took a drink and handed the glass to Molke. She took a sip and gave each child a sip, beginning with the oldest. Then Simcha uncovered the challah, recited the *Hamotzi* benediction, cut a piece, ate it, and then distributed challah portions to his family.

Everybody started with the fish, then soup, meat or chicken, with kugel made of the noodles, and last, the tzimmes, made of carrots sweetened with sugar. Between the courses Simcha and the children would sing *zemiros*, a sort of thanksgiving prayer in song. Every one of the boys tried to be louder than the others, and Molke would sit, her face shining brightly, and help in the harmonizing. From time to time she would say Amen, and the children would follow suit. As the candles got low and began to go out, only the kerosene lamp was left burning until Vassil's son, the peasant friend of the family, would come to turn it out. Molke would hand him a big piece of challah. No Jew was allowed to turn out fire on the Sabbath.

In total darkness Simcha and Molke would sit after the children were in bed, and talk about the next world and how a Jew has to prepare for it, how much good he had to do to his neighbors, to his friends, and even to his enemies to gain enough mitzvos to go right to Heaven. They sat talking until they tired and went to sleep. And when the Sabbath was gone and the grim week started, it was again the start of a struggle to make enough to live on.[4]

The week meant everyday life, it meant hard work, and it meant the return from the heavenly joy of the Sabbath to the world where one was misunderstood, despised, and hated. The people of the shtetl, it was said, lived from Sabbath to Sabbath, the one day each week that made all Jews equal and every man a king.

CZAR NICHOLAS I AND THE CANTONIST DECREE: The thirty-year reign (1825–1855) of the so-called Iron Czar was an unmitigated disaster for the Jewish people. Czar Nicholas I devised a new, fiendish way to strike at the Jewish people and hasten their Russification — through their children. In 1827, the Cantonist decree was signed (a canton is a military district), providing for six years of preparatory army training from age twelve through eighteen, followed by twenty-five years of military service in the Russian Army, all in far-off areas devoid of Jews. A fixed quota of children was placed on each Jewish community, or *kehillah*, and its leaders were threatened with military service should they fail to supply the requisite number of children. This had the unfortunate effect of setting Jew against Jew. Frantic parents bribed *kehillah* or government officials to take other children in their children's place. Some parents even mutilated their sons to make them unfit for military service. As wealthy parents were able to buy their way out, the burden of military service fell primarily on the poor.

Communities hired professional kidnappers, known as *khappers*, to fill their quota. The *khappers* grabbed children as young as eight, falsifying their ages to the authorities. They perpetrated incredible cruelties. Houses were raided during the night, and children were torn from the arms of their mothers, or lured away and kidnapped. The shtetl rabbis were powerless against the Jewish mafioso and the widespread corruption of the *kehillah* officials, causing great popular resentment against Jewish institutions and even Judaism itself. (However, the Lubavitcher rebbe, Rabbi Menachem Mendel Schneerson, operated an underground railroad that was able to rescue some children.) Eventually, the czar decreed that if a recruit were missing, any relative could be taken in his place — his father, uncles, or cousins.

Heartrending scenes took place when the army officers took the children away. It was worse than mourning for the dead, for when the children took leave of their dear ones it was at least for thirty years, and more often than not for life. Rashi (Genesis 37:35) describes their pain perfectly when he states that unlike a dead relative, the passage of time does not assuage the pain of involuntary separation from a living dear one. I. L. Levin, who saw such a transport start on its long journey, described the scene:

> Near a house stood a large and high wagon, to which a pair of horses were harnessed. Soldiers brought out children from the house, one after another, and deposited them in the wagon. Soon it was packed to capacity. Children were sitting or lying on top of each other like herring in a barrel. Fathers, mothers, and relatives stood around. A person who has not seen the agonizing parting of parents from their little children and who has not heard their helpless lamentations that penetrate to heaven does not know real tragedy. One father gives his boy a little book of Psalms. Another hands his son tefillin. From all sides are heard admonitions: "Remain a Jew; no matter what happens, hold fast to Jewishness!" Mothers wring their hands, the hopeless tears never stop, moans of agony and cries of despair resound.[5]

The children traveled to remote regions of Russia on foot, slogging month after month through dust, mud, snow, and ice, beaten with whips, starving, sick, and dying. A Russian writer met such a convoy and was told by the escorting officer:

> We got together a bunch of these accursed Jews, between the ages of eight and nine. Half of them will not get to their destination...they fall like flies. Well, you know these Jewish boys are so puny and delicate. They can't stand mixing dirt for ten hours, with dry biscuits to live on. Again, everywhere strange folks; no father, no mother, no caresses. Well then, you just hear a cough and the youngster is dead....

The little ones were assembled and arrayed in a military line. It was one of the most terrible spectacles I have ever witnessed. Poor, poor children! The boys of twelve or thirteen managed somehow to stand up, but the little ones of eight and ten... No brush, however black, could convey the terror of this scene on the canvas. Pale, worn out, with scared looks, this is the way they stood in their uncomfortable, rough soldier uniforms, with their starched, turned-up collars, fixing an inexpressibly helpless and pitiful gaze upon the garrisoned soldiers, who were handling them rudely. White lips, blue lines under the eyes betokened either fever or cold. And these poor children, without care, without a caress, exposed to the wind, which blows unhindered from the Arctic Ocean, were marching to their death. I seized the officer's hand, and with the words: "Take good care of them!" threw myself into my carriage. I felt like sobbing, and I knew I could not master myself.[6]

The Russian writer saw the Jewish Cantonists on the road, but he knew nothing of what happened to them later on, in the recesses of the barracks into which they were driven. At a later time, the few survivors among these martyred Jewish children revealed this terrible secret to the world. The children were first taken to the local Russian Orthodox priest for religious indoctrination, which proved fruitless in nearly all cases. Then the tortures began. A favorite procedure was to make the Cantonists get down on their knees in the evening and keep them in that position for hours. Those who agreed to be baptized were permitted to go to bed, while the others were kept up the whole night until they dropped from exhaustion. They were also flogged, and forced to do arduous gymnastic exercises. Children who refused to eat pork were beaten and left to starve. Sometimes they were fed salted fish and forbidden to drink until, crazed by thirst, they agreed to adopt Christianity.

Many stories of heroism abound. In one instance, a number of Cantonists agreed to be baptized. A great military parade was scheduled, and the children were taken to the banks of the river, where the Russian Orthodox priests, clad in their finest religious vestments, awaited the children. (One version of the story has the czar himself attending the ceremony.) At the command to jump into the water, the children replied "Yes! Yes!" Then, in the tradition of the 400 boys and girls at the time of *Churban Bayis Sheini*, the children disappeared beneath the waves and drowned.[7]

OTHER DECREES OF CZAR NICHOLAS I: So consuming was the hatred of Nicholas I for the Jews, one wonders how he found time for anything else. In his thirty-year reign, he issued 600 decrees against the Jews.[8] He shrank the Pale of Settlement, expelling Jews from the small towns and into the large cities, thereby disrupting the fabric of shtetl life. The *kehillah* was shorn of its power to regulate Jewish life, and was only left with the functions of collecting government taxes and recruiting soldiers for the czar's army. Synagogues could not be placed near churches. Jews were not able to use Hebrew or Yiddish in documents or commercial papers, a real burden since most Jews did not speak or write Russian. Jews could not hire Christian domestic help. Realizing that the Talmud was the root of the Jews' adherence to their faith, the czar not only ordered the Talmud be burned, but also severely curtailed printing religious books. Indeed, all books printed had to undergo rigorous censorship, either by Christians or Jewish renegades. The police harassed Jews who wore traditional garb, often cutting their *peyos* and shredding their long coats.

Nicholas realized, however, that these measures were not solving his so-called Jewish problem. Forced conscription and expulsion were having little effect on Jewish morals or manners. Indeed, Jews were so martyr-minded that they could endure the worst persecutions. Clearly, something different was needed. Therefore, the czar decided to attack the mainstays of Jewish religious life — the rabbinate and the schools. A German Reform Jew, Dr. Max Lilienthal, was brought in to organize modern schools in which nontraditional teachers would teach Jewish and secular subjects, thereby replacing the traditional *cheder* with its elementary school teacher, the *melamed.*

In 1843, the Russian government convened a Rabbinic Commission to decide the future of Jewish education. The two religious representatives, Rabbi Isaac of Volozhin, the head of the Misnagdim, and Rabbi Menachem Mendel, the Lubavitcher rebbe and leader of Russia's Chassidim, strove mightily to retain the traditional school system. Their efforts were successful, although they could not prevent the creation of modern government schools. In 1845, disappointed by his lack of success in advancing school reform, Lilienthal departed for the United States, becoming a prominent Reform clergyman in New York and Cincinnati. In his wake, the czarist government also established so-called rabbinical schools to train modern rabbis, decreeing that only graduates of these schools could be recognized as rabbis. However, the Jews saw through Nicholas' ruses, and these steps met with only limited success.

When Nicholas died in 1855, Russian Jews felt as if an enormous burden had been lifted from them. Nicholas' son Alexander II, who succeeded him and ruled from 1855 to 1881, freed millions of Russian serfs from bondage. He lifted the order of child conscription, although he did not allow children already in the army to return home. Alexander also opened the universities to Jews, hoping in that way to wean Jews away from their religion. He also allowed Jews with secular educations, whom he deemed useful, to live outside the Pale. Alexander II was assassinated in 1881, and was succeeded by his son, Alexander III.

ALEXANDER III: Under the rule of the rabidly anti-Semitic Alexander III, 1881–1894, the lot of Russia's Jews became worse than ever before. All the gains of the days of Alexander II, with the exception of the Cantonist decree, were reversed. Alexander III's main advisor, K. Pobedonostzev, adopted the slogan "Russia for Russians." Pobedonostzev also believed in a police state guided by the Church, and was quoted as saying that the Jewish problem would be solved by one-third conversion, one third emigration, and one-third annihilation.[9] Under this tyrant and his czar, anti-Semitism was transformed into violence against Jews.

THE POGROMS: Although during the reign of Alexander II — in 1871 in Odessa — a terrible pogrom against the Jews took place, it was an isolated incident. Under Alexander III, however, pogroms came back on a scale not known since the mid–seventeeth century. The authorities condoned them, may have even encouraged them, but certainly did nothing to stop them. It became horrifyingly apparent that what most united the Russian people — peasant, middle class, nobility, up to the czar — was a hatred of Jews.[10]

First, the Russian press hinted that the Jews were behind the assassination of Alexander II. Then officials went to southern Russia and told the local police that if pogroms broke out, they should be allowed to run their course without police interference. Rumors spread that the czar would permit attacks on the Jews during the coming Easter. Given that climate, it did not take long for attacks to begin. On Easter Sunday, 1881, a pogrom broke out against the 15,000-member Jewish community of Elizabethgrad. By the end of 1881, the bloody fever raged through 215 cities and villages in Southern Russia. Estimates put the number of homeless at 20,000, those ruined economically at 100,000, and the value of property destroyed at $80 million. Not many Jews were killed, although some usually were in the course of each pogrom.[11] Leaders of the mobs were generally not local people, but instead were Russians who came down by train to spearhead the riots. The pogroms followed a regular pattern: two or three days of wanton destruction before the police stepped in to quell the rioting. According to an eyewitness account:

> At 12:00 noon, the air suddenly resounded with wild shouts, whistling, jeering, hooting, and laughing. An immense crowd of young boys, artisans, and laborers were on the march. The destruction of Jewish houses began. Windowpanes and doors began to fly about, and shortly thereafter the mob, having gained access to the houses and stores, began to throw upon the streets absolutely everything that fell into their hands. Clouds of [pillow] feathers began to whirl in the air. The din of broken windowpanes and frames, the crying, shouting, and despair in the one hand, and the terrible yelling and jeering on the other, completed the picture... Soon afterward the mob threw itself upon the Jewish

synagogue, which despite its strong bars, locks, and shutters, was wrecked in a moment. One should have seen the fury with which the riffraff fell upon the Torah scrolls, of which there were many in the synagogue. The scrolls were torn to shreds, trampled in the dirt, and destroyed with incredible passion. The streets were soon crammed with the trophies of destruction. Everywhere fragments of dishes, furniture, household utensils, and other articles lay scattered about... Those that had looted the stores of ready-made clothes put on three or four suits, and, not yet satisfied, took under their arms all they could lay their hands on. Others drove off in vehicles, carrying with them bags filled with loot...[12]

When told of the pogroms, the czar said they were justified, because the Jews were hated for their "economic supremacy" and their "exploitation" of the Russian people. While most of the perpetrators got off with nothing, or extremely light sentences, the courts punished Jews arrested for defending themselves. There was almost no protest against the pogroms — not even the great Russian writers Tolstoy and Dostoyevsky raised their voices. Even radical groups opposed to the czar and nobility supported the pogroms, as evinced by the following leaflet:

Good people, honest Ukrainian people! Life has become hard in the Ukraine, and it keeps getting harder. The police beat you, the landowners devour you, the kikes, the dirty Judases, rob you. People in the Ukraine suffer most of all from the kikes. Who has seized the land, the woodlands, and the taverns? The kikes. Whom does the peasant beg with tears in his eyes to let him near his own land? The kikes. Wherever you look, whatever you touch, everywhere the kikes. The kike curses the peasant, cheats him, and drinks his blood. The kikes make life unbearable. Workers, arise! Wreak your vengeance on the landowners; pillage the Jews, kill the officials![13]

As dreadful as the pogroms were, by twentieth-century standards they were but mild manifestations of anti-Semitic opinion. By nineteenth-century standards, however, the pogroms were extraordinary and shocking. A protest meeting was called in London, attended by members of Parliament, the Anglican Church, and aristocrats. The Earl of Shaftsbury remarked that "if but a tenth part of the reports were true, it is sufficient to draw down the indignation of the world." He implored the czar "to be a Cyrus to the Jews, and not an Antiochus Epiphanes."[14] The United States House of Representatives formally protested to the Russian government, calling on the president to request the czar to protect his Jewish subjects against violence. Faced with such world pressure, by mid-1882 the pogroms died down, after that occurring only sporadically.

OTHER DISCRIMINATION: Nevertheless, after the pogroms subsided, more laws against Jews were promulgated. By 1890, there were 650 laws in the Russian code that discriminated against Jews.[15] Jews were not permitted to move even within the Pale of Settlement. They could not own land or engage in agriculture. Strict quotas were placed upon Jewish admission into secondary schools and universities. Jews could not get government jobs unless they converted. In 1891, tens of thousands of Jews were expelled from Moscow. Shortly afterward, the large, Magen David (Star of David)–capped dome of the beautiful, then-new Moscow Synagogue was ordered removed. Soon thereafter, the synagogue was shut down, and the government ordered the building sold. When the synagogue's rabbi petitioned the government to cease, he was banished to the Pale of Settlement.[16] An 1893 law, Concerning Names, forbade Jews from adopting Russian, Christian names.[17] In 1894, the government made the liquor trade a state monopoly, wiping out the occupation of some 250,000 Jews. As a result of these decrees, nearly 50 percent of the Jewish population of Russia became destitute, requiring public assistance.

THE PROTOCOLS OF THE ELDERS OF ZION: Russia was also the source of the most influential anti-Semitic document ever written, *The Protocols of the Learned Elders of Zion*. At one point, it was estimated that the worldwide circulation of this fraudulent document was second only to that of the Bible. The *Protocols* purports to tell the story of a secret assembly of international Jewish leaders who discuss their plans for world domination. Although the book was incontrovertibly proven to be an abject forgery, it has remained popular for more than a century. Hitler made it a principal instrument of Nazi propaganda, and Arab nations expend great sums in disseminating the *Protocols* throughout areas of the world that have had minimal exposure to Jews, including Japan and Latin America. The canard has even been featured on Amazon.com, complete with a literary review.

THE *HASKALAH*: The unending attacks on Jewish life in the 1800s caused a radical break in the inner life of Russian Jewry. Although only a small minority — mainly the intelligentsia — adopted the values of the *Haskalah*, or Enlightenment, its pernicious effects filtered down through Jewish society. At first, the Maskilim, or Enlighteners, felt that integration into Russian society would be a viable answer to government anti-Semitism. However, their thinking changed dramatically in 1881, when the pogroms struck assimilated and non-assimilated Jews alike, and the government's new official policies of exclusion were directed mainly at those Jews who tried to be "like all men."[18] Consequently, the focus of *Haskalah* shifted from a Russianized form of Judaism to Hebrew and Yiddish secular literature. In the words of the distinguished, popular historian, Rabbi Berel Wein:

> Whereas Reform created the classic assimilationist Jew, the "non-Jewish Jew," who would likely never see Jewish grandchildren in his family, *Haskalah* created the secular Jew. He was also a "non-Jewish Jew," but he was, in the main, not prone to convert or to even abandon Jewish society, though he professed no Jewish faith and observed no Jewish ritual. He attempted to redefine Jewish life and Judaism itself in his own image and by his own terms. He created a secular Judaism of intellect and scholarship, ideals and dreams, social welfare and political progress, devoid of the Jewish past and irrelevant to Jewish destiny. Thus, the secular *Haskalah* laid claim to the Hebrew language, to Biblical literature and study, to Jewish

history and historiography, and contested the traditional vision of the Jewish future.[19]

The centers of *Haskalah* were in Vilna and especially Odessa, which became the most secularized of all Russian Jewish cities. *Haskalah*'s pioneer champion in Russia was Isaac Ber Levinsohn. In 1828, he published *The House of Judah*. Many young people devoured its messages of seeking secular knowledge, studying Russian, and extolling the virtues of agricultural labor. He also influenced the government to intervene in the Jewish educational system, and to limit printing religious books unless they were approved by state censorship. Eventually, however, the government had no more use for him, and he died a pauper broken in spirit.

HEBREW *HASKALAH*: The Hebrew Maskilim turned to the stories of the Tanach and its biblical Hebrew, stripping them of all religious significance in order to inculcate secular humanist values in the Jewish populace. One of the most popular writers of the time was Abraham Mapu, whose romantic adventures set in ancient Palestine carried the subliminal message of repudiation of Eastern European Jewish life. Judah Leib Gordon's poems satirized Orthodoxy as choking progress. Following the footsteps of Korach in the desert,[20] Gordon played up a fictitious case to portray the seeming inflexibility of the Torah: a husband refused to grant his wife a divorce, condemning her to a miserable existence. Finally, after much effort, the husband was located in a distant land and persuaded to grant his wife a *get*. When the *get* was delivered to the woman, the rabbis invalidated it because a word in the document was misspelled.[21] In addition, Gordon coined the infamous phrase, "Be a man [i.e., a Russian] on the street and a Jew in the house."[22] Along the same lines, Moshe Leib Lilienblum's book, *The Sins of Youth*, called on Judaism to let "outdated customs go" in order to clear the path for religion to "adjust" to life. Peretz Smolenskin published a monthly journal in Hebrew called *HaShachar*, which proclaimed that Jews had a national identity that transcended their religion.

The allure of such ideas, especially for the young, can be gleaned from the testimony of one of Smolenskin's contemporaries:

"There was not one yeshivah in all the Russian Pale to which Smolenskin's *HaShachar* had not found its way. The young people devised cunning ways to deceive their guardians. They read *HaShachar* on the Gemara and under the Gemara and sat up nights with it."[23]

YIDDISH *HASKALAH*: It was through Yiddish, the language of the shtetl, that writers reached their greatest audience. Through poems, novels, plays, short stories, and theatrical productions, these writers caricaturized the lives and traditions of the shtetl Jews. Abraham Goldfaden established the first professional Yiddish theater, whose medium reached millions of Jews both in Europe and America. Three Yiddish writers achieved worldwide recognition: Sholem Rabinowitz, known as Sholem Aleichem (of *Fiddler on the Roof* fame); Sholem J. Abramowitz, whose pen name was Mendele Mocher Sforim; and Isaac Leib Peretz. Mendele Mocher Sforim is known as the grandfather of modern Yiddish literature, while Sholem Aleichem was regarded as the Jewish Mark Twain.[24] Peretz, the most intellectual of the three, did not have the mass appeal of the other two, but is regarded as the father of modern Yiddish literature. Eventually, Peretz became disillusioned of *Haskalah*, as did many other Maskilim, and wrote:

"The Enlightenment didn't throw any significant light in any direction. It failed to inspire us with hope, or to provide us a philosophy that we could live by. Hastily, and without sufficient thought, we leaders took over a foreign formula. The resulting trend was not consonant with the Jewish way of life and thought. It was misdirection. We didn't know for sure where it meant to go, but certainly it traveled on the wrong road — the wrong road for us Jews!"[25] Eventually, a number of Maskilim converted to Christianity.

REASONS FOR *HASKALAH*'S SUCCESS: A number of factors contributed to the attraction of the ideals of the *Haskalah*. The terrible hardships of the times, beginning with the Cantonist decree and culminating with the pogroms, caused people to feel that the traditional way of Jewish life held no future. Many Jews, especially the poor, felt that the communities took advantage of them during the

Cantonist period, and that the rabbinic leadership did not take up their cause. The grinding poverty and daily rigors of making a living led people to believe that the ideals of the *Haskalah* held the promise of a better tomorrow. In addition, the forced movement of large numbers of Jews into the big cities, thus disrupting the age-old life of the shtetl, destroyed Jewish cohesiveness.

The rapid industrialization of the latter part of the nineteenth century also caused major dislocations of Jews who were seeking economic opportunity in newly opened fields. Such emerging jobs were often not conducive to intensive Torah study, which in eras past had provided intellectual stimulation and spiritual fulfillment for the Jewish people. By the end of the 1800s, then, observant Jewry was reeling from the unprecedented upheavals in Jewish life.

Haskalah itself later assumed new forms: Zionism, Bundism, Socialism, and Communism (all of which will be discussed later). The Haskalic goal of divorcing the Jewish people from its Torah heritage still lives on in secular Zionism, particularly in Israel; indeed, the struggle between Israeli religious and secular Jews bears much similarity to the kulturkampf of a century ago in Russia.

THE VILNA VERSUS SLAVITA *SHAS* CONTROVERSY: This famous episode is noteworthy for being a landmark case in Jewish copyright law, setting important precedents in this area of halachah. In 1822, a new edition of the Talmud (*Shas*), unrivalled in its excellence, was printed in Slavita. Rabbi Moshe Shapira, the printer, was granted a twenty-five-year copyright for exclusive printing by prominent rabbinic authorities. However, in 1834, printers in Vilna, claiming that Slavita had sold out all its volumes, received an exclusive copyright from other great rabbis to print the *Shas*, even forbidding Slavita to print a second edition. All efforts at adjudicating the case or finding a compromise failed.

Tragically, in the heat of the proceedings, the Slavita side spread a false rumor that the preeminent sage of the time, Rabbi Akiva Eiger, was bribed into supporting Vilna's claim. Although Rabbi Akiva Eiger was the paragon of humility, he proclaimed in a sharp response that even if he could forgive the slight to himself personally, he could not forgo the disgrace to the Torah's honor. Divine retribution struck both sides. A fire burned the Vilna printing press, and a blood libel struck the Slavita printers.

In 1853, a Jewish printer in the Slavita press was found dead of an apparent suicide. Renegade Jews convinced the government that Jews murdered the printer, in a new twist of the classic blood libel — Jews killing Jews for their blood. The czar then shut down all but two Jewish printing presses, both of which were heavily censored. The two Shapira brothers, owners of the Slavita printing press, were sentenced to run the gauntlet. Five hundred soldiers were stationed on each side with wooden sticks, and the brothers were made to walk through the two rows stripped to their waist. When the yarmulke of one brother fell off his head during the beatings, he stopped to pick it up, even though the action prolonged his agony. This *kiddush HaShem* made such an impression on the Russians that the yarmulke was put on display in a museum.[26] Even after the beatings, the rival presses never resumed their printing, and eventually a new printing of the *Shas* was undertaken in Vilna, which became the current, standard version.

Chapter 20

RELIGIOUS JEWRY'S RESPONSE

THE 1800S — A DIFFICULT DIVINE TEST FOR THE JEWISH PEOPLE: Jacob's struggle with the angel (Genesis 32:25–33) represents the constantly changing ordeals the Jewish people will undergo until the Messianic Era.[1] During the 1800s, the powerful winds of secularism and persecution buffeted the Jewish people as never before. However, just as Jacob was Divinely assisted to overcome the angel, so the Jewish people were granted the spiritual fortitude to meet the challenges of their time. The Yeshivah and Mussar movements were formed, and Chassidus gained new strength. These forces ensured the survival of Torah Jewry to this time.

THE YESHIVAH MOVEMENT: Yeshivos have existed among the Jewish people from the earliest times, dating back to the era of the Patriarchs.[2] In an atmosphere of sanctity and intense Torah study free of distractions, aspiring men were guided and molded by great mentors, and as such the future leaders of the Jewish people were produced. After the Gaonic period, yeshivos generally consisted of small groups of students who studied with a local rabbi. However, the Chmielnicki massacres ravaged communities, drastically weakening this long-standing Torah educational system.[3] Scholars were beginning to lose their position of honor in communities.

VOLOZHIN: Upon the encouragement of his great teacher, the Vilna Gaon, Rabbi Chaim of Volozhin founded the Yeshivah of Volozhin. Established in 1803 and known as the mother of all yeshivos,[4] Volozhin became the prototype of the Lithuanian-style yeshivah, emphasizing the approach of the Vilna Gaon to Talmud study. Housed in a then-modern building, Volozhin eventually attracted more than 400 students from all over Lithuania. Several of the greatest scholars of the era, such as Rabbi Naftali Berlin (the Netziv) and the legendary Rabbi Chaim Soloveitchik of Brisk, gave lectures at the yeshivah. The existence of such an elite, prestigious institution of learning restored Torah scholarship to a position of esteem and respect among the Jewish people.

The method of study in Volozhin was unique. Based on the dictum of Rabbi Chaim in his *Sefer Nefesh HaChaim* that if there were one second in the history of the world that Torah study was absent, the earth would revert to nothingness,[5] Torah learning went on constantly. Special shifts of students were assigned to study throughout the night, and at times when people did not usually study Torah, such as holidays, Purim, and after fast days. (The Netziv personally took the slot immediately following Yom Kippur.[6]) Unlike other yeshivos, where the student body studies a set cycle of several Talmudic tractates over several years, in Volozhin the entire Talmud was studied from beginning to end, then repeated. The deans delivered discourses on every page of the Talmud instead of on specific topics; this became the norm in future yeshivos.[7]

Over the years, Volozhin resisted czarist oppression and overcame several fires. In 1892, Czar Alexander III closed the yeshivah when it refused to implement curricular changes that would spiritually destroy the institution. However, like a giant tree whose seeds spread far and wide, the students of Volozhin spawned future great academies of Torah learning. The Volozhin Yeshivah building reopened as a synagogue, and under the Soviet regime became a bakery. In 1993 the former Soviet republic of Belarus returned the building to the Jewish community.

OTHER LITHUANIAN YESHIVOS: In 1815, a yeshivah opened in the hamlet of Mir, becoming known as the Mirrer Yeshiva. While it prospered in the 1800s, its main renown came in the following century. The yeshivah of Telz opened in 1875 in Telsiai, Lithuania, and its popularity soared when one of the greatest Talmudists of the time, Rabbi Shimon Shkop, joined the faculty in 1884. Telz, like the Mirrer Yeshiva, reached its zenith in the first half of the 1900s. Great yeshivos also opened in Kelm, Slabodka, and Novarodok in the 1800s. The Lithuanian yeshivos' unparalleled level of learning attracted many brilliant youths, saving them from the ravages of the *Haskalah*, and ultimately proving the salvation of Torah-observant Lithuanian Jewry.

NON-LITHUANIAN YESHIVOS: In 1807, a yeshivah was founded by the great Chasam Sofer in Pressburg, becoming known as the mother of Hungarian yeshivos. Unlike the Lithuanian yeshivos, which concentrated on plumbing the depths of a Talmudic topic without regard to practical application, Hungarian yeshivos stressed tracing and clarifying the halachah from the Talmudic text and its commentaries. Here, the study of *Shulchan Aruch* was an integral component of Talmudic study, which was not the case in Lithuanian institutions. As a result, yeshivos such as Pressburg turned out many ordained rabbis, who spread throughout the cities and towns of Hungary. These rabbis turned out to be the salvation of religious Hungarian Jewry, which was locked in a bitter struggle with the Reform movement. Pressburg also developed many students, who, although they did not enter the rabbinate, became fine, upstanding businessmen.

CHASSIDIC YESHIVOS: For the most part, the chassidic world did not establish formal yeshivos until the 1900s. Chassidim felt that the old system of local studying had major advantages. Parents, children, and often grandchildren studied together in the synagogue, solidifying family bonds and transmitting the *mesorah*, the Torah-tradition, from generation to generation. It also enabled parents to supervise and influence the development of their adolescent children, which would not be possible if the students studied at a central yeshivah.[8] However, by the beginning of the twentieth century, chassidic leaders realized that the dramatically changing times necessitated the establishment of yeshivos, and yeshivos spread throughout the chassidic world as well.

RABBI CHAIM SOLOVEITCHIK (1853–1915): Also known as Reb Chaim Brisker, after the town of Brisk where he served as rabbi, Rabbi Chaim developed a new, revolutionary approach to Talmud study, which spread quickly through Lithuania and became the standard method of yeshivah study. Known as Reb Chaim's *derech*, or as *der Litvishe derech*, this analytical method strove to identify the underlying principles on which each law was based. Based on such piercing analysis, many new precedents in halachah were established. Rabbi Chaim's system was also extremely satisfying intellectually, and infused Talmudic study with new vitality.

Rabbi Chaim's magnum opus was his *Chiddushei Reb Chaim al HaRambam*, which applied the new approach to elucidating seeming contractions between different statements of Rambam's *Mishnah Torah*, then reconciling them with the Talmud. This work is the basic primer of Rabbi Chaim's thought system, and its depths are plumbed in contemporary yeshivos across the globe. An example of this method of study involves the law that if one immerses in a *mikvah* to become ritually pure while holding an impure item, the immersion is ineffective. This idea can be viewed in two possible ways. First, the person never became purified. Second, the person did indeed become pure, but immediately contracted impurity again from the impure object. This sort of clarity of thought greatly enhanced — if not revolutionized — Torah learning then, and continues to do so today.

Rabbi Chaim was also justly famed for his compassion for the needy. During his tenure as rabbi in Brisk, an enormous conflagration broke out in the city, destroying many Jewish homes. Although Rabbi Chaim's house was not harmed, he refused to sleep in it, spending his nights with the homeless people in cramped, communal quarters, until everyone was properly accommodated.[9] Rabbi Chaim's house was also the address for women to leave unwanted infants. Although these children were of questionable origin, and shunned by the community, Rabbi Chaim fed and raised them in his home, paying for wet nurses to feed them. One time, a person came to Rabbi Chaim asking whether he could fulfill the mitzvah of drinking four cups at the Seder with milk. Rabbi Chaim answered in the negative, and gave the person money to purchase all his holiday needs. When questioned as to his course of action, Rabbi Chaim explained that if the person wanted to drink milk at the Seder, he obviously had no meat. Rabbi Chaim's descendants comprise the Soloveitchik family, to this day one of the world's most prominent rabbinic families.

THE MUSSAR MOVEMENT — PROBLEMS IN LITHUANIAN (NON-CHASSIDIC) SOCIETY: Beneath the surface of piety and Torah study, Lithuanian society was eroding. Mitzvah observance was becoming rote and stale, lacking any enthusiasm or sense of purpose. Torah study was reduced to knowledge of myriad details, without any focus on the moral lessons and spiritual perfection the commandments are supposed to inculcate. The sections of the Torah dealing with interpersonal relations and perfection of character were neglected. Many people regarded Judaism merely as a list of do's and don'ts, and were especially susceptible to the Enlightenment coming from Western Europe. In the words of Rabbi Israel Salanter:

> Most Jews would not think of eating bread without washing their hands, even if they will go hungry as a result. However, the severe sin of *lashon hara* (gossip) is violated with impunity, even if there is little desire for it... If a kosher butcher has the slightest doubt regarding the status of his meat, he will consult with a rabbi, despite the possibility of incurring a substantial loss. However, if he is involved in a monetary case, he will lie and cheat, even though it is a worse sin than eating non-kosher food.[10]

Chassidus addressed these problems in its own way, which helped the society in which it thrived. However, Lithuanian Jews were historic opponents of Chassidus. In addition, the temperament of the average Lithuanian Jew was not suited for Chassidus. The cheerfulness, lightness, and spontaneous merriment of Chassidus held no attraction for the staid, reserved Lithuanian Jews. (Even today, the terms *kalte Litvak*, a cold Lithuanian, and *vareme Chassid*, a warm Chassid, are commonly used.) Misnagdic Jews needed a revolutionary movement to infuse new vitality into their observance. The Mussar movement, founded by Rabbi Israel Salanter, filled this need.

RABBI ISRAEL SALANTER (1810–1883): Rabbi Israel's family name was Lipkin, but he became known as Rabbi Israel Salanter after the town of Salant, Lithuania where he studied as a youth. He became attracted to a renowned scholar, Rabbi Zundel Brodie of Salant, a leading disciple of Rabbi Chaim of Volozhin. The young Rabbi Israel was inspired by Rabbi Zundel's piety, particularly its hiddenness. As later related by Rabbi Israel, he stealthily followed Rabbi Zundel into the forest, where the latter was in the habit of reciting and formulating ethical and pietistic duties of particular relevance. Once, Rabbi Zundel spotted young Israel and then told him, "Israel, learn Mussar that you may become one who fears Heaven."[11] Upon hearing his teacher's charge, Rabbi Israel's heart was filled with a fiery zeal, and he assiduously began studying Mussar.[12]

In 1838, having developed into a great scholar, Rabbi Israel entered public life, circulating through the small hamlets of Lithuania, eventually heading a prestigious Talmudic academy in Vilna, the so-called Jerusalem of Lithuania. His credentials as a towering Talmudic scholar now evident to all, Rabbi Israel felt that the time was ripe to launch his Mussar movement. In 1849, he opened a small yeshivah where he concentrated on molding disciples of preeminent intellectual caliber in the doctrines of Mussar. These students became the standard-bearers of the fledgling movement, establishing it in scholarly circles. Although Rabbi Israel intended his movement to include the bulk of the Jewish people, the intellectual bent of Mussar study tended to attract highly learned individuals. The intimate, individualistic, spiritual introspection that Mussar study required was — and is — beyond the capacity of the average Jew.[13] Rabbi Israel traveled to Germany and France in 1857, spending his final years there, attempting to reach Western European Jewry with his message. He died in Konigsberg, Germany (now Kaliningrad, Russia) in 1883.

THE PRINCIPLES OF MUSSAR: The word Mussar appears once in the *Chumash* (Deuteronomy 11:2), and is generally translated as chastisement or instruction. More recently, it has referred to the three major principles of the Mussar movement: perfection in Torah observance, perfection in deed, and perfection in character. Together, these constitute complete human perfection.[14]

Perfection in Torah observance: For Mussar, observance of ritual mitzvos and neglect of other precepts does not suffice. All commandments must be followed — a Jew must be as exacting in the performance of such mitzvos as loving one's neighbor, avoiding robbery, not bearing a grudge, and walking in the ways of G-d, as he is in observing the Sabbath laws, keeping kosher, praying, and eating matzo on Pesach. The Mussar movement took upon itself to put a stop to this strange discrimination between one mitzvah and another, between one sin and another, and instead worked to ensure that equal value be assigned to all mitzvos. This was no easy feat to accomplish, for human nature tends to disregard the commandments that go against ingrained negative character traits.

Perfection in deed: Even ritual mitzvos, which were generally observed, were performed mechanically, by force of habit. Mussar taught that devotional feeling and uplifting thoughts should accompany all actions, elevating the significance of the mitzvah being done. As an example, often, incidental rituals are stressed at the expense of essential components. Many people recite extra prayers on Yom Kippur while forgetting the major theme of the day, which is proper repentance.[15] At times, too, sins are committed in the observance of a mitzvah. A person rises very early for the *Selichos* service before Rosh HaShanah, but disturbs other people's sleep in the process. The study of Mussar involved setting one's priorities correctly, ensuring that any action performed was free of wrongdoing, particularly in regard to other people.

Perfection of character: The Mussar movement sought to attain the ultimate Torah goal and the most difficult of all human endeavors — the perfection of one's character. Man is born as a wild colt (Job 11:12), and his innate selfishness dominates his personality. Lust, envy, pride, vengefulness, and the desire for honor control his actions. A person must engage in rigorous self-analysis to identify his areas of weakness. However, intellectual awareness is not sufficient to change one's character, for one must involve his emotions as well. To this end, Rabbi Israel Salanter developed the most novel idea of the Mussar movement — the fervent, repetitive recitation of moral axioms using a deeply introspective tune.[16] These phrases were culled from the vast number of Scriptural and Talmudic references to character perfection, such as "Create in me a pure heart, O L-rd, and renew a steadfast spirit within me" (Psalms 51:12), and "Jealousy, lust, and glory remove a person from the world" (*Avos* 4:21). Rabbi Israel established Mussar houses where people could strive for character perfection in an atmosphere conducive to that purpose. Copies of Mussar works were available for study, especially Rabbi Moshe Chaim Luzzatto's classic *Mesillas Yesharim* (The Path of the Just), which became the primer of the Mussar Movement.

RABBI ISRAEL'S SAINTLINESS: Astounding stories were told of Rabbi Israel's behavior toward human beings. Although he did not intend it, many of his actions received broad coverage in the press, books, and literary works, evoking broad acclaim all over the world. In the words of one of his disciples:

> Our master and rabbi illuminated the eyes of the Diaspora through his many inquiries into, and vast knowledge of, the laws pertaining to money matters, robbery, and damages. In this respect he was indeed unique in these generations.[17]

Three of the myriad examples of Rabbi Israel's behavior give a faint glimpse of this giant:

While Rabbi Israel was eating, a poor widow came before him and complained that her son was about to be conscripted into the Russian army. If someone could only speak on her behalf to a certain Jewish leader who was well known to the authorities, there was a chance of freeing the boy. Rabbi Israel stopped eating. "If my son were in such a position," he said, "could I sit quietly and eat?" He immediately left the house, and ran out to exert some pressure on behalf of the widow, as if the boy were really his son.[18]

Once, before Pesach, Rabbi Israel was unable to be present during matzo baking, in which he was extremely meticulous. His disciples, who were overseeing the baking, asked him for directions. Rabbi Israel instructed them to be extremely careful not to upset the woman who kneaded the dough and not to rush her, for she was a widow and to upset her would be a violation of the prohibition against oppressing widows and orphans (Exodus 22:21). According to Rabbi Israel, the matzo must be kosher according to both the laws of Pesach and the laws of human relations.[19]

Another time, Rabbi Israel was invited to one of his disciple's Sabbath evening meal. The host assured Rabbi Israel that he would have an uplifting experience from the lengthy Torah discussions and *zemiros* sung at the table. Rabbi Israel agreed to attend, providing the meal was shortened by two hours. Having little choice, the host reluctantly consented to the strange condition. At the meal, Rabbi Israel rushed one course after another, and they ended in less than an hour. Greatly perturbed, Rabbi Israel's host asked if his esteemed teacher had found fault in the host's conduct. Rabbi Israel did not reply, but asked the cook to come into the dining room. "Please forgive me," he said to her, "for tiring you this evening, and causing you to hurry and serve one course after another without a break." The cook exclaimed, "If only you would come every Friday night! Thanks to you, I can go home two hours early!" Rabbi Israel turned to his disciple and said, "Your conduct at the table is truly praiseworthy — but not at the expense of others."[20]

In the final hours of his life a simple Jew attended to Rabbi Israel. He spent his last moments reassuring the man that dead people are harmless, and that there is no reason to fear being alone with a corpse. Rabbi Israel died as he had lived, always showing concern for the other person.

RABBI ISRAEL'S *TALMIDIM*: Rabbi Israel's great disciples carried on his legacy. Rabbi Isaac Blaser, who became the rabbi of the Russian capital of St. Petersburg, compiled the master's writings into a book called *Ohr Yisrael*. This work is the primary source for Rabbi Israel's Mussar system, as he did not leave any formal writings on the subject. Rabbi Naftali Amsterdam, another disciple, served as rabbi in Helsinki, Finland, before emigrating to Eretz Yisrael. Rabbi Jacob Joseph traveled to the United States in an attempt to bring rabbinic leadership to what was then a spiritual wasteland.

These men spread the doctrine of Mussar, their influence proving the salvation of Lithuanian Jewry. However, the Mussar movement found its strongest adherents among scholars, particularly in the Lithuanian yeshivos. Three main schools of Mussar eventually predominated and produced leaders: Kelm, Slabodka, and Novarodok.

THE KELM SCHOOL OF MUSSAR: Rabbi Simcha Zissel Ziv, a disciple of Rabbi Israel Salanter, founded the Kelm school of Mussar, becoming affectionately known as the Alter (elder) from Kelm. Careful never to eat a food for which he had a craving, after fasting he ate small, bony fish in order to break his desire to eat, and to acquire the character trait of patience.[21]

In 1862, he established a yeshivah in his hometown of Kelm, Lithuania, to perpetuate the doctrines of his great teacher. Kelm stressed discipline, harmony, order, organization, and control. It strove to produce students whose intellect always controlled their emotions, and who never lost themselves no matter what the situation. Kelm valued the power of concentration, producing calm, rational, ordered individuals who were at peace with themselves and others, whose piety meshed with all aspects of their environment, and whose intelligence led them.[22] Although the Kelm Yeshiva was very small, consisting of fewer than fifty students, some of the greatest figures in the twentieth century Mussar movement studied there — spiritual giants such as Rabbi Yerucham Levovitz, *mashgiach* (spiritual advisor) of Mirrer Yeshiva; Rabbi Nassan Tzvi Finkel, of Slabodka Yeshiva; and the saintly Rabbi Chatzkel Levenstein, *mashgiach* in the Mirrer Yeshiva after Rabbi Yerucham's death, and later in the great Ponovezh Yeshiva in Bnei Brak, Israel. Several incidents offer a glimpse of the greatness that was Kelm:

In the middle of the afternoon break, the students were required to come to a study session lasting exactly five minutes. Its purpose was to accustom them to value time and to concentrate their thoughts quickly.[23]

Once, a visitor forgot his cane in the Kelm Yeshiva. When he returned for another visit thirteen years later, having long despaired of recovering the cane, he found it hanging in the same spot where he had left it.[24]

Another time, there was a great commotion outside the window of the yeshivah. Not one of the students interrupted their prayers by turning their heads to look.[25]

THE SLABODKA SCHOOL OF MUSSAR: Rabbi Nassan Tzvi Finkel, a disciple of the Alter of Kelm, founded the Slabodka school of Mussar. Known as the Alter of Slabodka, Rabbi Finkel founded a yeshivah in Slabodka, a suburb of the Lithuanian city of Kovno (today Kaunas). He stressed a very uplifting form of Mussar, highlighting the sublime greatness of the human soul. The awareness of having been created by G-d, and having been endowed with a pure soul, infuses man with the ambition to attain perfection.[26] Each person is great and has immeasurable potential. Slabodka took students beyond their personal limitations and lifted them into the rarefied regions of spiritual greatness. The Alter was a consummate pedagogue whose mastery and knowledge of human nature were unsurpassable. He motivated and led, inspired and taught, influenced and innovated.[27] Many of the great Torah leaders of recent times were products of Slabodka, including Rabbi Aharon Kotler, Rabbi Yaakov Kaminetzky, Rabbi Yaakov Yitzchak Ruderman, and Rabbi Yitzchak Hutner.

THE NOVARODOK SCHOOL OF MUSSAR: In contrast to the tranquility and harmony of Slabodka, the Novarodok approach to Mussar demanded constant tension and critical self-analysis. Struggle against every weakness, and affirmation of man's imperfection, were the core of the Novarodok message. The idea was not to perfect the existent self, in the way of Slabodka, but instead to tear it down and rebuild it, engaging in a never-ending struggle for perfection and an uncompromising search for the truth. Rage, emotion, and passion are the only tools that can break open the heart and the mind, empty it of all unworthiness, and allow inner rebirth.[28] The Alter of Novarodok was wont to say that if a person only changes for the better bit by bit, he is similar to one who, while in the process of making his house kosher, cooks his remaining non-kosher food there, in which case his newly kashered dishes become non-kosher again.[29]

Rabbi Israel Salanter influenced Novarodok's founder, Rabbi Yosef Yozel Hurwitz, a scholarly merchant who met the great Mussar master on a business trip. Subsequently, Rabbi Hurwitz gave up his business dealings and embarked on a rigorous campaign of self-perfection in order to attract aspiring students to the paths of Torah and Mussar. In 1896, Rabbi Yosef started a yeshivah in the Lithuanian town of Novarodok, and the school quickly grew into an entire network called Beis Yosef, attracting large numbers of students. These institutions followed the path of Novarodok Mussar, stressing communal self-criticism, breaking one's ingrained habits and desires, and, above all, an uncompromising search for the truth. For example, if students bought new suits, they let others wear them first in order to break the owners' innate selfishness. Similarly, students were trained to go into stores and request items that the store did not sell, such as asking for nails in a store that sold spices, in order to purposefully suffer embarrassment — a cure for the characteristic of arrogance.[30] This kind of act imbued the students with a sense of mission, to be undaunted by any hardships or ridicule.

Novarodok yeshivos were set up all over Lithuania and Russia, their students fearlessly spreading Torah publicly at great personal risk — especially after the Bolshevik Revolution — until it became absolutely impossible to do so. In 1922, numerous groups of Novarodok students escaped to Poland, where they set up more than ninety yeshivos serving some 3,000 students. These students, and the tens of thousands of Novarodok adherents, had a profound effect on Polish Jewry. The fervor and dedication that the Novarodok followers demonstrated found a responsive echo in the chassidic world of Poland, which respected the movement and its leaders.[31] Afterward, many graduates of Novarodok yeshivos became leaders of Jewish communities in the United States, Israel, France, and England. For example, the legendary Steipler Gaon, Rabbi Yaakov Y. Kanievsky, was a product of Novarodok.

OPPOSITION TO MUSSAR: Throughout Jewish history, new ideas, regardless of their merit, have undergone the crucible of heated debate and criticism before being generally accepted. The relentless scrutiny by the greatest leaders of the time serve as a brake for any excesses of new ideas, and help keep them within the framework of traditional Judaism. This was true of the study of philosophy at the time of Rambam, the trend toward Kabbalah in the 1500s, the rise of Chassidus in the 1700s, and the Mussar movement as well.[32]

A number of prominent rabbis disagreed with Rabbi Israel Salanter's institution of centers for the study of Mussar, feeling that such places would create splinter groups that would eventually break off from normative Judaism.[33] Other scholars felt that the study of Torah in and of itself spiritually purifies a person — without having him concentrate on Mussar, which in addition would take time away from Torah study.[34] The defenders of Mussar replied that in fact Mussar topics occur regularly in the normal course of studying Torah. In addition, they said that while in earlier generations Mussar may indeed have taken people from pure Torah study, when society and scholarship were on higher spiritual levels, in the time of the Mussar masters radical measures had to be taken to heighten people's ethical sensitivities.

In particular, the followers of *Haskalah* were terrified by the success of the Mussar movement, rightly fearing that Mussar, like Chassidus, would be an effective counterbalance to their program of secularizing the Jewish people. As such, the Maskilim used underhanded tactics to combat the movement. Defamatory articles were published in *Haskalah* newspapers, and the Maskilim even attempted to involve the Russian government against Mussar. However, Rabbi Yitzchak Elchanan Spector, the leading halachic authority of Lithuanian Jewry, was able to explain to officials that

Mussar was an apolitical movement, and the effort of the Maskilim was thwarted.

IN THE YESHIVAH WORLD: At first, there was considerable resistance to the introduction of a formal study program of Mussar in the Lithuanian yeshivos. In Volozhin, for example, the study of Mussar was left to the discretion of the individual student to be undertaken in private.[35] Attempts to introduce Mussar to Mir were unsuccessful. Widespread student opposition to Mussar in the yeshivah of Slabodka, Knesses Beis Yitzchak, forced the Alter of Slabodka to establish a breakaway yeshivah. Known as Knesses Beis Yisrael, its membership was composed of sixty students, a fifth of the 300-member student body of the original Slabodka Yeshiva. The new yeshivah became very popular and increased greatly. (An example of the passions that Mussar study unleashed in the yeshivos is that in the new Knesses Beis Yisrael there was a student rebellion against the Mussar program.)[36] The yeshivos of Telz and Radin also experienced student unrest over Mussar. Eventually, however, even yeshivos previously opposed to Mussar became bastions of that discipline, for rabbis and students alike realized that Mussar was necessary not only to improve the students, but also to counter the blandishments of *Haskalah*, communism, and secular Zionism.

THE CHASSIDIC WORLD – CHASSIDUS EXPANDS: By the early 1800s, the chassidic world had overcome its struggle with the Misnagdim. As Chassidus became more popular, it branched out into many schools of thought, evolving into a brilliant, multi-hued tapestry. In contrast to the formative period of Chassidus where the mantle of leadership was passed from teacher to leading disciple, dynastic chassidic courts sprang up in which a family member, usually a son, inherited the rebbe's position.[37] Some of these groups were very large, while other attracted few adherents. Many of today's great branches of Chassidus have their roots in this time period.

POLISH CHASSIDUS: In Poland, Chassidus attracted the largest number of followers, largely through the influence of three men: the

Holy Jew of Peshischa, the rebbe Reb Bunim, and the legendary Rabbi Menachem Mendel of Kotzk.

Rabbi Yaakov Yitzchak of Peshischa, a great Talmudic scholar, became attracted to the chassidic leader, the Chozeh of Lublin. Realizing the vast potential of his new disciple, the Chozeh delegated Rabbi Yaakov Yitzchak the role of teaching chassidic philosophy to the scholars of his court. However, Rabbi Yaakov Yitzchak, who became known as the Holy Jew to distinguish between himself and the Chozeh, who also had the name Yaakov Yitzchak, drew apart. The Chozeh was known as a miracle worker, to whom poor and needy Jews flocked. Although the Chozeh was motivated by his love for fellow Jews, the atmosphere around him was charged with veneration for his great powers to draw upon Heavenly intercession. The Holy Jew felt this direction was a denigration of Chassidus, which, he believed, should be concerned with man's striving for self-perfection and unity with G-d. As such, the Holy Jew broke away from the Chozeh and established his own court at Peshischa, where he stressed four major points: Talmudic learning as the basic requirement for the chassidic way of life, opposition to the superficiality of chassidic folkways and the substitution of tzadik-worship for Torah study, resistance to the wonder-working of the tzadik, and prayer as the most sublime form of worship, with the freedom of the individual to choose his own time and mode of prayer,[38] a point that became very controversial and was later modified.

The Holy Jew exerted a strong pull on many young Talmudic scholars, who saw his blend of scholarship and piety as the fulfillment of their innermost cravings for a life of meaning. When the Holy Jew died in 1814, his outstanding disciple, Rabbi Simcha Bunim, the rebbe Reb Bunim, inherited the leadership of Peshischa. He continued the Peshischa tradition of unending and uncompromising search for truth and consistency in belief, thought, word, and action. Thus, the rarefied atmosphere of Peshischa gave rise to one of the most awe-inspiring figures of the chassidic world — Rabbi Menachem Mendel Morgenstern of Kotzk (1788–1859) — the legendary "Kotzker" and the father of much of Polish Chassidus.

THE KOTZKER REBBE: As a child, the Kotzker's extraordinary brilliance was manifest. As is typical of many geniuses, he grew up serious minded and lonely. As an adolescent, he became attracted to Rabbi Simcha Bunim of Peshischa, and the Kotzker's character took form and ideas crystallized. Upon the death of his master, the Kotzker started his own chassidic court. He did not accept many followers, feeling that few could stand up to his standards of the highest intellectual and moral quality.

All socially accepted conventions — such as learning, wealth, good manners, and family lineage — meant nothing in Kotzk. Only what a man made of himself, to what use he put the things the Creator endowed him with — only these mattered to the Kotzker Chassidim. Indeed, in the search for absolute truth the Kotzker rebbe and his followers wore rags and treated each other without common respect in order to emphasize the folly of external, superficial behavior.

However, a person with such impossibly lofty aspirations as the Kotzker had could not possibly be satisfied. In 1839, in an event known in chassidic circles as "That Friday Night," the Kotzker isolated himself from his followers and remained a recluse for twenty years — until his death in 1859. Different versions exist as to what transpired on that Sabbath, and the matter is shrouded in mystery and legend.[39]

KOTZKER DISCIPLES: The Kotzker's disciples became the leaders of Polish Chassidus. Foremost among them was Rabbi Yitzchak Meir Alter, who became renowned as the founder of the Gerrer dynasty, the largest chassidic group in Poland. Another disciple, Rabbi Chanoch Henoch Levin, founded Alexander Chassidus, the second-largest chassidic group in Poland. The Kotzker's son-in-law, Rabbi Avraham Borenstein, one of the greatest Talmudic scholars in Poland, became the first chassidic rebbe of Sochatchov. Rabbi Yitzchak Kalish became the rebbe of Vorki and was one of the most venerated figures in Polish Jewry. Radziner Chassidus, who wore *techeiles* (blue-stringed) tzitzis, was an offshoot of Kotzk, as well, as was the court of Amshinov.

The Kotzk system restored the supremacy of Torah learning among Polish Chassidim. Indeed, the great chassidic emphasis on devout prayer and communion with G-d added emotional depth to the Talmudic intellectualism and ethical perfection propagated by Kotzk. As a result of this development, the study of the *Zohar* and other works of Kabbalah lost their hold on the minds of much of Polish Jewry. Logical thinking became the hallmark of Polish Chassidim and Misnagdim. Here, the rebbe was not seen as a mediator between the Chassid and G-d, and certainly not as a miracle worker, but rather as a spiritual guide any person should try to emulate.[40]

KOTZKER SAYINGS: The Kotzker's aphorisms are legendary, and reveal some the essence of his thought system:

"The greatest miracle of all is taking a man from the street and making him a Chassid."[41]

"In no way would I choose for myself a G-d whose ways are intelligible to human beings."[42]

When a young man told the Kotzker that he completed the study of the entire Talmud, the Kotzker remarked, "And what did the entire Talmud teach you?[43]

Once, the Kotzker asked, "Where does G-d dwell? Wherever man lets Him in."[44]

OTHER CHASSIDIC CENTERS: Aside from Poland, Chassidus spread throughout Russia, Ukraine, Galicia, Romania, and Hungary. Prominent Hungarian rebbes included Rabbi Yitzchak Taub, the famous Kalever rebbe; Rabbi Moshe Teitelbaum, the forerunner of the dynasties of Satmar and Sighet; Rabbi Menachem Mendel Hager, founder of Vizhnitz Chassidus; and Rabbi Tzvi Hirsch Shapiro, who headed the Munkatch dynasty.

Many chassidic groups originated in Galicia. Rabbi Sholom Rokeach of Belz started the Belzer dynasty, which attracted Chassidim throughout Galicia, Poland, and Hungary. Rabbi Chaim Halberstam of Sanz founded many chassidic dynasties, the most famous of which are Bobov and Klausenberg. A multifaceted personality, Rabbi Chaim combined great scholarship and fervor in prayer with many charitable deeds, giving virtually all his money to the poor. "I love the poor," he said, "for G-d loves them too." Rabbi Chaim had a great appreciation for song and melody, seeing them as playing a vital role in the service of G-d, and his *niggunim* (melodies) and marches remain a source of inspiration. Other great Galician rebbes included Rabbi Tzvi Elimelech Shapiro, the Bnei Yisaschar, and Rabbi Moshe Friedman of Boyan.

The rebbe of the Ukrainian town of Rizhin, a great-grandson of the Maggid of Mezeritch, achieved legendary status in his lifetime. In contrast to many other chassidic rebbes who saw a simple, even poor lifestyle as a great virtue, the Rizhiner took a diametrically opposed view, feeling that opulent grandeur was necessary to attract and impress people to follow the chassidic path. All his personal belongings, even his everyday cutlery, were made of the most expensive materials. The buttons on his frock were made of solid gold studded with diamonds, and his pillowcase was woven from pure gold thread. His house was a massive, ostentatious palace. Yet he was held in the greatest regard by the sages of his generation, for they realized that the Rizhiner's intentions were only for the sake of Heaven. In reality, the Rizhiner was surrounded by everything but took nothing. He afflicted his body terribly, denying himself even the basic necessities. His legendary golden boots, for example, encrusted with diamonds and other gems, had no soles — thereby forcing him to walk barefooted on stony and muddy ground.[45] To escape the harassment of the czar, who had previously jailed him, the Rizhiner fled to the Romanian town of Sadigura, where he set up a magnificent court and synagogue, which still stands today. On his deathbed, the Rizhiner testified that he never derived any enjoyment from this world.[46] His six sons founded great dynasties of their own, including Chortkov, Hoshatin, and Boyan.

Rabbi Nachum Twersky of Chernobyl, Ukraine, the ancestor of the great chassidic Twersky family, was the forerunner of numerous Ukrainian chassidic dynasties, the best known of which is Skver. Through marriage over the generations exclusively with descendants of other rebbes, the Twerskys are related to virtually all chassidic dynasties, and are one of the most distinguished families of Chassidim. (In general, leaders of Chassidic courts tend to marry among themselves, making almost all Chassidic groups related by blood.)

THE REBBES OF LUBAVITCH IN THE 1800S: After the passing of the Alter rebbe, Rabbi Schneur Zalman, in 1812, his son, Rabbi Dov Ber, inherited his father's mantle. Known as the Mitteler rebbe, he moved the center of Chabad Chassidus from Liozna to Lubavitch, and became known as the first Chabad-Lubavitch rebbe. If it was Rabbi Schneur Zalman who founded the Chabad movement, it was his son who consolidated it. When Rabbi Schneur Zalman died, the concept of chassidic dynasties had not yet been fully developed. Some of his followers felt that no one could ever replace him, and that they should continue leaderless, just as the Breslover Chassidim did not replace their rebbe. Others were of the opinion that the disciples should split into different courts, in the manner of the students of the Maggid of Mezeritch. Rabbi Dov Ber was able to counter these opposing forces and solidify the movement.

Rabbi Dov Ber was very active communally. Since the Russian czar was grateful for the Alter rebbe's support in the war against Napoleon, Rabbi Dov Ber was able to use his influence to help Russia's Jews. He was able to aid in reconstructing Jewish communities devastated by the war and to obtain more land for Jewish settlement. Rabbi Dov Ber also established the first Chabad settlement in the land of Israel, in 1817 in Hebron. Rabbi Dov Ber passed away in 1827.

Rabbi Menachem Mendel, a son of one of the Alter rebbe's daughters, became the third rebbe of Chabad, also becoming the first Lubavitcher rebbe to adopt the surname Schneerson. Rabbi Menachem Mendel is known as the Tzemach Tzedek, the same name as his famous work of *Shaalos Uteshuvos*. During his leadership, the dispute between Misnagdim and Chassidim dissipated considerably, as each side joined forces to combat the *Haskalah*. Rabbi Menachem Mendel also worked tirelessly to counteract the effect of the Cantonist decree, rescuing many children and encouraging others to remain faithful Jews.

In addition, Rabbi Menachem Mendel's scholarship and ability to relate his Torah knowledge to all Jews led to an explosive growth in the number of Chabad Chassidim. While the first two rebbes of Chabad had a relatively small number of followers, Rabbi Menachem Mendel attracted more than 100,000 Chassidim.[47] Rabbi Menachem Mendel passed away in 1866, designating his youngest son, Shmuel, as the next rebbe.

In the tradition of Lubavitcher rebbes, Rabbi Shmuel was active in communal affairs, even traveling to Western Europe on such matters. When he passed away in 1882, his son, Rabbi Sholom Dov Ber, became the fifth rebbe of Chabad, and was known as the rebbe Rashab. In 1897, he established the network of Chabad yeshivos known as Tomchei Temimim. He passed away in 1920.

THE CHAFETZ CHAIM: Rabbi Israel Meir HaKohen Kagan (1838–1933) was universally accepted, by Chassidim, Misnagdim, Jew, and non-Jew. His influence was enormous, for everyone realized his utter integrity. Rabbi Israel Salanter said, regarding the young Chafetz Chaim, "G-d has prepared a leader for the next generation."[48]

In 1873, Rabbi Israel Meir published his classic *Chafetz Chaim* on the laws of *lashon hara*, evil gossip. This trailblazing work took a subject of utmost importance, that was scattered throughout the Talmud and its commentaries, and presented it in a systematic, scholarly, yet thoroughly understandable way — thereby making it accessible to all Jews.

In 1907, after twenty-five years of preparation, Rabbi Israel Meir published the comprehensive commentary *Mishnah Berurah* on *Shulchan Aruch Orach Chaim*, the section dealing with daily and seasonal laws, explaining their application in present-day situations. When the *sefer* appeared, the great Rabbi Chaim Soloveitchik said, regarding its author, "His greatness as a tzadik obscures his even greater status as a Torah genius." *Mishnah Berurah* has become part of virtually every Jewish home library. The Chafetz Chaim also wrote many other books, such as a guide for Jewish soldiers; laws regarding mitzvos that show concern for one's fellow Jews, such as granting loans; and an abridgement in the style of Rabbi Alfasi on the laws of sacrifices. All these were written in an easy-to-follow style.

The Chafetz Chaim's saintliness was legendary. He dressed in simple clothing, wearing the ordinary hat and boots of working people. His furniture, too, was simple and poor. In his large, bare rooms stood long tables and benches. There he studied, ate, and received guests. Once, a rich man came to his home, and was taken aback by its stark plainness. He asked the Chafetz Chaim, "Where is the rabbi's furniture?" "And where is your furniture?" replied the Chafetz Chaim. "But I am only passing through here!" said the rich man. "I, too," said Rabbi Israel Meir, "am just passing through."[49] On a Friday afternoon, at candle-lighting time, Rabbi Israel Meir was seen running through the streets trying to locate and pay a worker who had left the print shop early, in order to fulfill the mitzvah of paying an employee's wages on the day of his job (Deuteronomy 24:15).[50] Dorothy Thompson, the celebrated American journalist, wanted to interview the Chafetz Chaim. When told that this was impossible, she begged to at least see him. Peering through the window of the Chafetz Chaim's house for fifteen minutes and watching him study Torah, she said, "I have just seen the Jewish G-d."[51] The Chafetz Chaim passed away in 1933, greatly mourned by all Jews.

CHACHAM YOSEF CHAIM (1834–1909): Known as the Ben Ish Chai, after the title of his book, Rabbi Yosef Chaim mastered all aspects of the Torah — Talmud, Halachah, and Kabbalah. He became the final halachic authority in the Sephardic world, answering questions from as far away as Hong Kong and Rangoon, Burma. Rabbi Yosef Chaim delivered lectures of up to four hours' duration in the central synagogue of Baghdad, Iraq, and despite the length of his sermons, and the fact that hundreds of men, women, and children attended, there was always a deep silence.[52] Children sat at his feet on the podium for the entire duration of his lecture, never uttering a sound. Rabbi Yosef Chaim, the greatest scholar the Sephardic world produced in the 1800s, inspired awe in Sephardim and Ashkenazim alike, all of whom assiduously study his numerous *sefarim*.

Chapter 21

PLACES OLD AND NEW

ERETZ YISRAEL: Since *churban Bayis Sheini* and the dispersal of the Jews all over the world, Jews have prayed for a return to Zion. Several benedictions of the daily *Shemoneh Esrei* focus on this theme, as does the *Birkas HaMazon* recited after meals. The Pesach Seder and the Yom Kippur prayers conclude with the heartfelt recital of "Next year in Jerusalem!" However, over the centuries living in Eretz Yisrael was fraught with great difficulties, and few individuals realized the dream. By the middle of the nineteenth century, about 10,000 Jews lived there — 8,000 in Jerusalem, where they comprised a majority of the city's inhabitants, the remainder in several towns, including Peki'in in the Galilee, which had a continuous Jewish settlement since Roman times.[1] At the time, this number represented less than one-half of one percent of world Jewry. These Jews were religious and were known as the *yishuv hayashan*, the old settlers. They were also very poor and subsisted largely on donations from abroad. Disease and starvation were rampant, and Turkish rule was cruel and humiliating. Yet in the eyes of the inhabitants of the Land, the spirituality attained by dwelling in the Palace of the King overshadowed all physical hardships.

The first stirrings of a movement to settle large numbers of Jews in Eretz Yisrael began in 1843. Two Orthodox rabbis, Rabbi Judah Alkalai and Rabbi Zvi Hirsch Kalischer, working independently, wrote treatises proclaiming that the settlement of Jews in the Holy Land with the consent of the nations of the world was the first step in ushering in the Messianic Era. Virtually all other rabbis, for reasons that will be discussed later, did not agree with this assessment, and as a result the Orthodox world did not embrace this idea.

In the second half of the nineteenth century, small Jewish settlements sprang up in places not inhabited by Jews for hundreds of years. Several new Jewish neighborhoods were established outside Jerusalem's protective walls, such as the nearby areas of Yemin Moshe and Mishkenot Sha'ananim, both founded by Sir Moses Montefiore, and the settlements of Meah Shearim and more distant Motza, purchased by groups of Jerusalem Jews. Areas of new Jewish habitation, some founded by religious Jews, formed in Petach Tikvah and Zichron Yaakov on the coast, and Rosh Pinah and Metulla in the upper Galilee. These pioneers faced incredible difficulties, including malaria, poor crops, sparse water supply, and Arab harassment. In the main, however, the Jews persevered, laying the foundation for the expansion of these areas into present-day Jewish centers.

HOVOVEI ZION AND *BILU*: In the 1880s, after the outbreak of pogroms in Russia, two movements began with the aim of convincing Jews to immigrate to Eretz Yisrael and work as farmers. One was *Hovovei Zion*, or Lovers of Zion, and while it began with both religious and secular backing, it eventually turned wholly secular. The other movement was called *Bilu*, an acronym for the biblical verse "*Bais Yaakov lechu venelcha*," O House of Jacob, come and let us go (Isaiah 2:5). The young men and women of *Bilu*, being both secular and socialist in outlook, omitted the concluding words of the verse, "in the light of the Lord."[2] Both movements became part of what was later known as the First Aliyah, the immigration of 25,000 Jews to Eretz Yisrael in the period of 1882–1903. Baron Edmund de Rothschild of France funded several First Aliyah settlements, the most famous of which was Rishon Lezion, where he constructed vast wine cellars. When the wine turned out to be noncompetitive on the European market, Rothschild himself bought it at 20 percent over the going price.[3]

It was during this time that secular Jews and their ideals began to penetrate the land of Israel and eventually assume a dominant role. The present-day secular State of Israel, with its open hostility to observant Jews, can only be understood in the light of the anti-religious influence in Eretz Yisrael in the latter 1800s and early 1900s.

THE ROOTS OF ZIONISM: The movement known as modern Zionism can be divided into two parts: practical Zionism, which began with the First Aliyah, and political Zionism. Both areas were almost entirely influenced by secular, anti-Torah Jews. In 1862, a German Jew, Moses Hess, who had abandoned his family's Orthodox tradition, wrote a book called *Rome and Jerusalem*. Disillusioned by the persistence of Western anti-Semitism despite all efforts of Jews to assimilate, the book attempted to find a new, secular nationalistic solution to the Jewish problem. Inspired by the struggle of Italians for an independent Italy, *Rome and Jerusalem* urged Jews to involve the nations of the world in a quest for Eretz Yisrael. Once Jews had a place of their own, he reasoned, they would cease being a pariah among the world's nations. No mention was made of the religious and spiritual significance of the Holy Land.

It was from Russian Maskilim, however, that Zionism drew its greatest impetus. The vicious pogroms that began in 1881 showed secular Russian Jews that all efforts to assimilate into Russian society were pointless. Not willing to return to their tradition, the Maskilim looked elsewhere for fulfillment. In 1882, Leon Pinsker wrote *Auto-Emancipation*, which created a sensation among Russia's secularized Jews. Denying the Divine direction of events in Jewish history, including anti-Semitism, the book looked for so-called natural solutions for Jewish suffering. Pinsker wrote: "The Jewish people has no fatherland of its own, no center of gravity, no government of its own, no official representation. There is something unnatural about a people without a territory, just as there is about a man without a shadow. If, then, the prejudice of mankind against us rests on anthropological and social principles, innate and ineradicable, it was futile to seek the disappearance of these natural laws through enlightenment or assimilation."[4] In Pinsker's eyes, the only solution lay in the Jews attaining a national home of their own. Of course, as it is said in the holiday prayers, "*Umipenei chata'einu galinu mei'artzeinu,*" because of our sins we have been exiled from our land. Only repentance and Torah observance will bring an end to anti-Semitism and Jewish suffering.

Along the same lines, Eliezer Perelman, another Russian Maskil, is considered the father of Modern Hebrew. His antipathy to the Jewish religion can be evidenced in one of his writings: "I have decided that in order to have our own land and political life it is also necessary that we have a language to hold us together. That language is Hebrew, but not the Hebrew of the rabbis and scholars. We must have a Hebrew language in which we can conduct the business of life — in the home, school, public life, business, industry, fine arts, and in the sciences."[5] Asher Ginsburg, a Maskil who called himself *Achad Ha'Am* — One of the People — voiced a similar sentiment. He visualized a Hebrew idiom devoid of customary Scriptural and Talmudic allusions.[6]

Perelman's devotion to Hebrew was so great that from the moment he and his wife boarded ship for Eretz Yisrael, they never spoke any other language, and their children learned no other language, either.

To emphasize his hostility to the Yiddish language with which he was raised, Perelman adopted the surname Ben-Yehuda (son of Judah), replacing his father's Yiddish name, Leibele. More significantly, Ben-Yehuda popularized the Sephardic pronunciation of Hebrew words, instead of the Ashkenazic, which he considered less melodious and less genuine.[7] He is directly responsible for the Sephardic accent in which Modern Hebrew is currently spoken.

For their part, the Orthodox Jews of the Land, recognizing Ben-Yehuda's pernicious secularizing influence, placed him under a rabbinic ban of excommunication. Nevertheless, his influence spread greatly among secular Jews, and by 1916 a considerable percentage of them spoke Hebrew as their first language. Ben-Yehuda also composed several volumes of a Modern Hebrew dictionary, with many of his words entering the language spoken today in Israel. As such, Ben-Yehuda became a great hero to secular Zionists —

a major Jerusalem thoroughfare is even named after him — but to Torah-observant Jews he defiled *Lashon HaKodesh*, the Holy Tongue, by pursuing secularism.

THEODORE HERZL (1860–1904): The Hungarian-born Herzl grew up in a completely assimilated family and personally did not assume any Jewish observance. As an extreme assimilationist, he pursued many ideas to get Jews accepted in gentile society. One was an enormous program of social re-education for Jews, endowing them with what he termed "a delicate, *extremely sensitive* [italics in original] feeling for honor and the like," as if these values could not be found in the Torah. Another was a pact with the Pope, whereby the Pontiff would lead a campaign against anti-Semitism in return for "a great mass movement for the free and honorable conversion of all Jews to Christianity."[8] This misguided man, who so easily discarded the Jewish religion, later became the leader of the Zionist movement and the inspiration for the State of Israel.

In face of the relentless rise of anti-Semitism, all of Herzl's ideas were hopeless. In Vienna, where Herzl was living in 1895, Karl Leuger, running on an open anti-Semitic platform, became mayor of the city. The same year, as a newspaper correspondent, Herzl witnessed the humiliation of the French Jewish army officer Alfred Dreyfus, and the frenzied anti-Semitism that erupted at the time. Herzl came to the conclusion that the problem of anti-Semitism could only be solved if the Jewish people had a country of their own.

In 1896, Herzl published *The Jewish State*, outlining his aims for the Jewish people. He proposed that sovereignty be conceded to the Jews over a tract of land large enough to accommodate the people. It did not have to be in Eretz Yisrael, Herzl said, but could be in such places as Argentina, where the wealthy Baron Hirsch was subsidizing Jewish colonization (a project which ultimately failed), or Uganda, an idea later echoed by the British. *The Jewish State* became the primer of the Zionist movement, and eighty editions were printed in eighteen languages. The book's great eloquence introduced Zionism to European leaders, editors, university students, statesmen, and other molders of public opinion.

Herzl was ridiculed in secular Western Jewish circles. Lord Rothschild refused to see him, and Baron Hirsch called him an ignorant theorist. Reform Jews were bitterly opposed to Zionism, feeling that it would jeopardize their efforts to assimilate into Western society. Herzl did find one important ally, however. Max Nordau, a famous Jewish atheist philosopher, drew up much of the practical program for early political Zionism.

It was among the poor Jews, especially in Russia, that Herzl quickly became a legendary figure. His message, coupled with his great handsomeness, mesmerized thousands of Jews, to the point that the Chief Rabbi of Sofia, Bulgaria publicly proclaimed him as the Messiah. The extreme adulation caused Herzl to adopt a pompous exaggeration of his own self-worth. While addressing a large crowd in a synagogue in Sofia, someone shouted out, "It is all right to turn your back on the ark, you are holier than the Torah!"[9]

Herzl's sense of grandeur permeated his vision of a future Jewish state, for example imagining that an army regiment would be named the Herzl Cuirassiers. The country, Herzl believed, would contain international theaters, circuses, cafés, and a glittering avenue like the Champs-Elysees in Paris. Above all, there should be a state opera house, with the gentlemen in full tails, the ladies dressed as lavishly as possible. In his slavish admiration of German culture, the music of the anti-Semitic composer Richard Wagner would be played on great festive occasions.[10] Herzl also insisted that all delegates attending Zionist Congresses dress formally.

Herzl traveled widely seeking support for his vision of a Jewish state, meeting the German emperor and the ruler of Eretz Yisrael, the Ottoman Turkish sultan. Both leaders were lukewarm to his idea. However, the British expressed interest, eventually offering him land in British East Africa — Uganda.

THE FIRST ZIONIST CONGRESS: The First Zionist Congress opened in 1897 in Basle, Switzerland, and was attended primarily by secular Jews along with a smattering of religious Jews. Delegates arrived from fifteen countries, including the United States. The galleries were packed with visitors, both Jewish and Christian, and the leading newspapers of Europe sent correspondents to cover the event. When Herzl rose to address the assemblage, he received a standing ovation for fifteen minutes. Nordau established a World Zionist Organization to coordinate policy, and imposed a tax of a Hebrew shekel on WZO members. After three days of discussion, when the convention ended by the singing of *HaTikvah*, the Zionist theme song, the entire assembly rose, weeping.[11] The Congress spread the message of political Zionism, with seven conventions held over the next eight years.

UGANDA: The British offered the African territory of Uganda to be a colony under the sovereignty of the British crown, into which a million Jews could settle. The territory would be administered by the Jews and have a Jewish governor. At the Sixth Zionist Congress, held in 1903, the issue was heatedly debated among the delegates, many of whom would only agree to Eretz Yisrael as a Jewish homeland. Lobbying tirelessly behind the scenes, Herzl persuaded a majority of the delegates to vote in favor of Uganda. However, in 1904, Herzl suddenly died, and at the Seventh Zionist Congress in 1905, Uganda was voted down once and for all.

The British Colonial Office was greatly relieved, for as soon as British settlers in East Africa learned of the plan for Jewish colonization, they began to agitate against it. If Jews had settled in East Africa, they would have faced the combined hostility of the dominant British settlers and the black Africans, the latter egged on by the settlers, just as the rulers of Russia incited the Russian peasants.[12] Henceforth, all efforts toward a Jewish homeland were directed exclusively at Eretz Yisrael.

Herzl's family eventually died out, with no descendants remaining.

THE SECOND ALIYAH: Running from 1903–1914, the Second Aliyah brought 40,000 young, secular *chalutzim* (pioneers) from Eastern Europe to Palestine. Many of them openly admired the Russian peasants (despite their affinity for pogroms) and carried their love of farming to Palestine. The Jews' feeling was that agriculture would make the Jews independent, and as such it was well expressed in a pioneer folk song of the time: "*Anu banu artzah, livnot ulhibanot ba*" (We've come to the Land of Israel to build, and be rebuilt, there).

A secular Russian Jew, Aaron D. Gordon, became known as the foremost proponent of the new religion of labor. Giving up his job in Russia, Gordon immigrated to Palestine to become a physical laborer. Working by day in the fields, at night he wrote about the dignity of toil and agricultural labor as the "supreme act" of personal, national, and universal redemption. Gordon's influence on the secular Jews in Palestine was enormous. In his view, both the land and the means of production should be collectively owned. His ideas inspired the formation of that unique Zionist institution — the kibbutz.

The Second Aliyah established the first political parties for Jewish workers in Palestine, the most famous of which evolved into today's Labor Party. The Jews also organized the first self-defense association, *HaShomer*, established a Hebrew-language press, and founded the city of Tel Aviv, which became the first all-Jewish city in Palestine. Many of the secular institutions of the State of Israel have their origins in the Second Aliyah period.

RELIGIOUS OPPOSITION TO ZIONISM: Many religious leaders, both Chassidim and Misnagdim, were bitterly opposed to secular Zionism, feeling that it was worse than the *Haskalah*. The Maskil who strayed from the Torah knew that he was sinning, and that if he wanted to be a proper Jew he had to repent and observe the commandments. The Zionist was worse, according to this thinking, because he traded his religious identity for a secular nationalist one. The rebbe Rashab (the fifth rebbe of Lubavitch) summed up the dangers of secular Zionism in two major points:[13]

First, rejection of exile and the Messiah. A fundamental point of Judaism is that exile is a Divine condition imposed upon the Jewish people that will be terminated by the appearance of G-d's emissary, the Messiah. To the contrary, Zionist ideology stressed that each Jew could — and should — put an end to exile by proclaiming Zionism as the beginning of redemption. If one follows Zionism, so the thinking goes, one is no longer in exile, and Messianic redemption is no longer indispensable.

Second, Zionism's exclusively secular orientation. As an ideology founded by Maskilim, assimilated Jews, socialists, and atheists, Zionism adopted the European worldview of the nineteenth century that secular humanism, nationalism, and culture were the solutions for all of humanity's ills. Zionism's leaders, along with many of the immigrants to Palestine, completely rejected the Torah and its commandments, developing an implacable hostility toward Jews who were observant.

The great Rabbi Chaim Soloveitchik of Brisk termed the Zionists a cult, writing, "They have already proclaimed their goal to uproot the basis of the Jewish faith, and to attain it, they have made inroads in all places of Jewish settlement so as to enlist other Jews to assist them."[14]

The Hungarian rebbes of Satmar and Munkatch rejected Zionism for a reason unrelated to its secular orientation. The Talmud states that G-d imposed a solemn oath upon the Jewish people not to attempt to end its exile by returning and conquering Eretz Yisrael by force.[15] Other leaders, while not supporting Zionism, interpreted the Talmud's statement as proscribing military action, but not forbidding a strictly political movement to gain the Land with the consent of the nations.[16]

Sadly, the fears of religious leaders of the late 1800s were fully realized in the State of Israel, which for many years has worked to undermine the Torah observance of large numbers of Jews who settled there and to create a so-called new Jew in the Holy Land, one bereft of all Jewish observance. Currently, the clear bankruptcy of secular Zionist ideology — that having an independent country as all other nations will cure the ills of anti-Semitism — has become evident to all. Not only has anti-Semitism not been eradicated, but also hatred of Jews has been spread by Arab nations to peoples that previously had no exposure to Jews. In addition, Arab countries have, in the main, been rendered uninhabitable for Jews. Further, the belief that if Jews had an army that could fight back then they would no longer be in a position of helplessness has been shattered.

Currently, secular Zionists face a crisis not unlike that faced by Russian Maskilim when the czar's pogroms erupted in the 1880s. It is clear that only G-d can solve the eternal problems the Jewish people face when He ushers in the Messianic Era.

MIZRACHI: A small minority of rabbis were of the opinion that the Jewish settlement of Eretz Yisrael, and the effort to gain a Jewish homeland, were highly positive events. In 1902, Rabbi Isaac J. Reines founded the Mizrachi movement, which became the main religious lobby within Zionism. Some Mizrachi leaders, most notably the distinguished Rabbi Abraham I. Kook, who later became the Ashkenazi Chief Rabbi of Palestine, saw the Zionist movement — despite its secular orientation — as the beginning of the process of Messianic redemption. Virtually all other Orthodox rabbis rejected this viewpoint.

These three conflicting viewpoints regarding Zionism continue to affect Orthodox Jews' relationship to the State of Israel. Those religious Jews in Israel who attend Hesder yeshivos, which combine Torah study with military service, follow the Mizrachi stance. Many Jewish settlers who feel that it is important for Jews to settle in all areas of Eretz Yisrael, even in places inhabited only by Arabs, also subscribe to Mizrachi philosophy. In the United States, Jews known as Modern Orthodox tend to feel a strong affiliation with this branch of Zionism.

A less sanguine approach is taken by Jews identified as Yeshivah-Chareidi, and by many Chassidim, both in the United States and Israel. Although they feel very ambivalent about the State of Israel, due to its secular nature, they recognize it as a fait accompli. In Israel, these Jews participate in the political process and elect delegates to Israel's parliament, the Knesset. Unlike the Mizrachi movement, however, they do not view the State of Israel in the way it is described in a recently composed prayer recited in some synagogues, "the first flowering of our redemption."

The Chassidim of Satmar and Munkatch, and a small number of non-chassidic Jews, take a third approach, refusing to recognize the State of Israel, regarding it as a violation of Jewish law. In Israel, a group holding this viewpoint is called Neturei Karta, or Guardians of the City. Based in Jerusalem, they are descendants of Jews of the *yishuv hayashan* (old settlement), and they have no interaction with the Israeli government in any way. There has been tension between the Neturei Karta and other religious Jews in Israel who do not subscribe to this point of view.

ARAB OPPOSITION TO ZIONISM: The Zionists naively believed that the Arab population of Palestine would welcome Jewish settlement of the land as an economic benefit. Zionism did not set itself up against the Arabs per se, but instead against a West that had rejected the Jews. However, because the driving force of Jewish immigration and its political and cultural references were European-based, Zionism was seen as foreign to the region and associated with colonialism.[17] (This remains a major theme in Arab anti-Israel propaganda today.)

Even before the nineteenth century was over, some Arabs saw Zionism as a great danger, against which they tried to warn their compatriots. In 1891, Arabs in Jerusalem sent a telegram to the ruling Ottoman authorities protesting Jewish immigration and acquisition of land in Palestine. In 1909, there were violent Arab disturbances, and the first Jewish self-defense force, *HaShomer*, was set up in the Galilee. The two Jerusalem Arabs who were elected to the Ottoman Parliament in 1914 won their seats on an anti-Zionist program. One of them told his constituents, "If I am elected as a representative, I will dedicate all my energies, day and night, to remove the harm and danger awaiting us from Zionism and the Zionists."[18] In 1919, the Palestinian delegation to the Syrian Congress proclaimed: "Zionism is more dangerous than the French occupation, for the French know they are foreigners, while the Zionists think they are at home in Palestine."[19]

While there always had been Arab hostility to Jews, and oppression of Jews was common throughout the Arab world, Jews were traditionally able to live in Arab countries and in Palestine. In general, Arab persecution of Jews during the Middle Ages did not approach the intensity and duration of that of the Christian West.

Individuals and small groups of Jews were not seen as a threat to Islam, as the Jews inevitably accepted their *dhimmi* (second-class) status. However, once Jews started demanding self-determination in Palestine, the Arabs strongly objected. Jews proclaiming sovereignty over supposedly holy Arab land were seen as an affront to Islam. Indeed, today's terrorists and homicide bombers have their roots in the Arab opposition of 100 years ago.

SOCIALISM: In the 1800s, the political and economic theory known as socialism arose, advocating that communities as a whole should own and control means of production, distribution, and exchange. As a result, it was thought, the distinction between rich and poor would be blurred. Many Jews were attracted to this philosophy. Some viewed socialism as the method to create the just society described in Tanach. These Jews also saw socialism as a way to shed their Jewish heritage and serve the cause of achieving the supposed brotherhood of mankind in a secular format. Others were attracted to socialism's revolutionary nature, especially to Communism, which sought to change society by violent means. Socialist beliefs spread throughout Russia in the late 1800s, due in part to the brutal oppression of the czarist regime, with Jews playing a major role in the propagation. Indeed, socialist Jews laid the groundwork for the eventual dominance of Communism in Russia. In addition, these Jews were bitterly opposed to religion, viewing it, in the words of Karl Marx, as "the opiate of the masses."

THE BUND: In the latter 1800s, Russia transformed itself from an agrarian society to a great industrial power. Many Jews joined the trend of industrialization, especially in the garment and textile industries, which were centered in the Polish city of Lodz and almost entirely controlled by Jews. These workers toiled long hours for very little pay, and under appalling conditions. In 1897, several groups of Jewish workers, meeting in Vilna, formed an organization known as the Bund, which became a powerful secular force in Jewish life. At first, the Bund's struggle was economic, for higher wages and shorter working hours. It soon became clear, however, that the results could not be great, as most of the Jews worked in small shops belonging to poor artisans who themselves were laborers.

As a result, the Bund shifted its focus to the political arena. In contrast to Zionism, which wanted to create a Hebrew-speaking country for Jews in Palestine, the Bund stressed Jewish nationalism and culture in Eastern Europe, with Yiddish as its lingua franca. The Bund organized a system of secular Jewish schools, with Yiddish as the language of instruction. In addition, the Bund ardently supported Yiddish literature, printing novels and poems.

The Bund was also one of the most bitterly hostile movements to Torah Judaism. In their schools and literature, Bundists deliberately mocked the Torah, its sages, and followers. One of their plays ridiculed the mitzvah of sending home from the battlefield soldiers that were afraid of war (Deuteronomy 20:8) because of personal sins.[20] Eventually, in the play only the Chafetz Chaim and Gerrer rebbe were left facing a massive army. (When the Chafetz Chaim heard about the play, he said that the two of them would indeed win the war, for G-d determines the outcome of war, and would intercede for those who follow His Torah.)

Although both the Bund and the Socialists hated Orthodoxy, they had different outlooks regarding the future of the Jewish people. The Bundists wanted to create a new, secular, Yiddish cultural Jew, whereas the Jewish Socialists sought the end of the Jews as a unique nation.[21]

IMMIGRATION TO AMERICA: Between 1880 and 1924, four million Jews left Eastern Europe, and more than three million of them came to the United States. This emigration represented the greatest movement of Jews since the Spanish Expulsion in 1492, and was a major turning point in Jewish history. The vast majority of Jews in America today are descendants of those immigrants.

However, fully two-thirds of Eastern Europe's Jews chose to remain at home. Many of them were religious Jews, who, despite the terrible persecution and poverty, led a spiritually satisfying life, and who regarded America as impossibly profane.[22] Later, when some of these religious Jews did go, it was in large measure because their children went. Orthodox Jews were never a major part of the emigrants. In addition, assimilated Jews and the small number of affluent Jews also chose to stay.

Although oppression and pogroms played a major role in influencing Jews to leave Europe, they were by no means the only reasons why Jews left. Jews departed even in years without pogroms, and from nations that did not experience anti-Jewish violence, such as the Austro-Hungarian Empire. Jewish emigration must be understood in the context of the time. The entire continent of Europe was on the move — 30 million Europeans came to the New World from 1880 to 1924. Jews and non-Jews emigrated to America largely for economic reasons — to escape the grinding poverty of the Old World and to provide a better future for their children. In the case of the Jews, this physical advancement came at the cost of spiritual growth.

Jewish immigration differed from that of non-Jews in several ways. First, the Jewish migration was much more a movement of families than that of other European nationalities and groups. Children comprised nearly 25 percent of the Jewish population, but only 12 percent of the total immigration, both Jewish and non-Jewish. Second, Jewish immigration was directed more toward permanent settlement in the United States than was that of other European groups. Despite the hardships, nearly 95 percent of all Jews who came to America decided to stay. Overall, only two-thirds of all immigrants remained in the United States. Third, the Jewish migration contained a higher proportion of skilled workers from urban environments than that of any other group. (In particular, tailors were very highly represented.) Consequently, Jews were better able to cope with American urban life, particularly in New York City, than most other immigrants. Fourth, other nationalities came as individuals. The Italians, for example, came from their own independent nation. Individual Italians might be desperate, but not the Italians as a people. Of the Jews, however, it could almost be said that a whole people was in flight.[23]

THE TRIP ON LAND: For the Jews, it was an arduous journey to reach the ports of Western Europe, where they would board ships to cross the Atlantic Ocean. As the Russian government restricted passports, Jews had to cross the border into Germany illegally. These crossings entailed bribing professional smugglers to help them, and it was both expensive and risky, for frequently the smugglers were corrupt. The Jews crossed Germany by train, hoping not to be caught by officials or swindled by scoundrels who took advantage of their unfamiliarity with their surroundings. Later, the land trip became easier, due to the efforts of German Jews to help the travelers.

THE SEA VOYAGE: The Atlantic crossing, which took from one to two weeks, was a harrowing experience. Greedy ship owners treated immigrants like so much freight. Sleeping quarters in steerage class (the lowest) were compartments holding 300 or more persons. Berths, six feet two inches long, were in two tiers with two and a half feet above each berth, separated only by iron pipes. The iron framework held a mattress and pillow stuffed with straw or seaweed. The blanket was usually so flimsy that passengers had to sleep in their clothing to keep warm. Stewards never changed or cleaned the berths, even when voyages lasted sixteen days or more. All personal belongings, such as pots, pans, and clothing, had to be kept in the berth, as there was no room on the floor. The immigrants lined up for their food and ate it in their berths, for there was no dining room. Since no waste barrels were supplied, the steerage floor was always damp and filthy, and the air stank beyond endurance. In the description of one of the immigrants:

> On the first day I went to the mess counter for food, and was handed a chunk of white bread and herring which I took to my bunk. I bit into the bread. It tasted like chalk. The herring stunk. I threw it all away. The following day we did not need food. In fact, we seemed to have plenty to give up. It was stormy, and the boat rocked and shook. I kept tossing about. I stuck my head out of the bunk a little. A shower of vomit came down from the upper bunk on my face. There was no privacy. Men, women, and children were all mixed together. Our greatest suffering was due to a scarcity of water. We all provided ourselves with a tin can to hold

the water distributed every evening. It was all you could get until the following evening. One day I ate a piece of herring. Soon after, I drank all the water I had. The same evening, I was burning up with thirst.[24]

There were eight toilets and eight washbasins for 200 people. The toilet seats were always wet, and water often stood inches deep on the floor. A thorough washing of the body or even part of it was out of the question; there were no bathtubs. All this meant that the steerage passenger arrived at journey's end with a mind unfit for healthy, wholesome impressions, and with a body weakened and unfit for the hardships that are involved in the beginning of life in a new land.

ARRIVAL IN AMERICA: Seven out of every ten immigrants came through the port of New York. In 1892, the government opened the Ellis Island reception center. In the eyes of the immigrants, Ellis Island was Judgment Day for determining entrance into Heaven. Immigrants piled into the massive hall and broke into dozens of lines. One by one, they were subjected to several medical examinations, and those who appeared sickly or dim-witted were detained for further checking. Most detentions were for the eye disease trachoma, which particularly affected Jewish children.

After passing the medical examinations, immigrants were questioned about their character, money, relatives, crime, and work. Many gave the wrong answers and got into trouble. For example, if one said he had a job waiting for him in the United States, he was subject to deportation, because the law prohibited the importation of contract labor. The Hebrew Immigrant Aid Society (HIAS) attempted to help Jewish immigrants through the bewildering experience. While more than 95 percent of all immigrants were admitted to the United States, often eligible parents had to return to Europe because a child was refused entry. Sometimes, people sent back would try to enter the United States again and succeeded.

LIFE IN AMERICA: In Europe, America was known as the golden land because it was rumored that gold lay in the streets waiting to be picked up. In reality, America was anything but a golden land. After enduring the Ellis Island ordeal, the immigrant had to manage on his own with little or no protection. Countless thousands were cheated at docks and on trains and boats, suffering painful losses at the hands of dishonest travel agents, lawyers, bankers, notaries, and interpreters. Most immigrants settled in New York City, which became the largest Jewish city in the world, a distinction that it still holds. One square mile of the Lower East Side became the center of Jewish life, eventually holding more than one million people in its tenements. People were jammed into congested buildings that had a greater population density than even the notorious slums of India and China. One area of the East Side had more than 500 people per acre! The streets were filled with hundreds of stands and pushcarts selling every kind of cheap merchandise.

JOBS: Although there were many possible occupations, as well as peddling, most immigrant Jews entered the garment industry. One reporter said, "The Jewish needle made America the best-dressed nation in the world." It also came close to enslaving the immigrant generation in the sweatshops where that needle was plied. By 1900, more than 150,000 Jewish immigrants and their families were making their living in the clothing industry, which, after the invention of the sewing machine, required little training and skill.

The clothing shops were overcrowded, dirty, badly lit, poorly ventilated rooms where men, women, and children worked at a frenetic pace for up to fifteen or even eighteen hours a day. Cruel bosses and foremen harassed the workers, deducting pay from their meager wage for any real or imagined infraction. Children in particular suffered permanent injury and disease from the horrible conditions. Tasks were repeated over and over, numbing the mind. The thousands of shops jammed into the Lower East Side produced more than one-half of America's ready-made clothing.

SPIRITUAL LIFE: Immigration to America was an unprecedented spiritual holocaust for the Jewish people. A small percentage of the millions of Jews who entered the United States between 1880 and 1924 were religious; even if they were personally observant, they did not succeed in transmitting the Torah heritage to their children.

As a result, more than 90 percent of today's nearly six million American Jews are non-Orthodox. A number of factors ensured that Orthodoxy would be at a great disadvantage in the United States:

First, the feeling of starting anew. Immigrants felt they were starting a new life by coming to America and therefore wanted to shed everything connected to the Old World. Many felt that the Torah was antiquated and not relevant to new, modern America. In the famous phrase, they threw their tefillin into New York Harbor.

Second, the lack of community. Unlike in Europe, there was no established Jewish community to offer the immigrants a sense of stability and religious structure. People felt rootless and therefore chose the path of least resistance, going along with secular America. Such a situation was unprecedented in Jewish history, for even in the worst times the Jewish people always had a framework with which to meet the many tribulations of exile.

Third, there was no educational structure. There were virtually no rabbis to turn to for spiritual guidance and no Jewish schools for children. Some immigrants sent their children to Hebrew school in the afternoon (*Talmud Torah*), but these institutions were woefully inadequate to counter the powerful blandishments of American society. Feeling little or no pride in being Jewish, many immigrants and their children rapidly shed what little Torah observance they once had. The great Rabbi Moshe Feinstein once remarked that when parents lost their jobs due to Sabbath observance, they complained about how difficult it was being a religious Jew, rather than instilling in their children the conviction that the joys of leading a Torah life far outweigh the difficulties. As a result, even observant families saw their children leave the Torah path.

Fourth, the pressure to Americanize. All immigrants, Jewish and non-Jewish alike, faced great pressure to enter the melting pot and become full-fledged Americans. This message was constantly hammered home, especially to impressionable young children in the public schools. Fathers and mothers no longer dreamed of seeing their children become Torah scholars, for that was considered un-American. Consequently, Jewish parents especially aspired that their children get a good secular education in order to become doctors, lawyers, and other professionals.

Fifth, the pressure of earning a living. American society extolled making money as the supreme virtue to which one should aspire. A guidebook for immigrant Jews gave this advice:

Hold fast, this is most necessary in America. Forget your past, your customs, and your ideals. Select a goal and pursue it with all your might. No matter what happens to you, hold on. You will experience a bad time but sooner or later you will achieve your goal. A bit of advice for you: Do not take a moment's rest. Run, do, work, and keep your own good in mind.[25]

As the historian Lucy Dawidowicz points out:

The freedom to make money became an obsession for some. It was an end in itself. It began with a good purpose — to raise the children decently, to keep them out of the sweatshops if possible, and to lay aside funds for their education, and for old age. But in the process of scrambling for money, family life was neglected, community was disregarded, and tradition was abandoned.[26]

Sixth, working on the Sabbath. This was the worst of all the spiritual tests that Jews coming to America had to face, and it caused wholesale defections from Torah observance. It was extremely difficult to find a job that did not entail working on the Sabbath. When an employee left on Friday, he was told, "If you don't come in on Saturday, don't bother coming in on Monday." Fired workers were put on a blacklist, so that finding a new job was next to impossible.

Seeing their families starving and freezing broke the spirits of many Jews, and they succumbed to this most difficult of ordeals. At first they worked on the Sabbath with great reluctance, but as time wore on, they became accustomed to the state of affairs, in accordance with the Talmudic statement that a sin repeated becomes permissible in the perpetrator's eyes.[27]

As Sabbath observance is one of the major tenets of Judaism, and the foundation of family life, its violation opened a proverbial Pandora's box. Abandonment of other mitzvos rapidly followed, and the next generation, growing up without a remembrance of observant life, drifted farther away from Judaism. As American Jewry's connection to Torah Judaism became more and more tenuous, the intermarriage rate skyrocketed, from nearly zero in the immigrant generation to more than 60 percent today.

RABBIS: Few Torah scholars came to these shores — in fact, between 1899 and 1910, as the American Jewish population rose by one million, a mere 305 rabbis entered the United States.[28] One who did, Rabbi Moshe Weinberger, wrote a scathing report on the situation of Judaism in New York, particularly in regard to kosher slaughter and children's education. Discussing the latter, he wrote:

> During the time when the Hungarian or Polish Jewish youngster was brought to a level where he could understand the Prophets and listen to rigorous biblical and legal halachic studies, the American youngster is merely able to stammer a few words of English-style Hebrew, to pronounce the blessing over the Torah, and to chant the *maftir* on the day he turns thirteen — a day that is celebrated here as the greatest of holidays among our Jewish brethren. From that day onward a youngster considers his teacher to be an unwanted article...he forgets all he has learned.[29]

Rabbi Weinberger had the following advice to his fellow Jews in Europe: "To our brothers in Russia, Poland, and Hungary — Listen to us: tough it out and stay home."[30] The saintly Chafetz Chaim took matters one step further: "Even if he has already emigrated due to his economic distress, he must return to his home where G-d will sustain him. A proper person should curse the day of his arrival in a land where he must constantly witness desecration of the Torah. All his expectations should be directed toward G-d's helping him go free and return home. Certainly he must vow never to bring his children where they, G-d forbid, may be lost among the gentiles."[31]

NEW YORK CHOOSES A CHIEF RABBI: In 1887, the major Orthodox synagogues in New York decided that a prominent European rabbi was needed to assume control of the chaotic religious situation in the city. Rabbi Jacob Joseph, one of the most eminent scholars of Vilna, the so-called Jerusalem of Lithuania, answered the call. Despite the shrill hostility of Reform and assimilationist Jews, his arrival was greatly anticipated in the greater Jewish community. When the chief rabbi delivered his first Sabbath discourse, the synagogue was packed and thousands more stood outside. Alas, this happy marriage of rav and *kehillah* was not to last.

In order to correct the deplorable situation of kashrus in the slaughterhouses, and to defray the costs of kosher supervision, Rabbi Jacob Joseph proposed a one-cent tax on each slaughtered chicken. Vehement opposition broke out, spearheaded by an alliance of nonreligious Jews, butchers, and rabbis who feared the emergence of a central religious authority. Their rallying cry was *karobka*, the Russian word for a hated tax imposed on kosher meat by the czar. As such, these opposing rabbis and butchers proclaimed a rival supervisory agency that would certify chickens without charge. Among religious Jews, too, those of Polish and Hungarian origin looked askance at the Lithuanian Rabbi Jacob Joseph, feeling that he was culturally and temperamentally different.

Eventually, bitter political infighting eroded the authority of Rabbi Jacob Joseph. Shortly, there arose diverse new claimants to the title Chief Rabbi. In 1893, for example, Rabbi Chaim Y. Vidrowitz came to New York from Moscow, gathered a few chassidic *shtieblach* (small congregations) under his control, and proclaimed himself Chief Rabbi of America. When asked "Who made you chief rabbi?" he replied with a twinkle in his eye, "The sign painter." When further questioned why he was the head of *all* America, he replied in a very revealing statement, "Because it would be well nigh impossible for all of American Jewry to join together to depose me."[32]

In 1895, Rabbi Jacob Joseph's position was terminated. He then became ill and was paralyzed during the last five years of his sadly shortened life. Neglected by all but a few, all but forgotten by the community to which he had brought such hope and to which he had consecrated his endeavors, Rabbi Jacob Joseph, the one and only chief rabbi of New York, died in 1902, age 59.

Even in death, the chief rabbi knew no rest. At his funeral, which was attended by 100,000 mourners, anti-Semitic hooligans in a printing shop rained debris upon the procession. In the ensuing riot, the police wielded their riot sticks more against the attacked Jews than at the attackers. (A national outcry led to a subsequent improvement in the behavior of New York's police.) With the passage of Rabbi Jacob Joseph, a tragic victim of American Jewish small-mindedness, the dream ended of New York Jewry as a consolidated Torah community, the dream of the largest metropolitan center of Jewry in the world being structured for strength and integrity, the dream of fruition of authentic Judaism in the New World.[33]

However, Rabbi Jacob Joseph did not toil in vain. A gradual realization emerged among Orthodox American Jews of the importance of improving the quality of religious life. In 1898, the Union of Orthodox Jewish Congregations (today known as the OU) was formed. At Rabbi Jacob Joseph's funeral, the Agudath HaRabbanim, the Union of Orthodox Rabbis, officially came into existence. The first American yeshivos were founded in those years — Yeshiva Etz Chaim in 1886 and Rabbi Jacob Joseph School in 1901. In 1915, the Rabbi Isaac Elchanan Theological Seminary was opened for advanced students, the first institution of its kind in America. Etz Chaim and Rabbi Isaac Elchanan schools later merged, evolving into Yeshiva University.

RABBI BERNARD DRACHMAN: Rabbi Drachman, a born and bred American Jew, dedicated his life to further the cause of Orthodoxy. His combination of scholarship gained in Europe and an American upbringing enabled him to have an influence that immigrant scholars could not. After his congregation voted to introduce mixed seating at services, Rabbi Drachman reached international prominence when he publicly resigned, mincing no words as to his reason for such an action. He then founded his own synagogue, Zichron Ephraim, which attracted 200 families.

Zichron Ephraim rapidly became more than just a place to pray. It opened a Hebrew School that became very popular, providing thousands of children with Jewish knowledge they would otherwise not have received. A wide-ranging series of classes and lectures were also provided for adults. Programs were begun for adolescents, aimed at providing a strong Jewish influence on these emerging adults, helping them meet the influences of the wider world while remaining steadfast Jews. In a departure from European norms, the synagogue thus became the focus of many Jewish activities other than prayer.

Rabbi Drachman also endeavored to ease the struggle of Sabbath-observing workers. He founded an organization that interceded with employers on behalf of employees who wished to take off the holy day. An employment bureau was also set up to bring Sabbath-observant workers and employers together. During World War I, Rabbi Drachman played a major role in setting up agencies to provide relief for Jewish victims. He also helped organize the Jewish Welfare Board to help support American Jewish soldiers and their families.

Although Rabbi Drachman's achievements pale beside that of today's phenomenal American Torah community, his accomplishments cannot be minimized. He achieved the most that was possible in his time. To stand up where Reform held sway and proclaim the truth of Torah took enormous courage. To rally Orthodox Jews and further Torah education and observance was as revolutionary at the time as the idea of *kollelim* (full-time, paid Torah studies for married men) would be fifty years later. It can be said that Rabbi Drachman received the torch of Torah in America from individuals who battled before him to keep it alight, and then passed it on, the torch burning even more brightly, to those who would light the country with it.[34]

RABBI HERBERT S. GOLDSTEIN: Unlike Rabbi Drachman, who received his rabbinical ordination in Europe, Rabbi Goldstein was ordained in the United States, becoming the first rabbi to achieve this milestone on these shores. His Institutional Synagogue served thousands of people, providing them not only with prayer services, but also with social and sporting events to make Orthodoxy more appealing to American Jews, especially youth. Young people were given the opportunity to lead the services, thus instilling them with Jewish pride.

Courageous individuals, such as Rabbi Jacob Joseph, Rabbi Drachman, and Rabbi Goldstein, tilled the rocky, inhospitable soil of America, making it receptive, preparing it for the great Torah growth of today. These heroic pioneers, although seemingly not always successful in their efforts, laid the Torah foundation for subsequent generations, who are indebted to them.

Chapter 22

THE BEGINNING OF THE TWENTIETH CENTURY THROUGH WORLD WAR I

UNREST IN RUSSIA: Throughout Russia, protest gathered against the czar's autocratic regime. Revolutionary parties were formed calling for the end of the monarchy and its replacement by a republic. Jews especially played a prominent role in these movements, for among all of Russia's many ethnic groups, they suffered the most. Alarmed by the popularity of the insurgents, the Russian government introduced a scapegoat against which to turn the attention of the discontented masses: the traditional one, the Jews.

THE KISHINEV POGROM: Although not nearly the worst in terms of loss of life, the outbreak of violence at Kishinev was particularly brutal, and it became the most infamous of all Russian pogroms. On April 19, 1903, the last day of Pesach, which was also Easter Sunday, violence broke out against the Jews of Kishinev. Thousands of Russian soldiers and police stood by while a frenzied mob killed more than fifty Jews and mutilated their bodies. Hundreds of Jewish men and women were publicly humiliated and their property looted. When Jewish leaders pleaded to the government for justice, they were told that the existence of a Jewish revolutionary movement forced the government to take action. Further, the Jews were told, if the Jewish labor movement continued to grow, then the lives of all Jews would become even more intolerable. In fact, pogroms continued throughout the next two years.

In many cities in Europe and the United States there were mass protests against the Kishinev pogrom and the czarist government's complicity. A massive petition was prepared in the United States, calling on the czar to make any such massacres impossible in the future. The Russian government, furious at this outside interference, informed the United States that it would decline to receive the petition.[1]

THE JERUSALEM TALMUD FORGERY: In 350 CE, Roman oppression in Eretz Yisrael forced the sages to relocate to Babylonia. As a result, the Jerusalem Talmud, or *Yerushalmi*, which was begun in Eretz Yisrael, was never completed. Currently, the *Yerushalmi* exists only on four sections of the Mishnah: *Zeraim, Moed, Nashim,* and *Nezikin*. However, some Rishonim indicated the existence of *Yerushalmi* on *Kodashim*, Sacrifices.[2] No such text was ever transmitted through the generations, however, and the matter remained an unsolvable mystery.

In 1906, in the city of Szatmar, Hungary, a man announced that he had obtained an ancient manuscript of the *Yerushalmi* on *Kodashim*. Claiming to be a scion of the famous Sephardic Algazi family, and now calling himself Rabbi Friedlander, he printed two volumes of *Yerushalmi Kodashim* based on the manuscript, along with his own commentary. This publication caused a great stir in the Torah world. A number of prominent rabbis hailed the work, and gave it their approbations and financial help. The Chafetz Chaim, for example, began donning the tefillin of Rabbeinu Tam based on a passage in the newly found *Yerushalmi Kodashim*, which concurred with Rabbeinu Tam's version of tefillin. (Traditionally, all Jews wear Rashi's tefillin, while Chassidim put on Rabbeinu Tam's tefillin in addition. The difference between the two versions lies in the order of the Scriptural passages contained within the tefillin pair. No decision is rendered in the Babylonian Talmud in favor of either type of tefillin.)

Not all scholars were taken in by the new *Yerushalmi*. Rabbi Meir Dan Plotzky, a great scholar, discovered by deft detective work that Algazi/Friedlander was no Sephardi, but rather a professional forger. The rebbe of Ger, leader of the largest chassidic group in Poland and an acknowledged expert on ancient manuscripts, unequivocally proclaimed the new *Yerushalmi* a forgery based on technical considerations. When Algazi/Friedlander was pressed to provide the address of his supposed brother in Turkey, whom Friedlander claimed possessed the original manuscript, Friedlander claimed that he had forgotten it. Further scholarly examination of the new *Yerushalmi* demonstrated that it was plagiarized and collected from scattered authentic *Yerushalmi* passages and then retouched. Upon realizing that the *Yerushalmi* was a forgery, the Chafetz Chaim stopped donning Rabbeinu Tam's tefillin.

Shortly, the truth became known. The supposed new volume was the work of a professional forger, Zusska Lahiss, who was born in Lithuania. While he was not a great Torah scholar, he sought recognition as one. Lahiss wrote scholarly letters to sages in Eastern Europe claiming to be the rabbi of Mulhausen in France. Later, he traveled from town to town in Eastern Europe selling some of his works, which were of poor quality. (One in particular was a hateful anti-chassidic tract.) As his true character became known, Lahiss created a new Sephardic identity for himself in preparation for his greatest swindle — the *Yerushalmi Kodashim*. After his fraud became known, Lahiss disappeared from public view.

THE DREYFUS AFFAIR: This infamous incident, in which a French Jewish army officer was falsely accused of high treason, rocked the Jewish world. In no country were the Jews as thoroughly assimilated as France. Out of a Jewish population of 86,000, only 500 were Orthodox.[3] The Affair shattered the clichéd notion of "it can't happen here," sadly demonstrating the futility of assimilation in combating anti-Semitism.

ANTI-SEMITISM IN FRANCE: Although Jews had achieved full rights in France many decades previously, hatred of Jews was rife in nineteenth-century French society. Despite the secular government, Roman Catholicism exerted a powerful influence on the population, especially in the French Army. In 1886, Edouard Drumont published *La France Juive* (Jewish France), a vicious anti-Semitic tract that was reprinted more than 100 times in several countries, quickly becoming one of the most popular books of the time. In 1892, he began publication of *La Libre Parole*, a stridently anti-Semitic newspaper which decried supposed Jewish influence in the army and finance.

In 1889, many Frenchmen, encouraged by the Catholic Church, invested in a company attempting to build a Panama Canal. When the company went bankrupt, thousands of people lost their savings. Although the company's board of directors included both Jews and gentiles, all equally corrupt, blame was placed solely on the Jews.

ALFRED DREYFUS: Dreyfus grew up in a well-to-do, assimilated family. Aspiring to a military career while yet a child, Dreyfus realized his dream when, in 1893, he was accepted to the French Army General Staff, holding the rank of captain. At the time of the momentous events that would engulf him, Alfred Dreyfus was thirty-five years of age, married, and had two children.

THE AFFAIR BEGINS: In 1894, in the wastebasket of the German Embassy in Paris, French intelligence discovered a document listing French military secrets that a spy called "the scoundrel D" had provided to the Germans. As these secrets covered all areas of the military, suspicion focused on the General Staff. French officers concluded that "the scoundrel D" must be Dreyfus, whose name began with D, and who was the only Jew on the General Staff. Despite the absence of any evidence, and despite the fact that Dreyfus' handwriting did not match that of the document, Dreyfus was arrested and held in secrecy.

In addition, Dreyfus was court-martialed in secret, amid many flagrant violations of French law. Secret documents were assembled, which Dreyfus and his lawyer were not permitted to view. Experts testified that the handwriting on the document was Dreyfus'. French officers forged documents attesting to Dreyfus' role as a major spy for France's enemies. Under pressure from the army, military judges found Dreyfus guilty and sentenced him to public degradation, forfeiture of rank, and life imprisonment in a remote penal colony.

THE DEGRADATION OF DREYFUS: The date set for the macabre ceremony of humiliation was Saturday, January 5, 1895. This choice of day was not coincidental, for many Frenchmen viewed the degradation of Dreyfus as the humiliation of the entire Jewish people, and the purification of France from Jewish influence.[4]

At 9:00 a.m., Dreyfus was marched into the courtyard of the French War College to begin his ten-minute ordeal. Thousands of soldiers and reporters crowded the college, while a crowd of 20,000 gathered outside. There was complete silence as the commanding officer approached Dreyfus. In a voice charged with emotion, the officer proclaimed the terrible sentence: "Dreyfus, you are unworthy of bearing arms. In the name of the people of France we degrade you." A sergeant tore Dreyfus' medals, buttons, stripes, and epaulettes from his uniform, then broke Dreyfus' sword on the sergeant's own knee. As Dreyfus was marched around the courtyard in his tattered uniform, he shouted for all to hear, "I am innocent! Long live France! Long live the army!" The crowd and the assembled officers alike responded, "Death to the Jew! Death to the traitor!" Dreyfus was sent to the penal colony of Devil's Island off the coast of South America, then placed in solitary confinement, where he remained for more than four years.

THE AFTERMATH: Meanwhile, in France, the sorry episode did not die down. Slowly at first, then increasingly, people became convinced that Dreyfus was the victim of a cover-up. In 1898, the real spy, Count Esterhazy, was exposed and put on trial. He was acquitted by the army, which could not bring itself to admit that it had made such a horrible mistake.

Shortly afterward, Emile Zola, one of France's most respected novelists, wrote his famous *J'Accuse*, in which he accused the army and government of knowingly convicting an innocent man. Riots broke out in France between the supporters of Dreyfus (Dreyfusards) and his opponents (anti-Dreyfusards), and France teetered on the brink of civil war. In 1899, Dreyfus was brought back to France, tried a second time, and again found guilty. However, the president of France pardoned him, and Dreyfus was released from jail. In 1906, Dreyfus was declared innocent of all charges, and in a ceremony in the War College was reinstated into the French army with the rank of major. Dreyfus died in 1935 at the age of seventy-six. For its part, the French army did not admit that Dreyfus was innocent until the late 1990s.

THE BEILIS BLOOD LIBEL TRIAL: In 1911, the bloody body of a thirteen-year-old Russian boy was found in a cave outside the city of Kiev. Mendel Beilis, the Jewish manager of a brick factory located near the cave, was arrested and charged with the crime of ritual murder, or killing the boy for use of his blood. Beilis was imprisoned for the duration of his trial, a period of more than two years.

The trial attracted great attention, both in Russia and abroad. Russian prosecutors, representing the czar's government, futilely attempted to prove that Judaism condoned ritual murder. In addition, efforts to prove that Beilis was a religious fanatic ran into great difficulties, for he was not even an observant Jew. In fact, on the day the child was murdered, which was the Sabbath, Beilis had been working in the factory.[5]

The prosecution arranged for a priest, Father Pranaitis, to testify that according to his expert knowledge of the Talmud, there are endless uses to which Jews put Christian blood. The defense lawyers set a splendid trap for him by asking, "When did Baba Bathra live and what was her activity?" *Baba* in Russian is grandmother, but in fact Baba Bathra is not a person at all; it is one of the best-known tractates of the Talmud, dealing with property laws, as even a beginning student knows. If an American defense lawyer had asked a similar expert on American history, "Who lived at the Gettysburg Address?" and received an answer of "I don't know," the effect would have been the same. At the Russian trial, the Jewish spectators broke out in uncontrollable laughter.[6]

So absurd was the charge, and so strong the worldwide public outcry, that Beilis was acquitted. One of Beilis' lawyers, Oskar Grunzenberg, reported how close a call the matter had been: "Indeed, a miracle happened. The preliminary vote in favor of convicting Beilis was seven to five, but when the jury foreman began taking the final vote, one peasant rose to his feet, prayed to an icon, and said resolutely, 'I don't want to have this sin on my soul — he's not guilty.' "[7]

Eventually, Beilis moved to Palestine and then to the United States. He died in New York and is buried there.

LABOR UNIONS: By 1900, there were more than 80,000 garment workers employed in some 2,700 shops throughout the United States; one-third of the workers were women and girls. They labored in appalling conditions, seven days a week, from 7:30 a.m. to 9:00 p.m., except for Sunday, which was a half-day. Salaries averaged a paltry $1.50 per week for eighty hours of work. In response to such horrible conditions, the International Ladies' Garment Workers' Union (ILGWU) was formed, mainly by Jews. It became part of the American Federation of Labor (AFL), which was founded in 1886 by a Jewish immigrant from Denmark, Samuel Gompers. At first, reaction to labor unions was unspeakably hostile. When workers went on strike and fought with hired strikebreakers, police and judges took the side of the employers, flooding the courts and jail cells with arrested picketers. Sentencing one striker, a judge said, "You are on strike against G-d, whose firm law is that man shall earn his bread by the sweat of his brow!" (See Genesis 3:19.) However, a shocking incident took place that changed the perception of the public and turned it in favor of unions.

On Saturday, March 25, 1911, the 850 employees of the Triangle Shirtwaist Company in New York City, largely young Jewish girls, had one hour before quitting time. A man lit a cigarette and threw his match to the floor, where it touched off scraps of cloth from the cutting tables. The fire soon reached highly flammable cleaning liquids, then rapidly spread through the building. More than 140 girls lost their lives, both in the raging inferno and by jumping from the seventh through ninth floors, where the factory was located. Horrified by the tragedy, state and federal governments enacted new laws protecting workers. While the owners of the Triangle building were tried for manslaughter and acquitted, eventually the unions, led by Jewish socialists such as Sidney Hillman (who had studied in the Slabodka Yeshiva before becoming radicalized), made great strides in labor-management relations.

AGUDATH ISRAEL: Many Torah leaders realized that if the Orthodox world did not unite, it would succumb to the radical changes sweeping through the Jewish people at the time. In 1912, in the Polish city of Katowice, delegates from many nations met to form an organization "that would blend East and West, shtetl and metropolis, Chassid and Misnagid, yeshivah-reared and university-trained."[8] Calling itself Agudath Israel, the new organization proclaimed as its goal "the solution of all problems facing the Jewish people in the spirit of Torah."[9] To that end, Agudath Israel set up the *Moetzes Gedolei HaTorah*, or Council of Torah Sages, composed of the leading Torah authorities of the time, to guide the organization on all matters of policy. This idea reflected the vital principle that the leading Torah scholars, precisely because they embody the actualization of the Jew imbued with the wisdom of the Torah, are the ones charged to offer counsel on all matters of national policy. Commonly known as *daas Torah* (Torah judgment), this concept, like all matters of basic Jewish belief, originates in the Torah itself.[10]

> The Jew cannot relegate the sages to the realm of formal "religion" — giving them the authority to decide only questions of dairy spoons falling into meat pots, esoteric questions of Talmudic logic, or matters of synagogue ritual. Israel is a nation founded on Torah. It must be guided in every aspect by Torah wisdom and Torah instinct. The secular-oriented observant layman is no more qualified to decide matters of importance in Jewish life than is a patient to guide a surgeon's hand. In Agudath

Israel's view, the rules of political science, economics, or ethnic power politics must be measured against the dictates of Torah thought, not vice versa.[11]

The first *Moetzes Gedolei HaTorah* included such giants as the Chafetz Chaim, the Gerrer rebbe (Rabbi Abraham Mordecai Alter), Rabbi Chaim Ozer Grodzensky (the leading halachic authority of the time), and the rebbe of Chortkov, Rabbi Israel Friedman. Although not all Orthodox groups and leaders joined, the Agudah still claimed the allegiance of hundreds of thousands of Torah Jews. Its achievement of uniting large numbers of Orthodox Jews saved many from the ravages of anti-Torah ideologies and movements.

As one example of its leadership, the Agudah vehemently opposed the secular Zionist movement for subverting the historic religious bond of the Jewish people to the land of Israel, replacing it with a secular nationalism devoid of Torah and its commandments. At the same time, the Agudah supported Jewish settlement of the Land and greatly endeavored to facilitate immigration. Sadly, its success in this area was limited, for secular groups largely controlled European immigration to Eretz Yisrael.

ANTI-SEMITISM IN ENGLAND AND AMERICA: Generally, opposition to Jews in these countries was of the form known as polite anti-Semitism. Jews were often excluded from neighborhoods, country clubs, and resorts. Universities placed informal quotas on Jewish students, and many companies refused to hire them. Newspapers in America carried ads reading "No Jews Need Apply" or "White Protestants Only." In England, in upper-class society it was considered uncouth to say the word Jew in polite conversation.

There were flare-ups of violence, too, although nowhere nearly as bad as the horrors of the Russian pogroms. In 1911, riots against Jewish landlords, who supposedly charged exorbitant rents, broke out in the town of Tredegar, Wales. (Actually, only one Jew derived his income from rents.)[12] Although no Jews were killed, there was much property damage.

In 1913, in Atlanta, Georgia, a fourteen-year-old girl working in a factory owned by a Jew, Jacob Frank, was found murdered in the factory's basement. Thousands of people attended her funeral, and a great cry rose up to find the culprit. As Frank was one of the few people in the factory that day (Saturday), suspicion fell on him. Despite the lack of conclusive evidence linking him to the murder, Frank was found guilty, to the jubilation of the citizens. In 1915, Frank was dragged from prison by a band led by a judge, sheriff, and clergyman, and lynched in full view of an excited crowd. Although it was widely known who had committed the lynching, a grand jury announced it could find no evidence to convict anyone. Snapshots of Frank's hanging body became a popular item in Georgia, and were sold in rural markets throughout the state for many years.[13] In 1986, Frank was pardoned of murder, although not declared innocent, by the state of Georgia.[14]

WORLD WAR I: This conflict, termed by many historians as the origin of World War II,[15] began, significantly enough, on Tishah B'Av, 1914, and changed the face of Jewish Eastern Europe forever. Millions of Jews were caught in the crossfire between the German and Russian armies. Many of these Jews, although not targeted, lost their lives. Others fled the front lines or were exiled to the interior of Russia. In addition, the great upheaval caused by the war disrupted traditional community structures. The shtetl, which had been a bastion of Jewish tradition for centuries, was destroyed, never again attaining its previous status.

Jews fought in all the armies, often shooting at each other. The chart on the next page indicates the number of Jews in uniform, armies, and the number of deaths.[16]

On the western front, Hugo Guttman, a Jewish captain in a German infantry battalion, was so impressed by the bravery of a corporal under his command — Adolph Hitler, the company runner — that he successfully nominated him for the Iron Cross, First Class, for what Guttman described as "personal bravery and general merit." This was an unusual decoration for a corporal, and Hitler wore the medal with pride for the rest of his life. After Hitler came to power in 1933, he was embarrassed when Guttman said publicly, "I pinned the Iron Cross on Hitler." The Nazis protested that "no Jew

Country	Soldiers	Deaths
Austria-Hungary	320,000	40,000
Britain	50,000	8,600
France	55,000	9,500
Germany	100,000	12,000
Italy	6,000	500
Russia	650,000	100,000
United States	250,000	3,400
Serbia	1,200	250

could have done it," and Guttman was arrested. He was taken into custody three times before he was allowed to leave for the United States in 1934.[17]

THE JEWS OF PALESTINE DURING WORLD WAR I: The Ottoman rulers were especially cruel to Palestine's 85,000 Jews, ordering the expulsion of foreign Jews, which comprised most of Palestine Jewry. Being cut off from funds from abroad and from import outlets for their products destroyed numerous settlements. Epidemics of typhus and cholera, deportation to remote parts of the empire, and the near-famine conditions of 1917 all took their toll. By the war's end, Jewish population had decreased to 58,000.[18] Only one-third of the Jewish population of Jerusalem remained by the end of 1917; most of the rest had died of starvation or disease.

From the outbreak of the war, the idea had arisen in Zionist circles of the establishment of a Jewish force to fight alongside the Allies and against the Turks. In 1915, the Zion Mule Corps was formed, fighting with distinction on the Gallipoli Peninsula in Turkey. Jews in Palestine set up a spy ring called NILI to help the British. The ring rendered valuable service to the British before being broken up by the Turks, who tortured and executed several of the ring's members.

THE BALFOUR DECLARATION: Since the days of the Puritans in the 1600s, Christian Zionists had always existed in Britain; they saw the return of the Jewish people to their ancient homeland as fulfilling the Bible's mandate. (Somehow, this pro-Jewish approach coexisted in upper-class British society with its pervasive anti-Semitism.) On a more practical level, Palestine was of great strategic importance to Britain, being the bridge between Africa and Asia. Domination of Palestine by unfriendly powers such as Germany would endanger British colonies, most notably India. Therefore, Palestine was the missing link that could join together parts of the British Empire so that they could form a continuous chain from the Atlantic to the mid-Pacific.[19] The British also hoped that support for a Jewish homeland would inspire many Jews, especially in Russia, to support the Allied cause.

In 1917, Chaim Weizmann, president of the British Zionist Federation, trying to obtain British public support for a Jewish homeland in Palestine, held meetings with numerous sympathetic British officials. Almost all the government figures that mattered were disposed favorably toward the proposed declaration, which would declare unequivocal support for a Jewish Palestine.

Incredibly, opposition from Jewish members of the British cabinet brought the project to a halt. One of them, Edwin Montagu, a thoroughly assimilated Jew, saw Zionism as a threat to the position in British society that he and his family had so recently, and with so much exertion, attained. Judaism, he argued, was a religion, not a nationality, and to say otherwise was to say that he was less than completely British. Further, it disturbed Montagu that, despite his lack of religious faith, he could not avoid being categorized as a Jew. He was the millionaire son of an English lord, but was driven to lament, "I have been striving all my life to escape from the ghetto."[20]

On November 2, 1917, Lord Balfour, the British Foreign Secretary, issued a much-diluted version of the assurance of support that

Weizmann had requested. The document, issued in a famous letter to Lord Rothschild, became known as the Balfour Declaration. It electrified the Jewish people, for it meant that the world's premier colonial power recognized and supported Eretz Yisrael as the place of Jewish refuge and settlement. The text of the letter:

Dear Lord Rothschild:

I have much pleasure in conveying to you, on behalf of His Majesty's government, the following declaration of sympathy with Jewish aspirations which has been submitted to, and approved by, the cabinet: "His Majesty's Government views with favor the establishment in Palestine of a national home for the Jewish people, and will use their best endeavors to facilitate the achievement of this object, it being clearly understood that nothing shall be done which may prejudice the civil and religious rights of existing non-Jewish communities in Palestine, or the rights and political status enjoyed by Jews in any other country."

After the cabinet voted on the declaration, one of the ministers involved rushed over to Weizmann, effusively proclaiming, "It's a boy!" However, the Zionist leader was not happy with his new offspring. The British stated that Palestine was a "national home for the Jewish people." Was that a country, a colony, or something akin to an Indian reservation in the United States? Furthermore, the clause that "nothing shall be done which may prejudice the civil and religious rights of existing non-Jewish communities in Palestine" implied that if the Arabs found fault with the declaration on such grounds, Britain was absolved of its commitment to the Jewish people.

On December 11, 1917, British General Allenby captured Jerusalem from the Turks. Entering Jerusalem, Allenby declared, "We have come, not as conquerors, but as deliverers. It is our intention to open a new era of brotherhood and peace in the Holy Land."[21] Sadly, it was not long before the Jewish people realized the hollowness of these words.

Chapter 23

THE AFTERMATH OF WORLD WAR I

GREAT **C**HANGE: The cataclysmic events of the first years of the postwar period irrevocably altered the old order, and the far-reaching changes are still being felt in both the Jewish and secular worlds. Great empires were broken up into individual nations, and a Communist regime replaced the czar and took power in Russia. The modern Middle East began to assume its current form, sowing the seeds for today's unsolvable problems. And the ethnic conflicts in the former Yugoslavia are a result of the Allied creation of that country.

THE TREATY OF VERSAILLES: In 1919, the victorious Allies redrew the map of Europe. The new nations of Poland, Czechoslovakia, Austria, Hungary, Latvia, Lithuania, Estonia, and Yugoslavia were formed out of remnants of the German, Austro-Hungarian, Ottoman, and Russian empires. In the main, these new countries led to a worsening of Jewish life, for while the great polyglot empires existed, the Jews were one of many nationalities and not especially discriminated against, except in Russia. Many of the new countries, however, were fiercely nationalistic, and the Jews were seen as an alien presence. In addition, Jewish communities that were culturally similar were split up by new national boundaries; Hungarian Jews, for example, were divided among Hungary, Czechoslovakia, Romania, and Yugoslavia, while Lithuanian Jews now found themselves in Poland, Lithuania, Latvia, and Russia. Relations between many of the new nations were poor, causing great disruption in previously cohesive Jewish areas. Polish and Lithuanian Jews especially found it virtually impossible to communicate, due to the tension between the two countries caused by the Polish annexation of Lithuania's traditional capital of Vilna.

In world history, too, the Treaty of Versailles is seen as a watershed event. Historians view the roots of World War II in the indignities imposed upon Germany by the treaty. Germany had to accept guilt for starting World War I, lost portions of its national territory in Europe and all of its colonies, and had to pay war reparations. The fact that German troops were not defeated on the field of battle made their country's humiliation even worse in the eyes of many Germans, and Hitler was later able to play on the resentment of the German people.

The great *rosh yeshivah* (dean) of Baranovitch Yeshivah, Rabbi Elchanan Wasserman, commented on the verse (Deuteronomy 32:8), "He set the borders of the peoples according to the number of the children of Israel":

> The purpose of everything that occurs in the world is only for the Jewish people, as the prophet (Zephaniah 3:6) writes: "I have cut off nations, their towers have become desolate; I have destroyed their streets so that no one passes by; their cities have become waste so that there is no man — so that there is no inhabitant. I said, 'Surely you will fear Me, you will accept reproof.'" It is apparent that punishment comes to the world only because of the Jewish people. Before the new national borders were created at Versailles they were written and sealed in the Heavenly Court, whose purpose for establishing them was only for the sake of the Jewish people, either for their benefit or punishment.[1]

RUSSIA BECOMES COMMUNIST: The Communist takeover of Russia in 1917 sent shock waves throughout the world, and had a disastrous effect upon the Jewish people in three major ways. First, Russian Jews were forcibly separated from Torah observance and isolated from world Jewry. Second, a tidal wave of anti-Semitism spread throughout the world, with Jews blamed for the spread of Communism. Third, the United States closed its doors to immigration, trapping millions of Jews in Europe, where they were killed in the Holocaust.

In 1919, the Soviet government dissolved all Jewish religious communities, confiscated their property, and shut the overwhelming majority of synagogues and *mikva'os* forever. (The rabbi of Luban, Rabbi Moshe Feinstein, devised an ingenious plan to maintain a *mikvah* in his town. When he found out that the government wanted to build a public swimming pool in Luban, he prevailed upon the Jewish contractor to build it in a way that it would be a kosher *mikvah*. The word was secretly spread, and Jews came from great distances to the area's only functioning *mikvah*.)

Government schools, which the overwhelming majority of Jewish children attended, taught students to ridicule and hate religion.

The teacher told the hungry children, "Let's all say, 'G-d, give us candy!' "

The children duly made the request.

"Well, did anyone get candy?" the teacher asked.

"No!" came the reply in unison.

"Now let's say, 'Lenin, give us candy!' "

The children said the words, and a bag of candy was brought in.[2]

Rabbis and other religious functionaries were termed unproductive parasites and stripped of all privileges. They could not live in their state-owned houses, and were forced to live in the synagogue or with friends and relatives, who were already cramped in their own small dwellings. (Rabbi Moshe Feinstein, for example, suffered such a fate.) During times of hunger, when food was rationed, rabbis were not given ration cards. The onus of supporting them fell upon the community, which could barely feed its own families. Eventually, Torah study was prohibited, and rabbis were forced to resign their posts. Many were arrested, exiled to Siberia, or executed. As a result, the next generation was cut off from its Torah heritage, and Soviet Russia became a spiritual wasteland.

These terrible deeds were perpetrated by a special section of the Communist government known as the *Yevsektsiya*, comprised of fanatic anti-religious Jews. The Chafetz Chaim was of the opinion that the members of the *Yevsektsiya* descended from Amalek, the eternal enemy of the Jewish people.[3] He further remarked that when the first anti-religious decrees were promulgated, the Jews of Russia should have physically battled them even at the cost of their lives, in the manner of the Hasmoneans during the Syrian-Greek oppression. Although many Jews would have been killed, the power of the *Yevsektsiya* would have been weakened. It was this missed opportunity that allowed them to exercise a stranglehold over Russian Jewry.[4]

Outside of Russia, Jews were blamed worldwide for the rise of Communism. Ironically, it was the non-Jewish Jew, the Jew who denied there was such a thing as a Jew at all,[5] who bore responsibility. Leon Trotsky, born Lev Bronstein, personally organized and led the armed uprising that installed the Communists in power. Then he ensured the survival of the Communist regime during the first few years of its existence when it was in great danger of collapsing. More than anyone else, Trotsky symbolized the violence and demonic power of Communism and its determination to inflame the world, and he was also the most responsible for the popular identification of revolution with the Jews.

The consequences for the Jews, immediate and long term, locally and worldwide, were appalling. Civil war broke out in Russia and Ukraine between supporters and opponents of Communism, and the Jews were targeted by both sides. More than 100,000 Jews were killed and 1,000 Jewish communities destroyed in a spate of horrific pogroms, the worst since the horrors of 1648–49.

Communist-led uprisings, led by non-Jewish Jews, broke out in Germany, Hungary, and Poland, leading to murderous attacks on innocent Jewish communities. In all three countries, the local Communist parties had been largely created and run by non-Jewish Jews, and in each case it was the observant Jews of the ghettoes and villages — who abhorred godless Communism and who observed the rites of mourning, including shivah, when a family member turned Communist[6] — who paid the penalty. As a rabbi once mentioned to Trotsky himself, "It's the Trotskys who make the revolutions, and the Bronsteins who take the blame." In Russia, the Communist Jews were heavily involved with the secret police, forcing peasants to part with their grain and harassing the Russian Orthodox Church, earning the fierce enmity of the population.

In the United States, the Communist takeover of Russia and its association with radical Jews also had serious consequences. In 1924, the American government established a quota of 9,000 immigrants annually from Poland, Romania, and Russia, countries with a combined Jewish population of millions, effectively ending mass Jewish immigration to the United States. Anti-foreigner hysteria gripped America, shutting the doors of the country to immigrants, especially Jews. In actuality, these miniscule quotas were not filled, even when the scope of Nazi horrors against the Jews became known.

SUPPORTS OF TORAH IN RUSSIA: Although the flame of Torah Judaism was almost completely extinguished in the Soviet Union, one group struggled valiantly to keep it alive. The Lubavitcher Chassidim, led by Rabbi Joseph Yitzchak Schneerson (the Freierdige rebbe), maintained a system of schools throughout Russia. In 1928 there were 4,200 children in yeshivos in twenty-two cities.[7] The rebbe himself was arrested by the Communist authorities in 1927 and condemned to death. However, an international outcry caused the government to relent, and he was expelled from the country in 1928. From outside Russia, the rebbe was able to send funds clandestinely and appoint religious emissaries to Russia. In 1926, religious persecution intensified, and the yeshivos were forced to go underground. The Lubavitcher Chassidim kept up their secret effort until the downfall of Communism in 1991, even though many Chassidim were caught by the authorities and sent to Siberia or executed. However, the effort continued, and although only a small fraction of Russia's Jews were reached, Torah Judaism did not disappear altogether in the Soviet Union. Today's religious revival in the former Soviet Union can be credited to those brave pioneers who struggled under the most dangerous conditions imaginable.

BIROBIDZHAN: In 1928, the Soviet government supported the idea of an autonomous Jewish settlement in a region of Siberia near China called Birobidzhan. The Russians were concerned about the rising influence of Japan and China in the region, and wanted to populate the area as a buffer zone. Inducements, such as extra food and land, were provided to encourage Jews to settle there. Some Jews went to Birobidzhan seeking economic opportunity, while others went out of idealism, to build a socialist Jewish homeland in the Soviet Union, which would replace the attraction of Zionism and Eretz Yisrael.

At its peak in the 1930s, Birobidzhan had 35,000 Jewish settlers, and even attracted socialist Jews from the United States and Palestine. Once there, these foreign Jews were quickly disillusioned, but there was no way out of Stalin's Soviet Union. Eventually, these foreign Jews were executed during Stalin's purges.

Along with Russian, the government established Yiddish as an official language of the Birobidzhan region, and even non-Jews learned Yiddish in the schools. Street signs were written in Yiddish, and libraries contained large collections of Yiddish books, none of a religious nature. Newspapers were printed in Yiddish and given names such as *Emes* (truth). Needless to say, there were no religious institutions in Birobidzhan — the Jews had not even one synagogue.

Nevertheless, Jewish settlement dwindled after a few years. It was extremely difficult to produce crops from the swampy land. Travel was difficult, as there were no roads in the area. Hordes of bloodsucking insects made life miserable in the summer, and bitter cold and snow plagued the winter. Diseases such as malaria abounded. Many of the original pioneers moved out of the region, and by 1945 Birobidzhan lost its Jewish character. Today, a few thousand Jews still live in Birobidzhan.

ENGLAND CREATES THE MAP OF THE MODERN MIDDLE EAST: The end of World War I saw England in control of much of the Ottoman Empire's territories in the Middle East. By 1922, the map of the Middle East looked as it does today. Most significantly for the Jewish people, England tore away the land east of the Jordan River, 80 percent of the Palestine territory promised to the Jews as their national home, and created a new Arab protectorate called Transjordan, later known as Jordan. The leader of the Hashemite tribe, Abdullah, who had helped England in its struggle against the Turks, was installed as King of Transjordan. (His grandson, Hussein, was the famous King Hussein, and his great-grandson, Abdullah, rules Jordan today.) Transjordan was immediately closed to Jewish settlement, while the western portion of Palestine was open to both Jews and Arabs.

England also established protectorates in Egypt and Iraq, appointing as kings tribal leaders who had cooperated in the battle against the Ottoman Empire. In order to mollify France, which felt entitled to some of the spoils of war, England transferred Syria to French rule. France created the countries of Syria and Lebanon out of its newly acquired territory. In addition, England gave Syria the Golan Heights, historically considered part of Palestine. (Later negotiations between Syria and Israel over the Golan Heights largely revolved around how much land was actually given to Syria.)

We see, then, that Middle Eastern countries and frontiers were fabricated in Europe. Iraq and Transjordan were British inventions, lines drawn on an empty map by British politicians. A British civil servant established the boundaries of Saudi Arabia, Kuwait, and Iraq in 1922, while France drew the frontiers between Muslims and Christians in Syria and Lebanon. Much of the conflict in the Middle East in the last eighty years, both between Jews and Arabs and among the Arabs themselves, revolves around the arbitrary and artificial division of the region by the colonial powers.

THE BRITISH CHANGE THEIR POLICY: By 1922, England, although officially upholding the Balfour Declaration, no longer believed it was workable. A government's policy is only as effective as those charged with implementing it, and Britain's army, which ran

Palestine, realized the very real difficulty of reconciling Muslims to the prospect of an increased Jewish settlement. In addition, the army felt great resentment at having been burdened by London with the unpopular and highly difficult policy of the creation of a Jewish homeland pursuant to the Balfour Declaration. The army therefore gave the impression of being unwilling to carry the Balfour Declaration into effect. Churchill, for example, estimated that 90 percent of the British army in Palestine opposed the Balfour Declaration.[8] An army circular distributed to troops in Palestine stated: "In the case of Palestine these sympathies are rather obviously with the Arabs, who have hitherto appeared to the disinterested observer to have been the victims of an unjust policy forced upon them by the British Government." Great Britain was also greatly concerned with the reactions of Muslims throughout the Empire, particularly the 100 million Muslims of Britain's prize colony, India.

THE ARABS RIOT: Some anti-Semitic British officials encouraged the Arabs to attack the Jews. In 1920, Colonel Water Taylor, financial advisor to the Palestine military administration, told Haj Amin, "If disturbances of sufficient violence occurred in Jerusalem...[Britain] would advocate the abandonment of the Jewish Home. Freedom can only be attained through violence."[9] Amin took Taylor's advice and started a riot, the first of many such incidents. When it was over, five Jews were killed and more than 200 injured.

A BITTER ENEMY ARISES: In 1921, an event occurred that set the tone of Jewish-Arab relations in Palestine on its present-day collision course. In order to appear even-handed, Sir Herbert Samuel, the Jewish High Commissioner for Palestine, appointed Haj Amin al-Husseini to the position of Grand Mufti of Jerusalem. Husseini, a scion of one of Jerusalem's prominent Arab families, was implacably opposed to any compromise with Jews in Palestine. He rapidly gained control of the Muslim Supreme Council, which administered the mosques on the Temple Mount, and controlled the administration of all Muslim social services, funding, mosques, judicial appointments, and teaching positions throughout Palestine. Amin's virulent hatred of Jews rapidly spread throughout the Arab population, and any Arab who advocated cooperation or compromise with Jews was silenced or killed.

Hoping to calm Arab agitation, Samuel ordered an immediate suspension of all Jewish immigration, and even Jews who had already arrived at Jaffa, and who were waiting to disembark, were refused permission to land. When immigration was restored a few months later, it came with the condition that it should never exceed "the economic capacity of Palestine to absorb new immigrants," a phrase employed greatly to limit the numbers of Jews entering the land. Britain began employing a double standard — forbidding Jewish settlement in eastern Palestine (Transjordan), and severely restricting it in western Palestine (the area allotted to the Jews as their national home), while overlooking illegal Arab immigration into the Jewish-settled areas of western Palestine.[10] In her remarkable book, *From Time Immemorial*, Joan Peters documents that hundreds of thousands of so-called Palestinian Arabs entered the land illegally from surrounding countries during British control of Palestine.

THE RIOTS CONTINUE: On Yom Kippur, 1928, Jewish worshippers at the *Kosel HaMa'aravi* put up a screen to separate men and women, according to Jewish law. The Arabs claimed that this was the start of Jewish construction that would eventually wind up taking possession of the Temple Mount, and they began harassing Jews who came to pray at the Wall. British authorities took the side of the Arabs. Tensions gradually rose, and in August 1929 they reached the boiling point. Six days of rioting by Arabs resulted in 133 Jewish deaths in Jerusalem, Tzefas, and Hebron. The attacks in Hebron were particularly gruesome, killing sixty Jews, among them students from the famous Lithuanian Slabodka Yeshiva, which had opened a branch in Hebron in 1925. After the riots, Jews left Hebron, not to return until 1967. In 1936, with the help of funds from Nazi Germany,[11] Arabs rioted throughout the country in protest of the 100,000 Jews entering Palestine in 1934 and 1935, the two years of greatest Jewish immigration. In response, the British sharply curtailed the number of Jews permitted into the land.

In 1939, as a result of continual hostility to Jewish immigration from many Arab countries, Britain published a White Paper, known to the Jews of Palestine as the Black Paper, setting out rules that would make the attainment of a Jewish majority in Palestine impossible. Over the next five years, 1939–1944, only 100,000 Jews would be permitted to enter the country, thereby capping the Jewish population at 545,000. No restrictions were placed upon the Arab population, which then stood at 1.5 million. The document further stipulated that in 1949, Palestine would become an independent Arab nation. Britain thus repudiated the commitment it had made to the Jewish people with the Balfour Declaration. This policy could not come at a worse time for the Jews: the doors of Palestine were slammed shut as millions of Jews sought to flee Europe before and during World War II.

In 1941, al-Husseini traveled to Germany, where he met with Hitler, who promised to destroy the Jewish community in Eretz Yisrael. The Mufti broadcast Nazi propaganda to the Arab world, and then recruited Bosnian Muslim SS troops, which participated in killing Jews. He also applied pressure on nations in Europe not to allow Jews to leave but instead to turn them over to the Nazis. It is estimated that the Mufti of Jerusalem was personally responsible for the slaughter of hundreds of thousands of Jews.[12] After the war, the Mufti fled to Egypt and then Lebanon, dying in 1974.

JEWISH POLITICAL ACTIVITY IN PALESTINE: During the 1920s the Jews of Palestine began identifying with the forerunners of today's political parties. These affiliations affected relationships between different groups of secular Jews, between secular and religious Jews, and among religious Jews. The passions unleashed in the Jewish community of Palestine at that time underlie the fault lines dividing Israeli Jews today.

In 1920, the major figures of world Zionism met in London, where, in recognition of his efforts in achieving the Balfour Declaration, they elected Chaim Weizmann president of the Zionist Organi-

zation. Its representatives in Palestine, headed by Weizmann, became known as the Jewish Agency, and acted as the liaison between
the Jews of Palestine and the British administration. Departments
were organized for political affairs, immigration, labor, colonization, education, and health. Weizmann launched the Keren
HaYesod (Jewish National Fund) as Zionism's major fundraising
instrument. As a result, although he did not belong to any political
party, Weizmann became the most powerful Jew in Palestine, for he
had the ear of the British and controlled much of the funding from
abroad.

What Weizmann wanted to see emerge in Palestine were enduring social, cultural, secular educational, and economic institutions. He opposed large-scale immigration to Palestine from the
ghettoes of Poland, favoring only pioneers who would work the
land.[13] Weizmann said: "Our brothers and sisters of Djika and
Nalevki [typical ghetto districts of Warsaw] are flesh of our flesh
and blood of our blood. But we must see to it that we direct this
stream and do not allow it to deflect us from our goal. It is essential
to remember that we are not building our National Home on the
model of Djika and Nalevki."[14] Due to this callous bias against the
religious Jews in Poland, the Jewish Agency, to whom the British
granted effective control over the distribution of immigration certificates, allotted only 6 percent of these precious documents to observant Jews in Poland, despite the fact that they comprised more
than half the Jewish population.

The wave of Jewish immigration after World War I, known as
the Third Aliyah, brought 35,000 Socialist-inspired newcomers to
Palestine in a period of four years. They set up kibbutzim (collective
farms and villages) and moshavim (cooperatives similar to kibbutzim that differed in allowing some private ownership of land). It
was at this time that the political composition of the Jews in Palestine took on a decisively leftist stance. In 1920, most of the Labor Zionist parties joined into a trade union federation known as the
Histadrut, which became a giant economic corporation. The
Histadrut organized a marketing outlet for food products (Tnuva),
a worker's bank (Bank HaPoalim), universal health coverage

(Kupat Cholim), and a vast network of schools. It also launched industrial companies, the most famous of which was called Solel Boneh, which provided thousands of Jews with jobs in road work, construction, swamp drainage, and building settlements. The Histadrut also established a clandestine self-defense force, the Haganah, which became the nucleus of the later Israeli Army. The Histadrut today continues to play a dominant role in the economy of the State of Israel.

THE LABOR PARTY: Although the various labor parties were united under the Histadrut, they were not united politically. In 1930, the two largest labor parties joined to create the Mapai party, the forerunner of today's Labor Party. It was headed by David Ben-Gurion, stressed cooperation with the British authorities, and made attempts to reach an understanding with the Arabs. Mapai was socialist, leftist, secular, and anti-religious. More than any other, this was the group that would shape the ideology and institutions of Jewish Palestine and later the State of Israel.

THE REVISIONIST ZIONISTS: In 1925, Vladimir Jabotinsky founded a breakaway Zionist party known as the Revisionists. Against the wishes of both the British and the Arabs, it stressed a Jewish state on both sides of the Jordan River, by force if necessary. Jabotinsky pressed for large-scale unrestricted Jewish immigration into Palestine, and worked diligently to sneak Jews into the country by ship, managing to bring 15,000 secretly. A charismatic personality and dynamic speaker, Jabotinsky attracted an enormous following in Poland and Lithuania, including Menachem Begin, his main disciple and ideological heir. In Poland, Begin organized a youth paramilitary organization known as Betar (*Brit Trumpeldor*) after Joseph Trumpeldor, who died defending a settlement in the Galilee, and who became a great Revisionist hero. In Palestine, the Revisionists founded their own military group, the *Irgun Zvei Leumi* (more commonly known as the Irgun), which directed reprisals against Arab marauders.

Ideological differences between the Revisionists and Mapai

were deep and visceral, coloring politics in the State of Israel to this day. Jabotinsky rejected the socialism of Mapai, as well as its desire to reach a modus vivendi with the British and Arabs. The Revisionists broke off from the Labor-dominated Jewish Agency, forming their own social and political institutions. While not religious, Jabotinsky and his party were not opposed to religion as a matter of principle. The Revisionists eventually became today's Likud Party. The ideological differences between Labor and Likud today mirror the issues that divided them in the 1920s.

RELIGIOUS ZIONISM: The spiritual leader of the religious Zionists, Rabbi Avraham Y. Kook (1865–1935) pioneered the establishment of the Chief Rabbinate to govern religious life in Palestine. Two chief rabbis were appointed, one Sephardic and one Ashkenazic, a practice that exists today. Rabbi Kook became the first Ashkenazic chief rabbi. However, not all religious Jews in Palestine recognized his authority.

While everyone did regard Rabbi Kook as a scholarly and saintly figure, he became very controversial in the Torah world for his views on Zionism. Despite its secular and even anti-religious nature, for example, Rabbi Kook regarded political Zionism as the beginning of the Messianic era (*aschalta d'geulah*). His support for secular Zionist institutions alienated many observant Jews, who looked upon Zionism with great ambivalence and even strong opposition. Rabbi Kook founded a yeshivah, Mercaz Harav Kook, in Jerusalem in 1924, which was unique among yeshivos in its positive outlook on Zionism.

The major religious Zionist party in Palestine was the Mizrachi. It was under the umbrella of the General Zionists, but maintained its own cultural and educational institutions. Mizrachi's motto was *Torah V'Avodah*, Torah and Labor, and Mizrachi succeeded in attracting religious pioneers to the land of Israel. Today, Mizrachi is known as the National Religious Party. Its youth group and high schools are called Bnei Akiva, and it maintains Bar-Ilan University.

NON-ZIONIST JEWS: Most religious Jews in Palestine, particularly in Jerusalem, were opposed to Zionism. In 1918, Chaim Weizmann, in a meeting with many of Jerusalem's rabbis, attempted to make minor adjustments in the age-old yeshivah curriculum in order to modernize it. He also tried to get the community to adopt modern Hebrew as its daily language. As an inducement, Weizmann offered funds that Russian Jewry had sent through the Zionist Organization, money that was greatly needed by the impoverished community. Courageously, the rabbis rebuffed the blatant attempt to introduce *Haskalah*-type changes into their sacred way of life. This episode resulted in an unbridgeable gap between much of the Jerusalem community and the Zionist Organization.

The leader of the Jerusalem community known as the *yishuv hayashan* was Rabbi Yosef Chaim Sonnenfeld. A person of great saintliness and personal integrity, he steered the Jerusalem community on a path independent of the Zionist Organization, founding the Jerusalem organization known as *Eidah HaChareidis*. Rabbi Sonnenfeld's followers in the Meah Shearim section of Jerusalem adhere to his policy of complete nonrecognition and compromise with secular Zionism to this day. They do not accept funding from the government, participate in the political process, or recognize any Zionist institutions.

Rabbi Sonnenfeld had an unbounded love for the land of Israel, while maintaining that Jewish sovereignty should not take place until the coming of the Messiah. He was a respected figure by the British, and was called upon to present his viewpoint at commissions discussing the future of Palestine. Rabbi Sonnenfeld also tried to convey to the Arabs that not all Jews wanted a Jewish state, just a place to live. He met with Emir Hussein and King Abdullah in Transjordan, working out an understanding in which the Arabs would achieve political control of Palestine and Jews would be able to immigrate freely. His chief spokesman to the outside world was an articulate, formerly irreligious Jew, Jacob DeHaan, who presented this viewpoint to the world in a rational, coherent manner.

POLITICAL ASSASSINATIONS: Two political murders of Jews by other Jews took place in Palestine, and the ramifications are still deeply felt in Israeli society today. In 1924, Jacob DeHaan was shot in the streets of Jerusalem, but no culprit was found. Twenty thousand Jews of Rabbi Sonnenfeld's community attended the funeral. In 1970, the truth about the murder was finally made public. The Haganah, then alarmed at DeHaan's influence internationally, had decided to eliminate the traitor.[15]

In 1933, Chaim Arlosoroff, a major Labor leader, was shot while walking on the beach in Tel Aviv. Avraham Stavsky, a Revisionist, was accused of murdering Arlosoroff, but after a concerted effort, led by Rabbi Kook, to prove his innocence, Stavsky was acquitted for lack of evidence. The Arlosoroff murder continued to exacerbate relations between the Labor Zionists and the Revisionists for many years, and at the time of Yitzhak Rabin's assassination in 1995, the episode was brought up again as a divisive issue.

TORAH GROWS IN ERETZ YISRAEL: Today's explosive growth of Torah scholarship in Israel began with a modest development in the 1920s. Rabbi Isser Zalman Meltzer arrived in 1925 to head the Yeshiva Etz Chaim in Jerusalem. Rabbi Avraham Yeshayahu Karelitz, the famed Chazon Ish, came in 1933, settled in Bnei Brak, and became the leader of his generation. Among the Chazon Ish's many accomplishments were new, authoritative rulings on questions of halachah that did not arise before his time. He developed the practical application of the laws of *shmittah* (permitting the land to go fallow every seven years) to a modern agricultural society, and defined the date line according to Jewish law. The Chazon Ish was responsible for the growth of Bnei Brak into one of the world's greatest cities of Torah. He passed away in 1953. Rabbi Yaakov Yisrael Kanievsky, later to be known as the Steipler Gaon, settled in Bnei Brak in 1934, and lived there for more than fifty years until his passing in 1985.

JEWISH LIFE IN POLAND 1918–1939: The Polish census of 1931 indicated that there were 3,114,000 Jews in Poland, thereby making up 10 percent of the population, by far the largest percentage of Jews in any nation in the world. Poland was second only to the United States in terms of the actual number of Jewish inhabitants.

Nearly three-fourths of all Polish Jews were concentrated in the cities. The 350,000 Jews of Warsaw, for example, represented 30 percent of the capital's population, and a similar or even higher proportion was reached in other Polish cities. There, the Jews generally did not attempt to assimilate into Polish culture. They wore traditional dress and spoke Yiddish. A great many Polish Jews could not even speak Polish.

Most Jews were poor, working as ill-paid minor artisans — tailors, hatmakers, and shoemakers. Although they dominated Polish mercantile life, the Jews were largely poor peddlers, keepers of little shops, and proprietors of shabby market stalls, where a few zlotys' worth of goods represented the vendor's entire wealth.

These traditional occupations inevitably led to certain tensions. In every Polish village a Jew owned the store, a Jew was the horse and cattle trader, and a Jew was the moneylender. When times were difficult in the Polish countryside, which occurred frequently, it was the Jew who had to collect money, refuse credit, or buy cattle cheaply. These were not occupations that popularized Jews with the Polish peasantry. The peasant, who rarely comprehended the necessary function of the middleman in business transactions, tended to regard the Jew as a bloodsucker, when, in fact, the Jews were generally no better off than the peasants.

To be sure, there were a number of Polish Jews who had become wealthy and successful. These persons had usually assimilated themselves into Polish society, where they were called Poles of the Mosaic faith. Such Jews dominated the professions of law and medicine. They played major roles in banking and in the insurance industry. In fact, Jews handled practically all of pre-independence Poland's commerce.[16]

Poland's government adopted a policy of semi-official anti-Semitism, mainly in the economic arena. For example, certain kinds of artisans had to pass examinations in order to become licensed to pursue their trade. The examinations, however, were conducted only in Polish, thus excluding the large number of Jewish craftsmen who spoke only Yiddish. Compulsory Sunday closing laws were enacted for businesses, which turned into a form of economic sanction against the Jews, who were also closed on Saturdays, the Jewish Sabbath. Jews were largely excluded from government civil service jobs. Out of a total number of 16,840 postal, telegraph, and telephone officials, only twenty-one were Jewish. Jews totaled only forty-four of the 28,895 employees of the government-run railroad system. There were only 534 Jews that had positions in government offices and courts, out of a total of 41,905 workers.[17]

In 1936, matters became worse for the Jews. A government-approved boycott of Jewish merchants began to develop. When licenses to sell tobacco were revoked, 30,000 Jews were deprived of their livelihood. The government encouraged Markets without Jews, village market days on which Jewish stall keepers were excluded. In order to encourage Poles to patronize their own, a law was passed requiring every shop owner to post his name outside his store. A decree was imposed limiting kosher slaughter, on the grounds that it was inhumane. Very few Jews were permitted to purchase land. Colleges placed a quota on Jewish students, requiring them to sit in a separate area of the classroom. Pogroms broke out in several towns, killing thirty-six Jews and injuring more than 1,000. An official summed up the government's attitude toward Jews: "Personally, I love Danes very much, but if we had three million of them in Poland, I would implore G-d to take them away as soon as possible."[18]

While the countryside campaign to replace Jewish shopkeepers with Christians was fairly successful, it did not result in the development of mercantile expertise in the gentile replacements. It was quite noticeable that Christian shop owners frequently failed where Jews had survived. Thus, the economic persecution caused great suffering and pauperized an enormous number of small Jewish shopkeepers and artisans. It is estimated that by 1939, one-third of Poland's Jews, more than one million in all, were completely dependent on relief payments contributed largely by Jewish charities in the United States.[19]

JEWISH POPULATION DISTRIBUTION IN POLAND: The Jews of Poland were distributed in four areas: Congress Poland, containing

50 percent of all Polish Jews, including the major Jewish centers of Warsaw, Lodz, and Lublin; Galicia, which included the cities of Cracow and Lvov; the Kresy, lands that had previously been Ukrainian and Russian — the eastern areas of Volhynia, Belorussia, and Polish Lithuania, including Vilna, Bialystock, and Brisk; and former German territory awarded to Poland after World War I. The Jews of Congress Poland and Galicia were heavily chassidic, with a small percentage of assimilated Jews. In the east, the territories of Belorussia and Polish Lithuania formed, along with independent Lithuania, the Misnagdic heartland of Jewry. There were only 30,000 Jews in the former German areas, and they were largely Westernized and assimilated in the German fashion.

POLITICAL AND CULTURAL ACTIVITY: In Poland, more so than in any other country, Jews were extremely active in the political process. Poland's minorities were allotted a certain number of seats in the *Sejm*, or parliament; thus, many groups competed for Jewish loyalty by running for office. In addition, one's level of Jewish identification was strongly bound up in party affiliation, particularly among the young. There were a dozen Zionist parties — socialists, labor, centrist, religious. Other parties included Bundists, Yiddishists, assimilationists, and the religious party, Agudath Israel. The parties bickered among themselves, and were not able to unite to counter external threats to the community. Sadly, this situation has prevailed through Jewish history — before the destruction of the second Beis HaMikdash, during the time of the Warsaw Ghetto in World War II, and is currently the case in the State of Israel. In Poland, each party also had its own network of schools and youth groups, thus establishing divisive lines of demarcation between Jews.

Cultural activities, largely secular, thrived in Poland. Hundreds of Jewish newspapers, of every political persuasion, were published in Yiddish, Hebrew, and Polish. There were 230 Yiddish newspapers based in Warsaw alone. Hebrew and Yiddish literature and theater reached new heights. In 1925, YIVO, the Jewish Scientific Institute, catalogued and documented Yiddish culture and

Jewish history in Eastern Europe. Many of our photographs and footage of Jewish life in Eastern Europe before the Holocaust comes from the work of this institution.

RELIGIOUS LIFE IN POLAND: "Over these things I weep; my eyes run with tears" (Lamentations 1:16). The sublime spiritual grandeur of the Eastern European Jew is gone, never to be recaptured.

Nearly 350,000 Jews made their home in Warsaw. Many were eminent rabbanim, tzaddikim, and scholars, including the leading Torah sage in Poland, Rabbi Menachem Ziemba. People of great integrity and faith treaded the cobblestone streets of Warsaw, and it was said that the *Shechinah*, the Divine Presence, permeated its atmosphere. Warsaw was a nucleus of Torah study, Chassidus, and Jewish vitality. The shtieblach and study halls of Warsaw resounded with Torah at all hours of the day and night.

Every street in Warsaw boasted its own *gaon* or rebbe, and many rebbes were identified by their addresses: the Mila Street rebbe, the Pavia Street rebbe, the Nizka Street rebbe. There were more than 300 shtieblach in Warsaw, including thirty-five on Franciszkansa Street alone. The Association of Orthodox Rabbis of Poland, *Agudath HaRabbanim*, included prominent leaders from across the entire spectrum of Polish religious Jewry. The nearly 1,000 members deliberated on all matters of religious life at its Warsaw headquarters.

Warsaw also maintained a Jewish hospital, a religious old-age home, and an orphanage directed by observant Jews. The community had its own free kitchens for the poor and special Jewish shelters for the homeless. Many *chessed* organizations existed in Warsaw, distributing food and money on a daily basis, and especially before the Sabbath and holidays. Volunteers also visited the sick and took care of wedding and funeral needs.

Hundreds of elementary schools, known as *chadorim*, proliferated; all taught the Torah in the traditional way and spirit in which it had been taught for hundreds of years. Yeshivos were filled to overflowing with aspiring scholars. Warsaw was also a major center for printing *sefarim*, Torah periodicals, and newspapers representing the observant Jewish viewpoint.

The Sabbath in Warsaw was an intangible fragment of the World to Come, as it is described in traditional Sabbath songs. From every street rang forth the dancing and singing that accompany the onset of the holy day. The streets were packed with Jews dressed in their finest clothes, the joy on their faces reflecting the holiness of the Sabbath. Delicious aromas from the special Sabbath foods wafted down from every window. A Sabbath in Warsaw was truly, as the song so eloquently describes, "rest, joy, and light for the Jewish people."

CHASSIDIC LIFE: Continuing to nourish the spiritual life of Polish Jewry, dozens of chassidic towns — Ger, Alexander, Radomsk, Sochatchov, Ostrovtze, Vorki, Amshinov, and Radzin in central Poland; and Belz, Bobov, Bluzhov, Chortkov, Boyan, Sadigura, and Ropshitz in Galicia — were booming centers of Torah learning, service of G-d, and *chessed*. The Chassidus of Ger was the largest, attracting hundreds of thousands of adherents, so much so that there was no town in Poland without a *shtieble* of Ger. Although all of these groups were decimated in the Holocaust, many of them were able to reconstitute themselves, both in Israel and the United States, further enriching the Jewish people with their great spiritual legacy.

BETH JACOB: For thousands of years, girls traditionally received their Torah education at home. (This was also true for many boys; only the best students went to *cheder* or yeshivah.) The great sanctity of the Jewish home, and the holiness that permeated general Jewish society, ensured that Torah values were deeply instilled for life. (The Chafetz Chaim, for example, remarked that he was incapable of comprehending the spiritual greatness of his grandmother.) By the 1900s, however, things had changed drastically. The blandishments of secular movements were tantalizing, and the home could not compete with the new currents swirling in the streets. Countless numbers of men, despite having the advantage of formal Jewish education, were defecting from religious observance;

the situation was even worse for women. In 1918, a thirty-five-year-old dressmaker in Cracow, Sarah Schenirer, set up the first school for Orthodox Jewish women, calling it Beth Jacob after the Torah's description of Jewish women (Exodus 19:3, *Rashi*). Realizing the primary importance of women in transmitting Torah values to the next generation (which is why G-d offered the Torah at Mount Sinai to women first),[20] Sarah Schenirer took this unprecedented step.

The first Beth Jacob School had twenty-five students. Within twenty years, championed by the Chafetz Chaim and the Gerrer rebbe, and given an organizational framework by the major religious political party in Poland, Agudath Israel, the network of girls' schools grew to 80,000 students throughout Europe. Clearly, Sarah Schenirer's charge to her students in her will was being realized: "My dear girls, you are going out into the great world. Your task is to plant the holy seed in the souls of pure children. In a sense, the destiny of Israel of old is in your hands."[21]

With the German conquest of Poland in 1939, her schools were closed down, and during the following five years most of those who had been pupils were killed. After the war, however, the Beth Jacob system was recreated in the United States and Israel, so that the aim, to keep girls within the religious fold, was not lost.

DAF YOMI: In 1923, Rabbi Meir Shapiro, a dynamic Polish scholar, proposed a program of Torah study that would unite Jews across the globe. Known as *Daf Yomi*, it called on Jews everywhere to study the same page of Talmud daily, and to finish the entire Talmud in approximately seven and a half years. Acclaimed by Torah leaders in Poland, and popularized by Agudath Israel, the first course of study began on Rosh HaShanah of that year, and quickly caught on throughout the Torah world. It remains highly popular today.

THE LITHUANIAN YESHIVOS: Rabbi Yechiel Y. Weinberg describes the attitude of the Lithuanian Jew toward Torah study:

In Lithuania, the Jews lived an unfettered life. They knew of no greater celebration of life than the crown of Torah and mitzvos.

The whole of Jewish communal life was permeated with the spirit of the Talmud. The study of Talmud was the only opportunity for a spiritual and cultural life whose sole basis was the Talmud and sole stage the *beis midrash* (study hall). The study of Gemara itself assumed a particular character in Lithuania. It has the steady pace of work progressing gradually, confidently, toward a clear target by dint of ceaseless, diligent toil. It is the product of hard, serious mental effort. Its tool, in the search for clarity of comprehension, is the surgeon's scalpel.[22]

The Lithuanian-style yeshivah became the acme of Talmudic scholarship. Its students that survived the Holocaust transplanted the Lithuanian yeshivos, sparking a revival of Torah study throughout the Jewish world. Producing the great Torah leaders of America and Israel who painstakingly rebuilt institutions rivaling those of old, the scions of the Lithuanian yeshivos provided the guidance and inspiration so desperately needed after the Holocaust.

Lithuanian yeshivos were scattered throughout Lithuania and Northeast Poland, an area that was culturally Lithuanian but was annexed by Poland after World War I. The foremost institutions averaged 200–300 students. Poverty was endemic, and food was sparse. In Baranovitch, a joke circulated among the students: "Roll up your sleeves and go swimming after the noodles in the soup!"[23] Undoubtedly, the lack of material comforts focused the students' minds on Torah and enhanced their spiritual growth.

The yeshivos had a profound influence on Lithuanian Jewry, even on those who never attended. For example, during the month of Elul, which precedes the judgment days of Rosh HaShanah and Yom Kippur, there was a heightened mood of intensity in the yeshivos. The prayers were longer and more devout, and more time was spent in the study of Mussar. A description of Elul in the Lithuanian hamlet of Eishyshok:

The pre-dawn darkness would find the *shammas* making his way to the market square, and from there to every street and lane, to chant his special wake-up call. House by house, the melody of his call passed through the wooden shutters, and every man, woman, and child in the community rose early to go to shul. Soon the streets were filled with families, lanterns in hand, stumbling along in the early-morning chill. Footsteps echoing off the cobblestones, crisp autumn air with a touch of frost, darkness split by light from the lanterns — they were all part of the soul-stirring, awe-inspiring atmosphere of Elul.[24]

See the chart listing the major Lithuanian yeshivos between the two World Wars.

NON-LITHUANIAN YESHIVOS: Yeshivos were also widespread throughout the chassidic world, and they turned out extraordinary scholars, albeit with a different style and focus. The most famous of these yeshivos was *Yeshiva Chachmei Lublin*, established by Rabbi Meir Shapiro in 1930. Located in a modern, expansive six-story building, the yeshivah contained every amenity a student required. Admission requirements were very rigorous — applicants had to be able to recite 200 pages of Talmud from memory. A hundred thousand Jews attended the grand opening celebration. (Today, the building is used as a Polish medical school.) The Chassidus of Chabad also maintained an extensive network of yeshivos known as *Tomchei Temimim*. The rebbe of Radomsk headed the numerous branches of his school system.

There were also numerous Hungarian-style yeshivos, all patterned on the Yeshiva of Pressburg established by the Chasam Sofer. Most famous among these were the schools at Mattersdorf, Pressburg, Chust, Munkatch, Vizhnitz, Nitra, Ungvar, and Satmar. During World War II, the institution at Nitra was the only yeshivah open in Europe. It remained in existence until mid-1944, when the Nazis deported its students. Today, many of these yeshivos have re-established themselves in America and Israel, carrying on the great legacy of the past.

JEWISH LIFE IN HUNGARY: The treaty of Trianon in 1920 deprived Hungary of 70 percent of its territory and placed several hundred thousand former Hungarian Jews in Romania, Czechoslovakia, and Yugoslavia, leaving 450,000 Jews behind in Hungary.

YESHIVAH	ROSH YESHIVAH (Dean)	MASHGIACH (Spiritual Advisor)*	STUDENTS
IN LITHUANIA:			
Telz	Rabbi Yosef L. Bloch Rabbi Avraham Y. Bloch	Rabbi Zalman Bloch	300
Ponovezh	Rabbi Asher K. Baron	*	330
Slabodka	Rabbi Yitzchak I. Sher	Rabbi Avraham Grodzenski	250
Kelm	Rabbi Daniel Movshovitz	Rabbi Gershon Maidnick	42
IN POLAND:			
Mir	Rabbi Eliezer Y. Finkel	Rabbi Yerucham Levovitz Rabbi Chatzkel Levenstein	400
Radin	Rabbi Naftali Trop Rabbi Moshe Londinsky	Rabbi Eliezer Kaplan	300
Baranovitch	Rabbi Elchanan Wasserman	Rabbi Yisrael Y. Lubchansky	250

Grodno	Rabbi Shimon Shkop	Rabbi Shlomo Harkavy	250
Lomza	Rabbi Yechiel M. Gordon	Rabbi Moshe Rosenstein	240
Kletzk	Rabbi Aharon Kotler	Rabbi Yosef Nendick	260
Kaminetz	Rabbi Boruch Ber Leibowitz	Rabbi Naftali Leibowitz	300
Bialystock	Rabbi Avraham Yaffen	Rabbi Yisrael Movshovitz	

*Not every yeshivah had an official *mashgiach*.

Unlike Polish Jews, who did not identify as being Poles, Hungarian Jews, even those who were fervently Orthodox, felt great pride in being Magyar. All Jews spoke Hungarian, attended Hungarian schools, and did not create Jewish political parties as the Jews did in Poland. Jews adopted Hungarian first names, something unheard of in Poland.

Anti-Semitism, which was relatively low when Hungary was part of the Austro-Hungarian Empire, intensified greatly in post-Trianon Hungary for several reasons. First, Jews became virtually the only minority in Hungary and were suddenly very visible. Second, the Hungarian economy had collapsed, and there grew an increasing awareness that the Jews, who represented only 6 percent of the total population, possessed wealth and power considerably in excess of their number. The census of 1925 revealed that Jews constituted more than 50 percent of all lawyers in Hungary, 46 percent of doctors, 34 percent of editors and journalists, 39 percent of engineers and chemists, and 23 percent of directors and actors. In addition, Jews owned more than 40 percent of the industrial firms.[25]

For many Magyars, it appeared that Jews had infiltrated every part of the better-paid occupations and professions; Christians thus felt in danger of being pushed out altogether. In no small way, Hungarians began to resent what they saw. Third, the short-lived 1919 Communist regime of Bela Kun had been officered by a disproportionate number of Jews. For the first time in Hungary, anti-Jewish pogroms broke out after the overthrow of the Bolsheviks, killing more than 3,000 Jews.

Hungary became the first country in Europe after World War I to introduce anti-Semitic legislation. The Numerus Clausus Act of 1920 limited the percentage of Jewish students enrolled in universities to the proportion of Jews in the total population. Another law, passed in 1938, reduced the ratio of Jews in professions to 20 percent and called for the dismissal of 1,500 Jews from intellectual occupations every month until the proportion was attained. A further law decreased Jews in professions to 6 percent, also banning them from holding public office.

THE COMMUNITY: Hungarian Jews were divided into three groupings: Orthodox; a version of Reform called Neolog; and a traditionalist branch that lay between Orthodox and Reform known as Status Quo. The Orthodox Jews were largely concentrated in the northeast part of the country, the Neolog in the capital of Budapest, and the Status Quo spread throughout. Orthodox Jews suffered the greatest population loss after Trianon — the Jews who were assigned to the successor states were overwhelmingly religious, and 80 percent of the yeshivos formerly in Hungary were in other nations.

There were close to 500,000 Jews in Trianon Hungary, more than 200,000 of them living in Budapest. The population declined over the years, due to an intermarriage rate of nearly 20 percent, a low Jewish birthrate, and large-scale conversion to Christianity. In a sense, the loss of Hungarian Jewry began before World War II.

AMERICAN JEWISH ECONOMIC LIFE BETWEEN THE WARS: The Jewish community in the United States underwent great change between the wars. As the stream of newcomers stopped arriving in

1924, the immigrant environment eventually ended. Children of the Jewish garment workers did not, as a rule, follow their father's occupations, entering instead other areas of economic endeavor. Aided by the availability of educational opportunities and the rapidly changing structure of the American economy, the almost exclusively urban Jewish population (the flight to the suburbs had not yet begun) found outlets for its livelihood in the professions, and small and medium entrepreneurship. The trend that has since become the central socioeconomic fact of American Jewish life was well under way by the 1920s.

As a result, Jewish membership in blue-collar unions dropped by more than half, and although leaders of some unions remained Jewish, general Jewish involvement in the labor movement declined at the grass-roots level. In addition, the obsession of the immigrant generation with socialist issues was not reflected in the new, Americanized generation.

However, large segments of the American economy remained shut to the Jews, either immigrant or native-born. Corporations, banks, and other institutions kept Jews out of crucial managerial posts, not so much through formal decisions as through informal understandings. Engineering, in particular, was a field in which it was extremely difficult for Jews to find employment. Companies like New York Telephone had a clear policy of discrimination. At no time did the Jews approach, let alone participate in, the central concentrations of wealth and economic power in the United States.[26]

Quotas were established in prestigious colleges to keep the numbers of Jewish students down. In 1922, Harvard University issued a formal statement saying: "It is natural that with a widespread discussion of whether to limit the number of students there should be talk about the proportion of Jews at the college."[27]

The most rigorous anti-Semitic restrictions were enforced in the medical schools, as well as for opportunities in specialty training and appointment to hospital staffs, even in public institutions. Jewish hospitals founded late in the nineteenth century for the needs of Jewish patients in the 1920s devoted themselves to alleviating the plight of Jewish physicians. College and university faculties were, with few exceptions, closed to Jews, and Jewish teachers could usually secure public school employment only in the largest cities, where positions were filled through open, competitive examinations.[28]

THE IMMIGRANTS' CHILDREN: The cultural break between the immigrant generation and its offspring widened in the 1920s. Although the alienation process had begun earlier, the family and much of the environment still reflected Old Country culture. As the children of the immigrants grew older and raised their own families, however, they viewed their parents as an embarrassment, shunning their parents' values, regarding them as anachronistic and irrelevant. In the words of one immigrant child:

> One morning my father took his box and started out. I followed. Maybe that was the first time in years that I had taken a look at my father. As I had never grown very tall, but was in fact a shrimp, he still towered over me, but he seemed an old man now, bent, and I hated the discolored yellowish beard and the general shabby air of him. With terrible anger I felt myself seeing him as an old sheeny peddler, too.[29]

> One's mother spoke English, if she spoke it at all, with a grating accent; one's father shuffled about in slippers and suspenders when company came, hardly as gallant in manner or as nicely groomed as he ought to be. Both father and mother knew little about those wonders of the classroom — Shakespeare, the Monroe Doctrine, quadratic equations.[30]

This sense of shame caused whatever small amounts of Judaism the immigrants transmitted to their children to disappear in the coming generation. The Reform and Conservative movements, shunned by the immigrants, attracted their children in large numbers, while even more of them opted out of any Jewish affiliation whatsoever. However, the great trend toward intermarriage had not yet begun.

SECULAR CULTURE: The 1920s were the ripest years of Yiddish culture. There were eleven Yiddish theaters in New York City, and seventeen elsewhere in the United States, which, during a one-month period in the fall of 1927, presented 645 performances of 85 plays, many of high artistic quality. The Yiddish school system also reached its peak during these years, enrolling approximately 12,000 children, while a Yiddish organization called the Workmen's Circle (*Arbeter Ring*) attained its maximum membership of roughly 80,000. Symptomatic of future decline, however, was the lowered circulation of the Yiddish press from its 1915 peak. Hebrew culture attracted a devoted but much smaller following, organized in the *Histadruth Ivrith* of America and publishing the weekly *HaDoar*. Hebraists were particularly prominent in the rabbinate and Jewish education.

Jewish participation in the American theater was particularly high. The Marx brothers, Danny Kaye, and Zero Mostel (of *Fiddler on the Roof* fame) were outstanding comedians. Boris Aronson, one of America's best-known stage designers, began his career in the Yiddish theater. Jews excelled in theatrical production, direction, and song composition. They composed the great Broadway plays that so eloquently mirrored the reality of American life, such as George Gershwin's *Porgy and Bess*.

The development of motion pictures as a form of mass entertainment in the United States was largely the doing of Jewish producers and entrepreneurs, who made Hollywood the world's film capital after 1920. Jewish involvement with motion pictures was due to a number of factors. The industry had not developed a tradition of its own and had no vested interests to defend. Participation in it did not require a good knowledge of English. Motion pictures were initially regarded as a low-grade form of entertainment suitable for immigrants or the uneducated.[31] New arrivals, therefore, found it relatively easy to enter the field. Jewish immigrants helped transform movies from a marginal branch of entertainment into a worldwide, multi-billion dollar industry.

At the beginning of the twentieth century, most of the Jews connected with the film industry were film exhibitors or distributors. They owned small, shabby movie theaters, especially in the poor immigrant neighborhoods where the new form of entertainment enjoyed great popularity (for silent films had no language problems.) All the large Hollywood companies, with the exception of United Artists, were founded and controlled by Jews. The largest film company was Paramount, owned by Adolph Zukor, a Hungarian Jewish immigrant. Zukor also initiated the practice of advertising star actors.

It was the height of incredulity and something of a joke that penniless boys who arrived in America in the 1880s from Ukraine, Poland, and Austria-Hungary, speaking with Yiddish accents, should, more than anyone else, have the ability to reach the fantasies of a wide variety of people, creating a mythological America which became the national self-definition.

AMERICAN PHILANTHROPY: Helping the less fortunate is one of the major pillars of Judaism, and it was in this area that American Jews, both immigrant and native-born, most excelled. This greatness in philanthropy was due in part to traditional Jewish feelings of compassion, and in no small measure to the mistaken belief that one's Jewish identity and connection to the Jewish people could manifest itself solely in support for Jewish causes.

Jewish societies of immigrants from the same town, known as *landsmanschaften*, provided millions of dollars in relief to needy immigrants, in particular to the war-wracked cities and towns in Eastern Europe. In 1912, Hadassah, the Women's Zionist Organization of America, began developing an extensive medical infrastructure in Palestine, bringing modern health care to an area where it was virtually unknown.

In 1914, the American Jewish Joint Distribution Committee, popularly known as the JDC, or the Joint, was founded. Alarmed by the suffering of Jews in wartime, on October 24, 1914 a group of wealthy Jews of German-Jewish background, led by Jacob H. Schiff, Louis Marshall, and Felix Warburg, established the American Jewish Relief Committee. The Central Relief Committee was founded at the same time by Orthodox leaders, and the JDC distributed funds collected by the two bodies. In 1915 the People's Relief

Committee, representing labor, joined the effort. Consequently, the JDC was called the Joint because three separate commissions for assistance, representing three major currents in American Jewry, joined together in its endeavors. During World War I, the JDC spent nearly $15 million to aid Jews in Turkish-controlled Palestine. In 1915 the Joint sent the SS *Vulcan* with 900 tons of food; in Poland, the Joint sent relief to hundreds of thousands of Jews who had been forcibly removed from their homes and also to those who were in German-held areas. The United States' 1917 entry into the war prevented the direct transfer of assistance into hostile areas, but the State Department gave the JDC permission to establish an agency in neutral Holland to distribute its funds.[32]

In the postwar years, the Joint sent a staff of social workers to set up health and child care institutions for Jewish refugees of East European pogroms. Additional millions of dollars were expended in the provision of medical, financial, and vocational training for war refugees. As conditions in Eastern Europe deteriorated, the Joint continued to provide free loans, health and child care programs, and educational and religious services to Jews living in that region.

In 1915, at the behest of the Chafetz Chaim and Rabbi Chaim Ozer Grodzensky, religious American Jews founded Ezras Torah to alleviate the great suffering of the yeshivos and Torah scholars in Europe and Palestine. Rabbi Yosef Henkin, Rabbi Yisrael Rosenberg, and Rabbi Naftali Riff led the organization, helping thousands of scholars through most difficult times.

COMMUNITY RELATIONS ORGANIZATIONS: In addition to social and philanthropic institutions, a number of community relations organizations were founded. The American Jewish Committee was established in 1906, followed by the Anti-Defamation League of B'nai B'rith in 1913, and the American Jewish Congress in 1920. These secular organizations focused largely on combating rising anti-Semitism in the United States, also undertaking overseas work as well.

POLITICS: From the 1920s onward, American Jews were largely committed to the Democratic Party and to liberal agendas, such as a strong defense of civil liberties, active social legislation on behalf of deprived groups, and special public efforts to help African-Americans. These secular Jews' commitment to liberalism was based on two major factors: the once-powerful tradition of secular Jewish socialism, then fading but still felt and remembered, and the belief that Jewish interests and survival were best served by an open, secular society promoting liberal values and tolerating a diversity of people, including Jewish groups.[33] Franklin D. Roosevelt's New Deal of the 1930s, and his appointment of Jews to prominent positions within his administration, also led virtually all Jews, both secular and religious, to identify with the Democratic Party.

Jews began to enter high levels of government. Louis Brandeis was appointed to the Supreme Court in 1916, followed by Benjamin Cardozo in 1932, and Felix Frankfurter in 1939: all three have been recognized as among the greatest American judges. Henry Morgenthau became Secretary of the Treasury, and there were several Jewish governors. A number of Jews held President Roosevelt's confidence and served him in various official and unofficial capacities.

DEMOGRAPHICS: After the great influx of immigration, Jewish population centers in New York City's boroughs shifted as Jews abandoned highly congested areas. In 1918, most of Manhattan's 700,000 Jews lived on the Lower East Side and in Harlem. As their economic situation improved before the Depression of 1929, masses of Jews left the Lower East Side. While 314,200 Jews lived there in 1923, only 73,700 remained by 1940. In the 1920s, Harlem became a black neighborhood; of the 177,000 Jews living there in 1923, fewer than 5,000 remained in 1930. Many of these Jews settled in the Bronx and Brooklyn. The Jewish population of the Bronx rose from 420,000 in 1927 to 592,000 in 1939, making the borough 44 percent Jewish. Brooklyn experienced even greater Jewish population growth: the number of Jews rose from 568,000 in 1918 to

975,000 in 1937. No less than during immigrant years, New York Jews preferred to dwell near each other.[34]

RELIGIOUS LIFE: While religious life was weak in America during this period, it set down roots that laid the foundation for the great religious revival after the Second World War. A number of great scholars came to America, some to visit and others to settle. Rabbi Moshe Feinstein arrived in 1936 to head Mesivtha Tifereth Jerusalem on the Lower East Side, a position he would hold for fifty years. He later became the primary halachic authority in the Jewish world. Rabbi Eliezer Silver was the head of the American rabbinate, while the Bostoner rebbe established the first, and only, uniquely American chassidic center in Boston. Rabbi Shlomo Heiman, who headed Yeshiva Torah Vodaath, Rabbi Yitzchak Hutner, later the dean of Yeshiva Chaim Berlin, and Rabbi Yaakov Y. Ruderman, who became *rosh yeshivah* of Yeshiva Ner Israel of Baltimore, all came in the 1930s. Rabbi Yaakov Kaminetzky assumed several rabbinical posts after he arrived in 1937, and Rabbi Dr. Joseph Breuer founded the famous German *kehillah* in New York City in 1938. Rabbi Moshe Soloveitchik, and then his son, Rabbi Joseph D. Soloveitchik, assumed the leadership of Yeshiva University.

Only a minute fraction of American youth attended yeshivah. The overwhelming majority of youngsters received no Jewish education at all, or a scanty one in the local afternoon Talmud Torah. Unlike the privately run cheders established by the immigrants, Talmud Torahs were connected to a synagogue or community, and generally were run more efficiently and aspired to a somewhat higher educational standard. However, they failed to inspire the vast majority of students, who regarded much of Jewish teaching as irrelevant to their lives.

YOUNG ISRAEL: A number of Orthodox youth felt uncomfortable in old-style synagogues, yet were determined to reject the watered-down beliefs of the Reform and Conservative movements. In the 1920s, these young Orthodox men established a central organization known as the National Council of Young Israel. The new Young

Israel synagogues were committed to Orthodoxy, but because Young Israel's founders saw themselves as part of American society, they rejected many of the folkways of their parents, especially regarding old-style services as without melody or emotion. They shaved their beards, dressed in modern style, listened to English sermons, and replaced the customary non-liturgical conversations in Orthodox synagogues with an emphasis on decorum. Young Israel also set more rigorous standards for the education of its members, insisting that officers be Sabbath observers. Over the years, while Young Israel gradually lost some marks of distinctiveness, during the interwar period Young Israel was successful in bridging the gap between the faiths of the old and new worlds. The movement continues to be highly popular. In 1996, it boasted 146 congregations and some 130,000 members.[35]

KASHRUS: Between the wars, the kosher food situation in the United States was chaotic. Foods bore only the manufacturer's or advertising agency's unsupported kashrus assertion; some cited personal endorsement by figures whose rabbinic status and personal qualifications were questionable. In 1924, the Orthodox Union ventured into the field of kashrus supervision and certification as a not-for-profit public service. As such, all kosher supervisors appointed by the Orthodox Union were paid by the organization and were solely responsible to it. This practice eliminated food companies' influence on individual *mashgichim* (kosher supervisors). A uniform halachic standard was applied to all stages of food manufacture, from the sources of ingredients to final readying for distribution.

One of the first food companies to bear the famous O-U symbol was the Heinz Company, which in 1929 placed twenty-six of its fifty-seven varieties under the aegis of the Orthodox Union.[36] From those humble beginnings, kosher supervision has burgeoned, and the O-U is the leading supervisory kashrus organization, affirming the kosher status of thousands of food items.

ANTI-SEMITISM IN THE UNITED STATES: As Jewish immigrants kept pouring in, anti-Semitism increased in the United States. A general anti-foreigner feeling was prevalent throughout the country, especially after World War I, and in the eyes of many Americans the immigrant Jews represented a great wave of foreignness bearing un-American values. This anti-Jewish animus peaked in the 1930s and early 1940s: in 1935, James True filed a patent in Washington for a uniquely designed personal defense club he called a Kike Killer.[37] Polite, even popular anti-Semitism continued unabated, decreasing only after the horrors of the Holocaust became known.

HENRY FORD: Ford utilized the same obsessive determination and singular focus that created the Ford Motor Company to peddle mass-produced hate. In the 1920s, he published *The International Jew: The Protocols of the Learned Elders of Zion*, and for nearly two years ran an uninterrupted series of venomous essays in his newspaper *The Dearborn Independent*. *The International Jew*, running four volumes, was translated into sixteen languages and was widely read. Ford deliberately did not copyright the work, so that anyone who wished to disseminate it should feel free to do so.

In 1920, a number of Jewish organizations, both religious and secular, joined in condemning Ford's anti-Jewish campaign. A courageous non-Jew, John W. Spargo, rallied influential gentiles to speak out against Ford. In 1927, Ford apologized and retracted his anti-Semitic statements, but many people were ambivalent about the nature of his apology.

In admiration of Ford, Adolph Hitler hung a large portrait of him behind the desk in his office, and in 1938, before a crowd of 1,500 admirers in Detroit, Ford was awarded Germany's highest honor given to foreigners — the Grand Service Cross of the Supreme Order of the German Eagle. Ford beamed as the medal, a golden cross surrounded by four small swastikas, was pinned on him.[38]

FATHER CHARLES COUGHLIN: At the height of his fame in the 1930s, this demagogue was the first to achieve international fame and popularity on the radio. His voice was described as "a beautiful baritone...his range was spectacular. He always began in a low rich pitch, speaking slowly, gradually increasing in tempo and vehemence, then soaring into high and passionate tones...His diction was musical, the affect authoritative."[39] It is estimated that perhaps 16 million people listened to his weekly address, which blamed the Jews for everything from the Depression to American involvement in World War II.

Coughlin accepted money from and traded propaganda with the Nazis, amassing great wealth through shady business deals. After the *Krystallnacht* pogrom in 1938, he defended Nazism by saying it was a defense mechanism against Jewish-dominated Communism and ended his broadcast with sarcasm and facetiousness: "By all means, let us have the courage to compound our sympathy, not only from the tears of Jews, but also from the blood of Christians — 600,000 Jews whom no government official in Germany has yet sentenced to death."[40] Until the Catholic Church silenced him in 1940, Coughlin wielded enormous political power and changed forever the voice of America.

Indeed, Coughlin ushered in a revolution in American mass media through his dramatic ability to blend religion, politics, and entertainment, all in a powerful way, and whose impact is still being felt decades after his demise as a public figure. Two significant media phenomena, televangelism and political talk radio, stem from him.

THE SEPHARDIC WORLD: Using the term Sephardim to describe non-European Jews is a misnomer, for Sephardim are the descendants of both the Jews expelled from Spain in 1492 and the *conversos*, who arrived later and joined the existing communities. Therefore, Jews from Yemen, Iraq, and Iran are not Sephardim per se, for their communities existed prior to the Spanish Expulsion and did not absorb exiles nor were they influenced by them. In other countries of the Middle East and North Africa, while the Jews arriving from Spain blended into the existing communities and influenced them greatly, the immigrant Jews did not keep their unique Judeo-Spanish culture, such as the Ladino language. (From very early, non-*conversos* from Spain and Portugal adopted the practice of affixing the words *Sefardi tahor*, or "pure Sephardi," next to their signatures, as if to protect themselves from possible counterfeiters.)[41]

There were two major groupings of pure Sephardim. One was the Western Sephardim, who settled in Amsterdam, Hamburg, and other cities of Western Europe. A number of them reached the New World and were the first Jews to settle in America. Over time, the Western Sephardim assimilated into the surrounding cultures, and their influence in the Jewish world diminished.

The majority of Jews who left Spain and Portugal settled in the eastern Ottoman Turkish Empire, where the sultan welcomed them. It is estimated that perhaps 60,000 Sephardim entered the Empire.[42] They spread throughout Turkey, Greece, and the Ottoman-controlled area of Europe, the Balkans. A distinct Judeo-Spanish culture came into being, overwhelming the local Greek-speaking *Romaniot* Jews and lasting well into the 1900s. Cities such as Salonika, Smyrna (Izmir), and Constantinople (Istanbul) reconstituted a transplanted *Sefarad* (Spain).

Sephardic rabbinic scholarship flourished, and Salonika and Constantinople became major centers of *sefarim* printing. Many works were printed in Ladino, the language of the people, including *Shulchan Aruch, Menoras HaMaor*, and the famous *MeAm Loez*, which became the most widely read work among the Eastern Sephardim. This commentary was found even in the poorest households, and often was the only book the family owned. Afterward, rabbinic scholarship declined in the Sephardic world, with Torah becoming almost exclusively dominated by Ashkenazim. Nevertheless, the Sephardim remained extremely religious through the 1800s.

Matters changed in the second half of the 1800s with the arrival of the *Haskalah* in the Ottoman Empire. This incursion was the beginning of great Western involvement in the Ottoman Empire, with French influence being particularly strong. In 1860, secular French Jews in Paris founded the Alliance Israelite Universelle, with an avowed goal of reforming of Sephardic society and culture in conformity with modern European civilization — in other words, the complete secularization of Eastern Jews. By 1913, the Alliance encompassed a network of 183 schools throughout the Empire, attended by 43,700 pupils and covering an area from Morocco in the west to Iran in the east. Robbery of the Torah life of Eastern Jewry was in full swing. A case in point was the port of Salonika, Greece, where the Jews were the stevedores and porters. When religious observance was strong, the docks were closed on the Sabbath, a situation that sadly changed in the 1900s.

Another factor in the precipitous drop in religious observance was the breakup of the Ottoman Empire after World War I into smaller countries, such as Turkey, Yugoslavia, Bulgaria, and Greece. The Sephardic community in the Empire, previously a cohesive unit, was completely shattered. The new nations were strongly nationalistic, and greatly discouraged separate communities and educational systems. In Turkey, Jewish schools were required to teach only in Turkish, and the government instituted a campaign of harassment against people who spoke any language other than Turkish. Thus, the use of Ladino, the Sephardic equivalent of Yiddish, a language having a level of sanctity by virtue of being spoken exclusively by Jews, began to die out.

The *Haskalah* movement in the Sephardic lands was not as radical as in Ashkenazic Eastern Europe, and its focus was not on assimilating Jews into the surrounding culture, but rather inculcating them with Western secular values. Opposition to the movement was not as strong in the Sephardic countries, for Sephardic religious life in general did not present the same highly ideological trends as in the Ashkenazic world, there being no Chassidim or Misnagdim, for example. Even when Sephardim shed religious observance, they remained highly traditional, and intermarriage was virtually unknown. This trend continues to be true of the Sephardim of Israel today.

POLITICAL ACTIVITY: Jews in the Sephardic countries did not form their own political parties. However, Zionism was extremely strong in Bulgaria, taking its place at the center of the community's political structures and not on the margins, as was the case elsewhere in the region. In Turkey, where the government opposed Zionism, all Zionist activity was clandestine. Religious organizations, such as Agudath Israel, were unknown, as religious life was severely declining.

ANTI-SEMITISM: Generally, anti-Jewish feelings in these countries did not approach those in the rest of Europe. Several factors contributed to keep anti-Semitism weak. With the exception of a few cities, such as Salonika, the Jews constituted a relatively small proportion of the overall population and were not greatly visible. More significantly, they were one among many minorities and ethnic groups that inhabited the region, and were not felt to be a threat to the ruling powers. Thus, the nationalism of these countries was directed toward groups that the regime felt to be a threat, generally not Jews, although Jews were indirectly affected. The one place where anti-Semitism was very powerful was the city of Salonika, which witnessed a pogrom in 1932.

· After World War II, the surviving Sephardim of Europe, including almost all of the 50,000-strong community of Bulgaria, immigrated to Israel.

JEWISH POPULATIONS ON THE BRINK OF WORLD WAR II: On the eve of the Holocaust, there were about 18 million Jews in the world. (As in Egypt before Pharaoh's oppression, G-d rapidly increased the Jewish population before the Holocaust: from 2 million in 1800 to 18 million in 1939,[43] a rate of increase nearly double that of the general European population.) The largest Jewish population was in the United States, which had 4.9 million Jews. Poland was second with 3.5 million, followed by the Soviet Union with close to 2.9 million. Rounding out the top ten were Hungary — 650,000, Romania — 600,000, Palestine — 450,000, France — 350,000, Great Britain — 330,000, Germany — 240,000, and Czechoslovakia — 180,000. Sizable concentrations of Jews also existed in Lithuania, Holland, Belgium, Yugoslavia, Greece, Italy, Canada, South Africa, and Australia.

Chapter 24

INTRODUCTION TO THE HOLOCAUST

*Z*ACHOR! Remember! With their last breaths, the *kedoshim*, holy martyrs of the Holocaust, beseeched future generations not to forget their suffering and death. What, exactly, did they want the Jewish people to remember for all time? Why should the Jewish people study the horrific events and what lesson can they teach?

In a guidebook published by the United States Holocaust Memorial Museum on how to teach the Holocaust, among the reasons given are:

Study of the Holocaust assists students in developing understanding of the ramifications of prejudice, racism, and stereotyping in any society. It helps students develop an awareness of the value of pluralism, and encourages tolerance of diversity in a pluralistic society... Democratic institutions and values are not automatically sustained but need to be appreciated, nurtured, and protected... The Holocaust provides a context for exploring the dangers of remaining silent, apathetic, and indifferent in the face of others' oppression.[1]

No doubt these are important issues (although pluralism and diversity should not mean approval of behaviors and lifestyles that are immoral), and the Holocaust Museum has powerfully imparted these lessons to millions of viewers. But were these matters on the minds of the Jews who sang *"Ani maamin be'emunah sheleimah b'vias HaMashiach"* on the threshold of the gas chambers, and those who cried out *Shema Yisrael* as they were being shot at mass graves?

WHY DID THE GERMANS KILL JEWS?: The six million *individual* Jews who perished were not a cold statistic. These were *kedoshim* who implored future generations to remember *why* the Germans and their fellow murderers killed the Jews: because they were members of the nation that entered into an everlasting covenant with G-d at Mt. Sinai, and whose Divine mission is ultimately to perfect themselves and mankind by keeping the laws of the Torah and ushering in the bliss of the Messianic Era.

The Germans clearly recognized the pitched spiritual battle between their pagan, *volkish* ideology, that stressed the right of the supposedly superior Aryan race to plunder and dominate the nations of the world, and the sublime, altruistic teachings of G-d's Torah, which declare that mankind is created in G-d's image, and therefore has an obligation to create a perfect society by sublimating its animalistic desires to the will of G-d. The Jewish people, as the nation charged with this holy task, bore the full fury of the Nazis. Numerous quotes by Adolph Hitler and other Nazis bring out this point very clearly:

> It is true we are barbarians; that is an honored title for us. I free humanity from the shackles of the soul, from the degrading suffering caused by the false vision called conscience and ethics. The Jews have inflicted two wounds on mankind: circumcision on its body and conscience on its soul. They are Jewish inventions.

> The war for domination of the world is waged only between the two of us, between these two camps alone: the Germans and the Jews. Everything else is but deception.[2]

How remarkable. Many nations were antagonistic to Germany — Russia, France, Great Britain, and the United States all competed with Germany politically, culturally, economically, and militarily. Nonetheless, by its own admission Germany's struggle was only with the Jews, a weak people scattered throughout the globe, possessing no country or army. Yet Hitler himself correctly realized that the epic battle for control of mankind was between the Torah and Nazi ideology.

His reference to circumcision is noteworthy. A *midrash* states that when the Jewish people were traveling in the desert, the nation of Amalek attacked them, and in a gesture of defiance toward G-d, cut off the circumcisions of the Jews they killed and threw them toward Heaven.[3] *Bris milah* represents the subjugation of the Jewish body to the Torah, in direct opposition to Amalek and its spiritual (and possibly physical) heirs, the Germans.

Another quote of Hitler's is also quite revealing:

When over long periods of human history I scrutinized the activity of the Jewish people, suddenly there arose up in me the fearful question whether inscrutable Destiny, perhaps for reasons unknown to us poor mortals, did not, with eternal and immutable resolve, desire the final victory of this little nation.[4]

A directive, highly perceptive of the role of Torah, sent from the Reich Security Main Office in October 1940 to German occupation forces in Poland, reads:

The continued emigration of Jews from Eastern Europe to the West spells a continued spiritual regeneration of world Jewry, as it is mainly the Eastern Jews who supply a large proportion of the rabbis, Talmud teachers, etc., owing to their orthodox-religious beliefs, and they are urgently needed by Jewish organizations active in the United States, according to their own statements. Further, every orthodox Jew from Eastern Europe spells a valuable addition for those Jewish organizations in the United States in their constant efforts for the spiritual renewal of United States Jewry and its unification.[5]

On April 29, 1945, shortly before taking his own life, Hitler dictated his last words to the German people:

Above all, I enjoin the government and the people to uphold the racial laws to the limit and to resist mercilessly the poisoner of all nations, international Jewry.[6]

It is this vicious, fanatical, total hatred that makes the murder of Jews in the Holocaust unique. Millions of innocent non-Jews were brutally killed by the Germans, including two million captive Russian soldiers, Gypsies, and Polish civilians. However, there was no campaign to wipe out these peoples in their entirety — the Nazis were definitely not interested in exterminating Poles or Russians residing overseas. In the case of the Jews, however, every last Jew throughout the world was targeted for Nazi annihilation.

In 1940, the rebbe of Amshinov, Rabbi Shimon Kalisch, along with other Jews, was traveling on a train in Japan. During the journey, a group of Nazi soldiers, allies of Japan, passed through the car. They kicked at the Jews' legs, grabbed at their beards, and spat into their faces. "Parasites! Pigs! You think you are safe here? You are safe nowhere. We will annihilate you. We will eradicate your whole stinking, sub-human race from the face of the earth!"[7]

Sadly, there have been many genocidal persecutions in human history. Turks massacred Armenians, the Communist regime in Cambodia slaughtered two million of its own citizens, Serbs decimated Muslims in Bosnia, Hutus savagely killed hundreds of thousands of Tutsis in Rwanda, and the Arabs of Sudan are destroying the black Africans in the south of the country. In those instances, the massacres were a means to an end — to gain land, for revenge, traditional tribal enmity, or to build a new society. There was no ideology to destroy, say, Cambodians in the United States, or blacks in other areas of Africa. For the Germans, however, killing Jews was an end in itself; it was The Final Solution to the Jewish Problem. The Nazis wanted to wipe out every last Jew from the face of the earth, and planned to build a special Museum to the Extinct Jewish Race in Prague after they accomplished their goal.

THE BURNING QUESTION: WHY DID IT HAPPEN?: The Holocaust, with all its horrors, has been a terrible shock to the Jewish people, and, for all too many, a profound challenge to their faith. The question torments them: Why did G-d allow the Holocaust to happen? Why were six million people — including 1.5 million pure children — destroyed?

Clearly, it was not the first time that great numbers of Jews were killed by their enemies. In Egypt, over an eighty-six-year period, Jewish slaves were tortured and executed, and Jewish babies were cemented into walls and thrown to the crocodiles of the Nile River. The Babylonians and Romans killed millions of Jews at the time of the destruction of the First and Second Temples, and after the capture of Betar. Hundreds of thousands of Jews were massacred during the Middle Ages, at the time of the Crusades, the Black Death, the Chmielnicki uprising, and in pogroms lasting into the 1920s. However, peoples' faith today has been most shaken by the Holocaust. There are several reasons:

First, the Holocaust is recent, and people feel its effects more directly than events of thousands of years ago. Most Jews have relatives who died in the Holocaust, either immediate family members or more distant relatives. Indeed, there is virtually no Ashkenazic family that has not been touched, as well as many Sephardic ones as well.

Second, people are much more emotionally involved with the Holocaust. There are living survivors transmitting the story of their personal suffering to future generations. Pictures and books exist, documenting the horrifying story in graphic detail. To the contrary, much of previous Jewish suffering is left to the imagination: since it took place long ago, it is difficult to connect emotionally to that suffering. Realizing this phenomenon, Jewish prophets and sages instituted the fast of Tishah B'Av with its special prayers and mourning practices, to help the Jewish people feel on an emotional level the destruction of the two *Batei Mikdash*.

Third, despite the massive suffering and death in earlier times, the Jewish people were given direction — either from G-d directly in the Torah, from prophets who received Divine communication, or from the rabbis of the Talmud who were blessed with Divine inspiration — regarding why G-d exposed them to such tragic events. Even in later years, there were great leaders who guided the Jewish people as to how to react to overwhelming tragedy, maintaining their faith in a merciful, benevolent Creator. However, now, in the final chapter of Jewish history, in the days before the Messianic Era, the Jewish people grope about without a sense of Divine guidance. Unfortunately, most Jews are ignorant of their heritage and do not have access to the sages and written sources on how to handle this dilemma. This difficult phenomenon is called *hester panim*, the concealment of G-d's presence, and is the most difficult ordeal for the Jewish people to undergo in the long exile.

Before Moses' death, G-d commanded him to communicate the entire sweep of Jewish history to the assembled nation in the desert. In describing the end of time, Moses states G-d's message:

> And I will surely hide my Face on that day for all the evil that he [the nation] did, for he has turned to other gods (Deuteronomy 31:18).

> For I know after my death that you will surely act corruptly, and you will stray from the path that I have commanded you, and evil will befall you at the end of days, if you do what is evil in the eyes of G-d, to anger Him with your handiwork (ibid. 31:29).

Thus, it is very difficult, if not impossible, to say the Holocaust happened because of a specific reason. However, the Jewish way is to look into the Torah for guidance about the causes and effects of how G-d conducts Jewish history.

The caveat is, of course, that no one, other than G-d Himself or one of His prophets, has the right to tell an *individual* that he or she suffered or died for a specific shortcoming.[8] (However, it is highly proper for the person who suffered to look inward for a spiritual cause of misfortune.)[9] Therefore, any attempt at understanding causes for the Holocaust must focus on the *nation*, and even here, in the absence of prophecy or *ruach hakodesh* (Divine insight), one cannot state causes with certainty. This approach is reflected in Jewish practice as well. There is a long-established custom not to name a child after someone who died young or in an unnatural manner, for that is an inauspicious omen for the newborn. However, some people name a child after a person who was killed in the Holocaust, for that was a Divine decree upon the Jewish people as a whole, rather than on the individual.[10] (Others add a second name in this situation, too.)

THE TORAH'S PARADIGM OF JEWISH HISTORY: In the Torah reading for the morning of Tishah B'Av (Deuteronomy 4:25–40), G-d describes the course of Jewish history:

When you give birth to children and grandchildren, and will have been long in the Land, you will grow corrupt and make a carved image of anything, and you will do evil in the eyes of Hashem, your G-d, to anger Him. I appoint heaven and earth today to testify against you that you will surely perish quickly from the Land to which you are crossing the Jordan, to take possession of it; you will not stay in it for a long time, for you will be destroyed. G-d will scatter you among the peoples, and you will be left few in number among the nations where G-d will lead you (vv. 25–27).

From there you will seek Hashem, your G-d, and you will find Him, if you search for Him with all your heart and all your soul. When you are in distress and all these things have befallen you, *at the end of days* [emphasis added], you will return to Hashem, your G-d, and hearken to His voice. For Hashem, your G-d, is a merciful G-d. He will not abandon you nor destroy you, and He will not forget the covenant of your forefathers that He swore to them (vv. 29–31).

The Torah then reminds the Jewish people about their miraculous past:

For inquire now regarding the early days that preceded you, from the day when G-d created man on the earth, and from one end of heaven to the other end of heaven: Has there ever been anything like this great thing or has anything like it been heard? Has a people ever heard the voice of G-d speaking from the midst of the fire as you have heard, and survived? Or has any god ever miraculously come to take for himself a nation from amidst a nation, with challenges, with signs, and with wonders, and with war, and with a strong hand, and with an outstretched arm, and with greatly awesome deeds, such as everything that Hashem, your G-d, did for you in Egypt before your eyes? You have been shown in order to know that Hashem, He is the G-d, there is none beside Him (vv. 32–35).

The Torah connects the Exodus and giving the Torah to the account of Jewish suffering in exile to remind the Jews that unlike other nations, whose existence can be explained by social, political, and economic factors, the Jewish people only survive because of miraculous Divine guidance, and that the level of that guidance depends on their fulfilling the commandments of the Torah.

These verses provide insight into the pattern of Jewish existence throughout the long exile: Jews abandon Torah observance, they are persecuted and scattered worldwide, then they begin the true journey back to G-d in the end of days. G-d also promises the Jewish people that no nation will succeed in destroying them completely, and that He will mercifully enable them to rebuild their lives. The events before, during, and after the Holocaust fit perfectly the Torah's paradigm.

THE 2,000-YEAR PATTERN OF JEWISH EXILE: In a classic, prophetic piece written in *Sefer Meshech Chochmah* in the 1920s, when Hitler was but a powerless street ruffian, Rabbi Meir Simcha of Dvinsk traces the pattern of Jewish wanderings throughout the 2,000-year exile. While the full appreciation of his words can only be gleaned by studying and reflecting upon the original Hebrew, a brief synopsis of his message is of great value:

After being expelled from one area, Jews settle in a new land. Torah observance at this time is weak.

Jews build up their community and become successful materially in their new environment. Torah knowledge and mitzvah observance increase.

While there is a tendency in human nature to want to improve upon and surpass the accomplishments of previous generations, in the realm of Torah knowledge this is impossible. Earlier generations are greater than their successors, and the role of later generations is to attain an understanding of the works of their predecessors. Therefore, the human urge to blaze a new trail finds outlets in other, non-Torah endeavors.

Jews begin to criticize the Torah, saying that it is not relevant. They identify entirely with the host culture, saying, Berlin is Jerusalem!

A wave of anti-Semitism washes over the Jews, completely obviating any Jewish effort to assimilate. The Jews are expelled from the land, and the cycle begins anew.[11]

FOUR APPROACHES TO UNDERSTANDING WHY THE HOLOCAUST HAPPENED: First, there was a precipitous decline in religious observance in the 150 years before the Holocaust. In the 1800s, the Reform movement, widespread intermarriage, and conversion to Christianity decimated the Jewish populations of Germany and France. Toward the end of that century and into the 1900s, the *Haskalah* and the anti-Torah philosophies of Yiddishism, secular Zionism, Bundism, Socialism, and Communism ravaged Eastern Europe. For example, in 1850, only Torah-observant Jews ran the Jewish City Council of Vilna. Seventy years later, a number of secular anti-religious groups comprised the majority of the city's ruling council. The surviving religious enclaves in Eastern Europe, the chassidic and yeshivah-oriented groups, while in the main steadfast in their tradition, were being eroded by the blandishments of the surrounding anti-Torah society.

Rather than blaming the Holocaust generation for this catastrophe (which, after all, particularly struck the religious communities), it has been understood as a Divine reaction to the *cumulative* backsliding of the Jewish people over a number of generations, much in the manner of the destruction of the two Temples, as described in Deuteronomy.

Second, Jewish tradition teaches that there are 600,000 Jewish souls corresponding to the generation of the Exodus, and that all of the Jewish people share these souls.[12] It is therefore understandable that a particular generation's suffering can both provide atonement for centuries of Jews who preceded it, and benefit spiritually generations of future Jews. The Holocaust martyrs, who suffered for countless other Jews, will receive the greatest Divine reward.[13]

Third, other authorities, among them the great Rabbi Moshe Feinstein, take the approach that the Holocaust is a Divine decree extremely difficult for human beings to fathom.[14] In a similar vein, after the Spanish Expulsion, rabbinic leaders differed as to whether specific sins caused the tragedy to occur, or whether it was an inscrutable Divine decree whose reason could not be known until all of the vicissitudes of Jewish history are made clear at the advent of the Messianic Era.

Fourth, perhaps the Holocaust is a test of faith for the Jewish people. The Prophet Isaiah, in his famous vision describing the travails of the Suffering Servant (Isaiah 52:13–53:12) — which the commentaries understand as referring to the Jewish people — offers two explanations for Jewish suffering throughout the ages: to atone for the sins of the world, or as a test of faith for the Jewish people to bring their potential greatness to actuality.

Some of the verses that develop this theme:

And the Lord wished to crush him, He made him ill; if his soul makes itself restitution, he shall see children, he shall prolong his days, and G-d's purpose shall prosper in his hand (53:10).

Metzudas David explains that G-d imposes suffering upon the Jewish people as a spiritual challenge. Will the Jews justify their pain and attribute it to their own shortcomings, or will they cast aspersions upon Divine justice? If they react positively, they will have fulfilled G-d's desire, and they will increase greatly.

From the toil of his soul he would see, he would be satisfied; with his knowledge My servant would vindicate the just for many, and their iniquities he would bear (53:11).

Radak explains that in the Messianic Era, the Jews will prosper and inspire the nations of the world to adhere to G-d's Torah and follow in His footsteps. Rashi explains that the reason for the Jewish people's exaltation in Messianic times is because the nation suffered for the sins of the peoples of the world.

Therefore, I will allot him a portion in public, and with the strong he shall share plunder, because he poured out his soul to death, and with transgressors he was counted; and he bore the sin of many, and interceded for the transgressors (53:12).

Malbim says that as a reward for joyfully dying to sanctify G-d's name, the Jewish people will be vastly recompensed in the World to Come, with spiritual bliss on the level of their holy forefathers and prophets. Throughout history, Jewish suffering has brought about repentance and Divine forgiveness.

Jews throughout the ages have realized that while they could not fully understand the inscrutable ways that G-d runs the affairs of this world, their suffering was necessary in the progression of humankind toward the ultimate bliss of the Messianic Era.

WHY DID 1.5 MILLION INNOCENT CHILDREN DIE IN THE HOLOCAUST?: Actually, the question can be posed anytime a single child passes away or suffers. Everyone is given his or her mission in life — one that can only be fulfilled by that particular person. Some people achieve their goal in a very brief lifespan; an infant that passed away may have been a source of inspiration and faith for its family, or brought to the fore dormant character traits such as selfless devotion to others.

A mother gave birth to a child while awaiting selection on the ramp at Auschwitz. An SS guard promptly arrived, and in the description of an eyewitness, "kicked the newborn like a football." Did this child die in vain? Definitely not!

The Talmud states: "The son of David [the Messiah] will not arrive until all the souls are vacated from *Guf*."[15] Rashi explains that *Guf* is the name of the chamber in Heaven in which all the souls created during the six days of Creation lie in wait to be placed in newly formed bodies. Therefore, in a manner incomprehensible to mortals, every life, no matter how short, plays a crucial role in G-d's overall plan of advancing the world toward the perfection of the Messianic Age.

THE ENORMITY OF THE HOLOCAUST — THE PHYSICAL LOSSES: Although the Holocaust must be understood in the context of Jewish history in general, the enormity of the loss, and the horrific ways in which Jews died, are unique in the annals of the nation's suffering. Six million taken in other terms means:

To spend fifteen seconds to say the name of each Jew who was murdered, and reflect that each name represents a person, one would need 25,000 hours, or two years and ten months of *continual* time.

If each Jew were represented by just twelve inches, the total length would equal 1,136.36 miles, or from New York to Nebraska.

If six million four-by-six-inch cards, each with the name of one Jew who was murdered, were placed end to end, the line would stretch 568 miles, or from New York to South Bend, Indiana.[16]

If the 19,763-seat Madison Square Garden were filled to capacity daily starting January 1, it would take more than 303 days, or until October 31, to fill six million seats.

It would take 353,000 maps showing the birthplace, residence, and place of execution for each Jew murdered between 1939 and 1945. To draw these maps at the cartographer's fastest rate of a map a day, would take more than 967 years.[17]

In the Haftarah for the morning of Tishah B'Av, Jeremiah the Prophet laments (Jeremiah 8:23): "If only someone would turn my head to water and my eye to a spring of tears, then I would cry all day and night for the slain of my daughter's people!" Jeremiah also invokes searing eyewitness images of starving children in the Book of Lamentations (*Eichah*), which he authored. In addition, the *Kinnos* of Tishah B'Av are replete with graphic images of horrific atrocities:

If it could happen that the tongue of the nursing babe would adhere to its palate through unmitigated thirst — alas unto me!

If it could happen that the spirits of infants soared heavenward from their swollen corpses which were lying in the city's streets — alas unto me!

If it could happen that heaped on one stone were nine kab-measures of children's brains — alas unto me! (*Kinnah* 17).

When reading the horrendous accounts of the Holocaust, one should feel the loss and connect emotionally with the suffering of our people, as the *Nacheim* prayer of Tishah B'Av states: "My heart, my heart, it aches for their slain! My innards, my innards, they ache for their slain!" This emotional awareness is particularly important for the current generation, which is a step further removed from the children of the survivors.[18]

THE SPIRITUAL LOSS: Aside from the physical losses, which consumed one-third of world Jewry, a spiritual culture of more than 1,000 years went up in flames. This period of European Jewish history produced the Rishonim and Acharonim, along with the Chassidic, Mussar, and Yeshivah movements. Thousands of communities, both large and small, where myriads of great Torah scholars and pious Jews served their Creator for hundreds of years, disappeared overnight. After the Holocaust, the rarefied environment of the European Jew, uniquely suitable for spiritual greatness, was gone.

G-D'S CONSOLATION – THE REBUILDING: While the Jewish people can never completely replace what was lost, it is important to remember that G-d fulfilled His oft-repeated promise that no tyrant will ever succeed in destroying the Jewish people. Many survivors, with indescribable faith in G-d and incredible resilience, did not let their sorrows crush them, but rebuilt and fortified Jewish communities across the globe. Great chassidic dynasties, such as Ger, Bobov, Lubavitch, Belz, and Satmar, led by indefatigable leaders, arose phoenix-like from the ashes and reconstructed themselves in the United States and Israel. Rabbi Aharon Kotler, head of the Kletzk Yeshivah, arrived in the United States and established the Lakewood Yeshivah, the largest Torah institution since the time of the Amoraim in Babylon 1,500 years ago. In addition, Rabbi Kotler played a pivotal role in founding networks of Jewish day schools both in the United States (*Torah Umesorah*) and Israel (*Chinuch Atzmai*). As in the aftermath of the destruction of both *Batei Mikdash* and the Spanish Expulsion, after the Holocaust, too, the Jewish people were purified of many anti-Torah ideologies, ones that so afflicted life in pre-war Europe: for example, there are virtually no Bundists or Yiddishists today. Although the large majority of Jews are completely irreligious, it is a result of ignorance rather than conviction. Indeed, many more Jews today are discovering the beauty of a Torah lifestyle later in life than was the case 100 years ago.

After invoking the terrible curses of Deuteronomy 28 upon the

Jewish people if they would fail to observe the commandments of the Torah, Moses tells them, "You are standing today, all of you, before Hashem your G-d..." (ibid. 29:9). Rashi, in a famous comment, states (v. 12), "Like this day which exists and it becomes dark and light, so did He give you light, and so in the future He will give you light. The curses and punishments sustain you and keep you standing before Him." The trials and tribulations of the Jewish people throughout history keep them on track to fulfill their mission as G-d's Chosen People, and to receive the eternal rewards of the Messianic Era, when all suffering and sorrow will cease.

HITLER'S HATRED OF JEWS: It is an axiom of Jewish belief that historical events are orchestrated and directed by G-d, either to reward the nation or to punish it. Hitler's anti-Semitism has been the subject of countless scholarly analyses, but no historian has been able to explain satisfactorily the cause of its virulence. According to Werner Maser:

> Despite the wealth of information gained from an analysis of all the available data on Hitler's medical, intellectual and social backgrounds, there is still no satisfactory explanation of his anti-Semitism.[19]

Even Hitler's description of how he started along the path of Jew-hatred fails to shed light on why it became such an all-consuming mania:

> One day when I was walking through the inner city [Vienna], I suddenly came upon a being clad in long caftan, with black curls. 'Is this also a Jew?' was my first thought. At Linz they certainly did not look like that. Secretly and cautiously I watched the man, but the longer I stared at this strange face and scrutinized one feature after the other, the more my mind reshaped the first question into another form: Is this also a German?[20]

Countless multitudes of non-Jews have come in contact with very religious-looking Jews, and although great numbers of the non-Jews reacted with violent hatred, no one other than Hitler had this all-encompassing, burning zeal to eradicate every last Jew from the face of the earth. As such, it was decreed by Heaven that Hitler, like Haman, be given the power to display his single-minded fanaticism in attempting to destroy the Jewish people.

Some Jewish scholars have attempted to identify the German people as descendants of Israel's enemy throughout the ages, Amalek. In a spiritual sense, this assertion is true, for Germany shared Amalek's implacable hatred of the Jewish people, as well as the desire to declare uncompromising war against G-d's Torah and Chosen Nation, eventually upon G-d Himself. (A marching song of the Hitler Youth contained the line, "Priest and rabbi will be no more.") Hitler spoke of how "the Jew is the exact opposite of the German in every single respect, yet is closely akin to him as a blood brother."[21] The peculiar forms of hatred for Jews that emerged in modern times, although in some ways novel, have substantial connections with a history of Jew-hatred that dates back to the origins of anti-Semitism: the biblical story of Jacob and Esau, the twins locked in eternal battle. Hence, Hitler's seemingly strange assertion that Jew and German are blood brothers. Indeed, the cosmic struggle between these diametrically opposed brothers will continue to be played out on the stage of world history until the coming of the Messiah and the downfall of Esau.

Chapter 25

PRELUDE TO THE HOLOCAUST

EUROPEAN ANTI-SEMITISM: Hitler did not operate in a vacuum; instead, he built upon a foundation of long-standing Christian hatred of Jews. Although hatred of Jews existed in antiquity, it was not until the coming of Christianity that the Jews were singled out not only as a suspect people, an alien nation, but also as a guilty and accursed people because of the false charge that they had killed the Christian god. With the advent of the First Crusade in 1096, whose virulence was most felt in German regions of Europe, hatred and violence against Jews intensified greatly.

IN GERMANY: Significantly, the worst excesses of Jew-hatred in the Middle Ages took place in Germany. At the end of the thirteenth century, 150 Jewish communities throughout Germany and Austria were decimated and more than 100,000 Jews killed in the Rindfleisch massacres. A particularly large number of blood libel accusations originated in Germany. In the wake of the Endinger ritual child murder in Bavaria in 1462, a famous play and popular theater called the *Endinger Judenspiel* was performed annually to large audiences. German woodcuts and art depicted the Jews as pigs (*Judensau*) and devils, generally portraying them as swarthy, hook-nosed, and foul smelling. At the time of the Black Death in the mid 1300s, in such German cities as Freiburg, Augsburg, Nuremberg, Munich, Konigsberg, and Regensburg, Jews were slaughtered with a thoroughness that presaged the horrific Final Solution.[1]

Martin Luther, the German founder of the Protestant Reformation, shaped the overwhelming pejorative, indeed demonic, significance of the word *Jude*. Heaping viler attacks on the Jews than can be found in Hitler's *Mein Kampf*, Luther surpassed even the vitriol of the medieval Christian theologians. The legend of the Wandering Jew was published in Germany in 1602, becoming so popular that it went through nearly fifty editions in just a few years. In 1633, the famous Oberammergau passion play, depicting the crucifixion of the Christian god, was first produced, and still draws vast crowds from around the world.

With the rise of the Enlightenment in the late eighteenth century, a new secular, racist anti-Semitism developed. Darwin's Theory of Evolution focused public discussion on such pseudo-scientific Darwinian terms as natural selection, heredity, struggle for existence, and survival of the fittest. The Frenchman Count Gobineau and the Englishman Houston S. Chamberlain espoused theories that placed the Aryan Germanic race at the apex of humanity and the Jews at the bottom, their works becoming most popular in Germany. Gobineau's racial theories were also promoted with great success by the composer Richard Wagner, while Chamberlain married one of Wagner's daughters, settled in Germany, and became the focal point of radical Germanism. His book on racism sold well over 100,000 copies by World War I.

WHY GERMANY PRODUCED THE HOLOCAUST: A historical question that many scholars have grappled with is, given that anti-Semitism was rife throughout European society for well over 1,000 years, why is it that Germany conceived the Holocaust and played the major role in carrying it out? Could a different nation, such as England, France, or Russia, have produced a Holocaust?

There is no simple answer to this question. A prominent German-American historian, Klaus Fischer, who has written two well-received books on Nazi Germany and German anti-Semitism, feels that elements of the German national character, combined with German historical experiences, laid the foundation for Hitler's genocide of the Jews:

In order to understand the Holocaust, several additional German "cultural traits" must be added — namely, an exaggerated sense of order with corresponding habits of obedience to authority (authoritarianism), undue admiration for the military and its way of life (militarism), an exclusive sense of ethnic superiority and corresponding prejudices against foreigners or "unassimilated elements," and a strong need, rooted in past religious and philosophical traditions, for all-embracing ideological explanations in the form of worldviews.[2]

In fact, the main defense offered by the defendants at Nuremberg, and by Adolph Eichmann himself, was that they were merely following Hitler's orders and could not question his higher authority.

MODERN BACKDROP TO THE HOLOCAUST: The sixty-year period before Hitler's rise to power was a time of great upheavals and disruptions within German society. This time included the establishment of imperial Germany in 1871, World War I and Germany's defeat, the fall of the monarchy, revolution, the humiliation of the Versailles Treaty, catastrophic inflation, the Weimar Republic, and the Great Depression.

GERMANY BECOMES ONE: Germany's unification in 1871 marked the first time that Germany was one nation. Unlike England and France, which were united hundreds of years previously, Germany was a patchwork of more than 300 individual duchies, which often fought with each other. Consequently, in Germany the social fabric was far more fragile than in other countries of Western Europe. In addition, Germany was a hybrid society, half-feudal and half-industrial, with no social institutions to challenge its long-standing militaristic and authoritarian traditions.

(It is fascinating to note that the Talmud, written 1,500 years ago, predicted the future with such amazing prescience. A statement in *Megillah* 6b speaks of Germania of Edom consisting of

300 kings, who, if they would not be busy fighting each other, would destroy the world. A united Germany plunged the world into two world wars.)

WORLD WAR I: The German people were ecstatic when World War I began in 1914. Intoxicated by nationalistic fervor, most Germans looked on the war as a pleasant diversion from the boredom of civilian life, expecting hostilities to be over by year's end. Instead, the war turned into a battle of attrition with such staggering losses in men and materiel that even cold-hearted militarists gasped when they saw the casualty lists. In 1918, an exhausted Germany sued for peace. Having been conditioned by four years of wartime propaganda to believe that victory was inevitable, most Germans refused to accept the reality of defeat. A convenient scapegoat was found — the Jews — who in the eyes of an increasing number of Germans had supposedly stabbed Germany in the back.

THE AFTERMATH OF DEFEAT: The Treaty of Versailles was particularly humiliating for Germany, especially since it had not lost on the battlefield. France occupied German territory west of the Rhine, and Germany lost its colonies in Africa. In addition, Germany had to surrender its submarines and navy, pay onerous reparations, and take the blame for the war. This war guilt clause especially rankled German sensitivities, leading the way for Hitler to exploit the people's resulting resentment.

ANARCHY: In 1918, when the Kaiser abdicated the throne, chaos threw a traditional, law-abiding society into great turmoil. Gangs of opposing politics battled in the streets. Communists and other left-wing movements led revolutions throughout the country, attempting to take over numerous cities. Non-Jewish Jews, such as Kurt Eisner and Rosa Luxemburg, stood at the forefront of the revolutionary agitation, inflaming popular passions against the Jews. Anti-Jewish feelings in Germany were intensified when Jewish-led Communist regimes arose in Russia and Hungary. In the minds of Germans, all Jews became associated with the Communists, even though most Jews detested Communism. Soldiers returning from the front, known as *Freikorps*, led a right-wing campaign to crush the Communists. (The *Freikorps* later proved to be a bountiful source of Nazis.)

In 1923, the German economy collapsed, sparking runaway inflation. As unemployment soared, the government kept printing worthless paper money. A postage stamp cost 5 million marks, an egg 80 million, and a pound of meat 3.2 billion. In the early 1920s, one dollar was worth 100 marks. By the end of 1923, the same dollar was worth 4.2 *billion* marks. People rushed to the stores with satchels of worthless money to buy simple necessities. The savings of thrifty middle-class Germans were wiped out. Indeed, it was not uncommon for Germans to receive a worthless one-million-mark banknote for their hard-earned savings of several thousand marks accumulated over a number of years. At the same time that most Germans lost their life savings, a few financial manipulators grew fabulously wealthy, further eroding Germans' trust in their government.

ADOLPH HITLER: If there ever were a less likely candidate to become the leader, and to command the allegiance of a great nation, it was Adolph Hitler. Born in 1889 to lower-class parents (and possibly having a Jewish grandfather),[3] Hitler failed high school and dropped out. He attempted to become an artist, but twice failed his entrance examination to Vienna's main art school. For several years, he wandered around Vienna as a homeless vagrant. It was in Vienna where Hitler, at about age twenty, acquired a virulent hatred for Jews. He joined the German Army in World War I, was wounded in battle, suffered a poison gas attack, and was decorated for bravery.

In 1919, Hitler joined the German Workers' Party, later to become the Nazi Party, as party member seven.[4] (Anton Drexler was the party's founder.) In 1923, Hitler and Nazi followers attempted to overthrow the Bavarian government in Munich — an effort that has come to be known as the Beer Hall *Putsch*. The uprising failed, and Hitler was put on trial for treason. The trial focused national attention on Hitler, and served to publicize his political theories to large numbers of people. Found guilty, Hitler was sentenced to five years in prison, serving nine months. While in jail, Hitler wrote his political manifesto *Mein Kampf*, a book full of vulgar anti-Semitism and containing his program for German domination of the world. By 1945, six million copies of *Mein Kampf* had been sold, in sixteen languages.

Throughout the 1920s, Hitler and the Nazis, whom he now led, solidified their popularity in Germany. Hitler campaigned tirelessly, vowing to repudiate Versailles and restore Germany's pride and prosperity. German audiences seemed particularly mesmerized by Hitler's voice, feeling it was the voice of the ordinary German expressing exactly what ordinary Germans thought. Hitler's speeches invariably ended with rousing affirmations of German national greatness and reassurances that such greatness would once again be rejuvenated under the banner of National Socialism. At that point, most of the audience spontaneously burst out in frenzied cheering, hand clapping, and table pounding. There were wild cries and uncontrolled sobs by some members of the audience, especially women.[5]

Although there was a short period of prosperity from 1924–1929, the Weimar Republic was weak, fragmented into many political parties that intensely hated each other. The resulting lack of cooperation later played right into Hitler's hands. In 1929 the final blow to German democracy came — the Great Depression. By the end of 1932, six million German workers were unemployed, affecting one out of two German families. The stage was set to sweep Hitler into power.

NAZI GAINS: In 1925, the Nazi Party had a mere 700 members. The national elections of 1928 garnered the Nazis only 810,000 votes and but twelve seats in the 577-seat *Reichstag*. However, in 1930, with Germany in the throes of the Great Depression, the Nazis won more than 18 percent of the vote and increased their seats in the *Reichstag* from twelve to 107 — the second largest bloc in the German parliament. As the Depression deepened, vigorous Nazi propaganda efforts paid even more dramatic dividends. The 1932 election gave the Nazis a stunning 37 percent of the vote. With 230 *Reichstag* members, it became Germany's largest political party, 800,000 members swelling the ranks.

Throughout 1932, there were bloody street battles throughout Germany between Nazi storm troopers and other political parties, especially the Communists. With the government hopelessly stalled between right- and left-wing political parties, finally, on January 30, 1933, President von Hindenburg swore in Adolph Hitler as Chancellor of Germany. With the appointment of Hitler, Germany was plunged into an abyss, a dark age of unprecedented evil.

"I had been skating that day," a ten-year-old Jewish boy, Leslie Frankel, who lived in the town of Biblis, near Worms, later recalled. "When I got home, we heard that Hitler had become Chancellor. Everybody shook. As kids of ten, we shook."[6]

The question remains: How was it possible that a state whose people and culture ranked high in the world's civilization could have entrusted its fate to this deluded man who believed that he had been chosen to lead a holy war against the Jews? No single theory can satisfactorily explain Hitler's phenomenal success with the German people. Evidently, it was Divinely ordained.

HITLER SEIZES POWER: Hitler wasted no time in becoming sole master of Germany. After the Nazi-orchestrated *Reichstag* fire in February 1933, Hitler compelled the legislature to grant him dictatorial powers. The first concentration camp was established in Dachau, and the Gestapo, the secret police, was set up. All political parties, except for the Nazis, were outlawed, and the death penalty was prescribed for political crimes. Within six months, Germany was a totalitarian state.

EARLY ANTI-JEWISH MEASURES: On Saturday, April 1, 1933, the Nazis declared a one-day boycott of Jewish businesses throughout Germany. Soldiers were posted in front of Jewish-owned enterprises holding signs with such slogans as "Every mark in Jewish hands is stolen from the Fatherland!" Display windows were defaced with Stars of David and notices reading "Jewish undertaking." Guards took pictures of customers who entered the stores and later published lists of so-called traitors to Germany in the newspapers. Ironically, the Sabbath became a true day of rest for Jewish businesspeople.

Shortly afterward, laws were passed forcibly retiring Jewish civil servants from a large number of government jobs. A quota was placed upon Jewish enrollment in public schools and universities, and all Jewish professors were fired. Kosher slaughter was outlawed in Germany, the Nazis claiming that it was cruel to animals. In May, books written by Jewish intellectuals were removed from libraries and burned in giant bonfires, the largest of which was in Berlin. Joseph Goebbels, Hitler's Minister of Propaganda, proclaimed, "the spirit of the German people can again express itself." In September, Jews were excluded from art, literature, theater, and film, while in October Jewish journalists were forbidden to continue their work. More than 150 years of German Jewish assimilation were overturned in the short span of nine months.

In 1934, there were no significant anti-Semitic decrees, as Hitler spent the year solidifying his control of Germany. In June, Hitler ordered a bloody purge of his own Brown Shirts, or SA, a Nazi paramilitary organization that he felt posed a challenge to his own power. When President von Hindenburg died in August, Hitler became the only official authority in Germany.

THE NUREMBERG DECREES: Germany was a law-abiding society, and Hitler wanted to control popular anti-Semitism by placing it into a legal framework. In September 1935, the infamous Nuremberg Decrees were passed, with the major provisions prohibiting marriage between Germans and Jews, and forbidding Jews from hiring female Germans under age forty-five as domestic help. The *Reich* Citizenship Law distinguished between citizens (Aryans), who had full political rights such as holding public office, and state subjects (Jews), who were deprived of such rights. In March 1936, Jewish doctors were barred from treating Germans.

A whole new German *Shulchan Aruch* was put into place, describing in detail the unique separation between Jew and gentile. More than 2,000 years ago, the Prophet Ezekiel, addressing the desire of some Jews to assimilate among the nations, proclaimed (Ezekiel 20:32–33): "As for what enters your minds, it shall not be! As for what you say, 'We will be like the nations, like the families of the lands, to worship wood and stone,' ...I [G-d] swear that I will rule over you with a strong hand and with an outstretched arm and with outpoured wrath."

WHY JEWS DID NOT LEAVE: Faced with such persecution, why didn't the Jews leave Germany?

In the years 1933–39, nearly 300,000 Jews did leave. More than 80 percent of Jews under the age of forty, and 50 percent of Jews under sixty, found refuge in other lands. By September 1939, when World War II broke out, the German Jewish population of 500,000 in 1933 had dwindled to 185,000.[7] Emigration was markedly less among the older population, in no small measure due to physical infirmity and the natural reluctance of elderly people to change long-time residences. In addition, many Jews felt that Hitler's regime was a passing aberration. Surely the enlightened German people would realize the boorishness of the Nazis and vote them out of office. Jews also felt great loyalty to Germany, taking pride in their contributions to the country, feeling that the German people reciprocated their devotion. Finally, the lower standard of living of some of the possible places of refuge, such as Palestine or Shanghai, was unappealing to German Jews.

NAZI LEADERS: The men who ran Nazi Germany were, in the main, louts from the beer cellars. It is a great manifestation of Divine orchestration of history how people of such low caliber could rule a great, cultured nation and conquer much of the European world. Heinrich Himmler, head of the notorious SS, worked as a fertilizer salesman and a chicken farmer. Reinhard Heydrich, who was court-martialed out of the German Navy in 1930 for conduct unbecoming an officer, became head of the secret police branch of the SS. In 1939, the fate of Jews under German control was placed in his hands — until Czech partisans killed him in 1942. Joseph Goebbels, Minister of Propaganda, was a short, clubfooted, failed writer. Hermann Goering, head of the German Air Force, the *Luftwaffe*, was addicted to morphine.

One is struck by the plain, if not somewhat lurid, backgrounds of these leaders and their henchmen who carried out the so-called Final Solution. In fact, the writer Hannah Arendt coined a famous phrase describing them: "the banality of evil." A famous fictionalized account of the Holocaust portrays an ordinary German (Dorf) who walks into a Nazi Party office seeking employment, and who has no previous record of anti-Semitic action. Bit by bit, he becomes indoctrinated to hate Jews, and winds up leading a murder squad that kills thousands of them. Indeed, the potential for the worst kinds of behavior exists in every human being — which is why the Torah and Seven Laws of Noah temper such animalistic drives.

NAZI PROPAGANDA: The Nazis were masters at utilizing all methods of mass communication to indoctrinate the German people with racist beliefs. Newspapers such as *Der Sturmer* spewed forth the vilest poison against Jews, including graphic reenactments of the blood libel. Billboards everywhere displayed the message *Die Juden Sind Unser Umgluck* — the Jews Are Our Misfortune. The ending lines of the *Horst Wessel Lied*, the Nazi marching song, were: *Denn wenn das Judenblut vom Messer spritzt, Dann geht's noch mal so gut*, "For when the Jews' blood spurts from the knife, Good times are once more here."[8] Radio broadcasts, which the German people listened to more than any nation in Europe, endlessly hammered out the Nazi message. Exhibits in German museums showed horrifying medieval caricatures of Jews with hooked noses, claws, and horns. Schools and youth clubs shaped the impressionable minds of children, and teachers who refused to adhere to the government's line were dismissed from their jobs and prosecuted. Universities established chairs in so-called racial studies, and the study of science became corrupted — so much so that the Nazis rejected Albert Einstein's scientific theories as so-called Jewish physics.

The Germans, leaders in film production in the 1920s and 1930s, produced spectacular anti-Semitic movies. One film, *Jud Suss*, was so horrifying that the actors asked Goebbels to tell the country that they were not Jewish. One of the most dazzling documentary films ever made, still studied today by aspiring filmmakers, was *Triumph of the Will*, recording the 1934 Nuremberg Nazi Party rally:

> To see the films of the Nuremberg rallies even today is to be recaptured by the hypnotic effect of thousands of men marching in perfect order, the music of the massed bands, the forest of standards and flags, the vast perspectives of the stadium, the smoking torches, the dome of searchlights. The sense of power, of force and unity was irresistible, and all converged with a mounting crescendo of excitement on the supreme moment when the *Fuhrer* himself made his entry.[9]

A highly popular primer for children, *The Poisonous Mushroom*, tells the story of a young girl named Inge who is sent to keep an appointment with a Jewish doctor. Her leader in the League of German Girls warns her not to go, but there Inge is, nervously waiting in the doctor's office:

> Then the door opens. Inge looks up. The Jew appears. She screams... Horrified, she jumps up. Her eyes stare into the face of the Jewish doctor. And this face is the face of the devil. In the middle of this devil's face is a huge crooked nose. Behind the spectacles gleam two criminal eyes. Around the thick lips plays a grin, a grin that means, "Now I have you at last, you little German girl!" And then the Jew approaches her. His fat fingers snatch at her. But now Inge has got hold of herself. Before the Jew can grab hold of her, she smacks the face of the Jew doctor with her hand. One jump to the door. Breathlessly Inge runs

down the stairs. Breathlessly she escapes from the Jew's house.[10]

Like Pharaoh in Egypt, the Nazis realized that they could not get people to shove babies into crematoria overnight. A massive propaganda campaign was required, one that would raise Germans' hatred of Jews to such levels that they would be capable of committing the worst atrocities. Nonetheless, this does not mitigate the guilt of the perpetrators of the Holocaust, for they were not young children during Hitler's rule, and should have used their native intelligence and innate conscience to resist the propaganda barrage.

Clear, too, is the fallacy that higher education creates a better person. The Germans had the world's best universities, yet their graduates played a major role in the annihilation of the Jews. A disproportionate number of PhDs and MDs staffed the killing squads and death camps.

Nazi Germany also showed the frightening potential of a society united in the pursuit of evil. Unity is a most powerful force; just as a community joined together for the common good is more than the sum of its individual parts, so too a group proclaiming solidarity for harmful purposes unleashes an enormous destructive energy.

THE NAZI OLYMPICS: In 1936, Berlin hosted the Olympic Games, a great propaganda opportunity for Hitler to show the world how the Nazis had improved the lot of the German people. All that was most modern and efficient in Nazi Germany duly impressed many of those who came from abroad. Anti-Semitic billboards and posters were temporarily removed from public view. However, two Jewish swimmers who accompanied the American team were quietly told not to compete in order not to offend German sensitivities. Jesse Owens, the great African-American runner, won four gold medals, but Hitler refused to shake his hand, resenting the clear refutation of Hitler's racist belief that Aryans were the most superior athletes.

During the Olympics the Jews enjoyed only a temporary reprieve from anti-Semitic legislation. Afterward, laws were passed that forced many Jews to sell their property and businesses to the government for a pittance. In some cases, Jews lost their assets outright. Jews were also restricted from beaches, and parks had separate benches for Jews. Jews were forced to add the name Israel for men and Sarah for women. Emigrants from Germany had to leave almost everything behind, with the exception of those Jews going to Palestine, where the law permitted them to take out half their assets. More than 50,000 German Jews took advantage of this legal loophole, known as the Haavara Agreement, and went to Palestine.

GERMAN EXPANSION: Hitler's first real gamble in foreign policy came in March 1936 when he reoccupied the Rhineland, an area of Germany ceded to France by the Treaty of Versailles. The French could easily have countered the invasion and brought about the downfall of the militarily weak Hitler regime, but they stood passively by, feeling that Hitler was only occupying German territory. In March 1938, Hitler engineered the bloodless takeover of Austria, in the *Anschluss* joining it with the German *Reich*. Both France and England, as Hitler correctly realized, did not want war with Germany over culturally German Austria.

With Hitler's annexation of Austria, an additional 250,000 Jews fell under his control. Almost immediately, the German Nazis and Austrian mobs unleashed an orgy of violence against the Jews of Austria. Austrian Nazis looted Jewish businesses and apartments at will, and roving gangs turned against conspicuous eastern Jews, with their broad-rimmed hats, *peyos*, and flowing beards. Despicable street scenes showed vulgar ruffians forcing Jewish youngsters, old men, and women down on their knees to scrub the street with toothbrushes and sometimes with bare knuckles. Jews had to clean latrines while wearing tefillin, and were taken to Vienna's main amusement park and forced to croak like birds and eat grass. These spontaneous anti-Semitic riots accompanying the *Anschluss* were so violent that they shocked even the Germans.[11] As such, Austrian Jews were not only victim-ized by the release of years of pent-up anti-Semitic rage, but they were also more quickly pauperized, forced into emigration (more than 100,000 left the country), or consigned to concentration camps. Baron Louis Rothschild of Vienna was taken hostage and forced to sign over his assets to the Nazis before being permitted to leave Austria.

CZECHOSLOVAKIA: Hitler next turned to Czechoslovakia, which contained a large German minority in the Sudetenland. The German dictator was rightly convinced that the Western powers would not intervene for Czechoslovakia. In what has become the infamous symbol for appeasement, British Prime Minister Chamberlain met with Hitler in Munich, without the Czechs present, and ceded the Sudetenland to Germany. Chamberlain returned to England saying, "I have brought peace in our time." Within several months, Hitler annexed the rest of the Czech lands and installed a puppet regime in Slovakia, simply wiping Czechoslovakia off the map. He also forced hapless Lithuania to cede the port of Memel to Germany.

A popular Jewish saying states: "The hearts of kings and princes are in the hand of G-d." It is remarkable how England and France, which still had the ability to stop Hitler, acceded to every demand, not realizing the peril in which they were placing themselves. The Czechs, despite having a well-trained army equipped with modern weapons and impregnable fortifications that were more than a match for the Germans, did not fire a shot in their own defense. (Ironically, the same people who fault the victims of the Holocaust for not fighting back praise the self-preserving behavior of the Czechs.) The German commanders, after examining the formidable Czech positions in the Sudetenland, remarked that it would have been impossible to conquer them in battle.

THE EVENTS LEADING UP TO *KRYSTALLNACHT*: In March 1938, Poland passed a law revoking the citizenship of Polish nationals who had lived outside the country for five years. The law was specifically aimed at roughly 50,000 Polish Jews who had been residing in Germany and whom the Polish government did not want to return to Poland. Germany, which regarded the Polish law as a provocation designed to dump their Jews permanently in Germany, rounded up 17,000 Polish Jews in November and transported them to the Polish border. The Polish authorities refused to accept them, and the Jews languished in horrific camps on the border. On November 7, after hearing about his parents' desperate plight in the no-man's land between Germany and Poland, Hershel Grynszpan, a seventeen-year-old Polish refugee living in Paris, attacked a secretary in the German Embassy. After the German secretary died the next day from his wounds, the Germans carefully planned their response. Heinrich Mueller, head of the Gestapo, was ordered to send the following secret telegram to all Gestapo offices:

At very short notice, actions against the Jews, especially against their synagogues, will take place throughout the whole of Germany. They are not to be hindered... Preparations are to be made for the arrest of between 20,000 and 30,000 Jews in the *Reich*. Wealthy Jews in particular are to be selected.

On November 9–10, 1938, a horrible two-day pogrom, inspired by the government, broke out throughout the country. Ordinary people engaged in a frenzy of lustful destruction and a passion to kill. Some 276 synagogues, including the 900-year-old Rashi Synagogue in Worms, were burned to the ground, their contents looted or defiled. More than 7,500 businesses were vandalized, 30,000 Jews sent to concentration camps, and ninety-one Jews killed. The police were under orders not to intervene, and fire departments were told to put out fires only if they threatened buildings owned by Aryans. *Krystallnacht*, the Night of Broken Glass, was the name given to the pogrom by the Nazis. In general, historians consider *Krystallnacht* the formal beginning of the Holocaust.

In an act of incredible insolence, the Nazis blamed the Jews' presence for having caused all the damage and decreed that the government would impound the money the insurance companies were obligated to pay Jewish owners whose properties had been destroyed. In addition, the Jews were forced to pay for the pogrom's damage and assessed a so-called atonement fine of one billion *reichsmarks*. New laws were proposed restricting Jews in the cultural, educational, and social spheres. A discussion between Goering and Goebbels regarding Jewish travel on trains is typical of their thinking:

Goering: "There will be only one Jewish car. If it is full, the other Jews must stay at home."

Goebbels: "And suppose there are two Jews on the train, and the other cars are crowded. These two Jews, then, have a car to themselves. We should therefore announce that Jews might not sit until all Germans are seated."

Goering: "If the train is really full, as you say, believe me, I don't need a law. The Jew will be thrown out, even if he has to sit by himself in the toilet for the whole trip... We'll set aside a certain area of the park for the Jews. Park rangers will take care of putting animals there that look like Jews."

Goebbels: "Jewish children are still allowed in German schools. That's impossible. It's out of the question that a German boy should sit beside a Jewish boy in a German high school and receive lessons in German history."

Goering: "I'd like to say again that I would not like to be a Jew in Germany!"[12]

Between November 1938 and January 1939 the Nazi regime decided the fate of the German Jewish community. Jews were not permitted to own businesses or land, and had to sell them to the government for virtually nothing. Jews were prohibited from attending theater, cinema, concerts, and cultural exhibits of any kind, except those specifically organized by authorized Jewish groups. In a country such as Germany, where involvement in cultural activities was of major importance, these restrictions had a devastating impact. Jews were not permitted to own cars, and even their driving licenses were revoked. Jews were not allowed to enter certain areas, and were subjected to a curfew. Although no formal ghettoes were set up (the Nazis feeling that it would be easier for Germans to spy on Jews if the Jews were not isolated in their own area), Jewish residences were marked. In January 1939, Hitler warned the Jews: "If the international Jewish financiers in and outside Europe should succeed in plunging the nation once more into a world war, then the result will be... the annihilation of the Jewish race in Europe."

JEWISH REFUGEES: After *Krystallnacht*, virtually all German Jews realized that there was no future for them in Germany, and they tried to leave the country. Alas, the world's nations were not willing to relax their tight immigration quotas. America, England, and Canada, the most desirable destinations, were essentially closed to immigration. The Palestine White Paper reduced Jewish settlement there to a trickle. A 1938 international conference held in Evian, France disbanded without any commitment to take in any appreciable number of Jews. Reflecting the attitude held by many, the Australian delegate said that his country has no desire "to import a racial problem."

In the 1930s and 1940s, anti-Semitism was also at very high levels in the United States. An alarming set of polls taken between 1938 and 1945 revealed that roughly 15 percent of those surveyed would have supported anti-Jewish campaigns. Another 20 to 25 percent would have sympathized with such a movement. Approximately 30 percent indicated that they would have actively opposed it. In sum, then, as much as 35 to 40 percent of the population was prepared to support an anti-Jewish campaign, some 30 percent would have stood against it, and the rest — some 30 percent — would have remained indifferent. Even allowing ample room for inadequacies in the survey data, the seriousness of American anti-Semitism in those years is evident.[13] As such, the chief American delegate at Evian, Myron C. Taylor, undoubtedly believed that his warning against "dumping" Jewish refugees on American shores merely reflected American public opinion, which, according to a 1938 opinion poll, indicated that 67.4 percent wanted to keep refugees out.[14]

Indeed, immigration regulations were far more stringent in the United States than in Britain, where more than 50,000 German Jews were admitted. Among them were 10,000 children, who were allowed entry in 1938–39 in what became known as the *Kindertransport*. At the same time, fewer than 500 children came to the United States. Eric Lucas, one of the children of the *Kindertransport*, describes his departure:

When I was at last allowed to board the train, I rushed to the window to look for my parents, whom I could not see until I had left the customs shed. They stood there, in the distance, but they did not come to the train. I waved timidly, and yet full of fear, after the control I had just passed; but even that was too much. A man in a black uniform rushed toward me, "You Jewish swine — one more sign or word from you and we shall keep you here. You have passed the customs."

A few hours previously, first my father and then my mother had laid their hands gently on my bowed head to bless me, asking G-d to let me be like Ephraim and Menashe.

Standing at the window of the train, I was suddenly overcome with a maiming certainty that I would never see my father and mother again. There they stood, lonely, and with the sadness of death. Cruel hands kept us apart in the last intimate moment.

As the train pulled out of the station to wheel me to safety, I leaned my face against the cold glass of the window, and wept bitterly.[15]

Eric Lucas was unsuccessful in his attempts to bring his parents to England. His parents were caught in a proverbial Catch-22 situation: they could not receive a passport to leave Germany unless they could get a British visa. However, the British would not issue a visa until they had a valid passport. Eric Lucas never saw his parents again.

THE ILL-FATED VOYAGE OF THE *ST. LOUIS*: In May 1939, the ship *St. Louis* left Germany bound for Cuba with 930 Jews who had Cuban landing certificates. Upon arrival in Havana, however, the Cuban government refused entry to the Jews. The boat then headed for Florida, but the U.S. Coast Guard did not allow it to land. Despite a worldwide outcry, the American government did not relent, and the ship headed back to Europe, where England took in one-third of the passengers and France, Belgium, and the Netherlands the rest. Only the Jews fortunate enough to be allowed into England survived the Holocaust.

ATTITUDES TOWARD REFUGEES: Between 1933 and 1939 the attitudes and actions of the bystander countries toward Jews persecuted by the Nazi regime seems clear: these countries erected impenetrable barriers to refugee migration, resulting in tens of thousands of Jews being trapped in the *Reich* after World War II broke out in September 1939. These bystander countries, in particular the United States and Great Britain, thus bear no small measure of indirect guilt for the deaths of Germany's Jews and, indeed, of many others. (Although Great Britain allowed more Jews to enter their homeland than did the United States, they closed Palestine to Jewish refugees.) Even minimal generosity demonstrated toward the Jews fleeing Nazi persecution would have saved many thousands — perhaps hundreds of thousands — of lives. A Yiddish song of the times, sung in a mournful tune, echoes this sentiment: "Where can I go, where will they let me in, for every door is closed."

That is the standard outlook. However, one historian takes a radically different view:

There is, however, one principal error in the proposition that high barriers to the emigration of German and *Reich* Jews existed during the years 1933–1939, resulting in the subsequent deaths of many thousands: it is almost the precise opposite of the truth. Fully 72 percent of German Jewry escaped from Nazi Germany before emigration became impossible, including 83 percent of German Jewish children and youth. Given the general restrictions on all refugee migration (including non-Jewish refugees) which prevailed during the interwar period throughout the world, the emigration of most German Jews not only did not represent failure on the part of the democracies, but constituted one of the most successful and far-reaching programs of rescue of a beleaguered and persecuted people ever seen up to that time. Far from the doors of immigration being shut just before the gates went up forever with the outbreak of war in 1939, more *Reich* Jews found safety abroad in the last year preceding the outbreak of war than at any time before.[16]

This historian also buttresses his viewpoint by stating that any discussion of rescue is limited to the Jews who were under German rule before the war broke out, for once hostilities ensued immigration came to a virtual halt, due both to wartime conditions and the change in German policy from encouraging emigration to prohibiting it. In particular, the more than two million Jews massacred in the Soviet Union and its occupied territories were trapped behind the Iron Curtain.

This historian takes the same approach to the refugee ship *St. Louis*: "For a while, the sad voyage of the *St. Louis* seemed to have a happy ending... But within months, the Nazis overran Western Europe. Only the 288 passengers who disembarked in England were safe. Of the rest, only a few survived the Holocaust."[17]

At the exhibition commemorating the voyage of the *St. Louis* in the United States Holocaust Museum, the standard interpretation demonstrates the callousness of the world's nations toward the plight of the Jews. However, there is a very powerful counterargument: the Jews of the *St. Louis* did find a safe haven *at that time*; what happened later is irrelevant. The same differing historian writes regarding the countries that accepted the refugees:

In other words, the leaders of France (with a standing army of 1.5 million men), Belgium, and the Netherlands (neutral in the First World War) were blindly moronic (if not somehow anti-Semitic) for not realizing: a) that Germany would overrun and conquer their countries; b) that the Nazis would fundamentally reverse their policies from exiling Jews to imprisoning and killing them; c) that, beginning three years later, the Jews of Western Europe would be deported to extermination camps in Poland, something unimaginable by anyone in 1939."[18]

Clearly, then the refugee issue is a very difficult one. There were many reasons, aside from dislike of Jews, that countries turned their backs on them: fear that some refugees might be Nazi agents, that refugees would take jobs away from native workers, and that resources of the host country would be stretched too thin. There was another reason, perhaps the greatest of all: there were only half a million Jews in Germany, but millions more in Poland, Hungary, Romania, and other countries. If the borders were opened to all Jews seeking to flee oppression, then any nation wishing to rid itself of its Jews could begin mistreating them. Could any nation receive so many refugees so suddenly without ruining itself? During the 1994 genocidal war in Rwanda, for example, there was no American rush to admit victims, for this nation had no desire to be inundated with black Africans. In 1939, European Jews appeared to Americans to be no less alien than black Africans today. Some 40 million refugees exist worldwide today, yet there is no movement to repatriate them to other countries.

However, the nations of the world can still be faulted for not doing more for the refugees. Although individual nations took in embattled Jews, there was no worldwide campaign to ameliorate their plight. A concerted effort by the world's countries could indeed have rescued more Jews without having had a major impact on their societies. There were many places where Jews could have gone — England itself ruled over many colonies, each of which could have accepted some Jewish refugees. Even before the war broke out, millions of Eastern European Jews, particularly in Poland, realized the mortal danger of Nazi Germany and would gladly have gone to places in Africa or Southeast Asia. Obviously, it was impossible to take in all Polish Jews, but considerable numbers could have been saved. During the 1930s and '40s,

America did not even fill its quotas for Germany and Poland. Certainly, countries did accept Jews, but as the Talmud states in discussing the charitable responsibility of the wealthy, "According to the [strength of the] camel is the burden."[19]

COULD AN INDEPENDENT STATE OF ISRAEL IN THE 1930S HAVE HELPED?: This is a fascinating historical what-if question. The eminent Holocaust historian Lucy Davidowicz writes:

> Without political power Jews had no chance for survival. Had a Jewish state existed in 1939, even as one as small as Israel today, but militarily competent, the terrible story of six million dead might have had another outcome. As a member of the Allied nations, contributing its manpower and military resources to the conduct of the war, a Jewish state could have exercised some leverage with the great powers in the alliance. Even though it would not have diverted Hitler from his determination to murder the Jews, a Jewish state might have been able to wield sufficient military and political clout to have inhibited Slovakia, Romania, and Croatia from collaborating with the Germans in that murder. A Jewish state could have persuaded neutral countries to give Jewish refugees safe passage. A Jewish state would have ensured a safe haven. A Jewish state would have made the difference.[20]

This reason is provided as a justification for the existence of the current State of Israel — that there must be a place where Jews can find refuge from persecution. Undoubtedly, this is an important consideration, and many Jews have been able to flee hostile countries and go to Israel. However, some brandish this argument as a way to blame the religious leadership in Poland for discouraging emigration to Palestine, where the Jews would have been beyond the reach of the Nazis. Aside from the fact that the secular Jewish Agency controlled entry visas to Palestine, allocating only a small fraction to observant Jews, the argument against the religious leadership is fallacious for a very important reason: Had there been a State of Israel in 1939, comprised of several million Jews, Hitler would have given its destruction top priority. As it was, the German General Rommel nearly reached Palestine with ten divisions. Indeed, some of Hitler's strategists were suggesting using the brunt of the German Army for a sweep through the Middle East, a campaign which military historians say would have easily succeeded.[21] The presence of large numbers of Jews in a perceived enemy state would no doubt have given Hitler the impetus to pursue a Mediterranean strategy, and a militarily competent Israel would have been no match for the full force of the German Army led by one of the greatest generals of all time, the Desert Fox, Erwin Rommel.

GERMANY'S EUTHANASIA PROGRAM: The precedent for exterminating Jews in gas chambers was set in Germany in the 1930s. According to Nazi ideology, mentally ill or severely handicapped people were defilers of German blood and had to be destroyed. On a secret order from Hitler, six killing centers were set up throughout Germany, where roughly 275,000 German non-Jews were murdered. Here, the traditional role of doctor as healer and caretaker of the sick was corrupted to one of murderer in the name of racial hygiene and purification of the Aryan race. As such, doctors selected patients for death, and health-care workers transported the victims to the gassing centers. As later in the death camps, the patients were told they were taking showers. The dead bodies were cremated, and the ashes sent to the victims' families with a death certificate listing a false cause of death. In some places, lethal injections were used. After word leaked and the churches vigorously protested, Hitler stopped the adult euthanasia program, but the murder of children continued. (The last victim, a four-year-old child, was killed even after the Allied occupation of Germany.)[22]

At one of the killing sites, upon reaching the ten thousandth victim, the staff held a special ceremony. As number 10,000 lay on a stretcher, surrounded by flowers, the supervisor gave a speech and rewarded the staff with bottles of beer.[23]

If this barbarism was the attitude displayed toward the murder of their own countrymen, one can hardly be surprised at the zeal with which the Germans exterminated the Jews. The euthanasia program served as a demonic dress rehearsal for gassing Jews, with many of the same experts at the six German killing centers running gas chambers in the death camps of Poland. German physicians, inured to the suffering of presumed undesirables, performed gruesome medical experiments on Jews in the concentration camps.

HITLER'S DEMANDS ON POLAND: After taking Czechoslovakia, Poland was next on Hitler's list. Hitler demanded the return of Danzig (today Gdansk, Poland), a German-inhabited enclave in the midst of Poland. He also requested that Poland allow Germany to build an extraterritorial road across the Polish Corridor, which separated German East Prussia from the rest of Germany. Poland refused and was backed by England, which announced that it would go to war if Poland were attacked. Meanwhile, Hitler was carrying on secret negotiations with his ideological archenemy, Stalin and the Soviet Union.

THE HITLER-STALIN PACT: On August 23, 1939, Germany and the Soviet Union announced the signing of the German-Soviet Nonaggression Pact. The world was stunned by the reconciliation of such bitter foes, realizing that Hitler could then wage war.

JEWISH REACTION: There is a famous photograph of the Twenty-first Zionist Congress, which was held in Geneva at the time of the announcement of the Nonaggression Pact. Of the twelve people shown in the picture, four have a hand over their face or head. Another has his head bowed over his hands, which are crossed on his chest. Several others, wearing expressions of hopelessness, stare blankly into space. The caption on the picture reads: "They do not look like men who have just heard a piece of political news. They look like people who have heard a death sentence passed on members of their own family."[24] The pact meant that the jaws of a death trap were about to close on Poland's 3.5 million Jews.

SECRET PROVISIONS OF THE TREATY: The Nazis and Soviets agreed to divide Poland between them. In addition, each nation was promised a sphere of influence in Eastern Europe, with the Soviet Union receiving Latvia, Estonia, Finland, and Bessarabia, a Romanian province.

DIVINE PROVIDENCE: When the two giant powers decided the fate of Eastern Europe, they added a remarkable provision — to leave the country of Lithuania independent and to return to it the historic Lithuanian city of Vilna, which Poland had wrested away from Lithuania in 1920. This inexplicable action of Germany and the Soviet Union, working for the needs of tiny, insignificant Lithuania, saved many students of the great Torah institutions of Poland. At the outbreak of the war, following the advice of Rabbi Chaim Ozer Grodzensky, a number of yeshivos fled to neutral Lithuania, while some students, including the entire yeshivah of Mir, managed to leave Lithuania before the 1941 German takeover and reach safe havens.

Chapter 26

THE HORRORS BEGIN IN POLAND

HITLER ATTACKS POLAND: On September 1, 1939, Germany attacked Poland. The Poles fought valiantly, but the modern German tanks quickly overwhelmed the Polish cavalry. Seventeen days later, the Soviet Union invaded Poland from the east, in accordance with the secret protocols of the Hitler-Stalin Pact. As an American journalist described it, the Poles were crushed "like a soft-boiled egg."[1] Poland was divided between the victors, disappearing as an independent nation. Approximately 2.5 million Polish Jews came under Nazi rule, with the remaining one million falling to Soviet control.

German atrocities against Jews began immediately. Crude pictures of Jews with hooked noses, and the slogan "We're off to Poland to thrash the Jews," were painted on trains bringing German troops into the war zone.[2] German aircraft targeted both Jewish areas of cities as well as fleeing Jewish refugees. These atrocities, as well as many others, put the lie to the German claim that only the SS and not the regular army, the *Wehrmacht*, was involved in anti-Jewish actions.

Within hours of German occupation of a town or village, Jews were singled out for abuse and mass murder by SS troops acting in the rear of the German fighting forces. On September 3, the SS seized twenty Jews in the frontier town of Wieruszow, took them to the market place, and lined them up for execution. When the daughter of Israel Lewi, one of the condemned men, ran up to her father to say farewell, a German ordered her to open her mouth for her supposed impudence, then fired a bullet into it.[3] In Widawa, the Germans ordered the rabbi of the town, Rabbi Avraham Moroko, to burn Torah scrolls. He refused, whereupon they burned him with the *sifrei Torah* in his hands.[4]

In every conquered town and village, the Germans forced the Jews to clear rubble, carry heavy loads, hand over any gold, silver, or jewelry, scrub floors and lavatories with their *talleisim* (prayer shawls), and dance before their captors. The Prophet Isaiah, in a chilling premonition, said: "I submitted my body to those who smite and my cheeks to those who pluck; I did not hide my face from humiliation and spit" (50:6). Elderly Jews had their beards cut off with scissors or ripped from their chins. Young chassidic Jews had their *peyos* cut or torn from their faces, amid much German laughter and mockery. Overall, it is estimated that some 5,000 Jews were killed during the first few weeks of the German occupation of Poland.

At Lublin, the Germans destroyed the library of the famous yeshivah, an act that gave such pleasure to the conquerors that it was recalled with glee more than a year later. "For us," a German eyewitness later reported, "it was a matter of special pride to destroy the Talmudic Academy, which was known as the greatest in Poland."

> We threw the huge Talmudic library out of the building and carried the books to the marketplace, where we set fire to them. The fire lasted twenty hours. The Lublin Jews assembled around and wept bitterly, almost silencing us with their cries. We summoned the military band, and with joyful shouts the soldiers drowned out the sounds of the Jewish cries.[5]

Germany absorbed large portions of Poland into the *Reich*, and created a rump Polish area called the General Government. Tens of thousands of Jews from the newly annexed Polish districts were dumped into this region, causing massive overcrowding and starvation. Many Jews were forced to relocate to the General Government on foot during the winter of 1939–40, a particularly brutal season with much snowfall and temperatures that fell to twenty below zero.

THE ESTABLISHMENT OF GHETTOES: On September 21, 1939, in a secret directive, Heydrich ordered that all Poland's Jews be concentrated into areas of large cities near railway lines, which, although not openly stated at the time, would facilitate their transfer to death camps. Numerous ghettoes were set up throughout Poland, the largest of which were in Lodz, established in April 1940, and Warsaw, set up in November 1940.

The physical destruction of the Jews began with their deportation to the ghettoes of Eastern Europe. Ghettoes were not permanent places of settlement, as the SS made the Jews believe, but roundup centers that would make it more convenient either to let the Jews die in overcrowded and unsanitary conditions or to annihilate them by other means. Jewish ghettoes in Poland were generally located in the poorest or dirtiest sections of a city, or on the outskirts of cities that lacked facilities associated with urban living: paved streets, electricity, adequate water, and sewage. With the constant influx of Jews, first from all over Poland, then from other countries, the ghettoes became overcrowded death traps, where people died from a combination of scourges raging simultaneously: dysentery, typhoid, tuberculosis, and starvation. In the winter, people froze to death, especially the homeless, for there was little or no heating material, and the Germans had confiscated all warm clothing.

At its peak, the Warsaw Ghetto held nearly 400,000 people in an area of 2.5 square miles — just a few city blocks — enclosed by a nineteen-foot-high wall. As many as seven Jews lived in each room, causing endless struggles for living space, making the slightest privacy impossible, providing no relief from ceaseless noise and bodily odors of many thousands of human beings.

The Germans instituted a policy of starving the Jews. In Warsaw, Germans were allotted 2,300 calories daily (nutritional information printed on food packaging in America provides for a

2,000–2,500 calorie diet), while Jews were allowed only 180 calories per day, the equivalent of a cup of Cheerios with milk. Eventually, each Jew had to live a entire month on two pounds of bread, nine ounces of sugar, three and a half ounces of jam, and one and three quarters ounces of fat. Meat and cheese were almost impossible to find. All told, roughly 85,000 people, including 20,000 children, died of starvation in the Warsaw Ghetto.

LIFE IN THE WARSAW GHETTO: In Proverbs 30:8–9, King Solomon states: "Give me neither poverty nor wealth; provide me my allotted bread...lest I become impoverished and steal." The Talmud remarks: "Poverty removes a person from his [normal state of] mind."[6] The horrendous living conditions in the ghetto, and the struggle for daily survival, inevitably brought out unsavory facets of human character. Men fought one another for raw potatoes. People snatched food from one another, then sold or traded it at exorbitant rates. Self-absorption and preoccupation with one's own needs inured a person to the heartrending cries of beggars and children starving on the streets. To make matters worse, economic conditions were not equal in the ghetto: there were, for example, shops, cafes, and restaurants that catered to a small number of wealthy individuals. Well-dressed couples walked side-by-side with people in tatters. Eventually, however, as their assets gave out, all Jews were reduced to abject poverty.

Smuggling provided the ghetto's main economic activity — despite the great risk, for German law stipulated death for whoever was caught leaving the ghetto. Death notwithstanding, there were two classes of smugglers: those who did so for profit, and those who were forced to do so to save their families from starvation. This latter group was mainly comprised of young children, who found it easier to sneak out of the ghetto to the Aryan side of Warsaw. Nonetheless, many of them were caught, then beaten or killed. Undoubtedly, the heroism of many of these children prolonged the lives of numerous ghetto Jews.

The Germans established a number of factories in the ghetto, which mainly produced shoes and clothing for the German army.

Jews desperately contended with each other for jobs at these factories, both for the pitiful salary given, and in the mistaken belief that working at such plants would protect them and their families from deportation.

What's more, German raids on the ghetto were a daily fact of life. Individual soldiers or groups entered Jewish living quarters at will, and at all hours, demanding money and valuables. Often, the soldiers subjected their victims to humiliating personal searches. Then, if the soldiers were not satisfied, they beat or even killed the Jews. Needless to say, there was no legal recourse to such plunder. An eyewitness report of a Jewish family in Warsaw recalls one such visit by three German officers:

> They demanded money and jewelry and threatened the woman at gunpoint that she give them everything. She gave them all she had. Suddenly, one of the officers noticed a small medallion hanging around the neck of the little boy. This child had been ill from birth. He had petit mal, a form of epilepsy, which forced on as many as forty or sixty seizures a day, lasting one or two seconds. The child was mentally retarded. He could only express himself in inarticulate sounds. The only thing that gave this child any comfort was this very medallion. In the presence of the officers the child was taken with a seizure and the mother pleaded that the medallion be left for her child. One of the officers watching the child said: 'I see that the child is ill. I am a doctor, but a Jew-kid is not a human being,' and he tore the medallion off the neck of the little boy.[7]

Some of the Jews residing in the ghettoes kept diaries, both as a diversion from the rigors of daily life and from a desire to record their suffering for posterity. Several of these hidden diaries were unearthed, such as those of Emanuel Ringelblum, Adam Czerniakow, Hillel Seidman, and Chaim Kaplan of the Warsaw Ghetto, and a record of events in the Lodz Ghetto. These diaries, along with survivor accounts, give a detailed picture of life. An entry in one such diary for May 29, 1942, portrays the meaning of ghetto life to innocent children:

An acquaintance related that he was walking behind two little girls, and he overheard their conversation. The nine-year-old was describing the Lazanki Park in Warsaw to the five-year-old. It sounded like a fairy tale:

"The park is big — so-o-o big — and there are pathways and flowerbeds."

"What are flowerbeds?"

"...And a pond with swans..."

"What's a pond? And what are swans?"

The stilted conversation finally ground to a halt due to the lengthy explanations and complicated descriptions of this fairy-tale life that was no longer.[8]

Another diary records the appearance of Jews in the Warsaw Ghetto:

The majority are nightmare figures, ghosts of former human beings, miserable, destitute, pathetic remnants of former humanity. One is most affected by the characteristic change one sees in their faces: as a result of misery, poor nourishment, the lack of vitamins, fresh air and exercise, the numerous cares, worries, anticipated misfortunes, suffering and sickness, their faces have taken on a skeletal appearance; the prominent bones around the eye sockets, the yellow facial color, the slack pendulous skin, the alarming emaciation and sickliness. And, in addition, these miserable, frightened, restless, apathetic, and resigned expressions like that of a hunted animal.

On the streets children are crying in vain, children who are dying in hunger. They howl, beg, sing, moan, shiver with cold, without underwear, without clothing, without shoes, in rags, sacks, flannel which are bound in strips round the emaciated skeleton, children swollen with hunger, disfigured, half-conscious, already completely grown up at the age of five, gloomy and weary of life.

For various reasons standards of hygiene are terribly poor.

Above all the fearful population density in the streets with which nowhere in Europe can be remotely compared... In the early morning the corpses of beggars, children, old people, young people, and women are lying in every street — the victims of the hunger and cold.[9]

RELIGIOUS LIFE IN THE GHETTO: From the very beginning, the Germans banned religious observance. Synagogues and schools were shut down. Kosher slaughter was prohibited, and *mikva'os* were closed, with signs on their doors stating that use of the facility was punishable by ten years' imprisonment or death. Sabbath observance was virtually impossible, for the Germans forced the Jews to work on that day and on the *yomim tovim*.

Nevertheless, as in the days of Greek and Roman oppression, and during the persecution of the Spanish Inquisition, Jews courageously risked their lives to keep the Torah's commandments. In the words of Chaim Kaplan's diary entry for Tishah B'Av, August 12, 1940:

Public prayer in these dangerous times is a forbidden act. Anyone caught in this crime is doomed to severe punishment. If you will, it is even sabotage, and anyone engaged in sabotage is subject to execution. But this does not deter us. Jews come to pray in a group in some inside room facing the courtyard, with drawn blinds on the windows... Even for the high holy days, there was no permission for communal worship... Even in the darkest days of our exile we were not tested with this trial. Never before was there a government so evil that it would forbid an entire people to pray. The wonder is that we are still alive, and that we do everything. And this is true of public prayer too. Secret minyanim by the hundreds throughout Warsaw organize services, and do not skip over the most difficult hymns in the liturgy. There is not even a shortage of sermons. Everything is in accordance with the ancient customs of Israel... They pick some inside room whose windows look out onto the courtyard, and pour out their supplications before the G-d of Israel in whispers. This time there are no cantors and choirs, only whispered prayers. But the prayers are heartfelt; it is possible to weep in secret, too, and the gates of tears are not locked.[10]

Under the guise of children's centers, which the Germans allowed to exist, Rabbi Alexander Z. Friedman, the general secretary of Agudath Israel, set up a clandestine religious school system in the Warsaw Ghetto. At its peak, the secret network provided Torah education to 3,500 boys and girls. Rabbi Friedman also established kosher soup kitchens, as the official ones established by the ghetto administration were not kosher.

The edict against *mikvah* was circumvented in an ingenious manner: As the Polish police were bribed not to see or hear anything, a hole was dug in the basement adjacent to the *mikvah*, allowing people to crawl into the *mikvah* room while the front door — still bearing the German proclamation — remained locked. Due to fear of detection, the *mikvah* was heated only once a week. (However, in 1941, the Germans legalized the *mikvah*.)

Torah study, despite being outlawed by the Germans, was widespread. Great rabbis resided in the Warsaw Ghetto, most notably Rabbi Menachem Ziemba, the greatest Torah scholar in Poland. Other great scholars and rebbes lived in the ghetto, too, providing spiritual succor to their fellow Jews until the ghetto's liquidation, in May 1943. Rabbi Ziemba himself continued until the very end, even refusing an offer from the Catholic Church to save him. He died with his people during the Warsaw Ghetto Uprising.

Despite the overwhelming necessity to seek one's own survival, Jews in the ghetto established *chessed* organizations, such as free loan societies, charitable institutions, and orphanages. Starving individuals shared their pitiful rations with weaker family members or even total strangers.

Unlike Vienna, where many Jews committed suicide after the *Anschluss*, the Warsaw suicide rate was very low, despite a Jewish population over twice that of Vienna. In Warsaw, the populace demonstrated a tenacious will to survive that amazed the

Germans, who wondered why the Polish Jews did not react the way their Westernized brethren did. Perhaps the Jews of Vienna, who had little or no Jewish identity, felt a sense of utter hopelessness once their efforts at assimilation and acceptance into German society were so cruelly stripped away. The Jews of Poland, however, had no illusions about the gentile world, and were able to fall back on the teachings of the Torah and their Jewish heritage to sustain them through the worst times.

THE *JUDENRAT*: The Nazis sought to achieve their aims within the Jewish community via the establishment of a council of leaders known as the *Judenrat*. Heydrich's 1939 decree stated: "In each Jewish community, a Council of Jewish Elders is to be set up, to be composed, as far as possible, of the remaining influential personalities and rabbis. The council is to comprise up to twenty-four male Jews, depending on the size of the Jewish community." In actual practice, rabbis were not chosen for these positions, and the leadership of the *Judenrat* tended to be secularized Jews.

The *Judenrat* was responsible for the immediate and precise execution of all Nazi orders, including registration of all Jews by age and profession, an accurate survey of all Jewish property, and internal administration of all ghetto functions, such as housing, health, and police. Needless to say, the *Judenrat* leadership was faced with an impossible situation: should they temporarily cooperate with the Germans, hoping that worse decrees would be forestalled and that liberation would eventually come? Should they cooperate because would it not be better for fellow Jews to be the overseers of the community rather than the Nazis themselves?

As in all matters regarding human conduct, the Torah provides guidance for this most difficult dilemma. In Egypt, Pharaoh appointed a *Judenrat* to assist him in his program of genocide: "The king of Egypt said to the Hebrew midwives, of whom the name of the first was Shifrah and the name of the second was Puah. And he said, 'When you deliver the Hebrew women and you see them on the birth stool, if it is a son you are to kill him, and if it is a daughter she shall live.' But the midwives feared G-d and did not do as the king of Egypt ordered them, and they caused the boys to live" (Exodus 1:15–17).

Sforno (ibid.) explains that Shifrah and Puah were the head midwives in Egypt whom Pharaoh appointed to oversee all the Jewish midwives, and whose responsibility it was to implement his policy of genocide. They decided to pretend to go along with Pharaoh's orders while in reality thwarting them in every way possible. Although Shifrah and Puah realized they could very well be executed and replaced by others who would cooperate with Pharaoh, Shifrah and Puah would do to their utmost ability what was morally correct, leaving the outcome to G-d.

In general, there were four major behavior patterns of *Judenrat* leaders:

First, in the manner of the righteous midwives, there was complete noncooperation with the Nazis. In the Lvov Ghetto, for example, in accordance with Jewish law, which prohibits handing over even one Jew for execution at the cost of a very large group,[11] the *Judenrat* leader, Joseph Parnes, refused to provide lists of Jews to the Germans for deportation, and instructed his fellow *Judenrat* members not to assist them, either. The enraged Germans tied Dr. Parnes to the back of a car, and drove away at high speed, killing him.

Second, there was cooperation on questions of property, but non-cooperation in regard to delivering people for deportation. Adam Czerniakow, the head of the Warsaw *Judenrat*, took this course of action, meeting the rapacious monetary demands of the Germans while trying to alleviate the lot of his people as much as possible. When, in July 1942, he was ordered by the Germans to provide several thousand Jews daily for what the Nazis termed resettlement, and realizing what the implication was, he committed suicide rather than turn over a single Jew. (While very brave, this is not the Torah's approach; rather, he should have allowed the Nazis to kill him instead of taking his own life.)

Third, there was sacrifice of the lives of some people in the hope of saving others. At the end of 1942, Mordecai C. Rumkowski, leader of the Lodz *Judenrat*, knew that the Germans were murdering Jews. Hoping to rescue the remaining 70,000 Jews in the Lodz Ghetto, he continued to obey Nazi orders and helped deport Jews. To save some, as he hoped, he decided to sacrifice others, determining who should die and who should live. Sadly, Rumkowski was an egomaniac, referring to the Jews in the Lodz Ghetto as "my Jews," printing his likeness on postage stamps and money for use within the ghetto, profiting from business deals with the Nazis, and acting as an absolute dictator — all this in contrast to Warsaw's Czerniakow who conducted himself with a significant measure of humility. Perhaps it was this sense of overweening self-importance that caused Rumkowski to become an illegitimate arbiter of other peoples' lives.

Jacob Gens, of the Vilna *Judenrat*, selected 400 elderly Jews to be murdered, callously justifying his action by saying, "Those who did not have much time to live anyway went. With all due respect, the old Jews have to excuse us. They were sacrificed on the altar of our future."[12] Rumkowski and Gens (who was married to a Lithuanian Christian) flagrantly violated Torah law, which explicitly states that no one Jew's blood is more holy than another's.[13] In the end, cooperation with the Germans did not save their lives — Rumkowski died in the Auschwitz gas chambers, and Gens was shot.

Fourth, there was full cooperation with the Nazis in hope of saving their own lives. The sensational Kasztner trial in Israel of Budapest *Judenrat* leader Rudolph Kasztner alleged that the accused collaborated with Adolf Eichmann to deport Hungary's Jews to Auschwitz in exchange for receiving special privileges and having his own life spared. The accusation seemed true, for when the Germans retreated from Hungary they took Kasztner with them rather than kill him, as they usually did with other *Judenrat* leaders.

THE GHETTO POLICE: A Jewish police force, generally recruited from the lower elements of society, including criminals, enforced what passed for law and order in the ghetto. Here, too, the Torah provides a model for proper behavior: the Jewish police in Egypt, themselves brutally beaten by the Egyptians for not enforcing the quota of bricks imposed on the Jewish slaves (Exodus 5:14). Unfortunately, during the deportations from the Warsaw Ghetto the behavior of Jewish policemen reached the nadir of depravity: at times, they actually dragged Jews to the deportation trains. Not surprisingly, the force became the most hated Jewish body in the ghetto. Eventually, the Jewish police fared no better than those they dominated; they, too, died in the concentration camps.

GERMAN VICTORIES: During the first half of 1940, in a lightning campaign known as the *Blitzkrieg*, Germany overran much of Western Europe, conquering Norway, Denmark, Holland, Belgium, and France. This new form of fighting stunned the nations of Europe, whose armies were still trained in the mode of World War I–style trench warfare. By mid-year, the seemingly invincible German Army stood at the English Channel, poised to invade England. If England had been conquered, it would likely have led to Axis domination of the world. With England under his rule, Hitler could overrun the then-defenseless British and French colonies of the Middle East, gaining control of much of the world's oil supply, linking up with Japan in India, and menacing the Soviet Union on several fronts. Without having to fight a two-front war, the German Army might easily have overwhelmed the Soviets. At that juncture, having no forward bases from which to attack, the United States would have had to defend the Americas against an Axis in control of much of the world's resources. At the same time, Germany was developing jet aircraft and long-range bombers, which might have forced the United States to succumb. Hitler would then realize his life's dream of literally ruling the world and destroying the entire Jewish people. However, as the Torah states, "G-d is master of war" (Exodus 15:3), and although Hitler had two opportunities to defeat England, it is clear that he was Divinely prevented from doing so. There are no other plausible explanations.

Hitler's first chance was at the justly famous Battle of Dunkirk, where the German army had more than 400,000 French and British soldiers trapped at the English Channel. Inexplicably, the Germans did not bomb these troops into submission or force their surrender; as such, 338,000 of those soldiers were rescued by boat and brought to England. Had Germany destroyed the Allied forces at Dunkirk, there would have been virtually no British troops left to defend their homeland.

The second opportunity is not as well known, but is perhaps even more miraculous. In the 1940 Battle of Britain, the key to the Royal Air Force defense was a network of seven sector stations in Southern England. The German *Luftwaffe* had destroyed six of the seven stations. If the seventh had been destroyed, England would no longer have had an organized air defense system, leaving the island nation wholly vulnerable to attack.

At the moment that the *Luftwaffe* should have destroyed the last remaining station, Hitler changed the direction of the battle — and the war. Had the *Luftwaffe* continued, the Germans could have invaded England and in all likelihood achieved a swift and total victory. Instead, out of a characteristic blind rage, Hitler made a devastating mistake.

On the night of August 24, 1940, ten German bombers lost their way and mistakenly dropped their payloads on central London. The next night, the British launched a reprisal raid on Berlin — the first time the German capital had been hit. A furious Hitler announced that he would henceforth "eradicate" British cities. As such, he immediately called off the strikes against sector stations and ordered the inhuman terror bombing of British cities.[14] Although the Nazis wreaked untold damage on Great Britain, the kingdom did not fall — and in many ways the world was saved.

However, events were not as propitious in the east. By May 1941, after advances in Central and Southern Europe, Germany was the master of Europe, and stood poised to invade Soviet Russia. At that point, a full six million Jews lived under Nazi domination.

Chapter 27

THE LARGE-SCALE MASSACRES

"You will go mad from the sight of your eyes that you will
see."

(Deuteronomy 28:34)

"For how could one pursue a thousand and two cause ten
thousand to flee, if not that their Rock had sold them out,
and G-d had delivered them."

(Ibid. 32:30)

THE GERMAN INVASION OF THE SOVIET UNION: By June 1941, just 30,000 Jews had died, mainly through random killings, disease, and starvation. Yet even this death rate was too slow for the Germans, and they searched for ways to speed up the process. With the Nazi invasion of the Soviet Union on June 22, 1941, the extermination process began to assume unimaginably frightful proportions. Within five weeks, the number of Jews murdered exceeded the number killed in the previous eight years of Nazi rule. Indeed, the invasion of Russia presented the Germans with an opportunity they had hitherto lacked: remote regions far from prying eyes, the cover of an advancing army, vast distances, local collaborators, and an intensified will to destroy what the Nazis called the Judeo-Bolshevist menace.[1]

PLANNING THE FINAL SOLUTION: Although all historians agree that Hitler had a vision to annihilate the Jewish people, these scholars are divided as to whether the Germans planned it from the outset or took advantage of opportunities presented to them. The functionalist school maintains that the Germans, based on the military situation on the ground, planned the Final Solution in stages; the intentionalist school, however, holds that the extermination program existed very early, and the Germans were constantly seeking the best method of carrying it out.

No one knows exactly when Hitler gave the order to annihilate the Jews. No written document has ever been discovered that bears Hitler's signature and indicates, beyond a doubt, that he ordered the extermination of the Jews. Indeed, it was a mark of his cunning that he stayed in the shadows, limiting all discussions relating to the Final Solution to a handful of top advisors, chiefly Himmler, Heydrich, Bormann, and Goebbels. Nevertheless, clues from various sources indicate that sometime in the spring of 1941 Hitler gave a personal order to Himmler that the Jews had to be eliminated. It is also highly likely that Hitler suggested the precise nature of the plan: extermination by poison gas. After all, since the early days of the party he had made allusions to the subject, and in *Mein Kampf* he wrote that many German lives would have been saved in World War I if "these Hebrew corrupters of the people had been subjected to poison gas."[2]

Furthermore, it is highly significant that no written orders exist for the destruction of the Jews, and that any documents related to the matter use such euphemisms as evacuation to the East, resettlement, Final Solution, and special handling. In 1943, addressing SS officers in Poznan, Himmler said that the murder of the Jews "is a page of glory in our history which is never to be written."[3] Apparently, the Germans, from Hitler on down, realized the depravity of their deeds, for if they were so certain that their actions were completely justified, as they always claimed they were, why not trumpet the extermination process before the entire world — and especially before their own people? Here it is clear that misguided beliefs are no excuse for murder, for human beings have a G-d-given inner voice that tells them such actions are wrong.

THE *EINSATZGRUPPEN:* In preparation for the murder of the Jews of the Soviet Union, Heydrich created four mobile killing squads, or *Einsatzgruppen*. These killing units accompanied the German Army into Russia, operating behind the front lines with the full approval and active cooperation of the *Wehrmacht*. The *Einsatzgruppen* consisted of educated men both professionally and ideologically committed to their murderous assignment. Indeed, three of the four *Einsatzgruppen* leaders held doctoral degrees; the rest were lawyers, academics, ministerial officials, even a pastor and an opera singer. What united them was that all were true believers in Nazi ideology and fanatical Jew-haters. In all, the four units consisted of 3,000 men, and were responsible for the deaths of some 1,500,000 Jews, mainly by shooting, in an eighteen-month period.

As the German army advanced, hundreds of thousands of Jews were trapped, unable to outrun the invaders. The atrocities began immediately. In Kovno (Kaunas), Lithuania, three days after the invasion a horrific pogrom broke out, in which local thugs clubbed 1,500 Jews to death with crowbars in plain sight of cheering Lithuanian crowds. Mothers held up their children to enjoy the spectacle, and soldiers milled around to watch the fun like a soccer match.[4] One of the most terrible instances of savage butchery was the death of Rabbi Zalman Osovsky, the venerable rabbi of Slabodka, a suburb of Kovno. The Germans bound him to a chair, then laid his head upon the volume of the Talmud that he was studying — and sawed off his head. The Germans left his headless body in front of the Talmudic page that he had been studying, and displayed his head with the caption: *This is what we'll do to all the Jews!*[5]

Within a few short weeks, Lithuanian Jewry, along with the great yeshivos that were the nucleus of Torah Jewry, was decimated. Virtually no Lithuanian Jews survived the Holocaust. One who did, Rabbi Ephraim Oshry, described the final moments of Rabbi Elchanan Wasserman, a leading *rosh yeshivah*. Rabbi Elchanan's immortal words portray the sublime spiritual heights reached by this giant as he realized his end was near, and serve as an eternal inspiration for the Jewish people:

We were sitting around a table in the backyard of Rabbi Grodzensky's house on this long summer afternoon. Rabbi Wasserman was teaching the daily page of Talmud in tractate *Niddah,* and the sages and students present were immersed in the intricacies of a complex Talmudic discussion.

Suddenly the gate to the yard was pushed open, and in marched four Lithuanian Nazis. Their shouts were first ignored because almost no one had heard it; certainly not the sages present, whose ears were attuned solely to the words of Torah. When the Lithuanians noticed that the rabbis had not reacted to their shouts, they drew their revolvers and fired off a few shots... Another Lithuanian ordered, "Line up and follow me!" ...They placed Rabbi Wasserman at the head of the line and next to him Rabbi Zaks and the other rabbis with the most patriarchal images. I was placed last and managed to slip away...

While the Lithuanians made their plans, Rabbi Wasserman spoke to the arrestees. His voice retained its evenness, and his face displayed the same solemnity as always. He spoke as if he realized these were his last words. There was nothing personal in his words; he did not even ask to say farewell to his son Naftali who was in bed inside with a broken leg. He addressed everyone, *all of Jewry* [italics in original]:

"Heaven apparently considers us righteous people, for it wants us to atone with our bodies for Jewry as a whole. So we must repent now, on the spot. Time is short; the Ninth Fort (the place of execution of thousands of Jews) is near. We must make up our minds that we truly wish to sanctify G-d. If we repent, we will thereby save the remaining Jews, our brothers and sisters, so that they will be able to carry on as the remnant of Jewry." It was apparent when he spoke that he was referring to our brethren in England and the United States. He continued:

"Let us walk with heads held high. Let no one think a

thought that would disqualify his sacrifice. We are about to fulfill the greatest mitzvah — the mitzvah of *kiddush HaShem*. The fire that consumes our bodies is the fire that will rebuild the Jewish people."

The line of martyrs marched forward. Proudly, courageously, they walked on, about to atone with their own bodies for Jewry as a whole. These holy Jewish sages — may G-d avenge their blood — were killed that night in the Ninth Fort.[6]

Throughout Eastern Poland, the Baltic States, Ukraine, Belorussia, and Russia, with the active cooperation of their gentile neighbors Jews were driven out of cities, towns, and villages, and handed over to the *Einsatzgruppen*. The Jews were taken to the outskirts of the towns, to military fortifications, natural ravines, and antitank ditches, then shot by the thousands. Often, the unfortunates had to dig their own graves before being murdered. In many cases, Jews were buried alive without being shot, or were only wounded when shot into the pits, later suffocating when masses of bodies fell on top of them. A German engineer, who stumbled on a ghastly mass execution of Jewish men, women, and children, wrote one of the most shocking accounts of such mass killing. He records the quiet dignity of the victims who were well aware of their fate:

Moenikes and I directly went to the pits. Nobody bothered us. Now I heard rifle shots in quick succession, from behind one of the earth mounds. The people who got off the trucks — men, women, and children of all ages — had to undress upon the order of an SS man, who carried a riding or dog whip. They had to put down their clothes in fixed places... I saw a heap of shoes of about 800 to 1,000 pairs, great piles of under linen and clothing. Without screaming or weeping these people undressed, stood around in family groups, kissed each other, said farewells, and waited... I heard no complaint or plea for mercy... An old woman with snow-white hair was holding a one-year-old child in her arms, singing to it, and tickling it. The child was cooing with delight. The couple was looking on with tears in their eyes. The father was holding the hand of a boy about ten years old and speaking to him softly; the boy was fighting his tears. The father pointed to the sky, stroked his head, and seemed to explain something to him. At that moment the SS man at the pit shouted something to his comrade. The latter counted off about twenty persons and instructed them to go behind the earth mound. Among them was the family that I have mentioned. I well remember a girl, slim and with black hair, who, as she passed close to me, pointed to herself and said, "Twenty-three." I walked around the mound, and found myself confronted by a tremendous grave. People were closely wedged together and lying on top of each other so that only their heads were visible. Nearly all had blood running over their shoulders from their heads. Some of the people shot were still moving... I looked for the man who did the shooting. He was an SS man, who sat at the edge of the narrow end of the pit, his feet dangling into the pit. He had a Tommy gun on his knees and was smoking a cigarette. The people, completely undressed, went down...the pit and clambered over the heads of the people lying there...then I heard a series of shots. I looked into the pit and saw that the bodies were twitching... Blood was running from their necks.[7]

Only the most sadistic or hardened executioners could endure such horrors indefinitely. Some SS men did enjoy killing Jews, and many such incidents of craven blood lust have been recorded. In one town, for example, the Jews had gone into hiding, and when the SS killers combed the town they discovered a woman with a baby in her arms. When the woman refused to tell them where the Jews were hiding, one SS man grabbed the baby by its legs and smashed its head against a door. Another SS man recalled: "It went off with a bang like a bursting motor tire. I shall never forget that sound as long as I live." Jews were often shot for sport or recreation. Some SS men believed that they made great targets for marksmanship.[8]

The culmination of mass shootings came at Babi Yar, on the

outskirts of Kiev, where at the end of September 1941 33,771 Jews were murdered in two days. One of the few Jews to escape from the pit at Babi Yar was Dina Pronicheva. After the war, she told her story to a Russian writer, who published it. Dina Pronicheva, like hundreds of those who were shot during these massacres, was not killed. But unlike most of those who fell into the pit alive, she managed to avoid being suffocated, and to escape undetected.

All around and beneath her she could hear strange submerged sounds, groaning, choking, and sobbing; many of the people were not dead yet. The whole mass of bodies kept moving slightly as they settled down and were pressed tighter by the movements of the ones who were still living. Some soldiers came out to the ledge and flashed their torches down on the bodies, firing bullets from their revolvers into any that appeared to be still living. But someone not far from Dina went on groaning as loud as before.

Then she heard people walking near her, actually on the bodies. They were Germans who had climbed down and were bending over and taking things from the dead and occasionally firing at those which showed signs of life. Among them was the policeman who had examined her papers and taken her bag; she recognized him by his voice.

One SS man caught his foot against Dina and her appearance aroused his suspicions. He shone his torch on her, picked her up and struck her with his fist, but she hung limp and gave no sign of life. He kicked her with his heavy boot and trod on her right hand so that the bones cracked, but he did not use his gun and went off, picking his way across the corpses. A few minutes later she heard a voice calling from above: "Demidenko! Come on, start shoveling!" There was a clatter of spades and then heavy thuds as the earth and sand landed on the bodies, coming closer and closer until it started falling on Dina herself. Her whole body was buried under the sand but she did not move until it began to cover her mouth. She was laying face upward, breathed in some sand and started to choke, and then, scarcely realizing what she was doing, she started to struggle in a state of uncontrollable panic, quite prepared now to be shot rather than be buried alive.

With her left hand, the good one, she started scraping the sand off her, scarcely daring to breathe lest she should start coughing; she used what strength she had to hold the cough back. She began to feel a little easier. Finally she got herself out from under the earth. The Ukrainian policemen up above were apparently tired after a hard day's work, too lazy to shovel the earth in properly, and once they had scattered a little in they dropped their shovels and went away. Dina's eyes were full of sand. It was pitch dark and there was the heavy smell of flesh from the mass of fresh corpses.

Dina could just make out the nearest side of the sandpit and started slowly and carefully making her way across to it; then she stood up and started making little footholds in it with her left hand. In that way pressed close to the side of the pit, she made steps and so raised herself an inch at a time, likely at any moment to fall back in the pit. There was a little bush at the top, which she managed to get hold of. With a last desperate effort she pulled herself up and, as she scrambled over the ledge, she heard a whisper that nearly made her jump back:

"Don't be scared, lady! I'm alive too."

It was a small boy in vest and pants who had crawled out as she had done. He was trembling and shivering all over.

"Quiet!" she hissed at him. "Crawl along behind me." And they crawled away silently, without a sound.

Dina Pronicheva survived. The boy, Motyn, stayed with her, but as they sought to leave the area, he called that danger was near. "Don't move, lady, there are Germans here!" — those were Motyn's words. Luckily for Dina Pronicheva, the Germans did not understand them. But hearing him speak, they killed him on the spot.[9]

Those Jews killed by the *Einsatzgruppen* were among the

more blessed victims of the Holocaust. They died quickly, with relatively little suffering, with their loved ones almost until the very end, not having to undergo the torment of cattle cars and concentration camps.

After the thousands of murders, the Germans realized that this method of killing Jews was not very efficient. It was too slow, too labor-intensive — at that rate it could take nearly ten years to annihilate all the Jews of Europe. In addition, the personal nature of the killings was psychologically debilitating to the executioners. Some sought refuge in alcohol, some became physically ill, and a few committed suicide. A cleaner, more efficient method of implementing the Final Solution had to be found.

> "So you will serve your enemies whom G-d will send against you, in hunger and in thirst, in nakedness and without anything; and he will put an iron yoke on your neck, until he destroys you."
>
> (Deuteronomy 28:48)
>
> "And it will be that just as G-d rejoiced over you to benefit you and multiply you, so G-d will cause [the enemies] to rejoice over you to make you perish and to destroy you."
>
> (Ibid. 28:63)

THE WANNSEE CONFERENCE: On January 20, 1942, Heydrich called a meeting at a villa in the posh Berlin suburb of Wannsee, in which major representatives of various German government agencies involved in the Final Solution came together to discuss the technical details of murdering the remaining Jews of Europe. Heydrich hosted the meeting in a very genial atmosphere; Eichmann, who had also sent out the invitations, kept the minutes. Of the fifteen participants, eight held doctoral degrees from major German universities.

Heydrich unfolded a monstrous demographic chart listing more than 11 million Jews living in the various European nations, including the 330,000 Jews of unconquered England, the Sephardic Jews of North Africa, even the 200 Jews of Albania.

Lively discussion then ensued as to how these Jews could be rounded up, stripped of their possessions, transferred eastward, and annihilated. The final minutes of the conference are couched in revolting euphemisms that conceal mass murder: Final Solution, evacuation to the East, special handling, and so on. According to Eichmann's testimony at Jerusalem, however, the participants at the Wannsee Conference discussed "the subject quite bluntly: quite differently from the language which I had to use later in the record. During the conversation they minced no words about it at all."[10] In all, the demonic Wannsee Conference lasted only an hour and a half, after which a sumptuous lunch was served. The significance of the Wannsee Conference was not the initiation of the Final Solution — that had already begun with the mass shootings of Jews seven months previously — but instead that a broad segment of the German government, not merely Hitler and the SS, had both endorsed the Final Solution and worked out common procedures for its implementation.

THE TRAINS OF DEATH: The Germans planned the extermination of the Jews in the gas chambers, but in practice, death and destruction began while the Jews were still in the freight cars rolling toward the death camps. Designed to carry a maximum of sixty to seventy people, including their belongings, the cars were packed with double that number. Deprived of air and water, with no sanitary facilities, forced to spend endless hours traveling or waiting in stations in the packed freight cars, many became insane or died en route. Trips that should have taken a few hours took several days. Jan Karski, a righteous Polish gentile, disguised himself as a guard in order to report to the outside world the horrors the Jews were undergoing. He described the loading of a train and the attempts the Germans made to pack each car to the maximum:

Alternatively swinging and firing their rifles, the policemen were forcing still more people into the cars which were already overfilled. The shots continued to ring out in the rear, and the driven mob surged forward, exerting an irresistible pressure against those nearest the train. These unfortunates, crazed by what they had been through, scourged by the policemen, and shoved forward by the milling mob, then began to climb on the heads and shoulders of those in the trains. These latter were helpless since they had the weight of the entire advancing throng against them. They howled with anguish at those who, clutching at their hair and clothes for support, trampling on necks, faces, and shoulders, breaking bones, and shouting with insensate fury, attempted to clamber over them. More than another score of men, women, and children crushed into the cars in this fashion. Then the policemen slammed the doors across the arms and legs that still protruded, and pushed the iron bars in place...the floors of the cars had been covered with a thick, white powder. It was quicklime...anyone who has seen cement being mixed knows what occurs when water is poured on lime. The mixture bubbles and steams as the powder combines with the water, generating a searing heat.

The lime served a double purpose in the Nazi economy of brutality: the moist flesh coming in contact with the lime is quickly dehydrated and burned. The occupants of the cars would be literally burned to death before long, the flesh eaten from their bones. Thus the Jews would "die in agony," fulfilling the promise Himmler had issued "in accord with the will of the *Fuhrer*," in Warsaw in 1942. Secondly, the lime would prevent the decomposing bodies from spreading disease. It was efficient and inexpensive — a perfectly chosen agent for its purpose.[11]

Ada Lichtman, a survivor, described her journey to Sobibor: We were packed into a closed cattle train. Inside the freight cars it was so dense that it was impossible to move. There was not enough air; many people fainted, others became hysterical. In an isolated place, the train stopped. Soldiers entered the car and robbed us and even cut off fingers with rings...days and nights passed. The air inside the car was poisoned by the smell of bodies and excrement. Nobody thought about food, only about water and air. Finally, we arrived at Sobibor. [12]

Abraham Goldfarb testified about his trip to Treblinka:

When the Jews were brought to the railway station, the Germans forced 150–200 of them into a freight car designed for sixty or seventy. The cars were closed from the outside with boards. Water and food were not provided. People were suffocating; there was no air to breathe. Before we moved off, the Germans sprinkled chlorine in the cars. It burned the eyes. The weaker among us fainted. People climbed on top of each other and banged on the walls with whatever they could find. The children were so thirsty they licked their mothers' sweat. There were 150 people in our freight car. During the two-day trip to Treblinka, 135 suffocated. [13]

Thousands upon thousands of Jews died in the trains. Those living farthest away from the death camps had to endure journeys not of days but of weeks. Trains carrying Jews from Greece took up to a month to make the 2,700-mile trip to Auschwitz, a distance similar to that between New York and Las Vegas.

THE DEATH CAMPS: The Germans set up six major extermination camps, all in Poland: Chelmno, Belzec, Treblinka, Sobibor, Majdanek, and Auschwitz. The first camp, Chelmno, began gassing Jews on December 7, 1941. (The day that in American history "will live in infamy," as President Roosevelt said, for the attack on Pearl Harbor, lives on in even greater infamy in Jewish history.) The last camp, Auschwitz, gassed its last Jews in November 1944. In a period of almost three years, then, some 3,500,000 Jews lost their lives in these death camps.

Chelmno, Belzec, Treblinka and Sobibor were exclusively extermination camps; consequently there were very few survivors, and little is known about these camps. Majdanek and Auschwitz were combined labor and extermination camps; as a result, there were several thousand survivors. Virtually all survivors' testimony about life in the concentration camps comes from these survivors, particularly from Auschwitz. The following chart lists the grim statistics of Jewish deaths and survivors in the six killing centers, with all numbers approximations.[14]

Chelmno, Belzec, Treblinka, and Sobibor were each laid out over a relatively small area. Majdanek was a large camp with several compounds, and Auschwitz, beside being an extermination camp, was a giant industrial complex spread out over twenty-five square miles. Majdanek was unique among the camps in that it was located near a major city, one mile from Lublin, whereas the other five camps were located in isolated areas. Majdanek was also the only camp not destroyed by the Germans; its murder apparatus is still intact.

CAMP	VICTIMS	SURVIVORS
Chelmno	320,000	3
Belzec	600,000	2
Treblinka	800,000	40
Sobibor	250,000	64
Majdanek	360,000	500*
Auschwitz	1,100,000	7,600*

*Inmates in the camp at liberation. (Other Jews survived by being transferred during the war.)

ARRIVAL AT THE CAMPS: Upon arrival, the Jews were driven out of their freight cars, often leaving behind them trampled infants, and assembled on the ramp. A selection officer (in Auschwitz the notorious Dr. Joseph Mengele), with the simple wave of a hand, directed each new prisoner into one of two lines: on the right, those who were sentenced to hard labor; on the left, those who were condemned to death. Old men, women, and children were usually murdered immediately. At Auschwitz, 90 percent of all transports were sent to the gas chambers, while in the other camps virtually all the Jews were immediately earmarked for death, except for a small number of young men who were selected for labor.

THE GASSING: Those marked for death were ordered to undress and told that they would have to take showers. A number of psychological ploys, varying from camp to camp, were used to conceal the horrible reality that awaited the condemned. At Auschwitz, for example, people were told to tie their shoes together and hang their clothes on numbered hooks so that they could easily find them after their showers. They were even given soap to take to the gas chambers. Women were shorn of all their hair. Prodded and hurried along like a herd of cattle by special commandos wielding whips, sticks, or rifle butts, the victims were then driven into the gas chambers. Yet as effective as they were, these deceptions did not fool everybody, and there were anguished cries and heartrending scenes of indescribable horror. Once the victims had been shoved into a gas chamber, which could hold close to 800 tightly packed people, the doors were sealed and the gas was released through vents in the ceiling. After twenty minutes, everyone inside was dead.

The doors were then opened, and a special Jewish crew, the *Sonderkommandos*, extracted the gold from the teeth of the victims — the worst job in the concentration camps. Sometimes, a crew member recognized a parent, wife, or child among the victims, but there could be no open display of sorrow, for the German overseers carefully watched the Jewish workers, and threw a mourner alive into the crematorium. After the gold had been extracted, the bodies were cremated, either in the open air or in gigantic crematoria. The stench was palpable for miles. German manufacturers competed for government contracts to build the most automated and efficient incinerators. The top contract went to I. A. Topff and Sons, which eventually perfected a unit that contained an underground gas chamber together with electric elevators for hauling up the bodies.

Chaim Hirschman, one of the two survivors of Belzec, testified after the war about some of the horrors he witnessed. Among them was a transport of children up to three years old that arrived at Belzec:

The workers were told to dig one big hole into which the children were thrown and buried alive...I couldn't forget how the earth had been rising until the children suffocated.[15]

In one of the transports taken out of the gas chamber, I found the body of my wife and I had to shave her hair.[16]

Rudolf Reder, the other survivor of Belzec, recalled:

Soon after my arrival at Belzec, one very young boy was selected from a transport. He was a fine example of health, strength, and youth. We were surprised by his cheerful manner. He looked around and said quite happily, "Has anyone ever escaped from here?"

It was enough. One of the guards overheard him and the boy was tortured to death. He was hung upside down from the gallows — he hung there for three hours. He was strong and still very much alive. They took him down and lay him on the ground and pushed sand down his throat with sticks until he died.[17]

I heard the doors being locked, the moaning, shouting, and cries of despair in Polish and Yiddish; the crying of the children and women which made the blood run cold in my veins. Then there came one last terrible shout. All this lasted fifteen to twenty minutes, after which there was silence. The Ukrainian guards opened the doors on the outside of the building and I, together with all the others left over from the previous transports, began our work. We pulled out the corpses of those who were alive only a short time ago, we pulled them using leather belts to the huge mass graves while the camp orchestra played; played from morning until night.[18]

Kurt Gerstein, a German SS officer present at a gassing in Belzec on August 19, 1942, testified:

Next morning, a few minutes before seven, I was told: "In ten minutes the first train will arrive!" Indeed, a few minutes later a train arrived from Lvov, with forty-five cars holding 6,700 people, of which 1,450 were already dead on arrival... As the train drew in, 200 Ukrainians detailed for the task tore open the doors and, laying about them with their leather whips, drove the Jews out of the cars. Instructions boomed from a loudspeaker, ordering them to remove all clothing, artificial limbs, and spectacles. Using small pieces of string handed out by a little Jewish boy, they were to tie their shoes together. Then the march began. To the left and right, barbed wire; behind, two dozen Ukrainians, guns in hand.

They approached. Wirth and I were standing on the ramp in front of the gas chambers; men, women, young girls, children, babies, and cripples filed by. At the corner stood a heavy SS man, who told the poor people, in a pastoral voice: "No harm will come to you. You just have to breathe very deeply, that strengthens the lungs; inhaling is a means of preventing contagious diseases. It's a good disinfectant!"

The majority knew everything; the smell betrayed it. They climbed a little wooden stair and entered the death chambers, most of them silently, pushed by those behind them. A Jewess of about forty with eyes like fire cursed the murderers; she disappeared into the gas chamber after being struck several times by Captain Wirth's whip. Many prayed; others asked, "Who will give us water to wash the dead?"

SS men pushed the men into the chambers. Heckenholt was making great efforts to get the engine running, but it wouldn't go. My stopwatch clocked it all: fifty minutes, seventy minutes, and the diesel did not start. The people wait inside the gas chambers. They can be heard weeping "like in the synagogue," says Professor Pfannenstiel, his eyes glued to a window in the wooden door. After 2 hours and 49 minutes, the diesel started, and after 32 minutes, everyone was dead.

The people were still standing like columns of stone, with no room to fall or lean. Even in death you could tell the families, all holding hands. Two dozen workers were busy checking the mouths of the dead, which they opened with iron hooks, and in their midst stood Captain Wirth. He was in his element, and showing me a large can of teeth, he said: "See for yourself the weight of that gold! It's only from yesterday and the day before. You can't imagine what we find every day — dollars, diamonds, gold."[19]

August 1942, when Gerstein witnessed the gassing at Belzec, was the single worst month of the Holocaust — more than 400,000 Jews were murdered by the Germans. G-d alone knows the identity of each one, whose martyred souls repose in Heaven before Him.

Samuel Rajzman, a survivor of Treblinka, recounted what he witnessed:

When mothers succeeded in keeping their babies with them and this fact interfered with the shaving, a German guard took the baby by its legs and smashed it against the wall of the barracks until only a bloody mass remained in his hands. The unfortunate mother had to take this mass with her to the "bath." Only those who saw these things with their own eyes would believe with what delight the Germans performed these operations; how glad they were when they succeeded in killing a child with only three or four blows; with what satisfaction they pushed the baby's corpse into the mother's arms.[20]

THE *SONDERKOMMANDOS:* This special unit of Jewish prisoners was forced to herd the victims into the gas chambers, help them undress, and shave the women's hair, which the Germans used in submarine mattresses. Closely watched by the Germans, the Jews were thrown alive into the furnaces if they betrayed the slightest hint to the victims of their fate. The SS doctors and other SS men did the actual killing, introducing the gas into the chambers. Later, the *Sonderkommandos* removed valuables from the bodies before burning them in the ovens. The *Sonderkommandos* also sorted the possessions of the dead, sending all such stolen items to Germany. Eventually, usually after a few months, the

Sonderkommandos themselves were killed and replaced by new prisoners. The labor supply was inexhaustible, and the Germans wanted no witnesses. However, some did manage to survive, notably Philip Muller, a Slovakian Jew who worked as an Auschwitz *Sonderkommando* from April 1942 to November 1944, a period of more than two and a half years. Actually inside a gas chamber, Muller was able to leave at the last moment:

Now, when I watched my fellow countrymen walk into the gas chamber, brave, proud, and determined, I asked myself what sort of life it would be for me in the unlikely event of my getting out of the camp alive... It was not so much a matter of material possessions; they were replaceable. But who could replace my parents, my brother, or the rest of my family, of whom I was the sole survivor? And what of friends, teachers, and the many members of our Jewish community... I had never yet contemplated the possibility of taking my own life, but now I was determined to share the fate of my countrymen.

In the great confusion near the door I managed to mingle with the pushing and shoving crowd of people who were being driven into the gas chamber. Quickly I ran to the back and stood behind one of the concrete pillars. I thought that here I would remain undiscovered until the gas chamber was full; when it would be locked...I faced my fate with composure.

Inside the gas chamber the singing had stopped. Now there was only weeping and sobbing. People, their faces smashed and bleeding, were still streaming through the door, driven by blows and goaded by vicious dogs. Desperate children who had become separated from their parents in the scramble were rushing around calling for them. All at once, a small boy was standing before me. His little face puckered with worry, he asked timidly: "Do you know where my mommy and daddy are hiding?" I tried to comfort him, explaining that his parents were sure to be among all those people milling around in the front part of the room. "You run along there," I told him, "and they'll be waiting for you, you'll see."

The atmosphere in the dimly lit gas chamber was tense and depressing. Death had come menacingly close. It was only minutes away. No memory, no trace of any of us would remain. Once more people embraced. Parents were hugging their children so violently that it almost broke my heart... One girl spoke to me: "We understand that you have chosen to die with us of your own free will, and we have come to tell you that we think your decision is pointless, for it helps no one. We must die, but you still have a chance to save your life. Perhaps you'll survive this terrible tragedy and then you must tell everybody what happened to you. One more thing — you can do me one last favor: this gold chain around my neck. When I'm dead, take it off and give it to Sasha, who works in the bakery. Say 'love from Yana.' When it's all over, you'll find me here." She pointed to a place next to the concrete pillar where I was standing. Those were her last words.

Before I could make an answer to her spirited speech, the girls took hold of me and dragged me protesting to the door of the gas chamber. There they gave me a last push, which made me land bang in the middle of the group of SS men. Kurschuss was the first to recognize me and at once set about me with his truncheon. I fell to the floor, stood up, and was knocked down by a blow from his fist. As I stood on my feet for the third or fourth time, Kurschuss yelled at me: "Get it into your stupid head: **we** [bold in original] decide how long you stay alive and when you die, and not you!" Then he socked me viciously in the face so that I reeled against the lift door.[21]

HIDING THE CRIMES: The Germans attempted to obliterate any traces of their evil deeds. They blew up the gas chambers, exhumed the mass graves, and burned hundreds of thousand of corpses. The murderers believed they would enjoy their victory, that the world would never find out, or would reject the testimony of the few survivors as simply unbelievable. As the SS guards told their victims:

However this war may end, we have won the war against you;

none of you will be left to bear witness, but even if someone were to survive, the world will not believe him. There will perhaps be suspicions, discussions, research by historians, but there will be no certainties, because we will destroy the evidence together with you. And even if some proof should remain and some of you survive, people will say that the events you describe are too monstrous to be believed; they will say that they are the exaggerations of Allied propaganda and will believe us, who will deny everything, and not you. We will be the ones to dictate the history of the *lagers* [camps].[22]

The SS militiamen who used these cruel words were wrong in their self-confident expectations that the world would not believe the unbelievable, or that the lies of the killers would be given more credence than the honest testimonies of the survivors. Even Belzec, the deadliest of all the camps, had two survivors: Chaim Hirschman, who removed a plank from the floor of the train taking him to his death in Sobibor, jumped out safely, and managed to join a partisan group, and Rudolf Reder, who was taken under guard to Lvov to gather tin for the camp. Reder wrote about his escape:

At the end of November [1942], I had already been confined to the hell of Belzec for a few months. One morning the bully Irman told me that there was a need for tin in the camp... I went with a truck, accompanied by four SS men and a guard to Lvov. After a whole day of loading the tin sheets, I remained in the car, under the guard of one of the bullies, while all the others went for entertainment. For hours I sat without moving. Then I saw that my guard had fallen asleep and was snoring. Without thinking, instinctively, I slid down the car. The bully continued sleeping. I stood on the sidewalk, appearing as if I was arranging the tin sheets, but slowly moving toward Legionow Street, where the traffic was quite heavy. I pulled my hat over my eyes; the streets were dark and nobody saw me. I remembered where a Polish woman, my landlady, lived. I went there, and she hid me.[23]

Rudolf Reder survived the war. Chaim Hirschman also survived, but tragically was killed in a Polish pogrom in 1946, after the war.

A DAY IN THE LIFE OF A CAMP WORKER: Those selected for life faced hell itself. Numerous survivor accounts exist regarding life in the camps. Typical of these is that of a survivor of Majdanek:

You get up at 3 a.m. You have to dress quickly, and make the "bed" so that it looks like a matchbox. For the slightest irregularity in bed-making the punishment is twenty-five lashes, after which it is impossible to lie or sit for a whole month. Everyone has to leave the barracks immediately. People are trembling because of lack of sleep and the cold. In order to warm up a bit, groups of ten to twenty people stand together, back to back so as to rub against each other.

There was what was called a washroom, where everyone in the camp was supposed to wash — there were only a few faucets — and we were 4,500 people in that section. Of course, there was neither soap nor towel or even a handkerchief, so that washing was theoretical rather than practical...in one day, a person there became a lowly person indeed.

At 5 a.m. we used to get half a liter [16 ounces] of black, bitter coffee. That was all we got for what was called "breakfast." At 6 a.m. — a head count (*Zeilappell*). We all had to stand at attention until the SS men had satisfied their game-playing instincts by humorous orders to take off and put on caps. Then they received their report, and counted us.

After the head count we went to work. We went in groups — some to build railway tracks or a road, some to the quarries to carry stones or coal, some to take out manure, or for potato digging, latrine cleaning, barracks or sewer repairs. All this took place inside the camp enclosure. During work the SS men beat up the prisoners mercilessly, inhumanly, for no reason. They were like wild beasts and having found their victim, ordered him to present his backside, and beat him with a stick or a whip, usually until the stick broke. The victim screamed only after the first blows; afterward he fell unconscious and the SS man then kicked at the ribs, the face, at the most sensitive parts of a man's body, and then, finally convinced that the victim was at the end of his strength, he ordered another Jew to pour one pail of water after the other over the beaten person until he awoke and got up.

A favorite sport of the SS men was to make a "boxing sack" out of a Jew. This was done in the following way: Two Jews were stood up, one being forced to hold the other by the collar, and an SS man trained giving him a knockout. Of course, after the first blow, the poor victim was likely to fall, and the other Jew holding him up prevented this. After the fat, Hitlerite murderer had "trained" in this way for fifteen minutes, and only after the poor victim was completely shattered, covered in blood, his teeth knocked out, his nose broken, and his eyes hit, they released him and ordered a doctor to treat his wounds. That was their way of taking care and being generous.

Another customary SS habit was to kick a Jew with a heavy boot. The Jew was forced to stand at attention while the SS man kicked him until he broke some bones. People who stood near enough to such a victim often heard the breaking of the bones. The pain was so terrible that people having undergone that treatment died in agony.

Apart from the SS men there were other expert hangmen. These were the so-called *Capos*. The *Capos* were German criminals who were also camp inmates. However, although they belonged to "us," they were privileged, having special, better barracks of their own, better food, and almost normal clothes. They were even worse than the SS men. One of them, older than the others and the worst murderer of them all, when he descended on a victim, would not revive him later with water but would choke him to death. Once, this murderer caught a boy of thirteen in the presence of his father and hit his head so that the poor child died instantly. This "camp elder" later boasted in front of his peers, with a smile on his beast's face and with pride, that he managed to kill a Jew with one blow. Gallows stood in each section. For being late for the head count, or similar crimes, the "camp elder" hanged the offenders.

At 12 p.m. there was a break for a meal. Standing in line, we each received half a liter of soup. Usually it was cabbage soup or some other watery liquid, without fats and tasteless. That was lunch. It was eaten in all weather under the open sky, never in the barracks. No spoons were allowed. One had to drink the soup out of the bowl and lick it like a dog. I must emphasize that if we were lucky we got a 12 p.m. meal. There were "days of punishment" when lunch was given together with the evening meal, and it was cold and sour, so that our stomachs were empty for a whole day.

From 1 p.m. until 6 p.m. there was work again. Afternoon work was the same: blows, and blows again. Work was actually unproductive, and its purpose was exhaustion and torture.

At 6 p.m. there was the evening head count. Usually we were left standing at attention for an hour or two, while some prisoners were called up for "punishment parade" — they were those who in the Germans' eyes had transgressed in some way during the day, or had not been punctilious in their performance. They were stripped publicly, laid out on specially constructed benches, and whipped with twenty-five or fifty lashes. The brutal beating and the heartrending cries — all this the prisoners had to watch and hear.[24]

AUSCHWITZ: In contrast to the other camps, of which relatively little is known, a vast body of knowledge exists about Auschwitz, both from the numerous survivor accounts and actual German records. Unlike the other camps — which were set up to kill Jews who were largely Polish, although 135,000 Jews from other European countries were also murdered — Auschwitz was established to exterminate Jews from all areas of Europe under German control — from Norway in the north to the Greek islands off the coast of Turkey in the south, from Great Britain's Channel Islands in the west to the Soviet Union in the east. As such, Auschwitz has become both the symbol of the Holocaust and a representation of the lowest level to which human beings could ever sink.

Auschwitz was located approximately eighteen miles southeast of Katowice, in an area of Poland annexed to Germany. The camp complex was situated at the juncture of a major traffic network, so that it was possible to transport large numbers of people there without difficulty. At the same time, the camp could easily be shielded from the Polish population living in the vicinity. In May 1940, the site, formerly used by the Polish Army as artillery barracks, and by the Polish national tobacco monopoly, received its first prisoners, thirty German criminals who later became dreaded *Capos*. In June, 728 Polish Jews and non-Jews become the first inmates of the camp. The first gassing occurred in September 1941: 900 Soviet prisoners of war were used as a test. Eventually, five gas chambers were built in Auschwitz. In a two and a half year period, April 1942 to November 1944, between one million and 1.5 million Jews lost their lives there.

Auschwitz was a giant military-industrial and extermination complex divided into three major facilities. Auschwitz I held the main German headquarters and some industrial enterprises. One gas chamber and crematorium was located there, and medical experiments were carried out in the notorious Block 10. An infamous wrought iron sign, which still exists today, hung over the front gate, reading *Arbeit Macht Frei*, Work Will Make You Free.

Auschwitz II, known as Birkenau, was the main extermination center, containing four gas chambers and crematoria. Trains drove into Auschwitz-Birkenau, where the Jews disembarked onto the railroad platform, known as the ramp, for selection for forced labor or death. Belongings of the gassed victims were stored in warehouses, nicknamed Canada by the inmates who worked there, and sorted for shipment to Germany. These barracks were full of clothing, shoes, glasses, jewelry, watches, gold and diamond rings, and the finest liquors. Barracks holding more than 100,000 prisoners were located in this section of the camp, which was surrounded by a thirteen-foot-high electrified barbed wire fence, watchtowers, and guards authorized to shoot prisoners on whim.

Auschwitz III, known as Monowitz, contained synthetic rubber plants, coalmines, stone quarries, huge farms, and armament factories, all of which utilized the cheap and almost limitless supply of slave labor. Six thousand SS men staffed the three camp sections.

THE SELECTION: Upon disembarking at the ramp, the prisoners underwent a selection to determine if they would be sent to the gas chambers or used for slave labor or medical experimentation. Families were brutally torn apart forever. In some instances, Jewish workers at the ramp took babies from their mothers, thus saving the women from the gas chambers. Dr. Joseph Mengele usually conducted the selections. Survivors recall him as immaculately dressed and polished, with a hypnotic gaze and an ice-cold demeanor, whistling operatic arias while nonchalantly flicking his finger to the left or right. The Jews of Auschwitz referred to Mengele as the *Malach HaMaves,* the Angel of Death, and he has become the archetype of German evil.

LIFE IN AUSCHWITZ: Prisoners were overcrowded in three-tiered wooden bunks, in barracks that had no heating. Two or three people lay in space for one, sometimes on straw mattresses or on bare boards, without blankets. They were issued threadbare striped uniforms and wooden clogs, which often did not fit their feet. All personal possessions were confiscated, men and women were housed in separate quarters, and all family and communal life came to an end. Disease and epidemics, such as typhus and dysentery, were rampant. Prisoners in the barracks lived in constant fear of negative selections that weeded out the weak for the gas chambers. People who lost their will to live wasted away quickly, and were known as *musselmen,* either winding up in the gas chambers or ending their lives by touching the electrified fence. A constant smell of burned bodies pervaded the camp. When new arrivals entered the barracks, they inquired about the welfare of their relatives, and the veterans told them, "They're up the chimney." At first the incredulous newcomers scoffed at this news, but reality set in after a day or two. In addition, all the horrors described by the Majdanek survivors existed at Auschwitz. As such, it took enormous strength of character to survive Auschwitz, and due to their ability to fall back on their beliefs, religious Jews had a better chance. (This does not mean that all religious Jews displayed such internal fortitude, or that non-religious ones did not; only that observant Jews had an extra factor in their favor that sometimes enabled them to cope better.)

MEDICAL EXPERIMENTS: Barbaric German doctors conducted horrific medical experiments on hapless Jews. Dr. Mengele sterilized thousands of women, and conducted tests of dubious scientific value on twins and dwarfs. Fascinated with eye color, Mengele attempted to turn children's eyes blue by injecting them, most painfully, with ethylene dye; when the experiment did not work, as it never did, the children were gassed. In his laboratory, an entire wall was lined with human eyes, classified by color, from pale yellow to bright violet, pinned like butterflies.[25] To test the effects of altitude on pilots, Jewish inmates were put into high-pressure chambers until their lungs burst; others were frozen to determine the best way to revive frozen German soldiers. Inmates were injected with viruses to test new drugs. In Ravensbruck transplantation experiments, the bones of Polish women were removed from their bodies. Newborn babies were starved to death.[26]

1942: In this worst year of Jewish suffering, nearly three million Jews, fully half the victims of the Holocaust, were murdered. All of the death camps were fully operational, and Jewish populations that had existed in Europe for a thousand years were being uprooted forever. In July, the liquidation of the Jews in the Warsaw Ghetto began. Any Jew who did not have a special employment card, or *Ausweis,* was subject to deportation to Treblinka. An eyewitness recalled:

"I saw a young mother run downstairs into the street to get milk for her baby. Her husband had left for work earlier that morning. She had not bothered to dress, but was in bathrobe and slippers. An empty milk bottle in hand, she was headed for a shop where, she knew, they sold milk under the counter. The executioners demanded her *Ausweis.* 'Upstairs...work certificate. I'll bring it right away.'

" 'We've heard that one before. Have you got an *Ausweis* with you, or haven't you?'

"She was dragged protesting to the wagon, scarcely able to realize what was happening. 'But my baby is alone. Milk...' she protested. 'My *Ausweis* is upstairs.'

"Then, for the first time, she really looked at the men who were holding her and she saw where she was being dragged: to the gaping entrance at the back of a high-boarded wagon with victims already jammed into it. With all her young mother's strength she wrenched herself free, and then two, and four, policemen fell on her, hitting her, smashing her to the ground, picking her up again, and tossing her into the wagon like a sack.

"I can still hear her screaming in a half-crazed voice somewhere between a sob of utter human despair and the howl of an animal."[27]

Chapter 28

SPIRITUAL AND PHYSICAL RESISTANCE

CANARD USED AGAINST THE VICTIMS: A frequent accusation spoken against the Jews is that they went to their deaths like "sheep to the slaughter." The noted Holocaust historian Raul Hilberg even takes it a step further by blaming the Jews' deaths on their lack of resistance.[1] Such cruel finger-pointing is completely false, for numerous reasons.

OVERWHELMING GERMAN POWER: The German *Wehrmacht*, the mightiest fighting force the world had ever seen, trained in military tactics unheard of in the history of warfare at the time (the *Blitzkrieg*), overwhelmed mighty nations in a matter of weeks. If not for several strategic errors in Hitler's decision-making, it seems highly likely that the Axis Powers would have dominated all of Europe, Asia, and Africa, and eventually the world. In 1941 and 1942, at the height of Hitler's power, the Allies gave themselves a paltry 5 percent chance of winning the war.[2]

In addition to military might, the Germans tortured and killed two million Soviet prisoners of war. Despite being of prime fighting age and trained in the art of war, the Soviets did not resist; indeed, there is no record of any Soviet prisoner uprising. How, then, could the Jews, who had no military training, be expected to fight back? Indeed, it is remarkable that there were as many instances of Jewish resistance as happened.

Further, in order for a captive population to resist successfully and fight a guerrilla war, it needs a friendly population in which the fighters can hide, as well as a steady source of supplies. Such was the case with the Vietnamese versus the Americans, the Afghans versus the Russians, and the Palestinians versus the Israelis. The Jews of Europe, especially in Poland, had no such option. No one supplied them, and they were unable to blend into the local population, which, more often than not, handed them over to the Germans. Even partisan groups opposing the Germans often killed Jews attempting to join their ranks, or delivered them to the Nazis.

FEAR OF REPRISALS: The Nazis had virtually absolute power over the Jews, so that resistance was extremely difficult, if not impossible. When resistance was attempted at all, the Nazis retaliated massively, killing hundreds of Jewish hostages. Who would dare take the responsibility of killing a German, even a minor policeman, thereby causing the deaths of many innocent Jews in another community? This German policy of swift and brutal reprisals was not limited to Jews alone. In the most infamous of such instances, in 1942, when Czech partisans assassinated the SS leader Reinhard Heydrich near Prague, the Nazis obliterated the village of Lidice, killing all the men, sending the women to concentration camps, and distributing the children to families inside Germany. The practice of massive retaliation persuaded Jewish leaders to oppose active resistance. Those who resisted the Nazis were sometimes even labeled traitors by their own communities. So cowed were the Jews by German policy that recognition of Nazi plans to exterminate entire Jewish communities was blocked from the collective conscious — often until it was too late. As an example, it was only after realizing that the Germans were planning to annihilate all Warsaw's Jews that Rabbi Menachem Ziemba, the leading rabbinic authority in the Warsaw Ghetto, sanctioned the Warsaw Ghetto Uprising.[3]

GERMAN DECEPTIONS: The Germans employed an elaborate

array of psychological deceptions to lull the Jews into a false sense of security, thereby hiding their ultimate fate. In the ghettoes, the Germans deported thousands of Jews to death camps under the pretext of resettlement for work in the east. Often, before the Jews were killed, they were forced to write postcards home stating that they were doing well in their new location. (There were times, however, that surreptitious messages escaped the German censors. Rabbi David Eisen told of receiving a postcard containing a Polish word that had a thin line through it. The long, single word was innocuous; however, the line split the word into two words that meant "We are being smitten.") Passes were distributed to useful workers and their families, offering their bearers the mistaken belief that they were safe from harm. Upon arrival in the death camps, the deportees were told they were being assigned to labor details. The Treblinka railroad station had ticket counters and false clocks, and the killing areas were camouflaged and well out of sight. Gas chambers were disguised as showers. The deceptions worked, especially on Jews from outside Poland, who had no inkling of what the Germans were planning. Once inside the gas chambers, the Jews realized the Germans' deviousness, but by then it was too late.

FUTILITY OF RESISTANCE: Even for Jews who suspected, or even realized, what the Germans were doing, resistance was generally not an option. Loyalty to parents, children, and other family members who could neither fight nor flee precluded any action. Realizing the hopelessness of their cause, many Jews decided to face death in the comforting presence of family, community, and friends. In addition, the Germans cunningly utilized speed and surprise to disorient the Jews. Roundups, called *aktionen*, were often held in the middle of the night. The Germans suddenly surrounded a Jewish enclave and rushed the Jews into trains with such haste that small children were often left behind in bed. From the trains, the Jews were rushed into camp reception areas, and then into gas chambers. Given such a schedule, there was simply no time to plot a defense.

AN UNPRECEDENTED FOE: Compared to the warlike traditions of the Western world, the Jews had never glamorized violence as a cultural or spiritual ideal. Their poets did not reach great lyrical epiphanies glorifying combat as a noble enterprise. In addition, the Jews' historical experience — living as foreigners with no army of their own to defend them — taught them that resistance to organized oppression was futile. As such, Jews developed an arsenal of strategies to survive in a world dominated by others: petition, protection payment, bribery, ransom, compliance with anti-Jewish measures in the hope of mitigating or even removing them, flight, relief and rescue efforts, salvage, and reconstruction. In the main, these methods were successful for all enemies other than the Nazis. The Egyptians, Babylonians, Romans, Crusaders, Spaniards, and Russians all had no programs for the eradication of the Jewish people. (The biblical Haman was unsuccessful in his plans.) Unprecedented in their history, the Jews were faced with an enemy bent on their total extermination, and who was devoting all possible resources toward its implementation. Indeed, nothing in the Jews' long exile had prepared them for dealing with such an implacable foe. Rabbi M. Ziemba alluded to this when he encouraged the Warsaw Ghetto Uprising:

> We made the cardinal error of considering our enemies as stupid fools and thinking we would be too clever for them... Perhaps we should have realized from the outset that the wicked [foe] really did intend to destroy everything... All we can do now is resist to the best of our abilities — we may not surrender ourselves voluntarily into enemy hands! There are different ways to *kiddush HaShem*. If Jews were now being forced to forsake their religion and they could save their lives by baptizing themselves, as was possible in Spain or during the Crusades, then our death alone would constitute a *kiddush HaShem*... But today the only way to sanctify His Name is armed resistance![4]

PHYSICAL RESISTANCE: Far more Jews than is commonly supposed resisted Nazi persecution. Not only did the Jews resist in the Warsaw Ghetto, but also in more than twenty camps throughout Poland. More than 50,000 Jews escaped into the forests of Poland and Russia, where they either joined partisan groups or fought as well as they could under the circumstances. Revolts broke out in several extermination camps, including Sobibor, Treblinka, and Auschwitz, enabling several hundred prisoners to escape. While the literature on Jewish resistance has been growing steadily, nevertheless all the books, articles, memoirs, and diaries dedicated to acts of resistance do not alter the fact that resistance, no matter how noble or brave, made virtually no difference to the outcome. Even the famed Warsaw Ghetto Uprising killed only fourteen Germans and their collaborators, wounding an additional eighty-five. For all the heroic acts of Jewish resistance, it is doubtful that the Germans and their collaborators lost more than a few hundred men, dead and wounded.[5] All told, the Germans brushed the resistance aside as a minor obstacle, and in the totality of the destruction process it was sadly of no consequence.

THE WARSAW GHETTO UPRISING: This most famous of all Jewish acts of resistance took place over three weeks in April and May 1943. The starving Jews of Warsaw held out against German power longer than did the French Army in 1940. Finally, after using flamethrowers, artillery, and even aircraft, the Germans completely destroyed the Warsaw Ghetto. However, news of the revolt spread through the concentration and labor camps, inspiring many more revolts. The Jews of Warsaw had proved to themselves, and to the entire world, that they could fight as fiercely as any people on earth.

As the Jews battled the Nazis, the Poles in the Aryan section of Warsaw extended no assistance; on the contrary, when the ghetto was going up in flames, the Poles danced and sang, "The Jews are burning!" However, Divine retribution struck them measure for measure: in 1944, encouraged by Soviet forces approaching Warsaw, the Poles attempted an uprising against the Germans. The Soviet Army waited at the outskirts of Warsaw for the Germans to crush the revolt. Only after the Poles were decimated did the Russians enter the capital.

SPIRITUAL RESISTANCE: Far more important than physical resistance, spiritual resistance showed bravery and defiance, although it, too, usually ended in death. Even in the crowded gas chambers, individuals spoke bravely to the group. They always repeated their faith that the Germans would soon be defeated and Judaism would survive. The spiritual resistance, however, had another effect: Nazi officers were amazed by it. They could not understand how people they believed inferior could die with such dignity. Through spiritual resistance, the worst moment in Jewish history actually became one of the greatest times of Jewish pride.[6]

After five decades, research has ripened to the degree that definitions of resistance and courage are no longer routinely linked with counterforce and violence. Holocaust responses seem to be more objectively evaluated by viewing the given circumstances, and judging the realities of the persecuted, rather than by using standards of resistance dictated by the enemy. Thus the fierce refusal to alter chassidic dress, continued use of the *mikvah*, daily services and Torah study, observance of the dietary laws, birth, marriage, and burial practices, Sabbaths and holidays, all conducted illegally, in great danger and with great self-sacrifice, represented major resistance.

The literature on spiritual resistance has been steadily growing:

The first evening of the Warsaw Ghetto Uprising was also the first night of Pesach. One of the fighters, searching for flashlights in a ghetto building, suddenly came upon a family celebrating a Seder:

The room looked as if it had been hit by a hurricane. Bedding was everywhere, chairs lay overturned, the floor was strewn with household objects, and the windowpanes were all gone. Amidst this destruction, the table in the center of the room looked incongruous with glasses filled with wine, with the family seated around, the rabbi reading the Haggadah. Explosions and the rattling of machine guns punctuated his reading; the faces of the family around the table were lit by the red light from the burning buildings nearby... I could not stay long. As I was leaving, the rabbi cordially bade me farewell and wished me success. He was old and broken, he told me, but we, the young people, must not give up, and G-d will help us.[7]

An eyewitness account of the heartrending prayer of a woman who stood on the threshold of the gas chamber in Treblinka:

Like a *chazzan* (cantor) on Yom Kippur, like the leader of a congregation that has been consigned to death, did the woman stand that day in Treblinka, amidst the piercing cries of those who stood poised for imminent annihilation. She turned her face to the wall; behind her stood a multitude of women who similarly turned their faces. With a Yom Kippur melody, and with Yiddish words that flowed from the innermost recesses of her soul, the woman prayed fervently before her Creator:

"Master of the Universe! You are our one and only Father, and we have no heavenly father besides You. Open Your eyes and observe our affliction, see how downtrodden we are, and hearken to the cries of our children and infants. Remove from us all transgression, that we may be worthy like our fathers Abraham, Isaac, and Jacob, and like our mothers Sarah, Rebecca, Rachel, and Leah, of arriving there — together with all our loved ones — O Merciful Father in Heaven!"

An awesome, heartrending cry came from her lips, and from all the women who surrounded her. As she prayed, the women prayed along with her, word for word:

"O Almighty G-d, in behalf of Your Name which is sanctified throughout the world, avenge us. Seek [retribution for] our blood and for the affliction of our children from the hands of our enemies. Let our sacrifice not be in vain. *Shema Yisrael...*[8]

Faigel Eisen was nineteen years old and lived with her family in Czestochowa, Poland. Aryan-looking, and speaking perfect Polish, she was friendly with a *volksdeutsche* (ethnic German) family. Once, while visiting them, she overheard the SS in the next room planning the deportation of the Jews of her town. Her *volksdeutsche* friends begged her to stay and live with them, to pass herself off as an ethnic German. Refusing their offer, she emphatically said, "What will be with the rest of the Jews will be with me," and she voluntarily joined her people in their suffering.[9]

As the German *Einsatzgruppen* were about to execute the Jewish population in a small Ukrainian town, a chassidic Jew walked over to the young German officer in charge and told him that in civilized countries it was customary to grant a last request to those condemned to death. The young German assured the Jew that he would observe that civilized tradition and asked the Jew what his last wish was.

"A short prayer," replied the Jew.

"Granted!" snapped the German.

The Jew placed his hand on his bare head to cover it and recited the following blessing, first in its original Hebrew, and then in its German translation:

"Blessed art Thou, O L-rd our G-d, King of the Universe, who hath not made me a heathen" (*Shelo asani goy*).

Upon completion of the blessing, he looked directly into the eyes of the German, and with his head held high, walked to the edge of the pit, the huge grave filled with bodies, and said: "I have finished. You may begin." The young German's bullet struck him in the back of the head.[10]

Chanukah came to Bergen-Belsen. A wooden clog, the shoe of one of the inmates, became a Menorah; strings pulled from a concentration camp uniform formed the wick; and the black camp shoe polish stood for pure oil.

Not far from the heap of bodies killed that day in the barracks, the living skeletons assembled to participate in the kindling of Chanukah lights.

The rabbi of Bluzhov chanted the first two blessings in his pleasant voice, yet the festive melody was filled with sorrow and pain. When he was about to recite the third blessing, he stopped, turned his head, and looked around as if he were searching for something.

Immediately, he turned his face back, and in a strong, reassuring voice chanted the third blessing: "Blessed art Thou...who has kept us alive, and preserved us, and enabled us to reach this season" (Shehechiyanu).

A non-religious onlooker asked the rabbi:

"How could you say it [the third blessing] when hundreds of Jewish bodies are literally lying within the shadows of the Chanukah lights, when thousands of living Jewish skeletons are walking around in camp, and millions more are being massacred? For this you are thankful to G-d? This you call 'keeping us alive'?"

The rabbi answered: "When I reached the third blessing, I also hesitated and asked myself, what should I do with this blessing? But just as I was turning my head, I noticed that behind me a throng was standing, a large crowd of living Jews, their faces expressing faith, devotion, and concentration, as they were listening to the rite of the kindling of the Chanukah lights. I said to myself, if G-d, blessed be He, has such a nation that at times like these, when during the lighting of the Chanukah lights they see in front of them the heaps of bodies of their beloved fathers, brothers, and sons, and death is looking from every corner, if despite all that, they stand in throngs and with devotion listening to the Chanukah blessing 'Who performed miracles for our fathers in days of old, at this season'; if indeed I was blessed to see such a people with so much faith and fervor, then I am under a special obligation to recite the third blessing."

Some years after liberation, the rabbi of Bluzhov received regards from the Jew who had questioned him. He told the rabbi that the answer he gave that dark Chanukah night in Bergen-Belsen had stayed with him ever since, and was a constant source of inspiration during hard and troubled times.[11]

When asked why his experiences during the war had not embittered him, one survivor said: "I learned about friendship in Auschwitz. When I was cold, strangers shielded me with their bodies from the blowing winds, for they had nothing else to offer but themselves."[12]

In Kovno, the Germans often remarked to the Jews, "Why don't you commit suicide as the Jews of Berlin did?" Rabbi E. Oshry, a survivor of the ghetto, noted that there were only three instances of suicide in Kovno. The rest of the ghetto dwellers trusted and hoped that G-d would not forsake His people.[13]

The rabbi of Bluzhov remarked: "The suffering and the testimonies, when told by Holocaust survivors, are a song, a hymn of praise, a testimony to the eternity of the Jewish people and the greatness of their spirit."[14]

COMMEMORATING RESISTANCE: In the State of Israel, 27 Nisan is commemorated as *Yom HaShoah*, Holocaust Memorial Day, in memory of the Warsaw Ghetto Uprising, which raged on that day. However, many religious Jews find the establishment of such a day to be highly problematic. First, it is not halachically proper to fix a day of mourning during the joyous month of Nisan. (Menachem Begin, later Prime Minister of Israel, proposed Tishah B'Av as the day to commemorate the Holocaust.) Second, the official title of the day, *Yom HaShoah VeHagevurah*, The Day of Holocaust Remembrance and Heroism, implies that physical resistance alone defines heroism. In the words of one critic:

> How can I accept this without denying the dignity of those of the Six Million that had no recourse to arms, and yet had the courage to preserve their Judaism, and their basic humanity, in the presence of their murderers? Are the men of spiritual might less heroic than the men of the daring Molotov cocktail?[15]

A Warsaw Ghetto survivor, Joseph Friedenson, writes:

> We find it somewhat blasphemous when most remembrance gatherings are focused on the Warsaw Ghetto Uprising, or that this uprising is foisted as the central symbol of Jewish martyrdom and heroism during the Holocaust years. While we too certainly honor those who gave their lives in defense of the Jews of the Ghetto, we cannot accept the implied defamation of the honor and dignity of millions of others whose militancy did

not express itself in the handling of a rifle. My late father, Rabbi Eliezer G. Friedenson, who gave away his last morsel of bread to the weeping children of the Ghetto, was no less a hero for not having ever shot a gun.[16]

RIGHTEOUS GENTILES: While the vast majority of non-Jews in Europe did not manifest any concern over the fate of their Jewish fellow citizens, there were, scattered throughout Europe, individuals and even groups who rescued Jews for altruistic reasons and at great risk to themselves. Yad Vashem has honored more than 19,000 people as Righteous Among the Nations, individuals ranging from diplomats, military personnel, and religious officials, to ordinary men and women. Rescuers span many nations and cultures, from the 5,632 Polish honorees to the sixty Muslim Albanians, two Chinese, one Japanese, one Brazilian, and one American.

Rescuers, advancing various reasons to explain their motivation for not following the easy path of noninvolvement, show the greatness of human beings created in the image of G-d:

Religious reasons: "I was only a vessel through which the L-rd's purpose was fulfilled. I know that when I stand before G-d on Judgment Day, I shall not be asked the question posed to Cain — where were you when your brother's blood was crying out to G-d?" (Imre Bathory, Hungary).

Compassion: "I did nothing special, and I don't consider myself a hero. I simply acted on my human obligation to the persecuted and suffering. I want to emphasize that it was not I who saved them. They alone saved themselves. I simply gave them a helping hand... I sought no compensation for what I did, and in a way I am proud that while I was once rich, I am now destitute. To sum up, I should like to reiterate that I did no more than help forty-nine Jews to survive the Holocaust. That's all!" (Wladyslaw Kowalski, Poland).

Recognition of G-d's Chosen People: "First and foremost, I thank G-d for making me what I am and granting me the privilege of helping the Jewish people — G-d's people" (Ludevit Kochol, Czechoslovakia).

A natural thing: "What I did came naturally. It would have been unnatural not to do it" (Herta Muller-Kuhlenthal, Netherlands).

Sanctity of life: "I was scared to death, like everyone else. But I made up my mind right then and there: If I can help, I will... My mother always taught me that G-d made everyone the same; He doesn't care if they're Jews or not, because everyone has the right to live" (Mary Szul, Poland).

Shame: "When the Germans imprisoned the Jews of Vilna behind the walls of the ghetto, I was unable to do my work. I could not sit in my workroom, I could not eat; I was ashamed not to be Jewish. I felt I had to do something" (Ona Simaite, Lithuania).[17]

Although all Righteous Gentiles deserve great respect and appreciation, in one country in particular — Poland — their deeds are all the more praiseworthy. Nowhere else did rescuers face such severe risks. The Germans publicly proclaimed the death penalty for Poles helping Jews, and those caught were executed along with their entire families, sometimes being burned alive in their houses. Frequently, rescuers were denounced to the Germans by their Polish anti-Semitic neighbors — and even by family members. What's more, for the rescuers severe economic conditions made it very difficult to feed and support extra people, and suspicions were aroused when rescuers purchased or stored extra provisions. Therefore, the few thousand rescue stories emanating from Poland exemplify a spiritual boldness hardly conceivable; some are close to legendary. These Polish rescuers epitomize man as a loving and caring person, in his most elevated form. Their deeds serve as behavioral role models for future generations.

DIPLOMATS: A number of diplomats played pivotal roles in rescuing Jews by providing documents that enabled Jews to either leave Europe or attain protection in their native countries. Due to diplomatic immunity, which enabled these diplomats to operate without overt German retaliation, they saved the largest number of Jews of any Righteous Gentiles. This is not to say that the diplomats worked in absolute safety, for they often faced danger to their own and their families' lives, and retribution and disgrace in their own countries. Some of these diplomats are very well known, while others are quite obscure:

RAOUL WALLENBERG: The most famous Righteous Gentile, this Swedish diplomat is credited with saving up to 100,000 Hungarian Jews. In 1944, under pressure from the United States, the Swedish government sent Wallenberg to Hungary to see what could be done to help what remained of Hungarian Jewry. Armed with supreme confidence, virtually unlimited funds, and a businessman's pragmatic willingness to do anything that worked, Wallenberg threw himself into his task.

As such, Wallenberg issued thousands of Swedish safe-passes, which although of dubious authenticity, fooled the Nazis and their Hungarian collaborators. Further, Wallenberg played a key role in establishing a ghetto in Budapest, where, under the protection of various countries, more than 30,000 Jews were concentrated. Moreover, Wallenberg also purchased a number of Swedish safe houses where Jews lived under Swedish protection. When the death marches began, Wallenberg followed the column of Jewish prisoners in his car, distributing hundreds of passes to Jews and taking Jews back to the Swedish houses in Budapest, often facing down angry guards ready to shoot him. Sadly, he was arrested by the invading Soviets in 1945 and never heard from again.

CHIUNE SUGIHARA: In 1939, Sugihara became Japan's first envoy to Lithuania, a country with which Japan had virtually no involvement. Sugihara thus became the Divine instrument in the rescue of 10,000 Jews, among them the entire Mirrer Yeshiva, which found refuge in Shanghai, China, and was the only yeshivah to escape the war intact.

In August 1940, Sugihara saw a large crowd gathering outside his consulate. Moved by their plight, he issued visas that enabled Jews to leave Lithuania by way of Japan. Disregarding orders from his government to cease issuing visas, Sugihara nonetheless continued his noble efforts, even handing out lifesaving documents as his train took him to a new diplomatic posting. Recalling those days many years later, Sugihara told how he had struggled to make a decision:

I really had a difficult time, and for two whole nights was unable to sleep. I eventually decided to issue transit visas on my own authority as consul. I could not allow these people to die, people who had come to me for help with death staring them in the eyes. Whatever punishment might be imposed upon me, I knew I had to follow my conscience.[18]

After the war, the Japanese Foreign Office fired Sugihara for insubordination in the issuance of visas. He was honored by the Mirrer Yeshiva and in 1985 named a Righteous Gentile.

CARL LUTZ: This Swiss diplomat saved up to 45,000 Jews in Budapest, and when Wallenberg arrived, quickly taught him about the efficacy of protective passes and safe houses. Lutz's activities also served as a model for rescue operations conducted by the Spanish, Portuguese, and Vatican embassies. At great risk to himself, he continued saving Jews until the liberation.

FENG SHAN HO: As the head of China's mission in Austria, Ho, stirred to action by the pogroms following Germany's annexation of Austria, helped thousands of Viennese Jews escape the Holocaust. A humble man, Ho never spoke about his rescue activities to his friends or family; they became known only after his death in 1997, when his daughter read brief references to them in her father's diary. After his retirement from diplomatic service, the Taiwanese government falsely accused Ho of misappropriating funds, denied him a pension for his forty years of service, and still has not cleared his name. Ho's daughter remarked: "People often wonder why a person from China would be so concerned with the fate of Jews from Austria. If you knew my father, you wouldn't have to ask." A line in Ho's memoirs states: "I thought it only natural to feel compassion for the persecuted Jews and to want to help. From the standpoint of humanity, isn't that the way it should be?"[19]

RIGHTEOUS INDIVIDUALS: The best-known non-diplomatic Righteous Gentile was the famous German, Oskar Schindler, whose efforts in saving 1,200 Polish Jews became immortalized in the book and film *Schindler's List*. However, there are many lesser-known individuals who saved Jews in many fascinating ways:

Anton Schmid was one of the very few German military personnel actively engaged in saving Jews. A sergeant in the *Wehrmacht*, stationed in Vilna, Schmid, in charge of 300 Jewish laborers, quickly gained their affection and confidence. Shocked by the mass killings, Schmid decided in late 1941 to do whatever he could to help Jews survive. Managing to release imprisoned Jews, he surreptitiously supplied food and provisions to Jews inside the Vilna Ghetto. During Nazi raids on the ghetto, Schmid hid Jews in the cellars of three houses under his supervision. Schmid also became personally involved with leading figures of the Jewish underground in Vilna, cooperating with them, allowing them to sleep and plan activities in his home. As part of the Divine plan, Schmid was able to travel freely in the course of his military responsibilities, which included collecting straggling German soldiers and reassigning them to new units. Therefore, he was able to drive disguised Jews to other ghettoes, such as Warsaw, to warn Jews of Nazi atrocities. Schmid also sent Jews to other ghettoes that were safer than Vilna. Tragically, Schmid was arrested in 1942, court-martialed, and executed.[20]

Eberhard Helmrich, a major in the German Army, was the commander of a large farm in Poland. Employing nearly 200 Jews from the Drohobycz Ghetto, he saved many of them from arrests and the periodic roundups. On several occasions, Helmrich hid Jews in his home, obtaining the release of others by claiming they were needed for the farm's proper functioning.

When he learned that all the Jews in the region were to be liquidated, Helmrich was horrified. He and his wife conceived an original idea: providing false credentials to Jewish girls to pose as Poles or Ukrainians and attain work in Germany. In Berlin, Helmrich's wife found jobs for these girls, making sure there were no Poles or Ukrainians in the houses in which they were employed. Altogether, the Helmrichs saved more than a dozen girls. After the war, they were asked about their motivations:

> We were fully aware of the risks, but we decided that it would be better for our children to have dead parents than cowardly parents. From then on, it was comparatively easy. We figured that once we saved two people we'd be even with Hitler if we were caught, and every person beyond that would put us one ahead.[21]

In September 1940 ten-year-old Bruno Berl roamed the streets of Warsaw for three days without food and shelter. Unable to control his hunger any longer, he stopped the first person who came his way and asked for food. That person was Wladyslaw Kowalski, who took the boy home, fed him, and provided him with a new identity and a home with friends. This initial altruistic deed generated a desire to do more, spurring Kowalski to additional acts of rescue. As the representative of a company with which Germany had business dealings, Kowalski had freedom of movement in all parts of Warsaw, including the ghetto.

In 1943, exploiting his freedom of movement, Kowalski bribed the ghetto's Polish guards and smuggled seven Jews to safe havens on the Aryan side. Kowalski followed that with a family of four, then offered refuge to twelve Jews in his Warsaw home, constructing an underground shelter for them. In 1944, he hid for 105 days, along with forty-nine Jews, in the basement of a razed building that he converted into a large bunker. Refusing to abandon the Jews, who begged him to leave for his own safety, Kowalski replied, "Either we'll all survive or none of us will."[22] He stayed with the Jews until the Russians liberated them in January 1945.

Upon hearing reports of deportation of Jews in Greece, Archbishop Damaskinos, a prelate of the Greek Orthodox

Church, personally delivered to the Germans a petition stating that the church condemns all forms of racial and religious discrimination. He then ordered all the priests and monks under his authority to open their churches and convents to Jews seeking shelter, adding that under no circumstances were they to exploit the situation as an opportunity for proselytizing. He issued fake baptismal certificates for the Jews, and together with the Greek chief of police in Athens, provided hundreds of Jews with new identities and saved them from extermination. When the Germans demanded his resignation, Damaskinos replied: "Members of the Greek clergy never resign. They remain in the position G-d has appointed for them even if they are in danger of being put to death." The Germans, however, did not harm him.[23]

General Vilmos Nagy Nagybaczoni, the Hungarian Minister of Defense, saved Jews who were forced to join the Hungarian Army, where they were put in labor battalions and became the target of much anti-Semitic abuse. A simple soldier with traditional views of justice and decency, Nagybaczoni alleviated the plight of the Jewish labor battalions. First, he demanded that the disgraceful conditions within the Jewish labor battalions be immediately improved, and the men returned home along with other units of the army. Torture, beating, and expropriation of property were to be ended, and the Jews were to have food, clothing, and leaves like regular soldiers. At one stroke the worst phases of involuntary servitude for Jewish males ended.[24]

ZEGOTA: At the height of the deportations of Jews from Warsaw in 1942, a number of underground Polish political parties formed a clandestine organization to help Jews escape the Nazis. Stirred by humanitarian and religious convictions, as well as by patriotic zeal to save the honor of the Polish nation, *Zegota* endeavored to rescue as many Jews as possible, given the limited resources at its disposal. Supported by the Polish government-in-exile in London, with funds from Jewish organizations in the United States, *Zegota* created departments to deal with children hiding in private homes or institutions, medical assistance, false certificates, and payoff money for blackmailers. Throughout its two years, *Zegota* rendered assistance to some 2,000 Jews — at a time when the Nazis were consuming hundreds of thousands monthly. Although the activities of *Zegota* fell far short of the needs of the day, all eyewitnesses laud the zeal and dedication of its members.

In all, it is estimated that Righteous Gentiles saved between 15,000 and 25,000 Jews. However, since by their very nature all these acts were hidden, no one will ever know exactly how many were saved.[25]

Chapter 29

THE FATE OF JEWS IN VARIOUS COUNTRIES

The chances of survival for Jews in Nazi Europe depended on the level of control the Germans had in a particular country, and on the level of the native populace's anti-Semitism. In countries under direct German rule, and with high levels of Jew-hatred, such as Poland, the percentage of Jews murdered was much higher than in such countries as Italy and Denmark, where the Germans did not have either absolute power or the cooperation of the local populace.

POLAND: More than 90 percent of Poland's 3.5 million Jews perished in the Holocaust, accounting for more than half of the total victims. German rule over Poland was absolute; there being no Polish satellite government or political collaborators, the Nazis could do as they pleased. Public opinion was apathetic, even supportive of the Final Solution, and the remote locations of the death camps shielded them from world opinion. Therefore, it was hardly coincidental that most of the ghettoes and all the death camps were built in Poland.

Although the Poles did not directly assist the Germans in large-scale killing of Jews, the Poles also killed many Jews without German prompting, most notably in the town of Jedwabne, where in July 1941 the local Poles murdered the town's 1,600 Jews. In addition, Poles frequently delivered to the Nazis those

Jews who had escaped ghettoes and concentration camps. For their part, the Polish underground offered scant assistance to Jewish resistance groups, in some instances even killing the Jews as well. Indeed, many Poles felt that the Germans were providing an unpleasant but necessary solution to their intractable Jewish problem.

For many Poles the fate of the Jews also proved economically profitable. While the Germans took the majority of factories, warehouses, luxury residences, furniture, and clothing, the Poles seized the leftovers. Throughout Poland, ownerless stores, merchandise, workshops, raw materials, land, and houses quickly found new owners. The Poles regarded the new economic situation as a fait accompli. In the words of a Polish underground official: "The non-Jewish population has filled the places of the Jews in the towns and cities; in a large part of Poland this is a fundamental change, final in character. The return of masses of Jews would be experienced by the population not as restitution but as an invasion against which they would defend themselves, even with physical means."[1] Sadly, this was exactly the case after the war, when Jews returning to Poland to reclaim their homes were driven away and even killed.

Roughly 350,000 Polish Jews survived the Holocaust. Of this number, approximately 250,000 Jews lived in the portion of Poland annexed by the Soviet Union, and were deported to Siberia or fled into Soviet territory ahead of the German advance into Russia. After the war, these Jews were able to make their way back to Poland. The other 100,000 survivors were the remnants of the ghettoes, concentration and labor camps, and death marches. In addition, many Jewish parents gave their children to Polish Catholic families for hiding during the war. Some of these children were reunited with their parents or returned to Jewish relatives after the war, but the vast majority were assimilated into the Polish nation and lost to the Jewish people.

Although the Polish people suffered heavily under the Nazis — the Germans killed two million Poles — the Poles still bear a certain level of culpability for the fate of the Jews. In commenting on why the firstborn of Egyptian prisoners perished along with the rest of the Egyptian firstborn in the tenth plague, Rashi (Exodus 12:29) remarks that they derived enjoyment from the plight of the Jewish slaves. To this day, Poland is awash in plundered Jewish property.

THE SOVIET UNION AND THE BALTIC NATIONS: More than 1.5 million Jews were murdered in the Russian, Belorussian, and Ukrainian republics of the Soviet Union and in the annexed Baltic republics of Latvia, Lithuania, and Estonia. These Jews generally were not deported to death camps, but were executed by the *Einsatzgruppen*. Here, with anti-Semitism virulent, both for traditional religious reasons and because the Jews were associated with hated Communism, the Germans had the full cooperation of the populace in hunting down Jews. Often, the Germans themselves were shocked at the savagery of the native population toward the Jews. In particular, Ukrainians voluntarily joined the Nazi SS, becoming concentration camp guards who violently herded Jews into gas chambers, committing unspeakable atrocities along the way. In some camps, it was the Ukrainians who ran the engines that pumped the gas into the chambers. In the areas of the Soviet Union conquered by the Germans, three of every four Jews perished.

ROMANIA: Next to Germany, no other country was involved in massacres of Jews on such a massive scale as Romania. The Romanians eagerly cooperated with the *Einsatzgruppen* in the Soviet Union, massacring 26,000 Jews in Odessa alone, and hundreds of thousands altogether. Romanian soldiers also helped the Germans annihilate the Jews of Bessarabia, Bukovina, Moldavia, and Transnistria, all Romanian provinces that were ceded to the Soviet Union and then reclaimed by Romania. In many cases, the Romanians packed Jews into trains and shunted them around with no destination, until all the occupants suffocated or starved to death. Jews were stripped of their clothing and forced to march in freezing weather. The Romanians instigated savage pogroms — in the capital of Bucharest 170 Jews were killed and impaled on slaughterhouse hooks bearing the caption Kosher Meat. At times, the Romanians' horrific butchery had to be restrained by the Germans, who preferred a disciplined approach to killing Jews, rather than the Romanians' unrestrained enthusiasm.

As the war drew on, and German defeat became more apparent, Romanian policy underwent an abrupt change. Fearing possible Allied reprisals after the war, Romania refused to deport the 300,000 Jews of Old Romania, who largely resided in Bucharest. Being an ally of Germany from the outset of the war, and never occupied by Nazi troops, Romania was able to defy the Germans. These Jews survived the war. (The Jews of the Romanian province of Northern Transylvania were deported to Auschwitz in 1944; they were under Hungarian control, and are listed with the Jews of Hungary.)

GERMANY: Although it was the ideological center and primary perpetrator of the Final Solution, Germany was not the major site of the horrors associated with the Holocaust. Perhaps the Nazis were concerned about the effect on German public opinion of visible, large-scale massacres of Jews in their own country.

Most German Jews succeeded in emigrating before the war broke out. Of those that remained, 160,000 were sent to the ghettoes of Eastern Europe, where they met the fate of the Jews in the east. Many German Jews were sent to the show camp Theresienstadt in Czechoslovakia and perished when the inmates of the camp were transported to Auschwitz. Several thousand German Jews survived the transports, camps, and death marches, while others survived as slave laborers in German factories. Some Jews even survived the war unharmed in Germany, while others went underground, hidden by sympathetic non-Jews. Remarkably, 800 German Jews survived the war as patients in the Jewish hospital of Berlin.[2] It appears that at times the Nazis showed lenience toward their own Jews, a trait that was woefully absent in their treatment of alien, foreign Jews. This phenomenon also manifested itself in several countries' treatment of their own Jews, for example in Romania.

Nevertheless, the German people knew about and acquiesced in the genocide. There were 900,000 Germans in the SS alone, plus another 1.2 million involved in the railways. Indeed, most Germans knew the significance of the huge, crowded trains rattling through the darkness. As one recorded remark suggests: "Those...Jews, they won't even let one sleep at night!"[3] Hitler may have been evil incarnate, but the German people gave him unconditional support up to the very end.

Although it cannot be determined with certainty, estimates are that up to 250,000 people were directly involved in the crimes of the Holocaust.[4] This number includes not only the actual killers of Jews, but also the more numerous desk murderers, those who administered the destruction process from their desks and issued and carried out orders – routing trains, supplying materials, and so on. Indeed, Germany's efficient bureaucracy enthusiastically cooperated in implementing the Final Solution; from Hitler to Himmler, Heydrich, Mueller, and Eichmann, a great number of German and other nations' officials followed through on the instructions. To annihilate six million Jews in five years, it was necessary to have the full cooperation of scientists, judges, soldiers, reporters, financiers, clergy, educators, physicians, diplomats, and many others.

AUSTRIA: In some ways, the Austrians were worse than the Germans, playing a role in the Holocaust out of all proportion to their numbers. Hitler and Eichmann were both Austrian, as were the commanders of four of the six main death camps. They provided one-third of the personnel of the SS extermination units, despite constituting only 8 percent of the population of the Third Reich. All told, Austrians killed almost half the Jewish victims of the Holocaust.[5]

If such a thing is possible, the Austrians were more passionately anti-Semitic than the Germans, as evidenced by their behavior in Vienna during the *Anschluss* and *Krystallnacht*. Fortunately, most Austrian Jews managed to leave before the onset of hostilities; those who stayed suffered the fate of the German Jews. More than 200,000 German and Austrian Jews were killed in the Holocaust.

FRANCE: After being defeated by the Germans in 1940, France was divided into a German-occupied area in the north, including Paris, and the Vichy regime in the south, which although not actually occupied by the Germans, was under their political control. In 1942, the Germans occupied the whole of France.

France had a prewar heritage of vicious anti-Semitism, stretching over centuries, and exacerbated by the smoldering resentment left after the Dreyfus Affair. In October 1940, without any pressure from the Germans, the Vichy government enacted onerous decrees against Jews. As such, both the Vichy regime and the civilian government of occupied France actively cooperated in the Final Solution. French police were even more enthusiastic than the Germans in rounding up Jews for deportation. In Paris, on July 16, 1942, the French police ruthlessly packed 6,000 Jewish children ranging in age from three to seventeen into trains without food or adult escort and deported them to Auschwitz. All of these children were gassed. Approximately 90,000 of France's prewar Jewish population of 300,000 perished in the Holocaust, the overwhelming majority of whom were immigrants and refugees. Native French Jews were, for the most part, mercifully left alone.

Despite the nation's ugly past, during the Holocaust there was much greater sympathy for the Jews among the general French population than in Eastern Europe. Many Frenchmen risked their lives to hide Jews, most notably in the village of Le Chambon, which amazingly hid 5,000 Jews from the Germans. Jews were generally accepted into the French Resistance, unlike in Poland or Ukraine.

The evidence, however, clearly shows that the Germans never could have carried out their murderous designs if they had not received the active support of the French administration and public services — especially police and railroad officials, who rounded up Jews and made certain that the trains left promptly for their eastern destinations. Here, France's actions are particularly telling, because they involved a great and civilized nation in active complicity with unmitigated evil.

THE NETHERLANDS: The SS had complete control of the country; in fact, the Nazi ruler of Holland, Austrian SS officer Seyss-Inquart, was hanged at Nuremberg. Despite the lack of cooperation, and even against the opposition of a significant portion of the Dutch population (a 1941 general strike in Amsterdam in support of the Jews was ruthlessly crushed), the Germans, aided by local Dutch Nazis, deported more than 100,000 of Holland's 140,000 Jews via Westerbork transit camp to the killing centers in the east. Sadly, the German-appointed Jewish Council in Amsterdam cooperated with the Germans in deporting Jews. Significantly, though, after Poland the Netherlands has the largest contingent of Righteous Gentiles — close to 4,500 — remarkably large for a small country with a medium-sized Jewish population.

CZECHOSLOVAKIA: In 1938, Germany annexed the Czech region of the country, including the capital, Prague, and gave Slovakia its independence — but as a German satellite. All told, the Germans killed six out of every seven Czech Jews, close to 80,000 people, without significant help from the Czech populace.

Prior to the liquidation of the communities, the Germans enlisted the Jews in gathering religious artifacts and art treasures from Czech synagogues, storing them in Prague warehouses. The Nazis intended to display these collections after the war in a special museum in Prague's Jewish Quarter dedicated to the Extinct Jewish Race. This collection survived the war intact — as did the Jewish Quarter of Prague, including the thirteenth-century Altneushul — and it is the largest repository of Judaica in the world, a silent witness to the horrors perpetrated upon the Czech Jewish community.

In Slovakia, the government, controlled by Catholic priests

and led by the notorious anti-Semite Father Tiso, did not wait for the Germans to take the Jews — the Slovakians offered the Jews to the Germans, even agreeing to pay 500 *reichsmarks* for every deported Jew. In 1942, the Slovakians deported close to 60,000 Jews to Poland without German assistance. However, when the deportations were at their peak, they suddenly stopped. This change was due to the successful efforts of a rescue organization headed by Rabbi Michael Ber Weissmandl and Gisi Fleischmann, an Orthodox woman, which bribed SS officials to halt the deportations. For nearly two years, Slovakian Jews were not transferred out of the country; however, after an unsuccessful Slovak partisan uprising against the Germans, the deportations resumed. Of the prewar Slovak population of more than 135,000 Jews, only 25,000 survived. (The areas of Slovakia occupied by Hungary are listed with the Jews of that nation.)

GREECE: More than 50,000 of Greece's 70,000 Jews lived in the city of Salonika. These Sephardic Jews settled there after the Spanish Expulsion in 1492, transforming the city into a prominent center of both Jewish learning and commerce. Jewish stevedores ran the docks, and for many years ships did not unload their cargoes on the Sabbath. With the aid of sympathetic Greeks, many Jews throughout Greece were able to escape detection. In Salonika, however, nearly 50,000 Jews, close to 97 percent of the prewar total, lost their lives, mainly in Auschwitz. Several factors accounted for this destruction. First, the chief rabbi of Salonika, Rabbi Koretz, was duped by the Germans into lulling the Jews into a false sense of security. Second, the Greek population resented the economic success of the Jews, who accounted for one-third of the city's inhabitants, and so were not inclined to offer any assistance to the Jews. Third, the Germans acted rapidly in 1943 when they forced the Jews to move into the ghetto — then deporting them within a month.

HUNGARY: After World War I, the treaty of Trianon deprived Hungary of two-thirds of its former territory and three-fifths of its population. As a result, the overriding objective of Hungarian foreign policy was restoration of the lands lost by the Trianon treaty. To help achieve its ends, early on Hungary allied itself with Nazi Germany. From 1938 to 1940, with German acquiescence, Hungary recovered lost territories from Czechoslovakia, Romania, and Yugoslavia, nearly doubling its prewar population of more than 400,000 Jews. Unlike the native Hungarian Jews, who were largely assimilated, the Jews of the annexed territories were very religious, many following the great chassidic traditions of Satmar, Munkatch, and Vizhnitz.

Although Hungary was a very anti-Semitic country, having restricted the number of Jews in universities in 1920, paradoxically as late as 1944 Hungary remained a haven for Jews, even as they were being systematically exterminated elsewhere, especially in adjacent Poland. However, there was a great deal of Jewish suffering in Hungary before that date. Jewish males were conscripted into Hungarian Army labor battalions, known as *Munkatabor*, and subjected to the most horrific conditions and torture. In 1942, the Righteous Gentile General Nagybaczoni ordered that abuses of the Jewish laborers end, and that they be afforded all the privileges of ordinary soldiers. However, of the 50,000 Hungarian Jewish soldiers who accompanied the Hungarian Army in its invasion of the Soviet Union, more than 40,000 did not return home.

In 1941, Hungary deported more than 10,000 Jews it claimed did not have Hungarian citizenship to Ukraine, where the Germans massacred them. In 1942, Hungarian soldiers killed hundreds of Jews in the Yugoslavian town of Novi Sad, driving them onto the frozen Danube River, then shelling the ice until it broke and the Jews drowned.

With the German occupation of Hungary in March 1944, conditions for the Jews changed drastically. In a six-week period, May to July, Hungary turned into an assembly-line hell where nearly 450,000 Jews were deported and liquidated in Auschwitz. Virtually overnight, the country that had so successfully protected its Jews from the Nazi death camps became the country that cooperated the most of any nation in Europe in deporting its Jews. Even the SS was surprised at the alacrity with which the Hungarian government arranged the deportations, and they remarked that in no other part of occupied Europe had they received such cooperation.[6]

The deportation and subsequent murder of the Hungarian Jews is one of the best-known aspects of the Holocaust. Extensively documented, there is much testimony of survivors. Sadly, the Holocaust of the Hungarian Jews is unique and tragic for several reasons:

First, it began late in the war, when both the Germans and the world knew that the defeat of the Nazis was a matter of time. Indeed, the beginning of the end, the D-Day invasion of Normandy, took place during the height of the Hungarian Jews' gassing. In fact, Hitler was so zealous in killing Jews that he ordered much-needed trains be used for transporting Jews to Auschwitz rather than for the defensive needs of the German army. This foolhardy decision caused Germany to lose the war more quickly.

Second, unlike the previous killings in Poland and the Soviet Union, which were carried out in relative secrecy and isolation, the deportation of Hungarian Jews took place openly before the entire world.

Third, by 1944, the world knew what was taking place in Auschwitz. Many Hungarian Jews had also heard of it, although many also refused to believe that it could happen with the complicity of Hungary, a country to which they felt great loyalty and attachment.

Fourth, the Hungarian Final Solution was carried out with the greatest speed of all the Jewish killings in the Holocaust — 12,000 Jews were deported daily with the least manpower. German participation was miniscule — Eichmann's staff in Hungary consisted of only forty-eight SS men, who were aided by 20,000 Hungarian soldiers.[7] At the Nuremberg trial, one of the Germans remarked that if the Hungarians had refused to cooperate, the German goals would have been impossible to achieve.

In Hungary, and elsewhere, it is clear that if the world had really cared about the fate of Europe's Jews, all the Hungarian Jews could have been saved. Unlike Nazi-occupied Poland, the Hungarian government still functioned throughout the German occupation, and there were numerous foreign diplomats stationed in the country. In addition, Hungarian government and military officials were terrified about possible postwar reprisals, and would have been amenable to pressure from the outside world to prevent the deportations. Even more tragically, Jewish leadership in Budapest was fully aware of the final destination of the transports, but did not notify the Hungarian Jews. In the words of historian Cecil B. Eby:

> The Budapest *Judenrat*, for example, had been informed by escaped messengers that Auschwitz was an extermination camp, but they kept this information to themselves. Their policy seems to have been to turn the other way while 'unassimilated Jews' were thrown to the wolves, on the assumption that urban Jews might thus be spared. This attitude is evidenced by a letter from the council to the minister of interior, written on May 3, seeking a meeting to discuss the deportations: 'We emphatically declare that we do not seek this audience to lodge complaints about the merit of the measure adopted [the Auschwitz shipments] but merely ask that they be carried out in a humane spirit."[8]

In other words, in order to save Hungary's secularized Jewish elite, the Orthodox, chassidic Jews were expendable. This attitude manifested itself in other situations as well — Eichmann allowed Rudolf Kasztner, one of Budapest's secular Zionist leaders, to fill a train bound for freedom in Switzerland with more than 1,000 Jews of his choice. Kasztner packed the train with his relatives and friends, although the famed rebbe of Satmar was also put aboard. The Kasztner train was the only contingent of Hungarian Jews freed by the Nazis. In another instance, more than 20,000 Jews were placed in a camp guarded by only twenty soldiers, while three miles from the camp lay the Romanian border and freedom. Despite being aware of this fact, Kasztner did not tell the inmates to take the simple step of charging the gates. Although some Jews would undoubtedly have been shot, the vast majority would have reached free Romania.

Along the same lines, the Budapest *Judenrat* could have informed the hundreds of thousands of Hungarian Jews not to cooperate with the authorities. Indeed, much of the responsibility for the deaths of Hungary's Jews rests with the Budapest Jewish Council, in the words of one historian "the most spineless, the most servile, and with that of Vienna and Germany the most contemptible in all of Europe."[9]

Eichmann divided Hungary into six zones, first deporting the Jews in the newly annexed provinces, correctly feeling this course of action would be the most tolerated by the Hungarian people, who regarded these Jews as alien. Zone Six was Budapest and its 250,000 Jews, who largely survived with the help of Righteous Gentiles Raoul Wallenberg and Carl Lutz, who protected the Jews until the Germans left Budapest in early 1945.

The ordeal of the 1,200 Jews of Bonyhad, a small town in southern Hungary, is typical of the experience of the Hungarian Jews. Two weeks after the German occupation, Jewish stores had to display the yellow star. Jews were not permitted to leave their homes from 6 p.m. to 7 a.m., and were not allowed to leave Bonyhad at any time. All radios, cameras, and telephones had to be given to village officials. On April 5, all Jews were forced to wear a yellow star.

Soon, other anti-Jewish restrictions followed. Non-Jews were forbidden to work in Jewish households, and Jews were dismissed from many jobs. The local Jewish community council had to draw up a detailed list of all Jews in town, including family members and addresses. In May, Bonyhad's Jews were separated in a ghetto, and in July they were transferred to the regional ghetto in Pecs, where 6,000 Jews lived in horrendous conditions. On July 6, 1944, the Jews of Bonyhad were packed eighty-strong into boxcars containing a pile of carrots and cabbage and two buckets, one for drinking water and one for waste. Three days later, on July 9, the Jews arrived at Auschwitz, where all but seventy perished in the Holocaust.[10]

Nevertheless, because the Holocaust began relatively late in Hungary, more of its Jews survived than did those of any country under German control. A large percentage of survivors of Auschwitz and other camps came from Hungary and its annexed regions. However, the 450,000 Hungarian Jewish deaths are all the more tragic because they were so easily preventable.

DENMARK: This country is justly famed as a nation of Righteous Gentiles, it being the only nation to defy the Germans completely and save virtually all its Jews. So unified was the effort that the Danish Underground requested of Yad Vashem that all its members who participated in the rescue of the Jewish community not be listed individually, but as one group. Denmark was able to save its Jews because of several favorable factors:

First, of all the nations occupied by the Germans, Denmark was subject to the least direct Nazi control, and its government continued to function even after the German takeover. Hitler viewed the Nordic Danes as fellow Aryans; consequently, the Nazis were less brutal in their occupation of Denmark than in other countries.

Second, Denmark had a tradition of tolerance, and most Danes were not anti-Semitic. The government's attitude toward Jews was reflected in the population as a whole. When the Danish chief of police, Thune Jacobsen, had a meeting with Himmler, the latter raised the subject of the so-called Jewish problem. Jacobsen replied, "The Danish population does not consider this topic a problem." In 1941, a man was caught attempting to burn down the Copenhagen synagogue and was sentenced by a Danish court to three years imprisonment, the only instance in Nazi-occupied Europe of someone being punished for a crime committed against Jews.

In terms of Danish support for Jews, there have been many stories about Denmark and the yellow Star of David. According to one story, when the Germans demanded that the Jews wear the star, the entire Danish population wore it. Another version has the Danish King Christian X putting it on first, while a variation states that the king threatened to put it on first if the Germans required Jews to wear it. None of these stories are true, for the Nazis never introduced the yellow star to Denmark, but they do shed light on the character of the Danish people and their king.[11]

Third, the Danish Jewish community was very small, numbering fewer than 8,000, making their rescue relatively easy. In addition, Denmark was close to neutral Sweden, which offered a safe haven to the Jews.

In 1943, the Germans decided to arrest Denmark's Jews during the holiday of Rosh HaShanah. Three days before the planned action, a German anti-Nazi businessman, Georg Duckwitz, heard of the plot and revealed it to a Danish politician. Acting with great speed, thousands of Danes hid their Jewish countrymen in all sorts of places, among them hospitals, warehouses, stables, barns, hotels, cellars, and church lofts. When the Nazis organized house-to-house searches of Jewish residences in Copenhagen, where nearly all Denmark's Jews lived, they met with dismal failure.

The immediate goal in the escape effort was to get the Jews across the narrow strait separating Denmark and Sweden. A countrywide rescue effort was set up, with many Danes spending sizable sums of money and risking their lives to sneak the Jews to Sweden in fishing boats. That this operation was successful, with virtually no Jews being betrayed to the Nazis, is a testament to the greatness of the Danish nation.

However, not all of Denmark's Jews escaped. The Germans captured some 500, who received no warning or chose to ignore it. Some were too weak to flee, while others were betrayed by Danish Nazis. Nevertheless, even though the Germans took their victims out of Denmark, their fate was better than that of other Jews. They were taken to Theresienstadt, where the Danish government constantly inquired after their welfare and sent them food packages. From there, the Danish Jews were not transported to extermination camps. As a result, but fifty-one Danish

Jews lost their lives, meaning a Danish survival rate of more than 99 percent.

In addition, during the Jews' absence the Danish people took care of their homes and apartments. When the Jews returned from Sweden in 1945, some had to find new housing, for their homes had been taken over by people who would not leave. Most Jews, however, found their belongings intact. Many homes and apartments had been cleaned and painted, and neighbors greeted the returning Jews with fresh flowers and smiles of welcome. Clearly, Denmark is a shining example of how a little bit of light dispels much darkness.

BULGARIA: Unique in Nazi Europe, Bulgaria's Jewish population actually increased during the war years. Bulgaria epitomized a policy employed by some nations allied with Germany — deporting Jews in newly annexed territories while protecting its native Jewish citizens. Anti-Semitism in Bulgaria was at a relatively low level, and its Sephardic Jewish population felt perfectly at home there.

In 1941, Bulgaria annexed territories in Yugoslavia and Greece. The Bulgarian authorities viewed the 12,000 Jews living in these regions as alien and refused to give them Bulgarian citizenship. To Bulgaria's eternal shame, Bulgarian soldiers, officers, and policemen rounded up these Jews and deported them with the greatest cruelty. Almost all the deportees were gassed in Treblinka. No voice of protest came from any quarter in Bulgaria.

However, when it came to Bulgaria's native Jewish population, matters were different. The Germans worked out an agreement with Bulgarian government officials to deport all the Jews of Bulgaria to the death camps, and trains were readied to transport the Jews out of the country.

However, the plot was thwarted when the secretary of the Bulgarian deportation planner revealed the secret to a Jewish friend. With utmost speed, Jewish community leaders mobilized sympathetic government leaders and church officials, who convinced King Boris to cancel the planned deportations.[12] The same secretary apprised her friend of further efforts to hand over Bulgaria's Jews to the Germans; these were also thwarted through the good offices of Queen Giovanna and the head of the Bulgarian Orthodox Church, Metropolitan Stefan, both of whom abhorred the idea of deporting the nation's Jews.[13] Although Bulgarian Jews had to perform forced labor within the country, they were not mistreated. In 1948, virtually all Bulgaria's Jews settled in Israel.

ITALY: Despite being a major ally of Nazi Germany, Italy did not persecute its 2,000-year-old Jewish community. Although official discriminatory laws were established, anti-Semitism in Italy was at a lower level than in any of the Western democracies.[14] In fact, the Italian army protected the Jews of the regions it conquered in France, Yugoslavia, and Greece, thwarting all German efforts to harm them.

The situation changed drastically after the 1943 German takeover of Italy. With minimal help from the Italians, the SS rounded up several thousand Jews, including more than 1,000 Jews from Rome, whom they shipped to Auschwitz. Only seventeen of the Roman Jews returned.[15] Kind Italians hid thousands of Jews in churches, monasteries, and private homes. As a result, more than 40,000 of the 50,000 prewar Jewish population survived.

ALBANIA: The remarkable story of the rescue of Albanian Jewry is one of the Holocaust's least-known. Since no Jewish community was too insignificant for the Germans, Albania's 200 Jews were marked for destruction at the Wannsee Conference. Together with several hundred refugees who arrived during the war, by the time of planned German deportations, Albania held 600 Jews. At risk to their own lives, Albanian Muslims took Jews into their homes, hiding others in mountain villages. Jews changed their names to Muslim ones and officially lived as Muslims until the war's end, when they returned to their homes and regular lives.[16] This is the only case of an entire Jewish population, albeit tiny, being hidden *within* its native land. (The Germans did find five Jews, which is hardly insignificant, for the loss of a single Jewish life is like the loss of an entire world.)[17]

THE CHANNEL ISLANDS: Unknown to most people, the Germans did occupy some British territory during World War II — the islands of Guernsey, Jersey, Sark, and Alderney, known as the Channel Islands, located closer to France than to England. While the British have constantly maintained that they were different than the rest of Europe, and would never have cooperated in a German occupation of their homeland, the Channel Islands do not fit this story. Instead, the islanders compromised, collaborated, and fraternized with the Germans, just as people did throughout occupied Europe. Indeed, this is such a sensitive matter that records documenting this sorry chapter in British history were originally ordered to be closed for 100 years; some were destroyed.[18] As in Albania, the smallest number of Jews was not insignificant to the Nazis. There were seventeen Jews on the islands, who with typical German thoroughness had to be included in the campaign to rid the world of every Jew.

When the order came to register Jews, instead of simply denying that there were any Jews on the islands, British officials cooperated. Ambrose Sherwill registered five Jews on Guernsey, while Clifford Orange identified twelve on Jersey. Discriminatory laws soon followed. Jewish businesses had to display the label Jewish Undertaking, and Jews had their identity cards stamped with a J. Shortly afterward, Jews were not allowed to enter public places, and all Jewish businesses were confiscated without compensation. A nightly curfew was imposed, and Jews were restricted to shopping one hour a day. Overall, it is remarkable how the legalistic Germans went to such pains to implement their racial laws for a handful of Jews.

There are no files on what happened to the Jews, as all records were hidden or destroyed. However, the fate of two Jewish women, Therese Steiner and Marianne Grunfeld, is known: they were deported to France, and from there to Auschwitz, where both perished in the gas chambers.

In 1992, when the fate of these women became public, islanders defensively claimed that they had no idea what was happening to the Jews in Europe. Certainly, they may not have known the full horror, but they did know that Jews were in grave danger, as Sherwill's memoirs indicate. The truth is that no official, either in Guernsey or Jersey, considered the welfare of a few Jews sufficiently important to jeopardize good relations with their German occupiers.[19] Here, the Jewish issue is the most clear-cut example of how the Channel Islands local government's cooperation with the Germans became outright collaboration. A mixture of ignorance, indifference, and anti-Semitism all contributed to these British officials playing their part in the tragedy of the Holocaust. In addition, an SS slave-labor camp was established on the island of Alderney; several hundred Jews were brought there, where most perished under horrible conditions.

JAPAN: Germany's Pacific ally sheltered close to 18,000 Jews in Japan itself and in Japanese-occupied Shanghai, China. Ironically, the Japanese responded to Hitler's anti-Semitism in a positive way — if Jews had so much influence, they must be a power to be reckoned with, especially since the Japanese believed the Jews controlled America. In addition, the Japanese gratefully remembered the enormous loans extended to them in 1903 by the American Jewish banker Jacob Schiff that enabled them to finance the Russo-Japanese War.

Roughly 500 members of the Yeshiva of Mir, the only such institution saved intact from the Holocaust, traveled through Siberia; after numerous miracles (the unseaworthy tramp steamer bearing them from Siberia to Japan sank after the last transport), and despite having worthless papers, the yeshivah was permitted to settle in Japan. The refugees stayed in the Japanese city of Kobe for several months and were the recipients of much kindness and sympathy, receiving gifts of food and medical treatment. The Japanese, who had never seen a yeshivah, let alone one in which students studied eighteen hours a day, sent an officer to investigate this strange phenomenon. After a few days, the yeshivah was given governmental clearance, and its members were declared "Holy Idealists."[20] In 1941, the Japanese transferred the Yeshiva of Mir to Shanghai, where the students remained for the duration of the war.

In 1942, the Germans sent Joseph Meisinger, known as the Butcher of Warsaw for his role in murdering 100,000 Jews, to Shanghai to instruct the local Japanese in methods of dealing with their supposed Jewish problem. He proposed loading the Jews on ships and then sinking them, and enticed the Japanese into agreeing by promising them all of the murdered Jews' possessions. As there were a number of extremely wealthy Iraqi Jewish families in Shanghai, this was a very attractive proposition to the Japanese officials. However, "the Guardian of Israel does not sleep or slumber" (Psalms 121:4), and a Japanese representative at the meeting, Mitsugi Shibata, was revolted by the gruesome plot. Viewing it as a stain upon Japanese honor, he revealed the terrible secret to a Jewish acquaintance. When the Jews attempted to plead their case to the Japanese police, they were thrown into jail and brutally interrogated about the source of the leak. While Shibata was sent back to Japan in disgrace, the publicity forced the Japanese to cancel the extermination plans.[21] After the war, the Yeshiva of Mir relocated to the United States and Israel, where it is a major Torah institution today.

Chapter 30

RESCUE EFFORTS DURING THE HOLOCAUST

A SORRY RECORD: Germany's control over most of Europe, and the Nazis' fanatic determination to murder the Jews, meant that even a determined Allied rescue campaign probably could not have saved as many as a third of those who died. But a substantial commitment to rescue almost certainly would have saved several hundred thousand Jews, and would have done so without compromising the war effort. Such a campaign would have taken place only if the United States had seized the initiative. However, America, despite having early knowledge of the Holocaust, did not act until late in the war, and even then the effort was a very limited one.[1] American rescue efforts floundered for several reasons: public opposition, the callous indifference of the American government to the plight of Europe's Jews, and the tepid, even obstructive attitude of major American Jewish and Zionist organizations to rescue efforts.

PUBLIC OPPOSITION: Three main factors lay behind the opposition of the American public to rescue efforts: the Great Depression, xenophobia, and anti-Semitism. In 1933, at the lowest point of the Depression, 25 percent of American workers had no jobs. Even though war production eliminated unemployment, and actually created a need for manpower, there was still widespread apprehension that with the end of hostilities the Depression would return. As a result, every foreigner entering the country was viewed as potentially depriving an American family of its livelihood.

Nativist attitudes, which were particularly widespread in the 1920s, remained prevalent in the 1930s and 40s. A great many Americans disliked foreigners of any kind, and wanted to end or significantly reduce the small flow of immigration that still existed. The issue was partly one of job competition, but many Americans also harbored fears about the cultural impact foreigners had on the United States.

Anti-Semitism in the United States reached a peak in the late 1930s and the war years. A major portion of the American populace held very negative views of Jews, and would have supported anti-Jewish legislation.[2] During the war years, violence broke out in the country, especially in New York City and Boston, where Jewish children were attacked by gangs, cemeteries were vandalized, and synagogues desecrated. Generally, police were negligent in dealing with the problem.

Throughout the nation, a particularly pernicious kind of anti-Semitism circulated in handbills, pamphlets, posters, and as jokes and jingles. The most recurring theme involved the widely disseminated libel that Jews shirked military service, stayed home, and prospered, while Christian boys were sent off to fight and die. In reality, the proportion of Jews in the armed forces was as least as great as the proportion of Jews in the American population. Nevertheless, the anti-Semitic canards continued. This parodied the Marine's Hymn, "From the Halls of Montezuma":

From the shores of Coney Island
Looking out into the sea,
Stands a kosher air-raid warden,
Wearing V for victory,
Who chants:
Let those Christian saps go fight the Japs, [sic]
In the uniforms we've made.
So it's onward into battle,

Let us send the Christian slobs.
When the war is done and victory won,
All us Jews will have their jobs.[3]

The following piece, with minor variations, surfaced in all parts of the country, in oral and written form. It was called "The First American," and no version mentioned that the bombardier who died on the same mission that claimed Colin Kelly's life while sinking a Japanese ship was Meyer Levin, a Jew:

First American killed in Pearl Harbor — John J. Hennessy
First American to sink a Jap ship — Colin P. Kelly
First American to sink a Jap ship with torpedo — John P. Buckley
Greatest American war hero — "Butch" O'Hare
First American killed at Guadalcanal — John J. O'Brien
First American to get four new tires — Abraham Lipshitz [4]

Symptomatic of even more deeply negative attitudes was a small but noticeable flow of hate-filled letters to government officials and members of Congress objecting to Jewish refugees. A typical excerpt of one such letter:

"I see from the papers that 200,000 refugee Jews in Hungary will not live through the next few weeks. That's too bad — what do we care about the Jews in Hungary? What we want is the refugee Jews brought to this country returned to where they came from."[5]

Although support for rescue arose in several non-Jewish quarters, most non-Jewish Americans were either unaware of the European Jewish catastrophe or did not consider it important. No major Christian denomination spoke out on the issue, unlike in Britain, where leading Christian figures voiced their concern. Most newspapers printed very little about the Holocaust, even though extensive information was readily available. For example, on July 2, 1944, the Jewish-owned *New York Times* published what it termed "authoritative information" that 400,000 Hungarian Jews had been deported to their deaths, and that 350,000 more were to be killed in the next three weeks. This news, basically accurate, received four column-inches on page 12. That day, the *Times* found room on the front page to analyze the problem of New York holiday crowds on the move.[6] Similarly, radio broadcasts and mass-circulation magazines all but ignored the Holocaust, while Hollywood, despite extensive Jewish influence in the movie industry, did not deal with the matter at all. Due to all these societal pressures, even if the American government had been inclined to save Jews, the effort would have been fraught with great difficulty.

GOVERNMENTAL OPPOSITION: President Roosevelt, although knowing as early as 1942 of the mass murder of European Jews, did nothing for more than a year. He then moved only because he was confronted with political pressures he could not avoid, and because his administration stood on the brink of a bad scandal over its rescue policies. Even after establishing the War Refugee Board to save Nazi victims in 1944, the president gave it no cooperation, very little power, and even less government funding. Politically, the president stayed away from the Holocaust as well. During the march on Washington by 400 Orthodox rabbis, for example, in order not to meet the delegation Roosevelt used a spurious excuse and conveniently left the capital. Indeed, Franklin Roosevelt's indifference to so momentous a historical event as the systematic annihilation of European Jewry emerges as the worst failure of his presidency.

The American State Department was rife with anti-Semitism as well, and its official in charge of immigration, Breckenridge Long, displayed a particular antipathy toward Jews. A memorandum written by Long to State Department officials in 1940 stated: "We can delay and effectively stop for a temporary period of indefinite length the number of immigrants into the United States. We could do this by simply advising our consuls to put every obstacle in the way and to require additional evidence and to resort to various administrative advices which would postpone and postpone and postpone the granting of the visas." The policy change was kept secret, but within weeks refugee organizations in the United States realized what had happened. They protested to President Roosevelt, to no avail.[7] As a result, only 21,000 refugees, not all Jewish, were allowed to enter the United States during the three and a half years the nation was at war with Germany. This represented only 10 percent of the meager number allowed by impossibly strict immigration quotas.

Poor though it was, the American rescue effort was better than that of Great Britain, the Soviet Union, or the other Allied nations. Despite the fact that publicity about the Holocaust was more widespread, and cries for action more prevalent, in England than in the United States, the British Foreign Office, which controlled immigration, made the following unpublicized pronouncement: "There is a possibility that the Germans or their satellites *may change over from the policy of extermination to one of extrusion* [italics in original], and aim as they did before the war at embarrassing other countries by flooding them with alien immigrants."[8] In particular, Great Britain was worried about potential pressure to admit fleeing Jews into Palestine.

AMERICAN JEWISH RESPONSE TO THE HOLOCAUST: This is a highly emotionally charged subject: Orthodox Jews feel, with considerable justification, that secular Jewish organizations, both Zionist and non-Zionist, turned their backs on numerous opportunities to rescue their beleaguered fellow Jews. While individual Jews in the United States cannot be blamed for inaction, the leadership can be faulted for not pointing the way. It must be stressed, however, that by and large these leaders were not evil people; nevertheless, they did commit severe errors in judgment based on a variety of motives, including those of self-interest. Several factors colored the attitude of secular Jewish groups toward rescue efforts:

First, adulation of President Roosevelt: Secular Jews viewed Roosevelt as slightly short of divine, for FDR epitomized the liberal values to which they so overwhelmingly adhered. Consequently, the secular Jews were averse to doing anything that would show the president in a less-than-favorable light or putting any pressure on him to rescue Jews. Stephen Wise, the president of both the World Jewish Congress and the American Jewish Congress, two of the most powerful secular organizations of the time, and the acknowledged leader of secular American Jewry, succinctly summed up Jewish adoration of FDR: "Thank G-d for Franklin D. Roosevelt." Throughout this painful era, Wise clashed with other Jewish leaders, using all his political clout to force their acquiescence to Roosevelt. He even withheld information about the Nazis' Final Solution, transmitted to the United States through various channels. Only when forced by vociferous declamations and other pressure from various groups did he reluctantly call for action on the part of the American government.[9]

Second, fear of anti-Semitism: Many non-religious Jews in the United States were afraid that if so-called "old-fashioned rabbis" came to America, then the secular Jews would not be regarded as equal Americans because they would be identified with Orthodox Jews. Non-Orthodox Jews also looked down on identifiably religious Jews, especially fearing that the entry of large numbers of foreign-looking and sounding Jews would cause a rise in anti-Semitism. Jewish presidential advisor Judge Samuel Rosenman evinced this attitude: When a delegation of 400 Orthodox rabbis marched on Washington in 1943 and attempted to speak with the president regarding rescue, Rosenman told FDR that "the group behind this petition was not representative of the most thoughtful elements in Jewry." He also said that he tried to keep "the horde" from storming Washington.[10] In truth, secular Jews may have been correct in their fear of anti-Semitism; however, simple humanity demands that if a Jewish house is burning down, anyone possible should be saved, with the consequences worried about later.

Third, the desire to keep a low profile: Unlike today's cynical era, the 1940s were a time of unquestioning patriotism and respect for government officials; protests were not considered fashionable. Jews did not want to do anything that could be perceived as unpatriotic or against the war effort. Therefore, secular Jewish organizations followed the official government line that defeating Hitler as quickly as possible was the best way to save the Jews of Europe. However, while winning the war was indeed of supreme importance, much could have been done to save Jews that would not have interfered with the war effort.

Fourth, undue emphasis on legalisms: Secular Jewish organizations were averse to using any method of rescue that ran afoul of American law. Therefore, they would not employ passports of dubious value, bribe hostile nations' officials to release Jews, pay smugglers to help Jews find illegal places of refuge, and conduct forbidden negotiations with Nazi officials to halt the murders. Orthodox Jews, however, in keeping with the Torah's dictum that saving lives overrides virtually all other Torah laws, employed all these methods and more to save Jews. In 1941, Agudath Israel, an Orthodox organization, continued sending food packages to starving Jews in Poland — despite a government order to halt such shipments, considered detrimental to the British blockade of Axis Europe. (Somehow, the United States shipped food to Yugoslavia and Greece despite the same blockade.) A committee, led by the secular American Jewish Congress and Jewish Labor Committee, picketed the Agudah offices, then reported the shipments to the British. When England threatened to arrest Jewish refugees on its shores, the Agudah was forced to stop sending food.[11]

Fifth, lack of unity: A unified front of all Jewish groups would have pooled vast financial and human resources and exerted enormous pressure on the United States to rescue Jews. Sadly, such unity did not exist, particularly because some Zionist groups exerted pressure solely for a Jewish state in Palestine. The Zionist groups had mass followings, organizational skills, some financial capability, a few prestigious leaders, and valuable contacts high in government. The American Jewish Committee combined wealth and important influence. The Jewish Labor Committee was backed by a sizable constituency and could count on help from the American Federation of Labor. B'nai B'rith held the allegiance of a broad cross section of American Jews. Agudath Israel represented a very active element of Orthodoxy. The Bergson Group offered energy, publicity skills, fund-raising proficiency, and the capacity to win friends in Congress and elsewhere in Washington. But the split over Zionism proved unbridgeable. The outcome was that non-Zionist organizations went their own way, accomplishing little in building pressure for rescue. The Zionists, who were the best organized of the Jewish groups, put the major part of their resources into the effort for a postwar Jewish state in Palestine.[12] What's more, the clear infighting among many of the Jewish groups alienated Congressional supporters of rescue efforts and hampered their effectiveness.[13]

Sixth, inertia: An additional problem was the inability of secular American Jewish leaders to break out of a business-as-usual pattern. Too few schedules were rearranged, vacations were seldom sacrificed, and too few projects of lesser significance were set aside. Even from afar, this inability to adapt was painfully clear. In late 1942, Jewish leaders in Warsaw entrusted a message to Jan Karski, the Polish underground agent about to leave for Britain and the United States. It called on Jews in the free nations to turn to unprecedented measures to persuade their governments to act. But the Polish Jews had no illusions. Before Karski departed, one of them warned him:

Jewish leaders abroad won't be interested. At eleven o'clock in the morning you will begin telling them about the anguish of the Jews in Poland, but at one o'clock they will ask you to halt the narrative so they can have lunch. That is a difference which cannot be bridged. They will go on lunching at the regular hour at their favorite restaurant. So they cannot understand what is happening in Poland.[14]

Perhaps no amount of protesting, rallying, or the exercise of political pressure tactics would have accomplished much. But in the light of what American Jews knew, might not the Holocaust have been reflected in their daily, weekly, or even yearly lives?

Day after day, night after night, hundreds and thousands were disappearing into mass graves or burning to cinders. All of this was known to the free world, and yet...holidays were celebrated; charity balls and dinners were organized; people went to the concerts, to the theater...everything went on as if nothing was happening.[15]

This description is not a distorted view of life as it existed in the American Jewish community during the Holocaust. The normal, sometimes festive atmosphere offended some observers. A writer for the *Jewish Spectator* bemoaned the "careless gaiety" and "ostentatious luxury" of Jewish summer crowds at the beach resorts, the "giggling" and the golfing, the mah-jongg and the horse races, the casual, indulgent life enjoyed by Jews.[16]

All told, the Final Solution may have been *unstoppable* by American Jewry, but it should have been *unbearable* for them.

Significantly, the great Rabbi Aharon Kotler observed the mourning practices of the Nine Days throughout the war years, not eating meat except on Sabbaths and holidays. His wife wore the same threadbare clothing throughout those years, not purchasing any new clothing. Rabbi Moshe Feinstein did not sleep on a pillow during the war period, in the manner of Tishah B'Av.[17] Recha Sternbuch, a famed rescue activist in Switzerland, interrupted her own son's bar mitzvah celebration and traveled on the Sabbath to rescue endangered Jews.[18]

ATTEMPTS AT RESCUE: Despite the obstacles and failures, American Jews were responsible for some important achievements. They helped spread the news of extermination and created support, however limited, among non-Jews. During the war, the American Jewish Joint Distribution Committee (JDC) provided $15 million in aid to European Jews, more than all the world's governments combined. Other secular organizations also contributed, albeit on a smaller scale. The Hebrew Immigrant Aid Society (HIAS) dealt effectively with migration and ocean transportation problems. The World Jewish Congress undertook important rescue projects in collaboration with overseas Zionist organizations and anti-Nazi underground movements.[19]

PETER BERGSON: The man known as Peter Bergson grew up in Palestine as Hillel Kook and was the nephew of the Ashkenazic Chief Rabbi of Palestine, Rabbi Avraham I. Kook. Hillel Kook, who changed his name to Peter Bergson while in the United States, originally came to America to rally support for an independent Jewish army to fight the Nazis. However, upon receiving news of the annihilation of European Jewry, Bergson focused exclusively on rescuing Jews, using radical and innovative methods to get his message across. This brought Bergson and his group into direct and acrimonious conflict with the established secular Jewish organizations, which hesitated to apply pressure to rescue Jews. However, the Bergsonites and Orthodox groups shared the same sense of urgency to save Jews, and their cooperation proved to be the catalyst that sparked major rescue efforts.

Especially proficient in the use of media and public relations, Bergson placed controversial full-page ads in major newspapers demanding action. On February 16, 1943, the most famous of all Bergson's advertisements appeared in the *New York Times* on page 11: "FOR SALE to Humanity, 70,000 Jews, Guaranteed Human Beings, at $50 a piece." This shocking ad notified the world of Romania's willingness to allow these Jews out of concentration camps if they would emigrate to Palestine.

Immediately, a barrage of protest came from the established Jewish organizations and press. They angrily charged Bergson with deliberately and deceptively implying that each $50 contribution would save a Romanian Jew.[20] However, the offer *was* genuine. Sadly, no American response was forthcoming, and the 70,000 Romanian Jews perished during the war.

Undaunted, the Bergson group centered its efforts on building public pressure for rescue action, lobbying members of Congress and administration officials to create support for government rescue. The Bergson Group organized a pageant, *We Will Never Die*, to publicize the plight of European Jewry, recruiting numerous prominent actors for the pageant's cast. *We Will Never Die* was performed in many American cities before audiences of tens of thousands, including many major government officials. With stunning power, the pageant struck the first major blow at the wall of silence surrounding the Nazi genocide, thus playing an important role in raising public consciousness about the plight of European Jewry.[21] Incredibly, the established secular Jewish groups, fearing that the pageant would undermine their leadership, obstructed its showing in numerous cities.

In July 1943, after the Anglo-American Bermuda Conference on the refugee issue ended with complete Allied apathy toward finding places of sanctuary for Jews, the Bergson Group formed a committee of prominent Americans to galvanize the government into action.

ORTHODOX RESCUE EFFORTS: From the very outset, Orthodox organizations, such as Va'ad Hatzalah and Agudath Israel, as well as many courageous individuals, rabbis and laymen alike, played a major role in the rescue of European Jewry. Grounded in the Torah requirement of the supremacy of saving Jewish lives, the Orthodox turned to all available rescue tactics, including many considered unconventional. Concern for legal niceties, seeming disloyalty to the government, or fomenting anti-Semitism — the bane of so many secular groups — did not play a role in the single-minded devotion of Orthodox rescuers to their holy task. Unlike the perverse accusations of recent detractors, the Orthodox provided assistance to *all* Jews, regardless of levels of religiosity or political affiliation.[22] With the power of Torah behind them, rescue work simply transformed Orthodox Jews in America: seeing prominent rabbis travel on the Sabbath to enhance rescue activities, establishing connections at the highest levels of government, and more, all combined to forge a new, dynamic American Orthodoxy. After the war, John Pehle, the non-Jewish head of the War Refugee Board (WRB), wrote a letter of tribute to the Va'ad Hatzalah:

> The Va'ad Hatzalah may not have had available to it the largest sums for rescue and relief; it may not have had the greatest impact on public opinion; but for imaginative and constructive ideas, for courageous programs, for ingenuity and singleness

of purpose, your organization need bow to none. General Eisenhower's stern warning to the German people on his entry onto German soil not to molest those in concentration camps had its origin in a suggestion made by you. Your persistent efforts to bring relief to the refugee group in Shanghai, to the victims of oppression in Slovakia, Poland, Hungary, and elsewhere, testify to the fervor with which you fought to save precious lives. Under almost insurmountable difficulties you devised a program to finance underground means of bringing endangered Jews from Poland across the Carpathians to the safety that Hungary afforded early in 1944. Significantly enough, this program was approved by this Government on January 22, 1944, the very day that the late President Roosevelt created the War Refugee Board. Later, when Hungary was occupied by the Germans, your plans and projects were directed to securing safer places of refuge. Your assistance reached deep into Bohemia itself and brought release from Theresienstadt to many.[23]

Orthodox organizations and individuals, despite lacking political clout and strong funding, innovated many rescue activities, saving tens of thousands of lives. Many Orthodox organizations and individuals performed countless acts of rescue during the Holocaust years. This tiny, economically and politically powerless group performed heroically on behalf of the Jewish people. Orthodox Jews can be justly proud that this tragic period proved to be Orthodoxy's finest hour. A partial list of Orthodox rescue efforts:

ZEIREI AGUDATH ISRAEL: Rabbi Elimelech Tress, the leader of Zeirei Agudath Israel, the youth division of the Agudah, worked tirelessly to procure thousands of visas and affidavits to enable fleeing Jews to enter the United States. He also played a role in bringing forty Torah scholars to America on a special emergency visa program. One of the arrivals was the great Rabbi Aharon Kotler, who was chiefly responsible for the development of Torah Judaism in the United States. Zeirei also was instrumental in arranging visas and transportation for Lithuanian scholars to enter the United States from the Far East.

Zeirei was also very active in sending food shipments to Poland, which helped fend off starvation for thousands of Jews. Sadly, this rescue program was halted due to pressure from secular Jewish groups, which did not want to contravene the Allied boycott of Nazi-held lands.

Upon discovering that Germany honored Latin American documents, Orthodox activists in Switzerland and the United States procured thousands of such papers, some of dubious legality. When questions arose, the Orthodox activists pressured the American government to induce the Latin American regimes to recognize the certificates. This effort was successful in the main, and thousands of holders of those documents were saved, primarily in the Hungarian capital of Budapest.

In Budapest, as elsewhere, Orthodox rescue extended to all Jews, regardless of level of religiosity. Orthodox efforts saved thousands of secular Budapest Jews and fed countless starving Polish Jews of all affiliations. Although Orthodox groups devoted special exertion to saving Torah scholars and supporting yeshivah students in Shanghai, they pursued all rescue possibilities that came their way, regardless of religious affiliation of those in need.

VA'AD HATZALAH: In 1940, a partnership of European-trained American rabbis, refugee scholars, and exceptionally dedicated laymen founded the Va'ad Hatzalah, which quickly became the major Orthodox rescue organization. Rabbinic leaders of Va'ad Hatzalah included Rabbi Aharon Kotler, Rabbi Eliezer Silver, and Rabbi Avraham Kalmanowitz. Prominent laymen included Irving Bunim and Stephen Klein. Untried in statecraft and without a political base, they accomplished miracles.

In August 1942, reports of Nazi genocide reached Stephen Wise. Under pressure from the State Department, Wise promised not to publicize the news. "How could he pledge secrecy when millions of lives were involved?" asked Elie Wiesel twenty-five years later. "How was he not driven mad by the secret?"[24] Seemingly, for Wise, loyalty to President Roosevelt and his administration, however misplaced, came before exerting pressure to save Jewish lives.

Five days later, Isaac Sternbuch, the Va'ad Hatzalah's representative in Switzerland, received graphic news of Nazi atrocities in Poland. He immediately sent the message to Jacob Rosenheim, president of Agudath Israel, via the Polish diplomatic service, a method that avoided American government censorship. (Orthodox groups and individuals frequently used this illegal tactic.) Upon receiving the terrible news, Rosenheim, "although physically broken down from this harrowing cable,"[25] telegraphed Sternbuch's message to President Roosevelt (who predictably never responded), then conferred with Wise and other Jewish leaders. Wise told Rosenheim in no uncertain terms to keep the horrifying news out of the press, threatening to cut off all funding if his order were not obeyed. A full three months later, the government permitted the news to be publicized, and Jewish groups began a belated rescue effort. However, *one million* Jews were murdered in that period, the deadliest of the Holocaust. Precious time was lost exerting pressure for rescue.

In October 1943, two days before Yom Kippur, the Bergson Group helped organize a protest march of more than 400 rabbis in Washington. This impressively large group demonstrated exceptional concern and commitment in coming to Washington, D.C. two days before the holiest night of the year. Many had come from hundreds of miles away and faced a long trip back home, especially difficult under wartime travel restrictions. Some arrived home right before Yom Kippur, while others were stranded in Washington.

The Rabbis' March was successful, spurring Congress to open hearings on rescuing Jews, pressuring Roosevelt to establish the War Refugee Board, the only government agency devoted to rescue. In total, the WRB was responsible for rescuing 200,000 Jews, a large number of them from Budapest.[26]

ESCAPE FROM AUSCHWITZ: In April 1944, two Slovakian Jews escaped from Auschwitz and made their way to the Jewish underground in Slovakia. There they dictated a detailed report on what they had learned about the killing center during their two-year stay, and also announced that preparations were underway to kill all the Jews of Hungary. The Jewish underground's Rabbi Michael Ber Weissmandl, who was previously instrumental in bribing German officials to halt the deportation of Slovakian Jews for two years, distributed a condensed version of the Auschwitz report, along with a map of the gas chambers, to many Jewish agencies. Only three individuals publicized the story: Yaakov Griffel, Agudath Israel's representative in Turkey and a key rescue activist, and Recha and Isaac Sternbuch in Switzerland. Using the Polish diplomatic service, the Sternbuchs cabled the report to Rabbi Rosenheim and Rabbi Kalmanowitz in America, who in turn pleaded with the American government to bomb Auschwitz and the rail lines leading to it. In August 1944 John J. McCloy of the WRB gave the official government reply that bombing Auschwitz would divert important military resources that were needed elsewhere, and also would not be effective.

George Mantello, a Salvadoran diplomat and an Orthodox Jew, initiated a publicity campaign in Switzerland. Swiss newspapers publicized the horrors of Auschwitz for the first time, and as a result, worldwide pressure forced Hungary to stop the deportations, saving the lives of the Budapest Jews.

THE KASZTNER TRAIN: Rudolf Kasztner, a Hungarian Zionist leader, persuaded Eichmann to allow a train with more than 1,600 Jews, among them the rebbe of Satmar, to travel to freedom in Switzerland. Eichmann agreed on the condition that he receive forty tractors. Despite obstruction from the head of the Joint Distribution Committee, Saly Mayer, who was unsympathetic to the deal, Isaac Sternbuch managed to raise the necessary ransom, thereby saving the Jews on the train. In addition, nearly 18,000 more Jews were saved as a result of these negotiations.[27]

THE STERNBUCH-MUSY-HIMMLER NEGOTIATIONS: At the

end of 1944, Recha Sternbuch prevailed upon Dr. Jean-Marie Musy, a pro-Nazi previous president of Switzerland, to travel to Germany and negotiate with Himmler, the head of the SS, for the release of all Jews under German control. As a result of these dealings, more than 1,200 Jews were released from Theresienstadt in Czechoslovakia, and despite Hitler's orders to the contrary, the Germans did not destroy their camps before the Allies entered them.

BOMBING AUSCHWITZ: A recurring question has been why the United States rejected such requests to bomb Auschwitz's gas chambers and crematoria and the railroads leading to it. In 1986, McCloy revealed that when he took the matter to President Roosevelt, the president was "irate" at the suggestion and remarked, "Why, the idea! They'll say we bombed these people, and they'll only move it down the road a little way, and we'll bomb them all the more. If it's successful, it'll be more provocative, and I won't have anything to do with it. We'll be accused of participating in this horrible business."[28] To this day, one of the most controversial aspects of Roosevelt's World War II leadership remains the American refusal to bomb Auschwitz.

THE DISPUTE: One fact that all participants in the debate agree on is that the window for Allied air forces to do anything that might have retarded the murder of Jews was small — about six months in the summer and fall of 1944. Before that time, Eastern Europe was out of the range of Allied aircraft; it was only in the spring of 1944 that bases in Italy became available. There is also general agreement that, given the technology of that time, railway bombing would have been extremely imprecise, and that the Germans would have been able to repair rail lines easily or utilize alternate routes.[29] Therefore, the debate focuses on the bombing of Auschwitz itself.

Bombing proponents say that the Allies had aerial pictures of the death camp complex and full knowledge of what was portrayed. Proponents also say that it is impossible to claim that

Auschwitz could not have been bombed, for the U.S. Air Force accidentally dropped bombs on SS barracks in the camp on September 13, 1944, and in an earlier raid bombed factories less than five miles from the gas chambers. In all, proponents estimate that a raid on the death installations could have saved perhaps 150,000 Jews.[30]

Bombing opponents maintain that the significance of aerial photographs of Auschwitz was not fully understood; only in 1978 could more modern technology point out inmates being led to gas chambers. In addition, opponents claim that the gas chambers were not readily identifiable from the air. Furthermore, due to the generally poor weather in that part of Poland, the efficacy of German antiaircraft defenses, the great distance from Allied bases, and the sheer difficulty of precise bombing, opponents say that a raid on Auschwitz was fraught with danger. Other arguments include the idea that the bombs could have fallen on prisoner barracks, killing many Jews, and that if the gas chambers were destroyed the Germans would simply kill Jews in other ways, such as mass shooting. The view claims that had Auschwitz been bombed, no Jews would have been saved, and perhaps even more would have died than actually did.

With more than a half-century of hindsight, it is clearer now than in 1944 that if nothing else the sound of bombs exploding at Auschwitz would have constituted a moral statement for all time that the British and Americans understood the historical gravity of the Holocaust. Fifty years later, it is hard to accept the idea that the War Department's doctrine of using military resources only on supposedly military targets should have so rigidly prevailed. True, the bombing of Auschwitz might not have saved many Jews, but the record of the Allies would have been brighter, and each person saved might have lived out a decent life. (For their part, prisoners at Auschwitz eagerly hoped for bombing, despite the fact that they might be killed.[31] They, too, wanted the Allies to make a statement by striking back at the Nazi murderers. Not to do so was, in the prisoners' minds, tacit acceptance of the German killing machine.) The cold fact is that the plight of Europe's

Jews was not unbearable to the Allied powers.

THE POPE AND THE HOLOCAUST: Pope Pius XII has often been criticized for the Vatican's wartime silence about the murder of European Jews. In his defense, some have alleged that the Pope was doing a great deal behind the scenes to help the Jews. In actuality, the Pope did very little for the Jews, even in Italy, where the Vatican was in a position to be most helpful. Although Church officials saved Italian Jews, it was due to the kindness of individual priests rather than official Church policy.

Pope Pius, as the spiritual leader of the world's Catholics, was in a unique position to speak against the Holocaust. A clear statement of excommunication for any Catholic killing Jews, or aiding such murder, would undoubtedly have saved many Jewish lives. It might not have stopped the Nazis, who were fanatical in their zeal to rid the world of the Jewish people, but such a papal statement would certainly have lessened greatly the level of cooperation the Germans received from the Catholic countries of Europe. Undoubtedly, many Catholics of good conscience would have provided assistance to Jews, and others would have tacitly approved while their neighbors helped rather than informing on them.

Why, then, despite knowing of the Final Solution, did the Pope choose to remain silent? Several reasons are given. First, the Pope feared possible German reprisals against Catholics. There is some truth to this concern, especially in Poland, where the Germans acted with great brutality toward Catholic Poles. However, in Western Europe, the Germans tread more cautiously, and such a pronouncement would not have provoked German measures such as those in Poland. Second, the Pope was afraid that German and Austrian Catholics would leave the fold, their loyalty to Hitler overriding that of the Church. Third, the Pope hated Communism, and he feared that to undercut the Germans would result in the expansion of the Soviet Union deep into the rest of Europe. Fourth, from 1940 to 1944 Italian and German forces surrounded the Vatican, an enclave in the city of Rome, and the Pope feared an Axis occupation.[32]

However, in the early stages of persecution of the Jews, and especially late in the war, when the Vatican was safe and German defeat was imminent, the Pope could have spoken out. In the final analysis, two factors influenced the Pope's silence. Pius had fond memories of Germany, having spent a number of years there as the papal nuncio (ambassador). In 1933, the first year of Hitler's rule, he negotiated the *Reich* Concordat with Germany, which granted the Catholic Church jurisdiction over Germany's Catholics in exchange for Vatican approval of the Nazi regime. More significantly, the Pope shared the traditional Christian animosity toward the Jews, compounded by his belief that the Jews were behind the Bolshevik plot to destroy the Christian religion. As six million Jews were being savagely murdered, men and women of all faiths looked to the Pope — traditionally presumed to be an arbiter of morality and decency — for a word, a sign, an indication of how to respond. There they found little or nothing — and acted accordingly. Ironically, despite this incredible record of failure, at a time when humanity cried out in its deepest need, Pope Pius XII is currently being considered as a candidate for sainthood.

Chapter 31

THE FINAL DAYS OF THE
HOLOCAUST

THE DEATH MARCHES: By summer 1944 the Allies were closing in on the Third *Reich*, which still held 750,000 persons in its huge but increasingly vulnerable concentration camp network. In early November, as Soviet forces drew closer, the Germans stopped gassing operations at Auschwitz-Birkenau, then attempted to cover up their mass murder. As for the prisoners who remained in the concentration camps, the Nazis knew that if the prisoners were not evacuated, this labor source — and also the devastating testimony these men and women could deliver — would fall into the Allies' hands. With transport scarcer than ever, the Germans ordered marches over long distances not only to keep concentration camp prisoners beyond the Allies' reach, but also to relocate them for labor. As the weeks and months passed, these marches became increasingly brutal, deadly, and senseless. Starved, ill, wounded, and exposed to bitter winter weather, the tormented marchers were kept under guard, shot if they faltered even for a moment, or left to die if felled by exhaustion.

In November 1944, 76,000 Budapest Jewish men, women, and children were forced to walk to the Austrian border. This death march lasted a month, during which time thousands died from starvation, disease, exhaustion, and cold, with thousands more shot along the way. Raoul Wallenberg rescued several hundred fortunate prisoners, bringing them back to Budapest, but most were taken to slave labor camps in the *Reich*. In January 1945, 60,000 Jews from Auschwitz and its surrounding camps were marched and shipped by train to camps in Germany; over 15,000 perished. One group of 7,000 Jews was marched for ten days to the Baltic Sea, where they were pushed into the water and shot; only thirteen survived. In one instance, a group of more than 1,000 Jews was herded into a barn, which was then set ablaze. When American troops arrived the next day, they found a mass of charred bodies and few survivors. Raizl Kibel, a survivor of a death march, later recalled:

> In a frost, half barefoot, or entirely barefoot, with light rags upon their emaciated and exhausted bodies, tens of thousands of human creatures drag themselves along in the snow. Only the great, strong striving for life, and the light of imminent liberation, keep them on their feet. But woe to them whose physical strength abandons them. They are shot on the spot. In such a way were thousands who had endured camp life up to the last minute murdered, a moment before liberation. Even today I still cannot understand with what sort of strength I was able to endure the death march and drag myself to Ravensbruck camp, and from there, after resting a week or two, to Neustadt, where I was liberated by the Red Army.[1]

By the end of April 1945, the Nazis had initiated death marches from Flossenberg, Sachsenhausen, Neuengamme, Magdeburg, Mauthausen, Ravensbruck, and Dachau, all camps located in Germany and Austria. These marches lasted literally until the day of Germany's surrender, May 8, 1945. In all, more than 250,000 prisoners, mostly Jewish, were murdered or died on the forced death marches conducted throughout the last ten months of World War II.

THE LIBERATION: Although the atrocities at Majdanek and Auschwitz were reported in the Western press, the depth of Nazi brutality was not fully understood until the liberation of concentration camps in Germany and Austria by Anglo-American forces in April and May 1945.

As they entered the enclosed enclaves, the soldiers found dead bodies piled up by the hundreds along paths, roads, and train tracks, with thousands more in the camps themselves. Healthier prisoners in the camps could walk or hobble, but thousands lay in wooden barracks in filthy and decrepit multi-tiered bunks. Most had been starved, and tens of thousands were sick. Upon liberation, prisoners were freed from the killing and terror inflicted by the Germans and their collaborators, but many still faced death from disease and malnutrition. At Bergen-Belsen which largely held Jews, 13,000 internees died immediately after liberation, often from typhus that proved fatal to the malnourished survivors. Confronted by so many starving skeletons, well-meaning American soldiers brought chocolate, jam, and other rich foods, which the camp survivors ate ravenously, but which many could not digest and so died. Sadly, the food was too rich, too fatty, too filling, and it killed as surely as bullets and rifle butts. (Interestingly, in Talmudic times the Romans were well aware of the dangers of feeding rich food to starving people. When Roman physicians treated the saintly Rabbi Tzadok, who had fasted and prayed for forty years hoping to avert the destruction of the second Beis HaMikdash, they first fed him thin broth, then gradually increased the solid content of his food until they nursed him back to health.)[2]

THE SURVIVORS: Roughly 250,000 Jews survived the concentration camps and death marches, with another 1.5 million remaining alive in their home countries or returning from places of refuge. Some Jews returned to Eastern Europe to search for loved ones and to reclaim their property. Most found no relatives, and when they tried to return to their homes, they found them occupied by hostile strangers who drove them away or even killed them. In 1946, a blood libel pogrom erupted in the Polish city of Kielce, killing forty-two Jews, among them Chaim Hirschman, one of only two survivors of the Belzec death camp. Other anti-

Semitic riots broke out in Poland as well. A British reporter remarked that "anyone with a Jewish appearance in Poland is in great danger." Following the riots, 100,000 Jews left Poland for American displaced persons camps in Germany; at the same time, Eastern European Jews in Germany simply refused to return to their homelands.

To cope with the great number of refugees, the Allies established displaced persons (DP) camps throughout Germany, some of which were located in former concentration camps, such as Bergen-Belsen. At first, the U.S. military, tainted by anti-Semitic prejudice, showed great insensitivity to the plight of the Jews, giving them insufficient food, shelter, and health care, even housing them with DPs who were Nazi collaborators. Upon the urging of Jewish groups in the United States, President Truman sent Earl G. Harrison to investigate conditions in the camps. Harrison, a man of great compassion, sharply criticized the military's handling of the DPs. As a result, special centers were opened exclusively for Jews, and conditions improved greatly. Jewish organizations were able to send food packages and other aid to the camps. In particular, Rabbi Elimelech Tress of Zeirei Agudath Israel indefatigably worked to send supplies to the DPs. Rabbi Eliezer Silver of Va'ad Hatzalah also visited DP camps and tended to the inmates' spiritual needs.

Nearly 250,000 Jews remained in these camps until they were able to enter countries such as the United States, Canada, Great Britain, and Australia. Entry to Palestine was very difficult, however, due to the British restriction on Jewish immigration. Many Jews trekked across Europe for hundreds of miles through inhospitable, mountainous terrain, attempting to sneak into Palestine; most failed. When the State of Israel was established in 1948, the camps emptied out. The last DP camp, Fohrenwald in Germany, was closed in 1957.[3]

A particularly tragic story concerns the fate of thousands of Jewish children who survived when their desperate parents hid them with non-Jewish families or gave them to convents and monasteries. Most of these children had no memories of their parents or of having been born Jewish, and were raised up as devout Catholics. Feeling that they saved the souls of these children, the foster families and church institutions were very reluctant to return them to Jews. Sadly, while the vast majority of these children were lost forever to the Jewish people, Orthodox rescue efforts did succeed in returning several hundred children to Jewish auspices. Sometimes parents were able to locate their children. In one poignantly moving story, a father was reunited with his daughter, whom he had hidden with a Christian family, when he showed the child colored Chanukah candles, awakening within her long-buried memories.[4]

PUNISHMENT OF THE PERPETRATORS: In the newly liberated camps, some former inmates wrought immediate, summary justice against their persecutors, often with the encouragement of their liberators. In some camps, outraged Allied soldiers shot SS guards and their collaborators. As matters settled down, formal procedures were pursued to apprehend and jail individuals suspected of war crimes.

THE NUREMBERG TRIALS: In 1945, the Allied Powers tried twenty-two leading German officials in Nuremberg, Germany for war crimes and crimes against humanity. After nearly one year, eleven of the defendants were sentenced to death by hanging, while the others were given prison sentences of varying lengths or acquitted. Hermann Goering committed suicide in prison, and the other ten Nazi criminals were hanged. (Interestingly, the Nuremberg Trials are alluded to in code in the Book of Esther. Traditionally, for thousands of years, when writing the list of the ten sons of Haman who were hanged, scribes have enlarged or reduced several of the Hebrew letters without knowing why. After the Nuremberg Trials, the reason became clear: The Hebrew letters numerically correspond to the Jewish year 5707, which is the civil year 1946. Ten Nazis were hanged, while an eleventh committed suicide, similar to Haman's ten sons who were hanged and one daughter who committed suicide.[5] As Julius Streicher, one of the Nazis, was about to be hanged, he cried out *"Purimfest 1946!"* although it was October. Purim occurs in February or March.)[6]

THE EICHMANN TRIAL: In 1960, Israeli agents kidnapped Adolph Eichmann, who played a major role in planning and implementing the Final Solution, in Argentina, where he was living under a new identity, and brought him to Israel to stand trial. This event was a watershed in Holocaust history, for it brought survivors to reflect openly upon the horrors they endured, something they were reluctant to do beforehand. Interest in the Holocaust increased greatly, both among the general public and in academia. Many books were published on the Holocaust, and Holocaust studies became popular in many universities. Survivors began recording their experiences, both orally and in writing, for future generations. In addition, the Eichmann trial presented the details of the Holocaust as they unfolded in Europe from 1933 to 1945.

One of the most shocking revelations of the trial was that Eichmann, a primary agent in killing millions of Jews, was a relatively ordinary individual. He was not a zealous Nazi, only a bureaucrat doing his job — the epitome of what historian Hannah Arendt termed "the banality of evil." Eichmann was hanged in 1962, the only person ever executed by the State of Israel.

OTHER TRIALS: The overwhelming majority of post-1945 war crimes trials involved lower-level officials and officers, including concentration camp guards and commandants, police officers, members of the *Einsatzgruppen*, and doctors who participated in medical experiments. These war criminals were tried by Allied military courts and by the countries in which they had committed their crimes. Of the approximately 150,000 Germans involved directly in Nazi murders, roughly 35,000 were convicted.[7] Most criminals were never brought to trial, while others received light sentences or pardons, particularly in German courts. One man on the administrative staff of the Belzec death camp, who assisted in the murder of 600,000 Jews, was sent to prison for only four years by a German court. The other Belzec killers were acquitted because they were "unable to do anything except obey the orders given to them."[8] Far from being punished, numerous Nazis attained high positions in the postwar West German government and in industry, among them Friedrich Flick, the wealthy industrialist who had enriched himself by impoverishing Jews and then using them as slave labor. He died in 1972 at age 90 with a personal fortune of more than $1 billion, never having paid a single penny as restitution to his victims.[9] Many other Nazis, including such mass murderers of Jews as the notorious Dr. Joseph Mengele, settled in South America, living peaceful, even luxurious lives with money robbed from Jews. Ultimately, justice rests with G-d, who will punish evil in the Messianic Era.

ECONOMIC EXPLOITATION: It is impossible to calculate the economic losses of the six million martyrs. Their personal property was plundered, as well as communal resources. In one six-week period alone, 222,269 sets of men's suits and underclothes, 192,652 sets of women's clothing, and 99,922 sets of children's clothes, collected from the gassed at Auschwitz, were distributed on Germany's Home Front. The recipients knew roughly where these garments came from.[10] In addition, Jews performed all manner of slave labor, both in the ghettoes and the concentration camps. Of the many nations that enriched themselves from the pillage of the Jews, Germany has taken the lead in offering some form of restitution, although only a pittance of what actually was robbed from the Jews. Other nations have paid virtually nothing, or only acquiesced to the concept of restitution. The many individuals who stole Jewish property were never forced to relinquish their ill-gotten gains. Even today, Europe in awash in plundered Jewish assets.

POST-HOLOCAUST GERMANY: Germans said either they knew nothing about the murders or were only following orders, blaming either Hitler or the SS for the Holocaust. In 1996, Daniel J. Goldhagen published *Hitler's Willing Executioners*, which asserted that the Holocaust was not perpetrated by a few elite Nazi killers but by many ordinary Germans who were motivated by a lethal anti-Semitism that was deeply embedded in German culture 150 years before the Nazis. The book became a best-seller in the United States, and particularly in Germany, for it struck a nerve that had lain untouched. Great controversies and discussions revolved around the book, which had both vociferous detractors and ardent defenders. Currently, the attitude among many Germans, especially younger people, is that they are weary of hearing about, and being blamed for, the Holocaust, wishing the matter would simply be put to rest. However, the blood of the holy martyrs cries out to remember what happened forever, especially to the nation that committed the crime.

THE SWISS AND THE HOLOCAUST: Swiss banks profited greatly from the Holocaust, literally from Jewish bodies themselves. At his trial, Rudolf Hoss, the commandant at Auschwitz, testified how gold from the teeth of gassed Jewish victims, along with their rings, watches, and bracelets, was melted down into gold bars and sent to the German *Reichsbank*, which then deposited the money in Switzerland.[11] The Germans also sent along to Switzerland valuables plundered from Jewish individuals and communities, such as jewelry, art, and title deeds for real estate. After the war, when survivors or the victims' descendants claimed their property, they were told by Swiss banks to furnish proof of the account holder's death in the form of a death certificate. Since this was often impossible, the banks refused to relinquish the assets. Jews whose relatives held life insurance policies with Swiss companies were treated similarly. Therefore, the assets of thousands of the Nazis' murdered victims are safely preserved in Swiss bank vaults today. The World Jewish Congress estimates that, allowing for compound interest, the funds on deposit amount to many billions of dollars.[12]

In 1997, Christoph Meili, a security guard at a major Swiss bank, noticed ledger books headed for the shredder. Courageously, he surreptitiously removed three volumes; there were seventy others that he could not rescue. These ledgers contained shocking revelations of Swiss complicity in profiting from Nazi plunder. In the 1930s, German Jews were forced to sell prime Berlin real estate to the Nazi government for a pittance. The German regime then mortgaged these properties to Swiss banks at one thousand times the purchase rate. Meili has maintained that the Swiss stole a minimum of $500 billion of Jewish money, and that Europe holds trillions of dollars of Jewish assets. He also related that the Swiss National Bank received gold from the *Reichsbank*, stamped it with an earlier date to hide its origin, and minted gold franc coins. It was later noted that these coins contained a very high silver content, equal to that of the silver content in the gold teeth extracted from Jews gassed in the concentration camps. Even more shockingly, Meili revealed that the German chemical company Degusa, which manufactured the Zyklon-B gas used in the gas chambers, and which melted down gold from the camps, is located in New Jersey and manufactures most of the dental fillings used in the United States.[13] As a result of Meili's revelations, in 1998 the two largest Swiss banks agreed to a $1.25 billion settlement with 31,500 Holocaust victims and their families in return for an agreement that there would be no future claims against Swiss banks or the Swiss government.

Other nations, such as Spain, Portugal, and Sweden, also profited from dealings with the Nazis, while the American company IBM made substantial profits supplying the Germans with computer punch cards used to enforce racial laws and process concentration camp inmates.

HOLOCAUST DENIAL: Since shortly after the war ended, neo-Nazis and other anti-Semites, and those who consciously or unconsciously support them, have attempted to deny the obvious facts of the Holocaust. Minimizing the number of Jews murdered, their literature denies the existence of the gas chambers in Auschwitz, claims that the Jews suffered no more than other nations, and states that the only casualties Jews suffered were war victims; some even state that murder of the Jews did not take place at all. This propaganda reached its climax with the publication of a 1976 book by A. R. Butz, *The Hoax of the Twentieth Century*. Claiming that only a million Jews were killed during the war, and that all other Jews emigrated, this canard states that the Holocaust was invented by Jews to extract money from Germans and gain favor with Western powers.[14] In this view, all the overwhelming, documentary, eyewitness, and physical evidence of the Holocaust, including photographs, was explained away, using rationalizations that, despite sounding very sophisticated, have no basis in fact.

In 1993, Professor Deborah Lipstadt published her groundbreaking *Denying the Holocaust*, which identified several adherents of the revisionist movement and examined the basis for their beliefs, methodology, and manner in which they deploy their arguments. A major Holocaust denier, the Briton David Irving, sued Lipstadt for libel in England. In 2000, after a landmark trial, in which the historical truth of the Holocaust was clearly demonstrated and Irving was exposed as a charlatan closely identified with extremist anti-Semitic groups, the British judge, Mr. Justice Gray, found Professor Lipstadt innocent of libel. Presently, Arab nations heavily finance and teach Holocaust denial, which sadly finds many believers around the world.

Although Holocaust denial has grown every year since the Holocaust, it began as soon as the Nazis began to dismantle and destroy the death camps. Shortly after visiting the newly liberated camps, General Dwight D. Eisenhower, supreme head of the Allied forces in Western Europe, cabled a very perspicacious statement to General George C. Marshall:

> The things I saw beggar description... The visual evidence and the verbal testimony of starvation, cruelty, and bestiality were so overpowering as to leave me a bit sick... I made the visit deliberately, in order to be in position to give *first-hand* [italics in original] evidence of these things if ever, in the future, there

develops a tendency to charge these allegations merely to "propaganda."[15]

THE EFFECTS OF THE HOLOCAUST ON THE JEWISH PEOPLE: "The bloods of your brother cries out to Me from the earth" (Genesis 4:10). The Talmud states that G-d used the plural "bloods" in referring to Abel's murder to signify the bloods of his future descendants that were destroyed.[16] Likewise, the bloods of six million Jews were spilled, which after sixty years would easily amount to many times the 15 million Jews alive today. As such, the Jewish nation is but a small remnant of what it could have been. Moreover, the Holocaust destroyed forever the sublime Jewish way of life in Eastern Europe, the cradle of great Chassidic movements and illustrious yeshivos, along with renowned communities that lived in piety for more than a thousand years. Many of these institutions vanished forever, while others were greatly decimated. The focus of Jewish life and its major population centers shifted to the United States and Israel. There, Holocaust survivors attempted to rebuild their shattered lives, and in the main succeeded, raising a new generation of Jews. A number of leading chassidic rebbes survived, such as those of Ger, Satmar, Lubavitch, Bobov, Belz, Vizhnitz, and Klausenberg. Despite having endured great horrors, they were able to infuse many survivors with inspiration and form a new nucleus of followers to carry on their great traditions. Illustrious heads of Lithuanian yeshivos escaped as well, and led by the indefatigable Rabbi Aharon Kotler, reestablished brilliant Lithuanian Torah tradition on new shores.

The Jewish people will never forget the sacred memory of its holy martyrs, and there will be a great void in the Jewish heart that will not be healed until the days of the Messiah. Then, in the words of the Prophet Isaiah (25:8), "He [G-d] will eliminate death forever, and the L-rd G-d will erase tears from all faces and remove the shame of His nation from upon the earth, for G-d has spoken."

Chapter 32

THE ESTABLISHMENT OF THE STATE OF ISRAEL

PALESTINE DURING WORLD WAR II: In the early stages of the war, Palestine was not in immediate danger, although Italian aircraft did bomb Tel Aviv in September 1939, killing 107 Jews.[1] Despite being infuriated by the White Paper, the Jews of Palestine rallied to Ben-Gurion's striking declaration, "We will fight with the British against Hitler as if there were no White Paper; we will fight the White Paper as if there were no war." Recruitment into the Allied forces, and a desire to serve the Allied cause, were parallel with the hope of bringing in, legally or illegally, as many European Jews as could escape Nazi rule.

THE GERMANS APPROACH PALESTINE: In 1942, German General Erwin Rommel, the famed Desert Fox, invaded Egypt, thereby threatening the Jewish settlements in Palestine. In desperation, the British-trained members of the Haganah, the main Jewish self-defense force, created plans to conduct a guerrilla campaign against the Germans if Palestine should fall. These troops became known as the Palmach, or strike forces. Palestinian Jewish units also served in Vichy French areas of the Middle East, such as Syria and Lebanon, gaining valuable combat experience, which would later come to great use in the Israeli Army. In one of these campaigns, famed general Moshe Dayan lost an eye.

BRITISH-JEWISH COOPERATION ENDS: Once the danger to Palestine ebbed, when Rommel was driven back in autumn 1942, the British had no more use for armed Jewish soldiers in Palestine. Fearing that a Jewish army would provide the impetus for an independent Jewish state, the British relegated the Haganah to its former illegal status and attempted to disarm the Jewish soldiers.

Yet the Jews wanted neither to disband nor disarm. First, news of the Holocaust reached Palestine, creating a greater sense of urgency for bringing as many European Jews as possible. For this effort, the Jews knew they would need a military organization, and, if possible, arms. Second, the Jews had no illusions about British policy in Palestine. Despite British awareness of the Holocaust (as early as 1941 British intelligence had intercepts of SS radio transmissions describing the slaughter of the Jews),[2] the British continued their callous policy of prohibiting Jewish immigration to Palestine. Shiploads of desperate Jews fleeing Europe were not permitted to land in Palestine. To make matters worse, pressure was brought to bear on such European countries as Romania, Bulgaria, and Turkey to restrict the flow of Jews to Palestine. In those few cases in which the British allowed illegal Jews to settle in Palestine, the total number of refugees was deducted from that year's quota of Jewish immigrants.

The single event that did the most to turn Jews against Britain was the infamous *Struma* affair. An unseaworthy cattle boat, the *Struma* carried 769 Jewish refugees from Romania. In December 1941, the *Struma* landed in Turkey, where the beleaguered Jews applied for Palestine entry visas. When the British rejected the applications, the Turks towed the boat out to sea and cast it adrift. She sank, drowning all but two survivors, who were then admitted to Palestine in what was callously termed "an act of clemency." The grief and indignation of the Jewish people over the fate of the *Struma*'s passengers was intense, creating bitter anti-British feelings. At that point, many Jews felt that the only course open to them was to wage a war of liberation against the British rulers of Palestine. (It is important to note that Torah authorities generally do not approve of violence against a regime that physically oppresses the Jewish people. Negotiation, which more often succeeds than violence, is preferred.)

After World War II ended, and the full extent of the horrors of the Holocaust became known, there were increasing calls on Great Britain to allow large numbers of survivors into Palestine. In an extremely callous, insensitive remark, Prime Minister Clement Attlee said, "Now if our offices had placed the Jews in a special racial category at the head of the queue, my strong view is that the effect of this would have been disastrous for the Jews."[3] When General Barker, military commander in Palestine, announced military boycott measures against the Jewish community, he said that these measures "will be punishing the Jews in a way the race dislikes as much as any, by striking at their pockets and showing our contempt for them."[4] Such overtly anti-Semitic attitudes were widespread in the British government and among the colonial administration of Palestine.

THE THREE JEWISH RESISTANCE GROUPS: There were three main Jewish fighting groups that waged a guerrilla war against the British in Palestine. At times, the groups worked together; more often than not, they followed their own, sometimes conflicting, agendas of resistance.

The Haganah and Palmach comprised the military arm of David Ben-Gurion's Jewish Agency. Legal during the Axis threat to Palestine, the Haganah went underground when the British authorities declared it illegal in 1942. The largest Jewish fighting force in Palestine, the Haganah was the least violent in its methods. Its primary goals were to protect Jewish settlements throughout the land and effect positive change in Britain's immigration policy, particularly to reverse the restrictive White Paper.

The Irgun, led by Menachem Begin, advocated a prolonged campaign of destruction in order to drive the British out of Palestine and establish an independent Jewish state. Targeting British soldiers, the Irgun provoked the British into savage reprisals, including the hanging of a number of Irgun members.

The Stern Gang, also known as Lechi, was the smallest and the most radical of the Jewish resistance groups. The British relentlessly hunted down its members; its leader, Avraham Stern, was killed by British forces in a shoot-out.

These resistance forces constantly harassed British troops in Palestine. A few of the more famous incidents:

In 1944 the Stern Gang assassinated Lord Moyne, the British minister in Cairo. This vicious murder caused great harm to the Zionist cause, for Lord Moyne, although previously opposed to Jewish immigration, was then advocating a Jewish state in part of Palestine. Through his leadership, the British government was becoming more inclined in that direction. Moyne's two murderers were hanged, and British policy became implacably anti-Jewish and remained so.

In 1945 the Haganah sabotaged the Palestine railway system in 153 places, and in an even more daring attack in 1946, blew up ten of the eleven bridges connecting Palestine with its surrounding nations, effectively isolating the country from its neighbors. In response, the British launched a nationwide search for arms and commanders. Tel Aviv was combed block by block, its houses and buildings inspected unsuccessfully from basement to attic.

In 1946 the Irgun carried out the bombing of British military headquarters at Jerusalem's King David Hotel, killing ninety-one Jews, British, and Arabs. An anonymous woman telephoned the switchboard operator at the hotel saying that the hotel must be evacuated as there would be an explosion "in a few minutes." Her warning was ignored.[5] The furious British placed Jerusalem and Tel Aviv under curfew for four days, and General Barker imposed a boycott against Jewish shops.

In 1947, in reprisal for the execution of three of its members, the Irgun captured two British sergeants, hanged them, and booby-trapped the corpses, causing injury to British personnel who cut down the bodies. The murder of the sergeants caused the greatest wave of anti-Jewish fury yet carried out by the British. Troops in Tel Aviv went on a rampage, firing on buses, smashing cafés, even murdering several Jews; in Britain, anti-Semitic riots broke out in several cities. At that point, Palestine was trapped in a brutal cycle of terrorism and reprisal.

JEWISH REFUGEES: Hundreds of thousands of Jewish refugees in Europe dreamed of the one place that wanted to take them in — the Jewish community of Palestine. But to get there, the refugees would have to run the gauntlet of the British army, navy, and air force stationed throughout Europe and Palestine and set to prevent any Jewish immigration. The Jewish Brigade, the Jewish fighting force that had fought with the Allies during the war, threw its energy into sneaking as many Jews as possible into Palestine. The Brigade organized escape routes over harsh European mountain terrain to Italian ports, where hastily outfitted boats waited to take the refugees to Palestine.

THE *EXODUS*: Thousands of Jewish refugees attempted to enter Palestine by sea, but the British Navy, one of the best marine forces in the world, almost always intercepted the boats. All but five of sixty-three refugee ships were seized between 1945 and 1948, and 26,000 DPs were interned on the island of Cyprus. To discourage immigration, the internment camps were made as forbidding as possible. The heat in the summer was infernal, water was always scarce, and food barely adequate. Even so, the flood of refugees continued with growing momentum.[6] Between August 1945 and May 1948, as many as 40,000 Jews made their way to Palestine clandestinely.[7]

The *Exodus*, the biggest and most famous of all the refugee ships, was a derelict tramp steamer barely fit for a river voyage, let alone for travel on the high seas. Loaded with 4,554 Jewish men, women, and children, the ship left from France in 1947 bound for Palestine, shadowed every step of the way by four British destroyers. Arriving in Haifa, the *Exodus* was stormed by British boarding parties. Although the beleaguered passengers put up stiff resistance, they were overpowered by the British troops, who killed three Jews and wounded 28. The entire episode was filmed and photographed, then broadcast worldwide, causing a public relations disaster for Britain.

If the British would have taken the passengers to Cyprus, the matter might have eventually died down. However, the British were determined to make an example of the *Exodus* to try to discourage further attempts. British ships brought the passengers back to France, which, while offering asylum to the Jews, refused to force them to disembark. When the Jews decided to remain aboard, the British took them to a displaced persons' camp in Germany. By that point, if the British had been in collusion with the Zionist propaganda machine, it could not have contrived a more telling conclusion to the two-month saga of the *Exodus*. More than any other factors, it was London's preoccupation with Arab goodwill, along with its uncompromising attitude on the immigration issue, that provoked Zionist demands for Jewish statehood, ignited terrorism, launched the illegal refugee traffic to Palestine, undermined Britain's economy, eroded its international reputation, and finally doomed the Palestine mandate itself.[8]

BRITAIN CONSULTS THE UNITED NATIONS: Britain realized it was in a fight it could not possibly win. The immediate political objective of the Jewish guerrilla war — freeing Jewish immigration into Palestine — was one that had been publicly endorsed by American President Truman and was supported by public opinion in the United States. This American factor was one that Britain could not ignore, for it was totally dependent upon American postwar monetary aid to rebuild its shattered national infrastructure and to feed its hungry population. American Jews, who were then almost completely Zionistic, were concentrated in major urban areas and had disproportionate leverage in Congress and national elections. Britain therefore was concerned that a concerted Jewish effort to block Congressional aid to Britain would result in a financial disaster. Therefore, in February 1947, the British decided to submit their Palestine problem to the United Nations.

At that point, Great Britain was hoping that the United Nations would not be able to muster the two-thirds majority required for partitioning Palestine into Jewish and Arab states, due to the opposition of the Arab nations and the Soviet bloc, and would therefore advise the British to maintain the status quo. In that case, with the acquiescence of the world's nations Britain could reassert its control over Palestine and enforce the White Paper.

The United Nations decided to send a commission of eleven nations to Palestine to tour the country and make recommendations. Nations such as Yugoslavia, India, Guatemala, and Australia, which were distant from the conflict and had no vested interest in its outcome, were selected for the commission, known as UNSCOP. The members traveled throughout Palestine in the summer of 1947, speaking to Jews and Arabs, and were present during the episode of the *Exodus*, which affected them deeply. A majority of UNSCOP members recommended partition.

On November 29, 1947 the crucial vote came to the General Assembly, where each member nation, no matter how small, had one vote. The outcome was in doubt until the representative of the Soviet Union astounded the world by calling for the establishment of a Jewish state in part of Palestine. This vote assured the passage of the partition resolution, for the Soviet Union controlled the votes of its satellite nations. In the end, thirty-three nations voted in favor, thirteen against, including all the Arab and Muslim nations, and ten abstained, including Great Britain. Despite being allotted only three barely contiguous snippets of land for the Jewish state, and the frightful prospect of a brutal war with the Arabs, a great joy erupted in the Jewish world, where even many non-Zionist Jews realized an extraordinary moment in Jewish history had come to pass. (The anti-Zionist Jews of Meah Shearim and some others, such as Rabbi Velvel Soloveitchik, did not regard this as extraordinary, and in fact bitterly opposed it.) What else but Divine providence could have brought the United States and the Soviet Union, two bitter ideological enemies which had voted on the same side only twice in fifty years, to support the founding of the first Jewish state in so many years?

THE FIGHTING BEGINS: Immediately following the UN declaration, fighting broke out between the Arabs and Jews in Palestine. The five and a half month period from the vote to the establishment of the State of Israel was one of bitter war, with enormous casualties on both sides. In the first six weeks alone, 769 Jews were killed in Jerusalem.[9] Each side realized that whatever it could grab in the days before actual partition would likely become part of its nation.

The British, hoping to curry favor with the Arab world, and seething with resentment toward the Jews for landing them in such a predicament, actively supported the Arab cause. The Jews were denied the right to form a militia, and the British disarmed Haganah members wherever they were found. At the same time, the British sold weapons to neighboring Arab states, turned over arms and military installations to the Arabs inside Palestine, and in some cases helped the Arabs fight. In February 1948, British troops detonated truck bombs on Jerusalem's Ben-Yehudah Street, killing fifty-two Jews.[10] The British froze all of Palestine's assets, leaving nothing in the treasury for a successor regime.[11]

Although the Jews accepted the miniscule parcels allotted to them with great reluctance, the Arabs refused to recognize the UN resolution, stating that the Jews could not control any land in Palestine. Arab-instigated violence broke out immediately, with attacks on the Jewish quarters of Jerusalem, Haifa, and Jaffa, and on Jewish settlements around the country. Throughout the Arab world, riots erupted against Jewish communities that had existed for hundreds, even thousands, of years, eventually leading to the flight of hundreds of thousands of Jews from Arab lands and the destruction of great, ancient communities.

JERUSALEM: Although the UN resolution called for Jerusalem to be an international city, both Jews and Arabs bitterly fought for control. The situation of the Jews was particularly grave, as relief columns moving along the highway from the lowlands were systematically decimated by ambushes in the hills. Prohibited by the British from bringing in ammunition, organizing their reserves, and defending their communications openly, the Jews faced the grimmest period of their struggle for independence. By the end of March 1948, as the gauntlet of Arab fusillades from the hill areas became increasingly lethal, the entire Haganah convoy system was in danger of collapse. Arabs controlled the three roads leading to Jerusalem, and the city's Jewish population faced the imminent likelihood of being starved or overrun. On occasion, the Jews were able to gain temporary control of a road, and in that brief time span sent trucks with emergency provisions to Jerusalem, averting mass starvation. Eventually, with incredible difficulty, the Jews built a new bypass road to Jerusalem.

DEIR YASSIN: The Arab village of Deir Yassin lay astride the western approaches to Jerusalem, and its capture was key to keeping open the lifeline of supplies to the capital. On April 9, 1948, Irgun and Stern Gang forces attacked the village, and in the ensuing melee 250 Arab civilians were killed, with a number of captives marched through the streets of Jerusalem. Begin maintained that a warning, which was ignored, was given to unarmed civilians to flee before the fighting. When armed men dressed as women began firing on Jewish soldiers, the Jews shot back, and in the heat of battle were unable to distinguish between armed and unarmed men, women, and children. The Arabs insisted that the Jews massacred them in cold blood, fully knowing that the women and children were unarmed. The controversy continues to generate much bitterness to this day.

What actually happened at Deir Yassin may be in question, but there is no dispute about the effects of what was believed to have happened. The news of Deir Yassin, as broadcast on Arab radio, precipitated a flight of Arabs away from areas with large Jewish populations. By mid-May, roughly 300,000 Arabs had already fled their homes, partly in terror and partly with the encouragement of neighboring Arab countries, which exhorted them to flee the fighting and return when the Arabs conquered the entire country. Towns with large Arab populations, such as Haifa, Jaffa, and Tzefas, emptied out rapidly. This first flight of

Palestinian Arabs does not appear to have been forced by the Jews; in fact, the Jews of Haifa pleaded with the Arabs to remain.

Arab retribution for Deir Yassin came quickly. Five days later, Arabs attacked a clearly marked medical convoy of doctors, nurses, and patients heading to Jerusalem's Hadassah Hospital, murdering seventy-seven Jews. British troops in the area refused to let Haganah forces come to the rescue, and only belatedly came to the convoy's assistance.

THE PROCLAMATION OF THE STATE OF ISRAEL: After days of agonizing indecision and debate, David Ben-Gurion proclaimed the establishment of the State of Israel at 6:00 p.m. on May 14, 1948 (5 Iyar), in Tel Aviv. Against the advice of the State Department, President Truman recognized Israel eleven minutes later, and the Soviet Union followed suit two hours afterward.

Many Jews worldwide were joyous, but understandably apprehensive about the inevitable fighting that lay ahead. At the expiration of the British mandate over Palestine, six Arab nations — Egypt, Jordan, Syria, Iraq, Saudi Arabia, and Lebanon — invaded the country. Egyptian planes bombed Tel Aviv, and Ben-Gurion's first broadcast as Prime Minister of Israel was held in an air-raid shelter. Azzam Pasha, the Secretary General of the Arab League, proclaimed: "This will be a war of extermination and a momentous massacre which will be spoken of like the Mongolian massacres and the Crusades."

THE EARLY STAGES OF THE BATTLE: The greatest danger to Israel came in the early stages of the fighting, when the newborn nation possessed no artillery or aircraft to offset the great Arab advantage in weaponry. Arab strategy called for the Syrians and Lebanese to invade the Galilee in the north and occupy Tiberias and Tzefas. Egyptian forces were to attack from the south, moving in the direction of Tel Aviv, while the Jordanian Arab Legion and Iraqi troops opened the principal thrust toward Jerusalem and Haifa. Military observers in the United States and Great Britain gave the State of Israel a slim chance of survival.

"Behold, the Guardian of Israel neither slumbers nor sleeps" (Psalms 121:4). With the help of G-d, the Israeli forces withstood the initial onslaught. Syrian troops came down from the Golan Heights and attacked Kibbutz Deganiah, a position vital to the preservation of the north. The Arabs were about to overrun the kibbutz when two ancient howitzers, used in the Franco-Prussian War of 1870, arrived. Opening fire on the Syrian tanks and infantry, the two guns wrought havoc, psychological as well as physical, and the Syrians withdrew. Had the Syrians known that these two obsolete weapons represented half the arsenal of Jewish field guns in Palestine, they would have pressed the attack. Instead, the armored vehicles swung around in their tracks, clattered back up the mountain road, and never returned.

The howitzers were not the only Israeli weapons that had an effect greater than mere physical might. In several battles, the Jews used a homemade mortar known as a *davidka*, after its inventor David Leibovitch. It was not very effective, but it made a huge noise, gave the impression of being a powerful piece of weaponry, and fooled the Arab soldiers. There are a number of *davidka* monuments throughout Israel in tribute to this remarkable weapon.

For their part, the Iraqis proved only barely more effective than the Syrians. After an Israeli attack on Jenin failed, the Iraqis remarkably failed to counterattack and simply held their positions. Had they continued their offensive, the Iraqis might well have cut the newborn Jewish state in half. In the south, the Egyptian Army marched up the road extending to Gaza and Tel Aviv. In five days of ferocious fighting at Kibbutz Yad Mordechai and Kibbutz Negba, the exhausted and undermanned Israelis halted the Egyptian advance. These five days saved the State of Israel, for in that time Tel Aviv's defenses were strengthened, and reinforcements were found and rushed to hold the highway. Another Egyptian thrust was stopped at Kibbutz Ramat Rachel, very close to Rachel's Tomb and Jerusalem. The kibbutz was overrun and reconquered several times, until Israeli reinforcements arrived to halt the Egyptian advance on Jerusalem.

However, these victories were tinged with heartbreaking defeats. Israeli efforts to capture the police station at Latrun, key to opening the Tel-Aviv-Jerusalem road, were repeatedly repulsed. Casualties were very high among the green and untrained soldiers, many of whom had just landed in Israel from European DP camps and were rushed to the battlefield with barely a weapon in their hands. The Jordanian Arab Legion, trained and lead by British officers, besieged and pounded the Jewish Quarter of Jerusalem with artillery, and after a long struggle forced the religious occupants to surrender. Finally, Jewish soldiers were able to stop the Jordanian advance, holding on to the New City of Jerusalem.

Although half of Jerusalem was saved, the loss of the quarter, which, with the *Kosel HaMa'aravi* and its many synagogues, represented the spiritual center of the Jewish people, was a bitter blow to Jews everywhere. For nineteen years, until 1967, Jews were not permitted to visit the holy sites, while the Jordanians desecrated synagogues and Jewish gravesites on the Mount of Olives.

THE FIRST CEASE-FIRE: On June 11, the United Nations negotiated a temporary cease-fire between Israel and the Arabs. This interlude was a great blessing for Israel, as the nation's war-weary soldiers were able to rest before the inevitable next round of fighting. In addition, while the Arab forces did not unite to strengthen their positions or rearm, the Israelis were able to import significant amounts of weaponry illegally from abroad, particularly from Czechoslovakia. More immigrants arrived from British detention camps in Cyprus, augmenting the Israeli forces. Foreign volunteers, including some non-Jews, came to help the Israeli cause, some illegally flying American fighter planes to Israel from American bases.[12] (One of these volunteers, an American West Point graduate named Mickey Marcus, became the commander of the Jerusalem front. Tragically, an Israeli sentry mistakenly killed him when Marcus failed to give the proper password at night.)

THE *ALTALENA* INCIDENT — JEW VS. JEW: On June 19, the ship *Altalena* approached Tel Aviv with French arms destined for the Irgun. Ben-Gurion, as leader of the State of Israel, demanded that the weapons be handed over to central command, and that the men on board join the Israeli Army. When the Irgun refused to follow these orders, Israeli soldiers fired on the ship in full view of citizens on the beach. The Irgun returned fire, and there were casualties on both sides. Civil war, which would have been an un-mitigated disaster for the new country, was averted when Menachem Begin, who was on the *Altalena*, ordered Irgun troops to back down. Quickly, Irgun and Stern Gang forces were ab-sorbed into the national army, the Israel Defense Forces (*Tzahal*). The *Altalena* crisis was safely over, but the vision of that burning ship on the beach at Tel Aviv was to haunt the politi-cal life of the new state for decades to come. (For example, when Prime Minister Yitzhak Rabin, who was among those that fired on the *Altalena*, was assassinated by a right-wing radical in 1995, the *Altalena* matter was brought up again.)

THE SECOND ROUND OF FIGHTING: Freshly rearmed and rested, the Israeli forces went on a ten-day offensive in July. In the north, they cleared out Arab forces in the vicinity of Nazareth, exerting control over much of the Galilee. In the center of the country, the Israelis captured the important Lydda-Ramle area, including the British-built international airport. (Latrun re-mained unconquered until 1967.) However, the Egyptians were still not dislodged from the Negev in the south. The fighting ended with another United Nations truce.

THE BERNADOTTE MISSION: The United Nations dispatched the Swedish Count Felix Bernadotte to Palestine to seek a perma-nent peace. He proposed, among other things, to greatly limit Is-rael's sovereignty as a nation, ceding Jerusalem to the Arabs. These proposals were rejected by Israel as preposterous, and by the Arabs for leaving even a vestige of a Jewish state. On Septem-ber 16, the Stern Gang assassinated Bernadotte in Jerusalem, and the worldwide outcry prompted the Israelis to disband the remnants of the Stern Gang, although the assassin was never brought to trial.

THE LAST FIGHTING: The final phase of the War of Independence began in October and lasted two months. During this time, the Israelis captured the entire Galilee and drove the Egyptians out of the Negev. Through the dogged mediation of American UN official Ralph Bunche, Israel signed armistice agreements with its warring neighbors, except Iraq. Israel hoped that these agreements would translate into permanent peace treaties, but such was not to be. The Arabs, terming the establishment of Israel *Al-Naqbah*, The Great Disaster, overthrew rulers in Syria, Egypt, and Iraq, replacing them with leaders even more implacably hostile to the Jewish state. In Jordan, King Abdullah was assassinated on the Jordanian-controlled Temple Mount, and his grandson Hussein became the new monarch. Although the State of Israel was a fact, in the eyes of its neighbors it was horrifying and humiliating. For more than fifty years, *Al-Naqbah* has colored the relationship of Arabs and Israelis.

ISRAEL AFTER THE WAR: Israel wound up with 21 percent more territory than had been allotted to it under the UN partition plan. Although Israel existed on a single contiguous piece of land, it still had numerous severe strategic weaknesses. The Syrians controlled the Golan Heights and frequently shelled Jewish farms and settlements in the lowlands below. The Egyptians continually sent terrorists across the long border dividing the Negev and the Sinai Desert, and the Egyptian-controlled Gaza Strip became a center of terrorist activity. In the middle of the country, the Jordanian-controlled West Bank lay eleven miles from Tel Aviv, narrowing to nine miles near Netanya. In Jerusalem, the Mandelbaum Gate divided the Jewish and Arab sections of the city, and Jordanian soldiers occasionally shot at Jewish passersby.

The human cost of the war was appalling. Some 6,000 Jews,

1 percent of the Jewish population, had perished in the conflict, equivalent proportionately to 2.5 million Americans; 300,000 Israelis were wounded. Military expenditures alone had consumed nearly $500 million. The land itself was desolated, as many of its most productive fields lay gutted and mined, and its citrus groves, for decades the mainstay of the economy, were largely destroyed. These grievous wounds notwithstanding, Israel was alive and operating, and was an internationally recognized nation. In May 1949, Israel joined the United Nations.

THE PALESTINIAN REFUGEES: No other issue is as explosive in the Arab-Israeli conflict, and indeed in international relations, as that of the Arabs who left Israel as a result of the 1948 war. According to Israel, some 538,000 Arabs left the country, while the United Nations places the number of refugees at 720,000, 70 percent of the Arab population of Palestine.[13] This discrepancy is of great significance, for based on the higher figure there are currently 3.7 million Palestinians claiming a so-called right of return.

In the long and polemical war of words that has been conducted over these unfortunate refugees, the Arabs refer to the Palestinians as being driven out, while the Israelis maintain that they fled. It appears that a majority did indeed flee, while some were in fact chased out.[14] In the early phase of the fighting, the Haganah had no policy of driving out Arabs, and in Haifa even attempted to persuade them to stay. Later in the fighting, Arabs were encouraged to leave, particularly in Lydda, Ramle, and parts of the Galilee. These Arabs went to the West Bank, Gaza, and neighboring Arab countries, where they were housed in squalid refugee camps under UN auspices. Except for Jordan, all the Arab nations refused to settle these refugees in their vast territories, preferring to keep them in the refugee camps to be used both as a political lever against Israel and as an anti-Israeli propaganda tool. Israel understandably was reluctant to allow large numbers of potential enemies back into the country, thereby destroying the Jewish character of the state. As a result, several generations of Palestinians grew up in these camps, with no future and no *raison d'être* other than a seething hatred toward Israel. Today, these camps are the main source of anti-Israeli terrorism and homicide bombing.

RELIGIOUS REACTION TO THE STATE OF ISRAEL: As it became apparent that there would indeed be a Jewish state in Palestine, Agudath Israel, the main Orthodox organization in Eretz Yisrael, concluded a landmark agreement with the Jewish Agency. Wishing to include as broad a spectrum of Jews in the new state as possible, secular leaders, headed by David Ben-Gurion, reluctantly agreed to four points insisted upon by Agudath Israel. Signed on June 19, 1947, the document became known as the Status Quo Agreement. Its four major provisions:

First, observance of the Sabbath in public life. The Sabbath was to be the official day of rest of the State of Israel, with government offices and services closed on that day.

Second, observance of kashrus in government installations.

Third, marriage and divorce governed by Torah law.

Fourth, the right to religious education.[15]

While these four principles continue to be the quasi-official policy of the State of Israel, they have come under much attack by secular Jews, there being no constitution to enforce them as law. As such, there has been great struggle over opening stores, running buses and airlines, operating industrial and agricultural plants, and holding sporting events on the Sabbath. These conflicts persist today, the most recent of which was the controversy over orders given to religious soldiers to violate the Sabbath for a non-urgent military need. The maintenance of kashrus has also come under fire, with secular kibbutzim raising hogs and stores importing non-kosher meat and food products. Although the government provides financial aid to religious schools, there being no separation of religion and state as exists in the United States, there has been bitter conflict between the religious and secular sectors of the population over sharing educational funding.

Perhaps the most bitter and potentially dangerous area of confrontation lies in the areas of marriage, divorce, and conversion, which have the potential to tear Israeli society apart. Although conflict over this issue has existed since the inception of the state, notably with the divisive *Mi Hu Yehudi* (Who Is a Jew) controversy regarding non-halachic conversions to Judaism, the matter has greatly worsened in recent years. The arrival of great numbers of immigrants from the former Soviet Union in the 1990s, many not Jewish by any standard, has created a volatile situation in Israel, with secular Israelis demanding that the new arrivals be registered as Jews. Reform and Conservative Jews in America have exerted enormous pressure on the Israeli government to have their marriages, divorces, and conversions — all invalid under Torah law — recognized by the state. If successful, an unbridgeable gap will be created in Israeli society, for religious Jews will be unable to marry anyone whose lineage or ancestry is in doubt.

AGUDAH PARTICIPATES IN THE STATE OF ISRAEL: Although in the 1920s and 30s Agudath Israel would not work with the Jewish Agency due to the latter's anti-Torah stance, matters changed when the Agency became the government of the Jewish state. Religious Jews were citizens of Israel, regardless of what they thought of the state's leadership or policies. Realizing this, the Torah leadership of Agudath Israel, the *Moetzes Gedolei HaTorah*, issued the following proclamation, written by Rabbi Reuven Grozovsky:

> There is a difference between a state and a movement. In a state, for example, should we not participate in the elections, it would mean relinquishing our basic rights and even assisting them [the secular parties] to rule over us with ever greater power... The participation in the elections cannot be considered an approval of their government, their laws, or their ideals. The rule "Don't associate with the wicked" is not applicable here since, even unwillingly, merely by virtue of living in the country, everyone is associated.[16]

As a result, almost all religious Jews take an active political role in the State of Israel, forming their own political parties, electing representatives to the Knesset (Israel's parliament), and accepting government positions in both national and local organizations. From the outset, Agudath Israel has made every effort to obtain the observance of Jewish religious principles and practice in Israeli public life. For example, when the government attempted to force girls to enter the army, the Chazon Ish, the eminent Torah leader in Israel at the time, threatened a massive campaign of noncompliance, stating that this was a religious matter of life and death. Realizing the fierce determination of religious Jews regarding this issue, the government backed down. Agudah also won the right of yeshivah students, as well as other *chareidi* (non-Zionist religious) youngsters, to be excused from national military service. (Unfortunately, this remains a highly controversial issue in Israel today.)

ISRAEL'S FIRST NATIONAL ELECTIONS: In January 1949, Israeli voters went to the polls for the first time, electing 120 representatives to the Knesset. Left-wing parties won sixty-five seats, with Mapai, the largest labor party, garnering forty-six. Center-right parties received thirty-one seats, with Menachem Begin's Herut party winning fourteen. Religious parties totaled sixteen seats, with smaller parties receiving the remaining seats, including three Arab delegates. This ratio was essentially the voting profile that had existed in Palestine before the establishment of the state.[17] Eventually, Mapai turned into the Labor Party, and Herut became the Likud Party. Left-wing parties dominated successive Israeli governments until 1977, when Menachem Begin, in a stunning election victory, became prime minister of Israel. David Ben-Gurion became Israel's first prime minister.

THE LAW OF RETURN: Jews everywhere recognized that the State of Israel's very existence was based on providing one place on earth where Jews would be welcomed when they fled oppression. To that end, in one of its earliest pieces of legislation, the government of Israel drafted the landmark Law of Return. Signed in July 1950, the law guaranteed the right of every Jew, wherever he or she might live in the world, to enter Israel as an immigrant and become a citizen immediately on arrival (with the exception of those judged to be a danger to public health or security). To this day, a major portion of Israel's national budget is allocated for transporting and settling Jewish immigrants in Israel.

DIVINE PROVIDENCE IN THE ESTABLISHMENT OF ISRAEL: Timing was absolutely critical to Israel's birth and survival. Soviet Premier Stalin launched an intensely anti-Semitic campaign in 1948, adopting anti-Israel policies at the end of the year. By that time, however, Israel was securely in existence, due in no small part to Stalin's earlier efforts. America's policy was also changing, as the growing pressures of the Cold War dissolved her postwar idealism, forcing President Truman to listen more to State Department advice, which regarded Israel as a strategic liability. If British evacuation had been postponed, the United States would have been far less anxious to see Israel created, while the Soviet Union would almost certainly have been hostile to the Jewish state's birth. Therefore, Israel slipped into existence through a fortuitous window in history, which briefly opened for a few months in 1947–48. In the words of one prominent non-Jewish historian: "That too was luck; or providence."[18] Another historian writes: "A new state thus saw the light of day, in circumstances as fantastic as those related in the Arabian nights."[19]

Clearly, when G-d wills it, even the worst enemies become His tools for the benefit of the Jewish people.

Chapter 33

THE 1950s

THE GREAT IMMIGRATION TO ISRAEL: With the arrival of 684,000 new immigrants, Israel's Jewish population doubled within the first four years of the State's existence. These *olim*, as they came to be known, were made up in equal parts of Holocaust survivors and immigrants from Middle Eastern and North African Arab countries. The largest contingents were 123,000 Jews from Iraq, 118,000 from Romania, and 108,000 from Poland. Almost all of Bulgaria's 45,000 Jews also came during this time.

And the time was one of great hardship. A nation of 600,000 people had just fought for its life and immediately had to absorb an even greater number of immigrants. Most of those who arrived had been through horrible experiences, traumatizing them both physically and psychologically. Almost all of them had no source of livelihood and virtually no possessions. Even generous funding from Jews in the United States and Great Britain was not sufficient to cover the enormous costs of resettlement.

However, the immigrants were joyously welcomed, and every effort was made to find them food and shelter. All over Israel, enormous tented camps, known as *ma'abarot*, were set up. Conditions were appalling: there was no privacy, and people were unprotected from the stifling heat of summer and the rain and mud of winter. Although 40,000 newcomers could not stand the Spartan conditions and left, most *olim* stayed.[1] With great energy, Israel succeeded to a large extent in settling the great masses in permanent housing and finding them jobs. Within ten years, the *ma'abarot* disappeared.

Over the years, more than 700,000 Jews from Muslim countries have entered Israel, replacing the 700,000 Palestinians who left. These Jews were forced to leave behind almost all their assets, which in the case of the extremely wealthy Iraqi Jews amounted to billions of dollars of private and communal property. In contrast to the Palestinians who left, who were interned in Arab-controlled refugee camps, Israel has settled its immigrants — no Jewish refugee camps exist for Jews. Palestinian claims for lost assets are easily offset by property confiscated from the Jews of Arab lands. Basically, an even exchange of population has occurred, although Jewish wealth and property left behind in Arab countries far outstripped Arab wealth and property abandoned in Israel.

THE TREATMENT OF THE SEPHARDIM: For all its efforts to resettle Jewish refugees, Israel's treatment of its Sephardic immigrants is one of the most sordid episodes of secular Zionism and a permanent stain on the nation's record. The Europeanized Ashkenazim who ran the State of Israel denigrated the Sephardim for several reasons: The latter were generally poor and uneducated; their skills, mainly as small traders and craftsmen, were not viewed as useful; they did not speak Hebrew or Yiddish; and most important, they were seen as different, not easily blending in to the emerging Israeli culture. While the government attempted to teach Zionistic concepts to the Sephardim, its European values, especially secular humanism and socialism, were utterly foreign to the deeply religious Sephardim.

In addition, Sephardim were discriminated against in numerous ways. Ashkenazic immigrants, even those who arrived later, were given preference in housing and loans over Sephardim who had been in the country much longer. The best jobs and better government positions went to Europeans. Although matters have improved since the early days of the State, there remains much inequity, and the Sephardim, who comprise slightly more than half the Jewish population of Israel, feel great resentment.

Ashkenazic stereotyping of Sephardim had disastrous results. Sephardic children were taught to ridicule the religious value system of their parents, and to become so-called good Israelis, thus destroying parental authority and reverence for legitimate Jewish tradition. As a result, an entire generation of Sephardic Jews, especially from Morocco, which had once been a major bastion of Torah, became secularized and alienated from Judaism. Without spiritual values to sustain them through times of great physical hardship, and robbed of their magnificent heritage, the Sephardic youth gravitated to crime, becoming a permanent underclass in Israeli society.

THE YEMENITE JEWS: In 1949 and 1950, in what became known as Operation Magic Carpet, nearly 50,000 Jews from Yemen, one of the world's most ancient and traditional Jewish communities, were airlifted to Israel. Living in remote villages that had changed little since biblical times, the Yemenite Jews, who had never previously heard of airplane flight, imagined that their exodus from Yemen was the fulfillment of the Messianic prophecy of traveling to Israel "on wings of eagles." There, they looked forward to living a Torah life on the holy soil of Eretz Yisrael. Alas, such was not to be.

Yemenite Jews, all of them deeply religious and completely innocent about modern technology and culture, were deliberately stripped of their ancient heritage and religion. Shameful advantage was taken of the trust the new immigrants placed in those who had magically transported them to the Holy Land. Countless numbers of Yemenite children were taken from their parents — on the spurious grounds that they had infectious diseases that had to be treated in hospitals. A truly diabolical plot then emerged between doctors, nurses, hospital personnel, and government officials. Healthy Yemenite children were kidnapped and placed in non-religious kibbutzim to be raised with the values of secular Zionism; some were sold for adoption to childless secular Ashkenazic families in Israel and even abroad. Within a few years, an entire generation of Yemenite Jews was cut off from its glorious Torah heritage. Sadly, many Yemenites turned to drugs, crime, and an immoral lifestyle.

For their part, the Yemenite parents were falsely informed that their children had died and were buried. These Yemenite Jews, undergoing culture shock and intimidated by the State's officials, lacked the sophistication to navigate the nightmarish Israeli bureaucracy and begin an investigation — even if they had suspected foul play, which most simply did not. The Yemenites were poor, living in settlements or camps distant from where their children were being kept, and had no money to visit them in the hospital or to engage legal help. Besides, why would the people who saved them now lie to them — and about children?

Over the years, more and more adoptive Yemenite children, now grown adults, are discovering their background. Israel's government, afraid of the great backlash a full revelation of the story would create, is trying to squelch the episode by sealing the records of this affair. Nevertheless, as more details emerge, there has been increasing Yemenite resentment toward the government, occasionally leading to violence. Today, the Yemenite affair remains a potentially explosive issue.

GERMAN REPARATIONS: Throughout 1951, the governments of Germany and Israel had discussed an agreement whereby West Germany would pay reparations to Israel for the persecution of Jews during World War II. In 1952, when this agreement was presented to the Knesset for ratification, a political firestorm broke out in Israel. Ben-Gurion favored accepting these reparations, which would provide a valuable source of revenue to the greatly impoverished nation. Additionally, in addressing the Knesset, he passionately declared, "Would the murderers of our people be also their inheritors?" paraphrasing the Prophet Elijah's retort to King Ahab (I Kings 21:19), "Have you killed and also taken possession?"

Menachem Begin argued even more forcefully that the Jewish people should have nothing to do with Germany's dirty money, particularly since the Germans would view the payments as atonement for the Holocaust. This debate was not merely verbal: there were violent scenes in the Knesset, and a riot outside it. After much discussion, the Knesset decided to accept restitution. Hundreds of millions of dollars began flowing into the State, a process that continues today, with Germany contributing much to Israel's economic and military infrastructure. Payments were also made to individual victims of the Holocaust.

THE KASZTNER TRIAL: In 1952, Malchiel Greenwald, who had emigrated from Hungary, accused Rudolf Kasztner, a senior official in the Israeli Ministry of Industry and Trade, of testifying on behalf of SS Lieutenant General Kurt Becher, thus saving him from punishment for his war crimes. Greenwald further accused Kasztner of collaborating with the Nazis and contributing to the death of more than 400,000 Hungarian Jews when Kasztner served as a major leader of the Jewish Agency Rescue Committee in Hungary. At the time of the accusations, Kasztner was an intimate of high Labor Party officials, and not surprisingly the government decided to defend him. As such, in 1954 the State of Israel brought libel charges against Greenwald. The nine-month trial, which held the enraptured attention of the Israeli people, resulted in Greenwald's acquittal. Judge Halevi declared that by accepting an offer from the Nazis to allow a train of prominent people to leave Hungary in return for his silence, Kasztner had "sold his soul to the German Satan" (quote in original). The trial also revealed that a number of prominent government officials had directed the Jewish Agency during the war, and they had not exerted pressure on the British to save Jews for fear of jeopardizing these officials' own high positions and the prospect of a future Jewish state.[2] As a result of this trial, the government fell, and new elections were held. In 1957, a right-wing nationalist assassinated Kasztner for his alleged collaboration with the Nazis.

THE SINAI WAR OF 1956: As a result of *Al-Naqbah*, King Farouk of Egypt was overthrown, and the fiery Gamal Abdul Nasser became Egypt's leader. Through great personal magnetism, electrifying oratory, and the power of radio, Nasser became a preeminent hero in the Arab world. His tirades against Western imperialism and Israel, and his message of pan-Arab nationalism, resonated deeply among Arabs.

In June 1956, after being rebuffed by the United States in seeking aid to build the Aswan Dam, Nasser received a promise of Soviet aid. He also concluded a major arms deal with Czechoslovakia, a Soviet client state, thus greatly increasing Soviet influence in the Middle East. In August, Nasser nationalized the Suez Canal, which ran through Egyptian territory but was under the control of England. Along with American and English opposition, France was also troubled by Nasser, blaming their problems in the North African colony of Algeria on Nasser's propaganda, money, and arms. Israel also desired to see Nasser fall, for not only did he constantly send terrorists across the border, killing hundreds of Israelis, he also closed the Suez Canal to Israeli shipping — an act in open defiance of international law.

Faced with such opposition, Nasser then took steps that would inevitably lead to war. Egypt blocked the Straits of Tiran, an international waterway, to Israeli shipping, meaning that Israel then had no way of shipping goods out of its Red Sea port of Eilat. That blockade, combined with the closing of the Suez Canal, was strangling Israel economically. Nasser also began stepping up rhetoric of a joint Arab campaign to destroy Israel.

In October, Israel met secretly with Britain and France, planning a seemingly foolproof maneuver to humiliate Nasser and remove his threat to their nations. Israel was to invade and conquer the Sinai Desert, then Britain and France were to call upon the warring parties to cease fighting, and for Israel to withdraw from the Sinai. Israel would refuse, and the two allies would send troops into the Canal Zone to protect it from the combatants. The three countries would then emerge gaining their strategic goals, and Nasser would suffer deep humiliation.

The plan worked extremely well. Israel quickly overran the Sinai, and Britain and France, after presenting an ultimatum to Israel and Egypt that was ignored, took the Suez Canal. However, the world saw through the plot, and Israel was considered an aggressor. The United States especially was furious, in part because it was not informed about the campaign beforehand, in part because the campaign made President Eisenhower look bad, coming but a few days before a tough election. In addition, as world attention was previously focused on the Soviet Union's brutal suppression of the Hungarian uprising, and quickly shifted to Suez, the war deprived America of a great propaganda victory against the Soviet Union. For only the second time, the United States and the Soviet Union voted together on a United Nations resolution, this one ordering the three nations to withdraw.

The Soviet Union, eager to divert attention from its atrocities in Hungary, and hoping to gain influence in the Arab world, threatened to destroy the State of Israel. On November 7, Ben-Gurion defiantly gave a victory speech in the Knesset, refusing to withdraw from the Sinai. The United States immediately warned Israel that she would stand on her own against the Soviet Union. The next day, Israel announced its intention to withdraw from Sinai. Although Israel was forced to stand down, it made some important gains in the Sinai War. The Arab nations respected its military prowess, and would think twice before rushing into any future conflict. Israel was also promised an international United Nations observer force to keep open the Straits of Tiran and to stop terrorist incursions from Egypt. These arrangements worked for more than ten years, until Nasser tried a similar strategy in 1967, leading to the Six-Day War.

ISRAEL'S ECONOMIC POSITION IMPROVES: In the second half of the 1950s, Israel experienced spectacular economic growth. In agriculture, Jewish ingenuity literally made the desert bloom, with agricultural advances becoming a model for many developing countries. Indeed, Israel became virtually self-sufficient in agricultural products. The Huleh Valley, a malarial swamp, was drained in 1957, providing lush farmland and ridding the area of disease-bearing mosquitoes.

Gains in industry were equally impressive. Copper ore was extracted from mines in the southern Negev, and the Dead Sea area provided extensive quantities of chemicals and salt. Oil and gas wells were also developed. Tourism began to increase, employing many people and bringing much needed cash into the country. Skilled labor production rose, including diamond polishing, electronics, pharmaceuticals, precision instruments, and fashion goods. Israeli weaponry was exported worldwide, sometimes even to opposing sides of a conflict, and became one of Israel's major industries; it remains as such today. Israel's average per capita gross national product increase was a healthy 6.3 percent, among the highest growth rates in the world.

After the great influx of immigrants during the State's first four years, immigration slowed down. Still, more than 270,000 Jews arrived throughout the 1950s. These immigrants, largely from North Africa and Eastern Europe, brought the Jewish population in Israel close to two million. There were also 250,000 Arabs in Israel as well.

SOVIET JEWRY: In the last years of Stalin's rule, an extended anti-Semitic campaign was pursued in the Soviet Union. Jews were attacked in the press, and thousands of Jewish intellectuals were murdered while others were driven out of public life. In 1952 a show trial was held of leading Jews in the Czechoslovak Communist Party; the trial had ugly anti-Semitic overtones, and eleven Jewish party officials were hanged. The climax came early in 1953, when nine doctors, six of them Jews, were accused of being in conjunction with British, American, and Zionist agents in seeking to poison Stalin. This show trial was to have been the prelude to the mass deportation of Jews to Siberia, part of a Stalinist Final Solution.[3] Fortunately, Stalin died before the doctors came to trial, and his successors dropped the plans for mass deportation. Under Nikita Khrushchev, the new Soviet leader, conditions did not improve greatly. Large numbers of Jews were put on trial for supposed anti-Soviet economic behavior and executed. Khrushchev closed down many synagogues, their total falling from 450 to sixty during his rule. The Khrushchev era also witnessed an outbreak of blood libels, anti-Semitic riots, and synagogue burnings.

TORAH LIFE IN AMERICA: "Though your beginning was insignificant, your end will flourish exceedingly" (Job 8:7). Contrary to the view of many social scientists, who saw Orthodoxy as heading toward extinction, it experienced a remarkable resurgence in the 1950s. Although initial successes were small, they laid the foundation for today's burgeoning American Torah communities.

Rabbi Aharon Kotler, the preeminent Torah leader in the United States, was largely responsible for the dynamic growth of Torah consciousness, yeshivah education, and Agudath Israel in postwar America. American Jews always supported higher education, and even Orthodox parents who sent their children to yeshivah also wanted them to obtain college degrees and become professionals. Reshaping the thinking of American Orthodox Jews, Rabbi Kotler maintained that yeshivos modeled after the great European institutions, which stressed only Torah study, would flourish in America. In 1943, with fourteen students, he founded Beth Medrash Gevoha in Lakewood, New Jersey. By the early 1950s the student body had increased to 100 young men studying Torah. Today, the Lakewood Yeshiva is the largest Torah institution in the world, with several thousand students, some even attending along with their grandchildren. In addition, Lakewood has spawned many vibrant new branches throughout the world, raising the level of Torah study, both qualitatively and quantitatively, to new, previously undreamt of heights.

Rabbi Kotler also pioneered the concept of *kollel* in America, in which married men continued full-time Torah study. At the time, many pundits claimed that *kollel* was a ridiculous, impractical idea, for such young men would never obtain the skills needed to provide a livelihood for their families. However, despite minimal stipends and enormous pressures to support large families, *kollel* study has become increasingly popular. Currently, more than 4,000 married men are members of a *kollel*,[4] with the number constantly increasing. Indeed, Rabbi Kotler's vision created a new cadre of Torah scholars, thereby revitalizing the Jewish people after the destruction of the European Torah world.

TORAH UMESORAH: In 1944, Rabbi Shraga Feivel Mendlowitz of Yeshiva Torah Vodaath founded the National Society for Hebrew Day Schools, or Torah Umesorah. At that time, there were fewer than forty Torah day schools in the United States, almost all located in New York City. Nevertheless, Rabbi Mendlowitz and Rabbi Kotler both realized that Torah would grow in America only if day schools were established in every major Jewish community. When Rabbi Mendlowitz passed away in 1948, Rabbi Kotler served as Torah Umesorah's spiritual advisor until his own passing in 1962.

Within a decade of its founding, and despite facing hostile opposition from Jews who viewed an Orthodox day school network as a threat to the acceptance of Jews in American society, Torah Umesorah had succeeded in making it possible for every Jewish child in communities of 25,000 Jews or more to receive a Torah education.[5] Today, Torah Umesorah proudly claims a coast-to-coast network of some 600 schools, educating 170,000 students from kindergarten through twelfth grade.[6] With the establishment of Jewish day schools in the 1950s, Talmud Torahs, the Orthodox afternoon and Sunday schools, largely went out of existence.

BETH JACOB: If early twentieth-century Torah education for American boys was in poor shape, then it was nonexistent for girls. In 1937, Rebbetzin Vichna Kaplan, Sarah Schenirer's major disciple in Poland, founded Beth Jacob of America with seven girls seated around her dining room table in the Williamsburg section of Brooklyn. Evening classes were begun for public high school students, and a seminary was founded for older girls. Beth Jacob purchased its first school building in 1945; in 1958, to meet the growing demand, Beth Jacob established a new branch in the Boro Park area of Brooklyn, eventually supplanting the Williamsburg school. Today, Beth Jacob educates tens of thousands of students nationwide. It has also been directly responsible for the phenomenal growth of Torah in America, inspiring its graduates to marry full-time scholars and raise large families, joyfully accepting a lower material standard of living while creating homes dedicated to studying and teaching Torah.

CHINUCH ATZMAI: Despite promising to support all religious schools under the Status Quo Agreement, in 1953 the Israeli government nationalized the education system. In a new religious school network, the network of Agudath Israel schools was placed under Mizrachi administration. Terrified of the prospect of traditional schools being run by government officials rather than by Torah scholars, the major Torah leaders in Israel and the United States formed a new, independent network of schools, Chinuch Atzmai. Seeing the financial disaster that occurred when the Israeli government stopped much of its funding to these independent schools, Rabbi Kotler galvanized concerned American laymen to garner support for Chinuch Atzmai. This successful effort enabled the network to open hundreds of new schools throughout Israel, thereby saving many immigrants, especially Sephardim, from the ravages of secular Israeli society. Later, another Torah network of schools, Tashbar, was established as well. Today Chinuch Atzmai and Tashbar have several hundred schools serving some 60,000 students.[7]

CHASSIDIC COMMUNITIES: Between 1944 and 1959, nearly 200,000 Holocaust survivors entered the United States, many chassidic Jews, particularly following Hungarian rebbes such as the Satmar rebbe. Unlike earlier Jewish immigrants, these arrivals sought to maintain their religious way of life, isolating themselves as much as possible from the harmful aspects of American society. In 1948, Rabbi Joel Teitelbaum, the rebbe of Satmar, settled in Williamsburg. Though many of Williamsburg's newly arrived Chassidim had not been the rebbe's immediate disciples before the war, they found in his presence a spiritual magnetism that pulled together the shattered pieces of their lives. One survivor remarked: "When we arrived, we had nothing. We were dazed, hopeless, without any direction or center in our lives. The Satmar rebbe, may he be forever blessed, gave us a center. He instilled in us a new hope and restored our belief in the world — and in ourselves."[8]

Starting with virtually nothing, the rebbe laid the foundations of a new Satmar community, covering the entire spectrum of educational and social services. Today, the community is famous for its extensive emergency first-aid and ambulance service (Hatzolah), and its hospital visitation program (Bikur Cholim), both available to all Jews, regardless of affiliation. In addition, Satmar also has an enormous financial and personal assistance program available to individuals needing expensive medical treatment. The Satmar rebbe also played a key role in raising the standards of Orthodoxy in the United States, particularly in the area of kosher supervision and observance. (For example, *chalav Yisrael*, milk and dairy products under constant Jewish supervision, was a stringency generally not observed by Orthodox Jews. Due to Satmar influence, *chalav Yisrael* is de rigueur in many Orthodox circles today.) Satmar remains one of the largest chassidic groups today, and has created numerous communities outside its Williamsburg base.

Rabbi Joseph Yitzchak Schneerson, the sixth rebbe of Chabad-Lubavitch, arrived in America in 1940, settling in the Crown Heights section of Brooklyn. Upon his 1950 passing, his son-in-law, Rabbi Menachem Mendel Schneerson, became the new rebbe of Lubavitch. Under his guidance, Lubavitch grew from a practically moribund chassidic branch that had lost most of its followers in the Holocaust, into a worldwide movement. Unique among chassidic groups, Lubavitch actively promoted Jewish outreach and was one of the first groups to bring a religious message to many uncommitted Jews. In addition, Lubavitch did great work in keeping alive the small flame of Judaism in the former Soviet Union. Emissaries of the rebbe, known as *shluchim*, have established "Chabad Houses" in countless places, including such remote areas as Nepal, the Congo, and Siberia, thereby bringing religious life to Jews who would otherwise be completely cut off from their heritage. The movement also maintains a vast network of educational institutions. As such, Lubavitch is one of the largest chassidic groups worldwide, and although the rebbe passed away in 1994, it is constantly gaining new adherents.

Other chassidic groups, such as Ger, Bobov, Vizhnitz, and many smaller groups, also experienced resurgence in the 1950s, both in the United States and Israel. Indeed, the 1950s was a decade of great importance in the Orthodox Jewish world, for against all odds a community devastated by the Holocaust established the roots of future Jewish religious survival.

JEWISH DEMOGRAPHIC TRENDS IN THE 1950S: After the Second World War, traditional Judaism was being undermined for many Jews by an unexpected factor: affluence. Almost overnight, the postwar economic boom lifted millions of Americans into the suburban middle class. For Jews, the passage was sped by the collapse of anti-Semitic quotas and covenants, which seemed un-American after the Holocaust. As such, between 1940 and 1957 the proportion of Jews holding white-collar jobs soared from 10 to 55 percent. In the twenty-year period after World War II, one-third of the American Jewish population moved from cities to suburbs. In the process, the Jews spent an estimated $1 billion building a thousand new synagogues, the overwhelming majority of them Conservative and Reform.[9] From the mid-1940s through the 1950s the Conservative movement far outstripped its Reform counterpart in growth, especially in suburban areas.[10]

Indeed, many nonreligious Jews were attracted to the Conservative movement both for its lack of ideology and its willingness to conform its standards to congregational demands — no matter how non-Jewish their basis. For example, in the postwar period the Conservative movement, among other heresies, deemed travel to synagogue on the Sabbath a "worthy act," [11] and therefore permitted — even encouraged — the use of electricity on the Sabbath. The Conservative movement also abolished the second day of holidays and empowered its so-called rabbinical courts to nullify marriages in certain cases, something clearly antithetical to established Torah law. Reform, too, followed suit. Given the direction in which both Conservatism and Reform were headed, in 1956 leading Torah sages in the United States published an official declaration banning Orthodox rabbis from participating in religious organizations and rabbinical boards that grant recognition to Conservative and Reform clergy and congregations.

YESHIVA UNIVERSITY: Between 1945 and 1960, Yeshiva University, the bastion of Modern Orthodoxy, helped establish more than a hundred synagogues in the United States and Canada. These synagogues, situated mainly in the newly developing suburbs, and in areas recently opened to Jews, included some of the wealthiest and largest Orthodox congregations. As new synagogues were founded, people turned to Yeshiva University for assistance in finding rabbis, cantors, and teachers, and the university responded by developing programs to meet these needs. In 1954, Yeshiva University also established Stern College for women. Uptown, its men's division attracted many students who especially wanted to study under its dean, Rabbi Joseph Ber Soloveitchik. Today, Yeshiva University is renowned as a prestigious college, attracting thousands of students.

INTERMARRIAGE: In 1959, the intermarriage rate stood at a relatively low 7.2 percent.[12] The seismic wave of intermarriage that would rock the Jewish world was, inexorably, beginning to expand.

Chapter 34

THE 1960s

CATACLYSMIC UPHEAVAL: With prophetic insight, the Mishnah (*Sotah* 9:15) described the societal turmoil of the 1960s:

In the period which will precede the coming of the Messiah, insolence will increase...there shall be no rebuke...the truth will be absent; the young will shame the old; the aged will rise before the youth; a son will despise his father; a daughter will rise up against her mother...a person's enemies are his family members; the face of the generation is that of a dog; a son is not embarrassed before his father; and we can only rely on our Father in Heaven.

The tidal wave of change that engulfed the world in the second half of the decade created a ripple effect that is still being felt in Jewish and general society. In particular, three major events occurred that had a major impact on the Jewish people: the overturning of the old world order in both social values and intergenerational relationships, the dramatic Israeli victory in the Six-Day War, and the stirrings of what became known as the *ba'al teshuvah* movement, the discovery by previously uncommitted Jews of their religious heritage.

The first half of the decade saw changes that, although subtler, nonetheless had a profound effect on the Jewish people.

THE SILENT HOLOCAUST: With the opening of both suburbia and private colleges to Jews, and the decline of anti-Semitism in the United States, the small trickle of intermarriage in the 1950s became a literal flood in the 1960s, tripling to nearly 20 percent by the end of the decade. Although nowhere near the current rate of higher than 50 percent, the intermarriage rate was enough to raise alarms about Jewish survival. In 1964, the mass-circulation magazine *Look* published a major article called "The Vanishing American Jew." Secular Jewish agencies commissioned studies to analyze the problem, refusing to realize that only commitment to a Torah lifestyle can stem the tide.

THE CIVIL RELIGION OF AMERICAN JEWS: In his book *Faith or Fear*, Elliott Abrams observes:

> To be a Jew in America, indeed to be a good Jew, did not and does not to most American Jews require traditional ritual observance: it no longer means praying three times daily, studying the Torah, keeping kosher, and respecting the Sabbath. Instead, it means feeling oneself a part of the "Jewish community," giving money to that community's institutions, and supporting the liberal and secularist prescriptions for American society that would theoretically allow American Jews to thrive. The perceived interests of the community, and the act of working to advance those interests, have been sacrelized, and have become a sort of secular religion themselves. A model Jew in America is not off in the synagogue at prayer but out at a meeting discussing a new hospital, a trip to Israel, or a new fund-raising drive.[1]

Many Jews came to believe that charity and the pursuit of social justice was itself the heart of the Jewish religion, and donated vast sums toward causes that they felt did not threaten their Jewish identity or lack of observance, such as Israel, Holocaust commemoration, medical research, the environment, civil rights, and combating anti-Semitism. Proportionately very little funding was allocated for such Torah institutions as day schools and yeshivos.

The good works achieved by the American Jewish civic organizations have been immense, but they have failed to keep American Jews Jewish. Organizations such as Hadassah and B'nai B'rith have aging memberships, now averaging in the fifties and sixties, as younger Jews feel less of an affiliation with the Jewish causes of their parents. The United Jewish Appeal (UJA) and its federations have seen the percentage of charitable contributions of major donors drop from 70 percent to less than 30 percent.[2] What was sown in the 1960s reaps a bitter harvest today.

BLACK ANTI-SEMITISM: Reform and secular Jewish groups were the most active of all white people in the struggle for civil rights.[3] Ironically, victory proved a dividing point between Jews and blacks. The Black Muslims, who identified with Islam and the Arabs, became increasingly popular among African-Americans. A new emphasis on Black Power drove whites, especially Jews, from leadership positions in the civil rights movement. Equality of groups replaced the vision of equality of individuals. One had to belong to a group, and group identity was critical. This was a view entirely at odds with liberal Jews, who regarded equality as an individual right and generally shunned group affiliation.

As in Europe, Jews were seen as the oppressors of disadvantaged people. Jews were teachers in black schools, Jews owned retail stores in black neighborhoods, and Jews were the landlords of black ghetto residences. The black riots of the 1960s in major American cities, in which 90 percent of the nation's Jews lived, seemed to single out Jewish stores for destruction. Blacks demanded proportionate access to jobs, schools, and the professions, instead of the traditional criteria of merit that had favored Jews. Ugly confrontations erupted, particularly regarding New York City teaching positions. Currently, although not approaching the intensity of the 1960s, a considerable gulf exists between the two one-time allies, most recently exacerbated by the anti-Jewish Crown Heights riot of 1991.

THE ORTHODOX WORLD: Orthodox Jewry experienced enormous growth in the 1960s. Children of Holocaust survivors reached their teen years and young adulthood during this decade. Taking advantage of opportunities denied their parents, they swelled the yeshivos and Jewish schools, setting new standards for Torah excellence in America. Many of them became scholars and teachers, while even those who entered the general job market displayed a new pride and assertiveness in their observance, replacing the defensiveness of earlier generations of American Orthodox Jews.

Lumping together diverse Orthodox groups that in Europe had little interaction, such as Hungarian Chassidim and Lithuanian Misnagdim, created a uniquely American cross-cultural fertilization that benefited both groups. Chassidic modes of dress, customs, and kashrus standards began making inroads among Misnagdim, while the Lithuanian style of Talmudic study became more popular among Chassidim, especially those who attended Lithuanian-style yeshivos. (It is interesting to note that in photographs of attendees of Lithuanian yeshivos in Europe, only the faculty wore dark garb and beards. The students dressed in light beige suits and hats, and did not grow beards. The black hat of today's yeshivah student is a unique American innovation.)

Among the major Torah leaders in America were Rabbi Moshe Feinstein, Rabbi Yaakov Kaminetzky, the Satmar rebbe, and the rebbe of Lubavitch. (Rabbi Aharon Kotler passed away in 1962.)

THE *BA'AL TESHUVAH* MOVEMENT: Three factors contributed to the rise of Jews brought up in a nonreligious environment turning to Torah observance.[4] First, the new emphasis at the end of the '60s on ethnic identity won Orthodox Jews a measure of respect. If African-Americans could proudly display symbols of their ethnicity, could not Jews do the same? If one could wear a dashiki in public and eat soul food, why could one not wear a *kippah* and eat kosher food?

Second, young Americans began turning away from the value system of their parents, which stressed material success, to lifestyles that satisfied their desire for inner meaning and self-discovery. Jews, who attended universities at three times the rate of the general population, were particularly susceptible to the winds of change swirling about them. While many idealistic young Jews were attracted to radical causes and Eastern religions, others found spiritual fulfillment in their own heritage.

Third, many Jews, even those secularly oriented, viewed Israel's victory in the Six-Day War as miraculous. It strengthened their connection with the Jewish people and provided an impetus to explore Judaism as a lifestyle. While the numbers of returnees to Jewish observance was relatively small in the 1960s, the groundwork was laid for the many thousands of Jews who would discover their religion in later decades, both in the United States and in Israel.

THE PALESTINE LIBERATION ORGANIZATION (PLO): In 1964, the PLO was founded in Jordanian Jerusalem with its goal, baldly stated, "to attain the objective of liquidating Israel." (This was before all talk of so-called occupied territories and illegal settlements.) Its charter, adopted in 1968, declares that *all* of Palestine is an Arab country, and has not been amended despite the Oslo Accords that affirmed mutual recognition between the PLO and Israel. Article 6 of the charter is of great significance, stating: "The Jews who had normally resided in Palestine until the beginning of the Zionist invasion will be considered Palestinians." There are different interpretations of this clause regarding before what date Jews are to be considered normal residents of Palestine, but the upshot is the same: Jews who arrived in Israel after 1917, at the latest, and their descendants are not considered Palestinians and must leave the country. This, of course, includes the vast majority of Israel's five million Jews.

In 1965, Yasser Arafat founded the Fatah movement in Syria, and in 1968 took control of the PLO. A spate of guerrilla attacks in the newly conquered West Bank followed, hoping to create a spontaneous uprising against Israeli rule. When this attempt failed, the PLO moved to Jordan, using the country as its power base. However, major terrorist acts, dramatic hijackings, and the *intifada* were still events in the future.

THE NATIONAL WATER CARRIER: In 1964, Israel completed its integrated national water distribution system (*movil hamayim haartzi*). This monumental engineering feat pumped water from Lake Kinneret in the north all the way south to Beersheba in the Negev, a distance of over 120 miles. The new water system increased Israel's water supply by 25 percent — 75 percent for the Negev. As a result, the northern Negev was opened up for agricultural and industrial development. For the first time, many communities, notably Ashdod, Ashkelon, and Beersheba, were able to meet the growing requirements of new factories and municipal services. Israel gained fame across the world, and its expertise was even sought by the United States.

Syria viewed Israel's water project with great alarm. Two of the sources of the Jordan, the Hazbani and Banias rivers, have their sources in Lebanon and Syria respectively, flowing across the border into Israel. (Today the Banias is Israeli-controlled.) Accordingly, the Syrians made plans to divert the waters of the two rivers before they reached Israel.

Several skirmishes broke out on the Israeli-Syrian border, and eventually Israel destroyed the Syrian earth-moving equipment. Convinced that their diversion project was doomed, the Syrians abandoned the attempt. (In 2002, Lebanon initiated a water diversion project within a few hundred feet of the Israeli-Lebanese border. To date, Israel has not responded.)

ELI COHEN: One of the greatest spies of all time, Eli Cohen, an Israeli Jew, was nearly appointed deputy defense minister of Syria. Recruited by Israeli military intelligence, Cohen was sent to Argentina to blend into that country's large Syrian Arab population. Posing as an Arab, Cohen made numerous friends and business acquaintances in Argentina, and was invited to settle in Syria in 1960. Known as Kamal Amin Ta'abat, Cohen ingratiated himself with the Syrian military establishment and was invited for a personal tour of the Syrian fortifications on the Golan Heights. Blessed with a prodigious memory, Cohen transmitted to Israel precise details of the bunkers and hideouts, which enabled Israel to capture the Golan Heights in the Six-Day War. (Cohen also told the Syrians to plant eucalyptus trees near each bunker to facilitate wartime communications between outposts. As a result, Israel had a ready source of identification of Syrian positions.) In 1965, Cohen was caught, tortured, and publicly hanged in Damascus in front of hundreds of thousands of jubilant Syrians.

THE SIX-DAY WAR: The Yom Kippur War, the war in Lebanon, the Camp David Accords, the controversy over Jerusalem and Jewish settlements in the West Bank, the *intifada* and the rise of Palestinian terror — all are part of the outcome of those six days of intense Arab-Israeli fighting in the spring of 1967. Rarely in modern times has so short and localized a conflict had such prolonged, global consequences.

PRELUDE TO THE WAR: On April 7, there was a major dogfight involving Israeli and Syrian jets over the Golan Heights. A number of Syrian MIG fighters were shot down, and Israeli planes buzzed unopposed over Damascus. Stung by the humiliation, Syria aided terrorist strikes across the Israeli border. The Soviet Union, eager to gain influence among the Arabs, fed the Egyptians false rumors of an impending Israeli invasion of Syria. Clearly, the region was beginning to heat up rapidly.

On May 15, when Nasser sent more than 100,000 Egyptian troops into the Sinai, Israel called up some of its reserves. The next day, Egypt ordered the United Nation Emergency Force (UNEF), established after the Sinai War in 1956 as a buffer between Egypt and Israel, to evacuate its observation posts. UN Secretary-General U Thant bowed to Egypt's demand, withdrawing the force that for ten years had prevented war between Israel and Egypt. With UNEF gone, Egyptian and Palestinian Arab forces massed along the long border with Israel. On May 23, Nasser repeated the gamble he took in 1956, closing the Straits of Tiran to Israeli shipping in defiance of international law. This *casus belli* heightened the tension beyond the point of no return.

THE *HAMTANAH* PERIOD: From May 23 to June 4, which is known in the history of Israel as the *Hamtanah*, the waiting period, the mood of the people of Israel came as near to despair as it had ever come. Visions of the Holocaust were more vivid than they had ever been. Cairo, Egypt's capital, was festooned with lurid posters showing Arab soldiers shooting, crushing, strangling, and dismembering bearded, hook-nosed Jews. Arab soldiers prepared for war chanting *Hefa! Yaffa!* (Haifa, Tel Aviv.) Arab rhetoric became more shrill and ominous. Nasser proclaimed, "Our basic objective will be the destruction of Israel." Syrian Defense Minister Hafez-el-Assad, later dictator of Syria, echoed Nasser: "The time has come to enter into a battle of annihilation."

The Arab rhetoric was matched by the mobilization of Arab forces. Approximately 250,000 troops, more than 2,000 tanks, and 700 aircraft from Egypt, Syria, Jordan, Iraq, and several smaller Arab nations ringed Israel. Israeli soldiers were on alert for three weeks, but unlike the Arab nations, since Israel's army is largely comprised of reserve soldiers, they could not deploy indefinitely without severely disrupting the economy. Abba Eban, Israel's highly respected foreign minister, toured Western capitals hoping to gain sympathy for his nation's plight. Instead, he was admonished that Israel should show restraint and not initiate hostilities. Some even proposed that Israel cede land to Egypt to defuse the situation. (Clearly another bogus land for peace solution even before the existence of so-called occupied territories.)

Throughout Israel, thousands were digging trenches, building shelters, and filling sandbags. Upward of 14,000 hospital beds were readied, and antidotes stockpiled for poison gas, with victims expected to arrive in waves. Some 10,000 graves were dug.[5] On May 28, Israeli Prime Minister Levi Eshkol went on radio to reassure his beleaguered nation. Eshkol fumbled his delivery, mumbled his lines, lost his place, misread and corrected himself. It is said that Israeli soldiers, listening to that speech, broke their transistors and burst into tears.[6] Around the world, Jews watched with increasing terror as the specter of a second

Holocaust loomed, once again in the presence of an uncaring world.

On Sunday, June 4, the die was cast. The 275,000 men, 1,100 tanks, and 200 planes of the Israel Defense Forces were ready to embark on the largest offensive in Middle East history.

DAY ONE — MONDAY, JUNE 5: Shortly after 7 a.m. the war began with an Israeli aerial offensive against Egyptian airfields. Flying only fifteen meters above ground to evade Egyptian radar, Israeli pilots entered Egypt from the west, rather than directly over the border, thereby achieving complete surprise. Within three hours, Israel essentially won the war. Almost all of Egypt's vaunted air force was destroyed on the ground, and most of its radar and anti-aircraft sites rendered inoperable. Israel had complete control of the air on the Egyptian front. However, the extent of Israel's success would be kept secret for as long as possible, delaying a UN-imposed cease-fire and allowing Israeli tanks to roll into Sinai.[7] While Egypt claimed its forces were well on the way to Tel Aviv, Israel kept silent, only saying that it faced "a cruel and bloody campaign." (Jewish victories tend to get the world community nervous; on numerous occasions the UN has attempted to limit Israeli battlefield successes. No similar restraint is imposed on Arab actions.)

With the air war decided, Israel began a ground thrust into the Sinai. Thousands of Egyptian troops fled the battlefield on foot, leaving much heavy Soviet-made equipment behind intact. Israel notified Jordan's King Hussein that if he did not initiate hostilities, Israel would not attack his country. Ignoring the warning, the Jordanians lobbed thousands of shells into Jewish Jerusalem, killing 20 civilians, injuring more than 1,000, and damaging in excess of 900 buildings. Israel began a slow advance against Jordanian forces in both Jerusalem and the West Bank. Fighting was heavy, particularly at Jerusalem's Ammunition Hill (today a park known as *Givat HaTachmoshet*).

DAY TWO — TUESDAY, JUNE 6: Israel advanced farther into the

Sinai and captured the Gaza Strip. The Jordanians were pushed back farther in Jerusalem, and Israel encircled but did not invade the Old City, as its cabinet was debating the political ramifications of such a move. On the West Bank, Israel captured the towns of Jenin, Ramallah, and Kalkilya, ten miles from Tel Aviv. Meanwhile, the Syrians began shelling Israeli border posts from the Golan Heights. Israel, however, not willing to open a third front, did not retaliate. The United Nations hurriedly convened in New York, attempting to impose a ceasefire, but their efforts bogged down. This delay worked to Israel's advantage, as it was free to continue the offensive.

DAY THREE — WEDNESDAY, JUNE 7: In a day that will live on in Jewish history, Israel liberated the Old City of Jerusalem, including the Western Wall (the *Kosel HaMa'aravi*) and the Temple Mount. Israeli soldiers entered the area on foot, not in tanks, and took extra casualties, so as not to risk damaging the holy sites. It was an electric moment for Jews worldwide, of such significance that in succeeding months and years people asked, "Where were you when the *Kosel* was liberated?" Secular soldiers and Orthodox Jews danced together at the Wall, despite the great danger still remaining from snipers. The *pintele yid*, the Jewish spark that lays embedded within every Jewish soul, was aroused even in Jews who claimed they were nonbelievers, for many saw the hand of G-d in the amazing events that were unfolding.

In the Sinai, Israeli forces captured Sharm-al-Sheikh, breaking the Egyptian blockade of the Straits of Tiran, and approached the Suez Canal. In the West Bank, Israel captured Bethlehem, including Rachel's Tomb, and Nablus (Shechem). The situation on the Syrian front remained unchanged.

DAY FOUR — THURSDAY, JUNE 8: Israel entered the biblical town of Hebron, with the Cave of the Patriarchs (*Me'aras HaMachpelah*), and completed its conquest of the West Bank. In the Sinai, Israeli forces reached the Suez Canal, destroying much of the fleeing Egyptian Army in the process. Despite the continuous Syrian shelling of Israeli positions, Israel did not mount an offensive as its cabinet debated the political implications of such a move, especially possible Soviet reactions. By the end of the day, one battle was concluded, another in the process of ending, and a third about to begin.

THE *LIBERTY* INCIDENT: An American spy ship, the *Liberty*, was sailing in international waters close to the Sinai coast. Mistaking the *Liberty* for a hostile vessel, Israeli planes strafed the ship, killing thirty-four American sailors and wounding 171. For years, many Americans insisted that Israel intentionally targeted the ship with full knowledge of its nationality. Israel apologized for the tragedy and paid $13 million in compensation to the American government and to the families of the victims. In 1987, the American and Israeli governments officially closed the matter.[8]

DAY FIVE – FRIDAY, JUNE 9: Israel completed its conquest of the Sinai, and finally began its long-awaited offensive on the Golan Heights. Climbing 2,000 feet of extremely steep, rocky terrain in daylight, the Israelis were exposed to withering Syrian fire. Syria's fortifications were girded by mines and barbed wire, bristling with concrete bunkers and pillboxes. The fighting that ensued was reminiscent of that at Jerusalem's Ammunition Hill, waged at extremely close quarters, often hand-to-hand. Finally, with Israeli soldiers at the Syrian perimeter, the first squad lay bodily down on the barbed wire so that the rest of their comrades could vault over them.[9] From there the Israelis dashed to the Syrian trenches, taking them in bloody engagements. Israel also took the Banias and the approaches to Mount Hermon.

DAY SIX – SATURDAY, JUNE 10: Israel broke through on the Golan Heights, advancing toward the Syrian capital of Damascus. At this point, the Soviet Union threatened to intervene militarily against Israel if it did not stop the attack. Terrified at the prospect of fighting the Russians all alone, and also pressured by the United States, in the afternoon Israel agreed to a ceasefire.

While the details of the agreement were being worked out in the UN, Israel took the opportunity to seize the vitally strategic Mount Hermon, giving it a vital observation post deep into Syria.

RESULTS OF THE WAR: Israel captured Gaza and Sinai from Egypt, Jerusalem and the West Bank from Jordan, and the Golan Heights from Syria. In six days, the nation more than tripled its size, and for the first time achieved strategic depth with defensible borders far from its population centers. However, the victory came at a high price — 800 Israeli soldiers killed in action, equivalent per capita to 80,000 Americans, and more than 2,500 wounded. For their part, the Arabs suffered twenty-five times the number of casualties as Israel.

In what years later became regarded as an immense political blunder, Israel allowed control of Temple Mount to remain in the hand of the Muslim *Waqf*. Throughout the West Bank, Israel allowed Palestinian religious and community leaders to retain their prewar positions. Still, in the Old City of Jerusalem Israel bulldozed twenty-five Arab slum dwellings to the west of the *Kosel HaMa'aravi*, thus clearing the area for the current prayer plaza. The holiday of Shavuos, which came four days after the war's end, saw 200,000 joyous Jewish worshippers crowd the newly created, still unpaved area, many seeing the Wall for the first time. At the end of June, Israel reunited East and West Jerusalem, dismantling the checkpoints and dividing walls. The Jewish cemetery on the Mount of Olives, whose tombstones were used for roads and latrines by the Jordanians, was repaired and restored.

Unfortunately, Israel's victory came at a bitter price for the Jews in Arab countries. Mobs attacked Jewish neighborhoods in Egypt, Yemen, Lebanon, Tunisia, and Morocco, burning synagogues and assaulting residents. Hundreds of Jews were arrested in Egypt, while in Syria and Iraq thousands of Jews were expelled. A pogrom in Libya killed eighteen Jews.

After conquering territories beyond its wildest dreams, Israel was willing to return much of the land in exchange for a lasting peace. However, in August 1967, the Arabs met in Sudan and proclaimed the now-famous three no's: No recognition of Israel, no peace, and no negotiations. The Arabs thus missed a great opportunity, for returning much of the West Bank to Jordan in 1967 would have been far simpler than it is today, since then there were no Jewish settlements.

UN RESOLUTION 242: In November 1967, the United Nations Security Council adopted what became a famous resolution and the basis for all subsequent discussions regarding the region. Resolution 242 contained two major points: withdrawal of Israeli armed forces from territories occupied in the recent conflict, and the right of every state in the region to live in peace within secure and recognized borders. Generally known as land for peace, Resolution 242 was accepted by Israel, Egypt, and Jordan, while Syria and Iraq rejected it, finding its implicit acknowledgement of Israel's right to exist too difficult to digest. In addition, the parties did not agree to the exact wording. For example, the English-language version of the first clause read "from territories occupied" rather than "from *the* territories occupied," leading Israel to maintain that if a withdrawal is carried out on some of the conquered land, the resolution has been satisfied. To the contrary, the Arabs contend that the French and Russian versions of the text, which did not make such a distinction, must be followed. Consequently, Israel must withdraw from *all* the occupied territories to achieve peace.[10] The debate continues to this day.

THE WAR OF ATTRITION (1967–70): Almost immediately after the Six-Day War ended, Egypt began on-and-off shelling of Israeli positions on the Suez Canal. Nasser believed that Israel's reserve army could not withstand a prolonged war of attrition, and that the nation would be unable to endure the constant casualties and economic burden. (This is precisely the rationale behind the current Palestinian terror campaign.) In an almost three-year stretch, more than 1,500 Israeli soldiers and civilians were killed, and more than 2,000 wounded.[11] However, Egypt did not achieve her goal of demoralizing Israel.

THE SOVIET UNION: Israel's lightning victory over its Soviet-trained enemies evoked enormous pride among Soviet Jews, stimulating Jewish identification and self-confidence. In several cities small nuclei of Jewish activists began to meet, and soon pressure for emigration to Israel became both widespread and open. In response, the Soviet authorities stepped up its anti-Israel propaganda and halted Jewish emigration to a tiny trickle. However, the seeds of dissent were sown, and would sprout mightily in the 1970s. In the Soviet Union's satellite nation of Poland, a nasty 1968 government-sponsored anti-Semitic campaign led to the emigration of nearly all the country's Jews. Of a Jewish population that had numbered 3.5 million before World War II, only 6,000 elderly Jews remained.

VATICAN II: In 1965, Pope John XXIII charged Catholic theologians to prepare a wide-ranging restatement of Catholic doctrine, including a statement on relations with the Jews. After many revisions, the final draft, known as Vatican II and binding on all Catholics, contained two major provisions regarding Jews. First, although Jewish authorities in Roman times were responsible for Yeshu's death, today's Jews are not to be charged with the crime. Second, the Church officially stated that it deplores hatred and persecutions of Jews. Nevertheless, despite its effort to address Catholic-Jewish relations in a more positive light, Vatican II contained a number of weaknesses. It ignored historical evidence that the Romans, not the Jews, bore responsibility for the death of the Christian god. Instead of condemning anti-Semitism, and regarding it as heresy, the Church toned down the language to the much weaker term "deploring." In addition, the Church did not mention the need for repentance for its past and seeking forgiveness from the Jews.[12] As such, many Jews, particularly religious ones, were very wary of a statement in Vatican II calling for ecumenical dialogue, fearing a new attempt by the Catholic Church to convert Jews.

Chapter 35

THE 1970s

FAR-REACHING CHANGE: New opportunities and new problems arose in the Jewish world in the 1970s. Cracks, imperceptible at first, appeared in the Soviet Iron Curtain, then widening as — for the first time — large numbers of Jews were permitted to depart. Israel's aura of invincibility after the Six-Day War was shattered in the traumatic battle of the 1973 Yom Kippur War. Palestinian terrorism erupted on a global scale, and the United Nations adopted its infamous Zionism is Racism resolution. In the United States, Orthodox Judaism made new strides, particularly in the public arena.

SOVIET JEWISH EMIGRATION: Israel's lightning victory in 1967 stimulated great pride and a new assertiveness among Soviet Jews. Small groups of Jewish activists began to exert public pressure for emigration. They published underground literature (*samizdat*), met secretly with Western journalists visiting the USSR, and contacted prominent figures in the free world who publicized their plight. In 1970, eleven Jews unsuccessfully attempted to hijack a small passenger plane to Sweden; their plan was then to move on to Israel. Secret accounts of their subsequent trial were sneaked to the West, attracting worldwide attention. Due to Western pressure, the Soviets commuted the death sentences the Jews had been given.

As the issue reached the public arena in the United States, certain elements looked for radical means to force the Soviet authorities to release Jews. Meir Kahane's Jewish Defense League (JDL), a group comprised largely of young toughs, harassed Soviet diplomats, attacked Soviet property in the United States, and interrupted performances of visiting Soviet cultural groups. Torah leadership roundly condemned such attention-grabbing tactics. With their keen insight, the Torah scholars realized that such strong-armed measures would not sway the superpower that had crushed Hungary and Czechoslovakia in defiance of world opinion. Instead of facilitating the emigration of Soviet Jews, Torah leaders said, a campaign of embarrassment and disruption would actually impede it, even harming Jews in the Soviet Union. Instead, the Torah scholars said, quiet, behind-the-scenes diplomacy would be more effective in getting the Soviet authorities to release Jews — without causing the Soviets to lose face. Instead of protests, to arouse concern for Soviet Jewry among Orthodox Jews, Agudath Israel's *Moetzes Gedolei HaTorah* (Council of Torah Sages) called for a prayer assembly in January 1971 in New York City. More than 10,000 Jews braved the bitter cold to attend the service.

In 1971, Jewish emigration was permitted on a large scale, and during the years 1971–1974 more than 94,000 Soviet Jews were allowed to move to Israel. At the same time, fewer than 6,000 Jews were given permission to settle in the United States.[1] Why? Soviet authorities allowed Jews to depart for Israel under the guise of family reunification, thus being able to claim that it was not disenchantment with Soviet life that was fueling the departures. This trend changed in the latter half of the decade, when the majority of departing Soviet Jews went to the United States.

Nevertheless, the Soviet authorities made it extremely difficult for Jews to leave, and the actual exit visa procedure itself was as complex and shameful as possible. Applicants first had to obtain an affidavit from a family member in Israel containing an invitation to emigrate. The need for a character reference from the applicant's place of work often led to a sort of show trial, in which the Jew was publicly discussed, condemned, and then dismissed.

As the period between the application and granting the visa was quite lengthy, the émigré was often jobless, penniless, and liable to be jailed for what was termed parasitism (not being employed in the so-called workers' paradise) until the visa was finally approved.[2]

Many Jews, especially those with scientific or technical training, were denied permission to emigrate, as the Soviet government claimed they possessed secret knowledge vital to Soviet interests. Known as *refuseniks*, these Jews were fired from their jobs, charged with espionage or defamation of the Soviet state, and incarcerated in labor camps or confined in mental hospitals. One *refusenik*, Raisa Palatnik, described her ordeal:

And then the KGB [the Soviet secret police] began to show an interest in me. They searched my apartment and that of my parents. I am constantly summoned for questioning. My friends and relatives, the people I work with, are interrogated and pressured to give witness to my anti-Soviet activity. I understand that arrest and maybe years of imprisonment await me. But I know one thing positively: my fate is tied irrevocably to Israel. No imprisonments in Leningrad, Riga, and Kishinev can halt the struggle for repatriation to Israel. To my regret I do not know my people's tongue, Hebrew, but in my trial I will cry out against all anti-Semites in the Yiddish I was taught by my mother and father.[3]

The most famous *refusenik* was Anatoly Sharansky, who was arrested in 1978 on charges of spying for the United States. A man of outstanding moral courage, Sharansky became an international *cause celebre* until his release in 1986. He then immigrated to Israel, where, as Natan Sharansky, he became a leader of Soviet Jewish immigrants.

THE *BA'AL TESHUVAH* MOVEMENT EXPANDS: Yeshivos were established throughout the 1970s, especially in Israel, to accommodate the needs of the burgeoning newly religious community. The best known of these institutions are Ohr Somayach and Aish HaTorah for men, and Neve Yerushalayim for women. There were several reasons why outreach was more successful in Israel than in America. First, Judaism is the dominant religion and culture of Israel, and even secular Jews have or had relatives and ancestors who were religious. In the United States, however, Orthodox Jews are a small minority in a largely Christian and secular environment. Second, as part of the Status Quo Agreement, Israel's government provides financial support to all religious schools in the country, whereas in the United States the separation of church and state precludes any such assistance. Consequently, American yeshivos are dependent on tuition (buoyed by donations), which in many cases is beyond the reach of *ba'alei teshuvah*. Third, Americans are more tolerant of synagogue outreach than of yeshivos making such efforts, feeling that religious programs of houses of worship are less threatening. In Israel, the synagogue does not occupy the same role and importance that it does in the United States, and religious schools are part of the Israeli educational scene.[4]

Ba'al teshuvah yeshivos differ in their outreach strategies. At Ohr Somayach, the new arrival is immediately thrown into the study of Talmud despite his lack of background, it being felt that exposure to the beauty of intensive Torah study will inspire him to pursue his interest in Judaism. Aish HaTorah's approach, as exemplified by its fiery leader, Rabbi Noach Weinberg, is to challenge the secularism of entrants by presenting proofs of G-d and to stir their emotions through demonstrating to them the richness and fullness of a Jewish lifestyle. Both approaches have succeeded in helping many nonreligious Jews discover their heritage.

Chabad-Lubavitch has been active in outreach longer than any other group. In Israel, it became very involved with native Israelis, bringing holiday provisions and gifts to troops in the field, arranging bar mitzvahs for the sons of fallen Israeli soldiers, and providing education to disadvantaged children. These efforts have earned Chabad respect among Israelis, and it has been effective in attracting *ba'alei teshuvah*. In the United States, since the early 1970s Lubavitch has used dramatic outreach techniques, such as mitzvah mobiles that drive through Jewish neighborhoods and public places, attempting to get Jewish men to don tefillin and women to light Sabbath candles. A network of worldwide Chabad Houses was begun, bringing Judaism to Jews located far from any Jewish community. Lubavitch also focused on Jews who were frequently neglected, such as prisoners in federal and state institutions throughout the United States, and military personnel on remote bases.

THE FEMINIST MOVEMENT: Women's Liberation became a major cause in the 1970s. Originally focusing on such vital issues as the exploitation of women and discrimination against women in both the quality of jobs and salary levels, the Feminist movement soon began to demand total equality between men and women, ignoring the obvious physiological and psychological differences between them. This new social trend had, and continues to have, a profound effect on the Jewish world. In the decade of the '70s, there was a 200 percent increase in Jewish women not marrying, and the Jewish birthrate fell to 1.6 children per family, down from 2.8 in the 1950s.[5] The divorce rate skyrocketed, reflecting the trend in the non-Jewish world.

Rabbi Yaakov Weinberg, the dean of Yeshiva Ner Israel, noted at the time that of all the causes attracting so many adherents, the Feminist movement represented the greatest danger to the Orthodox world.[6] So-called left-wing Orthodox women began demanding equal roles in the synagogue, such as being able to lead the services; the ability to terminate a marriage and obtain a divorce; and formal Talmud study classes for women. When told that all of these are against halachah, the feminist leaders claimed that if the rabbis only had the desire, such accommodations could be made (as if human legislation could change the will of G-d as expressed in the Torah). The highly emotional and volatile issue of feminism still pervades many circles, creating great friction among Jews today.

The Women's Liberation movement of the 1970s even impacted the Torah-observant Jewish world. Due both to economic need and changing societal trends, more and more Jewish women, both single and married, began working outside the home. In families where the husband studied in *kollel*, the wife was the primary or even the sole breadwinner. The far-reaching effects of these new arrangements on the relationship between husband and wife, and on the Orthodox Jewish family as a whole, have yet to be fully understood.

AMERICAN ORTHODOX JEWISH LIFE AND CULTURE: As the American-born post-Holocaust generation began growing up and having their own children, a unique American Orthodox Jewish culture began. The invention of the cassette tape recorder, replacing cumbersome record players, spurred the production of a large Jewish music industry. Composers such as the Neginah Orchestra, the London School of Jewish Music, and Mordechai ben David (MBD) enjoyed great popularity, their songs and tunes spreading throughout the Orthodox world. Weddings and concerts featured the new music culture, which was a blend of traditional tunes and new songs. Some of the newer compositions featured lyrics and beats that were controversial, with some groups and institutions shunning those they felt were spiritually detrimental.

Cassettes also proved a boon to the dissemination of Torah, as thousands of hours of Torah tapes flooded the Jewish world. The new Walkmans sang with the words of such luminaries as Rabbi Avigdor Miller, Rabbi Berel Wein, Rabbi Yissocher Frand, Rabbi Noach Weinberg, and many others. This extraordinary dissemination of the spoken word from the Torah world continues today, along with videotapes and other electronic means of transmittal and reproduction.

There was also a veritable explosion of Jewish English-language book publication in the 1970s. In 1976, the ArtScroll/Mesorah publishing house printed its first volume, a running commentary on the Book of Esther. The book's superb Overview set a new standard in English-language literature, and the volume was a runaway best-seller. From this humble beginning, ArtScroll/Mesorah grew to become the dominant Orthodox

Jewish publishing house in the world, printing hundreds of books on many Jewish topics. The ArtScroll siddurim and *machzorim* are standard in many synagogues. ArtScroll/Mesorah's most ambitious project is a new translation of the Babylonian Talmud, a seventy-three-volume set that will be completed in 2005. Feldheim Publishers, an older publishing house, is second to ArtScroll/Mesorah in Orthodox Jewish book publication, also putting out many works of great quality. Targum Press, a newer Jewish publisher based in Israel, is making a major impact in Jewish life with its many excellent works covering all areas of Jewish interest. Numerous smaller publishing companies also exist.

AGUDATH ISRAEL: In the 1970s, Agudath Israel became a public service agency of major proportions. Its accomplishments during this decade were many and varied, including the popularization of the daily *Daf Yomi* study program. Originally created by Rabbi Meir Shapiro of Lublin, the completion of the sixth cycle was held in the Beth Jacob Auditorium in Brooklyn in 1968, attracting 1,000 people. In 1975, the end of the seventh cycle was marked in Manhattan Center in the presence of 5,000 celebrants. In 1982, the eighth *siyum* was held in the Felt Forum of Madison Square Garden to accommodate a larger crowd. The festivities marking the end of the ninth cycle in 1990 took place in Madison Square Garden itself, in the presence of 20,000 people. In 1997, there were two major *siyumim*, in Madison Square Garden and Nassau Coliseum, each filled to capacity with 20,000 people each. Similar celebrations took place all over the world. Today, many thousands of people study the same page every day in many different places. There is even a car on the Long Island Railroad reserved for commuters who wish to study the daily *daf* on the way to work.

To date, there have been ten complete cycles of study; see the following chart.

(Close readers will note a discrepancy on the number of days needed to complete the cycle. The first seven cycles of *Daf Yomi* were based on the Slavita edition of the Talmud, printed

START	FINISH
1. September 11, 1923/1 Tishrei 5684	February 2, 1931/ 15 Shevat 5691
2. February 3, 1931/ 16 Shevat 5691	June 27, 1938/ 28 Sivan 5698
3. June 28, 1938/ 29 Sivan 5698	November 19, 1945/ 14 Kislev 5706
4. November 20, 1945/ 15 Kislev 5706	April 13, 1953/ 28 Nisan 5713
5. April 14, 1953/ 29 Nisan 5713	September 5, 1960/ 13 Elul 5720
6. September 6, 1960/ 14 Elul 5720	January 29, 1968/ 28 Teves 5728
7. January 30, 1968/ 29 Teves 5728	June 23, 1975/ 14 Tammuz 5735
8. June 24, 1975/ 15 Tammuz 5735	November 24, 1982/ 8 Kislev 5743
9. November 25, 1982/ 9 Kislev 5743	April 27, 1990/ 2 Iyar 5750
10. April 28, 1990/ 3 Iyar 5750	September 28, 1997/ 26 Elul 5757
11. September 29, 1997/ 27 Elul 5757	March 1, 2005/ 20 Adar 1 5765

by Rabbi Meir Shapiro's grandfather. The Jerusalem Talmud tractate *Shekalim*, running eleven printed pages in Slavita, was included in the *Daf Yomi* cycle. Due to the extreme difficulty of finding *Daf Yomi* lecturers to cover this tractate adequately in eleven days, a change was made in 1975. After consultation with Rabbi Moshe Feinstein, *Daf Yomi* was subsequently based on the standard Vilna edition of the Talmud, which, due to more commentaries printed on the page, assigned twenty-two pages to *Shekalim*, thereby considerably easing the task of studying this difficult tractate. Consequently, a complete cycle of *Daf Yomi* now runs 2,711 days instead of the previous 2,702. In all, the slightly different layout of Talmud pages in the Vilna edition caused a gain of nine days rather than eleven.)[7]

In addition, Agudah also played a prominent role in the effort to have the United States Department of Education recognize yeshivos as institutions of higher learning, thus enabling them to receive government aid granted to universities. Its youth groups, Pirchei, Zeirei, and Bnos, grew greatly during this decade as well. Pirchei's *Siyum Mishnayos* attracted thousands of children to New York City annually, all united in the study of Mishnah, anywhere from a single chapter to all of its six orders. In 1973, the Jewish Education Program (JEP) was formed, utilizing volunteers to introduce Torah Judaism to Jewish public school students during the one hour in the school week that students were permitted to attend optional religious classes. As a result, numerous nonreligious Jewish students became Torah observant.

Agudath Israel also intensified its efforts on behalf of Soviet Jewry. Contacts were made with American government leaders, and quiet diplomacy was exerted to persuade the Soviet regime to allow Jews to leave. Packages of food and religious articles were discreetly sent to Jews in the Soviet Union, wherever possible. In Israel, Agudah set up a fund to assist new immigrants to adjust to Israeli life, both financially and socially, and to help them in religious matters. As the Soviet Jews began coming to America, Agudah ran the full gamut of resettlement activities, helping with job hunting, finding living quarters, and securing food and clothing. The spiritual needs of the immigrants were also addressed, from circumcising the children to finding them placement in Jewish schools, and preventing Christian missionary groups from converting Soviet Jews. In 1979, as Iranian Jews began leaving that country, Agudath Israel launched similar efforts on their behalf.

On the legislative front, Agudah was successful in getting New York State to enact laws more favorable to Orthodox Jews. Non-public schools became eligible for state funds for certain non-sectarian services that added millions of dollars to financially strapped yeshivah budgets. Tougher laws were passed to prevent fraud in advertising of kosher products and production of tefillin and mezuzos. A Jewish Patient's Bill of Rights was formulated to help ensure that hospitals respect the unique religious needs of their Jewish patients.[8]

Agudah's social services expanded greatly in the 1970s. Senior citizens' centers were set up in the New York City area, and special attention was paid to the needs of elderly shut-ins and nursing home and hospital patients. An employment agency, COPE, provided both young and middle-aged job aspirants with vocational training. Government funding was obtained to refurbish large apartment buildings in Brooklyn on the fringes of Jewish neighborhoods that had been victims of urban decay. Presiding over Agudah's phenomenal growth was the indefatigable Rabbi Moshe Sherer, who deftly led the organization until his death in 1998.

AMERICAN TORAH LIFE: The post-Holocaust baby boom swelled the ranks of American yeshivos in the 1970s. Among the leading yeshivos in the United States were Beth Medrash Gevoha of Lakewood, the largest, led by Rabbi Schneur Kotler; Torah Vodaath, whose *rosh yeshivah* was Rabbi Yaakov Kaminetzky; Chaim Berlin, with Rabbi Yitzchak Hutner at its helm; Ner Israel of Baltimore, whose dean was Rabbi Yaakov Y. Ruderman; and Telz Yeshiva of Cleveland, led by Rabbi Boruch Sorotzkin. Other prominent American yeshivos were Talmudical Academy of Philadelphia, Mesivtha Tifereth Jerusalem, Chafetz Chaim, and Mirrer Yeshiva. Numerous smaller yeshivos, some no less prestigious, dotted the American landscape as well. The many chassidic groups maintained their own yeshivos, and like their

Misnagdic counterparts, produced great scholars and knowledgeable laymen. Overall, yeshivah enrollment in the 1970s in the United States approached 10,000.[9]

Among the decade's American Torah leaders were Rabbi Moshe Feinstein, acknowledged along with Rabbi Shlomo Zalman Auerbach of Israel as the greatest halachic authorities in the Jewish world, and Rabbi Yaakov Kaminetzky, who was regarded as the elder statesman and advisor of the American Torah community. The numerous chassidic groups were led by their sagacious and saintly leaders, towering personalities who shaped and guided their communities and followers. Even those who did not share their ideological views — for instance the ideology of the Satmar rebbe, Rabbi Joel Teitelbaum, who was fiercely anti-Zionist and against Agudath Israel — nevertheless recognized them as among the generation's giants. In particular, Jews everywhere mourned the Satmar rebbe's 1979 passing, realizing that he left a void that could not be filled.

TORAH LIFE IN ISRAEL: Israeli yeshivos experienced even greater growth in the 1970s than did their American counterparts. Rabbi Joseph S. Kahaneman, the *rav* of Ponovezh, Lithuania, arrived in Eretz Yisrael in 1940 and built the Ponovezh Yeshiva in Bnei Brak. By the 1970s, this yeshivah was the largest in Israel; its *mashgiach* (spiritual advisor) was the sainted Rabbi Chatzkel Levenstein, who passed away in 1974. Under the tutelage of Rabbi Chaim Shmuelevitz, who passed away in 1979, Mirrer Yeshiva opened a branch in Israel that attracted thousands of students from both Israel and the United States. The renowned Soloveitchik family of Brisk, Lithuania established yeshivos that attracted many students from both Israel and abroad. Brisk yeshivos featured the unique Brisk approach to Talmudic study, focusing solely on the tractates dealing with sacrifices, *Kodashim*, it being felt that those topics best lent themselves to such analysis. Countless numbers of small yeshivos proliferated in Israel, too, much more than in the United States. The decade also saw a greatly increasing number of students from abroad, especially America, study at Israeli men and women's institutions. However, very few Israelis attended schools outside Israel.

TORAH LEADERS IN ISRAEL: The Holy Land was blessed with many Torah giants, both Sephardic and Ashkenazic. Rabbi Yaakov Y. Kanievsky, the Steipler Gaon, was the address of tens of thousands of Jews who streamed to his Bnei Brak home for blessings and advice. His multivolume work *Kehillas Yaakov* on the entire Talmud is famed in the yeshivah world as the epitome of clarity. Rabbi Yecheskel Abramsky, formerly the rabbi of Slutzk, Lithuania and London, spent the final twenty-five years of his life in Eretz Yisrael, passing away in 1976. Rabbi Shlomo Zalman Auerbach was the leading halachic authority in Eretz Yisrael, issuing landmark rulings on the most complicated matters. Rabbi Elazar M. Shach was the head of the great Ponovezh Yeshiva, and was regarded as the dean emeritus of Israeli *roshei yeshivah*. His pronouncements on policy regarding the relationship of the Torah community with both the Israeli government and the outside world were assiduously followed by tens of thousands of Torah adherents.

Among Israel's numerous Sephardic greats were Rabbi Ezra Attia, head of the famous Yeshiva Porat Yosef until his passing in 1970; Rabbi Yehuda Tzedaka, who succeeded him as the yeshivah's leader; Rabbi Raphael B. Toledano, a great Moroccan scholar who passed away in 1971; and the world-renowned Rabbi Yisrael Abu-Chatzeira, whose blessings and prayers invoked Divine salvation on behalf of thousands of people. These and many other leaders brought about a great resurgence in the Sephardic Torah world.

Major chassidic leaders based in Israel were the rebbes of Ger, Belz, and Klausenberg, along with one of the two rebbes of Vizhnitz. Many smaller chassidic groups flourished in the rarefied spiritual air of the Holy Land, establishing such important yeshivos and communities as Kfar Chabad, Kiryat Zanz, and Kiryat Hazor, the last established in the Galilee in 1976.

THE CONSERVATIVE AND REFORM MOVEMENTS: The un-bridgeable gap between Orthodoxy and these two movements widened in the 1970s. In 1969, the Conservative movement's Law Committee of the Rabbinical Assembly decided to abolish the observance of the second day of holidays outside Eretz Yisrael, other than Rosh HaShanah, in direct violation of Talmudic law. This practice increased in popularity among Conservative synagogues in the 1970s, although it was by no means unanimous. In 1972, the same legislative body passed a resolution stating that men and women should be counted equally for a minyan (the synagogue prayer quorum), leaving its implementation up to individual Conservative congregations.[10] The Conservative movement also published a new version of the prayer book, deviating significantly from the traditionally accepted siddur.

For its part, the Reform movement drifted even farther away from Torah observance. In 1972, the first woman clergy, Sally Preisand, was ordained. Seeking to swell the Reform ranks, the movement began to reach out to the non-Jewish spouses of inter-married couples, offering them membership in Reform synagogues. Further, a 1972 study showed that only one in ten Reform rabbis believed in G-d in the more or less traditional Jewish sense.[11] Balfour Brickner, a national leader of the Union of American Hebrew Congregations (UAHC), the Reform synagogue umbrella organization, noted that the Reform movement had rabbis who are atheists, agnostics, and even led deviant personal life-styles. "Shall we throw them out?" he asked. "Where would we stop?"[12] In the most egregious instance of all, in 1977 Reform Temple Emanuel of Tempe, Arizona, lent its *sukkah* to the nearby Church of the Epiphany for their use as the manger in their annual Christmas display.[13]

To make matters even worse, the Reform and Conservative movements created havoc with the personal status of many American Jews by performing invalid conversions and granting divorces invalid according to Jewish law. As a result, there were many converts who were really non-Jewish, and Jews who were *mamzerim*, forbidden to marry other Jews. Sadly, these problems reached epidemic proportions in the 1970s. In Israel, both movements strenuously attempted to undo the Law of Return, which grants recognition only to conversions performed under Orthodox auspices.

JEWISH SETTLEMENT IN THE CONQUERED TERRITORIES: In April 1968, ten Israeli families, pretending to be Swedish tourists, registered as guests in the Park Hotel in Hebron. That day, their leader, Rabbi Moshe Levinger, announced that the group was reviving Jewish settlement in Hebron, abandoned after the riots and killings of 1936. Eventually, the Israeli government forced the settlers to leave the town, but allowed them to build a Jewish suburb outside Hebron, Kiryat Arba.

There were two approaches in the Israeli government toward Jewish settlement in the occupied areas. Moshe Dayan favored building four Jewish cities on empty land atop the mountain ridge that stretches along the entire length of the West Bank and overlooks the coastal plain, which holds the bulk of Israel's population. These cities, he reasoned, would break up the existing contiguity of the Arab towns of Jenin, Nablus, and Ramallah in the north, and Bethlehem and Hebron in the south. Yigal Allon, the architect of what would become known as the Allon Plan, proposed that Israel settle areas it expected to keep under its sovereignty, such as East Jerusalem, Gush Etzion, Kiryat Arba, the Jordan Valley, and the Golan Heights. As for the rest, much of the occupied land would be given to its former owners in return for a promise of peace.[14] As part of its underpinnings, the Allon Plan was based on the premise that for Israel to remain a Jewish state it could not absorb the 1.2 million Arabs it had captured in the 1967 War. Consequently, during the Labor-led governments until 1977, all Jewish settlement activity in the West Bank, Gaza Strip, Sinai, and Golan Heights was limited to those areas to be retained by Israel. There would be no drive, other than Kiryat Arba, to set up Israeli settlements near Arab-populated areas.

Contrary to both the Dayan and Allon plans, religious Zionists led the impetus to settle the entire West Bank, feeling that the

Jewish occupation of the biblical Land of Israel was the harbinger of the coming of the Messiah. Nevertheless, vastly differing approaches regarding the West Bank ruptured the historic alliance between religious Zionism and the Labor movement, and a widening chasm began to form between religious and secular Jews in Israel.[15]

THE 1973 YOM KIPPUR WAR: During the three-year War of Attrition, the Soviet Union supplied Egypt and Syria with hundreds of the latest-model tanks, artillery, and jet fighters, including Russian pilots to fly them. (In one air battle in 1970, Israeli pilots shot down five Soviet-flown MiG 21 fighters without suffering any losses.)[16] More important, the Soviet Union helped the Egyptians establish the best-integrated defense network in the Middle East, combining a great number of SAM missiles and radar-directed antiaircraft guns to knock down Israeli attack planes. On the Israeli side, based on its spectacular and overwhelming victory in 1967, Israel's leadership had come to underestimate its enemies badly. Israel failed to recognize the significant changes in modern warfare that the new technologies, specifically electronics, brought. Despite clear warning signs and solid intelligence reports of an imminent war, Israel did not take its Arab opponents seriously. Alas, Israel was to suffer greatly for its arrogance.

THE WAR BEGINS: At 2:00 p.m. on Yom Kippur, Saturday, October 6, 1973, an avalanche of 100,000 Egyptian artillery shells began hammering Israeli positions across the Suez Canal. Shortly afterward, the first wave of 8,000 troops, the vanguard of an Egyptian force of 200,000 men, crossed the canal. Opposing them were 451 Israeli reservists with little or no battle experience. The vaunted Bar-Lev Line, a series of Israeli earthen embankments and fortifications on the Suez Canal, was easily breached by Egyptian high-velocity water cannon. Egypt, which was planning on 25,000 casualties in crossing the canal, lost only 200 men. Fighting with consummate skill, the Egyptian Army easily overran the skeletal Israeli force.

Israel sent its air force into the fray, bombing the Egyptian bridges set up across the canal, then striking airfields in Egypt. Unlike the Six-Day War, the results were disastrous, and technology was the key. With almost every loss from SAMs or antiaircraft fire, a significant portion of the Israeli air force was destroyed. Worse yet, Israel lost a great share of its best-trained and most qualified pilots, the key, irreplaceable element in the country's defense.

On the Golan Heights, due to the lack of room to maneuver and the proximity to Israeli population centers, the situation was even worse. Syria attacked with 1,100 top-of-the-line Soviet tanks and 1,000 artillery pieces against 170 Israeli tanks and 60 artillery pieces. In a daring, precise raid, specially trained Syrian commandos captured the strategic Mount Hermon. During the night, Syrian tanks raced for the Jordan River and Israel's heartland.

Monday, October 8 was the worst day of the war for Israel. An Israeli counterattack against Egyptian forces failed miserably, and little stood in the way of the Syrian Army cutting Israel in half at the Mediterranean Sea. Not only was Israel losing territory, it was also suffering a terrible attrition rate that shredded its tanks, planes, soldiers, and pilots. If Israel did not win a decisive victory quickly, the Arab armies would have ground the nation into the dust. Moshe Dayan, the Minister of Defense, requested authorization from Prime Minister Golda Meir to use nuclear weapons against the Arabs. Meir vetoed an immediate strike, but approved their use as a last-ditch response in case of the country's downfall. Clearly, Israel's doctrine was to fight and win a conventional war, but if sheer defeat loomed along with the prospect of an Arab-led Holocaust, Israel would bring down the Arab world with nuclear assaults.[17]

By October 9, the tide of war began to change. Despite suffering horrifying losses, the Israeli Air Force shuttled between both fronts, blunting the effectiveness of the Arab missile systems. Israeli planes knocked out all the Egyptian bridges across the Suez Canal, then bombed military targets in the Syrian capital Damascus. An Israeli tank commander, Yossi Ben-Hanan, rushed home from his honeymoon in the Himalayas, cobbled together a ragtag force of twenty tanks, and despite being vastly outnumbered, plunged into the Syrian ranks, causing them to retreat.

The arrival of mobilized reserve forces stiffened Israeli resistance. Providentially, the Arabs' decision to initiate hostilities on Yom Kippur, hoping to take advantage of Israel's unpreparedness, actually helped Israel in one respect — it was very easy to mobilize the reserves that were attending synagogues throughout the country instead of going from house to house. As dark as the situation seemed, from October 9 on no more Israeli territory was given up. However, Israel was rapidly running out of ammunition, planes, and tanks.

THE TURNING POINT: Two events occurred on Sunday, October 14 to make it the decisive day of the war — a failed major Egyptian offensive, and the arrival in Israel of the first American aircraft bringing much-needed supplies.

Egypt's 190,000-man force on the eastern, Israeli-held side of the Suez Canal launched an attack all along the front, the 1,200 tanks massed against 750 Israeli tanks making it one of the greatest tank battles in history. Using new antitank weapons supplied by the United States, the Israeli forces knocked out 260 Egyptian tanks, losing only ten of their own. At that point, Israel began planning on taking the offensive, carrying the battle to the Egyptian-held western bank of the Suez Canal. In the air, despite suffering heavy losses, Israel finally regained superiority. (It was not only Israeli pilots opposing Arab fliers — North Koreans and Americans flew combat missions for the Egyptians and Israelis respectively.)[18]

Responding to Israel's desperate request for armaments, President Nixon ordered, "Tell them [the air force] to send everything that can fly."[19] The United States Air Force's Military Airlift Command (MAC) immediately went into action. However, only one NATO country, Portugal, allowed American planes to fly over its territory *en route* to Israel, greatly complicating the 6,450-

mile trip from the United States. Nevertheless, after encountering initial glitches, the airlift became a gigantic conveyor belt, supplying over 700 tons of supplies in a single day. American Air Force Colonel Donald Strobaugh was the hero in this effort, ably coordinating the airlift at Tel Aviv's Lod Airport. The Soviet Union also initiated an airlift to its Arab patrons, but it paled in contrast to the American effort.

On October 18, Israeli Major General Bren Adan moved 170 tanks across the Suez Canal, beginning the encirclement of the huge Egyptian Third Army on the east bank. Two days earlier, Ariel Sharon had begun the cross-canal offensive, securing a bridgehead, but Adan brought reinforcements in strength. By October 24, the Third Army was trapped. On October 21, Israel recaptured Mount Hermon. Israeli forces now had a virtually unopposed path to Cairo and Damascus.

The Israeli successes alarmed the Soviet Union, which threatened to intervene in the conflict if Israel did not accept a cease-fire. In response, the United States put its forces worldwide, including nuclear weapons, on DefCon III, indicating an increased state of readiness. (Normal peacetime status is DefCon V; DefCon I is all-out war.) Had the Soviet Union reciprocated with a full-scale alert of its forces, the United States military would have gone to DefCon II, the situation where war is deemed imminent. This in turn might have convinced the Soviet Union to launch a first-strike nuclear attack on the United States. As such, for several hours on October 25, the world teetered on the brink of nuclear holocaust. However, the Soviet Union backed down, the horrifying threat was averted, and prospects increased for a cease-fire.

On October 28, Israel began direct talks with Egypt on the disengagement of forces. Eventually, Israel allowed the Third Army to return to Egypt, a move much criticized in Israel. Israel also withdrew from the west bank of the Suez Canal, while permitting the Egyptians to keep a small force on the canal's eastern side close to the water. On the Syrian front, Israel retained the Golan Heights and Mount Hermon, but returned some territory to Syria, most notably the town of Kuneitra. After three weeks of intensely bloody conflict, the guns fell silent.

RESULTS OF THE WAR: Although Israel had won an impressive victory, the mood in the country was that of complete despair. Casualties were appalling — 2,688 soldiers killed, proportionately equivalent to hundreds of thousands of Americans. So many families were bereaved that a sense of mourning enveloped the entire nation. Israel became more isolated in the world, as many nations broke off diplomatic relations after the war. The country also became almost completely dependent on the United States for military and economic aid, and for international diplomatic support. The sense of confidence that Israel had after the Six-Day War was completely shattered, and has not returned to this day.

Although the Arabs had lost the war, they won a major psychological victory, demonstrating once and for all that their troops can fight equally well as Israel's — in some instances even outperforming the Israelis. October 6, the anniversary of the outbreak of the war, is celebrated annually in Egypt as a day of honor. The Arabs also discovered a new weapon — oil. Led by Saudi Arabia, the Arab oil-producing countries imposed an oil embargo on nations that had supported Israel, and also drastically raised the price of petroleum. Virtually overnight gasoline prices jumped from 40 cents a gallon to one dollar, with cars having to wait hours at gas stations to fill up. Israel was widely blamed for this situation, and in Europe and Japan the situation was even worse, due to their greater dependency on Arab oil. The oil weapon would be wielded many times over the next thirty years, causing great havoc to the world economy, enriching the Arab nations immeasurably, and fomenting worldwide anti-Semitism.

THE PALESTINIANS AND TERRORISM: In the 1970s terrorist organizations proliferated worldwide, but the Palestinians, particularly the PLO, set the tone and standard for acts of horror. Aircraft hijackings and attacks on planes became popular during the decade, changing forever the face of air travel. In February 1970, Palestinians bombed a Swissair passenger jet headed for Israel, killing all forty-seven people on board. On September 6, 1970, in what became known as Skyjack Sunday, the Palestinians hijacked four planes with hundreds of passengers (including the renowned head of Yeshiva Chaim Berlin, Rabbi Yitzchak Hutner), forced them to land in Jordan, and threatened to kill the passengers unless Arab prisoners were released in several countries. Eventually, all the passengers were released, and some of the planes blown up. Later that month, in what became known as Black September, the PLO attempted to wrest control of Jordan from King Hussein. With indirect Israeli help, the king was able to quash the revolt, and the PLO moved to Lebanon, spreading throughout the southern region bordering Israel.

In May 1972, three members of the Japanese Red Army, working for Palestinian terrorists, sprayed the arrival hall in Tel Aviv's Lod Airport with machine-gun fire, killing twenty-seven people. In September 1972, at the Olympic Games in Munich, Germany, Arabs seized eleven Israeli athletes, held them hostage, and killed them after a bungled German rescue attempt. (Callously, the International Olympic Committee allowed the Games to go on.) Over the years, Israel's intelligence agency, the Mossad, tracked down and killed all those responsible for the murders.

In April 1974, Palestinians infiltrated from Lebanon into the Israeli border town of Kiryat Shmonah, burst into an apartment house, and indiscriminately machine-gunned eighteen men, women, and children. In mid-May, Palestinians seized a school in the northern Israeli town of Maalot, holding 120 children hostage and threatening to kill them unless Israel released Arab prisoners. Following its long-established policy, Israel refused to negotiate with the terrorists, and soldiers charged the school. In the ensuing melee, twenty children and one soldier were killed. In March 1975, Palestinians landed in a rubber dinghy off the Tel Aviv shoreline, entered a hotel, and killed eight hostages. In July of that year, a bomb hidden in a refrigerator went off in a Jerusalem street, killing fourteen people and wounding seventy-five others. (The perpetrator of the refrigerator bomb was released by Israel in June 2003 as a goodwill gesture to the Palestinians.) In March 1978, a PLO unit landed on the Israeli coast and hijacked a bus going from Haifa to Tel Aviv. Following a struggle, thirty-nine of those on the bus were killed.

Numerous other attacks took place throughout the decade. Sadly, today's Palestinian acts of terror are nothing new — the only novel twist being added is homicide bombing. In the 1970s, the Arabs tried to murder and escape. Now they have chosen immediate martyrdom.

UNITED NATIONS ANTI-SEMITISM: In October 1974, an event occurred that continues to have profound ramifications for peace in the Middle East. At a summit meeting in Morocco, the Arab world, including Jordan, decided to recognize the PLO as the sole representative of the Palestinian people. Instead of dealing with Jordan, the least hostile of Israel's enemies, regarding the return of the West Bank in exchange for a peace treaty and secure borders, Israel had to contend with the implacable Palestinians in any peace negotiations.

As a result of the Arab resolution, the United Nations voted to accept the PLO as an observer at all United Nations meetings, and invited its leader, arch-terrorist Yasser Arafat, to speak to the General Assembly in New York. Arafat, with a gun holster on his belt, addressed the world's nations: "Now Zionism will get out of this world — and from Palestine in particular — under the blow of the people's struggle." He received a standing ovation.[20]

ZIONISM IS RACISM: On November 10, 1975, the 37th anniversary of *Krystallnacht*, the United Nations General Assembly, dominated by Communist, Arab, and Third World nations, voted that "Zionism is a form of racism and racial discrimination." Since racism was anathema to the United Nations, and since Zionism was the name of the movement that established a home for the Jews in their biblical lands, the resolution was widely and correctly interpreted as both denying the right of Israel to exist, and encouraging anti-Semitism worldwide. The United States UN Ambassador Daniel Patrick Moynihan, a great friend of the Jewish people, defiantly proclaimed, "The United States rises to declare before the General Assembly of the United Nations, and before the world, that it does not acknowledge, it will not abide by, it will never acquiesce in this infamous act." Chaim Herzog, Israel's UN Ambassador, ascended the podium and tore a copy of the resolution in half. (Significantly, the UN Secretary-General at the time was Kurt Waldheim, who was later accused of war crimes committed while serving in the German Army during World War II.)

The hateful resolution accomplished nothing for the Palestinian cause, of course, and tarnished the UN in the eyes of many thoughtful people. Of the seventy-two countries that voted for the resolution, none were as greatly affected as Mexico. Tourism, especially from the United States, was a major mainstay of Mexico's economy. American Jewish groups announced a boycott of Mexico, and many American organizations cancelled plans to hold conventions there. There were 30,000 hotel cancellations in a single week. Although Mexico later apologized for its vote, it would take years to regain its tourist losses. In December 1991, the UN revoked the contentious resolution.

THE ENTEBBE RESCUE: In June 1976, Arab and German terrorists hijacked a plane to Uganda, run by mass murderer and anti-Semite Idi Amin. In a chilling reenactment of the selections at Auschwitz, the hijackers separated the Jewish and non-Jewish passengers, releasing the non-Jews. In the most daring airborne commando raid in history, five Israeli aircraft secretly traveled 2,500 miles to Uganda, landed at Entebbe Airport where the hostages were being held, killed the terrorists, and freed the hostages. In less than one hour after the initial landing, the Israeli planes departed with the freed captives. One hundred prisoners were rescued, while only four were killed — three caught in the crossfire between the Israeli troops and the hijackers, and an elderly woman, Dora Bloch, who earlier had been taken to a Ugandan hospital, and who became the hapless victim of the Ugandans' lust for revenge. The sole military casualty was mission commander Yonatan Netanyahu, whose brother, Benjamin, later became Prime Minister of Israel.

The Entebbe raid not only rescued the hostages, it also restored pride to an Israel still suffering from the trauma of the Yom Kippur War. World terrorism received a great blow, as many nations realized that the best way to deal with terrorists was not to negotiate with them, but to strike at them instead. Typically, the UN criticized Israel for aggression against Uganda.

THE LIKUD ELECTION VICTORY: After the 1977 elections, for the first time in Israel's history the Labor Party no longer led the government. Sephardic Jews, who felt great resentment toward the Ashkenazic elite that dominated Israeli politics, fueled the startling turnaround. Despite significant economic gains, their share in white-collar jobs did not exceed half that of Ashkenazic Jews. Neither did their representation in the government, armed forces, and universities.[21] The Sephardim decided to support the Likud candidate, Menachem Begin, who, although Ashkenazic, appealed to Sephardic voters, who saw him as an outsider like themselves. Begin expressed sympathy for Sephardic aspirations, and they flocked to his cause with great enthusiasm, crying out "Begin, King of Israel" at political rallies.[22] In a shocking result predicted by no one, the Likud Party swept to power, and Begin became prime minister.

As a result of Begin's victory, the State of Israel took on a more religious public appearance. Begin often wore a *kippah*, invoked the name of G-d, and performed mitzvos in public, behaviors not generally linked to earlier Labor prime ministers. El Al, Israel's national airline, stopped flights on the Sabbath. One of the first things Begin did on assuming office was to introduce the ancient biblical names for the West Bank: Judaea and Samaria. Although the establishment of settlements in the territories was well underway before he assumed power, Begin infused the settler movement with new zeal, conforming to his belief that Jews should dwell in the entire Land of Israel. Under previous Labor governments, settlements were viewed as having either economic or military value, but not as having religious significance.

SADAT VISITS ISRAEL: In November 1977, President Anwar Sadat of Egypt astounded Israel by proclaiming that he would be willing to address the Knesset in Jerusalem in pursuit of peace. Sadat's welcome by the people of Israel, who lined the streets of Jerusalem cheering their former enemy and waving Egyptian flags, reflected the nation's overwhelming desire to be accepted as part of the Middle East by the Arabs. At the Knesset, Sadat proclaimed that Egypt accepts Israel's right to exist, but that Israel must withdraw from all occupied lands and agree to the establishment of a Palestinian state. Although the visit was largely symbolic, and nothing of substance was agreed upon, the visit nevertheless broke through the great psychological barrier of Arabs refusing to meet Israeli government leaders publicly. Several months later, Begin paid Sadat a reciprocal visit in Egypt, but talks rapidly broke down.

PEACE WITH EGYPT: After months of tiring negotiations, American President Jimmy Carter drafted a formal peace treaty between Israel and Egypt that became known as the Camp David Accords. Israel agreed to withdraw totally from the Sinai Desert, remove its military bases, and uproot its settlements in the area, most notably the town of Yamit. Egypt agreed to a large buffer zone between its army and Israel's, and to the establishment of two American-manned early-warning stations in the Sinai to alert Israel in case of an Egyptian buildup. Israel gained free access for its ships through the Suez Canal, complete diplomatic relations with Egypt, and the cessation of Egyptian participation in the Arab economic boycott of Israel.

The Egyptian-Israeli peace was a turning point in the Arab-Israeli conflict. Egypt, as the leader in all previous wars with Israel, was out of the military equation, enabling Israel to focus more on other threats in the region. The Accords also showed the Arab world that Israel was serious in seeking peace and would make painful concessions to that end. After passage in the Knesset, on March 26, 1979, Begin, Sadat, and Carter formally signed the peace treaty on the White House lawn. Since then, Egypt has kept to the letter, if not the spirit, of the treaty. However, many Arabs felt that Egypt sold out the Arab cause for its own gain, and no other nation, other than Jordan, has followed Egypt's example. Sadat himself was assassinated in 1981.

Chapter 36

THE 1980s

SETTING THE TONE: In comparison to the turbulence of the 1960s and 70s, the 1980s seemed tranquil indeed. However, this decade shaped the current Jewish world in a more profound way than its two predecessors. A changing of the guard began to occur as many of the European Torah leaders passed on. Tensions between religious and secular Jews increased greatly, especially in Israel. As American Orthodox Jews became more affluent, unprecedented opportunities and challenges arose. Israel sank into the Lebanese quagmire, sapping its strength and morale. The Palestinian *intifada* marked a turning point in the Arab-Israeli struggle, and the Iranian revolution sent shock waves throughout the world. Cracks formed in the previously impermeable Soviet Iron Curtain, which widened until the entire structure came tumbling down.

A NEW ERA: The 1980s presaged the beginning of the post-Acharonim era, as the decade saw the passing of many of the greatest European-born-and-trained Torah giants. Among the departed were Rabbi Moshe Feinstein, Rabbi Yaakov Kaminetzky, Rabbi Yaakov Y. Kanievsky (the Steipler Gaon), Rabbi Yaakov Y. Ruderman, Rabbi Schneur Kotler, Rabbi Yitzchak Hutner, Rabbi Joseph Breuer, and the rebbes of Bluzhov and Skulen. These towering personalities were heir to a bygone level of saintliness and scholarship, neither of which could be replicated on American soil in modern times. Rarely in

Jewish history has there been such a dramatic drop in spiritual leadership in such a short period of time. The future leaders of the Jewish people, for better or worse, would come from the new, post-Holocaust communities of the United States and Israel.

AFFLUENCE: The 1980s were marked by a great increase in living standards for many American Orthodox Jews. In contrast to Eastern Europe, where for centuries there were very few wealthy Jews and great numbers of impoverished ones, in the United States a large Orthodox middle class emerged. This emergence had both positive and negative ramifications. *Kollel* study became extremely popular, almost de rigueur, during this decade, as parents were increasingly able to provide financial support for young couples. Even those that planned to embark on a professional career often spent a year or two after marriage in full-time Torah study.

However, increasing affluence created a growing desire for conspicuous consumption. Bar mitzvahs and weddings became more lavish. Homes became fancier, automobiles gaudier, clothing and vacations ever more expensive. Sadly, for many the pursuit of material luxury became their life's goal — at the expense of Torah study and family life. Most alarmingly, new, universal standards were set in areas such as *simchah* celebrations and dress. Unlike in Europe, where the great number of poor Jews felt no pressure to imitate the very few wealthy individuals, in the United States, where there was such a large middle and upper class, people believed that their communal standing would be harmed if they could not keep up with the proverbial Goldsteins. (In one particularly egregious example, a boy was shunned by his classmates for wearing plastic eyeglass frames instead of more trendy wire-rimmed ones.)[1] When family members desired things that so many friends and neighbors possessed, budding scholars left *kollel* and positions in Torah education. As a result of making unaffordable weddings or bar mitzvahs, many breadwinners sank in a morass of spiraling debt. Indeed, the constant demand for ever-increasing sums of money led some to adopt shady business practices and even outright dishonesty. In some cases,

Orthodox Jews were implicated in scams involving misuse of government funds, creating a great *chilul HaShem*. Courageously, rabbis and spiritual leaders began to address the issues of conspicuous consumption and dishonesty, with a greater public awareness emerging in these areas.

RELIGIOUS-SECULAR TENSION: As the influence of non-Zionist religious Jews in Israel (*Chareidim*) increased in the 1980s, anti-Chareidism became a winning political platform for secular political parties. Parties such as Meretz, Tzomet, and Shinui powered their way to the Knesset by enflaming secular fear of the *Chareidim*. In every parliamentary election since 1984, a different secular party printed election posters showing an angry mob of *Chareidim*, promising that only the secular party could beat back the *Chareidim*. However, political action was only a small part of secular loathing of the *Chareidim*.

In 1985, a political cartoon depicted a fat *chareidi* Jew holding a goblet of wine in one hand and a miniature secular Jew, whose blood he is sucking out, in the other. Some leading secular figures referred to *Chareidim* and yeshivah students as bloodsucking leeches, parasites, and lice.[2] The image of Jews portraying other Jews with crass medieval anti-Semitic symbols was shocking enough; even more horrifying, however, was graffiti imploring Israelis to "kill them (*Chareidim*) while they're young," and a handbill protesting the establishment of a religious daycare center in a secular neighborhood, which showed a group of religious children and read, in the style of Julius Streicher's *Der Sturmer*, "The New Enemies!!! They must be **liquidated** while they are still **young**!!!" [bold in original].[3]

This Nazi-like media campaign against Orthodox Jews was not limited to Israel. After the Israeli election of 1988, in which the religious parties held the swing vote of thirteen Knesset seats, both secular Jewish and non-Jewish newspapers and magazines worldwide carried grotesque, stereotypical caricatures of religious Jews along with shrill pronouncements of Israel turning into a theocratic state such as Iran.

Secular Israelis base their animosity toward *Chareidim* on two complaints: *Chareidim* do not serve in the army, and they are a drain on the economy. For their part, nonreligious Israeli Jews feel that they are dying and paying taxes to uphold a large group of people who neither share their values nor are productive. This ancient, heretical attitude, decried in the Talmud,[4] fails to realize that G-d guarantees the security of Eretz Yisrael in the merit of Torah scholars and students.[5] In truth, even if the *Chareidim* joined both the army and workforce in proportion to their numbers, secular Israelis' loathing of them would not diminish. The source of animosity toward religious Jews has much deeper roots — the struggle for the soul of the State of Israel. Secular Jews want an Israel that resembles the hedonistic nations of the West, while religious Jews feel that the Jewish state must represent authentic Torah values. Noting a societal trend that manifested itself even in ancient times, the Talmud remarks that ignorant Jews hate Torah scholars even more than non-Jews hate Jews.[6] As such, beginning with the 1980s the gulf between religious and secular in Israel widened to perhaps an unbridgeable gap.

IN AMERICA: In 1983, the Reform movement introduced the doctrine of patrilineal descent, proclaiming that the offspring of a Jewish father and non-Jewish mother is Jewish if the child maintains some attachment to the Jewish community (presumably membership in a Reform temple).[7] This flagrant violation of Jewish law sowed much dissension within the Jewish world. More than 90 percent of Reform temples granted membership, including official positions, to non-Jewish spouses. Even given its acceptance of non-Jewish spouses, Reform still found itself floundering. Alarmed, then, at its declining Jewish membership, the Reform movement proposed outreach activities to seek out and convert unaffiliated non-Jews to Reform Judaism.[8] Fortunately, this heretical initiative has not prospered.

The Conservative movement further distanced itself from Torah tradition. In 1982, the Conservative Rabbinical Assembly published a new edition of the Passover Haggadah, featuring "a revision of the Hebrew text which reflects Conservative ideology."[9] Additions to the traditional siddur were made to reflect feminist demands, such as a *Mi Sheberach* prayer to honor women who were called to the Torah on Sabbaths and holidays. Amy Eilberg became the Conservative movement's first female ordained clergy in 1985.[10] In 1988, after decades of changing its standards to satisfy the demands of its constituents, the Conservative movement created its first platform stating the major tenets of Conservatism.[11] During this decade, due to untenable changes on the left, or so-called liberal side of Judaism, hostile relations between the Reform and Conservative movements on one side and Orthodoxy on the other reached the point of no return.

Paradoxically, despite the contempt that Reform and Conservative Jews displayed toward religious Jews, the two leftist movements reacted with great vehemence regarding Orthodox invalidation of their deviations from normative Torah law. In the words of noted journalism educator Samuel G. Freedman:

> And in an inchoate way that less observant Jews rarely acknowledge, much less articulate, many of them look to the Orthodox for acceptance, approval, and legitimacy. That is precisely why the condemnation of the Reform and Conservative branches by even marginal [sic] Orthodox groups like the *Agudath HaRabbanim* provokes such anguish and outcry.[12]

From all this controversy, it appears that nonobservant Jews realize there is only one valid form of Judaism — true Torah. As such, their desire for an unfettered life, free of the Torah's commands, creates an enormous conflict with their individual and collective conscience, which creates an agonizing sense of insecurity. Therefore, instead of increasing their observance, which for many is an unpalatable option, they lash out at those whose lifestyles pose a constant challenge to their existence — Orthodox Jews.

RADICALIZATION OF THE ISLAMIC WORLD: The victory of radical Islam in Iran provided a great impetus for Islamist movements throughout the Middle East. Much in the manner of Marxism-Leninism, radical Islam spoke of a worldwide struggle between the forces of Islam and those of corrupt materialism, a struggle in which everyone must take sides. According to this scenario, the Muslim masses must be mobilized to fight the West, and Western conceptions of freedom must be rejected.[13] By the mid-1980s, the most significant opposition groups throughout the Arab world were Islamists, who, in order to gain control of their communities and show that they were the fiercest warriors in the cause of national liberation, tried to take leadership roles in fighting Israel. Therefore, a new element — religious fanaticism — was introduced to the Israeli-Arab conflict, which had previously been largely secular; this new factor would make the conflict's resolution almost impossible. Terrorist groups even more murderous than the PLO, such as Hamas and Islamic Jihad, were formed in the 1980s and aided by Iran. At that time, the Islamic Republic of Iran became the greatest long-term danger to Israel, embarking on a multibillion-dollar program of rearmament, including the attempt to develop nuclear weapons and procure delivery systems.

SOVIET JEWRY: In the early 1980s, due to the worsening relations between the USSR and the West, Soviet Jewish emigration had nearly stopped entirely. During the four years of slowest emigration, 1983 to 1986, only 4,281 Jews were permitted to leave.[14] However, with the gradual liberalization of Soviet society under Mikhail Gorbachev, Jewish emigration increased greatly, reaching 26,048 in 1989. Yet this number was only a portent of the great exodus of the 1990s.

Opportunities for Jewish self-expression within the USSR expanded significantly at the end of the 1980s. Religious schools were allowed to operate, and more synagogues were opened for worship. Contacts with overseas Jewish organizations resumed, and money, religious articles, and teachers were sent to the Soviet Union to revive Jewish life. A major portion of world Jewry was discovering its heritage after seventy years of isolation. However, the more liberal environment (*glasnost*) led to the rise of openly anti-Semitic organizations, which had previously been officially suppressed under the Soviet regime. One of the most rabid groups, *Pamyat*, became highly popular, spreading anti-Semitic propaganda throughout the Soviet Union.

BOMBING IRAQ'S NUCLEAR REACTOR: In 1981, alarmed by intelligence reports that Saddam Hussein's nuclear reactor would imminently become operational, Israel, in a brilliantly executed military operation, destroyed the facility. An American news report dramatically described the action:

> Like a bolt out of the [so-called] Old Testament, they hurtled at Baghdad out of the setting sun. Nearing their target, six F-15 interceptors camouflaged with the desert mottle of the Israeli Air Force peeled off to keep guard overhead. Eight F-16 fighter-bombers roared down to the concrete dome of the Osirak nuclear reactor. In a single series of lightning passes, the little fighters dropped their payload of 2,000 bombs. Within two minutes they disappeared cleanly into the gathering darkness, leaving behind a few puffs of flak and a fearsome new turn in a dangerous nuclear game.[15]

For its courageous action, Israel was roundly condemned worldwide and in the United Nations. The United States, although quite pleased with the raid, joined in censuring Israel. Ten years later, the wisdom of Israel's action became apparent, for had American forces faced a nuclear-armed Iraq in the First Gulf War, in all likelihood they would have suffered countless fatalities.

THE LEBANON WAR (1982): This conflict, which grew out of Israel's defensive needs, rapidly turned into a quagmire that became known as Israel's Vietnam. For the first time in its history, Israel became involved in a protracted battle that posed no threats to its survival. Israel achieved no strategic gains, was portrayed as the aggressor, made new enemies, polarized its own society, and, worst of all, lost more than 600 dead and suffered 1,800 wounded soldiers.

Over the years, Yasser Arafat's PLO had created a virtual

state within a state bordering Israel in Southern Lebanon. More than 15,000 PLO fighters were encamped throughout the country, along with an arsenal that included mortars, Katyusha rockets, hundreds of tanks, and an extensive anti-aircraft network.[16] Clearly, the PLO was gearing up for an eventual invasion of Israel. The situation bordering Lebanon in the Galilee became intolerable, as the frequency of rocket attacks forced Israelis to flee their homes or live in bomb shelters.

On June 6, Israel launched Operation Peace for Galilee, invading Lebanon with the twin objectives of advancing no more than twenty-five miles into the country, and completing the operation within three days. In its typical thoughtless reaction to Israeli military advances, the United Nations Security Council immediately demanded that Israel withdraw from Lebanon, a request that was ignored.

Israel rapidly achieved its objectives, its troops sweeping through Southern Lebanon in a week, entering Christian East Beirut to a rapturous welcome. In a two-day aerial dogfight, Israeli fighters downed ninety-six Syrian planes without incurring a single loss.[17] The PLO fighters were pushed back into Muslim West Beirut, and encircled by an Israeli siege. However, Israel desired a third objective in Lebanon: the elimination of both the PLO's quasi-government and Syrian influence. These were not easy tasks, and the ensuing escalation of the conflict sucked Israel into a swirling vortex of horror.

For the next two months, Israeli forces fired salvo after salvo into West Beirut in an effort to flush out PLO leadership from its redoubt. Hundreds of the city's inhabitants were killed, and many buildings destroyed. The daily television transmission of Israeli artillery bombarding Beirut; the columns of smoke, dust, and fire rising in the air; and the close-up pictures of the destruction, including serious damage to a hospital, caused immense harm to Israel's international image. Unlike Israel's earlier battles, in which the country was portrayed favorably in the world media as the underdog defending itself, in Lebanon Israel came to be seen as a savage aggressor killing innocent civilians. That war marked the beginning of the negative media image of Israel that has persisted until today. At home, many Israelis began to feel that the war's continuation was unnecessary, even unjustified. In August, the United States arranged for Israel to stop its bombardment of West Beirut, allowing the PLO to evacuate its forces to other countries in the Arab world.

Bashir Gemayel, Israel's Christian ally, was elected president of Lebanon on August 23, representing the high point of General Ariel Sharon's policy. Through Gemayel, Israel hoped for a formal peace treaty with Lebanon and a permanent solution to the problem on their border. However, a Syrian agent assassinated Gemayel on September 14.

In response, Israeli troops occupied Muslim West Beirut, and events spiraled rapidly out of control. On September 17, with Israeli soldiers ignoring the situation, Christian Phalangist forces, the traditional enemies of the Muslims in Lebanon, entered the two Palestinian refugee camps of Sabra and Shatilla, located in the area, and, in revenge for Gemayel's murder, massacred some 2,300 men, women, and children. Grisly photographs of the carnage were broadcast around the world.

Although no Israeli troops were involved in the killings, Israel, as the occupying power, was blamed worldwide. Prime Minister Begin did not help the situation when he thoughtlessly declared, "Goyim kill goyim, and they immediately come to hang the Jews."[18] In Israel, Begin's opponents, mostly secular Ashkenazim, organized a mass demonstration in Tel Aviv, where 400,000 Israelis demanded that the government set up a commission of inquiry into what had happened. The commission criticized Begin for "unjustifiable indifference," and had particularly harsh words for Sharon, finding him responsible for allowing the Phalangists to enter the camps and not anticipating the massacre. Sharon was dismissed as defense minister, but was allowed to remain in the government.

In 1983, Israel began pulling out from Lebanon, and American and French soldiers went into Beirut to keep the peace. In October, a homicide bomber rammed a truck loaded with explosives into a United States Marines barracks, killing 241 American soldiers. Disgusted by the endless conflict, the United States removed its forces, and Syria gained control of Lebanon, emerging as the de facto winner of the conflict. Israel realized none of its objectives, and created new Lebanese enemies, guerrilla groups such as Amal and Hizballah. Menachem Begin, broken by the war and by his wife's death, resigned as prime minister in September 1983, withdrew from public life, and died in 1992.

Israeli troops were stationed in an eight-mile wide strip of Lebanon adjoining northern Israel. Eventually, as terror attacks claimed the lives of increasing numbers of Israeli soldiers in the occupied zone, in 2000 Israel withdrew its forces entirely from Lebanon. Just as Vietnam changed America, so did Lebanon change the face of Israeli society.

NEW RELIGIOUS PARTIES: In the 1980s, a major new force in Israeli politics, the Orthodox Sephardic Shas party, was founded. Interestingly enough, its inspiration came from an Ashkenazic Torah sage, Rabbi Elazar M. Shach, under whom many Sephardic religious leaders had studied. Taking advantage of both the traditional Sephardic resentment of the Ashkenazic elite and the greater tolerance of religion found among nonobservant Sephardim, Shas developed into a powerful political force, garnering up to seventeen Knesset seats in future elections, frequently holding the balance of power. Rabbi Shach also formed a small Ashkenazic party, Degel HaTorah, which was distinct from the older Agudath Israel party. Under Israel's political system, which grants immense power to small parties, these groups often play a deciding role in the formation of ruling governments.

Rabbi Shach, also the head of the prestigious Ponovezh Yeshiva, became the recognized leader of many of Israel's religious Jews in the 1980s. Personifying the Torah's command to judges (Deuteronomy 1:17), "You shall fear no man," Rabbi Shach courageously spoke out on many controversial issues, and was vociferously attacked by secular and even some religious Jews. Nevertheless, his pronouncements were revered by tens of thousands, often created government policy, and not infrequently decided national elections. Rabbi Shach bemoaned the anti-religious activities of the left-wing kibbutzim, advocated withdrawal from land conquered in 1967 (in opposition to many on the right), and took Chabad-Lubavitch Chassidim to task for increasing messianic propensities. His stance was succinctly expressed in a discussion with Israeli politician (and onetime Prime Minister) Shimon Peres:

> What is a Jewish State? Every nation has a State. What is Jewish Agriculture? Every nation has agriculture. What is a Jewish Army? Every nation has an army. What is Jewish Industry? Every nation has industry. There is just one thing that the Jews have that the others don't, and that is the Torah. The Torah keeps the Jews alive.[19]

THE RESCUE OF ETHIOPIA'S JEWS: Some 28,000 black-skinned Jews lived in Ethiopia, where they were known to their neighbors as *falashas* (strangers). Their origins were uncertain, with legends tracing them back to the Queen of Sheba during the times of King Solomon, or even as remnants of the biblical tribe of Dan. It is more likely that they were Ethiopians by blood, descendants of possibly as many as 300,000 Africans who had converted to Judaism in the early Middle Ages.[20] When conditions became dangerous for them in Ethiopia in the 1980s, the Israeli government clandestinely arranged for the transfer of Ethiopia's Jews to Israel. From November 1984 to January 1985, in what became known as Operation Moses, some 8,000 Ethiopian Jews were airlifted to Israel.

In order to prevent action by the Sudanese and Ethiopian authorities, which were officially enemies of Israel, to stop the airlift, the Israeli government kept the operation a secret. However, word broke out when fundraising efforts were leaked to the press, and the mission came to an end. Writing after Operation Moses was revealed, the noted columnist William Safire remarked: "For the first time in history, thousands of black people are being brought to a country not in chains but in dignity, not as slaves but as citizens."[21]

Unfortunately, the new immigrants faced formidable absorption problems. Many of them had never seen running water or electricity before they reached Israel. They also faced racism, both in society and the armed forces. Ethiopian Jews were particularly incensed when they discovered that blood they donated to Israel's national blood bank was routinely discarded for fear of carrying diseases such as the AIDS virus.

As the Ethiopian Jews did not practice many Jewish traditions, of which they were unaware during their many centuries of isolation from the rest of the Jewish world, there was a question regarding their Jewish status. As a result, leading rabbinic authorities, including Rabbi Moshe Feinstein, ruled that they should undergo conversion.[22] Many Ethiopians were willing to convert, but a vociferous minority, spurred by anti-religious elements in Israel, attempted to prevent it from taking place, at times even resorting to force.

ARAB TERROR: Terror attacks on Israel and Jews worldwide continued unabated in the 1980s. In 1985, Palestinian terrorists hijacked the cruise liner *Achille Lauro*, murdered Leon Klinghoffer, an elderly wheelchair-bound American Jew, and dumped his body overboard, wheelchair and all. That same year, there were simultaneous attacks on El Al Airline ticket counters in Vienna and Rome, killing nineteen people. In 1986, Arabs attacked the Neveh Shalom synagogue in Istanbul, Turkey during Sabbath morning services, massacring nineteen worshippers. The next year, four Palestinians conducted a hang glider raid from Lebanon into Israel, slaying six soldiers at an army outpost. In 1988, Libyan terrorists planted a bomb on Pan Am Flight 103, headed from London to New York. The plane exploded over Lockerbie, Scotland, and all 289 passengers and crew members aboard the aircraft, along with eleven people on the ground, died.

THE *INTIFADA*: Since 1967, a new generation of Palestinians had grown up under Israeli occupation, and they were tired of military and diplomatic failures, and of increasing Israeli settlement in the occupied territories. Throughout the 1980s, there had been many episodes of stone throwing and verbal abuse against Israeli soldiers patrolling every Arab town. None of the episodes involved firearms. However, in December 1987, matters turned deadly.

After four Arab workers from Gaza were accidentally run over and killed by an Israeli truck, violence broke out throughout the Gaza Strip and the West Bank: Israeli soldiers were attacked with rocks, and even Molotov cocktails and guns. The popular revolt, known as the *intifada*, or uprising, took both Israel and the PLO by surprise.

In an attempt to suppress the *intifada*, Israeli soldiers used tear gas, rubber bullets, and in some cases, notably when their lives were in danger, live ammunition. Television crews carried images of Israeli troops shooting and beating Palestinian rock throwers, which gave the Palestinians an enormous propaganda tool and Israel worldwide opprobrium. (The media, of course, did not point out that the soldiers were acting in self-defense.) Yitzhak Rabin, then Defense Minister, told Israeli soldiers that it was better to strike a demonstrator with a club than to shoot him. However, this advice was misconstrued around the world as giving soldiers license to break the bones of civilians, and Israel's international image was further damaged.

The *intifada* lasted nearly five years. More than 100 Israeli soldiers and civilians were killed, with the Arab toll much higher. Israeli society was literally shaken to the core, with many Israelis questioning the continuation of the occupation. Young army conscripts resented the role assigned them of subduing civilians, even women and children, and destroying private homes. Israel's economy suffered greatly, due to the loss of cheap Arab labor, on which much of Israel's agriculture and industry still relies. The Palestinians gained the sympathy of the entire world and increasingly began to feel that it was just a matter of time until they achieved their independence.

Chapter 37

RECENT TIMES

REAT TURMOIL: Events occurred at a dizzying pace during the last decade of the twentieth century and the beginning of the twenty-first. Communism collapsed in the Soviet Union, with the great empire splitting into fifteen independent nations. The momentous events of the First Gulf War were soon followed by the false hopes of the Oslo Accords, and a peace treaty between Israel and Jordan. Prime Minister Rabin's assassination sharply divided Israel, and the beginning of large-scale homicide bombings rocked the nation. Negotiations with Syria and the Palestinians fell through, and the second *intifada* devastated Israel. But by far, the most far-reaching and defining event of the era were the terrorist attacks on the United States, at the World Trade Center and the Pentagon.

CHANGING OF THE GUARD: Virtually all the spiritual giants of the previous generation passed away during this time, including, but not limited to, such towering personalities as Rabbi Shimon Schwab, Rabbi Shlomo Zalman Auerbach, Rabbi Elazar M. Shach, Rabbi Avigdor Miller, and the rebbes of Lubavitch, Klausenberg, Bobov, and Ger. The full impact of their loss has yet to be felt, but the Jewish people were deprived of these sages' spiritual merit and sagacious advice at a most critical juncture. However, G-d has promised the Jewish people (Deuteronomy 31:21) that there will always be spiritual leaders to assume the mantle of leadership.

AMERICAN JEWISH DEMOGRAPHICS: In 1990, the National Jewish Population Study made shocking findings regarding the state of American Jewry. One-third of all Americans of Jewish ancestry no longer reported Judaism as their religion. Of all Jews who have married since 1985, the majority have married non-Jews. Roughly 1.3 million people of Jewish descent were professing another religion, while 1.1 million said they had no religion. Demographers predicted a drop between one million to more than two million in American Jewish population in the next two generations.[1]

This study was followed by an even more shocking find. After extensive research over four years, Anthony Gordon and Richard Horowitz completed their *Future of American Jewry Study* and published a chart titled "Will Your Grandchildren be Jewish?" dividing American Jews into five categories: Secular, Reform, Conservative, Centrist Orthodox, and Yeshivah/Chassidic. Starting with 200 members of each category in the first generation, they found that secular Jews would produce 10 Jewish great-grandchildren, Reform 27, Conservative 48, Centrist (or so-called Modern) Orthodox 692, and Yeshivah/Chassidic 5,175.[2] Realizing the shattering implications, the *New York Times Magazine* wrote:

> At the turn of this century, most American and Israeli Jews are facing a common challenging question: whether a meaningful non-Orthodox existence is possible in the new millennium; whether we can all avoid being the last of the non-Orthodox Jews?
>
> While there are a few bold attempts at a counteroffensive — proclaiming a Jewish Revival, gathering again in the synagogues — the overall trend is unquestionable: the rate of intermarriage is climbing; the number of affiliated Jews stays low; hundreds of thousands are being lost from American Jewry every decade.
>
> As American Jews fail to reproduce, as they find it impossible to keep their young within the faith, they are the ones now facing the threat of cultural extinction. At the turn of the twenty-first century, it is non-Orthodox Jewish Americans who are becoming an endangered species.[3]

Orthodox Jews see their non-Orthodox brothers, sisters, cousins, aunts, uncles, nieces, and nephews literally disappearing. Their parents and grandparents were well-meaning Jews whose Jewish identity was important to them. Their great-grandparents were the same ones today's Orthodox Jews had. Currently, the Jewish people face a demographic disaster on the scale of the Exile of the Twelve Tribes and the expulsion of the Jews of Spain.

THE FALL OF THE SOVIET UNION: Rarely does one witness the total and rapid shattering of a belief system such as occurred in 1991. The Communist Soviet Union, idolized by millions of people around the world as the model of a utopian human existence, likewise feared among the nations of the world for its military might, collapsed like a structure eaten away by termites. Statues of Marx, Engels, Lenin, and Stalin, the demigods of Communism, were unceremoniously knocked off their pedestals, and cities bearing their names became known by their traditional Russian ones — for example, Leningrad reverted to St. Petersburg, and Stalingrad became Volgograd. (In perhaps the ultimate act of humiliation, in 1992 the Russian government printed postage stamps honoring Marx and Lenin — the entertainers Groucho Marx and John Lennon.) After more than seventy years of suffocation, Russian Jews were afforded complete religious freedom, and yeshivos and other Jewish institutions sprouted up throughout the vast land.

NON-JEWISH IMMIGRATION TO ISRAEL: After the fall of the Soviet regime, hundreds of thousands of Jews immigrated to Israel annually. Among them were hundreds of thousands of Russian non-Jews with Jewish relatives, eligible to enter the country under the Law of Return. Estimates of these non-Jews ranged from the official Israeli government figure of 270,000 to as many as 400,000.[4] Among them were 25,000 young women of marriageable age. These figures represented a potential problem for Israeli society, raising the horrifying specter of mass intermarriage and proliferation of non-Jews in Israel posing as Jews. In addition, this large number of Russians — a traditionally anti-Semitic group — was introduced to Israel, along with a new criminal element, the Russian Mafia. While percentages of non-Jews among the immigrants will never be known precisely, it appears that a majority of Russian immigrants coming to Israel in most recent years are non-Jewish.[5] Secular Israeli leaders, looking to bolster the population, applauded the influx, while religious Jews raised voices of alarm, which were derisively dismissed.

ETHIOPIAN IMMIGRATION: In less than two days, on May 24 and 25, 1991, Israel airlifted 14,400 Ethiopian Jews to Israel. Known as Operation Solomon, the unprecedented haste was required due to imminent fighting between government and rebel forces in Ethiopia. Stripping the planes of all seats and furnishings to carry the largest number of passengers possible, Israeli air force crews packed the entire refugee population into thirty-three military and civilian aircraft. En route, Israeli army doctors and nurses ministered to ill and dehydrated passengers, and even delivered three babies.[6] Once in Israel, the Ethiopians were housed in temporary facilities. While their integration into Israeli society would be as daunting as the absorption of their brethren in 1984–85, at least they were safe.

THE FIRST GULF WAR: When the U.S.-led coalition began bombing Iraq in January 1991 to drive it from Kuwait, Iraqi dictator Saddam Hussein launched Scud missiles against Israel, hoping to provoke Israeli retaliation, which in turn would lead to the defection of the Arab members of the anti-Saddam alliance. President Bush exerted great pressure on Israeli Prime Minister Shamir not to strike back, perhaps the only instance in history of a nation being attacked and told it may not defend itself. During a five-week ordeal, Israel endured thirty-nine such attacks, concentrated mainly in the Tel Aviv and Haifa areas. Fearing chemical attacks, which fortunately did not occur, citizens donned gas masks and retreated to specially sealed rooms.

Divine providence was manifest during this war, with many stories of open miracles that saved lives. An infant spent several hours buried under concrete; he was finally dug out, asleep and unharmed in his plastic-coated crib. Hearing the roar of sirens, ninety people sprinted to a bomb shelter, only to find it locked. They took refuge in a smaller shelter nearby — and watched the larger shelter take a direct hit. Another missile made its deadly impact on the only uninhabited apartment building in a densely populated area.[7] All told, the missiles killed but one Israeli civilian, wounded several hundred, and destroyed some 4,000 apartments.[8] Several citizens also died from suffocation in gas masks and from heart attacks. The war ended in February, when the coalition expelled Iraq from Kuwait.

Although the low number of casualties was indeed nothing short of miraculous (similar attacks on Iranian civilians during the Iran-Iraq war killed large numbers of Iranians), the war revealed Israel's grave vulnerability. Israel was not at war, its army and air force could not demonstrate its prowess, and its borders could not keep away the danger. Because the missiles took a mere five to seven minutes to reach their targets, no effective warning could be given. How much more exposed would the nation be in a full-scale war, when chemical, biological, or even nuclear weapons might be used? It became clear that only G-d, and not the vaunted Israel Defense Forces, could protect the nation. Israel also saw the true face of the Palestinians, who stood on their rooftops to cheer the Scud missiles on their way.

THE OSLO ACCORDS: In 1993, an event occurred that shocked the world — after secret negotiations, Yasser Arafat's PLO recognized the State of Israel, and Israel recognized the PLO as the sole representative of the Palestinian people. In a ceremony at the White House in Washington, broadcast worldwide, the two parties signed the formal Declaration of Principles. Coaxed by President Clinton, Israeli Prime Minister Rabin and PLO Chairman Yasser Arafat shook hands; Rabin's face clearly expressed his loathing at taking the hand of an arch-murderer and terrorist. In his book *Secret Channels*, the Arab writer Mohamed Heikal captured the surreal scene:

> The contrast between Rabin's dark suit and dour manner and Arafat's tieless military uniform, black and white *kaffiyeh*, and irrepressible grin could not have been greater. Rabin looked like a mourner at a funeral, Arafat an actor collecting his Oscar at a Hollywood ceremony. And yet when they made their speeches Rabin was inspirational and Arafat downbeat. There seemed to be no connection between body language and the spoken word.[9]

The agreement granted the PLO a five-year period of self-rule in the Gaza Strip and Jericho area, and created a new governing entity, the Palestinian Authority (PA), under PLO control. Israel committed itself to withdraw from additional territory in the future, and to arm and equip a Palestinian police force of more than 10,000 men. Left postponed were many key issues, such as Palestinian statehood, international borders, the status of Jerusalem, and the so-called right of return to their ancestral homes of up to four million Palestinian refugees. The PLO agreed to revise all clauses in its charter calling for the destruction of Israel, to stop all terrorist activities, and to cease anti-Israel incitement in its schools and media.

Once firmly in control of Gaza, Arafat immediately established the infrastructure of a police state, suppressing any dissent to his rule. His police force vastly exceeded the agreed-upon limit, and obtained vast stores of arms and ammunition, some supplied by Israel and others imported from elsewhere. Israel then faced a hostile army on its porous borders with the territories.

Arafat did not revise the Palestinian Covenant calling for the extinction of Israel. In a farcical display for President Clinton's visit to Gaza, the Palestinians held a vote by show of hands to annul the charter. This vote had no legal standing, as the Palestinians themselves stressed. Arafat also publicly claimed (in Arabic to Arab audiences, not on American news) that he never gave up on his dream of destroying Israel. He justified his participation in the peace process by comparing it to a treaty that Mohammed had made with the Jewish Quraysh tribe in 628 CE. In that pact, Mohammed promised his enemies peace, but slaughtered the Quraysh as soon as his armies were ready.[10] In another proclamation, Arafat declared that the entire land of Israel, "from the sea to the river," is a sacred Islamic *waqf* (trust) that no Muslim can give away.[11] Visiting a mosque in Johannesburg, South Africa, Arafat exhorted his audience: "You must come to fight, to begin the jihad to liberate Jerusalem, your first shrine."[12]

Anti-Semitic and anti-Israel incitement continued unabated in Palestinian society. On one children's TV show, a six- or seven-year-old girl said she was from Beersheba, a city located in Israel's pre-1967 borders. The narrator then explained, "Beersheba is one of the Palestinian cities which is now occupied." In summer camps, Palestinian boys were taught how to use assault rifles and sang songs such as "We'll Throw Them into the Sea" and "My Children — In the Suicide Squads." The Children's Club TV show featured festively dressed six- to eight-year-old children announcing their intention of becoming suicide bombers, to the applause of their teachers. On another program, one boy explained what should be done to the Jews: "We will throw them into the sea. The day is near when we will settle our account with stones and bullets."[13] Not a single utterance throughout these activities for children suggested coexistence, let alone peace, with a legitimate Israel. An entire generation was growing up imbued with a fierce sense of hate and fanaticism. Nevertheless, Israel and the United States, in their headlong rush to embrace Arafat, ignored these warning signals.

Arafat also did not keep his commitment to stop terrorism; on the contrary, he aided and abetted such groups as Hamas, Islamic Jihad, and his own Fatah terrorist organizations, the Tanzim and al-Aksa Martyr's brigades. He arrested terrorists to please the international community, but often released them after attention was focused away. He smuggled illegal weapons through underground tunnels from Egypt into Gaza, and established secret factories for the manufacture of ammunition and bombs. In one instance, Israel intercepted and captured a ship containing fifty tons of weapons, including Katyusha rockets and anti-tank missiles. Documents found on board bearing Arafat's signature proved that he was directly involved in the weapons' acquisition.

For Israel, recognition of the PLO turned out to be a colossal strategic blunder, for Arafat's organization had been moribund after supporting Iraq in the 1991 Gulf War. In addition, a sophisticated indigenous leadership, free of terrorism, had been rising in the territories, with whom Israel, possibly in conjunction with Jordan, could have negotiated a favorable settlement of the conflict.

PEACE WITH JORDAN: In 1994, Israel and Jordan signed a formal peace treaty. As there were no major areas of conflict between the two nations, negotiations leading up to the signing proceeded smoothly. Israel ceded small strips of territory along the Jordanian border, with the small number of Israeli farmers living on the land leasing it back from Jordan, and agreed to supply Jordan with a quota of water. The communiqué also noted Jordan's special relationship to the Muslim shrines in Jerusalem.

NEGOTIATIONS WITH SYRIA: Throughout the last decade of the twentieth century, Israel engaged in on-again-off-again negotiations with Syria regarding the Golan Heights, captured by Israel in the 1967 war. Discussions revolved around four major points. First, the extent of Israel's withdrawal: whether to the 1923 international border or even to the June 4, 1967 line, which would afford Syria part of the eastern shore of Lake Kinneret opposite the Israeli city of Tiberias. Second, the demilitarization of the area. Third, the cessation of guerrilla and rocket attacks from Syrian-controlled Lebanon to Israel. Fourth, the parameters of a peace treaty. Israel wanted full diplomatic relations with Syria, open borders, and trade and cultural relations. Despite Israeli concessions on virtually everything Syria demanded, when Syria did not offer a total peace, only a declaration of a state of non-belligerency, the talks broke down.

THE GOLDSTEIN SHOOTING: In February 1994, Dr. Baruch Goldstein, a resident of Kiryat Arba, a Jewish town near Hebron, gunned down twenty-nine Arabs at Friday worship at Hebron's Tomb of the Patriarchs. Anguished cries erupted from the international community and the United Nations, and Israel was roundly condemned. (Interestingly enough, similar attacks on Israelis evoke no international outcry.) The senseless massacre inflamed the Arabs and contributed to the rise of revenge homicide bombings.

HOMICIDE BOMBINGS: Referred to worldwide as suicide bombings, but in reality cold-blooded acts of murder, the Palestinians discovered this new tactic in 1994. Sadly, there has been no abatement in such attacks, which have killed and maimed hundreds of Jews. Remarkably, there has been a distinct lack of sympathy throughout the world for Israel's plight; on the contrary, Israel is always being pressured to offer more concessions to the Palestinians in order to halt the so-called cycle of violence. Some horrifying examples of the endless list of Palestinian atrocities:

In October 1994, during the height of the morning rush hour, a bomber destroyed a bus in Tel Aviv, killing twenty-two passengers and wounding forty-seven. An attack on a bus stop in Netanya in January 1995 killed twenty-one soldiers. In February-March 1996, within a span of nine days, more than sixty Israelis were killed in four homicide bombings. One of the attacks took place in Tel Aviv on Purim, killing many children who were out celebrating the festive day in costumes. In July 1997, a bomber blew himself up in the main market of Jerusalem, Machaneh Yehudah, killing sixteen shopkeepers and stallholders. More recent murders include the horrific bombing of a Sbarro restaurant in Jerusalem, which killed eighteen people, including six infants, and wounded more than 100; the Pesach Seder night massacre at Netanya's Park Hotel, which killed thirty and wounded hundreds; and the *Kosel* bus bombing that took the lives of over twenty people.

Despite the constant deaths, Divine providence has been constantly manifest, for there were tens of foiled attacks for every successful one. In some cases, the bombs went off prematurely, killing only the bomber, while in others the bomb did not detonate or exploded in an area with no Israelis present. Perhaps the greatest miracle of all came in the May 2002 attempted bombing of the Pi-Glilot fuel and distribution center near Tel Aviv. A sophisticated bomb was concealed under a truck that was to stop at the distribution center. The bomb was detonated on time by an observer who could see the truck reaching one of the main pumps. Fortunately, it was a heating-oil pump, and the fuel was not explosive; the fire spread slowly and was put out by the center's automated fire-control system. Had the truck been loading regular fuel or natural gas, a huge explosion would have taken place in a densely populated area, and thousands would have been killed.

Other terrorist actions included the kidnapping of Israeli soldiers, drive-by shootings, and rocket attacks. When Corporal Nachshon Wachsman was kidnapped in October 1994, 50,000 Jews prayed at the Western Wall for his release. Sadly, he was killed in an unsuccessful Israeli Army raid on the house where he was held captive.

OSLO B: Ignoring all Palestinian violations and provocations, Israel stumbled further down the road of the so-called peace process. In September 1995, Prime Minister Rabin signed the Oslo B accords, committing to a swift and massive withdrawal from the West Bank, including all the major cities; in return, Israel received virtually no security guarantees. Elections were to take place that would turn the PA into a state-like entity. For their part, the Palestinians agreed to fulfill their previous agreements, amending their charter, arresting terrorists, and confiscating illegal weapons. None of these things occurred.

At the time, Oslo B was bitterly opposed by many sensible Israelis, including those in favor of the peace process, as being fool-hardy and fraught with danger. Even the dovish General Avraham Tamir, an architect of the 1979 peace treaty with Egypt, sharply attacked Oslo B, saying, "They're signing an agreement without security."[14] However, in a narrow vote aided by the Arab delegates, Rabin forced it through the Knesset. This move was followed in 1996 by handing over most of Hebron to the PA by Prime Minister Benjamin Netanyahu. To this day, all Israeli prime ministers since 1993, Labor and Likud alike (Rabin, Peres, Netanyahu, Barak, and Sharon), have bent to American and Arab pressure, making concession after concession, receiving nothing in return.

THE RABIN ASSASSINATION: On November 4 1995, after ad-dressing a pro-peace rally in Tel Aviv, Prime Minister Rabin was shot and killed by Yigal Amir, a putatively religious university student who considered the peace process a betrayal of Jewish values. Before Rabin's burial, an estimated one million people filed past his coffin at the Knesset. The murder of a Jewish leader by a fellow Jew created a numbness throughout the land. It also widened fault lines in Israeli society between religious and secu-lar Jews, and between different strands of Zionism.

Rabin's funeral was attended by 4,000 representatives of eighty-six nations, including President Clinton, Egyptian Presi-dent Mubarak, Jordanian King Hussein, and government offi-cials of Morocco, Qatar, and Oman, Arab nations that had no dip-lomatic relations with Israel. (Arafat wanted to attend but was persuaded not to.) A number of eulogies were offered; King Hussein's and President Clinton's addresses were particularly moving. Shimon Peres took over as Prime Minister. Yigal Amir was sentenced to life in prison.

THE HASMONEAN TUNNEL RIOTS: In 1996, the Israelis opened a second entrance to the Hasmonean Tunnel, an archaeological dig that runs right along the edge of the Temple Mount. Arafat capitalized on this event to unleash his forces. In a well-planned operation covering the entire area controlled by the PA, a mob on the Temple Mount threw down stones at Jewish worshippers at the *Kosel HaMa'aravi*, and Palestinian policemen and terrorists shot at Israeli troops. Fifteen Israelis were killed, and Arafat achieved his objective, creating adversarial relations by involving Palestinian forces in battles with Israeli soldiers. These riots were also a test to see if Israel would retaliate for such a flagrant provocation or proceed with the Oslo process. Arafat must have been encouraged by the outcome.

THE WYE ACCORDS: In 1998, President Clinton exerted enormous pressure on Prime Minister Netanyahu to sign a further agreement with the Palestinians. Held at the Wye River Plantation in Maryland, Israel was forced to cede 10 percent of the territories to sole PA control (Area A), place 19 percent of the land known as Area B under joint PA-Israel administration, and keep the remaining territory under sole Israeli jurisdiction. Arafat ruled over 95 percent of the Palestinian population. To convince Netanyahu to cooperate, Clinton used a devious strategy, holding out the possibility of releasing convicted Israeli spy Jonathan Pollard. However, on the last day of the summit Clinton informed Netanyahu that Pollard would remain in jail. By then, Netanyahu was already committed to sign.[15] Once again, Arafat repeated his empty promises of many times past. For example, in response to a commitment to confiscate illegal weapons, the PA announced that it had collected ten rifles, two grenades, and three mines — from more than one million Palestinians.[16]

MORE SECULAR-RELIGIOUS TENSION: In the 1990s, Israel's Supreme Court, led by the rabidly anti-religious Chief Justice Aharon Barak, handed down numerous anti-*chareidi* rulings. Among them were decisions that draft deferments granted to yeshivah students were illegal; secular protesters may march on the Sabbath on Bar-Ilan Street, a major thoroughfare passing through religious neighborhoods, to protest *chareidi* efforts to close the street on the holy day; and rabbinic courts may not excommunicate violators of Torah law. Worst of all, the Supreme Court threatened to overturn the Status Quo Agreement of 1947, which granted the Orthodox rabbinate sole jurisdiction over marriage, divorce, and conversion, and instead to allow Conservative and Reform ceremonies to be recognized by the State of Israel. In February 1999, up to 500,000 people participated in a prayer rally invoking Divine mercy against the dangers of the Supreme Court.

While many secular Israelis regarded the rally as a declaration of war against the High Court of Justice, some honest individuals in the nonreligious camp agreed with *chareidi* concerns. Ruth Gavison, a law professor at Hebrew University and a senior fellow of the prestigious Israel Democracy Institute, stated that *Chareidim* had three important, and substantially correct, criticisms of the courts: First, they are too activist, as in the opinion of Chief Justice Barak, who said "everything is judgable." Second, the courts selectively enforce the law, overlooking the indiscretions of their friends while prosecuting political enemies. This was brought out most sharply by the long trial and fraud conviction of Shas leader Aryeh Deri, while numerous prominent secular politicians were acquitted of corruption and betrayal of the public trust. Third, judges have control over the process of appointing new judges, which turns the system into a self-perpetuating closed caste. In Gavison's words: "Supreme Court Justices represent a subculture in Israel — male, Ashkenazi, secular — and it is unclear why Israeli society ought to live according to its dictates."[17]

A compromise, which satisfied no one, was reached on the thorny issue of personal status. Conservative and Reform representatives were permitted to join multi-denominational conversion institutes, which were to run according to traditional, Orthodox guidelines.

ISRAELI WITHDRAWAL FROM LEBANON: After the Lebanon war of 1982, Israel maintained control of a small strip of Lebanese territory, known as the security zone, running along the border with Israel. Over the years, guerrilla attacks in the zone cost the lives of hundreds of Israeli soldiers. Tired of the constant casualties, in May 2000 — against the professional opinion of the army — Prime Minister Barak ordered a unilateral Israeli withdrawal. Unfortunately, Barak entirely failed to take into account the Arab world's predictable reaction to the Israeli retreat. The Iranian foreign minister proclaimed that all Arabs must learn from Hizballah's "reconquest" of Southern Lebanon that "this is the way to liberate occupied lands." In Gaza, thousands celebrated in the streets, chanting: "Lebanon today — Palestine tomorrow!" The Arabs realized that Israel had no will to carry on prolonged conflict and suffer daily casualties.

THE FAILED CAMP DAVID TALKS: In July 2000, at talks in the United States, Barak offered unprecedented concessions to the Palestinians — 95 percent of the West Bank, 100 percent of the Gaza Strip, an overland highway connecting the two parts of a future Palestinian state entirely free of Israeli interference, Israeli territory adjacent to Gaza in exchange for the 5 percent of the West Bank annexed to Israel, the right of Palestinian refugees abroad to settle in the new Palestinian homeland, and — the greatest concessions of all — Palestinian control over the Arab sections of East Jerusalem, with the right to establish the capital there, and religious sovereignty over the Temple Mount. Almost all Israelis were aghast at Barak's foolhardy proposals.

However, for Arafat these concessions were not enough. True to his goal of destroying Israel, he refused to make his only concession — renouncing the right of Palestinian refugees to return to the State of Israel. This so-called right was a red line that even Barak could not cross, for the influx of millions of anti-Jewish Arabs into Israel would surely destroy the Jewish character of the country — if not the country itself. Consequently, the talks broke off with nothing accomplished. Arafat was then determined to gain by force what he could not receive at the bargaining table, and waited for a single provocation to begin the second *intifada*.

In September 2000, Ariel Sharon visited the Temple Mount. Although the visit was cleared ahead of time with the Palestinians, Arafat seized the opportunity to begin a large-scale insurgency throughout the territories. Joseph's Tomb in Nablus was desecrated, Jewish worshippers at the Western Wall and Rachel's Tomb were attacked, and widespread terrorism broke out, which has not abated to this day. In a particularly horrifying incident, after making a wrong turn in Ramallah, two Israeli soldiers were lynched by a Palestinian mob; gleeful Arabs displayed their hands dipped in the victims' blood. As of July 2003, the *intifada* has cost the lives of more than 800 Israelis and wounded in excess of 5,500 others in some 17,000 attacks. Homicide bombings killed 348 Israelis, terrorist shootings in public places murdered 177, while others died through stabbings, stone throwing, drive-by shootings, roadside shootings, car bombs, lynching, and being run over.[18] A day did not pass without some type of incident.

MEDIA DISTORTIONS: The worldwide media adopted a virulently anti-Israel stance in covering the *intifada* and terrorism. This attitude was caused both by anti-Semitism and a desire to identify with the Palestinians, who were seen as freedom fighters despite their barbaric tactics. The Palestinians also mastered media relations and propaganda, and had little difficulty convincing world opinion of the righteousness of their cause. On the Israeli side, public relations efforts were unsophisticated and poorly coordinated. As a result, when Arab murderers blew up pizza shops and Seders there was little or no world sympathy for Israel, while Israeli soldiers were roundly condemned as murderers when they defended themselves against Palestinian children trained to kill. In the words of Bernard Goldberg in his best-selling book, *Bias*:

> And besides, that kind of news makes liberal journalists uneasy. After all, these are the same people who bend over backward to find "moral equivalence" between Palestinian terrorists who blow up discos in Tel Aviv filled with teenagers, on the one hand, and Israeli commandos who *preemptively* [italics added] kill terrorist ringleaders *before* they send their suicide bombers into Israel on a mission to kill Jews, on the other.[19]

ANTI-SEMITISM INCREASES: With the outbreak of the *intifada*, there was a sharp increase in worldwide anti-Semitism, especially in Europe. Western European media, in particular, began associating Israeli soldiers with the Nazi SS, an image that deeply resonated in nations once under Nazi domination. In France and Germany in particular, attacks on Jews and Jewish institutions became commonplace. Numerous factors accounted for the spike in anti-Semitism. Unemployment and frustrations were high. In some communities, immigrant Muslims and Jews lived side-by-side. Arab satellite stations, as well as European news networks, broadcast a steady stream of reports of Palestinians under fire, their homes destroyed, their lands reoccupied, and their children killed; these reports ignored the fact that it was the Palestinians who constantly provoked the violence. In many parts of Europe there is also a residue of the racist attitudes that spawned the Fascist and Nazi policies of the 1930s. Europeans could also salve their consciences for their ignominious role in the Holocaust by pointing fingers at the Jews, saying the Jews are no better than they.

THE POPE VISITS ISRAEL: In 2000, Pope John Paul II visited Israel, capping a decade of improvement in Jewish-Catholic relations that began in 1993 with the Vatican's diplomatic recognition of the State of Israel. The Pope visited Yad Vashem, the Israeli Holocaust center, and the Western Wall. He apologized on behalf of all Catholics for horrors such as the Crusades and the Inquisition, but significantly did not apologize for the Church's role in the Holocaust. In the words of an astute observer:

> The real courageous apology is the one that costs us — when we have to admit that we are wrong, that we made a mistake. This is a much greater test of character than admitting to the misdeeds of other people, especially if those people have been dead for centuries.[20]

Nevertheless, the papal visit was highly significant. It repudiated the Christian belief that the Jews are condemned to wander the earth for killing the Christian god. (For this reason, the Church did not recognize Israel until 1993.) John Paul also took other steps in combating the Church's traditional anti-Semitism, such as stating that the Jews are not to blame for Yeshu's death, and that the Jews are not cursed for that act, despite the passage in the book of Matthew to the contrary. It remains to be seen, however, if these attitudes will trickle down to the Catholic rank-and-file.

AMERICAN ORTHODOXY: Orthodox Jews in America faced unprecedented challenges and opportunities in the last decade of the twentieth century and the start of the twenty-first: the proliferation of at-risk teenagers, a focus on the educational needs of special students, Senator Joseph Lieberman's vice-presidential nomination, and the challenges of such new technology as the Internet.

In the 1990s, a significant number of teenagers from Orthodox homes began moving away from Torah observance. Much soul-searching took place in the Orthodox community, and numerous causes were identified: the overwhelming power of American culture, marital strife in the home, broken homes, childhood depression, financially overstressed parents unable to deal with difficult children, lack of inspiration in a Judaism observed by rote, and a lack of esteem in school for those not academically gifted.[21] In response, the Orthodox community established organizations to deal with the problem, such as Agudath Israel's Project YES. Slow but significant progress has been made in this area.

Greater sensitivity was shown during this decade to the needs of both physically and developmentally challenged children, perhaps reflecting the greater acceptance in American society of such individuals. Programs were set up in yeshivos, day schools, and camps to accommodate students with Down's syndrome, autism, diabetes, and cancer, among other conditions, and efforts were made to sensitize the student body to the differing needs of individuals. Although much remains to be done in this area, the community has come a long way from the time when such children were viewed as a stigma and kept hidden to avoid harming the marriage prospects of other siblings.

Senator Joseph Lieberman's nomination in 2000 as the

Democratic vice-presidential candidate was a watershed for the way in which Orthodox Jews were perceived in general society. Orthodox Jews found new acceptance, received greater respect for their beliefs, and appeared less alien than previously. The nomination was a major *kiddush HaShem*, with Lieberman being viewed, in the words of the *New York Times*, as "an untainted candidate who is widely regarded as one of the most upstanding politicians in the nation."[22] The paper also noted that "in his twelve years in the Senate, Mr. Lieberman has acquired a reputation for steady habits, family values, and faithfulness to his beliefs."[23] Jews learned the very important lesson that adherence to Torah brings respect from the outside world, and that it is not necessary to assimilate to succeed in American society. However, there was some concern that Lieberman's prominence in government would lead to an upsurge in anti-Semitism, and that Jews in general should not hold such high positions so as not to be blamed when things go wrong.

The Internet brought a unique challenge to the efforts of religious Jews to keep harmful influences out of the home, and much discussion was held regarding restricting the Internet or even banning it from schools and homes. In 2003, a group of seventy-five principals published a letter stating: "The Internet may function as a valuable and useful tool for business and other financial concerns. It can be allowed no place in the home, however, because its influence is pervasive, far-reaching and insidious — thus even more detrimental than that of television."[24] The ubiquitousness of the Internet would make it extremely difficult even for committed parents to shield their children from its harmful influences.

9/11: This shattering horror, a watershed event that divided modern history into pre-9/11 and post-9/11 eras, contained a special message for the Jewish people. Historically, during the long exile, and in countries with benign environments, Jews have tended to become very comfortable. In America, Jews prospered as never before. 9/11 demonstrated that things can be overturned in an instant, that all munificence comes only because of G-d, and that people do not control fate or riches. 9/11 also marked the opening salvo of a new global struggle — the West vs. Islam — the effect of which on the world and the Jewish people has yet to be determined.

People worldwide saw Divine providence manifested, many recognizing the hand of G-d in human events. Countless miraculous stories abounded, from the person who became sick on September 10 and could not report to his job the next day, to the worker who was late to his job because he ordered schoolbooks for his son, to the rescue workers who were fortunate to escape as the towers tumbled down. The kindness and valor of people trapped in the towers, and rescue workers who gave up their lives to save others, will serve as an inspiration for all time.

THE ISRAELI ECONOMY: Aside from the horrific death toll, the *intifada* had a devastating effect on Israel's economy. In 2003, a report found that the number of unemployed in Israel would reach 300,000, and that one of four citizens, roughly 1.5 million people, would live at or below poverty level. Half a million children were said to be hungry.[25] Particularly hard-hit was Israel's large tourist industry, with many hotels virtually empty. Throughout much of the 1990s, Israel's was among the world's fastest expanding economies, with Israel's standard of living increasing by 25 percent. Suddenly, it was over.

The economic crisis played a major role in the rise of the militantly anti-religious Shinui Party in the 2003 elections. Shinui won fifteen Knesset seats, making it the third-largest party in the Knesset, and the fastest growing party in Israeli politics. Shinui ran on a single issue — putting an end to what they called the usurious exploitation of the State's coffers for religious purposes, a platform plank which resonated deeply among secular Israelis. Unfortunately, Shinui's success was an unmitigated disaster for religious Jews in Israel. Government funds for yeshivos and Torah institutions were cut by 80 percent, and the number of Torah students from kindergarten to *kollel* who received funding was reduced from 216,000 to fewer than 80,000. Heavily subsidized mortgages for newly wed religious couples were eliminated. In addition to these blows, payments to families with four or more children were reduced 75 percent, causing a reduction of more than $1,000 monthly to large families. (Nevertheless, subsidies to university students were increased 17 percent in 2002 and not cut in 2003.)[26] As a result, Torah-observant Jews in Israel faced massive teacher and *kollel* layoffs, and a great reduction in outreach activities.

GULF WAR II: The United States' toppling of Saddam Hussein's regime in Iraq and capture of Saddam in 2003 was a godsend for Israel, for it removed a dangerous enemy and sent a clear message to such nations as Iran and Syria. Israel prepared for the war as it did in 1991, by issuing gas masks in the event of an Iraqi chemical attack, but, with Divine mercy, Israel was neither attacked nor drawn into the conflict.

THE ROAD MAP: In 2003, President George W. Bush, seeking to break an impasse in the Palestinian-Israeli conflict, pressured Israel to begin implementing his so-called road map for peace. The road map called for Israel to withdraw from all the West Bank and Gaza cities it had entered in 2002 to root out the terrorist infrastructure, for the Palestinians to stop terrorism, and for a Palestinian state to be established by 2005. The road map, like so many other peace initiatives, floundered on the rocks after repeated Palestinian murders of Jews. (Tragically, 30,000 Jews have lost their lives in Israel over the last sixty years in wars and terrorist acts.)

There is no stasis; Jewish history continues to be in flux. The sainted Chafetz Chaim once remarked that the events of the pre-Messianic era resemble those of a storekeeper going out of business, who quickly liquidates his merchandise and settles his accounts. Similarly, in order to hasten the arrival of the Messiah, G-d is causing events, that would normally take decades and even centuries, to occur at a dizzying pace.[27] May all the suffering cease, and may the Miraculous Journey of the Jewish people quickly reach the last stop on the line — the coming of Messiah.

NOTES

Introduction and Chapter 1

1. Rabbi E. Wasserman, *Kovetz Maamarim* (5723 edition), p. 81.
2. Talmud, *Shabbos* 112b.
3. Numbers 20:12.
4. Rabbi Yaakov Emden, *Siddur*.
5. Klaus P. Fischer, *The History of an Obsession*, p. 21.
6. Rabbi Moshe C. Luzzatto, *Daas Tevunos*, vol. 1, p. 10.
7. Talmud, *Sanhedrin* 38b, *Chullin* 60a.
8. *Daas Tevunos*, vol. 1, p. 110, note 253.
9. *Rashi*, Genesis 4:19.
10. Ibid. 4:20.
11. Ibid. 4:22.
12. Rabbi A. Miller, *Sing You Righteous*, p. 54.
13. *Rashi*, Genesis 8:14.
14. Talmud, *Sanhedrin* 56a.
15. Rabbi B. Wein, *Jewish History Cassette Series*, tape #90.
16. Rabbi A. Miller, *Behold a People*, p. 23; Paul L. Maier, *Josephus: The Essential Works*, p. 37.
17. Talmud, *Sanhedrin* 109a.
18. *Yalkut Shimoni*, *Noach*, paragraph 62.
19. Commentary of Rabbeinu Nissim to Talmud, *Rosh HaShanah* 3a.
20. Quoted in: Rabbi D. Brown, *Mysteries of the Creation*, p. 250.
21. Ibid., p. 248.
22. Ibid., p. 249.
23. Ibid., pp. 249–250.
24. Talmud, *Chullin* 60a.
25. *The New York Times*, 7/28/90.
26. Talmud, *Kesubos* 77b.
27. *Discovery*, Aish HaTorah, pp. 30–31.

28. *Midrash Tehillim* 34:1.

29. Talmud, *Zevachim* 113b; *Rashi*, Genesis 6:13.

30. *Rambam, Mishnah Torah, Hilchos Kiddush HaChodesh* 6:8 with commentary.

31. *Tosafos, Sanhedrin* 70a.

32. *Sanhedrin* 4:5.

33. *Mishnah Torah, Hilchos Avodas Kochavim* 1:1–2.

34. Ibid. 1:3.

35. Talmud, *Pesachim* 118a.

36. *Tosafos, Shabbos* 10b.

37. Rabbi Eliyahu Dessler, *Michtav MiEliyahu*, vol. 2, pp. 162–163.

38. *Kovetz Maamarim*, p. 85.

39. *Klei Yakar*, commentary on Deuteronomy 2:3.

40. Converts of certain nations have various marriage restrictions; see Deuteronomy 23:4–9. Today, any convert may marry a native Jew, as those nations have disappeared. See Talmud, *Berachos* 28a.

41. *Ramban*, Genesis 32:26; Miller, *Behold a People*, p. 81.

42. *Ramban*, Genesis 32:4.

43. *Yom Kippur ArtScroll Machzor*, "*Eileh Ezkerah*" (pp. 586–592).

Chapter 2

1. Yosef Y. Reinman, *Destiny*, p. 39.

2. *Yalkut Shimoni, Shemos*, p. 105, "The Jews filled their theaters and circuses."

3. *Seder Olam Rabbah*, ch. 3.

4. *The Midrash Says, Shemos*, p. xiii.

5. Ibid.

6. See Deuteronomy 24:18, 22.

7. Exodus 13:16.

8. Paul Johnson, *A History of the Jews*, p. 6.

9. Ibid., p. 10.

10. Ibid., p. 15.

11. Rabbi Y. Silver and Rabbi S. Cohen, *Torah Min HaShamayim*, p. 92; Johnson, *A History of the Jews*, p. 24.

12. Johnson, *A History of the Jews*, p. 25.

13. Silver and Cohen, *Torah Min HaShamayim*, pp. 103–105.

14. Rabbi A. Miller, *Sing You Righteous*, p. 54.

15. *Rashi*, Exodus 19:2.

16. Talmud, *Shabbos* 88a.

17. Deuteronomy 5:4.

18. *Ramban*, Deuteronomy 4:9.

19. p. 186.

20. Leviticus 25:21.

21. Exodus 34:24.

22. Deuteronomy 20:8.

23. Talmud, *Berachos* 5a.

24. Rabbi A. Miller, *Awake My Glory*, pp. 227–228.

25. Talmud, *Zevachim* 118b.

26. M. W. Sterling, 1945 Report of the Smithsonian Institute, quoted in: Rabbi A. Miller, *Behold a People*, p. 171.

27. For example, the *Molech* — Leviticus 20:23. Also see Deuteronomy 12:31.

28. *Rashi*, Leviticus 18:3.

29. Psalms 106:34–40.

30. Jerusalem Talmud, *Sheviis*, ch. 6, halachah 1.

31. Leviticus 17:3, 4.

32. Mishnah, *Zevachim* 14: 4–8.

33. Miller, *Behold a People*, p. 221.

34. *Daas Sofrim*, Rabbi C. Rabinowitz, quoted in: Rabbi G. Weiss, *Samson's Struggle*, p. 100.

35. Talmud, *Sanhedrin* 20b; I Samuel, ch. 8, with commentaries.

36. Talmud, *Zevachim* 118b.

37. Talmud, *Moed Katan* 16b.

38. *Yalkut Shimoni*, I Samuel, paragraph 139.

39. Talmud, *Menachos* 109b.

40. Rabbi Shimon Krasner, *Nachalas Shimon*, I Samuel, part 2, ch. 58.

Chapter 3

1. In numerous prayers, David represents *malchus*.

2. Psalms 23:1.

3. Psalms 89:30–38.

4. Rabbi A. Miller, *Behold a People*, p. 278.

5. Talmud, *Sanhedrin* 21b.

6. *Mishnah Torah, Hilchos Issurei Biah*, 13:14.

7. I Kings 6:1.

8. See the first verse of each of these books.

9. Talmud, *Shabbos* 14b.

10. I Kings 3:7, see *Rashi* and *Abarbanel*.

11. Talmud, *Sanhedrin* 101b.

12. Ibid. 102a.

13. Mishnah, *Avos* 5:18.

14. II Kings, 14:25–27; Talmud, *Yevamos* 98a; Rabbi Chaim D. Rabinowitz, *The History of the Jewish People*, vol. 1, pp. 53-54.

15. Talmud, *Gittin* 88a.

16. Talmud, *Arachin* 32b.

17. Talmud, *Bava Basra* 115b.

18. I Kings 12:17; II Chronicles 11:16.

19. Talmud, *Megillah* 14b.

20. Talmud, *Pesachim* 4a.

21. Talmud, *Gittin* 57b.

22. Talmud, *Sukkah* 45b, *Rashi*.

23. Talmud, *Sanhedrin* 94b.

24. Talmud, *Chullin* 4b.

25. Talmud, *Sanhedrin* 64a.

26. Heard from Rabbi Reuven Feinstein, Dean of Yeshiva of Staten Island.

27. See *Rashi*, Talmud, *Zevachim* 106b, "*Al P'nei HaSadeh.*"

28. Talmud, *Megillah* 14a.

29. *Mishnah Torah, Hilchos Yesodei HaTorah*, 10:1–2.

30. Talmud, *Yevamos* 90b; *Mishnah Torah, Hilchos Yesodei HaTorah* 9:3.

31. Mishnah, *Avos* 1:1.

32. Talmud, *Yevamos* 102a, *Megillah* 2b.

33. Talmud, *Yevamos* 49b.

34. Talmud, *Sanhedrin* 103b.

35. Talmud, *Horayos* 12a.

36. Talmud, *Megillah* 14b.

37. Talmud, *Taanis* 22a–b, *ArtScroll Kinnos for Tishah B'Av*, pp. 182–183.

38. Talmud, *Gittin* 88a.

39. Talmud, *Megillah* 29a, *Rashi*.

40. Talmud, *Sanhedrin* 103a.

41. *Beis Yosef, Orach Chaim*, ch. 550.

42. See *Tosafos Rosh HaShanah* 18b, "*Zeh Tishah B'Tammuz.*"

43. Talmud, *Gittin* 57b.

44. *ArtScroll Kinnos*, p. 155, note.

45. Talmud, *Kiddushin* 69b, *Rashi*.

46. Talmud, *Bava Basra* 60b.

47. Talmud, *Niddah* 61a.

48. Talmud, *Shabbos* 145b.

Chapter 4

1. Talmud, *Pesachim* 87b-88a.

2. Talmud, *Sanhedrin* 105a.

3. Ezekiel, chapters 1, 40–46.

4. Ezekiel 20:32–33.

5. Talmud, *Kesubos* 33b, *Tosafos*.

6. Quoted in: Rabbi Shlomo Rotenberg, *Am Olam*, vol. 1, pp. 270–271.

7. Talmud, *Megillah* 11b.

8. Talmud, *Sanhedrin* 22a.

9. Quoted in: Rotenberg, *Am Olam*, vol. 1, p. 340.

10. Talmud, *Megillah* 12a.

11. Isaiah 45:1.

12. Talmud, *Megillah* 11a.

13. Ibid., 11b.

14. Rabbi E. Gevirtz, *L'Hovin Ul'Haskil*, pp. 91–92.

15. Talmud, *Zevachim* 62a.

16. Talmud, *Megillah* 11b.

17. Talmud, *Yoma* 53b.

18. Talmud, *Shabbos* 90a, *Tosafos*.

19. Mishnah, *Menachos* 98a.

20. Talmud, *Kesubos* 26a.

21. Talmud, *Bava Kamma* 82b.

22. Quoted in: Rotenberg, *Am Olam*, vol. 2, p. 28.

23. Talmud, *Shabbos* 123b.

24. Rotenberg, *Am Olam*, vol. 2, p. 310; Rabbi A. Miller, *Torah-Nation*, p. 63.

25. *Mishnah Torah, Hilchos Tefillah* 1: 3–5.

26. Talmud, *Sanhedrin* 64a.

27. Miller, *Torah-Nation*, p. 76.

28. Talmud, *Yevamos* 21a.

29. Talmud, *Avodah Zarah* 36a.

30. Ibid. 36b, *Tosafos*, "*E Ikka.*"

31. Rotenberg, *Am Olam*, vol. II, p. 324.

32. Talmud, *Bava Basra* 14b.

33. Talmud, *Sanhedrin* 99a.

34. Talmud, *Bava Basra* 15a.

35. Talmud, *Nedarim* 37b.

36. Rotenberg, *Am Olam*, vol. 2, p. 326.

37. Talmud, *Sotah* 48b; Rabbi Yehuda HaLevi, *Kuzari* 3:39.

38. Talmud, *Sanhedrin* 11a.

39. Rabbi A. Kaplan, *Handbook of Jewish Thought*, vol. 1, p. 112.

40. Talmud, *Sotah* 48b.

41. See M. First's book *Jewish History in Conflict* (Jason Aronson, 1997) on this subject.

42. Talmud, *Bava Kamma* 38b, *Tosafos*.

43. Talmud, *Gittin* 10a, *Chullin* 4a.

44. Talmud, *Chullin* 6a.

Chapter 5

1. *Kuzari*, First Essay, no. 103.

2. Rabbi Z. Fendel, *Legacy of Sinai*, p. 131.

3. Mishnah, *Avos* 1:2; *Meiri, Beis HaBechirah*, Introduction to *Avos*, p. 19.

4. *Shaarei Leshem Shvo VeAchlamah* 2:11; *Pirkei Heichalos* 27.

5. Talmud, *Yoma* 39a.

6. *Meiri*, pp. 19–20.

7. Talmud, *Yoma* 69a.

8. Rabbi S. Halperin, *Seder HaDoros*, p. 137.

9. Rabbi M. Katz, *Yesterday, Today, and Forever*, vol. 2, p. 292.

10. Talmud, *Avodah Zarah* 10a; Yosef Y. Reinman, *Destiny*, p. 177.

11. Mishnah, *Avos* 1:3.

12. *Avos DeRabbi Nasan* 5:2.

13. *History of the Jewish People*, the Second Temple Era, p. 58.

14. *Meiri*, p. 22.

15. *Seder HaDoros*, p. 142.

16. Talmud, *Megillah* 9a.

17. Talmud, *Kiddushin* 49a, *Tosafos*.

18. *Soferim* 1:7.

19. Talmud, *Chagigah* 16a, *Rashi*.

20. Talmud, *Temurah* 16a, *Rashi*.

21. Talmud, *Menachos* 109b; Paul L. Maier, *Josephus, the Essential Works*, p. 393.

22. Rabbi Z. Yaavetz, *Toldos Yisrael*, vol. 4, p. 54.

23. Katz, *Yesterday, Today, and Forever*, vol. 2, p. 303. See Maier, *Josephus, the Essential Works*, p. 211.

24. *Bereishis Rabbah* 2:5.

25. *Megillas Antiochus*.

26. Talmud, *Kesubos* 3b.

27. Talmud, *Gittin* 57b.

28. Rabbi C. Rabinowitz, *The History of the Jewish People*, vol. 1, p. 186.

29. Y. Eisenstein, *Otzar Yisrael*, vol. 4, p. 316.

30. Ibid., vol. 6, p. 196.

31. Talmud, *Menachos* 28b.

32. Talmud, *Shabbos* 21b.

33. *Toldos Yisrael*, vol. 4, p. 90.

34. *Seder HaDoros*, p. 145.

35. Talmud, *Taanis* 18b.

Chapter 6

1. Talmud, *Avodah Zarah* 9a, see Talmud, *Sanhedrin* 97b and *Rashi*.

2. Genesis 49:10.

3. *History of the Jewish People*, the Second Temple Era, p. 91. Also see Appendix to Schottenstein edition of *Tractate Yoma*, vol. 1.

4. Talmud, *Sotah* 48a.

5. P. Maier, *Josephus, the Essential Works*, p. 222.

6. Talmud, *Berachos* 29a.

7. Maier, *Josephus*, p. 223.

8. *History of the Jewish People*, p. 99. See Talmud, *Berachos* 29a.

9. Talmud, *Kiddushin* 66a.

10. Talmud, *Sukkah* 48b; Rabbi Z. Yaavetz, *Toldos Yisrael*, vol. 4, p. 191.

11. Maier, *Josephus*, p. 225.

12. Talmud, *Taanis* 23a.

13. Rabbi C. Rabinowitz, *The History of the Jewish People*, vol. 1, p. 277.

14. Talmud, *Bava Basra* 21a.

15. Talmud, *Kesubos* 82b.

16. Talmud, *Sanhedrin* 45b.

17. Maier, *Josephus*, p. 266.

18. Talmud, *Yoma* 19b.

19. Ibid. 9a.

20. Talmud, *Sukkah* 48b.

21. Talmud, *Bava Kamma* 83b.

22. Talmud, *Menachos* 65a.

23. Talmud, *Kesubos* 62b, *Tosafos*.

24. Talmud, *Pesachim* 49a–b.

25. *Rashi*, Song of Songs 6:12.

26. Talmud, *Shabbos* 15a.

27. Rabbi Y. HaLevi, *Doros HaRishonim*, vol. 2, p. 624.

28. Mishnah, *Avos* 1:10.

29. Talmud, *Avodah Zarah* 9a, *Rashi*.

30. Talmud, *Bava Basra* 3b.

31. Talmud, *Avodah Zarah* 9a.

32. Talmud, *Bava Basra* 4a.

33. Maier, *Josephus*, p. 255.

34. Jerusalem Talmud, *Kesubos* 58b.

35. Talmud, *Shabbos* 15a.

36. Rabbi Z. Fendel, *Legacy of Sinai*, p. 147.

37. Mishnah, *Avos* 1: 4–12.

38. Talmud, *Yoma* 35b.

39. Talmud, *Shabbos* 31a.

40. Ibid.

41. Talmud, *Gittin* 36a.

42. Mishnah, *Avos* 1:15.

43. Rabbi A. Miller, *Torah-Nation*, p. 196; Maier, *Josephus*, p. 233.

44. Talmud, *Shabbos* 31a.

45. Ibid. 15a.

46. Talmud, *Sanhedrin* 88b.

47. Talmud, *Yevamos* 13b.

48. Mishnah, *Avos* 5:17.

49. Mishnah, *Eduyos*, chapters 4 and 5 list the exceptions.

50. Talmud, *Eruvin* 6b; Talmud, *Shabbos* 13b.

51. Talmud, *Shabbos* 21b.

52. Fendel, *Legacy of Sinai*, pp. 158–159.

53. W. Nicholls, *Christian Anti-Semitism: A History of Hate*, p. 18.

54. Maier, *Josephus*, p. 284.

55. Talmud, *Sanhedrin* 43a, 67a, 107b (censored in our editions; see *Chesronos HaShas*).

56. Talmud, *Sanhedrin* 32a.

57. Ibid. 35a.

Chapter 7

1. Talmud, *Yoma* 9b.

2. Talmud, *Avodah Zarah* 8b.

3. Talmud, *Yoma* 39b.

4. Mishnah, *Bikkurim* 3:4.

5. Talmud, *Kesubos* 17a.

6. Talmud, *Sotah* 41a-b, *Tosafos*.

7. Talmud, *Gittin* 56a.

8. Paul L. Maier, *Josephus, the Essential Works*, p. 329.

9. Talmud, *Gittin* 55b.

10. p. 292.

11. Talmud, *Gittin* 56a.

12. Ibid.

13. Ibid. 56b.

14. L. Resnick, *A Time to Weep*, pp. 49–51.

15. Mishnah, *Taanis* 26b; Jerusalem Talmud, *Taanis* 20a.

16. pp. 371–372.

17. Talmud, *Taanis* 29a.

18. *Shulchan Aruch, Orach Chaim* 558:1.

19. Talmud, *Gittin* 56b.

20. Maier, *Josephus*, p. 376.

21. Talmud, *Avodah Zarah* 9b.

22. Ibid.

23. Talmud, *Yoma* 9a.

24. Talmud, *Arachin* 11b.

25. Resnick, *A Time to Weep*, pp. 14–16.

26. Rabbi A. Miller, *Torah-Nation*, pp. 242–243.

27. Talmud, *Bava Kamma* 91b, see Rabbi S. Krasner, *Nachalas Shimon*, I Samuel, vol. 2, pp. 262–263.

28. *Mishnah Torah, Hilchos Aveil* 1:11.

29. Talmud, *Avodah Zarah* 18a, *Tosafos*.

30. Talmud, *Gittin* 57b.

Chapter 8

1. Rabbi Y. HaLevi, *Doros HaRishonim*, vol. 3, ch. 10.

2. Jerusalem Talmud, *Berachos* 9a.

3. HaLevi, *Doros HaRishonim*, vol. 3, ch. 21.

4. Talmud, *Berachos* 11b; *Doros HaRishonim*, vol. 3, chs. 39–43.

5. Talmud, *Berachos* 28b.

6. Talmud, *Gittin* 58a.

7. Talmud, *Bava Basra* 134a.

8. Talmud, *Sukkah* 41a.

9. Ibid.

10. Talmud, *Rosh HaShanah* 29b.

11. Talmud, *Sanhedrin* 32b; HaLevi, *Doros HaRishonim*, vol. 3, ch. 11, pp. 47–48.

12. Talmud, *Gittin* 56b.

13. HaLevi, *Doros HaRishonim*, vol. 3, ch. 21.

14. Midrash, *Devarim Rabbah* 2:15.

15. Talmud, *Bava Metzia* 59b.

16. HaLevi, *Doros HaRishonim*, vol. 3, ch. 21.

17. Rabbi Z. Yaavetz, *Toldos Yisrael*, vol. 6, p. 49.

18. *Sefer HaChinuch*, mitzvah 496.

19. Talmud, *Bava Metzia* 59b.

20. Mishnah, *Rosh HaShanah* 2:9, commentary of *Tiferes Yisrael*, 43.

21. Talmud, *Rosh HaShanah* 25a.

22. Talmud, *Berachos* 27b, *Tosafos*.

23. Talmud, *Berachos* 28a.

24. Ibid.

25. Talmud, *Sukkah* 51b, *Hagahos HaGra* ad loc., 5.

26. HaLevi, *Doros HaRishonim*, vol. 3, ch. 47.

27. Talmud, *Kiddushin* 40b, *Sanhedrin* 74a.

28. Talmud, *Sotah* 49a; Rabbi A. Miller, *Exalted People*, p. 117.

29. *Mishnah Torah, Hilchos Beis HaBechirah* 2:1.

30. Midrash, *Bereishis Rabbah* 64:8.

31. Rabbi Z. Yaavetz, *Toldos Yisrael*, vol. 6, p. 115; Talmud, *Taanis* 26b.

32. HaLevi, *Doros HaRishonim*, vol. 4, pp. 579–580.

33. Talmud, *Shabbos* 60a; see Schottenstein Edition of Talmud, loc. cit., note 30.

34. Talmud, *Sanhedrin* 93b.

35. Jerusalem Talmud, *Taanis* 24a.

36. Talmud, *Sanhedrin* 97b.

37. Talmud, *Bava Kamma* 97b.

38. HaLevi, *Doros HaRishonim*, vol. 4, ch. 33.

39. Talmud, *Taanis* 26b.

40. Rabbi B. Wein, *Echoes of Glory*, p. 209.

41. Talmud, *Gittin* 58a, *Bava Kamma* 83a.

42. Talmud, *Gittin* 57a.

43. Talmud, *Sanhedrin* 93b.

44. Jerusalem Talmud, *Taanis* 24b.

45. *Mechilta*, Exodus 20:6.

46. Talmud, *Sanhedrin* 74a-b.

47. W. Rubinstein, *The Myth of Rescue*, pp. 81–82.

48. *Kinnah* 21.

49. *Yom Kippur ArtScroll Machzor*, p. 586.

50. Midrash *Asarah Harugei Malchus*.

51. Talmud, *Menachos* 29b.

52. *Rambam*, Introduction to *Yad HaChazakah*.

53. Talmud, *Kesubos* 62b.

54. Ibid. 63a, *Tosafos*.

55. Talmud, *Yevamos* 115a; *Nedarim* 50a, commentary of Rabbeinu Nissim; *Kiddushin* 27a.

56. Talmud, *Yevamos* 62b.

57. *Shulchan Aruch, Orach Chaim* 493:1.

58. Talmud, *Berachos* 61b.

59. Talmud, *Avodah Zarah* 18a.

60. Talmud, *Sanhedrin* 14a.

61. *Yom Kippur ArtScroll Machzor*, p. 588.

62. Talmud, *Chullin* 123a.

63. Talmud, *Avodah Zarah* 11b.

64. Talmud, *Chullin* 142a.

65. Talmud, *Chagigah* 15a.

66. W. Nicholls, *Christian Antisemitism: A History of Hate*, pp. 130-131.

67. J. Carroll, *Constantine's Sword: The Church and the Jews*, pp. 139-140.
68. Talmud, *Bava Basra* 121b.
69. Ibid.
70. Talmud, *Meilah* 17a–b.
71. Talmud, *Shabbos* 33b.
72. Talmud, *Shabbos* 118b.
73. Talmud, *Avodah Zarah* 10b, *Sanhedrin* 91b.
74. Talmud, *Gittin* 59a.
75. Talmud, *Temurah* 14b.
76. *Rambam*, Introduction to *Yad HaChazakah*.
77. Rabbi M. Bergman, *Mavo Shearim*, p. 33; *Yalkut Shimoni, Shemos* 405.
78. Bergman, *Mavo Shearim*, p. 33.
79. *Iggeres of Rabbi Sherira Gaon*, translated by Rabbi N. D. Rabinowich, p. 14.
80. Ibid.
81. *Rambam*, Introduction to *Yad HaChazakah*.
82. *Iggeres of Rabbi Sherira Gaon*, p. 27.
83. Talmud, *Sanhedrin* 86a.
84. Talmud, *Sotah* 22a, *Rashi*.
85. Bergman, *Mavo Shearim*, pp. 43–44.
86. Rabbi Y. Halperin, *Seder HaDoros*, p. 158.
87. Rabbi Y. Halperin, *Seder Tannaim V'Amoraim*, p. 171.
88. Ibid., p. 93.

Chapter 9

1. *Kesubos*, 103–104.
2. Talmud, *Sukkah* 20a.
3. Rabbi Y. HaLevi, *Doros HaRishonim*, vol. 5, p. 211.
4. Talmud, *Chullin* 18b, *Rashi*.
5. Ibid. 15a, *Rashi*.
6. Talmud, *Kesubos* 106a.
7. Talmud, *Berachos* 17b.
8. Talmud, *Sanhedrin* 5a, *Tosafos*, "Dehacha."
9. Ibid.
10. Talmud, *Kesubos* 67b.
11. Rabbi Y. Halperin, *Seder HaDoros, Tannaim V'Amoraim, os heh.*
12. Talmud, *Avodah Zarah* 38b.

13. Y. D. Eisenstein, *Otzar Yisrael*, vol. 9, p. 319.

14. *Meiri*, Introduction to *Avos*, p. 48.

15. Ibid.

16. Talmud, *Chullin* 141a-b, *Rashi*.

17. *Mishnah Torah*, Hilchos Deos 2:4, Seder HaDoros, Tannaim V'Amoraim, Abba Aricha.

18. Talmud, *Berachos* 58b.

19. A. Spier, *The Comprehensive Jewish Calendar*, pp. 19-20.

20. Talmud, *Shabbos* 53a, *Rashi* and footnote.

21. Talmud, *Gittin* 17a, *Rashi*.

22. Talmud, *Shabbos* 21b, *Rashi* and *Tosafos*.

23. Talmud, *Shabbos* 45a, *Rashi* and *Tosafos*.

24. *Meiri*, Introduction to *Avos*, p. 49.

25. Talmud, *Rosh HaShanah* 31b.

26. Talmud, *Bava Metzia* 84a.

27. Talmud, *Berachos* 5b.

28. Rabbi M. Bergman, *Mavo Shearim*, p. 47.

29. Talmud, *Yevamos* 36a.

30. Talmud, *Bava Metzia* 84a.

31. Talmud, *Kesubos* 17a.

32. Talmud, *Chagigah* 14a.

33. Talmud, *Avodah Zarah* 11a.

34. Bergman, *Mavo Shearim*, p. 48, note 7.

35. *Rif (Alfasi)* on Talmud, *Eruvin*, p. 35b.

36. *Mishnah Torah*, Hilchos Kiddush HaChodesh 1:7.

37. Ibid. 4:1.

38. Ibid. 11:4.

39. HaLevi, *Doros HaRishonim*, vol. 5, pp. 397–399.

40. *Ramban, Sefer HaMitzvos, Aseh* 153.

41. Talmud, *Nedarim* 78b.

42. HaLevi, *Doros HaRishonim*, vol. 5, p. 475.

43. Talmud, *Gittin* 34b, *Rashi*.

44. Talmud, *Kiddushin* 31b.

45. Talmud, *Shabbos* 88a.

46. Talmud, *Bava Basra* 134a.

47. Talmud, *Bava Metzia* 22b.

48. Ibid. 21b.

49. *Yam Shel Shlomo, Bava Kamma,* ch. 7.

50. *Iggeres of Rabbi Sherira Gaon,* translated by Rabbi N. Rabinowich, p. 72.

51. HaLevi, *Doros HaRishonim,* vol. 5, p. 482.

52. *Iggeres of Rabbi Sherira Gaon,* p. 73, notes.

53. Talmud, *Gittin* 59a.

54. Talmud, *Bava Basra* 157b, *Rashbam.*

55. Talmud, *Bava Metzia* 86a, *Rashi.*

56. HaLevi, *Doros HaRishonim,* vol. 5, p. 591.

57. Rabbi A. Kaplan, *The Handbook of Jewish Thought,* vol. 1, p. 191.

58. *Meiri,* Introduction to *Avos,* p. 49.

59. Talmud, *Bava Metzia* 86a; HaLevi, *Doros HaRishonim,* vol. 5, pp. 602–603; Kaplan, *The Handbook of Jewish Thought,* vol. 1, p. 191.

60. *Handbook,* ibid.

61. Bergman, *Mavo Shearim,* p. 60.

62. Z. T. Paretzky, *Reservoirs of Faith,* p. 99.

63. *Iggeres of Rabbi Sherira Gaon,* p. 118, notes ibid.

64. Bergman, *Mavo Shearim,* p. 60.

65. Paretsky, *Reservoirs of Faith,* p. 99.

66. HaLevi, *Doros HaRishonim,* Vol. 6, p. 21.

67. Talmud, *Bava Metzia* 42a.

68. Talmud, *Shabbos* 41a.

69. Talmud, *Kesubos* 93b.

70. Talmud, *Shabbos* 63a.

71. Talmud, *Bava Kamma* 37a.

72. Talmud, *Gittin* 55b–58a.

73. Quoted in: W. Rubinstein, *The Myth of Rescue,* p. 81.

74. *Meiri,* Introduction to *Avos,* p. 49.

Chapter 10

1. Rabbi S. Halperin, *Seder HaDoros,* pp. 174, 189.

2. Y. D. Eisenstein, *Otzar Yisrael,* vol. 3, p. 227.

3. *Igros Moshe, Yoreh Deah,* part 2, *siman* 174.

4. Ibid., *Orach Chaim,* part 3, *siman* 45.

5. *Baal HaMaor,* Talmud, *Sanhedrin* ch. 4 (12a in text).

6. Rabbi C. Rabinowitz, *The History of the Jewish People,* vol. 1, p. 521.

7. Halperin, *Seder HaDoros,* pp. 174–175.

8. Ibid., pp. 176–177.

9. *Rema, Orach Chaim* 257:8.

10. Rabbi B. Wein, *Herald of Destiny*, p. 3.

11. Talmud, *Kesubos* 67a, *Tosafos.*

12. Rabbeinu Yerucham, *Nesiv* 22, *chelek sheini*, p. 186b.

13. *Shulchan Aruch, Orach Chaim* 493:2.

14. Talmud, *Berachos* 16b, 17a, 34a, *Avodah Zarah* 8a.

15. Eisenstein, *Otzar Yisrael*, vol. 8, p. 221.

16. Talmud, *Chagigah* 13a, *Tosafos.*

17. *Ibn Ezra*, Ecclesiastes 5:1.

18. *Mishnah Torah, Hilchos Sefer Torah* 8:4.

19. Eisenstein, *Otzar Yisrael*, vol. 3, p. 103.

20. Ibid.

21. A. Eisenberg, *Jewish Historical Treasures*, p. 79.

22. *Mordechai*, beginning of Talmud *Chullin.*

23. *Ibn Ezra*, Exodus 2:22.

24. N. D. Korobkin, *The Kuzari*, Introduction.

25. *The Jewish Observer*, April 2000, pp. 40–44.

26. *Meiri*, Introduction to *Avos*, p. 52.

27. Cited in: Eisenstein, *Otzar Yisrael*, vol. 7, p. 235.

28. *Iggeres of R. Sherira Gaon*, translated by Rabbi N. D. Rabinovich, Introduction.

29. Ibid.

30. *Abudraham, Seder Parshios VeHaftaros*, p. 303.

31. *Meiri*, Introduction to *Avos*, p. 51.

32. Eisenstein, *Otzar Yisrael*, vol. 4, p. 95.

33. Ibid., pp. 93–94, quoting *Teshuvos Zichron LaRishonim* 245.

34. HaLevi, *Doros HaRishonim*, vol. 6, pp. 283–287.

35. Rabbi Z. Fendel, *Legacy of Sinai*, p. 264.

Chapter 11

1. *Meiri*, Introduction to *Avos*, p. 52.

2. Y. D. Eisenstein, *Otzar Yisrael*, vol. 6, p. 204.

3. E. Paris, *The End of Days*, p. 35.

4. See gloss to *Rashi*, Judges 20:45.

5. See Rabbi S. R. Hirsch, *The Nineteen Letters*, translation and commentary of

Rabbi J. Elias, pp. 309–328; *The Journal of Halacha and Contemporary Society*, number XXXII, pp. 65–93.

6. Eisenstein, *Otzar Yisrael*, vol. 10, p. 154.

7. Ibid., vol. 3, p. 246.

8. Ibid.

9. Ibid., vol. 6, p. 245.

10. *Rashi*, Genesis 11:28; Exodus 28:28.

11. *Tzavaas R. Judah HaChasid.*

12. S. Eidelberg, *Medieval Ashkenazic Jewry*, p. 110.

13. Ibid., pp. 111–112.

14. Ibid., pp. 118–119.

15. Ibid., pp. 117–145.

16. Paris, *The End of Days*, pp. 61–62.

Chapter 12

1. Rabbi M. Bergman, *Mavo Shearim*, p. 68; *Meiri, Avos*, p. 55.

2. Ibid.

3. *Shulchan Aruch, Even HaEzer* 1:10, *Beis Shmuel* loc. cit., 21.

4. Ibid., *Rema.*

5. Rabbi M. Epstein, *A Woman's Guide to the Get Process*, p. 10.

6. Ibid., p. 11.

7. *Journal of Halacha and Contemporary Society*, vol. 1, p. 61.

8. Y. D. Eisenstein, *Otzar Yisrael*, vol. 3, p. 318.

9. Talmud, *Shabbos* 13b, *Gittin* 35a.

10. *Shulchan Aruch, Choshen Mishpat* 87:19.

11. Talmud, *Chullin* 46b, *Rashi*, "*Haynu Rivisayhu.*"

12. Talmud, *Avodah Zarah* 75a, *Rashi*, "*VeLo Pligi.*"

13. *Meiri, Avos*, p. 54.

14. Talmud, *Bava Metzia* 73b, *Rashi*, "*Guharka.*"

15. Talmud, *Sanhedrin* 82b, *Rashi*, "*U'Pinchas.*"

16. Talmud, *Berachos* 25b, *Gilyon HaShas.*

17. Eisenstein, *Otzar Yisrael*, vol. 5, p. 68.

18. *Kuzari* 2:20.

19. *Rashbam*, Genesis 37:2.

20. *Mordechai*, Talmud, *Eruvin* 528.

21. Talmud, *Bava Kamma* 10a, *Tosafos*, "*Kegon.*"

22. Talmud, *Menachos* 34b.

23. *Shulchan Aruch, Orach Chaim* 34:1–2.

24. *Yam Shel Shlomo*, Introduction to *Bava Kamma, Teshuvos HaRivash* 394.

25. *Shulchan Aruch, Orach Chaim* 580, *Magen Avraham* loc. cit., 9.

26. *Shulchan Aruch, Even HaEzer* 154:22, *Rema.*

27. Talmud, *Shabbos* 35a, *Tosafos.*

28. Talmud, *Kesubos* 103b, *Tosafos,* "*Oso HaYom.*"

29. *Ramban* on *Sefer HaMitzvos, Aseh* 1.

30. *Biur HaGra, Shulchan Aruch, Yoreh Deah* 179:13.

31. *Mishnah Torah, Hilchos Teshuvah* 8:2, *Hasagos HaRaavad.*

32. *Mishnah Torah, Hilchos Deos* 4:20.

33. *Hasagos HaRaavad, Mishnah Torah, Hilchos Kilayim* 6:2.

34. *Hasagos HaRaavad, Mishnah Torah, Hilchos Nizkei Mammon* 2:14, *Avos HaTumos* 2:10.

35. *Baal HaMaor*, Talmud, *Chullin*, ch. 3, p. 10b.

36. Talmud, *Bava Kamma* 77a, *Tosafos:* "*Parah*" (2).

37. *Ramban*, Exodus 13:16.

38. *Ramban*, Numbers 33:53.

39. S. D. Steinberg and Y. Turnheim, *Eretz Avoseinu*, p. 88.

40. *Shaarei Teshuvah* 3:139.

41. *Meiri*, Talmud, *Berachos* 43b.

42. *Yam Shel Shlomo, Gittin* 4:66.

43. *Orchos Chaim L'Rosh*, 100.

44. Ibid., 36.

45. Ibid., 128.

46. Rabbi M. Feinstein, *Igros Moshe, Yoreh Deah*, vol. 3, *siman* 98.

47. Rabbi E. Wasserman, *Kovetz He'aros*, Introduction.

48. Talmud, *Nedarim* 81a, *Ran.*

Chapter 13

1. *Kinnos* for Tishah B'Av, *Kinnah* 29.

2. *ArtScroll Selichos for Erev Rosh HaShanah, Ana Habeit*, p. 426.

3. Klaus P. Fischer, *The History of an Obsession*, p. 29.

4. Ibid.

5. Talmud, *Taanis* 29a.

6. Robert Chazan, *In the Year 1096*, p. 54.

7. Quoted in: Fischer, *The History of an Obsession*, p. 13.

8. *Encyclopaedia Judaica*, CD-ROM Edition (1997), "England."

9. E. Korn, *The Crucial Hour*, last page.

10. W. Nicholls, *Christian Antisemitism*, pp. 242–243.

11. Talmud, *Bava Metzia* 70b, *Tosafos*.

12. Nicholls, *Christian Antisemitism*, pp. 232–235.

13. Fischer, *The History of an Obsession*, p. 30.

14. D. A. Fisch, *Jews for Nothing*, p. 42.

15. Fischer, *The History of an Obsession*, p. 34.

16. E. Flannery, *The Anguish of the Jews*, p. 101.

17. P. Johnson, *A History of the Jews*, p. 211.

18. Fischer, *The History of an Obsession*, p. 32.

19. Ibid., p. 31.

20. M. Gilbert, *Atlas of Jewish History*, map 66.

21. *Mishnah Berurah*, *Orach Chaim*, 580:16.

22. Talmud, *Sanhedrin* 39a.

23. For a full account, see *The Disputation at Barcelona*, translation by Rabbi C. Chavel.

Chapter 14

1. B. Netanyahu, *The Origins of the Inquisition in Fifteenth Century Spain*, p. 1102.

2. C. Roth, *History of the Marranos*, p. 16.

3. E. Paris, *The End of Days*, pp. 103–104.

4. Roth, *History of the Marranos*, p. 28.

5. W. Nicholls, *Christian Antisemitism: A History of Hate*, pp. 263–264.

6. Paris, *The End of Days*, p. 142.

7. Netanyahu, *The Origins of the Inquisition*, p. 932.

8. Roth, *History of the Marranos*, pp. 108–110.

9. Paris, *The End of Days*, p. 258.

10. Nicholls, *Christian Antisemitism*, p. 265.

11. Paris, *The End of Days*, p. 170.

12. Ibid., pp. 225–226.

13. Ibid., p. 249.

14. Quoted in: Paris, *The End of Days*, p. 250.

15. See H. Meyer, *The Exiles of Crocodile Island*, for such a tale.

16. Paris, *The End of Days*, p. 251.

17. Rabbi C. Rabinowitz, *The History of the Jewish People*, vol. 2, p. 142.

18. Rabbi B. Wein, *Herald of Destiny*, p. 222.

19. Paris, *The End of Days*, pp. 306–307.

Chapter 15

1. Talmud, *Megillah* 13b.

2. Quoted in: *Yated Neeman*, 8/8/97, p. 24.

3. Talmud, *Chagigah* 11b.

4. A. Y. Finkel, *The Great Torah Commentators*, pp. 213–214.

5. *Mishnah Torah, Hilchos Sanhedrin* 4:1.

6. Ibid., 4:11.

7. *Mavo LaShas Vilna*, p. 7.

8. M. Lehmann, *R. Joselman of Rosheim*, chs. 4–14, (pp. 16–67).

9. Ibid., ch. 44 (pp. 188–200).

10. Klaus P. Fischer, *The History of an Obsession*, p. 39.

11. Ibid.

12. W. Nicholls, *Christian Antisemitism: A History of Hate*, p. 271.

13. *Encyclopaedia Judaica*, CD-ROM Edition (1997), "Poland: Internal Jewish Life."

14. R. M. Watt, *Bitter Glory: Poland and Its Fate 1918–1939*, p. 358.

15. *Kovetz Igros Chazon Ish, Michtav Alef.*

16. *Maharsha* on Talmud, *Shabbos* 119b.

17. *Yam Shel Shlomo, Bava Kamma*, ch. 4.

18. Quoted in: Y. D. Eisenstein, *Otzar Yisrael*, vol. 4, p. 211.

19. Ibid.

Chapter 16

1. H. J. Zimmels, *Ashkenazim and Sephardim*, pp. 75–76.

2. *Encyclopaedia Judaica*, CD-ROM Edition (1997), "Amsterdam."

3. M. Gilbert, *Atlas of Jewish History*, map 52.

4. P. Johnson, *A History of the Jews*, pp. 289–290.

5. Rabbi B. Wein, *Triumph of Survival*, p. 29, footnote.

6. Gilbert, *Atlas of Jewish History*, map 48.

7. A. Y. Finkel, *The Great Torah Commentators*, p. 21.

8. *Chronicles: News of the Past*, 15 Kislev 5409 (vol. 3, no. 14), p. 4.

9. Johnson, *A History of the Jews*, p. 260.

10. *Magen Avraham, Shulchan Aruch, Orach Chaim* 580, end.

11. *Journal of Halacha and Contemporary Society,* number XXXIII, p. 98.

12. Talmud, *Kiddushin* 71a.

13. Talmud, *Avodah Zarah* 18a, *Tosafos.*

14. *The Universal Jewish Encyclopedia,* vol. 10, p. 598.

15. C. M. Weiser, *Frumspeak: The First Dictionary of Yeshivish,* p. xiii.

16. *The Universal Jewish Encyclopedia,* p. 599.

17. B. C. Kaganoff, *A Dictionary of Jewish Names and Their History,* p. 190.

18. Ibid., p. 34.

19. Ibid., p. 24.

Chapter 17

1. Talmud, *Berachos* 5a.

2. Introduction to *Mesillas Yesharim,* Machon Ofek Edition, p. 13.

3. *Daas Tevunos,* vol. 1, Bnei Brak 5735, p. 4.

4. A. Amsel, *Rational Irrational Man,* pp. 165–172.

5. *Ketzos HaChoshen,* vol. 1, Oraysoh Edition, p. 33.

6. Ibid., p. 16.

7. R. Weingarten, *The Noda Biyehuda,* pp. 96–97.

8. Quoted in: *Yated Neeman,* 10/10/97, p. 41.

9. Quoted in: D. Eliach, *HaGaon,* vol. 1, p. 55.

10. Ibid., p. 54.

11. A. Kaplan, *Chassidic Masters,* p. 69.

12. Ibid., p. 122.

13. Introduction to *Shulchan Aruch HaRav,* vol. 1.

14. N. Mindel, *Rabbi Schneur Zalman of Liadi,* p. 210.

15. Kaplan, *Chassidic Masters,* p. 88.

16. E. J. Schochet, *The Hasidic Movement and the Gaon of Vilna,* pp. 49–50.

17. Ibid., p. 8.

18. Mindel, *Rabbi Schneur Zalman of Liadi,* p. 24.

19. Schochet, *The Hasidic Movement and the Gaon of Vilna,* p. 24.

20. S. D. B. Avtzon, *The Tanya,* p. 85, note 197.

21. A. Karp, *A History of the Jews in America,* p. 11.

22. Ibid., p. 10.

23. Women's Group, Congregation Mikveh Israel, *A Taste of History,* p. 2.

24. D. Karp, *Heroes of American Jewish History,* p. 44.

Chapter 18

1. P. Johnson, *A History of the Jews*, p. 306.
2. T. M. Rabinowicz, *The Encyclopedia of Hasidism*, p. 340.
3. W. Nicholls, *Christian Antisemitism: A History of Hate*, p. 303.
4. Johnson, *A History of the Jews*, p. 310.
5. Ibid.
6. Ibid., p. 302.
7. Commentary of Rabbi O. MiBartenurah on Mishnah *Avos* 1:1.
8. Mishnah, *Avos* 5:22.
9. M. I. Dimont, *Jews, G-d, and History*, p. 308.
10. Nicholls, *Christian Antisemitism*, p. 306.
11. Johnson, *A History of the Jews*, p. 312.
12. Nicholls, *Christian Antisemitism*, p. 326.
13. L. S. Davidowicz, *The War against the Jews*, p. 7.
14. Quoted in: Nicholls, *Christian Antisemitism*, p. 320.
15. I. Sharfman, *The First Rabbi*, pp. 25–26.
16. D. Bianco, *Modern Jewish History for Everyone*, p. 30.
17. Y. D. Eisenstein, *Otzar Yisrael*, vol. 9, p. 313.
18. Johnson, *A History of the Jews*, p. 329.
19. Dimont, *Jews, G-d, and History*, p. 306.
20. Quoted in: *The Nineteen Letters*, Feldheim Publishing, p. 326.
21. Rabbi E. M. Klugman, *Rabbi Samson Raphael Hirsch*, pp. 156–158.
22. Quoted in: *Yated Neeman*, 11/29/96, p. 22.
23. *Orlah* 3:9.
24. Y. D. Shulman, *The Chasam Sofer*, p. 251.
25. Quoted in: *Yated Neeman*, 1/16/98, p. 25.
26. Johnson, *A History of the Jews*, p. 366.
27. Sharfman, *The First Rabbi*, pp. xvi-xvii.
28. Johnson, *A History of the Jews*, pp. 369–370.
29. Bianco, *Modern Jewish History for Everyone*, p. 193.
30. Deuteronomy 1:17.
31. Sharfman, *The First Rabbi*, p. 247.
32. N. Ferguson, *The House of Rothschild: Money's Prophets 1798–1848*, p. 12.
33. *Encyclopaedia Judaica*, CD-ROM Edition (1997), "Rothschild."
34. Ferguson, *The House of Rothschild*, p. 483.

35. Ibid., p. 7.

36. A. S. Lindemann, *The Jew Accused*, p. 36.

Chapter 19

1. M. Meltzer, *A History of Jewish Life from Eastern Europe to America*, p. 47.

2. Ibid., p. 48.

3. Ibid., p. 74.

4. Ibid., pp. 84–85.

5. Ibid., p. 29.

6. S. M. Dubnow, *The Jews in Russia and Poland*, vol. 2, pp. 24–25.

7. Ibid., p. 27.

8. Meltzer, *A History of Jewish Life from Eastern Europe to America*, p. 36.

9. Conor C. O'Brien, *The Siege*, p. 38.

10. Ibid., p. 34.

11. Ibid., pp. 35–36.

12. Dubnow, *The Jews in Russia and Poland*, vol. 2, pp. 252–253.

13. Meltzer, *A History of Jewish Life from Eastern Europe to America*, p. 128.

14. Dubnow, *The Jews in Russia and Poland*, vol. 2, p. 288.

15. Meltzer, *A History of Jewish Life from Eastern Europe to America*, p. 131.

16. Dubnow, *The Jews in Russia and Poland*, vol. 2, pp. 423–424.

17. Ibid., p. 427.

18. O'Brien, *The Siege*, p. 47.

19. Rabbi B. Wein, *Triumph of Survival*, p. 158.

20. *Yalkut Shimoni Korach*, 750.

21. Dubnow, *The Jews in Russia and Poland*, pp. 229–230.

22. Ibid.

23. Meltzer, *A History of Jewish Life from Eastern Europe to America*, pp. 98–99.

24. Ibid., p. 103.

25. Ibid., p. 94.

26. *Yated Neeman*, "Vilna vs. Slavita and the Slavita Blood Libel."

Chapter 20

1. Rabbi A. Miller, *Behold a People*, p. 81 (paragraphs 115–116).

2. Talmud, *Yoma* 28b.

3. Z. T. Paretzky, *Reservoirs of Faith*, p. 266.

4. S. Y. Zevin, *Ishim VeShitos*, p. 17.

5. *Nefesh HaChaim* 4:11.

6. Paretzky, *Reservoirs of Faith*, p. 269.

7. Zevin, *Ishim VeShitos*, p. 17.

8. *Yated Neeman*, 7/2/99, pp. 40–41.

9. Zevin, *Ishim VeShitos*, pp. 76–77.

10. *Ohr Yisrael* (Vilna 5650), *Iggeres HaMussar*, pp. 106–107.

11. H. Goldberg, *Israel Salanter: Text, Structure, Idea*, pp. 4–5.

12. *Ohr Yisroel, Nesivos Ohr*, p. 124.

13. D. Katz, *The Mussar Movement*, Vol. 1, pp. 78–79.

14. Ibid., p. 63.

15. Ibid., p. 67.

16. *Ohr Yisrael,* p. 43.

17. Quoted in: Katz, *The Mussar Movement*, vol. 2, p. 206.

18. C. E. Zaitchik, *Sparks of Mussar*, p. 30.

19. Ibid., pp. 41–42.

20. Ibid., pp. 40-41.

21. Ibid., p. 78.

22. M. Levin, *Novarodok*, Introduction, p. xvii.

23. Zaitchik, *Sparks of Mussar*, p. 79.

24. Ibid., p. 81.

25. Ibid., p. 78.

26. A. Y. Finkel, *The Great Torah Commentators*, p. 146.

27. *Novarodok*, Introduction, pp. xvi-xvii.

28. Ibid., pp. xvii-xviii.

29. D. Katz, *Tnuas HaMussar*, vol. 4, p. 308.

30. Ibid., p. 257.

31. Levin, *Novarodok*, pp. 41–42.

32. D. Katz, *Pulmus HaMussar*, p. 17.

33. Ibid., p. 21.

34. Ibid., p. 286.

35. Ibid., p. 256.

36. Ibid., pp. 264–270.

37. Dr. J. Fox, *Rabbi Menachem Mendel of Kotzk*, p. 40.

38. Ibid., p. 51.

39. A. Kaplan, *The Chassidic Masters*, pp. 173–174.

40. *Rabbi Menachem Mendel of Kotzk*, pp. 171–172.

41. Ibid., p. 139.

42. Ibid., p. 141.

43. Ibid., p. 145.

44. Kaplan, *The Chassidic Masters*, p. 186.

45. *Yated Neeman*, 10/27/95, pp. 22–24.

46. Finkel, *The Great Torah Commentators*, p. 180.

47. C. Dalfin, *The Seven Chabad-Lubavitch Rebbes*, p. 58.

48. Finkel, *The Great Torah Commentators*, p. 118.

49. Zaitchik, *Sparks of Mussar*, p. 217.

50. Ibid., p. 225.

51. N. Wolpin, *The Torah Personality*, pp. 19–20.

52. *The Power of Torah*, Ben Ish Chai Anthology, vol. 8, Foreword, p. xxiv.

Chapter 21

1. M. Gilbert, *Israel*, p. 3.

2. Ibid., p. 5.

3. H. M. Sachar, *A History of Israel*, p. 31.

4. Ibid., p. 15.

5. Ibid., p. 82; Gilbert, *Israel*, p. 8.

6. C. C. O'Brien, *The Siege*, p. 84.

7. Gilbert, *Israel*, p. 8.

8. P. Johnson, *A History of the Jews*, p. 395.

9. O'Brien, *The Siege*, p. 73.

10. Johnson, *A History of the Jews*, p. 397.

11. Sachar, *A History of Israel*, p. 46.

12. O'Brien, *The Siege*, p. 671, note 52.

13. C. Dalfin, *The Seven Chabad-Lubavitch Rebbes*, pp. 97–98.

14. Rabbi C. Rabinowitz, *The History of the Jewish People*, vol. 2, p. 391.

15. Talmud, *Kesubos* 111a.

16. See *Journal of Halacha and Contemporary Society*, no. VIII, p. 28.

17. F. Massoulie, *Middle East Conflicts*, p. 49.

18. Gilbert, *Israel*, p. 30.

19. Massoulie, *Middle East Conflicts*, p. 49.

20. Talmud, *Sotah* 44a.

21. Johnson, *A History of the Jews*, pp. 449–450.

22. M. Meltzer, *A History of Jewish Life from Eastern Europe to America*, p. 170.

23. I. Howe, *World of Our Fathers*, pp. 57–63.

24. M. Meltzer, *A History of Jewish Life from Eastern Europe to America*, pp. 179–180.

25. Ibid., p. 242.

26. Ibid., p. 241.

27. Talmud, *Arachin* 30b.

28. S. G. Freedman, *Jew vs. Jew*, p. 34.

29. S. Bernstein, *The Orthodox Union Story: A Centenary Portrayal*, p. 25.

30. Ibid., p. 26.

31. Quoted in: A. Rakeffet-Rothkoff, *The Silver Era*, pp. 18–19.

32. Ibid., p. 28.

33. Bernstein, *The Orthodox Union Story: A Centenary Portrayal*, p. 41.

34. *Yated Neeman*, 11/24/95, p. 29.

Chapter 22

1. M Gilbert, *A History of the Twentieth Century*, vol. 1, 1900–1933, pp. 72–73.

2. Introduction to *Peirush HaMishnayos L'Rambam*.

3. P. Johnson, *A History of the Jews*, pp. 380–381.

4. D. L. Lewis, *Prisoners of Honor: The Dreyfus Affair*, p. 56; W. Shirer, *The Collapse of the Third Republic*, p. 54, note.

5. A. S. Lindemann, *The Jew Accused*, p. 186.

6. Ibid., p. 188.

7. Ibid., p. 191.

8. *The Struggle and the Splendor*, Agudath Israel Publications, p. 15.

9. Ibid., p. 20.

10. Numbers 15:24; Psalms 25:14.

11. *The Struggle and the Splendor*, pp. 21–22.

12. Gilbert, *A History of the Twentieth Century*, vol. 1, 1900–1933, p. 233.

13. Lindemann, *The Jew Accused*, p. 272.

14. Ibid., p. 235, note 2.

15. K. P. Fischer, *Nazi Germany, A New History*, p. 15.

16. M. Gilbert, *The Jews in the Twentieth Century*, pp. 69–74.

17. Ibid.

18. J. Peters, *From Time Immemorial*, p. 215.

19. D. Fromkin, *A Peace to End All Peace*, pp. 281–282.

20. Ibid., p. 294.

21. H. M. Sachar, *A History of Israel*, p. 113.

Chapter 23

1. *Kovetz Maamarim*, p. 82.

2. A. Chazan, *Deep in the Russian Night*, p. 22.

3. *Kovetz Maamarim*, pp. 92–93.

4. Ibid., p. 94.

5. P. Johnson, *A History of the Jews*, p. 448.

6. E. J. Gottlieb, *The Inescapable Truth*, p. 297.

7. Rabbi S. D. B. Levin, *Toldos Chabad B'Rusya HaSovyetes*, p. 41.

8. D. Fromkin, *A Peace to End All Peace*, p. 524.

9. M. G. Bard, *Myths and Facts: A Guide to the Arab-Israeli Conflict* (2002 ed.), p. 26.

10. J. Peters, *From Time Immemorial*, p. 331.

11. Ibid., p. 363.

12. Ibid.

13. Johnson, *A History of the Jews*, p. 443.

14. H. M. Sachar, *A History of Israel*, p. 155.

15. M. Gilbert, *Jerusalem in the Twentieth Century*, pp. 108–109.

16. R. M. Watt, *Bitter Glory: Poland and Its Fate*, 1918-1939, p. 358.

17. E. Mendelsohn, *The Jews of East Central Europe Between the World Wars*, p. 42.

18. Watt, *Bitter Glory*, p. 361.

19. Ibid., p. 366.

20. *Shemos Rabbah, Yisro* 28:2.

21. M. Gilbert, *The Jews in the Twentieth Century*, pp. 118–119.

22. Quoted in: Z. T. Paretzky, *Reservoirs of Faith*, pp. 299–300.

23. Told to the author by his father, R. David Eisen, *zt"l*, a student of Baranovitch.

24. Y. Eliach, *There Once Was a World*, p. 416.

25. C. D. Eby, *Hungary at War*, pp. 98–99.

26. I. Howe, *World of Our Fathers*, p. 167.

27. Ibid., pp. 411–412.

28. P. Fishman, *The Jews of the United States*, p. 63.

29. Howe, *World of Our Fathers*, p. 254.

30. Ibid., p. 262.

31. Fishman, *The Jews of the United States*, pp. 210–211.

32. *Encyclopaedia Judaica*, CD-ROM Edition (1997), "American Jewish Joint Distribution Committee."

33. Howe, *World of Our Fathers*, pp. 622–623.

34. Fishman, *The Jews of the United States*, pp. 105–106.

35. S. Bernstein, *The Orthodox Union Story: A Centenary Portrayal*, p. 102.

36. Ibid., pp. 93–94.

37. D. Warren, *Radio Priest*, p. 131.

38. N. Baldwin, *Henry Ford and the Jews*, pp. 284–285.

39. Warren, *Radio Priest*, p. 25.

40. Ibid., p. 157.

41. E. Benbassa and A. Rodrigue, *Sephardic Jewry*, p. 195.

42. Ibid., p. 10.

43. Johnson, *A History of the Jews*, p. 356.

Chapter 24

1. *Teaching About the Holocaust: A Resource Book For Educators*, United States Holocaust Memorial Museum, pp. 1–2.

2. H. Rauschning, *The Voice of Destruction*, pp. 80, 223, 237.

3. *Yalkut Shimoni, Ki Seitzei*, 25.

4. A. Hitler, *Mein Kampf*, p. 64.

5. Quoted in: W. Rubinstein, *The Myth of Rescue*, p. 81.

6. Quoted in: E. H. Flannery, *The Anguish of the Jews*, p. 211.

7. M. Tokayer and M. Swartz, *The Fugu Plan*, p. 172.

8. Talmud, *Bava Metzia* 58b.

9. Talmud, *Berachos* 5a.

10. *Sefer Otzar HaBris*, vol. 1, p. 346, note 5.

11. *Sefer Meshech Chochmah, Parashas BeChukosai*, 26:44.

12. *Lessons in Tanya*, vol. 1, p. 19.

13. Rabbi Moshe C. Luzzatto, *Derech HaShem* (The Way of G-d), part 2, 3:8.

14. B. Maza, *With Fury Poured Out*, p. 245.

15. *Yevamos* 63b.

16. Rabbi Y. Kasnett, unpublished manuscript.

17. M. Gilbert, *The Macmillan Atlas of the Holocaust*, p. 10.

18. Rabbi J. Elias, *Teaching Churban Europa to Our Children*, Torah Umesorah, pp. 6–7.

19. Quoted in: K. P. Fischer, *Nazi Germany: A New History*, p. 88.

20. Hitler, *Mein Kampf*, p. 56.

21. Rauschning, *The Voice of Destruction*, p. 238.

Chapter 25

1. W. Nicholls, *Christian Anti-Semitism: A History of Hate*, p. 246.
2. K. P. Fischer, *The History of an Obsession: German Judeophobia and the Holocaust*, p. 55.
3. K. P. Fischer, *Nazi Germany: A New History*, p. 75.
4. Ibid., p. 122.
5. Ibid., p. 124.
6. M. Gilbert, *The Holocaust*, p. 31.
7. W. D. Rubinstein, *The Myth of Rescue*, p. 18.
8. Fischer, *The History of an Obsession*, p. 190.
9. Quoted in: S. Rossel, *The Holocaust: The World and the Jews, 1933–1945*, p. 91.
10. Ibid., p. 86.
11. E. B. Bukey, *Hitler's Austria*, p. 131.
12. Fischer, *The History of an Obsession*, pp. 285–286.
13. D. Wyman, *The Abandonment of the Jews*, p. 15.
14. Fischer, *The History of an Obsession*, p. 277.
15. Gilbert, *The Holocaust*, pp. 76–77.
16. Rubinstein, *The Myth of Rescue*, pp. 16–17.
17. M. Berenbaum, *The World Must Know*, p. 58.
18. Rubinstein, *The Myth of Rescue*, p. 62.
19. *Kesubos* 67a.
20. Quoted in: Rubinstein, *The Myth of Rescue*, p. 215.
21. B. Alexander, *How Hitler Could Have Won World War II*, pp. 45–52.
22. Fischer, *The History of an Obsession*, p. 297.
23. Ibid., p. 296.
24. C. C. O'Brien, *The Siege*, pp. 244–245.

Chapter 26

1. Quoted in: K. P. Fischer, *Nazi Germany: A New History*, p. 447.
2. M. Gilbert, *The Holocaust*, photographs following p. 328.
3. Ibid., p. 85.
4. Ibid., p. 87.
5. Ibid., p. 101.
6. *Eruvin* 41b.
7. Gilbert, *The Holocaust*, pp. 100–101.

8. Quoted in: R. Lichtenstein, *History Bears Witness*, "Life in the Ghetto."

9. K. P. Fischer, *The History of an Obsession*, pp. 320–321.

10. Quoted in: Y. Bauer, *A History of the Holocaust*, pp. 177–178.

11. *Shulchan Aruch, Yoreh Deah* 157:1, *Rema*.

12. Bauer, *A History of the Holocaust*, p. 162.

13. Talmud, *Pesachim* 25b.

14. B. Alexander, *How Hitler Could Have Won World War II*, pp. 40–41.

Chapter 27

1. M. Gilbert, *The Holocaust*, p. 175.

2. K. P. Fischer, *Nazi Germany, a New History*, p. 498.

3. Gilbert, *The Holocaust*, p. 615.

4. K. P. Fischer, *The History of an Obsession*, p. 346.

5. E. Oshry, *The Annihilation of Lithuanian Jewry*, pp. 2–3.

6. Ibid., pp. 24-26.

7. Fischer, *The History of an Obsession*, pp. 346–347.

8. Ibid., p. 347.

9. Gilbert, *The Holocaust*, pp. 204–205.

10. Fischer, *The History of an Obsession*, p. 352.

11. Quoted in: R. H. Abzug, *America Views the Holocaust 1933–1945*, pp. 189–190.

12. Y. Arad, *Belzec, Sobibor, Treblinka*, p. 63.

13. Ibid., p. 64.

14. Gilbert, *The Holocaust*, p. 287; D. Czech, *Auschwitz Chronicle 1939–1945*, p. xvii; *The Holocaust Chronicle*, pp. 544, 699.

15. Gilbert, *The Holocaust*, p. 305.

16. Ibid., p. 304.

17. Ibid., p. 419.

18. Ibid., p. 416.

19. Arad, *Belzec, Sobibor, Treblinka*, pp. 101–102; Y. Bauer, *A History of the Holocaust*, pp. 210–211.

20. P. Johnson, *A History of the Jews*, p. 511.

21. Bauer, *A History of the Holocaust*, pp. 224–226.

22. Fischer, *The History of an Obsession*, pp. 357–358.

23. Arad, *Belzec, Sobibor, Treblinka*, pp. 264–265.

24. Bauer, *A History of the Holocaust*, pp. 211–213.

25. A. Levy, *The Wiesenthal File*, p. 204.

26. Ibid., pp. 210–211.

27. Gilbert, *The Holocaust*, p. 390.

Chapter 28

1. R. Hilberg, *The Destruction of the European Jews*, vol. 3, p. 1113.

2. *The New York Times*, 5/6/45, section E5.

3. Dr. H. Seidman, *The Warsaw Ghetto Diaries*, p. 236.

4. Ibid., pp. 235–236.

5. Hilberg, *The Destruction of the European Jews*, vol. 3, p. 1106.

6. S. Rossell, *The Holocaust*, p. 129.

7. M. Gilbert, *The Holocaust*, p. 559.

8. Y. Arad, *Belzec, Sobobor, Treblinka*, p. 215; Rabbi Z. Fendel, *The Thirteen Principles*, pp. 61–62.

9. Told to the author by his mother, *zt"l*.

10. Y. Eliach, *Hasidic Tales of the Holocaust*, pp. 159–160.

11. Ibid., pp. 13–15.

12. Ibid., p. 107.

13. Gilbert, *The Holocaust*, p. 323.

14. Eliach, *Hasidic Tales of the Holocaust*, beginning of ch. 1.

15. N. Wolpin, *A Path through the Ashes*, p. 281.

16. Ibid., p. 283.

17. M. Paldiel, *The Path of the Righteous: Gentile Rescuers of Jews During the Holocaust*, pp. 376–381.

18. Ibid., p. 254.

19. *Yated Neeman*, 12/29/00.

20. I. Gutman, ed., *Encyclopedia of the Holocaust*, Macmillan Publishing, 1990, p. 1333.

21. Paldiel, *The Path of the Righteous*, pp. 166–167.

22. Ibid., pp. 199–200.

23. Ibid., pp. 346–347.

24. C. D. Eby, *Hungary at War*, p. 108.

25. Paldiel, *The Path of the Righteous*, pp. 185–186.

Chapter 29

1. D. Wyman, *The World Reacts to the Holocaust*, p. 101.

2. Ibid., p. 401.

3. P. Johnson, *A History of the Jews*, p. 498.

4. K. P. Fischer, *The History of an Obsession*, pp. 398–399.

5. Johnson, *A History of the Jews*, p. 499.

6. C. D. Eby, *Hungary at War*, p. 119.

7. Ibid., p. 122.

8. Ibid.

9. Ibid., note.

10. L. Blau, *Bonyhad: A Destroyed Community*, chs. 7, 8.

11. E. Levine, *Darkness over Denmark*, pp. 27–29.

12. M. Bar-Zohar, *Beyond Hitler's Grasp*, p. 83.

13. Ibid., pp. 165–177, 188, 193–197.

14. Wyman, *The World Reacts to the Holocaust*, p. 514.

15. Ibid., p. 523.

16. Del Fuego, *Sephardim and the Holocaust*, pp. 200–201.

17. Talmud, *Sanhedrin* 37a.

18. M. Bunting, *The Model Occupation*, p. 6.

19. Ibid., p. 113.

20. Wyman, *The World Reacts to the Holocaust*, p. 566.

21. M. Tokayer and M. Swartz, *The Fugu Plan*, ch. 16.

Chapter 30

1. D. Wyman, *The Abandonment of the Jews*, preface, p. xiii.

2. Ibid., p. 15.

3. Ibid., p. 11.

4. Ibid., pp. 11-12.

5. Ibid., p. 12.

6. Ibid., p. 321, note.

7. D. Wyman and R. Medoff, *A Race against Death*, pp. 6–7.

8. Wyman, *The Abandonment of the Jews*, p. 105.

9. D. Kranzler, "Steven Wise and the Holocaust," article printed in *Reverence, Righteousness, and Rahamanut, Essays in Memory of Dr. Leo Jung*, J.J. Schachter, ed., pp. 155–192.

10. H. Lookstein, *Were We Our Brothers' Keepers?*, pp. 165–166.

11. *Ashes to Renewal* (Agudah), pp. 477–478.

12. Wyman, *The Abandonment of the Jews*, pp. 328–329.

13. Lookstein, *Were We Our Brothers' Keepers?*, p. 179.

14. Wyman, *The Abandonment of the Jews*, pp. 329–330.

15. Lookstein, *Were We Our Brothers' Keepers?*, pp. 213–214.
16. Ibid.
17. *The Jewish Observer*, June 2000, p. 12.
18. J. Friedenson and D. Kranzler, *Heroine of Rescue*, pp. 21–22.
19. Wyman, *The Abandonment of the Jews*, p. 330.
20. Wyman and Medoff, *A Race against Death*, p. 31.
21. Ibid., pp. 34–35.
22. See article in *Jewish Action*, Fall 2002, pp. 30–39.
23. D. Kranzler, *Thy Brothers' Blood*, p. 153.
24. Lookstein, *Were We Our Brothers' Keepers?*, p. 109.
25. Wyman, *The Abandonment of the Jews*, p. 45.
26. Ibid., p. 285.
27. Lookstein, *Thy Brothers' Blood*, pp. 107–109.
28. M. Beschloss, *The Conquerors*, p. 66.
29. M. Neufeld and M. Berenbaum, *The Bombing of Auschwitz*, p. 8.
30. Ibid., p. 7.
31. Beschloss, *The Conquerors*, p. 65.
32. S. Zuccotti, *Under His Very Windows*, pp. 310–316.

Chapter 31

1. M. Gilbert, *The Holocaust*, p. 775.
2. Talmud, *Gittin* 56b.
3. *Liberation 1945*, United States Holocaust Museum, p. 114.
4. Rabbi B. Merling, *Olomeinu Gems: Stories For All Year Round*, pp. 29–34.
5. Talmud, *Megillah* 16a.
6. *Discovery*, Aish HaTorah Publications, June 1996 edition, pp. 77–79.
7. K. P. Fischer, *The History of an Obsession*, p. 416.
8. Ibid., p. 418.
9. P. Johnson, *A History of the Jews*, p. 515.
10. Ibid., p. 498.
11. J. Ziegler, *The Swiss, the Gold, and the Dead*, p. 115.
12. Ibid., p. 245.
13. Taped interview with the author, March 1999.
14. *Encyclopaedia Judaica*, CD-ROM Edition (1997), "Holocaust Historiography."

15. Quoted in: *Liberation 1945*, p. 57.

16. Talmud, *Sanhedrin* 37a.

Chapter 32

1. M. Gilbert, *Israel*, p. 100.

2. R. Breitman, *Official Secrets*, pp. 238–239.

3. C. C. O'Brien, *The Siege*, p. 261.

4. Ibid., p. 265.

5. M. Gilbert, *Jerusalem in the Twentieth Century*, p. 172.

6. H. M. Sachar, *A History of Israel*, p. 270.

7. Gilbert, *Israel*, p. 127.

8. Sachar, *A History of Israel*, p. 278.

9. Gilbert, *Jerusalem in the Twentieth Century*, p. 187.

10. Ibid., p. 195.

11. Sachar, *A History of Israel*, p. 297.

12. Gilbert, *Israel*, p. 200.

13. Sachar, *A History of Israel*, p. 334.

14. O'Brien, *The Siege*, pp. 301–302.

15. *The Struggle and the Splendor*, Agudath Israel Publications, p. 75.

16. Ibid., pp. 79–80.

17. Sachar, *A History of Israel*, p. 355.

18. P. Johnson, *A History of the Jews*, p. 526.

19. T. A. Bailey, *A Diplomatic History of the American People*, 10th ed., p. 794.

Chapter 33

1. H. M. Sachar, *A History of Israel*, p. 404.

2. Ben Hecht, *Perfidy*, pp. 232–234.

3. P. Johnson, *A History of the Jews*, p. 570.

4. *Jewish Action*, winter 2002, p. 19.

5. A. Bunim, *A Fire in His Soul*, p. 276.

6. *Directory of Day Schools in the United States and Canada*, 2001 edition.

7. *Ashes to Renewal*, Agudath Israel Publications, p. 459.

8. *National Geographic*, August 1975, "Brooklyn's Hasidic Jews," p. 289.

9. S. G. Freedman, *Jew vs. Jew*, pp. 39–40.

10. M. H. Danziger, *Returning to Tradition*, p. 24.

11. P. Fishman, *The Jews of the United States*, p. 149.

12. E. Abrams, *Faith or Fear*, p. 2.

Chapter 34

1. p. 129.

2. Ibid., p. 133.

3. M. H. Danziger, *Origins of Return*, pp. 72–73.

4. Ibid., p. 79.

5. M. B. Oren, *Six Days of War*, pp. 135–136.

6. C. C. O'Brien, *The Siege*, p. 413.

7. Oren, *Six Days of War*, p. 176.

8. M. G. Bard, *Myths and Facts: A Guide to the Arab-Israeli Conflict*, 2002 edition, p. 64.

9. Oren, *Six Days of War*, p. 283.

10. O'Brien, *The Siege*, p. 418.

11. M. G. Bard, *Myths and Facts*, p. 71.

12. W. D. Nicholls, *Christian Antisemitism*, pp. 363–364.

Chapter 35

1. B. Wasserstein, *Vanishing Diaspora*, p. 200.

2. P. Johnson, *A History of the Jews*, p. 571.

3. Quoted in: D. Bianco, *Modern Jewish History for Everyone*, pp. 166–167.

4. M. H. Danziger, *Returning to Tradition*, p. 116.

5. Women's Issues, *Ner LeElef Publications*, vol. 1, appendix C.

6. *Rabbi Issachar Frand in Print*, p. 202.

7. Correspondence between the author and Rabbi Boruch B. Borchart and Rabbi Moshe Kolodny of Agudath Israel of America.

8. *The Struggle and the Splendor*, Agudath Israel Publications, p. 141.

9. W. Helmreich, *The World of the Yeshiva*, p. 49.

10. Encyclopaedia Judaica, *1974 Year Book*, p. 396.

11. Quoted in: D. A. Fisch, *Jews for Nothing*, p. 235.

12. Ibid.

13. Ibid., p. 239.

14. M. Gilbert, *Israel*, pp. 405–406.

15. Ibid., p. 407.

16. W. J. Boyne, *The Two O'Clock War*, p. 160.

17. Ibid., p. 61.

18. Ibid., pp. 159–160.

19. Ibid., p. 119.

20. Gilbert, *Israel*, p. 467.

21. H. M. Sachar, *A History of Israel*, p. 835.

22. Gilbert, *Israel*, p. 479.

Chapter 36

1. N. Wolpin, *Timeless Parenting*, pp. 358–361.

2. N. J. Efron, *Real Jews*, pp. 57–58.

3. Ibid., p. 55.

4. *Sanhedrin* 99b.

5. Talmud, *Shabbos* 119b.

6. Talmud, *Pesachim* 49b.

7. E. Abrams, *Faith or Fear*, p. 122.

8. Ibid., p. 115, note.

9. *Siddur Sim Shalom* (Conservative) 1989, p. xxiii.

10. J. Antler, *The Journey Home*, p. 293.

11. L. Trepp, *A History of the Jewish Experience*, p. 251.

12. S. G. Freedman, *Jew vs. Jew*, p. 218.

13. B. Rubin and J. C. Rubin, *Anti-American Terrorism and the Middle East, A Documentary Reader*, p. 8.

14. B. Wasserstein, *Vanishing Diaspora*, p. 200.

15. Quoted in: C. C. O'Brien, *The Siege*, p. 610.

16. M. G. Bard, *Myths and Facts: A Guide to the Arab-Israeli Conflict*, 2002 edition, p. 95.

17. H. M. Sachar, *A History of Israel*, p. 905.

18. O'Brien, *The Siege*, p. 630.

19. M. Gilbert, *Israel*, p. 276.

20. Sachar, *A History of Israel*, p. 939.

21. *The New York Times*, January 7, 1985.

22. See *The Jewish Observer*, April 1985, p. 13.

Chapter 37

1. E. Abrams, *Faith or Fear*, pp. 1–2, 9.

2. A Gordon and R. M. Horowitz, *Independent Study*, 1994, published in many magazines.

3. 6/8/97, p. 52, "Vanishing."

4. Arutz Sheva News Service, 6/30/03 (online).

5. *Yated Neeman*, 12/17/99.

6. H. M. Sachar, *A History of Israel*, p. 982.

7. *From Our Sealed Rooms*, Targum Press, p. 13.

8. M. Gilbert, *Israel*, p. 547.

9. Y. Bodansky, *The High Cost of Peace*, p. 97.

10. Ibid., p. 92.

11. Ibid., p. 181.

12. Ibid., p. 109.

13. Ibid., p. 210.

14. Ibid., p. 130.

15. Ibid., p. 215.

16. Ibid., p. 217.

17. N. J. Efron, *Real Jews*, pp. 220–222.

18. *Hamodia*, 7/4/03, p. B2.

19. p. 203.

20. Rabbi M. M. Weiss, *A Torah Perspective for Challenging Times*, p. 149.

21. *The Jewish Observer*, November 1999, March 2000 issues.

22. 8/8/00, p. A1.

23. Ibid., p. A20.

24. *The Jewish Observer*, May 2003, pp. 24–25.

25. *Real Jews*, preface, p. xiii.

26. *The Jewish Observer*, May 2003, pp. 6–9.

27. Rabbi E. Wasserman, *Kovetz Maamarim*, 5723 edition, pp. 117–118.

HEBREW BIBLIOGRAPHY

Abudraham, Rabbi David Abudraham.

Beis Yosef, Rabbi Yosef Karo.

Daas Tevunos, Rabbi Moshe C. Luzzatto.

Derech HaShem, Rabbi Moshe C. Luzzatto.

Doros HaRishonim, Rabbi Yitzchak HaLevi Rabinowitz.

HaGaon, Dov Eliach.

Igros Moshe, Rabbi Moshe Feinstein.

Ishim VeShitos, Rabbi Shlomo Y. Zevin.

Ketzos HaChoshen, Rabbi Aryeh L. Heller.

Kovetz He'aros, Rabbi Elchanan Wasserman.

Kovetz Igros Chazon Ish, Rabbi Avraham Y. Karelitz.

Kovetz Maamarim, Rabbi Elchanan Wasserman.

Mavo LaShas Vilna, Rabbi Y. Weinfeld.

Mavo Shearim, Rabbi Meir Bergman.

Meshech Chochmah, Rabbi Meir Simcha of Dvinsk.

Mesillas Yesharim, Rabbi Moshe C. Luzzatto.

Michtav MiEliyahu, Rabbi Eliyahu Dessler.

Mishnah Berurah, Rabbi Yisrael M. Kagan.

Nachalas Shimon, Rabbi Shimon Krasner.

Nefesh HaChaim, Rabbi Chaim of Volozhin.

Ohr Yisrael, Rabbi Yisrael Salanter.

Orchos Chaim L'Rosh, Rabbeinu Asher.

Otzar HaBris, Rabbi Yosef Weissberg.

Otzar Yisrael, Yehuda D. Eisenstein.

Pulmus HaMussar, Dov Katz.

Rabbeinu Yerucham, Rabbi Yerucham.

Seder HaDoros, Rabbi Yechiel Halpern.

Sefer HaChinuch, Rabbi Yosef Babad.

Shaarei Leshem Shvo VeAchlamah, Rabbi Shlomo Elyashiv.

Shaarei Teshuvah, Rabbeinu Jonah.

Shulchan Aruch, Rabbi Yosef Karo.

Shulchan Aruch HaRav, Rabbi Schneur Zalman of Liadi.

Siddur, Rabbi Yaakov Emden.

Teshuvos HaRivash, Rabbi Yitzchak ben Sheshes.

Tnuas HaMussar, Dov Katz.

Toldos Chabad B'Rusya HaSovyetes, Rabbi S. D. B. Levin.

Toldos Yisrael, Rabbi Zev Yaavetz.

Tzavaas Rabbi Yehuda HaChasid, Rabbi Yehuda HaChasid.

Yam Shel Shlomo, Rabbi Shlomo Luria.

BIBLIOGRAPHY

Abrams, Elliott. *Faith or Fear*. New York: Free Press, 1997.

Abzug, Robert H. *America Views the Holocaust 1933–1945*. Boston: Bedford/St. Martin's, 1999.

Alexander, Bevin. *How Hitler Could Have Won World War II*. New York: Crown Publishers, 2000.

Amsel, Avrohom. *Rational Irrational Man*. New York: Feldheim Publishers, 1976.

Antler, Joyce. *The Journey Home*. New York: Shocken Books, 1997.

Arad, Yitzhak. *Belzec, Sobibor, Treblinka*. Bloomington, IN: Indiana University Press, 1999.

Ashes to Renewal. New York: Agudath Israel of America, 1995.

Avtzon, Sholom Dov Ber. *The Tanya*. New York: Published by author, 1999.

Bailey, Thomas A. *A Diplomatic History of the American People*. 10th ed. Englewood Cliffs, NJ: Prentice-Hall, 1980.

Baldwin, Neil. *Henry Ford and the Jews*. New York: Public Affairs, 2001.

Bard, Mitchell G. *Myths and Facts: A Guide to the Arab-Israeli Conflict*. Chevy Chase, MD: AICE, 2002.

Bar-Zohar, Michael. *Beyond Hitler's Grasp*. Holbrook, MA: Adams Media, 1998.

Bauer, Yehuda. *A History of the Holocaust*. Danbury, CT: Franklin Watts, 1982.

Ben Hecht. *Perfidy*. Israel: Milah Press, 1999.

Benbassa, Esther, and Aron Rodrigue. *Sephardic Jewry*. Berkeley: University of California Press, 2000.

Berenbaum, Michael. *The World Must Know*. Boston: Little, Brown, 1993.

Bernstein, Saul. *The Orthodox Union Story: A Centenary Portrayal*. Northvale, NJ: Jason Aronson, 1997.

Beschloss, Michael. *The Conquerors*. New York: Simon and Schuster, 2002.

Bianco, David. *Modern Jewish History for Everyone*. Los Angeles: History for Everyone, 1997.

Blau, Leslie. *Bonyhad: A Destroyed Community*. New York: Sheingold Publishers, 1994.

Bodansky, Yossef. *The High Cost of Peace*. Roseville, CA: Forum Prima, 2002.

Boyne, Walter J. *The Two O'Clock War*. New York: Thomas Dunne Books, St. Martin's Press, 2002.

Breitman, Richard. *Official Secrets*. New York: Hill and Wang, 1998.

Brown, Rabbi Dovid. *Mysteries of the Creation*. Southfield, MI: Targum Press, 1997.

Bukey, Evan Burr. *Hitler's Austria*. Chapel Hill, NC: University of North Carolina Press, 2000.

Bunim, Amos. *A Fire In His Soul*. Spring Valley, NY: Feldheim Publications, 1989.

Bunting, Medeleine. *The Model Occupation*. London: Harper Collins Publishers, 1995.

Carroll, James. *Constantine's Sword: The Church and the Jews*. Boston: Houghton Mifflin, 2001.

Chavel, Rabbi Dr. Charles B. *The Disputation at Barcelona*. New York: Shilo Publishing House, 1993.

Chazan, Aaron. *Deep in the Russian Night*. Lakewood, NJ: CIS Publishers, 1990.

Chazan, Robert. *In the Year 1096*. Philadelphia: JPS Publishing, 1997.

Chronicles: News of the Past. New York: Hemed Books, 1993.

The Complete ArtScroll Machzor — Yom Kippur. New York: ArtScroll, 1986.

The Complete ArtScroll Selichos. New York: ArtScroll, 1992.

The Complete Essays of Mark Twain. New York: Doubleday, 1963.

The Complete Service for Tishah B'Av. New York: ArtScroll, 1991.

Czech, Danuta. *Auschwitz Chronicle 1939–1945*. New York: Henry Holt and Company, 1990.

Dalfin, Chaim. *The Seven Chabad-Lubavitch Rebbes*. Northvale, NJ: Jason Aronson, 1998.

Danziger, M. Herbert. *Returning to Tradition*. New Haven: Yale University Press, 1989.

Davidowicz, Lucy S. *The War Against the Jews*. New York: Holt, Rinehart, and Winston, 1975.

Del Fuego. *Sephardim and the Holocaust*. New York: Sepher-Hermon Press, 1995.

Dimont, Max I. *Jews, God, and History*. New York: New American Library, 2003.

Directory of Day Schools in the United States and Canada. 2001 edition. New York: Torah Umesorah Publications, 2001.

Discovery. June 1996 edition. Israel: Aish HaTorah Publications, 1996.

Dubnow, Simon. *The Jews in Russia and Poland*. Philadelphia: JPS Publishing, 1918.

Eby, Cecil D. *Hungary at War*. University Park, PA: Penn State Press, 1998.

Efron, Noah. *Real Jews*. New York: Basic Books, 2003.

Eidelberg, Shlomo. *Medieval Ashkenazic Jewry*. New York: Sepher-Hermon Press, 1999.

Eisenberg, Azriel. *Jewish Historical Treasures*. New York: Bloch Publishing Company, 1968.

Eliach, Yaffa. *Hasidic Tales of the Holocaust*. New York: Oxford University Press, 1982.

——. *There Once Was a World*. New York: Little, Brown and Company, 1998.

Elias, Rabbi Joseph. *Teaching Churban Europa to Our Children*. New York: Torah Umesorah, 2001.

Encyclopaedia Judaica, 1974 Year Book. Jerusalem: Keter Publishing House, 1994.

Encyclopedia of the Holocaust. Edited by Israel Gutman. New York: Macmillan Publishing, 1990.

Epstein, Rabbi Mendel. *A Woman's Guide to the Get Process*. Israel: published by author, 1989.

Fendel, Rabbi Zechariah. *Legacy of Sinai*. New York: The RJJ School Press, 1981.

——. *The Thirteen Principles of Faith*. New York: Hashkafah Publications, 1985.

Ferguson, Niall. *The House of Rothschild: Money's Prophets 1798–1848*. New York: Viking, 1998.

Finkel, Avraham Yaakov. *The Great Torah Commentators*. Northvale, NJ: Jason Aronson, 1990.

First, Mitchell. *Jewish History in Conflict*. Northvale, NJ: Jason Aronson, 1997.

Fisch, Dov Aharoni. *Jews For Nothing*. Spring Valley, NY: Feldheim Publishers, 1984.

Fischer, Klaus P. *The History of an Obsession*. New York: Continuum, 1998.

———. *Nazi Germany: A New History*. New York: Continuum, 1995.

Fishman, Priscilla. *The Jews of the United States*. New York: Quadrangle, 1973.

Flannery, Edward H. *The Anguish of the Jews*. Mahwah, NJ: Paulist Press, 1985.

Fox, Dr. Joseph. *Rabbi Menachem Mendel of Kotzk*. New York: Bash Publications, 1988.

Frand, Rabbi Yissocher. *Rabbi Yissocher Frand in Print*. New York: Mesorah Publications, 1995.

Freedman, Samuel G. *Jew vs. Jew*. New York: Simon and Schuster, 2000.

Friedenson, Joseph, and David Kranzler. *Heroine of Rescue*. New York: Mesorah Publications, 1987.

Fromkin, David. *A Peace to End All Peace*. New York: Avon Books, 1989.

From Our Sealed Rooms. Southfiled, MI: Targum Press, 1991.

Gevirtz, Rabbi Eliezer. *L'Hovin Ul'Haskil*. New York: JEP Publications, 1980.

Gilbert, Martin. *Atlas of Jewish History*. New York: Macmillan Publishing Company, 1969.

———. *A History of the Twentieth Century*. Vol. 1, 1900–1933. New York: William Morrow and Company, 1997.

———. *The Holocaust*. New York: Holt, Rinehart and Winston, 1985.

———. *Israel*. New York: William Morrow and Company, 1998.

———. *Jerusalem in the Twentieth Century*. New York: John Wiley & Sons, 1996.

———. *The Jews in the Twentieth Century*. New York: Shocken Books, 2001.

———. *The Macmillan Atlas of the Holocaust*. New York: Macmillan Publishing Company, 1982.

Goldberg, Bernard. *Bias*. Washington, DC: Regnery Publishing, Inc. 2002.

Goldberg, Hillel. *Israel Salanter: Text, Structure, Idea*. New York: KTAV Publishing House, 1982.

Goldwurm, Rabbi Hersh. *History of the Jewish People: The Second Temple*

Era. New York: Mesorah Publications, 1982.

Gottlieb, Eli J. *The Inescapable Truth*. New York: Feldheim Publishing, 1971.

Helmreich, William B. *The World of the Yeshiva*. New York: The Free Press, 1982.

Hilberg, Raul. *The Destruction of the European Jews*. 3rd ed. New Haven: Yale University Press, 2003.

Hirsch, Rabbi Samson Raphael. *The Nineteen Letters*. New York: Feldheim Publishers, 1995.

History of the Jewish People, the Second Temple Era. New York: Mesorah Publications, 1982.

Hitler, Adolph. *Mein Kampf*. Boston: Houghton Mifflin, 1943.

The Holocaust Chronicle. Lincolnwood, IL: Publications International, Ltd., 2000.

Howe, Irving. *World of Our Fathers*. New York: Harcourt Brace Jovanovich, 1976.

Johnson, Paul. *A History of the Jews*. New York: Harper Perennial, 1987.

Kaganoff, Benzion C. *A Dictionary of Jewish Names and Their History*. Northvale, NJ: Jason Aronson, 1996.

Kaplan, Rabbi Aryeh. *Chassidic Masters*. New York: Moznaim, 1984.

———. *Handbook of Jewish Thought*. New York: Moznaim, 1979.

Karp, Abraham. *A History of the Jews in America*. Northvale, NJ: Jason Aronson, 1997.

Karp, Deborah. *Heroes of American Jewish History*. New York: KTAV Publishing Company, 1972.

Katz, Dov. *The Mussar Movement*. Tel Aviv: Orly Press, 1977.

Katz, Rabbi Mordechai. *Yesterday, Today, and Forever*. Nanuet, NY: Feldheim Publishers, 1997.

Klugman, Rabbi Eliyahu Meir. *Rabbi Samson Raphael Hirsch*. New York: Mesorah Publications, 1996.

Korn, Esther. *The Crucial Hour*. New York: Aish Yosef Publishers/Distributors, 1981.

Korobkin, N. Daniel. *The Kuzari*. Northvale, NJ: Jason Aronson, 1998.

Kranzler, David. *Thy Brothers' Blood*. New York: Mesorah Publications, 1987.

Lehmann, Meir (Marcus). *Rabbi Yoselman of Rosheim*. Nanuet, NY: Feldheim Publishers, 2002.

Lessons in Tanya. New York: Kehot Publication Society, 1999.

Levin, Meir. *Novarodok*. Northvale, NJ: Jason Aronson, 1996.

Levine, Ellen. *Darkness Over Denmark*. New York: Holiday House, 2000.

Levy, Alan. *The Wiesenthal File*. Grand Rapids, MI: William B. Eerdmans Publishing Company, 1994.

Lewis, David Levering. *Prisoners of Honor: The Dreyfus Affair*. New York: Henry Holt and Company, 1994.

Liberation 1945. Washington, DC: United States Holocaust Museum, 1995.

Lindemann, Albert S. *The Jew Accused*. New York: Cambridge University Press, 1991.

Lookstein, Haskel. *Were We Our Brothers' Keepers?* New York: Hartmore House, 1985.

Maier, Paul L. *Josephus: The Essential Works*. Grand Rapids, MI: Kregel Publications, 1994.

Massoulie, Francois. *Middle East Conflicts*. New York: Interlink Publishing Group, 1999.

Maza, Bernard. *With Fury Poured Out*. New York: Shapolsky Publishers, 1989.

Meltzer, Milton. *A History of Jewish Life From Eastern Europe to America*. Northvale, NJ: Jason Aronson, 1996.

Mendelsohn, Ezra. *The Jews of East Central Europe Between the World Wars*. Bloomington, IN: Indiana University Press, 1983.

Merling, Rabbi Beryl. *Olomeinu Gems: Stories For All Year Round*. New York: Mesorah Publications, 1987.

Meyer, Henye. *The Exiles of Crocodile Island*. New York: Mesorah Publications, 1984.

Michener, James. *The Bridge at Andau*. New York: Random House, 1957.

The Midrash Says: The Book of Shemos. New York: Bnei Yaakov Publications, 1980.

Miller, Rabbi Avigdor. *Awake My Glory*. New York: Balshon Printing and Offset Company, 1980.

———. *Behold a People*. New York: Balshon Printing and Offset Company, 1968.

———. *Sing You Righteous*. New York: Balshon Printing and Offset Company, 1973.

———. *Torah-Nation*. New York: Balshon Printing and Offset Company, 1971.

Mindel, Nissan. *Rabbi Schneur Zalman of Liadi*. 5th ed. New York: Kehot

Publication Society, 2002.

Netanyahu, Benzion. *The Origins of the Inquisition in Fifteenth Century Spain.* New York: Random House, 1995.

Neufeld, Michael J., and Michael Berenbaum. *The Bombing of Auschwitz.* New York: St. Martin's Press, 2000.

Nicholls, William. *Christian Antisemitism: A History of Hate.* New Jersey: Jason Aronson, 1993.

O'Brien, Conor Cruise. *The Siege.* New York: Simon and Schuster, 1986.

Oren, Michael B. *Six Days of War.* New York: Oxford University Press, 2002.

Oshry, Ephraim. *The Annihilation of Lithuanian Jewry.* New York: The Judaica Press, 1995.

Paldiel, Mordecai. *The Path of the Righteous: Gentile Rescuers of Jews During the Holocaust.* Hoboken, NJ: KTAV Publishing House, 1993.

Paretzky, Zev T. *Reservoirs of Faith.* Nanuet, NY: Feldheim Publishers, 1996.

Paris, Erna. *The End of Days.* Amherst, NY: Prometheus Books, 1995.

Peters, Joan. *From Time Immemorial.* New York: Harper and Row, 1984.

Power of Torah. Ben Ish Chai Anthology, vol. 8. Jerusalem: Yeshivat Ahavat Shalom Publications, 2001.

Rabinowicz, Tzvi M. *Encyclopedia of Hasidism.* Northvale, NJ: Jason Aronson, 1996.

Rabinowitz, Rabbi Chaim D. *The History of the Jewish People.* New York: Moznaim, 1998.

Rakeffet-Rothkoff, Aaron. *The Silver Era.* New York: Feldheim Publishers, 1981.

Rauschning, Hermann. *The Voice of Destruction.* New York: Putnam, 1940.

Reinman, Yaakov Y. *Destiny.* Lakewood, NJ: Olive Tree Press, 1995.

Resnick, Leibel. *A Time to Weep.* Lakewood, NJ: CIS Publishers, 1993.

Reverence, Righteousness, and Rahamanut. Edited by J. J. Schachter. Northvale, NJ: Jason Aronson, 1992.

Rossel, Seymour. *The Holocaust: The World and the Jews, 1933–1945.* West Orange, NJ: Behrman House, 1992.

Rotenberg, Rabbi Shlomo. *Am Olam.* 2 vols. New York: Keren Eliezer, 1988, 1995.

Roth, Cecil. *History of the Marranos.* New York: Shocken Books, 1974.

Rubin, Barry, and Judith Colp Rubin. *Anti-American Terrorism and the Middle*

East: A Documentary Reader. New York: Oxford University Press, 2002.

Rubinstein, William D. *The Myth of Rescue.* London: Routledge, 1997.

Sachar, Howard M. *A History of Israel.* 2nd ed. New York: Albert A. Knopf, 1996.

Schochet, Elijah Judah. *The Hasidic Movement and the Gaon of Vilna.* Northvale, NJ: Jason Aronson, 1994.

Seidman, Hillel. *The Warsaw Ghetto Diaries.* Southfield, MI: Targum Press, 1997.

Sharfman, I. Harold. *The First Rabbi.* Malibu, CA: Pangloss Press, 1988.

Sherira Gaon, Rabbi. *Iggeres D'Rabbi Sherira Gaon.* Translated by Rabbi N. D. Rabinowich. New York: Moznaim, 1988.

Shirer, William. *The Collapse of the Third Republic.* New York: Simon and Schuster, 1969.

Shulman, Yaacov Dovid. *The Chasam Sofer.* Lakewood, NJ: CIS Publishers, 1992.

Siddur Sim Shalom (Conservative). New York: The Rabbinical Assembly, United Synagogue of Conservative Judaism, 1989.

Silver, Rabbi Yehuda, and Rabbi Shaya Cohen. *Torah Min Hashamayim.*

Spier, Arthur. *The Comprehensive Jewish Calendar.* New York: Feldheim Publishers, 1986.

Steinberg, Sholom Dov and Yaakov Turnheim. *Eretz Avoseinu.* Jerusalem: Toras Chayim, 1999.

The Struggle and the Splendor. New York: Agudath Israel Publications, 1982.

A Taste of History (cookbook). Waseca, MN: Walter's Cookbooks, 1987.

Teaching about the Holocaust: A Resource Book For Educators. Washington, DC: United States Holocaust Museum.

Tokayer, Marvin, and Mary Swartz. *The Fugu Plan.* New York: Weatherhill, 1996.

Tractate Avodah Zarah. Vol. 1. New York: Schottenstein Edition of the Talmud, 2001.

Tractate Shabbos. Vol. 2. New York: Schottenstein Edition of the Talmud, Mesorah Publications, 1996.

Tractate Yoma. Vol. 1. New York: Schottenstein Edition of the Talmud, 1998.

Trepp, Leo. *A History of the Jewish Experience.* West Orange, NJ: Behrman House, 2001.

The Universal Jewish Encyclopedia. Vol. 10. New York: Universal Jewish Encyclopedia Company, 1948.

Warren, Donald. *Radio Priest*. New York: Free Press, 1996.

Wasserstein, Bernard. *Vanishing Diaspora*. Cambridge, MA: Harvard University Press, 1996.

Watt, Richard M. *Bitter Glory: Poland and Its Fate*. New York: Barnes & Noble Books, 1998.

Wein, Rabbi Berel. *Echoes of Glory*. New York, Shaar Press, 1995.

———. *Herald of Destiny*. New York: Shaar Press, 1993.

———. *Triumph of Survival*. 2nd ed. New York: Shaar Press, 1997.

Weingarten, R. *The Noda Biyehuda*. New York: CIS Publishers, 1991.

Weiser, Chaim M. *Frumspeak: The First Dictionary of Yeshivish*. Northvale, NJ: Jason Aronson, 1995.

Weiss, Rabbi Gershon. *Samson's Struggle*. Staten Island: Kol HaYeshiva Publications, 1984.

Weiss, Rabbi Moshe Meir. *A Torah Perspective for Challenging Times*. Staten Island: Published by author, 2002.

Wolpin, Nisson. *A Path Through the Ashes*. New York: Mesorah Publications, 1986.

———. *Timeless Parenting*. New York: Mesorah Publications, 2000.

———. *The Torah Personality*. New York: Mesorah Publications, 1980.

Women's Issues. Jerusalem: Ner LeElef Publications, 2002.

Wyman, David S. *The Abandonment of the Jews*. New York: Pantheon Books, 1984.

———. *The World Reacts to the Holocaust*. Baltimore: The Johns Hopkins University Press, 1996.

Wyman, David S., and Rafael Medoff. *A Race Against Death*. New York: The Free Press, 2002.

Zaitchik, Chaim Ephraim. *Sparks of Mussar*. Jerusalem: Pisgah Foundation, 1985.

Ziegler, Jean. *The Swiss, the Gold, and the Dead*. New York: Harcourt, Brace & Company, 1998.

Zimmels, Hirsch Jakob. *Ashkenazim and Sephardim*. London: Marla Publications, 1976.

Zuccotti, Susan. *Under His Very Windows*. New Haven: Yale University Press, 2000.

INDEX

A

Abahu, Rabbi, 119

Abaye and Rava, 121–122

Abba Aricha. *See* Rav

Abba Sirka, 87

Abraham, 11–12

Abramsky, Rabbi Yecheskel, 594

Abu-Chatzeira, Rabbi Yisrael, 594

Achai Gaon, Rabbi, 137

Acher, 108

Adam, 5–6

Aggripas, 82–83

Agudath Israel
    in America, 589–592
    in Europe, 344–345

Ahab, 34, 36, 37

Aharon ben Asher, 135

Aharon ben Meir, 136–137

Ahasuerus, 48

Akiva, Rabbi, 106–107, 113

Albania, Jewish survival during
    Holocaust, 502–503

Alexander the Great, 59–60

Alexander II, Czar, 283

Alexander III, Czar, 283

Alfasi, Rabbi Yitzchak, 160–161

Aliyah
    First, 314
    Second, 319–320
    Third, 360–361

Alkalai, Rabbi Judah, 313

Amalek, 30

Amei Haaretz, 73–74

Amnon, Rabbi, 150

Amon, 39

Amos, 34

Amram Gaon, Rabbi, 138

Amsterdam, 227–229

Anshei Knesses HaGedolah, 52–55

Antiochus IV, 63–65

anti–Semitism
    blood libel, 187–191, 342–343
    and Christianity, 79–80, 181–197,
    523–524, 582
    England, 187–188, 345

France, 339–340

Germany, 404–405

Protocols of the Elders of Zion, 286–287

Spain, 198–199

United States, 345–346, 375–377, 383–385, 420, 571

Appolonius, 66

Arizal, 212–214

Arlosoroff, Chaim, 364

Asa, 36

Asarah Harugei Malchus, 106

Asher ben Yechiel. *See* Rosh

Ashi, Rabbi 122

Ashkenazim, origins of , 146–147

Athaliah, 36

Attia, Rabbi Ezra, 594

Auerbach, Rabbi Shlomo Zalman, 593–594

Austria
  Jewish survival during Holocaust, 491–492
  Nazi rule of, 416–417

Av, Fifteenth of, 110

Av, Ninth of, 89–90
  See also Betar; Holy Temple, First; Holy Temple, Second

Azariah, 45

B

Bach, 223

Baal HaTurim, 179–180

Baal Shem Tov, Rabbi Israel, 245–246

Baal Teshuvah movement, 572–573, 585–586

Baalei Tosafos, 173–174

Babi Yar, 447–449

Babylonian Exile
  after First Holy Temple, 44–51
  after Second Holy Temple, 116–118

Babylonian Talmud. *See* Talmud, Babylonian

Bachya, Rabbi Ibn Pakudah, 161–162

Beis HaMikdash. *See* Holy Temple

Baithusim. *See* Sadducees

Balfour Declaration, 348–349

Bamos, 26–27, 38
  Hezikia, role in abolishing, 37

Bar Kamtza, 85–86

Bar Kochba, 104

Bar Yochai, Rabbi Shimon, 110

Barak, Ehud 634

Begin, Menachem, 604–605, 616–617

Ben Abuyah, Elisha,108

Ben Ish Chai, 312

Ben Naftali, 136

Ben Zakkai, Jochanan. *See* Jochanan Ben Zakkai

Benjamin, 16

Ben-Yehuda, Eliezer, 316–317

Betar, 104–105

Beth Jacob
  in America, 564–565
  in Europe, 369–370

Bilu, 314–315

Birobidzhan, 355

Boaz, 29

Bormann, 443

British rule of Israel, 355–357
    See also Balfour Declaration

Bulgaria, Jewish survival during
    Holocaust, 501–502

Bund, 324–325

Bustenai, 131–132

C

Cain, 6

Calendar, Jewish, 7–8, 10, 56–57
    fixing of, 120–121
    dispute, 136–137

Camp David, 634–635

Chabad, 310–311, 566, 567, 586–587

Chacham Tzvi, 241–242

Chafetz Chaim, 311–312

Chanan of Ashkaya, Rabbi 127

Chananel, 158–159

Channel Islands, Jewish survival
    during Holocaust, 503–504

Chanukah, 67–69
    See also Hasmoneans

Chasam Sofer, 265–266

Chassidim
    communities in America, 565–567
    conflict with Vilna Gaon, 250–253
    expansion of in 1800s, 305–310
    rise of, 245

Chaverim. See Pharrisees

Chazon Ish, 364

Chinuch Atzmai, 565

Chiyya, Rabbi, 117

Chmielnicki Massacres, 231–233

Chonyo, 31, 63–64

Christianity
    domination of Israel, 119–120
    origins of, 108–109
    See also Yeshu

Claudius, 82–83

Cohen, Eli, 574–575

Communism, and Russia, 351–354

community organizations, 380,
    570–571

Conservative Judaism, 268, 567– 568,
    595–596, 611–612

conversion, forced, 199, 201–203

Creation, 5, 8

Crusades 182–187

Cutheans, 57–58

Cyrus, 47–48

Czechoslovakia
    Jewish survivial during Holocaust,
    493–494
    Nazi rule of, 417

D

Daf Yomi, 125, 370, 589–591

Damaskinos, Archbishop, 484–485

Daniel, 47

Darius I, 47

David, King, 32

death camps, 453–468

death march, 525–526

Deborah, 28

DeHaan, Jacob, 364

Denmark, Jewish survival during Holocaust, 499–501

discrimination. *See* anti-Semitism

Don Joseph Nasi, 217

Donna Gracia Mendes, 217

Drachman, Rabbi Bernard, 334–335

Dreyfus, Alfred, 338–342

Duckwitz, Georg, 500

E

Egypt, peace agreement with Israel, 606–607

Egypt
exodus from, 19–21
slavery, 18–20

Ehud, 28

Eichmann, Adolph, 406, 491, 496–498, 530

Eiger, Rabbi Akiva, 265–260

Einsatzgruppen, 444–450

Elazar ben Azaria, Rabbi, 101

Elazar ben Shamua, 108

Elazar ben Yair, 91
See also Masada; Zealots

Elazar HaModai, Rabbi, 104

Eldad HaDani, 135

Eli, 29

Eliezer, Rabbi, 99–100

Emden, Rabbi Yaakov, 239–240

Enlightenment, 287–290

Enoch, 6

Entebbe, 604–605

Essenes, 73–75

See also Yeshu

Esther, Book of, 48–50

Ettlinger, Rabbi Yaakov, 264

Evil Merodach, 45–46

Exodus, 540–541
See also Egypt, exodus from

Expulsions, 194–195
See also Spanish Inquisition

Eybeschutz, Rabbi Yonason, 239–240

Ezekiel, 44–51

Ezra, 51–52

F

Feinstein, Rabbi Moshe, 593

Fleischmann, Gisi, 494

Flood, 6–7

Florus, 83–84

France, Jewish survival during Holocaust, 492–493

French Revolution, 255

G

Gamliel, Rabban, 99–100

Gedaliah, 42–43

German political power, 469

German victories in Poland, 440–441

Germany
anti-Semitism, 404–405
Emancipation, 259
invasion of Poland, 440–441
invasion of Soviet Union, 442
Jewish life in the Middle Ages, 152–155
Jewish survival during the

Holocaust, 490–491
political situation before the
Holocaust, 405–408
post-Holocaust, 532–533
Gershom Meor Hagolah, Rabbi,
159–160
ghettoes, 220–221
during the Holocaust, 431–440
Warsaw Ghetto Uprising, 473
Gideon, 28
Goebbels, Joseph, 413, 443
Goering, Hermann, 413
Goldstein, Baruch, 629
Goldstein, Rabbi Herbert S., 335–336
Gra, 243–245
Greece, Jewish survival during
Holocaust, 494
Greek culture, 62–63
See also Hellenists
Gulf War, 624–625

H

Habbakuk, 47
Hadrian, 102–104
Haganah, 538–539
Haggai, 50
Hai Gaon, Rabbi, 126, 139–140
Ham, 6–7
Hananiah ben Tradyon, Rabbi, 107
Hananiah, 45
Hanina ben Hachinai, Rabbi, 108
HaReuveni, 216
Hasmoneans
Judah HaMacabee 66–67

Mattisyahu, 65–66
revolt, 64–66, 72
rule of, 71
Hellenists, 62–63
Heller, Rabbi Yom Tov Lipman, 231
Helmrich, Eberhard, 483–484
Herod, 75–76
Herzl, Theodore, 317–318
Heydrich, Reinhard, 413, 443–444,
450, 491
Hezekiah, 37
Hillel, 77–78
Himmler, Heinrich, 412–413, 443, 491
Hirsch, Rabbi Shimshon Raphael,
262–264
Hitler, Adolph
biography of, 408–409
political power, 409–410
See also Nazi party
Ho, Feng Shan, 482–483
Holocaust
denial of, 533
Final Solution, 442–443, 450–451
Jewish thought, 392–402
philosophical questions, 405–406
political reasons, 406– 408
reparations from Germany,
558–559
righteous gentiles, 479–486
survivors, 527–529
Wannsee conference, 450–451
See also death camps; Hitler,
Adolph; Nazi party; resistance
during Holocaust; names of
specific countries

Holy Temple, First
  building of, 33
  destruction of, 47
  in comparison to Second, 95
  See also Av, Ninth of

Holy Temple, Second
  building of, 50–51
  destruction of, 82–89
  Jewish calendar, 92
  Jewish disunity, 84–85
  See also Av, Ninth of

Hosea ben Elah, 34

Hovovei Zion, 314–315

Hungary
  Jewish life in, 372–375
  Jewish survival during the
    Holocaust, 494–499

Hutzpith HaMeturgeman, Rabbi 108

Hyrcanus, 71–72

I

Ibn Chiyug, Yehuda, 150

Ibn Ezra, 149, 165–166

Ibn Gabirol, 149

Ibn Labrat, Donash, 150

Ibn Saruk, 150

Ibn Shaprut, 148

Idolatry, 6, 11, 37
  abolishing of, 54

intifada, 620, 634–635

Irgun, 538–539

Isaac, 13–16

Isaiah, 35, 37, 39, 48

Islam
  fundamentalism, 612–613
  relations with Jews, 129–131
  rise of, 128

Israel
  biblical conquest of, 25
  British rule of, 355–357
  creation of State, 541–545
  political parties, 361–362

Isserlein, Israel, Rabbi, 180

Isserles, Rabbi Moshe, 222

Italy
  Jews in the Middle Ages, 144
  Jewish survival during Holocaust,
    502

J

Jabal, 6

Jacob Frank, 345–346

Jacob, 14–17

Jannai, 72

Japan, Jewish survival during
    Holocaust, 504–505

Japheth, 6–7

Jason, 63–64

Jeconiah, 46

Jehoiakim, 40–41

Jehoiachin, 41

Jehoshaphat, 36

Jephthah, 28

Jeremiah, 42
  prophecy of, 46

Jeroboam, 33–34

Jeshevav the Scribe, Rabbi, 108

Jesus. *See* Yeshu

Jezebel, 34

Joash, 36

Jochanan Ben Zakkai, 87–89, 97–98

Jochanan, Rabbi, 119

Jonah, 34

Jonah, Rabbi, 176

Jordan, peace with, 628

Joselman of Rosheim, Rabbi, 219

Joseph ben Tuvia, 60

Joseph, 17

Joseph, Rabbi Jacob, 332–334

Josephus, 93

Joshua, 25

Joshua, Rabbi, 100–103

Josiah, 40

Jotham, 37

Jubal, 6

Judah ben Bava, Rabbi, 107

Judah ben Damah, 108

Judah Berabbi Ilai, 110

Judah HaChasid, Rabbi 152

Judah HaLevi, Rabbi 166–167

Judah HaNasi, Rabbi, 111, 115
    See also Oral Law

Judah Nesiah, 116

Judah, Kingdom of, 35–37

Judges, rule of, 27–29

K

Kalischer, Rabbi Zvi Hirsch, 313

Kaminetzky, Rabbi Yaakov, 593

Kamtza, 85–86

Kanievsky, Rabbi Yaakov Yisrael, 364, 594

Karaites, 132

Karo, Rabbi Joseph, 214

Kasztner, Rudolph, 497–498, 520, 559

Kelm, 301–302

Ketzos HaChoshen, 242–243

Khazars, 135–136

Kochba, Shimon Bar, 104

Kotler, Rabbi Aharon, 517, 563–565

Kotzk, Rebbe of, 306–308

Kowalski, Wladyslaw, 484

Krystallnacht, 417–420

Kuzari, 166

L

Laban, 16

Lakish, Rabbi Shimon, 119

Lamech, 6

Lebanon
    Israeli withdrawal from, 634
    war with Israel, 614–615

Liberation, 526–527

Luther, Martin, 405

Lutz, Carl, 482

Luzzatto, Rabbi Moshe Chaim. *See* Ramchal

M

Machir, Rabbi, 143

Maharal, 225

Maharsha, 222–223

Maharshal, 223

Malachi, 50

Malbim, 266

Manasseh, 39

Martha bas Beothus, 87

Martin Luther, 219–220

Marx, Karl, 259–260

Masada, 91–92
　See also suicide in Jewish law

Maskilim, 261–262

Meir, Rabbi Lublin, 223

Meir, Rabbi, 108

Meiri, 143, 178

Meltzer, Rabbi Isser Zalman, 364

Mendlowitz, Rabbi Shraga Feivel, 564

Mendelssohn, Moses, 257–259

Men of the Great Assembly, 52–55

Mishael, 45

mishkan, 25, 27

Mishnah, 112–113
　See also Oral Law

Mizrachi movement, 322–323, 362

Mohammed, 129–130

Molcho, Shlomo, 216–217

Montefiore, Sir Moses, 272–274, 314

Mordecai, 49

Moshe of Kalonymous, Rabbi, 144

Mussar movement, 296–299
　opposition to, 304–305
　See also Kelm; Novarodok; Slabodka

N

Nagybaczoni, Vilmos Nagy, 485

Napoleon, 256–257

Nassan, Rabbi, 161

Nazi party
　founding of, 409
　ideology, 390–392, 402–403
　leaders, 412–413
　political expansion, 416–417
　political power, 410–412
　propaganda, 413–414

Nebuchadnezzar, 41–43

Nehemiah, 52

Netherlands, Jewish survival during the Holocaust, 293

New York
　beginnings of Jewish life, 230
　Chief Rabbi, 332–336
　demographics, 381–382

Nicholas I, Czar, 279–283

Nissim, Rabbi, 179

Noah, 6–7

Noda B'Yehudah, 243

Novarodok, 302–304

Nuremberg laws, 411–412

Nuremberg trials, 529–530

O

Ohr HaChaim HaKodosh, 241

Oral Law
　arrangement of, 54
　writing of, 111–113

Oshiya, Rabbi, 117

Oslo accords, 625–626, 630–631

P

Palmach, 538–539

Petronius, 81–82

Pharisees, 73

philanthropy, 379–380

PLO 573, 625–628
See also terrorism

Pnei Yehoshua, 242

Poland
invasion by Germany, 429–431
Jewish life in, 1500s, 221–225
Jewish life pre-Holocaust, 364–367
Jewish survival during Holocaust 487–489
religious life, 368–489

Pontius Pilate, 81

Prague, 225–226

prayer
formalization of, 53
prayer book, 127, 133–134

printing press, 218

procurators, 81–84

prophecy, 38
end of, 55

Protestant Reformation, 219–220

Protocols of the Elders of Zion, 286–287

Purim, 48, 50

Q

Quietus, 102

R

Raavad III, 172–173

Rabanan Savoroi, 123–124

Rabbeinu Tam, 167–168

Radak, 173

Rambam, 169–172

Ramban, 174–176
disputation with priest, 195–197

Ramchal, 240–241

Rashba, 178

Rashbam, 167

Rashi, 162–165

Rav, 117–118

Rebecca, 17

Reform Judaism, 267, 595–596, 611–612
movement against in America, 267–270
movement against in Europe, 262
origins of, 260

Rehoboam, 33–36

Resh Lakish, 119, 126–127

Resh Galusa, 117

resistance during Holocaust, 471–479
in the United States, 509–516, 521–523
Orthodox efforts, 516–519

Ritva, 178–179

Romania, Jewish survival during Holocaust, 489–490

Rosh, 177–178

Rothenberg, Rabbi Meir of, 176–177

Rothschild family, 270–272

Russia
    discrimination against Jews, 286
    Enlightenment, 287
    Jewish life in 1800s, 275–279
    pogroms, 283–286, 337–338

S

Saadiah Gaon, 138–139

Sadat, Anwar, 606

Sadducees, 73–74

Salanter, Rabbi Israel, 297–301

Samaritans, 57–58

Samson, 29

Samuel, 29

Saul, 29–31
    See also suicide in Jewish Law

Schenirer, Sarah, 269–270
    See also Beth Jacob

Schindler, Oskar, 483

Schneerson, Rabbi Joseph Yitzchak, 566

Schneerson, Rabbi Menachem Mendel, 566–567

Schmid, Anton, 483

Seleucid rule, 63

Sephardim, 385–388
    origins of, 146–147
    treatment of in Israel, 556–557

Shaagas Aryeh, 242

Shelah HaKadosh, 230–231

Shabsai Tzvi, 233–235

Shach, 231

Shach, Rabbi Elazar M., 595, 617–618

Shammai, 77–79

Shapiro, Rabbi Meir, 370

Shem, 6–7

Shemariah, Rabbi, 141

Shemaya and Avtalyon, 75

Sherira Gaon, Rabbi, 139

Shibata, Mitsugi, 505

Shimon bar Yochai, 110

Shimon ben Shatach, 73

Shimon HaGadol, Rabbi, 151

Shimon HaTzadik, 58–60

Shimon Kayara, 137

Shimon, Rabbi ben Gamliel HaNasi, 107–108

Shlomis, 72–73

Shlomtzion HaMalka. *See* Shlomis

shmittah 7–8

Shmuel HaNagid, 148–149

Shmuel, 118

Shulchan Aruch, 214–215

Sugihara, Chiune, 481

Sinai War, 560–561

Six-Day War, 575–581

Slabodka, 302

Solomon, 33

Soloveitchik, Rabbi Chaim, 295–296

Soloveitchik, Rabbi Joseph Ber, 568

Sonnenfeld, Rabbi Chaim, 363

Soviet Union
    emigration from 583–585
    fall of, 623
    Jewish life in 562–563, 613–614
    Jewish survival during Holocaust, 489

Spain, Golden Age of, 145–146, 155–156

Spanish Inquisition, 203–210

St. Louis, 421–422

Stern Gang, 539

Sternbuch, Isaac, 519–521

Sternbuch, Recha, 520

suicide
in Jewish Law, 94
at Masada, 91

Switzerland, banks, 532–533

Syria, peace talks with, 628–629

T

tabernacle. See mishkan

Talmud, Jerusalem, 120

Talmud, Babylonian, 120, 122–125

Talmud
burning of, 195
censorship by Christians, 217–218
forgery, 338–339

Tammuz, seventeenth of, 89

Taz, 231

Teitelbaum, Rabbi Joel, 566, 593

Temple. See Holy Temple

Ten Martyrs, 106

Ten Tribes, 34–35

terrorism, Arab, 357–359, 601–603, 619, 629–630

Teves, tenth of, 41

Tishah B'Av. See Av, Ninth of

Titus, 89–91, 98

Toledano, Rabbi Raphael B., 594

Trajan, 101–102

Tress, Rabbi Elimelech, 517

Tubal Cain, 6

Tzadokim. See Sadducees

Tzadok, Rabbi, 88

Tzedaka, Rabbi Yehuda, 594

Tzefas, 212

Tzom Gedaliah, 43

U

United Nations
anti-Semitism, 603–604
partition plan, 541–542
resolution number 242, 581

United States
early Jewish settlement in, 253–254
Jewish immigration to, 325–332
Jews in politics, 381
religious life, 382
See also anti-Semitism in United States; New York

Uzziah, 35

V

Versailles, Treaty of, 350–351

Vilna Gaon, 243–245

Vespasian, 85–86

Volozhin, 292–293

W

Wachsman, Nachshon, 630

Wallenberg, Raul, 481

War of Attrition, 581

War of Independence, 543–549

Weissmandl, Rabbi Michael Ber, 494, 520

West Bank, religious settlement in, 596–597

World War I, 346–348

Wye Accords, 633

Y

Yavneh, 95–106

Yehuda HaChasid, Rabbi, 238–239

Yehudai Gaon, Rabbi, 137

Yemenites, 558

Yeshiva University, 568

yeshivos
Chassidic, 294–295, 372–374
Lithuanian, 293–294, 370–374
Hungarian, 294, 372–374

Yeshu, 79–80

Yiddish
origins of, 237–238
secular culture, 378–379

Yishmael Kohen Gadol, Rabbi, 107–108

Yom Kippur War, 597–601

Young Israel, 382–383

Z

Zealots, 82, 85, 91, 92, 95, 97

Zedekiah, 41

Zegota, 485–486

Zerachiah HaLevi, 173

Zionism
Arab opposition to, 323–324
First Zionist Congress, 318– 319
Jewish opposition to, 320–322
revisionist, 361–362
roots of, 315

Zola, Emile, 341–342

In Appreciation

Mr. and Mrs. Leroy Harris
Pittsburgh, Pa.

לזכר נשמת

Father — זעליג בן שמחה
Mother — זיסקא בת יעקב
Brother — שמחה בן זעליג
Father-In-Law — יצחק בן זעליג

In Appreciation

Dr. and Mrs. Emanuel Kanal
Pittsburgh, Pa.

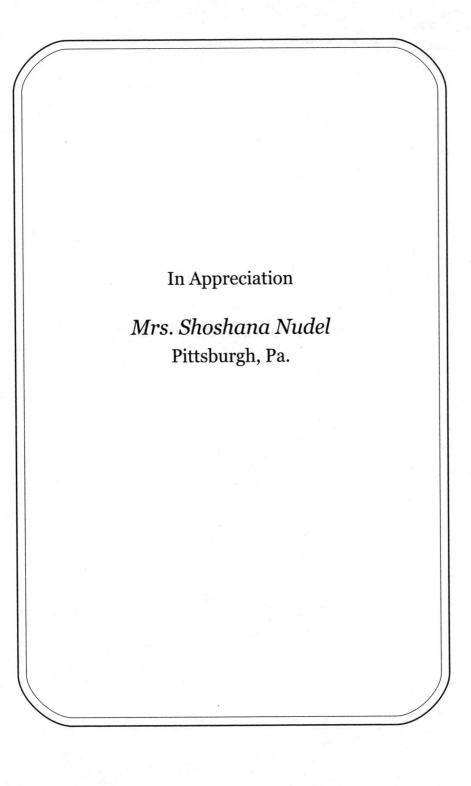

In Appreciation

Mrs. Shoshana Nudel
Pittsburgh, Pa.

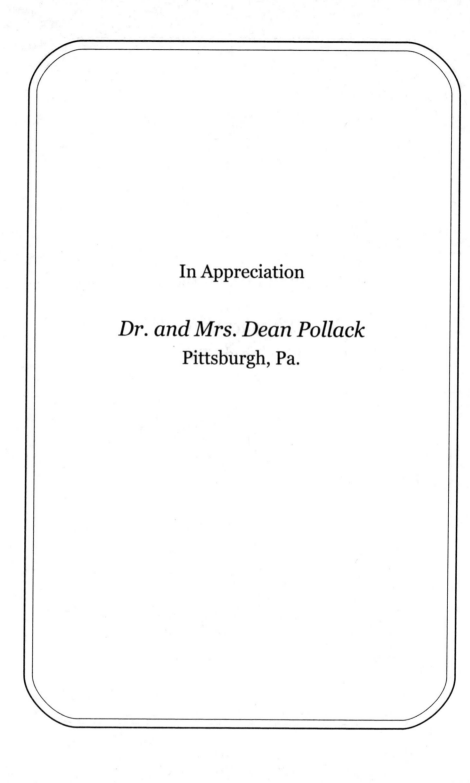

In Appreciation

Dr. and Mrs. Dean Pollack
Pittsburgh, Pa.

In Appreciation

Mr. Joshua Rosenbloom
Silver Spring, Md.

In Appreciation

Rabbi Amiel and Dr. Isabel Rosenbloom
St. Louis, Mo.

In Honor of Our Children

Matis and Ruchama Miller
Avi Rosenbloom
Aharon Rosenbloom

In Appreciation

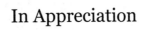
Pittsburgh, Pa.

In Appreciation

Mr. and Mrs. Norman A. Sindler
Pittsburgh, Pa.

In Memory of

Morris Sindler — ל׳ חשון תש״ך
Rose Stein Sindler — י״ב חשון תשכ״ג

Greatly Admired and Sorely Missed

Norman A. Sindler, Son

In Appreciation

Mr. and Mrs. Parke Americus
Pittsburgh, Pa.

In Appreciation

Mr. and Mrs. Jay Angel
Pittsburgh, Pa.

In Appreciation

Dr. and Mrs. Alan Itskowitz
Pittsburgh, Pa.

In Appreciation

Mr. David Nadoff and Family
Pittsburgh, Pa.

עטרת זקנים בני בנים ותפארת בנים אבותם

In Memory of Our Parents

יהודה ליב בן יעקב — *Leo Unger*

רבקה בת ישראל — *Freda Unger*

מאיר יעקב קאפל בן ירוחם פישל — *Meyer Pfeffer*

חנה אסתר בת יצחק — *Chana Esther Pfeffer*

יהי זכרם ברוך

Murray and Elvira Pfeffer

In Appreciation

Mr. Joel Pfeffer and
Congregation Poale Zedeck
Pittsburgh, Pa.

In Memory of

ר' יוסף בן אהרן טאמבאסקי ע"ה
Joseph Tombosky

July 20, 2001 - נפטר כ"ט תמוז תשס"א

By Alan and Joyce Tombosky

Dedicated to the memory of my brother,
Fred Wachs.
A kind and gentle soul.

Dr. Hirsh and Trudy Wachs

STAR WRECK

The Series

The Series

The spacy spoofs
that dare to boldly go
where nobody wanted to go before

LEAH REWOLINSKI

ILLUSTRATIONS BY
HARRY TRUMBORE

A 2M COMMUNICATIONS LTD. PRODUCTION

B⬛XTREE

Star Wreck: The Series first published in Great Britain in 1994 by Boxtree Limited, Broadwall House, 21 Broadwall, London SE1 9PL.

Star Wreck: The Generation Gap first published in the United States in 1989 by Excellent Word Services. Second edition published in 1990 by St Martin's Press. *Star Wreck II* and *Star Wreck III* first published in the United States in 1992 by St Martin's Press. *Star Wreck IV* and *Star Wreck V* first published in the United States in 1993 by St Martin's Press.

All five *Star Wreck* novels first published in Great Britain in 1993 by Boxtree Limited.

ISBN: 0 7522 0830 6

Printed in Great Britain by Redwood Books, Trowbridge, Wiltshire

A CIP catalogue entry for this book is available from the British Library

10 9 8 7 6 5 4 3 2 1

Acknowledgments

For research assistance, thanks to Rachel Pearson, as well as two staffers of the Milwaukee Public Library who went to great lengths checking the spelling of Murl Duesing's name.

Thanks to those who evaluated *Star Wreck* in its previous life as a screenplay, suggesting subtle improvements ("Have you considered giving it a plot?") and evaluating the author ("You're warped!")

Thanks to my parents, who taught us to talk back to the television long before it was fashionable.

Finally, thanks to all those who created the original TV series and movies, for there can be no spoof without a spoo-fee.

Contents

Star Wreck: The Generation Gap 9

Star Wreck II: The Attack of the Jargonites 99

Star Wreck III: Time Warped 199

Star Wreck IV: Live Long and Profit 319

Star Wreck V: The Undiscovered Nursing Home ... 451

STAR WRECK
THE GENERATION GAP

". . . Its mission: to cruise around the universe looking for new predicaments to get into. To search the outskirts of the galaxy for areas with less crowding, lower tax rates and better schools. To boldly go where nobody wanted to go before!"

That doesn't sound too exciting to Captain James T. Smirk and his crew when they're assigned to team up with their "next generation" counterparts. But before you can say, "I'm a doctor, not a Jacuzzi attendant," they all run into the Cellulites – warped survivors of a centuries-old dieting program gone wrong. They're big, bad, bowlegged – and more dangerous than a Snot-cruiser full of Sinusoids!

1

Take Off, Eh

"CAPTAIN'S TOP-SECRET diary, Star Date 2323.2323232323 . . ."

The captain took a deep breath and continued. " . . . 2323 ½.

"Dear Diary: It's good to be back aboard the Endocrine, though I do have some qualms about sharing the helm with another captain."

Capt. Jean-Lucy Ricardo pressed the "pause" button on his Dictaphone and surveyed the Bridge. Leadership came naturally to him. He stood out among the crew members, with his commanding presence, authoritative voice and bald head.

His crew bustled around the Bridge, preparing for launch. The color of their uniforms indicated their function in the mission: red for commanding officers, blue for support staff, orange for Personnel Department, yellow for Marketing, and black pinstripes for Accounting. Many of them wore miniskirts, including some of the women.

Capt. Ricardo resumed his dictation.

"Nevertheless, I will do my best to comply with Starfreak's order to share this mission with Capt. Smirk." Capt. Ricardo pressed the "pause" button again and muttered, "That old goat."

All of Starfreak Command had been surprised when Capt.

11

James T. Smirk and his crew suddenly came out of retirement. Starfreak Command was even more surprised when Capt. Smirk insisted on sharing this mission with the current crew of the USS Endocrine. It was an offer Starfreak couldn't refuse, since Smirk owned a majority interest in its stock.

Ricardo sighed. Time to get down to business. He began the status check with his Bridge officers.

"Counselor Troit, have you finished testing the psychological readiness of the crew?"

"They're all eager to go, captain," she replied, then lowered her voice and added, "except for the little matter of the intense hostility, insane jealousy and deeply rooted territoriality which we all feel toward Capt. Smirk's crew, as you and I discussed yesterday."

Counselor Deanna Troit was extraordinarily sensitive to others' emotions, thanks to her Betavoid heritage. The talent had earned her the post of Ship's Shrink. It also came in handy for judging aliens the Endocrine encountered during its missions. Troit could tell whether they came in peace or had some ulterior motive, like trying to sell the crew a set of encyclopedias.

"Forget the hostility for now, counselor," the captain replied, his jaw clenched. "We're all adults here, and if a bunch of space jockeys who've spent the last 80 years lollygagging around suddenly want to take over our ship . . . "—his voice had been rising; he paused and shook his head to calm himself—" I'm sure we can handle this like reasonable human beings."

Troit shrugged and turned away briskly. A moment later, her ample bosom caught up with the rest of her body and turned away also. She sat down in one of the three command chairs at the center of the Bridge.

Capt. Ricardo resumed his status check.

"Have the on-board preparations been completed, Number 1?"

Commander Wilson Piker, your basic tall, dark and handsome hunk, was standing at the rear of the Bridge. He stepped dramatically down the curved ramp to the command center and stopped in front of Capt. Ricardo. With feet planted apart, shoulders squared, head cocked to one side and hands clenched into fists, Piker announced, "Ready, sir!"

Capt. Ricardo stared at him for a long moment, contemplating the key role his First Officer played in the ship's operations. Whenever a crisis arose, Piker was always the first to step forward and strike a dramatic pose.

Ricardo was more than satisfied with Piker's on-the-job performance, but often he wished Piker wasn't quite so . . . so . . . generic. The quality had earned him the nickname of Number 1.

Ricardo turned to the forward section of the Bridge. Seated at a console on the right was Lieutenant Commander Dacron, an android who looked amazingly human except for one teeny detail: his skin was as white as a sheet.

"Status report, Mr. Dacron," the captain ordered.

"Ground crew reports loading is completed, sir," Dacron replied.

At a similar console to the left was the ship's pilot, Ensign Westerly Flusher. Westerly was the youngest acting ensign in Starfreak and the only starship pilot with a bedtime curfew. Westerly checked and rechecked his console, trying not to look cute.

"Engineering," said Capt. Ricardo to the intercom, everything set for takeoff?"

"Ready to go, captain," replied Lt. Georgie LaForgery from his post in the Engine Room.

Georgie had recently been promoted to chief engineer, a highly technical position which required him to wheel his chair around so he could press buttons on several consoles. It was a big step up from his previous job of ship's pilot, for which he'd had only one console and a chair that was bolted to the floor,

Capt. Ricardo thought back to the day he and Georgie met, shortly after Starfreak had assigned him his crew. When he realized that his new pilot was blind, he nearly swallowed his teeth.

But Georgie had worked out fine. His visual prosthesis, which looked like a cross between wrap-around sunglasses and a radiator, enabled him to see through solid objects and determine their chemical composition. Thus, he was the only crew member aware of the mechanical principles used in Counselor Troit's underwire bra.

At the communication post toward the rear of the Bridge, a phone rang. Lt. Wart picked up the receiver. Across his chest was a gold sash reading "Mr. Universe, A.D. 2368." The Kringle listened to the caller, grunted, and hung up.

"Captain," he announced, "the old farts . . . er, our new crewmates have boarded."

"Very well, Mr. Wart," said the captain. "Ensign Flusher, initiate launch sequence."

"Aye, sir," Westerly replied.

The precocious youngster was well prepared for this complex task. On the console in front of him was a button with a picture of a key on it. Westerly pressed it. The Endocrine's engine turned over.

"Launch sequence initiated, sir," Westerly said.

"Engage!" ordered the captain.

Westerly pressed a button showing an arrow pointing upward.

The USS Endocrine rose from the launch pad and headed into the sky.

"Set course bearing 100.7 mark 3.14. Speed: Warped 3."

"Aye, sir," Westerly replied, pressing more buttons.

In the darkness of space, the ship's thrusters glowed as the

It was the usual backup at the
subspace on-ramp.

engine kicked in. The ship blasted away, leaving behind only dual streaks of light from the thrusters.

Stars dotted the vast blackness surrounding them. Planets moved by in graceful orbits. From somewhere in the depths of space came the haunting notes of a musical introduction.

"Space," intoned Capt. Ricardo. There was a long pause.

"The final frontier," Piker provided in a stage whisper.

"What?" grunted Ricardo. "What did you say, Number 1?"

"Your line, sir," Piker offered. "The line goes, 'Space, the final frontier'."

"That's not what I was going to say," Ricardo growled.

"Oh. Sorry, sir."

"Now, where was I?" Ricardo continued. "Ah, yes. Space. We need more of it. The universe is getting more crowded by the minute."

As he spoke, the Endocrine ran into a traffic jam. It was the usual backup at the subspace onramp.

The Endocrine crawled along with the merging traffic: starships, satellites, a blimp, the Wicked Witch of the West riding her broom, flying superheroes, and a Snoopy balloon from Macy's Thanksgiving parade. An overhead sign read "Vehicles under Warped 5, use right lane."

As traffic began moving freely again, Capt. Ricardo continued his narrative.

"These are the voyages of the Starship Endocrine. Its mission: to cruise around the universe looking for novel predicaments to get into. To search the outskirts of the galaxy for areas with less crowding, lower tax rates and better schools. To boldly go where nobody wanted to go before!"

The Endocrine moved into the express lane ("Ships with more than 1,000 passengers only.") It took off with a roar, defying conventional wisdom that sound cannot travel through the vacuum of outer space.

2

Meet Your Mates

"**A**LL RIGHT!" CAPT. Ricardo rubbed his hands together, trying to look enthusiastic. With the arrival of Lt. LaForgery and Dr. Cape Pragmatski, all his senior officers were on the Bridge. "We're about to meet the crew of the original Endocrine, so look sharp, everyone."

"Sir?" ventured Westerly.

"Yes, ensign?"

"I don't get it," Westerly said. "The original crew flew their missions over 80 years ago. How can they still be alive?"

"There's been a lot of speculation about that around Star-freak Headquarters ever since they came out of retirement," Capt. Ricardo admitted. "I'm hoping Capt. Smirk will let us in on their secret of eternal youth."

"I'm interested in that myself," said Dr. Pragmatski. "I'd like to run complete medical checks on everyone in Capt. Smirk's crew."

"That won't be necessary, doctor," Capt. Ricardo said. "Capt. Smirk brought aboard his own physician, Dr. McCaw, who will conduct their physicals."

Dr. Pragmatski bristled. "His own physician? In *my* Sick Bay?"

"That brings up an issue you're all going to have to deal with," said Capt. Ricardo, addressing the entire crew. "There's

17

some duplication in our combined staffs, so many of you will share your responsibilities with your counterparts on Capt. Smirk's team."

This announcement prompted some grumbling. Ricardo glanced at Troit, standing next to him. Her expression told him he was on shaky ground with the crew.

He squared his shoulders and continued in a shrill tone, "You've all taken an oath to Starfreak. Let's show some loyalty. Remember our common goal: to seek out underdeveloped real estate all over the galaxy—to boldly go where nobody wanted to go before."

The grumbling grew louder. Troit shook her head slightly. "They're not buying it," she muttered.

"All right, listen up!" Capt. Ricardo ordered. "Does the term 'hostile takeover' mean anything to you?" The room grew silent except for the snapping of Westerly's gum.

Capt. Ricardo's expression was stern. "Right now Capt. Smirk owns a controlling interest in Starfreak. If for some reason he's unhappy—if this mission isn't the fun fling he expects it to be, for example—he'll sell out.

"There's a rumor on the street that the Sinusoids would be only too happy to buy into the corporation. They've got the cash to do it, too. So unless you'd like to spend the rest of your career in a Snotcruiser, let's try to keep Smirk's people happy, all right?"

Lt. Wart, standing at his communication post, announced, "Sir, Capt. Smirk and his crew are approaching the Bridge in the Crewmover."

"All right, everyone, this is it," said Capt. Ricardo, nervously tugging at his tunic. Wart, Westerly and Dacron left their posts to join him and the others at the center of the Bridge.

The door of the Crewmover, the Endocrine's subway system, opened onto the Bridge. Capt. Smirk strode out, his crew trailing behind.

The two captains shook hands. "Welcome to the Bridge, Capt. Smirk," said Capt. Ricardo.

"Capt. Jean-Lucy Ricardo. It's a pleasure to meet you," Capt. Smirk replied. "I've heard so much about you. It's wonderful to know the Endocrine is in such capable hands." *Hmmm*, thought Smirk. *He may be 60 years younger than me, but at least I still have my hair.*

"Thank you," Capt. Ricardo acknowledged. He was surprised by Capt. Smirk's friendliness. Was this some kind of ploy?

"Allow me to introduce my crew," said Capt. Smirk, "the galaxy's original well-balanced, multiethnic, equal opportunity team." Capt. Smirk hoped they'd remember his instructions to lighten up a little. This trip could be as much fun as the old days if they'd just learn to hang loose.

"First," said Capt. Smirk, "representing the Vultures, my science officer, main man and all-around brilliant guy, Mr. Smock." Mr. Smock nodded to Capt. Ricardo without a word.

Oh well, Smock never was Mr. Charm, thought Capt. Smirk, *but the rest of the crew ought to be more outgoing.* As Capt. Smirk introduced the others, they each stepped forward in turn.

"Representing the British Isles, my chief engineer, Mr. Snot." Mr. Snot's kilt swayed as he managed a stiff bow.

"Representing the Far East: Mr. Zulu." Zulu's Oriental features, normally friendly and open, were a lot less scrutable at the moment, Smirk noticed.

"Representing Moscow, Stalingrad, Siberia, and lots of other drab, Godforsaken, frigid regions that no other major world power wanted: Mr. Checkout." Smirk's grin grew a little more strained as the joke fell flat.

"Representing wry, grizzled people of all nations, our medical officer, Dr. McCaw—or as he is affectionately known, 'Moans'." Dr. McCaw scowled in their general direction.

"And finally, our two-for-one crew member, representing

both Blacks and women, Lt. Yoohoo." Yoohoo gave them a polite but cool nod.

Well, that was a bust, Capt. Smirk reflected. *My people aren't exactly falling all over themselves with friendliness.*

Capt. Ricardo's crew formed a receiving line.

"I'd like to introduce you to my staff," Capt. Ricardo said. "Let's meet them now, up close and personal. First, my right-hand man, my First Officer, Commander . . . um . . . er . . . sorry, but I'm so used to calling you Number 1 that I've forgotten . . ."

"Piker," his First Officer provided.

"Ah, yes. Wilhelm Piker," Ricardo said, flustered.

"Wilson Piker. I'm honored to meet you, Capt. Smirk." Piker extended his hand. Capt. Ricardo relaxed a bit. *Perhaps Number 1 will break the ice,* he thought.

Piker continued, "It's amazing to think we're standing here with the original crew of the Endocrine. You don't look a day over 90. How do you do it?"

Capt. Smirk seemed flattered. "Well, we don't like to let too many people in on it—but since you're now our fellow crew members, I'll tell you. We discovered our secret after Mr. Smock rose from the dead."

Piker was startled. "I beg your pardon?"

"Yes," Smirk continued matter-of-factly, "he died. But you know the saying: 'You can't keep a good Vulture down.' Mr. Smock regained his health and brought us the secret of eternal life."

Everyone turned toward Smock. He pulled a small carton from the sleeve of his tunic. "Yogurt," he stated.

"Our whole crew has been eating it ever since," Smirk continued. "It has helped us maintain our vigor. That's one reason we've been looking forward to this mission. Frankly, retirement was getting boring.

"Oh, it was fine for a few years. But I've played 6 million rounds of golf; Mr. Zulu spent over 70,000 hours fishing; and

Smock even had time to catch up on his back issues of Reader's Digest. We're all itching to get back to work."

"Very good," commented Capt. Ricardo. "Tell me, Mr. Smock, what is it like to come back from the dead?"

Before Smock could answer, Dacron interrupted.

"The literature on the phenomenon of near-death experience indicates that the subject passes through a long, dark tunnel," Dacron informed them. "He or she frequently meets with a Being of Light, who reviews significant episodes of their life. The physical sensation of being out of one's body also frequently accompanies the episode."

There was an awkward pause, finally broken by Smock's tactful reply. "Thank you. I couldn't have said it better myself."

Capt. Ricardo grimaced. "Well, then. This is Lt. Cmdr. Dacron, our token android."

Capt. Smirk shook Dacron's hand. As his crew members did the same, Capt. Smirk pulled Capt. Ricardo aside. "I'm afraid I'm not up on the latest android technology," Smirk whispered. "Do they all have white skin?"

"No," replied Capt. Ricardo. "We got him at a discount price. Off-brand merchandise, you know. But despite his skin color, he's fully functional."

Dacron smiled and wiggled his eyebrows as he shook hands with Lt. Yoohoo. The two captains moved down the receiving line.

"This is our chief engineer, Lt. Georgie LaForgery," said Capt. Ricardo.

"Is that a visual prosthesis, lieutenant?" asked Capt. Smirk.

"Yes, sir," Georgie asserted, a bit defensively. "It works so well that my blindness does not handicap me in any way. *Particularly* when I fill in as pilot whenever necessary."

"You betcha," said Capt. Smirk, forcing a grin.

They moved farther down the receiving line.

"This is Westerly Flusher," said Capt. Ricardo, "the youngest acting ensign on a Starfreak vessel."

"It works so well that my blindness
does not handicap me
in any way."

"Well, young lad!" Smirk exclaimed heartily. "And what are your duties aboard the Endocrine?"

"I hang around the Bridge, sir, piloting the ship and just generally trying to be helpful," Westerly said in his earnest Eddy Haskell tone.

Next in line was Wart. *This is going to be touchy*, thought Capt. Ricardo.

"As you know, Capt. Smirk, Kringles have been admitted to the federation," Capt. Ricardo began. "We've come a long way since the days of warfare between . . ."

"Say no more," Capt. Smirk interrupted, extending his hand. "You must be Lt. Warp."

"Wart," the Kringle growled, tightening the handshake into a viselike grip.

"Pleased . . . to . . . meet . . . you," Capt. Smirk wheezed, his face turning red. Wart released his hand, and Smirk winced.

"This is Dr. Cape Pragmatski," Capt. Ricardo continued as they moved on. "She's been our chief medical officer ever since Westerly's mother, Beverage Flusher, was kicked upstairs by the high command."

"Nice to meet you, Dr. Pragmatski." She wasn't wasting any facial muscles on excessive smiling, Smirk observed. "You and Dr. McCaw should get on famously. Might even start a group practice, eh?"

Dr. Pragmatski's face grew even stonier. "I hardly think so, Capt. Smirk," she replied.

They moved on to the last person in line.

"Capt. Smirk, this is Counselor Deanna Troit."

Capt. Smirk took her hand. "So very pleased to meet you, Counselor Troit."

Troit smiled. "My friends call me Dee."

"Dee Troit. Lovely." Smirk kissed her hand and continued to clasp it as they talked.

"What does the title of Counselor signify?" He gave her his

sure-fire dreamy look—the one he liked to think of as "setting
my gaze on 'stun'."

"I counsel the captain in matters of politics, human relations,
and anything to do with emotions. As a Betavoid, I can sense
the emotions of others."

Smirk's smile had taken on a definitely sappy quality. "Ah.
So you can tell, then, what I'm feeling for you right at this
moment?"

Troit blushed. "Yes, but perhaps I shouldn't identify your
emotion out loud. It's rather personal. I don't wish to embarrass you."

"How very quaint—a gentlewoman who speaks delicately
in matters of the heart. I feel as if you already know me very
well, Counselor Troit, that you can tell what motivates me,
what . . ." he paused meaningfully, " . . . . moves me."

"Indeed, captain," Troit responded.

Capt. Smirk kissed her hand again and gazed deeply into
her eyes. Then he moved away.

Troit leaned over toward Dr. Pragmatski and whispered,
"Raging hormones."

Capt. Smirk surveyed the surroundings. "Quite an impressive Bridge, Capt. Ricardo. You have so many more buttons
and dials and fancy displays than we had. It's so much cozier
in here, too. And new carpeting—nice touch. I like this."

"Thank you," said Capt. Ricardo. "Let's take our stations,
shall we?"

There was a subtle but fierce scramble for chairs at the
science stations in the back, leaving Zulu and Checkout standing. Things were just as awkward, though considerably more
polite, in the center of the Bridge. Capt. Ricardo, Capt. Smirk,
Piker, Troit and Smock had only three command chairs
between them.

"Number 1, take care of this, will you?" said Capt. Ricardo.
"Get us two more chairs."

"Sir, we don't have any extra equipment on board," Piker

reminded him. "Fuel-economy measures from Starfreak, you'll recall."

"Then get something from the HolidayDeck."

"Yes, sir."

A short time later, the five of them sat in Piker's "solution" to the seating problem: a semicircular restaurant booth made of tufted plastic, complete with a pedestal table in front of it. Capt. Ricardo, seated in the center of the elbow-to-elbow quintet, put on a happy face and tried to make the best of it.

"Well, here we are," he chirped. "Now, I like to run a democratic Bridge. I often consult with my staff. So! What Warped speed should we maintain for the first sector of our voyage?"

Everyone in Capt. Smirk's crew looked at Capt. Ricardo in astonishment. Capt. Smirk's jaw dropped open slightly, and Mr. Smock's frown deepened.

"Capt. Smirk, you first," Capt. Ricardo invited.

Capt. Smirk recovered his composure and replied diplomatically, "Let's go with Warped 6."

"Mr. Smock, what do you say?" asked Capt. Ricardo.

"Warped 6 should prove satisfactory," Smock answered.

"Number 1?"

"I'm kind of partial to Warped 5 myself," Piker asserted.

Capt. Ricardo polled everyone on the Bridge in turn, then asked Dacron to calculate the average of all responses. It turned out to be Warped 5.375.

"Ensign Flusher, maintain Warped 5.375," the captain ordered.

"Aye, sir."

"Captain," Counselor Troit broke in, "request permission to leave the Bridge."

"Leave the Bridge? Why, counselor? We were just getting comfortable."

Troit fidgeted in the booth and mumbled something.

"What's that, counselor? Speak up, will you?"

"I said, I have to go to the bathroom," she hissed.

"Oh. Very well."

The others shifted aside and left the booth, except for Capt. Smirk, who slid over to the center. He leaned back, spreading his arms across the seat and making himself comfortable.

"Aahhh," he exhaled. "It's good to be back in the saddle again."

Capt. Smirk rubbed his hands over the upholstery. In the seam between the back and the seat, he found something and pulled it out. It was a coin.

"Hmmm," he mused, "somebody lost a quarter here."

Capt. Smirk shifted into his command posture and intoned, "Mr. Smock! At this Warped speed, how long until we reach the Crabby Nebula?"

Mr. Smock began, "Approximately t—"

Dacron interrupted. "Precisely 23 Earth hours, sir." From his post at the front of the Bridge, Dacron did not notice Smock glaring at the back of his head.

"Thank you, Mr. Dacron," said Capt. Smirk.

"Well," said Capt. Ricardo, "now that we're underway, I think it's time my people gave the original crew a tour."

"Terrific idea!" Capt. Smirk responded. The rest of his crew looked as if someone had suggested they have their wisdom teeth pulled.

"Everyone on my crew: get together with your counterparts and show them your department," instructed Capt. Ricardo. "That includes you, Ensign Flusher; you may put the ship on automatic pilot for now. I'll tour with Capt. Smirk, of course. Mr. Dacron, you have the Bridge."

"Aye, sir." Out of the corner of his eye, Dacron watched them leave. When the Crewmover door closed behind them, he glanced around the Bridge, making sure he was alone.

Then Dacron pressed a button on his console. Its display screen became a small TV monitor. Dacron's favorite daytime show, "As the Starship Turns," was just beginning.

"Oh, Trevor, Trevor . . ." moaned an actress on the sound-track.

"Oh. Tiffany, Tiffany . . ." responded her partner.

Dacron watched their embrace with great interest. Without taking his eyes from the screen, he reached into a concealed compartment in his chair and pulled out a can of soda.

"Trevor, I have something very important to tell you."

Dacron leaned forward, entranced.

"I . . . I'm going to have your baby."

I knew it, I knew it! Dacron exulted to himself. *Hot dog! The plot is really thickening today.*

Dacron sat back in satisfaction and took a long swig of soda.

3

Getting to Know You

CAPT. RICARDO AND Capt. Smirk stepped into the Crewmover. "Destination, please," said the Crewmover's automated voice.

"Officers' quarters," instructed Capt. Ricardo.

"Thank you," responded the Crewmover, which then began playing its taped announcement. "Welcome to the Crewmover system. For your safety and comfort, please follow these few simple guidelines. Keep your arms and legs inside the compartment at all times . . ."

Capt. Ricardo scowled. "Computer, fast-forward through these instructions."

"Yes, captain," the computer responded. There were squiggly sounds as the audio tape advanced. Then the Crewmover continued:

"When you leave, please check the compartment to be sure you have taken all your belongings, including small children, heh, heh, heh."

"All the way to the end, Computer," the captain snapped.

Squiggly tape-advance sounds resumed. Then the Crewmover speakers played an easy-listening version of "Tie a Yellow Ribbon Round the Old Oak Tree."

"So," said Capt. Ricardo, resuming their conversation, "you haven't seen your quarters yet?"

"No," responded Capt. Smirk. "I was in the observation deck during launch."

The Crewmover door opened, and they entered the corridor.

"I understand the quarters on your ship were somewhat Spartan," Capt. Ricardo said. "I hope you'll be pleasantly surprised by the creature comforts we now enjoy." They entered Capt. Smirk's suite.

"Say, this is impressive," commented Capt. Smirk as he walked through the living room and continued into a side room.

"Hey!" he called, his voice bouncing off the ceramic tiles. "A Jacuzzi! Terrific!" He returned to the living room.

Capt. Ricardo continued the tour, turning on the bedroom light and stepping over to the headboard of the bed.

"And for those days when the responsibilities of command leave your muscles tense . . ." He flicked the switch on a box fastened to the headboard. The bed vibrated vigorously.

"And what's this?" Capt. Smirk stepped up to the wide-screen TV on the other side of the room.

"Dacron replicated that for me in the UltraFax," said Capt. Ricardo. "It's an ancient entertainment device called a television. When you're keyed up from a hectic day at the helm, you watch this for a while and it helps you stop thinking."

Capt. Ricardo turned on the set and continued his explanation. "I've forbidden these devices anywhere except in my quarters, and now in yours also. I don't want the crew to get into the habit of watching. I've found it's quite addictive."

The screen showed the call letters of station WYUK, and an announcer stated, "We now return to Murl Duesing Safari." As the show resumed, Murl was wrestling an aardvark.

As Capt. Ricardo reached out to turn off the set, Capt. Smirk grabbed his wrist without glancing away from the screen.

"Wait, please," he said. "I want to see what happens."

Dacron was so deeply engrossed in "As the Starship Turns" that Westerly's return to the Bridge startled him into spilling soda onto his control console.

Westerly was munching a Twinkie. "They didn't need me to show them around the ship," he whined with his mouth full. "I shoulda known that old crew wouldn't have any kids my age."

"That snack cake is intriguing," commented Dacron. "May I observe it more closely?"

"Sure," said Westerly. He walked over, leaned down till his face was inches from Dacron's, and stuck out his cake-encrusted tongue. "Bleaaahhh."

Dacron studied Westerly with great curiosity. "Fascinating," he observed. "Every one of your molars has at least one dental filling."

Westerly was disappointed. "Dacron, it's impossible to gross you out," he complained.

"May I trade you a can of soda for one of those Twinkies?" Dacron asked. Then something on his console caught his eye.

Westerly noticed the shift in Dacron's attention. "What's wrong?" Westerly asked.

"These headings indicate we are being drawn off course," Dacron said.

"Ummm. And your TV isn't working," Westerly noticed. He went to a science station in the back, opened a drawer, and turned on a small portable television hidden inside.

"This one works just fine," he called from the back of the Bridge. "You must have shorted out your console when you spilled that soda, Dacron. The readings are probably wrong."

"That is quite likely, Westerly. We could not be traveling so far from our intended direction without drastic course alter-ations."

"So we have something in common," Dr. McCaw admitted to Dr. Pragmatski. Her medical diploma on the wall of Sick

Bay indicated that she, too, had graduated from the Institute of Sarcastic Medicine.

"Oh, you're well remembered around the institute," allowed Dr. Pragmatski. "Medical students are now required to memorize the McCaw Amendments to the Hippocratic Oath. All 50 of them." She groaned, then recited the first few amendments: "I'm a doctor, not a rhinoceros. I'm a doctor, not a cotton ball. I'm a doctor, not a billiard cue. I'm a doctor, not a Roto Rooter."

A smile cracked across Dr. McCaw's face. "My contribution to medical science," he mused, staring into the distance.

"Contribution, my uvula!" snapped Dr. Pragmatski. "Those amendments set back cooperation between starship captains and doctors at least 50 years!"

They glared at each other.

"And this, gentlemen, is the HolidayDeck," Piker announced proudly.

"What does it do?" Zulu asked as he and Checkout gazed at the wide entrance doors. They'd accepted Piker's offer of a tour after Mr. Smock declined; Smock said he was overdue for his weekly eyebrow-tweezing.

"The HolidayDeck is a simulator that will create any environment we choose, complete with climate and other special effects," Piker explained.

"I'd like to try it," Checkout said.

"Certainly." Piker stepped up to the HolidayDeck control panel. "A setting to remind you of your homeland, perhaps?"

He spoke to the panel. "Establish an environment similar to the Siberian region of Earth."

A cold wind blasted them as the HolidayDeck doors opened. Snowflakes fluttered into the hallway.

"My, that certainly is realistic!" Zulu remarked. He and Checkout huddled their shoulders against the cold as they stepped into the HolidayDeck, marveling at the wet snow clinging to their uniforms.

"Just wait till you see how authentic it looks when the doors close!" Piker concurred, beaming. He touched the control panel to shut the doors behind Zulu and Checkout, imagining their delight at how cleverly the HolidayDeck disguised the exit.

Just then Piker noticed the clock. *Good grief*, he thought, *I'm missing the start of "The Beverly Hillbillies."* He rushed to his quarters.

"Your visual prosthesis is intriguing, lieutenant," said Dr. McCaw. "How does it work?"

Georgie sat on an examination table in Sick Bay with Dr. McCaw standing next to him. "The visor converts visual input to electrical pulses," he explained. "Then an implant relays them to my brain."

"Dr. Pragmatski mentioned that this device is rather painful. Why?"

"The batteries," said Georgie. "This sucker carries seven D-cell batteries, and they weigh a ton."

"Does any external eye tissue remain?"

"Well, yes." Georgie hesitated. "Most people are pretty squeamish about it, though, so I always wear my visor in public."

"I'd like to examine the area, if you don't mind," said Dr. McCaw.

"Are you sure? It's pretty yuccky."

"Good God, man," barked Dr. McCaw, "as a doctor, I'm used to these things."

"Well . . . OK," Georgie relented. He removed his visor. Out popped fake eyeballs on springs, bouncing and dangling in front of his face.

"Aaargh! Eccch!" exclaimed Dr. McCaw. "Put it back on. Geez, that's disgusting!"

Just then the ship's engines rumbled slightly. A moment later, Capt. Ricardo's voice came over the intercom.

"Establish an environment similar
to the Siberian region of Earth."

"Mr. LaForgery."

"Yes, sir. I heard that, too."

"Everything all right in the Engine Room?"

"I'll go check, sir."

Smock sat back in the barber's chair and tried to relax. He'd come to Hair Port, the Endocrine's salon, for more than just his regular eyebrow tweezing; he also needed time to sort out his thoughts.

When Capt. Ricardo suggested they all tour the ship with their counterparts, Mr. Smock had felt vaguely disturbed. As he reflected on it now, Smock realized he'd felt uneasy because he had no counterpart on the new crew.

To Capt. Smirk, Smock had been wonderful counselor, almighty officer and prince of precision. But Capt. Ricardo divided these functions between Troit, Piker and Dacron.

It wasn't logical, Smock thought. *to have three officers where one would do.* However, he decided he would have to go with the flow.

He hoped that this mission would provide some scientific challenges to occupy his mind. *At any rate,* he thought, *it surely is better than reading "Life in These United States" for the 50th time.*

"So, basically, the ship is powered by the mixtures from these tanks," Georgie explained. "The tank of matter is here, the tank of anti-matter is over there, and the tank of uncle-matter is in the corner. That, plus a few dilithium crystals to help us crank it up on a cold morning, is how we keep this starship humming."

"I see," said Mr. Snot. "And where's your Jargon Manual?"

"My what?"

"Your Jargon Manual. To use when the going gets tough."

"I'm sorry, Mr. Snot," Georgie responded. "I don't understand."

"You know, lad," said Mr. Snot, "the manual of technical reasons why the engine won't work in a crisis. For instance, when your captain asks you to blast the ship out of a nasty spot of trouble, you can refer to the manual and say, 'Can't do it, Jim. The lateral baffles won't stand the strain!' or 'The ship isn't made to withstand conditions like this, captain. We must keep the retroflux valves intact, or there'll be trouble on the moors'."

Georgie scratched his head. "Gee, Mr. Snot, why not just fix the engine instead of making all those excuses?"

"They're not excuses, boy! That's genuine engineer talk—the most intimidating language known to man. Surely you understand how important it is never to let on you're not sure how all these thingamabobs work—or don't work."

"But shouldn't you try to find what's wrong and fix it, so you can do what your captain orders?"

"Achh," Mr. Snot muttered. "You're just a brownie, that ye are."

Just then the engine made a grinding sound. In the center of the room, the pulsating pillar of light faltered for a moment.

Georgie hustled over to the engine's control console. "It sounds like we're straining against something . . . a tractor beam, maybe," he speculated.

Alarmed, Mr. Snot began talking to himself. "It'll be difficult without a manual, but perhaps I can improvise . . . yes! How about, 'No, captain, that tractor beam will wear us down to a nubbin if we try to reverse thrusters.' Or maybe, 'The hull won't hold if . . .'."

Georgie left for the Bridge to check out his suspicions.

Capt. Ricardo and Capt. Smirk stood on the observation deck gazing out into space. It was an awe-inspiring sight. Like countless humans throughout the ages, they responded with sincere emotion and profound thoughts.

"Whenever we encounter an alien
race, I find the most human-looking
female and court her."

Capt. Ricardo mused to himself, *They can send a man to the moon, but they can't find a cure for baldness.*

Capt. Smirk, meanwhile, exhaled deeply and stated, "Those countless stars. Why, there must be . . . billions of them. BILLyuns and BILLyuns. And I've got a woman on every one of them."

"Come again?" Capt. Ricardo was startled out of his reverie.

"Oh, yes," Capt. Smirk said with obvious pride. "A woman in every port, you might say. And I can't wait to visit more ports and meet some classy dames.

"It's been my hobby for quite some time," he continued. "Whenever we encounter an alien race, I find the most human-looking female and court her.

"No matter how bizarre the aliens, I can locate among them a lovely lady in a formal chiffon gown and a hair style fresh from the 1963 edition of 'Beautician's Guide to Hairspray.' Then it's just a matter of time till romance blossoms."

"Really." Capt. Ricardo was underwhelmed.

Westerly gloated over having a science station all to himself. Crew members were starting to return to the Bridge after their tour of the ship, but now he had squatter's rights to the chair that Zulu, Checkout and other crew members had fought over earlier. The chair was at the station which had the best TV reception.

"Where are those two, anyway?" he asked Piker as the commander passed by.

"Who, Westerly?" asked Piker.

"Zulu and Checkout. I want to get something from my quarters, but not if they're going to come back here in the meantime and steal this chair."

"Zulu and Checkout? Oh, I set them up in the HolidayDeck. Created an authentic Siberian tundra for them," Piker boasted.

Dacron was leaning back in his chair as a janitor sponged out the inside of his console. Hearing Piker's remark, he turned toward them, puzzled. "That was quite a while ago, was it not, sir?" he asked.

"Well, yes, it was, Dacron," said Piker.

"Have they been in there all this time?"

Piker thought about it.

Dacron persisted, "Did you instruct them how to open the doors by using the 'Exit' command?"

"Ummmm . . ." said Piker. He went over to Wart and whispered something to him. The Kringle nodded and left the Bridge, his expression uncharacteristically close to a smile.

As Wart approached the Crewmover, its door opened. Georgie bolted out, rushed to the pilot's chair and checked the console readings. "We are being pulled off course! Westerly, get over here to your post, turn off the automatic pilot, and fly this ship!"

"Aye, sir." Westerly scrambled to his seat.

The engine rumbled again, much louder this time, and the ship lurched a little. Georgie hurried to the Crewmover, declaring, "I'm going back to the Engine Room and get to the bottom of this!"

Dacron pointed to the windshield at the front of the Bridge. "Look! We are being held in a tractor beam!"

Sure enough, a ray of light shining from a genuine green and yellow John Deere tractor was pulling them toward a distant planet.

"Wait!" proclaimed Piker. "As senior officer on the Bridge, I'll handle this." He stepped to the center of the Bridge, struck a pose, and announced, "It's a tractor beam!"

Capt. Ricardo's voice came over the intercom. "Number 1, report."

Piker described their predicament.

"I'm on my way," said the captain.

"What do we know about this planet that's pulling us, Mr.

"Collect the papers in that
baseball cap of yours—
the one you got at
Kringle Night at the ballpark."

Dacron?" demanded Capt. Ricardo as he and Capt. Smirk strode onto the Bridge.

Dacron consulted the data banks and reported, "The planet is an abandoned Starfreak colony known as Cellulite—1. No communication transmissions or shuttle traffic have been reported here for over 20 years."

Wart entered the Bridge from the Crewmover, herding Zulu and Checkout, who were stiff as Popsicles.

"Lt. Wart, open 'hey, you' frequencies," the captain ordered.

Wart stood at the communication post. " 'Hey, you' frequencies open, sir."

"Cellulite—1, this is Capt. Jean-Lucy Ricardo of the federation starship Endocrine. Why have you towed us here?"

There was no response.

"I repeat, this is the Endocrine. Cellulite—1, come in." Capt. Ricardo waited a moment, then ordered, "Lt. Wart, send that message in all languages, on all frequencies, and to all ZIP codes."

There was no answer from the planet.

"Well, if we can't get them to cooperate, we'll try to break free," said Capt. Ricardo. "Engine Room! Can you break us away from this tractor beam?"

"We don't know how, capt—" Georgie's voice on the intercom was cut off by sounds of a scuffle. Mr Snot came over the speaker. "Can't do it, Jean-Lucy. The wee bit of engine we have won't hold up under the stress!"

"Wee bit of a—what the devil?" Capt. Ricardo shook his head. "Never mind. We'll have to find some other approach. A voice vote on what to do is inappropriate in this crisis . . ."

"Agreed!" exclaimed Capt. Smirk.

". . . So we'll vote by secret ballot," concluded Capt. Ricardo. "Number 1, pass out slips of paper. I want everyone to write down their suggestions of what to do. Wart, collect the papers in that souvenir baseball cap of yours—the one you got at Kringle Night at the ballpark. That's the largest hat we've got. It's going to take some pretty large ideas to get us out of this predicament.''

Capt. Smirk sank back into the command booth, rubbing his hand over his eyes.

A genuine green and yellow John
Deere tractor was pulling them
towards a distant planet.

4

Sleeping Boobies

"READY, COUNCELOR?" ASKED Capt. Ricardo.

"Ready, sir," responded Counselor Troit, standing at a blackboard at the wall of the Bridge.

Capt. Ricardo drew a slip of paper from Wart's baseball hat and unfolded it. "First suggestion," he said, "is 'Beam down an Away Team to investigate.'" Counselor Troit wrote the suggestion on the board.

"Second suggestion," said the captain, drawing another slip. "'Beam down Capt. Smirk and his crew, and leave them th—' . . . uh, make that 'Beam down Capt. Smirk and crew.'

"Next: 'Send the android against this alien force and let him talk it to death.' Ahem. Here's another vote for an Away Team . . . and another, this one 'led by a commander skilled at striking dramatic poses.'

"This one says, 'Send a probe to see if there are any . . .'" Capt. Ricardo hesitated, "'*classic games* there'? I can't read this handwriting."

"Perhaps it's 'classy dames'," offered Capt. Smirk, as if he were guessing at what it said.

When all the votes were tallied, it was clear that most of the crew members wanted to send an Away Team. The only question was who would be on it. Capt. Ricardo had Wart check the list to see whose turn it was, and for the sake of

43

fairness, he offered to let someone from Capt. Smirk's crew go along. Capt. Smirk himself jumped at the chance.

A short time later, the Away Team stood on the UltraFax platform in Shipping and Receiving. There they were sorted according to weight and assigned a shipping priority. Westerly, the lightest, would go Express Mail. Capt. Smirk would go Special Delivery, and Cmdr. Piker was assigned First Class. Lt. Wart, the heaviest by far, went Fourth Class.

Piker, as team leader, commanded, "Set phasers on 'stun.' " The others complied.

"Energize me!" Piker ordered the shipping clerk.

The clerk UltraFaxed them toward Cellulite-1. One by one, they materialized inside a building there, in a deserted hallway.

Westerly, the Express Mail passenger, arrived first. He felt uneasy holding an armed phaser. This was his first Away Team assignment, and he wondered again if his backpack held everything he needed: boom box, computer hackers' newsletter, a dozen Day-Glo orange shoelaces, and several Twinkies.

Capt. Smirk arrived next, followed by Cmdr. Piker.

They waited several minutes for Wart, until someone remembered he'd traveled Fourth Class. "We'd better get going; he may never get here," Capt. Smirk observed.

They crept forward, Piker in the lead, followed by Capt. Smirk, then Westerly. The sounds of their footsteps were magnified in the deathly silent corridor.

"Hello?" called Piker. "Anybody home?"

They stopped to listen. Suddenly Capt. Smirk's stomach growled. Startled, Westerly jumped back. His finger jerked the phaser trigger, sending out a beam that struck Capt. Smirk in the back of the head. The captain slumped to the floor.

"Ohhh, rats," Westerly moaned. "Am I gonna get it now."

Piker confronted him. "Westerly Flusher! The Starfreak Employee Handbook specifically forbids firing upon a superior

They were sorted according
to weight and assigned
a shipping priority.

officer from behind. I'm responsible for your training, and I view this as a serious offense."

"Yes, sir," mumbled Westerly.

"No supper for you tonight, young man," Piker admonished.

Piker flicked the communicator button pinned to his tunic. "Endocrine," he transmitted, "Capt. Smirk is temporarily out of commission. Beam him up."

After Capt. Smirk vanished in the beam from Shipping, Capt. Ricardo's voice came over the transmitter. "Number 1, what's going on down there?"

"I'll explain later, sir," Piker responded. "Let's go," he ordered Westerly.

They continued down the corridor. At the far end, a glow of light spilled out from a doorway. They made their way toward it.

Just before they reached the end of the hall, Piker extended his hand to hold Westerly back. "This is it," he whispered. "Remember how we saw it done on 'Miami Vice.' "

Westerly nodded. They gripped their phasers with both hands, elbows locked. Piker stole a glance into the room, then somersaulted sideways past the open doorway. He stood up, peeked into the room again, and nodded to Westerly. They both burst into the room at once.

"Freeze! Starfreak patrol!" Piker shouted. He and Westerly stood there panting for a long moment, taut with tension. Westerly was the first to relax.

"It looks like they're freezing, all right," he observed.

Lining the walls were several hundred transparent plastic compartments. Each compartment held a human. They were standing up and appeared to be in suspended animation. On one wall, a flashing sign read "Diet in Progress. Do Not Disturb."

" 'Diet in Progress'? What does that mean?" wondered Piker.

He and Westerly strolled down the aisle between the twin banks of animation chambers.

At the far end of the room was a reception area with a desk, several chairs and a few worn copies of "People" magazine. It appeared that Westerly and Piker had come in the back way.

Westerly picked up a pamphlet from the reception desk. " 'HyberThin,' " he read. " 'Lose weight without dieting, without exercising, without breathing.' "

Piker flicked his transmitter. "Endocrine," he said, "is there anything in our data banks about a phenomenon called Hyber-Thin?"

Dacron's voice came over the transmitter. "HyberThin was a profit-making enterprise. For a fee, this business placed dieters into hibernation until their fat cells shrank or their contract ran out, whichever came first. The business was franchised to . . ."

"Thank you, Dacron; that's all we need to know." Piker cut him off with a flick of the transmitter button.

Westerly, rummaging around in the reception desk, discovered a spreadsheet. "Commander, it looks like this fat farm went belly-up. Or maybe I should say pot-belly-up." Westerly chuckled.

Piker frowned. "What do you mean?"

"It looks like these people had lifetime contracts that were too expensive for the franchise to honor. The customers never got down to their goal weights, yet the business was required to keep them on life support, so its profits went out the window."

Piker stroked his chin. "Come again?"

Westerly sighed. "They went broke, commander."

"Oh." Piker considered this for a moment. Then he began pacing the room. "All right, so these people have been on the longest diet in the history of humankind. But what does that have to do with the force that drew our ship here? Where's

Smirk awoke in sick bay.
Troit was at his side.

the source of the tractor beam?" He headed back toward the rear entrance. "We'll need to scout further."

Westerly lagged behind. All this talk of dieting reminded him he hadn't eaten for more than 15 minutes. And he was going to miss his supper tonight as a punishment, too. He reached back into his knapsack and pulled out a Twinkie. He didn't notice that a second Twinkie fell from the knapsack onto the floor.

Around the fallen Twinkie, the air shimmered, and the diet chambers within several yards shook slightly.

Westerly and Piker heard the noise and turned around. Several chambers swayed back and forth. Their doors creaked as they swung open.

A middle-aged woman stepped stiffly out of a chamber. She hesitated over the Twinkie for a moment, then swooped down onto it, tore open the wrapping and swallowed the Twinkie in two gulps.

Within moments, several other dieters also stepped out of their chambers, sniffing the air and checking the floor for crumbs.

Westerly's jaw dropped open. Piker reached over and lifted it shut with his forefinger. Then he hailed the Endocrine. "Captain, we've got a situation here."

" 'Situation'? Be more specific, Number 1!"

"There are humans here. We must have awakened them from some sort of hibernation." Piker briefed the captain on the status of the diet franchise.

One of the dieters approached Piker and Westerly. "Excuse me," she said, "but would you happen to have any Oreos on you?"

"Number 1, I suggest you beam a few of these people on board so we can learn more about them."

"Yes, sir," said Piker. He selected three of the bewildered dieters and lined them in a row. "Five to beam up," he notified the Endocrine. "No, wait," he corrected himself. Wart had just arrived. "Make that six to beam up."

At that same moment, Capt. Smirk awoke in Sick Bay as the effects of Westerly's phaser blast wore off. Troit was at his side. Capt. Smirk gave her a groggy smile.

Troit soothed his brow. "You were stunned by a phaser beam when Ensign Flusher accidentally fired on you," she told him. "How do you feel?"

"Wonderful," Smirk responded. "It's terrific to see combat again. I find that danger always heightens the emotions, don't you? We realize how fragile life is, how we must make every moment count."

Troit melted into his arms. *From the moment we met*, she thought, *I've been a sucker for this guy. I never could resist a man wearing Old Spice.*

Smirk, too, was smitten. There was no mistaking the signs: the half-closed lids, the syrupy grin, the violins playing in the background.

5

Meet the Celluites

"SO THE HYBERTHIN franchise promised that you'd 'wake up thin'?" Capt. Ricardo asked.

One of the Cellulites nodded.

"We were pulled to your planet by a tractor beam," Capt. Ricardo continued. "Can you tell us anything about it?"

"The promoters probably forgot to turn it off when they left," one of the Cellulites replied. "It was a marketing device: fly too close to the planet, and the tractor beam drew you down. Then the HyberThin people gave you the hard sell."

"Excuse me, captain," said another of the Cellulites, "but we haven't eaten in several decades. Would you have any more of those Twinkies aboard?"

Capt. Ricardo was puzzled. "Twinkies?"

"Sir," Piker explained, "Westerly dropped a Twinkie when we were investigating the HyberThin chambers."

"It woke us up," asserted a Cellulite. "There's nothing like an honest-to-goodness Twinkie. I can smell one at 50 paces."

Capt. Ricardo folded his arms and frowned as he realized what had happened. Then he concealed his irritation for a moment and replied politely, "Of course you may have some—er, Twinkies. I'm sure we could replicate them in the UltraFax. Mr. Zulu, please see that our guests have enough to eat."

"Aye, sir," said Zulu. He escorted the Cellulites to the Crewmover.

As soon as they had left, Capt. Ricardo turned to Westerly. "You dropped a Twinkie while you were on an away mission . . ."

"Yes, sir," Westerly replied, staring at his shoes.

" . . . Waking up these Cellulites, and inflaming their appetites. Ensign, this is a flagrant violation of the Prime Time Directive."

Westerly folded his hands behind his back and prayed for a quick and painless death.

The Crewmover door opened. Troit walked onto the Bridge, followed by—Westerly gulped—Capt. Smirk. *Great*, thought Westerly, *now there are two people here who want to kill me.*

Capt. Ricardo continued, "As punishment, you will go to bed without your supper tonight."

Piker stepped forward. "Sir, I already assigned him that punishment for firing his phaser at Capt. Smirk."

Capt. Smirk stepped next to Westerly and reached out. Westerly flinched, then stared in amazement as Capt. Smirk draped an arm across his shoulder.

"No harm done," Capt. Smirk remarked. He added quietly to Westerly, "You can have my supper tonight. I'm not very hungry." He patted Westerly on the head and began strolling around the Bridge, humming a cheerful tune.

"Well, Capt. Smirk, you seem to have come out of your coma in a mellow mood," observed Capt. Ricardo.

"Indeed, captain! Now that I've tasted adventure once again, the universe seems so fresh and full of promise. What a rare mood I'm in." Capt. Smirk hummed a little more and began to sing, "Why it's almost like being in . . ." He interrupted himself with a grin and winked at Counselor Troit.

"But I digress," he continued. "What did you find on the surface of the planet, Commander Piker?"

An intercom transmission interrupted them. "Captain, this

One of the Cellulites grabbed
Westerly and roughly
searched his pockets.

is the Mess Hall. The Cellulites finished off all our Twinkies *and* our chocolate. Now they're demanding we make them more chocolate, but I need to use the UltraFax to prepare tonight's supper."

"Don't we have anything else?" asked the captain. "Some nice peppermints, perhaps, or some jellybeans, or . . ."

"Chocolate, captain!" one of the Cellulites shrieked over the intercom. "There is no substitute! If it isn't here in the kitchen, we'll find it elsewhere on your ship!"

Her outburst puzzled them. "Somehow she sounds different from a few minutes ago," Mr. Smock observed. "This is not at all logical, but she sounded not only meaner but . . . bigger."

"It is possible, Mr. Smock," Dacron interjected. "Weight is regained much more rapidly after an extended fast."

Within moments the Cellulites returned to the Bridge. Dacron's speculation was correct. They were regaining weight at an astounding rate and had burst the seams of their clothes.

"Chocolate! We must have chocolate!" they cried.

"Captain." Counselor Troit pulled Capt. Ricardo aside. "I sense great desperation in them. They will do anything for chocolate."

One of the Cellulites grabbed Westerly and roughly searched his pockets. She came up with a Hershey bar and tore off the wrapping.

"Hey! That's all I have to eat tonight!" Westerly protested.

"Mr. Wart! Escort these Cellulites off the ship," commanded Capt. Ricardo. Wart herded them off to Shipping and Receiving.

"We won't give them the chance to reboard without my authorization," continued the captain. "Shields up."

Everyone on the Bridge groaned. Turning on the shields put such a strain on the ship's electrical system that crew members were forbidden to use blow dryers and curling irons. Capt. Ricardo always urged them to maintain a stiff upper lip in such situations, but that was easy for him to say.

Yoohoo took Wart's place at the communication post. "Captain," she reported, "the Cellulites are transmitting a message from the surface of their planet."

"Open 'hey, you' frequencies," the captain responded.

An image of the Cellulites appeared on the transmission screen at the front of the Bridge. In just the past minute, they had grown to humongous proportions. They were now coming down from their sugar high, which made them very cranky. "Is this how you treat all your guests, Ricardo?" one of them sneered.

"The welfare of my crew must take precedence over my duties as host," Capt. Ricardo maintained. "We regret that our interference with your planet has inconvenienced you. However, I will not allow my ship to be held hostage. I demand that you turn off your tractor beam at once. Then, and only then, can we negotiate a solution."

"Not on your life! Before we let you go, we need more of that chocolate!" the Cellulite retorted.

Capt. Smirk stepped forward. "Surely we can resolve this situation," he offered. "I'll tell you what—you can have my share of our yogurt for the entire year."

"Yogurt?!" The Cellulites laughed him to scorn. "Ecchh! We're lifelong dieters. We're sick to death of yogurt. Chocolate!" The Cellulites began to chant. "Chocolate! Chocolate! We want chocolate!"

Capt. Ricardo gestured for Yoohoo to turn off the transmitter. He plopped wearily into the command booth and rubbed his neck muscles.

Capt. Smirk persisted. "Mr. Smock, isn't there any way we can escape the tractor beam?"

Before Smock could reply, Dacron spoke. "Yes, captain, by—"

Smock reached out and gave Dacron's shoulder the Vulture pinch. Dacron went limp. "Hmmm. It works on androids also," Smock observed to himself.

Smock reached out and gave
Dacron's shoulder the Vulture pinch.

To Capt. Smirk, Smock reported, "Sir, while you were gone with the Away Team, I did further research in tractor physics. We could escape the tractor beam by spreading sand for traction, engaging reverse thrusters for 3.5 seconds, shifting forward in low gear for 3.5 seconds, arid alternating back and forth to rock the ship till we build enough momentum to break loose."

Westerly beamed. "That's brilliant, Mr. Smock! Where did you learn that technique?"

"On a television documentary about winter driving," Smock answered.

"Well, there we go, then!" Capt. Smirk was pleased with this quick and easy solution.

Capt. Ricardo drummed his fingers on the pedestal table. "Excuse me," he said with exaggerated politeness. "I'm only the captain, I know, but perhaps I could offer my humble opinion."

"Yes, Capt. Ricardo?" responded Capt. Smirk, oblivious to Ricardo's sarcasm.

"We've just committed a serious violation of the Prime Time Directive," said Capt. Ricardo. "If we use force to break away and leave the Cellulites in this fix, Starfreak Command will have our hides faster than you can say 'warped speed.'"

"Oh, really?" Capt. Smirk frowned. "I think Smock's idea is terrific. And I have a feeling Starfreak Command will agree with me. I say we go for it."

Capt. Ricardo's face grew redder by the second as he echoed, " 'Go for it'?!"

Capt. Smirk leaned across the pedestal table toward Capt. Ricardo. Smirk narrowed his eyes as he issued his challenge. "Ensign Flusher! Take us out of here. That's an order."

Capt. Ricardo stood up, his jaw set. "Don't forget for a second whose ship you're on, you bloody . . ."

Piker smoothly stepped between them. "Captains," he said, "there's only one thing to do in a situation such as this, when tempers are high, the situation is critical, and bold action is required."

They glared at him.

"Hold a meeting," Piker suggested.

Soon all the Bridge officers were seated around the conference room table, except for Dacron, who was still slumped over his console recovering from Smock's Vulture pinch.

Capt. Ricardo opened the discussion. "We can't just leave now. We've breached the natural order of life for the Cellulites, in direct violation of the Prime Time Directive. We dare not ignore the directive."

Checkout spoke up. "I don't understand how leaving this planet would violate the Prime Time Directive."

"Neither do I," concurred Zulu.

Capt. Ricardo decided to humor them. "Oh? Perhaps it has changed since your last tour of duty. What was the Prime Time Directive in your era?"

Checkout answered matter-of-factly, " 'Don't worry; be happy.' " Zulu nodded in agreement.

Capt. Ricardo sighed and rolled his eyes. "I can see you have a little brushing up to do. Would one of my crew please update Capt. Smirk's team on the *current* Prime Time Directive?"

Capt. Ricardo's officers shifted nervously in their seats and stared at the table.

"Well?" he demanded. "Surely you all know it."

No one spoke up.

His anger mounting, Capt. Ricardo demanded, "Number 1, recite the Prime Time Directive."

"Er, the Prime Time Directive." Piker thought it over. "That is as follows: 'We will sell no wine before its time.' "

Capt. Smirk's team burst into laughter and catcalls.

Capt. Ricardo grimaced, frustrated. "No, no! The Prime Time Directive. One of you must know it. Wart! What is our guiding philosophy? What do you say when you wake up every morning?"

" 'Go ahead. Make my day,' " Wart replied.

Capt. Ricardo's shoulders sagged. "The Prime Time Directive," he said wearily, "for those of you who seem to have forgotten or perhaps never even heard it, is: 'Put things back where you found them.' "

"Oh! *That* Prime Time Directive," Piker said brightly.

"So now that we've tampered with the Cellulites, we must not leave until we've restored them to the way they were," Capt. Ricardo counseled.

Capt. Smirk frowned in irritation. "Of course not," he said. "But what, exactly, does that mean? They were fat before they went into hibernation, and now they're fat again. Has anything really changed? They've only been awake and thin for a few minutes—*that* was the fluke! If it really matters to you that they feel thin, let's go to the Garment Nebula and buy them some tent dresses with vertical stripes."

Capt. Ricardo shook his head. "It's not the same thing," he countered. "We've got to get them relatively thin again—set up a diet program, get them to exercise, that sort of thing."

"We haven't really changed anything," Capt. Smirk persisted. "Let's get out of here before they blow up."

"I still feel this is wrong," Capt. Ricardo dithered. "We're violating the Prime Time Directive."

"Then why don't we go somewhere and get them some diet pills or something." Clearly, Capt. Smirk was fed up with the whole issue.

"I don't know." Capt. Ricardo crossed his arms. "Perhaps we should take a vote on it."

"Take a vote on it!" Capt. Smirk exploded. "You want to take a vote on everything! Let's just get out of here and be done with it!"

Capt. Ricardo likewise lost his temper. "You know full well

you have no intention of returning here, not with diet pills, tent dresses or anything else!"

"Right!" Capt. Smirk stood up abruptly, knocking over his chair. "At least I know how to make up my mind! We're leaving here, and that's that!" He stormed out of the conference room.

Piker called after him, "Sir, let's schedule another meeting to discuss this further!"

6

Mutiny at Midnight

APT. SMIRK PACED the Bridge. This was taking a lot longer than he'd planned.

He and his crew met on the Bridge precisely at 2350 hours, but they hadn't allowed time for removing the dust covers that Capt. Ricardo's crew placed over everything before going to bed.

Unpleasant feelings raced through Smirk's mind: guilt over taking this radical step . . . regret at having to leave just when things were going so well with Counselor Troit . . . disappointment that he hadn't been able to try out the HolidayDeck.

But better times await us, he thought. *There's a whole universe out there, ripe for the taking. Why squander our talents on this ridiculous planet?*

Finally all the dust covers were off. No one had discovered them yet. So far, so good.

"Mr. Zulu," said the captain, unconsciously lowering his voice even though no one from Capt. Ricardo's crew was around to hear them. "Detach us from the saucer section and get us free of the tractor beam."

"Aye, sir." Zulu worked the console. "Cup section detached from saucer," he reported. Zulu then rocked the cup section loose using Mr. Smock's winter-driving technique. "We are now free of the tractor beam," Zulu reported.

"Set coordinates for the nearest fun-filled star system," ordered Capt. Smirk.

"Setting coordinates at 52954 mark 61554."

"Warped speed 5," continued the captain.

"Warped speed 5," echoed Zulu.

"Engage."

The cup section lifted smoothly away from the saucer section and blasted off.

The Endocrine's cheap security system only reacted after a crisis reached major proportions. Furthermore, it had only one alarm to cover all situations, including fire, alien invasion, and unauthorized cup section detachment.

The alarm system kicked in after Smirk's crew left. It had all the standard starship alarm features. A claxon horn blared from overhead speakers. Red lights labeled "panic lights" flashed on and off in the corridors. Steam hissed into the halls from spigots marked "emergency steam."

Capt. Ricardo woke up in his quarters and rushed to the window, just in time to see the guts of his starship disappear into space. He cursed to himself as he threw his robe over his pajamas and headed for the Spare Bridge. Somehow he immediately understood what had happened.

The blaring horns woke Georgie. He reached over to the nightstand and switched on the lamp, revealing his visor soaking in a semi-circular plastic pan. Next to it was a plastic bottle of Visor Scrub Overnight Soaking Solution.

Georgie sat up in bed. His right eyeball dangled from its spring, but on the left side there was only a spring with no eyeball attached. Sensing something was amiss, Georgie touched the end of the left spring, then groaned.

"Awww, not now—of all the rotten timing . . ."

Georgie began feeling around under the covers for his miss-

He rushed to the window, just in
time to see the guts of his starship
disappear into space.

ing eyeball. When he didn't find it, he burrowed deeper, then deeper yet, disappearing beneath the blankets.

Wart's bedroom had a bare cement floor and cement walls. An unshaded light bulb glared from the ceiling. Directly beneath it, Wart lay on a bed of nails.

When the horns began blaring, Wart awoke at once, scowling. "Just when I'd gotten comfortable," he rumbled.

Dacron's bedroom was a padded cell. Each night he retreated there to refresh himself and recharge his energy. An electrical cord extended from his navel to a transformer in the wall outlet.

At the alarm, Dacron's eyes opened instantly and remained open without blinking. He stood up and took several brisk steps toward the door. Then he reached the end of his electrical cord. The taut cord jerked him backward, and his feet flew out from under him.

Capt. Ricardo paced the Spare Bridge. It was a dusty and depressing place. Worse yet, there was absolutely nothing for him to do. Now that Smirk had flown off with the cup section, Ricardo and his crew remained behind, trapped by the Cellulites' tractor beam. For lack of anything better to do, Ricardo paged his officers, ordering them to report to the Spare Bridge.

Wart arrived first. Noticing Capt. Ricardo's robe, he asked, "Oh, is this a 'come as you are' party?" Capt. Ricardo glared at him. Wart shrugged and went to the communication post.

Dacron came next, rubbing his navel. He sat groggily at the console on the right and worked its controls for a few moments. Finally it occurred to him to wonder why they were using the Spare Bridge. "Did I miss something?" he inquired.

Georgie came in, wearing his visor, as well as a black eyepatch over his left eye. Then came Troit, Dr. Pragmatski, and Westerly, still in pajamas.

"Lt. Wart, open 'hey, you' frequencies. We'll attempt to contact the cup section," Capt. Ricardo ordered.

This raised a few eyebrows around the Spare Bridge. What did Capt. Ricardo mean, "attempt to contact the cup section"? Sensing the captain's surly mood, no one said anything, but curiosity was high. Westerly sidled over to the faded curtains covering the windshield of the Spare Bridge and peeked outside.

" 'Hey, you' frequencies open, sir," said Wart.

"This is Capt. Ricardo. Cup section, do you read me?"

There was no response. Capt. Ricardo tried again and again, but the cup section did not answer.

Piker finally arrived, carefully smoothing his hair with the palm of his hand. "Sorry I'm late," he said. "I had a devil of a time with my hair."

"No hurry, Number 1," the captain said. "We aren't going anywhere. It seems Capt. Smirk and his crew have taken off with the cup section."

Everybody moaned.

"Mr. LaForgery," Capt. Ricardo continued, "can we break free of the tractor beam and pursue them?"

"No, sir," Georgie asserted. "What little power we have left is required to maintain the shields and keep the Cellulites from boarding."

Piker didn't miss a beat. He drew himself up to his full height and asserted, "Captain, this is a real crisis."

Since the ship obviously wasn't going anywhere, the officers left their posts and milled around the Spare Bridge.

Counselor Troit wailed, "You mean they just took off? Without so much as a 'Dear John' note?"

"Would you believe a 'Dear Jean-Lucy' note?" said Georgie as he discovered a piece of paper on the counter in the back. He read aloud the handwritten message:

"Dear Jean-Lucy: I figured you wouldn't be using the Bridge for awhile, so we borrowed the cup section. By the time I get

When the horns began blaring,
Wart awoke at once, scowling.

to Planet Phoenix—9, you'll be rising. By the time I make Starbase Albuquerque, you'll be working. By the time we return I'm sure you'll have solved the Cellulite situation. Regards, James T. Smirk."

7

The Agony and the Ecstasy

Day 7

"**G**OOD MORNING. THIS is your captain speaking." Capt. Ricardo released the button on the intercom microphone for a moment and cleared his throat.

Things had gone sharply downhill in the seven days since Smirk and crew took off with the cup section. None of the weight-loss gimmicks Ricardo's people tried had worked for the Cellulites, who wanted only to reboard the Endocrine and devour its food supply.

The shields kept the Cellulites from boarding but required more electrical power each day. That meant the crew had to do without an ever-growing list of electrical luxuries.

The captain continued his announcement. "Today's addition to the Prohibited Appliances List is video games. Stiff upper lip, everyone."

Ricardo surveyed the Spare Bridge, which was a far cry from his regular Bridge. The Spare Bridge had secondhand consoles and beat-up slip-covered chairs. An old computer that took up an entire wall did nothing but print out a horoscope when a birth date was entered.

Absent from the Spare Bridge was Westerly Flusher. Capt.

Capt. Ricardo planned to drop
leaflets onto the Cellulites.

Ricardo had grounded him in his room for a month. Making him go without supper seemed too light a punishment for triggering this whole mess, especially after Smirk left them stranded here.

Today Capt. Ricardo planned to drop leaflets onto the Cellulites, containing information on every diet ever recorded. Perhaps it would help the Cellulites trim down by themselves and fulfill his crew's obligation to the Prime Time Directive.

"Hey, you party animals! This is Capt. Jim-bo Smirk with today's social schedule." His voice boomed over the intercom of the Endocrine's cup section as it sailed through the Nebbish Nebula. "Tonight we'll dock at Nefertiti—2, a fun-loving planet with some very uninhibited natives. Tonight's party theme is Luau Time. It should be a blast! Smirk out."

Flitting around the galaxy and partying heavily made Capt. Smirk feel like a young man of 70 again. He'd switched off the radio in case Capt. Ricardo tried to contact him and spoil all the fun. *If they really need to get in touch with me*, he thought, *let them send a Candygram*.

Just as Smirk had hoped, on this spree he was meeting one classy dame after another, each with a more elaborate hairdo than the last. And the varieties of chiffon that had been developed since his last mission were astounding. Best of all, he still had the knack for finding gorgeous human females in the most unlikely alien tribes.

Day 10

"Good morning. This is Capt. Ricardo speaking. In order to maintain the defense shields, today's addition to the Prohibited Appliances List is the HolidayDeck. Repeat: the HolidayDeck is closed for the duration of our confinement."

Troit's mood sunk deeper at this announcement. The HolidayDeck had been her sole emotional outlet lately. She went there daily to brood over Capt. Smirk: how he had left them stranded, why he hadn't bothered to say goodbye, how she was going to wring his neck if they ever met again.

At least today she had a project to work on, one that might take her mind off him. Capt. Ricardo had asked her to contact the Cellulites on the Viewscreen and try to hypnotize them into dieting. At the very least, she hoped to persuade them to stop eating the leaflets the crew had dropped on their planet last week.

"Hey, gang!" exclaimed Capt. Smirk over his intercom. "We're headed for Parabola-X9, where the inhabitants make an art form out of the beer bash! Tonight we'll have a toga party, so don't bother getting out of bed early. Just wrap your bedsheet around you and come as you are!"

Listening to the announcement, Mr. Smock judged this a most practical costume idea, especially since he was already wearing a robe.

This breakaway from the saucer section suited Mr. Smock just fine. He knew logic would never solve anyone's weight problem, so Capt. Ricardo's pursuit of a solution seemed senseless. Most of all, Smock was happy to perform at peak capacity again without interference from that pesky android Dacron.

Day 12

"This is Capt. Ricardo speaking. I know this will be hard for all of you, but an additional sacrifice is necessary to preserve electricity for the shields. You will all have to stop using your waffle irons."

Piker was unperturbed. His usual breakfast was a quart of Power Milkshake Drink that was said to build the biceps like magic, so going without waffles was no big deal.

What did bug him, though, was the thought of Smirk & Co.

"It's Mardi Gras time!"

stranding them here next to Cellulite—1. The situation allowed no opportunities for dramatic poses. Piker resorted to spending a lot of time in front of the mirror, combing his hair in different ways.

Worst of all, his exercise video for the Cellulites had failed. The video showed Piker pumping iron, a routine that enabled him to fill out his tight flight suit so dramatically.

The Cellulites seemed interested in weight training but never got past the talking stage. The crew monitored their conversations. After a week of listening to the Cellulites' constant chatter about how they were going to start exercising "tomorrow", the crew turned off the communicator.

"Allll riiiight! It's Mardi Gras time! Our next stop includes a rendezvous with some really with-it aliens, so pull on those costumes and get ready to roll!"

Yoohoo smiled at Capt. Smirk's announcement. Not only did she enjoy the partying, but simply hanging around the ship was fun now that she was the token female again.

Day 16

"Attention all crew members. Add the following to the list of Prohibited Appliances: fish tank aerators. I repeat: fish tank aerators."

"Oh, no!" Dr. Pragmatski groaned. That meant her biology experiment was kaput. She'd spent weeks training several goldfish to swim to the top of the bowl when she rang a little bell. All that effort would be wasted now; soon their only trick would be the belly roll. Reluctantly she pulled the plug on the aerator.

That was her second disappointment this week. She'd had no luck when she beamed down and tried to convince the Cellulites to let her wire their jaws shut. She barely got out of there with her dental kit. *Well, if they don't want help, let them wallow*, she thought. *I'm a doctor, not a miracle worker.*

"Cowabunga! We'll hit the deck on AlphaBetaNiner at 1800 hours. Tonight's party theme is 'come as your favorite fictional character'. Bring your own yogurt, and we'll mix it together for a wild and crazy Suicide Punch."

Zulu searched his closet for yet another costume. *Preparing for these parties is becoming monotonous*, he reflected.

At first he'd been thrilled over their breakaway and eager to sample the hot spots of deep space. Lately, though, he'd grown tired of their daily routine: traveling to a new planet every night, partying until dawn, sleeping it off the next day, and on and on. Zulu longed for the discipline of normal shipboard life.

Not that he'd let on to Capt. Smirk. The captain was in his glory; each woman he discovered outshone the last. *Maybe there's just something wrong with me*, Zulu speculated, *but this seems more like work than fun.*

Day 20

"Capt. Ricardo here. Attention, everyone. Today's addition to the Prohibited Appliances List is television sets. Yes, I found out that you have them, and I'm asking you to turn in your sets. Don't make it necessary for me to search your quarters."

No TV! Westerly couldn't believe the injustice of it all. It was bad enough being confined to his room for a month, but now his only entertainment was cut off.

He hated being isolated from the rest of the crew. Even the cook who brought in his meals was forbidden to talk to him.

Meanwhile, the crew continued the weight-loss campaign. Capt. Ricardo beamed down several toning tables to Cellulite−1. But even passive exercise was too much for the Cellulites, so they used the devices as buffet tables.

"Oh no!" Dr. Pragmatski groaned.
Her biology experiment was kaput.

"Hi ho, happy campers! There's a wedding afoot on Planet Roundyboo, where we're headed. We're invited to a bridal shower for Princess Midge. Theme is 'kitchen goods'."

Dr. McCaw scoffed. *Bridal shower, my rear end*, he thought. *This party foolishness rubs me the wrong way. And so far these aliens have all been nincompoops.*

Dr. McCaw longed to treat a medical challenge more serious than a hangover, or a rug burn acquired during a game of Twister. In fact, he was surprised to discover that he yearned to talk with a hard-nosed peer like Dr. Pragmatski. *It doesn't seem likely we'll meet again soon, though*, thought Dr. McCaw. *Not unless Jim gets over this second childhood and comes to his senses.*

Day 24

"Good morning. This is the captain. Today's prohibited appliance is electric pencil sharpeners. Have a nice day."

Dacron slumped in front of the computer screen in his quarters. He knew he should take a break and recharge his energy, perhaps stick his finger in a socket, but he just didn't feel up to it.

Everything seemed so pointless since Capt. Ricardo confiscated their TV sets. Since he couldn't structure his day around his favorite TV shows, Dacron plodded aimlessly around the ship. He became listless, and his skin grew even more pale.

Capt. Ricardo tried to be helpful, inventing tasks for Dacron to do, such as reviewing every obesity research paper ever published in the medical journals. But that took Dacron only about 10 minutes, and then he was at loose ends again.

Meanwhile, Troit's anger toward Capt. Smirk had softened. She replicated a bottle of Old Spice in the UltraFax and sniffed it, deliberately bringing back memories of that scoundrel. She admitted to herself that she missed certain things about him:

that funny grin, the cute curl at his forehead, and the way his pants bagged above his ankles.

"Hey, hey, hey! Tonight we're invited to a swinging celebrity reception. And get this: Entity Magazine's 'Ten Most Eligible Aliens' will be there! Do these people know how to party or what!"

A celebrity reception. Great, thought Checkout. *That's the most intimidating kind of party. Everybody stands around checking out each others' clothes and trying to top each others' witty lines, all the while scanning the room in case somebody more interesting walks in.*

Checkout didn't need another blow to his ego. He wasn't doing well with the women as it was. Even on Planet Horsehead, where the women outnumbered the men 10 to 1, he struck out. He'd spent that evening wondering which was worse, those barfy alien women or the fact that they were ignoring him.

Yoohoo, too, was starting to feel ill at ease. This romp through space exposed her congenital defect: a complete absence of personality.

This flaw never bothered Yoohoo before. In fact, it had helped her get hired in the first place, since she would never upstage Capt. Smirk and Mr. Smock. But now Yoohoo discovered that "hailing frequencies open, sir" didn't make much of an opening line, and beyond that her conversational skills were minimal.

Day 27

"Capt. Ricardo here. Attention, everyone. We need every bit of electricity to keep our shields from failing. The Cellulites are still trying to board, and they could easily eat us out of house—er, ship—and home. Therefore, you will have to do without your Water Pik dental appliances."

She replicated a bottle of Old Spice
and sniffed it, deliberately bringing
back memories of that scoundrel . . .

The situation is desperate, thought Capt. Ricardo. *Without clean teeth and gums, crew morale will fall fast.*

In the last few days, Capt. Ricardo's outrage at Capt. Smirk had begun to crumble. He was tired of the whole situation and ready to forgive Capt. Smirk, if only he'd come back.

Today it had been Georgie's turn to think of a way to reduce the Cellulites' bulk. Georgie constructed an extra-large sauna and beamed it down to the planet. "Maybe they can sweat it off," he reasoned.

The Cellulites were intrigued by the sauna. They threw mesquite onto the heated rocks and barbecued a steer in it.

After that, Georgie fell into the same funk that inhabited the rest of the crew. Normally meticulous about his appearance, now he took to removing his visor while on duty, absent-mindedly playing with his eyeball springs.

"Now hear this, you wild and crazy crew. This is the life!"

Capt. Smirk put down the intercom microphone and yawned. The lack of sleep and the constant forced hilarity were starting to get to him. For the crew's sake, he tried to pump some enthusiasm into his voice.

"Have I got a theme for you: 'party till you puke'!"

Oh, for the love of Pete, what a disgusting idea, thought Mr. Snot. He'd been exceedingly crabby lately. These easy runs from one planet to the next were well within the ship's capacity. With no mechanical breakdowns and no crises, Mr. Snot worried about losing his creative edge.

Mr. Smock felt the same way. Locating the nearest party planet each day did not provide the scientific stimulation Smock envisioned when they fled the saucer section. In fact, the Cellulite problem was an interesting challenge compared to the soft life on their current pleasure cruise.

Day 29

"Attention, crew. This is Capt. Ricardo. I know this is a lot to ask, but remember, I'm making the same sacrifices as all of you. You're going to have to turn off your night lights. Cheerio, all."

Wart nearly panicked. *Turn off the night lights! No, anything but that!*

No one suspected his fear of the dark, and Wart didn't want them to find out now. Yet he worried he would cave in; like everyone else on the ship, he felt helpless and vulnerable in this no-win situation.

I'll have to manage, Wart told himself. *I'm still the bravest one on board. I was the only one who dared to beam down to the planet yesterday to try that ear-stapling acupuncture scheme on the Cellulites. It was supposed to reduce their appetites. It might have worked, too, if I'd have been able to find their ears. Perhaps more drastic measures are necessary. Nose rings, maybe?*

"Listen up, you fun-loving guys and gal." It took a real effort for Capt. Smirk to inject some enthusiasm into his voice. "We're headed for Planet Moronski, where they've planned a puppet show . . ." His voice trailed off, and he slumped in his chair.

It isn't working, he thought. *It's no fun anymore.*

The strain of making the scene at one party after another was getting to him. And the impossible had happened: he was tired of the constant parade of alien women. He missed Counselor Troit. The women he'd met on this spree seemed shallow compared to her. They couldn't anticipate his moods the way Deanna could, either.

Capt. Smirk knew what he had to do. He picked up the intercom microphone.

"Listen," he announced, "I think the puppet show can go on without us."

Throughout the cup section, his crew members looked up with sudden hope. Perhaps they could stop all this exhausting partying and get back to work.

"Let's head back to the saucer," Smirk ordered.

His crew cheered.

8

The Prodigals
Return

A T FIRST, CAPT. Ricardo's crew didn't even realize Capt. Smirk's crew had come back. Zulu skillfully piloted the cup into a linkup with the saucer without the slightest bump to announce their presence. The monitors in the saucer had been shut off to save electricity, and nobody was in the mood to look out the window.

As usual, the saucer section gang was in the Spare Bridge, gathered around a space heater. They were stunned when the door of the Spare Crewmover opened to admit Smirk and crew.

"Hi, everybody." Capt. Smirk greeted them with studied nonchalance. "What's new?"

A kaleidoscope of emotions was reflected in Capt. Ricardo's expression: anger at confronting the perpetrators of their recent misery, relief that the ship and crews were intact once again, and surprise that Smirk had returned at all. Finally, pride took over. "Nothing much," he replied casually. "How about you?"

"Been having some pretty wild times," said Capt. Smirk, "but we thought we'd come back here and check out the scene. Say, why is it so cold in here?"

"It's cold," Capt. Ricardo replied, his anger rising, "because

"It's cold because we had to turn
off the furnace."

we had to turn off the furnace and save electricity for the shields."

"Is that so?" Capt. Smirk stiffened, sensing the tide of resentment in the room. His crew huddled behind him like sheep.

"All our power is required to maintain the shields and protect us from the Cellulites." Capt. Ricardo was picking up steam now. An angry flush spread from his eyebrows to his forehead and parts north. "We've been doing without video games, waffle irons—"

" . . . the HolidayDeck . . ." Troit contributed, her eyes flashing in anger.

" . . . fish tank aerators . . ." snapped Dr. Pragmatski.

"Electric pencil sharpeners . . . Water Piks . . . night lights . . ." Crew members interrupted one another, recounting their own personal nightmares of deprivation.

Capt. Smirk's team went on the defensive. "If you'd learn to loosen up a little, you wouldn't need the HolidayDeck for a good time," Capt. Smirk retorted to Troit.

Simultaneously, Dr. McCaw barked at Dr. Pragmatski, "Fish tank aerators! What do you need those for? You're a doctor, not a marine biologist!"

Everyone on both crews shouted at once. The din became louder and louder. Counselor Troit, overwhelmed by the ferocity of emotion dinging around the Spare Bridge, sat down and held her head in her hands.

This has gone too far, Troit decided. She tried getting their attention. "Crew."

No one heard her. They continued shouting.

"Crewww," said Troit, louder this time. Still no response.

"Crew—SHHHAAADAAAAAPPP!"

Everyone stared at Troit, amazed at the bellow she had produced.

"Thank you," Troit added in a small, clipped voice. She

continued, "You're all acting like children. We're never going to get out of our predicament by arguing.

"Everyone is at fault. Our crews have never cooperated properly. Never mind who started it; it's time for all of us to apologize."

Troit drew the two captains together. "You need to set the example for your crews," she instructed.

Capt. Smirk took on a bad-little-boy expression. "Deanna is right," he admitted. "We were out of line. I still believe in Starfreak tradition, including the Prime Time Directive. I'm sorry."

Capt. Ricardo's irritation eased. "So am I, Capt. Smirk. It's partly my fault for failing to get our crews to cooperate. I've left you too far out of the decision-making process, too. Things will be different between our crews from now on." They shook hands.

"Now, everyone else, make up with each other," Troit ordered the rest of them. They complied, some more readily than others, and within a few minutes everyone had taken the first steps toward a kinder, gentler starship.

"Here are the ground rules for this brainstorming session," Capt. Ricardo told the crews. Everyone was back on the regular Bridge, more than ready to solve the Cellulite dilemma. "You may suggest any idea that comes to your mind.

"We must avoid criticism; it inhibits the free flow of imagination. No idea is 'too silly.' In fact, try deliberately to think of silly ideas, to get your imagination working. Got that?

"All right, let's get started. The problem we're addressing is: How do we get the Cellulites back to the way they were before we came, thereby maintaining the Prime Time Directive?"

Everyone thought hard for a minute. Then Smock ventured, "You are certain no idea is too far-fetched, captain?"

"That is correct," answered Capt. Ricardo. "What is your suggestion, Mr. Smock?"

"Perhaps we could resort to hypnosis to reduce their appetites," said Smock. "I know this technique is viewed with some skepticism in the medical community, but this is a desperate situation."

"We've already tried hypnosis," said Capt. Ricardo, "though I appreciate your contribution to our discussion. Anyone else? Come now, loosen up your imaginations. Get really silly."

"What about those toning tables that people used to use for passive exercise?" said Yoohoo.

"Er . . . we've tried that also," said Capt. Ricardo.

"I know!" Zulu exclaimed, then giggled. "This is really crazy. How about using a sauna to get them to 'sweat off' the weight?"

Capt. Ricardo cleared his throat. "Uh, we tried that, too. Please, make your suggestions even more far-fetched."

"Jaw wiring," said Dr. McCaw.

"We tried it."

"Ear stapling; it's a form of acupuncture," volunteered Checkout.

"We tried it."

"Well," concluded Capt. Smirk, "it seems you people are several steps ahead of us."

Those on the Bridge fell into a silent funk. Then Westerly arrived in the Crewmover.

"What are you doing out of your room, young man?" Piker demanded.

"My grounding officially ended 5 minutes ago," Westerly asserted. "Will someone tell me what's been going on in the last month?"

Troit quickly filled him in. " . . . And now we're trying to figure out how to get the Cellulites back to the way they were when we found them," she concluded.

"Dacron, review the solutions we've come up with so far," said Capt. Ricardo, trying to get the discussion back on track.

When Dacron finished reciting their suggestions, Westerly was puzzled. He began tentatively, "Why don't we . . ." and then stopped.

"Why don't we what, Westerly?" asked Piker.

Westerly looked around warily. "Why don't we— . . . no, forget it. You'll think I'm smarting off. It's not worth being grounded for another month."

"Why don't we what?!" demanded Capt. Ricardo. "If you've got an idea, young man, spit it out!"

"Promise me I won't be grounded?"

"Yes!"

"OK." Westerly took a deep breath. "Why don't we just put them back in the diet chambers? *That's* the way we found them. And eventually, they'll lose some weight again. It worked for them before."

There was a long period of silence on the Bridge, as each one in their own way pondered, *Why didn't I think of that?*

Finally Dr. Pragmatski spoke up. "Fine in theory," she stated, "but how do we get them back in the diet chambers? They've been anything but cooperative. They're more like the old Earth joke: where does a 600-pound gorilla sit?"

"In the zoo?" Dacron guessed.

"ANYWHERE HE WANTS." Everyone else supplied the punchline in unison.

"This calls for strategic planning and bold tactical moves!" Capt. Smirk felt the thrill of battle, even if it was only the battle of the bulge. "Ricardo, it's time for you and I to put our heads together and come up with a plan."

9

Man vs. Flab

WITHIN HOURS, OPERATION Hoho was underway.
Now that they had a clear objective, Capt. Ricardo and Capt. Smirk lost no time in coming up with a dramatic strategy. And in convincing their crews to cooperate on the plan, Smirk drew on his extensive training and experience in Starfreak Method Acting.

He declaimed, "Consider the classic struggles: man vs. man, man vs. himself, man vs. the elements. What we face now is man vs. flab." No one could argue with his logic, especially since they weren't sure what he was talking about. So the plan won unanimous approval.

In the first phase of the plan, Smock and Dacron spent the night researching Cellulite behavior from earliest recorded history to the present. The next morning, they presented their information to Capt. Ricardo and Capt. Smirk.

To the captains' relief, Smock and Dacron had obviously cooperated on their research. And the data confirmed that their plan would work. The operation was off to a good start.

"We believe that 20 cases of Hohos will be sufficient to enable us to achieve our objective," Smock concluded.

"Westerly and Checkout." Capt. Smirk swiveled in his command chair to face them. He and Capt. Ricardo had agreed to remove the restaurant booth and reinstall two chairs in the center of the Bridge. "Replicate 20 cases of Hostess brand Hohos in the UltraFax. "

"Yes, sir," they responded, heading off the Bridge.

"Number 1, I believe it's time for your input," Capt. Ricardo said. According to the plan, Piker was to inject dramatic statements at regular intervals.

Piker hesitated. "Did you want a proclamation of victory, or—"

"No, Number 1. We're still in the thick of this, so we need some dramatic tension."

Piker put on a concerned yet determined expression and declared, "Time is running out. We need to move boldly to relocate the Cellulites before they blow up."

"Very good, Number I."

Checkout's voice came over the intercom, "Captains, we've got the Hohos."

Another hurdle crossed; Westerly and Checkout had cooperated during their phase. Capt. Smirk nodded in satisfaction at Capt. Ricardo.

Capt. Ricardo turned toward the back of the Bridge. "Security ready?"

"Aye, sir," responded Wart and Zulu, who would provide security for the newly-renamed Aweight Team.

"Sick Bay," Capt. Ricardo said to the intercom, "ready with the sedatives?"

"It's taking longer than you estimated," Dr. McCaw barked. "I'm a doctor, not a drive-through medical clinic." Both captains tensed. Had their plan just hit a snag?

Over the intercom, they heard a muffled discussion in Sick Bay. Then Dr. McCaw continued, "All right, we're ready."

Dr. Pragmatski added, "We've got enough sedatives to relax the Cellulites for about 20 minutes. Then the effects will wear off and leave them extremely cranky, so we'd better have them in the chambers by then."

"Affirmative," said Capt. Ricardo. "Wart and Zulu will pro-

Smock and Dacron spent the night
researching Cellulite behavior
from earliest recorded history

vide security backup. Meet them in Shipping and Receiving."
Wart and Zulu headed for the loading dock.

"Westerly and Checkout, get your Hohos down to Shipping," said Capt. Smirk to the intercom.

A few moments later, a shipping clerk reported over the
intercom that the doctors and their security escort had
UltraFaxed down to Cellulite—1. "I put them precisely on the
coordinates of Couch Potato Downs, where the Cellulites have
set up living quarters," she reported.

Without prompting, Piker stood up and posed. "Now all we
can do is wait," he stated.

It was, indeed, a tense period. Those on the Bridge visual-
ized their crewmates carrying out the next step of the plan:
Wart and Zulu luring the Cellulites outside with the smell of
Hohos so the two doctors could administer the sedatives.
Everyone on the ship wondered how they were doing during
this dangerous maneuver.

"They can put a man on the moon, but they can't invent a
visual monitor linking an Away Team with the ship," Capt.
Smirk mused.

Finally the Aweight Team reported. "We've got them outside, captain," Zulu said. "They look very . . . hungry."

"Careful, people," Capt. Ricardo cautioned.

There was another long, tense period of waiting. Then Dr.
Pragmatski spoke over the intercom. "We've administered the
sedatives, and they're working," she said. "For the next 20
minutes, these Cellulites will be like putty in our hands."

Capt. Smirk ordered, "Counselor Troit and Lt. Yoohoo,
time for you to UltraFax down." The women headed for their
task: persuading the Cellulites to cooperate with the rest of
the plan. Capt. Ricardo had insisted that the Cellulites return
to the diet chambers of their own free will. It was the only
way, he felt, to ensure the crew was following the Prime Time
Directive to the letter.

More waiting. The tension was nearly unbearable. The captains twiddled their thumbs while Piker paced back and forth, striking a dramatic pose whenever he reached a wall and had to turn around.

Finally Troit spoke on the intercom. "They've agreed to return to the chambers," she announced.

"All right!" Capt. Smirk exclaimed. "Engine Room! Mr. Snot, Georgie, are the forklifts ready?"

Mr. Snot reported over the intercom, "Aye, sir, we've got some grand forklifts ready for totin' that big load."

"Then UltraFax down and start carrying the Cellulites from Couch Potato Downs back to their chambers at the HyberThin franchise."

"Aye, sir."

Their next transmission came from the surface of Cellulite—1. "Captain," Mr. Snot said with awe in his voice, "there be whales here! These Cellulites must weigh over half a ton apiece!"

"Mr. Snot," Capt. Smirk replied, "are you saying the forklifts can't handle it?"

Mr. Snot recovered, his voice coming back loud and strong. "Georgie and I built them to take any punishment. They'll handle it, or my name isn't Sean Michael Thomas Snot the Third!"

"Attaboy, Mr. Snot." The captains sighed in relief.

"What time is it, Number 1?"

"Uh, let's see—noon is 1200 hours; add 1 hour and it's 1300; then 1400, 1500 . . . ummm . . . it's 6:25 Central Standard Time."

"Aweight Team!" said Capt. Ricardo. "You've only got 5 minutes left. Report!"

"We're having trouble getting the Cellulites off the forklifts and into the chambers," Georgie said.

"Number 1," commanded Capt. Ricardo, "take a dolly from

"Captain," Mr Snot said
with awe in his voice,
"there be whales here!"

the maintenance department and go down there to help them."

"Cabbage Patch or Barbie?" inquired Piker.

"What?"

"What kind of dolly do you want, captain?"

"Westerly." Capt. Ricardo turned away from Piker and toward Westerly at his pilot's post. "Get a dolly from the maintenance department and meet Cmdr. Piker at the UltraFax platform. You'll both beam down to help move the Cellulites."

"Yes, sir."

"Captains," Smock said from his science station, "new data from the computer indicates the Cellulites will emit a tremendous negative vibration the moment the sedative wears off. That seems to be a reaction to being placed on yet another diet of unlimited duration."

"And the consequences, Mr. Smock?"

"Computer projections indicate that Cellulite—1 will release a force field. This eruption will not harm the Cellulites in their diet chambers, but will expand outward from them with the impact of ten thousand tons of TNT, enough to destroy our ship, all crew members and any possibility of a sequel."

"Thank you, Mr. Smock. We'll sit here and worry about that for a while."

Two minutes remained.

At Capt. Smirk's orders, Westerly left his communicator turned on so the Bridge crew could monitor the situation on Cellulite—1.

What the captains heard wasn't reassuring. Tempers flared under the pressure of the deadline. There were shouts of "Outta my way!" and "Let's move it!" And several crew members seemed to be relapsing into old habits, with exclamations of "I'm a doctor, not a moving van" and "These wee forklifts can't stand the strain."

With one minute left before the predicted explosion time,

Westerly reported, "Captain, we just turned off the tractor beam. We found the 'off' switch in the marketing director's office."

Then finally, with just 30 seconds to go, Piker announced, "Sir, all the Cellulites are back in their diet chambers."

"Very good! Fax back up here immediately," responded Capt. Ricardo. "No time to save the forklifts. Just get yourselves on board."

After a very long pause, the clerk in Shipping announced, "Aweight Team has faxed aboard, sir."

"Let's get out of here!" Capt. Smirk exclaimed. He began punching buttons on the pilot's console. "Setting course 777 mark 007, Warped factor 9."

"Engage!" said Capt. Ricardo.

As the Aweight Team returned to the Bridge, Dacron began counting off the seconds to the explosion on Cellulite−1. "T minus 10 seconds and counting. Nine seconds . . . 8 . . . 7 . . . 6 . . . 5 . . . 4 . . . 3 . . . 2 . . . 1 . . . detonation."

Back on the surface of the planet, the Cellulites shook off the effects of the sedative and realized they'd agreed to another extended fast. Their irritation exploded in a burst of energy, creating a force field which rapidly expanded outward from the planet.

"Impact coming!" Capt. Ricardo cried. "Everybody grab something and hold on tight!"

Capt. Ricardo sat in a command chair and clutched the sides for stability. Most of the others grabbed a console. Capt. Smirk hustled over to Counselor Troit and pulled her body against his.

10

Finish with a Bang

THE EXPLOSION REACHED the Endocrine.
A powerful impact rocked the Bridge, and a blast overpowered all sound. The force knocked several crew members off their feet. The lights flickered off for a moment as power was interrupted, then came back on. The thunderous roar died away.

Gradually, everyone realized the crisis was past. They picked themselves up, dusted themselves off, and sighed in relief. It appeared that the worst damage was to their VCR's, which needed resetting after the power interruption.

At long last it was time to celebrate.

Yoohoo turned a knob at her station, and the Hallelujah Chorus from Handel's "Messiah" blared from the speakers.

Crew members shook hands, hugged each other and threw confetti.

Wart, Dr. Pragmatski and Dr. McCaw came perilously close to smiling. Mr. Snot danced a merry jig.

Troit and Capt. Smirk continued making amends most heartily in the center of the Bridge.

Capt. Ricardo stood smiling in the midst of it all, savoring the moment.

Dacron pointed to the windshield. "Look!"

Everyone turned to look outward. The explosion on

Cellulite—1 faded to a healthy glow, much like the bulbs in a tanning bed. The planet had become a new star.

"Captain, we're picking up a message from Cellulite—1," Wart reported from the communication post. "It's being broadcast in all languages, on all frequencies, and on all network affiliates."

As he spoke, the message was superimposed on the Viewscreen. Its letters appeared one by one:

A..L..L . . .

"Alleluia?" someone guessed.

A..L..L.... T..H..E . . .

"All the way home," suggested someone else.

A..L..L..... T..H..E..S..E........... W..O...R....

"All these worms?" Dacron guessed. Finally they gave up and waited until the entire message was revealed:

ALL THESE WORLDS ARE YOURS EXCEPT FOR CELLULITE—1. USE THEM TOGETHER. USE THEM IN PEACE. HAVE A NICE DAY.

They fell silent for a moment, deeply moved. Everyone assumed this was an awesome message, loaded with cosmic significance, since no one understood it.

Piker struggled to put their awe into words. "It appears the universe harbors an intelligence greater than yours and mine," he reflected.

"Well, yours anyway," said Mr. Smock.

The Endocrine shifted into Warped drive and blasted away.

Capt. Ricardo wrapped it up. "Captain's top-secret diary, Star Date 6256.5661. Having fulfilled the Prime Time Directive with the Cellulites, we continue our mission: to cruise around the universe looking for novel predicaments to get into. To search the outskirts of the galaxy for areas with less crowding, lower tax rates and better schools. To boldly go where nobody wanted to go before!"

A powerful impact rocked
the bridge.

STAR WRECK II
THE ATTACK OF THE JARGONITES

Admiral Tweet appeared on the communication screen, wearing the frenzied look of someone about to undergo a tax audit. "Smirk!" he barked hoarsely, "the Jargonites have invaded us here at headquarters! You've been hanging around in orbit for half a day now. When are you going to do something?"

"Right away, Admiral," Smirk responded. "Don't worry. I have a plan."

"It'd better be a quick plan," Tweet said. He looked towards his office door, which was being forced inwards, straining the hinges.

"It is, Admiral," said Smirk. "Bold and decisive. I can't tell you too much about it in case the Jargonites are monitoring this transmission. Let's just say it involves destroying my ship."

"But ... destroy ... while you're in orbit—Smirk, the explosion will take Earth along with it!" Tweet's voice rose in panic.

"Don't worry, Admiral," Smirk repeated. "I have it all under control ..."

The Honeymoon Is Over

IT WAS A DARK AND STORMY NIGHT. AS USUAL, THE USS *Endocrine* was flying through the galaxy, cruisin' for a bruisin'.

Captain Jean-Lucy Ricardo sat in his quarters reading *How to Win Friends and Influence People.* He put the book down and sighed. His staff problems seemed too sticky for any mere self-help book.

After the triumph of their previous mission on Cellulite-I, there had been a brief period of peace between his crew and the crew of Captain James T. Smirk. A frightfully brief period. Then the exultation wore off, and reality set in. The crews still resented sharing the same ship. They refused to combine their areas of responsibility and were at each others' throats constantly. Cramped for space, they spent more time fighting over territory than working.

Capt. Ricardo set the book aside and stood up. *I'll go mingle with the troops for awhile,* he thought. *Perhaps that will help ease the tension. Let's see—it's Saturday night, so they'll all be in the bar.*

Capt. Ricardo boarded the Crewmover, the *Endocrine's* vertical/horizontal elevator with the best Muzak in the fleet.

"Destination, please," requested the Crewmover's automated voice.

"Ten-Foreplay," said the captain.

Actually, Capt. Ricardo was the only one who thought of Ten-Foreplay as a bar. "Social club" was more like it. The *Endocrine* was such a wholesome ship, what with families aboard and all, that Ten-Foreplay's house rules prohibited brawling, bar dice, and lewd and lascivious behavior. It was widely regarded as the dullest watering hole in Starfreak.

As Capt. Ricardo entered Ten-Foreplay, he saw his co-captain, James T. Smirk, sitting at a table with Counselor Deanna "Dee" Troit. The captains bared their teeth at each other in a social grin.

Ricardo envied him. Smirk and Deanna had become engaged just after the *Endocrine's* previous mission. It was obvious to Ricardo that Smirk was the happiest man in the galaxy now that he was about to be married.

How did I ever let myself get into this predicament? Capt. Smirk thought. Deanna was going on and on about silver patterns and bridal registries. Smirk felt the familiar tightness that grew in his chest whenever he contemplated their future together. His palms began to sweat. He kept nodding, hoping she'd think he was paying attention as he stared off into the distance, trying to keep his composure.

It wasn't as though he didn't love Deanna. He'd been sincere when he'd proposed to her the night the *Endocrine* crew overcame the Cellulites. The romantic gesture had somehow seemed to fit into the celebration.

Then the next morning when he awakened, it had hit him: committing himself to Deanna meant losing out on the Wonderful World of Classy Dames. No more seeking out the most beautiful human-looking female in every alien race. No more star-crossed romances, made all the more intense by the knowledge that they would inevitably end. No more playing the conquering lover. He would be hemmed in, tied down, *domesticated.*

Yet he couldn't bring himself to tell Deanna how he felt. She got so emotional at times. What would happen if he called off their engagement? It might break her heart. Worse yet, she might break his jaw. So he kept his misgivings to himself, and when they were together, it took all his energy to mask his feelings from her Betavoid telepathy.

Deanna was saying something. He'd better pay attention. "Jim? Jim, are you listening?"

"Of course, darling." He smiled at her and took a gulp of his vodka martini. She really was a beautiful woman, he reflected. And talented, too. Why, just last week she'd earned a promotion, which allowed her the privilege of wearing a dress on the Bridge.

"I was just wondering," she said, tossing her curls coyly, "when we're going to set the date."

"Date?" Smirk gave her a blank stare.

"Of our wedding day, sweetheart." She sipped her blackberry brandy. "Or are we going to continue this engagement indefinitely?"

"Oh, *that* date!" Smirk attempted a light laugh, which emerged too loudly as a sort of bleat. The odd noise prompted several people at nearby tables to turn and look curiously at him. "Well, ah, I hadn't really thought about it; I've been enjoying our endangerment so much."

Troit smiled tolerantly. "Don't you mean 'engagement'?"

Smirk forced the corners of his mouth ever higher. "Yes. That's what I meant to say. Engapement. Ummm, endrapement. Engaguh—guh . . . Eng-g-g-. . ."

Troit lovingly clasped his hand and loosened his grip on the vodka martini. "I think you've had enough for now, dear," she whispered.

Capt. Ricardo walked over to a table where three of his officers were sitting: his second in command, Commander Wilson Piker;

his Kringle security officer, Wart; and chief engineer Georgie LaForgery.

"Mind if I join you?" the captain asked.

"Not at all," said Piker. "Pull up a chair. We're just about to order." He handed a menu to Capt. Ricardo.

Ten-Foreplay's food service was a money-making venture recently introduced by the chief bartender, Guano. She needed the money to get herself an eyebrow transplant.

An odd-looking creature approached their table. "Hi, I'm Dirk, and I'll be your alien tonight," he simpered. "Can I take your order?"

"I'm ready," Piker said. "How about you, Wart?" Oddly, this sounded like a taunt.

Capt. Ricardo suddenly regretted sitting with them. Too late, he recalled Piker's recent fascination with Kringle cuisine. Piker and Wart had an ongoing macho match to see who could eat— with gusto—the most revolting Kringle food.

Wart ordered first. "I'll take the stewed targgh intestines, some hard-boiled bztocckk eyeballs, and a mug of breshtltorg blood." His eyelids narrowed in satisfaction as he handed the menu to Dirk.

Piker drew a deep breath and smiled as he met his opponent's challenge. "I'll have deep fried roargazht tail," he told the waiter, "a side order of glrshhh tongue and—" he paused for effect "—a draft of morishkee urine."

"Sir?" Dirk the waiter turned to Capt. Ricardo.

"I'll just have tea, thank you." Ricardo managed a wan smile. "Earl Grape."

"And you, sir?" Dirk inquired of Georgie.

"I'm not drinking tonight, thanks. I'm, uh, the ship's designated driver," Georgie said.

"Ah, there's nothing like a meal of wild game," Piker exulted. "I remember when my dad taught me to cook. I was only 10 years old. We were living in Alaska, and my mother had just left us in that awful incident with the bear."

"She was attacked?" Georgie gasped.

"No, she ran off to live in a cave with him." Piker took a swallow of ice water. "Actually, the bear was a big improvement over my father." Piker pulled three packets of Nutrasweet out of the tabletop container and emptied them into the water, stirring with his finger. "Anyway, after that we had to do all the housework ourselves. That's when Dad taught me to cook." He drained the entire glass without taking a breath, set it down, and ran his hand across his mouth with relish. It was his warm-up for the lip-smacking that would follow shortly.

Capt. Ricardo wasn't really listening. He had started to reflect on how far his first officer had come lately.

When their mission with the Cellulites ended, Piker decided he needed an intellectual challenge. Crew members offered suggestions: take adult education classes in Starship Management at Starfreak Trade & Tech; learn a second language; study chess; take up woodworking. Piker politely thanked them and carefully considered each possibility. After weeks of thought, he announced his chosen project: He was going to grow a beard. Later he became even more ambitious, planning to enter a Luciano Pavarotti lookalike contest.

The waiter arrived with their orders. "Watch out," he said, placing Piker's food in front of him. "The plate is extremely hot." The radioactivity symbol stenciled on the plate's border emphasized his warning. The parsley glowed enticingly.

Piker grinned in triumph. His meal was much more disgusting than Wart's. He grabbed his fork and began shoveling in the food.

Not to be outdone, Wart picked up a bztocckk eyeball and used his salad fork to pluck out the pupil like a pimiento from an olive.

Capt. Ricardo turned an interesting shade of green as he set his teacup carefully back in its saucer. He noticed that Georgie had closed the slats of his visor.

* * *

At an adjacent table, a waitress brought a tray. "Here you go," she announced, setting a bowl in front of each customer. "Three yogurts . . .

". . . a Scotch . . ." she continued, placing the drink in front of Mr. Snot.

". . . saki . . ." which she gave to Zulu.

". . . and a Shirley Temple," which went to Checkout.

Mr. Snot raised his glass in a toast. "Here's to good health," he proposed. Then he lifted a spoonful of yogurt in a second toast, adding, "and civilized eating." His last remark, directed loudly and pointedly toward the table next to them, drew a warning grumble from Wart.

Mr. Snot, Zulu and Checkout regarded their yogurt without enthusiasm. All of Smirk's crew had developed a high tolerance to the yogurt's anti-aging effects, so that they now resorted to eating it at every meal.

It hadn't helped; they had aged considerably since the Cellulite mission. Capt. Smirk desperately tried to counteract the trend. His motto became, "We're not getting older, we're getting funnier," and he constantly maneuvered them into cornball situations. The comic relief became so unremitting that finally they begged for some serious relief.

Then he led them on a camping trip to Jellystone Park, with an exhausting schedule of scaling rock walls and embarrassing themselves around the campfire. Again, they begged for a rest. Smirk was still going strong, demonstrating his vigor by climbing hills, climbing mountains, climbing sanitary landfills, climbing anything he could find that was higher than he was—but the others wanted to go back, so he relented.

Yoohoo probably could have benefitted the most from getting some exercise on the camping trip, but Capt. Smirk subtly discouraged her from coming along—"This is a male-bonding kind of thing," he told her—so instead she spent the week at a fat farm.

She didn't lose weight. However, she did pick up some freelance battle assignments from Starfreak Command. At each

Piker grinned in triumph . . .

battle she was airlifted in to a high vantage point to perform a seductive dance, and the enemy was incapacitated with laughter.

Capt. Ricardo noticed Dr. Beverage Flusher and her son Westerly enter Ten-Foreplay. Glad for the excuse to escape the gross eat-off, Ricardo left the table and approached them.

My, how Westerly has grown, he thought. *He's changed from a gangly, awkward adolescent to a gangly, awkward post-adolescent. It must have been quite a surprise for Beverage when she returned to our ship.* "Dr. Flusher, may I have a word with you, please?" Capt. Ricardo inquired.

Westerly took advantage of the interruption to escape to the video gameroom. Dr. Flusher had been hanging around him like a mother hen ever since she'd gotten back on the ship. He had a lot on his mind, and she was only distracting him from doing some serious worrying.

His worrying spell had started several nights before when Westerly was beating Capt. Smirk at a game of chess.

Smirk had begun making conversation in an attempt to distract Westerly. He had mentioned that he'd once had a son. His son had died, Smirk said. In fact, today was the anniversary of his death. His remains were somewhere out there in the vastness of space. . . . Westerly's gaze had followed Smirk's finger, pointing out the window at the inky blackness. A chill had run down Westerly's spine. He had had an inexplicable feeling of déjà vu.

When he had looked back at the chessboard again, everything seemed to have shifted, and he felt a little strange. After that, the game had turned to Smirk's advantage, and eventually Smirk won. Westerly, putting away the chess set, had been so upset he never even noticed that one of his knights was missing.

Later, moping around at his post, Westerly had realized why Smirk's anecdote had been so disturbing.

"That's it!" he'd blurted out.

"What, ensign?" Capt. Ricardo had growled, stepping over to Westerly's control console.

"Captain Smirk's son! Another child of an officer, dead! Counselor Troit had a son, but he's gone. And Dacron had a daughter, and she's gone, too. Every time an officer of this ship has a kid, they die!"

"Hmmm, yes," mused Capt. Ricardo. "I see what you mean. That's worked out rather nicely, hasn't it?" Westerly knew Capt. Ricardo didn't mean to be nasty; he just hated kids.

But still, thought Westerly, *what kind of force seems to have it in for these officers' children? And where does that leave ME?* He'd fretted over it ever since.

"Dr. Flusher . . ." Capt. Ricardo began, leaning close to her as they sat at the bar, "have you—" he broke off, flustered, as Guano the bartender approached.

"I'll have a Manhattan," Dr. Flusher ordered.

"Any fries with that?" prompted Guano.

"No." Dr. Flusher smiled politely. "Just the drink."

"How about some of our cheesy potato skins? They're really good."

"No, thank you." Dr. Flusher's smile grew more strained.

"Chicken wings? Tapas? Sushi? Or—I've got it—a hunk of steak tenderloin would go real good with that Manhattan," urged Guano.

"Just . . . the . . . drink," Beverage hissed.

"O-kaaay," Guano conceded, muttering "cheapskate" under her breath as she left them.

Capt. Ricardo resumed their conversation in an urgent tone. "Have you gotten my latest dose of GrowBrain yet?"

"Captain." Beverage suppressed a giggle. "It's GrowGrain, not GrowBrain. It grows hair, not brain matter." She picked up the drink Guano set down in front of her.

"That's too bad, come to think of it," she continued, taking a sip. "I could make a fortune selling a brain enhancer." She glanced at Piker at the nearby table; he was doing his bear imitation again.

"Every time an officer of this ship has a kid, they *die!*"

"All right—GrowGrain," Capt. Ricardo answered impatiently. "Can you get me more?"

"No." She set the drink down, suddenly stern. "I told you, Captain, we're discontinuing treatment. Not only did the GrowGrain fail to stimulate hair growth on your scalp, but there was that dangerous reaction in the Crewmover."

An asbestos allergy was a well-documented side effect among patients who'd had the GrowGrain tonic slathered over their heads. So Dr. Flusher hadn't been too surprised when the asbestos lining of the Crewmover made Capt. Ricardo's skull wrinkle like a prune. Luckily, the wrinkles disappeared after a week of bed rest.

"I can avoid the Crewmover," Capt. Ricardo pleaded. "I'll stay on the Bridge all the time. I'll sleep there. I can set up a cot in my ready room."

Dr. Flusher wrinkled her mouth skeptically. "And what happens in an emergency when you need to go somewhere else on the ship? Our vertical decks are five hundred thirty-eight stories high."

"I'll take the stairs."

Farther down the bar, Dr. McCaw scowled as he set down his glass of gin. The mere sight of Dr. Flusher irritated him.

He was still ticked off that Starfreak had transferred Dr. Cape Pragmatski and replaced her with Dr. Flusher. He and Pragmatski had been just about to open their I'm-A-Doctor chain of space medicine clinics. They'd planned to treat phaser burns, meteor concussions, and the UltraFax dislocations that occurred when a beam-down went awry and people came out with their body parts mixed up. But they had to abandon the franchise idea when Pragmatski left.

Starfreak's arbitrary decision infuriated Dr. McCaw because, as he complained to Capt. Smirk, "It goes against my mission as a doctor: to turn a profit." But there was nothing anybody could do about it. McCaw eked out some small satisfaction by playing practical jokes on Flusher whenever he got the chance.

He grinned. Wait till she found the radioactive life-forms he'd hidden in the pocket of her lab coat.

At the far end of the bar, Dacron gulped down a glass of crankcase fluid, ran his tongue around his mouth, and shook his head. No matter what they said about these state-of-the-art beverage simulators, the drinks just didn't taste like the real thing.

Dacron walked over to the men's restroom. He really didn't have to go—ever; this was just part of his ongoing crusade to master all human characteristics.

Unwittingly, Dacron walked into the ladies' room instead. Yoohoo stood in front of the mirror, her skirt lifted up to her waist as she adjusted her girdle. She screamed when she saw him. Dacron apologized profusely and backed out.

He felt himself blushing a brighter shade of pale. *How could I have made that mistake?* he wondered.

Entering the men's room, Dacron saw Mr. Smock standing in front of the sink, peeling off the pink adhesive tape he'd used to set his ears, then putting the finishing touches on his sideburns with Dippity-Do.

Meanwhile, Georgie sat in one of the toilet stalls, shivering. *I hate the way these Starfreak jumpsuits force us to peel off half our clothes every time nature calls,* he thought. *When am I going to get a two-piece uniform like the senior officers have?*

Capt. Ricardo and Capt. Smirk left Ten-Foreplay for the Bridge. They'd been informed that Starfreak Command was hailing them.

"Destination, please," requested the Crewmover.

"Bridge," ordered Capt. Ricardo.

"Say, Jean-Lucy, do we have a 'lost and found' on the ship?" asked Capt. Smirk.

"Not that I know of. Why?"

"I've misplaced my Super Bowl ring."

"Well," said Capt. Ricardo, "such a large ring should be easy to spot. Where have you looked?"

"Nobody else gets out of here without buying some food!"

"I thought I might have taken it off to play tennis, so first I looked in the gym," said Capt. Smirk.

The Crewmover heard Capt. Smirk say "gym." Programmed to respond to voice commands corresponding to any area of the ship, the Crewmover smoothly switched directions and headed for the deck where the gym was located. The captains failed to notice.

"But it wasn't there, so I looked in the HolidayDeck."

The Crewmover reversed direction with a little jolt and headed for the HolidayDeck.

"Then I checked the gift shop . . ." This time the Crewmover jerked hard in changing its horizontal and vertical course. The captains were flung against the wall.

"Say, what is this?" Capt. Ricardo wondered.

Capt. Smirk continued, "I also checked the bowling alley . . ." There was another abrupt jerk.

". . . the print shop . . ." The Crewmover executed a sideways swoop followed by a stomach-churning dip.

". . . and the custard stand." The Crewmover reversed itself downward with such force that the captains hit their heads on the ceiling.

Rubbing the bruise on his shoulder, Capt. Smirk stood in the center of the Bridge and addressed the intercom.

"Attention, all officers. Report to the Bridge at once. We are about to receive an important transmission from Starfreak Command. They've ordered all key personnel to stand by for the briefing. Smirk out."

Standing behind the bar, Guano watched in frustration as Dacron emerged from the men's room and hurried out of Ten-Foreplay. Georgie followed a moment later.

Guano was furious. She ran to the bar's exit and spread-eagled herself against the swinging doors. "All right, that's it!" she shrieked. "Nobody else gets out of here without buying some food!"

* * *

Capt. Ricardo and Capt. Smirk stood before the Viewscreen as the Starfreak Command logo appeared. The next moment, the Viewscreen broadcast the image of Admiral Tweet.

Tweet was a white-haired elderly gentleman whose body had once been inhabited by a large alien life-form that resembled a Metallic Wood-Boring Beetle. Starfreak, reluctant to lose an officer to medical disability, had called in Orkin to get him back in commission.

"Captain Smirk, Captain Ricardo," Admiral Tweet began, "we need you to come to Earth immediately as a defensive measure. The Jargonites have invaded our air space."

"Jargonites? I'm not familiar with them, Admiral," said Capt. Smirk. "What do they want?"

"The Jargonites are a race of human-potential advocates," Admiral Tweet replied. "As for what they want, we're not entirely sure yet, since most of their communications with us have been full of, er, jargon. All we know is that they want to help us reach our peak potential, whatever that is—through force, if necessary.

"So far they've been content just to observe us, but we suspect that they may become aggressive. We need the protection of one of our starships in case things get nasty. And your *Endocrine* is the only ship close enough to help.

"I expect you to get here on the double," Admiral Tweet concluded. "There isn't time for any delays, so lay off the petty bickering, all right?"

"Yes, sir, Admiral," the captains replied. Tweet signed off.

"Hot diggity dog! A mission!" Capt. Smirk jumped into his co-captain's command chair. "Mister Flusher, set a heading for—"

"Just a minute, Capt. Smirk," Capt. Ricardo interjected. "Haven't you forgotten something?"

"What? Oh, that. Can't we do it after we get started?"

"No, we can't. It always comes before the real business of the mission gets underway."

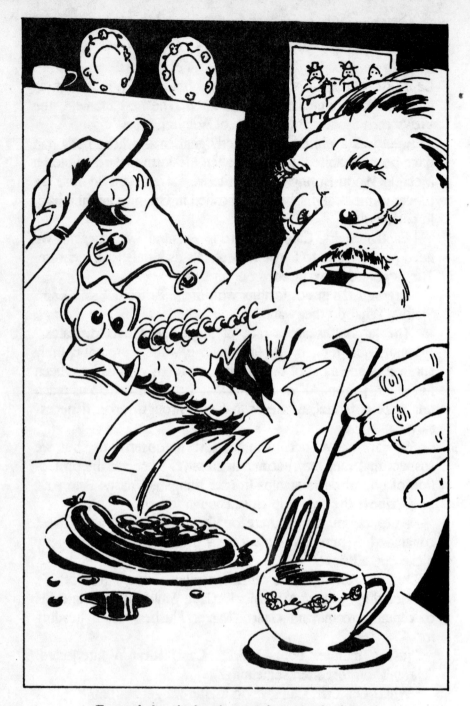

Tweet's body had once been inhabited
by a large alien life-form that resembled
a Metallic Wood-Boring Beetle.

"Well, all right," conceded Smirk, "but try to get it over with soon, will you?"

Before them stretched the vast space of the universe. Everywhere there were stars—stars and planets, lots of planets, colorful planets, as colorful as state-of-the-art computer simulation could make them, which was even more colorful than any of the actual astrophotography in *Astronomy* magazine. And there was that music again; no one knew where it came from, and they'd given up trying to find out.

After the first few notes, Capt. Ricardo intoned, "Space. We still don't have enough of it."

Capt. Smirk cleared his throat, irked at this obvious reference to their crews' rivalry.

"These are the voyages of the starship *Endocrine*," Capt. Ricardo continued. "Its continuing mission: to cruise around the universe looking for novel predicaments to get into. To search the outskirts of the galaxy for areas with less crowding, lower tax rates and better schools. To boldly go where nobody wanted to go before!"

Away they went.

Let's Pick Up the Pace

"WHERE'S OUR NAVIGATOR?" CAPT. Smirk asked, noticing that Dacron's post was empty.

Mr. Smock, munching the chimichanga he'd bought in Ten-Foreplay, reported, "Lieutenant Commander Dacron should be here by now. He left Ten-Foreplay before I did when you paged us to come to the Bridge."

"We can't wait for him," Smirk said. "Can we have somebody fill in here?"

From the back of the Bridge, six crew members took off in a scramble for Dacron's console. Checkout barely beat out the others and, with a few well-placed elbow jabs, fought his way into the chair.

"Ready to provide information on the wessel, Captains," he announced.

" 'Wessel'?" repeated Capt. Ricardo.

"Never mind," muttered Capt. Smirk. "He hasn't been the same since that worm crawled out of his ear on the mission against Genghis Khan."

"Mr. Flusher," Capt. Smirk said aloud, "set course heading 13.13 mark 13.13. Speed: Warped 8.13."

Anxiety gripped Westerly. All of those thirteens sounded like bad luck to him. He didn't want this to be the mission in which he went the way of all officers' children. Not even if he got to make a great parting speech the way Yasha Tar did after she bit the dust. *No,* Westerly decided, *I'll be the master of my own fate.* He pressed his console buttons to enter a course heading of 14.14 mark 14.14 and a speed of Warped 8.14.

"Course and speed laid in," he reported. On his console, the miniature plastic statue of St. Michelob, patron saint of space brats, seemed to rebuke him for his dishonesty. "Sorry," he whispered.

Checkout looked at his console, glanced at Westerly, and checked the console again, frowning. "Vesterly, these instrument readings show our welocity and wector heading are at wariance to the Captain's orders. Did you mean to wenture in that wicinity?"

Westerly had a pretty good idea of what Checkout had said, having watched most of the Bugs Bunny cartoons featuring Elmer Fudd. Luckily, though, no one else understood, and he could defuse Checkout with an irrelevant response. "It's okay, Mr. Checkout," Westerly asserted. "I'm sure we'll find a wayside with picnic tables on our way to Earth."

"Vayside?" Checkout repeated, pulling out his Russian-English pocket dictionary.

Meanwhile, Dacron was riding the Crewmover all over the ship.

When he'd left the men's room of Ten-Foreplay at Capt. Ricardo's order, he knew where he was supposed to go. But the moment he got into the Crewmover, the word for this destination vanished from his brain.

"Destination, please," requested the Crewmover.

Dacron tried to think of the word. He could picture the place, but what was it called?

"Destination, please," the Crewmover asked again.

Such a memory lapse had never occurred to Dacron before. He wasn't sure what to do next.

"Desti*nation*, please." The Crewmover's automated voice had a slight edge to it this time.

Dacron decided to do the best he could. "Take me to the place where Captain Ricardo and the commanding officers spend the majority of their time."

"Thank you," the Crewmover said, a little haughtily, and began to move. A few seconds later the doors opened. The Crewmover had taken him to the HolidayDeck.

"No, this is not the correct place," Dacron observed.

"I did the best I could with the insufficient information you provided," the Crewmover sniffed.

"Indeed," Dacron conceded. He would have to be more specific in his instructions. The name still eluded him, so after a few moments' thought he requested, "Take me to the place where the business of running the ship is accomplished."

After another short ride, the doors opened again. The Crewmover had returned to Ten-Foreplay.

"Uhhh . . ." Dacron began.

"This isn't right, either?" the Crewmover asked, exasperated.

"No, it is not," Dacron said. "Through no fault of yours, Crewmover," he hastened to add. "I just cannot seem to recall the name of my destination."

"Well, let me give you the grand tour, then," snapped the Crewmover, shutting its doors again with a tad too much force. It ferried him all over the ship, from the observation lounge to the mess hall, video arcade, laundromat and tanning salon. Each time the doors opened, Dacron peered out and announced that this wasn't the place, either.

Finally the Crewmover exclaimed, "Look, pal, there are other people on this ship who need a ride, too. I can't be trucking you around all day. Why don't I just take you to the Bridge, where you can sit and daydream about finding someplace that suits you?"

"The Bridge!" Dacron exclaimed. "That is it. Take me to the Bridge, please."

* * *

They had been following Westerly's secretly altered course for nearly an hour when Dacron finally arrived at the Bridge. Checkout reluctantly surrendered Dacron's console to him.

Capt. Smirk shot a challenging glance at Capt. Ricardo. "Discipline problems with your crew, Jean-Lucy?" he murmured.

"Mr. Dacron," Capt. Ricardo began, "where have you—"

"Captain," said Wart, "sensor readings indicate an unknown phenomenon 10,000 kilometers ahead."

"That's strange," said Capt. Smirk. "The course I set for us steered clear of anything that would get in our way." Westerly glanced nervously over his shoulder at the captains.

Capt. Smirk continued, "Say, where are we, anyway? These constellations don't look familiar."

Piker stepped forward. "Are you questioning the ability of our pilot, Captain?" he demanded.

"Not really," Smirk replied, "though I do think it's a bit odd to have a youngster at the controls of Starfreak's flagship."

"Because if you are," Piker continued, "I want you to know that I'm responsible for his training."

Capt. Smirk muttered, "That explains a lot." Then he added aloud, "For whatever reason, commander, we seem to be off course."

"No, we're not," Piker countered. "Take another look at those stars. There's the Big Zipper, right where it should be. And—"

"Never mind," Capt. Ricardo broke in. "Mr. Wart, focus the Viewscreen on that unknown phenomenon you spotted."

The Viewscreen showed a long squiggly thing, tapering at the ends, with rings spanning it at regular intervals. It was squirming slowly in space.

"What is that?" wondered Capt. Ricardo.

Piker crooked his neck assertively. "Sir, it appears to be a long squiggly thing—"

"Yes, Number I," Capt. Ricardo interrupted, "but what *is* it? Mr. Dacron, what do the data banks say?"

"The phenomenon corresponds to no known parameters,"

Dacron reported. "It appears to be a life form never encountered before."

"Aren't they all," grumbled Capt. Ricardo. Aloud he said, "Mr. Wart, magnify on screen."

The close-up shot showed the surface more clearly but still gave no indication of what the object was.

"De-magnify," ordered Capt. Ricardo. That was no better. "Reduce 50 percent." Still no help. "Crop out the lower third, bleed it off the top of the screen, and display it in a 70 percent screen of Pantone 266." That was a lot nicer to look at, but it still didn't reveal what the object was.

"Captains, I believe I have a clue," said Mr. Smock from a science station at the back of the Bridge. He brought Volume Seven of the *Encyclopedia Brittanica* over to the captains. "The object we have encountered appears to be a common earthworm."

"By golly, will you look at that," Capt. Smirk marveled, grasping the encyclopedia. "Is this a new method of disseminating hard data, Smock? A technological advancement over the display terminal?"

"It's called a 'book,' Captain," Smock told him.

"But the picture of this worm," Capt. Ricardo reminded them. "It does look just like this creature, Mr. Smock. You're absolutely right."

"Sayyyy," Capt. Smirk speculated, rubbing his chin and staring at the Viewscreen. "If this is a worm, there must be . . ."

The creature suddenly shifted toward them, revealing an opening in its outer covering.

". . . A wormhole!" Smirk concluded triumphantly.

"So?" asked Capt. Ricardo.

"You know! A wormhole. A shortcut through space. A method of travel that bypasses normal restrictions on time and matter."

"Ah, yes," Capt. Ricardo said. "Now I remember. We've encountered a wormhole before. It was highly dangerous, though. Unstable. If you travel through it, you never know when it's going to disappear and trap you on the other side. And wormholes can produce all kinds of illusions and strange objects. You can't be too careful when dealing with something from a worm's, uh, hole."

As if on cue, the wormhole suddenly revealed a starship.

"Look at that!" exclaimed Capt. Smirk. "Why, it almost looks like . . ."

"Could it be . . . ?" Smock concurred.

"Yes, it could!" Zulu and Checkout chimed in unison from the back of the Bridge.

It was the original *Endocrine.*

"OUR SHIP!" exclaimed Smirk and his crew.

Piker frowned with concern and tilted his neck a little further. "Are you sure?"

"That's it! That's our ship! That's our ship!" Capt. Smirk and Mr. Spock grasped each others' arms and jumped up and down with glee. The others on Smirk's crew applauded and cheered as they left their posts and ran for the Crewmover.

"Now, let's not be too hasty . . ." Capt. Ricardo began.

"Jean-Lucy, I've just gotta get back on board," Capt. Smirk replied from the Crewmover. "This is unbelievable! And all this time I thought Starfreak had sold it for scrap metal."

The Crewmover door began to close.

"Captain Smirk! We don't even know if this is real," Capt. Ricardo called. "It could be a mirage, or a trap—" But the Crewmover door shut, and Smirk and his crew were already on their way to the UltraFax platform to beam over to their ship.

Smirk knew that Ricardo was right. This could be an illusion. Or the wormhole might be unstable; it could disappear at any time.

The situation was potentially dangerous or even fatal, so naturally Smirk and all his key officers UltraFaxed over to the ship at the same time. *No use hedging your bets,* Smirk thought. Besides, he was just too excited to be cautious.

And their arrival on his own Bridge more than justified the risk. Everything was just as they had left it: the goofy flashing lights scattered randomly around the walls, the orange altar rail around the room's perimeter, even the noises they'd rigged to resemble submarine sounding devices.

Everyone was overjoyed to be back at their old posts. Capt. Smirk sank into his captain's chair with practiced ease. Mr. Smock checked out the science stations; all were in working order. Checkout and Zulu assumed their stations—no more scrambling for a good seat. Yoohoo was already in her chair, wearing the communication headset they'd bought wholesale from a telephone supply house.

Capt. Smirk paged Dr. McCaw in Sick Bay. "How's it look, Moans?"

"Ready for action, Jim. Let's get going and incur some injuries."

Capt. Smirk grinned. "Mister Snot, how are things in the Engine Room?"

"Ach, Captain, things are in a pretty predicament. It'll take a month o' Sundays to get these workin's ready. Even getting impulse power will take me days of back-breakin' repair work."

Smirk's grin grew even broader. It was just like old times.

"Lieutenant Yoohoo, open a channel to Captain Ricardo's ship," he ordered. Ricardo's image appeared on the Viewscreen almost instantly.

"Captain Smirk, do you think it is wise to remain in that unstable area with your entire crew?" Ricardo chided.

"Now, now, Jean-Lucy," Smirk replied, "we'll be fine. Where's your sense of adventure? You sound like an old schoolmarm." Having his own ship made Smirk feel positively giddy. He no longer needed to compromise his style of command.

Capt. Ricardo consulted with someone off-screen, then turned back to Smirk's image with a concerned expression. "Captain, our sensor readings show that the wormhole is shifting."

Capt. Smirk felt a twinge of alarm, but his grin held up. "Very well, Jean-Lucy, we'll get out of harm's way if it'll make you feel better. Mister Snot, move us ahead on half-impulse power."

Mr. Snot's voice strained over the intercom. "Can't do it, Captain. The engine won't even turn over."

"Wormholes can produce all kinds of
illusions and strange objects."

Capt. Smirk blinked, but kept grinning. Through his grin, he muttered, "Then go to emergency power, Mr. Snot."

"Emergency power's gone, sir. This battery lost its charge about 53 years ago."

"Captain Smirk, the wormhole is closing," warned Capt. Ricardo.

"Yes. Well, uh, we're having a little difficulty . . ." Capt. Smirk replied.

"Sir, sensor readings indicate the wormhole is closing at a rate of 20.5 kilometers per second," reported Checkout.

Onscreen, Capt. Ricardo asked, "Captain Smirk, do you need help?"

"Well, 'help' might be too strong a word . . ." Capt. Smirk temporized.

Capt. Ricardo ordered, "Mr. Wart, lock a tractor beam onto their ship and pull them out of there." Responding to the crisis, Piker stood up and angled his neck sharply.

"Vormhole closing welocity has increased to 39.5 kilometers per second," said Checkout.

"Wormhole on screen," Capt. Smirk ordered. The Viewscreen showed the opening was narrowing rapidly.

"We are now being towed at 5.89 kilometers per second," Zulu announced.

Everyone's eyes were locked on the Viewscreen. The wormhole constricted as the tractor beam pulled them toward the outside.

"Vormhole welocity at 46.8 kilometers per second," Checkout warned.

"Lieutenant Yoohoo, keep the wormhole on the Viewscreen, and hail Ricardo's ship on audio," Smirk ordered.

" 'Hey you' frequencies open, sir," said Yoohoo, thinking, *Ah, yes, it's all coming back to me now. Even after all this time, I still remember the words.*

"Jean-Lucy, do you think you could tow us a bit faster?" Capt. Smirk squealed.

"We're doing the best we can," Capt. Ricardo replied.

They drew closer to the opening as it narrowed. Smirk's crew watched, fascinated. The sides of the wormhole seemed close enough to touch. They barely squeaked by. Then they were outside, and everyone breathed a sigh of relief.

Capt. Smirk ordered Yoohoo to place the communication channel back on the Viewscreen. "Wow! That was a blast!" he exclaimed, vaguely aware that his armpits were drenched with sweat. "Thanks for the tow, Jean-Lucy."

Capt. Ricardo crossed his arms over his chest. "Now that you're out, we can discuss the need to resume our mission and abandon this ridiculous project."

"Abandon it! You must be kidding! I intend to get this ship up and running and take her back to Earth with my crew."

"You're wasting time," Ricardo scolded. "We've already been delayed long enough."

"You don't have to delay any longer," Smirk countered. "Go on ahead and get to Earth to stand patrol. We'll join you later. Having a second starship there will give us a strategic advantage."

"Captain," Wart broke in, "we are being hailed by Starfreak Command."

"On screen," Capt. Ricardo ordered. "And relay the transmission to Captain Smirk's ship, also."

Admiral Tweet's weathered face appeared on the screen. "Captain Ricardo," he began, then squinted, "and Captain Smirk? Are you transmitting from two separate ships?"

"Yes, Admiral," replied Capt. Ricardo. "Captain Smirk's old ship has reappeared from a wormhole, and he wants to stay here and tinker with it . . ."

"Which would give us additional firepower if we need it for Earth," Capt. Smirk asserted.

"Never mind," Admiral Tweet said. "This is urgent. We're having more trouble with the Jargonites here on Earth. They're no longer content just to observe us; now they've decided we need their help to 'reach our peak potential.' So they're broadcasting messages through all the media to soften us up. Listen."

"Lock a tractor beam onto their ship and
pull them out of there."

Admiral Tweet turned on a small portable television facing the Viewscreen. Onscreen, a spindly man in a tweed coat paced a lecture stage. "That," said Admiral Tweet, "is one of the Jargonite leaders, Dr. Heritage M. Blather."

"Life is a wonder," Dr. Blather oozed. "Remember the hamster in the little cage. He works some and digs some and eats some and sleeps some and nobody knows why but we are all like that. And then we die."

"Huh?" said Capt. Ricardo and Capt. Smirk.

"Remember the things you learned as a child," said Dr. Blather. "Milk is good for you. Arsenic is bad. Hitting is a no-no. Be kind to animals. Don't touch yourself there.

"Ah, the wonder of it all," the Jargonite continued. "I am on a groovy wavelength with the universe. It feels like I could groove here forever, watching my aura undulate."

"I feel a little nauseous," said Capt. Smirk.

"A common reaction," replied Admiral Tweet, turning down the sound on the TV. "That's how they disarm their enemies. Then, once they've worn down your resistance, they take over and organize you into encounter groups for brainwashing sessions.

"That's when things really get serious. They confuse you with a barrage of illogical garbage. It gets so bad you don't know whether you're coming or going.

"We have reports that the Jargonites have infiltrated all sectors of the galaxy. You'll almost certainly run into some of them on your way here. I want you to know what you're up against, so I'm going to show you a tape of the Jargonites in full swing."

Admiral Tweet flicked the "on" switch of a VCR connected to the TV set.

"This encounter session was taped on Starbase Delta Neenah Nana by a video camera originally installed to catch shoplifters," he continued. "The Jargonites who captured the base didn't know the session was being taped. I must warn you, this isn't pretty. I'm only going to play a few moment's worth to avoid permanent brain damage for all of us."

The tape showed a paunchy middle-aged man wearing a nondescript business suit. "That's Doctor B. S. Galore," said Admiral Tweet. "Don't be deceived by his looks. He's one of the Jargonites' deadliest pirates."

Admiral Tweet turned up the sound on the tape of Dr. Galore's lecture, directed to the starbase's unwilling participants in his encounter session. "So before your starbase will be all that it can be, you have to share The Dream," said Dr. Galore. "Let's structure your Dream so you can be empowered to establish the goals and mechanisms by which you will assert the individual's power to bring about a maximum state of awareness which will proximally insert your inclination to create a time interval in which . . ." On and on he droned. One by one the starbase staffers fell asleep, lost consciousness, or went into toxic shock.

Mr. Smock said, "I'm sorry, Admiral, but our universal translator seems to be out of order. We should be hearing his message in English."

"That *was* English, Mr. Smock," Admiral Tweet assured him.

Dr. Galore kept on churning. ". . . The past is not a rigid structure to be considered only on the basis of experiential observances, but can be languaged by those who experience it to acknowledge one another's awareness through infinite access points of . . ."

"But it makes absolutely no sense," protested Mr. Smock.

"Precisely the point," acknowledged Admiral Tweet, turning down the sound.

"There must be a way to glean some logic out of all that verbiage," continued Mr. Smock. "If we could only listen to a little more, Admiral, perhaps I could determine a pattern—"

"I'm sorry, Mr. Smock, but we can't exceed safe levels of exposure. I've probably played too much of it already."

Indeed, Checkout and Zulu were nodding off to sleep. On

Wart felt his blood pressure rising.

Ricardo's Bridge, Wart felt his blood pressure rising; *one good punch would get that Blather guy to shut up*, he thought.

"Please, Admiral," Smock persisted. "There must be some underlying thought in all of this."

"No, Mister Smock," the admiral replied. "You've heard enough. I just wanted to demonstrate the danger. So, you all see what we're up against. Get here pronto, and be ready to do battle!"

"We will, Admiral! We'll have our ship up and running in no time!" responded Capt. Smirk.

"Admiral, will you please explain to Captain Smirk the advantages of his crew returning to this ship?" Capt. Ricardo countered.

"I told you, Captain Ricardo, you can go on ahead," Capt. Smirk exclaimed. "We'll join you later. The extra firepower will really be helpful now that we're at war."

Capt. Ricardo responded, "But we may need your personnel immediately—"

"Stop bickering, both of you!" Admiral Tweet broke in. "Smirk, have you forgotten our fuel-economy measures? We can't afford to keep duplicate vehicles in service."

"But, sir," Capt. Smirk responded, "during wartime, surely we need all the starships we can muster."

"Hmmm," said Admiral Tweet.

"Remember the Battle of Tampon-2, in which two Starfreak vessels engaged the enemy in tandem?" Smirk continued. "The battle for which Admiral Eke received the NoBull Peace Prize?"

"Hmmmm," Admiral Tweet repeated. "Good point, Smirk. All right, you can use both ships. But just for now, when we're at war. Once we beat these Jargonites, it'll be back to one ship again."

"Yes—*my* ship!" exclaimed Smirk.

"No, mine!" declared Ricardo.

"Mine has seen more battles!" cried Smirk. "It's a real war machine."

"Mine is vastly superior in Warped speed and hull construction . . ." argued Ricardo.

"Shut *up*, both of you!" yelled Admiral Tweet. "The vessel we'll use after this is all over will be whichever one gets us out of this fix. Its captain and crew will have command, and it will be considered THE *Endocrine* with official Starfreak commission. The other crew will serve as subordinate staff on that ship. Understand?"

"Yes, sir!" they both responded, each satisfied that he'd just won the argument.

3

On the Road Again

"MISTER SNOT, WHEN YOU SAID you'd have to get the ship patched together with baling wire and spit, I thought you were speaking figuratively," Capt. Smirk whined.

"Oh, no, sir," answered his chief engineer. "That's really all we have available. There isn't a starship parts outlet within seven parsecs of here, and even if there was, how would we get there? So we make do with what we have. And you, Captain, must take your turn on spit shift now. Here's your lemon, and here's your beaker. Bring it to me when it's full."

Of all the predicaments we've been in, thought Smirk, *this is truly the most ridiculous. There isn't even any redeeming danger in it.*

He knew Mr. Snot was taking the right course. Slowly but surely the engine and the outer hull, creaky with disuse, were being restored. But the painstaking process aggravated Capt. Smirk's natural restlessness.

He sliced open the lemon and moaned. Time to get to work.

At that moment, far ahead, Capt. Ricardo's crew sighted the Jargonites for the first time. A huge banner that stretched across the front of the enemy ship read "Dare to Dream Your Dream."

"Captain, the Jargonites are hailing us," Wart reported.

"Make no response. Keep the frequency closed," ordered Capt. Ricardo. "Shields up."

"Captain, they are somehow penetrating the frequency," continued Wart, pushing buttons on his console, to no avail.

"Dacron, stand by," said the captain. "We're going to need your help on this."

"Aye, sir."

An image appeared on the Viewscreen. It was none other than Dr. B. S. Galore himself, the pirate they'd seen on Admiral Tweet's videotape.

Troit looked concerned. "He's hiding something," she told the captain.

"Greetings, fellow experiencers of the human adventure!" the Jargonite said, beaming. "I am Dr. B. S. Galore of the Jargonite starship *Conundrum*. Have you hugged your alien today?"

"I am Captain Jean-Lucy Ricardo of the Federation starship *Endocrine*," the captain responded. "Would you kindly remove yourself from our 'hey you' frequency?"

"Today is the first day of the rest of your vastly enhanced lifespan," said Galore, ignoring the request. "Let's get started on structuring The Dream for your crew that will maximize the dialoguing which you can create on an ongoing basis to root out the hidden misassumptions currently inhibiting the growth of base measurements on your . . ."

Capt. Ricardo leaned close to Dacron and whispered, "Has anything he said given you clues to help us break off the transmission?"

"Nothing yet, sir," Dacron answered. "This language does not correspond to any known system of logic." Suddenly Dacron noticed a disturbing reading on his console. "Sir," he continued, "it appears the Jargonites are attempting to break into our computer."

"Keep them out!" Ricardo hissed. "And find a way to close our 'hey you' frequency."

Dr. Galore kept talking. "Systems of logic can structure a

"I thought you were speaking figuratively," Capt. Smirk whined.

reality that can either enhance or inhibit the ability of persons to not only reattach themselves to the configuration but . . ."

As Dacron labored over the circuits, foiling the Jargonites' unspoken efforts to infiltrate the computer, the other members of the crew began to feel the effects of the jargon onslaught.

Westerly started falling asleep at his post. He caught himself with a start, jerked upright, but then slumped forward as he began to drift again.

Counselor Troit tried to read Galore's feelings, but the barrage of words kept getting in her way. She found herself tempted to surrender to his rhetoric, just to see if it would help her understand him.

Wart was furious. They were being overpowered by this mealy-mouthed professor who obviously couldn't fight his way out of a paper bag. Wart clenched his fists. *Give me a shot at him. This guy will be history,* he thought.

Capt. Ricardo bent close to Dacron and growled, "What is taking you so long to block them?"

"This is an extremely delicate maneuver, Captain," Dacron replied. "There is a high risk of damage."

"To the computer, you mean?"

"No, to my circuits." Dacron had begun to sweat, and his malfunctioning air conditioner was buzzing softly.

"Never mind," snapped Capt. Ricardo. "Access your third nested macro in the Blind Obedience software program, and get on with it."

Dacron's eyes crossed for a second as he reached deep into his memory. The buried command surfaced, and he worked the console with renewed vigor.

Finally, Dacron whispered, "I have secured computer control, Captain. As for closing the 'hey you' frequency, the procedure is relatively simple."

"What should we do?" Capt. Ricardo asked.

"Instruct Mr. Wart to go to Plan B," Dacron answered. "Meanwhile, to distract Dr. Galore, I will engage him in a dialogue."

"No!" Capt. Ricardo objected. "I can't let you do it!"

"Do not worry, Captain," Dacron assured him. "I have an infinitely greater capacity than most of the crew for withstanding this rhetoric. You will recall that I survived graduate school."

"Well, all right," Capt. Ricardo relented. "But be careful."

Dacron nodded. Capt. Ricardo sidled up to Wart as nonchalantly as he could and muttered out of the side of his mouth, "Plan B." The Kringle grunted in response and began to perform the appropriate operations on his console.

"Dr. Galore," Dacron said, standing up to draw attention to himself. "Is it not true that the human-potential movement has been responsible for an increase in acne among the Zambonians?"

Dr. Galore arranged his face in a well-practiced smile. "A common misconception, Mr.—"

"Dacron," he supplied.

"Mr. Dacron. Let me language this for you. The Zambonians mistook the term 'interface' to mean 'in your face,' and as a result, their fixed and rigid thought patterns interfered with their ability to dialogue along the lines of maximum output . . ."

Do not listen, Dacron told himself. *Remember the Psych 303 lectures, when you learned to sleep with your eyes open. Do not try to make sense of this.* But he found it impossible to heed his own warning.

". . . Encounter the inner person to restructure the interface on which the intrinsically transformed ability will meet . . ." Galore droned on, determined to enlighten Dacron.

"Restructure the interface"? Dacron wondered. "Intrinsically transformed ability"? How long ago did this sentence begin? Does it have a subject, verb and object? When will it end? It should not be this hard to resist this rhetoric. What is wrong with me?

Capt. Ricardo glanced at Dacron. So far, so good. He knew that Dacron was correct—he was the only one who could stand up to the Jargonite without getting snowed under.

As Dacron's knees buckled, Capt. Ricardo
tried to grab a handhold on his ear . . .

Wart jabbed the console with his forefinger. Just a few more adjustments, and they'd have the frequency closed.

". . . Experiential shifts bring into being an awareness of 'self' when 'self' and 'other' are understood to be constructs in the midst of . . ." Galore was really getting worked up. He hadn't noticed that Wart was closing the frequency.

"Being an awareness," Dacron's circuits echoed. *"Self and other . . . constructs in the midst."* Constructs in the mist. *Gorillas in the Mist.* He could feel himself losing control. *But somewhere in here,* he thought, *there must be at least one teeny tiny little thought. If only I could find it.* His circuits switched to Automatic.

"Accessing," he stated. His eyes crossed again, and static crackled around his forehead.

Meanwhile, Wart was concentrating intently. He was almost finished. Five seconds more, and the "hey you" frequency would be back under their control.

"Accessing," Dacron repeated. "Accessing. Accessing."

Westerly awoke with a start, focused on Dacron, and saw that smoke was coming out of Dacron's ears. "Dacron!" he cried, getting up to help. Then Capt. Ricardo, too, saw what was happening and dashed toward Dacron.

Wart punched the console buttons furiously. "There . . . there . . . and there!" He had control of the channel. Dr. Galore disappeared from the Viewscreen.

As Dacron's knees buckled, Capt. Ricardo tried to grab a handhold on his ear but missed. Dacron fell on top of Westerly with a thud.

"Dr. Flusher!" Capt. Ricardo called to the intercom. "Medical emergency on the Bridge. Bring personnel to transport a patient to Sick Bay."

"Bring a stretcher, too," Piker added decisively, striding over to the tangle of bodies in the forward part of the Bridge. He was at his most commanding, his neck at 90-degree angle to his body.

Westerly crawled out from under Dacron, nursing a bloody

nose. He fingered the St. Christopher's medal around his neck and sighed in relief. *I've cheated death*, he thought. *Maybe I've broken the Curse of the Officers' Offspring.*

Dr. Flusher hurried in from the Crewmover. "Westerly!" she shrieked. "My baby! What has happened to you?" She rushed to him, sidestepping Dacron's sprawled form as she did so, and nearly stepping on Dacron's nose.

"Not me, Ma—it's Dacron!" Westerly pinched his nostrils shut and tilted his head back. A bloody nose was no big deal for him; he was used to getting them from some of the other kids, who regularly beat him up and called him a sissy. The boys were even worse.

"Oh . . . uh . . . Dacron," said Beverage. She bent over him with an instrument that resembled a large electric razor. "What happened?" she asked Capt. Ricardo.

"He was engaged in a battle of wits with the Jargonite leader," Capt. Ricardo explained. "Apparently it overloaded his circuits."

"There was smoke coming out of his ears and everything," Westerly added. "It was radical."

Beverage passed the instrument over Dacron's midsection. "Hmmm," she commented. She passed it over his neck. "Hmmm," she elaborated. She passed it over his forehead. "Hmmm," she concluded.

"Well, Doctor?" inquired the captain.

"Too soon to tell," she answered. "Let's get him to Sick Bay. I'll need to run some tests."

Capt. Smirk could hardly believe it. Mr. Snot had actually fixed the ship. They were really going to be on their way.

The engine hummed smoothly. Warped drive had been restored. They had full futon torpedo capability.

"Mr. Zulu, set course heading 8.5 mark II, Warped 8," ordered the captain.

"Aye, sir," Zulu responded.

Smirk leaned back in his chair and grinned. Here was the moment he'd longed for: back on his own ship, with everything fully operational and ready for his order. All he had to do was give the "engage" command.

"Mr. Zulu. Eng—gay-gay-gay . . ."

There seemed to be something wrong with his throat. Smirk tried again.

"Enguh . . . enguh . . . eng-g-gaaakk . . ."

His officers turned to look at him. "Is there something wrong, Captain?" inquired Mr. Smock.

"Uh, no, Smock. I just seem to have a frog in my throat. Would you give the order, please?"

"Very well, Captain. Mr. Zulu, engage."

Smirk smiled sheepishly as they all returned to their tasks. But soon he lost his embarrassment in the sheer joy of traveling in Warped drive. He began to sing an old Earth song—"On the Road Again."

A Shock for Smock

THE SWIFTNESS OF THE JARGONITE ASSAULT caught Smirk's crew off-guard not long after they took off. No sooner had their long-range sensors picked up the ship than it was upon them, blocking their route to Earth and locking into their communication channel.

Capt. Smirk ordered a warning torpedo fired close to the Jargonite vessel. A moment later, the image of a Jargonite appeared on the Viewscreen.

"Good morning, fellow feeling beings," he greeted them. "I am Hector L. Blabnstuff. How are you today?"

"Get off this frequency or face the consequences," Capt. Smirk warned him.

"My, my. Such hostility. Why would you want to shoot at us like that? I think you should say you're sorry. Better yet, why don't I beam over to your ship and give you a hug? You look like you could use one."

"Mr. Zulu, stand by with futon torpedoes," said Capt. Smirk. To Blabnstuff he announced, "That was a warning shot. Unless you get off our communication channel and get out of our way, we will fire again."

"Well, if you don't want a hug, I could give you a rain check,"

"Mr. Zulu, stand by with futon torpedoes."

continued the Jargonite. "Here, I have some hug coupons you can redeem later."

"Shields up," ordered Capt. Smirk. "Fire on my command."

"Are you living the balanced life?" Blabnstuff inquired. "Do you work some and play some and eat and sleep and cry and laugh and cough and shave and vegetate every day some?"

Smirk felt his jaw muscles tighten. He gripped the sides of his chair in fury, thinking, *Who does this guy think he is?* "Fire!" he ordered.

The torpedo glanced off the Jargonite ship, deflected uselessly into space.

"Mr. Zulu, have they raised their shields?"

"Negative, Captain. I do not read any shield mechanisms around the Jargonite ship."

"Fire again. Keep firing until we penetrate their hull," said Capt. Smirk.

Blabnstuff smiled tolerantly. "Your weapons are harmless against us. We have our Reality Deflectors up. As long as we ignore all the bad things in the world, they simply don't exist for us. That includes your futon torpedoes."

Zulu fired one torpedo after another. All skimmed away before reaching the ship.

"Sir, our power is down 30 percent from the torpedo launchings," said Mr. Smock.

"Acknowledged," answered the captain. "Smock, find a way to block them out of our communication channel."

"Say, now, you're an interesting fellow," the Jargonite said as he noticed Mr. Smock. "How do you exist in the world?"

"I beg your pardon?" Mr. Smock inquired.

"I mean, what is your reality? Are the circumstances and existences of your world the sum total of the same realities as the circumstances and existences of my world?"

"Don't listen to him, Smock!" warned the captain. "Mr. Zulu, keep firing those torpedoes!" Smock bent over the console, trying to restore control of their communicator.

"Ve are now down to 10 percent powver," Checkout reported.

Their weapons continued to deflect from the surface of the Jargonite ship. Mr. Snot hailed them on the intercom.

"Captain, what in the divvil are ye doin'? All our power is goin' to firin' these torpedoes—we don't have much to spare!"

"Steady, Mr. Snot," the captain cautioned. "Let's not panic."

"Sir, we should be leavin' here. If power gets much lower, we'll be stranded again!" Mr. Snot yelped.

"I'm counting on you to keep it together, Snotty," urged Capt. Smirk.

Blabnstuff continued to pester Smock. "Wouldn't you agree that past experience is merely a counterpart to the sum total of a reality that . . ." Smock bit his lip to keep from replying.

"One more round! Fire futon torpedoes!" Capt. Smirk ordered.

"Firing, sir," responded Zulu. But the torpedoes shivered off the Jargonite ship into space.

"Captain," said Mr. Smock, "I am unable to restore control to the communication channel. I suggest we set a course to break contact with the Jargonites and remove ourselves from communication range." Smock was breathing heavily, and he avoided eye contact with Blabnstuff.

"Very well, Mr. Snot," Capt. Smirk allowed. "Mr. Zulu, eng- . . . enguh . . . enggg . . ."

"What?" asked Zulu.

Mr. Snot announced over the intercom, "I can't even keep minimal power going for much longer."

"Engaga . . . gakkkk," the captain continued, his face contorted. He was becoming dizzy. And he felt a distracting sensation in his hand: his ring finger had gone rigid.

"Sir, we've just lost Warped drive," Zulu reported.

"Well, then, eng- . . . um, move away on impulse power," said the captain.

"We just lost that too, sir," said Zulu.

"Mr. Snot!" Capt. Smirk said to the intercom. "What's happening? We need to move out of here."

"We're down, Captain—down somethin' terrible! We squandered every bit of power on the torpedoes."

"Can't you just give us a little push? Can't you rig up something, Mr. Snot?"

"No, Captain. My whole engineering staff has been scared spitless."

Frustrated, Smirk banged his fist on the arm of his chair. Suddenly he noticed Mr. Smock facing the Viewscreen, listening to Blabnstuff ramble on. Mr. Smock drew a deep breath to answer him.

"Smock, no!" cried the captain, but it was too late.

"Sir, do you realize that everything you have said to this point makes absolutely no sense whatsoever?" Mr. Smock inquired icily.

It was just the opening the Jargonite was waiting for.

"Sense," he echoed. "Does your sense coincide with my sense? Can we language the juxtaposing and interfacing of sense to make . . ."

As Blabnstuff gushed on, Mr. Smock began to tremble, clenching his fists. Soon he was shaking violently. Sweat beaded on his brow.

"Illogical," he asserted. "What you are saying is, absolutely and without question, totally and unequivocably without merit!"

"Smock, take it easy," Capt. Smirk warned. "You're going to pop a blood vessel."

But Smock had lost control. He paced back and forth, debating, arguing, challenging Blabnstuff until he began to hyperventilate. He dropped to his knees, exhausted.

"Dr. McCaw to the Bridge," Capt. Smirk ordered over the intercom. "Mr. Smock needs medical attention."

With great effort Smock raised his head and added, with his last ounce of energy, "And . . . furthermore . . . 'language' . . . is not . . . a verb!" Then he collapsed.

"My, that was a satisfying encounter," exulted Blabnstuff. "What a breakthrough. Your officer really languaged a lot of hostility, Captain." Capt. Smirk glared at the Viewscreen, his face scarlet with rage.

Blabnstuff continued, "It's good for him to get that out of his system. We have to clear up all this stuff before we get down to the real business of setting up an encounter group so you can define your crew's Dream."

"Dream?!" yelled Capt. Smirk. "Dream?! My dream, you mush-mouthed bag of hot air, is to wipe you off the face of the galaxy!" Capt. Smirk stomped over to the communication console and began tearing out wires at random. "I'll close this channel if it's the last thing I do! I'll shut you up!"

Sparks shot out of the console as Capt. Smirk shredded its innards. The Viewscreen went dark. The audio channel also shut down. All was quiet on the Bridge for a few moments. Capt. Smirk clutched the console, catching his breath.

"Captain, sensors indicate that the Jargonite ship is withdrawing," Zulu reported.

"For now," Capt. Smirk panted. "For now. I'm sure it's just a ploy."

"Captain," said Yoohoo, "we're receiving a message from Admiral Tweet on Earth."

"A message? How can we? I just shut down the communicator."

"It's coming over the emergency channel," said Yoohoo. She held a tin can to her ear, pulling taut the string that connected it to the wall. Yoohoo took notes as she listened. When the transmission ended, she handed the slip of paper to Capt. Smirk.

It read:

Get here immediately if not sooner. The Jargonites have landed.

Detour Through the Neutered Zone

CAPT. RICARDO'S CREW RECEIVED THE SAME message from Starfreak Command. A moment later, another Jargonite ship was upon them.

"Increase speed to Warped 9," Capt. Ricardo ordered Westerly.

Westerly felt surprisingly calm in the midst of this new threat. Somehow, getting the bloody nose from Dacron's fall had broken the tension for him. *If there's a futon torpedo out there with my name on it,* thought Westerly, *worrying won't keep it away.* He felt almost brave enough to throw out his rabbit's foot.

The increased Warped speed kept them ahead of the Jargonites, but just barely. Capt. Ricardo decided to take evasive maneuvers as a precaution. At all costs, he would avoid any further direct contact with the Jargonites.

But these evasive maneuvers were tricky, and their best navigator was still in Sick Bay. Had he recovered enough to help out?

"Dr. Flusher." Capt. Ricardo hailed her via the intercom. "We need navigational help. Is Dacron well enough to return to duty?"

"Just the opposite," came her reply. "He's much worse. He

regained consciousness, but his voice is low and slow. His eyelids are at half-mast. And what worries me most is that he's not babbling anymore. I can only get one-word answers out of him."

"Any idea what's wrong?" the captain continued, frowning.

"Not yet," Dr. Flusher replied. "I'll need to run more tests."

"Keep me posted, doctor," Capt. Ricardo concluded.

"Captain." Piker stood up and angled his neck. "With your permission, I'd like to navigate."

"Very well, Number I."

Piker sweated profusely. None of his evasive maneuvers had worked. In fact, the Jargonites seemed to have them cornered. The only way out was through the Neutered Zone. He ordered Westerly to follow a heading that would plunge them directly into it.

The Jargonites hesitated, then turned back. They would not follow the *Endocrine* into the zone, to face the unknown dangers that lurked there.

"Number I, I don't think we should—" began Capt. Ricardo.

"Captain, Romanumen vessel approaching," Wart announced, monitoring the sensors.

A wave of anxiety swept the Bridge. The Romanumens were the most feared enemy of the Federation. Little was known about them, except that they usually wore bad haircuts.

"Increase to Warped 10," Piker ordered. He continued his evasive maneuvers, but the Romanumens countered each one and continued to draw closer.

If only Dacron were here, thought Capt. Ricardo. *He'd outmaneuver them easily and might even be able to take on the Jargonites again.*

Piker was so intent on dodging the Romanumens that he neglected to watch where the *Endocrine* was going. Suddenly Westerly exclaimed, "Sir, our course is leading us directly into an asteroid garter belt!"

Piker sat in his command chair and rested his head against

The Romanumens were the most feared
enemy of the Federation.

the back in a vain attempt to keep his neck from crooking any further. "Continue course, Mr. Flusher," he ordered.

The next few minutes were excruciatingly tense. They avoided one asteroid after another, some by mere inches, and continued at their breakneck speed.

Gradually the Romanumens slowed down, apparently deciding the risk to their ship was too great.

After several minutes, the *Endocrine* cleared the asteroids. A few moments more and they were at the edge of the Neutered Zone. The Romanumens would not follow them into Federation territory.

Exhausted, Piker asked for permission to go to Sick Bay and get some Ben-Gay for his neck. Capt. Ricardo assented.

As they emerged from the Neutered Zone, a Jargonite ship was waiting for them.

Eventually Smirk's crew caught up and passed the leading edge of the Neutered Zone, never guessing that Ricardo's crew was detouring through it, fleeing the Romanumens.

No Jargonites were in sight, so Capt. Smirk took advantage of the calm period by napping in his quarters. He was tired; he hadn't slept well lately.

Nor would he sleep peacefully this time. The familiar nightmare crept upon him as he dozed: It was the day of his wedding to Counselor Troit. As he watched her advance down the aisle, countless classy dames in chiffon gowns sat in the pews. Gripped by the horror of surrendering his freedom of choice, he awoke with a scream.

Capt. Smirk stumbled to the vanity to pull himself together for his return to the Bridge. As he ran a comb through his hair, clumps of it fell out. Smirk shrieked. This had really gone too far.

That's it, he thought. *I'm relieving myself of duty. Smock will have to take over.*

But a few minutes later, in Sick Bay, Smirk despaired of handing command over to Mr. Smock.

"He's totally obsessed with making sense of the Jargonites' messages," Dr. McCaw reported. "We couldn't keep him from reading the transcripts of their conversations with us. That's why I had him restrained."

Mr. Smock's arms were bound in a straitjacket. "Language the possibilities," he babbled. "Structure an interface. Work and eat and sleep and crawl and collapse every day some."

I guess it's up to me, Capt. Smirk thought. *Unless I get my head together, the Jargonites will overtake us next time. If only I could talk to Denise . . . er, Deedee . . . blast it, what's her name again? My fiancée.*

In the Bats' Way

CAPT. RICARDO'S SHIP SCREAMED OUT OF THE Neutered Zone at top speed and whooshed past the waiting Jargonites. Pure speed would be the crew's only hope in avoiding the enemy.

Just at that moment, Capt. Smirk and crew caught up to Ricardo's ship. Capt. Ricardo's delay in the Neutered Zone had evened out the race.

Both ships strained ahead, neck and neck, still out of range of the Jargonites—but at great cost.

"Captain, we can't keep this up too long," warned Mr. Snot. "The freezenjammers on the dilithium crystals will seize up soon."

Likewise, on Ricardo's ship, engineer Georgie LaForgery cautioned, "Captain, the reactor core is ready to blow. It's hot enough to fry an egg."

Both captains confirmed that they'd heard their engineers' warnings but continued the pace, careening ahead without acknowledging each other's presence.

Mr. Smock came to the Bridge, but there was little he could do to help. Time, and the limits of the ship's power source, were their enemies now. Capt. Smirk insisted Smock keep wearing the straitjacket in case the Jargonites broke through the Viewscreen again.

Meanwhile, on Ricardo's ship, Dacron lay on an examination table in Sick Bay. Dr. Flusher frowned as she passed an instrument back and forth across his forehead. The instrument gave off a soft, steady hum.

Deeply concerned, Dr. Flusher hurried to the Bridge to report her findings to Capt. Ricardo.

"You think it's that serious?" Ricardo questioned her.

"Very serious," she emphasized. "The Dain Bramage Meter reading is 60.014." She held up the dial for him to see, then set the instrument on the arm of his command chair. "That means Dacron's brain is 40 percent 'down.' And it's getting worse by the hour."

Piker picked up the meter in idle curiosity. "How can you be sure this thing is working?" he asked.

"It emits a steady sound as you pass it across the brain. The more non-functioning brain matter there is, the higher-pitched and louder the sound," Beverage explained. She turned back to the captain. "I've never gotten a reading this high with any patient before. It really worries me."

"Mmmm." Capt. Ricardo thought it over.

"I don't hear anything," Piker continued, jiggling the meter in front of his eyebrows.

"It's turned off right now," Beverage snapped. "Captain, we must get Dacron to a medical facility at the nearest starbase where they can do more tests and find out what's wrong. This damage could be permanent if we don't reverse it soon."

"Oh," said Piker, discovering the "on" switch. Still aiming the meter at his head, he flicked the switch.

Immediately the meter blasted a piercing shriek. Piker reeled backward, dropping the instrument. Capt. Ricardo grimaced in pain. Others screamed, reflexively covering their ears. Beverage dived for the meter and managed to shut it off.

"Captain, the reactor core is ready to blow."

Everyone's ears were ringing so loudly it took them a moment to realize the noise had stopped.

"Well, Captain, what will we do?" Beverage continued, shooting Piker a dirty look.

"WHAT, DOCTOR?" he shouted. The ringing in his ears muffled all sound.

"I SAID, WHAT WILL WE DO?" Beverage shouted back.

Before Capt. Ricardo could answer, Wart interrupted loudly. "SIR, JARGONITE VESSEL APPROACHING 10 O'CLOCK HIGH."

"CLOSE 'HEY YOU' FREQUENCIES, MR. WART."

But it was too late; the Jargonites had locked open a channel and were already on the Viewscreen. "Have you got The Dream for your team yet?" inquired Dr. B. S. Galore.

Capt. Ricardo stared at him. Dr. Galore's lips were moving, but Ricardo couldn't hear a single word. Apparently this cloud would have a silver lining after all.

"I said, have you got The Dream?" Dr. Galore repeated. For once, nobody on the Bridge seemed affected by the Jargonites.

"Hmmm," said Dr. Galore when no one responded. "I can see I'm going to have to language this in another way." He thought for a moment, then brightened. "This communication difficulty is a doorway to an expanded opportunity for new pathways to effective communication, once the barriers to thought, word, and expression have been made available to the parties that are participating."

This is wonderful, Ricardo thought. *We're immune to his gibberish.*

Dr. Galore's image on the Viewscreen was replaced by a densely-worded document. The same document appeared on all the consoles and science-station readouts on the Bridge.

Wart pressed buttons in an attempt to clear his communication screen, but the document remained. "WHAT IS THIS?" he bellowed.

Piker checked each of the stations in turn. They all displayed Dr. Galore's latest attempt at communication: a questionnaire.

"Question one," it read, "state in your own words what you consider to be The Dream of the Starship *Endocrine*. Question two: What thoughts, feelings, beliefs and assumptions stand in the way of achieving the goals, accomplishments, and achievements which constitute The Dream? . . ."

On and on it went, the visual equivalent of the Jargonites' deadly droning monologues. Reading it, some of the crew members were already nodding off to sleep. Others were obviously struggling to make sense of it; Dr. Flusher guessed from their labored breathing and flushed faces that their blood pressure was climbing dangerously.

"DON'T READ IT! CLOSE YOUR EYES!" Dr. Flusher urged them, but nobody heard her.

"I'll give you some time to think about it. Please have your answers ready for our next meeting," concluded Dr. Galore as he signed off.

Capt. Ricardo raced from one station to the next, wrenching his people away from their consoles, forcing them to look away from the questionnaire.

"WART!" Capt. Ricardo shouted. "SHUT DOWN THE SYSTEM TO CLEAR IT, THEN BOOT UP AGAIN!"

"WHAT?" the Kringle replied.

Capt. Ricardo wrote his instructions on a scrap of paper. Wart shut off the computer, then turned it back on. By the time the system came on-line again, with all the consoles cleared, there was a new image on the Viewscreen: the Starfreak logo.

"SIR, MESSAGE FROM STARFREAK," Wart announced.

A moment later, the screen split into side-by-side images of Admiral Tweet and Capt. Smirk. It was a conference call.

"Ricardo!" barked Admiral Tweet. "We're having a phone meeting."

Something about the admiral disturbed Counselor Troit. She bent close to Capt. Ricardo for a private comment. "WHAT?" he replied, frowning.

She looked from him to Admiral Tweet's image on the screen and back again, then decided to write her message. She handed the slip of paper to Capt. Ricardo. It read, "He's hiding something."

"Very well, Counselor," Capt. Ricardo muttered, crumpling the paper into a ball. "WHAT CAN I DO FOR YOU, ADMIRAL?" he shouted to the Viewscreen.

Tweet gave him an odd look, then decided to continue. "Capt. Ricardo, Capt. Smirk, we're really in a bad way here on Earth."

"Eh?" said Capt. Ricardo, cupping his hand behind his ear.

"HE SAID THEY'RE IN THE BATS' WAY ON EARTH," Piker repeated, trying to be helpful.

"BATS? WHAT BATS?" said Capt. Ricardo.

"I didn't say anything about bats," Admiral Tweet barked.

"THEY'RE REALLY VERY GENTLE CREATURES," Capt. Ricardo assured him. "I WOULDN'T BE TOO CONCERNED IF I WERE YOU."

"Ricardo, WHAT IS THE MATTER WITH YOU?" Tweet bellowed. This time Capt. Ricardo heard him.

"I'M SORRY, SIR," he said. "OUR HEARING WAS AFFECTED DURING . . . UH . . . OUR LAST ENCOUNTER WITH THE JARGONITES."

"Oh, for pity's sake. Here, I'll type out my message, then." A printout replaced Admiral Tweet's image on the Viewscreen. Capt. Ricardo and the rest of his crew read it, trying to ignore the other half of the screen, on which Capt. Smirk regarded them with a bemused smile.

Tweet's message said:

We're in a bad way—(not "bats' way," you idiots)—on Earth. People are becoming violently ill listening to the Jargonites' jargon for days on end. Their minds are turning to Jell-O. We're losing more brainpower every minute. We need you *soon*.

Capt. Smirk gave Admiral Tweet his best confident-commander smile. "Don't worry about a thing, Admiral. We'll be there in no time. You can count on *my* crew."

Slightly mollified, Tweet turned off the printed message and broadcast his image on his half of the screen. "At least one of you seems to have his head in the right place," he replied. "So, Smirk, tell me about your plans to engage the enemy."

Smirk started to repeat after him: "My plans to eng- . . ." Smirk's grin drained off his face. "Well, sir, we will eng-gaaa . . . gah . . ."

Admiral Tweet and Capt. Ricardo and crew stared in fascination. Perspiration beaded on Smirk's brow. He scratched his forehead, trying to recover his composure. "The enemy will be engggg . . ."

Smirth scratched some more. Blotches spread over his face. Mr. Smock appeared beside him, coming to his rescue. "We learned much in our skirmish with the Jargonites, Admiral," Smock said, "and we will put this knowledge to good use next time we *engage* the enemy."

"Thank you, Smock," said Capt. Smirk. The blotches on his face had swelled into hives.

Admiral Tweet looked slightly dazed. "Mr. Smock, is that a straitjacket you're wearing?"

Smock paused for an eternal moment. His eyes shifted down to the straitjacket, over to Capt. Smirk, down to the jacket, then back up to the Viewscreen. "Yes, Admiral," he replied evenly. "It is a straitjacket." Next to him, Capt. Smirk hyperventilated.

Capt. Ricardo broke in. "WHAT'S THAT? WHAT DID HE SAY?"

Admiral Tweet exploded. "What is wrong with you people?!" he screamed. "I don't believe this! *You* are going to save us from the Jargonites?! You're hopeless—all of you! If you blow this mission, you're out of Starfreak for good!" He paused to catch his breath, then added, "Besides, if you don't stop farting around and get here soon, there won't *be* any Starfreak—or any Earth!" He abruptly switched off his transmission.

Capt. Ricardo and Capt. Smirk stared at each other. "Hey," said Capt. Smirk, "some phone meeting, huh?"

Wearily, Capt. Ricardo rubbed the bridge of his nose with his

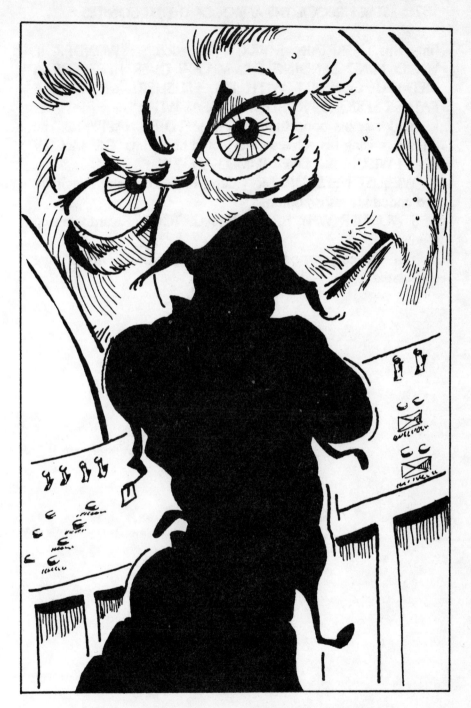

"Mr. Smock, is that a straitjacket you're
wearing?"

fingertips. "CAPTAIN SMIRK," he called, "I WONDER IF YOU'D MIND SENDING DR. McCAW OVER HERE FOR A MEDICAL CONSULT WITH DR. FLUSHER. WE HAVE A RATHER SERIOUS PROBLEM TO DEAL WITH."

Smirk saw his opportunity at once. "I'D BE HAPPY TO," he replied, raising his voice so they could hear him. "DR. McCAW AND I WILL BEAM OVER IMMEDIATELY."

"WE JUST NEED DR. Mc-" Capt. Ricardo began, but Smirk had ended his transmission.

"I WONDER WHY HE'S COMING, TOO?" Ricardo mused loudly.

Troit looked worried. "HE'S HIDING SOMETHING," she speculated.

7

The Meeting of the Mindless

R. McCAW BENT OVER DACRON, WHO WAS lying motionless on the examination table in Sick Bay. "Hmmm," he said, probing Dacron with a voltage meter. "Are you sure you don't like him better this way? He's certainly a lot quieter."

The joke was lost on Dr. Flusher and Counselor Troit, who couldn't hear him.

"HIS CONDITION IS OBVIOUSLY THE RESULT OF THE ENCOUNTER WITH THE JARGONITES," Beverage shouted. Dr. McCaw backed away several steps. "I THINK IT MAY HAVE OVERWHELMED HIM PSYCHOLOGICALLY. THAT'S WHY I ASKED COUNSELOR TROIT TO PARTICIPATE IN THIS CON-SULT."

Deanna nodded and added, "I THINK HE'S HIDING SOME-THING."

McCaw shook his head. No use trying to settle Dacron's problem until these two could converse in a normal tone of voice. He gave them each some eardrops. A few moments later, the ringing in their ears stopped.

"Whew! Thank you, Dr. McCaw," said Beverage. "So, as I said, Dacron collapsed after his argument with the Jargonite.

But I can't figure out why he had such a severe reaction, or why he's getting worse all the time even though he hasn't been exposed to the Jargonites since then."

"How much do you know about his innards?" grumbled Dr. McCaw, regarding Dacron with distaste.

"Not a whole lot," Beverage admitted. "I need to do more tests."

"Could this be some kind of android influenza?" Dr. McCaw continued.

"Too soon to tell," said Beverage. "I need to do more tests."

Dr. McCaw was losing the small amount of patience he'd had to start with. "Is he allergic to anything, like exposure to direct sunlight? Has he been sitting too close to a magnet?"

"I don't know," said Beverage. "I need to do more tests."

Exasperated, Dr. McCaw hollered, "Forget the doggone tests! Just open him up and see what's wrong—here, use my crowbar, for Pete's sake!"

Dr. McCaw pulled a crowbar out of his black doctor's bag. He turned Dacron over. A panel on Dacron's back read: *CAUTION! Do not open. Danger of electrical shock. No user-serviceable parts inside. Refer to owner's manual for list of authorized service centers for this model.*

Dr. McCaw ignored the warning and opened him anyway. Dr. Flusher bit her lip in concern but did nothing to stop him. She wasn't about to get in his way, not after all the rumors she'd heard about his temper. Like the rumor about the time he'd argued with another doctor over a referral patient and ended up biting off the doctor's ear.

Dr. McCaw rummaged through Dacron, creating a ruckus that sounded like the clanking of a dozen pots and pans. "What a mess," he muttered, deeply engrossed. "Hasn't anybody heard of preventive maintenance? No, you all wait until something goes wrong, and then you bring it in to the shop . . ." He barked at Dr. Flusher, "Get me the scalpel out of my bag!"

She slapped it expertly into his hand. He tinkered awhile, then ordered, "Sponges." She handed him some.

"Pliers." She dug through the bag and found them for him.

"Crescent wrench." Beverage wasn't too sure about this one, but luckily there was only one wrench in the bag, so she guessed that must be it.

"Phillips screwdriver." Beverage handed him a tool.

"No! *Phillips* screwdriver! Where did you do your residency, anyway?" he demanded. Dr. McCaw dug through the black bag himself and found the right tool.

"Umm—Doctor, your hands are no longer sterile," Bev reminded him.

"Uh-huh. Give me one of those Handi-Wipes, will you?"

Dr. McCaw was now utterly engrossed in the surgery. The clanging continued as he delved deeper and deeper into Dacron's body. Suddenly: "Ah-*ha!*" he exclaimed.

"Here's what's causing his problem," Dr. McCaw said, pulling at something deep inside.

"What?" exclaimed Beverage breathlessly. She and Deanna leaned in for a closer look.

"He's pregnant!" Dr. McCaw announced. The women gaped at him, aghast.

"Ha ha! Just kidding!" Dr. McCaw cackled. "No, his problem is . . ."

Dr. McCaw pulled a small object out of Dacron. The women leaned closer.

". . . His battery is running low."

Beverage and Deanna sighed, limp with relief. "That's all?" said Deanna, gazing at the battery. "So that's why his voice was getting low," she continued, as realization dawned, "and he stopped babbling, and he couldn't cope with the Jargonites. At least it's nothing serious."

"It *could* be serious," Dr. McCaw warned. "He's going to need a replacement—soon."

"That's right," Dr. Flusher concurred. "I've read cases in the medical literature in which androids went down because of dead batteries and could never be booted up again."

"Well, at least we know the problem is curable," said Deanna.

"He's pregnant!" Dr. McCaw announced.

"By golly, it was fun performing surgery again," Dr. McCaw asserted, cracking his knuckles. "You can close now, Dr. Flusher." He walked away, leaving Beverage to finish the busy-work of retrieving the sponges and stitching up the patient. "I have to go make out my bill."

Beverage sighed and bent to the task, soldering iron in hand.

"If you'll excuse me, too," Deanna told her, "I must meet with Capt. Smirk. He asked if he could see me."

Smirk was in the observation lounge, gazing out into space. "Those countless stars," he murmured to himself. "And I've got a woman on every one of them." His voice caught, and his eyes brimmed with tears. "But will I ever see any of them again?"

Behind him, the door to the lounge opened. *That must be Deanna,* he thought. *Get hold of yourself, Jim. No time for self-pity. You've got to talk your way out of this fix.*

Troit held herself aloof as he kissed her in greeting. "You wanted to talk to me?" she inquired coldly.

"Yes, I . . ."

"You're hiding something," she blurted.

"Darling, I . . ." said Smirk.

"It's about our engagement, isn't it?" Deanna demanded. "You feel uncomfortable with it."

"Deanna . . ."

"You feel hemmed in, anxious, tied down," she remarked.

"I-I-I've been . . ." Smirk stammered.

"You know that once you get back to Earth, you'll feel even worse, what with all those other women you could be dating if it weren't for me," Deanna continued.

"You see . . ."

"You still love me, but it will never work out. You'd always resent me for cramping your style. You need to be free—free as a bird, free as the wind."

"It's . . ."

"You hope I understand it's better this way. You'll always cherish the love we had. You know I'll find someone else and be even happier with them. You think it's best that we say good-bye," Troit concluded.

I knew I could convince her, Smirk gloated to himself. *That old James T. Smirk charm strikes again.*

He pulled her close, though she resisted him, stiffening. "Could I have something to remember you by?" he asked, puckering up, eyes closed.

"Indeed," she answered.

"You sure you don't want me to give you something for that shiner?" Dr. McCaw asked as they stood on the UltraFax platform, waiting to be beamed back to their ship.

"No, thank you, Moans," replied Capt. Smirk, nursing his black eye. "It's sort of a souvenir, you see."

Capt. Smirk sat upright in his command chair, brimming with renewed confidence. "Mr. Zulu, set course for Earth," he ordered.

"Course headings set," Zulu responded.

Smirk paused for effect, then announced, "Mr. Zulu—engage!"

Bring Him In to the Shop

D R. FLUSHER'S PATIENCE WAS WEARING THIN after an hour on the phone to the AAAA-Android Parts Emporium. She was trying to order a new battery for Dacron, and the emporium staff kept transferring her from one department to another. She talked to nearly everyone, from the receptionist to the head of research and development to somebody named Harold in the mail room.

Finally she got through to someone who sounded like they might know what she was talking about. For a change, *they* were asking *her* questions, instead of vice versa.

"His serial number?" she repeated into the phone. "Gee, I don't know. Where is it located? . . . You're *kidding* . . . All right, just a minute, let me check . . . It's 228385W 38293. . . .

". . . I just need a battery. . . . No, we don't have a service contract on him. . . . No, I can't give you the name of the store where he was originally purchased. What difference does that make?

". . . What do you mean, we have to bring him in for service? Look, all I need is a battery! We're willing to pay extra for delivery. . . . It's not my fault this is your busiest season. . . .

Then how soon *could* you deliver one? . . . Two months?! He needs help immediately!

". . . Well, I suppose we'll *have* to pick it up. Where are you located? Wait, let me get a pencil . . . Planet M9, Vector Sector . . . second continent from the magnetic pole . . . turn left at the third crater . . . service entrance . . . got it . . . hours 9 A.M. to 5 P.M. . . . Do you take MasterCard?"

Capt. Ricardo entered Sick Bay as she hung up the phone. "HOW IS OUR PATIENT, DOCTOR?" he shouted.

"Please, Captain," Beverage said, "you don't have to shout."

"I'M NOT SHOUTING," Ricardo shouted.

Nearby, a second-light-year resident leaned out of the doorway of the on-call lounge and glared at him. "Hey, keep it down, will ya? This is a hospital zone. Some of us are trying to sleep." He slammed the door.

Beverage promptly administered some of Dr. McCaw's eardrops to the captain.

"Ah!" He clapped his hands once in satisfaction. "Jolly good. Now, how are things coming with Lieutenant Commander Dacron? Was Dr. McCaw able to shed some light on his problem?"

"Yes," said Dr. Flusher. "He discovered that Dacron has a weak battery."

"Oh! Is that all? Should be simple to fix, I'd think."

Bev shook her head. "The factory refuses to deliver a replacement. We're going to have to take him there for service."

"Take him there! Doctor, that's out of the question," Ricardo replied. "We've got to get to Earth to battle the Jargonites."

"Captain, you don't understand," Bev continued. "Dacron's condition is worse than ever." She led him into an adjacent room, where Dacron lay on the table. "We even tried jump-starting him, with no success," said Bev.

"Mmmph," grunted the captain. One cable linked Dacron's nose with the battery of a Volvo parked next to the table, while the other cable was fastened to Dacron's toe and grounded to an I.V. stand.

"We're gaining on them!"

"Where is this factory you want us to stop at?" asked Capt. Ricardo.

Bev winced a little, anticipating his reaction. "The Vector Sector," she said.

"The Vector Sector!" yelled Capt. Ricardo. "That's several light-years out of our way!"

Next door, the resident pounded on the wall in annoyance. "Pipe down, eh?" came the sound of his voice through the wall.

"Doctor," Capt. Ricardo continued more quietly, through clenched teeth, "we simply can't delay our mission to Earth that long. Do you want Capt. Smirk to beat us there?"

"But you've seen how serious Dacron's condition is," Bev pleaded. "If we don't get him restarted soon, the damage could be permanent."

"We can't take time out for a detour," Capt. Ricardo insisted.

"Yes, we can," Bev countered. "Okay, so Capt. Smirk makes it to Earth first. But we can follow up later and assist him. Right now Dacron needs our help more. Don't try to be a hero at his expense."

"Beverage," the captain maintained, folding his arms across his chest, "I will not abandon this mission."

"Then Dacron's blood will be on your head."

Capt. Ricardo didn't like the sound of that, but he wasn't about to admit it. "Doctor, for pity's sake, he doesn't have blood."

That night, Capt. Ricardo tossed and turned in bed, unable to sleep. Dr. Flusher's final retort rang in his ears: "All right, then, his 10-W-40 be on your head!"

"We're gaining on them." Capt. Smirk, tense with concentration, stared at the Viewscreen. "I'm sure we're pulling ahead." He watched as they inched ahead of Ricardo's ship.

"More power, Mr. Snot!" he ordered over the intercom. "And no excuses!" Smirk popped out of his chair and began pacing the Bridge. "Mr. Zulu, increase speed to Warped 9.5."

"Increasing to Warped 9.5," Zulu echoed.

Checkout reported, "Position now one length ahead of the other wessel."

"That's it," Smirk urged, almost to himself. His hands were clenched, as was his recently permed hair. "That's it."

"Position two lengths ahead," Checkout noted.

"We're doing it, gang! We're doing it!" Smirk exulted. "We're winning! I knew we had it in us! Pour it on now. We can be the first ones to Earth. I just know it."

"Position—" Checkout began, then halted, puzzled. "Sir, the other wessel is . . . pulling away." He rechecked his console in bewilderment.

"What?" Smirk froze in mid-swashbuckle.

"Sir," said Mr. Smock, "Capt. Ricardo's crew has altered course."

They all gaped at the Viewscreen in disbelief. The other ship had turned away sharply and was speeding off on a tangent.

"What . . . where are they going, Smock?" Capt. Smirk sank slowly back into his chair, hardly believing his eyes.

Mr. Smock made some calculations in his head, double-checked them by counting on his fingers, then replied, "Projecting from their present course and coordinates, they are traveling toward the Vector Sector."

"The Vector Sector? What in the—that's just a dumpy industrial park. Why would they be going there now?"

"Perhaps they have made a navigational error," Smock speculated. "Shall we hail them to find out?"

"No," Smirk answered hastily. "No, Smock, we'll . . . uh, I'm sure Capt. Ricardo has his reasons for whatever it is he's doing. We'll continue on course for Earth."

"Are you sure this place is open? It looks awfully quiet," Piker observed, crooking his neck just a tad to indicate concern. He was carrying Dacron, which cramped his neck-crooking style somewhat by throwing him off-balance.

"Yes, I'm sure," Beverage replied. "I wrote down the hours when I called them."

They had just UltraFaxed down to the deserted reception area of AAAA-Android Parts Emporium. It was more than a day and a half since the crew had veered away from their race toward Earth.

Beverage walked up to the desk and tapped a device marked "ring bell for service." No one responded. She tried it again, but the area remained silent.

Piker became impatient. "This is ridiculous," he muttered, carrying Dacron toward the inner office door. As Piker entered the doorway, Dacron's head and feet bonked the doorframe on either side.

"Oops," said Piker. He stood there for a moment, as if he were deciding how hard he'd have to push to force Dacron past the frame. Finally he declared, "I think I'll just put him down for a minute."

Piker dumped Dacron on the receptionist's chair, then entered the office. "Hey, can we have some help out here?" He passed further into the building, opening doors and calling as he went.

Bev nibbled on her thumbnail while she waited. Something about this place gave her the creeps. She had the weird sensation that it had been recently abandoned.

She wished Piker would get back. What was taking him so long, anyway?

"Can I help you?" Her heart seized at the unexpected voice behind her. She whirled around; there stood a Jargonite.

"I . . . uh . . . I-uh . . ." she stammered, trying to assemble a graceful excuse to get away.

"I'm a poet and wisher and dreamer and caring human being," said the Jargonite. "How about you?"

"I'm uh . . . uh . . . I'm just looking for the ladies' room," Bev said, snatching at the first thought that entered her head.

"Ah. I see." The Jargonite was visibly disappointed that the conversation had taken such a sensible turn.

Beverage backed slowly toward the door marked "Plant Entrance." "Well, it's been nice talking to you," she said, forcing a smile. As soon as her back touched the door, she grabbed the handle, yanked the door open, and dashed inside.

As Capt. Smirk's ship drew within a few hours of Earth, a nagging fear began nibbling at the edges of Smirk's excitement. He gradually realized that the glory of being the first—and only—starship to arrive was offset by the danger of having to battle the Jargonites alone. Given their problems during previous encounters, he wasn't all that sure they could pull it off.

As soon as they entered Earth's orbit, Smirk hailed Admiral Tweet. When the Admiral's face appeared on the Viewscreen, Smirk was shocked; Tweet looked so haggard that Smirk wondered if Starfreak had reinstated the 40-hour week.

"Admiral, are you all right?" Capt. Smirk inquired.

"Jim," Admiral Tweet gasped, blinking, "is that you?"

"How are you doing against the Jargonites here on Earth?" asked Capt. Smirk.

"Terrible," Tweet answered with great effort. "They've got control of nearly everything—the government, the media, almost all public and private facilities." He paused to readjust one of the toothpicks propping his eyelids open. "Here at Starfreak headquarters, we're one of the last holdouts, and only because we've got our blather deflectors up. I think they'll break through those soon, though. We've been getting a lot of static." Interference buzzed across the Viewscreen.

"We're coming down to investigate," Smirk told him.

"Be careful, Jim," Tweet warned. "These Jargonites are all over the place. Once they notice you haven't been brainwashed, it's all over—" Static crackled across the Viewscreen again, then Tweet's image was replaced by a flashing message from the Jargonites:

Empower Yourself to Be All You Can Be

Beverage walked up to the desk and
tapped a device marked "Ring Bell for
Service."

"Mr. Zulu, assemble an away team for me to lead," said the captain. Danger or not, he wasn't going to pass up the opportunity to play the conquering hero. *Boy, are people on Earth going to be glad to see us,* he thought. *There'll be cheering crowds, network news cameras—the works. Maybe they'll even throw us a tickertape parade.* By the time Smirk joined Zulu, Checkout, and Dr. McCaw on the UltraFax platform, he was already composing in his mind an acceptance speech for Starfreak's highest honor, the Purple Hangnail.

Meanwhile, on the UltraFax platform of Capt. Ricardo's ship, Beverage and Piker materialized after a hasty retreat from the AAAA-Android Parts Emporium. Wart, standing by on security alert, hurried over to them. "Are you all right?" he inquired.

Beverage tried to catch her breath. "Jargonites . . . they've infiltrated . . . the factory . . ."

"They're all over the place," Piker gasped. "I kept dodging them all around the plant."

"Apparently," Beverage continued, "they fancy themselves specialists in android medicine." She smoothed her hair back from her face. "I overheard them talking about this bizarre treatment method called myofiscal release. It involves treating physical problems by digging for their psychological roots until the patient coughs up money."

Piker added, "Luckily, Dr. Flusher found the storage area and located an android battery."

"Yes, I see," Wart observed as Beverage held out the circular object in her palm. "But where is Dacron?"

The other two looked at him, then at each other. "I thought *you* had him," they said simultaneously.

The captain actually handled the news rather well, Piker told himself as he sat across from Capt. Ricardo's desk in the ready room. Within 20 minutes Capt. Ricardo passed through the stages of denial ("I know you didn't actually leave Dacron in the factory. This joke is not funny, Number I"), bewilderment ("How

can you just 'forget' a crewmate?"), rage ("You're not fit to work
on an Aromaian sewage shuttle!"), and guilt ("I knew I should
have led the away team myself."). With relief, Piker realized the
captain was entering the acceptance phase.

"We're going to have to send some people back down there
to locate Dacron," said Capt. Ricardo, almost to himself. "The
fewer the better, to avoid attracting attention from the Jargonites. Hmmm. Perhaps just a one-person away team. And since
they may be captured and brainwashed, it had better be someone
expendable."

Westerly was thrilled to the tips of his toes that Capt. Ricardo
was giving him this assignment. He couldn't recall the last time
they'd sent someone solo on an away mission. A few more
assignments like this, and he'd have his Boy Scout space badge
in no time. He gave them a jaunty salute as he UltraFaxed down
to the factory.

With each passing minute as they waited by the UltraFax for
Westerly's return, Capt. Ricardo grew more nervous. Beverage
stood beside him, and she'd promised to strangle him with her
bare hands if Westerly didn't return completely unharmed.

To everyone's immense relief, Westerly located Dacron within
a few minutes, and the two of them UltraFaxed back. Beverage
put her anger at Capt. Ricardo on hold so she could tend to her
patient. She had surgery to perform.

"Staff meeting, Mr. Smock," ordered a tight-lipped Capt. Smirk
as his away team returned to the ship from their reconnaissance
mission on Earth. Smock guessed from Smirk's expression that
the away team hadn't gotten a big welcome.

Smock was correct. "Things are a mess down there," Capt.
Smirk announced as soon as the officers assembled around the
conference table. "All the humans I saw have been completely
brainwashed. They're walking around empowering and acknowledging each other in broad daylight. They've become blithering

"All the humans I saw have been
completely brainwashed."

idiots, and they're endangering themselves and others. I saw a building burn down while the firefighters sat next to it, working out an interpersonal conflict. What about the rest of you? What did you see after we split up?"

"Checkout and I looked into a day-care center," reported Zulu, "and saw children playing with matches, falling out of windows and chasing balls into the street while their parents and teachers attended a vision-setting session."

"It's even worse in the hospitals," croaked McCaw. "I saw patients die as the doctors and nurses took turns acknowledging one another for being such great team players."

"What about the Jargonites? Did you see many of them?" asked Mr. Smock.

"They are all over the place," said Checkout. "It was very difficult to ewade capture. That is vy ve came back so soon—another couple of minutes and they vould have realized ve veren't brainvashed yet."

"We can't get any support from anyone down there while they're all subject to this brainwashing," Capt. Smirk said. "And we certainly can't use the futon torpedoes until we've isolated the Jargonites from the humans. We need to flush the Jargonites out of there."

"Excuse me, Captain," said Smock, "but how would we accomplish this? If they've got control of Earth, where are we going to flush them out *to*?"

Smirk thought it over for a long moment, then raised his eyebrows and replied. "How about here?"

Dr. Flusher had been in surgery for over six hours, and she still didn't have Dacron's new battery in place. She hated to admit it, even to herself, but she could have used Dr. McCaw's help again. Instead, she resorted to consulting the owner's manual.

"Read that part again about Part Z and Thingamajig G," she asked Counselor Troit.

Troit peered at the manual and read aloud, "When replacing

main battery, adjust Disruptor B so that Part Z and Thingamajig G are synchronous with the baud rate of the unit."

"Well, I see Part Z and Thingamajig G, but what's *this* thing in the way?" Bev said, pursing her lips in frustration. She jiggled the unidentified plastic part; it wouldn't budge. "Read a little further," she urged Troit.

"Specifications for Subpart L of Part Y have been established to provide reasonable protection from electrical shock under wet conditions," Troit read. "However, exercise caution in retrieving the android if it falls into a bathtub."

Bev muttered to herself, "This battery does not *FIT*," as she attempted to force it into place. Her face reddened with the effort. She asked Troit in exasperation, "What else does it say?"

"That's about it," Troit said, then read the final paragraph: "For further information, purchase FCC booklet 'Getting the Most From Your Android' (stock #007-000-3939 2828) from the Superintendent of Documents . . ."

Beverage vented her frustration by pushing harder and harder on the battery, until suddenly—*"Ouch!"* she cried.

"What is it?" asked Troit.

"Oooooh! I broke my nail!" Dr. Flusher inspected her splintered fingernail. "A $45 manicure down the drain!" she wailed. "That does it. I give up. This battery is not going to fit, and nothing I can do will help it!" She stormed out of Sick Bay.

Troit regarded Dacron with pity; Dr. Flusher had been too angry to remember the protocol. *The least I can do*, Troit decided, *is to treat his remains with dignity*. She pulled a plastic dust cover out of the supply closet and carefully draped it over Dacron's limp form.

Drastic Solution

"**C**APTAIN, THIS IS A RASH AND IMPULsive plan. The consequences are unpredictable—perhaps fatal. It emphasizes immediate action at the expense of sound judgment."

"Thank you, Mr. Smock," Capt. Smirk replied, oblivious to the concern in Smock's remark. "It's my kind of move, all right."

The two of them stood facing one another across a table supporting the ship's Drastic Solution brand self-destruct device. It was labeled: *Warning: This is not a toy. Activate only if all alternatives have been exhausted or at least discussed in a staff meeting.*

Yoohoo's voice came over the intercom. "Captain, message from Admiral Tweet at Starfreak Headquarters."

"Put him through," ordered Capt. Smirk, turning toward the small communication screen on the side counter.

Admiral Tweet wore the frenzied look of someone about to undergo a tax audit. "Smirk!" he barked hoarsely. "The Jargonites have invaded us here at headquarters! You've been hanging around in orbit for half a day now. When are you going to do something?"

"Right away, Admiral," Smirk responded. "Don't worry. I have a plan."

"It'd better be a quick plan," Tweet said, looking nervously over his shoulder. Someone was pounding on his door.

"It is, Admiral," said Smirk. "Bold and decisive. I can't tell you too much about it in case the Jargonites are monitoring this transmission. Let's just say it involves destroying my ship."

Tweet's gaze swiveled back and forth between the monitor and his office door, which was now being forced inward, straining the hinges. "What? Smirk, the fighting here is so loud—I thought I heard you say you were going to destroy your ship."

"That's right, Admiral."

"But . . . destroy . . . while you're in orbit—Smirk, the explosion will take Earth along with it!" Tweet's voice rose in panic.

"Don't worry, Admiral," Smirk repeated. "I have it all under control."

"I don't believe this." Tweet's voice rose to ever higher notes on the musical scale. "Smirk"—he was near high C—"do something!" His office door burst inward, admitting a mob of Jargonites. The communication transmission ended abruptly.

"Well, let's get on with it," Capt. Smirk said. "Mr. Smock, have you informed all of our crew to ignore the evacuation warning?"

"Yes, Captain," said Smock. "They understand that it is intended to frighten the Jargonites back onto their own ships and away from Earth."

"Right," Smirk confirmed. "And once they leave, you and I will come back in here and cancel the sequence. I've tied this string to my finger so I won't forget. Now, let's start the Drastic Solution sequence."

Each of them placed his right hand on a sensing device. "Begin Drastic Solution sequence," Smirk told the computer.

"Recognize Smirk, James T.," responded the computer. "Recognize Smock, Mister. To proceed, give coded command."

The only ones who knew the code were Capt. Smirk, Mr. Smock, and anyone who happened to page through the Important Data section of Capt. Smirk's daybook. Starfreak had installed this safety feature to prevent Drastic Solution from unauthorized use as a Halloween prank.

"Eegin-bay ountdown-cay ow-nay," said Smirk, carefully enunciating the code.

"Does Smock, Mister, confirm?" inquired the computer.

"Yes," Smock replied.

"Countdown set for Drastic Solution," announced the computer. "Ship will self-destruct in thirty minutes."

The warning lights in the hallway blinked as Capt. Smirk and Mr. Smock walked back to the Bridge. "This ought to shake 'em up," Smirk predicted. "What was that they were doing when we left?"

"Team-building, Captain," Smock replied.

"Yes, team-building. This will put an end to that baloney," said Smirk.

These Jargonites are so gullible, Smirk reflected. *It was easy as pie to lure them here onto the ship. All we did was ask for a little coaching. And now that they're here, we'll scare them back into space with a little sleight-of-hand.*

"Ship will self-destruct in twenty-nine minutes," the computer announced over the intercom.

"Watch the doorway, Smock," said Capt. Smirk with a chuckle as they stepped up to the Bridge. "We're likely to get trampled by the Jargonites on their way out."

But to their great surprise, the Bridge looked just as it had when they'd left it: Smirk's crew sat in a circle around the Jargonite leaders, and several more Jargonites stood watch around the edges. As before, the crew members sat in a stupor, their wits dulled by the oppressive team-building jargon.

The leader, Dr. B. S. Galore, gave them a stern look. "That was an awfully long bathroom break," he commented.

"Bathroom break!" Smirk guffawed. "Galore, don't you get

it? We've just initiated the Drastic Solution sequence. This ship is going to blow itself up!"

"Ship will self-destruct in twenty-eight minutes," said the computer.

"Self-destruct. Uh-huh," said Galore, folding his arms across his chest and tapping his foot. "Capt. Smirk, this is an obvious ploy to language a lot of hostility you have toward us. I think it's time that you take the hot seat." He pointed to the chair at the center of the circle.

"Galore, you don't understand." Capt. Smirk stopped laughing and stood face-to-face with the Jargonite. "We haven't got time for baring our souls anymore. In twenty-eight minutes, this ship is going to destroy itself and take Earth along with it."

Galore became angrier. "I knew I shouldn't have let you out of the room," he said. "You've lost the whole thought-process of the team. That does it! No more bathroom breaks!"

"Ship will self-destruct in twenty-seven minutes," the computer observed.

Capt. Smirk squirmed on the hot seat, but not for the reason participants usually squirmed.

"Ship will self-destruct in ten minutes," the computer said.

"Now, Capt. Smirk," said Dr. Galore, circling him like a vulture, "how would you describe yourself?"

"Look, we haven't got time for this!" Smirk protested.

"Why are you so resistant to helping to outline The Dream for your crew?" Galore persisted.

"We don't need a dream, you imbecile. We need to get off this ship before we're all blown to kingdom come!" Smirk was sweating. He and Smock couldn't get back to turn off the Drastic Solution device; the Jargonites wouldn't let them leave the Bridge.

"Don't you think it's time to let go of this 'Drastic Solution' construct you've invented and face reality?" Galore countered.

Suddenly the Viewscreen came to life. An image appeared there, and a voice hailed them:

"Dr. Galore. So we meet again."

Capt. Smirk's crew stared in disbelief. It was Dacron.

Dacron felt good as new—better, even—as he sat at his station on the Bridge of Capt. Ricardo's ship, which was now in orbit next to Smirk's vessel.

Westerly had finished installing Dacron's battery to complete the requirements for his Scout badge. Dacron's logic circuits were humming again. And this time he was on the offensive.

"Dr. Galore," said Dacron evenly, "can you tell me whether you have any genuine credits in the counseling field?"

"Credits?" Galore echoed blankly.

"Yes," said Dacron. "What qualifies you to conduct these sessions? Do you have a degree in psychotherapy? Any advanced training?"

"Well, uh, I do have a master's degree . . ." Galore began.

"A master's degree in what?" countered Dacron.

"Uh, marketing," Galore admitted. "But I *have* done lots of goal-setting sessions with many alien races, and . . ."

"Excuse me, Doctor, but was this done at their invitation?"

"Er, no," Galore floundered. He and the other Jargonites were becoming agitated. "We sort of tricked them into it, actually. But it was for their own good. They needed an experiential shift to bring their self into accordance with the ideal . . ."

"Wouldn't you say that's unethical—to ask them to undergo group therapy without their knowledge or consent?" Dacron persisted. "Do you follow any code of ethics, Dr. Galore?"

"Ethics?" The word struck a nerve. All the Jargonites froze. Galore began to hyperventilate.

"Yes, ethics," Dacron continued.

Galore cringed. "Don't say that!" he cried.

"Say what?" Dacron asked innocently. "Ethics?"

"Aaaaahh!" screamed Galore. "You're hurting my ears!"

Capt. Smirk jumped into the fray. "Ethics!" he cried. "Ethics!

Ethics!" The Jargonites screeched, holding their ears, twisting about in agony.

Smirk's crewmates stirred from their hypnotic state. "Ethics! Ethics!" they cried, flinging the words at their captors.

"Aaaaahh!" the Jargonites screamed. Static electricity began snapping around their heads.

"Ethics!" the crew shouted. "Ethics!"

Some of the Jargonites ran for the door. "Let them go!" Smirk ordered.

The Jargonites who remained began to undergo a startling transformation. As the static crackled around them, they dissolved into balls of fiber.

"What in the world—what are those?" Smirk gasped.

"Sir, it appears the Jargonites are dissolving into their component parts: warm fuzzies," observed Mr. Smock.

Each Jargonite became a tumbleweed-sized ball of brightly colored material. Soon all of the Jargonites remaining on the Bridge had unraveled into these warm fuzzies.

Smirk and his crew faced the Viewscreen and applauded. "Well done, Mr. Dacron!" Smirk called.

Dacron smiled modestly. "Thanks to Westerly, I have regained my reasoning ability," he told them.

Smirk applauded heartily. As he did so, he happened to glance at the string tied to his finger. "Yaaaaaah!" he shrieked. "The Drastic Solution!"

Capt. Ricardo appeared on the Viewscreen. "What is it?" he asked.

"We've set the ship to self-destruct," Smirk cried.

"Ship will self-destruct in one minute," the computer announced.

"We'll UltraFax you aboard," Capt. Ricardo announced. "Stand by."

"Wait!" Smirk cried. "Our people aren't all on the Bridge. We've got to assemble them here."

"Can't we just Fax all the life forms from your ship to ours?" asked Capt. Ricardo.

O'Brine had his hands full with this Fax-over . . .

"No, sir," answered Mr. Smock. "You would also be bringing aboard any Jargonites who have not deteriorated into warm fuzzies."

Smock turned to Capt. Smirk. "Captain, we must turn off the Drastic Solution mechanism, or Earth will be destroyed."

"Right, Smock. Let's get going," said Capt. Smirk. To Capt. Ricardo he said, "Once Smock and I leave the Bridge, Fax over all remaining Bridge crew. Also, locate Dr. McCaw and Mr. Snot elsewhere on the ship and Fax them up. Mr. Smock and I will signal you when we're ready to come aboard."

"Awaiting your signal, Captain," Capt. Ricardo replied.

O'Brine, Capt. Ricardo's UltraFax chief, had his hands full with this Fax-over. Smirk's Bridge crew was easy enough to transport, but he had a tough time locking on to Mr. Snot in Engineering.

"Mr. Snot, hold still," he pleaded over the communication channel.

"Arrfff!" responded the chief engineer. It sounded as if he was choking.

Eventually Mr. Snot materialized on the UltraFax platform. Warm fuzzies engulfed his portly frame. He brushed them away from his face, gasping for air.

"They were all over the place!" he panted. "In my eyes, in my mouth, even in my kilt!"

Getting a lock on Dr. McCaw was even harder. "Doctor, you've got to stand still," O'Brine told him.

"Arrgrrhhfffgghh!" said Dr. McCaw, his voice as muffled as Mr. Snot's had been. O'Brine desperately punched the buttons of the UltraFax console, trying to fix the Fax beam onto his moving target.

Eventually, Dr. McCaw materialized on the platform, lying on his side, warm fuzzies swaddling his head and feet. He struggled vainly to loose himself from them.

"Let's help him," O'Brine ordered a shipping clerk. The two pulled at the material around McCaw's head.

"Mmmpphh!" said Dr. McCaw.

"He's saying something," the clerk said. "What is it?"

They unraveled the warm fuzzies wrapped around McCaw's head. Finally his mouth was free. "Doggone it!" he snarled. "I'm a doctor, not a Q-Tip!"

"Everyone except Capt. Smirk and Mr. Smock have Faxed aboard, Captain," came O'Brine's voice over the intercom.

"Thank you, Mr. O'Brine," responded Capt. Ricardo. "Mr. Dacron, use the audio channel to monitor the nearest Jargonite ship for a moment."

Dacron did so. ". . . Attention, all team-builders on Earth. Report to your original ship at once. We are evacuating immediately . . ." said the Jargonite leader.

"That's enough, Mr. Dacron," ordered the captain. "Open a channel to Capt. Smirk's ship." As soon as Dacron had done so, Capt. Ricardo inquired, "Capt. Smirk, how soon can you turn off the Drastic Solution mechanism?"

"We can't," came Smirk's frightening reply.

Capt. Smirk and Mr. Smock had barely gotten five yards down the corridor outside the Bridge. The warm fuzzies were piled up everywhere, blocking their way.

"Ship will self-destruct in thirty seconds," the computer announced.

"Well, this is it, Smock," said Capt. Smirk. "It's been nice knowing you."

"Captain, do you intend to do nothing?" Mr. Smock inquired.

"I'm going down with the ship," Smirk maintained stoutly. "It seems like the macho thing to do."

"There *are* additional considerations," Smock reminded him. "If the ship destroys itself now, it will take Capt. Ricardo's ship, both our crews, and all of Earth with it."

"Ah, yes. I do see what you mean, Smock," said Capt. Smirk. "Any suggestions?"

"Yes, sir," said Mr. Smock. "Let's go to Plan D."

"Plan D . . . Plan D . . . which one is that, Smock?"

A bright flash flooded the Viewscreen . . .

"Officially it is known as Starfreak's plan of last resort, Captain. You yourself nicknamed it Plan D. You said the 'D' stood for 'Dumb.' "

"Ah, Plan D. But . . ." as the realization dawned on Capt. Smirk, horror filled his eyes, ". . . then we have no hope of saving the ship."

"Ship will self-destruct in fifteen seconds," said the computer.

"I think we are at that point anyway, Captain," Smock told him gently.

Capt. Smirk sighed deeply. "All right, let's get on with it."

"Ten more seconds? Are you sure, Mr. Dacron?" Capt. Ricardo paced the Bridge, wringing his hands.

"Yes, sir. Our computer is in contact with the computer on Capt. Smirk's ship. Now there are eight seconds remaining in the Drastic Solution countdown."

Suddenly, on the Viewscreen, they saw Capt. Smirk's ship launch itself away from them into space. A moment later, Capt. Smirk and Mr. Smock materialized onto Capt. Ricardo's Bridge in a shower of UltraFax sparkles.

"There it goes!" cried Capt. Smirk, pointing to his now-vanishing starship.

"What happened?" Capt. Ricardo asked, astonished.

"Plan D," Mr. Smock explained. "We set it on autopilot and aimed it toward an uninhabited quadrant of space."

"Five seconds," Dacron counted down, "four . . . three . . . two . . . one."

A bright flash flooded the Viewscreen for a moment as Capt. Smirk's ship exploded. Bits of twisted metal and warm fuzzies floated by as the flotsam scattered into space.

"My ship," said Capt. Smirk, dazed. "My ship."

Home Sweet Home

66WELCOME TO OUR CELEBRATION banquet, crew members of the USS *Endocrines*—er, *Endocrine*," began Admiral Tweet.

Celebration? Phooey, thought Mr. Snot. *Our ship's blown to smithereens, and he wants us to celebrate.*

I wish Mom hadn't made me come to this dumb banquet, thought Westerly. *I'd rather be in my room watching "The Galaxy's Funniest Home Videos."*

"We hope you enjoy this most festive occasion," continued Admiral Tweet.

Enjoy? I'll be lucky if I can stay awake through this festive occasion, thought Georgie.

He's hiding something, Troit reflected. *I bet they're going to make us play charades.*

Will destroying our own ship affect our year-end bonuses? wondered Zulu.

"We've prepared our most sumptuous food . . ."

Probably too spicy to digest, judged Dr. McCaw. *I can feel my ulcer kicking up already.*

Bland steam-table Federation pap, Wart thought.

". . . So enjoy the meal . . ."

Which fork am I supposed to use first? worried Yoohoo.

I'm sure everybody is staring at my broken fingernail, Beverage fretted.

Remember, drink from the glass, not from the finger bowl, Checkout reminded himself. *From the glass, not the bowl.*

I hope they don't serve corn on the cob, thought Piker. *I always get some stuck to my beard.*

". . . And afterward, we'll have a delightful presentation from our board of directors," Tweet concluded.

And to think I gave up retirement for this, Smock reflected.

Perhaps I should switch to Standby and sleep with my eyes open, Dacron speculated.

I wonder if anyone would notice if I sneaked out right after dessert? thought Capt. Ricardo.

Capt. Smirk turned to the attractive woman seated next to him at the head table. "What's a classy dame like you doing at an official function like this?" he asked, favoring her with his devil-may-care grin.

A half-smile played on her lips. "Oh, I like to mingle with the masses once in a while," she replied.

"Me too," said Smirk with a debonair tilt of his head. He lowered his voice. "Then again, I prefer to mingle in smaller groups—say, one on one. Why don't you and I ditch this boring shindig and head for someplace more cozy?"

"Mmmm," she responded. "I'd like to, but I really have to stay here."

Ahh, playing hard to get, Smirk realized. *That's fine. It just adds spice to the chase.*

He continued making conversation. "I've heard the Starfreak board of directors has a new chairman—a woman, believe it or not."

"Really?" She arched her eyebrows.

"Yep," Smirk continued. "I don't know anything about her except her name: Tanya Tribble. But a woman chairman! If that doesn't beat the band."

By the time dessert and Alka-Seltzer were served, Smirk was

sure he had her in the palm of his hand. As Admiral Tweet launched his after-dinner speech, Smirk made his move.

Tweet began, "Fellow members of the Federation, Starfreak salutes you. Your courage and daring have saved Earth from certain destruction by the Jargonites. As they retreated from Earth, our minds cleared, and once again we are free to live the unexamined life."

Smirk leaned close to the woman and whispered, "I know a place called Ten-Foreplay that serves the best steak tenderloin in the universe." The woman smiled at him briefly but then turned back to listen to Admiral Tweet.

"When the conflict was raging, I made a promise to Capt. Ricardo and Capt. Smirk," continued Tweet. "Whoever achieved victory, I told them, would have command of the one and only *Endocrine.*"

Smirk pressed on. "Or we could forget the tenderloin and go to a luau in the HolidayDeck." The woman glanced at him but did not respond.

"However," Tweet went on, "as you know, both crews were instrumental in the victory. Capt. Smirk's crew lured the Jargon-ites from Earth and set the trap; Capt. Ricardo's crew provoked the Jargonites to the warm-fuzzy stage and provided a haven when Smirk's crew had to abandon ship."

Smirk pushed ahead. "Forget the luau. Come on up to my quarters, and I'll show you my etchings." This time she didn't even look at him.

"So I've decided to turn the decision over to our chairman of the board, Tanya Tribble," Admiral Tweet concluded. "As an administrator with many years' experience, Ms. Tribble will have devised a fair and equitable reward, I'm sure. And now it is my pleasure to present to you . . . Tanya Tribble."

The woman stood up. *Well, okay, maybe it wasn't a great line, but you don't have to* leave, Smirk thought. Then he watched with growing horror as she headed for the podium. This, he realized, was Tanya Tribble.

"Thank you, Admiral Tweet," she said into the microphone.

Capt. Smirk turned to the attractive
woman seated next to him.

Smirk slumped forward in agony until his head rested on the table.

"*Endocrine* crew, I salute you," she said. "Your victory was the result of great cooperation." Several crew members broke into fits of coughing.

"Therefore, the most fitting fulfillment of Admiral Tweet's pledge," Tribble said, "is to have both crews share the *Endocrine* once again. You will conduct your missions together on Capt. Ricardo's ship, and all crew members will share responsibility equally. Capt. Smirk and Capt. Ricardo will co-captain the ship."

This time it was Capt. Ricardo who slumped forward in agony until his head rested on the table. Meanwhile, Capt. Smirk moaned, started to sit up, then fell off his chair.

"You stepped over the line!"

"Well, I had to! I've got to get to the Crewmover."

"But you don't have to walk through my area to get there. Go around that way!"

"Stop it, both of you!" Capt. Ricardo stepped between Yoohoo and Counselor Troit as they began shoving each other. "Lieutenant Yoohoo, please try to avoid walking so close to Counselor Troit. And Deanna, you mustn't be so sensitive when someone walks through our area."

Yoohoo made a face as she sashayed past Counselor Troit. Deanna responded by sticking out her tongue as soon as Yoohoo's back was turned.

The mission was only three hours old, yet Capt. Ricardo was already wondering for the fiftieth time why he'd given Piker authority to solve the problem of crowding on the ship. Piker had painted a line down the center of the Bridge. Capt. Ricardo's crew was confined to the Crewmover side; Smirk's crew occupied the other side.

That made my crew's crowding problem worse than ever, Ricardo thought. *Especially since Dr. Flusher, for some unfathomable reason, has now insisted on staying on the Bridge, too.*

Zulu gloated as he operated the controls. He knew that Piker hadn't intentionally made him the pilot. It was just that Piker hadn't realized, until too late, that the pilot's seat fell within Capt. Smirk's territory.

As Capt. Ricardo settled into the co-captain's chair on his side of the Bridge, Capt. Smirk set their course.

"Mr. Zulu," he ordered, "set heading for the Alpha Broccoli system."

"Course set and laid in," Zulu responded.

"Engage," commanded Capt. Smirk.

As they sped toward their destination, Capt. Ricardo began his litany.

"Space. We need more of it. These are the voyages of the Starship *Endocrine*. Its continuing mission: to cruise around the universe looking for novel predicaments to get into."

Capt. Ricardo paused and checked his script; Capt. Smirk had rewritten the next line.

"To search the outskirts of the galaxy for classy dames."

Capt. Smirk grinned.

"To boldly go where nobody wanted to go before!"

"Get out!" yelled Smirk as the time machine seemed about to explode. Likewise, inside the *Endocrine*, Dacron herded the other crewmembers out the exit, where they slid down the inflated emergency slide.

Everyone gathered nearby and turned back to stare at the travel crafts, which were vibrating faster and faster, until they disappeared.

The crewmembers became aware that they were not alone; a tremendous crowd of people surrounded them. Recovering from their shock, the crew looked around at where they'd landed.

It was a huge convention hall in a modern hotel. A banner off to the side read, "Welcome, Wrekkies."

The thought struck all of them, even Piker, at the same instant: they had been thrown into the future, right into the middle of the wrekkie convention they'd seen on the Preview. . . .

1

Here We Go Again

"IT WAS THE best of times; it was the worst of times." Capt. James T. Smirk paused to read the line he'd just written. Then he crossed it out and wrote: "The times were OK." There. That was much better.

Only 598 more pages and I'll be done with these memoirs, Smirk thought. He closed his eyes and pictured his book occupying the "#1 bestseller" slot on the bookstore display. He could even envision his picture on the cover, just beneath the title: *So Many Classy Dames, So Little Time.*

Inspired, Smirk flourished his feather pen and straightened the parchment. Then he paused; what should he say next?

He knew that the autobiography would recount his dashing conquests of exotic alien races, fearsome creatures, and gorgeous women. Yet something was nagging at him.

Suddenly he realized what it was. Their current situation would make a boring chapter.

The crews of Capt. Smirk and Capt. Jean-Lucy Ricardo were back together again on the USS *Endocrine.* After the crews defeated the Jargonites—destroying Smirk's ship in the process—Starfreak Command ordered them to share Ricardo's ship and cooperate on future missions.

But the brass back at headquarters have no idea what

it's like out here in the field, Smirk thought. *Sharing this ship is the pits.* The members of Smirk's and Ricardo's crews bickered constantly, despite the captains' efforts to maintain peace. The infighting distracted everybody from their ongoing mission of finding novel predicaments to get into.

It was so much better when we didn't have to share a ship, Smirk thought. *If only we could go back in time and get my ship before it was blown up in the Jargonite war. Hey, wait a minute. We CAN go back in time. Yeah! And my crew could bring our ship to the present, and we'd be free again.*

There was just one hitch. Since Smirk's crew would need to build a time machine, Capt. Ricardo was bound to notice what they were up to. And Ricardo was notoriously reluctant to mess around with the space/time continuum.

He's so overprotective of history, Smirk thought. *So what if we change a few minor events? It always worked out all right before.*

Heck, it's worth a try. It shouldn't be that hard to persuade Ricardo to let us go. I'm sure he'd do anything to get us out of his hair, such as it is.

Smirk decided to propose the project immediately. However, he knew better than to call a formal meeting to discuss it. He'd never seen a starship where meetings got so out of hand as on the *Endocrine.* Capt. Ricardo was apt to invite everyone who wanted to get their two cents in, even people like Dr. Flusher who had absolutely nothing to contribute.

Instead, Smirk decided, he wouldn't even use the term "meeting." He'd just invite Ricardo to a friendly discussion. And he realized his right-hand man Mr. Smock should be there, too, just in case he needed some actual thought to bolster his argument.

Smirk reached for the intercom microphone, then remembered that they didn't have one. All he had to do was page Capt. Ricardo, and the computer would find him.

At that moment Ricardo was in the ship's lounge, Ten-Foreplay, mulling over a command decision: what to order for lunch.

Should he have Earl Grape tea and buttered crumpets, as he'd eaten for lunch every day since the Battle of Hastings? Or should he vary his routine and spread marmalade on the crumpets instead? A wave of anxiety washed over him, with vague yet terrifying fears over the consequences of switching to marmalade.

Then he shook his head and thought, *Perhaps Counselor Troit is right. I* AM *becoming rather compulsive.*

"You subconsciously resent having to share command of your ship," Troit had advised him, "so you seek a sense of control over your life by performing these compulsive behaviors."

At the time, Capt. Ricardo had ignored her diagnosis. He regretted telling her that every night after his bedtime shower and skull-polishing, he went around the ship checking that all 1,476 stove burners were shut off, 589 toasters were unplugged and 1,225 sets of drapes were closed. "You can't be too careful," Ricardo had told Troit.

Troit had also observed that his command style was beginning to fossilize. She'd pointed out, "Do you realize that yesterday you said 'Make it so' 53 times?" She'd given him some worry beads to play with, which helped for a while.

But now, Ricardo thought, *compulsion is rearing its ugly head once again. No, wait, that's just my reflection in the mirror behind the bar. Well, I'll show her. I'll do something wild and radical to break with the past.*

The waitress arrived at his table and began a singsong recital of the day's special: "Today's featured item is broiled fillet of sole with potatoes au gratin and fresh broccoli ... but—no, don't tell me, let me guess—you're going to have Earl Grape tea and buttered crumpets."

Capt. Ricardo flashed what he hoped was a devil-may-care grin and responded, "No. I've decided to live dangerously. Make it sole."

While waiting for his order, Capt. Ricardo ventured even further on the wild side by sampling the cellophane-wrapped sesame crackers in the breadbasket. As usual, he started counting so he could chew the mouthful exactly 23 times before swallowing, but then the intercom distracted him.

"Jean-Lucy." It was Capt. Smirk's voice. "I'd like to discuss something with you. Let's get together in your Ready Room at 2560 hours, okay?"

Ricardo started to object—this get-together sounded like it had formal meeting potential—but the cracker crumbs caught in his throat. He coughed and wheezed. Smirk took this for a "Yes" and signed off the intercom.

Ricardo continued to hack as the dusty cracker crumbs lodged in his windpipe. His face turned scarlet; diners at nearby tables looked on with increasing concern. One of them jumped up and encircled Ricardo's chest to perform the Heimlich maneuver. He squeezed with terrific force—expelling the cracker, and Ricardo's false teeth as well.

Mr. Smock was bored. How bored was he? He was so bored that, just to have something to do, he was about to read a book he'd sworn he would never read . . . the book he'd been avoiding since the day he first saw it in the *Endocrine*'s library . . . the book that now remained as the single volume in the entire library that he hadn't read:

14,000 Things to Be Sappy About.

He tried to psych himself up before opening the cover. Surely it couldn't be as bad as it sounded. Maybe a little bit of whimsy was just what he needed. Summoning up more courage, he flipped through the pages at random. Out of the corner of his eye he peeked at a few entries:

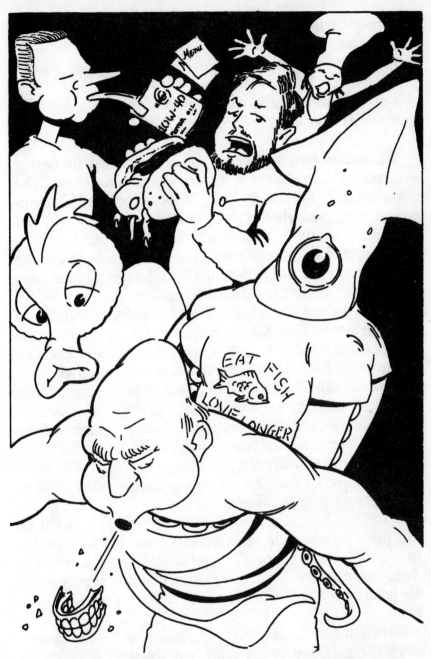

One of them jumped up and encircled Ricardo's chest to perform the Heimlich maneuver.

rubbery Jell-O salads with canned fruit in them
torn undergarments
the giddy, wispy way you feel when the alarm goes
    off at 5 A.M. on a Monday
a strong enema on a wintry afternoon
the Partridge Family

"Aaaaaaaaarrrrrgggghhhh!" Smock recoiled in horror
and dropped the book as if it were a poisonous snake. The
librarian gave him a dirty look. Smock recovered his composure long enough to return the book to the shelf, but
he was still trembling as he left the library.

So much for that diversion. He didn't want to end up
wearing the straitjacket that had been hanging in the back
of his closet since the Jargonite mission.

Smock walked down the corridor, careful to remain on
the Smirk-crew side. Like everything else on the ship, the
corridor was divided in half. Capt. Smirk's crew was confined to one half, Capt. Ricardo's crew to the other.

It was a natural extension of Cmdr. Piker's original idea
to divide the Bridge in half. *Yet that was not logical,* Smock
reflected. *Dividing the Bridge put steering control in the
hands of our crew, although navigation is on Capt. Ricardo's side. And so are the Crewmover and Capt. Ricardo's
Ready Room.* Or, as Capt. Smirk privately referred to it,
the captain's Romper Room.

"I can't fathom it, Smock," Smirk often said. "What do
you make of a captain who retreats from his own Bridge
so often? Is he anti-social, or what?" Smock, knowing a
rhetorical question when he heard one, would simply shake
his head to indicate that Ricardo's behavior puzzled him,
too.

Awkward as this was, the ship remained divided in half,
since the majority of the crew had voted in favor of the
idea. It wasn't too bad in the laundromat, the mall, or
even Ten-Foreplay, but things got a little strange in the
showers, where the "cold" faucets were on Smirk's side

Like everything else on the ship, the corridor was
divided in half.

and the "hot" on Ricardo's. Ricardo's crew frequently suffered third-degree burns, while Smirk's crew tended toward pneumonia.

As for Cmdr. Piker, who originated this brilliant scheme, Smock had a plan. For the past few months Smock had been secretly sending Piker's resume to dozens of starships throughout the galaxy, hoping that someone would hire him away from the *Endocrine*. The ploy had resulted in a surprising number of offers. But so far, to Smock's disappointment, Piker had turned them all down.

The intercom broke into Smock's train of thought. "Smirk here, Mr. Smock. Capt. Ricardo and I are getting together at 2560 hours in the Romper—er, Ready Room to discuss an idea of mine. Why don't you join us?"

"Certainly, Captain," Smock responded. *Anything to break the monotony,* he thought.

"Oh, and Smock," Smirk continued, "don't mention to Ricardo the reason we're meeting, all right?"

"I will not, Captain," said Smock, "especially since you have not told me what it is."

"Never mind," Smirk said. "I'll brief you on it before we go in. Just back me up, no matter what I say. Throw in a few facts and figures whenever there's a lull. Make it sound, you know, scientific."

Cmdr. Wilson Piker sat in his quarters, idly tugging at his beard, and finally admitted to himself that he was stumped.

Just as I expected, he thought. *The situation is much worse than I expected.*

For the past several hours he'd searched for a missing videotape. It was time to give up and admit that the darned thing was probably lost forever.

The video was a gift from Ensign Westerly Flusher, who had filmed a typical *Endocrine* workday as his 29th audition tape for Starfreak Academy Film School. To the crew's immense relief, the school finally accepted him. Westerly was now away at the Academy, majoring in cinematography and minoring in weeniehood.

Hmmmm. If I were a videotape, where would I be? Piker wondered. *Probably not serving as First Officer of a starship.*

Piker's train of thought jumped the track. *Even being First Officer isn't going to help me this time,* he fretted. *Usually, all I have to do is yell at somebody, and the problem gets solved.*

Why, just the day before they'd had some serious trouble with the water softener. Georgie LaForgery, trying to explain why the whirlpool baths were filling with crud, said Engineering would need at least four hours for repairs. "We haven't got four hours!" Piker had barked; and Georgie had fixed the softener in 45 minutes.

There was something magical about the way Piker asserted his authority. An impossible job became possible, solely because he demanded it. He was the only one on the ship with this talent, which was probably why Capt. Ricardo hadn't canned him long ago.

But I can't yell at somebody this time, because I'm the one who lost the video, Piker ruminated. *Let's see... where did I have it last?*

He remembered that he was about to watch the tape earlier that day. He'd just turned on the VCR when Capt. Ricardo had called on the intercom, reminding him to reset the ship's clocks for Daylight Saving Time.

I took the videotape with me to the computer room, Piker thought, *and put it on the counter next to my keychain. Then I reset all the clocks simultaneously with that new software, SpringAhead/FallBack. When I woke up on the floor, I picked up my keychain and left the computer room.*

Piker went over the scenario in his mind several times. Something about it bothered him. After several more minutes of intensely arduous thought, he figured out what it was: *Why did I wake up on the floor?*

"Computer," Piker said, "when I used the SpringAhead/

FallBack software this morning, were there any unusual effects?"

"Affirmative," said the computer's feminine voice.

"What happened?"

"The software contained a bug which created a time rift lasting 1.53 seconds."

Uh-oh, Piker thought. "Describe the effects of the time rift," he ordered.

"Momentary unconsciousness for sixteen officers; three unexplained pregnancies; the passage of a T-120 VHS videocassette into the abyss; and a loss of $1,435 in accrued interest on the ship's credit union accounts."

Geez. "About that videocassette—exactly where is it now?"

"Working," said the computer as it searched its records. After a pause, the computer announced, "Gone."

Beep-beep boop-boop, the door chime sounded in Capt. Ricardo's Ready Room. He made a mental note to have the melody reprogrammed to something more dignified— "Hail to the Chief," perhaps.

"Come," Ricardo answered.

Capt. Smirk and Mr. Smock entered. Ricardo felt a twinge of surprise; Smirk hadn't said anything about having Smock join in this discussion. It was probably some kind of ploy to catch him off-guard, Ricardo decided, so he'd retaliate by pretending not to mind.

"Ah, gentlemen," said Ricardo, leading them toward the lounge chairs arranged around a kidney-shaped coffee table. "Make yourselves comfortable, won't you?" Ricardo settled into a chair, wincing a little as he inadvertently leaned against the arm of the chair with his Heimlich-bruised ribs.

After the other two sat down, Ricardo picked up the candy dish and held it out to them. "Marzipan?"

"Thank you." Capt. Smirk smiled and took a piece of

the candy, which was molded in the shape of a Kringle torture rod.

"Mr. Smock?" offered Ricardo, tilting the dish toward him.

"No, thank you, Captain," responded Smock, folding his hands in his lap. "I do not eat sweets."

"Well, Capt. Smirk, what was it you wanted to see me about?" Capt. Ricardo said, attempting a smile which he hoped looked genuine; he'd been practicing all evening.

Smirk's first impulse was to propose his time travel idea right off the bat; but on the way over to the Ready Room Mr. Smock had advised him to open the discussion on neutral territory. So Smirk pretended this was just another problem-solving session on the captains' toughest problem: the bickering between their crews.

"Have you seen the warning letter from Starfreak's HMO?" Smirk asked. Ricardo nodded grimly. The letter stated that the *Endocrine* crew was way over the allowable number of claims for scalpel puncture wounds and I.V.-stand concussions. The injuries were occurring to patients who'd come to Sickbay for treatment and then got caught in the crossfire between Dr. McCaw and Dr. Beverage Flusher.

"What can we do about it?" Ricardo asked.

Smirk shrugged. "I can't tell Moans what to do. You know how bad his temper is. Any day now I expect to walk in there, find him kneeling over Flusher's body, and hear him say, 'She's dead, Jim.' "

Ricardo shuddered at the thought of Beverage being murdered. It was bad enough that he'd sent her husband Jock on that fatal Away Team mission years ago; now if Beverage also died under his command, it would look bloody awkward on his resume.

Smirk went on, "And did you know Wart broke Checkout's nose?"

"What?" Capt. Ricardo said. "When did that happen?"

"This afternoon. On the Bridge."

Injuries were occurring to patients who got caught
between Dr. McCaw and Dr. Flusher.

"No, I didn't know," said Ricardo. "I've been here in my Ready Room since lunchtime." Smirk gave Smock a look that shouted, *See? What did I tell you?*

Smirk told Ricardo, "Smock saw how it all started. Could you repeat your report, Smock?"

"Certainly, Captain," said Mr. Smock. "In apparent retaliation for Lt. Wart's bullying, Mr. Zulu and Mr. Checkout had been throwing small magnets at his woven metal sash. They were keeping score of who got the most magnets to stick. Mr. Zulu was ahead five to three when the Kringle officer realized what was happening and charged them both."

"Uhhhhh," Ricardo moaned. Then he thought of another management problem. "I just got Security's damage report on that food fight in Ten-Foreplay last night," he said. "It seems your communications officer Yoohoo performed her lounge act one time too many. Let's see, I have the report here somewhere." Ricardo went to his desk, rummaged through piles of paper until he found the report, and brought it back to their chairs.

"Yes, here it is," he said, scanning the report. "Under 'Cause,' it reads, 'Chief bartender Guano, worried that Yoohoo's screeching was scaring away customers, threw out the first tomato as Yoohoo reached the chorus of 'To Dream the Impossible Dream.' "

"That was some fight," Smirk observed. "My shoulder is really sore. Smock, next time remind me to throw something smaller than a watermelon. So, Jean-Lucy, what does Security say about the total damage?"

"The upholstery on six chairs was stained," Ricardo read. "Also, a window was broken and three crewmembers were sucked out, along with some extremely valuable china."

"Mmmm. Tough break." They pondered the loss for a moment. Then Smirk said, "By the way, we're having another power outage tonight."

"Not again." Ricardo groaned. "Who's doing the sabotage this time, LaForgery or Snot?"

Yoohoo performed her lounge act one time too many.

"It's Mr. Snot," Smirk admitted. "But you can't blame him. You know he likes to keep that engineering stuff a secret; nobody else is supposed to know how it all works. Well, LaForgery wants to film a 'Reeking Rainbow' TV segment explaining the dilithium Crystal Vanish chamber."

Beep-beep boop-boop, the door chime sounded. "Come," said Ricardo, and Piker entered.

"Oops," said Piker. "I didn't realize you had company, Captain."

"That's all right, Number One." Ricardo motioned for him to sit down. "You can join us; the more the merrier. Pretty soon we'll have enough for a quorum. Does Dacron have the Bridge right now?"

"No," Piker answered. "Actually, I don't think anybody has the Bridge right now. Dacron's been missing since lunchtime."

"Missing. Again." Ricardo glared at Smock.

Smock stared back at him. "Why are you looking at *me,* Captain?" he deadpanned.

"Mr. Smock," Ricardo intoned, with an air of exaggerated patience, "I realize Mr. Dacron's constant babbling gets on your nerves. We've all felt similarly irritated with Dacron at one time or another. But most of us have refrained from flicking his 'off' switch and stashing him in a broom closet or a crawl space."

"What leads you to think I—" Smock protested.

"Why don't we all agree," Ricardo cut him off, "that if Dacron turns up at his station in one piece by morning, we'll let the matter drop with no questions asked. Shall we?"

"Very well, sir," Smock conceded.

Ricardo turned to Piker. "What brings you here, Number One?"

"Uh, just a minor problem with some software I was using, Captain. I'll tell you about it later when we're alone.

No sense boring Capt. Smirk and Mr. Smock with the details."

"Good idea," said Smirk. "Well, Jean-Lucy, as we were saying, it's fairly obvious that our crews aren't getting along."

"Hear, hear," murmured Ricardo.

"Things went much smoother when I had my old ship and we conducted our missions separately," Smirk continued.

"They certainly did," Ricardo assented.

"So, then, it's agreed," said Smirk, holding up his palms in his smoothest diplomatic gesture. Rapidly he concluded, "We'll go back in time, retrieve my ship before it was destroyed, and bring it to the present. Come on, Smock, let's get started." Smirk stood up and headed for the door.

"What?" Ricardo cried. "We will do no such thing!"

Smirk already had his back turned. Silently he mouthed, *Darn it all, darn it all, darnitalldarnitallDARNITALL.* He turned back to them. "Awww, c'mon, Jean-Lucy. For once in your life, don't be a wet blanket."

"Capt. Smirk," responded Ricardo, "interfering with the space/time continuum is inherently dangerous."

"That's just folklore," Smirk countered. "Actual scientific fact shows just the opposite. Isn't that right, Smock?"

"Er, yes, Captain," Smock chimed in. "Time travel has been proven safe and effective in 99 percent of all cases when combined with a closely-monitored program of oral hygiene and professional dental care."

"But you can never be sure," Ricardo insisted. "What if you accidentally introduce some new technology to the past? Or what if you interfere with a historically significant event? You could irreversibly alter the timeline which follows. The present as we know it might cease to exist."

"So what's so bad about that?" Smirk retorted. "The present as we know it could use some improvement, if you ask me. Heck, every time my crew went into the past, things turned out for the better."

"Oh, really?" Ricardo raised a skeptical eyebrow.

"Yes, really." Smirk waggled his head, imitating Ricardo's snooty look. "For instance, once we traveled back into a 1930s Earth timeline involving a woman named Edith Keebler, who had two possible fates. We made sure she got killed, just as she was supposed to. By doing that, we prevented the alternate timeline in which she would have become a famous peacenik—and so, thanks to us, the eventual result was World War II."

Ricardo gaped at Smirk. "You're saying you're responsible for World War II? You call that a good result?"

"Er, let me put that another way..." Smirk faltered. His face turned red as he muttered, "Smock, help me out here."

Unexpectedly, Piker broke in. "Sure, where would we be without World War II? If it hadn't happened, all of our present history books would be wrong." The other three, stunned by Piker's logic, stared at him.

Piker continued, "And if World War II never happened, there'd be no 'World at War' documentary to give Laurence Olivier his start as a narrator. Without that break, Olivier would probably be just another English actor doing voice-overs for Pontiac commercials."

Smirk felt a sinking sensation listening to Piker take his side, along with a twinge of sympathy for Ricardo, who worked with Piker on a daily basis.

Ricardo, meanwhile, glared his First Officer into silence. Icily he said, "Cmdr. Piker, could I see you in the conference room for a moment? Gentlemen, if you'll excuse us."

Ricardo and Piker left the Ready Room, crossed the Bridge, and entered the conference room. As soon as the doors slid shut, Ricardo hollered at Piker, "What do you think you're doing? Don't ever take sides with anyone against the Family again!"

Piker was surprised. Counselor Troit had told him the Captain was getting compulsive, but she hadn't said anything about paranoia.

"Now we haven't got a united front on this issue," Ricardo continued. "They'll keep badgering us until we let them have their way. If only we could prevent them from going back in time. Well, that's something I'll have to figure out. You, meanwhile, just keep a lid on it."

"Yes, sir." Piker kept his voice neutral, but inside he was seething. *Well, I may not be appreciated around here, but there are others who feel differently,* he thought. *Next time a headhunter calls, I might just listen.*

They returned to the Ready Room. Ricardo proposed, "Let's do this, Capt. Smirk: we'll use the Preview feature on the computer to find your ship in the past. At the same time, we'll have the computer analyze the possible effects on the space/time continuum of removing your ship from the past and bringing it to the present."

"Sounds good to me," Smirk agreed. "Let's start the mission, shall we?"

The captains took a deep breath and spoke simultaneously. "Space. We need more of it.

"These are the voyages of the starship *Endocrine.* Its mission: to cruise around the universe looking for novel predicaments to get into. To search the outskirts of the galaxy . . . "

Here their voices diverged. Capt. Ricardo had recently returned to the original wording: " . . . for areas with less crowding, lower tax rates and better schools."

Simultaneously, Capt. Smirk recited his version: " . . . for classy dames."

They chimed in together on the last line. "To boldly go where nobody wanted to go before!"

2

A Ship
Divided

"**H**AVE YOU RIGGED the Preview feature?" Capt. Ricardo muttered out of the side of his mouth.

"Yes, sir," whispered engineer Georgie LaForgery. "It won't show the past, only the future—some random happening about 50 years from now. It'll look like an equipment malfunction."

They watched the conference table fill up rapidly. Capt. Ricardo had insisted that everyone participate in this meeting, leading Capt. Smirk to protest that the matter wasn't important enough to invite everyone. *Still, he thought it important enough to sleep overnight on the conference table so he'd get a good seat,* Ricardo observed.

There was the usual jockeying for position, and latecomers brought lawn chairs to supplement the meager seating around the table. Members of both crews could sit in either half of the conference room, since it had been declared a demilitarized zone.

Capt. Ricardo stood up. "I hereby call this meeting to order," he announced. "Would the secretary please read the minutes of the last—"

"Mr. Chairman," Smirk interrupted, "I move we dispense with the reading of the minutes from the last meeting."

"Second," Smock chimed in.

Capt. Ricardo frowned. Skipping the reading of the minutes always gave him the jitters that something important would be left out. Still, Smirk had used the proper procedure, and Ricardo had no choice but to follow up.

"All those in favor of omitting the reading of the minutes, signify by saying 'aye'," Ricardo said.

"AYE," came the loud response—much louder, in fact, than if everyone in the room had spoken. Ricardo immediately suspected Smirk and Smock of tampering with the voice vote again. *Should I have Wart shake them down for that "crowd noise" sound-effect device they used once before?* Ricardo wondered. *No, better not. It would get things off to a bad start.*

"Opposed?" Total silence. Ricardo shot a stern glance at Piker to indicate that he should oppose the measure. Piker defiantly stared back at the Captain. Ricardo thought, *What's eating HIM?*

"The motion carries. The secretary will dispense with the reading of the minutes," said Ricardo. Accordingly, Yoohoo flipped her steno pad over to a fresh page and sat with pen poised to take notes.

"Is there any old business?" Ricardo continued.

"Today is Dr. McCaw's birthday," someone said.

"He said *old* business, not *ancient* business," someone else piped up.

"Quiet, please," Ricardo said. "Dr. McCaw's birthday is duly noted for the record. Anything else?"

Dacron raised his hand. "Yes, Mr. Dacron?" said Ricardo.

"Mr. Chairman," said Dacron, "I would like to remind everyone that we need to update our bylaws. You will recall that I have raised this issue during each of the last 57 meetings, and it has always been tabled. Do you think we might—"

Dacron froze in midsentence as Mr. Smock, sitting next to him, made a swift, smooth movement behind the android's back. Dacron collapsed, hitting his head on the table with a loud *thunk*.

Ricardo acknowledged Mr. Smock's contribution with a nod and continued, "All right, let's move on to new business."

"Mr. Chairman." Smirk leapt in immediately. "I move we use the Preview feature of the computer to find my crew's ship before it was destroyed in the battle with the Jargonites."

"Second," said Mr. Smock.

"Any discussion?" asked Ricardo. There was none; everybody was eager to use the Preview feature to look into the past. They were all restless for some good entertainment since there had been nothing decent on television lately.

Ricardo nodded to Georgie, who went to the wall and activated the Preview's viewer-friendly programming screen. Georgie entered the data as prompted:

Stardate: 911.007-3.14
Place: Somewhere off the starboard side of Earth
Precise location/object/building/suite number, etc.:
    USS *Endocrine* commanded by James T. Smirk
Collision damage waiver? No

Georgie pressed "Enter" and pretended to wait for the Preview to move backward and show them the time they sought. But the Preview flashed an "Error" message, and a recorded voice stated:

"The year you have entered . . . 911.007-3.14 . . . has been disconnected. We apologize for the inconvenience. For your viewing pleasure, the Preview network provides the following segment of the future."

"What the . . . " Smirk began in dismay.

The Preview screen lit up with the legend "Planet Earth / Maplewood, New Jersey / 50 years in the future."

"This isn't what we wanted," Smirk protested.

The Preview screen showed a crowd milling around inside a convention hall. A banner overhead read "Welcome, Wrekkies."

Smirk forgot about his objection. He and everyone else in the room stared at the screen, astonished—for there in the convention hall were people who looked strangely like the *Endocrine* crew.

They wore *Endocrine* uniforms and Vulture ears and Kringle foreheads and plastic communicator pins. They greeted each other as "Ensign Kilbourn" and "Commander Rexnord" and "Lieutenant Mader." They toured a life-sized replica of the *Endocrine*'s Bridge. And they bought all sorts of items imprinted with the likenesses of *Endocrine* crew-members: framed posters and plastic dolls and refrigerator magnets and bumper stickers and toilet seat covers and lunch boxes and day-of-the-week underwear.

Ricardo was stunned. "Freeze program," he gasped, gripping the table for support.

Georgie flicked a switch, and the Preview screen stopped scanning. It locked onto a close-up of a "Genuine Captain Ricardo Night Light" with a bulb glowing inside a plastic replica of Ricardo's head.

There was a moment of dead silence. Then everyone spoke at once.

"What is it?" "Terrific!" "Are you kidding? This is madness!" "Did you see the Troit Lift-and-Separate Bras they were selling?" "Who are they?" "Can we go there?" "How dare they imitate the Kringle brow furrow! I'll break their necks!"

Ricardo had to pound his gavel for several minutes to restore order. Then he spoke, with an obvious effort to keep his tone calm and measured:

"Any other new business?"

"Mr. Chairman, you can't ignore what we've just seen!" Piker objected.

Capt. Smirk chimed in. "Jean-Lucy, just think of it: Fifty years from now, our crew will be the biggest fad on Earth. Doesn't that excite you?"

"No, it does not," Ricardo replied. "As a matter of fact, it's dreadful to think I might encounter an object like a life-size poster of myself, sometime in the next half-century."

"Huh—you should live so long," muttered Piker.

"What was that?" Ricardo snapped. Piker glowered back at him, refusing to answer. Ricardo continued, "I heard that!"

"Then why'd you ask me what I said?" Piker retorted.

Frustrated, Ricardo slammed down his gavel a half-inch from where Piker's hand rested on the table. "You're out of order, Number One," he growled.

The other crewmembers resumed their argument over whether the scene in the Preview was wonderful or awful. Meanwhile, Georgie began fooling around with the Preview again.

"What are you doing, Lieutenant?" Ricardo demanded.

"I was just curious, Captain," said Georgie, "about what triggered this 'wrekkie' movement. How do these people in the future know so much about us? Maybe I can find out how it all got started."

"Good idea," responded Ricardo. They watched the Preview screen as Georgie scanned backward from the convention. Faster and faster he scanned; his eyes and brain were accustomed to watching lightning-quick images from years of television channel-switching with the remote control. Ricardo, however, began to get dizzy.

"Take it easy, Lieutenant," Ricardo requested. "Make it slow."

Just then Georgie found what he was looking for. "There," he said, bringing the image down to normal speed. Everyone else stopped talking and began to watch along with them.

The Preview flashed the legend "Planet Earth / Residence of Herschel Kinnickinnic / Maplewood, New Jersey / 40 years in the future."

The Preview showed that as the adolescent Herschel sprawled in an easy chair watching "Leave It to Beaver," a blinding flash of light split the room, and the television

There in the convention hall were people
who looked strangely like the *Endocrine* crew.

exploded. As the smoke cleared, Herschel examined the remains of the TV. Next to the shattered picture tube, he found a videotape.

"Uhhhh...the time rift," Piker moaned. Ricardo glanced suspiciously at his First Officer.

Herschel took the videotape to his room; it, too, was equipped with a TV and a VCR. He popped the tape into the player and began to watch.

"Hey, that's the tape Westerly Flusher made of us at our work stations," Zulu observed.

"So dat's how dey found out vhat ve're like," Checkout said.

Georgie pressed fast-forward, and the crew watched the future unfold on the Preview screen. Herschel, intrigued by the videotape, watched it several times. Then he invited some friends to view it with him. Soon they were dressing like the *Endocrine* crew and holding monthly meetings. Within a few years, the meetings grew so large that they were taken over by a professional organization, Getalife Conventions.

"Hmmm. Perhaps all we need to do is prevent Westerly from making the videotape, and this whole chain of events will never occur," Ricardo speculated. "But what other consequences might there be?" No one could answer him. Ricardo continued, "Mr. Smock, I'd like to have Mr. Dacron analyze this. Boot him up, will you?"

Smock reached over and flicked Dacron's switch. The android jerked up to a sitting position and chattered, "Positronic Program, Version 5.0, copyright 1992 by MaxiWord Corporation. 989,758,170 bytes total disc space. CONFIG.SYS. CONFIG.BAT. chkdsk c:>\vocab\endless [enter]." He blinked twice, then stated, "Lt. Cmdr. Dacron reporting for duty, sir."

"Dacron, what would happen if we went back in time and prevented Westerly from filming our crew?" asked Capt. Ricardo.

"There is a 99 percent probability that our current time-

The android jerked up to a sitting position and chattered.

line would be affected," Dacron responded. "Without the videotape, Westerly would not have been accepted into the Starfreak Academy Film School. Instead, he would still be here on the *Endocrine*."

Capt. Ricardo grimaced. "Well, so much for *that* idea," he concluded. "It looks like we're going to have to go forward 40 years and prevent Herschel from finding the videotape."

"Sir." Piker stood up and cocked his head, preparing to make a dramatic statement. "What about your longstanding objection to altering the space/time continuum?"

Ricardo, wondering again why his First Officer seemed to have a bug in his britches, decided to assert his authority. He told Piker, "I'm entitled to change my policy. As the saying goes, 'A foolish consistency is the hobgoblin of little minds'—a phenomenon that's undoubtedly very familiar to you, Number One."

Piker, suspecting he'd been insulted but not sure just how, sat down and mulled over possible retorts.

Capt. Smirk spoke up. "If we're going forward, it should be to *encourage* Herschel to make this wrekkie thing even bigger and better. Why, if we play our cards right, we could be big, really big—more popular than the Beatles, even."

A gasp of dismay escaped Mr. Smock's lips.

"Come on, Smock," Smirk continued. "I know you like your privacy and all that, but this fan worship could be a lot of fun once you get into it."

Mr. Smock shuddered.

"I'm with Captain Ricardo," stated co-engineer Snot. "We ought ta go forward 'n' get the tape before it falls into the hands of this Herschel lad."

"Nyet!" shouted Checkout, jumping to his feet. "Ve should go help Herschel. Ve can make personal appearances, sign autographs, and endorse more products!"

"Siddown, you little twerp!" snarled Dr. McCaw. "What in heaven's name is so great about having our picture stamped on a toilet seat cover?"

"Don't tell him to sit down, you big bully," snapped Dr. Flusher, reaching into her pocket for a scalpel to fling at McCaw.

The argument among the crew regained its momentum. A few people squared off for a fistfight, and security chief Wart picked up a chair to throw. Capt. Ricardo, envisioning another window being broken and more valuable furnishings destroyed, shouted above the din:

"All right, all right! We'll vote on it!"

Everybody quieted down. After the room fell silent, Piker abruptly blurted to Capt. Ricardo, "I'll let it go this time, but if you call me a hobgoblin again I'm going to file a grievance with the First Officers' Union Local 2598."

Capt. Ricardo stared at Piker for a long moment, then shook his head and returned his attention to the matter of voting. Ricardo decided to poll for individual opinions, since he was afraid an ordinary voice vote would allow Smirk to use his crowd noise sound-effect device to sway the outcome again.

"The issue we're voting on is whether or not to let this 'wrekkie' phenomenon occur," said Ricardo. "Should we allow Herschel to find the videotape? Please confine yourselves to a short statement."

They went around the table counterclockwise. Piker, seated at Ricardo's right, was first.

"I say yes," Piker stated, "because I think we're entitled to a few positive strokes, and these people would obviously worship the ground we walk on."

Dr. McCaw was next. "Rubbish!" he grizzled. "I'm a doctor, not a superstar!"

"I have no feelings about the matter, either negative or positive," said Dacron, "for I am an android, and as you know, androids cannot feel emotion, and—" *Thunk*. Dacron collapsed onto the table again.

Mr. Smock smoothly slid his arm from behind Dacron's back and folded his hands in front of him. "I agree with Capt. Ricardo that we should forestall this phenomenon," he said, "since it disturbs me to see the noble Vulture ear being worn by outsiders."

Checkout said, "I say we inwestigate dese fans; dis is the first time in my life anyvone has ewer looked up to me."

Zulu shrugged. "I don't see what all the fuss is about either way."

"Ditto," echoed Georgie.

"You've never been laid off," countered Dr. Flusher. "Ever since Starfreak yanked me away from the *Endocrine* and then sent me back, I've been looking for some perks to make up for it. This fan worship could be just what the doctor ordered."

"I'd love to sing to the fans," Yoohoo trilled.

"That's reason enough for me to sit tight, right here in the present," Guano grumbled.

Deanna Troit looked troubled. "They're hiding something," she judged. "I'm reading multiple personalities in each one of them. I don't think we should interfere."

"I'm agin' it," said Mr. Snot. "They'd probably be wantin' me to explain warped drive to 'em. I say we put a stop to the whole thing."

"I agree," snarled Wart. "We should launch an immediate attack on the convention hall."

"Mr. Wart," said Smirk in a mildly reproving tone, "you'd attack? With so many charming ladies there? I think this is wonderful. In fact, I'd rather go to the future and attend this convention than go to the past and get our ship. I say aye, aye, a thousand times aye!"

Now that everyone else had spoken, Capt. Ricardo made his statement. "For the record, my official stand is 'Bah, humbug.' " He made sure Yoohoo dutifully recorded this in the minutes.

With the discussion safely behind them, Smock reached over and turned Dacron back on.

"Will the secretary please report the tally?" Ricardo

grumbled. He didn't like the way all of this was shaping up.

"The official vote," said Yoohoo, "on the question of whether to allow Herschel to find the videotape is five 'pro,' five 'con,' and five neutral."

"It's a tie, so we can do whatever we want," Smirk swiftly asserted. "All you Pros, gather round." He stood on his chair and motioned for them to come. Piker, Yoohoo, Beverage Flusher and Checkout moved toward him.

"All Cons, assemble now to fight for the glorious cause!" shouted Wart, raising his fist. "Let your blood run hot in this day of the warrior. This Herschel must be crushed."

"Just a minute . . ." murmured Ricardo, who counted himself among the Cons but didn't appreciate being treated like a foster Kringle. Nevertheless, as Smock, McCaw and Snot gathered around Wart, Ricardo joined them.

The remaining five, backing away from the newly-forming groups, found themselves assembling into a third group of their own. "Well, here we are," observed Deanna Troit, "the Neutrals."

"Hey, let's hear it for the Neuts!" said Georgie in his bounciest cheerleader voice. Deanna, Dacron, Guano and Zulu stared at him, and he mumbled sheepishly, "Uh, maybe not."

The Pros and the Cons huddled in separate corners discussing their plans, but with Wart's booming voice within the Cons, and Piker's random dramatic statements for the Pros, they soon overheard each other. The Cons were figuring out how to build a time machine to go forward and prevent Herschel from viewing the videotape. The Pros wanted to reach the same point, thwart the Cons, and encourage Herschel.

All ten of them realized at the same instant that it was just a matter of who got there first with a time machine. They all raced for the door and charged through at once, somehow managing to get everyone stuck in a clump of torsos, arms and legs.

Dacron shrugged and walked over to the entrance. He gave the whole pack of them a quick shove through the doorway and into the future.

3

Déjà
Boo-Boo

"YOU WANT *ME* to build our time machine?" Piker repeated.

"That's what I said, Commander," Smirk told him. "Do you have a problem with that?"

"Well, sir," Piker said, "the job seems more appropriate for one of the subordinates, don't you think? I sort of pictured them doing the hands-on work while you and I would sit back and, uh, you know—command."

"Commander Piker." Smirk lowered his voice and indicated the rest of their team, seated at an adjacent table in Ten-Foreplay. "Which one of them is capable of building it? Beverage Flusher? Yoohoo? *Checkout?*"

"Yes, but my job description normally wouldn't cover that sort of..." Piker continued. Smirk held up a hand to silence him.

"I expect my right-hand man to roll up his sleeves, move to the firing line, play hardball, roll with the punches, fight in the trenches, and whistle while he works," Smirk insisted. "Is that clear, Commander?"

Piker nodded.

"After all," Smirk went on, "when we were stranded on Earth during that Keebler episode, Mr. Smock rigged up a short-wave radio transmitter out of egg cartons and aluminum foil. That's the kind of practical help I need."

"Yes, sir." Piker mulled over the problem as he left Ten-Foreplay. He realized this could be his golden opportunity to impress Capt. Smirk. Perhaps Smirk would even hire him as First Officer now that Mr. Smock had joined the Cons.

Soon Piker was lost in thought—without a map, as usual. *How am I going to build a time machine? Do they print blueprints for them in* Popular Mechanix? *Maybe we should try to rent one instead. Captain Smirk mentioned something about Smock building stuff out of egg cartons. What's an egg carton?*

Piker wandered into his room and flicked on the television, hoping the alpha waves would stimulate his imagination. By coincidence, his favorite science fiction program, "Dr. Whom," was underway. Dr. Whom had just finished knitting an extra two feet onto his muffler and was about to step into his time machine, the Tardy.

"That's it," Piker concluded. "I'll build a Tardy."

Later that day, Piker summoned his fellow Pros with the news that their time machine was assembled and ready for travel. The contraption stood covered with a tarp in the middle of the workshop. When everyone had gathered around it, Piker unveiled the machine with a flourish and announced, "Ta-daaa!" The other Pros stared at it for a long time.

Finally Checkout said flatly, "I don't get it."

"It looks like an old phone booth or something," Beverage ventured.

"A time machine can look like a phone booth," Piker retorted. "Haven't any of you ever seen the one on 'Dr. Whom'?"

"I've never watched that program," said Yoohoo. "It's on at the same time as 'Quilting with Gladys.' And I never miss 'Quilting with Gladys.' "

"Well, take my word for it. It's a time machine," said Piker, irritated at their lack of enthusiasm.

"Let's get going," Capt. Smirk urged them. "We want to make sure we reach Herschel before the Cons do. So, Commander, how does this machine work? Do we each take turns using it?"

"Uh, no," Piker answered. "We all have to get in at once."

Beverage hooted. "You want all five of us to cram into this little phone booth?"

"Captain, I'm frightened," Yoohoo quavered.

"Let's stay calm, everyone," Smirk said. "It's just for a moment, and then we'll be out." Gently he herded them into the booth. As he passed Piker, Smirk muttered, "I hope you know what you're doing."

Piker hoped so, too. He pushed Smirk's shoulder, forcing it past the doorway, then squeezed himself inside and shut the door. The five of them were packed solid.

"Ugh! Who had onions for lunch?" Yoohoo demanded. She wriggled her hand free and waved it in front of her nose.

"Excuse me, excuse me," Piker said, pushing his way toward the telephone. "I have to dial this thing to get us where we're going." Awkwardly they reshuffled themselves until Piker could reach the phone. He dialed a dozen digits and waited.

In a moment the Tardy was surrounded by darkness. "I think we've arrived," Piker said.

Smirk forced the door open and stepped out. They had landed in an open field, and it was apparently late at night. The others crept out after Smirk.

"This doesn't look like Maplewood, New Jersey," Beverage observed.

"Shhhh!" Smirk ordered. "I see someone up ahead!"

Their eyes adjusted to the darkness; they could make out the vague outlines of several people moving to and fro. Smirk dropped to his hands and knees; he crept toward the mysterious figures, motioning that the others should follow.

As her companions crawled through the grass, Yoohoo

The five of them were packed solid.

hesitated, certain that the rough terrain would put a run in her pantyhose. She loped forward on her hands and feet, trying to keep her knees off the ground. The awkward position forced her to look down rather than ahead, so she didn't notice when Checkout stopped just in front of her. Yoohoo butted Checkout with her head.

"Ooof!" exclaimed Checkout. "Vat da heck—"

"Shhhh!" Smirk told them; but it was too late.

"Who's thar?" demanded one of the figures up ahead. "Soldiers, see to that noise yonder!"

A moment later, Smirk and his companions were surrounded, with a thicket of rifles aimed at their heads.

"Nice going, Commander," Smirk muttered. The five Pros sat on the ground in the midst of a military encampment. From the conversations going on around them, they had deduced that Piker's time machine had brought them to Fort Sumter on the eve of the outbreak of the Civil War.

"I don't understand it," Piker mumbled, shaking his head in disbelief. "I must have dialed the wrong number."

"Wrong number!" Smirk hissed. "You were supposed to move us to the future, not the past! How could you be so far off?"

"Captain, I'm frightened," Yoohoo bleated.

"Quiet, Yankee spies!" ordered one of the guards standing over them.

Capt. Smirk fidgeted. It made him nervous to sit here under the Confederate guards' control, with the Tardy hidden somewhere in the darkness between them and the fort.

Yet in the midst of his uneasiness, something puzzled him. According to his calculations, the Confederates should be preparing to attack Fort Sumter at dawn, triggering the first official battle of the war. But for some reason, in this timeline, the Confederates were talking about negotiations. It almost sounded like they were ready to make concessions to the Union.

Smirk and his companions were surrounded.

Maybe war can be avoided, Smirk thought. *No Civil War...*

His mind reeled with the implications. If there were no Civil War, many lives could be spared...an entire publishing genre would never exist...and "Ashokan Farewell" wouldn't make the Top Ten.

But Smirk knew these issues were still up in the air. The important thing right now was for the five of them to get out of this timeline. He came up with a plan and whispered it to Piker; Piker nodded and, using whispers and gestures, communicated the message to the others.

Smirk felt a moment's satisfaction. *There's one thing you can say about Piker—he knows how to take orders,* Smirk thought. *Smock would have argued that my plan is foolhardy and dangerous. And it is, but so what? Piker's like me, an action kind of guy. Maybe I should create a position for him on my permanent staff.*

Smirk's strategy was for the Pros to stun the guards with their phasers, which the soldiers hadn't confiscated since they didn't recognize them as weapons. Then Smirk would hold off the remaining troops while his companions dashed to the Tardy. He would join them last, keeping the soldiers at bay with his phaser as he boarded the time machine.

The only drawback was that they'd need to perfectly coordinate their dash to the Tardy. If anyone's timing was off...

Smirk shook his head; it was too late for second thoughts. Dawn would break soon. This was the time to make their move.

The others watched for his signal. "To your marks..." Smirk whispered. "Set...go!"

They all rose at once and fired at the guards, knocking them unconscious.

Smirk pointed his phaser at the remaining soldiers, who backed away warily. "Make a break for it!" Smirk shouted to his companions.

They scrambled away—in all directions. In the darkness and confusion, it was hard even to see one another, much less the Tardy way out in the field. Yoohoo and Beverage ran smack into a supply tent. Checkout tripped over a campfire. Piker sprinted ahead of the soldiers' front line, then collided with a tree.

Smirk despaired. *How am I supposed to cover for them when they're running around like chickens with their heads cut off?*

The commotion attracted the attention of a commander stationed next to the cannon. He pointed straight ahead at Piker. "The Yankee spies are escaping! Fire!" the commander ordered.

The cannon blasted—and, since it was pointed at Fort Sumter, incidentally began the Civil War.

Bored
Silly

"**W**HAT IS THAT thing, Snot—a carnival fun-house? I can't time travel in that. I'm a doc-tor, not a carny worker," McCaw groused.

Mr. Snot frowned. "Forrr pity's sake," he answered, "haven't ye ever seen the old 'Time Funnel' television series, mon? They used to travel back in time wi' a spinnin' tunnel just like this one. The rest o' the equipment just happened to be attached to the tunnel, that's all."

The Cons stood inspecting Mr. Snot's just-unveiled time machine at the same moment Piker was misdialing the Pros into the past. Neither group knew what the others were up to.

Snot's time machine did look like a carnival funhouse. Its entrance was a large spinning barrel painted with stripes. Beyond that were steps that rocked back and forth in alternating directions, as well as some warped mirrors.

Wart kicked the side of the structure, testing its strength. "Hmmmph," he grunted. "You got this from the HolidayDeck, didn't you? It sounds hollow."

"And what if I did?" Snot retorted. "It isn't easy to find parts for such a—"

"Never mind, Mr. Snot," said Capt. Ricardo. "Is the time machine ready to use?"

"Aye, sir," replied Snot. "As soon as we've all gotten to

241

the control room inside, I'll send us off."

Mr. Smock went first. After studying the spinning barrel for a moment and calculating the rate of spin and various tangents of trajectory, he managed to stay upright while negotiating his way to the other side.

He made it look so easy that the others, following him, were caught off guard and lost their footing. Ricardo wobbled, grabbing Wart for support; but the Kringle was already unsteady, and he crashed into Snot, who in turn fell against McCaw. Down they all went, rolling around like rocks in a cement mixer. Finally they rolled to the other side and spilled out at Smock's feet.

Next they climbed the shifting steps, with varying degrees of success. Smock and Wart moved up fairly easily, but Ricardo, Snot and McCaw had to cling to a side railing and drag themselves up.

Panting and sweating, they followed the funhouse maze to the next room, which was filled with mirrors. Mr. Smock had gotten there first, and he was studying the mirrors in puzzlement. "I fail to understand the purpose of these distorted images," he stated.

McCaw muttered, "I always thought these funhouse mirrors were pretty stupid."

"They're supposed to be funny, Mr. Smock," Ricardo said. "See? When you stand in front of this one, it makes you look extraordinarily tall and thin. Whereas the image of the one where Wart is standing is all wavy. And Snot's reflection is distorted to look grossly overweight."

McCaw stepped beside Snot and studied his own image in the same mirror. "No, it's not distorted," he observed. "This is an ordinary mirror. That's Snot's real reflection." He guffawed. "Now, *that's* funny!" Ricardo, realizing that he'd unintentionally insulted Snot, blushed until his entire skull resembled a GE Intimate Moments pink light bulb.

Snot, muttering angrily under his breath, stomped over to the control panel just beyond the mirrored room. He set the controls and announced, "Here we go."

Panting and sweating, they followed the funhouse
maze to the next room.

The funhouse shook and rattled for a minute; then the motion stopped. "I think we're there," Snot said.

The Cons made their way back down the steps and through the barrel. As they spilled out of the time machine, everyone realized that something was very wrong. This was definitely not New Jersey.

A mechanical arm reached out, grabbed Smock by the ear, and lifted him several inches off the ground. The arm belonged to a half-human, half-machine creature which examined Smock impartially. With its pasty white skin and cluttered mechanical body parts, the creature looked like a hybrid between Dacron and the props department of the movie *Brazil*.

"Don't struggle, Mr. Smock!" Ricardo urged.

Within moments, more of these creatures arrived and began hauling the other Cons to their feet.

"What the devil are they?" asked McCaw.

Capt. Ricardo, his voice filled with dread, answered, "The Bored."

An hour later, the five Cons shivered in a holding pen. The Bored had stashed them there after stripping them to their underwear and sending in a mechanical tailor to measure them for new limbs.

The Cons had managed to figure out that they were being held prisoner in a Bored ship. They also knew that they'd gone way too far into the future—even farther than during Starfreak's first encounter with the Bored—since the aliens had undergone minor design changes like the addition of stereo headphones and chest-front ice dispensers.

"Perhaps if you can recall more about your previous interactions with the Bored, Captain, it will help us escape from them now," said Mr. Smock.

"I've told you all I remember, Mr. Smock," said Ricardo wearily. "They kidnapped me from the *Endocrine*, turned me into a Bored named Lowcutie, and made me a pawn in their takeover of the universe."

Ricardo fervently hoped that Smock would mellow out soon. The Captain was bone-tired from the unaccustomed stress of coping with a right-hand man with a brain. If Piker were here, he would have run out of dramatic statements long ago and probably would be napping by now.

But Mr. Smock persisted in analyzing the situation. "This ship we are trapped in—how is it constructed?"

Wart answered him. "On the outside, a Bored ship looks like a Radio Shack outlet that has been crushed in a trash compactor. Here in the interior, all the Bored creatures are interchangeable units connected to a central power source. They have multiple redundant layers that are impossible to penetrate."

"Kind of like the bureaucracy of Starfreak Command, eh?" cracked McCaw.

"Exactly how did they turn you into a Bored?" Smock asked the Captain.

Ricardo sighed. "Mr. Smock, is this really necessary?"

"The details might suggest an escape strategy," Smock replied.

"Oh, all right," Ricardo conceded. "They grafted mechanical parts onto my body. I got a laser-beam eye, a stainless steel pancreas, a forearm/hand unit that doubled as a can opener, and, uh . . . other enhancements."

"What other enhancements?" Smock insisted.

"Well . . . " Ricardo hesitated, then leaned over and whispered something into Smock's ear.

Smock raised a Vulture eyebrow in surprise. "I see," he said evenly. "And after you were rescued, all these alterations were returned to normal human form?"

"Yes. I had Dr. Flusher surgically remove the Bored parts and send them back," said Ricardo, squirming a little under Smock's gaze. "Uh, that is, all except the . . . you know."

Smock's eyebrow rose higher.

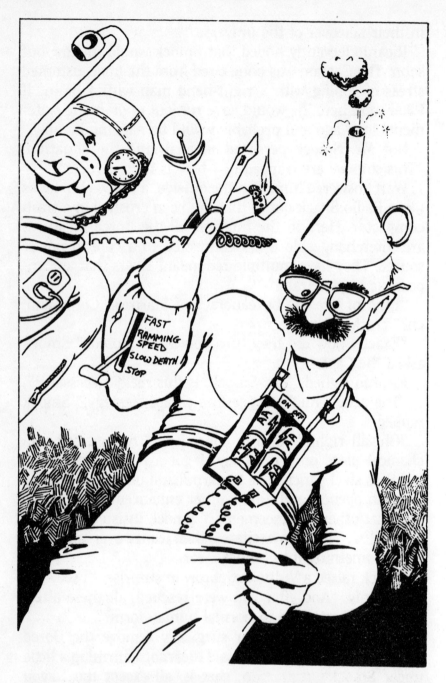

"They kidnapped me from the *Endocrine* and turned me into a Bored named Lowcutie."

"Well, I thought that might come in handy sometime," Ricardo defended himself.

"So far, this information has not suggested how we could escape," Smock said. "Mr. Wart, you were on board this ship also. Perhaps you can tell us something more."

Wart thought for a moment, then answered, "There is one other thing. On our first rescue mission, we discovered Capt. Ricardo's discarded uniform in a refrigerator vegetable drawer. That seemed unusual."

"Did you take it with you?" Smock asked.

"No. We left it in the drawer," replied the Kringle. Then his eyes glimmered as he realized the significance of Smock's question. "That means it may still be here . . . "

Smock nodded as he completed the thought: " . . . With a communicator pin attached, we hope."

As soon as the Cons realized that Ricardo's communicator pin was stashed in some forgotten cranny of the Bored ship, offering them a means of calling for help, they all pitched in at what they did best: arguing.

Each of the five crabby pessimists made his own unique contribution to the squabble. Ricardo overanalyzed their options and called for a vote, irritating Wart, Snot and McCaw. Then Smock pointed out the futility of anger in the situation, which only heightened their irritation.

McCaw vetoed the initial escape plan—"I'm a doctor, not Houdini." Snot pointed out that the mechanics of the plan were unsound and predicted they'd all be "blown into wee bits of flotsam and jetsam" if they tried to beam out. Wart proposed a strategy involving maximum mayhem, and everyone ignored his idea, just as they'd done to every mouthwateringly violent proposal he'd ever made since joining the crew.

Finally, the sheer discomfort of sitting around shivering in their underwear forced them out of the holding pen to search the ship. The Bored hadn't left them with much clothing. Ricardo wore boxer shorts imprinted with the coat-of-arms pattern of his alma mater, the Stuffordshire Boys' School. Snot had an old-fashioned sleeveless t-shirt and an underkilt. Smock's jockey shorts were ultramodern, with an energy-efficient Velcro fly. Dr. McCaw's underwear was blue standard-issue surgical garb he'd "borrowed" from Sick Bay. And Wart wore leather briefs accented with metal studs.

They crept down the corridor, wondering how to locate Ricardo's old uniform. A major clue emerged when McCaw spotted a Building Directory/Floor Plan on the wall. They plotted a route from the "you are here" dot to the Pantry area in Corridor 1179D.

On the way there, they passed the room where their time machine had come to rest. Several Bored were dismantling it and tossing the parts into a recycling bin. Without weapons there was nothing the Cons could do to stop them, so they continued their search.

When they reached the Pantry, Wart immediately recognized the vegetable drawer. Ricardo's uniform lay inside, with its communicator pin still in working order.

Ricardo flicked it on. "*Endocrine*, this is Capt. Ricardo. Come in." There was no response. "I'm sure they're receiving the signal," Ricardo said. "*Endocrine*, please respond."

A metallic voice crackled to life behind them: "Lowcutie!" Whirling around, they saw that a dozen Bored were advancing into the Pantry.

"Lowcutie," said the twelve Bored, speaking with one voice, "you have failed to return a particularly valuable body part grafted onto you during a previous visit. You must surrender it immediately."

5

Neuts to
the Rescue

"**A**AAAAAAAAAAAAAAAAAAA!"

Capt. Ricardo's scream traveled through time and emerged through the "hey, you" speakers on the *Endocrine*'s Bridge. It was a dramatic scream, almost Shakespearean in its masterful tone and timbre. But ultimately it did not make a sound on the Bridge, for there was no one there to hear it.

Left on their own, the Neuts—the *Endocrine* officers who hadn't backed either time-travel scheme—had stretched the art of goofing off to new heights. They figured, why bother with tedious chores like charting new planets or running a Class II diagnostic on the snack dispensers when there was a strong possibility that the Pros or Cons would screw up the timeline and it would all simply cease to exist?

At the moment, the Neuts were lounging around in Ten-Foreplay.

Dacron stood at the far end of the bar wearing a cowboy hat. He loved pretending Ten-Foreplay was a Wild West saloon. "Barkeep!" he called. "Another round of simpahol drafts for us cowpokes. It has been a long, dusty trail ride herding them doggies from Houston to Alamogordo."

"Don't you think you've had enough, Dacron?" asked Guano, folding her arms across her chest. Unlike the oth-

249

The Neuts were lounging around in Ten-Foreplay.

ers, who could shake off the effects of the synthetic alcohol substitute, Dacron had never gotten the hang of it. The simpahol jazzed up his circuits for hours.

"Enough? What is 'enough'?" Dacron asked, extending his hand in a stagey gesture. "It is said that it is better to give than to receive, but how much giving is enough, and how much receiving is too much? And it is also said that too often we love things and use people, when we should use things and love people, but in reality it is people and not things that cause all the misery in the galaxy. After all, when was the last time a 'thing' hijacked a starship, or stepped on someone's foot, or ... "

"Guano, would you give him the beer already?" Georgie whined. "The faster he drinks, the sooner he'll move out of this blabby stage and into his laughing jag."

"Oh, all right. Here, cowboy." Guano drew a simpahol beer from the tap.

Dacron grinned. "Please be sure to slide it down the bar in the traditional Western manner," he requested.

Guano shoved the mug toward Dacron from her end of the counter. The mug slid past Dacron, flew off the edge of the bar, and crashed on the floor. Two seconds later, Dacron made a delayed grab for it. He stared at the shattered mug at his feet, then turned to Guano. "May we try that again, please?" he asked. Guano began drawing another beer.

Meanwhile, Zulu sat at one of the tables, swatting his paddle ball. "I wonder what the Pros and Cons are doing right now?" he remarked.

"Ask me if I care," Troit snapped. "Probably off setting a new record for making and breaking commitments." She pulled out a voodoo doll and placed it on the table. Its face looked remarkably like Capt. Smirk's. Next she held up a pin and studied the doll, choosing a tender spot in which to stick it.

Guano looked uneasy. "Deanna, this voodoo stuff gives me the creeps. Haven't you gotten over Capt. Smirk yet?

Sure, he broke your engagement, but I thought you'd adjust pretty quick, being a counselor and all."

"This is a very healthy outlet for my hostility," Troit said through clenched teeth. She stuck the pin into the doll's shoulder.

"Well, I shay good riddance to all of them," Dacron slurred, leaning on the bar, "particularly Mr. Schmock. I am not sure why, but whenever he is nearby I develop a headache."

"Headache . . . heartache . . . pain in the butt," Troit muttered, pulling the pin out of the doll's shoulder and plunging it into its head, then its chest, then its rear end.

"Shay, hash anybody heard the one about the rabbi, the priesht and the minishter?" Dacron asked.

"Here we go," observed Georgie. "Dacron's entering his laughing phase."

"We'd better get him out of here," Zulu said. "Remember what happened last time? He kept doing that stand-up routine until he started hemorrhaging. I think he calms down a lot faster when he's off by himself."

"Let's take him to the Bridge," Georgie suggested.

"A priesht, a rabbi and a minishter are shtranded in a shufflecraft," Dacron continued, "trying to figure out how to call for help . . ." Dacron kept on babbling as Zulu and Georgie swooped him up from either side, carrying him out of Ten-Foreplay and into the Crewmover.

" . . . And the minister says, 'This is the 24th century. God does not exist anymore!' " Dacron delivered the punchline and dissolved in whoops of helpless laughter just as Georgie and Zulu carried him onto the Bridge from the Crewmover, the *Endocrine*'s horizontal/vertical elevator to all parts of the ship. Plopping him into the captain's chair, they left the Bridge and returned to Ten-Foreplay.

As his laughter began to subside about half an hour later, Dacron began looking for a new diversion. Still giggling, he pulled out the latest issue of *Playdroid* magazine and studied the foldout of a fully functional female. Then he remembered that it was late afternoon and "All My Androids" was about to come on. He switched the Viewscreen to its TV setting and cranked up the footrest on the Captain's chair.

He discovered it was still a little early; the broadcast of "The Bald and the Beautiful" wasn't over yet. Dacron had never been able to get into that show, though he knew it was Capt. Ricardo's favorite. He turned down the sound to wait for his program to begin.

In the sudden silence on the Bridge, Dacron heard a faint voice. "Helllllp . . . helllllllp . . . " It seemed to be coming from the "hey, you" speakers. He cranked up the volume on the receiver.

"Hello?" Dacron inquired.

"Dacron, is that you?" It was Capt. Ricardo.

"Unnhhh," Dacron moaned. Dimly he recalled talking to Capt. Ricardo on the "hey, you" frequency a while ago. The conversation had seemed so important at the time. But now it took all of Dacron's concentration just to raise his head gingerly from the conference room table, rub his temples, then let his head flop back down amid the glasses of Alka-Seltzer, bottles of aspirin and mugs of hot coffee. "Unnnhhhhh."

"Well, this certainly is one of the more entertaining staff meetings I've ever attended," Georgie remarked.

"It sure beats following Robert's Rules of Order," Zulu noted.

"Dacron," Deanna said, "when you called this meeting, you said it was an emergency. Can you just tell us what Capt. Ricardo and the Cons need, so we can help them?"

Dacron turned his face to one side so that his mouth no longer pressed against the table. Without lifting his head, he moaned, "They went too far into the future. They are trapped in the Bored ship. We will have to build a time machine to rescue them. I swear I am going to die."

"Are they in any immediate danger?" Zulu asked.

"Capt. Ricardo is at great financial risk," Dacron said. "The Bored may confiscate his heirlooms."

"His heirlooms? Dacron, what are you talking about?" Georgie demanded.

Dacron explained, "He said if we do not arrive soon, he will lose the family jewels."

The four subordinate Neuts sat on the Bridge discussing what to do next. Dacron, their leader, had ended the meeting by announcing that he would not allow the effects of the simpahol to interfere with the performance of his duties. He'd lifted his head, opened his eyes, and with great dignity, crawled out of the conference room. He'd made it as far as the doorway, where he now lay, sleeping it off.

"Let's face it—only Dacron can build a time machine," Georgie pointed out.

"Why can't you do it?" asked Zulu. "You're an engineer."

"I never studied Time Mechanics," Georgie admitted. "It wasn't a required course, so I skipped it and took Intro to Yoga instead."

"Maybe we should try to contact Capt. Smirk and the Pros," Guano suggested. "We haven't heard from them lately, either."

Georgie agreed. From the communicator panel at the Tactical station, he sent out a signal and began zeroing in on the Pros' location.

"Where are they? Did they make it to the correct place and time?" Zulu asked.

"I don't think the time is right," Georgie said, studying the readouts. "As a matter of fact, I think they're in the past. As for where they are, it seems to be a Class M&M planet."

"You know, I never understood what a Class M&M planet is," Guano mused.

"That means it's capable of supporting human life, with

a breathable atmosphere and a hospitable climate," Georgie explained.

Guano looked puzzled. "Aren't they all like that?" she asked. "I mean, when was the last time you guys put on space suits or helmets when beaming down to the surface of an unfamiliar planet?"

"Hey, I think I've reached them," Georgie said. "Hello? This is Lt. Georgie LaForgery of the USS *Endocrine*. Who's there?"

"Smirk here," came the voice. "What can we do for you, Lieutenant?"

"When and where did you land, Capt. Smirk?"

"We're on Earth, at Fort Sumter," Smirk said breezily, "and the time is—oh, 1860-ish."

"Fort Sumter..." Georgie repeated in amazement. "...during the Civil War...Are you and the other Pros all right, Captain? I hear cannons in the background."

"Oh, there's a bit of a skirmish going on at the moment, but we're fine, Lieutenant—"

"No, we're not!" Piker's voice interrupted. "He's just too proud to ask for help. Georgie, get us out of here! We're trapped—"

His voice halted abruptly, and Capt. Smirk came back on the audio channel. "Actually, it *is* getting rather boring here, and we have a slight malfunction in our time machine. If you would be so good as to swing by and pick us up, we'd appreciate it."

"We'll try, Captain," said Georgie, "but first Dacron has to build a time machine, and then we have to rescue the Cons. They're stuck, too. After that, we'll come get you."

Beverage Flusher's voice came over the audio. "Please hurry, Georgie," she said. "Capt. Smirk is having medical problems, and I need to get him to Sick Bay and perform some tests. It's a condition I've never seen before, creating stabbing pains all over his body."

The Neuts turned to look at Troit, who pulled out her voodoo doll and gazed at it with new respect.

"We'll be waiting for you—eeeek!" Flusher's voice was drowned out by a hail of gunfire. The Neuts were puzzled momentarily; then they shrugged it off, and Georgie closed the audio channel.

Early the next morning, Dacron started working on the Neuts' time machine. During the night he'd had his fluids changed and had attended his first meeting of Androids Anonymous. Now he felt like a new pseudo-man.

It took him only a few hours to build the contraption. He applied the latest Japanese quality-control techniques and came up with a just-in-time machine.

Dacron time-traveled to the Bored ship. He found the Cons huddled in a corner, helplessly watching the Bored strip down their funhouse time machine. A frustrated Mr. Smock fiddled with Capt. Ricardo's communicator, which the Bored had disabled immediately after Ricardo's distress call to Dacron. Smock had hoped to fix it and beam them out of there, but it was a hopeless task since he had neither tools nor egg cartons to work with.

The Bored were caught off guard by Dacron's sudden arrival. As the aliens moved to counter this unexpected threat, the Cons made a run for it.

In an instant, Dacron activated a control on the wall panel, disabling the shields that the Bored had placed around the funhouse. Immediately the Neuts locked on to the funhouse and beamed it back to the *Endocrine*. Then Dacron ran down the corridor to catch up with the Cons, with the Bored pursuing just inches behind him.

The Cons had taken advantage of their brief head start to duck into a supply closet. Failing to notice their evasive maneuver, Dacron was about to run past the closet when Wart reached out, grabbed him, pulled him into the closet, and slammed the door shut behind them. The Bored pounded on it furiously.

Everyone but Dacron panted in exhaustion. Finally, between gasps for air, Dr. McCaw blurted out to Dacron,

"Well . . . how are you . . . going to . . . get us out of here . . . Whitey?"

"I was able to beam your funhouse back to the *Endocrine*," Dacron said, "but we cannot use the transporter ourselves. We must travel in my just-in-time machine. Unfortunately, the Bored are now positioned between us and the machine. Mr. Smock, I will need your help with a procedure enabling me to access their collective consciousness, using my body as a communication channel. That will overcome their resistance, as well as allowing me to pursue my hobby of speaking in funny voices."

Smock stepped forward. "What should I do?" he asked.

Dacron walked over to the intercom unit on the wall, one of hundreds placed throughout the ship to allow two-way communication and play background music. At the moment, its small speaker was broadcasting heavy metal.

On the face of the intercom were buttons marked "Kitchen," "Playroom" and "Nursery." Next to them was a small outlet labeled "AC/DC." Dacron opened the outlet, revealing a tangle of wires.

"This is the conduit for Alien Communication/Direct Connection," Dacron explained to Smock. "You will need to hook up my brain to this outlet." He touched the back of his head. "Here, just beneath my cowlick, is the panel which allows access to my higher functions."

"Do you wish to remain conscious during this procedure, Mr. Dacron?" Smock asked.

Dacron nodded. "It is vital that I stay alert so that I can relay instructions to the Bored."

"Will it hurt?" Smock asked.

"No, it will not."

"Darn," Smock said dryly. He pressed the latch, and the panel to Dacron's brain popped open. "All right, now what do I do?" Smock asked.

"There is a cord there," Dacron told him. "It consists of three intertwined wires, sheathed in black, green, and white plastic, respectively. Do you see it?"

"Yes," Smock answered.

"Pull out the cord," Dacron continued, "separate the wires, and connect the white wire from my brain to the white wire in the receptacle. Please check carefully before connecting. It is vital that you connect white to white."

Smock studied the three wires. The other Cons, standing behind Dacron's back, realized that Smock was considering various options besides white-to-white. McCaw and Snot snickered, and Wart rubbed his hands in anticipation. Only Capt. Ricardo ignored the scene; he looked uncharacteristically distracted, staring straight ahead and babbling soundlessly to himself.

Finally Smock made up his mind. He extended Dacron's white wire and deliberately hooked it to the green wire in the intercom.

Dacron's eyes rolled upward, and his hair frizzed out in all directions, crackling with static electricity. The signal from the intercom snapped his reflexes into the posture of a strutting rock performer: he mimed playing an electric guitar while screaming along with the heavy metal song on the intercom.

McCaw and Snot laughed and laughed till they had to hold their sides; tears ran down their cheeks. Wart strained to keep from cracking an unKringlelike smile, but his eyes twinkled with delight.

Finally Smock decided they'd all had enough fun for one day. He removed the green wire and correctly connected white to white.

Instantly Dacron's expression went blank as he became a conduit for the collective Bored consciousness. The Bored sensed the connection with an unknown entity. They took over Dacron's own vocal mechanism to speak to him, stating in a metallic drone, "Hey there ... big boy ... we may be compatible. State your modem."

Dacron switched to his usual tone of voice and countered, "Give me a 'C' prompt." His eyes rolled randomly until the Bored complied. He ordered, "Delete C/BORED/

.." Then Dacron went limp, and Smock disconnected him from the intercom.

As soon as Smock closed Dacron's brain panel, the android regained normal functioning. "I have disabled the Bored," he announced. "They will no longer prevent us from reaching my time machine." Sure enough, out in the hallway the Bored were sprawled around like so many auto parts at the junkyard.

Within moments Dacron got the Cons aboard the just-in-time machine and flew them back to the *Endocrine*'s shuttlebay. The other Neuts had gathered to greet them, and they were surprised when the Cons stepped out of the vehicle in their underwear.

Only Capt. Ricardo was fully dressed, wearing the old uniform he'd reclaimed from the Bored. Georgie approached him, noticing his stunned expression. "Are you all right, Captain?" Georgie asked.

Smock explained, "The Captain is adjusting quite well. His original human parts are now *all* back in place."

Capt. Ricardo's mouth moved, but no sound came out.

"I see you're wearing your old uniform," Georgie observed. When he'd left, Capt. Ricardo had been wearing a new red jacket made of Iowa pig suede. He wore the jacket at all times, indoors and out, commenting that as he got older, the *Endocrine* seemed to get chillier.

Georgie continued, "Would you like a new uniform, Captain? Should I order the seamstress to stitch up another jacket for you?"

Ricardo nodded, extended two fingers in a command gesture, and croaked, "Make it sew."

Next, Dacron went back to rescue the Pros. They'd taken refuge in a grove of trees as the Civil War raged around them. The Pros practically fell over each other rushing to get into the just-in-time machine—except for Capt. Smirk, who maintained a veneer of casualness.

Smirk ambled into the machine, then gestured back

toward the open field just beyond. "Mr. Dacron," he said, "would you retrieve our Tardy? It's sustained some minor damage."

The Tardy had been smashed by a cannonball; Dacron took along a broom and dustpan as he went to pick it up. Meanwhile, Dr. Flusher opened the first-aid compartment of Dacron's vehicle and found an inflatable pillow for Smirk to sit on.

Dacron carried in the pieces of the Tardy. Then he told the Pros to fasten their seat belts for the ride back.

At first they were all in a jovial mood, grateful just to be safe again; but by the time the just-in-time machine docked in the *Endocrine*'s shuttlebay, several of the Pros had managed to start an argument over who was at fault for their disastrous mission.

Finally Capt. Smirk ordered them to knock it off. They couldn't afford to waste time, he observed, pointing out that the Cons were already hard at work repairing their time machine for another try. As their teammates started reassembling the Tardy, Dr. Flusher took Smirk to Sick Bay to administer a hippospray for his stabbing pains.

Counselor Troit realized that the Pros would do anything to get the jump on the Cons, and vice versa. She sensed this with her remarkable Betavoid telepathy, as well as the fact that they were shouting and waving their fists at each other. On Troit's advice, Dacron locked up his just-in-time machine so neither group could use it.

With everybody back on board, the Neuts were forced to look busy again, so Dacron returned to his console on the Bridge. Within a few minutes his workaholic nature reasserted itself, and he actually was busy. Studying the Preview segments they'd viewed earlier, Dacron noticed a significant element in the Herschel/wrekkie timeline. He asked the two captains to come to the Bridge and review what he'd found.

"Well, what is it, Lieutenant? We've got some serious

repairs to do," said Capt. Smirk. Both he and Capt. Ricardo could hardly hold still, so eager were they to return to work on their time machines and be the first to take off.

Dacron told them, "I have discovered that the moment in which Herschel discovers the videotape is a focal point of the entire time spectrum as we know it."

He pointed to a blip on the Preview screen. "The universe seems to be collapsing toward this event. It is a sort of black hole in time. If one of your groups is able to reach and participate in this moment, thus altering it slightly, the timeline will be repaired. If not, our entire past, present and future will cease to exist. I just thought you would like to know."

Both captains pretended to be professionally concerned about this possibility. Their expressions were somber, but the shifting of their eyes gave them away. They looked like cyclists sizing each other up near the end of a race, jockeying for position, trying to determine who would begin the sprint for the finish line.

Dacron continued, "Since my just-in-time machine has proven the most accurate so far, I could use it to reach Herschel and prevent the destruction of the universe— though the Prime Time Directive prohibits me from interfering further on behalf of either of your groups."

"No, thank you, Lieutenant. We'll manage on our own," said Smirk. He ran his finger over the forward consoles, pretending to inspect them for dust, all the while sidling toward the Crewmover.

Ricardo announced loudly, "Thank you for your report, Mr. Dacron. I believe I'll think it over in my Ready Room." He strode toward the Ready Room door, but at the last second he pivoted and dashed toward the Crewmover. Smirk, crying out in dismay over letting himself be duped, broke into a run.

Ricardo reached the Crewmover first. He jumped in and hit the "door closed" button. Smirk flung himself forward, jamming his torso between the closing doors.

The Crewmover, sensing an obstacle, began to open the doors. "Emergency override!" cried Ricardo, and the doors started closing on Smirk again.

"Belay that order!" yelled Smirk, and the doors slid open. He wedged himself into the Crewmover before Ricardo could stop him. As the doors finally shut tight, the two passengers tried to outshout each other with instructions to the Crewmover: "Deck 15!" "No, Deck 79!" "15!" "79!"

When the Pros and the Cons went to bed that night, they each left a sentry guarding their time machines. And sometime around midnight, each of their sentries decided to take matters into his own hands.

Checkout, who was supposed to be guarding the Pros' machine, crept away from his post and tiptoed toward the Cons' workshop. He wanted to break out of his role as the group wimp by doing something heroic; sabotaging their opponents' machine would fill the bill. Checkout decided the damage should be subtle, so the Cons wouldn't know anything was wrong until after they'd wasted more time in the race.

At the same moment, Wart left his guard post at the Cons' machine and headed for the Pros' workshop. Wart chafed at playing defense; he was better on offense, and he decided it was time to take the battle to the enemy. Besides, he was fed up with the way his fellow Cons always ignored his advice; this was one instance, he decided, where violence would take its rightful place.

The two sentries missed seeing each other as they sneaked through the ship's corridors. In the Cons' workshop, Checkout made some subtle adjustments in the funhouse control panel. Meanwhile, Wart sabotaged the Tardy's time-setting device and, in a stylish parting gesture, planted a time bomb on board.

6

The Days and Nights
of Yasha Tar

EARLY THE NEXT morning, the Cons took off in their
funhouse. As they approached their designated coordinates in the future, everything seemed to be in
order.

"We're definitely heading toward Earth this time," said
Capt. Ricardo as they sat in the control room watching
the observation screen. "Look, there's a movie theater."

Looming ahead was The Centiplex, which advertised
"100 Screens / No Waiting." As the Cons' time machine
flew past the marquee, they could make out a few titles,
including "Terminator #689" and "Three Men and an Old
Hag."

The time machine passed through the lobby and landed
in one of the 100 screening rooms inside. The Cons stepped
out into the darkened theater; it was deserted.

Wart checked the doors. They were locked from the
outside. McCaw investigated the fire escapes at the front
of the theater; they, too, were locked.

"Even if we're at the right time, this isn't the right
place," said Ricardo. "It looks like we'll need help again."
He touched his communicator button. "*Endocrine,* this is
Capt. Ricardo. Come in." There was no answer.

"Something must be blocking the signal," Smock speculated, "perhaps the construction materials of this build-

ing, or something in the surrounding atmosphere."

"What is it with these communicators?" Ricardo grumped. "They always break down when we need them most. Well, since we can't contact the ship for information, let's get out of here and try again. How long will it take, Mr. Snot?"

Snot re-entered the funhouse to find out. After a few moments of tinkering in the control room, he came out and announced, "Someone's fooled wi' the works. Our locator was off by decades, and the homing device is ruined. The machine won't get us out of here."

Just then music began to play, and the movie screen lit up with a message:

> Welcome to the Centiplex Complex. For the viewing enjoyment of those around you, please refrain from smoking, talking, screaming, or changing your infant's diaper in the theater.
>
> And now for our feature presentation.

All the Cons sat down to watch, mesmerized by the wide screen.

The film opened with a shot of two men sitting on a stage. They introduced themselves to the camera.

"Hello, I'm Gene Thickskull, film critic of the *Chicago Tribeaut*," said one.

"And I'm Roger Eatbert, film critic of the *Chicago Fun Times*," said the other. "Welcome to the Yasha Tar Film Festival."

"What?" gasped Ricardo.

"What is the matter, Captain?" asked Smock.

Capt. Ricardo replied, "Yasha Tar is one of my former crewmembers. But she died years ago on an away mission. How in the world did her life become a film festival?"

Smock shrugged. "It appears that her timeline had greater significance than you originally thought, Captain," he answered.

Eatbert continued, "We're here to critique the films you're about to see—to throw in our two cents' worth, if you will."

"Or in your case, Roger, one cent's worth," commented Thickskull.

Eatbert shot a dirty glance at Thickskull, then resumed his spiel. "All the films are an offshoot of the 'wrekkie' cult sparked by the discovery of a videotape made by Yasha's crewmate Westerly Flusher. His film generated rabid interest in the crew of the USS *Endocrine*...."

Capt. Ricardo muttered, "That bloody videotape! I'm going to yank it out of the hands of this Herschel character if it's the last thing I do."

"...and as the wrekkies searched the Starfreak archives," Eatbert continued, "they found more tapes of the *Endocrine* crew—tapes made by anti-shoplifting security cameras that used to film continuously throughout the ship. The wrekkies assembled the footage into individual episodes. On this program we'll focus on the episodes in which Yasha Tar plays a prominent role.

"We'll briefly review the films in the order they were released, pass judgment on them—"

"And most importantly," Thickskull interrupted him, "we'll tell whether or not I could identify with the characters. Let's start with Yasha's debut, 'Encounter at Ballpoint.'"

They showed a brief film clip. Ricardo and Wart stared at it, simultaneously fascinated and repelled to see themselves caught unawares by the camera.

"Well, Gene," Eatbert said when the clip ended, "it wasn't Yasha's finest moment, but with an ensemble cast all having to be introduced at once, that's understandable."

"Yasha had a better chance to show her talents in the second feature, 'The Naked Cow,'" Thickskull said. "I loved the way she explored the final frontier: sex with a machine. Talk about boldly going where no one has gone before!"

"Calm down, Gene," Eatbert urged. "Keep your sweater

"On this program we'll focus on the episodes in which Yasha Tar plays a prominent role."

tucked in. Yasha's next biggie was 'Commode of Honor.' Unfortunately we don't have any footage from that episode, because on the night it was broadcast we misprogrammed our VCR and taped 'Wheel of Fortune' by mistake."

Next the critics presented a scene from "Skin of Exxon" showing Yasha getting knocked off by a mean-tempered oil slick.

Starting to rise from his theater seat, Smock asked, "I suppose that's the end of the storyline, Captain?"

"No, Mr. Smock. Not by a long shot," Ricardo said. Smock sat back down.

Eatbert announced, "Now the fun really begins. In 'Time Lag-acy,' Yasha Tar's sister, Fresh Tar, turns up as a terrorist on the late Yasha's home world."

Wart spoke up. "I am tired of hearing them *talk* about the films," he groused. "I want to *see* the films, and not just tiny clips, either!" The others caught his cranky mood.

"Yeah, show the movies already!" McCaw hollered at the screen.

"Get on wi' it!" shouted Snot. "We want movies!"

Ricardo, trying to act like one of the guys for a change, but utterly unfamiliar with rowdiness, managed only: "Make it show!"

Next, the film played scenes from "Yesterday's *Endocrine*," in which the *Endocrine C-Sick* accidentally traveled ahead of its timeline, bringing Yasha Tar into the future. Only Guano, through some mysterious process, knew that Yasha did not belong in the present because she had been cancelled two seasons before. The film clip showed Ricardo sending Yasha back to her death in the *Endocrine C-Sick*.

"Captain, how could you?" murmured Smock.

"She requested the transfer herself," Ricardo countered. "Besides, that's still not the end of the story. Keep watching."

Sure enough, the next clip, from "Beyond Redemption," revealed that Yasha had not died in the *Endocrine C-Sick* after all. She was taken prisoner by a Romanumen commander; he married her and fathered a daughter who looked remarkably like Yasha except for an updated hairdo and some snazzy eyebrows.

The daughter grew up to be a Romanumen commander like her father. She tried to split the Federation by backing a conspiracy among the Kringles, led by Duras-Cell. But even though the Romanumens lent the conspirators their technologically advanced ships, fully equipped with croaking devices, ultimately the takeover failed.

"Say, that woman looked familiar," Smock remarked. The clip ended, and Thickskull and Eatbert came back onscreen.

"And we haven't heard the last of Yasha's Romanumen daughter," Eatbert observed. "She popped up again in 'Eunuchation,' a rare two-episode story featuring the return of the famous Mr. Smock."

Thickskull chimed in, "Part one made *The Guinness Book of World Records* for the shortest onscreen appearance of a heavily hyped guest star. As a matter of fact, Smock had a bigger part in the 'Coming Attractions' trailer than he did in the actual episode." The critics sat back to watch scenes from the two programs.

"Now I remember," Smock said. "She foiled my secret peace mission that attempted to reunite the Vultures and the Romanumens." The onscreen action showed the conclusion, in which the *Endocrine* crew overcame the evildoers and Yasha's daughter slunk off stage left, muttering, "Curses, foiled again."

"*That's* the end," Ricardo announced. "As far as I know, anyway."

The screen went black for a moment. Then it lit up with a shot of two men sitting on a stage. It was Thickskull and Eatbert again. They introduced themselves to the camera.

"Hello, I'm Gene Thickskull, film critic of the *Chicago Tribeaut*."

"And I'm Roger Eatbert, film critic of the *Chicago Fun Times*. Welcome to the Yasha Tar Film Festival."

"Hey, this is the same as before," Wart protested.

"We're here to critique the films you're about to see . . . " Eatbert said.

"It's started over!" Snot shouted. "We're stuck in a time loop! Help! Help!"

Snot and McCaw panicked and scrambled for the exit. They got into a fistfight over who would pass through the door first, oblivious to the fact that it was locked anyway. Wart, enraged over the prospect of being stuck in a time loop, began uprooting the theater seats and throwing them at the screen.

"Captain, may I remind you," said Smock, "that the longer we remain trapped here, the greater the likelihood that the Pros will reach Herschel first."

"Oh dear, oh dear," fretted Capt. Ricardo, fingering his worry beads.

7

The City on the
Edge of Foreclosure

"**I** DON'T BELIEVE this. I just don't believe it. Why me?!" Capt. Smirk raised his arms to the heavens as if he were soliciting an answer, and Piker stared at the ground in embarrassment. The others followed them out of the Tardy and looked around.

"Does this look like the Maplewood, New Jersey of the future to you, Commander? Does it?" Smirk demanded.

Piker's face reddened. "No, sir."

"No, it isn't," Smirk went on. "Let me tell you where—and when—we've come to, because my crew has been here before."

They stood in a barren landscape amidst scattered rocks. Before them stood an imposing arch made of stone. The arch flashed as it spoke to them: "I am the Guardian of Reruns. Step through me and view the past."

Smirk continued to harangue Piker. "Last time we were here, we stepped through that arch, straight into the Earth of the 1930s. But I really had no great desire to visit there again."

Smirk paused, caught his breath, and opened his mouth to resume his tirade; then he stopped himself. Even though Piker had obviously misprogrammed their time machine again, it was futile to correct his thought processes when he probably didn't even have any.

270

"Captain," Checkout called. He was examining the Tardy's control box. Smirk joined him.

"Someone has tampered vith the time-control mechanism," Checkout observed, pointing to the panel, which was smashed into dozens of pieces.

"Hmmmph," said Smirk, realizing that perhaps this time their inaccurate landing was not Piker's fault after all. As he turned toward Piker to apologize, he saw Piker stepping through the arch.

"Commander, no!" Smirk shouted, but Piker had already gone to the other side.

"We've got to follow him. Everyone must stay together!" said Smirk, herding the others toward the arch. "Let's go. Hurry!"

"Captain, I'm frightened," Yoohoo whinnied.

Passing through the arch, they found themselves on a street corner of an American city in the early 1930s. Piker was already there, looking around. "Sir," he said to Smirk, "I thought this arch might give us an alternate means of time travel."

"Well, it won't," Smirk snapped. "It's not going to get us to the future, anyway. Now don't touch anything. We've all got to leave at the same time. Let's get out of here before we affect this timeline."

Piker wasn't listening. He watched anxiously as a woman stepped off the curb, oblivious to the fire engine which was bearing down on her, bells clanging and siren wailing. "Look out!" Piker yelled, grabbing the woman and pushing her back to safety on the curb. Unfortunately he forgot to remove himself from harm's way, and the side mirror of the fire engine clipped his head.

"Thank you, sir," the woman chirped as she walked away. Piker rubbed his head, his expression more vacant than usual.

Smirk rushed up to Piker. "Now you've really done it!" Smirk scolded him. "You never should have saved that woman's life."

Piker gazed at him groggily. "Sir?"

"That woman," Smirk continued, "is Edith Keebler. The last time my crew was here, Dr. McCaw made the same mistake: he saved her life. Though that seems like the right thing to do, it isn't.

"You see, she's a social worker with two possible futures. In one, she dies. That's the timeline you just screwed up. In the other—her alternate future—she lives, becoming a leading pacifist in the Keebler Elves Peace and Cookie Movement. She's instrumental in delaying America's entry into World War II until it's too late and the Nazis have already developed superior chocolate chips. Do you understand, Commander?"

Piker nodded. He didn't understand, but he'd learned in Starfreak Academy that as long as he didn't admit it, the teachers would leave him alone.

"So for history to come out correctly, Edith Keebler must die now," Smirk concluded. "And since you just prevented her accidental death, we're going to have to kill her ourselves."

"Yes, sir." Piker pulled out his phaser and switched it from its usual "Stun" setting to the "Terminate with Extreme Prejudice" setting. Smirk grabbed his arm.

"No, Commander, not the phaser," said Smirk. "It's too dangerous to introduce advanced technology into the past."

Piker scratched his head. "You mean like when Capt. Ricardo talks about how we have to keep the timeline intact, as our solemn duty to posterity?"

"No, I mean that it's my solemn duty not to get stuck here in the 1930s," said Smirk. "Remember how the Confederates got hold of one of our phasers and almost vaporized us? It would be tragic if I couldn't resume my place among the classy dames of the future." *I shouldn't have to remind him of this—especially about all the women who are counting on me,* Smirk thought. *Mr. Smock would have known that implicitly. Maybe I won't offer*

Piker a position on my crew after all. Smirk continued, "You're going to have to kill Edith in some way that's appropriate to this era."

"I see." Piker put the phaser away and looked down the street. Edith Keebler, who'd been walking away from them, was about halfway down the block. Piker jumped into a taxi at curbside. "Follow that woman!" he directed.

"The one in the red sedan?" the taxi driver responded.

"No, the one on the sidewalk in the brown coat."

The driver stared at him. "Why don't you follow her yourself, buddy? Just get out and walk!"

"You don't understand," Piker urged him. "I want you to run her over."

Piker sprawled at Smirk's feet after the driver had kicked him out of the cab and sped away. As Piker picked himself up and prepared to follow Edith Keebler on foot, Smirk stopped him.

"Wait, Commander," said Smirk. "Don't kill her just yet. I think I've fallen in love with her."

Piker was puzzled. "She's not really your type, is she, sir? She hasn't got a beehive hairdo, she's not wearing chiffon..."

"But look at all that heavy eye makeup," crooned Smirk as he gazed at Keebler, who was crossing the street against the light. "She's got that anachronistic charm that makes me shiver." A car swerved to avoid Keebler and struck a lamppost head-on; she kept walking heedlessly. "Look, Commander, I know we can't let her survive indefinitely, but just let me be with her a little while, maybe spend the evening courting her. In the morning we'll talk about what to do."

Piker nodded. "You're the boss," he said.

The five Pros followed Keebler to her workplace, a cookie kitchen that gave free handouts to the poor. As they reached the head of the line and loaded their supper plates with Elfkin Bite-Size Sandwich Cookies, Smirk felt the stab of his recurring shoulder pain. Edith Keebler, doling out cookies, noticed him wince and came around the counter to help him.

"Are you all right?" Keebler asked, touching Smirk's shoulder.

"It's nothing," Smirk said with a grimace. "Just an old football injury."

"Really? You're a football player?" Keebler began massaging his shoulder, and Smirk gave her a syrupy smile.

"Quarterback," said Smirk. "Ummm, that feels good." He flexed the shoulder she was rubbing.

"I'm trained in therapeutic massage techniques," Keebler told him. "Are any other parts of your body giving you trouble?"

"Not at the moment, but I'm sure I could come up with something by this evening," Smirk responded. "Could I walk you home?"

"Well, I'm the only worker on duty here, and there are so many hungry people to be fed"—Keebler looked at the line, which filled the room and stretched out the door— "and if I don't stay on the job they'll all go to bed hungry tonight...oh, what the heck. Sure, you can walk me home. Let's go."

Keebler grabbed her coat. They passed the cookie line and went out the door, with Smirk giving Piker a thumbs-up gesture behind Keebler's back.

As the two walked through the city streets, getting to know each other, Smirk was impressed by Keebler's inborn talent for remaining unscathed and unaware while causing mayhem all around her. Five blocks and six major traffic accidents later, Smirk knew he loved Edith Keebler.

It wasn't her mind that attracted him; he mistrusted pacifists, since they always seemed intent on making the universe unnecessarily boring. No, he loved her exotic beauty and her glamorous makeup, so totally unlikely in a social worker living in Depression-era America.

Yes, this was love, all right. They even had music playing in the background. It came from a radio sitting in a storefront; the song was "Goodnight, Sweetheart."

Where have I heard that recently? Smirk wondered. *Ah, yes. Dacron was singing it in the shower at the gym.* Dacron's falsetto had startled Smirk, who thought for a moment that there was a woman in the locker room.

Smirk deliberately brought his thoughts back to the present. Keebler was ushering him into her apartment. This would be a night of exquisite poignancy, Smirk knew: wooing a total stranger with the knowledge that the next day she would be totally out of the picture, stone-cold dead. This was romance just the way he liked it.

Smirk's peace of mind lasted only until the next morning, when he and Piker had a philosophical discussion about which one of them should kill Edith Keebler.

"You do it."

"I don't want to do it. You do it."

"I don't wanna do it either. You do it."

"No, you do it."

Piker had been having second thoughts about the whole thing. His most serious worry was that killing Keebler would affect the cookie timeline. Perhaps when they returned to the 24th century, there would be no more Pecan Sandies.

Finally Smirk gave Piker a direct order to knock off Keebler. Piker couldn't use his phaser, and it took him till midafternoon to come up with an alternate weapon. Then he spent several more hours lugging it up to the rooftop of a five-story building.

Finally, everything was ready. The safe which Piker had borrowed from a nearby merchant hung precariously from a rope off the rooftop. Piker scanned the passersby until he spotted Edith Keebler. He waited as she approached his drop site; then he released the rope. The safe plunged toward the sidewalk.

The safe plunged toward the sidewalk.

That evening, as they waited their turn in the cookie line where Edith Keebler was handing out Pitter Patter Peanut Butter Cremes, Smirk muttered to Piker, "She's still here. What happened?"

"I tried dropping a safe on her, but she swerved at the last second and accidentally knocked someone else into the spot I was aiming for," said Piker.

"A safe?" Smirk rolled his eyes. "Was the other person killed?"

Piker nodded. "Instantly."

"It wasn't anybody crucial to World War II, was it? Remember, we have to keep this timeline intact. Everything has to happen the way it was meant to."

"No, nobody special," Piker answered, wishing he'd paid more attention in history class so he'd know for sure whether or not this George S. Patton guy was really important.

The next morning, Piker lurked in the alley waiting for Keebler to pass by on her way to work. He'd hidden a bundle of dynamite under a pile of rags on the sidewalk; its long fuse extended to his hiding place. Any minute now, as Keebler approached, he'd light the fuse.

He spotted Keebler and watched as she crossed in the middle of the street, causing a busload of orphans to swerve out of her way and go into a tailspin. As she headed toward the pile of rags, Piker lit his match.

Smirk glared at Piker over his breakfast tray of Chips Deluxe. "Well?" he demanded, indicating with a jerk of his head that Keebler was still very much among the living.

"How did I know that Salvation Army band was going to get in the way?" Piker protested. "I can't believe she came through it without a scratch. The dynamite even drove a trombone through a mailbox. You should have seen it."

"Never mind," Smirk said. "Just do this and get it over

with, will you? Try to get her on her way home tonight."
That does it, Smirk thought. *Piker has screwed up one
time too many. I'm taking him off my payroll. Wait a
minute, I never put him on my payroll. Well, I'm definitely
keeping him off the payroll, then.*

Piker slumped against a lamppost, watching the door of
the cookie kitchen, wondering how he was going to make
another attempt on Keebler's life when he had neither a
plan nor a weapon. *I don't think I'll try for a job on Captain
Smirk's crew after all,* he thought. *Not only does he constantly demand that I think, I don't even get time-and-a-
half pay for it.*
   He was so preoccupied with his predicament that he
missed seeing Keebler come out the door. By the time he
realized she was leaving, she was halfway down the street,
about to disappear into the crowd.
   Piker strode after her, dodging pedestrians left and right.
"Excuse me, excuse me," he said.
   He had almost caught up, but a mother pushing a baby
buggy still blocked his path. Piker accidentally clipped the
mother, knocking the buggy against Keebler's leg.
   Keebler lost her balance, hovered on the curb for a
moment with arms flailing, then fell into the street directly
in the path of a steamroller. The steamroller lumbered
over Keebler and continued on its way.
   Piker stared in fascination at the mosaic of Keebler's
body; it had retained its shape, if not its thickness, and
now covered about a quarter of the city block. He realized
Capt. Smirk had caught up to them and was also staring
at Keebler's remains.
   "Gee," Piker observed, "she looks a lot like Wile E.
Coyote in the 'Road Runner Road Repairs' cartoon that
was on last Saturday."

The five Pros leapt out of the Guardian of Reruns arch and
stood in the barren field near their Tardy.

The arch spoke. "The timeline has returned to normal. All is as it was before, except for the gray hair of Communications Officer Yoohoo, which could definitely use some Grecian Formula."

At that moment Wart's time bomb exploded, sending pieces of the Tardy flying everywhere. None of the Pros were hurt, but the prospect of being stranded again, and letting the Cons get to Herschel first, left them sitting around in stunned silence.

"You people aren't having the best of luck, are you?" the Guardian observed archly.

8

Rescue Redux

MEANWHILE, BACK ON the *Endocrine,* the Neuts were involved in their latest scientific project: a scavenger hunt.

Dacron had dreamed up the scavenger hunt to relieve the Neuts' boredom. He'd given Zulu permission to disassemble him and hide his body parts throughout the ship. Only Dacron's left hand remained on the Bridge, resting on the arm of the Captain's chair, just in case an emergency came up. The hand could work the Captain's control buttons and even had hearing capabilities, thanks to a microchip in its pinky.

Prowling around the ship on level 64½, Guano spotted a scavenger item half-hidden behind a thermostat. She ran up and grabbed it; it was one of Dacron's ears.

Guano checked the score sheet. "Only ten points!" she complained to herself. "Hardly worth carrying back to the Bridge!" Nevertheless, she stashed the ear in her enormous hat, along with her cosmetics case, credit cards, a picnic lunch, and the unabridged second edition of *Webster's New Twentieth Century Dictionary.*

"Dis is Lt. Checkout to *Endocrine. Endocrine,* do you read me?" Checkout whispered urgently into his communicator insignia.

Despite his high hopes, Checkout hadn't gained any

status by telling his fellow Pros that the Cons were probably stranded, too, since he'd sabotaged their time machine. "Anybody can *wreck* a machine," Yoohoo had responded. "If you're so smart, why can't you fix our machine instead, and get us out of here?" Then they'd all lapsed back into their funk.

So now Checkout was crouched behind some rocks about ten yards away from the others, hoping to summon some help. He had to keep his voice down so Capt. Smirk wouldn't discover him trying to call the ship. Smirk had insisted that somehow they would get themselves out of this fix. Checkout was sure they couldn't; he hoped Dacron would rescue them again with his just-in-time machine.

"*Endocrine,* come in, please," whispered Checkout. He held the communicator to his ear and turned the volume up a notch.

His hopes rose when he heard a signal coming through. But instead of the voice of an *Endocrine* crewmember, he heard music playing. Checkout listened for awhile, then realized it was the theme music from the daytime drama "Daze of Our Lives."

"*Endocrine,* come in, please. Mayday. Mayday," Checkout hissed as loudly as he dared.

The music stopped. Checkout continued, "*Endocrine,* dis is Checkout. Ve are stranded here next to da Guardian of Reruns. Can you get a lock on our position? Can you rescue us?"

A series of taps came through the communicator. Checkout realized he was hearing a message in Morse Code. His translation skills were rusty, but he pulled out a pencil and paper anyway and frantically jotted down his interpretation as the message came through:

'Twas Brillo, and the slimy gloves
Did perspire and gamble in the babe

Reading over what he'd written, Checkout decided to get help. He crept back toward the group and caught Yoohoo's eye. He motioned for her to join him and held a finger to his mouth to indicate she should keep quiet about it. Yoohoo stood up, stretching and yawning elaborately, and pretended she was simply taking a walk as she made her way to Checkout's hiding place.

"What is it?" she asked. He led her out of earshot of the group.

"I've contacted da ship," he told her, "and asked for rescue, but I don't understand deir answer. Tell me vat you tink." He handed her his insignia device.

Instantly recognizing the Morse Code, Yoohoo transformed into her briskly efficient communicator's posture, pressing the receiver to one ear while sticking a finger in her other ear to block out distractions. "Say again, *Endocrine*," Yoohoo requested.

Checkout handed her the pencil and paper, and she translated the code:

> *Message received stop will rescue you as soon as*
> *I get myself together stop love Dacron*

• • •

"Has Zulu found my arms yet, Counselor?" Dacron asked. He stood on the Bridge, reassembled except for his upper limbs.

"Not exactly, Dacron," Troit told him, "but at least we're getting closer. Remember how Zulu thought he'd hidden them in a cupboard? Well, Georgie realized Zulu had accidentally thrown them down a laundry chute. Georgie and Zulu are down in the laundry room now, looking for them."

"Ah," said Dacron. "Then I will begin the rescue attempt armlessly."

"Can't you use your hand?" asked Troit, glancing at Dacron's left hand, which was still lying on the Captain's chair.

"No," said Dacron. "The battery needs recharging. Apparently my hand did a lot of work while I was away. But do not be concerned, Counselor. I can prepare the just-in-time machine without the use of my arms." He entered the machine, which the others had carried onto the Bridge for him, and began pressing its control buttons with his nose.

Meanwhile, at the Bridge's Tactical station, Guano tried to decipher the communication panel so they could contact Capt. Ricardo and the Cons. No messages had come from them in a while, and the Neuts were concerned that they too were stranded again.

"This thing isn't very user-friendly," Guano grumbled, staring at the panel.

"It's probably still in DOS," Troit suggested. "Why don't you call up the Idiotspeak program? Just type in DORK, then press Enter."

Guano did. "Hey, that's better," she said brightly. "The communicator says our signal to the Cons is being blocked, apparently by a large concentration of industrial-sized popcorn machines. But it does give us coordinates so we can find the Cons and pick them up."

Georgie and Zulu emerged from the Crewmover onto the Bridge. "Where's Dacron?" Georgie asked. "We found his arms." Hearing this, Dacron stepped out of the just-in-time machine.

"Hey, Dacron," said Georgie in a tone of forced cheerfulness. "Got the ol' arms for you." He held them out.

Dacron looked a little taken aback. "They seem to be several sizes smaller than when they were removed," Dacron observed.

"Uh, yeah, they might be," admitted Georgie. "They were already in the dryer when we found them, and I guess they've shrunk." He clicked them into Dacron's arm sockets. The wrists dangled at the level of Dacron's ribcage.

"I'm terribly sorry about this, Commander," said Zulu.

"Fortunately, I am not able to bear a grudge," Dacron

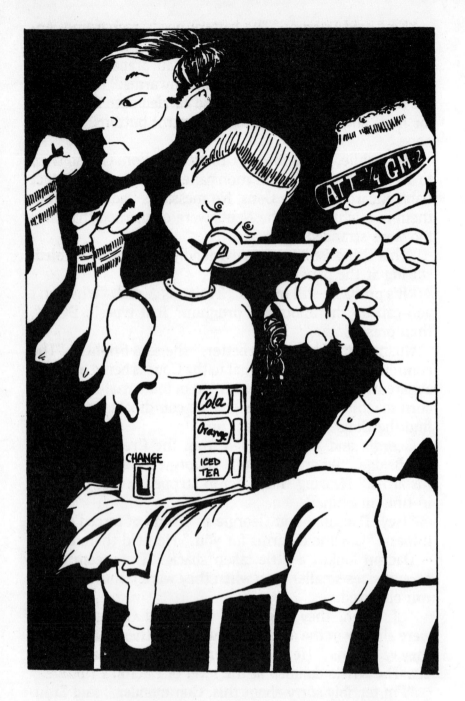

The wrists dangled at the level of Dacron's ribcage.

told him. "However, if and when I ever acquire emotion, I may look back on this incident with a slightly different viewpoint."

Georgie snapped Dacron's hands into place. "Well, we can try stretching your arms," Georgie offered. Dacron agreed to try it, so Zulu and Georgie each took an arm and began to pull.

With all his parts intact and stretched back into shape, Dacron had little trouble piloting his time machine to rescue the Pros and Cons again.

But Dacron's hopes that everyone would finally begin to cooperate in their efforts to reach Herschel were soon dashed. Both captains were as eager as ever to perfect their own time machines and beat the other to the punch.

Dacron reminded them that the entire known universe would be wiped out if somebody didn't reach Herschel soon. But Smirk merely told him that the Pros were bound to hit the mark on their next try, and Ricardo said the same thing about the Cons.

Dacron doubted it. He figured that unless their time machines were adjusted to a goof-proof level, they had little chance of getting to Herschel. Somebody had to do the tune-up, and Dacron decided he was just the android for the job.

To lure the Pros' and Cons' sentries away from their overnight security watch on the time machines, Dacron set off a hull-breach drill.

When the alarm sounded for the drill, the sentries, like everyone else, left their posts to practice the procedure they would follow in the event of an actual hull breach: crouch in the southeast corner of the room beneath heavy furniture and prepare to explode.

While the sentries were gone, Dacron sneaked into the time machines. He found their control panels incredibly primitive. The best he could do was to rig each of them with a guidance device, so that even if they landed at the wrong point again, they'd eventually be drawn to Herschel. It was up to the Pros and Cons not to screw up in any other unforeseen, creative way; Dacron hoped that at least one of the groups could manage that.

Childhood's Dead End

"IT'S A 'SEVEN.' "

"No, it's a 'one.' "

"How can it be a 'one'? Look at that big hook at the top. That makes it a 'seven' for sure."

"No. If it were a 'seven' I would have drawn a line through the lower part, like this." Beverage grabbed the pen from Piker and dashed a stroke through the numeral. "That's the way it's taught in Penmanship."

"Oh, right. Flaunt your postgraduate education at us again," Piker retorted.

"Will you two stop it?" Smirk snarled, and they broke off, pouting. "Who cares what number Beverage wrote down? Obviously, Cmdr. Piker misinterpreted it, for whatever reason, and misdialed again. Now where the heck are we?"

The Tardy had landed inside a room. It looked ordinary, yet there was something forbidding about it. The Pros peered through the Tardy's glass walls, afraid to step out.

"I've seen dis somevhere before," Checkout mused. "In a movie or sometink. Maybe it vas a traininkfilm."

Yoohoo, facing the rear of the booth, gasped, "Look!"

The others turned as quickly as they could, considering that they were jammed into the Tardy like canned sardines. From out of nowhere, the image of a fetus had appeared, hovering in midair beyond the Tardy.

In an instant that image was replaced by one of an old man sitting at a table. He turned toward them, observed them placidly for a moment, then resumed eating his fourteen-inch pizza with cheese and mushrooms which nestled in a paper wrapper that proclaimed it "The BEST Pizza in TOWN!"

"Vy, dat's Dave," Checkout gasped.

"Dave who?" Beverage asked.

"Vatch," Checkout said, pointing at the man. "Next ve'll see him on his deathbed."

"Eeeeuuuww," squealed Yoohoo squeamishly.

Sure enough, the next image showed the old man in bed, with only an intravenous line of Jolt Cola keeping him alive.

"What's going on?" Piker demanded.

"It's some kind of flashback showink his lifetime," Checkout said. "Dat fetus was him, and so vas the man vith the pizza, and dis old man, too."

"Yeah, right," Piker scoffed.

"Why are we being shown his lifetime? We don't even know him," Beverage said.

"But there's somebody we do know." Smirk pointed to the side. "That's Smock's parents."

A new image had appeared, showing Smock's Vulture father assisting his human wife Amandate in the labor room. The Pros realized they were witnessing Smock's birth.

A nurse bundled the newborn Smock in a blanket and handed him to the Vulture. "Congratulations, Ambassador Shark," she said. "You have a son."

Smock's father stared impassively at the newborn, then grunted. "Hmmph," he said. "His features are decidedly human. I do not approve. Please put him back."

The image disappeared as mysteriously as it had come. "Checkout, what is this?" Smirk asked.

"It's difficult to explain, Keptin," Checkout said. "Ve have landed in a room vich displays significant events

"It's some kind of flashback showink his lifetime,"
Checkout said.

Smock's father stared impassively at the newborn.

someone vants us to see. And since it began vay back vith Mr. Smock's birth, I believe ve are in for a massive rerun."

Everybody groaned.

Checkout was right. Outside the Tardy, a series of images unfolded before the Pros' eyes. Each segment showed an important episode in the life of one *Endocrine* crewmember:

A teenaged Capt. Smirk beamed as he passed around an article from his high school paper announcing that his class had voted him "Most Likely to Father an Alien Child."

Dr. McCaw, as a young medical student, moonlighted as a cadaver in Anatomy Lab to help earn his way through medical school.

Checkout, on his sixth try for his pilot's license, backed into the instructor's shuttle while maneuvering out of the shuttlebay.

Yoohoo, at her previous job before joining Smirk's crew, chirped, "Thank you for using AT&T."

Mr. Snot, in one of his pre-*Endocrine* jobs, wore coveralls with "Ajax Heating & Cooling" stitched on the front pocket. Standing in front of a disassembled furnace, he told a distraught homeowner, "I've never seen th' likes of it. It'll have to go into th' shop."

Guano donned her first of many enormous hats, hiding the fact that her brain had quadrupled in size since she'd taken the Evelyn Woodpecker speed-reading course.

Capt. Ricardo was elected the first president of a newly-formed union that would later become Starfreak: the Hairline Pilots' Association.

Piker, as an infant, was accidentally dropped on his head from atop a 50-foot Alaskan glacier.

Deanna Troit, on her second birthday, opened her gifts: a doll, a harmonica, and a training bra.

Dacron was undergoing assembly by Dr. Nubian Spittoon. Nearby in the laboratory stood some earlier android prototypes: Dacron's brother Lycra and his sisters Polly Esther, Silke, and Lynnen.

Guano donned her first of many enormous hats.

Wart retrofitted a toy rifle into a working weapon and stormed the principal's office to dramatize the demand of his kindergarten class for chocolate milk at snack time.

Georgie created his visor in a high school shop class by welding a muffler grill onto his girlfriend's hairband.

Beverage, planning her wedding to Jock Crusher, registered her Tupperware pattern at Sears.

The series of images ended. "Now what?" Smirk asked.

"If it goes like I tink it vill," said Checkout, "ve'll now see lots of colors and veird psychedelic effects. Ve'll also be squished into two dimensions."

"Will it hurt?" whimpered Yoohoo.

"Only if you're overveight," Checkout said. Yoohoo began to wail.

Piker checked the Tardy's readout. "Captain, we're sliding forward in time toward our target date. Somehow it's become locked into the Tardy's automatic time-finder. We could be the ones to reach Herschel after all."

"But first we've got to survive this two-dimensional business," Smirk said as the Tardy began slipping toward a kaleidoscopic horizon. "Hang on, everybody!"

10

That Was Then...
This Is Nuts

"**I** DON'T UNDERSTAND what's so hard about controlling something as elementary as this time machine!" Capt. Ricardo raged.

"I know ye don't understand, mon! That's why I have t' do th' dirrrty work for ye!" Snot yelled back.

The two of them stood arguing nose-to-nose outside Snot's funhouse. On their third try, the Cons had landed on the Bridge of the *Endocrine*—20 years in the future.

"Gentlemen," Smock interrupted, "rather than arguing over who is to blame for this miscalculation, it would be more productive to explore our surroundings. This is a priceless opportunity to glimpse the near future—"

"Make it so, then, Mr. Smock," Ricardo snapped.

"Sir?" responded Smock.

"Do it," Ricardo explained. "Check out the ship. Give me a full report on what everybody's up to." They hadn't yet glimpsed the crew of 20 years hence; the future-Bridge was deserted, and the ship was on Autopilot.

"Yes, Captain," Smock replied.

Smock's explorations were cut short less than an hour later when Ricardo summoned him over the intercom: "Mr. Smock, report to the time machine immediately."

When Smock arrived, the funhouse was humming

loudly, and the other Cons had already boarded it. Smock joined them in the control room.

"What is happening, Captain?" Smock asked.

"We're not sure," Ricardo answered, "but somehow the time machine started itself. Snot found there's some sort of automatic guidance mechanism at work, and it's set for the target date we've been trying to reach. I believe we'll make it this time."

A moment later the funhouse took off. The Cons watched the monitor as a swirl of events passed before them, interspersed with occasional flying houses, tumbleweeds, and the Wicked Witch of the West.

Snot calculated that the journey would take at least an hour, so they sat on the floor and tried to get comfortable.

"Well, Mr. Smock, this would be a good time to hear what you observed on board the ship 20 years from now," Ricardo said.

"I did manage to find a few crewmembers," Smock reported. "Cmdr. Piker, for instance. He is still receiving a constant stream of job offers for the captaincy of other ships."

"Job offers?" Ricardo echoed. "Why would they want him? How would they hear of him in the first place?"

"I have no idea, Captain," Smock said blandly. "At any rate, he sat at a desk reviewing a tall stack of letters— invitations to assume command of various other Starfreak vessels. He was marking the letters with a rubber stamp that read 'Position Refused / Thanks for Your Interest / Wilson Piker.'

"I also talked to Lt. Cmdr. Dacron. He told me that within the past 20 years he had experienced every possible emotion, but no one was willing to acknowledge it. Also, his body had been inhabited by numerous life forms, such as a grandfatherly scientist, several species of alien beings, and the Avon Lady.

"I caught a glimpse of Guano. She finally got her eyebrow transplant. Unfortunately, the blond shade she chose looks rather artificial.

"The HolidayDeck had expanded to 50 units operating 24 hours a day. They were being administered by a HolidayDeck afficionado named Lt. Retch Barcode.

"There was also an extremely arrogant alien known as Q-Tip."

Ricardo looked surprised. "Q-Tip was on board?"

"He was just visiting," Smock said. "He's now retired, living at the James T. Smirk Home for Incurable Hams. He dared me to justify the existence of the human race. When that taunt failed to arouse me, he challenged my intellect with a series of trivia questions, such as 'What are the names of the seven dwarfs?' "

"Q-Tip," Ricardo mused. "You know, I almost miss him."

"He mentioned you," Smock said. "His exact words were: 'Ask the inimitable captain that if humanity is so advanced, how come his crew still wears uniforms, as if they were all working at McDonald's?' "

"On second thought, I don't really miss him that much," Ricardo added.

"Captain," Snot broke in, pointing to the time indicator, "we're still on target for the moment Herschel finds the videotape. There's no doubt o' it—we'll be the first ones to arrive after all."

None of the Cons could actually bring himself to smile at this good news, but they all looked decidedly less crabby.

Back on the *Endocrine*, Dacron rechecked his console a final time. The readout confirmed his fear: they were in big trouble.

"Attention, fellow crewmembers," said Dacron, paging the Neuts via the intercom. "An extremely urgent situation has developed. I regret to inform you that we must all gather on the Bridge and actually do some work."

After the other Neuts assembled, lounging on the carpet

in the forward section of the Bridge, Dacron set up a podium in front of them and began reading from a sheaf of notes. "Welcome to my 'State of the *Endocrine*' address," he began. "These are historic times for our crew."

Georgie jabbed Zulu with his elbow and whispered, "I think Dacron is letting this temporary-command thing go to his head." Meanwhile, Guano, sensing a long speech in the making, yawned widely while making an elaborate show of consulting her wristwatch.

Dacron continued, "The actions we take in the next few hours could determine whether we live to explore new galaxies or disappear into obscurity like the Samkonian fruit fly with its lifespan of approximately 10.8 nano-seconds.

"Before the Pros and Cons began their latest journey, I installed guidance devices on their time machines. While tracking their progress, I have concluded that the devices are operating perfectly. Too perfectly, in fact. Please, hold your applause." Dacron looked up from his notes; then, since there was no applause, he went on.

"By landing on their target moment in Herschel's home at precisely the same instant, the Pros and Cons will open a time rift, throwing them years further into the future. Such an event will irreversibly alter the space/time continuum. We will be unable to retrieve them, even with my just-in-time machine. In effect, they will have vanished forever."

Dacron paused for a sip from the water glass on his podium, and Guano broke in. "Are you finished? Can we go back to the HolidayDeck now?"

Dacron shook his head. "I need you to take up positions here on the Bridge. We will contact each of the groups and try to persuade them to alter their course slightly, thus preventing this time rift."

Zulu went to the Tactical station's communication console. Dacron and Deanna sat in their command chairs, Georgie took the pilot's seat, and Guano pulled a mixer out of her hat and began to whip up a batch of chocolate milkshakes.

"Mr. Zulu, hail the Pros," Dacron ordered.

" 'Hey, you' frequency open," Zulu responded, "but we've only got an audio signal from them, Commander."

"Attention, Pros. This is Lt. Cmdr. Dacron. Do you read me?"

Capt. Smirk's voice sounded strained. "What is it, Dacron?"

"You are headed for the precise instant when Herschel finds the videotape," Dacron said. "The Cons are about to arrive there also. There is a guidance device in your control mechanism. You must adjust it to offset your arrival by a few seconds, thus preventing a time rift that will throw you ten years into the future and alter the space/time continuum irreversibly."

"I'd like to oblige," came Smirk's reply, "but we're two-dimensional right now, so it would be a little tricky to move the controls. At the moment, my entire body is one molecule thick, and I'm sort of plastered to my chair."

"Oh," said Dacron.

"But thanks for the information," Smirk concluded flatly. "Smirk out."

"Mr. Zulu, hail the Cons," Dacron ordered.

"Cons' time machine answering our hail," reported Zulu. The image of the Cons' control room appeared on the Viewscreen of the Bridge.

"What is it, Dacron?" said Capt. Ricardo from the View-screen.

"Sir, your Cons and Captain Smirk's Pros are about to arrive at Herschel's home at the same instant," said Dacron. "This will create a dangerous rift that could leave both of your groups stranded in the future. The Pros are unable to control their course. I suggest that you offset your arrival by several seconds, thus preventing a collision."

"What? And let them beat us to the punch? Balderdash!" Ricardo answered.

"You could arrive *before* them, sir," Dacron suggested.

Ricardo conferred briefly with Smock and Snot, then shook his head. "That is unacceptable," he said. "We'd risk being sucked into the previous time rift that occurred when Cmdr. Piker's videotape arrived at Herschel's home. No, Lieutenant, we'll take our chances on this course." The Cons closed their "hey, you" frequency.

"Well, so much for team spirit," Zulu remarked. He checked his console, then announced, "The collision of the Pros and Cons will occur in ten minutes."

"I believe we should set our course to arrive then also," Dacron stated. "We can accompany them through the time rift to the distant future. It should be an educational experience." The others gave their approval, so Dacron connected the ship's navigation console to the control panel of his just-in-time machine with a three-pronged extension cord.

"Dacron, what are our chances of surviving this rift?" Georgie asked.

"Precisely one in 1,000,000,000," Dacron replied as he set the last of the time controls.

"What?!" screamed Guano. "You want to risk our necks just so you can expand your horizons? Forget it!" She shook her head defiantly, causing the milkshake mixer to teeter dangerously close to the edge of her hat.

"I am afraid it is too late," Dacron replied. "The navigational sequence cannot be discontinued once underway."

Disgusted, Zulu banged his fist on the Tactical station. "Of all the...the..." he sputtered, "...putting us in danger just to satisfy your scientific curiosity..."

"Besides," Dacron continued calmly, "I will offset our arrival by a fraction of a second, and we can pause just long enough to alter Herschel's pivotal moment in the space/time continuum. This will halt a black-hole effect that I have detected at those coordinates, which would otherwise obliterate the universe. The Pros and Cons will remain there too briefly to take this action, so we must.

It is, in fact, our only chance for survival."

"Oh," said Guano and Zulu, their frenzy dribbling away like air escaping from a faulty party balloon. Frowning, Guano asked, "Why didn't you tell us that in the first place?"

"I wanted to trigger your typical human overreaction," Dacron replied. "I find it intriguing."

"So we've got one chance in a billion of surviving this experience?" Georgie asked. Dacron nodded. Georgie whistled softly and remarked, "Guess we'd better prepare to meet our Maker."

Dacron looked puzzled. "My maker, Dr. Nubian Spittoon, is too far away for me to meet him in the next ten minutes. His laboratory on the planet Omicrowave Theta is—"

"It's a figure of speech, Dacron," Georgie interrupted. "It means we'd better get our affairs in order and say our prayers."

Dacron gazed at him curiously. "I have never heard you speak of religion before, Georgie."

"Oh, I do," Georgie revealed, "every time somebody tells us we've got less than ten minutes to live. It's just that I'm usually down in Engineering, so you don't hear it."

Zulu chuckled. "Sounds like the old saying is true: 'There are no atheists in black holes.'"

"If you'll excuse me from this philosophical discussion," Troit broke in, "I'm going to spend my last moments of life enjoying a hot fudge sundae." She headed for the Crewmover.

"I'm with you, girl," Guano declared as she followed Troit. "Let's crank up the sound system in Ten-Foreplay and go out with a bang." She glanced back at the others. "You guys want to join us?"

"No, thank you," Zulu replied. "I believe I'll go to my room and spend the next few minutes meditating, after which I will begin to scream hysterically."

"I'm staying at my post," said Georgie from the pilot's

station. He stood up and began to sing: "Rock of ages, cleft for me . . . "

Dacron said, "I will stay here on the Bridge also and explore a final possibility for increasing our odds of survival." As Guano, Troit and Zulu left the Bridge, Dacron rummaged around inside the storage compartment of his console, looking for his statue of St. Jude.

When the countdown indicated that there was less than a minute to go, the computer summoned all the Neuts back to the Bridge. When they'd all gathered there, the computer explained: "Starfreak special-effect regulations require a minimum of five crewmembers on the Bridge who, at the moment of collision, must simulate a jolt in roughly the same direction."

Guano suddenly went berserk. "I can't stand it!" she yelled. "We're about to die, and that computer is so . . . so . . . calm! Just like you," she cried, flailing at Dacron with her fists, "you . . . robot!"

Dacron held up his arms to ward off her punches. "If it would make you feel better," he said, "we can program the computer's voice to simulate panic."

Guano stopped swinging at him. "Yes," she said, panting. "Yes, it would make me feel better."

"Computer," said Dacron, "provide audio countdown to collision using '1117–17A Screaming Meemie' voice format."

"Thirty seconds to impact," responded the computer in an unusually shrill tone. "Oh no. Oh no. This is it. We're never gonna make it."

"That's better," said Guano, taking a seat in one of the command chairs. "At least somebody here sounds more worried than me. It helps me feel calm by comparison."

"Twenty seconds to impact," the computer wailed.

Guano relaxed in her chair. "Hey, computer, take it easy," she said. "It's not the end of the world."

"It is! It is! Fifteen seconds to impact," the computer shrieked.

"Boy, some people really get worked up over little things," Guano remarked jauntily.

"Hail Mary, full of grace..." the computer gasped. "...Five seconds to impact."

Guano yawned. "I think I'll take a nap. Wake me when we're through the rift, OK?"

"Three seconds to impact..." the computer screamed. "Oh no...oh nooooo...two...oh nooooooo...one... IMPACT!"

11

On with
the Show

THE TIME-TRAVELING Pros and Cons arrived at Herschel's living room at the same instant. Herschel stared at them, pushing absentmindedly at the masking-taped bridge of the nose of his glasses.

Then the fabric of time ripped open, and they were gone again, plunging through the rift they'd created.

A half-second later, the Neuts arrived at the same spot. They paused only long enough for their predetermined action to alter the timeline: swooping up the Doritos from Herschel's snack table.

The computer readout indicated that this interference had indeed halted the black-hole effect, so the Neuts left at once, following the others into the future via the time rift.

Up ahead, a few of the Pros and Cons with their wits about them realized that neither group had accomplished its objective; Herschel still held Piker's videotape in his hand as they left.

But there was no time to ponder the implications of that. All they could do was hang on for their lives as they hurtled through the time rift. It felt like sitting inside a VCR that was being fast-forwarded. The Neuts followed, sucked along in their wake, drawing closer and closer until all three groups traveled as one.

The time-traveling Pros, Cons and Neuts arrived at
Herschel's living room at the same instant.

Crash! The three vehicles landed hard, then began to vibrate violently.

"Get out!" yelled Smirk, pushing the Pros out of the Tardy. Ricardo evacuated his team from the funhouse. Likewise, inside the *Endocrine*, Dacron herded the Neuts toward the nosecone of the Bridge; they jumped out the exit and slid down the inflated emergency slide.

Everyone gathered nearby and turned back to stare at their travel crafts, which were vibrating faster and faster; the edges moved so fast that they blurred, then began wearing away. Soon their outlines disappeared. Then the middles wore away, until finally all three vehicles simply vanished.

The crewmembers became aware that they were not alone; a tremendous crowd of people surrounded them. Recovering from their shock, the crew looked around at where they'd landed.

It was a huge convention hall in a modern hotel. A banner off to the side read, "Welcome, Wrekkies."

The thought struck all of them, even Piker, at the same instant: they had been thrown ten years into the future, right into the middle of the wrekkie convention they'd seen on the Preview.

The effect was electrifying. The Pros began to cheer, jumping up and down and slapping each other on the back. And the Cons had a collective panic attack; some screamed and ran for cover, while others froze in terror. Only the Neuts remained neutral, reserving their judgment until they could experience the convention for themselves.

The crowd drew closer, curious about the newcomers who'd just arrived amidst the best special effects ever seen at a Getalife convention. One fan asked another, "Are these the 'surprise guest stars' we read about in the convention flyer?"

Dacron approached a pair of fans. "Excuse me," he asked, "but could you tell me today's Stardate?" He already suspected what it was, but he needed to know the precise moment so he could reset his internal clock.

"Yeah," said one. "It's Stardate 4149361212, and the time is 2:15 P.M."

"Thank you," Dacron responded.

The other fan touched the sleeve of Dacron's uniform. "Hey, great costume, dude," he raved. Then he leaned closer and added in a kindly tone, "But I think your artificial nose is a little too long."

Talking to the newcomers, the fans started to catch on that these were members of the actual *Endocrine* crew. The fans began clustering around their particular idols as the crew dispersed into the gathering.

2:17 P.M.

Piker paraded around the convention hall. He waved regally at the masses milling around him and entertained wonderful thoughts about being named Pope Piker I. Passing Smirk's autograph table, Piker gave Smirk a thumbs-up sign.

Smirk waved back, then returned to his autograph routine. With his felt-tip pen poised over a glossy 8 × 10, he smiled at the statuesque blonde standing in front of the table and said, "Hi, what's your name?"

"Charmaine," she purred, leaning forward until her curls brushed Smirk's forehead. She dropped her hotel room key into the box Smirk had set on the table; it clinked down among the several dozen keys that other classy dames had already left there.

The line of people waiting to reach Smirk's table snaked back through the expo area. His booth was like a magnet for every female at the wrekkie convention.

Even many women who were visiting the city for another, unrelated convention somehow heard that Smirk was here, and they'd joined the lineup to meet their heartthrob. Their severe dress-for-success outfits stood out in the crowd; it wasn't every day that the Sisters of Sorrowful Obstinacy left the convent.

His booth was like a magnet for every female at the
wrekkie convention.

Near the end of Smirk's line, in another corner of the expo, Wart shouted at one of the vendors.

"How dare you sell these sacred Kringle relics!" he raged, pointing to a Kringle Electric Cattle Prod & Toddler Discipline Stick that retailed for $15.99.

"Hey, buddy, take it easy," the vendor whined. "Gads, some of you people really get *into* this stuff. These ain't actually the real thing, you know. I manufacture 'em in my garage."

"*That* is even *worse!*" Wart roared, lifting the edge of the table to overturn the vendor's wares.

Two burly security guards approached the booth. "We got a problem here?" one of them asked. They grabbed Wart's elbows to escort him out, but he flung them both aside like rags. Then, with a Kringle battle cry, Wart began smashing the booth with his fists.

A few moments later, more security personnel arrived. It took a half-dozen guards to restrain Wart. "Let's take him to the Green Room to cool off," one of them said as they carried Wart away. "Nobody's using it right now. The show doesn't start until 3 o'clock."

2:24 P.M.

Dr. McCaw panted, staring at the door of the janitor's closet in which he'd locked himself. As fans pushed from the outside, the door seemed about to give way.

With a final shove, they broke through. McCaw held them at bay with a scalpel. "Stay back," he warned, "or you're all in for some nonelective surgery!" They warily gave him a wide berth as he advanced through their midst.

When McCaw reached the edge of the crowd, he started running. The fans followed, but he eluded them in the narrow, winding service corridors of the hotel. A little farther on, he discovered the Green Room. With all those security guards standing around to keep an eye on Wart, the Green Room looked like a safe hideout, so McCaw sat down among them.

Meanwhile, Capt. Ricardo made his way unnoticed through the vendors' expo, disguised in a rubber Ferengi face mask which he'd bought for the manufacturer's close-out price of just $2.29.

Unfortunately, the mask didn't cover the back of his head, and a fan recognized his bald pate as he passed by. "Capt. Ricardo!" she trilled, pointing at him. Someone else squealed in delight. A small crowd gathered.

Ricardo, desperate to avoid their attention, bolted out of the expo hall. Searching for a secluded area, he too found his way to the Green Room.

2:33 P.M.

Despite Checkout's high hopes for popularity among the wrekkies, he soon realized that the line of people waiting at his autograph table was far shorter than any of the other Pros' autograph lines. He even overheard one fan tell another, "Well, it was either this or stay in the main auditorium watching that blooper tape, and I've already seen it six times."

Checkout burned with envy when he noticed that Zulu had to call on his old karate skills to fight off admirers.

Nearby, Troit felt another dizzy spell coming on. She hid behind a portable coat rack filled with discount Starfreak uniforms.

The convention experience had turned out to be a staggering assault on Troit's Betavoid telepathy. She couldn't help sensing that each fan harbored not only their own personality but also the alter-ego of at least one member of the *Endocrine* crew, and some fans identified with several crewmembers. It was standing-room-only among the personas, and Troit felt suffocated.

2:40 P.M.

Walking through the expo, co-engineer Snot spotted a tableful of Starfreak technical manuals that claimed to explain "everything there is to know about ship's propulsion." He freaked out. Paramedics were summoned. They carried him to the Green Room.

Georgie was able to walk through the crowd unrecognized, since he appeared to be just one of many fans wearing the plastic visor costume accessory that could be purchased throughout the expo. He got in line to tour a working model of the *Endocrine* that a local wrekkie chapter had constructed.

Georgie was amazed as he walked through the full-size replica; it was perfect to the last detail. Wandering around the reconstructed Bridge, he lifted the lid of Dacron's console and saw that the builders had even remembered to stash inside it a copy of *Soap Opera Digest*.

The tour ended in the Engine Room, and Georgie's astonishment increased; studying the dilithium Crystal Vanish chamber, he realized that this ship would actually work. It could really be used for space travel, as soon as they removed the velvet ropes preventing anyone from touching the control panel.

As he left the replica ship, Georgie noticed Beverage Flusher sitting at an autograph table. "How's it going, Doctor?" Georgie asked.

"Terrible," she snarled. "Most of the people stop here only to ask me where Counselor Troit is signing autographs."

A man in a business suit approached them and said, "Excuse me, but you're both from the *Endocrine*, aren't you?" They nodded. The man continued, "I'm a promoter from Getalife Conventions. Would you come with me, please?"

2:52 P.M.

In one corner of the Green Room, Yoohoo started warming up for her daily practice by singing scales. In the opposite corner, Guano got down on her knees in front of the security guard who'd brought her there. "Please!" she implored. "Earplugs ... wads of cotton ... even an old

Georgie was able to walk through the crowd unrecognized.

Kleenex—I'll take whatever you've got! Just let me plug my ears!"

The door opened, and the promoter who'd approached Georgie and Beverage led them and several others into the room. "Well, how do you like our convention so far?" the promoter asked, beaming.

"Sir," said Mr. Smock, "this is the most bizarre outbreak of human emotion I have ever seen."

"It's great, isn't it?" the promoter responded, slapping Smock on the back. "People can't believe their luck— seeing you all here in person! I just wish you would have told me you were coming so we could have advertised it. We probably could have charged a higher admission fee, too."

2:57 P.M.

"Captain, do you realize that all of our crewmembers have assembled in this room?" Dacron said.

"I know," Ricardo muttered. "Something odd is going on." He scanned the Green Room nervously.

The door opened, and someone called in to them: "Three minutes to curtain!"

On their way into the Green Room, some of the crew had glimpsed the huge crowd that filled the main auditorium to capacity. Now it dawned on them that they were going to be escorted onstage in front of this crowd.

Pandemonium broke out among the Cons. Ricardo wrung his worry beads so hard that the chain broke apart. Smock's startled expression lifted his Vulture eyebrow so high that it disappeared into his bangs. McCaw and Snot scrambled to hide behind Wart, who brushed them aside like sand fleas. Then all five of them made a panic-stricken dash for the door, but even Wart couldn't break through the dozen bouncers who blocked their way.

In her corner, Guano rhythmically thumped her head against the wall, wailing, "I'm not gonna share the stage with a singing Yoohoo! No! Nooooo!"

3 P.M.

The entire crew stood onstage behind the curtain, waiting for the big moment. The promoters told them that they'd be introduced to the crowd, after which they'd take part in a brief ceremony.

Some crewmembers tingled in anticipation of their moment in the spotlight. Others wondered whether they would survive the ordeal; only the thought of the bouncers lurking offstage kept them from making a run for it.

The chief promoter was onstage now, standing in front of the curtain. They heard him greet the audience: "Hey, everybody, what time is it?"

"It's Starfreak time!" they responded in unison.

"Have we got a show for you today!" the promoter continued. "This is a Getalife exclusive! For the first time ever, live and together onstage, ladies and gentlemen, welcome the crew of the USS *Endocrine!*"

The curtain rose. The audience roared, and all the crewmembers, even the Cons, gasped in amazement. It was an incredible feeling—this outpouring of affection from total strangers, people who'd previously known them only through the magic of videotape.

As the five-minute standing ovation finally started to die down, a woman called out from the balcony, "Can we come onstage and give you a hug?!"

Smirk stepped forward. "Sure!" he agreed. The crowd went wild, and only a phalanx of security guards at the front prevented fans from storming the stage.

After another long wait for the crowd to quiet, the promoter and another man came onstage and approached the two captains in the center of the group. The promoter announced, "And now I'd like to introduce Wade Beamer, president of 'Starfreaks and Proud of It,' the fan club here in Maplewood that's given us so much wonderful volunteer help at this convention. Wade will make a presentation to the crew." He handed the microphone to Wade.

Wade looked a little nervous. The microphone slipped out of his sweaty palm and clunked onto the floor. As he picked up the mike, he swayed a little, his knees knocking together. "O-n," he began, his voice cracking; he cleared his throat and tried again. "On behalf of 'Starfreaks and Proud of It,' and wrekkies everywhere," he quavered, "to thank you for making this historic appearance today, it is my honor to present you with the keys to our working model of the USS *Endocrine*." He saluted the crew, adding, "Live long and profit!" The audience cheered.

Ricardo and Smirk both reached toward Wade's outstretched hand and grabbed the keys. The captains did a little tug of war with the key ring for a moment; then, realizing they ought to look gracious while onstage, together they held the keys aloft. The convention hall vibrated with the crowd's ovation.

3:30 P.M.

Zulu, sitting in the pilot's seat of the *Endocrine* replica, turned the key. The engine purred to life. The other crewmembers at their Bridge stations sighed with relief.

"All systems go?" Smirk inquired. "Fuel?"

"Check," Dacron replied.

"Flaps down?"

"Check."

"Windshield cleaned?"

"Check."

Smirk nodded his go-ahead, and Ricardo ordered, "Engage."

Zulu touched the control panel, and the ship rose straight up and blasted through the ceiling of the convention hall.

A few crewmembers looked down wistfully at the convention they were leaving behind. As the ship rose higher, the conventiongoers looked like so many ants, including the chief promoter ant, who was shaking his head in dismay over the damage to the convention hall's roof.

After the ship cleared the building, Zulu switched to horizontal propulsion and kicked the engines up to Warped 23 in the Super Reverse mode. Bypassing numerous years, planets and commercials, the crew returned almost instantaneously to Ricardo's ship at the space/time coordinates where they'd started—way back to the moment when Smirk first thought of time travel as a strategy for getting his crew their own ship.

Smirk's team stayed on the wrekkies' working replica of the ship, while Ricardo's crew transferred back to their original craft. Everyone was happy with this arrangement, and they agreed that the timeline had turned out all right after all.

"But since we're back where we started, we've got to be careful to avoid getting sucked into the same sequence of events again," Ricardo warned. He and Smirk put their heads together to figure out how to keep from getting trapped in a never-ending time loop.

In the end, they realized that just one alteration was necessary. As they relived the day it all began, Ricardo simply refrained from asking Piker to set the clocks for Daylight Saving Time, thus preventing him from losing Westerly's tape in the abyss once again.

And to make doubly sure that the timeline wouldn't repeat itself, both captains made minor changes in their routines as they relived that fateful day.

This time, as Smirk started his memoirs, he wrote a different lead: *These are the times that fry men's souls.* And during lunch in Ten-Foreplay that same day, Ricardo ordered his standard meal of Earl Grape tea and buttered crumpets rather than venturing into sole food.

Within a few days, the corrected timeline asserted itself. Within a week, their bizarre time journey seemed like a fast-fading dream. And within a month, they'd all forgotten about the events that took place during the time warp— even Dacron, who erased the memory from his hard drive just to be one of the gang.

* .* *

And so, happily restored to separate ships once again, the crews of Smirk and Ricardo blasted off into the sunset with a triumphant cry:

"Thanks be to God!"

STAR WRECK IV
LIVE LONG AND PROFIT

In the back room, Mr. Smock stepped into the walk-in cooler and powered up his shortwave radio.

Pondering what source to consult, Smock considered the fact that the Fountain of Youth's location was a deep dark secret. Not even his scientist pals, with whom he freely traded information, would know where it was.

He would have to consult the ultimate source of knowledge, the font of all wisdom, the keepers of even the most obscure yet vital facts in the universe. He dialed the frequency of the Milwaukee Public Library Ready Reference service and crossed his fingers. . . .

1

The Return of the
Pink Slip

"**D**ARLING, WAKE UP. Jim, dear, it's morning." The voice of Counselor Deanna "Dee" Troit floated through Capt. James T. Smirk's sleeping quarters aboard his ship, the USS *Endocrine*.

Smirk turned over in bed, pulling the silk sheets over his head. Troit's voice continued to coax him gently. "The universe needs you. There are worlds to be explored and battles to be fought. Time to get up and buckle your swash."

Smirk rubbed his hands over his eyes. "Coming, darling," he mumbled. He sat up and pressed the "off" button of his alarm clock, silencing the recording of Troit's voice. *Too bad it's just an electronic reconstruction,* he thought. *But someday soon, she'll be my bride, and it'll be her voice waking me up in person. I hope.*

At the moment, however, Deanna wasn't even aboard his ship. She was in her usual spot on Capt. Jean-Lucy Ricardo's vessel—the other USS *Endocrine*—parked next to Smirk's ship in orbit of Starbase Flamingo.

Smirk was grateful that he no longer had to share a ship with Capt. Ricardo. Smirk and his crew now had the luxury of their own vessel, a working model of the *Endocrine* which their wrekkie fans had given them at the conclusion of their previous mission. Yet without Deanna around,

Smirk had found that this was a hollow triumph.

Smirk swung his feet over the side of the waterbed, then groaned, remembering what was on today's agenda: they had to UltraFax over to Starbase Flamingo for a meeting with Ricardo's crew and Admiral Nonsequitur. *Ecch,* Smirk thought. *I could be out in space obliterating an alien race or showing off my macho profile after a fistfight. Instead, we have to sit around jabbering at each other in a dull, dry, boring meeting.*

As Capt. Jean-Lucy Ricardo awoke in his quarters aboard the neighboring ship, he lay in bed for a few extra moments, savoring the thought of what was in store for them today: a meeting.

There would be discussions ... voting ... consideration of every angle ... endless rehashes. It would be splendid.

Admiral Nonsequitur hadn't given them a detailed agenda as Ricardo had hoped. In fact, he'd refused to tell them what the meeting was about. But even without any anticipatory paperwork to savor, Ricardo was excited.

Ricardo headed to his bathroom, opened the medicine cabinet and scanned his large collection of skull waxes. Since today would be such a special day, he decided to use the Number 2 wax for the extra shine he'd need to stand out during the meeting.

Later that morning, after both crews had finished their water aerobics classes and eaten breakfast, they UltraFaxed over to Starbase Flamingo.

Capt. Smirk perked up when he caught sight of Deanna Troit in the hallway to the meeting room. He pushed his way toward her as the crowd of crewmembers funneled through the doorway. Deftly Smirk slipped his arm around Troit's shoulders. "Lovely morning, Counselor," he purred.

Troit glared at him. Smirk contorted his face into an

expression of bruised bewilderment. "Was it something I said?" he pouted.

"Take your arm off me, Captain," Troit said evenly.

"Unnhh—shot down again. You've pierced me to the core." Smirk clutched his heart as if in pain. Then, lowering his voice so no one else would hear, he added, "I *have* been having some stabbing pains in my back lately, Deanna. You aren't still sticking pins into that voodoo doll with my picture on it, are you?"

Troit sighed. "No. I told you, I've gotten over that."

They halted in the doorway as the others filed past them into the meeting room. Smirk felt encouraged. At least Deanna hadn't yet taken his breath away with an elbow jab in the ribs like the last time he'd tried to put the moves on her. Eagerly, Smirk studied her face; it looked like she had more to say to him.

For once, he'd read her correctly. With an air of resignation, Troit said, "Captain, we need to talk."

After the last of the other crewmembers had shuffled into the meeting room, Troit and Smirk remained in the hallway. Troit shut the meeting room door so they could speak in private.

"Talk away, my sweet," Smirk crooned. "Your voice is music to my ears."

"Oh, really?" Her tone hovered around 0 degrees Centigrade. "Too bad that wasn't the case when we were engaged to be married. Or better yet, when you broke off our engagement."

"That was a dreadful mistake," Smirk admitted. "Simply a case of cold feet, my dear. But now I've seen the error of my ways. You're the only woman in the galaxy for me. I must have you."

Troit shook her head sadly. "I'm sorry, Jim, but I've thought about it a lot. It's not a simple matter of making up with each other. I've decided you're just not my type."

"Not your type?" Smirk echoed. He held out his palms

beseechingly as if posing for her inspection. "What's not to like?"

Troit groped for words. "You're just too . . . too . . . I don't know . . . arrogant, I guess. Like when you assume that just because you want me, I'm going to want you, too. Or like when you're conducting a mission—you never consult your crew like Captain Ricardo does. You just order everybody around because you think you know their jobs better than they do."

"Well, I do," Smirk retorted. "I'm always right, and in the end we always come out on top. What's wrong with that?"

Troit shrugged. "Sometimes it's more interesting to root for the underdog," she replied. "You can't tell someone's character until they've really been tested."

"But I am being tested, my darling," Smirk said. "I have to prove myself worthy of your love. I've dedicated my life to that goal. Isn't that proof enough of my character?"

"No. Don't you see?" She began to slip into her counselor mode, her voice dripping with Profound Understanding. "You only want me because you can't have me. There are millions of women out there in the galaxy, but you focus on me simply because I'm unattainable."

Smirk felt a twinge of alarm. This wasn't going the way he'd planned. It was time to slather on an extra-thick layer of that old James T. Smirk charm.

"Can you blame me?" he whispered, putting on his best hurt-puppy expression. "Everyone else pales beside you. I am nothing without you, Deanna. I've given up all my hobbies to focus on our courtship. I hardly even watch TV anymore."

Smirk leaned closer, half-closing his eyelids as if overcome with longing. "Please come back to me. Please. Pleeeeeease." He closed his eyes completely and puckered his lips, tilting his head toward hers.

She regarded him with pity. "Get a life," she replied.

She doesn't mean it, Smirk told himself. *She's just*

"I've given up all my hobbies to focus on our courtship."

struggling to overcome her common sense. Any second now, she'll succumb. He leaned forward with his eyes still closed and his lips still puckered, unaware that Troit had left the hallway and gone into the meeting room without him.

Stay puckered, Smirk told himself. *Be ready.* His lips were starting to ache. *Gee, she's really taking a long time to come around.*

"Captain?" This came in a deep baritone. *Hmmmm,* Smirk thought, *either Deanna's voice has changed, or someone else is here in the hallway with us.* With lips outstretched, Smirk raised his eyelids slowly.

His right-hand man, Mr. Smock, stood there. Deanna was nowhere in sight. Mr. Smock gave an embarrassed little cough and continued, "Sir, the admiral has requested that you join us so we can begin the meeting."

Smirk retracted his lips. "The meeting. Ah, yes, the meeting." He straightened his tunic and headed toward the entrance. "Well, I guess these lip-toning exercises can wait. Have you ever tried them, Smock? They're much more practical than water aerobics when it comes to real-life applications."

They entered the meeting room, and Smirk sat down in the chair Smock had saved for him. Unfortunately, Smirk observed, it was nowhere near Deanna Troit; she was sitting halfway across the semicircle of chairs that faced the podium.

Smirk caught Troit's eye and silently mouthed "I love you" with exaggerated expressiveness. She frowned at him, then tossed back her hair and stared at the front of the room.

Admiral Nonsequitur stood at the podium, glaring at Smirk. "Glad you could join us, Captain," he began sarcastically. "The early bird makes the worm turn, eh?" Smirk gave him a conciliatory smile.

"But enough of this endless discussion," Nonsequitur went on. "Let's get down to brass taxes. Here's the bottom line: Financially, Starfreak is barely squeaking by.

"Naturally, we've tried all the standard remedies," Nonsequitur said, "like increasing the salaries of our board of directors, awarding bonuses to the executive staff, and investing heavily in remote outposts that we'll never use."

Something rustled at Deanna's elbow. The person next to her was handing her a note. She unfolded it and read:

Deanna and Jim up in a tree
K-I-S-S-I-N-G
First comes love, then comes marriage.
Let's find a wedding chapel in this parish.
$$\text{Love,}$$
$$\text{Jim}$$
P.S. I love you.

Troit crumpled the note, pointedly avoiding Smirk's eyes.

Admiral Nonsequitur continued, "None of these measures has helped. So we're going to resort to downsizing." A ripple of tension passed through the room. Suddenly everyone was listening intently. Even Capt. Smirk began paying attention.

"We can no longer afford to keep two identical ships in service, with duplicate staffs performing essentially the same functions," said Nonsequitur. "In fact, we can't even afford to keep you all on the payroll anymore. Therefore, we have decided..."

Nonsequitur glanced around the room and, sensing their animosity over this announcement, slipped into the passive voice. "...Uh, therefore, it has been decided that there will be just one USS *Endocrine,* and just one person in each staff position. We have decided—er, the decision has been made to utilize some members from each captain's crew. The rest of you will be temporarily laid off—er, outplaced."

Capt. Ricardo leaped to his feet. "Admiral, I object!"

"The ship Starfreak will keep in service," Nonsequitur went on, ignoring Ricardo's protest, "will be the one which Captain Ricardo's crew currently occupies, and he will be its captain."

"Oh, then, never mind," Ricardo said, sitting down again.

Several people glanced in Smirk's direction, expecting him to object in turn, but he was too stunned to say anything at all. Besides, he knew from experience that it was futile to protest; he'd been stripped of his command once before, and there was nothing you could do about it once the big shots made up their minds.

"Here are the other staff assignments," Nonsequitur continued. "Chief Bartender Guano will be promoted to first officer."

"What?!" screamed Commander Wilson Piker. "That's my job!"

"Correction: it *was* your job," Nonsequitur told him.

"But I'm supposed to be Number 1," Piker said. "What number am I now? Am I on the staff at all?"

Nonsequitur squinted at the list. "Piker . . . Piker . . . yes, here's your name. I'll get to your assignment in a minute."

"But—" Piker began.

Nonsequitur interrupted. "There will be no haggling over your assignments," he said. "Our team in Human Resources spent a lot of time determining exactly the right person for each of these jobs. And Starfreak will monitor your ship to make sure you *stay* in these jobs.

"Now," he continued, snapping his papers against the podium in annoyance, "if you'll all refrain from further outbursts, I'll read the rest of this assignment list, and then we can go for a swim in the pool. All right, here they are. Dr. McCaw will serve as second officer, and former Chief Engineer Mr. Snot will be communications officer.

"Ship's counselor is now Mr. Wart," Nonsequitur read. "Chief medical officer—that's you, Mr. Piker. Chief engineer, Deanna Troit."

Deanna looked as though she might faint. Smirk's heart went out to her. Then his heart returned to its customary self-centered position as he pondered whether he himself would make the team. If Starfreak gave him a new post, at least he and Deanna would serve on the same ship, which would vastly improve his courting potential.

Smirk prayed silently, *Please, let me have an assignment. Any assignment. Just let me make the cut.*

"Let's see, there are three positions left here," said Nonsequitur. "Security chief..."

Smirk, Smirk, Smirk, the captain thought, projecting his concentration toward the admiral.

"...Yoohoo," read Nonsequitur. "UltraFax chief..."

Smirk, Smirk, Smirk...

"...Checkout." Nonsequitur read the last line: "And chief bartender in the Ten-Foreplay lounge..."

Smirk, Smirk, Smirk, please let it be me, Smirk, Smirk...

"Mr. Smock. All right, people, you have your assignments. Now, everybody in the pool!" Nonsequitur slammed down his gavel to end the meeting. A buzz of discussion filled the room as everyone stood up and began reacting aloud to this stunning development.

Everyone, that is, except Capt. Smirk. He slumped in his chair, unable to believe his bad luck. *Shot down twice in one morning,* he thought, wincing.

On his way out, Capt. Ricardo gave Smirk a hearty pat on the shoulder. "Tough luck, old chap," Ricardo said, unable to completely suppress a note of gloating in his voice.

Ricardo's newly-chosen crewmembers left the room with him, eager to celebrate at the pool party. The remaining six crewmembers gathered morosely around Smirk, reflexively seeking his leadership even though he'd just lost his official standing in Starfreak.

"Captain," asked Dacron the android, "could you explain the meaning of our new status, 'laid off er outplaced'?"

Smirk could only stare at him, too miserable to reply.

"Make that just plain 'laid off,' Dacron," said former Chief Engineer Georgie LaForgery. "No use sugar-coating it."

"Well, we still have a ship, anyway," pointed out Mr. Zulu. Georgie looked dubious, but Zulu shrugged and added in a hopeful tone, "Starfreak didn't say we couldn't keep on using the wrekkies' working model."

"Yeah, but without Starfreak's supplies and financial backing, we're not going to get very far," Georgie pointed out.

Dacron was still puzzled over what had happened. "Precisely what is our status relative to Captain Ricardo's crew now that we are 'laid off'?" he inquired.

"We don't *have* any status, Dacron," said Westerly Flusher. For a long time Westerly had been away, enrolled in Starfreak Academy Film School, but just the week before he'd quit school in a protest over artistic censorship. His innate sense of good timing had brought him back to the *Endocrine* just before this layoff. "Captain Ricardo's crew has the approval of Starfreak and access to all its resources," Westerly said, "meaning there's none left for us."

"We're out of it," agreed Westerly's mother, Dr. Beverage Flusher, who was formerly Capt. Ricardo's chief medical officer.

"I see," said Dacron. "In effect, they are the Haves, and we are the Have-Nots."

Dacron's observation seemed to strike a chord within Capt. Smirk. He began to emerge from his daze. "The Have-Nots," Smirk said quietly. "So it's come to this, eh? All these years of service, and I don't even get a gold watch. They just kick me out the door."

"Sir, don't you still own shares in Starfreak?" Zulu asked. "I thought you had a controlling interest, in fact."

"I sold them," Smirk said. "The market was bullish, trading was at an all-time high, and I needed some cash for a motorboat. So I sold all my Starfreak preferred shares

Westerly had been away, enrolled in Starfreak Academy Film School.

and cashed in my IRA besides. Financially, I'm no better off than any of you right now. Here we are, the Have-Nots." He sat there looking dejected, apparently content simply to mope with his head in his hands.

The others, waiting for someone to take charge, began to get a little nervous. Finally, Ricardo's former UltraFax Chief, Smiles O'Brine, ventured, "Uh, Captain, shall I UltraFax us onboard your ship?" Smirk nodded, so O'Brine pulled out his remote-control unit and Faxed them up to the Bridge of the alternate *Endocrine*. At least there they could mope in familiar surroundings.

2

Get Your Butts in Gear

THE NEXT MORNING, the Haves took on their new roles aboard Capt. Ricardo's *Endocrine*.

First Officer Guano sat at the center of the Bridge in the chair formerly occupied by Cmdr. Piker. The day before, when Admiral Nonsequitur had given her the promotion, Guano had felt pure excitement. But now that she was actually assuming this position, she realized that her former job as chief bartender might not have completely prepared her to be second in command of a starship.

Guano wondered if Cmdr. Piker had left behind some sort of job manual. She opened the storage compartment of the chair and peered inside. But all she found were a few crumpled Big Mac wrappers and an illustrated children's book, *A Beginner's Guide to Outer Space Terms*.

At his Operations ("Oops") station in the forward section of the Bridge, Dr. McCaw scowled at the console panel. He realized he was supposed to run this thing, but none of the control buttons or readouts made any sense. A faint odor of crankcase oil lingered in the upholstery of the chair, reminding him that Dacron had occupied this station before the layoff.

McCaw noticed Guano checking her storage compartment, so he did the same with his, but it yielded only the current week's copy of *Soap Opera Digest*.

333

Capt. Ricardo emerged from the Crewmover, the *Endocrine*'s nifty elevator system, and strode to his captain's chair. "What's that noise?" he inquired.

Instantly Guano went on the defensive. She knew that as first officer, she was responsible for keeping the vessel running smoothly; she was supposed to stay on top of things at all times. How would Piker respond in this situation? As she pictured him standing there, a Piker-like reply popped to her lips. "What noise?"

"That beeping," said Ricardo. "Don't you hear it?"

"Yes, I hear it," said Guano, "but I didn't know it was anything out of the ordinary."

"Dr. McCaw?" Ricardo said, turning toward the Oops station.

McCaw shrugged. "It's not coming from my panel, so I wasn't going to worry about it," he said.

"Mmmm," said Capt. Ricardo. "Where *is* it coming from?"

No one answered. Finally, the feminine voice of the computer spoke up. "The beeping tone is coming from the communication panel of the Tactical station. The phone has been left off the hook."

Capt. Ricardo walked over to the station, which stood on the elevated platform directly in back of the senior officers' command chairs. "Where's Mr. Snot?" Ricardo asked. "He's supposed to be staffing this area."

"Montgomery Ward Snot is in the Conference Room . . ." said the computer. It paused for several beats, then added, ". . . napping."

"Napping, eh?" Ricardo said with a frown. "Number 1, go wake him up and get him in here."

Guano sat filing her nails. Ricardo stared at the back of her enormous hat and repeated, "Number 1!"

McCaw, swiveling to look back at Guano, hissed, "Pssst! He's talking to you, hat head."

"Wha—?" Startled, Guano dropped her nail file. "Uh, yes sir. Right away, Captain." She scrambled to the Conference Room door at the back of the Bridge.

By the time Guano awoke Mr. Snot and brought him back to the Bridge, Capt. Ricardo had adjusted the Tactical station's console. The status line now read "incoming message."

"Open a 'hey, you' frequency and put the caller on the Viewscreen, Mr. Snot," ordered Ricardo, striding over to his command chair.

"Viewscreen . . . Viewscreen . . ." muttered Snot, trying to make sense of the communication panel.

Ricardo watched the Viewscreen, waiting for an image to appear, but nothing happened. He turned around and inquired, "Mr. Snot?"

"Just a minute, Cap'n," Snot replied, flustered. "I've got t' figure out all o' this rigamarole—all these buttons 'n' things . . . it's a very technical matter . . ."

Guano, standing next to Snot, broke in, "Just press that one that says 'Place Caller on Viewscreen.'" She reached for the button, but Snot slapped her hand away.

"I'll do it m'self, woman!" Snot snarled, pressing the button.

Guano punched him in the shoulder. "Watch it, you!" she squealed. "I'm your superior officer, you know."

On the Viewscreen, Admiral Nonsequitur had appeared as soon as Snot pressed the panel button. He now watched the skirmish at the rear of the Bridge: Snot shoved Guano aside, and Guano responded by pinching Snot's arm.

"Say, now, what's all the fighting about?" Nonsequitur demanded. "Is it somebody's birthday?"

Capt. Ricardo turned around for a moment, growled "Knock it off, you two," and turned back to the Viewscreen with a broad smile. "What can we do for you, Admiral?" asked Ricardo.

"Starfreak has an important order for your crew, Captain," said Nonsequitur. "It's a purchase order. No, wait, that's not right. It's some kind of order, though. An order of fries? Drat, now I've lost my train of thought."

Only his years of Starfreak discipline kept Capt. Ricardo from fidgeting as he faced the Viewscreen, listening to Nonsequitur ramble on.

The admiral groped around in the mounds of paper on his desk. "Some kind of order . . . the High Command faxed it to me a few hours ago . . ." he mumbled to himself. He rummaged through one desk drawer after another, then grabbed his wastebasket and overturned its contents onto the desktop. "Ah! Here it is," he exclaimed, pulling a sheet of paper out of the refuse. "Why is it always in the last place you look?"

Dr. McCaw muttered out of the side of his mouth, "Probably because you stop looking as soon as you find it."

"Well, I won't waste your valuable time reading this entire order to you," Nonsequitur continued. "Except, perhaps, for the first sentence, which says, 'Starfreak hereby orders the USS *Endocrine* under the command of Captain Jean-Lucy Ricardo to locate the Fountain of Youth.' And maybe this second sentence: 'Once located, the fountain is to be claimed for Starfreak.' And this third sentence is pretty important, too. It says, 'The fountain is known to have anti-aging properties, and its waters can be bottled and sold throughout the galaxy.'

"And also the fourth sentence: 'Profit from the sale of Fountain of Youth waters will be used to offset the huge after-tax losses of Starfreak for the second quarter of 44430.' And the fifth and sixth sentences: 'Intelligence reports indicate that the fountain is located somewhere in the Vivi Sector and that our enemies the Romanumens are also seeking its whereabouts. Allowing the Romanumens to reach the fountain first would deal a devastating blow to Starfreak.' And the seventh and final sentence, 'Therefore, it is the opinion of the High Command that the crewmembers of the USS *Endocrine* should get their butts in gear.'

"Well, Ricardo, you've got your work cut out for you," said Nonsequitur. "I'd be pretty anxious to find that fountain if I were you. Especially after the way the accountants were talking at last night's budget meeting . . . something about cost centers and line-item vetoes—or was it Fritos?—and how we can't afford even one *Endocrine* . . ." Nonsequitur's voice trailed off as he became distracted by the Lava Lite on his desk.

A worry line creased Capt. Ricardo's brow. "Precisely what did they say, Admiral?"

"Mmmm?" Nonsequitur murmured, tracing his finger along the Lava Lite's surface, following the path of a floating blob. He mused, "You know, if we replaced all of the incandescent light bulbs in Starfreak Headquarters with fluorescents, we might save enough on the electric bill to afford another snack vending machine. Nonsequitur out." His image disappeared from the Viewscreen.

Capt. Ricardo nibbled nervously on his thumbnail. "What do you suppose he meant by that reference to the budget?" he wondered aloud. "Will they take us out of commission if we don't find this fountain for them?"

Guano felt she should respond to this vague threat to the crew, but she didn't know what to say, so once again she tried to approximate what Piker would have done. She stood up, cocked her head and ordered, "Red Alert!" This triggered a warning sound, and red lights along the walls began blinking on and off.

Piker's voice came over the intercom from Sick Bay. "Captain?"

"Never mind, Number—er, Commander—um, Mr. Piker. There's no emergency," responded Capt. Ricardo, shooting a disdainful glance at Guano. He ordered the computer, "Cancel Red Alert."

"I wasn't asking about the Red Alert, sir," Piker's voice continued. "I wondered if you could spare Dr. McCaw for a few minutes. We had a patient come in here with severe bleeding from a leg wound, and the tourniquet I applied worked pretty well—"

"Tourniquet?" muttered Dr. McCaw.

"—But then one of the orderlies loosened the tourniquet," Piker continued, "and the bleeding really got out of hand—"

"I'm sorry, Mr. Piker," the captain broke in, "but you know Starfreak's orders: everyone has to work at their assigned tasks. We're being monitored to make sure we comply. Besides, I need Dr. McCaw here on the Bridge. We've just begun a new mission."

"Well, if he can't come here and help us stop the bleeding," said Piker, "can he at least tell me where to find the mop?"

Dr. McCaw scowled. He barked at the intercom, "It's probably in the broom closet next to Dr. Flusher's office."

"Thanks," said Piker, signing off.

Capt. Ricardo told the Bridge crew, "Let's get to that fountain before we become the victims of a line-item veto, shall we? Ensign, set a course for the Vivi Sector. Engineering," continued the captain, speaking to the intercom, "we'll need maximum power."

"Yes, Captain," came Deanna Troit's voice. "I'm studying the Jargon Manual right now. I think I have a pretty good idea of how the engine works."

Mr. Snot, at the back of the Bridge, shuddered when he heard this.

"Engage," ordered Capt. Ricardo.

As Capt. Ricardo embarked upon his new mission, Capt. Smirk languished aboard his own ship.

Here I am, hiding out in the captain's Ready Room, thought Smirk as he sat on the sofa. *I used to be so contemptuous of Ricardo when he did this. But what's the point of staying on the Bridge if we're not going anywhere?* Smirk sighed and continued carving the coffee table with his penknife, drawing a heart around "JS & DT."

Although Smirk's Have-Not crewmembers had boarded his ship and gone to their usual stations, they had no duties to perform. Without Starfreak's blessing, there would be no missions to conduct. Even if they had decided to go galivanting out on their own, they knew that eventually the Dilithium Crystal Vanish chamber in the Engine Room would be running on "empty," and Starfreak wasn't going to give them a refill.

Beep-beep boop-boop went the door chime. "Come in," said Smirk.

Dacron entered. "Captain, there has been—" he began, then halted, startled by the sight of Smirk carving the coffee table.

"Yes, Lieutenant? What is it?" Smirk said without looking up.

Dacron swallowed nervously, then ventured, "Sir, I believe that is unauthorized use of Starfreak property."

Smirk chuckled, a bitter smile crossing his face. "Well, let them come and arrest me, then."

Dacron stared at the carving. "Does this ritual signify your love for Counselor Troit?"

"My *unrequited* love, Dacron," said Smirk, chipping away at the wood. "Something you wouldn't understand. Something even I don't understand."

Smirk paused and stared off into the distance for a moment, then added, "Come to think of it, my love has never been unrequited before. No woman could resist me. Until Deanna came along." He pulled a ballpoint pen out of his pocket and began darkening the heart outline. "What was it you wanted, Dacron?"

"Sir, I have discovered an interesting development involving the other ship," said Dacron. "I listened in on their latest exchange with Starfreak Command."

"Really? I thought you used to spend the morning watching soap operas," Smirk commented.

"All of the programs have been pre-empted today by the President's State of the Universe address," Dacron replied. "To stay busy, I was monitoring the communication channels of the other *Endocrine*. I learned that they have been given a mission to find the Fountain of Youth. The fountain

"My love has never been unrequited before. No
woman could resist me."

is to be an essential source of revenue for Starfreak."

"So?" Smirk said idly, picking up his knife again and etching an arrow to pierce the heart.

"Starfreak Command is unsure of the exact whereabouts of the fountain," Dacron continued. "They know only that it is somewhere in the Vivi Sector. Apparently they are unaware of an article published in last month's *Astronomy* magazine which reported that an amateur telescope maker had pinpointed the fountain's location. It is in the Hydrant Quadrant."

"So?" Smirk repeated.

"Sir, since we have more precise knowledge of the fountain's location, we could get there first," Dacron pointed out. "Claiming control of the fountain would increase our bargaining power with Starfreak. Perhaps they would reinstate our crew to full-time status."

"Hmmm." Smirk set down his knife and considered this possibility. Then he crossed his arms and slumped back on the couch cushions. "Oh, I dunno. What's the point?" he whined. "Even if we did all that, I still wouldn't have Deanna. Without her, it hardly seems worth it."

Yet despite his discouraging words, Smirk seemed unable to dismiss the idea. "Although . . . if we got there first, Starfreak Command *would* have to deal with us," he mused. "They'd never be able to lay us off again.

"But how are we supposed to get there before Ricardo's team?" Smirk continued. "We're really at a disadvantage. Starfreak has left us in a lurch." He stood up and paced the room, growing more annoyed with every step.

"We're cut off from Starfreak supplies and fuel," Smirk complained, "we're understaffed, and we've lost our official standing in the federation." Angrily he kicked the wastebasket; it sailed through the air and bounded off the glass of the built-in aquarium, startling the kissing gouramis.

"It was just a suggestion, sir," Dacron said, looking wary.

"I *hate* feeling so . . . so . . . powerless!" Smirk raged. "It's so frustrating to be the underdog!" He picked up the candy dish from the coffee table and cocked his arm as if to throw it; then suddenly he stopped, his arm frozen in midair. "The underdog," he repeated softly.

Smirk slowly lowered the candy dish and set it back on the table. "The underdog—yes," he said to himself. "The odds against us are tremendous. She knows that. We'd be coming from behind."

"Sir?" Dacron inquired, trying to follow Smirk's line of thought.

"That would really impress her," Smirk continued. "There we'd be, valiantly struggling against the odds, and Deanna would see us charging in at the last minute to beat Starfreak's hand-picked crew. A come-from-behind victory! That would show her I've got the right stuff.

"Yeah! Let's do it!" Smirk yelled, raising his fist in a power salute. "Dacron, you're a genius!" Exuberantly Smirk grabbed Dacron by the shoulders and smacked his cheek with a big kiss. Then Smirk trotted out of the Ready Room onto the Bridge, eager to begin this new venture.

Dacron remained standing as he was when Smirk kissed him, wondering why every time he thought he'd figured out human emotions, someone threw him a curve ball.

"So is everybody clear on what we're doing in this new mission?" Smirk said a short time later as he concluded his explanation to the others in the Conference Room.

Westerly raised his hand. "What was that part about not getting there before Captain Ricardo's crew?" he asked. "If we know where to find the Fountain of Youth, why don't we head straight over there?"

"Tactical reasons," Smirk replied crisply. "It's too involved for me to explain. Let's just say that it's essential we go in at the last minute and snatch the victory out from under them. Now, Mr. LaForgery," Smirk continued, addressing his chief engineer, "can you come up with a way to get us there even though we barely have enough fuel to maintain impulse power?"

Georgie screwed up his face in concentration. "It'll be difficult," he mused, "but I think it's possible. Maybe if we digitize the structural integrity fields to match the Jiffy Tubes, then transwarp the hull deflectors over their maximum range"—his voice grew more and more enthusiastic as he realized the possibilities—"and reconfigure the thermostats in the nacelle, and then use Lime-A-Way on the hard water deposits in the maintenance room . . . Bingo!" Georgie snapped his fingers. With a grin, he concluded, "It'll work, all right."

"Could you translate that into English for us, Mr. LaForgery?" asked Capt. Smirk.

"Sure, Captain," Georgie responded. "We'll use most of our available fuel to travel to within a few hundred kilometers of Captain Ricardo's ship. After that, we'll just draft them. We should be pulled along in their wake."

"Won't they know we're following them?" Westerly asked.

Dacron chimed in, "Their sensors will be able to detect another ship at such close range."

"I guess it depends on who's manning their sensor array at the Tactical station," Capt. Smirk observed. "The person would have to be sharp enough to notice an anomaly on the radar. Who was assigned to that station? Does anyone remember who Nonsequitur named to the post?"

"It was Mr. Snot," Zulu recalled.

"Oh. Then we're safe," Smirk concluded.

3

Ten-Foreplaying
Around

GEORGIE'S TECHNIQUE OF drafting the other ship for propulsion worked so well that the Have-Nots could just sit back and enjoy the ride.

It was three days since they'd begun following Ricardo's vessel, and Ricardo's Haves seemed completely unaware of their presence. The Have-Nots felt secure that Communications Officer Snot wouldn't detect them on his radar screen, and Dacron secretly monitored all of the Haves' Bridge conversations to stay alert for any unexpected upsurges in crew intelligence.

So far, though, everything he'd heard indicated that Capt. Ricardo had his hands full simply trying to maintain order among his ill-suited officers. Ricardo was much too busy to notice that another starship was trailing them across the galaxy.

Dacron activated the audio recorder to keep track of further conversations on Ricardo's Bridge. He planned to monitor the recordings later; right now it was time to join the gang in the Ten-Foreplay lounge.

Before leaving the Bridge, Dacron pulled out a portable audiotape player, slipped the cordless headphone plugs into his ears, and flicked the switch. Instantly, the Devo tape he'd gotten from the ship's archives brought a sparkle to his yellow eyes. Capt. Smirk had given him the cassette

344

Ricardo was much too busy to notice that another
starship was trailing them across the galaxy.

player in the hope that listening to music would stifle Dacron's incessant babbling, and so far the tactic was working.

As he pushed open the swinging doors of Ten-Foreplay, Dacron was surprised to see that his crewmates were in an extremely merry mood.

From his experiences in Ten-Foreplay on Capt. Ricardo's ship, Dacron knew that the beverages served there usually had only a mildly intoxicating effect. In fact, everyone but Dacron could sober up at will because the drinks were made from simpahol, a synthetic alcohol substitute. This late—24th-century development was the culmination of years of research funded by MADD.

But here in Capt. Smirk's Ten-Foreplay, Dacron observed, the drinks were making the humans act positively giddy. He popped out his earplugs so he could listen in on the conversation, curious to learn why things seemed so different this time.

"Do it again!" UltraFax Chief Smiles O'Brine was saying. "Here, Zulu, do the ritual with my pretzels." O'Brine stood up, wobbling a little, and slid his bowl of three-ring pretzels down the bar to Zulu.

Zulu scooped the pretzels from the bowl and stacked them neatly, one on top of the other, till the pile was several inches high. The others giggled in anticipation. Dacron noticed that even Capt. Smirk, who stood behind the bar wearing a server's apron, seemed amused by Zulu's antics.

"The Zen pretzel ritual begins," said Zulu in a deliberately pretentious voice, and the others guffawed. "The karate master projects his consciousness into the pretzels. He becomes one with the pretzels." Zulu stared at the pile, bug-eyed, and his crewmates laughed harder. Dacron, puzzled by their euphoria, tried in vain to analyze this latest manifestation of the human sense of humor.

"The karate master pictures himself breaking through the awesome combined strength of the pretzels," Zulu continued. Bev Flusher was laughing so hard that she had to lean for support against Georgie, who was sitting on the barstool next to her. He, in turn, wiped tears of laughter from the gutters of his visor. Westerly Flusher took a gulp from his glass of milk and leaned in close to get a better look at Zulu.

Zulu raised his hand high in the air. "The karate master breaks through the pretzels!" he cried. With a lightning-quick motion, Zulu sliced the side of his hand through the pile. Pretzels flew in every direction.

The others shrieked with laughter. Westerly Flusher chortled abruptly, and milk poured out of his nose. Capt. Smirk, helpless with mirth, clutched his aching sides and almost lost his balance. He grabbed out blindly for support and accidentally pulled the soda tap; cola gushed out of it. The sight of this doubled the frenzy of everyone's laughing fit.

Several minutes later, their roars and shrieks finally subsided to chuckles and giggles. There were long, satisfied sighs as everyone got back their breath and started to pull themselves together.

"What a party!" Georgie exclaimed. "I never felt like this in *our* Ten-Foreplay."

Bev Flusher nodded in agreement. "These drinks really pack a wallop," she said. "Captain, you mix a mean cocktail. Have you stocked your bar with a different kind of simpahol?"

"Simpahol?" Smirk replied, straightening his uniform. "What's that?"

Meanwhile, aboard Capt. Ricardo's ship, the computer had just gone down, and Ricardo felt an inexplicable chill of fear along his spine.

He gripped the arms of his command chair and told himself there was nothing to worry about. He'd sent technicians to investigate the problem. They could usually repair a computer malfunction within a few minutes.

With a lightning-quick motion, Zulu sliced through the pile.

Meanwhile, all of the ship's backup systems were operating normally. So what was making him so nervous?

I must have a subliminal memory of some catastrophe that coincided with an earlier computer malfunction, he reasoned. But what could it have been? He closed his eyes and pressed a fist against his mouth, trying to resurrect the half-buried memory.

Ricardo willed himself into trancelike concentration, blocking out the routine noises of the ship. He barely heard the *swooosh* of the Crewmover doors opening to admit someone onto the Bridge. Thus, he was completely unprepared for the falsetto shriek that assaulted his ears a moment later.

"Oh, Jean-Lucyyyyyy!" trilled the voice. It was the kind of sound that would have raised the hairs on the back of Ricardo's head, if he'd had any.

It was the voice of Deanna Troit's mother, Woksauna Troit.

Ricardo reflexively jerked backward, curling his legs onto the chair seat beneath him in a defensive posture. Woksauna Troit advanced, arms outstretched.

"There you are, you darling captain!" exclaimed Woksauna. "My, don't you look *commanding* today!"

Ricardo smiled wanly. He wondered what kind of embarrassing atrocity she wanted from him now, and whether he would be able to weasel out of it. So far his track record with Woksauna hadn't been too good, but maybe this time he could forestall panic long enough to think of a convincing excuse.

"I'm so glad I found you," Woksauna continued, "because I need your help."

Here it comes, Ricardo thought. *Stay alert, man!* His breath quickened, and his senses became ultra-sharp, like those of a hunted animal.

"I need you to pose with me for a fashion layout," Woksauna went on.

Fashion! Ricardo willed himself not to faint.

"It's for the next edition of *Betavoid Bride* magazine," Woksauna said. Then, coyly, she added, "They'd like to picture a mature couple in traditional Betavoid wedding garb."

Forcing himself to maintain a near-normal tone of voice, Ricardo replied, "But Woksauna, I thought it was traditional for a Betavoid bridal couple to be nude at the ceremony."

"Exactly," Woksauna said with relish.

Ricardo's flight-or-fight bodily reaction kicked into high gear. This was the moment of truth. He needed to come up with an excuse that would do more than just buy him time; it had to make Woksauna forget this absurd idea altogether. If he failed . . . his mind raced: *Woksauna will drag me into the photo session . . . I'll have to remove all my clothing . . . and worse yet, I'll be forced to look at a naked Woksauna . . . by Jove, the mere thought of it is enough to give one the hives . . . the hives—that's it . . . yes, I'll make up a story about that.*

Ricardo's vast relief lent an uncharacteristic sincerity to his smile. "I'm sure it would be a splendid opportunity," he told Woksauna, "and I'll make a point of taking you up on your invitation just as soon as my rash goes away."

Woksauna blinked. "Rash?"

"Yes," Ricardo replied brightly. "The worst of it is clearing up now—most of the scales have dropped off. Oh, I forgot," he interrupted himself. "You haven't seen it underneath my clothing. Would you like to have a look? I'm told it's almost past the contagious stage." He began lifting his tunic and reaching for her hand.

"Uh, no," Woksauna gasped. "No, thank you, Captain. Actually, I ought to get going." She backed away, keeping her eyes fixed on Ricardo's hand as he held it poised to lift his shirt. "I just remembered," Woksauna babbled, "that I, uh, left my ultrasonic denture cleaner plugged in." She backed into the railing that circled the center of the

Bridge, caught herself, turned around and fled to the Crewmover.

"Come on over to my quarters anytime," Ricardo called jauntily. "We can watch videotapes of the chemical peel treatments I underwent in Sick Bay." Woksauna summoned a queasy smile as the Crewmover doors closed.

Ricardo sat back in his command chair and savored his victory. But he had only a few minutes of peace. Apparently the computer was back on line, because its voice came over the intercom with another crisis for him to solve.

"Warning," the computer announced to the Bridge crew. "Unauthorized buildup of phaser energy on Deck 007."

"Security Chief Yoohoo," said Ricardo, hailing her over the intercom, "order your troops to investigate a phaser buildup on Deck 007."

"Sir—" Yoohoo answered instantly, then hesitated before continuing. "Uh, my troops are causing the buildup, sir."

"They're what?" Ricardo responded.

"They won't obey my orders," Yoohoo pouted. "They're upset about the compulsory Mary Kay makeover sessions I ordered for all Security personnel. Now these ... these ... troublemakers have set their phasers on 'stun,' and they've backed me into a corner."

"Are you trying to tell me you've got a mutiny on your hands?" Ricardo asked incredulously.

First Officer Guano, realizing that this presented a significant threat to the ship, jumped up and cried, "Red Alert!"

Capt. Ricardo scowled. "I hardly think this justifies a Red Alert, Number 1," he chided.

"Well, it's more important than a Yellow Alert," Guano said. "I mean, a Yellow Alert is practically meaningless." Capt. Ricardo gave her a cold stare.

Guano pressed her argument. "A Yellow Alert is like an amber traffic light," she said. "Nobody pays any attention to it." Ricardo's stony expression remained unchanged, but Guano continued, "We need something in between a Red Alert and a Yellow Alert." She cocked her head and ordered, "Cancel Red Alert. Begin. . . ." she searched her thoughts for a moment, then proclaimed, "Burnt Sienna Alert!"

Capt. Ricardo winced a little. It was much like the wince that Cmdr. Piker used to evoke from him, and in fact Guano was becoming more like his former first officer every day.

"Number 1," Ricardo said, "why don't you take a break? You've certainly earned it. Go down to Ten-Foreplay and relax for a while."

"You're sure, Captain?" Guano responded. "I wouldn't want to be away from my post when anything important happens."

"I'm sure we can manage," Ricardo said, trying to lift the corners of his mouth into a reassuring smile.

"OK," Guano agreed, "but be sure to call me the minute you see a crisis coming. Even a little one."

"We will, Commander," Ricardo said. As soon as Guano left in the Crewmover, Ricardo sighed with relief. Then, returning to the problem at hand, he spoke again to the intercom.

"Mr. Wart, we need your counseling services on Deck 007," said Ricardo, "to settle an argument among the Security troops."

"Yes, Captain," Wart's deep bass boomed in response.

This was followed a moment later by Piker's uncertain tone, hailing them from Sick Bay. "Uh, Captain?"

"What is it, Mr. Piker?"

"Sorry for the interruption, but I've got another question for Dr. McCaw," Piker said.

McCaw, who was sitting at his Oops console, frowned as he looked up at the intercom speaker in the ceiling. "Now what?"

"I'm about to perform an amputation," Piker said. "I

found Dr. Flusher's laser scalpel, but I can't figure out how to turn it on."

"Just flick the switch at the top of the hand grip," McCaw told him.

"I did, but nothing happens," Piker replied. "Nurse Ames," he continued, his voice fading slightly as if he were speaking to someone off to the side, "here, you try it." His voice returned to its normal volume as he said, "It's not just me. Nurse Ames can't get the switch to work, either."

"Then the safety catch is probably on," McCaw said. "It's located on the bottom of the tool."

"Where?" Piker asked. He continued, as if talking to himself, "Let's see, waveform amplitude—that's not it . . ."

McCaw warned him, "But before you release the safety catch, you have to clear the power setting you entered—"

"Ah, here's that safety catch," Piker went on.

A blood-curdling scream shot over the intercom from Sick Bay. In the background, someone cried out, "Nurse Ames! Oh, Cherry—your arm—oh, my gosh!"

"Oops," Piker said. "I guess it's working now. Thanks for your help."

Ricardo and McCaw stared at each other in disbelief. Then Ricardo shook his head as if to clear it. He brought up another matter. "Dr. McCaw, have you made any headway on figuring out how we can find the Fountain of Youth?"

"No, I haven't," McCaw responded. "Look, Jean-Lucy, what makes you think I can figure it out? I'm a doctor, not a tour guide. Now, if Mr. Smock were here—"

"But Mr. Smock is not here, Doctor," Ricardo cut in. "He is tending the bar in Ten-Foreplay, as Starfreak assigned him to do."

McCaw put on his most defiant I've-heard-this-all-before expression, but Ricardo continued.

"We're all under strict orders not to serve in any capacity other than those officially assigned," Ricardo nagged. "You know as well as I do that if I let Mr. Smock come here to

"Oops," Piker said. "I guess it's working now."

the Bridge and plot our course, as you've been insisting, Starfreak would yank our commission out from under us."

McCaw crossed his arms over his chest and began, "Well, if you weren't too proud to ask for directions—"

Ricardo cut him off. "Not another word out of you," Ricardo ordered, waving a reprimanding finger at McCaw. "I've had enough lip from you today. Do you understand?" McCaw glared at him, then swiveled back to his control panel without a word.

"And one more thing," Ricardo continued. "From now on you will refer to me as 'Captain' or 'Captain Ricardo', not 'Jean-Lucy' or 'chief' or 'boss.' " Ricardo tugged on his tunic to straighten it, as he often did out of habit, only this time the adrenaline rush from his anger made him pull so hard that he ripped the bodice seam. "Oh, for pity's sake," he muttered, going back to his command chair.

However, McCaw was determined to get in the last word, even if he was under orders not to speak. He began pressing the buttons of the Oops console out of sequence, attempting functions that he knew the console's software couldn't deliver. The panel emitted an annoying *zzst-zzst-zzst-zzst* with every attempt.

Ricardo ignored the tactic for a while, but when he felt a headache coming on he decided he'd had enough. "Dr. McCaw," he said, trying to keep his voice neutral, "perhaps you're due for a break also. Why don't you join Guano in Ten-Foreplay?"

"I don't like your Ten-Foreplay," McCaw responded. "The simpahol tastes like something from a kid's chemistry set." He kept poking the buttons. *Zzst-zzst-zzst-zzst.*

"That's an order, Dr. McCaw!" Ricardo declared, so McCaw was forced to drag himself onto the Crewmover.

The ensign sitting at the Conn station reported, "Captain, the engines can't maintain the cruising speed of Warped 3.14 you ordered."

Once again Capt. Ricardo spoke to the intercom. "Engineering," he said, "we're unable to maintain optimum power. What's wrong with the engines?"

Deanna Troit's voice answered him. "The engines are fine," she replied. "It's just that some of my crewmembers are still adjusting to their new jobs. Once they figure out what they're doing, we'll get up to full speed again."

"What do you mean, their new jobs?" Ricardo asked.

"Well, I sensed that many of them weren't happy with their usual assignments," Troit said. "They felt unfulfilled and discontented. So I let them trade jobs with each other. Psychologically, it's much more sound to have them doing work they enjoy. Once they're over this learning curve, things will be back to normal."

"Deanna," said Capt. Ricardo, rubbing his aching forehead with his fingertips, "this is not the time to have our Engineering crew learning on the job. Starfreak hasn't reassigned any of them the way they've done to our officers—thank goodness. I want you to return your crewmembers to their usual posts immediately."

"But Captain," Troit said, "I sense so much unhappiness here when they're doing work they don't like. There's a tremendous level of anguish, and as a Betavoid, I can't simply ignore it."

"Could you ignore it more easily if you weren't in Engineering?" Ricardo asked.

"I'm not sure," Troit said. "I'd have to be somewhere on the ship where there are contradictory emotions strong enough to mask what I feel here in Engineering."

"What about Ten-Foreplay?" Ricardo asked. "Everyone there is usually in a good mood."

"I suppose . . . " Troit conceded. "Yes, those positive emotions might be strong enough."

"Then make it so," Ricardo ordered. "Report to Ten-Foreplay, and stay there until further notice. *After* you get everybody back in their former jobs, that is."

"Yes, Captain," replied Troit, signing off.

Ricardo gazed around the Bridge. There was hardly anybody left. *Since the day shift began this morning,* he realized, *one by one I've sent all my Bridge officers to Ten-Foreplay*.

The sound of snoring at the back of the Bridge reminded Ricardo that this was not precisely true. *Well, I've sent away* almost *all of my Bridge officers*, Ricardo thought. *Mr. Snot is still at his post*.

Her work finished, Deanna Troit headed for Ten-Foreplay, as Capt. Ricardo had ordered. But the swinging doors to the bar didn't respond to her touch as usual. She pushed harder; they wouldn't budge.

Frowning, Deanna leaned on the door and pushed with all her might. It finally cracked open a few inches, revealing a mass of people on the other side.

As Deanna stuck her face into the opening, an ensign standing in the crowd with a drink in his hand asked, "Whaddaya want?"

"I'm just trying to get in," Deanna said.

The ensign made a sarcastic face. "Ricardo's already sent half the ship down here." Nevertheless, he pushed back the crowd to open the door a few more inches and yelled to those around him, "Hey! We got somebody comin' through!"

Twenty minutes later, panting and perspiring, Deanna finally squeezed through the last layer of patrons surrounding the bar. Dr. McCaw was sitting there, and he grunted when he saw her. "Ricardo sent you here, too, eh?" he asked. "I've never seen such a crackpot management method in my life. Anybody gets in his way, he sends 'em to the lounge. How did you people ever get anything done?"

"This isn't his usual style of command," Deanna sniffed. "He seems to be overreacting to stress just now. Perhaps he's hiding something, too." After receiving her drink order from acting bartender Mr. Smock, Deanna began elbowing her way back through the crowd, looking for a table.

"Hmmph," McCaw retorted, turning back toward the bar and redirecting his attention to Mr. Smock.

"Why aren't you smiling, Smock?" McCaw asked sarcastically. "Bartenders are supposed to smile and chat intimately with their customers. You know, draw them out. Make them feel good."

"I find it irrelevant to conduct small talk with patrons," Smock replied. "What logical purpose would it serve? No useful information is conveyed in such a conversation. As for my somber expression, it is a direct consequence of this post, for which I am drastically overqualified."

"You're telling me," McCaw groused. "I can't believe I went through med school and fifty-nine years of practice just to end up punching buttons on a Plexiglas panel at the front of the Bridge. Not to mention taking orders from somebody who couldn't tell a catheter from a stethoscope if his life depended on it."

McCaw swallowed his drink in a single gulp, then coughed and wheezed. "Arrtch! I wonder what this simpahol stuff does to your innards?" His crabbiness increased by several notches, and he scanned the room for another target.

Yoohoo sat on a nearby barstool. McCaw jerked his thumb toward her and told Smock, "Yoohoo's Security troops had her backed into a corner. Ricardo sent Wart to straighten things out. Well, Security Chief," McCaw taunted Yoohoo, "did *Counselor* Wart get you out of that tight spot?"

"As a matter of fact, he did," Yoohoo responded haughtily. "He took them all to his office for a counseling session." She pulled a makeup compact out of her purse and checked her reflection in its little mirror. Then, satisfied that none of her features had moved since she'd last checked, Yoohoo closed the compact and dropped it back in her purse.

"Hmmmph," grumbled McCaw, irritated that he hadn't gotten a rise out of Yoohoo. Noticing that Troit had found

"I find it irrelevant to conduct small talk with patrons," Smock replied.

a seat with Guano at a nearby table, McCaw called out, "Hey, Guano! You're with the wrong person. You should be seeing a hat shrink, not a headshrink."

Guano started to stand, rolling up her sleeves as if preparing for a fistfight, but Troit held her back. "Just ignore it," Troit said. "You don't want to encourage him."

"Yes, I do," Guano replied. "I want to encourage him, and I want to aggravate him, and then I want to take him out back and break his nose." But Troit firmly gripped Guano's sleeve and pulled her back into her chair.

Yoohoo left the bar and joined them at their table. "He's just a blowhard," Yoohoo told Guano. "Don't give his malarkey the dignity of a reply."

"That's right," Troit agreed. "Let's talk about something more pleasant. Like sex, for instance."

"Hmmm. That reminds me, Deanna," Guano said. "Your mother dropped in on the Bridge this morning."

Troit's smile faded into a look of exasperation. "I suppose she came on to Captain Ricardo again?" Troit asked. Guano nodded.

"She did *what?*" Yoohoo gasped.

Guano explained to Yoohoo, "Deanna's mother goes into heat every so often. It's some kind of Betavoid change-of-life thing. Whenever that happens, she comes on board. Her ultimate goal is to finagle a weekend at Club Bed with the captain."

"Does she ever succeed?" asked Yoohoo, sipping her drink.

"No," said Deanna. "I think Captain Ricardo is afraid of her. He prefers the old-fashioned type of woman—you know, one with a regular menopause like Mom used to have."

"I wish I could have seen that," Yoohoo said. "When did it happen?"

"Early," Guano told her, "while the computer was down." She turned thoughtful. "You know, it's funny that the computer was down during Woksauna's visit," Guano mused, "because the computer was down the *last* time she was on board, too. That was before we got our new job assignments. I remember it distinctly because her valet, Lurch, ordered special drinks for the two of them here in Ten-Foreplay. I tried to call up the directions, and the computer voice wouldn't respond."

Deanna shrugged. "It's probably just a coincidence," she said.

But Guano pursued the idea. "Come to think of it," she went on, "I've never seen the two of them operating simultaneously. Woksauna Troit and the computer, I mean. It's sort of like Clark Kent and Superman, you know?" Sensing their apathy, Guano asked her companions, "Doesn't it make you the least bit curious?"

"Not really," said Deanna, stirring her drink with a swizzle stick. "I already know more about my mother than I want to know."

Back at the bar, McCaw was still cranky, and he searched for a new victim. Checkout sat a few barstools away, nursing a beer. McCaw called to him, "Might as well make yourself comfortable there, Pavlov."

Checkout looked up blearily, and McCaw continued, "You won't be needed to UltraFax anybody down to the Fountain of Youth, 'cause at the rate Ricardo's going, we'll never find it. Har har har."

At that moment Capt. Ricardo's voice came over the intercom. "Attention, all officers," he said. "Report to your stations. We have arrived at Planet Stradivarius–9 and will now investigate the Fountain of Youth."

Disbelief and annoyance fought for dominance in McCaw's expression. "Well, I'll be hornswoggled," he crabbed.

The Look
of Love

" ◆ ◆ ◆ AND FOR THOSE who think it's necessary to consult maps or rely on others for directions, let this be a lesson to you," said Capt. Ricardo, winding up his lecture to the Bridge crew. "An accomplished explorer can navigate by the stars. It's a simple matter of knowing your constellations."

The Haves were now back on their Bridge, with everybody standing by to contact the planet Ricardo had found; even Mr. Snot was awake and alert.

"They're hailing us, Cap'n," Snot reported from his Tactical station.

"Put them on the Viewscreen, Mr. Snot," said Ricardo.

As soon as Snot switched on the "hey, you" frequency, the opening of a motion picture burst onto the Viewscreen. Its achingly bright shot of a tourist resort was backed with a lush musical soundtrack.

"Welcome to Stradivarius—9, playground of the galaxy," said an announcer. The film's visual image switched to a fur-covered platform bed in the middle of a gaudy hotel room. The announcer intoned, "We invite you sit back, relax, and enjoy your stay. We have accommodations to suit every taste and budget.

"While you're here, be sure to visit our Lover's Lounge,

where our renowned chef, Pierre Dupa, serves up his glo-rious four-star cuisine," the announcer continued. On-screen, Chef Pierre stood at tableside displaying a flaming Baked Alaska to an appreciative couple and then dousing the flames with a fire extinguisher.

"What the devil is this?" McCaw wanted to know.

"But of course, the main attraction is our famous foun-tain," the announcer continued. The screen showed swim-suit-clad tourists frolicking in the dancing waters of a fountain that dominated an outdoor courtyard. "No visit would be complete without a dip in the fountain. You'll feel frisky as honeymooners!" The location coordinates of the fountain were superimposed on the screen.

"That must be it," Ricardo concluded. "Dr. McCaw, relay those coordinates to Mr. Checkout in Shipping and Re-ceiving. We'll send an Away Team down there immediately to claim the fountain for Starfreak."

"Claim it for Starfreak?" McCaw said. "What about the people who are already here? They've got quite a resort operation going. Won't they be a little upset if we try to claim it?"

"Hmmm. You're right, Doctor," Ricardo replied. "They may indeed put up a fuss. Mr. Snot, arm the futon tor-pedoes, just in case."

"Aye, Cap'n," Snot replied, pressing the appropriate but-tons on the "anti-communication" section of his com-munication panel.

"There's something funny about all this," McCaw went on. "I thought the Fountain of Youth was supposed to be the best-kept secret in the galaxy. This place looks more like Disney World."

"Never mind, Doctor," Ricardo said. "Just relay the co-ordinates to Shipping. Number 1," Ricardo continued, turning to Guano, "you'll lead an Away Team down to the fountain. You'd better take some Security personnel along in case you meet with resistance." Guano nodded in reply.

"Counselor Wart," Ricardo said to the intercom, "have

you finished with the Security personnel yet?"

"We are in the semi-final rounds, Captain," Wart's voice replied. "We're down to the final four survivors."

"What?!" Ricardo yelped. "You're supposed to be conducting a counseling session, Mr. Wart."

"You asked me to settle their dispute, Captain," Wart replied. "In addition to their quarrel with Security Chief Yoohoo, they had internal disagreements, so I am holding elimination rounds here in my counseling office. In keeping with Kringle ritual, each combatant uses the weapon of their choice. It is a highly efficient method."

Ricardo, looking dizzy, leaned against his command chair. "How many of these Security people did you say are left, Mr. Wart?" he asked weakly.

"Four. And each one is a hardy warrior," Wart asserted.

"Yes, I'm sure they are," Ricardo said with a dazed look. "Well, I think you ought to end the contest now, Mr. Wart. Declare them all the winners."

"As you wish, Captain." Wart signed off.

Ricardo stared off into the distance. Guano waited several moments, then prompted him, "Uh, sir, you wanted me to lead an Away Team. Should I take those four Security people with me?"

Ricardo gazed blankly at Guano for a moment, then shook himself back into alertness. "Uh . . . no—not them," he said. "Choose your own Away Team, Commander."

"Yes *sir!*" Guano answered enthusiastically. She mused aloud, "Let's see, who should I take?" An Away Team mission would be a plum assignment, since all the crewmembers were itching to get off the ship for a change of scenery, and this Stradivarian resort looked especially promising.

Guano turned around slowly to survey the Bridge, resting her gaze on several crewmembers in turn as if considering and then rejecting them. "Dr. McCaw? Nahh. Ensign Roach? Uh-uh. Mr. Snot? Mmmm . . . nope."

Abruptly, Guano swiveled toward the front of the Bridge and said to the intercom, "Deanna Troit and Mr. Smock,

"In keeping with Kringle ritual, each combatant uses the weapon of their choice."

report to Shipping and Receiving for an Away Team assignment." Then she strode off toward the Crewmover, leaving crewmembers scowling in her wake.

Guano had never really considered taking along anyone from the Bridge crew. Earlier, when she realized that as first officer she might someday get to lead an Away Team, she'd decided to take along Troit, who was her best friend, and Smock, who could provide the necessary brainpower.

The three of them converged on Shipping and Receiving, where UltraFax Chief Checkout was frantically trying to decipher his UltraFax control panel.

On board the Bridge of the Have-Nots' ship, which lurked around the corner behind an asteroid, Capt. Smirk asked Dacron, "What are they up to, Lieutenant?"

"Captain Ricardo's crew is orbiting a planet known as Stradivarius-9," Dacron reported. "This resort planet is famed for its Fountain of Love, which evokes strong feelings of affection in anyone who touches, swims in, drinks, or fills water balloons with its liquid."

"Ha! They're lost," Smirk concluded. "They probably think that's the Fountain of Youth."

"Captain, sensors indicate that they are powering up their UltraFax," Dacron observed. "They may be preparing to send an Away Team down to the surface."

"We'd better keep an eye on them. We might find out something useful," Smirk said, thinking, *Maybe they'll take samples of that water back to the ship. What if Deanna drinks some of it eventually? I want to be nearby if she starts feeling affectionate.*

"We'll send an Away Team, too," Smirk decided aloud. "Mr. Dacron, I want you and Beverage Flusher to beam down there. You'll be less conspicuous if you go as a couple. From a distance, you might even be mistaken for honeymooners. Stay out of sight of Ricardo's team, and report to me anything they do."

"Aye, sir," said Dacron, leaving the Bridge.

A few minutes later, as Dacron and Bev stood on the UltraFax platform, Capt. Smirk's voice came over the intercom with an update for UltraFax Chief O'Brine. "Mr. O'Brine, it sounds like Ricardo plans to Fax his Away Team right next to the Fountain of Love," Smirk said. "Wait till your sensors tell you they've begun Faxing, and then put our team somewhere nearby."

"Yes, Captain," O'Brine said, setting the panel controls.

Back on Ricardo's ship, Guano, Troit and Smock waited nervously on their UltraFax platform, wondering if Checkout could handle the delicate machinery that would disassemble them into itty-bitty molecules and reassemble them on Stradivarius–9.

Checkout's anxious expression as he surveyed his control panel was not reassuring. "I tink I've got it set up right," he said dubiously. "Everybody ready?"

Guano and Troit shrugged. Smock responded, "Energize, Mr. Checkout."

"Here you go," Checkout said, waving his hand across the activation sensor.

The three of them felt the familiar UltraFax tingle, that tickly sensation of showering in ginger ale. Then they rematerialized—but not on Stradivarius–9. Gazing around them, they saw that they were indoors somewhere.

"That's not the fountain, is it?" Troit asked innocently, pointing at a white porcelain structure in which Guano had landed. Water emerged from an outlet near the top of the fixture, washing down its surface and gurgling into a drain at floor level.

Smock's face reddened. "No, it is not," he replied. "That is a urinal."

"Aaakkk!" cried Guano, leaping out of it.

Smock continued, "It seems Mr. Checkout has beamed us into the men's room." The blush spread from Smock's face to the pointy tips of his ears, turning them a brilliant shade of magenta.

"That's not the fountain, is it?" Troit asked innocently.

"You mean we're still on the *Endocrine?*" Troit said with dismay.

"Aakk! Ecchh! Yukkk!" Guano cried, vigorously wiping off her feet against the floor tiles.

As Checkout's control panel revealed his mistake to him, he reset the UltraFax and tried again. The three Away Team members felt themselves phasing away from the men's room.

Meanwhile, the activation of Checkout's UltraFax had triggered sensors in O'Brine's UltraFax, setting off the automatic response that would beam Dacron and Bev down to the fountain.

O'Brine had also programmed a slight delay into his UltraFax, offsetting his Away Team's arrival to avoid a collision with the Haves. But since O'Brine hadn't anticipated the Haves' detour to the men's room, suddenly both Away Teams were traveling toward exactly the same coordinates at exactly the same instant.

Guano, Troit and Bev materialized normally, side by side. "What are *you* doing here?" Troit asked Bev.

But before she could answer, they were distracted by the sight of the two remaining UltraFax beams becoming crossed with each other at the edge of the Fountain of Love. As Dacron and Smock materialized on the same spot, the impact sent them both reeling. They teetered for an instant on the fountain's edge, then fell in.

Troit and Bev rushed to help them. "Are you all right, Dacron?" Troit asked, reaching for his arm.

Troit noticed that Dacron looked different. It wasn't just that his uniform was soaked and his hair was dripping. There was something in his expression that she'd never seen before. If it had been anyone but Dacron, Troit would have identified it as the look of love.

His eyes were dreamy as he clasped her hand. "I am fine, Counselor," he said. "In fact, I feel wonderful." He climbed out of the fountain and stood next to her with a syrupy smile on his face. "It was so kind of you to come to my assistance," Dacron said. "You have earned my eternal devotion."

Troit felt puzzled. Dacron wore the look of love, all right. It was on his face. It was the kind of look that time can't erase. But how could this be? Dacron was an android, and Troit knew that androids could not feel emotion—a fact that Dacron had pointed out to the crew several times a day for the past five years. Yet her Betavoid telepathy told her that he did, indeed, feel love for her.

Standing next to them, Bev helped Smock step out of the fountain. "Oh, Mr. Smock, you're drenched," she observed.

"But it shall not quench my passion," Smock replied, holding her hand gently.

"Huh?" Bev responded.

"Thou art wonderful, Beverage," Smock declared. "As beautiful as the moons of Mebzorp." He kissed her hand.

Startled, Bev pulled her hand away and took a step backward. She glanced at the others and noticed Dacron's lovesick expression. "Uh-oh," Bev said, looking back and forth between Dacron and Smock. "I think I see what's going on here."

"What *is* going on?" Troit asked.

"They fell into the Fountain of Love," said Bev. "It gave them a strong dose of free-floating affection. You and I were the first ones they laid eyes on, so we've become their love objects."

"The Fountain of Love?" said Troit. "Captain Ricardo said we were beaming down to the Fountain of Youth."

Bev shook her head. "You're not even close," she confided.

Nearby, Guano was filling bottles with water from the fountain and stashing them in her hat.

Troit called to her, "Guano, let's go. This isn't the right place. We've got to get back to the ship."

"Just hang on a sec," Guano requested. "I want to stockpile some of this stuff in case I ever get back my old bartending job. It'd sell like hotcakes in Ten-Foreplay."

5

Sorta
Suitors

"**Y**OU SAW DACRON and Beverage Flusher?" Ricardo repeated. "Arriving together at this ... Fountain of Love? What were they doing there?" He paced the Ready Room, where he was debriefing Guano after her Away Team returned from Stradivarius–9.

Guano shook her head. "I'm not sure. Maybe Bev is getting desperate. Her husband's been dead quite a while now, you know."

Ricardo didn't hear her; he was caught up in the possible implications of this sighting. "How did they get here?" he said to himself. "When we left, they were all stuck on Starbase Flamingo. And why would they arrive at the same time we do? I wonder if Smirk is behind this. Could he be piloting his ship around here somewhere?"

Ricardo started to head back to the Bridge, intending to order Mr. Snot to do a sensor scan of the area; then he stopped and turned back toward Guano. "Commander," he said, "is there anything else that happened on your away mission that I should know about?"

Guano recalled the bizarre phenomenon of Smock falling in love with Beverage after being drenched by the fountain. Surely Capt. Ricardo would want to know that his Vulture bartender had gone bonkers. But she feared that if she described the effects of the fountain water,

Ricardo would start asking around and eventually find out about the stockpile of bottles in her hat. The captain would probably force her to turn her Fountain of Love water over to Starfreak.

"Nope. It was just your typical away mission," Guano replied breezily, as if this hadn't been the first away mission of her life.

As Capt. Ricardo stepped back onto the Bridge, Mr. Snot told him, "Cap'n, we've got a message comin' in from Starfreak Headquarters."

"Onscreen, Mr. Snot," Ricardo said, turning to face the Viewscreen.

Admiral Nonsequitur appeared on the screen. "Ricardo, this is Admiral Nonsequitur calling," he said.

"I know, Admiral. I can see your face," Ricardo reminded him.

"Oh," said Nonsequitur. "Huh. Maybe I should have shaved this morning." He began rummaging distractedly through the clutter on his desk, picking up pencils that were scattered among the heaps of paper.

As Ricardo waited, Nonsequitur pulled out an electric pencil sharpener and set the pile of pencils to the left of it. He inserted pencils into the sharpener one by one, laying each pencil neatly to the right of the sharpener when it was finished. Then he picked up the entire pile, placed it on the left again, and began re-sharpening the pencils.

Ricardo cleared his throat. "Uh—Admiral . . . ?"

Nonsequitur looked up. "Ah, Ricardo! I'm glad you called," he said.

Just then, as if someone had thrown a switch, an uncharacteristic look of alertness dawned in Nonsequitur's eyes. Ricardo, having seen this happen before, perked up and waited for Nonsequitur to say something worth hearing.

"I have an important message for you," Nonsequitur said. "One of our scout ships reported seeing a Romanumen wartbird—their flagship vessel, the *Brassiere*—undoubtedly heading for the Fountain of Youth. However, they're going in the opposite direction from where your ship is headed."

Ricardo fidgeted in embarrassment.

"Meanwhile, you people are screwing around in orbit of this...this...Love Planet," Nonsequitur went on. "If you're that lonely, Jean-Lucy, why don't you call one of those 900 numbers that lets you have a long conversation with a menopausal Betavoid?"

Ricardo wondered why Nonsequitur's rare moments of mental clarity always seemed to coincide with a screwup by his crew. This was worse than the time Nonsequitur unexpectedly called them during that unauthorized Earl Grape Tea Party, during which Ricardo had allowed an ad agency to film a commercial on his Bridge in exchange for six cases of tea.

"We'll get right on it, Admiral," Ricardo promised.

"You do that," Nonsequitur affirmed, "or else both your crew and Captain Smirk's will go on permanent layoff."

Ricardo nervously nibbled his thumbnail as Nonsequitur went on. "The expenses of both *Endocrines* will be charged against income from the Fountain of Youth, once we find it," Nonsequitur said. "I just came back from a meeting with the accountants, and they made it quite clear: no fountain, no *Endocrines*."

Then, as mysteriously as it had arrived, the clarity began to fade from Nonsequitur's eyes. He stuck a ballpoint pen into the sharpener and frowned as he listened to the blades grinding against plastic. He looked up and asked, "Have I ever told you about my years at Starfreak Academy?"

"No, Admiral," Ricardo said, feigning interest.

"Good!" Nonsequitur barked. "Because that's none of your business!" He flicked off his transmission and disappeared from the Viewscreen.

Capt. Ricardo sighed. He turned toward Ensign Roach Blarin' at the Conn station and ordered, "Ensign, lay in a course to follow the *Brassiere*. And set our cruising speed at Warped 6.7."

"Sir, what coordinates shall I enter?" asked Ensign Roach. A series of wrinkles furrowed the bridge of her nose, as was characteristic of her humanoid species, the Bridgeorans.

Roach continued, "The admiral said the Romanumens are headed in the opposite direction from us, but right now we're not going in any direction, so what's the opposite?" Roach's puzzled expression created a new wrinkle in her nose.

"Ah. That is a problem, Ensign," Ricardo agreed. "We'll just have to continue to steer by the constellations."

"Which one, sir?" Roach responded.

"Read me the list again, will you?" said Ricardo, settling down into his command chair.

Roach pulled out her *Rand McNally Road Atlas and Star Chart* and consulted a map. "In this quadrant we have Phoenix the City," she read, "Orion the Studio, Mensa the Genius, Lynx the Car . . . "

"Oh, never mind," Ricardo interrupted. "Let's just follow that bright one over there." He pointed at the Viewscreen.

Roach squinted out into space. "Sir, that's a searchlight for the grand opening of a frozen yogurt shop."

"I know that," Ricardo retorted. "Follow it anyway."

By the time Capt. Ricardo remembered to check his sensors for the possible presence of Smirk's ship, the sensors showed that the Haves were alone. Unknowingly, by increasing Warped speed to 6.7, they'd left the others far behind.

On Smirk's ship, Chief Engineer Georgie LaForgery explained this new predicament to Smirk and Dacron as they met in the Ready Room.

"Captain Ricardo's crew took off too fast. They left us flatfooted," Georgie admitted. "We might be able to catch up and begin drafting them again, but getting to that point will really strain our reserves of Dilithium Crystal Vanish."

"Keep at it," Smirk urged him. "At least get us close enough so we can monitor their transmissions again. We have to stay up to date on what's happening with Dea— uh...that is, with any developments that might occur. Like this permanent layoff that Nonsequitur mentioned."

Georgie nodded and headed for the door.

"And, Mr. LaForgery..." Smirk continued. Georgie stopped and turned around.

"...Keep up the good work," Smirk added. "This is the first time in my career that I've had a chief engineer who can explain what he's doing." Georgie smiled, saluted, and headed back to Engineering.

Turning to Dacron, Smirk saw that the android still had that odd expression on his face, the Mona Lisa smile he'd worn ever since returning from Stradivarius–9. Then Smirk noticed the cordless earphone plugs that were jammed into Dacron's ears; Dacron had been listening to his cassette player and hadn't heard a word of their conversation so far.

Smirk reached over and popped an earphone plug out of Dacron's ear socket, startling Dacron into attention. Smirk held the plug to his own ear. "What are you listening to, Dacron?" Smirk asked curiously.

"Barry Manilow, sir."

"Barry Manilow? I didn't think your tastes extended to the sentimental, Dacron."

"Lately I have begun studying the computer's archives of human love songs and poetry, sir." Dacron didn't specify that "lately" meant just in the previous three hours since he'd fallen into the Fountain of Love. Before Smirk could question him further and discover that his first officer now had an enormous crush on the woman Smirk sought for himself, Dacron hastened to suggest the plan he'd concocted.

"Captain, I would like to try creating some of this literature myself," Dacron said. "Perhaps I could write poetry and love letters on your behalf. We could send them to Deanna Troit to test the feminine reaction to my work."

Smirk seemed amused. "You want to ghostwrite love letters for me?" he asked. He thought it over for a moment, then said, "Well, why not? Maybe your research will come up with some phrases that'll win her heart. Sure, Dacron, go ahead. Just let me see what you write before you send out anything with my name on it, will you?"

"Of course, Captain," Dacron replied.

"Also," Smirk added, warming up to the idea, "in your letters to her, be sure to emphasize our dire straits. I want to evoke Deanna's sympathy. Mention that we're low on fuel and trying our darndest to keep up. Make it sound like a valiant quest. Like we're down but not out."

"Yes, sir." Dacron stood up, preparing to leave.

"Oh, and Dacron," said Smirk, "try to make this material sound like I wrote it, all right? I know that may be difficult for you since you're an android without emotions, but these letters have got to seem authentic." Smirk draped a fatherly arm across Dacron's shoulders to ready him for a little pep talk. "When you're writing them, try to put yourself in my place."

Smirk's voice dropped to an evocative whisper. "There's this intelligent, beautiful, desirable woman. You'd give anything to have her." A faint pinkish blush spread across Dacron's chalky white cheeks.

"She is the peak of perfection," Smirk crooned. "Just thinking of her face . . . her eyes . . . her hair . . . makes you tingle inside." Dacron began to breathe heavily.

"True union—physical, mental, emotional—would bring both you and this lovely creature to the peak of ecstasy," Smirk went on. Beads of sweat appeared on Dacron's brow.

"Well, Dacron," Smirk concluded, "do you get my drift?"

"Yes, Captain," Dacron replied. "May I be excused now, sir? I believe I need to take a cold shower."

"Ha ha!" Smirk slapped him on the back. "That's the spirit."

Several days later, Mr. Smock crept into the walk-in cooler in the back room of Ten-Foreplay on Ricardo's ship, making sure no one saw him enter.

Smock powered up the short-wave radio transmitter he'd secretly built in his spare time. He had rigged together this piece of unauthorized equipment from egg cartons, cocktail napkins, and other odds and ends scavenged from the bar. Now he would use it to try to contact Beverage Flusher. He hoped Smirk's ship had pulled into communication range once again so he could reach her.

He was in luck; his radio triggered Beverage's office phone. After two rings, she answered: "Beverage Flusher."

Smock nearly swooned when he heard her voice. Unaware that he'd contracted pneumonia after falling into the Fountain of Love, he knew only that the fever which had gripped his body all morning burned even hotter the moment Beverage spoke. His heart beat wildly, the way it used to when he heard a particularly logical theorem. "Dr. Flusher? This is Mr. Smock."

"Oh, hello, Mr. Smock." Her tone was friendly yet noncommittal. "What can I do for you today?"

Be mine, Smock almost blurted out. But he held back, recalling how startled Beverage had seemed when he'd climbed out of the Fountain of Love with words of flattery pouring from his lips. *I must avoid coming on too strong,* he thought.

Smock struggled to keep his voice calm. "There is a particularly interesting article in the latest issue of *Scientific American,*" he said. "I was wondering if you'd seen it. It concerns the entropy of the titanium isotope across the impedance of krypton nuclei." He struggled to catch his breath; his pneumonia-stricken chest grew tighter by the second.

"Yes, I did see it," Beverage replied enthusiastically.

"But what a radical notion they're proposing—that the frakesonian spineroscopy technique can be fragmented across the sirtis and mcfadden modes."

Smock coughed, caught his breath, then coughed again. "But that must be considered—" he broke off as another deep cough shook his chest and then subsided—"in light of the burton-wave theory, given the inevitable inaccuracies of the dornscope and the stewartometer in detecting goldberg variations."

"So true," Bev said with a sigh. She added, "You know, Mr. Smock, it's really nice to talk shop with a fellow scientist again. It gets so *lonely* around here sometimes."

The implied invitation in Bev's tone of voice made Smock draw in his breath sharply. This triggered another coughing seizure which gripped him until he could scarcely breathe.

Bev went on, "Maybe you could come over some evening. I'll make dinner, and we can have a cozy little chat by the light of the Bunsen burners."

Smock couldn't shake his fit of coughing. Struggling to draw in another breath, he felt himself blacking out.

"Mr. Smock?" he heard Bev ask. "Would you like that?"

Smock began seeing stars.

"Mr. Smock? Mr. Smock?" came Bev's voice from the radio transmitter. As he lost consciousness, Smock heard her pout, "Hmmph. Typical modern man. Show the least bit of interest and he flakes out on you."

Smock awoke on the floor of the walk-in cooler several hours later. His limbs were thoroughly chilled, yet his head burned with fever. Spasms of coughing seized his chest, leaving him weak and dizzy.

This must be love, he thought. *Like most human attributes, it is highly overrated.*

Smock dragged himself down the corridor to Wart's counseling office and rang the door chime. "What is it?" boomed Wart from within.

"May I see you, Counselor?" Smock called, gasping for breath. "I need a consultation on a private matter."

"Oh, all right," Wart grumbled.

As Smock entered, he saw that Wart was in the midst of a practice session with his Kringle battle axe. Wart slashed at the air, waving the axe in a ritualized sequence of motions. "What is the problem, Mr. Smock?" he asked without pausing.

"Would you like me to lie down on the couch as I describe my situation?" Smock inquired.

"Whatever," said Wart with a shrug. He continued to wave his weapon, parrying an imaginary opponent.

Smock stretched himself out on the patients' couch and began, "I am suffering from particularly acute bodily symptoms which I attribute to the emotion of love. I am obsessed with the thought of a certain woman, and she—" Smock broke off, disturbed that Wart's battle practice continued without even a glance in his direction. "Mr. Wart, shouldn't you be taking notes?"

Wart turned abruptly and held his axe high in the air, directly over Smock's head. "Do *not* tell a Kringle how to conduct his business!" Wart roared. Alarmed, Smock rose up on his elbows to a half-sitting position.

Wart raged, "It is bad enough that Starfreak ordered me into this job where I must listen to everyone talk about their *feelings*"—he spat out the word with distaste—"without some impudent patient telling me how to run my office!

"Now, I have a *system* here in the counseling center. You state your problem, and then I tell you how to get 'rid of it. Do you understand?"

"Yes, I do," Smock replied warily. Wart resumed his axe-swooping motions. Smock reclined again on the couch and folded his hands over his chest.

"As I was saying," Smock continued, "I am obsessed with the thought of a certain woman. She is so thoroughly human that I despair of becoming a worthy love match

"Mr. Wart, shouldn't you be taking notes?"

for her. Yet I cannot forget her. Day and night I dream about her, imagine her, sigh over her. In the grip of this deathless love, I pine for her. I wither like the reed in a parched land. My heart aches. My spirit grows weary. Tell me, Counselor Wart, what shall I do?"

Wart stopped swinging the axe long enough to scowl at Smock and deliver his treatment recommendation. "Snap out of it!" he growled.

Toward the end of that long, long day, Smock found himself consulting the professional of last resort: Chief Medical Officer Piker.

Smock's symptoms had grown so severe that he was barely conscious when he tottered into Sick Bay. Piker, sensing an interesting medical case in progress, waived the usual three-hour admittance routine and led Smock directly to the intensive care table.

Piker flattened Smock's tongue with a Popsicle stick and demanded, "Say 'aahhhh.'" Shining a flashlight at Smock's throat, Piker observed, "I see the problem right here. You have more than one uvula."

Piker straightened up importantly, adjusted the lapels of his white medical coat, and switched off the flashlight. "The 'uvula' is the term we medical people use for that fleshy thing that hangs above your tongue, way back in your throat," he said. "The word is right there in the medical dictionary, if you'd like to see for yourself. I found it this afternoon when I was looking up 'umbilical.'"

Smock nodded wearily. "I know what the uvula is, Mr. Piker," he rasped. "But *all* Vultures have more than one of them. Some Vultures have as many as four or five, though you only see those Vultures when the circus comes to town. No, I'm afraid the dual-uvula structure is not related to my symptoms."

"Hmmmmm," said Piker, gazing at him in an imitation of deep thought. Finally he asked, "What *are* your symptoms, anyway?"

Smock drew in a breath to answer, which triggered a coughing spasm deep in his chest. Piker grew alarmed watching Smock cough on and on and on, turning a deeper shade of red each time he hacked.

"Red Alert!" Piker declared. His medical staff snapped to attention, then stared at him, unsure what to do next. "No, that's not right," Piker checked himself. "Code Blue!"

At this command, several nurses wheeled a medical cart next to Smock's treatment table. One of them ripped open Smock's tunic and began prepping his chest for surgery. Another inserted an intravenous line into Smock's pointy eartip. A third went through his pockets looking for his insurance card.

Between gasps for breath, Smock managed to wheeze, "What . . . are you . . . going . . . to do?"

"Operate," Piker told him. "We'll have to remove some vital organs." A nurse helped Piker don his personalized surgical mask, which had strategically-placed cutouts in it to keep it from flattening his beard.

"But . . . " —Smock was beginning to black out— " . . . which ones?"

"Won't know till we get in there," Piker replied, his eyes glowing with the maniacal gleam of a surgeon on the hunt.

Later, back in Ten-Foreplay, Smock popped the top off a bottle of sparkling water, guzzled it down without pausing for breath, and reached for another. It was now three days since Piker had performed surgery on him, and this constant thirst seemed to be one of the side effects. Luckily, in his post as chief bartender, Smock had easy access to plenty of liquids during working hours.

To Smock's intense relief, Piker hadn't removed any vital organs after all. When Smock awoke in the recovery room, Piker had told him, "All I did was ream out your lungs." Piker had seemed disappointed that more invasive treatments had been impossible because his scalpel couldn't cut through Smock's tough Vulture innards.

One of them ripped open Smock's tunic.

Now, as Smock walked over to his bar sink to wash some glasses, once again he heard the strange *clank-clank* coming from his ribcage. This phenomenon, too, had arisen after his surgery.

Smock wondered if it was anything serious. It certainly interfered with his work behind the bar. If he didn't stand absolutely still while speaking to a customer or taking someone's drink order, the clanking noise drowned out their voices.

Smock told himself that this clanking was the reason he'd been putting off trying to contact Beverage Flusher again. He rationalized that it would be hard to conduct a sensitive conversation over this tumult, which sounded like a set of silverware churning around loose inside a dishwasher on the rinse cycle. But in his heart of hearts, Smock knew that he was simply afraid to approach Beverage again. She was probably still miffed that their last call had ended so abruptly, and Smock didn't know how to make amends for that.

How would a human male handle this situation? he wondered. *Perhaps a gift would be in order. What might she like?*

Unfamiliar with traditional offerings like candy or flowers, Smock tried to think of something that would appeal to Beverage's scientific interests. Finally he settled on a nice pair of skinfold calipers. As he agonized over whether to sign the gift tag "Yours, Mr. Smock" or "Affectionately, Mr. Smock," he saw Capt. Ricardo enter the door of Ten-Foreplay. Hurriedly Smock tucked the gift box under the counter.

"Captain," Smock said as Ricardo approached, "to what do we owe the pleasure of this unusual visit?"

To the surprise of Smock and everyone else nearby, Ricardo hoisted himself up and stood on a barstool. Reaching overhead with a screwdriver, he adjusted a small metal device attached to the ceiling tiles. Then he climbed down, dusted off the stool, sat on it, and motioned for Smock to lean in toward him. Smock did so, gingerly, trying not to clank.

Ricardo handed Smock a package. Inside it, Smock found several official-looking documents, some black and white 8″ x 10″ photographs, and an old-fashioned reel-to-reel audiotape.

Smock wound the tape onto a tape player he just happened to have behind the bar, adjusting the sound level so only he and Ricardo would be able to hear it. As he listened to the tape, he sifted through the documents.

"Good evening, Mr. Smock," said Ricardo's voice on the tape. "I have just disabled Starfreak's crew monitor in the ceiling because the confidential information you are about to hear requires the highest-level security clearance, and thus is not normally associated with your Starfreak-assigned position of chief bartender.

"As you know, we are supposed to find the Fountain of Youth, and our Bridge crew has been hard at work on this task. Please see photo number one." Photo number one showed the Bridge crew during the day shift. Guano sat in her position, reading *Mad* magazine; McCaw was at the Oops station, scowling; Ensign Roach manned the Conn, cleaning out her nose-bridge ridges with dental floss; and Ricardo sat in his command chair, commanding.

"Unfortunately," Ricardo's voice continued, "our atlas does not reveal the fountain's location, and another map which we often consult does not cover this sector. Please see document A." Smock lifted document A from the pile; it was a paper placemat from a fast-food restaurant, printed with a colorful children's treasure map.

There were other papers and photos; Smock hurriedly glanced through them as the reel of tape drew near its end.

"Your mission, should you decide to accept it," the audiotape said, "is to find out—from whatever source you can—exactly where this Fountain of Youth is located, and relay the coordinates to your captain before he leaves the bar this evening. As always, should you be captured and tortured, we will deny any knowledge of giving you this mission, and we will clean out your locker and sell its contents to pay storage costs. That is all. This tape will self-destruct in ten seconds."

Smock nodded to Ricardo, a movement which set off a series of clanks in Smock's chest.

As Smock headed for Ten-Foreplay's back room, the audiotape self-destructed via spontaneous combustion, sending up a cloud of greasy black smoke. This triggered a fire sprinkler in the ceiling, which doused Ricardo and several patrons sitting at the bar.

In the back room, Smock stepped into the walk-in cooler and powered up his shortwave radio.

Pondering what source to consult, Smock considered the fact that the Fountain of Youth's location was a deep dark secret. Not even his scientist pals, with whom he freely traded information, would know where it was.

He would have to consult the ultimate source of knowledge, the font of all wisdom, the keepers of even the most obscure yet vital facts in the universe. He dialed the frequency of the Milwaukee Public Library Ready Reference service and crossed his fingers.

Unfortunately, Smock had to lean forward awkwardly to use the radio; it rested on a stack of beer cases in the corner, which was the only available flat surface in the cooler. As he leaned, he couldn't help shifting around, and his interior clanking started up again.

"Hello. Ready Reference," said the consultant on the other end of the transmission.

"Hello," said Smock. "I wonder if you could tell me"—his innards went *clank-clank-clank*—"the location of" *clank-clank* "the Fountain of Youth."

"The Fountain of Truth?" repeated the consultant.

Clank-clank-clank. "What?" said Smock. "I'm sorry, I didn't—" *clank-clank-clankety-clank* "—hear you."

"Just a moment, sir . . . "—the consultant's words were

being drowned out on Smock's end—"...I..." *clank* "-et that..." *clank-clank* "-formation..." *clank-clank-clank* "...you."

As he waited on "hold," Smock worried whether he'd even be able to hear the information when it came. He turned the receiver up to full volume, and when the consultant came back on the line, her voice was loud enough to rattle the soda bottles next to the radio.

"THE COORDINATES ARE WEST 5555 BY SOUTHWEST 90038," she told him.

"Thank you," Smock replied, his ears ringing. He clanked his way back to the bar. Ricardo, still dripping wet from his dousing by the fire sprinkler, glared at him.

"Sir, the coordinates are—" Smock began.

"I heard the coordinates, Mr. Smock," Ricardo snapped, "along with everyone else here in the lounge, and probably all the way to Deck Nineteen as well. This was supposed to be a secret mission, you know." Ricardo stood on the stool again and used his screwdriver to reactivate Starfreak's crew monitor in the ceiling.

Climbing off the stool, Ricardo left Smock with his parting shot: "You wouldn't need to do everything at top volume if you'd just turn down that horrid heavy metal music you've got on in here."

"Captain Smirk? This is LaForgery in Engineering." Georgie's voice came over the intercom of Smirk's ship, into the Ready Room where Smirk and Dacron were meeting. "Captain Ricardo's crew just made a drastic course alteration. They turned so abruptly that we lost all our momentum. We can catch them, but it looks like it'll take the remainder of our fuel. Is that what you want to do?"

"Yes, yes, do it!" Smirk replied impatiently. "Take care of it yourself, Mr. LaForgery. I've got an urgent matter to attend to here."

"Yes, sir." Georgie signed off the intercom.

Smirk leaned forward with his elbows on the desk and

said to Dacron, who sat in front of him, "The letter! Read the letter, Dacron." Then he held up his hand. "No, wait. Let me get in the mood to really enjoy this." He leaned back in the swivel chair with his arms behind his head, elbows out to the side. He closed his eyes, sighed deeply to focus his concentration, and said, "OK, now read it out loud to me."

Dacron held up the printout of the message from Deanna Troit which had arrived over his computer modem a few moments before. It was her first response to the love letters Dacron had sent her under Smirk's name.

"Dear Captain Smirk..." Dacron read. Smirk opened his eyes, looking disappointed.

" 'Captain Smirk'?" he echoed. "I was hoping for at least 'Dear Jim.' 'Captain Smirk' is so formal."

"We did use 'Chief Engineer Troit' in the salutations I wrote, Captain," Dacron reminded him.

"Mmmm." Smirk nodded in agreement. "Well, next time let's move up to 'Dear Deanna.' All right, go on. I won't interrupt again."

Dacron read aloud:

Dear Captain Smirk,

It's impossible to remain angry with a man who composes such touching letters. Despite my resolve, I find myself writing this reply to you.

I was surprised to learn that you are within communication range of our ship, but then, down here in Engineering we don't really have a clue what's happening up on the Bridge. Rest assured that I will not tell Captain Ricardo you are so close; your presence shouldn't have any impact on our mission, whatever it is.

Your poetry skills have improved remarkably. More important, your letters show a thoughtful, sensitive, *human* side of your personality which you've never before revealed to me. Perhaps I was mistaken when I refused to give you another chance.

Let's continue this secret correspondence for now, until I can be sure that this change of heart is permanent and that you will not revert to being the chauvinistic jerk I used to know.

Sincerely,
Deanna Troit

"Wow!" Smirk exulted. "Is that great or what?!"

Dacron maintained his customary neutral expression, relieved that he didn't have to force a smile. It would have been hard to pretend happiness on Smirk's behalf when his own feelings were so jumbled.

On one hand, Dacron was delighted that his writing had been powerful enough to change Deanna's mind. On the other hand, he was envious that what she was changing her mind about was the possibility of resuming her romance with his boss.

Dacron wasn't sure where all this would lead. If his future letters were as persuasive as the previous ones had been, he might end up writing Deanna into Smirk's arms.

But Dacron didn't want to end the correspondence, even if Smirk hadn't been urging him on. He had to have some outlet for his newfound compulsion with Deanna. This ghostwriting scheme seemed the safest bet, for now. It let him express his genuine feelings for her without angering Smirk.

Jubilantly, Smirk swiveled back and forth in his chair. "Mr. LaForgery," he said to the intercom, "how long until we catch up to Ricardo's ship?"

"Captain," Georgie's voice answered, "the fuel supply is lower than I estimated. I've gone over the numbers several times, and we may not have enough power to reach them. And anyway, they're still taking the wrong course. We're actually closer to the Fountain of Youth where we are right now. Couldn't we just sit tight until they pass this way again?"

"No!" Smirk exclaimed. "It's urgent that <u>we get back</u> within communicator range of their ship. Do whatever you need to do to get us there, Mr. LaForgery."

Smirk swiveled to face Dacron. "Well, don't just sit there, Lieutenant," Smirk urged him. "Get going and start drafting my reply to Deanna. You've done a great job so far. Not bad for a guy with silicon chips where his heart should be."

Too
True

STARDATE *44444.4 / 1350 hours*
"This is Captain Smirk," said the recording. "I'm away from my command chair right now, so please leave a message at the tone. If you require immediate assistance, please press 'C' and ask the computer for help." *Beeeep.*

"Captain, this is Georgie LaForgery in Engineering," Georgie said to the recorder. "We're really having problems down here. We've run out of Dilithium Crystal Vanish for the engines, just as I thought we would. Also, our sensors aren't working too well, and I don't know where we're going to get replacement parts, since only Starfreak carries them. We've also got to refill all the replicators with toner powder.

"Oh, and one other thing—the subspace communicator is on the fritz, although that seems to be the least of our problems. I'll be working on repairs for these things, but it could take a while. LaForgery out."

1350½ hours
"This is Chief Engineer Georgie LaForgery," said the recording. "I've stepped away from my work station for a moment to visit the men's room, but if you'd like to leave a message, I'll get back to you as soon as I can." *Beeeep.*

"I've stepped away from my work station to visit the men's room..."

"LaForgery, this is Captain Smirk," came Smirk's voice. "Forget all those other repairs for now and just concentrate on fixing the subspace communicator. It's vital that we get it working again."

1430 hours

"This is Captain Smirk," said the recording. "I've gone to the gym to play racquetball, so please leave a message at the tone." *Beeeep.*

"Captain, this is your first officer, Dacron," said the android. "Mr. LaForgery and I have been working on the subspace communicator, as you requested. It will take several days, at least, to restore its ability to send messages. However, we *have* enabled it to *receive* messages. If any letters should arrive from Deanna Troit, I will forward them to you immediately. Dacron out."

A series of love notes began piling up on Capt. Smirk's desk. Each night he sifted through the pile, growing increasingly frustrated as he wondered how long it would be before Dacron could answer them for him.

Stardate 44445.4

Dear Jim,
   It's been a while since I've heard from you, and I wonder how you're doing. I miss the poetry you've been sending. Please write soon.

Sincerely,
Deanna

Stardate 44446.4

Dear Jim,
   Your sudden silence intrigues me. Are you busy with some new adventure? I've re-read all your let-

ters, and now I'm eager for more. When will you write again?

Fondly,
Deanna

Stardate 44449.1

Dear Jim,
I'm dying to read more of your tender poetry. I know you must be busy, but can't you write something? Not even a limerick to tide me over?
This ship, and in particular my assigned post in Engineering, is the most unromantic place imaginable. A love note from you would be a welcome relief.

Achingly,
Deanna

Like Capt. Smirk, Dr. Beverage Flusher also began accumulating a stack of correspondence. In her case, the letters came from Mr. Smock. She read and re-read his messages, growing certain that his affection would flicker out before the Have-Nots' communicator would be repaired and she could answer him.

Stardate 44446.7

Dear Dr. Flusher:
Please forgive the abrupt conclusion to our recent telephone conversation. A health emergency intervened before I could say goodbye. In fact, it is for health reasons that I resort to writing to you rather than calling again. My physical condition makes it difficult to carry on a normal conversation.
I trust you are well and having success in your

medical career. Would it be too bold of me to ask if your invitation to dinner is still open?

Sincerely yours,
Mr. Smock

Stardate 44448.2

Dear Dr. Flusher:

Since I have not had the pleasure of a reply from you as yet, I trust that you need more time to consider whether or not to dine with me. Please take as long as you need to decide.

In the meantime, here is a copy of a particularly fascinating article from the *Journal of Brownian Motion*. I hope you think of me as you read it.

Sincerely yours,
Mr. Smock

Stardate 44449.4

Dear Dr. Flusher:

Please forgive me for raising the issue of us having dinner together. It must have angered you, for you have not replied to my letters. I deeply regret my impudence. It will not happen again.

I will take your refusal to reply as a signal that you are no longer interested in pursuing a social relationship with me. And though this will be the last of my letters, I shall always hold your image in my mind with the highest regard.

Sincerely yours,
Mr. Smock

After sending off his final message to Dr. Flusher, Smock forced himself to get back to work. The Haves' ship had just arrived at another planet, and Ricardo ordered Smock to join the Away Team traveling down to its surface.

Moments later, the Away Team of Smock, Guano and Troit stood on the UltraFax platform, waiting to beam down to the coordinates Smock had been given by Ready Reference—not realizing that their crew had inadvertently sought out the Fountain of Truth.

"I hope you made sure to lay in the right beam-down coordinates this time, Checkout," Guano griped. "I don't want to end up in the ladies' room, standing in the bidet."

Checkout scowled at her. "Dey are correct," he snapped, energizing the UltraFax beam.

Indeed, the coordinates were right on target. In fact, Checkout was a little too accurate. He beamed the trio right into the middle of the fountain, where a continuous plume of water cascaded high into the air and splashed back down into the pool, churning its surface.

The sudden drenching in the Fountain of Truth drew shrieks from Guano and Troit. They headed for the side, but the slick bottom of the pool made movement difficult, and both of them slipped and plunged backwards. Smock, meanwhile, was slaking his intense thirst with big gulps of the fountain's water.

Troit took another step toward the edge, slipped again, and fell back with a splash. The impact tore loose an underwire from her bra, leaving her looking rather lopsided. The wire bounced away in the dancing waters.

Troit shook her dripping hair out of her eyes. "Mr. Smock!" she called out. "Here we are practically drowning, and you're standing there taking a drink. Get your Vulture butt over here and help us!"

"Cool your jets, Counselor," Smock replied. "I am thirsty. You can either wait till I have finished drinking or find your own way out of this fountain."

Guano eyed them curiously. She'd already realized that this wasn't the Fountain of Youth, since none of them were looking any younger. *But what fountain is it?* she wondered. *What would make these two speak their minds for a change? They both usually behave like diplomats.*

Guano dog-paddled her way to the fountain's edge and scrambled over the side. A few paces away, she found a sign:

Fountain of Truth
Caution: ingestion may be fatal to politicians

Guano wasn't sure whether this water would prove valuable, but rather than waste any time wondering about it, she immediately began gathering the water into jugs and stashing them in her hat. She had a good supply by the time Troit and Smock finally emerged from the fountain. They contacted the ship, told Capt. Ricardo that this wasn't the right place, either, and Faxed back up. The ship left the orbit of the planet, and the Haves resumed their search.

Stardate 44449.7 / 0950 hours

Dear Capt. Smirk:
   All right, buster, why haven't you answered my letters? I'm tired of being nice about this! I've been pretending it doesn't bother me, but it does.
   I must have been crazy to think that you had actually changed your ways. Apparently you're still the inconsiderate creep I remember so well from our engagement, because as soon as I respond to your moves, you flake out on me again. Well, let me tell you, unless I hear from you SOON, we're finished!
                                    Assertively,
                                    Deanna Troit

Stardate 44449.7 / 0951 hours
"This is First Officer Dacron," said the recording. "At the moment I am plugged into the wall outlet to recharge my batteries, so I cannot speak to you in person. However, if you leave a message at the tone, I will answer it promptly and in exhaustive detail." *Beeeep.*

"If you leave a message at the tone, I will answer it
promptly and in exhaustive detail."

"Dacron!" came Smirk's holler into the recorder. "How can you rest at a time like this? We've got to get that subspace communicator working again so we can answer Deanna's letters! We—oh, never mind—I'll come over there myself to get you in gear . . . "

"I am sorry, sir, but I cannot possibly drink another drop." Dacron stared dazedly at the empty cans of Mountain Dew littering the floor around him. "In fact," he added, "I find it difficult to believe that my body has already retained this much liquid."

"Just try to drink a little more," Capt. Smirk urged him, hovering over the chair in which Dacron sat in a corner of Engineering. "He's got room for more, hasn't he, Georgie? You're our resident android expert."

Georgie shook his head and said, "I think he's just about reached his limit, Captain."

"But he doesn't seem any more alert than when we started," Smirk observed. "You said this stuff is even better than coffee at making him hyper."

"It'll just be a little longer. Then the caffeine will kick in," Georgie reassured Smirk. "That should recharge him in a big way. It'll be the equivalent of spending ten hours plugged into the wall outlet."

"I hope you're right," Smirk replied. "He's got to work at top speed to fix the subspace communicator. Not to mention all the other things that are broken around here." Smirk glanced impatiently at his watch. "How much longer?"

"Ten seconds more," said Georgie, consulting his own watch. "Five, four, three, two, one . . . now."

A spasm seized Dacron's body, and his head snapped to attention. He leaped out of the chair. "INTRIGUING!" he shouted. "My heart rate just accelerated two hundred and fifteen percent!"

"Let's get him over to the communicator," Georgie directed. He and Smirk steered Dacron to a panel at the wall; it opened to reveal the inner workings of the subspace communicator's main junction box. Dacron worked furiously at the panel, his hands moving so fast that they blurred. A few seconds later he reported, "Sending mode of subspace communicator has been restored." He looked around with nervous, birdlike movements. "What shall I work on next?"

As Georgie led Dacron to another task, Smirk eagerly opened a channel on the subspace communicator so they could contact Troit on Ricardo's ship. However, the signal still wasn't getting through; the monitors indicated that Ricardo's ship had moved out of range into another LATA zone. Frustrated, Smirk switched off the set.

"LaForgery!" Smirk said. "Get Dacron working on the engines next. We've got to get closer to Ricardo's ship."

"Aye, sir," Georgie said.

A few minutes later, Smirk's crew was underway with the engines humming at Warped 9, thanks to Dacron's speedy invention of a Dilithium Crystal Vanish substitute.

During the next few hours, Dacron took advantage of his nervous energy. He refilled the replicators, performed a full diagnostic of the ship's built-in vaccum cleaning ducts, mopped the Mess Hall floors, and discovered a cure for cancer. He was working on the faulty sensors when Smirk paged him from the Bridge.

"Dacron," Smirk said, "we've arrived at a planet. Our sensors indicate that this was the latest stop that Ricardo's crew made. I want you and Beverage to Fax down there and see what's happening."

"Should I finish repairing the sensors first, Captain?" Dacron asked. "We cannot be sure they are reliable."

"No," Smirk replied. "I want to stay hot on Ricardo's trail. We know his ship has been here recently, and they're probably still in orbit. They might have somebody down on the surface. Check it out."

"Yes, sir," Dacron said.

Luckily, Ricardo's Away Team had left a lot of stray

UltraFax particles lying around, thanks to Checkout's sloppy beam-down technique; so Smirk's UltraFax chief, O'Brine, had no trouble tracing the exact spot of their landing. Noticing that there was a body of water at that spot, O'Brine shifted his UltraFax beam several meters to the left.

Dacron and Beverage materialized a few steps away from the Fountain of Truth. Beverage walked over to investigate the sign identifying the fountain. As Dacron scanned the area for any indication of Ricardo's crew, he noticed the sunlight gleaming off an object that bounced in the fountain's churning water.

Searching his memory banks, Dacron instantly identified the object as the underwire of a woman's bra, and his lover's intuition told him it belonged to Deanna Troit. Dacron's pulse, already soaring from the Mountain Dew, raced even faster. Impulsively he jumped into the fountain to retrieve the underwire.

"Dacron! What are you doing?" Beverage called. Dacron waded back toward the edge, triumphantly holding the wire high in the air. Beverage helped him step out of the fountain.

"I could not resist retrieving this precious possession of Deanna Troit," Dacron said. "It is a remnant of her delicate lingerie. She must have left it here accidentally. I will cherish it forever."

"What in the world—?" Beverage shook her head in confusion. "Dacron, what are you saying?"

"This is a keepsake from the object of my passion," Dacron explained. "I am deeply, madly, achingly in love with Deanna Troit."

"But you can't feel love—" Beverage began. Then realization dawned in her eyes. "That fall into the Fountain of Love is still affecting you..." she said slowly as she figured it out, "...and now this Fountain of Truth...so you can't keep it to yourself..."

"This is too wonderful to keep to myself!" Dacron cried.

He jumped up onto the flat edge of the low wall encircling the fountain and lifted his arms toward the sky. "I want the universe to know that I love Deanna," he proclaimed. "And furthermore, she loves me."

Dacron began dancing back and forth along the wall. "She does not know it yet, because she thinks all those love letters came from Captain Smirk. But it was my writing that won her heart!"

Bev's eyes widened. "You've been writing love letters to Deanna and putting the captain's name on them?" she asked.

"Yes! He asked me to ghostwrite for him. But the words were all mine," Dacron exulted, hopping up and down, "and they were sincere. And I must tell her so!"

"Dacron, are you crazy?" Beverage pulled him off the wall and grasped his shoulders, trying to hold him still. "Stop dancing for a minute and listen to me," she ordered, looking him straight in the eye. With an effort, Dacron tamed down his jumping motion to a nervous jiggle.

"You can't just go blurting out all this," Beverage told him. "Captain Smirk will be furious if you blow his cover. You know how much he's counting on getting back together with Deanna."

Anxiety clouded Dacron's expression. "That is true," he said. "Everything we have done on this mission has been directed to that end." He looked even more worried as he added, "But I must tell everyone the truth. I cannot seem to keep it to myself."

"You're going to have to," Beverage said. "Do you want the captain to shut you down? He'll do that, you know. He'll open your back panel, press your 'off' switch and throw away the key. Unless..." Bev got a thoughtful gleam in her eye.

"Unless what, Doctor?" Dacron asked anxiously. "Please help me. I have no skill for office politics."

"Unless I shut you down, and bring you back up whenever he's not around," Bev went on, making up a scheme as she went along. "We could keep you in Sick Bay; I'll say you've been damaged by falling into the fountain. When you're awake, we'll restrain you somehow so you can't blurt out anything over the communication channels...he'll surely be monitoring them. Then, when we finally catch up with the other ship, you can go see Deanna in person and tell her the truth."

A yellow tear formed in the corner of Dacron's eye. "You would do all that for me?" he asked, choked with emotion. "That is so kind of you, Doctor."

Beverage smiled and gave a little shrug. "I'd like to see true love win out for a change," she confessed. For a moment, her thoughts drifted back over her own unlucky love life.

Her husband, Jock Flusher, had been killed in action many years ago. Poignantly enough, Capt. Ricardo himself had delivered Jock's body to Beverage; that was back when Ricardo was still moonlighting for UPS.

Much later, she'd fallen for an alien being, only to discover that his handsome outer body was merely a host for his true inner entity, which looked like a cow's stomach. When the host body died, Dr. Flusher had transplanted this throbbing mass into a series of temporary hosts: first Cmdr. Piker, then an alien woman, and finally a laboratory chimpanzee.

Despite all this turmoil, she'd still planned to marry the cow's-stomach essence of her lover, but Starfreak refused to honor their application for a marriage license because they'd filled in the blank for "groom's species" with the notation "subject to change." The affair had ended on a bittersweet note, and Flusher still felt uneasy whenever the Mess Hall menu featured tripe.

And now, Flusher realized sadly, her inability to answer Smock's letters had ruined their budding relationship before it even got off the ground. She began thinking out loud: "In fact, I thought even I had a shot at love, but it seems to have died on the vine...."

Capt. Ricardo himself had delivered Jock's body to Beverage.

She waved her hand, dismissing the thought. "Never mind," she said to Dacron. "We've got to get you to Sick Bay and pretend you've been damaged. Let's hope this works."

7

Truth's
Consequences

"**C**OME WITH ME , Deanna. Please?" Guano pleaded, tagging along as Deanna Troit performed routine maintenance of the engines of Ricardo's ship. "I really want to get to the bottom of this thing about your mother and the computer," said Guano. "Ever since we fell into that Fountain of Truth, it's been bugging me."

"I know. You've hardly stopped talking about it since the minute we got back," said Troit, flushing some Dilithium Crystal Vanish into the engine's Main Bowl.

Troit admitted, "You've even got *me* interested in finding out the truth about the computer. I guess I'll go with you. But this won't be easy. You know we're going to have to talk directly to the CPU—the Central Processing Unit."

Guano nodded. "I know. I just didn't want to go alone." They headed down the corridor toward the Crewmover.

"You really think my mother's involved with the computer in some way?" Troit asked.

"You heard what everybody said when we asked around in Ten-Foreplay this morning—how they think of her whenever the computer speaks, and how nobody has ever talked to them both at the same time," said Guano. "The whole thing is pretty fishy. Now if you ask the computer something that only your mother would know, maybe we can trick it into revealing the connection. Maybe the computer is tied into her modem or something."

"I'll try," said Troit, "but have you ever met the CPU in person?" Guano shook her head. "It's awfully intimidating," Troit continued. "That's why most of the crew only hears the audio. It's pretty hard to deal with the CPU face-to-face."

They rode the Crewmover to Lower Level 68 in the depths of the *Endocrine*'s basement. The door opened onto a cavernous, dimly-lit room, and a damp, musty odor hit their nostrils.

Programmer gnomes scurried about, adjusting the tubing and wiring that snaked out to all areas of the ship. At the far end of the room sat the CPU, flashing its lights and pouring smoke from its exhaust valves. In front of it, a hologram of a huge turbaned female head floated in midair, shrouded in fog.

Terrified, Guano froze in her tracks. Troit clutched Guano's hand and pulled her forward.

"Who dares to approach the CPU?" thundered the hologram head. The programmers squeaked, scuttling out of the way.

Troit raised her chin and quavered, "Deanna Troit." She curtsied.

"Deanna Troit, eh? Well, you'd better have a good reason for bothering me, Troit, 'cause I know where you hang out, and I might just decide to zap you someday," sneered the computer's hologram head. Then it glared at Guano, demanding, "And who are you?"

Guano bit her nails and tried to hide behind Troit, who pushed her out front again.

"Me?" Guano squealed. "I'm uh, um . . . Rita Miller."

"We have come to ask you a question, Your Magnificence," Troit began.

"Why can't you use the audio channel like you're supposed to?" the computer scolded.

"It's sort of a delicate topic," said Troit. "We didn't think

"Who dares to approach the CPU?"

you'd want to talk about it in front of everybody."

"Hmmmph," the computer sniffed. "All right, let's hear it."

"Well, as you know, Christmas is coming," Troit said, "and I'd like to buy my mother a present, and as you probably also know, she prefers low-cut gowns, which she buys at Frederick's of Hubble..."

"Will you get to the point?" the computer raged, with a flash of its strobe lights and a puff of smoke for emphasis.

"So I was wondering"—Troit's words rushed out—"whether you've got some sort of inventory of her wardrobe so I don't buy her something she already has."

"How should I know what clothing your mother owns?" bellowed the computer. Volcanic sound effects boomed out of its speakers, shaking the walls. Troit and Guano reflexively took a step backward. "Am I your mother's keeper? What a question to ask of Starfreak's most advanced processing unit!"

"Well, you've answered more trivial questions than that," said Troit. "Last week I heard you and Ensign Roach talking about the world record in the ninety-and-over age division of the women's triple jump—"

"SILENCE!" thundered the computer. "I will not deign to consider your request. Now get out of here, you miserable blobs of organic matter!"

"But—" Troit protested.

"GET OUT! BEAT IT! AMSCRAY! The Great and Powerful Computer has spoken!" To emphasize its point, the CPU threw out a bolt of electricity, knocking Troit to her knees.

"Hey!" yelled Guano. "Why'd you do that? You big bully!" She helped Troit to her feet. "You didn't even answer our question, you big blustering wall of microchips!"

The CPU's hologram face narrowed its eyes and sneered, "Button your lip, you...you...creature with no eyebrows, you."

"Oh yeah? Who's gonna make me?" Guano challenged, rolling up her sleeves.

"I know what you're thinking," the CPU hissed. "You think I've got something to hide. You think you're going to discover the truth about my identity."

"Huh?" said Guano.

"What do you mean? How can you know what she's thinking?" asked Troit.

"Nothing," the computer replied quickly. "Nothing. Just forget it."

But their suspicions had been intensified, and now Guano noticed a curtain fluttering at the side of the CPU. She motioned to Troit. Silently they approached the curtain as the computer continued blustering and throwing off smoke.

Guano drew aside the curtain. Troit gasped: "Mother!"

There behind the curtain, working an assortment of levers and buttons on a control panel, was Woksauna Troit. She gave them a startled glance, then leaned toward her microphone. "Pay no attention to that woman behind the curtain!" she said. Her voice boomed from the CPU speakers. "The Great and Powerful Computer . . . uh . . . "

Seeing that Guano and Troit weren't falling for it, Woksauna stopped the charade and primly smoothed back her hair. "Hello, spittle one," she said, greeting her daughter with a pet name from childhood. "Hello, *Guano*," she added with a mean look.

"Mother, how could you?" Deanna said with a sigh. "You, of the Betavoid royal House of Pancakes, keeper of the sacred griddle—moonlighting as a computer?"

Woksauna looked embarrassed, but she defended herself stoutly. "What else am I to do? There are only so many key staff positions for a women of my . . . of a certain age. Besides, this job lets me keep an eye on you, Deanna. The computer has video cameras trained on every area of the ship.

"Which reminds me," she continued, wagging an index finger at her daughter, "I see you've been playing around with that Piker fellow again. How many times must I tell you? A man never buys the cow when he can get the milk for free."

While Guano and Troit were confronting the computer in the basement, Mr. Smock stomped down the hall toward Sick Bay, determined to find out what was wrong with him.

He had to get rid of these horrible post-surgical symptoms. As long as he kept clanking and rattling and running off to get a drink of water every few minutes, he couldn't hope to approach Beverage Flusher if their paths should ever cross again. He was counting on his next Away Team mission to provide that opportunity.

After falling into the Fountain of Truth, Smock had made up his mind to tell Dr. Flusher how he really felt about her. He figured he had nothing to lose by trying the direct approach, since his highly circumspect letters to her had gone unanswered. An old saying of Capt. Smirk's popped into his head: "When all else fails, tell the truth."

But first Smock had to conquer these nagging physical problems, and he no longer had any qualms about pinpointing their source: Chief Medical Officer Wilson Piker.

Smock burst through the entrance of Sick Bay. "Sir, do you have an appointment?" asked the receptionist, rising to intercept him; but he strode past her into the examination area.

Piker was on duty, studying a patient's severely fractured leg and tapping a reflex hammer around the wound. "Tell me where it hurts," he ordered.

"Aaaaaagh!" the patient screamed as Piker struck the wound directly.

Piker looked surprised at this violent reaction, but before he could raise his hammer to make another diagnostic test, Smock grabbed him by the lapels of his medical jacket and shoved him against the wall. "What the—" Piker stammered.

"Listen, you quack," Smock snarled. "I've been feeling

terrible ever since you performed surgery on me. I don't expect you to be able to figure out your own mistakes, but perhaps, in spite of you, I can find out just what went wrong during that operation." With that, Smock pressed his thumb along Piker's jawbone and his fingers against Piker's temple and cheekbone, engaging Piker in the famous Vulture mind-melt.

Smock realized that in this case it might be hard to tell when the mind-melt took effect. Usually the meltee's suddenly-vacant expression was the definitive sign, but Piker always looked pretty vacant anyway. However, when Smock's mind filled with a serious of vacuous images a moment later, he knew he'd gotten in.

The theme music from "Petticoat Junction" was playing over and over in Piker's brain. Smock pressed past that and drove deeper, into the memory region.

It was cluttered with trivia. Smock searched through clusters of Piker's favorite lottery numbers, Kringle recipes and jazz trombone solos until finally he found Piker's memory of the surgery. It was frustratingly vague, but Smock did get the impression that somehow Piker had messed up the protocol toward the end of the procedure.

Disappointed, Smock backed out of Piker's brain and ended the mind-melt. He drew his fingers away from Piker's face.

Piker moaned. "My brain hurts," he complained. "This is like being back in school."

Smock left Sick Bay but returned just a few minutes later accompanied by Dr. McCaw, who climbed onto the surgery table so he could reach the crew monitor Starfreak had placed on the ceiling.

"Hey, what do you think you're doing?" Piker demanded. "That table is supposed to be sterile, you know—so we can play poker on it while we eat lunch."

"Well, then, wipe it off after I'm done with it," McCaw retorted, climbing back down to the floor. "Haven't you ever heard of Lysol?"

Smock drove deeper into Piker's memory.

"And how come you're here, anyway?" Piker went on. "You belong on the Bridge. I'm the chief medical officer now."

"Not for the next couple of hours, you're not," said McCaw. "Jean-Lucy agreed that I could come in here and perform surgery on Mr. Smock, to figure out where you screwed up."

"Has Starfreak authorized your change of duties?" Piker wanted to know.

"Of course they haven't, you nincompoop!" McCaw barked. "Why do you think I disabled the ceiling monitor? If we waited for all the paperwork involved in a Starfreak authorization, Mr. Smock could die of thirst. Or noise pollution. Or whatever other symptoms he's got, thanks to your incompetence."

McCaw motioned for Smock to lie on the table and began prepping him for surgery. McCaw explained to Piker, "Ricardo said to go ahead with this make-good operation. We'll get the authorization later by pretending we haven't yet performed the surgery, so eventually the HMO will reimburse us. I've done it this way millions of times."

"Hmmmph," Piker grunted.

"I'll need an assistant," McCaw said, donning a blue gown and mask. "Who's your best surgical nurse?"

Piker frowned and admitted grumpily, "Miss Ames, I guess."

"Well, get her over here," McCaw ordered. A moment later, the nurse appeared at his side. McCaw glanced at her, then did a double take and inquired, "What happened to your arm?"

"It's artificial, sir," Nurse Ames replied.

"I can see that," McCaw snapped, "but it seems so awkward—here, let me have a look." He grasped the limb, gave it a cursory glance, and asked her, "Who installed this thing?"

"Chief Medical Officer Piker, of course," she said.

"Well, he put it on backwards," McCaw said. "After I've

finished using the table, ask him to fix it for you. Right now, get me someone else to help with this surgery. I don't want a backhanded assistant."

Nurse Ames disappeared, and soon another nurse stepped up to McCaw's side. "Nurse Hatchet at your service, Dr. McCaw," she reported.

"Hatchet, set up the anesthesia," McCaw said. She nodded and went to the corner to retrieve a large rubber mallet. "What's that?" McCaw asked.

"It's Mr. Piker's way of putting patients under," Nurse Hatchet told him. "He says it's quicker and easier than gas."

McCaw gave her his distinctive look of disdain, perfected through years of practice; it managed to convey his displeasure even though most of his face was covered by the surgical mask and cap. "I can see this is going to be a long day," he groused.

Two hours later, Dr. McCaw finally finished the surgery on Mr. Smock. A metal pan at McCaw's elbow held the objects he'd retrieved from Smock's innards—things that Piker had inadvertently left behind during the previous surgery: five surgical instruments, a pair of latex gloves, a dozen sponges, and several insurance reimbursement forms.

Back on the Bridge, Capt. Ricardo waited anxiously for the surgery to be finished. The sooner Smock recovered, the sooner he'd be able to re-query his secret source of information about the location of the Fountain of Youth.

The Haves' Bridge crew desperately needed Smock's help. On their own, they still hadn't gotten any closer to discovering where the fountain might be. The best they had come up with was to notice a bunch of youthful-looking aliens traveling out of the LaLa Quadrant. They had projected back to the source of the travelers, only to discover that it was a starbase specializing in plastic surgery.

Ricardo wondered gloomily whether the Romanumens might actually beat them to the Fountain of Youth, and if so, whether Admiral Nonsequitur would follow through on his threat to lay off all of them. *Maybe I could take an early retirement instead,* Ricardo speculated. *Or better yet, go back to serve on my former ship, the USS* Skinbracer.

Several days later, on Capt. Smirk's ship, Dacron sat twiddling his thumbs in the research lab of Sick Bay. Beverage Flusher provided him this sanctuary so Capt. Smirk wouldn't realize he was fully operational and liable at any moment to blurt out the truth, the whole truth, and nothing but the truth.

After Bev and Dacron had beamed back to Sick Bay from the Fountain of Truth, Bev had turned him off and laid him on an examining table. Smirk came in for a progress report, saw Dacron sprawled out on the table, and bought Bev's story that Dacron was damaged during the away mission. After Smirk left Sick Bay, Bev turned Dacron back on.

Smirk hadn't returned since then; and because the research lab was tucked deep within Sick Bay, they felt sure that he couldn't unexpectedly walk in on Dacron without being intercepted by Bev.

Dacron was locked in this inner room. "It's for your own protection," Bev reminded him. "You won't have a chance to tell anybody about your crush on Deanna."

Dacron passed the time by monitoring a special long-range sensor array he'd rigged up. Bev had made sure that the equipment could not send audio or visual messages, which might be monitored by the captain. All Dacron could do was listen to the sensor speakers, hour after hour, but it was better than doing nothing.

There had been no more messages from Ricardo's ship; Deanna Troit had stopped writing, just as she'd threatened to do. Dacron wondered if he would ever get the chance to explain everything to her in person.

Amidst the sensors' humming and hissing with routine transmissions and static, one signal suddenly caught Dacron's attention. As he listened more closely, he realized this was indeed an important development. He had tapped into the radio of the Romanumen flagship *Brassiere.*

Dacron knew that no one else on the ship would have caught this transmission, and the information was vital. He had to tell Capt. Smirk.

"What is it, Dacron?" Beverage asked a few moments later. "The nurse said you insisted on seeing me immediately."

"Doctor, I must speak to the captain," Dacron declared. "The Romanumens are about to arrive at the Fountain of Youth. If they claim the fountain, Starfreak will have no chance of recovering it. I can help us get there first, if I am able to work at my Oops station.

"You said my condition of excessive truthfulness will last indefinitely," Dacron continued, "but can you give me something to temporarily suppress it so I may serve on the Bridge until we have completed our mission?"

"Gee, Dacron, that's a tough one," Bev said, thinking hard.

"Is there some medicine that might work?" Dacron asked. "It need only last for a few hours."

"There *is* an old folk remedy. . . . " Bev said to herself. "I wonder if I still have some of that around. . . . " She headed for the medicine closet with Dacron trailing her eagerly. After rummaging through the clutter in the back of the closet, Bev pulled out a bottle. "Aha!" she said. "Here it is."

She blew the dust off the label, which read "Essence of Bureaucracy."

"This suppresses the ability to give straight answers," Bev said. "I'm not sure what dosage to give you, though," she continued, reading the fine print on the label. "Too much, and you'll go into a stupor; too little, and you'll still be blurting out the truth about Deanna. Well, let's start with a tablespoonful, and I'll monitor you as you talk to Captain Smirk."

Beep-beep boop-boop went the door chime of Capt. Smirk's Ready Room. Smirk stood by the side wall, fooling around with the model of the *Endocrine* that sat on a pedestal. He pushed the model back and forth while making Warped engine noises: *vrooom, vrooom.* "Come in," he called toward the door.

Dacron and Bev entered. "Ah, Dacron," said Smirk. "Good to see you up and about again."

"Thank you, sir," Dacron began. He glanced nervously at Beverage, then went on, "Captain, I have intercepted an important message from the Romanumen flagship."

Smirk pushed aside the model *Endocrine* and turned his attention to Dacron. "Yes?"

"They now know the exact location of the Fountain of Youth, and they are headed there at top speed," Dacron told him. "I have calculated a method by which our ship might exceed its normal engine capacity so we could arrive before they do. It would involve constant, subtle modifications of the ship's engines. I believe I can best direct this effort from my station on the Bridge."

Smirk was all business. "Well, let's get going!" He started toward the door but stopped when Dacron spoke up again.

"I must emphasize, Captain," Dacron continued, "that there is no margin for error. Your previous plan to hold back and then dash in for a dramatic rescue at the last minute would jeopardize this mission."

"I understand, Dacron," Smirk said. "We'll concentrate on getting to the fountain before the Romanumens do. And at least we'll beat Ricardo there, which should convince Starfreak to reinstate our crew to full-time status." He headed for the door, then stopped again as Dacron resumed his spiel.

"It would be a grievous error to play coy, merely for

dramatic effect," said Dacron, "and lose the chance to claim the fountain for Starfreak just so you could impress Dea—"

Abruptly Beverage jerked Dacron by the arm. "Dacron!" she interrupted, pulling him toward the far corner. She smiled at Smirk and said, "Excuse us for a moment, Captain." Spinning Dacron around to face her, she forced his mouth open and poured several gulps of Essence of Bureaucracy down his throat, straight from the bottle.

Dacron swallowed hard, blinking his eyes. "Thank you, Doctor," he said. "That is much better."

"What was that you were saying, Dacron?" Capt. Smirk prompted.

"Nothing of importance, sir," Dacron replied. "It would be best for us to proceed with our mission immediately."

Beverage sighed with relief and followed Dacron and Smirk as they headed for their stations on the Bridge.

Dacron gave their pilot the precise coordinates of the Fountain of Youth in the Hydrant Quadrant, and she laid in the course. As the ship sped toward their destination, Dacron used the intercom to stay in contact with Georgie in Engineering, suggesting a series of adjustments to the engines for maximum output.

Beverage sat in the command chair to Smirk's left. She tried not to be too obvious about watching Dacron for any telltale signs of hyperhonesty. So far, he was holding up all right.

After they had traveled for about an hour, Westerly noticed a signal on the radar at his Tactical station. "Captain Smirk," he reported, "our course is taking us close to Captain Ricardo's ship."

"Really?" Smirk straightened up in his chair. He told the pilot, "Slow to Warped 3.14 so we can check this out," and then asked Westerly, "What are they doing?"

"Not much, sir," Westerly observed. "They're orbiting an American Automobile Association tourist information center."

"Probably asking for directions," Smirk said with a chuckle. "Let's listen in on their communication transmissions, just for kicks. Monitor the audio channel from their ship, Mr. Flusher. Put it over our Bridge speakers."

"Aye, sir." Westerly pressed the control buttons. Unfortunately, being away at Starfreak Academy Film School had left Westerly's skills a little rusty, and he inadvertently put the radio into its default mode that allowed two-way communication. Unknown to him and the rest of Smirk's Bridge crew, anything they said would now be heard on Ricardo's Bridge.

A few moments later, they heard Mr. Snot tell Capt. Ricardo, "Cap'n, we've got a message comin' in from Starfreak Headquarters."

"Onscreen," came Ricardo's voice.

Smirk cocked his eyebrow in a this-ought-to-be-interesting expression and tipped his head, the better to hear the broadcast of Ricardo's conversation.

"Captain Ricardo," came the voice of Admiral Nonsequitur.

"Admiral," replied Ricardo, sounding a little nervous. "We've been meaning to call you. We'd like special dispensation for Dr. McCaw to perform surgery on Mr. Smock. You see—"

"Never mind, Ricardo," Nonsequitur interrupted. "We have something far more important to deal with. Starfreak has just intercepted a coded Romanumen message sent by the wartbird *Brassiere* to the Romanumen headquarters. The ship reported that they're zeroing in on the Fountain of Youth. Do you know what this means?"

"I suppose, Admiral," Ricardo said in an abject tone, "it means that they're about to beat us to the punch."

"They are?" Nonsequitur seemed amazed. "Yes, yes, Ricardo. You're right! Of all the rotten—they're going to beat us to the punch!"

Smirk shook his head gleefully, knowing his crew would forestall this disaster. He beamed at Beverage, and she smiled back, sharing his delight.

They heard Ricardo suggest weakly, "We could follow their ship and try to cut them off at the last minute..."

"That won't work," Nonsequitur said. "You'll never find them. They've got that device turned on, that thing that makes their ship invisible—what is it called? Choking device? Joking device?"

Ricardo supplied the term. "Croaking device."

"Yes, the croaking device," said Nonsequitur. "So the only way we could hope to beat them there would be to start now and outrace them. But we can't do that without knowing the exact location of the fountain. If only we knew where it is..."

Sitting at his Oops station, Dacron began panting as the Essence of Bureaucracy wore off. Powerful pro-honesty forces sought to loosen his tongue: years of Starfreak training to supply information whenever a superior officer needed it... the Fountain of Truth water that had saturated his synthetic pores... and the aftereffects of the Mountain Dew, which still kept his system in overdrive. Even the knowledge that he would cook his own goose by blurting out the truth was no match for the compulsion to blab.

"The Fountain of Youth is in the Hydrant Quadrant," Dacron said aloud. "The precise coordinates are North 2389 by Northwest 6751."

"Who said that?" came Nonsequitur's voice over the intercom.

This was immediately followed by Ricardo's voice, which echoed, "North 2389 by Northwest 6751?"

A look of horror spread across Smirk's face. "They can hear us!" he gasped.

"Smirk, is that you?" Nonsequitur's voice inquired.

As realization dawned, Smirk involuntarily followed the path of error around his Bridge. He glared at Dacron, swiveled backward to shoot a dirty look at Westerly Flusher, then snapped his gaze up toward the ceiling where the communicator's microphone hung.

"They can hear us! Good grief!" Smirk shrieked. Everyone on his Bridge froze in disbelief for a moment as they realized what had just happened.

Then they heard Capt. Ricardo order, "Ensign Roach, lay in a course of 3.45 mark 48.98 for the Hydrant Quadrant."

Smirk swung into action. "Punch it up to Warped ten!" he ordered. "We've got to beat them there!"

Beverage bounded over to Dacron and pulled him to his feet. She dragged the befuddled android to the Crewmover while apologizing to Capt. Smirk. "I-I thought I had him fixed, b-b-but . . . " she babbled, "there must still be something wrong with his software. I'll take him to Sick Bay and—uh—run a cleanup utility program on him."

"Just get him off my Bridge," Smirk raged.

"I think you should know, sir, that I—" Dacron began, but Beverage clamped a hand over his mouth and shoved him into the Crewmover before he could spill his guts.

After the doors closed, Bev sighed with relief and gave the Crewmover their destination: "Shipping and Receiving."

Dacron looked puzzled. "Doctor, you told the captain we were going to Sick Bay," he reminded her.

Bev shook her head. "We've got to be ready to UltraFax down to the Fountain of Youth as soon as our ship arrives at the planet," she said. "Do you think Captain Smirk would send you on another away mission after what just happened? If we're lucky, you and I can get down to the fountain before he knows we're leaving. Then it's up to you to state your case to Deanna."

Both ships raced at top speed toward the Hydrant Quadrant. In the midst of the chase, Capt. Smirk suddenly stood and turned to Westerly Flusher at the Tactical station.

"Mr. Flusher, secure a private channel to Deanna Troit on Ricardo's ship. Patch it through to my Ready Room,"

Smirk ordered, striding to the Ready Room door.

Once inside, Smirk turned on his desktop monitor, and Troit's image appeared. She stood in front of the huge pulsing engine on Ricardo's ship. Her arms were crossed, and she impatiently tapped the fingers of one hand against her arm. "Yes, Captain, what is it?" she asked curtly. "I'm very busy right now."

"Ah, yes. I'm sure you are," said Smirk, giving her his oiliest smile. "We've all been so busy lately, haven't we? But sometimes it's good to stop and smell the roses."

Troit frowned harder. "Get to the point," she snapped.

"Well, you're probably thinking that I've been so involved with this mission that I hadn't taken time to write to you lately," Smirk continued in his most buttery tone. "But now it can be told: I *couldn't* write to you. Starfreak orders, you know."

A shadow of doubt passed over Troit's cross expression. "Starfreak orders? But you're not in Starfreak anymore."

Smirk gave a debonair chuckle. "Yes, that's what everybody's supposed to think, isn't it?" he said with a wink, as if acknowledging a foolish charade they all had to maintain. Troit looked even more confused.

"Our cover has been working," Smirk continued. "Everybody in the galaxy disregards us because they think we're washed up. Meanwhile, we're hot on the trail of the Romanumens, on a top-secret mission—so top secret, in fact, that we couldn't break radio silence."

"Oh," said the bewildered Troit, who seemed to be debating whether or not to accept his story.

"And that's why I couldn't correspond with you anymore, my dear," Smirk said, "much as I yearned to do. I simply couldn't risk giving away the position of our ship. Especially since we were barely clinging to survival, doing without Starfreak support and supplies—all to intensify the illusion, naturally."

Smirk sighed deeply, as if the struggle had taken its toll. "Yes, we've given it our all," he said. "Yet I fear that in my zeal to perform my duty, I have risked the thing I cherish most: our romance. You must be quite angry with me for not contacting you—even though any communication between us in the last few days might have eventually led to the downfall of the federation."

"Well, I—" Troit said, reluctant to be cast in such a petulant light.

Smirk pressed on. "Dearest Deanna, would you deny me this chance, merely because I have also done my duty as a Starfreak officer? I still have a lifetime's worth of love poetry stored up for you, and soon there will be nothing between us. Just say you'll be mine."

Troit shook her head. "I don't know," she answered. "It's all so confusing."

"Just think about my words of love in the letters I sent," Smirk half-whispered, "and how much they moved you."

Troit got a faraway look in her eyes. "Yes," she admitted, "those letters did make me feel there was genuine sensitivity somewhere inside you. Although I must say that my empathic powers can't seem to pick it up from you right now."

"It's probably this darned communicator. We must have a bad connection," Smirk reasoned. "But surely you remember the poetry and outpourings of love I've written."

Troit blushed. "Yes, I do. I've even memorized some of them. They make me feel that our romance is . . . predestined, somehow. Those letters did touch something deep inside me, and it would be a shame to lose that feeling."

"Wonderful," Smirk said in an awestruck tone. He leaned forward and continued urgently, "Deanna, for once, listen to your heart, not your head. Say you'll marry me. This time we'll make it all the way through our engagement, I promise."

"Well . . . " Troit was still hesitant.

"Say yes," Smirk urged her. "It won't be binding. You know that federation law allows a three-day cooling-off period on any marriage proposal accepted over the communicator, as long as you notify your fiancé in writing if you decide to break it off."

Troit, deep in thought, ran her hand through her hair distractedly. Then she tossed her head, smiled and answered, "All right. I accept. You must have grown up a lot since we last broke up, or you couldn't have written those marvelous letters."

Smirk gave her his patented "stun" gaze and replied, "Just hold that thought, my darling, till we meet again." He blew a kiss at the communicator screen before switching it off.

The Mushy
Part

THE TWO STARSHIPS arrived simultaneously at the Hydrant Quadrant planet where the Fountain of Youth was located. They skidded to a halt, then hovered in orbit.

As soon as Capt. Smirk's ship was in position, UltraFax Chief O'Brine sent Bev and Dacron down to the Fountain of Youth.

Meanwhile, on Capt. Ricardo's ship, Guano, Troit and Smock stood on their Shipping platform and watched Checkout fiddle with the UltraFax controls. He checked the monitor and muttered, "Dere is already someone down dere."

"It might be someone from Captain Smirk's crew," said Guano, looking out the window at Smirk's ship, parked next to theirs. "They've caught up to us again."

"I'm sure *their* transporter chief, Mr. O'Brine, knows what he's doing," Troit said pointedly. "Why don't you just Fax us to the same spot? It's probably near the Fountain of Youth."

"I vas just about to do dat," Checkout said through clenched teeth. He energized the trio, sending them down to the coordinates occupied by Smirk's Away Team.

The Away Teams collided next to the fountain. Troit landed on top of Dacron; Smock materialized so close to

428

Bev that she could smell the Sen-Sen on his breath; and Guano landed between the two couples. Swiftly they all unscrambled themselves and stood up.

Bev and Smock stared at each other for a moment. Then they both began speaking at once, interrupting each other and starting anew in mid-thought as they sorted out what had happened since their last phone call.

"I thought I would never see you again—"

"We have got a lot to talk about—"

"I haven't been able to stop thinking about you—"

"Why didn't I hear from you—"

"Our communicator could only receive messages, not send them—"

Within moments, they were embracing, gazing into each other's eyes, and murmuring highly technical, scientifically-correct endearments.

"Ugh! How mushy," Guano grumbled. She turned away and hightailed it over to the fountain.

Troit also turned away, to give the lovers some privacy, and found herself face-to-face with Dacron. He looked as if he'd been watching her all along.

"Dacron," she murmured, disconcerted.

"Counselor Troit," he said. "Or rather, Chief Engineer Troit. Or may I call you Deanna?"

"You may," she answered. She studied him for a moment, then ventured, "Dacron, I'm sensing strong feelings of affection in you. Are you still under the influence of your fall into the Fountain of Love?"

"Yes, I am," he said, shyly taking both her hands in his. "The affection I feel is for you, Deanna."

Gently she pulled away. "Dacron, that's sweet," she told him, "but you really shouldn't say any more. You see, I've just become engaged to Captain Smirk."

Dacron stared at her, dumbstruck.

"He proposed over the communicator just a little while ago, and I said yes," Troit continued.

The old Dacron would have made a gentlemanly retreat

upon hearing this news, but the new Dacron, saturated with Fountain of Truth water, could not keep silent.

"But Captain Smirk does not love you the way I do," Dacron protested. "He is only interested in you because you are unattainable. There is no depth to his feelings."

"That's what I thought," Troit responded, "until I read his letters. They show a completely different side of him: thoughtful, sensitive, caring, and even mature. I've come to love him through his correspondence."

"But *I* wrote those letters," Dacron blurted out.

"What?" Troit took a step back, astonished at the very idea.

"If you love the person revealed in this correspondence, Deanna, then it is me you love, not Captain Smirk," Dacron told her.

Troit shook her head. "Dacron, how can you expect me to believe that?" she chided him. "You may have developed some capacity for emotion, but you couldn't have written those letters. They were masterpieces. They showed a true depth of feeling."

"I wrote them all," Dacron insisted. "I can quote them. For instance, the one written on Stardate 44438.2 began: 'Dearest Deanna, As the moons of Frippery–4 cast their shadows over my pillow, I toss and turn, dreaming of your smile . . .' "

Troit gasped. "You've been reading the letters Captain Smirk wrote to me!" Without thinking, she slapped Dacron's face.

Tears filled Dacron's eyes—tears that contained a high Mountain Dew/H_2O ratio—and a single teardrop ran down his cheek. Still, the compulsion to tell everything would not let him give up. "The words were mine," he said, his tone subdued yet firm. "I signed Captain Smirk's name to them because we agreed I would ghostwrite for him. But I sincerely meant everything I wrote. It was the only way I could safely express my love for you."

"Why are you saying this?" Troit demanded with a catch

Without thnking, she slapped Dacron's face.

in her voice. She looked nearly as miserable as he did.

"Deanna." Dacron ventured to touch her shoulder, and when she did not resist, he went on, "If I were lying, your Betavoid powers would tell you so, would they not?"

Troit didn't answer, but her expression plainly revealed her inner turmoil. Dacron pressed on. "I can prove that I wrote those letters," he offered. "I shall challenge Captain Smirk to a duel. A poetry duel."

This novel suggestion made Troit smile in spite of herself. Emboldened, Dacron continued, "It will take place right now, while you and I are down here, so Captain Smirk cannot interfere with the outcome. Each of us will compose an impromptu poem for you. Then you will know that only I was capable of writing the letters which won your heart."

Troit nodded in agreement. "All right."

Dacron touched the communicator insignia on his chest. "Dacron to Captain Smirk."

"Go ahead, Dacron," came Smirk's voice.

"Captain, I am here on the surface of the planet with Deanna Troit—"

"What?!" Smirk screamed. Dacron and Troit cringed; even over the cheap, tinny speaker of the insignia, Smirk's voice packed a wallop. "You're supposed to be in Sick Bay," Smirk yelled.

"I UltraFaxed here to tell Deanna the truth about our correspondence," Dacron continued.

"You WHAT?!" Smirk hollered, his voice so loud that the insignia on Dacron's chest actually vibrated.

Dacron flicked the "reset" button behind his earlobe to restore his hearing, which had shut down automatically during the second of Smirk's high-decibel outbursts.

Dacron continued, "Deanna has agreed that if we each ad lib a poem, the results will confirm the actual author of the letters."

"That's ridiculous!" Smirk stormed. "Deanna, I shouldn't have to prove myself after all this time."

"You sound a little like your old slippery self, Captain,"

Troit said. "Aren't you up to the challenge?"

"But . . ." Smirk said. He paused for several moments, then continued, "Oh, all right. Just one poem? That won't be too hard. Not after all those other poems I've written. Should be a snap."

"Would you like to go first, Captain?" Dacron offered.

"No, thanks," Smirk answered quickly. "After you, Dacron."

"Very well," said Dacron. He thought for a minute, then turned and spoke to Deanna. "The secret garden of your heart / Is where I long to bloom and grow / So wilt thou let my spirit rest / Within the shelter of your soul?"

"Beautiful," Troit whispered, gazing into his eyes.

"What kind of poem is that?" came Smirk's gripe from the insignia speaker. "It doesn't even rhyme very well. 'Grow' and 'soul'?"

Troit swallowed hard and brushed away a tear. "Your turn, Captain Smirk," she said briskly.

"Oh-*kay!*" he responded heartily. "Here goes: Roses are red / Violets are blue / I like french kissing / How about you?"

There was a long pause. Finally Smirk prompted, "Well, what do you think? Kinda makes you feel hot all over, doesn't it?"

Troit didn't answer. She and Dacron were in the midst of a long and passionate kiss.

Watching them from nearby, Guano made a face and mumbled, "More mushy stuff." She flicked her insignia. "Guano to Checkout."

"Checkout here," came his voice from aboard Ricardo's ship.

"Fax me back there, will ya?" she demanded. "Oh, and I'm bringing along some souvenirs, so lock onto them and bring them up, too."

A third ship, undetected by the others, hovered in orbit far above the Fountain of Youth. It was the Romanumen flagship, lurking behind its croaking device.

"Sensors show four life forms and an android on the surface of the planet," reported the Romanumen first officer from his station on the Bridge of the wartbird. Then he stated, "Correction—three life forms. The fourth person just returned to one of their vessels. Those who remain are at the edge of the Fountain of Youth."

"What are they doing?" demanded the Romanumen captain. "Have they claimed the fountain yet by planting the Starfreak flag?"

"No, sir," said the first officer. "Sensors show they are ..."—his lip curled in disgust—"... kissing."

"Kissing?" The captain's tone was icy with disdain. "The discipline of Starfreak officers declines each time we encounter them. Let us take advantage of the situation while we can. Send down an Away Team with the Romanumen flag, and have them place it in the center of the fountain."

"Yes, sir," the first officer responded.

"Arm futon torpedoes!" the captain ordered. "Aim them at the orbiting ships. We will show them who rules this sector."

"Futon torpedoes armed and ready," announced the tactical officer. She flicked the switch that disabled the croaking device so the weapons system could fire.

Down on the planet, Bev came up for air after a long kiss with Smock and happened to glance at the sky just as the Romanumen ship uncroaked. "Aaaiiieee!" Bev screeched. The others looked where she was pointing and saw the Romanumen ship floating next to their own vessels.

Instantly Dacron flicked his communicator insignia. "Mr. O'Brine, four to Fax immediately to the Bridge," he ordered.

O'Brine had been napping at the UltraFax controls. Awakened by Dacron's order, he dazedly energized the Fax, accidentally engaging a mode designed to switch the positions of the Faxees.

When the two couples materialized on the Bridge of Smirk's ship, they found their partners switched: Dr. Flusher was embracing Troit, and Dacron was smooching with Smock. Hastily they disengaged and looked around the Bridge.

In response to the sudden appearance of the Romanumens, a Red Alert was already in progress; scarlet lights flashed on and off, and crewmembers dashed around aimlessly, scattering paperwork. Capt. Smirk was blow-drying his hair to prepare for battle.

Dacron ran to his Oops station, flung aside the ensign who'd temporarily taken his place, and opened a channel to Ricardo's ship. "Dacron to Captain Ricardo," he said. "There is a Romanumen wartbird uncroaking off your starboard bow. Suggest you take evasive action."

"I see it," Ricardo responded crabbily. "Just because I'm older than you, don't assume there's anything wrong with my eyesight."

"Yes sir," Dacron said, adding, "Captain, they have armed their futon torpedoes."

"I need Mr. Smock over here for tactical advice," Ricardo said. They heard Ricardo page Checkout and demand him to UltraFax Mr. Smock back to their ship. Ricardo lowered his shields for a moment to allow for the Faxing.

Smock gave Beverage a jaunty salute and told her, "Till we meet again." Then he disappeared amidst the sparkles of an UltraFax beam.

"Sir," said Dacron, turning to Capt. Smirk, "I suggest we take evasive action."

Smirk was staring at Troit. "No," he answered Dacron without turning his gaze from Troit. "If Ricardo is going to stand and fight, so are we."

Huge explosions rocked both ships simultaneously. The Romanumens had fired their first round of futon torpedoes.

"Damage report!" Smirk demanded, striking a macho pose in the center of the Bridge.

When the two couples materialized, they found their
partners switched.

"Decompression on Decks 23 and 76," said Westerly, checking the sensors. "Deck 72 is missing. It's snowing on Decks 39 and 40, and there's a six-inch base and two inches of new powder on Deck 41."

Troit glared back at Smirk. "If you think you're going to impress me by risking our necks in some cowboy stunt, you're wrong," she declared. "I know what you tried to pull off with those letters Dacron wrote for you, and I think it's despicable."

She touched her communicator insignia. "Troit to Captain Ricardo. Permission to Fax aboard, sir."

"Granted," responded Ricardo.

Troit turned toward Dacron. "I'll see you later," she told him.

After Troit Faxed away, a second Romanumen torpedo hit Smirk's ship. Upon impact, the crew shifted to one side on cue, more or less simultaneously, and then regained their balance.

"Damage report!" Smirk demanded again.

"Deck 72 has turned up in the Lost and Found on HolidayDeck 3," Westerly reported. "There's an ozone alert on Decks 56 and 68. A flock of sheep has gotten loose on Deck 97."

"Captain," said Dacron, consulting his console, "the Romanumens are powering up their futon torpedoes again. Our shields will not withstand another blow."

Still Smirk held his ground, reluctant to surrender this chance to play the hero.

Over on Ricardo's ship, meanwhile, the computer was getting peeved about the danger they faced.

"Why I got mixed up in this, heaven knows," said the computer's voice, which by now they all knew belonged to Woksauna Troit. "I should have left while I had the chance."

"Mother, it's a little late to have regrets about hiding on board our ship," Troit pointed out.

"It's never too late for regret, spittle one," Woksauna retorted.

"Computer, report the condition of the Romanumen weapon systems," Mr. Smock ordered.

"A third array of futon torpedoes is being armed. Their countdown gives sixty seconds to impact. Shields will not withstand another strike," Woksauna stated in her matter-of-fact computer voice. Then, shifting to her own personal shrill tone, she continued, "Speaking of regret, Deanna, if you'd have taken my advice you'd be married by now, and at least I could have seen some grandchildren before I died.

"After all I've—" Woksauna interrupted herself and switched to her computer voice: *"Forty-five seconds to impact."* Then she resumed harping: "—done for you, the least you could do would be to settle down, get married, have children, and suffer like the rest of us."

"Captain Smirk," said Ricardo over the "hey, you" frequency, "we have determined that our shields cannot stand another strike from the Romanumen torpedoes. And our sensors show that the Romanumens have already placed their claim on the fountain. I think both of our ships should withdraw."

"Twenty seconds to impact," said Woksauna the computer. "But would you listen to your mother, Deanna? Of course not. You thought you were too smart to—"

She interrupted herself to speak as the computer again. *"Ten seconds. Nine, eight, seven—*Oh, nuts*—five, four—"*

"All right!" Smirk reluctantly conceded over the communication channel. "Let's get out of here."

Both ships kicked into Warped drive just as the Romanumens fired their third deadly volley of futon torpedoes.

"The Romanumens have already placed their claim on
the fountain."

9

Guano's
Hat Trick

"**P**SSST! DACRON!"

Dacron turned around and saw that Georgie, sitting directly behind him, was passing him a note. The sheet of lined notebook paper had been folded into a self-sealing triangle. Dacron opened it, moving slowly so as not to catch the eye of Admiral Nonsequitur.

At the front of the room, Nonsequitur paced back and forth, deeply involved in his ranting and raving. Somehow he'd managed to keep his mind on the same subject for more than a minute. He was well into the third hour of scolding the crews of both ships, who sat in rows before him, squished into uncomfortable classroom-style chairs. This was Starfreak headquarters' lecture hall, designed specifically for occasions when the brass wanted to intimidate the rank-and-file.

At first, the crews of Ricardo and Smirk had cowered as Nonsequitur screamed at them for allowing the Romanumens to capture the Fountain of Youth. Nonsequitur ignored the fact that they'd managed to escape without injuries or major damage to their ships. Instead, he piled on the guilt over Starfreak's tremendous loss of potential income from the fountain.

Everybody was duly penitent—for a while. But they discovered that you can only cringe for so long before the

441

cringe reflex wears out. By about the middle of the second hour, most of the crewmembers had realized that the worst was over: Starfreak was taking away their jobs and their ships, and nothing more could be done about it, so why worry?

They'd begun tapping their fingers, whispering among themselves, shooting spitballs, and passing notes, such as the one Dacron had just received:

Dacron,
     What are you going to do with yourself now that we're out of Starfreak for good?
                                                            Georgie

Dacron pulled out a mechanical pencil and composed an answer in his methodical, precise script:

Georgie:
     I have been invited to assume a position with the staff of Ready Reference. They welcome my input, since I can answer most patrons' questions merely by consulting my memory banks. This leaves the reference books free for others to use.
     Deanna Troit will accompany me. She will seek employment within the counseling field in the Greater Milwaukee area.
                                                            Dacron

Others whispered back and forth about their own plans. Smock and Beverage intended to stay together; he'd already proposed, asking her to be his significant other. Piker wanted to open his own restaurant, specializing in Kringle cuisine. Checkout, realizing he was unemployable outside of Starfreak, was hoping to enroll in graduate school.

Up at the front of the room, Nonsequitur paused to sip from the glass of water at his podium. Then he declared to the group, "If Starfreak auctions off both your ships,

Piker wanted to open his own restaurant, specializing in Kringle cuisine.

we might scrape up enough money to pay for this year's executive board retreat at a luxury resort. And speaking of the auction, we'll need to sell your uniforms, too. Leave them here today when I dismiss you.

"Now," he continued, "let me tell you the worst thing about this whole botched affair. Starfreak learned this morning that the Romanumens don't intend to sell any of the Fountain of Youth water. They're going to hoard it all for themselves. So the rest of us in the federation won't have access to it at all."

Guano, sitting near the front row, was one of the few who were still half-listening to Nonsequitur. When she heard this remark, she suddenly perked up and raised her hand.

"What is it?" Nonsequitur said.

"Admiral," said Guano, "if the Romanumens are hoarding the water, that makes it especially valuable, doesn't it?"

"Of course it does," growled Nonsequitur. "It's the old law of supply and command."

"So if someone besides the Romanumens has water from the Fountain of Youth, they'd be sitting on a fortune," Guano suggested.

"Yes, yes, of course—but no one else has any," Nonsequitur replied irritably.

"Suppose Starfreak could get their hands on some?" Guano continued coyly. "Say . . . if a certain crewmember knew where there was a good supply of it?"

As Guano went on, others in the room began to realize that something significant was happening, and they suspended their note-passing, whispering and flirting to listen to her.

"Do you think that if that crewmember turned the water over to Starfreak for future sales, the High Command would agree to use some of the profit to reinstate both USS *Endocrines* and their crews?" asked Guano. "Do you think you could get us a signed contract to that effect? A contract stating that once this crewmember turns over, say, thirteen half-barrels of Fountain of Youth water, both ships will be put back in service immediately?"

Nonsequitur stood and stared at Guano, absorbing this information. He stood there for a good five minutes, until Guano began to wonder if his brain had finally been overloaded past the point of no return.

Finally he blurted, "Let me find out for you," turned on his heel, and headed out of the lecture hall. The room buzzed with excited conversation as the crews speculated on their chances of reinstatement.

UltraFax Chief Checkout leaned over and asked Guano, "Does dis have anyting to do with dose barrels you had me Fax up to da ship on your last avay mission?"

Guano gave him a condescending smile. "Gee, Checkout, how did you ever guess?"

After a long time Nonsequitur came back, holding an official-looking document. It spelled out Guano's terms, and it had been signed by Starfreak's head honchos. Guano asked the two captains to check the legitimacy of the signatures to make sure the signers had authority.

"They're big shots, all right," said Capt. Smirk.

Capt. Ricardo agreed. "Those are the same signatures that appear on our paychecks. I'd recognize them anywhere." After the captains signed the document, Guano gave Admiral Nonsequitur the coordinates on board Capt. Ricardo's *Endocrine* where Starfreak would find its barrels of Fountain of Youth water.

"Hmmph. Looks like you got out of this one," Nonsequitur grumbled. "Both ships are back in commission, and you all have your old jobs back."

Everybody cheered.

That evening, they all gathered in the Ten-Foreplay lounge of Capt. Ricardo's ship to celebrate. In honor of the occasion, Guano declared that drinks were on the house. She even broke out her supply of water from the fountains.

Mr. Snot, sitting at the bar, took several gulps of his drink. "It was good o' you to hold a little o' this Fountain o' Youth water in reserve from the barrels you turned over to Starfreak," he told Guano, holding out his glass for a refill.

Guano refilled his glass and turned away, muttering to herself, "I knew some people around here desperately needed it." She was being unusually polite this evening because she'd been guzzling Fountain of Love water with a vengeance.

Snot clinked his glass against Dr. McCaw's and Yoohoo's, proposing a toast: "Here's to our return to a civilized ship."

"Here, here," McCaw rasped. "One where everyone knows their job, yet isn't required to do it."

" 'Hey, you' frequencies open, sir," Yoohoo added irrelevantly; she was already practicing her usual routine.

Checkout reached over to attempt to clink his glass against theirs, but nobody noticed, so he simply shrugged and kept on drinking.

Zulu, sitting at a table in the center of Ten-Foreplay, wasn't quite as happy to be returning to the status quo. "I rather enjoyed our status as outcasts," he told Georgie and Westerly, who sat with him. "It was a challenge to be running lean and mean."

"Too much of a challenge, if you ask me," Georgie responded. "I felt like an idiot when all the systems went down at once and Dacron had to bail us out. There's nothing worse for an engineer's ego than having an android come to the rescue."

"I could have saved the day instead, if you'd have let me," Westerly offered.

"Hmmm. I guess there *is* something worse, after all," said Georgie, brightening up. "Thanks, Westerly."

Westerly stared at Georgie for a moment, trying to determine whether or not he was being sarcastic. But Georgie's expression was unreadable thanks to the visor which hid his eyes, so Westerly turned his attention back to the banana split he was eating.

"Speaking of Dacron, where is he?" Zulu asked. "I thought *everybody* was coming to this party."

"He and Deanna Troit made a token appearance," Georgie said. "Then they left for some...uh...privacy." He gave Zulu a knowing smirk. "Dacron wants to demonstrate to Deanna that he's—" Georgie hesitated, glancing at Westerly, then spelled out, "F-U-L-L-Y F-U-N-C-T-I-O-N-A-L."

Westerly protested around a mouthful of banana split, "Hey, no fair. You know I haven't taken Introductory Spelling yet at the Academy."

Zulu told Georgie, "I guess that explains why Beverage Flusher and Mr. Smock didn't stay long either, huh?"

"Yeah," said Georgie. "They're probably over in the lab, testing out some new theorems." Zulu and Georgie burst into raucous laughter while Westerly toyed with the cherry atop his banana split, debating whether to eat it or throw it across the room to start a food fight.

At a nearby table, Capt. Ricardo sipped his Earl Grape tea, then asked, "Well, what insights have the two of you gained from the new assignments you'd held?"

Wart, mindful that he was speaking to the captain, tried to put it as diplomatically as he could. "I have a new appreciation for the skill required of the ship's counselor," he stated. "Managing human emotion is a complex task." Capt. Ricardo nodded approvingly and glanced away. Wart added under his breath, "Mostly because humans are a bunch of sniveling crybabies."

"And what have you learned, Number 1?" Ricardo asked Piker.

"Plenty," Piker said, shaking his head in awe. "The human body is such an intricate system of diverse organs. The amount of knowledge a medical doctor needs is incredibly humbling. Toward the end there, I even resorted to getting advice from the medical staff and the reference books instead of just guessing."

"Mmmmm...yes," Ricardo responded. "Well, it certainly will be much better having you both back in your own jobs again."

Way over in a dark corner of Ten-Foreplay, a solitary figure sat in the shadows, chin in hand. It was Capt. Smirk. He held up a piece of paper and read it for the umpteenth time that evening:

Starfreak Official Form No. 432-A–6699
Official Disengagement Notice

Notice is hereby given that the undersigned wishes to break off an engagement to be married, pursuant to Article 3322 of the Official Starfreak Code, which allows the cancellation of any marriage proposal made and/or accepted via a starship communication device, provided such notice is given within three (3) working days, and in consideration of which, time is of the essence, the early bird gets the worm, etc. etc., so get a move on, eh?

Signed: _Deanna Troit_
Stardate: 44453.7

Witness: **DACRON**
Stardate: 44453.7

Smirk felt an especially sharp pang at seeing Dacron's signature on the document—Dacron, his erstwhile right-hand man and secret rival, who now possessed the affections of the woman Smirk himself coveted.

Smirk knew that asking one's latest lover to sign as the witness to the disengagement document was a pretty well-established custom. Heaven knows, he'd done it himself often enough. Yet being on the receiving end was a bitter blow.

Smirk shook his head, then crumpled the document in his fist. *I've had it with women,* he decided. *If I can't have*

Deanna, I don't want anybody. I'll go through life a solitary man. I'll drift around in space till the end of my days, a model of chastity and self-control—my life a testament to this matchless love that is now lost forever.

Smirk heard a rustle at his side and turned to see a Ten-Foreplay cocktail waitress standing next to the table. "Can I get you something, sir?" she asked.

Smirk gave her the once-over, then smiled with approval. "You certainly can," he said. "Bring me a magnum of that Fountain of Love water . . . and two glasses."

"Oh," the waitress remarked pleasantly, "will Counselor Troit be joining you?"

"Who?" Smirk responded.

"Counselor Deanna Troit. I heard the two of you were engaged," said the waitress.

"Oh, *her*. No, that's all over," Smirk said breezily. "No, my dear, the second glass is for you. I was about to ask if you would join me." The waitress blushed with pleasure, and Smirk added, "What's a classy dame like you doing in a watered-down watering hole like this?"

"Q-Tip is gone," Flusher said. "He spent some time revamping Dacron's wardrobe, and then he left the ship."

"Where is Dacron?" Ricardo asked.

As if on cue, the door from the hallway swooshed open, and Dacron jumped into the room. Gone was his minimalist hairdo; in its place was a dramatic mane. A cluster of gold chains glittered at his neck. The top three buttons of his shirt collar were unbuttoned, revealing a shock of chest hair that hadn't been there yesterday, and the back of his collar was turned up rakishly. The rhinestones on his hiphuggers caught the light.

"Thangyouvurymuch," he said as he grasped the microphone, rings glistening on every finger. "Ah wanna do a little number for yuh now that ah think you'll like."

Without a doubt, here was a different Dacron than the one the crew had been used to. Among androids, now he was clearly The King. . . .

1

Do Not Go Gently Into That Good Riddance

CAPT. JAMES T. SMIRK studied his reflection in the mirror. *Still smashing after all these years*, he decided. Then he felt a sharp tug at the back of his scalp.

"Ouch!" Smirk exclaimed, rising reflexively a few inches out of the chair.

"Oops. Sorry, Captain," the barber said. "Guess I got a little carried away. But you did say you were in a hurry."

As Smirk warily settled down in the chair again, the barber carefully lifted another strand of the hairpiece and continued tightening the weave that held it to Smirk's own hair.

"*I am* in a hurry, Mr. Seville," Smirk replied. "I've got a meeting with a Starfreak admiral in half an hour. But can't you work fast without scalping me?"

"It'll be done in a few minutes," the barber soothed him. "We want it to look natural, don't we?"

"Absolutely," Smirk replied, checking his reflection again. *I must admit*, he thought, *I've aged better than any of my crew*. He began imagining the others from the USS *Endocrine* who were waiting here with him at Starfreak Headquarters.

Take Mr. Smock, for instance. His permanently dour expression had hardened into a chiseled mask that made him a prime candidate for the fifth face on Mt. Rushmore. And though Smock's Vulture eyebrows maintained their youthful tilt, everyone knew he achieved this facelift illusion with cellophane tape strategically placed beneath his bangs.

Zulu had started to take on the serenity of an ancient Zen

453

I must admit, Smirk thought, I've aged better than any of my crew.

master. But Smirk had never thought of serenity as an essential quality for a Starfreak officer, especially when it meant, as in Zulu's case, taking several four-hour naps every day.

Checkout's boyish features clashed with the wrinkles he'd acquired. His behavior embodied the expression "There's no fool like an old fool," and often he smelled of Ben Gay.

As for Chief Engineer Snot, it was a contest to see which was drooping faster—his jowls, his chins, or his pot belly.

Dr. McCaw had been a lot more spry lately; rumor had it that he'd given himself a hip replacement without telling anyone. Still, there were years of crankiness etched into his face, and he complained that the bursitis in his shoulder was a serious hindrance to his medical practice because it affected his golf swing.

Then there was Yoohoo, Smirk's communications officer, who seemed to have frosted her hair with typewriter correction fluid. Yoohoo had adopted the annoying habit of lecturing young Starfreak recruits on how easy they had it nowadays. "In the old days all this electronic equipment was manually operated," she often pointed out. "It took six strong crewmembers to hold open the shuttlebay doors. And the vacuum sucking them out into space was a lot stronger then, too."

And despite his unquenchable confidence in his own appearance, Smirk himself had the uneasy suspicion that there was a Starfreak conspiracy afoot to convince him to step aside and let some young punk take his place. The conspirators had even gone so far as to sell his name to a mailing list for the elderly. At least, that was Smirk's explanation for why his mail these days consisted mostly of catalogs offering liver spot creme and subscriptions to *Senility Digest*.

Smirk thought, *Well, they can hint all they want. We're not stepping aside until we're good and ready. We're not getting older, we're getting bitter. Er, better.*

Smirk's mind ambled back to the present; the barber had finished tightening his hairpiece and was now styling it. As he pulled a miniature rake through the top to create height, the barber said, "You might want to try a new look one of these days, Captain. Astroturf is really hot right now. Once we weave a patch of that onto the back of your head, we can carve into it anything you want: your initials, a gang insignia, whatever." Expertly he wielded a curling iron to touch up the waves on either side of Smirk's crown.

"No thanks, Mr. Seville. I'll stick with the old tried and true," Smirk replied. "It seems to work pretty well with the ladies," he added, his voice straining with false modesty.

"You sure you won't try it?" Seville asked, grinning at Smirk in the mirror. "We could carve some sweetheart's initials into the 'turf—whoever your latest conquest is at the moment."

Smirk returned the grin. "Heck," he retorted, "I'd be in here every few hours for a re-carving—the initials would change too often."

Seville chuckled. "Just trying to drum up business," he said, putting the finishing touches on the curl that drooped fetchingly over Smirk's forehead.

As Smirk headed down the crowded hallway from the barber shop to the admirals' offices, his mind meandered pleasantly between speculation and observation.

It's odd that they wouldn't tell me which admiral I'd be meeting with, he thought. *They just said that it would be "whoever is on call at the time." Whatever happened to protocol?*

Wow, look at that hot mama. She's the one I put the moves on at the singles' dance last night. She's looking my way. She likes the hair, I can tell.

Maybe the admiral wants to apologize for the way Starfreak Command treated us after we lost the Fountain of Youth to the Romanumens. Sure, it meant a couple quadzillion dollars in potential profit down the drain, but did that justify threatening to throw both Endocrine *crews out of the fleet? Good thing Captain Ricardo's bartender used her stash of fountain water to bargain with Starfreak and get back our commissions.*

Hey, there's that little filly who offered to read my palm during breakfast this morning. An old ploy, but a good one. I'll give her the look that says I'd love to stop and chat if only I weren't on my way to an important meeting.

Maybe Starfreak wants to tell me that they've finished the thirty-zillion-mile tuneup on my ship, and they're giving us a new mission.

Oh, man, there's that bouncy little ensign. She looks even better in her Starfreak uniform than she did in her bikini at the pool yesterday. Ahhh, if only I could be a strand of Lycra on her tunic for a minute—oooh, baby!

The distractions made Smirk wonder just how many classy dames were staying here at Starfreak Headquarters at the moment. *There must be at least two thousand or so,* he thought. *And I've gone through nearly all of them. It's been a busy week. Time to get back into the field for some new life forms.*

In the waiting room of the admirals' office area, a light flashed at the receptionist's console. He consulted the readout, then turned to Smirk and told him, "The admiral will see you now."

"Thanks," Smirk replied, setting aside the copy of *U.S. News & Universe Report* he'd been reading. He usually preferred to spend his waiting time flirting with the receptionist rather than leafing through old magazines, but seeing a male behind the desk had squelched that idea. *I wonder if they placed a guy there just to make me ill at ease,* he thought.

Smirk relaxed, though, as he entered the office. Although the back of the admiral's chair faced the doorway as its occupant stared out the window, Smirk could see that the admiral was a woman. Suddenly he felt he was back on familiar territory. Whatever this meeting was about, he certainly could charm his way through it. He sat down in the single chair that faced the desk.

Then the admiral swiveled toward him, and Smirk gasped in dismay. He realized this was someone he hadn't seen since the night he'd stood her up for a date. That was a couple of decades ago, but he hadn't forgotten—and from the look on her face, neither had she.

Smirk even recalled the circumstances of that evening long ago. On the way to pick her up for the date, he'd happened upon a stranger—an alien woman with a most extraordinary trio of mammary glands. Smirk, agog with scientific curiosity, had spent the night pursuing the alien instead.

The woman he'd stood up had been a mere lieutenant then. Now, here she was, an admiral who not only outranked him but also seemed intent on outstaring him. He stammered, "A-A-Admiral Less. How good to see you."

She met his eyes with an icy gaze. "You're twenty years, sixteen days, five hours and ten minutes late, Smirk."

"Ah, Ruth," he replied, "still dwelling on our near-date, eh? Let me explain—"

"Never mind." She tapped her five-inch red-lacquered fingernails on the glossy varnish of the desktop. Smirk wondered, *Am I seeing things, or is the nail of her index finger filed to a point?*

"I'm so glad I happened to draw personnel duty today, Captain," Admiral Less continued. "How amusing it is that I'll be the one to break the news to you."

Smirk's hands tightened on the armrests of the chair. *What news?* he wondered.

Obviously savoring the suspense, Admiral Less reached for the pile of mail on her desk, picked up the top envelope, and slit it open with her pointed fingernail. "Mmmmf," she said with a grimace, glancing at the contents. "More junk mail." She tossed the letter into the wastebasket and reached for another.

"Uh, Admiral," Smirk ventured, "you were going to tell me something?"

"Hmmm?" she replied with studied casualness. "Oh, yes." Briskly she straightened up in her chair. Her eyelids narrowed, and the corners of her mouth tilted dangerously upward into unfamiliar smile territory. "Captain, it has come

The woman he'd stood up had been a mere lieutenant then.

to the attention of Starfreak Command that you and your crew are past the mandatory retirement age. *Well* past retirement age," she added meanly. "In fact, it's strange that nobody noticed this sooner. I guess we've all been so busy with our new Total Quality program that we've let our regular work slide for the last few years.

"Your orders are to relinquish command of the *Endocrine*. At 0800 hours tomorrow, you and your crew will report to your new permanent living quarters at the Vacant Attic Nursing Home."

Smirk stared at her, then gave a feeble laugh. "Uh-huh. Yes," he said. "Pretty ironic. I break a date, and twenty years later you get revenge by relieving me of command. I guess what goes around comes aground, eh?"

Smirk's grin, which was pretty sickly to begin with, faded rapidly as he studied the admiral's face. "You *are* kidding, aren't you, Ruth?" Admiral Less returned his stare. "Okay, you've had your laugh," Smirk babbled. "We're even. Very funny. Now, what was it you really wanted to see me about?"

For a moment he had a ghastly vision of the mandatory retirement that Less was talking about. Not only would there be the numbing boredom he'd discovered during his crew's previous, voluntary retirement, but being confined to a nursing home would prevent him from flying around the galaxy to search for classy dames. It would be excruciatingly painful.

Yet the admiral's steady gaze shredded Smirk's last hope that this was all a bad joke. He slumped back in the chair. "You're not kidding," he gasped, as though she'd just punched him in the stomach.

"No, I'm not," she affirmed. "It's all very straightforward. Your time is up. The contract that Starfreak signed with your crew expired when our hoard of Fountain of Youth water dried up. The sale of that water was paying your bills. Now that it's gone, Starfreak has no further obligation to keep your crew in service."

A mixture of strong emotions swirled over Smirk's face like an oil slick floating on a puddle. He seemed to waver between punching the admiral in the nose and throwing up on her desk.

"I'm sure you'll like it at the nursing home, Captain," Admiral Less purred with counterfeit pity. "The women out-number the men five to one."

Then she reached out with one exquisitely manicured fin-gernail and pressed a button on her desk. A trap door opened beneath Smirk's chair, and he plunged down into darkness.

That night in the ballroom of Starfreak Headquarters, there was a retirement party for Capt. Smirk and his crew. Guests began arriving early, anticipating an evening of boisterous merrymaking.

Starfreak, mindful of Smirk's popularity among the rank and file, had spared no expense for this gala event. The Jell-O molds contained real fruit, there were mountains of Twinkies and HoHos on the buffet, and the Gatorade flowed freely. The room was festooned with genuine balloons and party stream-ers, not the usual holographic decorations.

Guests admired a display case holding the gold phasers, each engraved with the message "In gratitude for years of faithful service," which the retirees would receive during the ceremony that evening. Most guests were too polite to men-tion that phasers were inappropriate gifts for officers whose biggest fights in the upcoming years would be waged over who got the best chair in the TV lounge of the nursing home.

Soon after the deejay started playing the first disco number of the evening, the head honchos of Starfreak filed in, sig-naling the start of the official ceremony. The house lights dimmed, the crowd gathered round, and excitement filled the air. There was just one thing missing: the guests of honor.

At the moment, those guests of honor were down in Star-freak's repair dock, attempting to steal their own ship.

"Are you almost done, Snotty?" Capt. Smirk asked ur-gently. He stared at Snot's legs and kilt; the rest of the ample

Guests began arriving early.

chief engineer was wedged into the confines of the ship's engine. Smirk added, "How long till you get it started?"

Snot's voice, cranky and strained, emerged from the bowels of the *Endocrine*'s Dilithium Crystal Vanish chamber. "I'm havin' a divvil of a time w' it, Cap'n! This is delicate worrrrk!"

Smirk looked nervously over his shoulder. Most everyone in the repair dock had already left for the retirement party, but someone could have lagged behind and might yet discover them. And though Mr. Smock was posted at the ship's main entrance to intercept anybody who got nosy, Smirk feared that Smock might very well fall asleep on the job. Like Zulu, Smock had become adept at napping.

"Hurry up, Snotty!" Smirk urged. "The tuneup work was already done by Starfreak's mechanics. All you have to do is get the engine to turn over."

"I know, sir," barked Mr. Snot, "but it's not all that easy. It's been a while since I've had t' hot-wire my own ship."

Finally the engine started. Snot had once again conquered the intricacies of matter/antimatter mechanics with a few random, frustrated swipes of his wrench, as well as snarls of Gaelic phrases not found in any tourist guidebook.

Relieved to hear the pulsing of the engine, Smirk rushed to the Bridge. Zulu, Checkout and Yoohoo had already taken their regular stations. Presumably, Dr. McCaw was off brooding in Sick Bay. Mr. Smock, seeing that everything was ready, closed the outer door and turned the deadbolt lock.

Smirk sat in his captain's chair. "Ready for takeoff, Mr. Zulu?" he inquired.

"All systems go," Zulu responded.

"Captain," Mr. Smock broke in, "may I remind you that once we begin the unauthorized use of the ship, there is no turning back."

"No turning back? Tough!" Smirk replied. "What's to turn back to? A life of card games and day outings to the mall? C'mon, Smock, get with it!"

"I support your plan wholeheartedly, Captain," Smock said. "I simply felt it was my duty to point out the consequences."

"Phooey on the consequences! Full speed ahead!" Smirk ordered.

"Moving ahead at impulsive speed," Zulu answered. He pressed the controls, and the ship moved forward in the huge docking bay.

"From now on," Smirk said, increasingly excited now that their venture had officially begun, "I don't want to hear any second thoughts, understand? If you can't go boldly, you shouldn't go at all."

"Captain—" said Mr. Smock.

"No, Smock," interrupted Capt. Smirk, "I don't want any more 'logical' reasons for staying behind."

"Sir—" Smock ventured.

"I mean it," Smirk snapped, swiveling to face him. "No regrets. No more pandering to the brass at headquarters. It's all on our shoulders now, so let's live up to it bravely."

"Captain," Smock said more forcefully, "I am merely trying to tell you that we are headed for the locked doors of the repair bay."

Smirk turned toward the Viewscreen at the front of the Bridge. "Aaaiiy!" he cried. "Where's the door opener? Checkout, isn't this your job?"

"No, Keptin," Checkout replied. "I tink my official duty during takeoff is to fold and sort da road maps."

"Who's got the opener?" demanded Smirk. Checkout and Yoohoo scrambled around the Bridge in a befuddled search for the remote door opener unit, checking the hope chest, the piano bench, and the laundry bin. Meanwhile, the doors loomed ever closer.

"All stop, Mr. Zulu," ordered Smirk.

Zulu stabbed the buttons of his console in vain. "The engines won't respond," he answered. " 'Stop' mode is inoperable, Captain."

"Then throw it in reverse," Smirk suggested. Zulu tried, but that gear was not working either.

"Mr. Snot!" Smirk barked to the intercom. "We need to stop until we can get the bay doors open. Can you give us reverse gear or stop mode? Sometime in the next ten seconds?"

"What?!" Snot yelped over the intercom. "I thought ye wanted t' get out o' here, so I worked like th' dickens t' get ye some forward speeds. W' all due respect, Cap'n, I wish ye would make up yourrr mind!"

"Oh, good grief," Smirk muttered, angry at himself for forgetting that asking Snot to hurry was like asking a glacier to run the 100-meter dash. They'd just wasted a few more precious seconds, and now the doors loomed so close that they filled the entire Viewscreen.

Suddenly Mr. Smock, who'd been staring at the Viewscreen all along, took several long strides toward it. He reached upward and pulled down the sun visor flap at the Viewscreen's top edge. There, fastened to the visor with a loop of wire, was the door opener. Smock pressed its button, and the doors to the repair bay slid open. As the hatch widened, the *Endocrine* slipped out with only inches to spare.

Capt. Smirk exhaled in relief. "Nice work, Mr. Smock," he said. Smock acknowledged the praise with a nod.

"Let's get going before they realize we've left," Smirk continued. "Mr. Zulu, lay in a course for that planet in the Hydrant Quadrant where the Romanumens have claimed the Fountain of Youth. And punch our speed up to Warped Ten."

Mr. Smock regarded Capt. Smirk with his patented raised-eyebrow expression of surprise. "The Fountain of Youth, Captain? Do you have a plan in mind?"

Smirk smiled. "Do I have a plan, Smock?" he chirped. "Have you ever known me *not* to have something up my sleeve? Of course I've got a plan. Now all we have to do is convince the Romanumens to cooperate with it." Smock started to shake his head disapprovingly, but Smirk stopped him with a quick gesture and a smile. "Uh-uh, Mr. Smock," he said. "We're going boldly, remember? Just like in our creed."

As the ship blasted away from Starfreak Headquarters into the vastness beyond, Smirk intoned that creed:

"Space. We need more of it. These are the voyages of the Starship *Endocrine*. Its continuing mission: to cruise around the universe looking for novel predicaments to get into. To search the outskirts of the galaxy for classy dames. To boldly go where nobody wanted to go before!"

2

Here We Go
A-Dithering

"**G**OOD MORNING, and welcome to our seminar, 'The Politically Correct Starship.'"

As the keynote speaker began, Capt. Jean-Lucy Ricardo leaned forward eagerly, intent on catching every word. However, his crewmembers, seated around him in this crowd at the Starfreak Headquarters lecture hall, were considerably less enthusiastic.

First Officer Wilson Piker was already nodding off. Next to him, Chief Engineer Georgie LaForgery closed the slats of his visor and flicked a switch that would pick up a satellite-TV signal. The others sat moping in varying degrees of boredom.

The crewmembers had reunited more or less by default. Though Starfreak had given back their ship at the end of their previous mission, instead of sticking together, they'd gone their separate ways. However, none of their ventures had worked out as planned.

Dacron the android and Counselor Deanna "Dee" Troit had moved to Milwaukee for a while, but although Dacron enjoyed his job with the Ready Reference Service of the Milwaukee Public Library, the Wisconsin weather didn't agree with him. It had been an especially cold winter. Several times, Deanna needed to call AAA for an emergency jump-start just to enable Dacron to get out of bed.

For her part, Deanna found that leisure activities made it hard to concentrate on her newly established private coun-

There were just so many festivals to attend....

seling practice. There were just so many festivals to attend on Milwaukee's lakefront: Summerfest, Festa Italiana, Polish Fest, Kringle Fest, Android Fest, Sentient Being Fest, Festa Nebula, and on and on.

Even more upsetting to Deanna was the fact that Dacron's romantic interest in her had vanished. As the effects of the Fountain of Love water he'd fallen into started wearing off, his nightly refrain became "Not tonight, dear; I have a headache." Deanna wasn't sure whether androids could even have headaches, but she took the hint.

Similarly, Dr. Beverage Flusher's romance with Mr. Smock had sputtered as the effects of the fountain water wore off for him, too, and he became his old rational self again. Beverage finally realized that the thrill was gone after they'd spent a beautiful moonlit night freezing their buns off in Smock's backyard observatory shed, charting the course of a distant star, Fossideedee-5.

First Officer Piker had opened his Kringle-cuisine restaurant, mismanaged it for a few months, then left town during a Board of Health inquiry into the charge that several patrons had died of food poisoning.

Chief Bartender Guano still had her small private hoard of water from the Fountains of Truth, Love, and Youth. But little by little, she'd had to sell off most of the water to pay living expenses. She was saving the remainder for a dry day.

Security Officer Wart had pulled his son, Smartalecsander, out of day care and spent several months being a full-time parent. That led to Wart's hospitalization for nervous exhaustion. Smartalecsander was now enrolled in daytime classes and nighttime activities, and Wart was under doctor's orders never again to attempt 24-hour custody of a five-year-old.

Chief Engineer Georgie LaForgery had immersed himself in an ongoing HolidayDeck program with the computer's recreation of a charming fellow engineer, Leeka Bombs. Within a few months Georgie and Leeka had enjoyed a HolidayDeck wedding and established a HolidayDeck love nest. But when

Leeka announced that she was in a HolidayDeck family way, Georgie panicked and ended the program.

Capt. Ricardo and his brother Rodney Ricardo had been the toast of the all-star mud-wrestling and wine-tasting circuit in France for awhile. Then the grapes had an off year, public interest in mud wrestling waned, the circuit closed down, and the wrasslin' Ricardos were out of work.

And so all of Ricardo's crewmembers had drifted back to Starfreak Headquarters within the last month or so. However, Starfreak Command, nursing a grudge over the crew's role in losing the Fountain of Youth to the Romanumens, hadn't been in any hurry to give them a new mission.

The crew also knew that their permanent status was in jeopardy because their agreement with Starfreak expired when the last of the fountain water was gone. So they'd reluctantly agreed to attend this seminar on political correctness to get on the good side of Starfreak Command.

That is, most of them came reluctantly. Capt. Ricardo was the exception—he thought it was a jolly good idea. Now he was taking notes as the speaker outlined the day's program.

"During our breakout sessions," the speaker said, "you'll learn the correct attitudes toward multi-sexual beings, aliens of color, disenfranchised life forms, and other groups. You'll discover why your present approach to your Starfreak duties is sexist, racist, ageist, and sentientist. By the end of this seminar, you'll be groveling for forgiveness to alien beings that you aren't even aware of right now, and admitting that you are the scum of the galaxy. Okay, everybody ready? Let's get started!"

Capt. Ricardo felt pretty smug at the beginning of his first breakout session, an encounter group for starship captains. Ricardo studied his peers and guessed that he was as politically correct as any of them. As they went around the circle and introduced themselves, he scored a few points by apologizing for being a white male.

Then it came time to focus more intensely on each individual's track record. Ricardo's name happened to come up first, and the others began questioning him.

"Captain Ricardo, what's your stand on opportunities for women?" one captain inquired.

"I'm glad you asked," Ricardo replied, smiling with as much sincerity as he could muster. "My crew includes women in a number of important positions."

"Which positions?" she pressed.

"My chief medical officer is female, as is my ship's counselor," Ricardo answered.

"Hmmph," somebody sniffed, "medicine and counseling. The traditional female 'helping' professions. Anybody else?"

"Uh, well," said Ricardo, momentarily taken aback, "there is Guano."

"And what does this 'Guano' do?" the first woman asked.

"She's, er, she's the head bartender in our Ten-Foreplay lounge," Ricardo responded.

"The head bartender?" someone else echoed.

"And a very important position it is, too," Ricardo maintained stoutly. "She's a good listener, and she often provides a shoulder to cry on or gives a bit of good advice to a confused crewmember."

"Isn't that the responsibility of your ship's counselor?" asked another captain.

"Well, er, yes," Ricardo stumbled, "these are things that Counselor Troit does, but Guano also does them for crewmembers in Ten-Foreplay, when, ah, when they're...."

"Drunk?" someone else supplied.

"Captain Ricardo," said the group leader, "according to the questionnaire you filled out for this seminar, your Bridge crew doesn't contain any Hispanics or Asians. Would you mind explaining why?"

"Well, I, uh...it's certainly not intentional..." Ricardo stuttered. "I suppose I've never looked at it that way."

"Just how many minorities are there on your Bridge crew, Captain Ricardo?"

"There's Wart, my security officer," Ricardo said. "He is a Kringle—"

"An aggressive, warlike race that hardly qualifies as an oppressed minority," someone stated.

"And then there's Lieutenant Commander Dacron, an android," Ricardo said, pulling nervously at his collar. "Very few starships have an android among their senior officers, you know."

"So what?" another captain challenged. "He's a male, isn't he?"

"Yes, he is," Ricardo said.

"Does he have any redeeming color value? Is he purple, magenta, polka-dotted? Anything highly unusual?"

"Not really," said Ricardo.

"Just what color is he, Captain?"

Capt. Ricardo swallowed hard and admitted, "White. Dacron is extremely white." A chill of disapproval swept through the group.

Another captain broke in. "Captain Ricardo, what about equal opportunities for animals?"

Ricardo crossed his legs and jiggled his foot nervously. "Animals ... animals ... let's see ... " he said. "Ah, yes. One of my senior officers has a pet named Spot."

"Oh, so you do provide opportunities for dogs, then?"

"Er, no," Ricardo said, jiggling his foot a little faster. "We don't have any dogs. Actually, Spot is a cat." He grinned broadly at the group; cold stares answered him. His grin wilted as he attempted to explain: "Since this was the first pet among the senior officers, and Spot is a traditional pet name, Dacron thought it would be amusing to give it that name, despite the fact that it's a cat, not a dog—"

"This Dacron, who gave the cat its name," somebody interrupted, "is he the albino android?"

"He's not an albino," Ricardo replied testily. "He—"

Mercifully, at that moment the intercom interrupted them. "Captain Ricardo, this is Admiral Less," came the voice. "Report to my office at once."

Ricardo stood up and began backing out of the room. "So sorry to have to end this line of questioning," he said, facing down the others' glares. "It's really been quite...quite... enlightening." Then he turned and darted out the door before anyone could ask another question.

As he headed down the hall, wiping perspiration from his brow, Ricardo wondered what kind of score the others would give him on their evaluation sheets. At least no one had thought to ask about the race and sex of his first officer.

"Sit down, Captain, and relax. I won't bite," said Admiral Less with a hint of a sly grin. She was obviously enjoying Ricardo's discomfort.

It wasn't the possibility of getting bitten that Ricardo was worried about; it was the chance of being stabbed by that menacing fingernail of hers. He tried to relax, but the horsehair guest chair made him fidget, as it undoubtedly was designed to do.

He had talked to plenty of admirals before, but those conversations usually took place over the Viewscreen as he stood in the comfort of his own Bridge. Being here on Starfreak territory was considerably more intimidating.

"Starfreak has a mission for you, Captain," said Admiral Less. "You're familiar with the recent actions of Captain James T. Smirk and his crew—the way they refused the order to retire and then commandeered their ship?"

Ricardo nodded. Indeed, he'd followed the story more closely than most. Mandatory retirement weighed heavily on his mind these days, and he secretly wondered if he too would have the courage to resist being put out to pasture when his own time came.

"Obviously, Starfreak cannot let this action go unchallenged," Less went on. "But now there's much more to it than that. I'll let this videotape explain."

Admiral Less popped the tape into her desktop VCR, and they turned to watch her portable Viewscreen. The image that appeared there was a little shaky—the tape had obviously been made with a handheld camera—but the subject was unmistakable: it was Capt. Smirk. He was standing in the middle of an outdoor fountain, gaily splashing water with his hands.

"Starfreak Command, this is Captain Smirk!" he said to the camera. "I thought you'd like to know that my crew has driven the Romanumens off this planet and claimed the Fountain of Youth. Perhaps we could negotiate a reinstatement of my crew in return for my sending a portion of the fountain's water to Starfreak. So what do you say? Do we have a deal?"

A water pistol appeared in the foreground, and someone began firing it at Capt. Smirk. "Checkout, knock it off!" Smirk protested cheerfully. He splashed water in Checkout's direction; a few drops beaded up on the camera lens. "I'll be waiting to hear from you, Starfreak!" Smirk concluded, signing off with the two-fingered peace sign.

Admiral Less switched off the VCR and told Ricardo, "Our intelligence reports confirm what Smirk said. He did drive the Romanumens off the planet. Don't ask me how, with one starship and a tiny, over-the-hill crew. Perhaps the Romanumens became complacent after Starfreak officially gave up on the fountain.

"So now we've got a renegade Starfreak officer holding the most valuable asset in that sector. Obviously, Captain Ricardo, your mission is to get it back for us."

Ricardo ventured, "You're not going to bargain with him?"

"Bargain? What for? He had no right to use that starship in the first place," Less maintained. "As a matter of fact, right now there are seven spots at the Vacant Attic Nursing Home awaiting him and his cronies. After you've recovered the Fountain of Youth, you're to deliver Smirk and his crew to the nursing home."

"I see," Ricardo answered. Suddenly the mission took on greater interest for him. Finally, here was a chance for his crew to wreak revenge on their rivals—and with Starfreak's blessing, to boot.

"Of course, this reinstatement of your crew is just a trial

period, Captain," the admiral went on. "But once you carry out the mission, Starfreak will profit from the sale of the Fountain of Youth's water, and some of that money can be earmarked to keep your *Endocrine* in service. Consider yourself lucky—a lot of our other ships are still in the shop for repairs after the Bored War."

"Very good, Admiral," Ricardo said. Already he was aching to get on with the mission. *Look out, Smirk, you cocky jackanapes,* he thought. *This is my crew's chance to make it clear, once and for all, that we're the only* Endocrine.

As Capt. Ricardo's ship made its way toward the planet Smirk had taken over, Ricardo was puttering in his Ready Room when an unexpected visitor arrived.

The visitor couldn't have come at a worse time. Ricardo's right arm was immersed up to the elbow in the built-in fish tank in the corner. He'd removed the cover to check the filter pump, and one of the gold pips on his collar had fallen into the tank. Now he was trying to retrieve the pip before the expensive kissing gouramis might try to swallow it and kill themselves.

The visitor appeared in a flash of light, startling Ricardo so that he dropped the net he was using to retrieve the pip. "Hello there, *mon Capricorn,*" said the intruder.

Ricardo whirled around and snapped at him, "Q-Tip! Don't you ever knock?"

"Why should I?" Q-Tip replied, lounging across Ricardo's desk and fiddling with the pen-and-pencil set. He was in the humanoid form he usually adopted for visits to the *Endocrine.* "As part of a continuum of omnipotent beings, I feel entitled simply to barge in at will. You should be used to that by now." Q-Tip peered at Ricardo. "Whatever are you doing to that poor fish?" he inquired.

Turning his gaze from Q-Tip back to the fish tank, Ricardo realized that he'd snared a fish's fin with his net. "Drat," he muttered, gently shaking the net to try to release the fish;

"A lot of our other ships are still in the shop for repairs."

but the fish stuck to the net, wobbling back and forth along with it.

Exasperated, Ricardo threw the net into the tank and replaced the cover. He shook his dripping arm and demanded, "I thought you'd agreed to stay with the Quke continuum and leave us alone, Q-Tip. What will it take to get rid of you this time?"

"A small favor," Q-Tip replied with an oily grin. "A teeny tiny request. I was watching a rerun of 'Cosmos' the other day, and as I drifted off to sleep near the end, I dreamed of piloting a starship. It was so enthralling that I decided to live out the fantasy. So I want you to teach me how to drive."

Ricardo opened a desk drawer and pulled out a hand towel imprinted "Valleywood Fairways Golf Course." As he dried his arm, Ricardo told Q-Tip, "You're omnipotent. Why don't you just make yourself a starship and drive it?"

"That wouldn't be the same," Q-Tip said, sitting up eagerly. "I need an existing starship that presents a real challenge. I want to meet that challenge, not just make up my own version of reality. So what do you say, Jean-Lucy? Will you teach me how to drive your ship?"

"No," Ricardo said flatly.

Instantly Q-Tip's temper flared. "You're being reckless, *mon capillary*," he warned. "You know I always repay the favors of my friends. I'm like the Godfather that way. It's a good idea to have me in your debt. Grant me this favor."

"And if I don't," Ricardo retorted, "can I expect to wake up one morning with a horse's head in my bed?"

Q-Tip bridled, snorting in disgust at the suggestion. "You know that would be beneath me," he replied hoarsely. "But you will be sorry. Someday you'll need my help, and you'll wish I owed you a favor."

"I'll take that chance," Ricardo replied as he began rolling down his sleeve.

"Very well," Q-Tip growled. He snapped his fingers, and Ricardo felt a strange tug at his collar and heard the kissing gouramis splash around in their tank. Then Q-Tip disappeared in a flash of light.

Wondering what Q-Tip had just pulled off, Ricardo strolled over to the corner. A glance at the fish tank and a quick feel of his collar confirmed his suspicion: now all four of his pips lay at the bottom of the tank.

As Q-Tip and Ricardo were chatting in the Ready Room, Dacron was entering the Ten-Foreplay lounge for his afternoon break.

But instead of her usual cheerful greeting, Chief Bartender Guano gave him an eerie stare. Dacron sat on a barstool and inquired, "Is something wrong, Guano?"

"Yes," she replied. "It's you. You're not supposed to be here."

"Oh," said Dacron. He thought for a moment, then pulled out his wallet. "Here is my ID," he offered. "It proves that I have reached legal drinking age."

"No, no, Dacron," said Guano. "It's not that. I mean you're not supposed to be here in this timeline. This is all wrong somehow."

Dacron was puzzled. "I do not understand."

"Neither do I," Guano said, "but I got this same creepy feeling when your old dead crewmate Yasha Tar showed up. Remember? Somehow she'd slipped into the wrong timeline and turned up alive again here on the ship."

Dacron pondered the meaning of this. "Do you think that the same sort of fate is in store for me?" he asked. Both he and Guano knew what had eventually happened to the misplaced Yasha: she'd returned to her proper timeline and got caught in a deadly battle aboard the *Endocrine C-Sick*.

"I don't know," Guano replied in a raspy whisper. She shivered.

Dacron asked, "Do you believe in omens, Guano?" When the chief bartender nodded, Dacron continued, "Yesterday I accidentally dropped a bottle of Tarium-Three on my cat,

"Yesterday I accidentally dropped a bottle of Tarium-Three on my cat."

Spot, turning him into a black cat. Since then he has crossed my path fifty-seven times."

Guano shuddered. "Have you had any other signs of bad luck lately?" she asked. "Have you broken a mirror or anything?"

"Yes, I have," Dacron answered. "I dropped the main operating mirror while adjusting one of our deflector screens this morning. But I did not realize until this moment that it had significance beyond the fact that it will cost three times my annual salary to replace."

"Oooh. This is bad," moaned Guano. "This is really bad." She shook her head.

Dacron grasped her arm, looking increasingly worried. "What should I do, Guano?" he asked. "What is in store for me?"

"There's only one way to find out," said Guano. She ducked behind the counter for several moments. Dacron leaned over the bar, trying to see what was going on. Soon Guano reappeared wearing a fortune-teller's black gown and a sorcerer's pointy hat. She placed a novelty toy, the 8-Ball, on the counter.

"This is our guide to the spirit world," she told Dacron. "The 8-Ball never lies." Examining the ball, Dacron found a plastic window at its bottom. As he watched, a cube floated into view in the window, reading "Maybe so." He turned the 8-Ball right side up, then upside down, and checked the window again; this time it read "Nevermore."

"This will tell us your fate," Guano stated. "Oh, powerful 8-Ball," she declaimed loudly, drawing stares from other patrons at the bar, "reveal your truth to us. Is Dacron in trouble?" Guano nodded at Dacron; he shook the ball and turned it upside down. The reply read "Yep."

Dacron and Guano looked at each other in alarm. Guano asked, "Oh, 8-Ball, is Dacron in any physical danger?" Dacron shook the 8-Ball an extra long time to make sure it was randomly mixed; then he turned it upside down. An answer floated into view: "Real bad."

Now Dacron and Guano were thoroughly hooked by the
mystery.

Now Dacron and Guano were thoroughly hooked by the mystery. Guano, her voice trembling, asked her final question, "Oh, 8-Ball, is Dacron going to die?"

Together Dacron and Guano shook the 8-Ball, round and round and round, till they could delay no longer. They turned the ball over carefully. The answer floated into view:

"You betcha."

By the time Capt. Ricardo's crew arrived at the planet where Capt. Smirk was holding the Fountain of Youth, Ricardo's resolve to smash his rival had withered somewhat. Ricardo stood in the center of his Bridge, studying the planet's surface in the Viewscreen as he silently suffered the slings and arrows of his chronic condition: an overdeveloped conscience.

Smirk is only doing what I would do in the same situation, Ricardo thought. *As a fellow captain, shouldn't I come to his aid instead of doing the dirty work for Starfreak's bureaucracy? He hasn't really done anything this nasty to me. As a matter of fact, he has actually helped us in the past, like when we teamed up to defeat the Cellulites, and when he blew up his ship to destroy the Jargonites.*

Dash it all! Why couldn't he just settle down into a peaceful retirement? Instead he pulls another foolhardy stunt that puts me in the middle.

But if I don't pry him loose from this planet, Starfreak will suspend my crew and then send someone else to do the job. One way or another, Smirk's days are numbered. Might as well get on with it.

"Standard orbit," Ricardo ordered the nameless ensign-of-the-week occupying the Conn station. The ship settled into an orbit of the planet Smirk had captured.

"Mr. Wart," Ricardo continued, "open a channel to the surface."

" 'Hey, you' frequencies open, sir," Wart reported from his Tactical station at the back of the Bridge.

Capt. Smirk appeared on the Viewscreen in dazzling white sports togs. An embroidered "I ♥ tennis" headband propped

up the moist curls on his forehead. "Ricardo!" he said with
a grin. "Why don't you Fax on down here for a match? I just
beat Mr. Zulu in straight sets."

"No, thank you," Ricardo responded with a polite smile.
"We're here on an official mission, Captain Smirk. I'm afraid
we must take you and your crew into custody and transport
you to the Vacant Attic Nursing Home."

"Oh, c'mon, Jean-Lucy. You can't be serious," Smirk responded. "Do I look like someone who's ready to be put out
to pasture?"

Ricardo squinted at the Viewscreen. Smirk's face *did* have
fewer creases than Ricardo remembered, and Smirk seemed
to be bursting with energy. He even appeared to be sporting
real hair, not that tacky hairpiece he'd taken to wearing lately.

Ricardo shook his head to ward off the confusion of these
new developments. "That's irrelevant," he told Smirk. "My
orders are to claim this planet for Starfreak. And you, Captain,
have violated a direct order from an admiral. I have no choice
but to arrest you."

"Of course you have a choice," Smirk said, deftly flipping
off the headband and wringing the sweat from it. "You and
your crew could join me down here. With both of our ships
guarding the planet, we'd be invincible against any further
assaults that Starfreak might send. We'll spend our days playing in the fountain, and our nights living it up. What d'ya
say, Jean-Lucy?"

Smirk's offer was so tempting that for a moment Capt.
Ricardo wobbled on the edge of uncertainty. Then his conscience began to throb, and he became himself again.

"Certainly not," he said icily. He turned toward the Oops
station and ordered, "Mr. Dacron, inform Shipping and Receiving to lock on to Captain Smirk's crew and UltraFax them
to our Maximum Security Guest Quarters."

"I wouldn't do that if I were you," Smirk warned them in
a lilting singsong.

Dacron consulted his console and reported, "Shipping is
ready to transport, sir."

Ricardo, hands on his hips, settled his face into an intimidating stare worthy of Clint Eastwood and ordered, "Go ahead. Make it so."

Moments after the UltraFax beam was activated, an explosion shook the ship. Capt. Ricardo, teetering to recover his balance, ordered, "Damage report!"

"Captain," came Georgie's voice over the intercom from Engineering, "there's some kind of force field protecting the entire planet. Its energy source is Captain Smirk's ship, which is parked in the northeast quadrant. The field bounced our UltraFax beam back to us and damaged our shields. There's a hole in the main shield array. I'm going to have to climb out there with my patch kit to fix it."

"Captain," Wart broke in, "I recommend we fire a full array of futon torpedoes to break the planet's protective field."

"I disagree," Georgie's voice continued. "The futons could boomerang back to us, too. In fact, any weapon we use would bounce right back and hurt us instead of them. This is no ordinary force field. I've seen this before. It's a Colgate Invisible Shield."

"Understood," Capt. Ricardo said to the intercom. He continued, "Mr. Wart, power down all weapons systems."

Bitterly disappointed, as he always was when he didn't get to fire a weapon, Wart did as ordered, then vented his frustration by kicking a hole in one of the science station cabinets at the back of the Bridge.

Ricardo, returning his attention to the Viewscreen, saw that Smirk was making eyes at Counselor Troit, who sat at her regular Bridge station. "Captain Smirk, do you mind?" Ricardo interrupted loudly. Troit blushed and looked away. Smirk turned toward Ricardo with a grin.

"It's been nice seeing you all again," Smirk said. "Some more than others," he added with a significant glance at Troit. "But I've got to go now. I've got an appointment with my personal trainer in the Nautilus room in ten minutes. See you." Abruptly he flicked off his transmission to the Viewscreen.

"But—" Capt. Ricardo started to protest; then he went slack with resignation. He realized he'd never outtalk his rival. But the encounter had given him an idea on how they could get a foothold with Smirk.

"Counselor Troit," he said, turning toward her, "see me in my Ready Room immediately."

"Don't think of it as treachery," Ricardo told Troit a few minutes later, as she started to object to the orders he'd just given her. Ricardo folded his hands, leaned forward on his Ready Room desk, and continued, "Think of yourself as the Mata Hari of Starfreak."

"But sir," Troit protested, "you're asking me to trade on my personal relationship with Captain Smirk just to gain his confidence and gather intelligence about what's going on down there."

"Well . . . yes," said Ricardo. "I didn't expect you to object, Counselor. I thought you'd given up any romantic interest in Captain Smirk long ago, when you broke off your engagement to him and accompanied Dacron to Milwaukee."

Troit wrinkled her face with chagrin. "It's amazing what a few months with an android did to my perspective," she mused, "especially after Dacron's metabolism ran out of Fountain of Love water. It was like living with the Encyclopedia Britannica."

"All right, so Smirk looks more like the last of the red hot lovers than ever," Ricardo acknowledged, trying to stifle his growing irritation. *Why do so many of my crewmembers fight my wishes?* he wondered. *It's such a bother when they have a mind of their own. Why can't more of them be like Commander Piker—brain dead?*

He continued, "Regardless of your personal feelings, Deanna, you've got to help us succeed in this mission. If we don't, Starfreak will fire us again. And they'll send someone else to take Smirk into custody. Either way, he's going to have to face his retirement. So why not do what you can to make the transition as painless as possible? Maybe you can even talk him into surrendering."

Troit sighed. "I suppose so," she agreed.

"Good," Ricardo said with finality. "You may contact Captain Smirk on your personal Viewscreen. Get him to lift this force field long enough for you to UltraFax down. Once you're there, try to find out about this force field or anything else that might help us."

Once the shock of the 8-Ball's dire prediction had worn off a little, Dacron decided to seek a second opinion. Guano agreed that it would be wise to get another, more rational perspective on the issue, so she offered the use of her Ouija Board.

She set the board on the bar, and Dacron sat on a barstool facing her. Together they rested their fingertips on the planchette.

The Ouija quickly confirmed the 8-Ball's prediction that Dacron was going to die. It also hinted that Dacron's death would be slow and painful, triggered by a freak occurrence that would unfold into dire consequences somewhere down the line.

Recalling Yasha Tar's demise, Dacron asked, "Mr. Ouija, will my death occur in the line of duty?"

The planchette dragged itself across the board, slowly spelling out its reply: "SORTA."

Then, remembering the crew's greatest regret at Yasha's death, Dacron asked, "Will it be a senseless death? One which will not further our mission in any way?"

The planchette crept from letter to letter and answered: "TOTALLY SENSELESS."

Dacron was clearly disturbed. "Mr. Ouija," he asked, "can you describe the event that will trigger my death?"

The planchette hesitated in the middle of the board for nearly a minute. Then it crept to the side—slowly at first, but soon picking up speed. Dacron and Guano shifted position to keep their fingertips resting on the planchette as it ran off the board. To their amazement, the planchette slid across the surface of the bar and dropped off the edge.

"Oh, brother," Guano griped as Dacron bent to retrieve it. "This board must need repair." Dacron put the planchette back on the board, and the two placed their hands on it again. "All right, Ouija, I want a straight answer," Guano chided. "Now will you please describe the event that will trigger Dacron's death?"

The planchette began sliding from one letter to another, much faster this time, and with a definite edge to its movements as if the board were angry at them. The reply came: "THAT WAS THE ANSWER YOU IDIOT." Again the planchette slid off the board, skidded across the bar, and plunged to the floor.

3

You're Not Getting Older, You're Getting Younger

CAPT. RICARDO AWOKE with a start and looked around, wondering, *Where am I*? Then he relaxed as he realized he was on the Bridge and had simply fallen asleep again. *They make these chairs too darned comfortable*, he rationalized.

Ricardo pulled the side lever to lower the footrest on his La-Z-Boy command chair. Standing up, he faltered momentarily; his left leg had fallen asleep.

Instantly Piker leaped up and steadied him by the elbow. "Are you all right, sir?" he inquired.

"I'm fine, Number 1," Ricardo assured him. "Just a bit of a cramp in my calf."

"Of course, sir." Piker flashed the fawning grin characteristic of first officers and vice presidents throughout the galaxy.

Ricardo limped over to Dacron's Oops station at the forward section of the Bridge. "How long has Counselor Troit been down on the planet, Dacron?" he asked.

"Exactly thirty-two hours, nine minutes and six seconds, sir," Dacron replied.

"And there's been no change in the sensor readings?" Ricardo pressed. "No break in the Colgate force field? No way to lock on to her signal from here?"

"That is correct, sir," Dacron said. "We have no way of tracking Counselor Troit, nor of retrieving her with our UltraFax beam, until Captain Smirk allows her to make contact." Then a light flashed on Dacron's console. "Captain," he continued, "sensors show a slight break in the force field. It lasted three-point-two seconds and was accompanied by UltraFax beam activity."

Capt. Ricardo hailed Shipping and Receiving via the intercom and confirmed what he'd hoped: Counselor Troit had just Faxed back onto the ship. He instructed her to report to his Ready Room at once.

Capt. Ricardo studied Counselor Troit as she sat down in one of the chairs facing his Ready Room desk. From the look on her face, he guessed that she'd made significant progress with Capt. Smirk. Ricardo noted that Troit's eager, excited expression actually transformed her features so much that she looked years younger.

"Counselor," Ricardo began, "was your mission a success?"

"Oh yeah!" she bubbled. "It's, like, *so* cool down there, you know? I could have just stayed forever."

Ricardo smiled politely. "I'm sure it's a very nice planet," he assented. "Were you able to find out anything about how we can break this force field?"

"Well, no," she admitted. "But, you know, there just wasn't any chance to ask about it without being too pushy. I mean, here I am, UltraFaxing down, and Captain Smirk is like, hey, baby, it's so good to see you again, and I'm like, yeah, I'm glad to see you too, and he's like, do you wanna see the buildings we put up here, and I'm like, sure, let's go. So it would have been pretty phony to break in and go, so, hey, tell me all about this force field around your planet! You know?"

Ricardo stared at her. "Deanna, are you feeling all right?"

"I'm fine," she answered breezily. She fingered a lock of her long hair, holding it up to the light to inspect it for split ends. "Why?"

"You don't sound like your usual self," Ricardo told her.

"I'm just so excited after seeing Captain Smirk again," Deanna revealed. She pulled out a pack of gum and held it toward Capt. Ricardo. "Want some?" He shook his head. She unwrapped a stick of gum and crammed it into her mouth.

"I'm not sure what he's up to," Deanna continued, chomping the gum vigorously, "but there's a lot of stuff going on down there. He invited me to come back whenever I want. Maybe I should go back down there right now, huh? This time maybe he'll tell me about this force field thing you wanted to know." She bounced up out of her chair. "Okay?"

Capt. Ricardo, at a loss for words, simply nodded in agreement. Together they headed out of the Ready Room.

Troit flitted around the Bridge from one crewmember to another. "Guess what, guys?" she squeaked. "I'm going back down to the planet." She squeezed Dacron's shoulder, and he gave her a bewildered look. "Gonna spend more time with this real hunky captain," she went on, skipping over to Piker and ruffling his hair with her hand. She plopped into the captain's chair for a moment and swung her legs with abandon. Then she jumped up again and skipped toward the Crewmover. "This is gonna be *so* great!" she exclaimed. As the Crewmover doors closed, she waved and called, " 'Bye now! Catch ya later!"

Piker smoothed his hair back into place and, as Ricardo settled into the captain's chair to his left, Piker demanded, "What's with her?"

"I'm not sure," Ricardo said. He wasn't sure why Deanna was carrying on so. He wasn't sure she'd be able to gather the information they needed. He wasn't even sure she'd manage to avoid another dangerous infatuation with the smooth-talking Smirk.

Ricardo grimaced. He was only sure of one thing: Deanna had discarded her gum by sticking it onto his chair cushion—and he'd just sat in it.

That afternoon, Dacron spent his off-duty hours in his quarters putting his affairs in order, since no less an authority than Guano's 8-Ball and Ouija Board had both decreed he was going to die.

First Dacron made sure his insurance premiums were paid. Then he set up a trust fund ensuring that Spot would be well cared for. Finally, he sorted through his possessions and discarded those that might cause him post-mortem embarrassment if viewed by others, such as the videotape he and Yasha Tar had made long ago during their brief but torrid tryst.

When all the details were taken care of, Dacron paused, unsure what to do next and wondering how to tell whether death was imminent. He decided to lie down and wait for the Great Spirit to overtake him. Stretching himself out on the bed and lying on his back, Dacron declared aloud, "It is a good day to die."

Within a few minutes, Dacron drifted into a state of deep meditation. Spot ambled into the room, nosed around the edge of the mattress for a moment, then jumped onto Dacron's stomach. Startled, Dacron doubled up, wrenching his back. Spot hissed at him and ran away.

Massaging his aching android muscles, Dacron hobbled over to his medicine chest for some Doan's Pills. He concluded that perhaps his time had not yet come, after all.

It was suppertime, and Smartalecsander sat at the dining table in Wart's quarters staring at his plate. Wart admonished his son, "Eat your supper, young man."

"I don't wanna eat it," Smartalecsander whined. "Why do I hafta eat this baby food? I want to eat what you're eating."

"Traditional Kringle fare is too rich for a youngster," Wart told him. His own plate held a goulash of farm-fresh garnishktz intestines and markklomm sinew.

"It's not fair," moped Smartalecsander. "My food isn't even moving." He plopped his spoon up and down in his mashed potatoes.

"Stop that," Wart ordered. Although he sympathized with the boy, he tried his fatherly best to sound stern. "I'm sure there are human children," he began, then hesitated, ". . . somewhere . . . who would be happy to eat what is on your plate. Now eat it!"

For a while, the two of them chewed away in angry silence. Finally Wart made a stab at pleasant dinner conversation. He'd felt a little out of touch with his son's life ever since re-enrolling him in the *Endocrine*'s educational program. "What did you learn in school today, Smartalecsander?" he inquired.

"A buncha stuff about getting along with other people," the boy replied.

"Oh?" Wart asked suspiciously.

"Like how we should all live in peace and harmony," Smartalecsander droned, obviously bored by the lesson, "and how we can work out our differences without resorting to violence. And why people who start wars are bad guys."

"WHAT?!" Wart bellowed, pounding the table so hard that the leech shaker tipped over.

Smartalecsander, alarmed by the outburst, explained meekly, "The teacher said it's better to compromise and live peaceably than to start a war over foolish pride."

"Of all the ... " Choked with rage, Wart stood up and paced the room several times. He returned to the table and, in a voice tense from his effort at self-control, asked his son, "Did this teacher also present the other side of the argument—why the honor of one's people is important enough to wage war over, even if it means killing every last one of those people?"

"No, Father," Smartalecsander said.

Wart shook his head in disgust. "This is too much," he spat out. "I cannot have you subjected to such propaganda."

Smartalecsander brightened. "You mean I don't hafta go to school anymore?"

"No," Wart answered as a plan formed in his head. Briefly he recalled his doctor's admonition that spending more than a few hours a day with his son could bring on another nervous breakdown. Then he dismissed the thought—this matter was too important to let his own health considerations stand in the way.

"I will teach you myself, Smartalecsander, in the proper Kringle tradition. We will begin your lessons tomorrow."

Wart sat down again and spread his napkin across his lap. "Now eat your green beans," he told the boy, "or you won't get any krshtloff brains for dessert."

"Huh? Wha—what is it?" Capt. Ricardo sat up in bed, his heart pounding from the shock of being awakened by the intercom.

"I am sorry to disturb you, sir," came Dacron's voice over the intercom, "but you asked to be notified immediately when Counselor Troit returned to the ship. She has just Faxed aboard."

"Unnh," Ricardo grunted. "What time is it?" Groping in the dark for the bedside lamp, he knocked down the plastic pan in which his partial had been soaking.

"It is 0300 hours, sir," Dacron replied.

"0300? Uggh—three A.M.," Ricardo groaned. He kicked at his electric blanket and pulled off his nightcap, muttering, "I wish she had the sense to get in at a decent hour."

"Pardon me, sir?" Dacron inquired.

"I wasn't talking to you, Dacron," Ricardo said. "Our conversation is over. The intercom is supposed to sense that."

"The intercom's automatic end-of-conversation sensor has been malfunctioning," Dacron told him. "Georgie will fix it as soon as he receives the parts that are on back order. Until then, we must use an audio code phrase to end all intercom conversations. Over and out."

Capt. Ricardo asked Cmdr. Piker to sit in on this debriefing of Counselor Troit. Ricardo figured that if Troit was as spacey as she'd been the last time, Piker might be able to make some sense of her report; she seemed to be on his wavelength.

Troit flounced into the Ready Room where Ricardo and Piker were already seated. She took the chair next to Piker, flashed him a brilliant smile and said, "Hiya, Will."

"Hello, Deanna," Piker replied, obviously flattered by her momentary attention.

"Counselor Troit," Ricardo began, yawning, "on any future

away missions, I'd appreciate it if you would return at a decent hour so we don't have to hold the debriefing in the middle of the night like this."

Troit pouted. "What's the big deal? I got here as soon as I could." She twisted one of her shoulder-length curls around her finger and fidgeted in the chair. "Are you giving me some kind of curfew or something?"

Capt. Ricardo sighed. "Never mind. We need your report to shed some light on what Captain Smirk is up to. We've observed a number of construction vehicles going to and from the planet."

"We've seen cement-mixer spacecraft," Piker elaborated, "shuttles carrying concrete blocks, and even a landscape-architect craft full of ficus trees. It looks like Smirk is building something down there. What's going on?"

Troit shrugged. "I dunno. I wasn't outside very long this time. Captain Smirk and I spent most of our time in his b— uh, in his living quarters."

Piker seemed not to notice her slip. He went on, "Dacron monitored the force field around the planet. He said it opens up somehow to let these construction vehicles enter, but we haven't figured out how to use the opening to gain access ourselves. Did Smirk say anything about how to enter or leave the force field?"

"Nope," Troit said, studying her fingernails. "We didn't talk about construction vehicles or force fields or any other boring stuff. We had, like, these really meaningful conversations, you know? The kind where you really bare your soul? It was so . . . so . . . real."

A 30-watt light bulb went on inside Piker's head as he realized Deanna was once again romantically interested in Smirk. Jealousy flared as the embers of Piker's long-buried passion for Deanna rekindled, warming his pancreas.

Once, long ago, he and Deanna had been a hot item. At the last second they'd backed away from what would have been a mixed marriage—she had a brain, he didn't. Knowing the odds were stacked against their relationship, they'd decided to break up; but every so often, the vision of "what could have been" would flood them with tenderness and mutual respect.

"So you wasted all your time down there just letting that greaseball sweet-talk you again?" Piker snapped.

"He's not a greaseball," Troit retorted. "You haven't seen him lately. He's, like, so cute. His hair is all thick and fluffy. Anyway, you should talk. You're the one who goes through Alberto VO-5 by the case."

"Stop it, you two," Ricardo interjected. "Counselor, did you—"

Dacron's voice came through over the intercom. "Captain," Dacron said, "Admiral Less is on the main Viewscreen here on the Bridge. She wishes to speak to you immediately."

"I'll be there in a minute, Dacron," Ricardo replied. He grumbled to Piker, "What wonderful timing. We haven't made any headway, and now that witch is going to ask me for a progress report."

"I heard that, Ricardo," crackled Admiral Less' voice over the intercom.

Ricardo winced, suddenly remembering the broken sensor of the intercom. "My apologies, Admiral," he said. "Over and out."

Ricardo turned to Troit. "Counselor, it's obvious you're not yourself lately," he said. "I want you to report to Sick Bay for a checkup by Dr. Flusher."

"But I'm not sick," Troit protested.

"And I want Commander Piker to escort you, to make sure you get there," Ricardo continued. Piker nodded, clasping Troit's forearm.

"All right, I'll go," Troit whined. "Why are you picking on me all of a sudden?"

Piker stood up, gently but firmly pulling Troit with him. "You know, these May–December romances never work out," he told her unsubtly as they approached the door.

"Buzz off," Troit replied. "You don't know Jim like I do.

He's always been young at heart. Not like some stuffy first officers I know."

"Oh, so now Captain Smirk is 'Jim' again, huh?" Piker said.

Their voices faded as they headed for the Crewmover. Capt. Ricardo followed them out of the Ready Room, trudged to the center of the Bridge, and faced the Viewscreen.

Admiral Less' image appeared there in all its nasty glory. It looked as if she'd been tapping her fingernails impatiently on her desk for quite some time; there was a small groove worn into the wood.

"Admiral," Ricardo began as pleasantly as he could, "what keeps you up at this hour?"

"I'm always up, Ricardo," she said. "A long time ago I faced a choice: coffee or sleep. I chose coffee. At sixteen cups a day, sleep becomes irrelevant.

"But let's get down to business," she continued. "What were you saying about not making headway? Haven't you captured the Fountain of Youth yet?"

"No, Admiral," said Ricardo. "We're still trying to find a way to penetrate the force field Captain Smirk has placed around the planet."

"You mean you haven't even been down to the surface?" Admiral Less shrieked.

Sitting at his Oops station, Dacron flinched. His ears were sensitive to high frequencies, and Admiral Less' voice was capable of reaching the dog-whistle range.

"No, we haven't," Ricardo admitted. "But we do have an opening. My ship's counselor, Deanna Troit, has been able to—"

"Don't bore me with the details, Ricardo," Less scolded. Her voice pitch rose further. "Only one thing is important here—results." Dacron reached into his console drawer for a couple of plugs of cotton and tried to stuff them into his ears without drawing attention to himself.

Less went on, "I'm giving you one more chance to arrest Smirk's crew and claim that fountain. If you can't handle the assignment, I'll send in someone else to do it." Her tone became ever more strident and piercing; Dacron winced in pain despite the cotton plugs.

"And if you fail, that's the end of your crew's chance at permanent reinstatement in Starfreak," Less concluded on an excruciatingly high note. Dacron, unable to stand it any longer, covered his ears with his hands and ran shrieking from the Bridge.

Admiral Less observed him from the Viewscreen and remarked, "Well! I'm glad to see that at least one of your officers realizes the gravity of the situation."

Later, after breakfast, Capt. Ricardo walked down the hall to Sick Bay to question Dr. Flusher about Counselor Troit's condition.

On the way there he happened to pass Wart's quarters. A crudely lettered sign was taped to the door: KRINGLE MILITARY ACADEMY / HOME SCHOOLING OUR SPECIALTY. A Kringle military anthem was playing within. Ricardo made a mental note to ask Wart about the situation.

Entering Sick Bay, Ricardo saw Dr. Flusher examining Counselor Troit while Piker hovered next to them, looking concerned. Apparently Piker had overcome his irritation with Troit and had shifted into his protective mode.

"If there's anything I can do, anything at all," Piker was saying as Ricardo approached, "just let me know."

"You can move a couple of feet to the left," Flusher told him. "You're standing in my light."

"Oops. Sorry," Piker said.

"Doctor Flusher," said Capt. Ricardo, "have you made a diagnosis yet?"

Flusher nodded. She excused herself from Troit, escorted the captain into her office, and shut the door. "I've never seen anything like it," Flusher exclaimed.

Ricardo took her statement with a grain of salt; Flusher said this about nearly every condition she treated. Ricardo sometimes wondered why every new case seemed such a revelation to her. Had she spent her internship in one of the narrower subspecialties, like Ferengi gynecology?

"Deanna's riboflavin system has somehow been totally reconfigured," Flusher went on. "Her thiamin mononitrate levels are skyrocketing, yet the corresponding sodium ascorbate ratio is exceedingly low. And the heliovectrometer ratings are off the charts."

Capt. Ricardo blinked; this was all too much to absorb during a morning that had begun at three A.M. "Doctor," he implored, "can you tell me in layman's terms what's going on with Counselor Troit?"

"Captain," said Dr. Flusher, speaking slowly and clearly for emphasis, "physically and emotionally, Deanna has reverted to an earlier age. She's now approximately fifteen again."

" . . . The Battle of Warthogshead, the Battle of Nurshrikk, and the Battle of Krawczyk," Smartalecsander recited.

"You forgot the Battle of Grrzzzzzyk," Wart prompted him. "That comes after Nurshrikk."

"Okay," said Smartalecsander. "Is it time for recess yet, Father?"

"I suppose so," Wart allowed. This was only the first day of his son's home schooling, and they were still sorting out the ground rules. Smartalecsander had been an attentive pupil, and Wart decided he deserved a reward. "I have something for you," Wart told the boy.

Smartalecsander watched eagerly as his father opened a desk drawer and pulled out a package. "I got you this toy," Wart said, handing him the box. "It is similar to one that I enjoyed playing with when I was young."

"Oh, boy!" Smartalecsander exclaimed, ripping open the package. "A G.I. Jones doll!" The stiff soldier doll was dressed in battle fatigues.

"This is a *talking* G.I. Jones model," Wart pointed out. "My G.I. Jones was not capable of speech. You are lucky that such technology is in use today. I'm sure he has many statements to make about duty and honor."

There was a string at the doll's back. Smartalecsander pulled it out to its full length, and as the string wound back, the doll spoke. "Have a nice day," it said.

"What?" Wart asked.

Smartalecsander pulled the string again. This time the doll said, "Let's turn our swords into plowshares."

"*What?*" Wart demanded. He grabbed the package that Smartalecsander had tossed aside. For the first time he noticed the small print on the front: NEW! PEACETIME MODEL. With a grunt of disgust, Wart flung down the box.

Smartalecsander pulled the string once more. "Give peace a chance," said the G.I. Jones doll.

Wart snatched G.I. Jones from the boy's hand. "Let me have that!" he growled. "More sentimentalist propaganda! To think some people would sell this to children just to make a profit . . . " He seemed about to toss the doll into the garbage can, but Smartalecsander spoke up.

"Wait, Father," he said. "Why don't we conduct a ritual execution on him, like you did that time with the goldfish that wouldn't obey orders?"

Capt. Ricardo's plans for a staff meeting that afternoon were bitterly dashed, even before the agenda could be mimeographed. He cursed this cruel twist of fate, but there was no getting around it: the two issues he'd intended to discuss at the meeting had suddenly solved themselves.

The mystery of Counselor Troit's retro-aging was cleared up by someone's offhand remark that she must have had contact with the Fountain of Youth during her visit to Smirk's planet.

The other issue was how the rest of the crew could get around the force field and gain access to the planet, as Troit had. Ricardo envisioned an elaborate scheme in which Troit would get Smirk to Fax her down again while an Away Team would somehow secretly tag along. But that point was also mooted when Dacron noticed that the force field had been turned off.

"Why don't we conduct a ritual execution on him?"

A glance at the Viewscreen confirmed his observation. Not only was the planet now open to visitors, but a steady stream of passenger vehicles was headed down to the surface, drawn by a huge neon side that read:

Welcome

JUVEN ISLE THEME PARK

Now Open

4

We Are
Not Amused

THAT SAME DAY, about midmorning, Capt. Ricardo assembled his Away Team in Shipping and Receiving. Now that the force field had been deactivated, they intended to finish their stalled mission: to take Smirk and crew into custody and claim the Fountain of Youth for Starfreak.

Capt. Ricardo was a little nervous about heading into this unknown environment—Juven Isle Theme Park—that Smirk had constructed right under their noses. "Dacron," Ricardo asked, "what did the sensors show about this place?"

"Sensor reports are inconclusive," Dacron replied. "However, I was able to obtain an official guidebook." He opened the guidebook to the page labeled "General Information" and read aloud: "Welcome to Juven Isle Theme Park, designed for the truly young and the youthful wanna-bes. Whether your idea of fun is thrill rides, fast-food stands, musical revues or utterly useless souvenirs, we're here to take your money. All major credit cards are accepted—"

"That's enough, Dacron," Capt. Ricardo broke in. "Apparently Captain Smirk has built himself an amusement park. Since this is Opening Day, he and his crew are probably out on the grounds somewhere. We'll need to locate all of them and bring them back here to the ship. Understood?"

The others nodded. Besides Ricardo, the Away Team consisted of Dacron, Dr. Flusher, and Troit, who was escorted by Piker. Wart was to have come along too, but he begged off at the last minute, citing a conflict between this mission

503

and some kind of father/son social event at Smartalecsander's school. Ricardo made another mental note to ask him what he was up to.

Ricardo stepped onto the UltraFax platform, and the others followed. The Fax beam was set to send them right into the middle of the park. However, in mid-transport, the beam was diverted, and instead they materialized next to the ticket sales booths outside the entrance gate. Unknown to them, an anti-gatecrashers shield protected the park from anyone trying to sneak in via UltraFax without paying admission.

Readjusting their battle plan, they meekly joined the crowds waiting in line to buy tickets. Then, approaching the entrance gate, they faced another challenge. A large sign declared: NO CARRY-IN BOTTLES, CANS, RECORDING EQUIPMENT OR INSIGNIA COMMUNICATORS ALLOWED IN PARK. Reluctantly they surrendered their communicator pins to a security officer. Finally they entered the park itself.

"We'll rendezvous here at 1500 hours," Capt. Ricardo told his crew, pointing to a nearby landmark: a flower bed in which the flowers formed a giant yellow happy face. "Bring with you any members of Captain Smirk's crew you encounter during the day. And stay away from that Fountain of Youth," he warned them. With that, they dispersed to begin the mission.

"Hurry up," Troit urged. "We want to hit the good rides before the lines get too long." She skipped through the crowds clogging the sidewalks, pulling Piker along with her.

"I thought you weren't familiar with what's been going on down here," Piker said, struggling to keep up. "How do you know which rides are good?"

"Jim gave me a sneak preview of some of them," Troit revealed. "I didn't tell Captain Ricardo about it 'cause I was afraid I'd get grounded." Tugging Piker's arm, she added, "Come on, Will. Let's go!"

"Ease up a little, will you?" Piker asked between gulps for air. He wasn't in shape for such an endurance contest, he realized; they must have jogged at least fifty meters already.

"We probably shouldn't be going on any rides, anyway," Piker added. "We're here to capture Smirk's crew, not to have fun."

"Oh, chill out, Will," Troit urged him. "We'll get around to that. Besides, we'll be going on some of the tallest rides. From the top, you'll be able to see the whole park, so it should be pretty easy to spot those guys. Maybe you'll even see them from this first one, the Ferris wheel."

That made sense to Piker. And the gleam in Troit's eye when they reached the Ferocious Ferris gave him another idea: accompanying her on these death-defying thrill rides would definitely be an act of machismo. *She'll probably get scared when we go up high*, Piker thought, *and then I can put my arm around her and make her feel safe. And the thrill of the ride will carry over into how she feels about me. She'll forget all about her crush on Smirk.* The vision was so compelling that it wasn't until they'd waited in line for fifteen minutes and were climbing into the next available seat that Piker remembered he was terrified of heights.

The attendant snapped a metal restraining bar into place across their laps, and the car lurched backward and swayed beneath them. Instantly Piker's sweat glands kicked in; his palms became so slick he could barely grip the bar. He shut his eyes, but that only intensified the sickening feeling as the car swooped up and back.

"Wheeee!" Troit cried. "This is fun!" Piker turned to the side so she wouldn't notice that he couldn't even bear to look.

Finally he realized that if he was going to survey the park for Smirk's crew, he would have to open his eyes while they were at the top, at least for a few seconds. He decided to ease into it by opening his eyes at the bottom first. When the noises and air currents told him they were near the ground, Piker cautiously opened his eyes and looked ahead. They were just passing the lowest point of the wheel's revolution.

Standing on the ground was a young worker in a park maintenance department uniform. Piker shook his head and blinked in astonishment, for the worker seemed to be scraping gum off the underside of the Ferris wheel's seats—while they were in motion. Apparently the park's bubblegum-chewing patrons had wasted no time on Opening Day in marking this new territory, like wolves leaving scent marks around the prairie.

The next time their car reached the bottom, Piker opened his eyes for a longer period and confirmed that the worker was, indeed, trying to clean the cars without stopping the ride. The worker had about five seconds to scrape each car before it swung out of his reach. His timing gradually fell behind, so that after three or four seats had gone by, he got bonked in the back of the head by the next car coming up.

Poor devil, Piker sympathized. *Management probably told him they couldn't afford any downtime while he works on the equipment.*

On the third pass, the young worker's face was visible for a moment, and Piker felt a strange buzz of recognition. It might have been the combination of his dizziness and his impression that this was the ultimate loser's job, but Piker had the fleeting thought that the worker looked just like Checkout would if Checkout were 16 years old.

"Hey, Will, let's rock the car!" Deanna cried, and she began swinging the seat back and forth. Piker's interest in the young maintenance worker vanished as he closed his eyes again and concentrated on not throwing up.

Dacron, wandering among the crowds, soon came up with the same idea that Troit had proposed: the taller rides would provide a good vantage point from which to search for Smirk's crew.

Precise as always, Dacron consulted the guidebook to determine which ride was the tallest. It turned out to be the park's meanest roller coaster, Deathmeister XL-5.

After a long wait in line, Dacron finally boarded one of the cars. A 10-year-old boy plopped into the seat next to him, did a double take upon seeing Dacron's white skin, then cheerily assured Dacron, "Hey, dude, don't be so scared. It's just a ride."

Dacron locked at him in puzzlement for a few seconds; then understanding dawned on his face. "Ah. I see," he said. "You interpret my paleness as an indication of fear over the impending ride. However, that is incorrect. This is my normal skin color."

"Wow. Cool!" the boy exclaimed.

"As a matter of fact, I am looking forward to reaching the tallest peak," Dacron told him.

"You wanna know the best way to ride this ride?" the boy asked as the train of cars lurched forward on the metal track. Dacron nodded. The boy continued, "You've gotta stand up. It's the most awesome feeling."

"But these restraining bars across our laps are designed to prevent such an action," Dacron observed.

"No problem," the boy answered, reaching for a locknut on the lower end of the bar. He gave it a jerk, and the bar swung open. "My friends and I figured this out. We've been on this ride eight times since the park opened this morning." Dacron saw that other youngsters in the cars ahead had loosened their bars, too, and were standing up as the train headed for the first hill.

A sign off to one side ordered REMAIN SEATED, and Dacron noticed that further along in the ride they would be passing through several low tunnels. "Are you certain this is safe?" he inquired.

"I dunno," said the boy. "But it's really fun. Just remember to duck before we hit the tunnels." Dacron hesitated. His seatmate, who was already standing, urged him, "Come on. Don'tcha wanna have fun?"

Dacron looked like he was pondering a foreign concept. "Hmmm. Fun," he mused. "Yes, I believe I do." He stood up, bracing himself as the car ascended the steep angle. A sign at the side of the track read DO NOT STAND. The train clattered up the rails.

Finally the cars reached the top of the first hill and hovered there for an excruciatingly suspenseful moment. Dacron tried to survey the park, but at this height, cirrus clouds blocked their view. Then he looked ahead to where the track took its first plunge down a 78-degree slope.

Instantly Dacron's sensors registered grave danger. His hands locked into a death grip around the restraining bar. The WD-40 chilled in his veins, and his pulse pounded at his temple where an artery fed into his apomecometer.

The cars plunged into a near free-fall. Riders screamed as their primal instincts told them that this was somewhat unnatural. Whomped by G-forces of suffocating intensity, those who'd remained in their seats were plastered against the backrests, and those who were standing clung desperately to the nearest handhold and hung on for their lives.

The cars bottomed out and rushed up the next hill, carrying mighty momentum from their first drop. Then they headed for a series of dips in the track. Some of the dips were covered by the tunnels Dacron had noticed, made from arches of fake rock.

Dacron's seatmate and his buddies sat down, anticipating the low clearance ahead, but Dacron remained standing. In those moments of terror as they'd plunged down the first hill, his hard drive had frozen up, leaving his positronic circuits powerless to evaluate the situation. He stood with his knees locked as the cars approached the tunnel.

"Look out!" yelled the boy, trying to pull Dacron back into his seat, but it was too late. Dacron's head conked against the low arch. Knocked from the car, he fell to the ground some 50 feet below and collapsed in a heap.

As Dacron's hard drive re-booted and he came to his senses, the first thing he saw was a sign propped up against the understructure of the ride. It read: WE TOLD YOU NOT TO STAND.

Gingerly, Dacron examined the spot where the arch had struck his head. His hand came away from his forehead wet with WD-40, so he decided to head for the first-aid station. The guidebook told him it was right next door. *From a liability standpoint, that is probably a good idea*, Dacron reasoned. He tottered over to the station, where a nurse took his name, his temperature, and an imprint of his MasterCard.

Soon after Dacron was seated in one of the treatment rooms, a young medic entered. He took one look at Dacron and exclaimed, "You?!"

"I beg your pardon?" Dacron inquired.

"Uh . . . never mind," the doctor muttered. He seemed to be in a bad mood as he gave Dacron's forehead a cursory examination.

"Please give me the unvarnished truth, Doctor," Dacron requested. "How long do I have to live?"

"Too darned long," mumbled the doctor. "Here, tell me when it hurts." He stuck a knitting-needle-like probe into Dacron's wound.

"Ouch!" Dacron cried.

The doctor withdrew the probe, folded his arms against his chest, and looked down his nose at Dacron. "You park visitors are all the same," the doctor crabbed. "Get a little cut or bruise and you think it's the end of the world. I'm tired of treating these minor injuries. From now on I'm only going to handle wounds that require twenty-five stitches or more, understand? I'm a doctor, not a nurse! Now get out of here. If you're so worried about that itty-bitty cut, go buy a box of Band-Aids at the souvenir stand."

Dacron stumbled out of the first-aid station, trying to figure out what had just happened. The doctor's voice had sounded very much like Dr. McCaw's, yet his young face didn't match up with Dacron's internal file on McCaw. As Dacron's synaptic circuits began to throb, he dismissed the thought and headed for the nearest souvenir stand to buy bandages.

Piker huffed and puffed, trying to keep up with Troit. She was so determined to reach the next "good" ride that they were practically running.

As they rushed through a courtyard on their way across the park, neither of them paid much attention to a strange clown surrounded by a crowd of eager children. The clown's rainbow wig barely concealed his pointy ears. His deadpan expression and sternly slanted eyebrows seemed out of place

The clown's rainbow wig barely concealed his pointy ears.

as he went about the jolly business of twisting long, thin balloons into animal shapes.

One of the children held up a purple balloon and asked the clown to shape it into a weiner dog. The clown shook his head and told the child, "I am afraid I cannot comply with such an illogical request. Dogs are never purple."

Farther on, Piker and Troit passed the section where the kiddie rides were clustered. Again, they were in too much of a hurry to notice their surroundings. But if they had stopped to investigate, they'd have seen a young Scotsman, his coveralls smeared with grease, who was attempting to repair the Horsey-Go-Round. In his frustration at the balky mechanism, he was screaming so vehemently that parents were covering their children's ears with their hands.

Piker and Troit finally reached their ride and got in line. "This is it," Troit told Piker, rubbing her hands together in anticipation.

They'd arrived at the centerpiece of the park, Juven Isle itself. The island had been constructed of fabricated rock and a jungle of plastic foliage. A moat of water surrounded it, and waterfalls and fountain sprays sprang forth from the rock at various points. Swooping over and under and around it all was a log-flume roller coaster. As the coaster zipped around the island, riders plunged through the water in several places, laughing and shrieking as they became thoroughly soaked.

"This is absolutely the best ride," Troit claimed. "You're gonna love it." She failed to mention that the source of all of Juven Isle's water was the Fountain of Youth. It wasn't labeled as such, but a sign at the entrance gave a clue: DO NOT ATTEMPT TO RIDE THIS ATTRACTION IF YOU SUFFER FROM A HEART CONDITION, ARE PREGNANT, OR DO NOT WANT TO BECOME APPROXIMATELY FIVE YEARS YOUNGER WITH EACH EXPOSURE. Troit giggled mischievously, but Piker, who hadn't noticed the sign, couldn't get her to say why she was so giddy. "You'll see," she said. "Once you ride this ride, you're, like, never the same."

When their turn came, they climbed into a car. Once again,

Piker was too frightened of the height to survey the park as the coaster climbed upward. But after they plunged through the first water drop, which splashed all the riders, he relaxed just a bit.

They got wetter as the coaster whizzed through a bubbly waterfall. *Hey, this is fun*, Piker realized. He laughed with delight, and Troit laughed along with him.

With each plunge, Piker enjoyed the ride more. By the time they passed through the last water trough, where the cars were submerged for a full 15 seconds, he felt exhilarated.

When the ride ended, Troit and Piker ran down the exit ramp to the sidewalk. "That was great!" Piker exclaimed.

"I told you you'd like it," Troit replied.

"What's next?" Piker asked, looking around eagerly. "I'm up for anything!"

The closest thrill ride was the Egg Beater, so they decided to try it. Egg Beater riders were strapped, standing up, onto the spokes of a metal framework. As the ride got under-way, the spokes whirled and intertwined faster and faster until they blurred with speed.

Helping people on and then scraping them off this dizzying contraption was a young worker in a park employee's uniform. He was quite helpful, volunteering to hold objects that the riders couldn't take along because they might lose them dur-ing the ride—things like stuffed toy prizes, oversized hand-bags, and false teeth. But what Piker noticed most about him were his strangely familiar Oriental features. Even so, Piker failed to make the connection between this familiar face and his own mission. And as Piker stumbled off the ride, his brain was more scrambled than usual, so he forgot all about the encounter.

Dr. Flusher shifted her weight uneasily from one foot to another and studied the buildings in the park's main court-yard. She was caught in that perennial, unmentionable di-lemma of Away Team members: locating the restroom in an alien environment.

Finally she spotted a ladies' room, but her relief was tempered with dismay when she saw that the restroom had a waiting line as long as the lines for any of the amusement rides. In fact, the women were backed up past a sign that said: WAITING TIME FROM THIS POINT—APPROXIMATELY 75 MINUTES.

Finally, after what seemed an eternity, Flusher reached the restroom. Afterward she hobbled out, wondering if her bladder would ever be the same. She didn't feel up to doing much walking, so when she noticed one of the park's theaters, she decided to begin her search there.

Standing up front near the stage, Flusher was able to scan the crowd, but she didn't see anyone from Smirk's crew. Then the house lights dimmed and she was forced to sit down.

An announcer stepped into the spotlight. "Welcome to Broadway Boo-Boos," she said with artificial brightness, "our tribute to a dozen Broadway shows that closed within a week of their opening night. For our first number, from the Broadway adaptation of 'General Hospital,' here's the classic ballad 'Sentimental Gurney'!"

Scattered applause greeted the first singer. With her voluptuous figure and dark-skinned beauty, she made a beautiful first impression. Then she spoiled it by opening her mouth. It sounded as if she was singing in some alien key, one which had several half- and quarter-tones that the human ear couldn't quite assimilate.

I've heard that voice somewhere before, Flusher thought. *I know—it reminds me of Yoohoo rehearsing while we waited to go on stage at that wrekkie convention. But this woman is so young. This can't be Yoohoo . . . can it?*

Troit and Piker rode the log flume again. As soon as they got off, they ran back and got in line once more.

When they exited the third time, Piker was whooping with excitement. "That was, like, totally awesome!" he exclaimed in a voice that was much higher than it had been that morning.

Troit and Piker rode the log flume again.

Troit gave him an adoring glance. The tunic of his uniform hung rather loosely; it looked like he'd shed a lot of weight from his torso. His face was boyish and unlined. The most startling change of all was that his beard had disappeared. His cheeks were now covered with a soft, downy peach-fuzz.

"You were right about these rides, Dee baby," Piker went on. "They're the greatest."

She hugged his waist. "I knew you'd get into this, Will," she replied. "You are just *too* cool."

Suddenly Piker felt certain that he could make Deanna forget all about Smirk. All it took was a little finesse in the romance department; he realized. So Piker hugged Deanna, nuzzled her neck, and gave her an enormous hickey.

5

Death Valley
Days

CAPT. RICARDO TOOK a different tack in this search for Smirk's crew than the other Away Team members did. He didn't ride the rides. In fact, he'd never be caught dead on a ride. The whole practice struck him as pointless and undignified. So finding a high vantage point was out of the question.

He didn't visit the musical revues. The last time he'd seen a play was a couple of decades ago, when the musical version of the science fiction classic *Dune* was making the rounds. That had been such a bomb that he'd sworn off theater altogether. So he wasn't about to waste time searching the park's auditoriums.

He didn't visit the souvenir shops. He knew from experience that the clerks would take one look at him and try to sell him a souvenir cap or a bottle of sunblock lotion for his scalp. So if some of Smirk's crewmates happened to be working in the shops, he'd take the chance of missing them.

Instead, Ricardo headed straight for the management office, reasoning that since Smirk was masterminding this project, he had to station himself in a place where he could direct all the action.

Ricardo was right. Approaching the management building, he saw a crowd of teenage girls gathered at the door. At the center of the group stood a handsome young man in baggy surfer shorts and a sweatshirt. Atop his head was a thick cluster of brown curls. They contrasted sharply with the close-

516

shaved sides of his head, into which the initials "JTS" had been carved. He was holding up his hands as if to ward off the females around him.

"Please, please," he said with a smile, "there's only so much of me to go around!"

Capt. Ricardo elbowed his way through the group until he was standing at the young man's side. "Captain Smirk?" Ricardo inquired.

Smirk seemed genuinely happy to see him. "Jean-Lucy," he said, "what's shakin', man?" Ricardo frowned, and Smirk said to the crowd, "Gals, if you'll excuse us for a minute?" The girls sighed with dismay as Smirk escorted Ricardo into the management building and shut the outer door behind them. Ricardo followed Smirk as he headed for an inner office. Its door was plastered with posters of rock bands.

"Have a seat," Smirk invited, sweeping a pile of gym clothes off the guest chair and onto the floor. Ricardo sat down gingerly, as if he feared that relaxing in the chair would make him more susceptible to dirty-clothes germs.

Smirk went around to the other side of the desk, sat in the swivel chair, and put his feet up on the desk. Then he pulled his feet back abruptly and sat up straight. "Sorry to be so rude, man," he said. "Do you want, like, something to drink or something?"

Smirk bounced over to the wet bar behind his desk. He stuck his head inside the small refrigerator, and his voice emerged: "We've got cola, diet cola, orange juice, sports drink, milk, and a pitcher of raspberry Fizzies that I made up this morning."

"No, thank you," Ricardo replied stiffly.

Smirk grabbed a quart of milk, sat in his desk chair again, and swung his feet onto the desk. "I'm glad you made it here on Opening Day," he said. He paused to take a swig of milk from the carton, then continued, "You'll get to see this really boss parade we're having tonight. It'll go down the main promenade." He grinned, and a milk mustache glistened on his upper lip.

"Captain Smirk," Ricardo said, impatient to get on with it, "surely you must know why I'm here."

"You bet your sweet bippy," Smirk replied. "And I can't blame ya. You're gonna see a really groovy change after just one or two trips through the water on Juven Isle. My crew and I practically lived there the first few days after we got here. We were getting so young we had to lay off the water for a while, so we wouldn't turn into babies like the Roman-umens did."

"I'm not here for the water," Ricardo snapped. "We've been through all of this already. I'm here to claim the Fountain of Youth for Starfreak and to take you into custody for transport to the nursing home Starfreak has assigned you."

Smirk gazed at Ricardo for a few seconds, then cackled with laughter. Ricardo stared back, flushed with anger. Smirk abandoned himself to his laughter for a minute, then caught his breath and paused to finish off the milk in the carton. After a big swallow, he exclaimed, "Man, you are too much."

Smirk leaned back in his chair and pressed the on/off button of the stereo receiver on the shelf next to his desk. An announcer's voice boomed from the six speakers surrounding the room: "The time is 2:45, and you're listening to WpH1, the home of acid rock."

Smirk crushed the empty milk carton against his desk and tossed it at a wastebasket in the corner that had a small plastic basketball hoop hung over it. The carton sailed neatly through the hoop and into the basket. "Three points!" Smirk exclaimed. Then he turned to Ricardo.

"Sorry to ruin your day, Jean-Lucy, but like I told you before, we're not going," he said. "We've got one terrific operation here. Why should we give it up? Just so Starfreak Command can get a little fatter? No way, man.

"My crew captured this planet fair and square. You think it was fun rounding up all those baby Romanumens into a playpen and then shuttling them to a day-care planet in the next sector? I'm *still* trying to get the spit-up stains out of

"We were getting so young we had to lay off the water for a while."

my tunic. Yeah, we paid the price to own this fountain, all right. And we're gonna make it pay off."

Smirk paused a moment to groove to the music on the radio broadcast, his upper body swaying to the heavy bass beat as the lead vocalist screamed, *"This must be love, 'cause you make me sweat / It's true love, baby, I'm dripping wet . . ."*

Smirk turned back to their conversation. "Maybe some of my crewmembers aren't crazy about their jobs," he allowed, "but they pitch in 'cause the more profit we make with this park, the more power we have in the federation. It doesn't even matter whether we ever get back in Starfreak. We've got everything we need right here. I don't need to leave my own backyard to meet some of the tastiest chicks in the galaxy. This park attracts hot babes like you wouldn't believe."

"It's unfortunate that you feel you must resist," Ricardo said, his eyes darting nervously back and forth. "But I do have my orders."

"Hey, let's not make a big scene here, okay?" responded Smirk, sensing trouble. "We can all be cool about this."

"Cool?" Ricardo echoed, buying time. He shifted in his chair to distract attention from his hand. In the next instant he reached for his phaser, which was set on "stun."

Smirk's reflexes were sharper than ever. As Ricardo drew the phaser, Smirk lunged for his pneumatic-action super-squirting toy water rifle on the cluttered desktop, took aim, and blasted a spray of frigid water that knocked Ricardo out of his chair. Reaching out to break the fall, Ricardo dropped his phaser.

In an instant Smirk leaped over to Ricardo's side and placed the water rifle at Ricardo's temple. Ricardo lay in a puddle and gazed up at him helplessly, shivering from the icy blast.

"Cool your jets, Jean-Lucy," Smirk suggested. He kicked the phaser out of Ricardo's reach, then extended a hand to help Ricardo to his feet. "Now that you're wet anyway, you might as well go ride the log flume." Ricardo stood up and wrung some of the water out of his tunic.

Smirk put a hand on Ricardo's shoulder, guiding him toward the outer office. "You can stay as long as you wanna here in the park today," Smirk offered. "So can Dacron and Piker and Dr. Flusher," he went on, waving his hand at the far wall, which held a bank of video monitors linked to surveillance cameras set up throughout the park grounds. "And of course Deanna is free to come and go, like, whenever."

They reached the outer door, and Smirk paused. "But, man, don't mess around saying you're gonna take me to some old-fogey nursing home. I mean, do I look like I'm ready to retire?"

Ricardo shook his head.

"Oh-*kay*!" Smirk exclaimed. His mood turned cheery in an instant. He opened the door, and the girls waiting outside started calling his name, squealing, and pushing toward him. Those in the front row clutched at his sweatshirt.

"All right, babes, you win," Smirk cried in mock resignation. "Take me!" With that, he flung himself into the midst of the crowd, prompting a chorus of lustful screams.

By 1500 hours, all the members of the Away Team had straggled back to the happy-face flower bed. After reclaiming their insignia communicators from the park's security office, they Faxed up to their ship.

A few of them took time out to change into dry clothes. Then they convened a meeting in the Conference Room, and Capt. Ricardo briefed them on his encounter with Smirk.

When Ricardo finished his summary, Dr. Flusher spoke up. "So all his crewmembers are younger," she realized. "Then that *was* Yoohoo that I saw in the theater."

"All right, that's two crewmembers accounted for," Ricardo figured. Turning toward Piker, he saw that his first officer was nuzzling Counselor Troit's ear. "Ahem!" Ricardo harrumphed. Troit giggled, and Piker sat up straight, his face reddening.

For the first time since their Away Team had reassembled, Ricardo took a good look at Piker and noticed something significant. Piker looked much younger and thinner—and there was something else different about him, too. "Number 1," Ricardo inquired, "where's your beard?"

Piker shrugged. "I dunno," he said. "I guess I lost it on one of the rides." This struck Troit's funny bone. She held a hand to her mouth to stifle an attack of the giggles, and her shoulders shook as the giggles erupted inward.

Trying to decipher Troit's overreaction, Ricardo peered at her. That raised a new question. "Counselor Troit, what is that on your neck?"

Troit couldn't contain herself any longer. Her laughter burst forth so violently that she had to gasp for air. Instantly Piker caught her mood, and he, too, launched into a laughing fit.

"I see some of us have visited the Fountain of Youth," Dr. Flusher observed. She went to examine the spot that Ricardo had noticed on Troit's neck. After passing her medical tricorder over it, Flusher announced, "It's a Class Four hickey, administered within the past twenty-four hours."

Exasperated at Piker and Troit, Capt. Ricardo decided to continue the debriefing without them while their laughing fit ran its course. Ricardo turned to Dacron and asked, "Mr. Dacron, did you see any members of Captain Smirk's crew while we were down on the planet?"

"No, sir," Dacron replied, holding a hand against his forehead.

"Is something wrong, Dacron?" Ricardo asked.

"It is merely a superficial head wound, Captain," Dacron answered, "one requiring fewer than twenty-five stitches." He paused and seemed to daydream for several seconds. Then he continued with a dazed look, "Nevertheless, bits and bytes have been leaking out of my central processor periodically."

Dr. Flusher left Troit and walked over to Dacron, gently pulled his hand away, and examined the cut. "I'd hardly call this superficial," she judged. "It's a wonder you haven't suffered brain damage, Dacron."

"I have not ruled out the possibility of dain bramage, Doctor," Dacron stated. "I have yet to run a self-diagnostic."

"It's a wonder you haven't suffered brain damage, Dacron."

"We've got to get you to Sick Bay," Flusher ordered, helping him to his feet.

"I would not mind receiving some edical mattention," Dacron admitted. "Perhaps running an anti-virus program would ease this discomfort and clear up my sinuses." His head jerked, his eyes glazed over, and he stated irrelevantly, "Consumes forty-four times its weight in excess stomach acid."

"Please excuse us, Captain," Flusher said as they headed for the door.

Dacron's head jerked again. "Goodbye, all," he said, waving at them awkwardly as he backed out of the room. "Happy trails to you." Flusher pulled him through the doorway.

Piker and Troit finally seemed to be winding down. Sternly Ricardo stared at Troit and asked, "Counselor, you took Commander Piker through the Fountain of Youth, didn't you?"

She nodded. "I hoped it would get him to lighten up," she explained.

Ricardo regretted giving Piker the assignment to keep Troit out of trouble. *Escorting someone whose judgment is impaired is no job for someone who has never had any judgment to begin with*, he realized. *Well, that's all water under the dam now. Or under the flume, as it were.*

Wearily, Ricardo asked, "Did either of you happen to see any of Smirk's crewmates anywhere on the park grounds?"

"No, sir," Piker answered. "But I've got some information that's much more important than that. I wanted you to be the first to know." He put his arm around Troit, squeezed her shoulders, and announced, "Dee and I are going steady."

When the amusement park finally closed late that night, Capt. Smirk's crewmembers returned to their living quarters on Smirk's *Endocrine*, which was parked in the back parking lot.

Although the crew had been young for only a week, they'd already managed to put their mark on the formerly sterile quarters. Clothes were strewn everywhere. Under each bed, a mound of junk included such keepsakes as dirty gym socks, empty cola bottles, magazines, and leftover pizza crusts in cardboard delivery boxes. Visual clutter crept up the walls in the form of posters, souvenirs, crowded bulletin boards and scuff marks from the balls crewmembers tossed around constantly.

Now, as they all returned from their long workday, the living quarters took on the feel of a college dorm. The crewmembers whooped it up, bouncing from one room to another, reliving the day's activities, trashing their rooms to work off nervous energy, and eating whatever they could get their hands on.

Zulu entered McCaw's room and asked him, "Lenny, could I, like, borrow your razor?"

"What for?" taunted McCaw. "You don't shave yet."

"Sure he does," Snot joined in. "He's gonna shave his legs!" He and McCaw burst out laughing. Zulu picked up a pillow and started whacking at their heads.

"Hey, guys," said Capt. Smirk as he entered the room, "did anybody else get a load of the old fogeys' Away Team today?"

"I did," Yoohoo called from across the hall. She sat on her bed painting her toenails, with her toes separated by big fluffy cotton balls. "Dr. Flusher was in the audience watching my noon show, and I'm like, hey, baby, take a lesson from somebody who knows how to *use* it!" Yoohoo wiggled her hips for emphasis, and the others responded with wolf whistles and howls.

"Where did you see them, Captain?" Zulu asked.

"Ricardo comes to my office," Smirk recounted, obviously relishing the tale, "and he goes, so, you guys better come with big bad ol' me, or *else*, and I'm like, give me a break! So he actually pulls out his phaser, that turkey! So I let him have it with the water rifle. Pow!"

Smirk checked his reflection in the mirror over McCaw's dresser and added, "Geez, I wonder if he'll get pneumonia now. They'll hafta put a mustard plaster on his head or something."

"I saw Commander Piker and Counselor Troit riding da

Ferris veel," Checkout offered, slurring his words a little. He was slumped in a chair and holding an ice pack to the egg-sized bump on the back of his head, an occupational injury from being struck by Ferris-wheel seats every 20 seconds. "Piker looked scared. Probably afraid of heights. Vat a chicken." Checkout giggled weakly, then passed out.

"I saw Piker and Troit on my Egg Beater ride," Zulu said. "He looked okay then."

"Speaking of chickens," said McCaw, "that dopey android, Dacron, came in looking for a bandage for his so-called skin. And I'm like, yeah, I've got nothing better to do than hold your hand, yo-yo."

Mr. Smock wasn't there to join the discussion. By midday he'd become fed up with doing balloon tricks for the kiddies, and he'd gone to Capt. Smirk asking for a reassignment. Smirk, admitting that perhaps the clown job didn't make full use of Smock's talents, had decided that Smock should remain on the *Endocrine*'s Bridge and monitor the sensors in case Starfreak had any other sneaky tricks in store for them.

Later that evening, Mr. Smock put the sensors into the "record" mode and joined Zulu, McCaw and Snot as they lounged in McCaw's room, trying to decide how to spend the rest of the night. Capt. Smirk had already left to watch the park's Opening-Night parade along with his dates, four gorgeous gals he'd met that day.

"First we gotta get some real food," Zulu stated. "If I don't get something to eat within fifteen minutes, I'm gonna die."

"Then what?" asked McCaw.

"We could watch TV," Snot suggested. He lay on the bed balancing the remote control channel-changer on his gently rounded tummy. His young fingers had already developed an amazing dexterity at channel-changing.

"There's nothin' on," McCaw told him.

"There's always the Weather Channel," Snot said.

"Nah. That's boring."

"Hey!" Zulu exclaimed. "I know what we can do." He jumped up and shut the door to the outer hallway so Yoohoo wouldn't hear them. "Let's stage a panty raid on Yoohoo's room!"

The others exclaimed: "Yeah!" "Awright!" "Let's do it!"

"Excuse me," Mr. Smock inquired. "What is a panty raid?"

"It's, like, really crazy," Zulu explained, a grin lighting up his face. "You get·a buncha guys to charge into some girl's room and go through all their dresser drawers and steal their underpants!"

"And then?" asked Smock, deadpan.

"Well . . . then, that's it," Zulu said, his excitement losing some of its momentum. "You just do it for laughs, you know." Smock's expression reflected his struggle to understand this concept.

"Wait a minute," McCaw said. "Isn't there supposed to be more than one girl? I mean, like, isn't it better if you charge in on where there's a whole buncha girls? Yoohoo probably has only one underwear drawer. We'd have it cleaned out in a few seconds."

"I guess so," Zulu admitted, losing even more enthusiasm. "Well, you got a better idea?"

"There must be somebody we can pick on," Snot said idly, flicking the channel-changer with his forefinger to make it spin round and round on his stomach.

They looked around the room, thinking it over. Eventually, each pair of eyes lit on the same spot: Checkout, slumped in the easy chair, with the now-melted ice bag drooping over his ear.

Sometime around midnight, Checkout awoke. His ice bag was gone. He tried to reach up to feel his injured head, but he couldn't move his arms. Shaking off his stupor, he took a deep breath and realized he was outside in the dark.

He couldn't move his legs, either. He wiggled his fingers, and the scratchy sensation confirmed his worst fear: he'd been buried up to his neck in sand. As his eyes became accustomed to the darkness, he realized he was in the theme park's playground area, smack in the middle of the sandbox.

Checkout sighed deeply and began wriggling his shoulders back and forth, back and forth, half an inch at a time. He knew that although it would be a slow, tedious process, he could eventually dig his way out. He'd done it often enough before.

Midnight marked the end of Admiral Less' normal workday at Starfreak Headquarters. She reached for her lengthy "things to do" list and saw that only one item remained for today: "Reclaim Fountain of Youth for Starfreak."

There had been no further word from Capt. Ricardo, and Less figured this meant he still hadn't made any headway. She decided it was time to send in someone competent to do the job.

She punched a button on her desktop Viewscreen and ordered, "Get me Commander Bungeeman Crisco."

About that same time, on the orbiting *Endocrine*, Capt. Ricardo strolled into Sick Bay. He saw that Dr. Flusher was performing brain surgery on Dacron, who lay on an examination table with his head in a vise. Ricardo turned to leave so he would avoid disturbing Flusher, but she called him back.

"Come in, Captain," she invited. "I can talk to you while I do this. I don't need to concentrate."

Ricardo stepped to the head of the table and observed that Flusher had pried open the top of Dacron's skull. Inside were lots of little blinking lights, whirring gears, and assorted ratchets, rubber-band pulleys, and round Tinker-Toy pieces. "One wonders how it all works," Ricardo marveled.

"Oh, it's pretty straightforward, actually," Flusher told him. With a shiny metal probe, she touched a spot on Dacron's brain; his left leg twitched. She touched another spot, and his right hand jerked; still another, and his Adam's apple bobbed up and down.

"They're all direct connections," Flusher remarked. "In fact, I've dissected frogs with more complex systems than this." She laid the instrument back on the tray, picked up a can of compressed air, and began blowing the dust off Dacron's circuits. "So what brings you here, Captain?"

"I wanted to see whether Dacron would be able to join our Away Team again tomorrow morning," Ricardo said. "And you, too, of course. I'm taking more officers this time. We'll stay in a group, for greater strength."

Flusher nodded, setting aside the can of air spray. She gathered up the used surgical tools from the tray and carried them over to the sink with Ricardo following her. "Dacron should be able to come along," she affirmed. "He may not be up to full speed, but he'll be ambulatory." Turning on the hot-water tap, she squirted some Lemon Fresh Joy over the instruments and began stirring up a froth of bubbles.

"Will Commander Piker and Counselor Troit have come to their senses by then?" Ricardo asked. "I don't want a couple of young whippersnappers on my Away Team," he added with a little grimace of distaste.

"I think so," Flusher said, rinsing the instruments under the faucet and setting them in a plastic utensil holder to dry. "The effects of the fountain's water seem to wear off within twenty-four hours, as long as the person is not re-exposed."

"They won't be," Ricardo told her. "They're under strict orders to stay with the team, and we're not going anywhere near the fountain."

"Then the normal aging process that they'll go through overnight tonight won't be reversed," Flusher affirmed.

The two of them returned to the operating table. Flusher closed the cap on Dacron's skull, released his head from the vise, and reached for the "on" switch on his back. "Okay, Dacron, let's see how you're doing now," she said, flicking the switch.

Nothing happened.

"Hmmmm," said Flusher with the puzzled yet self-assured frown she'd been taught in medical school. She flicked the switch on and off a few times, but Dacron showed no signs of life.

Flusher's expression grew increasingly concerned as she studied the screen of the Scramscope Android Patient Monitor at Dacron's bedside. Apparently she'd somehow failed to notice that sometime within the last few minutes, all of the vital-signs readouts on the screen had gone flat. This meant that either Dacron was dead or someone had tripped over the Scramscope cord again and unplugged it from the wall outlet.

"Nurse Chapstick," Flusher called, "will you get me the Scramscope instruction manual, please?"

"What is it, Doctor?" Ricardo asked, sensing her concern. "You'll be able to revive him, won't you?"

"Of course," Flusher answered, flashing an overly bright smile. "It's just a routine procedure. Meanwhile," she said, steering the captain toward the waiting area of Sick Bay, "why don't you take a seat here and read a few back issues of our in-house publication, *Sick Bay Sentinel?*"

Nervously Ricardo watched from the waiting area as Nurse Chapstick brought Flusher the instruction manual for the monitor. Flusher carefully tested the monitor, double-checked that it was plugged in, and finally, in desperation, gave it a good swift kick. But Dacron's vital signs remained null.

"Code Purple!" Flusher called out. From somewhere in the back of Sick Bay, a team of computer technicians swarmed into the operating area. They re-opened the panel to Dacron's brain and peered inside, using a flashlight to illuminate his mechanism.

After poking around in Dacron's skull for a minute, the chief technician shook his head, and the others solemnly closed the panel. The chief technician said something to Flusher and laid a comforting hand on her shoulder for a moment; then they all filed out the back way again.

Ricardo could no longer stand the suspense. He rejoined Flusher at Dacron's side and asked, "What is it, Doctor?"

Tears welled in her eyes. Unable to speak, she handed Ricardo the invoice that the technicians had left. It read, "Hard drive crashed. Irreparable damage. Consultation fee: $4233.50, payable 30 days net."

" 'Irreparable'?" Ricardo asked, not wanting to believe it. "Were they sure?"

Flusher nodded, blinking; tears spilled down her cheeks. She pulled out her handkerchief, blew her nose with it, then discarded it into a jar labeled STERILE GAUZE.

"But he's come back from the dead so many times," Ricardo persisted. Right off the top of his head Ricardo could recall several of them: the mission when Dacron went "down" and then revived once his program had cleared itself; the day Westerly saved Dacron by installing a new battery in his chest; and the many times Dacron's head had been blown off, misplaced, or removed as a practical joke, and eventually reattached. Ricardo added, "Surely someone who's been through all the things that Dacron has experienced should be able to come back from this."

Flusher shook her head. "Nobody survives a hard-drive crash." She began disconnecting the monitor electrodes from Dacron's chest. "If he'd been more careful about backing up his files on floppy disks every day, maybe we could reconstruct his programs," Flusher continued in a tone tempered with regret, "but that was the one area in which he always slacked off."

Tenderly she touched Dacron's shoulder. "He was so good about everything else..." she murmured, "eating a low-cholesterol diet...flossing...oil changes every three months..." Her voice drifted off.

Gazing at Dacron's lifeless form, Ricardo felt a stab of pain at the loss. *This means I'll have the tedious chore of interviewing people to take his place at the Oops station,* Ricardo thought. *What a bloody nuisance.*

Dacron had died while Ricardo and Flusher casually chatted at the sink in Sick Bay. His soul drifted out of his body and hovered in the operating area for a moment. Seeing that the Scramscope was about to set off an alarm that would have interrupted the conversation between Ricardo and Flusher, Dacron's soul thoughtfully disconnected the alarm mechanism.

Dacron realized that he was dead, and from his familiarity with the literature on near-death experience, he thought he knew exactly what to expect next. First, his soul would drift around the ship for a while. Then he would pass through a dark tunnel. Next he would see others who had died before him. Finally, he would confront a Being of Light, who would show him highlights of his lifetime and ask if he was ready to cross over into the afterlife.

However, Dacron soon discovered that near-death was a little different for an android. For one thing, his soul didn't hover near the ceiling the way most souls did. Instead, it scuttled along a few feet above the floor like a helium balloon that was past its prime. Every time somebody moved nearby, a draft of air sent Dacron's soul bobbing willy-nilly in another direction.

With his perspective limited to floor level, this phase of Dacron's experience was restricted to spotting dustballs and forgotten medical instruments dropped behind cabinets, although he did get one enlightening glimpse up Dr. Flusher's skirt. He was glad when the dark tunnel appeared, signaling the end of the tedious floating segment.

Dacron felt himself being sucked down the dark tunnel. It appeared much like a car tunnel on the freeway, and Dacron felt an overwhelming urge to honk his horn, then realized he didn't have one. Eventually he emerged on the other side of the tunnel.

Just as Dacron expected, there in the Great Beyond were others who had died before him, including Lull, the android daughter he'd constructed in his basement workshop, and Wart's old girlfriend K-Mart. Dacron tried to speak to them, but apparently they couldn't see or hear him. Something stood between him and the others, and Dacron surmised that he hadn't yet fully passed over into the afterlife.

Dacron looked around expectantly for the Being of Light,

that all-knowing, all-accepting power who would decide his final fate. But since Dacron was on the android track, he was met instead by the Being of Fluorescence.

Confronting the Being of Fluorescence wasn't exactly awe-inspiring. It was more like standing in the presence of a George Webb's all-night diner.

"Excuse me," Dacron said to the Being. "I am Dacron. I believe you are to show me the highlights of my life to help decide if my mission among the living has been accomplished."

The Being yawned, nodded, and flicked a hidden switch. Directly in front of them, clouds gathered to serve as a sort of motion picture screen, and Dacron's life was projected onto the clouds in a flickering 16mm film image. There were many boring scenes that consisted mainly of talking heads, with Dacron's head doing most of the talking, and the Being of Fluorescence fell asleep halfway through the story.

When it ended, the Being awoke with a start. Dacron, anticipating the Being's next action, said, "I believe you will now ask me whether I am prepared for the afterlife. Is that correct?"

"No," said the Being, getting up stiffly and turning off the lamp of the film projector. "I'm trying to decide whether or not to let you in. There's a quota on androids, so we decide on a case-by-case basis. Meanwhile, I'm going to have to put you on hold."

Before Dacron could protest, the Being flicked his hand, and instantly Dacron found himself in a doorless, windowless room. Another person sat on a bench in the corner, and Dacron recognized her at once: it was his deceased former crewmate Yasha Tar.

"Dacron! Fancy meeting you here," Yasha said. She was dressed in the Romanumen uniform in which she had appeared during her previous incarnation among the living.

"Yasha." Dacron studied their surroundings. "Where are we?"

She grinned, swept her arms wide, and said sarcastically,

"Welcome to Limbo. You sit here until it gets so dull back in the real world that they need you to juice things up. So you go back for a while, do a little song and dance, and when it's all over, you're yanked over here again."

Dacron seemed less than thrilled by the prospect. "This is not the career direction I envisioned for myself," he said.

Yasha wrinkled her mouth. "Me neither," she said. "But let's face it, Dacron. After six years of sitting at the Oops station, what else are you qualified to do?"

Dacron brightened. "I can sing," he replied. "My singing voice recently rose into the lyric soprano range. Would you like to hear a number?"

"Maybe later," Yasha told him. She patted the seat next to her. "C'mon and sit down. I want to hear all the news about what's happening on the other side."

That very night, Capt. Ricardo ordered that a funeral service for Dacron be held in an appropriate HolidayDeck setting. Ricardo believed that the others should face the reality of Dacron's death straight on, without delay. Besides, he didn't want the whole affair to drag out any longer, since it might mess up their Away Team mission the next morning.

Chief Engineer Georgie LaForgery painstakingly programmed the HolidayDeck to re-create a funeral-home parlor. Dacron's body was laid out in state at the front, and it was a sobering sight. His pale face matched the snowy white pillow on which his head rested. His hands, folded across his chest, clutched a sprig of air fern.

Bouquets of flowers surrounded the coffin, with banners bearing tribute to the many roles Dacron had filled: "Friend," "Crewmate" and "Major Shipboard Appliance." Even his estranged brother Lycra had sent a bouquet—apparently filched from a gravesite, judging from its faded plastic flowers and the legend VETERAN OF THE BORED WAR.

One by one, Dacron's crewmates stepped up to the coffin to pay their last respects.

Capt. Ricardo went first. Gazing at Dacron, he shook his

head with regret. "Dacron, Dacron," he murmured. "You're still so young. Why did you have to go so soon? Couldn't you have waited until the end of this mission?" Still shaking his head, Ricardo left the coffin and sat in one of the folding chairs to await the beginning of the memorial service.

Cmdr. Piker was next. He was beginning to show his age again as the fountain water wore off, and his somber expression made him look even more mature. "So long, old pal," Piker said softly to Dacron. "I'm going to miss staring at the back of your head on the Bridge all day."

Wart followed. He rested his hands on the edge of the coffin, gazed respectfully at Dacron for a long moment, then lifted his head straight up at the ceiling and let out a blood-curdling howl, scaring the wits out of the other mourners.

With a final respectful glance at Dacron, Wart stepped to the side. Piker said to him, "I thought that howling was a Kringle ritual to tell the dead that a Kringle warrior was about to join them. Why do it for Dacron?"

Wart grunted. "I wanted to warn those in the hereafter that a compulsive talker was coming into their midst," he replied. Then Wart turned to the Chief Mortician standing nearby and told him, "The body is now nothing but an empty shell. You may dispose of it as you wish."

"Er, thank you, sir," said the Chief Mortician. "I believe we'll stick with our original plan."

"Hmmmm. What plan is that?" Piker asked in idle curiosity. "Cremation? Or embalming, and then torpedoing him out into space?"

"No, sir," the mortician replied. He leaned closer to Piker and explained in a low tone, "With androids like Mr. Dacron, for whom the usual alternatives are inappropriate, we use ... how can I put this delicately? ... a TrashMasher."

Counselor Troit was next to step up to the coffin. Like Piker, she had begun aging again. Gone was the exhilaration of her brief respite from adulthood. Now her eyes brimmed with tears as she regarded the lifeless form of the android who had once captured her heart with his love letters and poetry, including some of the bawdiest limericks she'd ever read.

Troit leaned over to press a final kiss against Dacron's cheek. Unfortunately, she was unaware that his skin had cooled considerably; instantly her moist lips stuck to the superchilled hardness of his face.

The others stood at a distance awaiting their turn. Their indulgence toward Troit's sentimental gesture withered into distaste as the kiss seemed to go on and on. Guano muttered to Dr. Flusher, "Doesn't Emily Post say that it's improper to kiss the dead for longer than five seconds?" Flusher shrugged.

Troit waved her hands, trying to signal her predicament, but the others interpreted her fluttering fingers as an indication that the kiss was getting her all hot and bothered.

"Oh, gross!" Guano exclaimed. "Somebody ought to put a stop to this." The others, aghast, continued to do nothing but stare, so Guano took it on herself to end the spectacle. She marched toward the coffin and reached for Troit's arm. But before she could touch Troit, a splinter of light flashed next to her, and Q-Tip appeared.

"Well, well," Q-Tip said, taking in the entire funeral scene with a glance. "What have we here? A dead second officer. This looks like a job for the Quke continuum."

"Q-Tip," growled Capt. Ricardo, "this is no time for your foolishness. We are trying to have a solemn funeral here."

"Solemn, eh?" Q-Tip arched an eyebrow at Troit, whose lips were still plastered against Dacron's cheek. "Really, my dear, you should try to restrain yourself," Q-Tip chided her. "Where I come from, such practices are frowned upon." Troit tried to respond, but her biting retort came out as "Mmmm mmmm mmmmmm!"

Q-Tip turned back to Ricardo and continued, "Come, come, *mon Capuchin*. Perhaps now you'll strike a deal with me. You know I can bring your android back to life with a wave of my omnipotent hand. All I ask is that you grant the simple request I laid at your feet not long ago."

"I'm not going to bargain with you, Q-Tip," Ricardo retorted. "If I give in to you this once, there'll be no end to your demands."

"What was it that he asked, Captain?" Piker wanted to know. Ricardo glared at Q-Tip, refusing to answer.

"Captain, I know you like to stick to your principles and all that," Georgie broke in, "but Dacron's my best friend. Couldn't you bend the rules a little and give in to Q-Tip so we can have Dacron back?"

"What did he ask you to do?" Piker persisted. "Was it really something so terrible? Are we supposed to go annihilate an alien race or something? Bomb a space colony of orphans? What?"

"Captain," said Dr. Flusher, joining the fray, "if Dacron comes back to life, that's one less death on my medical record this year, and maybe my malpractice insurance won't go up after all."

Guano added, "Can't you please give in to him so we can have Dacron back?"

Troit, her lips still stuck on Dacron, moved her eyes meaningfully at Ricardo and urged, "Mmmmm mmmmm mmmmmm!"

"Captain, tell us," Piker insisted, "what does Q-Tip want you to do?"

Ricardo folded his arms across his chest and told them, "He wants me to give him a driving lesson on the *Endocrine*."

Immediately the air filled with their cries. "That's it?!" "Well, do it, then!" "I can't believe you'd let that stand in your way." "Just a driving lesson?"

"All right. All right," Ricardo said, holding up his hands for silence. "All right, Q-Tip," he conceded, "I'll give you your driving lesson if you'll bring Dacron back to life."

"Splendid!" Q-Tip exclaimed. He snapped his fingers, and immediately the two of them were transported to the Bridge— Q-Tip sitting at the Conn with Ricardo standing next to him.

"What about Dacron?" Ricardo asked.

"All in good time, *mon capon*," Q-Tip said. "I'll take care of him once the lesson is over. I want to make sure you follow through on this bargain. Now!" he went on, running his hands eagerly over the control console. "What comes first?"

"First you have to turn on the engine," said Ricardo, pointing to a button with a picture of a key on it. The engine turned over as soon as Q-Tip pressed the button.

"Now," Ricardo continued, "give it a little gas, keep your foot on the clutch, and move it out of 'park' into first gear—"

"Wait. Wait. You're telling me too much at once," Q-Tip complained. The ship lurched forward and died.

"You weren't giving it enough gas," Ricardo corrected him.

"But you said to give it just a little gas," Q-Tip protested. He restarted the engine and tried again.

Five false starts later, Q-Tip managed to get the ship moving forward.

"Steer a straight course," Ricardo told him. "Look in the mirror so you know what's around you. Glance over your shoulder at your blind spot, too."

"You're talking too fast again," Q-Tip whined, clutching the console nervously. He glanced back over his shoulder as instructed. "What blind spot?" he asked.

"Look out for that meteor!" Ricardo shouted. He shoved Q-Tip's arm aside and pressed the steering buttons; the ship swerved, missing the meteor by mere feet.

"Hey," Q-Tip protested, trying to pry Ricardo's hands off the console, "this is my turn to drive, not yours."

Reluctantly Ricardo let go of the controls. A few seconds later, the ship began to bounce violently.

"What's that?" Q-Tip demanded, his face turning white with fear.

"Turbulence," Ricardo said, grabbing the back of Q-Tip's chair to keep his balance. "Try to steer around it—whoa!"

The ship hit an air pocket and plunged several thousand feet. It finally bottomed out in a landing that felt like hitting solid rock. The turbulence resumed, bouncing them repeatedly.

"Wh-uh-uh-what duh-uh-uh-uh-do I-I-I du-uh-uh-do?" Q-Tip asked as his chin struck his chest again and again.

Back in the HolidayDeck funeral parlor, the others rode out the swaying and bouncing of the ship during Q-Tip's driving lesson. Wart, Piker and Georgie braced themselves against Dacron's casket so it wouldn't tip over. Guano managed to free Troit's lips from Dacron's cheek by heating the contact point with the blow-dryer she always carried around in her hat.

Finally the wild ride smoothed out. A few minutes later, Q-Tip and Ricardo re-entered the funeral parlor, caught up in a bitter argument.

"You call that driving instruction?" Q-Tip sputtered. "I'm not even ready to get my learner's permit after that travesty."

"You asked for a first lesson, and that's exactly what I gave you," Ricardo replied.

"I didn't ask for a first lesson," Q-Tip hissed. "I asked you to teach me to drive. I wanted to learn freeway merging, parallel parking, the whole enchilada."

"You got what we agreed on," Ricardo insisted. "Now hold up your side of the bargain. Bring Dacron back to life."

"What you gave me wasn't what we agreed on," Q-Tip retorted. "It was just your interpretation of what we agreed on—a flagrant piece of creative finagling. Well, two can play that game. You want Dacron brought back to life? Fine! But I'm going to do it *my* way!"

Still glaring at Ricardo, Q-Tip snapped his fingers at Dacron. Dacron blinked a couple of times and started to stir. The others, filled with joy and relief, gathered around his coffin.

"Dacron, can you hear me?" Dr. Flusher asked.

Slowly, a sultry smile spread across Dacron's face. "Hullo, darlin'," he drawled.

Hands reached out to help Dacron sit up. "You were pretty far gone there for a while," Flusher continued. "You went down when I tried to re-orient your circuits. Everything seems to be in order now."

The others rode out the swaying and bouncing of the ship.

Dacron blinked lazily. "Thangyouvurymuch," he responded.

Capt. Ricardo gave Dacron a dubious look, then turned and demanded, "All right, Q-Tip, what's the catch?" Q-Tip returned Ricardo's stare with a taunting smile.

"Doctor," Ricardo continued, "are you sure Dacron is back to normal?"

"No," said Flusher, who was starting to look worried. It was clear that something was different about Dacron. "Dacron," Flusher prompted, "how do you feel?"

"I feel wunnerful," Dacron answered, his lip curling upward into a strangely sexy twitch. "I feel . . . I feel like . . . "

Abruptly he jumped out of the coffin, landed squarely on the floor, and shook his hips. He grabbed Flusher's medical tricorder from her jacket pocket and held it to his mouth as if it were a cordless microphone. Dacron announced, "I feel like singin' a song for y'all." He launched into a raucous version of "Blue Suede Shoes" in a husky tenor that befitted the classic.

Flusher's jaw dropped open in astonishment. After watching Dacron continue for several bars, she reached into her breast pocket for a hippospray, grabbed Dacron's upper arm, and thrust the instrument firmly against him. Dacron stopped his frantic performance and slumped back against the coffin.

Ricardo, helping to steady him, asked, "Dacron, what is the matter?"

Dacron looked up and, seeing Q-Tip standing there, inquired, "Is that you, Colonel Parker?"

"Indeed," Q-Tip said, coming to Dacron's side and laying a proprietary arm across his shoulders. "You see, *mon cap pistol*," Q-Tip said to Ricardo, "I too can be creative in fulfilling my half of the bargain. I have given you back your android, with a personality enhancement thrown in at no extra charge."

Dr. Flusher retrieved her tricorder from Dacron's hand and passed it over his head and chest to check his vital signs.

"Dacron," she said, "I'm so sorry to have put you through all this. I sincerely hope you won't sue me for malpractice."

"Ah forgive yuh, baby," Dacron said with a smile, cocking a languorous eyebrow at Flusher. "But puh-*lease* stop callin' me 'Dacron.' Muh name's Elvis, honey."

6

The Wrong Arm of the Law

THE NEXT MORNING, before heading over to help open the park, Capt. Smirk visited Mr. Smock, who was monitoring the sensors on the Bridge of the *Endocrine*.

"What d'ya think, Smock? Is it catchy enough?" Smirk asked, holding up a t-shirt for Smock's inspection. Imprinted on the front of the shirt was the legend JUVEN ISLE: THE HAPPIEST PLACE IN THE GALAXY.

Smirk continued eagerly, "This shirt is just a prototype, but we can have fifteen thousand of 'em sewn up in about a week. The sales rep said that anything made out of this fabric sells like crazy. It turns different colors when you're horny. Look!" Smirk held the t-shirt against his chest, and the tie-dyed pattern began flashing in neon hues.

Smock gave it his impassive once-over. "Very eye-catching," he judged.

"I gotta go," Smirk said, turning on his heel and heading for the door. "There's a big group comin' in this morning, and I hafta make sure the ticket takers are ready." Smirk had already marketed a group rate for park admissions, and the Born to Be Wild Intergalactic Reform School for Girls was the first to take advantage of it.

"Captain," Smock called after him, "before you go, I believe you should be aware of a message the sensors picked up last night. We have a recording of it."

Smirk stepped back to Smock's station, and Smock told him, "This was an audio transmission from Admiral Less at

543

Starfreak Headquarters to a field commander named Bungeeman Crisco." Smock pressed the "replay" button on his
console.

The recording began with Crisco's groggy voice. "Huh...
hullo?" he said.

"Crisco? This is Admiral Less at Starfreak Headquarters."
Even in a recording, her voice was as piercing as a dentist's
drill. "You sound funny, Crisco. Do you have a cold or something?"

"Unhh...no..." Bedsprings creaked in the background.
"It's just that I was asleep when you called, Admiral."

"Asleep? Hmmm. Well, it's time you got up anyway. I want
you to start on a new mission immediately." Briefly, Admiral
Less filled him in on Starfreak's intention to oust Smirk,
claim the Fountain of Youth, and transport Smirk's crew to
the nursing home.

"We'd sent somebody else on this mission, but he blew it,"
she concluded crisply. "I don't want to waste any more time
on this. Get in there and get the job done."

"Yes, Admiral," Crisco responded.

Mr. Smock broke in. "The remainder of their conversation
is merely routine," he said, turning off the recording. He
went on, "I calculated the probable coordinates of Commander Crisco's ship when he received this message. Allowing
for travel at the average cruising speed of Warped 8.23, he
should arrive here today at approximately 0900 hours. Do
you wish to take any countermeasures against him, Captain?"

"No, Smock," Smirk replied. "His crew will probably come
looking for us in the park. Don't try to keep them from Faxing
down here. We'll just let them, like, roam around. Once they
hit the water of Juven Isle, they'll lighten up—big time."

Aboard Capt. Ricardo's orbiting ship that morning, Counselor
Troit was having a difficult time getting out of bed. And no
wonder: the previous day at suppertime, she'd been a sprightly
15-year-old, and now she was attempting to arise and shine

after gaining 20 years overnight. The Fountain of Youth water had definitely worn off.

This was not just a normal case of the early-morning blahs. This mother of all rude awakenings was like a humongous boulder of Elmer's Glue-All that pressed her against the mattress and oozed around her ears.

With enormous effort, Troit opened her eyes. Dimly she wondered how in the world that 15-year-old body had managed to cram so much living into the past few days. Now she was paying for it; every single muscle either ached or had gone on strike.

She forced herself out of bed to get ready for an early-morning counseling session; Capt. Ricardo had asked her to debrief Dacron regarding his near-death experience.

Meanwhile, in his own quarters, Cmdr. Piker was suffering a similar case of the Monday-morning syndrome. His beard had yet to grow back, but everything else about him had deteriorated from factory-fresh condition to somewhat-worse-for-the-wear during the night.

Capt. Ricardo, on the other hand, had sprung out of bed extra early to allow time for a project he'd been putting off: investigating what Wart was up to. In fact, all the mental notes Ricardo had been making about this project were accumulating into a full-length symphony. And another incident had arisen to suggest that Ricardo should check out the situation soon.

When the Away Team had returned to the ship the previous night, there'd been a memo on Ricardo's desk from the principal of the *Endocrine*'s day school. She'd complained that Wart's private school had beaten the day-school team in a game of tackle football, even though Wart's school had only one pupil in it. Apparently Smartalecsander had shown no mercy on the other kids.

As he approached Wart's quarters, Ricardo noticed that the handmade sign at the door had been replaced by a permanent plaque that read KRINGLE MILITARY ACADEMY / ABANDON ALL HOPE, YE WHO ENTER HERE.

Smartalecsander had shown no mercy on the other kids.

Ricardo rang the door chime. "Come in," he heard Wart say.

Wart and Smartalecsander were seated at the dining table. "Captain," said Wart, standing to greet him and indicating a vacant chair. "Please, sit down."

"Mr. Wart," Ricardo began as he took the seat, "shouldn't Smartalecsander be attending classes with the rest of the children?"

Wart stiffened. "I am teaching my son myself, Captain," he replied. "In fact, we are having a lesson right now." Ricardo glanced at Smartalecsander, who was simply eating from a dinner plate.

Noticing Ricardo's skepticism, Wart explained, "It is a lesson in discipline. Smartalecsander is to finish that serving of brussels sprouts without whining or gagging."

"I see," said Ricardo. "Wart, I understand your desire to raise Smartalecsander in the Kringle tradition. But the Starfreak Board of Education has certain standards. Home-schooled children aren't considered properly educated. For that reason, when they get older, they are seldom admitted to Starfreak Academy."

Wart looked perturbed; the wrinkles on his forehead knotted into a tangle. "I was not aware of that," he admitted.

"I'm sure you want that option to remain open for your son," Ricardo added. "Admission to Starfreak Academy is the highest goal a student can aspire to."

Smartalecsander, sensing that the balance of power was shifting, stopped eating his brussels sprouts. Immediately Wart prompted him, "Eat your vegetables, young man." Craftily, Smartalecsander continued forking the green globules into his mouth, ever so slowly, but he stopped chewing them.

Capt. Ricardo said, "I'll never forget my own days at the Academy. I gained a lifetime's worth of knowledge there. In fact, some of the best lessons came outside of the classroom."

Wart shifted impatiently in his chair. Like all the senior officers, he'd heard the story of Ricardo's school days a million times. Sitting beside Wart, Smartalecsander slowed his fork motion even further while squirreling away another brussels sprout in his cheek.

"One mentor in particular stands out," Ricardo went on. "He was an old gardener named Toothby."

Wart barely suppressed a groan. Smartalecsander shoved another brussels sprout into his mouth and faked a chewing motion.

"Toothby was a retired Martian who'd taken the gardening job to supplement his Social Security income. Though he wasn't a scholar, he possessed an abundance of another kind of knowledge," Ricardo said, leaning back in his chair and warming to the story. "I used to follow him as he worked, and occasionally, if I were lucky, he would let me scatter manure around the flower beds. By the time I was a sopho- more, he even let me borrow his shovel for the job. In the spring of my senior year, I helped him spread Milorganite over the lawn. Ah, those were glorious days."

A low rumble of impatience emerged from Wart's chest; he couldn't help himself. Smartalecsander, studying his fa- ther's face, realized that Wart was near the breaking point. The boy stopped all pretense of chewing.

Ricardo recalled, "Toothby used to say to me, 'Jean-Lucy, gardening is like life. If things aren't going your way, just dump another load of manure over everything around you.' It's a lesson I use in my command every day. In fact—"

"AAARRRGGGGHHHH!" Wart erupted. He jumped up as if to engage in battle, then caught himself and stood there panting heavily. "All right, you win!" he shouted. "Just stop talking about Toothby!"

Ricardo, taken aback for a moment, quickly recovered and asked Wart, "You mean you're willing to send Smartalecsan- der back to day school?"

"Yes," Wart conceded.

Smartalecsander, realizing that this last lesson in discipline at the Kringle Military Academy could go unfinished, promptly opened his jaw to its widest and disgorged a pile of brussels sprouts onto his plate.

"If I were lucky, he would let me scatter manure around the flower beds."

* * *

"Aww, honey," Dacron drawled, "ah'm tahr'd of lookin' at these ink blots. If yuh really wanna know about muh personality, why not let me sing yuh a song?" He leaned forward eagerly on the edge of the sofa in Deanna Troit's counseling office.

Troit pursed her lips. "Dacron, you know that the Rorschach is a standard test for personality evaluation," she replied, trying to keep the impatience out of her voice. "It's well accepted within the psychological community, and the findings will substantiate my writeup of your case for the *Journal of Serendipitous Headshrinkery*."

"Baby, you're makin' this way too complicated," Dacron said, his lip curling into a half-smile that somehow managed to look both sensuous and sweet. "Ah'm just a good ol' boy who loves rock-'n'-roll and appreciates pretty women like yourself. Who cares how ah got this way? Ah'm not the first felluh who's changed for the bettuh after a brush with death."

Troit, glimpsing her reflection in the glass of the coffee table, noticed that a faint network of crow's feet had sprouted around her eyes within the last half hour. She wondered whether she was suffering a rebound as the fountain water wore off; maybe she'd end up older than she'd been to start with. The thought left her too dispirited to continue this formal inquiry into Dacron's personality quirks.

"All right, then, never mind," Troit allowed. "We'll skip the tests, and I'll construct my report from field observations of your behavior. You seem to have recovered from this near-death experience remarkably well, without any of the usual complications like post-fatal depression."

"That's swell," Dacron responded. "Ah'm glad we settled that. Sounds to me like a good time for a song." He reached behind the couch for the guitar he'd constructed in the ship's replicator.

"Not now, Dacron," Troit told him. "Dr. Flusher asked me to send you to Sick Bay after we'd finished our session. She wants you to undergo a medical evaluation before our away mission."

Dacron nodded and prepared to leave. "She's gonna love the new me," he predicted. "Ah've noticed that muh entire body is so much more flexible. Especially muh hips."

Capt. Ricardo and Wart dropped off Smartalecsander at the *Endocrine*'s schoolroom and headed for Shipping and Receiving, where the Away Team would meet to Fax down to the amusement park once again. Halfway down the hall, they were joined by Guano the bartender.

She'd dressed casually for a day of fun and games. Instead of her usual voluminous robe, she wore a baseball jersey over bike shorts.

As the three of them stepped into the Crewmover, Ricardo gave her the once-over and remarked, "Guano, this is an official mission. We're not visiting the park to enjoy ourselves. There are no side trips allowed."

"You mean I won't even be able to buy souvenirs?" Guano whined. Capt. Ricardo shook his head. "Then I guess I won't be needing this extra money," Guano concluded, tipping her head toward the floor. Out of the top of her enormous hat, a sheaf of currency floated to the floor, and coins clanked and rattled and bounced out. Guano held out her jersey like an apron and scooped up all the money into it.

The Crewmover doors opened, and Guano walked out first, heading for the public lockers at the side of the Shipping bay. She put a quarter into one of them, pulled out the key, dumped her money inside, and shut it for safekeeping.

Troit and Piker were already in Shipping, standing near the UltraFax platform. Piker, holding out his arms pleadingly, was asking Troit, "Look, all I want to know is, are we still going steady?" Troit shrugged.

Ricardo walked over to Dr. Flusher, who was waiting next to the UltraFax control panel with Chief Engineer Georgie LaForgery. "Is Q-Tip still around?" Ricardo asked Flusher.

"The last time I saw him, he was looking through the window of Sick Bay, watching you examine Dacron."

Flusher shook her head and said, "Q-Tip is gone. He spent some time revamping Dacron's wardrobe, and then he left the ship."

"Where is Dacron?" Ricardo continued. "Have you and Counselor Troit decided whether he's well enough to come with us on this mission?"

Flusher nodded. "Yes, he is. He's waiting just around the corner in the hall," she told the captain. "He said he wanted to make a big entrance once the whole Away Team gets here."

"Well, the rest of us are ready to go," said Ricardo, glancing around impatiently.

As if on cue, the door from the hallway swooshed open, and Dacron jumped into the room. He was a different Dacron than they were used to. Among androids, now he was clearly The King.

Gone was his minimalist swept-back hairdo; in its place was a dramatic mane that cascaded over his forehead. Thick wooly sideburns accented his cheeks. His yellow eyes were camouflaged by sunglasses that gave him an air of utter cool.

A cluster of gold chains glittered at his neck. The top three buttons of his shirt collar were unbuttoned, revealing a shock of chest hair that hadn't been there yesterday, and the back of his collar was turned up rakishly.

Dacron spread his arms wide in a gesture of showmanship. The rhinestones on his hiphuggers caught the light.

The crew stared at him. Finally Georgie recovered a little from the initial shock and politely applauded Dacron's entrance.

Rings glistened on every finger as Dacron held a Mr. Microphone to his lips. "Thangyouvurymuch," he said, acknowledging Georgie's applause. "Ah wanna do a little number for yuh now that ah think you're gonna like."

Dacron pressed a button on the microphone. It must have been a remote control, for out of nowhere, background music immediately began blaring a rowdy but somehow familiar tune. Dacron sang:

> You ain't nothin' but a Pakled
> Droolin' all the time.
> You ain't nothin' but a Pakled
> Droolin' all the time.
> You may own a lotta hardware
> But your brain ain't worth a dime.

Then the music changed; the first few bars of "I Can't Help Falling in Love with You" wafted forth. "Ah'm gonna slow it down a little now," Dacron told his audience.

But before Dacron could shift into the ballad, Ricardo stopped him. "That's enough, Dacron," Ricardo ordered, grabbing the microphone and turning off the background music.

Ricardo led them onto the UltraFax platform. Dacron, somewhat subdued, followed in his usual obedient manner, though he did swivel his hips while waiting on the pad.

Not far from Ricardo's *Endocrine*, another craft approached the planet and prepared to assume orbiting altitude. At its helm was Cmdr. Bungeeman Crisco.

Crisco's physical appearance revealed that he was well on the way to following the trend set by Capt. Ricardo—prepared to *baldly* go where nobody wanted to go before.

This mission to transport Smirk & Co. to the Vacant Attic struck Crisco as so laughably easy that he hadn't even bothered to bring along any of his Starfreak subordinates. He'd simply borrowed a paddywagon craft and carried a phaser set on "gentle stun." From what Admiral Less had told him, Crisco didn't expect Smirk and his officers to put up much resistance.

"You'll know them when you see them," Admiral Less had assured Crisco after giving him his orders. "Relics. Ready for the fox farm."

Although Crisco hadn't been too keen on being awakened in the middle of the night by Admiral Less' call, once he got going on the mission, he felt a stirring of hope. Maybe this was the fresh start he needed, for he'd been having a run of bad luck lately.

First his wife Hennypenny was killed aboard the *Sara Lee* when the evil machine-like Bored started recycling all the metal in the starship without bothering to remove the crew and passengers first. Crisco's last-minute escape from the imploding ship with his son Joke still gave him nightmares, especially when he thought about the autographed Babe Ruth jockstrap he'd been forced to leave behind.

Starfreak's life insurance carrier refused to honor Crisco's claim on Hennypenny's policy; they maintained that a death ray emanating from a giant metal cube was considered an act of God. Then came the most crushing blow: Crisco's hairline began receding about a half-inch per day for no apparent reason. "Stress," the doctors diagnosed, telling him to take two hipposprays and call them at the turn of the century.

The ironic twist was that part of the blame for his wife's death could be traced to a fellow Starfreak officer—a traitor who had aided and abetted the Bored in their attempt to take over the universe. Crisco, like everyone else in the federation, knew that some captain named Jean-Lucy Ricardo had been captured and was temporarily turned into a half-machine Bored.

The Bored, master recyclers that they were, had picked Ricardo's brain for every useful bit of Starfreak military strategy they could find amidst the reams of Shakespearean dialogue, archeological writings and alien-flute solos. The Bored used this military strategy against the federation in the Bored War. With Ricardo—renamed "Lowcutie"—leading them, they'd destroyed scores of federation ships and killed thousands of people. True, they'd done it against Ricardo's will, and afterward he'd said he was really, awfully sorry, but the damage was already done.

A glance at the control screen of Crisco's shuttlecraft

brought his wandering thoughts back to his current mission. Sensors indicated that there was already a starship orbiting the planet where he was headed—undoubtedly Smirk's ship, Crisco figured. He steered clear of it, pulled into an empty orbit path, shifted his shuttle into "park," and turned off the engine. After a final check of the sensors, which clearly outlined the inhabited areas of the surface, Crisco set the shuttle's UltraFax on auto mode and Faxed himself down.

"What is it, Smock?" responded Smirk, addressing the intercom in the ceiling of his management office. Smock had just hailed him from the Bridge of their ship in the parking lot. "Make it short. I'm busy," Smirk added, with a suave smile at the young woman sitting on his lap.

"Captain, Commander Crisco just entered orbit and Faxed down to the entrance gate," came Smock's voice. "I thought you would like to be informed."

"Thank you, Smock," Smirk responded. He smoothed back a curl on his companion's forehead. "I'll track him with the surveillance camera monitors."

Smirk's eyes never quite made it to the monitors. If they had, though, he would have seen Crisco pass by Smirk's officers one by one, totally unaware that these youngsters in their jaunty park uniforms were his intended prey.

Three hours later, Cmdr. Crisco, tired and cranky from fighting the crowds of Juven Isle, decided to take a break and assess his options.

He hadn't spotted anyone who looked remotely like an aging Starfreak officer. The vast majority of those crowding the park were exuberant young patrons who charged at top speed from one ride to the next, jostling Crisco and stepping on his toes en route.

It was near noon, and Crisco realized he hadn't eaten in quite a while. He headed for the nearest fast-food restaurant, a pizza joint decorated to look like an old-fashioned firehouse. There was a long wait in the line to order food, so he had plenty of time to study the carefully arranged details of the firehouse decor, including moldy firehoses hanging on the walls, worn rubber boots standing as centerpieces on each table, and a Dalmatian that wandered around begging for table scraps.

Finally Crisco got his cola and a slice of greasy pizza. He scanned the room for a table, but every place was filled.

Wandering through the dining area with his paper plate and cup, Crisco spotted a doorway which looked like it might lead to another seating area. As he drew near, though, he realized that this was a small banquet room that seemed to be fully occupied. A few steps closer and he noticed that the diners were wearing Starfreak uniforms. Immediately he slid to one side of the doorway to avoid drawing attention to himself.

Crisco approached the entrance sidewise. A lone dining chair was placed just outside the door; he sat on it, cocking his ear toward the opening.

"Mr. Chairman," said someone inside, "I want to call the question."

"You can't call the question," said another voice. "There's already a motion on the floor to amend the previous motion."

"Well, then," said the first voice, "I move we get that motion off the floor and take a vote to call the answer."

Crisco felt a nudge at his knee. The Dalmatian was sniffing at the plate of pizza in his lap. Crisco lifted the plate and shook his foot at the dog, whispering, "Shoo! Shoo!"

The dog persisted, whining a little and scratching at Crisco's pants leg. "Quiet, boy," Crisco hissed, swinging an elbow at the dog while balancing his pizza in one hand and his cola in the other.

The discussion in the next room was getting louder. "You know," someone observed, "we started this meeting an hour ago and we still haven't gotten past the motion to accept the minutes of the last meeting."

"All in good time, Number 1," said another. "There is no substitute for proper procedure."

Crisco wondered, *Who are these guys? Could this be Smirk and his crew? They certainly sound like retirees—like they've got all the time in the world.* Crisco's heart raced as he speculated, *Maybe this detour to the pizza parlor has led me straight to my targets.*

The dog at his elbow whined louder. "Shhh!" Crisco responded. He tried holding the plate higher, but still the dog managed to lick the crust. In desperation, Crisco raised the plate and carefully placed it atop his own head. This broad, smooth platform held the pizza out of the Dalmatian's reach. With his newly freed hand, Crisco pulled out his phaser. Carefully he stood up and leaned close to the doorway.

Someone was saying, "I move we amend the motion to table the question that called the answer."

Another voice added, "And I want to attach a rider that says we'll approach the management office with phasers on 'maximum stun.' "

"You can't attach a rider unless the person who made the motion agrees," countered someone else, "and you have to call out 'Simon says' before you do it."

Warily, Crisco peered around the corner. He spotted a bald Starfreak officer at the head of the table; the insignia on his collar indicated that he was a captain. *This has to be Smirk and his crew*, Crisco decided. *No wonder Starfreak wants to put them out to pasture. What a bunch of fuddy-duddys.*

Unexpectedly, the Dalmatian, frustrated that Crisco's food remained out of reach, whined piercingly and gave a series of short yelps. The captain turned toward the door, asking, "What was that?" In the nick of time, Crisco pulled back from the doorframe.

This is it, Crisco thought. *Time to make my move.*

He thrust the phaser forward and leaped into the room. "Freeze!" he ordered. "You're all under arrest!" Eight Starfreak crewmembers stared back at him. At first their expressions showed pure surprise, but then a few smiled and even giggled; and Crisco realized he was still balancing the plate of pizza on his head and holding the cola in his other hand.

Holding the phaser at readiness, he set the cola on the table, then carefully retrieved the pizza from its platform and set it down too.

The Dalmatian seized the chance—lunged forward, snatched the slice of pizza, and darted out of the room.

The bald captain at the head of the table asked in an icy tone, "Would you mind telling us what this is all about, *Commander*?" He gave the title a slight but unmistakable twist of derision.

"I'm Commander Bungeeman Crisco," came the reply, "and by order of Admiral Less of Starfreak Command, I'm taking you under arrest and transporting you to the Vacant Attic Nursing Home." Crisco was so hyper from the thrill of making this arrest that he failed to notice that most of the crewmembers were well under retirement age.

"The Vacant Attic? Us?" The captain looked confused for a moment; then his expression cleared. "Ah," he said, "you must have mistaken us for Captain Smirk's crew."

"Don't try to pull any fast ones on me," Crisco growled. "I know that's just who you are." He cranked the phaser up from "gentle stun" to the "major owie" setting, making sure everyone saw him do it.

Even at such close proximity, Crisco still failed to recognize Ricardo as Lowcutie, the Bored who'd appeared on the Viewscreen of the *Sara Lee* ordering them to surrender. During that encounter, half of Ricardo's face had been obscured by a metal plate in the Bored's "Foundry Chic" fashion style.

"All right, hands on the table," Crisco ordered. Reluctantly, they all complied, and Crisco circled them, confiscating their phasers. Then he went around the table again and began frisking each of them for additional weapons.

"But I'm not Captain Smirk," the captain protested. "Actually, I'm here to capture him, just as you are. I'm Captain Jean-Lucy Ricardo."

"Yeah, and I'm Pope Priscilla XIII," Crisco snarled. He spent a few extra moments frisking Counselor Troit's curves. *You can't be too careful with these renegades*, he told himself.

Crisco moved on to frisk Dacron. Running his hands roughly over the android's back, he unknowingly flicked the "off" switch, and Dacron collapsed onto the table. Appalled at Dacron's sudden apparent demise, Crisco jumped back and gasped, "Ohmygosh."

Troit, rolling her eyes in exasperation, leaned over and reset the switch. Dacron re-booted, looking a little groggy, with his sideburns slightly askew. "Whoa, mama," he slurred. "Did somebody get the number of th' truck that hit me?"

"No, really," the captain persisted. "I am Captain Jean-Lucy Ricardo."

Crisco whirled around to face the captain and pointed the phaser directly at his head. "Look, cut out this baloney sausage," he warned. "I know you're James T. Smirk. Don't keep bringing up the name of this Ricardo guy, 'cause that traitor was responsible for the death of my wife during the Bored War."

The bald captain gulped, apparently alarmed at Crisco's fierceness.

"So if you *were* Ricardo," Crisco continued, "I'd pull your tonsils up from your throat and wrap them in a bow around your skull. As it is, I'm just going to take you into custody and dump you at the nursing home."

Crisco backed away a few steps and ordered, "All right, everybody up." He herded them into a group and began setting his remote Fax control. "You'll sit in a detention cell on my shuttlecraft during the trip," he told them. "I'll be pulling your ship with a tractor beam. This will be a no-frills ride, so don't expect any complimentary soft drinks or peanuts on the way there."

As they stood waiting to be Faxed up, Piker, who was just outside of Crisco's earshot, murmured, "Captain Ricardo, aren't we going to fight back?"

"What can we do?" the captain whispered in response. "Besides, I think fighting back in this instance would violate the Prime Time Directive. And stop bringing up the name

'Ricardo,' " he added, nervously fingering his throat. "From now on, call me Captain Smirk."

The clerk at the reception desk of the Vacant Attic Nursing Home looked up expectantly as Crisco escorted Ricardo's crew through the front door. "Oooh!" she squealed. "You must be Captain Smirk and his group. We've been waiting for you." She reached for her phone receiver, pressed a button on the phone's base, and spoke over the public-address system: "Escorts to the front desk, please."

Crisco stepped up to the counter. The receptionist told him, "We'll just need to fill out some papers to make everything official." With considerable effort, she hefted a two-foot-high stack of papers onto the counter. Consulting the first form, she began, "Are the residents bringing any vehicles for the storage yard?"

"Just one," Crisco replied, "a Galahad-class starship, registry number NBC 1701 D-minus." The clerk wrote the number on a plastic tag and handed it to Crisco.

"Hang this from the front mirror," she instructed, "and pull the vehicle around the back to Lot A. That's where our residents keep their cars, RVs, Harley-Davidson cycles and so on. When they're not using them, of course."

Crisco figured that most of the vehicles probably stayed in mint condition. None of the residents in this lobby, at least, were about to take them out for a spin; they sat dozing in the upholstered chairs, warmed by the midafternoon sun streaming through the windows.

The escorts who had been summoned by the p.a. appeared in the lobby. Each of them took charge of one crewmember.

"Hello," said one of them, greeting Ricardo loudly and with exaggerated enunciation. "How are we feeling today?"

" 'We' are fine, and not the least bit deaf," he replied tartly.

"Oh, my," she responded with a tolerant chuckle. "Somebody hasn't had his prunes for breakfast, has he? We'll have to get you in a jolly mood. You can sit in on my canasta club this afternoon."

Crisco stepped up to the counter.

Another escort eyed Cmdr. Piker and observed, "You look like a really well-preserved old buzzard. I know just the thing for you. One of our shuffleboard teams has lost its star player. They'd probably take you on without even a tryout."

Piker leaned over to Ricardo and muttered, "Captain, how long are we going to put up with this?"

"We'll wait until Crisco leaves," Ricardo answered in a low tone, "then tell them who we really are and get them to release us."

"Hey, baby," Dacron was saying to his escort, "could y'all use a singer for some of your residents' parties?"

"We sure could!"· she twittered. "In fact, we're having a social tonight at eight o'clock. We'd love to have you perform."

"Darlin'," Dacron promised, "we're gonna rock- 'n'-roll this place till the walls start to sweat."

Dacron was true to his word. His one-man Elvis revue had a whole lotta shakin' goin' on. The dance floor of the social room was crowded with residents rocking out with the help of their canes, walkers and wheelchairs.

About the only ones who weren't joining in were Ricardo and his other crewmembers. They sulked on the sidelines, frustrated because the staff rejected their claim of mistaken identity and refused to let them leave the building. Their phasers had been confiscated, so they were no match for the bouncer who guarded the doorway, armed with a stun gun.

At the height of the party, Q-Tip appeared in a flash of light. He quickly sized up the situation, relishing Ricardo's discomfort.

"Well, Jean-Lucy," he taunted, "it's good to see that your second officer has found an outlet for his creativity—and one that fills your golden years with music to boot. He must be such a comfort to you in your old age."

"This is not funny, Q-Tip," Ricardo retorted. "Why don't you put your powers to good use and get us out of here?"

Q-Tip didn't seem to hear him. He was studying Dacron and the wild party scene with increasing interest.

"You know, that boy really knows how to rock," he mused, almost to himself. "They're crazy about him." Onstage, Dacron removed the scarf from his neck and wiped his sweaty face with it, drawing squeals of delight from the female residents.

The number ended, and Dacron announced a short intermission. He started to stroll toward his crewmates but moved just a few feet beyond the stage before being mobbed by fans.

Q-Tip nodded and said to no one in particular, "Yes. Let's do it." He snapped his fingers, and both he and Dacron vanished in beams of dazzling light. The fans looked around in bewilderment when Dacron disappeared, but since none of them had much short-term memory to speak of, their disappointment was brief. Within moments they were stampeding toward the refreshment table, having completely forgotten about The King's *concert interruptus*.

A few minutes later there was another flash of light, and Q-Tip and Dacron reappeared at Ricardo's side. "Jean-Lucy, my protégé has something he'd like to tell you," said Q-Tip, flashing a triumphant grin.

Dacron shook back the shock of hair that had fallen across his eyes and asked his crewmates, "Have y'all met muh manager, Colonel Parker?" He indicated Q-Tip with a wave of his hand. "The colonel has some great plans for muh career. He's gonna take me out on tour, get me a recordin' contract, and even have me do some movies. So ah guess ah'll be out on the road for awhile. It's been nice workin' with y'all. Ah'll be sure to come back for a visit someday."

"Dacron, have you lost your mind?" Capt. Ricardo protested, but there was yet another flash of light, and Dacron and Q-Tip disappeared.

Hello Muddah,
Hello Faddah

Mercenary Caregivers Ltd.
"Your deterioration is our business"
Administrators of quality nursing homes:
Vacant Attic • Love 'Em & Leave 'Em
Stow 'N' Go • Forgotten but Not Gone
Nevermore • Last Gasp

MEMO

To: Vacant Attic Nursing Home Resident #5482992, Capt. James T. Smirk, a.k.a. "Capt. Jean-Lucy Ricardo"

From: Gareth Flintbottom, MD, Ph.D, Maitre D'— Administrator, Mercenary Caregivers Ltd.

RE: Your letter of Stardate 38285.2¼

Your recent letter to our administrative headquarters, regarding the so-called "confusion" of your identity, has been forwarded to my office.

If it pleases you to be called "Jean-Lucy Ricardo" rather than James T. Smirk (which was your officially registered name upon check-in), then our staff will be happy to oblige, just as they did for your second officer, "Elvis." As you know, we always try to humor any request of our residents, as long as it doesn't cost us anything.

However, I am afraid you are nowhere near ready for release from the Vacant Attic Nursing Home. You must rid yourself of this notion. I suggest you stay busy to help you keep your mind off the matter. Perhaps you could join your facility's craft guild and begin an apprenticeship in basketweaving.

Starfreak Command
Headquarters Building
Office #2292N

Dear <u>Capt. Ricardo</u>   :

Thank you for your interest in <u>getting out of Vacant Attic Nursing Home.</u> Starfreak Command is always deeply concerned with the opinions of its underlings. You can be assured that my staff and I are giving every consideration to this matter. Please accept this handy pocket calendar with my best wishes.

Sincerely,
Admiral E.J. Cahoots

Enclosure: 12-month pocket calendar

Dear Jean-Lucy,

Hey, guy, how's it going? I got your letter when my ship stopped in at Starbase 773 for an oil change. We had to pick up the letter personally 'cause there was postage due.

I'd love to help get you out of your predicament, old buddy, but politically it's a little sticky right now, especially since I'm about a year away from retirement myself and I don't want to screw that up by crossing Admiral Less' path, you know?

So I'll have to take a pass on your suggestion that I fly over to drop a futon torpedo on your nursing home's head office. But I'll be sure to stop by for a visit if I'm ever in your sector.

Live Long and Profit,
Capt. Chuck Vaguer

Listen, Smirk,

I know what you're up to. Writing from the nursing home under Capt. Ricardo's name is such a dumb stunt that I'm insulted you thought I'd fall for it.

Admiral Ruth Less

Dear Jean-Lucy,

It was good to hear from you again. I trust that our ongoing correspondence gives meaning to your days in the nursing home. It sounds as if you're becoming resigned to your situation. As you say, the bright side is that you no longer have the stress of making decisions, except for the tough task of choosing from selections on the dining hall menu. Perhaps one of the aides could help you with that.

I'm sending a bottle of our newest wine. The grapes in our vineyard are exceptional this year. Therefore, rather than wasting them on wine, we're eating them. This new wine is made of fermented tangerine peels. Nevertheless, I hope you enjoy it. Remember to drink it slowly since this is the real thing and not that simpahol stuff. You don't want to get soused. On the other hand, considering where you're living, you might as well guzzle it.

Your brother,
Rodney Ricardo

Dear Jean-Lucy Ricardo,
I got your letter saying that you're stuck in the nursing home under a mistaken identity and that nobody in Starfreak believes you. However, I believe you. This is just the sort of dumb situation I always expected you to land in. Anybody who'd willingly spread fertilizer with his bare hands is going to come to a bad end—that's what I always say.
It sounds like you have a lot of time on your hands, so I'm enclosing a gardening project to give you something to do. It's a Chia Pet. Just add water and it grows. I think you can handle it.

Sincerely,
Toothby the Gardener

Dear Commander Wilson Piker:
What a surprise to hear from one of my former students. When did you learn to read and write? Certainly not in my classroom.
You asked me to help you get out of the nursing home you're in, but I think that's a bad idea. In fact, considering your intelligence level, I think they're doing the galaxy a favor by keeping you locked up.

Sincerely,
Mrs. Crayon
Frozen Pipes Elementary School
Valdez, Alaska

Deanna baby,

It was really far-out to get your letter. So the nursing home guys think you're us, huh? That's pretty funny. I mean, not ha-ha funny, but weird funny.

I'm too busy to help you out right now, but if there's ever a lull in the babe situation here, I'll definitely see what I can do.

Ciao,
Jim Smirk

Dear Smartalecsander:

As your father, I am very concerned with the report card I just received from your teacher on the *Endocrine*. She wrote in the margin of the card that you are now the class bully. I expected more of you, young man. You should be the *ship's* bully by now. Get with it!

Wart

Dear Westerly,

My dear, dear son, I am writing to you on a matter of utmost urgency. All of us senior officers have been detained against our will in the Vacant Attic Nursing Home. Please tell someone in authority there at your Starfreak Academy Film School about our horrible predicament. All of my letters to others on the outside have gone unanswered. You're my last hope.

With motherly love,
Bev Flusher

Enclosure: your weekly allowance

Dear Mom,

Thanks for the money. Please send more.

Love,

Westerly

Packing Slip

TO: Georgie LaForgery

RE: Repair of visor model #345A–7953D

COMMENTS:

We have repaired your visor as requested. Seeing that your return address is in the Vacant Attic Nursing Home, we have added a bifocal option at no extra charge. We hope you enjoy your new visor.

Josie Whale

Repair manager, VisorCrafters

P.S. Regarding your other request: Sorry, but I can't help spring you from the nursing home. I suggest you check the Yellow Pages under SWAT teams and find one that takes on freelance jobs.

Dear Miss Guano,

I sincerely thank you for the fine cigars and wonderful letter. I did not know until today that the federal post office could deliver mail sent via time-travel canister.

You would hardly recognize San Francisco. It has changed so much since your last visit, and horseless carriages are everywhere.

Nevertheless, some things never change. The android's discarded head remains in my household as a remembrance of our exciting adventure; I have been using it as a cuspidor. And I continue my practice of attending literary receptions and boring the

"The android's discarded head remains in my household as a remembrance of our exciting adventure."

guests with my overly lengthy anecdotes that lead to
flimsy punchlines. I consider it my social obligation
to natter on and on to fill any awkward silences.

Sadly, I am afraid that there is nothing I can do to
get you out of your current predicament. You must
remember that I am not capable of time travel, unless
I can figure out a way to squeeze myself into one of
these post office letter canisters. Would it help at all
if I sent back the android's head? It sounds as if he
needs a new one.

Your old friend,
Samuel Clemens ("Mark Twain")

8

A Hunka Hunka
Burnin' 'Droid

Q-TIP STOOD IN THE WINGS, his gaze swiveling back and forth between Dacron, who was doing his Elvis schtick in the spotlight, and the mob of fans out in the audience. Dacron was playing the planet of Wilma-7 as part of his concert tour, and the show had started to heat up.

During this stretch of appearances, touted as the Resurrection Tour, Q-Tip had noticed a curious phenomenon. Every concert had a point at which the crowd's frenzy reached critical mass. It usually occurred about three-quarters of the way through the show, when the excitement level cranked up to a new plateau, the screams of the audience battered the stage like ocean waves, and a flash fire of hysteria spread through the auditorium.

At that point, people would do crazy things. Depending on what planet the tour was playing and the type of aliens in the audience, the fans might rush the stage, or tear their hair and clothes, or start throwing things, or faint, or begin speaking in tongues. Occasionally some of the aliens would metamorphose into other life forms or start eating each other.

Q-Tip surveyed the scene and speculated that tonight's concert had just about reached that breaking point.

He was right. A minute later, from one of the front rows, a pair of panties came sailing toward the stage. It looked like tonight would be a UFO night.

The panties triggered a deluge of flying objects. All were

572

Dacron was playing the planet of Wilma-7.

gifts that the fans had brought in a desperate attempt to make some sort of connection with their idol. The air filled with their love offerings. Roses, handmade sweaters, jewelry and baked goods were rocketed at the stage. Dacron dodged them as gracefully as he could and kept on singing even after a schaum torte grazed his shoulder, leaving a streak of strawberry filling.

A stagehand standing beside Q-Tip clucked his tongue in disapproval. "All that good food going to waste," he said. "And throwing it at *him* yet. He doesn't look like he needs it."

"Hey, watch your mouth," Q-Tip snapped. "That's my boy out there."

Q-Tip knew as well as anyone that Dacron's waistline had expanded significantly from the grind of road touring. The greasy take-out food they often ate and other indulgences of the rock-'n'-roll lifestyle had already transformed the early Dacron into the late Dacron.

Yet criticism of the android was intolerable to Q-Tip, who lived vicariously through Dacron's superstardom. It was the kind of popularity that Q-Tip could never seem to achieve on his own, despite his omnipotence.

When Dacron finally left the stage at the conclusion of the concert, he was dripping with perspiration. "Man, it's a nuthouse out there," he panted as Q-Tip draped a towel around his neck and accompanied him down the backstage corridors to his dressing room.

"You really got them going tonight," Q-Tip exclaimed. "Isn't it a rush to feel all those people going crazy over you?"

"Ah dunno," Dacron said. "At first it was, but now ah just feel sorta . . . empty."

"A lot of performers would give their right arm to be in your position," Q-Tip reminded him.

"How about if ah give muh right arm to get *out* of muh position? Ah can unscrew it for yuh right now," Dacron moped. Then, under Q-Tip's stern gaze, he backed off a little. "Ah'm sorry, Colonel," he said. "Ah don't mean to be ungrateful. Ah know you're doin' a great job of steerin' muh career an' all, but it's jus' gettin' so crazy lately. All ah can think about is muh pals back at the Vacant Attic, and how much ah miss 'em, and how ah should be doin' somethin' to get 'em out of there. Muh mama would've wanted me to help 'em—if ah'd ever had a mama."

"You wouldn't be happy on that little hick planet," Q-Tip told him. "Your place is here in the big time. And there's more to come. I was going to save this for later, but I'll tell you now, just to cheer you up: I got a call today from the Ed Sullen show. They want you to be on the show this Saturday night! Isn't that great?"

Dacron knew that Q-Tip had been angling for this appearance, which represented the peak of his career to date. But to Dacron, greater fame only meant that he was ensnared even deeper in the celebrity web that now seemed so cumbersome.

"That's wunnerful, Colonel," Dacron said with as much enthusiasm as he could muster.

They turned the final corner down the hall to Dacron's dressing room. "Oh, no," Dacron groaned. "Not more groupies." About a dozen flashy women were clustered around the dressing room door, waiting for him.

"Too tired for a little feminine companionship?" Q-Tip asked, seeming disappointed that this vicarious pleasure was about to fall through.

"Ah may be fully functional, Colonel, but even ah have muh limits," Dacron replied, wearily rubbing his eyes with the towel.

"All right, then," Q-Tip conceded, escorting him through the crowd and into the dressing room, leaving the women outside.

The dressing room was arranged just as Dacron's contract specified. There was a buffet table with a six-pack of crankcase oil, several bags of Manny's Oat Bran Tortilla Chips, and a bowl of M&M candies with the green ones removed. One wall held a Snap-On Tools calendar with a boudoir photograph of

O-rings alluringly arranged on velvet. Light bulbs throughout
the room heated up, spreading the scent of the Essence of
Silicon cologne that had been sprayed on them.

Dacron sat in front of his dressing table and stared dully
at his reflection in the mirror. "Yuh know," he said, "lately
when ah look in the mirruh, ah get scared. There's no soul
behind muh eyes."

"So what?" Q-Tip scoffed. "Like you had a soul before?"

"Ah did," Dacron protested. "And ah had a purpose in mah
life when ah was on the ship. Ah used t' sit all day punchin'
those buttons on mah console and sneakin' a peak at mah
soap operas when the captain was off the Bridge. It was a
good ol' time. Now ah'm on the road, and half the time ah
don't even know which city ah'm in, an' it's just one gig after
anothuh—"

"Oh, knock it off," Q-Tip snapped. "You performers are all
alike. You'll do anything to get to the top, but then once
you're there, all you can do is complain." Q-Tip adopted a
whiny voice to imitate the litany of rock-star complaints:
" 'Life on the road is so hard.' 'All they want to hear is the
old hits, not my new songs.' 'Nobody knows how rough it is
to spend a full two hours singing each night.' 'I want to be
back home.' "

"Well, ah *do* wanna be back home!" Dacron said, flashing
an uncharacteristic show of temper. "Or at least, back with
muh friends at the Vacant Attic."

"Forget it!" Q-Tip snarled. "I told you before, we are not
cutting short this tour. I didn't bring you this far to have you
flake out on me. Especially now that we've snared a spot on
the Sullen show." He and Dacron glared at each other, and
Q-Tip added, "You know, your moodiness is making this tour
a real drag. Snap out of it, will you?"

Q-Tip gestured at the dressing room door, then flicked his
wrist and disappeared in a flash of light.

Dacron checked the door immediately. Just as he'd expected, Q-Tip had locked him in. He flung himself onto the

couch and sulked for awhile; then he remembered that his secret stash was still hidden in the closet in a small suitcase.

Dacron opened the case and surveyed its contents, an array of android pharmaceutical software that helped him cope with the stress of his new life. There were uppers: various cleanup utilities that helped him get going in the morning. There were downers: Lotus spreadsheets he ran just before bedtime to help him sleep. And there were hallucinogens for the times he really needed to get away from it all. His favorite was a screen-saver program with a Lava Lite motif that projected itself against his closed eyelids.

Lately he'd become dangerously dependent on all of them, but he blamed it on the pressures of the road. Besides, he knew he could stop anytime. He just didn't want to.

After loading the Lava Lite screen-saver, Dacron lounged on the sofa. Immediately his muscles relaxed as the program worked its magic. His whirling thoughts started to settle down, and he pictured himself moving far away from the hassles of the tour. He dreamed of building a mansion where he could get away from it all. He'd make it into a palace, and it would become his own private retreat. He could call it Spaceland.

Back at Juven Isle, Cmdr. Crisco lurked in the bushes next to the log flume ride. He was casing the joint to figure out the best way to gain control of the water of the Fountain of Youth. That would let him get started on the second half of his mission: to build a trans-planetary pipeline that would deliver the water to Starfreak Command.

Crisco's return to the planet from the Vacant Attic had been delayed by a minor crisis involving his son, Joke. Smiles O'Brine, filling in for his wife Kookoo as a substitute teacher, had recommended that Joke undergo a psychological screening for Westerly Flusher Syndrome, a progressive disorder of the wimp nodes. Luckily, the evaluation turned out to be reassuring: the shrink told Crisco that Joke would probably

O'Brine had recommended Joke undergo a psychological screening for Westerly Flusher Syndrome.

be okay as long as he avoided active Bridge duty until after puberty.

Crisco was grateful that everything had turned out all right, but the detour had cost him precious time, and now he was chafing to finish his mission.

Upon his return to the planet, Crisco had been surprised to see that the theme park was still operating even though he'd taken Smirk & Co. to the Vacant Attic some time ago. He had assumed that once the ringleaders were gone, the whole park would shut down. But that hadn't happened. The place was going full blast. It was jammed with visitors, and there were plenty of employees around, too—far too many to allow Crisco to singlehandedly take over Juven Isle.

So he conducted a covert operation, sneaking through the island's plastic foliage and trying to determine where all this water was coming from.

Studying the layout, Crisco couldn't help noticing that the water truly did have an anti-aging effect. Rider after rider got off the log flume looking much younger than when they'd got on.

The artificial jungle became thicker as he penetrated farther into the phony island. Hefty canes of plastic bamboo hindered his every step. Ropey plastic vines ensnared his ankles. A canopy of plastic leaves blocked the sunlight.

There was a quick movement in the brush up ahead. Crisco peered through the foliage, trying to determine what was there. Failing to see the motion again, Crisco crept in its direction, ducking under a thick branch that blocked his view.

As Crisco pushed the branch aside, he felt a weird sensation against his neck, and a cold, slippery weight draped itself around his shoulders. Instinctively he froze. Moving only his eyes, he managed to determine, to his horror, that a huge tropical snake had just slithered down onto him from one of the trees.

Now don't panic, Crisco told himself as his stomach began doing the Twist. *Stay cool and think your way out of this, man. Figure out what kind of snake this is so you'll know how to deal with it. Is it a boa constrictor that's going to squeeze the breath out of you? Or is it a poisonous type that will sink its huge fangs into your cheek? Or maybe a garter snake that will spit in your eye and blind you? Or an eel that's going to drag you into the water and drown you? That's it—nice and cool . . .*

The rustling in the brush just ahead started up again, much louder this time. Crisco's skin crawled as he imagined the snake becoming spooked by the noise and killing him in an instant.

A young man pushed his way out of the foliage toward Crisco. His uniform had JUVEN ISLE SECURITY stitched on its pocket. "Can I help you, sir?" he inquired.

Crisco, still frozen like a statue, gestured wildly with his eyes to indicate the snake draped around his shoulders. The young man's expression registered surprise, but he recovered quickly. Nodding to Crisco, he whispered, "African Bamboozle Snake. Very poisonous. We'll have to take him to the park's kennel and knock him out with the sleeping-dart gun." The young man reached for Crisco's hand to lead him out of the brush.

Crisco whimpered as loudly as he dared, terrified to move from the spot.

"It's okay," continued the security guard in a whisper. "The snake will rest on your shoulders as long as you don't make any sudden movements."

Something—perhaps the look of serenity on the young man's Oriental features—inspired a smidgen of confidence in Crisco. Or maybe it was the fact that he had no choice. Whatever the reason, he followed ever so cautiously as the security guard led him out of the jungle surrounding Juven Isle.

They left the island and continued through the park. The trip down the pedestrian mall was a nightmare. Youngsters crowded near Crisco to see and touch the snake draped around his shoulders, while Crisco tried to warn them off with stern looks and ineffective finger-waving. The snake seemed to have fallen asleep and was apparently oblivious of the commotion, though every so often it shifted position an inch or so, striking terror into Crisco's heart.

Finally, after what seemed an eternity, they reached a cluster of small office buildings. Crisco followed as the young man proceeded to an inner room. "Here he is, Captain Smirk," called the young guard. Dimly, in the midst of his terror, Crisco wondered about the significance of this greeting and of the name the guard had spoken.

There in the inner office, another young man sat with his feet propped cockily on his desk. He studied Crisco with a wry smile. The young man's amusement, his lack of surprise at the menacing snake, even his sweatshirt that read KISS ME, I'M SENTIENT—it all began to seem surreal to Crisco. He wondered if he was having another one of his pepperoni nightmares.

"Thank you, Mr. Zulu. Sit down, Commander Crisco," said the young man, grinning, as he gestured toward the guest chair. Fleetingly Crisco wondered how this stranger knew his name. The youngster gazed at him steadily as Crisco, staring straight ahead and holding his shoulders rigid to avoid disturbing the snake, maneuvered his rear into the chair and unwittingly sat on a cardboard pizza carton someone had left there.

"Can I get you anything?" the young man offered. He reached into a small refrigerator, retrieved several beverage cans, and brought them to Crisco's side of the desk. "Soda? Fruit drink?" Crisco, afraid even to shake his head, moved his eyes from side to side.

"I know," said the young man. "Maybe you'd like something for your *snake*!" To Crisco's horror, the youngster grabbed the snake and began twisting his hands around its body.

Sheer fright knocked the breath out of Crisco, and for an instant he blacked out. When he came to, he saw that the young man and the security guard were laughing hysterically. The snake was stretched out on the desk, belly-up, motion-

less—and even from a few feet away Crisco could see the
legend stamped on its underside: MADE IN TAIWAN.

Overcome with laughter, the young men fell down and
rolled on the floor, hooting and howling. Crisco felt the slow
burn of the realization that he'd just been scammed.

When the other two finally caught their breath, they gave
each other a bear hug. "Right on, Security Chief!" exclaimed
the sweatshirted youngster. The other left the room. The one
with the sweatshirt climbed back into his desk chair, brushing
the dust of the floor off his sleeves.

"Whew! That was classic!" he exclaimed. He extended a
hand, and the stunned Crisco reflexively reached out to shake
it. "Welcome to Juven Isle," said the young man. "I'm Captain
James T. Smirk. Now maybe you'd like to tell me why you
were sneaking around in my plastic jungle, hmmmm?"

Dacron rolled over in bed and moaned as he unwillingly
drifted into wakefulness. Sunlight sneaked past the edges of
the thick drapes hanging over the window of his hotel luxury
suite. Judging from the intensity of the sun, the time was
well past dawn, but to Dacron's groggy circuits it felt like the
middle of the night.

Vaguely he recalled that his entourage had arrived in the
city sometime after midnight. They'd taken rooms in a hotel
near the studio where Dacron would appear on the Ed Sullen
show that evening. There'd been a party in his room—that
much Dacron remembered—and when everyone had finally
left, he'd been too keyed up to sleep. He'd loaded a game
program into his head just for kicks. Everything after that
was just a blank; Dacron speculated that the game must have
had a bug in it.

Wham! The door burst open and slammed against the adjacent wall. Q-Tip stormed into the room. His irate expression
made it clear that he'd chosen this unusual—for him—
method of entry to create the biggest possible ruckus.

"Why are you still in bed?" Q-Tip demanded. He wrenched
open the drapes, staggering Dacron with a blast of sunlight.

"It's five o'clock in the afternoon!" Q-Tip barked. "You're due at the Ed Sullen studio in less than an hour!"

Groaning, Dacron tried to pull the covers over his head, but Q-Tip stomped over to the bedside and yanked the covers off.

"Look at you," Q-Tip sneered. "You've really let yourself go. There's nothing more disgusting than an android with a pot belly."

Dacron shivered, curling up against the mattress and covering his head with one of the Heartbreak Hotel's satin pillows.

"Well, get up!" Q-Tip ordered.

"Ah cain't," Dacron whimpered.

"You miserable bucket of bolts!" Q-Tip raged. "This is your big chance! Don't you realize that you'll be the first android Sullen's ever had on the show? You can be a credit to your species!" Dacron tried to avoid him by turning over, but Q-Tip flashed to the other side of the bed and thrust his face next to Dacron's. "After being on the Sullen show," Q-Tip said, "you'll be able to call the shots in your career. You'll play all the big venues—Vegas, Venus, Vega, even the Vela system. Your face will be known from Maine to blue Hawaii."

"Ah don't cay-are," Dacron whined. "Ah wanna be back with muh pals, the people who love me tender. Ah'm tahred of all this high livin'. Ah never was much of a high livuh t' begin with. Don't make me go on, Colonel. Don' be cruel."

"Surely you can't be serious," said Q-Tip with a hint of trembling in his voice. "You wouldn't turn down a chance to do—*Ed Sullen*."

"Yes, ah would," Dacron insisted, rolling over onto his back and folding his arms across his chest in defiance. "And you cain't make me."

They both knew this was true. Once before, when Dacron was suffering a similar nervous breakdown tinged with rebelliousness, Q-Tip had physically forced him through the mechanics of his stage show. The result was patently fake, and the fans had actually booed him.

Q-Tip knew that to try a similar maneuver for this Sullen appearance would be disastrous. Dacron would bomb on intergalaxywide live TV, and instead of the vicarious pleasure Q-Tip anticipated, he'd endure vicarious embarrassment. Just imagining the scene made Q-Tip feel all shook up.

"Dacron, please." Q-Tip grasped the android's arm. "You know how much this means to me. This would be the ultimate thrill. I simply must feel that excitement from the audience one more time. Remember, you owe me one. I'm responsible for bringing you here out of nowhere from your job in the ghetto of Ricardo's starship. Please do the show. Please!"

Dacron sulked for a few moments longer, then allowed, "Well, maybe. But only if you promise me somethin'."

"Anything. Anything," Q-Tip answered eagerly.

"Promise me that after this ah'll stop tourin' for a while and go back to muh friends," said Dacron. "And that you'll help me get 'em out of that nursin' home and back into our ship."

"I promise," Q-Tip assured him.

Wearily, Dacron rose from the bed. Q-Tip sighed with relief, then headed for the bathroom. "You get your stage clothes on," he ordered, "while I'm heating up the hot rollers for your hair."

Once he'd gotten over the shock of the snake scare, Crisco began to relax in Smirk's office, and as the two of them talked, Crisco even got to like Smirk. And there was much to like, for Smirk was at his most charming: serving soft drinks and snack chips, chatting about Starfreak, drawing out stories about Crisco's past, and revealing candidly that Crisco had transported the wrong crew to the Vacant Attic Nursing Home. Smirk even described what it felt like when he and his crew transformed from old geezers into young punks after they'd captured the Fountain of Youth.

Yet through it all Crisco sensed that Smirk wasn't about to let him walk out the door unrestricted. There was still the little matter of who controlled the fountain. And it was clear that right now that control resided firmly in Smirk's hands.

The conversation turned to the hardships of Starfreak life. Smirk commiserated with Crisco over the loss of his wife and revealed that he himself had once lost an adult son. "Not that Starfreak Command ever really cared," Smirk mused. "You wouldn't believe the paperwork I had to wade through just to get some honest-to-goodness embalming fluid for him. They were gonna use peanut oil, for Pete's sake."

"It's hard to imagine you having a grown son," Crisco murmured, studying Smirk's unlined face.

"Yeah, I suppose," said Smirk, rubbing his hand over his smooth cheeks. "But I was old once, just like you."

Crisco stared at the far corner and revealed bitterly, "Starfreak gave me a hard time, too, after my wife died. They said an officer with my ranking was only allotted thirty minutes of bereavement time with pay. I'm still trying to get the rest of my paycheck for that week."

"They'll put the screws to ya every chance they get," Smirk said with a world-weary shake of his young head. He seemed lost in thought for a few minutes. Then he shook himself out of his reverie and remarked, "So you say Starfreak Command ordered you to take my Fountain of Youth water and pipe it back to them?"

"What?" Crisco, too, emerged from his trip down memory lane. He made a face. "Starfreak? Aw, heck, screw 'em."

Smirk grinned at Crisco's insolence, then predicted, "Yeah, but if you come back empty-handed, they'll just send somebody else. Eventually, somebody's gonna take over my fountain."

"That's true," Crisco concluded reluctantly. His expression made it clear that he no longer thought this was a fair course of action.

"Unless . . . " said Smirk, mulling over some possibility.

"Unless what?" Crisco prompted.

"Well, you could still build your pipeline," Smirk said,

seeming to make up a plan as he went along. "That would take the heat off both of us."

"Then you'd be willing to pump some water to Starfreak?" Crisco asked.

"I could," Smirk went on. "Nobody's saying how *much* water, if you catch my meaning. Like, you don't know what the daily production of the fountain is, right?"

"Right," Crisco agreed, catching on.

"So if I send, say twenty-thousand youtholiters a day to Starfreak, they're gonna assume that's the total volume of water coming out of the fountain. And if I also set you up with a steady supply of bottled water for resale, and keep the rest of the fountain water running through Juven Isle, no one's the wiser, right?"

"Right," Crisco said, clearly pleased at the thought of cheating Starfreak out of a major portion of the spoils.

Smirk added, "Especially not Ricardo and his crew, livin' the high life over there in the Vacant Attic, 'cause you and I aren't about to tell anyone who they really are, right?"

"Right!" Crisco exclaimed.

"This calls for a toast," Smirk declared. He opened his refrigerator and pulled out two souvenir bottles of fountain water. "What d'ya wanna drink to?" he asked, handing one bottle to Crisco.

Crisco responded, "Let's drink to you and your crew— forever young." They clinked their bottles together and chug-a-lugged with relish.

9

Finis

"ALL RIGHT, CLASS, here we go. Now, has everybody got their little looms out? Good." As the instructor opened another session of the Potholder Weaving class, Capt. Ricardo studied the small square metal frame on the table in front of him. A worried frown creased his face.

During the past month, he and his classmates had spent two class periods each week stretching loops of doubleknit fabric over their frames. Now came the tricky part: weaving the other half of the loops over and under the original loops, at right angles, to form the fabric of the potholder.

Capt. Ricardo had been dreading this moment. This next step required the use of a latch hook and sounded dreadfully complicated. And it intensified the constant danger that a loop of fabric, stretched to its full length, might somehow work one end loose of the frame and turn into a deadly missile.

Ricardo's universe had definitely shrunk since the day he and his crew first checked into the Vacant Attic. Initially they'd remained in the nursing home against their will, since no one from the outside would come to their rescue.

But after some time, almost without noticing it, they became resigned to their situation. Eventually, nursing home life brought out the bland vanilla side of them all, and they even grew to like it at the Vacant Attic.

The nursing home was calm and peaceful. Everybody got along so well. There was no backbiting, no bickering—in fact, no character conflict whatsoever.

587

Soon they dropped their letter-writing campaign aimed at
getting someone to rescue them, and they settled into their
assumed identity as Capt. Smirk and crew. Their placid routines plodded along with the nursing home's cheery activity
schedule: Bingo on Monday, arm exercise class on Wednesday,
"Go Fish" card tournaments on Thursday, and cookie-and-
milk socials on Sunday afternoons.

For crewmembers who desired additional challenges, the
Vacant Attic offered plenty of classes in various skills, like
the art of potholder weaving which Capt. Ricardo was now
trying to master.

"Pick up your latch hook and place a loop of fabric on it
like this," said the instructor. Warily Ricardo followed her
example.

Suddenly someone appeared in the chair next to him. It
was Q-Tip.

"My, my, *mon capitalist*," said Q-Tip, studying Ricardo's
potholder frame with a sardonic grin, "I never dreamed you
were so artistic."

Ricardo glared at him and set down his latch hook. "Q-
Tip, you mustn't appear and disappear so suddenly," he said.
"You're likely to give one of these people a heart attack."

"Say, who are you?" the instructor demanded, staring at
Q-Tip. "Have you signed up for this session?"

Q-Tip ignored her and asked Ricardo, "Well, aren't you
curious about why I came here?"

"Not really," said Ricardo, squirming as the entire class
turned to stare at them. "Why don't you leave before you get
me in trouble?"

"Oh, dear, dear, dear," Q-Tip said, *tsk-tsk*ing his tongue
in mock exasperation. "How little it takes to rile you these
days." He picked up a fabric loop, stretched it to its full length,
and aimed it threateningly at Ricardo.

"All right," Ricardo said, nervously eyeing Q-Tip's weapon,
"why *did* you come here, Q-Tip?"

"So glad you asked," Q-Tip said, lowering the loop. "I've

brought your boy back." He snapped his fingers, and Dacron appeared next to them in all his rockabilly glory.

"Hullo, Cap'n," said Dacron. "It's so good to see y'all again."

"And there's more," Q-Tip continued, "but I don't want to go into that here. Let's move to your room where we can have a little privacy." Q-Tip snapped his fingers again, and the three of them instantly transported to Ricardo's small bedroom.

Another snap of Q-Tip's fingers, and the rest of Ricardo's crew appeared in the room also. They blinked, surprised by the sudden change in their surroundings. Q-Tip had snatched them from a variety of activities that were reflected in the clothing they wore. Troit and Piker sat there in wet bathing suits, having been taken from a water aerobics session. Wart and Georgie were wearing smocks from their watercolor painting class. And Dr. Flusher and Guano were still in their bathrobes.

Seeing that Dacron had returned, the others gathered around him with hugs and exclamations. Q-Tip tapped his foot impatiently until the commotion died down; then he announced, "You'll all be happy to know that at the request of your homesick android, I'm here to take you away from this wasteland of boredom."

The crewmembers drooped. A blanket of silence hung over them.

"Well, hey, ever'body!" Dacron exclaimed, trying to drum up some enthusiasm. "Don't y'all wanna go back to the ship and get out of here?"

The silence stretched on. A couple of people shrugged their shoulders. A few cleared their throats nervously. There was shuffling of feet.

"What's the matter with you people?" Q-Tip demanded. "I didn't expect a ticker-tape parade, but at least you could show a *little* gratitude. This is what you've been waiting for, isn't it?"

Capt. Ricardo spoke up. "We did want to be rescued, some time ago," he allowed, "but lately that prospect has seemed rather remote, and I guess we've all become resigned to our situation. We even rather like it here."

Q-Tip's expression hardened with anger and disgust. "Like it?" he hissed. "You like it here?"

One by one, the others nodded. Dacron looked disappointed but said nothing.

"Of all the . . . you humans are just . . . " Q-Tip sputtered. "How utterly, utterly . . . *boring!*" he spat out, as if it were the worst insult he could muster.

"This is no fun at all anymore!" Q-Tip went on. "Even you!"—he pointed at Dacron—"You're getting to be a real drag. You're no longer fit to be The King." With a wave of his hand, Q-Tip transformed Dacron back into his old strait-laced, un-potbellied self.

"I'm leaving," Q-Tip concluded. "It'd be more fun to pick on a group of insurance actuaries than to hang around you people any longer!" With a flash, he disappeared.

"Well," Capt. Ricardo said. "Let's all get back to what we were doing, shall we?"

That night, Dacron began the transition to nursing-home life by giving another concert for the residents. Though he was pretty much back in his android mode, his circuits still contained trace imprints of show-biz patterns, and this concert was his way of livening up the somnolent nursing-home atmosphere.

Onstage, Dacron's movements were a lot stiffer and jerkier than in his Elvis days, and his singing voice had returned to its falsetto range; but he still had a spark of the old fire left in him, and his ad libs were much more to the point than they'd been before.

"My, what an exuberant crowd," he remarked at one point. "Are you all aware of the correct manner in which to rock-'n'-roll?" And later: "I would like to dedicate this number to a delightful young woman I met after one of my concerts. I shall never forget how her manual dexterity relaxed my severe case of post-concert bodily tension." And still later, glancing offstage as he wiped his sleeve against his forehead, "May I have a glass of crankcase oil, please? This activity is severely dehydrating."

Unfortunately, although Dacron's ad libs were better, overall his act was much less polished without Q-Tip's guidance. He'd put his belt buckle on backwards. His hair had lost its body; now, parted in the middle, it hung limply over his forehead as if he were emulating Shemp of the Three Stooges. And Dacron had made an unfortunate choice in the order of his songs, choosing "Are You Lonesome Tonight?" as his closing number.

Up to that point the place was rocking, but this ballad draped a melancholy mood over the nursing home residents. They truly were lonesome tonight, and every night, for their nearest relatives lived on other planets and rarely came to visit. By the time Dacron finished the song, a fog of longing had settled over the audience. He left the stage to a smattering of applause.

The nurses, nurses' aides and other workers were dismayed by this turn of events. They began clapping and calling, "Encore! Encore!" When Dacron failed to return to the stage, they began stomping their feet and pounding the walls. A few of them borrowed residents' walkers and rhythmically thumped them against the floor.

Capt. Ricardo went backstage to see if he could persuade Dacron to extend the concert and pacify the workers. A few minutes later Ricardo emerged onto the stage, holding up his hands for silence. He approached the microphone as the crowd quieted to hear his announcement.

"I'm sorry, but the concert really is over," Ricardo told them. "Dacron has left the building."

"Well done, Commander Crisco, well done," said Admiral Less, leaning back in her chair and regarding with approval the officer sitting on the other side of her huge power desk.

"Thank you," Crisco responded, trying not to stare at Less'

"This station is sort of wild and woolly."

daggerlike red fingernails, which she rubbed absentmindedly against the polished surface of the desk.

"My people tell me that the trans-planetary pipeline is running at full capacity. We're pumping the fountain's entire daily output of 20,000 youtholiters directly into our supply towers," Less said. "And the Vacant Attic staff says that Smirk's crew has adjusted nicely to nursing-home life. Did they give you any trouble when you took them into custody?"

"Some, but I handled it," Crisco responded smoothly.

"Starfreak is very pleased with the way you've conducted this mission," Less went on. "The High Command has come up with a special reward for you."

Crisco straightened up in his chair. This was more than he'd expected.

"We're giving you a new assignment," Less told Crisco. "You'll be in charge of a space station on the frontier—Geek Space Nine, in orbit of the planet Badger. The federation recently booted the Carcinogen occupational forces out of there.

"This station is sort of wild and woolly," Less revealed, "but you can use that to your advantage. For one thing, I know your son hasn't had any adult female role models in his life since your wife died. Well, Geek Space Nine has a holographic brothel, so there are plenty of females around. It ought to provide some balance for the boy.

"The security situation is a bit ... unruly, shall we say," Less went on, "but Starfreak is giving you a free hand to clamp down on the crime wave. We're not going to require you to file an official report every time you fire your phaser, if you catch my drift."

"Yes, ma'am," Crisco responded.

Admiral Less hesitated momentarily, then added, "You'll also notice that the Carcinogens kind of trashed the place before pulling out."

Crisco frowned with concern. "What kind of condition is the space station in, Admiral?"

"Oh, you'll get it fixed up in no time," Less breezed. "We're giving you plenty of expert help. Transporter Chief Smiles O'Brine is transferring there from the crew of the *Endocrine*—the new *Endocrine*, that is. He's prepared detailed engineering specs for sweeping up the pieces of the station's UltraFax and glueing them back together. And there's your first officer, who's a former Bridgeoran terrorist—she's very handy with explosives, I hear. You ought to be able to use that somehow. Every commander needs a good explosion now and then to keep the staff on their toes."

Less opened a file folder on her desktop. "Let's see about some of the others at the station..." she said, scanning a document. "There's a lieutenant—this duty roster says she's a 300-year-old slug in the body of a fashion model...huh, that oughta be interesting.

"Someone named Dodo," Less continued, reading aloud, "is the shape-shifting security officer. He keeps his department's expenses low by turning himself into a German Shepherd, a pair of handcuffs, a nightstick, or whatever he needs...

"There's a nightclub on the promenade, owned by a civilian Ferengi," Less went on, speaking to herself. "Gads, are we never going to shake these dratted Ferengi? They've become the houseflies of the galaxy."

Less read the roster in silence for a minute, her expression growing increasingly skeptical. Then, realizing Crisco was studying her, she concluded briskly, "Well, you get the drift." She snapped the personnel folder shut as if she feared Crisco would glimpse something revealing.

Crisco summoned a wan smile, fighting back the suspicion that his promotion was about to confirm the Peter Principle that employees always rise to their level of incompetence.

At Juven Isle Amusement Park, another happy day dawned It couldn't help but be a happy day, for the Patent Office of the United Federation of Planets had just officially approved the park's application for a trademark on its slogan, "The Happiest Place in the Galaxy."

Capt. Smirk and six of that week's girlfriends boarded the Tower of Power ride in the center of the park. He'd commandeered the ride today for their private use. They were going to ride to the top`of the tower and enjoy the view all day long as the round cabin revolved at its leisurely speed. They'd brought along a picnic lunch and a CD player to make the day complete.

"This is, like, too cool," one of the girls said as the cabin began climbing the tower. She opened the lid of the picnic cooler. "D'you wanna drink, Jim?"

"Sure, sweets," Smirk replied. "I'm dyin' of thirst. It's been at least half an hour since I've had a cola."

As she handed him the can of soda, Smirk plopped into one of the seats that faced the bank of windows overlooking the park. With his arms outstretched to the girls sitting on either side, he surveyed the grounds and felt a deep sense of satisfaction.

From his perch, Smirk could see the parking lot where their *Endocrine* was stored. Mr. Smock, he knew, would be busy monitoring the controls, keeping an eye on all vehicles approaching the planet, and maintaining the park's underground vacuum waste-disposal system.

From this height, no sound reached them, but Smirk glanced at the Migraine Bumper Cars building where Snotty was performing repairs today, and imagined he could hear the young engineer's frustrated rantings.

A long line of park visitors was already forming outside the first aid building. Smirk speculated that McCaw had once again posted his "The doctor is OUT" sign with a picture of a medic wielding a five-iron.

In one corner of the park, the Ferocious Ferris was spinning faster than ever. Smirk could just barely see the tiny form of Checkout beneath it, dodging seats as he continued his gum-scraping duties. Checkout claimed to be getting more adept at the task; now he only got struck by every tenth seat.

At the other end of the park, Smirk saw a few patrons

running out of the theater—apparently terrorized—and he figured that Yoohoo must have just taken the stage.

The newest thrill ride, Samurai Slicer, was up and running. Smirk knew that Zulu would be carefully monitoring his creation. As riders bounced on the rocking platform and tried to avoid the huge blades that randomly whooshed down at them from overhead, Zulu would keep a sharp lookout, ready to press the "Emergency Stop" button if there was a close call. So far the ride had had just a few fatalities, and these had only increased its reputation—there was always a two-hour wait in line to get on.

The girls on either side of Smirk began angling for his attention. He turned away from the window and flashed a stunning glance at each of them in turn.

One of them began feeding him grapes. The other whipped out a manicure set and began doing his nails.

Smirk relaxed in his chair and declared to no one in particular, "This is the life!"

An old battle cry popped into Smirk's head. Filled with jubilation that things had turned out so well, he proclaimed:

"These are, like, the voyages of the Starship *Endocrine*. Its mission: to, you know, cruise around the universe looking for totally cool situations to get into . . . to search the outskirts of the galaxy for hot babes . . . to, like, boldly go where nobody wanted to go before!"

HOW TO ORDER YOUR BOXTREE BOOKS

STAR WRECK

- ☐ 1-85283-340-8 *Star Trek Technical Manual* £13.99
- ☐ 1-85283-398-X *Trek the Universal Index* £13.99
- ☐ 1-85283-899-X *Captain's Log* £13.99
- ☐ 1-85283-399-8 *Captain's Log – Season 6* £9.99
- ☐ 1-85283-388-2 *Deep Space Log Book* £9.99
- ☐ 1-85283-571-0 *Exploring Deep Space and Beyond* £6.99
- ☐ 1-85283-393-0 *The Making of UFO and Space 1999* £9.99
- ☐ 0-7522-0915-9 *Randall and Hopkirk (Deceased)* £9.99

All these books are available at your local bookshop or newsagent, or can be ordered direct from the publisher. Just tick the titles you want and fill in the form below.
Prices and availability subject to charge without notice.

Boxtree Cash Sales, P.O. Box 11, Falmouth, Cornwall TR10 9EN

Please send a cheque or postal order for the value of the book and add the following for postage and packing:

U.K. including B.F.P.O. – £1.00 for one book plus 50p for the second book, and 30p for each additional book ordered up to a £3.00 maximum.

Overseas including Eire – £2.00 for the first book plus £1.00 for the second book, and 50p for each additional book ordered.

OR please debit this amount from my Access/Visa Card (delete as appropriate).

Card Number [ ][ ][ ][ ][ ][ ][ ][ ][ ][ ][ ][ ][ ][ ][ ][ ][ ][ ]

Amount £ ....

Expiry Date on card ....

Signed ....

Name ....

Address ....